# BOOK-KEEPING AND ACCOUNTS

SPICER AND PEGLER'S

# BOOK - KEEPING
# AND ACCOUNTS

*Seventeenth Edition*

by

W. W. BIGG, F.C.A.

and

R. E. G. PERRINS, F.C.A.

HFL (PUBLISHERS) LTD
9 BOW STREET, COVENT GARDEN,
LONDON WC2E 7AL

| | |
|---|---|
| First Edition | 1908 |
| Second ,, | 1910 |
| Third ,, | 1913 |
| Fourth ,, | 1919 |
| Fifth ,, | 1920 |
| Sixth ,, | 1924 |
| Seventh ,, | 1927 |
| Eighth ,, | 1931 |
| Ninth ,, | 1934 |
| Tenth ,, | 1938 |
| Eleventh Edition | 1945 |
| (Second Impression) | 1946 |
| (Third Impression) | 1947 |
| Twelfth Edition | 1950 |
| Thirteenth ,, | 1952 |
| Fourteenth ,, | 1956 |
| (Second Impression) | 1956 |
| (Third Impression) | 1958 |
| Fifteenth Edition | 1959 |
| (Second Impression) | 1961 |
| Sixteenth Edition | 1963 |
| (Second Impression) | 1964 |
| (Third Impression) | 1965 |
| (Fourth Impression) | 1966 |
| (Fifth Impression) | 1967 |
| (Sixth Impression) | 1968 |
| (Seventh Impression) | 1969 |
| (Eighth Impression) | 1970 |
| Seventeenth Edition | 1971 |

This Edition © HFL (PUBLISHERS) LTD
1971

ISBN 0 372 11620 5

*Printed in Great Britain at*
THE STELLAR PRESS, HATFIELD, HERTS

# PREFACE

In preparing this new edition the opportunity has been taken to review the whole of the text in order to keep abreast of current trends and legislation.

Our thanks are due to the Institute of Chartered Accountants in England and Wales for their kind permission to include appropriate sections of their Recommendations on Accounting Principles. The first statement of *Standard Accounting Practice* was published too late to be incorporated in the main body of the text but has been reproduced as Appendix IV. We are also grateful to the officers of the various companies whose permission was readily given to the reproduction of their accounts which appear in the Appendix.

We also have to thank Mr A. K. Moir, F.C.A., Mr L. J. Northcott, F.C.A., Mr D. W. Beckett, A.C.W.A., A.A.C.C.A., and the tutors of H. Foulks Lynch & Co. Ltd, for the assistance given to us in the preparation of this edition.

W. W. BIGG
R. E. G. PERRINS

*March 1971*

# TABLE OF CONTENTS

## Chapter I
### DOUBLE ENTRY BOOK-KEEPING

PAGE

§ 1. Introduction .. .. .. .. .. .. .. 1
2. The Theory of Double Entry .. .. .. .. .. 1
3. The Various Classes of Assets and Liabilities .. .. .. 3
4. Capital and Revenue Expenditure .. .. .. .. 4
5. The Books of Prime Entry .. .. .. .. .. 5
6. Cash Books .. .. .. .. .. .. .. 6
7. The Petty Cash Book .. .. .. .. .. .. 10
8. Day Books .. .. .. .. .. .. .. 11
9. The Journal .. .. .. .. .. .. .. 13
10. The Ledgers .. .. .. .. .. .. .. 15
11. The Trial Balance .. .. .. .. .. .. 17
12. The Trading and Profit and Loss Account .. .. .. 17
13. The Balance Sheet .. .. .. .. .. .. 19
14. The Accounts of a Sole Trader .. .. .. .. .. 21
15. Methods of dispensing with Day Books and Personal Ledgers .. 26

## Chapter II
### TOTAL (OR CONTROL) ACCOUNTS AND SECTIONAL BALANCING

§ 1. Total (or Control) Accounts .. .. .. .. .. 29
2. Sectional Balancing or Self-balancing Ledgers .. .. .. 36
3. The Location of Errors.. .. .. .. .. .. 37

## Chapter III
### PROVISIONS AND RESERVES, DEPRECIATION ETC.

§ 1. Definitions of Provision, Reserve and Reserve Fund .. .. .. 39
2. Provision for Bad Debts .. .. .. .. .. 39
3. Provisions for Cash Discounts .. .. .. .. .. 42
4. Outstanding Liabilities .. .. .. .. .. .. 43
5. Payments in Advance .. .. .. .. .. .. 44
6. Definition of Depreciation; Considerations necessary to assess its rate.. 44
7. The Necessity of Providing for Depreciation .. .. .. 45
8. The Principal Methods of Providing for Depreciation .. .. 49
9. The Treatment of Repairs, Renewals and Replacements .. .. 64
10. The Operation of Sinking Funds for the Repayment of Loans .. 66
11. Secret Reserves .. .. .. .. .. .. 68
12. Suspense Accounts .. .. .. .. .. .. 70

### Chapter IV

## MANUFACTURING ACCOUNTS; RECEIPTS AND PAYMENTS ACCOUNTS AND INCOME AND EXPENDITURE ACCOUNTS; THE PREPARATION OF ACCOUNTS FROM INCOMPLETE RECORDS

PAGE

§ 1. Manufacturing Accounts .. .. .. .. .. 72
2. Receipts and Payments Account and Income and Expenditure Account 77
3. The Preparation of Accounts from Incomplete Records .. .. 81

### Chapter V

## GOODS ON SALE OR RETURN, CONSIGNMENT ACCOUNTS ETC.

§ 1. Treatment of Goods sent on Sale or Return .. .. .. 89
2. Consignment Accounts .. .. .. .. .. .. 92
3. Entries in the Consignor's Books .. .. .. .. 93
4. Entries in the Consignee's Books .. .. .. .. 101
5. Accounts with Agents .. .. .. .. .. .. 102

### Chapter VI

## BILLS OF EXCHANGE, PROMISSORY NOTES ETC.

§ 1. Definitions .. .. .. .. .. .. .. 106
2. Stamp Duty on Bills of Exchange and Promissory Notes .. .. 107
3. Specimen Forms of Bills of Exchange and Promissory Notes .. .. 108
4. Forms of Bill Books .. .. .. .. .. .. 110
5. Accommodation Bills .. .. .. .. .. .. 117
6. Dishonoured Bills, Retired Bills, Short Bills etc. .. .. .. 121

### Chapter VII

## PARTNERSHIP ACCOUNTS

§ 1. The Nature of Partnership .. .. .. .. .. 125
2. The Partnership Agreement .. .. .. .. .. 127
3. The usual Adjustments necessary in Partnership Accounts .. .. 129
4. Partners' Fixed Capital Accounts; Current Accounts; Loan Accounts .. 133
5. Goodwill in Partnership Accounts .. .. .. .. 134
6. Outgoing Partners .. .. .. .. .. .. 153
7. Sleeping, Quasi and Limited Partners .. .. .. .. 164
8. Dissolution of Partnerships .. .. .. .. .. 166
9. Joint Venture Accounts .. .. .. .. .. .. 187

### Chapter VIII

## COMPANY ACCOUNTS
### PART I
*General legal considerations and accounting for Share Capital etc.*

§ 1. The Distinctions between Partnerships and Limited Companies .. 196
2(**a**). Private Companies .. .. .. .. .. .. 200

## COMPANY ACCOUNTS (*Continued*)

|  |  | PAGE |
|---|---|---|
| § 2(b). | Unlimited Companies | 202 |
| 3. | The Memorandum and Articles of Association | 202 |
| 4. | The Statutory Books and Returns | 203 |
| 5. | The Various Classes of Share Capital | 210 |
| 6. | The Application and Allotment of Shares | 213 |
| 7. | Forfeiture of Shares | 226 |
| 8. | The Share Books | 231 |
| 9. | Preliminary and Formation Expenses | 233 |
| 10. | Mortgages and Debentures | 237 |
| 11. | The Purchase of a Business by a Limited Company | 251 |
| 12. | Bonus Shares | 271 |
| 13. | Payment of Interest out of Capital | 273 |
| 14. | The Preparation of a Company's Books and Accounts for Audit | 274 |

### PART II

*Balance Sheet and Accounts – disclosure requirements*

| 15. | The Balance Sheet and Accounts of a Company | 275 |
|---|---|---|

### PART III

*Interpretation and Accounting Ratios*

| 16. | Interpretation and Accounting Ratios | 320 |
|---|---|---|

### PART IV

*Amalgamations, Reconstructions and Reduction of Capital*

| 17. | The Amalgamation of Companies | 348 |
|---|---|---|
| 18. | The Absorption of one Limited Company by another | 365 |
| 19. | Reduction of Capital | 374 |
| 20. | Reconstructions and Reorganizations | 382 |

### Chapter IX

## THE ACCOUNTS OF HOLDING COMPANIES

| § 1. | Holding Companies | 387 |
|---|---|---|
| 2. | Definition of Subsidiary Company | 389 |
| 3. | Group Accounts | 390 |
| 4. | Consolidated Balance Sheet | 395 |
| 5. | Consolidated Profit and Loss Account | 428 |
| 6. | Holding Company's Profit and Loss Account framed as a Consolidated Profit and Loss Account | 437 |
| 7. | General Illustration | 440 |
| 8. | Accounting for the Results of Associated Companies | 445 |

## Chapter X

## DEPARTMENTAL ACCOUNTS; BRANCH ACCOUNTS

PAGE

§ 1. Departmental Accounts .. .. .. .. .. 446
2. Branch Accounts .. .. .. .. .. .. 451
3. Branches for which the whole of the accounting records are kept at head office .. .. .. .. .. .. .. 451
4. Branches which maintain separate accounting records .. .. 475
5. Foreign Exchanges .. .. .. .. .. .. 492
6. Foreign Branches .. .. .. .. .. .. 494

## Chapter XI

## MECHANIZED AND ELECTRONIC ACCOUNTING SYSTEMS

§ 1. Principles .. .. .. .. .. .. .. 508
2. Writing and Copying Devices .. .. .. .. .. 509
3. Adding and Calculating Machines .. .. .. .. 514
4. Ledger Posting Machines .. .. .. .. .. 520
5. Punched Card Systems .. .. .. .. .. 523
6. Electronic Computers .. .. .. .. .. 530

## Chapter XII

## BANKRUPTCY, LIQUIDATION AND RECEIVERSHIP ACCOUNTS

§ 1. General Principles .. .. .. .. .. .. 542
2. The Preparation of a Statement of Affairs in Bankruptcy .. .. 543
3. Bankruptcy of Partnerships .. .. .. .. .. 554
4. The Accounts of a Trustee in Bankruptcy.. .. .. .. 556
5. Deeds of Arrangement .. .. .. .. .. .. 556
6. The Preparation of a Statement of Affairs of a Company in Compulsory Liquidation.. .. .. .. .. .. .. 557
7. The Accounts of a Liquidator in Compulsory Liquidation .. .. 566
8. The Accounts of a Liquidator in Voluntary Liquidation .. .. 566
9. Return to Shareholders.. .. .. .. .. .. 569
10. The Accounts of a Receiver .. .. .. .. .. 572

## Chapter XIII

## MISCELLANEOUS ACCOUNTS

§ 1. Hire-purchase Agreements, Agreements to pay by Instalments and Rental Agreements .. .. .. .. .. .. 575
2. Mine etc. Rents and Royalties etc. .. .. .. .. 600
3. Farmers' Accounts .. .. .. .. .. .. 605
4. Fire Claims for Stock .. .. .. .. .. .. 608
5. Loss of Profits Insurance (Consequential Loss) Policies .. .. 609
6. Contract Accounts .. .. .. .. .. .. 614
7. Bankers' Accounts .. .. .. .. .. .. 618
8. Voyage Accounts .. .. .. .. .. .. 620
9. Marine Insurance Accounts .. .. .. .. .. 621

## MISCELLANEOUS ACCOUNTS (*Continued*)

PAGE

§ 10. Ledger Accounts for Investments .. .. .. .. 623
11. Tabular Ledgers .. .. .. .. .. .. 631
12. Stock Exchange Transactions .. .. .. .. .. 635
13. Professional Accounts .. .. .. .. .. .. 648
14. Insurance Companies .. .. .. .. .. .. 660
15. (Treatment of Scrip Profits etc.) – Underwriters' Accounts .. .. 666
16. Accounts of Containers .. .. .. .. .. .. 668
17. The Accounts of Building Societies .. .. .. .. 672

## APPENDICES

I Specimens of Published Accounts .. .. .. .. 678
II *Companies Act 1967* – Schedule 2 .. .. .. .. 727
III Prescribed forms applicable to Bankruptcy, Liquidation and Receivership .. .. .. .. .. .. .. 737
IV Statements of Standard Accounting Practice –
1. Accounting for the results of associated companies .. .. 752

CHAPTER I

# DOUBLE ENTRY BOOK-KEEPING

## § 1. Introduction

A simple definition of book-keeping is 'the art of recording all money transactions so that the financial position of an undertaking and its relationship to
both its proprietors and to outside persons can be readily ascertained'. Gone
are the Dickensian days when Ebenezer Scrooge's clerk 'Bob Cratchit' sat at his
sloping desk embellishing gigantic ledgers with a quill pen for 15 shillings (£0·75!)
per week; modern business, subject to keen competition in which clerical labour
is in short supply and expensive, requires accurate detailed information quickly;
much clerical drudgery formerly done manually is now performed by costly
machinery. The object of this book is to outline some of the book-keeping and
accountancy problems facing modern business and suggest their solutions.
Book-keeping cannot be clearly distinguished from accountancy; broadly speaking, the book-keeper writes up books and makes accounting records, whilst
the accountant designs and controls the book-keeping system and utilizes the information it produces to prepare financial statements and advise managements.

The accountant is responsible for directing and co-ordinating the work of the
book-keeping staff, and for designing and maintaining accounting systems
adequate to the needs of the particular business. It is part of his duty to prepare
periodical accounts of profit and loss and financial statements in a form which
will be of assistance to the management, not only in appraising past results, but
in formulating future policy. By careful and scientific analysis of accounting
records he can bring to light significant facts which will enable errors in management and policy to be rectified and reforms and economies to be introduced. He
must be competent to devise and consolidate the accounting records of branches
and subsidiaries, install and direct costing systems and generally to advise the
management and give effect to their policy on all matters affecting the business
in its financial and accounting aspects.

The principles of double entry book-keeping are described and illustrated fully
in Spicer and Pegler's *Practical Book-keeping and Commercial Knowledge* and
are only outlined in this book, which is devoted mainly to more advanced
accountancy.

## § 2. The Theory of Double Entry

Double Entry Book-keeping recognizes that every transaction which can be
recorded in terms of money involves the receiving of value by one or more persons and the giving of equivalent value by another or others. The system accordingly requires entries to be made in the books of a business to give effect to
both aspects of the transactions.

The principal book of account is the LEDGER, and although normally a

1

number of subsidiary books are also necessary, it is the Ledger in which all transactions are ultimately recorded in double entry form. The Ledger is divided into 'accounts', each being devoted solely to transactions with a particular person, or of a particular kind. Accounts dealing with persons are called 'PERSONAL ACCOUNTS' and those in which transactions are recorded from the viewpoint of the business, 'IMPERSONAL ACCOUNTS'. The Impersonal Accounts are further subdivided into 'REAL ACCOUNTS' which are concerned with things (e.g. plant and machinery, buildings etc.) and 'NOMINAL ACCOUNTS' in which the various kinds of expense, income, profit and loss are recorded.

The simplest form of ledger account is divided vertically into two sides, that on the left being called the 'debit' and that on the right the 'credit' side of the account. Accordingly, an entry on the left-hand side of a ledger account is called a debit, and one on the right-hand side a credit to that account.

The fundamental rule of double entry may now be concisely stated, as follows:
The account which RECEIVES value is DEBITED;
The account which GIVES value is CREDITED.

Thus, if XY & Co sell goods of the value of £100 on credit to AB & Co in the books of XY & Co the personal account of AB & Co is debited and the impersonal account for Sales is credited with £100, AB & Co having received the value, and Sales Account being the account in which the 'giving' of value in the form of sales is recorded. When, later, AB & Co pay the £100, their account is credited, because they 'give' the value, and Cash Account is debited, because this account 'receives' it.

It must be observed that the value received by, and consequently debited to, an account is not always something tangible, such as goods or cash. The payment of wages, for example, is made as consideration for a *service* received by the business, viz. the labour of employees, and must be debited to Wages Account, which represents that type of service. The value received may even be of a negative character, and constitute a loss, such as a bad debt which, when sustained, must be debited to the account which 'receives' the loss, viz. Bad Debts Account, and credited to the account of the defaulting debtor, which yields it.

Again, the account which gives the value may be an impersonal one, representing the *source* of a benefit, such as income from investments; the amount received is therefore debited to Cash Account and credited to Income from Investments Account, the account of the source from which the income is derived.

The rule of double entry stated above, may be amplified as follows:

| Type of Account | Debit | Credit |
|---|---|---|
| Real Accounts | Property acquired, e.g. Plant, Fixtures etc. | Property disposed of or sold |
| Personal Accounts | The Receiver | The Giver |
| Nominal Accounts | Expenses/Losses | Income/Gains |
| Cash Book | Receipts | Payments |

The advantages of double entry can be stated as follows:

1. It provides a complete record of every transaction, from both its personal and impersonal aspects.

2. It provides an arithmetical check on the records since the total of the debit entries must equal the total of the credit entries, and consequently the total of the debit *balances* must equal the total of the credit *balances*.

3. From the Personal Accounts the amounts owing to and by each person with whom the business deals can at any time be ascertained.

4. The balances of the Nominal Accounts can be collected together in a Profit and Loss Account, which discloses the results of the operations, i.e. the profit or loss for any given period.

5. By means of a Balance Sheet, in which the balances of accounts representing capital, assets and liabilities are set out, the financial position of the business at any given moment, can be ascertained.

6. With a reliable system of internal organization, it reduces the risk, and facilitates the detection of, errors and fraud.

### § 3. The Various Classes of Assets and Liabilities

Assets may be classified as follows:

(*a*) *Fixed Assets* are those which are acquired for retention in the business and not for conversion into cash. The life of such assets usually extends over some years, and the operations of many accounting periods derive benefit from them. The cost of fixed assets, therefore, represents capital expenditure, which, instead of being charged wholly against the revenue of the period in which it is incurred, is spread over the effective lifetime of the assets, by charging a proportion of cost against the revenue of each of the years in which they are used. Examples of fixed assets are buildings, plant and machinery, fixtures and fittings, goodwill etc.

(*b*) *Wasting Assets* are for earning revenue, but are gradually consumed or exhausted in the process of earning revenue, e.g. a mine, a cemetery.

(*c*) *Current* (*or Floating or Circulating*) *Assets* are acquired for resale, and consist of assets in the various stages of conversion into cash, such as debtors and cash itself. Such assets are termed 'circulating assets' because they are constantly changing in form by being 'turned over' in the process of trading. Thus cash may be applied in buying goods, goods may be sold and replaced by book debts, book debts are turned into cash, and so on. It is by the turnover or circulation of current assets that profits or losses are made.

Current assets less current liabilities are termed 'the working capital' of a business.

Cash, and assets that are capable of immediate realization, e.g. Bills Receivable, short term investments or debtors may be termed 'liquid assets'.

(*d*) *Fictitious* (*or Nominal*) *Assets* are debit balances resulting from expenditure of an exceptional nature, which is not represented by present value, but has not been written off. Examples are preliminary expenses (in the case of a limited company), and deferred revenue expenditure, e.g. special advertising, the benefit of which will extend to future accounting periods and which it would be inequitable to charge against the revenue of any one period. Such assets have no intrinsic value, and it is therefore desirable to write them off as soon as possible.

Assets may be classified as 'tangible' or 'intangible*: tangible assets have material existence, such as stock, cash, plant etc.; intangible assets have no tangible form but represent the value of a right, e.g. goodwill, patents, book debts etc. The use of these expressions is not recommended, as there is a tendency to depart from the literal interpretation of the terms. Intangible assets, e.g. goodwill and patent rights, must not necessarily be regarded as fictitious; they may be of considerable value, whereas a fictitious asset is valueless.

Liabilities are amounts owing by a business; current liabilities are those which theoretically must be met within one year from the balance sheet date; bank overdrafts are normally shown as current liabilities because the amount due to the bank is fluctuating and is usually repayable within a short period. Liabilities which need not be met for over a year are often classified as 'fixed' or 'long term' liabilities. The ratio of 'current liabilities' to 'current assets' is important since it indicates the adequacy of the working capital in a business.

## § 4. Capital and Revenue Expenditure

Capital expenditure may be defined as expenditure incurred in the acquisition of fixed assets required for use in the business and not for resale; or in the alteration or improvement of assets, for increasing their earning capacity in the business.

Revenue expenditure is expenditure incurred in the maintenance of fixed assets, in the acquisition of assets required for conversion into cash, in selling and distributing goods, and in administering the business.

The distinction between capital and revenue is of great importance since it affects the amount of profit or loss, and the correctness of the Balance Sheet.

Since capital expenditure results in a long term benefit to the business, it is written off piecemeal, the proportion unexpired at the end of each accounting period being carried forward to continue to form part of the capital employed in the business. Revenue expenditure, on the other hand, contributes only once to the earning of profit, and except when it is represented by unsold stock and payments in advance, is wholly exhausted and written off against revenue in the period in which it is incurred.

For the financial health of the business, capital expenditure should be provided for by long term capital, i.e. capital contributed by the proprietors, or raised in the form of mortgages or debentures, which are not repayable at an early date. Although it may be desirable for revenue expenditure also to be provided, at least partially, by long term capital, it may be financed in part by bank overdrafts and credit received from creditors, so long as the current assets are maintained at a figure sufficient to meet the current liabilities as they become due, and to leave an adequate margin of working capital to meet current expenses and contingencies.

## § 5. The Books of Prime Entry

Although the principle of double entry requires a debit and a credit to be made in the ledger for every transaction, it is necessary first to sort out the transactions, according to their nature, by entering them in subsidiary books, or 'books of prime entry', from which they can conveniently be transferred, or 'posted' to the ledger. Any number of books of prime entry may be employed, according to the needs of the particular business. Those usually found in a trading business are cash books, day books, and the journal.

### Cash Book

A cash book serves the dual purpose of a book of prime entry and a ledger account. It is ruled, like a ledger account, with debit and credit sides, all cash received being debited and cash paid credited. In order to complete the double entry for cash transactions, items are posted from the debit side of the cash book to the credit side of ledger accounts, and from the credit side of the cash book to the debit side of ledger accounts. A cash book is a ledger account for cash transactions; an entry in a cash book constitutes one part of the double entry, and it only remains to make the other part.

In a large business there may be a number of cash books, according to the number of cash accounts which it is necessary to maintain. In any event there will usually be, in addition to the general cash book, a petty cash book, in which small incidental expenses, such as postages, fares, carriage etc. are recorded.

### Day Books

In a day book all transactions of a particular kind are entered up preparatory to being posted to the ledger; a day book should be written up daily, whereas the ledger is only written up periodically or at the end of an accounting period. Separate day books will usually be found for purchases, sales, returns outwards, returns inwards, and for any other classes of transactions which are sufficiently numerous to justify the use of a separate book. As will be seen later, the double entry in the ledger for transactions first entered in a day book is usually made by posting each item to the debit or credit of the personal account of the debtor or creditor concerned, and the periodical total of the transactions to the credit or debit of the appropriate impersonal account in the ledger. For example, each item in the sales day book is posted to the debit of the account of the customer who receives the goods, whilst the periodical total of the sales is posted to the credit of the Sales Account, which 'gives' the value.

### The Journal

Formerly, the journal was the only book of prime entry, and every transaction, of whatever kind, was recorded in it before being posted to the ledger. In modern book-keeping, the journal has been supplanted, to a large extent, by the day books (which are, in effect, special journals) so that the use of the journal is now restricted to miscellaneous transactions and adjustments, for which no other book of prime entry is available. The journal is a memorandum book; it does NOT form part of the double entry.

## § 6. Cash Books

### (a) *Form of Cash Book where receipts are banked, and all payments are made by cheque.*

In order to minimize the risk of misappropriation of cash, all cash received should, if possible, be paid into a bank account intact, and all payments, apart from petty disbursements, should be made by cheques drawn on the bank account. The cash book should contain columns on either side for *Details* and *Bank*, each sum received being entered on the debit side in the *Details* column and the amount of each lodgment with the bank (which should agree with the amount appearing in the bank paying-in slip) extended into the *Bank* column. On the credit side, the amount of each cheque drawn on the bank account is entered in the *Bank* column, so that the *Details* column need only be used where one cheque is drawn to provide for two or more payments. As has been already explained, entries on the debit side of the cash book are posted to the credit side of the corresponding accounts in the ledger, and entries on the credit side of the cash book to the debit side of the ledger accounts.

Where cash discounts are allowed and received, additional columns must be provided on each side of the cash book – discount allowed on the debit side and discount received on the credit side.

CASH DISCOUNT is an allowance made from the amount of an account if it is paid before a stipulated date or within a specified period. The discount is deducted by the debtor from the sum due, when making the payment. When a cash discount is allowed by the business, it is entered in the *Discounts* column on the debit side of the cash book, and posted, together with the cash to which it relates, to the credit side of the account of the payer. Similarly, discount received is entered in the *Discounts* column on the credit side of the cash book, and posted, together with the cash paid, to the debit of the account of the payee. On balancing the cash book, the *Discount* columns are cast and ruled off, the total of the *Discounts Allowed* column being posted to the *debit* side, and the total of the *Discounts Received* column to the *credit* side of the Discount Account in the ledger.

The discount columns in the cash book are memoranda columns only and must be posted in the same way as totals from the day books to the ledger at the end of the accounting period. Discount allowed to debtors for paying on or before a certain date is debited since it is an expense of financing the business. Often it is cheaper to allow debtors a discount than to pay bank overdraft charges. Discount received is credited in the ledger since a gain is being achieved by paying creditors early, the cost of purchases being reduced.

Cash discount must be distinguished from trade discount; trade discount is deducted from the invoice before any entry is made in the books; it does not form part of the double entry.

TRADE DISCOUNT is an allowance made for trade purposes, e.g.

1. When a wholesaler supplies a retailer with goods invoiced at retail prices.
2. When a customer buys goods in bulk.

3. When catalogue prices have been reduced but the catalogue has not been reprinted.

4. When there are price reductions to sell surplus stock (e.g. the January and July sales in the clothing trade).

**Illustration**

## CASH BOOK

| Date | Particulars | Folio | Dis-count | Detail | Bank | Date | Particulars | Folio | Dis-count | Detail | Bank |
|---|---|---|---|---|---|---|---|---|---|---|---|
| 19.. Jan. 1 | Balance　b/f. | | £ | £ | £ 400 | 19.. Jan. 1 | F. Robertson | | £ 4 | £ | £ 196 |
| | J. Jones　.. | | 2 | 98 | | | Sundries: | | | | |
| | F. Smith　.. | | 1 | 49 | | | Salaries　.. | | | 15 | |
| | | | | | 147 | | Petty Cash | | | 5 | |
| | | | | | | | | | | | 20 |
| | | | | | | | Balance c/d. | | | | 331 |
| | | | £3 | | £547 | | | | £4 | | £547 |
| Jan. 1 | Balance b/d. | | | | 331 | | | | | | |

*Note*: The account of J. Jones will be *credited* with £100 and that of F. Smith with £50, whilst Discount Allowed Account will be *debited* with £3. The account of F. Robertson will be *debited* with £200, Salaries Account with £15 and Petty Cash Account with £5, whilst Discount Received Account will be *credited* with £4.

## (b) Form of Cash Book for mixed Cash and Bank transactions

In small businesses part of the cash takings is often used to pay for purchases and expenses, and the balance is banked. When this is done, the cash book should have columns on either side for CASH and BANK, the CASH columns representing, in effect, the ledger account for cash and the BANK columns the ledger account with the bank. Notes and coin received should be entered on the debit side in the CASH column; cheques received should be entered on the debit side in the BANK column. Payments in notes and coin should be entered on the credit side in the CASH column; payments by cheque should be entered on the credit side in the BANK column. Alternatively cheques when received can be debited in the CASH column and credited in the CASH column when banked, the BANK column being debited. When notes and coin are drawn from the bank the BANK column is credited and the CASH column debited. The balance of the CASH column will always represent notes and coin in hand and can be checked by physical verification; the balance of the BANK column will show the balance standing to the credit of the business, or overdrawn, as the case may be, at the bank.

**Illustration**

On January, 1st the following amounts were received:
　　Cheque from J. Jones £20; Discount allowed £1.
　　Cash from F. Smith £40; Discount allowed £2.
　　Dividend on investment paid direct to Bank £10.

and the following payments were made:

Paid T. Robinson by cheque £33; Discount allowed £2.

Drew £20 from Bank for cash.

Paid Wages £18 from cash.

Private drawings of partner £10, from cash.

Cash banked £45.

Record the above transactions in a convenient form of cash book, the commencing balances being £25 cash in hand and £300 at the bank.

## CASH BOOK

| Date | Particulars | Folio | Discount Allowed | Cash | Bank | Date | Particulars | Folio | Discount Received | Cash | Bank |
|---|---|---|---|---|---|---|---|---|---|---|---|
| 19.. Jan. 1 | Balances b/f. | | £ | £ 25 | £ 300 | 19.. Jan. 1 | T. Robinson | | £ 2 | £ | £ 33 |
| | J. Jones  .. | 1 | | | 20 | | Cash   .. | Contra | | | 20 |
| | F. Smith  .. | 2 | 2 | 40 | | | Wages   .. | | | 18 | |
| | Dividend | | | | | | Drawings  .. | | | 10 | |
| | from | | | | | | Bank   .. | Contra | | 45 | |
| | investment | | | | 10 | | Balances c/d. | | | 12 | 322 |
| | Bank   .. | Contra | | 20 | | | | | | | |
| | Cash   .. | Contra | | | 45 | | | | | | |
| | | | £3 | £85 | £375 | | | | £2 | £85 | £375 |
| | Balances b/d. | | | 12 | 322 | | | | | | |

In large businesses, cash receipts are often recorded by one or more clerks, and cash payments by others, separate cash books being employed for receipts and payments respectively. Periodically (e.g. daily, weekly or monthly) the totals of these books are entered in a Total Cash Account kept either in the impersonal ledger or in a separate book. If this book is under the control of a senior official it enables secrecy to be maintained, so far as the ordinary staff is concerned, about the cash position of the business.

The volume of transactions of the business may necessitate several cash received books being kept, e.g. one for each department, and an efficient system of control, in such cases, is indispensable.

Again, it may be desired to deal with such confidential payments as directors' fees, managers' salaries, partners' drawings etc. separately from the routine expenditure, and in such cases it is customary to have a private cash book with a separate bank account, sums being transferred periodically to this account from the general bank account.

### (c) The Bank Reconciliation Statement

It rarely happens that the balance of the cash book agrees exactly, at any given date, with the balance shown by the bank pass book or statement. The difference may be due to any of the following causes:

1. Cheques drawn in favour of creditors and credited in the cash book may not yet have been presented by the creditors for payment.

2. Cheques paid into the bank for collection and debited in the cash book may not have been entered by the bank on the bank pass book or statement.

3. Payments made by or to the bank against bankers' orders may not have been entered in the cash book, e.g. credit transfers and standing orders.

4. Dividends, bills receivable etc., collected by the bank may not have been entered in the cash book. Similarly, bills payable may have been paid by the bank, but not yet entered in the cash book.

5. Bank interest and charges entered in the bank pass book or statement may not have been entered in the cash book.

6. Cheques dishonoured may have been entered on the bank pass book or statement but not in the cash book.

It is necessary, therefore, to complete the writing up of the cash book for items not yet recorded therein, and then to prepare a statement reconciling the difference between the final cash book balance and the balance shown by the bank statement. Having checked entries in the cash book against those on the bank pass book or statement, the items not ticked on both sides of the cash book will represent those not yet passed through the bank. The items not credited by the bank should be added to the balance shown on the bank statement, and the cheques outstanding deducted. If the account is overdrawn, the items not credited by the bank will be deducted from, and the cheques outstanding added to, the balance shown by the bank pass book or statement. The balance should then equal the balance shown by the cash book.

Reconciliation statements reconcile the pass book or bank statements at a specific date. When preparing a reconciliation statement any time after that date, cheques outstanding can be split between 'cheques not yet presented' and 'cheques presented after date'. When future reconciliation statements are prepared it may not be necessary to check all the entries in the cash book against those in the bank statement but it must be proved that all cheques outstanding at the previous reconciliation have been presented; this analysis will help spotlight stale cheques and draw attention to 'window dressing' – creditors might be reduced and balance at the bank per the cash book reduced, or the overdraft increased, to camouflage the correct amount due at the Balance Sheet date to creditors.

**Illustrations**

1. On checking the bank statement with the cash book on August 4th, it was found that the balance standing to the credit of the business at the bank was £722 on July 31st, whereas there was a balance (DR) on the cash book of £700. Cheques paid in but not yet credited by the bank were: Black £40, White £60; cheques drawn in favour of Jones £20, and Smith £32 had not been presented; a cheque in favour of Robinson for £70 was presented on August 2nd. Prepare the reconciliation as at July 31st.

Reconciliation of Bank Statement with Cash Book at July 31st.

|  | £ | £ |
|---|---|---|
| Balance at Bank per statement |  | 722 |
| *Add* amounts not yet credited – Black | 40 |  |
| White | 60 |  |
|  | — | 100 |
|  |  | —— |
| Carried forward |  | 822 |

|  |  | £ | £ |
|---|---|---|---|
| Brought forward |  |  | 822 |
| *Less* cheques not yet presented – Jones |  | 20 |  |
| Smith |  | 32 |  |
|  |  | — |  |
|  |  | 52 |  |
| cheques presented after date |  |  |  |
| – Robinson |  | 70 |  |
|  |  | — | 122 |
|  |  |  | — |
| Balance as per Cash Book |  |  | £700 |

2. Assuming the facts as in the previous illustration, with the exception that the balance at the Bank was £6, and the *overdraft* as per Cash Book £16, the reconciliation statement would be as follows:

Bank Reconciliation Statement as at July 31st.

|  |  | £ | £ |
|---|---|---|---|
| Balance at Bank per Bank Statement |  |  | 6 |
| *Add* Amounts not credited – Black |  | 40 |  |
| White |  | 60 |  |
|  |  | — |  |
|  |  |  | 100 |
|  |  |  | — |
|  |  |  | 106 |
| *Less* Cheques not yet presented – Jones |  | 20 |  |
| Smith |  | 32 |  |
| Cheques presented after date |  |  |  |
| – Robinson |  | 70 |  |
|  |  | — | 122 |
|  |  |  | — |
| *Overdraft* as per Cash Book |  |  | £16 |

## § 7. The Petty Cash Book

Petty cash transactions may conveniently be recorded in a columnar petty cash book, an example of which is given below. Receipts of cash are entered in the receipts column (the *Bank* column in the general cash book being credited); whilst payments are entered first into a total payments column, and then extended into columns analysed under the most convenient headings. The totals of the various analysis columns are posted at each balancing period to the debit of the respective impersonal accounts, with the exception of the *Ledger* column, which is reserved for all items for which there is no specific analysis column. These items are posted in detail to the appropriate accounts. This form of petty cash book eliminates the necessity of posting each payment separately to the ledger.

When an analysed petty cash book is used there is no necessity to keep a petty cash account in the impersonal ledger, as the petty cash book is itself a ledger account and forms part of the double entry. Sometimes, however, a Petty Cash Control Account is opened in the impersonal ledger, and all amounts paid to the petty cashier are debited to that account. At regular intervals the totals of the analysis columns of the petty cash book are entered on the credit side of the

Petty Cash Control Account from which postings are made to the various expense accounts. In this manner the petty cash book becomes merely a memorandum book, and forms no part of the double entry.

**Illustration**

PETTY CASH BOOK

| Receipts | Folio in Cash Book | Date | Particulars | Voucher Number | Total Payments | Travelling Expenses | Stationery | Postage | Sundry Expenses | Ledger | Folio |
|---|---|---|---|---|---|---|---|---|---|---|---|
| £ 20 | 31 | 19.. Jan. 1 | Cash | | £ | £ | £ | £ | £ | £ | |
| | | | Envelopes | 1 | 1 | | 1 | | | | |
| | | | J. Jones – Bristol Expenses | 2 | 3 | 3 | | | | | |
| | | 2 | Postage | | 2 | | | 2 | | | |
| | | | Office Furniture – Stool | 3 | 6 | | | | | 6 | 27 |
| | | | Cleaning Carpets | 4 | 4 | | | | 4 | | |
| | | | | | 16 | 3 | 1 | 2 | 4 | 6 | |
| | | | Balance c/d. | | 4 | L. 49 | L. 25 | L. 19 | L. 81 | | |
| £20 | | | | | £20 | | | | | | |
| 4 | | 3 | Balance b/d. | | | | | | | | |

## The Imprest System of Keeping Petty Cash

The imprest system is a method of keeping cash or petty cash, whereby the cashier is provided with a fixed sum, and at each balancing period is given a cheque for the exact amount of his disbursements, thus restoring the petty cash balance to the original figure. The amount of the periodical disbursements is thus kept prominently before the notice of the person controlling the bank account, and enables a closer check to be imposed on petty cash expenditure. The petty cash book should always be thoroughly checked when expenditure is reimbursed, and ruled off or initialled up to that point. The petty cashier can at any time be called upon to produce vouchers, the total of which, together with the cash in hand, should equal the amount of the imprest.

## § 8. Day Books

The most important day books are those used for purchases, sales, returns inwards (sales returns) and returns outwards (purchase returns).

The following is a suitable ruling for a simple form of purchases day book:

PURCHASES DAY BOOK

| Date | Invoice No. | Particulars | Ledger Folio | Amount |
|---|---|---|---|---|
| 19.. Jan. 1 | 18 | A. Wilson | W. 62 | £ 44 |
| | 19 | J. Smith | S. 104 | 50 |
| | 20 | A. Lucas | L. 22 | 18 |

The particulars of entries in the purchases day book are obtained from the invoices received for the goods purchased. Invoices should be numbered and filed in numerical order, the serial number of each invoice being entered in the appropriate column in the purchases day book. No difficulty should then be experienced in referring to any invoice, if particulars of the purchase are required.

The amount of each item in the purchases day book is posted to the *credit* of the account of the supplier. Periodically the purchases day book is cast, and the total posted to the *debit* of Purchases Account.

The sales day book, returns inwards book and returns outwards book are in similar form, the double entry in the ledger being effected as follows:

Sales Day Book:
    *Debit* each sale to the personal account; *credit* periodical totals to Sales
    Account.

Returns Inwards Book:
    *Credit* each return to the personal account; *debit* periodical totals to Returns
    Inwards Account.

Returns Outwards Book:
    *Debit* each return to the personal account; *credit* periodical totals to Returns
    Outwards Account.

It is usual for Day Books to relate only to:

(*a*) goods on credit, *and*

(*b*) goods in which the business trades.

Separate day books can also, however, be kept for allowances, commissions, fees, bills receivable and bills payable, and other purposes, according to the needs of the business.

### Columnar Day Books

It is occasionally convenient to have a form of purchases and expenses day book that will record all inward invoices, whether they relate to purchases or expenses

A *Total* column is provided, and as many subsidiary columns as necessary. The amount of each invoice is entered in the *Total* column (from which it is posted to the credit of the creditor's account), and extended into the proper subsidiary column or columns. The totals of these columns are posted periodically to the debit of the respective impersonal accounts, thereby eliminating the need to post each item separately to the impersonal ledger.

The following is a suitable ruling for such a book:

### COLUMNAR PURCHASES AND EXPENSES DAY BOOK

| Date | Invoice No. | Particulars | Fo. | Total | Purchases | Freight | Trade Exps. | Ledger | Fo. |
|------|-------------|-------------|-----|-------|-----------|---------|-------------|--------|-----|
|      |             |             |     | £     | £         | £       | £           | £      |     |

The ledger column is used for items for which no special column is provided. Items in this column are posted in detail and not in total.

Similar forms can be used for sales day books, returns books and the like, where it is desired to analyse the items under different headings, e.g. classes of goods, departments, travellers, ledgers etc.

## § 9. The Journal

Since the vast majority of transactions are capable of being assigned to one or other of the day books or special journals, the use of the journal or ('journal proper') is now confined to items such as:

1. correcting and adjusting entries;

2. opening and closing entries;

3. transfers from one account to another;

4. the purchase and sale of fixed assets, when columnar purchases and sales day books are not kept.

The journal is provided with debit and credit columns to correspond with the sides of the ledger. Entries in the debit column of the journal are posted to the debit side of the ledger, and entries in the credit column of the journal to the credit side of the ledger.

There must be appended to each entry in the journal an explanation of the transaction, or *narration*, without which the origin of, and reason for, the entry might not be apparent. The narration should contain full information as to the nature of the transaction and the dates of contracts, minutes, resolutions etc. giving rise to it, so that the authority for the transaction as well as the origin of the entry will be shown.

A journal entry shows first the name of the account to be debited, with the amount in the debit column. The name of the account to be credited follows on the next line (the amount being entered in the credit column), prefixed by the word 'To' (in practice, the use of the word 'To' is frequently dispensed with). Sometimes a journal entry will be a composite one, in which more than one account is debited or credited. The totals of the debits and credits must, however, be equal in amount.

**Illustrations**

(1) Record by journal entry purchase of Electrical Generator, £600, from B. Jones & Co.

JOURNAL

| | | | | | | | £ | £ |
|---|---|---|---|---|---|---|---|---|
| Plant and Machinery Account .. | .. | .. | .. | .. | .. | *Dr* | P.L.  3 | 600 | |
| To B. Jones & Co  .. | .. | .. | .. | .. | .. | | B.L.  27 | | 600 |
| Purchase of one electrical generator | | | | | | | | | |

*Note*: From the above entry £600 will be posted to the debit of Plant and Machinery Account and £600 to the credit of B. Jones & Co.

(2) Record by journal entry transfer of £50 from B. Jones & Co's account in the bought ledger to their account in the sales ledger, to set off a purchase against a sale.

## JOURNAL

| | | | £ | £ |
|---|---|---|---|---|
| B. Jones & Co　..　..　..　..　..　..　.. | Dr | B.L. 27 | 50 | |
| To B. Jones & Co　..　..　..　..　..　.. | .. | S.L. 22 | | 50 |
| Balance of Bought Ledger Account transferred to Sales Ledger on contra account. | | | | |

*Note*: B. Jones & Co's account in the bought ledger is debited and their account in the sales ledger credited, thereby setting off the purchase against the sale.

(3) Record by journal entry interest at 5 per cent. per annum for one year on A. & F. Smith's capitals of £1,000 and £500 respectively.

## JOURNAL

| | | | £ | £ |
|---|---|---|---|---|
| Interest on Capital Account　..　..　..　..　..　.. | Dr | P.L. 64 | 75 | |
| To Current Accounts— | | | | |
| A. Smith – 5% on £1,000　..　..　..　..　..　.. | | P.L. 10 | | 50 |
| F. Smith – 5% on £500　..　..　..　..　..　.. | | P.L. 15 | | 25 |
| Interest at 5 per cent. per annum for the year ended December 31st, 19.., on Partners' Capitals. | | | | |

*Note*: Interest on Capital Account is debited with £75, A. Smith's Current Account being credited with £50 and F. Smith's with £25.

(4) Record by journal entry the opening entries of B. Smith, who started business on January 1st, 19 . ., with the following assets and liabilities:

|  | £ |
|---|---|
| Debtors　..　..　..　.. | 200 |
| Bills Receivable　..　.. | 100 |
| Cash at Bank　..　.. | 500 |
| Stock　..　..　.. | 800 |
| Creditors　..　..　.. | 150 |
| Bills Payable　..　.. | 50 |

## JOURNAL

| 19..Jan. 1 | | | £ | £ |
|---|---|---|---|---|
| | Debtors　..　..　..　..　..　..　..　.. | Dr | 200 | |
| | Bills Receivable　..　..　..　..　..　..　.. | .. | 100 | |
| | Stock　..　..　..　..　..　..　..　.. | .. | 800 | |
| | Cash　..　..　..　..　..　..　..　.. | .. | 500 | |
| | Creditors　..　..　..　..　..　..　.. | .. | | 150 |
| | Bills Payable ..　..　..　..　..　..　.. | .. | | 50 |
| | B. Smith: Capital Account　..　..　..　.. | .. | | 1,400 |
| | Assets, Liabilities and Capital at this date　..　..　..　..　.. | | £1,600 | £1,600 |

*Note*: The above entry is necessary to open the books of B. Smith's business on double entry principles. Each asset received by the business is debited to the appropriate asset account, and each liability credited to the appropriate liability account. The excess of the aggregate amount of the assets over that of the liabilities represents the value which the business has received from the proprietor, B. Smith, i.e. the capital which he has invested in the business, and is credited to his Capital Account.

(5) How would the following errors in the books of a business affect the accounts? Show corrective journal entries:

£35　for goods sold to H. Jones posted to the debit of General Expenses Account.

63　cash posted to the credit of H. Brown, a partner, instead of to H. Brown, a customer.

£120   posted to Office Expenses Account for the purchase of a safe.

1   posted to debit of Stationery Account, instead of to T. Wildsmith in payment of his account.

390   for wages to workmen for installing the firm's new machinery, charged to Wages Account.

30   cost of repairing roof of a shed, charged to Buildings Account.

## JOURNAL

| | | £ | £ |
|---|---|---|---|
| H. Jones          ..        ..        ..        ..        ..        ..        ..        ..        ..        Dr | | 35 | |
|     To General Expenses Account     ..        ..        ..        ..        ..        ..        .. | | | 35 |
| Transfer to H. Jones of amount debited in error to Expenses | | | |
| H. Brown, Current Account          ..        ..        ..        ..        ..        ..        ..        Dr | | 63 | |
|     To H. Brown (Sales Ledger)     ..        ..        ..        ..        ..        ..        .. | | | 63 |
| Transfer to customer of amount posted in error to credit of H. Brown's Current Account. | | | |
| Office Furniture Account          ..        ..        ..        ..        ..        ..        ..        Dr | | 120 | |
|     To Office Expenses Account     ..        ..        ..        ..        ..        ..        .. | | | 120 |
| Transfer to Furniture Account of cost of safe charged in error to Office Expenses. | | | |
| T. Wildsmith    ..        ..        ..        ..        ..        ..        ..        ..        ..        Dr | | 1 | |
|     To Stationery Account   ..        ..        ..        ..        ..        ..        ..        .. | | | 1 |
| Transfer of amount posted in error to Stationery Account. | | | |
| Plant and Machinery Account          ..        ..        ..        ..        ..        ..        Dr | | 390 | |
|     To Wages Account     ..        ..        ..        ..        ..        ..        ..        .. | | | 390 |
| Wages incurred in installing new machinery. | | | |
| Repairs Account          ..        ..        ..        ..        ..        ..        ..        Dr | | 30 | |
|     To Buildings Account   ..        ..        ..        ..        ..        ..        ..        .. | | | 30 |
| Cost of repairing roof of shed charged in error to Buildings Account. | | | |

The rectification of these errors will increase the profit by £516 as follows:

Decreased debits on expense accounts:

|  | £ |
|---|---|
| General Expenses   ..          ..          ..   35 | |
| Office Expenses   ..          ..          ..   120 | |
| Stationery ..          ..          ..          ..   1 | |
| Wages   ..          · ..          ..          ..   390 | |
|  | 546 |
| *Less* Increase in debit for Repairs   ..   30 | |
| Increase in Profit   ..          ..          ..£516 | |

## § 10. The Ledgers

Until now the ledger has been referred to as one book, and in a small business it is possible that all ledger accounts could be accommodated in one volume. In a business of any size it is necessary for the ledger to be subdivided, because of the large number of accounts, and also to enable a number of clerks to be engaged in posting to ledger accounts at the same time.

In a trading business it is usual to have a sales ledger, a bought ledger and a nominal or impersonal ledger. Further subdivision may be necessary according to the size and requirements of the business. For example, the sales ledger may be divided into a number of books, each containing accounts of customers whose names begin with a particular letter, or a letter within a particular group.

Thus there may be a ledger for names beginning with any of the letters A to G, another for names beginning with H to O, and another for P to Z. Alternatively, the ledgers may be divided according to geographical areas, or departments, or agencies. The bought ledger may be similarly divided.

The impersonal ledger may contain all the real and nominal accounts. This ledger may be divided into a nominal ledger, and a private ledger, containing partners' capital and current accounts, loan accounts, investment accounts and any other accounts of a private and confidential character.

### Loose-Leaf and Card Ledgers

Within recent years the use of loose-leaf and card systems of ledgers has become increasingly common.

In a *Loose-leaf ledger*, the leaves are not bound together in the ordinary way, but are inserted in binders with a locking mechanism so that they can be withdrawn, or new leaves inserted, by a very simple operation.

A *Card ledger* consists of a number of cards containing one for each ledger account, which are filed away in alphabetical order in cabinets. As the cards have to be withdrawn from the cabinets for entries to be made on them, it is not possible to take the same precautions against loss or substitution as in the case of loose-leaf ledgers, where the key of the ledger can be kept under the control of some responsible official, and therefore strict supervision must be enforced. Card ledgers are indispensable in mechanized accounting.

The following advantages can be derived by the adoption of these systems:

1. The ledgers are continuous, since additional pages or cards can be inserted as required, and it is therefore unnecessary to open new ledgers altogether at any one time. Moreover, all leaves relating to one person can be kept together, which is usually not possible in a bound ledger, no matter how carefully it is 'spaced out' when opened.

2. Closed and dead accounts can be withdrawn from the ledger, and filed separately. This avoids the necessity of keeping such a large number of accounts in the current ledgers.

3. When extracting balances, preparing statements or checking postings, the sheets or cards can, if necessary, be divided between a number of clerks.

The disadvantages of these systems are:

1. When additional leaves are inserted, the ledgers cannot be folioed in the ordinary manner, although this can be done to a partial extent under the heading of each letter.

2. The possibility of sheets or cards being accidentally lost or destroyed; cards can also be misplaced in the cabinets after use. This disadvantage is overcome by a sound system of internal control.

3. There is a danger of a fraudulent substitution of one sheet or card for another, in order to conceal defalcations; or sheets or cards might be destroyed intentionally for a similar reason. Again the internal control should eliminate these possibilities.

4. It has been contended that loose-leaf or card ledgers might not be admitted as sufficient evidence in a court of law, owing to the possibility of substitution, but this need not be regarded as a serious disadvantage, since some additional evidence for the entry would usually be required, apart from the record in the ledger.

Section 436 of the *Companies Act 1948* provides that any register, index, minute book or book of account required to be kept by a company may be kept either by making entries in bound books or by recording the matters in question in any other manner. Where bound books are not used, adequate precautions must be taken for guarding against falsification and facilitating its discovery, and where default is made in complying with this requirement, every officer of the company who is in default may be liable to a fine not exceeding £50, and to a default fine.

## § 11. The Trial Balance

A Trial Balance is a list of all the balances standing on the ledger accounts and cash books of a concern at any given date. It is clear that if a debit and a credit have been made for every transaction, in the absence of clerical errors the total of the debits should equal the total of the credits, and if the accounts are balanced off, and the balances carried down, the total of the debit balances should equal the total of the credit balances.

Although the agreement of the two sides of a Trial Balance provides *prima facie* evidence of the accuracy of the book-keeping, it is not conclusive proof of the absence of error, since the following classes of mistake would not cause a disagreement in a Trial Balance:

1. The complete omission of a transaction; neither a debit nor a credit being made.

2. Posting to the correct *side* of the ledger but to the wrong account.

3. Compensating errors, e.g. errors on one side of the ledger compensated by errors of the same amounts on the other side; or underpostings on one side compensated by overpostings on the same side.

4 Errors of principle, e.g. where transactions have been dealt with in a fundamentally incorrect manner, such as revenue expenditure treated as capital, or vice versa, e.g. motor expenses charged to Motor Vehicle Account.

The objects of a trial balance are:

1. To prove the arithmetical accuracy of the books;

2. To provide an analysis from which, subject to adjustment, the final accounts can be prepared.

When the difference on a trial balance is a round number of pounds and it is divisible by 9, it will usually be a transposition of figures, e.g. 43 written as 34.

## § 12. The Trading and Profit and Loss Account

In order to ascertain the profit or loss made during a period, where books are kept by double entry, it is necessary, on the final date of the period, to transfer the balances of the nominal accounts to a Profit and Loss Account, in which the expenses and losses are set against the gains to show the net profit or loss.

Where the business comprises the buying and selling of goods, the Profit and Loss Account is normally divided into three sections, viz. Trading Account, Profit and Loss Account, and Appropriation Account.

The object of the Trading Account is to find the amount of the gross profit on sales, i.e. the excess of the realized proceeds of goods sold over their cost, before taking into account the expenses incurred in selling and distributing the goods, and in running the business.

THE TRADING ACCOUNT is accordingly debited with the value of the stock of goods on hand at the beginning of the period (transferred from the Stock Account), with the cost of the goods purchased (transferred from Purchases Account) and with any other expenses incurred in bringing the goods to a saleable condition (e.g. inward freight, import duty, purchase tax, and possibly certain buying, packing or grading expenses which have to be met before the goods arrive at the condition and place where they will be sold). The Trading Account is then credited with the proceeds of the goods sold (transferred from the Sales Account) and with the stock on hand at the end of the period, for which the corresponding debit is to the Stock Account. Alternatively, the value of the closing stock may be deducted on the debit side of the Trading Account from the sum of the opening stock and purchases, in order to show the cost of the goods actually sold. The balance of the Trading Account will now represent the gross profit on sales, and is carried to the credit of the Profit and Loss Account.

The bringing into account of the closing stock is important. If the account dealt with quantities only, the stock on hand at the beginning, plus the purchases, would equal exactly the sales plus the stock on hand at the end. Generally, however, the Trading Account deals only with values, though strictly the quantities are presumed to balance in the manner indicated. In effect, the Trading Account, having been debited with all the goods that have come in and credited with all the goods that have gone out, gives back to the Stock Account the goods which remain, the value of which must accordingly be credited to the Trading Account and debited to the Stock Account.

In order to ensure that the gross profit disclosed by the Trading Account is not overstated by the inclusion of any unrealized profit, or by omitting to make allowance for any ascertained loss, the unsold stock should in no circumstances be credited to Trading Account at a value in excess of its actual cost, or its current realizable value, if that is lower than cost. Furthermore, if at the close of the accounting period the stock could be replaced at a lower figure than both the actual cost and the realizable value, the replacement value should be substituted.

The amount of any loss caused by stock being damaged or stolen is NOT a loss arising in trading and does not affect the gross profit on trading, and therefore any such losses should be credited in the Trading Account and debited in the Profit and Loss Account.

**Illustration**

Business is commenced on January 1st when £100 worth of goods are purchased. During the year ended December 31st no sales are made but £40 of goods are stolen.

TRADING ACCOUNT FOR THE YEAR ENDED DECEMBER 31st, 19..

| | £ | | £ |
|---|---|---|---|
| Purchases .. .. .. | 100 | Profit and Loss Account – Goods stolen | 40 |
| | | Closing Stock at cost .. .. .. | 60 |
| | £100 | | £100 |

PROFIT AND LOSS ACCOUNT

| | | | |
|---|---|---|---|
| Trading Account – Goods stolen | £40 | Net Loss .. .. .. .. .. | £40 |

The principles to be observed in valuing stock and work in progress in the accounts of industrial and commercial undertakings are fully considered in a memorandum issued by the Council of the Institute of Chartered Accountants in England and Wales, extracts from which are given in Chapter VIII, § 15 (*j*) in connection with the accounts of limited companies.

The PROFIT AND LOSS ACCOUNT is credited with the gross profit brought in from the Trading Account, and with any other revenue items, such as discounts receivable, rents receivable, income from investments etc. arising during the period; and debited with all the expenses incurred in selling and distributing the goods, and in the general administration of the business. The balance of the Profit and Loss Account represents the net profit or loss for the accounting period which, in the case of a sole trader, is transferred to his Capital or Current Account. In the accounts of other concerns the net profit or loss is carried to an APPROPRIATION ACCOUNT, in which also appear, in the books of a company, any balance brought forward from the previous period, and appropriations of profit in the form of transfers to reserves, and dividends; and in a partnership, any interest on capital and partners' salaries. The final balance of the Appropriation Account in a partnership is divided between the partners, and their respective shares are transferred to their Capital or Current Accounts. In the case of a company the balance is carried forward and appears as a reserve in the Balance Sheet.

The Profit and Loss Account of a non-trading concern, such as an investment or property company, or club, is usually called a REVENUE ACCOUNT or an INCOME AND EXPENDITURE ACCOUNT.

## § 13. The Balance Sheet

The Balance Sheet is a classified summary of the balances of the accounts remaining open in the ledgers after the balances of the nominal accounts have been transferred to the Profit and Loss Account, but including the balance of that account. The Balance Sheet does not relate to a period, but sets out the book values of the assets, liabilities and capital 'as at' a particular date, so that such a heading as 'Balance Sheet for the year ended' is wrong.

The Balance Sheet does not profess to show the current monetary worth of the undertaking at the date on which it is drawn up, since the values at which many of the assets appear may be far removed from the prices they would realize if sold, while certain intangible assets, such as goodwill, although of considerable value to the business as a going concern, may be completely ignored. In fact, the Balance Sheet merely shows, as a rule, the unexpired residue, after allowing for depreciation through use, effluxion of time, or other cause, of the original cost of the assets, ignoring any change that may have taken place in the purchasing power of money since the expenditure was incurred or to the amount of money it would now cost to replace them.

The Balance Sheet therefore is a statement showing on the one hand the amount of capital sunk or employed in the business and the sources from which it is derived (e.g. capital provided by the proprietors, loan capital, retained profits etc.), and on the other, the form in which such capital is employed, i.e. the unexpired expenditure, at the date of the Balance Sheet, on the various assets by which the total capital fund is represented.

In the Balance Sheet the fixed assets are normally valued at cost, less provision for depreciation, and the current assets at cost or net realizable value, whichever is the lower.

It is customary in England, where the 'horizontal' form of Balance Sheet is used, for the credit balances to be entered on the left-hand side of the Balance Sheet, and the debit balances on the right-hand side, these being the reverse of the sides on which they appear in the ledger.

It is common for companies to dispense with the 'horizontal' form and to present the Profit and Loss Account and Balance Sheet to their members in the 'vertical' form, as mentioned in Chapter VIII, § 15 ( *i* ).

Although there is no statutory order for marshalling the items in the Balance Sheet they should be grouped under suitable sub-headings to render intelligible the most important aspects of the financial position to people who know little about accounts. For limited companies, the best modern practice is exemplified by the specimen Balance Sheets reproduced in Appendix I. On the assets side, separate groupings and sub-totals are given of fixed assets, investments and current (or floating) assets, full details being supplied of the assets comprised in each group. On the liabilities side, the capital is shown first, reserves and undistributed profits being added thereto to disclose, in an extended total, the amount of the proprietors' interest in the net assets. Separate headings and sub-totals are then given of debentures and other long-term liabilities, provisions and current liabilities respectively. Sometimes the total of the current liabilities is deducted from the total of the current assets, in order to reveal the net amount of the working capital at the disposal of the business.

Columns may also be provided to show the corresponding figures for the previous year, This is compulsory for companies registered under any of the Companies Acts.

## § 14. The Accounts of a Sole Trader

**Illustration**

Henry Williams commenced business on February 1st, with cash at bank £500. The following transactions took place during the month:

| | | | | | | £ |
|---|---|---|---|---|---|---|
| 19 .. | | | | | | |
| Feb. | 1. | Bought Goods from W. Martin | .. | .. | .. | 250 |
| | | Purchased Warehouse Fittings for Cash | | .. | .. | 40 |
| ,, | 2. | Sold Goods to T. Crown .. | .. | .. | .. | 80 |
| | | Drew Cheque for Petty Cash | | .. | .. | 20 |
| ,, | 3. | Paid W. Martin on Account | .. | .. | .. | 150 |
| ,, | 4. | Sold Goods to W. Wilson .. | .. | .. | .. | 100 |
| ,, | 5. | Received Cheque from T. Crown | .. | .. | .. | 77 |
| | | Allowed him Discount .. | .. | .. | .. | 3 |
| ,, | 6. | Drew cheque for Wages .. | .. | .. | .. | 7 |
| ,, | 8. | Bought Goods for Cash .. | .. | .. | .. | 30 |
| ,, | 9. | Sold Goods to L. Robinson | .. | .. | .. | 170 |
| ,, | 10. | Purchased Goods from F. Pearson | .. | .. | .. | 130 |
| ,, | 11. | Paid W. Martin in settlement | .. | .. | .. | 95 |
| | | Discount allowed by him .. | .. | .. | .. | 5 |
| ,, | 12. | Paid Carriage on Goods Sold | .. | .. | .. | 2 |
| ,, | 13. | Drew cheque for Wages .. | .. | .. | .. | 7 |
| ,, | 14. | Bought Goods from W. Martin | .. | .. | .. | 150 |
| | | ,, ,, for Cash .. | .. | .. | .. | 40 |
| ,, | 16. | Sold Goods to W. Wilson .. | .. | .. | .. | 180 |
| ,, | 17. | W. Wilson paid on Account | .. | .. | .. | 200 |
| ,, | 18. | Purchased Goods from H. Wood | .. | .. | .. | 75 |
| ,, | 19. | Sold Goods for Cash .. | .. | .. | .. | 92 |
| ,, | 20. | Drew cheque for Wages .. | .. | .. | .. | 7 |
| ,, | 21. | Sent Cheque to H. Wood .. | .. | .. | .. | 72 |
| | | Discount allowed by him .. | .. | .. | .. | 3 |
| ,, | 22. | Sold Goods to T. Crown .. | .. | .. | .. | 130 |
| ,, | 23. | Bought Goods from W. Martin | .. | .. | .. | 240 |
| ,, | 24. | Bought Goods for Cash .. | .. | .. | .. | 73 |
| ,, | 25. | Sent Cheque on Account to W. Martin | .. | .. | 200 |
| ,, | 26. | Received from T. Crown on Account | .. | .. | 100 |
| ,, | 27. | Drew cheque for Wages .. | .. | .. | .. | 7 |
| ,, | 28. | Paid Electric Lighting Account | .. | .. | .. | 5 |
| | | Paid Rent .. .. | .. | .. | .. | 8 |
| | | H. Williams drew for personal use .. | .. | .. | 15 |

Petty Cash Expenditure for the month was:

| | | | | £ |
|---|---|---|---|---|
| Purchases | .. | .. | .. | £4 |
| General Expenses | | .. | .. | 7 |
| Carriage Outwards | | .. | .. | 3 |

Stock on Hand at February 28th, £325.

All cash received was paid into the bank and all payments (other than petty cash expenditure) were made by cheque.

Enter the above transactions in the proper books of prime entry and post to the Ledgers. Prepare Trial Balance, Trading and Profit and Loss Account and Balance Sheet.

## CASH BOOK

Fo. 1

| 19.. | Particulars | Fo. | Discount | Bank | 19.. | Particulars | Fo. | Discount | Bank |
|---|---|---|---|---|---|---|---|---|---|
| | | | £ | £ | | | | £ | £ |
| Feb. 1 | Capital Account | I.L. 1 | | 500 | Feb. 1 | Warehouse Fittings .. | I.L. 11 | | 40 |
| ,, 5 | T. Crown .. | S.L. 1 | 3 | 77 | ,, 2 | Petty Cash .. | I.L. 12 | | 20 |
| ,, 17 | W. Wilson .. | S.L. 2 | | 200 | ,, 3 | W. Martin .. | B.L. 1 | | 150 |
| ,, 19 | Sales .. | I.L. 3 | | 92 | ,, 6 | Wages .. | I.L. 5 | | 7 |
| ,, 26 | T. Crown .. | S.L. 1 | | 100 | ,, 8 | Purchases .. | I.L. 4 | | 30 |
| | | | | | ,, 11 | W. Martin .. | B.L. 1 | 5 | 95 |
| | | | | | ,, 12 | Carriage .. | I.L. 6 | | 2 |
| | | | | | ,, 13 | Wages .. | I.L. 5 | | 7 |
| | | | | | ,, 15 | Purchases .. | I.L. 4 | | 40 |
| | | | | | ,, 20 | Wages .. | I.L. 5 | | 7 |
| | | | | | ,, 21 | H. Wood .. | B.L. 3 | 3 | 72 |
| | | | | | ,, 24 | Purchases .. | I.L. 4 | | 73 |
| | | | | | ,, 25 | W. Martin .. | B.L. 1 | | 200 |
| | | | | | ,, 27 | Wages .. | I.L. 5 | | 7 |
| | | | | | ,, 28 | Lighting .. | I.L. 7 | | 5 |
| | | | | | ,, 28 | Rent .. | I.L. 8 | | 8 |
| | | | | | ,, 28 | Drawings .. | I.L. 2 | | 15 |
| | | | | | ,, 28 | Balance c/d. | | | 191 |
| | | | £3 | £969 | | | | £8 | £969 |
| | | | Fo. 9 | | | | | Fo. 9 | |
| Mar. 1 | Balance b/d. | | | 191 | | | | | |

## SALES DAY BOOK

Fo. 1

| Date | Particulars | Fo. | Amount |
|---|---|---|---|
| 19.. | | | £ |
| Feb. 2 | T. Crown .. .. .. .. .. .. .. .. | S.L. 1 | 80 |
| ,, 4 | W. Wilson .. .. .. .. .. .. .. .. | ,, 2 | 100 |
| ,, 9 | L. Robinson .. .. .. .. .. .. .. .. | ,, 2 | 170 |
| ,, 16 | W. Wilson .. .. .. .. .. .. .. .. | ,, 2 | 180 |
| ,, 22 | T. Crown .. .. .. .. .. .. .. .. | ,, 1 | 130 |
| | | | £660 |
| | | | Fo. 3 |

## PURCHASES DAY BOOK

Fo. 1

| Date | Particulars | Fo. | Amount |
|---|---|---|---|
| 19.. | | | £ |
| Feb. 1 | W. Martin .. .. .. .. .. .. .. | B.L. 1 | 250 |
| ,, 10 | F. Pearson .. .. .. .. .. .. .. .. | ,, 2 | 130 |
| ,, 14 | W. Martin .. .. .. .. .. .. .. .. | ,, 1 | 150 |
| ,, 18 | H. Wood .. .. .. .. .. .. .. .. | ,, 3 | 75 |
| ,, 23 | W. Martin .. .. .. .. .. .. .. .. | ,, 1 | 240 |
| | | | £845 |
| | | | Fo. 4 |

## IMPERSONAL LEDGER
## HENRY WILLIAMS CAPITAL ACCOUNT

Fo. 1

| | | | | 19.. | | | | £ |
|---|---|---|---|---|---|---|---|---|
| | | | | Feb. 1 | Bank .. .. .. | C.B. 1 | | 500 |

## HENRY WILLIAMS CURRENT ACCOUNT

Fo. 2

| 19..<br>Feb. 28 | Bank ..  ..  .. | C.B. 1 | £<br>15<br>22 | 19..<br>Feb. 28 | Net Profit  ..  .. | I.L. 20 | £<br>37 |
|---|---|---|---|---|---|---|---|
| | Balance c/d.  ..  .. | | | | | | |
| | | | £37 | | | | £37 |
| | | | | Mar. 1 | Balance b/d.  ..  .. | | 22 |

## SALES ACCOUNT

Fo. 3.

| 19..<br>Feb. 28 | Trading Account  .. | I.L. 20 | £<br>752 | 19..<br>Feb. 19<br>,, 28 | Bank ..  ..  ..<br>Sundries  ..  .. | C.B. 1<br>S.D.B.1 | £<br>92<br>660 |
|---|---|---|---|---|---|---|---|
| | | | £752 | | | | £752 |

## PURCHASES ACCOUNT

Fo. 4.

| 19..<br>Feb. 8<br>,, 15<br>,, 24<br>,, 28 | Bank ..  ..  ..<br>,,  ..  ..  ..<br>,,  ..  ..  ..<br>Petty Cash  ..  ..<br>Sundries  ..  .. | C.B. 1<br>,,<br>,,<br>I.L. 12<br>B.D.B.1 | £<br>30<br>40<br>73<br>4<br>845 | 19..<br>Feb. 28 | Trading Account  .. | I.L. 20 | £<br>992 |
|---|---|---|---|---|---|---|---|
| | | | £992 | | | | £992 |

## WAGES ACCOUNT

Fo. 5.

| 19..<br>Feb. 6<br>,, 13<br>,, 20<br>,, 27 | Bank ..  ..  ..<br>,,  ..  ..  ..<br>,,  ..  ..  ..<br>,,  ..  ..  .. | C.B. 1<br>,,<br>,,<br>,, | £<br>·7<br>7<br>7<br>7 | 19..<br>Feb. 28 | Profit and Loss Account .. | I.L. 20 | £<br>28 |
|---|---|---|---|---|---|---|---|
| | | | £28 | | | | £28 |

## CARRIAGE ACCOUNT

Fo. 6.

| 19..<br>Feb. 12<br>,, 28 | Bank ..  ..  ..<br>Petty Cash  ..  .. | C.B. 1<br>I.L. 12 | £<br>2<br>3 | 19..<br>Feb. 28 | Profit and Loss Account .. | I.L. 20 | £<br>5 |
|---|---|---|---|---|---|---|---|
| | | | £5 | | | | £5 |

## LIGHTING ACCOUNT

Fo. 7.

| 19..<br>Feb. 28 | Bank ..  ..  .. | C.B. 1 | £<br>5 | 19..<br>Feb. 28 | Profit and Loss Account .. | I.L. 20 | £<br>5 |
|---|---|---|---|---|---|---|---|

## RENT ACCOUNT

Fo. 8.

| 19.. | | | | £ | 19.. | | | | £ |
|---|---|---|---|---|---|---|---|---|---|
| Feb. 28 | Bank .. | .. | C.B. 1 | 8 | Feb. 28 | Profit and Loss Account .. | | I.L. 20 | 8 |

## DISCOUNT ACCOUNT

Fo. 9.

| 19.. | | | | £ | 19.. | | | | £ |
|---|---|---|---|---|---|---|---|---|---|
| Feb. 28 | Sundries .. .. | | C.B. 1 | 3 | Feb. 28 | Sundries .. .. | | C.B. 1 | 8 |
| | Profit and Loss Account .. | | I.L. 20 | 5 | | | | | |
| | | | | £8 | | | | | £8 |

## GENERAL EXPENSES ACCOUNT

Fo. 10.

| 19.. | | | | £ | 19.. | | | | £ |
|---|---|---|---|---|---|---|---|---|---|
| Feb. 28 | Petty Cash .. | .. | I.L. 12 | 7 | Feb. 28 | Profit and Loss Account .. | | L. 20 | 7 |

## WAREHOUSE FITTINGS ACCOUNT

Fo. 11.

| 19.. | | | | £ | | | | | |
|---|---|---|---|---|---|---|---|---|---|
| Feb. 1 | Bank .. | .. | C.B. 1 | 40 | | | | | |

## PETTY CASH ACCOUNT

Fo. 12.

| 19.. | | | | £ | 19.. | | | | £ |
|---|---|---|---|---|---|---|---|---|---|
| Feb. 2 | Bank .. | .. | C.B. 1 | 20 | Feb. 28 | General Expenses | .. | L. 10 | 7 |
| | | | | | | Carriage | .. | L. 6 | 3 |
| | | | | | | Purchases | .. | L. 4 | 4 |
| | | | | | | Balance c/d. .. | .. | | 6 |
| | | | | £20 | | | | | £20 |
| Mar. 1 | Balance b/d. .. | .. | | 6 | | | | | |

## STOCK ACCOUNT

Fo. 13.

| 19.. | | | | £ | | | | | |
|---|---|---|---|---|---|---|---|---|---|
| Feb. 28 | Trading Account | .. | L. 20 | 325 | | | | | |

## SALES LEDGER
## T. CROWN

Fo. 1.

| 19.. | | | | £ | 19.. | | | | £ |
|---|---|---|---|---|---|---|---|---|---|
| Feb. 2 | Sales .. | .. .. | S.D.B.1 | 80 | Feb. 5 | Bank .. | .. .. | C.B. 1 | 77 |
| ,, 22 | ,, .. | .. .. | ,, | 130 | ,, 5 | Discount | .. .. | ,, | 3 |
| | | | | | ,, 26 | Bank .. | .. .. | ,, | 100 |
| | | | | | ,, 28 | Balance c/d. .. | .. | | 30 |
| | | | | £210 | | | | | £210 |
| Mar. 1 | Balance b/d. .. | .. | | 30 | | | | | |

Fo. 2.

## W. WILSON

| 19..<br>Feb. 4<br>„ 16 | Sales .. .. ..<br>„ .. .. .. | S.D.B.1<br>„ | £<br>100<br>180<br>£280 | 19..<br>Feb. 17<br>„ 28 | Bank .. .. ..<br>Balance c/d. .. .. | C.B. 1 | £<br>200<br>80<br>£280 |
| Mar. 1 | Balance b/d. .. .. | | 80 | | | | |

Fo. 3.

## L. ROBINSON

| 19..<br>Feb. 9 | Sales .. .. .. | S.D.B.1 | £<br>170 | | | | |

Fo. 1.

## BOUGHT LEDGER: W. MARTIN

| 19..<br>Feb. 3<br>„ 11<br>„ 11<br>„ 25<br>„ 28 | Bank .. .. ..<br>Discount .. ..<br>Discount .. ..<br>Bank .. .. ..<br>Balance c/d. .. .. | C.B. 1<br>„<br>„<br>„ | £<br>150<br>95<br>5<br>200<br>190<br>£640 | 19..<br>Feb. 1<br>„ 14<br>„ 23 | Purchases .. ..<br>„ .. ..<br>„ .. .. | B.D.B.1<br>„<br>„ | £<br>250<br>150<br>240<br>£640 |
| | | | | Mar 1 | Balance b/d. .. .. | | 190 |

Fo. 2.

## F. PEARSON

| | | | | 19..<br>Feb. 10 | Purchases .. .. | B.D.B.1 | £<br>130 |

Fo. 3.

## H. WOOD

| 19..<br>Feb. 21<br>„ 21 | Bank .. .. ..<br>Discount .. .. | C.B. 1<br>„ | £<br>72<br>3<br>£75 | 19..<br>Feb. 18 | Purchases .. .. | B.D.B.1 | £<br>75<br>£75 |

## TRIAL BALANCE: February, 28th 19..

| Fo. | | Dr | Cr |
|---|---|---|---|
| | | £ | £ |
| I.L. 1 | Capital Account .. .. .. .. .. .. .. .. | | 500 |
| „ 2 | Current Account .. .. .. .. .. .. .. .. | 15 | |
| „ 3 | Sales .. .. .. .. .. .. .. .. .. | | 752 |
| „ 4 | Purchases .. .. .. .. .. .. .. .. | 992 | |
| „ 5 | Wages .. .. .. .. .. .. .. .. | 28 | |
| „ 6 | Carriage .. .. .. .. .. .. .. .. | 5 | |
| „ 7 | Lighting .. .. .. .. .. .. .. .. | 5 | |
| „ 8 | Rent .. .. .. .. .. .. .. .. | 8 | |
| „ 9 | Discount .. .. .. .. .. .. .. .. | | 5 |
| „ 10 | General Expenses .. .. .. .. .. .. .. | 7 | |
| „ 11 | Warehouse Fittings .. .. .. .. .. .. .. | 40 | |
| „ 12 | Petty Cash .. .. .. .. .. .. .. .. | 6 | |
| C.B. 1 | Cash at Bank .. .. .. .. .. .. .. .. | 191 | |
| B.L. 1 | W. Martin .. .. .. .. .. .. .. .. | | 190 |
| „ 2 | F. Pearson .. .. .. .. .. .. .. .. | | 130 |
| S.L. 1 | T. Crown .. .. .. .. .. .. .. .. | 30 | |
| „ 2 | W. Wilson .. .. .. .. .. .. .. .. | 80 | |
| „ 3 | L. Robinson.. .. .. .. .. .. .. .. | 170 | |
| | | £1,577 | £1,577 |

## TRADING AND PROFIT AND LOSS ACCOUNT
### for Month ended February 28th, 19..

Fo. 20.

| | | | £ | | | | £ |
|---|---|---|---|---|---|---|---|
| Purchases | L. 4 | | 992 | Sales | L. 3 | | 752 |
| *Less* Stock at Feb. 28th | L. 13 | | 325 | | | | |
| | | | 667 | | | | |
| Balance, Gross Profit c/d. | | | 85 | | | | |
| | | | £752 | | | | £752 |
| Wages | L. 5 | | 28 | Gross Profit b/d. | | | 85 |
| Carriage | L. 6 | | 5 | Discount | L. 9 | | 5 |
| Lighting | L. 7 | | 5 | | | | |
| Rent | L. 8 | | 8 | | | | |
| General Expenses | L. 10 | | 7 | | | | |
| Net Profit, carried to Current Account | L. 2 | | 37 | | | | |
| | | | £90 | | | | £90 |

## BALANCE SHEET AS AT FEBRUARY 28th, 19..

| | | £ | | | | | £ |
|---|---|---|---|---|---|---|---|
| H. Williams: | | | Fixed Assets: | | | | |
| Capital Account | | 500 | Warehouse Fittings | | | | 40 |
| Current Account: | | | | | | | |
| Net Profit | £37 | | Current Assets: | | | | |
| *Less* Drawings | 15 | | Stock | | | £325 | |
| | | 22 | Sundry Debtors | | | 280 | |
| | | 522 | Cash at Bank | | | 191 | |
| | | | Cash in hand | | | 6 | |
| Current Liabilities: | | | | | | | 802 |
| Sundry Creditors | | 320 | | | | | |
| | | £842 | | | | | £842 |

## § 15. Methods of dispensing with Day Books and Personal Ledgers

The imperative need nowadays of exercising the greatest economy in the field of business administration is prompting firms, even where a mechanized system of accounting has not been installed, to dispense with the use of day books and personal ledgers, and substitute a system under which original documents, or carbon copies, are employed to serve the functions hitherto performed by these books of account. The following is an outline of such a system:

### (a) Purchases and Expenses

1. All suppliers' invoices and credit notes, after being checked as to quantity, description and price, are filed in a folder or other container, in alphabetical order. The greatest care must be taken to prevent the possibility of any being lost or mutilated.

2. At the end of each month, all invoices and credit notes received from each individual supplier during the month are arranged in order of date, and checked with the statement of account rendered by him.

3. Each supplier's invoices and credit notes for the month are then attached to his statement of account, and the whole produced to the director or principal when the cheque in payment of the account is presented to him for signature.

4. The Cash Book contains on the credit side analysis columns for purchases of goods, capital expenditure, rent, rates etc. and each principal classification of expenditure. Payment to creditors entered therein are numbered consecutively, the corresponding numbers being entered on the creditors' statements which, with the official receipts (if any) attached, are filed away in numerical order. The amount of each payment is entered in the Cash Book in the total column and extended into the appropriate analysis column, the periodical totals of which are posted to the debit of the relevant accounts in the impersonal ledger.

This system can only be employed where accounts are settled at regular intervals, and the greatest care must be taken in filing the invoices and credit notes received, and in checking them with the creditors' statements, if it is to operate effectively. When, for any reason, an invoice is not paid on its due date, it should be filed with the invoices for the following month, and a list should be made at the end of each month, of all invoices outstanding, so that none will be overlooked.

When preparing the Profit and Loss Account and Balance Sheet at the end of an accounting period, the total amount of the invoices outstanding for purchases and other expenses, must be debited to the Purchases Account, or the relevant expense accounts, as the case may be, and carried down therein as credit balances to the beginning of the new period. The accounts for the old period will thereby be charged with the whole of the expenditure incurred for that period, whilst the credit balances carried down will represent outstanding liabilities, and will be included in the amount of the creditors in the Balance Sheet. These credit items will automatically be balanced off when the accounts are paid and the postings made from the columnar Cash Book in the new period.

### (b) Sales

In businesses where the transactions with individual customers are relatively few in number and the payment of accounts within a short period of credit can be rigidly enforced, it may be possible to dispense altogether with a Sales Day Book and Sales Ledger, folders containing carbon copies of invoices etc. taking the place of personal accounts.

Three or more copies of each sales invoice (or credit note) are prepared simultaneously, one being sent to the customer, another placed in the current folder or other receptacle maintained for him, and another used in building up the total figures for posting to the impersonal ledger. Other copies, if required, can be used for further analysis or statistical purposes.

When a customer sends a remittance the invoices and credit notes discharged thereby are withdrawn from the folder and filed permanently. The balance owing by the customer at any time will thus be the sum of the invoices (less credit notes) remaining in the folder. (If desired, the amounts of all invoices, and credit notes issued to the customer may be entered on the inner page of the folder as a 'recapitulation statement'. When an account is paid, the amount of the remittance is deducted from the total amount due, the balance outstanding being thus clearly indicated.)

To enable the appropriate entries to be made in the impersonal ledger, detailed lists will be prepared (probably by means of an adding and calculating machine) of each day's sales invoices and credit notes, and the net total of sales (less credits), as computed by the machine, posted to the debit of the Debtors Control Account and to the credit of Sales Account. The daily totals of cash received and discounts allowed, as shown by the Cash Book, will be credited to the Debtors Control Account, the balance of which, at any time, will then be the total of the outstanding debtors for sales, and should be capable of reconciliation with the balances disclosed by the customers' folders.

## CHAPTER II

# TOTAL [OR CONTROL] ACCOUNTS
# AND SECTIONAL BALANCING

## § 1. Total [or Control] Accounts

A Total Account is an account to which are debited and credited the total amounts of all the transactions which have been debited and credited in detail to individual ledger accounts. A Total Account in respect of a particular ledger therefore operates as a control account for that ledger, since the balance of the Total Account at any time should equal the sum of the balances of all the individual accounts within that ledger, and provides a check on the accuracy of such balances. Total Accounts are alternatively referred to as Control Accounts.

In a business of any magnitude, it is desirable to raise Total Accounts in respect of debtors and creditors ledgers for the following reasons:

1. Since the balances of the Total Accounts at any time should represent the totals of the balances appearing in the debtors and creditors ledgers, if it is desired to prepare interim Profit and Loss Accounts and Balance Sheets, the balances of the Total Accounts can be entered in the Trial Balance, thus obviating the time and labour involved in extracting schedules of the balances of the individual Debtors' and Creditors' Accounts.

2. If kept under the control of a responsible official, and not made accessible to the ledger clerks whose duty it is to post to the debtors and creditors ledgers, the Total Accounts operate as a control over those ledgers, and constitute a valuable feature of the system of internal check.

3. Where the two sides of a Trial Balance do not agree, with the aid of Total Accounts the difference may be located to the particular ledger or ledgers in which the errors exist, and the work of checking can be confined to that ledger or ledgers, thus avoiding waste of time in balancing.

The Total Accounts may, if desired, be kept in the impersonal ledger, from which it will then be possible to extract a Trial Balance without reference to the personal ledgers, since the Total Accounts will provide the totals of the personal account balances. It is preferable, however, to keep the Total Accounts in a separate book under responsible control, so that a check can be imposed upon the personal ledgers, whilst making it unnecessary to expose the impersonal ledger to the clerk in charge of the Total Accounts.

### (a) Total Debtors Account

This account is debited with the sum of all the items which have been debited in detail to individual personal accounts in the sales ledgers, and credited with the sum of all the items which have been credited to such accounts. The balance of the Total Debtors Account should therefore be equal to the sum of all the balances appearing in the sales ledgers.

It must be remembered, however, that the sales ledgers may contain a few accounts showing credit balances, and the balance of the Total Debtors Account will only represent the difference between the total of the debit balances and the total of the credit balances (if any) in the sales ledgers. When, therefore, the balance of the Total Account is agreed with the schedule of balances extracted from the sales ledgers, balances should be brought down on both sides of the Total Account, representing respectively the total of the debit balances and the total of the credit balances in those ledgers.

The Total Debtors Accounts will contain on the debit side the totals of:
1. Opening debit balances.
2. Sales made during the period.
3. Dishonoured bills and cheques (if any).
4. Cash paid to debtors (if any).
5. Transfers and other items (if any).

And on the credit side:
1. Opening credit balances (if any).
2. Cash received from debtors during the period.
3. Discounts allowed to debtors.
4. Returns inwards, and allowances.
5. Bills receivable.
6. Bad debts written off.
7. Transfers and other items (if any).

The opening balances will be brought down from the previous period, and will agree with the total of the last schedule of debtors.

The total amount of sales for the period will be obtained from the sales day book, the totals of which should be posted monthly or at other periodical intervals to the Total Debtors Account.

Dishonoured bills will be obtained from an analysis of the journal (see (c) below). This should not involve any serious difficulty, as the number of such items will probably not be great. Should any of the dishonoured bills have been discounted, the entries debiting the personal accounts in the sales ledger will probably have been made direct from the cash book. In such cases the adjusting entries in the Total Debtors Account should have been made simultaneously with the cash postings. The whole of these dishonoured bill items can easily be checked, however, as the *Remarks* column in the bills receivable book should show at a glance all bills which have been discounted, and all which have been dishonoured.

The total amount of cash received from debtors which has been posted to the sales ledgers during the period will be obtained from the *Sales Ledger* column in the cash book and posted to the Total Debtors Account at monthly or other intervals.

Discounts allowed will be obtained from the totals of the *Discount* column on the debit side of the cash book, and from the *Cash Discount* column (if any) in the bills receivable book. Where no such column is provided in the bills receivable book, the discount will either have been entered in the *Discount* column in the cash book, or a separate journal entry will have been made for each item. In the latter case the total will be obtained from an analysis of the journal.

Returns inwards will be obtained from the totals of the sales returns book, which will be posted to the Total Debtors Account periodically. Allowances will be obtained from the analysis of the journal.

Bills receivable will be obtained from the total of the bills receivable book, which will be posted periodically to the Total Debtors Account.

The bad debts written off will be obtained from an analysis of the journal.

### (b) Total Creditors Account

This account operates as a control account of the bought ledgers and should disclose a balance equal to the total of all the individual balances in those ledgers. The account is raised in a similar manner to the Total Debtors Account.

On the credit side will be found:

1. The opening credit balances.
2. Purchases during the period.
3. Transfers and other items (if any).

And on the debit side:

1. Opening debit balances (if any).
2. Cash paid to creditors during the period.
3. Discounts received.
4. Returns outwards.
5. Bills payable.
6. Transfers and other items (if any).

The opening balances will be brought down from the previous period, and will agree with the total of the last schedule of creditors.

The total amount of goods purchased during the period will be obtained from the purchases day book.

The total amount of cash paid to creditors during the period will be obtained from the *Bought Ledger* column in the cash book.

Discounts received will be obtained from the totals of the *Discount* column on the credit side of the cash book, and from the *Cash Discount* column (if any) in the bills payable book. If no such column is provided in the bills payable book, and the items have not been passed through the *Discount* column in the cash book, the total will be obtained from an analysis of the journal.

Returns outwards will be obtained from the totals of the purchases returns book.

Bills payable will be obtainable from the totals of the bills payable book.

### (c) *Journal*

In any system of Total Accounts it is essential to pass every item through a book of prime entry before posting it to the ledger. The journal is consequently of considerable importance for the purpose of recording those items for which no special book of prime entry is provided.

The following is a convenient ruling of a journal used solely to record transfers.

**Illustration (1)**

TRANSFER JOURNAL

| Date | Account to be debited | Folio | Amount | Folio | Account to be credited | Date |
|------|----------------------|-------|--------|-------|------------------------|------|
|      |                      |       | £      |       |                        |      |
|      |                      |       |        |       |                        |      |

Where there are not too many ledgers, the transfer journal may be incorporated in the ordinary journal, which may be ruled so that the required totals can be arrived at without additional analysis, as shown in the following illustration:

**Illustration (2)**

## JOURNAL

| Date | Particulars | Folio | Bad Debts £ | Sundries £ | Sales Ledgers A-K £ | Sales Ledgers L-R £ | Sales Ledgers S-Z £ | Bought Ledgers A-L £ | Bought Ledgers M-Z £ | Folio | Sundries £ | Sales Ledgers A-K £ | Sales Ledgers L-R £ | Sales Ledgers S-Z £ | Bought Ledgers A-L £ | Bought Ledgers M-Z £ |
|---|---|---|---|---|---|---|---|---|---|---|---|---|---|---|---|---|
| | | | | | | DEBITS | | | | | | | CREDITS | | | |
| July 15 | Bad Debt – Jones .. | | 15 | | | | | | | | | 15 | | | | |
| | Transfer – Smith .. | | | | | | 140 | | | | | | | | | 140 |
| Dec. 31 | Correction – drawings charged to Personal Account Mr Brown .. | | | 50 | | | | | | | | 50 | | | | |
| | Allowance from B.M.X. Ltd .. .. | | | | | | | 10 | | | 10 | | | | | |

**Illustration (3)**

On January 1st, the sales ledger balances were £16,000 debit and £64 credit, and the bought ledger balances at the same date £8,760 credit and £59 debit.

During the six months ended June 30th, sales amounted to £46,000; purchases to £39,340; cash received from debtors £42,240; cash paid to creditors £39,552; discount allowable £1,760; discount receivable £1,648; returns inwards £850; returns outwards £620; bills receivable £1,780; bills payable £2,740; dishonoured Bills £190; discount allowed to debtors, but subsequently disallowed £10; bad debts written off £320; a debit balance in the bought ledger transferred to the sales ledger, £13.

The sales ledger balances at June 30th amounted to £15,208 debit and £9 credit; and the bought ledger balances to £3,559 credit and £65 debit.

From these particulars prepare a Total Debtors Account and a Total Creditors Account, bringing down the balances as at June 30th.

### TOTAL DEBTORS ACCOUNT

| | | | £ | | | | | £ |
|---|---|---|---|---|---|---|---|---|
| Jan. 1 | Balance b/f. | | 16,000 | Jan. 1 | Balance b/f. | | | 64 |
| June 30 | Sales | | 46,000 | June 30 | Cash | | | 42,240 |
| | Dishonoured Bills | | 190 | | Discount Allowable | | | 1,760 |
| | Discount disallowed | | 10 | | Returns Inwards | | | 850 |
| | Transfers | | 13 | | Bills Receivable | | | 1,780 |
| | Balance c/d. | | 9 | | Bad Debts | | | 320 |
| | | | | | Balance c/d. | | | 15,208 |
| | | | £62,222 | | | | | £62,222 |
| July 1 | Balance b/d. | | 15,208 | July 1 | Balance b/d. | | | 9 |

### TOTAL CREDITORS ACCOUNT

| | | | £ | | | | | £ |
|---|---|---|---|---|---|---|---|---|
| Jan. 1 | Balance b/f. | | 59 | Jan. 1 | Balance b/f. | | | 8,760 |
| June 30 | Cash | | 39,552 | June 30 | Purchases | | | 39,340 |
| | Discount Receivable | | 1,648 | | Transfers | | | 13 |
| | Returns Outwards | | 620 | | Balance c/d. | | | 65 |
| | Bills Payable | | 2,740 | | | | | |
| | Balance c/d. | | 3,559 | | | | | |
| | | | £48,178 | | | | | £48,178 |
| July 1 | Balance b/d. | | 65 | July 1 | Balance b/d. | | | 3,559 |

*Notes to Illustration:* The accuracy of the Total Accounts should be tested by drawing up a Trial Balance, including the balances on these accounts in lieu of the totals of the schedules of debtors and creditors. If this Trial Balance agrees it may be assumed that the Total Accounts are correct, but it is advisable to check all postings to the impersonal ledgers to avoid the possibility of compensating errors.

### (d) Columnar Books

Where only a small number of personal ledgers is kept the books of prime entry should be ruled with columns to correspond with the personal ledgers in order to provide the totals of amounts posted to each ledger. In a case where there are two sales ledgers and one bought ledger the rulings shown in the following illustration would suffice.

**Illustration**

## CASH BOOK

| Dr. | | | | | | | | | | | | | | | | | | | | Cr. |
|---|---|---|---|---|---|---|---|---|---|---|---|---|---|---|---|---|---|---|---|---|

**Dr.**

| Date | Particulars | Folio | Discount £ | Details | Bank £ | Sales Ledger Town — Discount £ | Sales Ledger Town — Amt. £ | Sales Ledger Country — Discount £ | Sales Ledger Country — Amt. £ | Impersonal — Amt. £ |
|---|---|---|---|---|---|---|---|---|---|---|

**Cr.**

| Date | Particulars | Folio | Discount £ | Details | Bank £ | Purchases Ledger — Discount £ | Purchases Ledger — Amt. £ | Impersonal Ledger — Amt. £ |
|---|---|---|---|---|---|---|---|---|

## SALES DAY BOOK

| Date | Name | Particulars | Folio | Total £ | Sales Ledger Town £ | Sales Ledger Country £ |
|---|---|---|---|---|---|---|

## PURCHASES DAY BOOK

| Date | Name | Particulars | Folio | Amount £ |
|---|---|---|---|---|

### (e) Separate Day Books or Subsidiary Analyses

Where the number of ledgers is too large to make the above system of analysis practicable a different method must be employed. In some cases it may be advisable to keep a separate set of books of prime entry for each ledger, or for each group of ledgers. In the latter case, each book will be analysed in the manner set out above.

In other instances, it may be expedient to use only one set of books, but to prepare periodical analyses thereof on separate sheets. To facilitate this analysis, each ledger must be given a distinguishing letter or symbol, which should be entered in the folio column of the day book in respect of items posted to that ledger. This method is explained more fully in § 2 below.

Where the number of ledgers is considerable, it will usually be found that a system of machine accounting is employed, and the machines themselves will accumulate totals as postings proceed. These totals can be entered in the Total Accounts, thus obviating the necessity for analysis.

### § 2. Sectional Balancing or Self-balancing Ledgers

The separate proving of individual ledgers forms an important part of a system of control. Where none of the methods of analysis described above can conveniently be adopted the following scheme of sectional balancing may be used:

1. A prime entry should be made for each transaction. No transfers from one ledger to another should be made without the entry first being passed through the journal. This rule should be most rigidly enforced, as otherwise great difficulty may be experienced in agreeing the balances of the particular ledger with the Total Account applicable to that ledger.

2. In the books of prime entry posting references should be made as follows: each ledger should be distinguished by a particular letter, which should be written boldly just outside the folio column in the book of prime entry in every posting reference to that ledger. The folio column will, of course, contain merely the page of the ledger concerned, and by glancing down the pages of any of the books of prime entry, the letters denoting the ledgers to which the postings have been made will be apparent.

3. At the end of each month or other interval lists should be extracted of all the items posted to each ledger from each book of prime entry.

The totals of these lists referring to any book of prime entry should agree with the total of that book for the period.

4. When such lists have been checked, the amounts thereof should be entered into a summary book, which should have a separate column or page for each ledger in use. The summary book will thus contain particulars of all the entries in the books of prime entry correctly analysed, so that, with the balances brought forward from the previous period, a Total Account will result for each ledger.

5. The clerks who extract the ledger balances should take no part in the postings to those ledgers, and no ledger balances should be taken out by the clerk who prepares the analysis sheets for entry in the summary book.

6. The summary book should be under the immediate control of a responsible official, and no ledger clerk should be allowed access to it.

Ledgers are commonly mis-named 'self-balancing' where counterparts of the Total Accounts in the impersonal ledger are kept in the personal ledgers themselves for the purpose of enabling an independent Trial Balance to be prepared from each ledger. The Total Accounts, being equal but opposite, cancel each other out in the Trial Balance of the books as a whole. This practice is, however, unnecessary and undesirable, as it not only involves the Total Accounts being prepared twice merely to serve a theoretical purpose but nullifies a valuable feature of the system of internal check, by making the total figures available to the ledger clerks.

The following is an illustration of a sales ledgers summary book, ruled for a business having five sales ledgers.

**Illustration**

SALES LEDGER SUMMARY BOOK

| Date | Particulars | Ledgers | | | | | | Date | Particulars | Ledgers | | | | | |
|---|---|---|---|---|---|---|---|---|---|---|---|---|---|---|---|
| | | A | B | C | D | E | Total | | | A | B | C | D | E | Total |
| 19.. Jan. 1 „ 31 | Balance b/f.   .. Sales ..            .. Dishonoured Bills Discount Transfers Cash ..            .. Balance c/d.   .. | | | | | | £ | 19.. Jan. 1 „ 31 | Balance b/f.   .. Cash ..            .. Discount Allowed Returns Inwards Bills Receivable Bad Debts Transfers        .. Balance c/d.   .. | | | | | | £ |
| 19.. Feb. 1 | Balance b/d.   .. | | | | | | | 19.. Feb. 1 | Balance b/d.   .. | | | | | | |

*Notes to Illustration:* A separate page in the summary book could be allotted to each ledger if desired.

The total column will be found useful for purposes of checking with the monthly totals in the books of prime entry, and can be used as a Total Debtors Account.

## § 3. The Location of Errors

If it is found that the Trial Balance agrees when the balance of a Total Account is inserted, but that the list of ledger account balances does not agree with the balance of the Total Account for that ledger, it may be that there is a compensating error in the impersonal ledger. For example, if the Sales Account is overstated owing to an error in the cast of a day book, since the same inaccurate amount of sales will have been debited to the Total Debtors Account, the Trial Balance will agree, but the list of balances in the sales ledger will not agree with the balance of the sales ledger Total Account. In some instances it may be found that the Trial Balance would agree if the total of the schedule of balances were inserted instead of the balance of the Total Account. If such is the case, the error is *prima facie* an omission of a total in posting to the Total Account, or the posting of an incorrect figure thereto.

If it is found that the total of the balances on a particular ledger does not agree with the balance of the Total Account relating thereto, the following steps should be taken to locate the cause of the difference:

1. Check the additions of the books of prime entry relating to the ledger concerned, paying particular attention to 'carry forwards'.
2. Check the analysis columns in all the books of prime entry.
3. Re-check the postings to the Total Accounts.
4. Check the postings made in the ledger.
5. Re-check the balances extracted from the ledger.
6. Re-cast the list of balances.
7. Check the opening list of balances with the accounts in the ledger concerned, seeing that the balances are properly brought down.

If these steps fail to bring the error to light, it will be necessary to analyse the ledger and agree the totals of the books of prime entry with the analysis.

If the Trial Balance disagrees, apart from the Total Accounts, or if no Total Accounts are kept, the procedure for the discovery of the cause of difference will be on the following lines:

After the Trial Balance has been re-cast, the items should be scanned to see whether the amount of the error is capable of being interpreted as a mis-posting. Thus, if the difference is £9, it may arise through £54 being posted as £45, and all items of that amount in the books of prime entry should be subjected to scrutiny. This, however, is a very fortuitous test, and not much time should be spent on it.

If the amount of the error is divisible by two, it is possible either that a posting of half the amount has been made to the wrong side of the ledger, or that a balance of half the amount has been entered in the wrong column of the Trial Balance.

If these tests do not reveal the error, the balances should be re-checked in detail on to the Trial Balance.

If the error still remains undetected, the whole of the books of prime entry must be cast, and, if necessary, the postings to the ledger re-checked. All carry forwards must be watched, since transposed figures may be the cause of the discrepancy. In casting the ledgers, exceptional care should be taken to see that the correct balances have been carried down, and that the accounts actually balance; and it may be necessary to check the opening balances from the previous Balance Sheet and schedules.

If Total Accounts have not been kept, these may, in the last resource, be compiled, and with their aid the error should certainly be located.

## CHAPTER III

# PROVISIONS AND RESERVES, DEPRECIATION ETC.

### § 1. Definitions of Provision, Reserve and Reserve Fund

As will be seen in Chapter VIII, definitions of the expressions 'provision' and 'reserve' are given in the *Companies Acts 1948* and *1967*, and are required to be used in the accounts of limited companies.

A 'provision' means an amount written off to provide for depreciation, or diminution in value, of assets, or retained to provide for a known liability, the amount of which cannot be ascertained with any substantial accuracy. A 'reserve' must *not* include an amount set aside for any such purpose and must therefore, by implication, represent undistributed profits or surplus assets. In the interests of consistency these interpretations of the Companies Acts are used to define these expressions throughout this work.

Provisions, made for expected losses and contingencies, are charges against profits, since the true profit can only be ascertained after such provisions are made. Reserves are appropriations of profit, the assets by which they are represented being retained to form part of the capital employed in the business.

Provisions are usually shown in the Balance Sheet by way of deductions from the assets in respect of which they are made. General reserves and reserve funds are shown as part of the proprietors' interests.

A Capital Reserve is one which is not regarded as available for distribution through the Profit and Loss Appropriation Account, e.g. premiums on the issue of shares, profits on re-issue of forfeited shares, profits on sales of fixed assets, a surplus arising on the revaluation and writing-up of fixed assets and profits earned prior to incorporation.

A 'reserve fund' is a reserve which is represented by investment outside the business. The Institute of Chartered Accountants recommends that, unless the reserve is represented by specifically earmarked investments, in securities or other assets, realizable as and when required, at not less than the amount of the reserve, the term 'fund' is inappropriate. Sinking Fund investments for the repayment of loans and insurance policies are instances of specific reserve funds.

### § 2. Provision for Bad Debts

When a debt is found to be irrecoverable, it should be written off as a loss by means of a journal entry debiting Bad Debts Account and crediting the account of the defaulting debtor. At the end of the accounting period the Bad Debts Account is closed by transfer to the Profit and Loss Account. Should a debt which has been written off as bad be subsequently recovered, in whole or in part, the debtor's personal account should be debited and Bad Debts Account credited, the cash received then being credited to the debtor's account. This is preferable to posting the amount recovered direct from the Cash Book to the credit of the Bad Debts Account without making any entry in the debtor's personal account, since it is desirable, for future reference, that this account should contain a full history of the occurrence.

After all debts which are known to be irrecoverable have been written off, there may still be some doubtful accounts for which it would be prudent to provide. A provision for bad or doubtful debts may be calculated either by reference to the amounts of the specific debts which are regarded as doubtful, or by way of a percentage on the total debts outstanding. In many businesses experience shows that the percentage of bad debts to outstanding debtors does not fluctuate widely from year to year and in such cases this method may, as a rule, quite safely be employed.

When the actual bad debts are written off, they should be transferred to the debit of Bad Debts Account, and when the final accounts for the period are prepared, the necessary provision may be debited and carried down to the credit of this account, the balance being transferred to Profit and Loss Account.

### Illustration (1)

The outstanding debtors of a business at January 1st, 19.., are £20,000, and at December 31st, 19.., £25,000. Provision is made for doubtful debts at 4 per cent. on the outstanding debtors. Bad debts written off during the year amount to £750. Show the Bad Debts Account for the year, and the amount to be written off to Profit and Loss Account.

### BAD DEBTS ACCOUNT

| 19.. | | £ | 19.. | | £ |
|---|---|---|---|---|---|
| Dec. 31 | Debts written off  ..    .. | 750 | Jan. 1 | Provision b/f. 4% on £20,000  .. | 800 |
| | Provision c/d. 4% on £25,000  .. | 1,000 | Dec. 31 | Profit and Loss Account .. | 950 |
| | | £1,750 | | | £1,750 |
| | | | 19.. | | |
| | | | Jan. 1 | Provision b/d.  ..    ..    .. | 1,000 |

Alternatively, a separate account may be kept for the provision for doubtful debts, the balance of which is adjusted at the end of the accounting period to the amount of the provision it is desired to carry forward, by a transfer either to the Bad Debts Account or direct to Profit and Loss Account.

### Illustration (2)

Assuming the facts as stated in the previous example:

### BAD DEBTS ACCOUNT

| 19.. | | £ | 19.. | | £ |
|---|---|---|---|---|---|
| Dec. 31 | Sundry Debtors (detailed)    .. | 750 | Dec. 31 | Profit and Loss Account .. | 950 |
| | Provision for Doubtful Debts Account: | | | | |
| |     Increase in Provision  ..    .. | 200 | | | |
| | | £950 | | | £950 |

## PROVISION FOR DOUBTFUL DEBTS ACCOUNT

| 19.. Dec. 31 | Provision c/d., 4% on £25,000 .. | £ 1,000 | 19.. Jan. 1 Dec. 31 | Provision b/f. 4% on £20,000 .. Bad Debts Account .. .. | £ 800 200 |
|---|---|---|---|---|---|
| | | £1,000 | | | £1,000 |
| | | | 19.. Jan. 1 | Provision b/d. .. .. .. | 1,000 |

*Note:* If preferred, the increase in the provision can be transferred direct to Profit and Loss Account, in which the bad debts written off and the increase in the provision will be debited thus:

Bad Debts written off    ..       ..       ..       ..    £750
Provision for Doubtful Debts – Increase    ..       ..    200
                                                    ———   £950

The following illustration incorporates the recovery of debts previously written off as bad:

### Illustration (3)

At January 1st, a company had a Provision for Doubtful Debts of £500, against specific debtors, made up of B, £120; C, £100; D, £60; K, £60; L, £5; M, £61; N, £94. During the year to December 31st, the following debts proved to be bad: A, £15; B, £240; C, £210; D, £60; E, £90; F, £180. Debts were recovered for amounts written off as bad in previous years, viz. G, £70; H, £110. Of the debts provided for at January 1st, the following were paid during the year: K, £34; L, £5; M, £50, and the balances of K's and M's Accounts, were written off. At December 31st, the following debts were deemed doubtful, and a provision was created against them: N, £47; P, £140; Q, £155; R, £10; S, £320. Show the Bad Debts Account and how the amounts would appear in the Profit and Loss Account.

### BAD DEBTS ACCOUNT

| 19.. Jan/Dec | Debtors – amounts written off as bad: | | £ | 19.. Jan. 1 | Balance – provision b/forward: .. | | £ |
|---|---|---|---|---|---|---|---|
| | | A    15 | | | | B   120 | |
| | | B   240 | | | | C   100 | |
| | | C   210 | | | | D    60 | |
| | | D    60 | | | | K    60 | |
| | | E    90 | | | | L     5 | |
| | | F   180 | | | | M    61 | |
| | K (60-34) | 26 | | | | N    94 | |
| | M (61-50) | 11 | 832 | | | | 500 |
| Dec. 31 | Balance – provision carried down: | | | Jan/Dec | Debtors – bad debts recovered: | G    70 | |
| | | N    47 | | | | H   110 | |
| | | P   140 | | | | ——— | 180 |
| | | Q   155 | | | | | |
| | | R    10 | | Dec. 31 | Profit and Loss Account: Bad Debts written off *less* recoveries £(832—180) | 652 | |
| | | S   320 | 672 | | Increase in provision £(672—500) .. .. | 172 | |
| | | | | | | ——— | 824 |
| | | | £1,504 | | | | £1,504 |
| | | | | 19.. Jan. 1 | Balance – provision b/down .. .. .. | | 672 |

The provision for doubtful debts reduces the estimated realizable amount of book debts and is shown on the Balance Sheet as follows:

| *Current Assets:* | | £ | £ |
|---|---|---|---|
| Debtors    ..      ..      .. | | × | |
| *Less* Provision for bad debts .. | | £672 | |
| | | —— | × |

## § 3. Provisions for Cash Discounts

Where cash discounts are allowed and received, the amounts of the debts and liabilities received and paid will be less than the amounts appearing in the books, but opinions differ whether provision should be made for discounts to be allowed on outstanding balances when preparing the final accounts. On the one hand, it may be contended that unless the discounts allowable and receivable on outstanding debtors and creditors are taken into account, the book debts and liabilities will be overstated in the Balance Sheet which will not, therefore, disclose the true position of affairs. The counter argument is that as cash discount is an allowance for payment within a specified time, it is analogous to interest on loans and should enter into the computation of profit for the period which enjoys, or is deprived of, the use of the money. The point is unimportant, and so long as the same procedure is followed consistently, no objection can be taken whichever method is employed. No credit should, however, be taken for discount to be received from creditors unless provision is made for the discount to be allowed to debtors.

Where provision for discounts is made, it may either be carried down in the Discount Account or recorded in a Provision for Discounts Account, which should be operated in the same way as a Provision for Doubtful Debts Account.

Provision for discount allowable will be calculated on:

(*a*) good debts (i.e. debts outstanding after provision for bad debts); *and*

(*b*) on debts which can be expected to be paid within the stipulated period of credit.

In the Balance Sheet the provisions for discounts should be deducted, inset, from the trade creditors and debtors respectively.

### Illustration

Discounts allowed to customers during the year were £1,800; discounts received from creditors were £800; the debtors at the close of the year were £12,000 and creditors were £6,000. A provision for bad debts of £800 has been made; the time during which discount was receivable and discount allowable is granted had not yet expired either for the debtors or for the creditors. Provide for discount allowed and discount received at $2\frac{1}{2}$ per cent.

### DISCOUNT ACCOUNT

| | | | £ | | | | | £ |
|---|---|---|---|---|---|---|---|---|
| Cash Book – discounts allowed | .. | .. | 1,800 | Cash Book – discounts received | .. | .. | | 800 |
| Balance c/d $2\frac{1}{2}$ % on | | | | Balance c/d $2\frac{1}{2}$ % on | | | | |
|     Debtors £11,200 (12,000—800) | .. | .. | 280 |     Creditors £6,000 | .. | .. | .. | 150 |
| | | | | Profit and Loss Account | .. | .. | .. | 1,130 |
| | | | ———— | | | | | ———— |
| | | | £2,080 | | | | | £2,080 |
| Balance b/d | .. | ..    ..    .. | 150 | Balance b/d | .. | ..    ..    .. | | 280 |

Alternatively – separate accounts could be opened for discounts allowed and discounts received respectively; Profit and Loss Account would then be debited with £2,080 for discounts allowed and credited with £950 for discounts received.

## § 4. Outstanding Liabilities

It usually happens that at the date of balancing the accounts certain liabilities which have become due or are accruing have not been recorded in the books. These may include such items as rent or rates, charges for gas, water, electric light, telephone, or similar items consumed or incurred during the period, for which no account has yet been received.

All such items must be brought into account by debiting the nominal account concerned and either carrying down the outstandings in the nominal accounts themselves or by crediting a Sundry Creditors' Account (sometimes called an Outstanding Liabilities Account).

The former method is more usually adopted, and the following illustration shows how the accounts are affected.

**Illustration**

The books of a manufacturer are closed at December 31st, and the following debit balances appear in the Trial Balance:

        Rent and Rates     ..         ..         ..         ..     £765
        Gas, Electric Light and Water         ..         ..     £112

One quarter's rent, amounting to £145, is due but not yet paid. A demand note for local rates for the half-year ending March 31st following, amounting to £90, has been received but has not been paid. There are outstanding liabilities not yet brought into account for gas, £16; water £9.

Show the accounts as they will appear when the books are closed off.

### RENT AND RATES ACCOUNT

| 19.. Dec. 31 | Expenses paid (detailed)     ..<br>Balance Outstanding c/d.     ..<br>Rent     ..     ..     ..<br>Rates (1 Quarter) ..     .. | £145<br>45 | £<br>765<br><br><br>190 | 19.. Dec. 31 | Profit and Loss Account     ..     .. | £<br>955 |
|---|---|---|---|---|---|---|
| | | | £955 | | | £955 |
| | | | | 19.. Jan.  1 | Balance b/d.     ..     ..     .. | 190 |

### GAS, ELECTRIC LIGHT AND WATER ACCOUNT

| 19.. Dec. 31 | Expenses paid (detailed)     ..<br>Balance Outstanding c/d.:<br>Gas     ..     ..     ..<br>Water    ..     ..     .. | £16<br>9 | £<br>112<br><br>25 | 19.. Dec. 31 | Profit and Loss Account     ..     .. | £<br>137 |
|---|---|---|---|---|---|---|
| | | | £137 | | | £137 |
| | | | | 19.. Jan.  1 | Balance b/d.     ..     ..     .. | 25 |

It will be seen from the foregoing illustration that the charges to Profit and Loss Account are increased to the extent of the sums outstanding; and the balances brought down are, for the purpose of the Balance Sheet, treated as liabilities.

When the charge is paid during the succeeding period, it will be debited to the nominal account, but will be offset by the balance brought down, so that it will not be included in the charge to Profit and Loss Account for that period.

The same principle can be applied to any nominal accounts; but where purchases are concerned it is better, where possible, to pass all the invoices through the purchases day book (where one is kept) during the period to which they relate.

Where the system of debiting the nominal accounts and crediting Sundry Creditors' Account (or Outstanding Liabilities Account) is adopted, at the commencement of the succeeding accounting period, the Sundry Creditors' Account must be debited and the relevant nominal accounts credited.

## § 5. Payments in Advance

It frequently happens that payments for expenses such as rent, rates, insurances etc. made during a period refer wholly or partly to a succeeding period. The treatment of such items is similar to that of outstanding liabilities.

**Illustration**

The books of a manufacturer are closed at December 31st, and included in the Trial Balance is a debit balance of £260 for Rent and Rates Account.

The sum of £40 for local rates for the half-year ending March 31st following was paid on December 1st.

Show the adjustment on the nominal account for the purpose of the Balance Sheet.

### RENT AND RATES ACCOUNT

| 19.. | | £ | 19.. | | £ |
|------|------|------|------|------|------|
| Dec. 31 | Expenses (detailed)  ..  .. | 260 | Dec. 31 | Balance c/d.. | |
| | | | | One Quarter's Rates, paid in advance | 20 |
| | | | | Profit and Loss Account  ..  .. | 240 |
| | | £260 | | | £260 |
| 19.. | | | | | |
| Jan. 1 | Balance b/d.  ..  ..  .. | 20 | | | |

It will be seen from the foregoing illustration that the charge against profit for the current period is reduced by the amount carried forward to the succeeding period. This amount will appear in the Balance Sheet as an asset and will increase the charge to Profit and Loss Account in the succeeding period. Where there are several items of expenditure paid in advance, it is common for the total to be included in the Balance Sheet under a composite description such as: 'Prepayments' or 'Amounts paid in Advance'.

## § 6. Definition of Depreciation; Considerations necessary to assess its rate

Depreciation is the exhaustion of the effective life of a fixed asset owing to 'use' or obsolescence. It may be computed as that part of the cost of the asset which will not be recovered when the asset is finally put out of use. The object of providing for depreciation is to spread the expenditure, incurred in acquiring the asset, over its effective lifetime; the amount of the provision, made in respect of an accounting period, is intended to represent the proportion of such expenditure, which has expired during that period.

The term 'use' has been employed in the above definition of depreciation to cover not only the wear and tear, but also exhaustion of the contents of wasting assets such as mines and quarries, and the effluxion of time in the case of assets such as leases, for which there is a time limit of ownership.

Obsolescence occurs when it becomes beneficial to replace an asset, before the end of its normal effective life, by a new and improved type of asset or process, which will perform the same or a similar service more efficiently and more economically. Obviously, it is difficult to provide for obsolescence, as it is an element which cannot be foreseen with accuracy; a new invention may arrive most unexpectedly.

Depreciation is sometimes divided broadly into two classes:
(a) Internal, and (b) External.

Internal depreciation arises from the operation of any cause natural to or inherent in the asset itself, e.g. wear and tear of plant and machinery.

External depreciation arises from the operation of forces apart from the asset itself, e.g. obsolescence of plant and machinery.

The term 'depreciation' must not be confused with 'fluctuation', which implies a temporary change in market value quite distinct from any depreciation which may occur.

In order to assess the rate of depreciation, consideration must be given to three factors: the cost of the asset, its effective life (by which is meant the period during which the asset will give profitable service to the business) and its probable residual value when its effective life comes to an end. The last two factors are not capable of precise calculation and can only be determined by estimation.

In estimating the effective life, the various forces operating to cause depreciation must be carefully distinguished. It is usually possible to forecast the depreciation by use, such as wear and tear, with reasonable accuracy, given experience and knowledge of the business concerned; but the external forces such as obsolescence are so uncertain that often they are ignored until the actual loss caused by them has been ascertained.

Consideration must be given to the state of repair in which it is intended to keep the assets (some machines can have their life time considerably extended by periodical renewal of certain components), and the skill of the operators using the assets. The effective life has been defined as 'the period beyond which it does not pay either to keep the asset in use by repair, or to renew a part of it'.

### § 7. The Necessity of Providing for Depreciation

At the end of its effective life, the asset ceases to earn revenue, i.e. the capital value has expired and the asset will have to be replaced or a substitute found.

Provision for depreciation is the setting aside, out of the revenue of an accounting period, the estimated amount by which the capital invested in the asset has expired during that period. It is the provision made for the loss or expense incurred through using the asset for earning profits, and should therefore be charged against those profits as they are earned.

If the whole of the profits were withdrawn during the life of the asset, without providing for depreciation, monies would not be accumulated out of revenue, for replacing it; consequently, when it became necessary to replace the asset new capital would have to be found.

If depreciation is not provided for, the books will not contain a true record of revenue or capital. If the asset were hired instead of purchased, the hiring fee would be charged against the profits; having been purchased, the asset is, in effect, then hired by capital to revenue, and the true profit cannot be ascertained until a suitable charge for the use of the asset has been made. Moreover, unless provision is made for depreciation, the Balance Sheet will not present a true and fair view of the state of affairs; assets should be shown at a figure which represents that part of their value on acquisition, which has not yet expired.

It is beyond the scope of this book to discuss whether or not a limited company is under any legal obligation to provide for depreciation on its fixed and wasting assets. From the standpoints of business finance and accountancy it is argued that, since depreciation occurs irrespective of the financial results of a business, it should be recorded like any other transaction, if the books are to show a true and fair view.

Under the simplest methods of providing for depreciation, the amount of the provision is credited to the Asset Account and debited to a Depreciation Account, which in due course is transferred to the debit of Profit and Loss Account.

The effect of writing off depreciation in this way is illustrated in the following simple Balance Sheets:

A is a sole trader whose summarized Balance Sheet, before providing for depreciation, is as follows:

| | £ | | £ |
|---|---|---|---|
| Capital .. | 11,000 | Sundry Assets .. | 7,000 |
| Creditors .. | 2,000 | Machinery | 6,000 |
| Profit and Loss Account | 3,000 | Cash .. | 3,000 |
| | £16,000 | | £16,000 |

If A provides £600 for depreciation, he will see profits available for withdrawal of £2,400:

| | £ | | £ |
|---|---|---|---|
| Capital .. | 11,000 | Sundry Assets .. | 7,000 |
| Creditors .. | 2,000 | Machinery | 5,400 |
| Profit and Loss Account | 2,400 | Cash .. | 3,000 |
| | £15,400 | | £15,400 |

If these profits are withdrawn, £600 will be retained in the business in the form of cash. If the same provision for depreciation is made annually during a ten years' effective life of the asset, there will be £6,000 cash available for replacing machinery; the capital outlay has been made good, as its value expired, out of revenue.

If A were consistently to withdraw the whole profits, without providing for depreciation, his Balance Sheet on the expiry of the life of the asset would be:

| | £ | | £ |
|---|---|---|---|
| Capital | 11,000 | Sundry Assets | 7,000 |
| Creditors | 2,000 | Profit and Loss Account: | |
| | | Loss on Machinery | 6,000 |
| | £13,000 | | £13,000 |

In that case, in order to replace the machinery, fresh capital would have to be introduced.

Provision for depreciation is normally based upon the original capital outlay plus the cost of any major renewals, which increase the revenue-earning capacity of the asset (but not those which merely maintain it), less the estimated scrap value.

Strictly, depreciation of an asset, which is acquired during an accounting period, is calculated on a time basis, from the date of acquisition to the date of the Balance Sheet. However, where several fixed assets of about the same value are acquired at different dates during an accounting period, the average date of their acquisition is often taken for computing the depreciation of them all. Moreover, in some businesses it is customary to charge a full year's depreciation on the assets in use at the end of an accounting year, irrespective of the date on which they were acquired.

The treatment of obsolescence depends upon the facts. It may be shown, from past experience, that important developments or changes in particular types of assets can be expected at fairly regular intervals. If so, this factor should be taken into consideration in estimating the effective life. Usually, however, obsolescence occurs unexpectedly, and should be provided for as and when it arises. Frequently the loss through obsolescence is so large that it cannot be met out of the revenue of any one period, and must be provided for either out of capital or by being written off gradually over a period of years as an abnormal loss.

Another question, to which increasing emphasis has been given in recent years, is the impact of inflation on the replacement cost of assets and whether, in times of rising prices, it is desirable and proper to base the provision for depreciation, not upon the actual historical cost of assets, as has been the practice in periods of relative price stability, but upon estimated expenditure that will be incurred in replacing the assets for which the provision is made.

The provision for replacement of assets and the measurement of profits are complementary problems and the combined effect of the steep rise in price levels and heavy taxation have caused doubt to be thrown on the validity of the methods of ascertaining profit hitherto generally followed. Broadly, it is contended that the capital employed in a business should be measured, not by the amount of money contributed by the proprietors, including profits left in the business, but by the capacity of that money to purchase goods and equipment. Accordingly it is maintained that the true profit can only be ascertained after providing out of revenue the funds necessary to replace stocks and fixed assets at the sums which will have to be expended for that purpose. It is pointed out that where the revenue itself is inflated by the rise in price levels, the charges against revenue should be measured by a similar yardstick if true profits are to be ascertained.

The suggestion has been made, and strongly advocated in some quarters, that the values at which fixed assets appear in the Balance Sheet should be written up to the estimated present cost of replacing them by identical assets in a comparable condition, and that thereafter depreciation charged against profits should be calculated on the written-up values. A more recent suggestion is that the accounts prepared on traditional lines should be accompanied or followed by supplementary accounts in which items representing forms of wealth other than money are translated into monetary units of current purchasing power. The supplementary accounts would thus show the effect on the undertaking of changes in the value of money in which the accounts are expressed.

The Council of the Institute of Chartered Accountants in England and Wales published in 1952 a memorandum wherein, whilst recognizing the urgent need for the maintenance of industrial efficiency by the making of adequate provision for the replacement of lost capital, they indicated that they saw no need to modify the advice previously given that the charge for depreciation should be based on historical cost, and that any amounts set aside to finance increased costs should be treated as transfers to reserve. The Council considered that the proposal to base the charge for depreciation on other than historical cost is at variance with the accountancy practice hitherto generally followed, of treating as charges to revenue the actual monetary cost of stocks consumed and capital expired, and would lead to inconsistency and confusion. It was pointed out that the logical application of the method advocated by those who desire a change would require them not only to make charges against revenue on new bases for stocks and fixed assets, but also to provide for the diminished purchasing power of cash and other liquid assets to be used in the business. It would be illogical, in ascertaining profit, to treat as a necessary charge the cost of maintaining the purchasing power of money provided by the issue of fixed preference or loan capital, whilst ignoring the corresponding reduction in the obligation, expressed in terms of purchasing power, to the holders of that capital. If the new conception were adopted, the holders of preference shares might be deprived of dividends without acquiring any capital benefit.

The Council recommended directors of companies to consider the effects of the rise in price levels and the relative merits of (a) relying upon the company's ability to raise new capital as and when it may be required for meeting increased replacement costs, and (b) the desirability of setting aside and accumulating out of profits such sums for this purpose as may be practicable. These considerations may be a matter of major importance in determining the amount of profits which, from the standpoint of financial prudence, should be regarded as available for dividend.

The Council further recommended that in order to emphasize that, as a matter of prudence, the amount set aside is, for the time being, regarded as not available for distribution, it should normally be treated as a specific capital reserve for increased cost of replacement of assets. For Balance Sheet purposes fixed assets should not, as a general rule, be written up on the basis of estimated replacement costs, especially in the absence of a measure of stability in the price level.

The Council of the Association of Certified and Corporate Accountants, on the other hand, came down on the side of the advocates of the replacement value basis. They recommend that the charge for depreciation be divided into two parts:

(a) the basic charge, calculated on recorded cost and designed to recover such cost over the life of the asset; and

(b) a supplementary charge for the difference by which the basic charge falls short of the amount which would appear as an expense if it were calculated on a basis homogeneous with maintenance, repair and other expenses.

They pointed out that the practical application of this principle would not create great technical difficulties. The system of accounts would remain unchanged up to and including the Trading or Manufacturing Account, where the basic depreciation would be accounted for. The balance – the trading profit – could be brought to a Depreciation Adjustment Account where the supplementary depreciation could be charged. The balance would be carried to Profit and Loss Account. The basic depreciation would continue to be deducted from the book value of the assets in the Balance Sheet and the supplementary depreciation brought to a special replacement provision account.

In the methods of providing for depreciation described and illustrated in the succeeding section, it is assumed that the charge to Profit and Loss Account for depreciation is based on the original monetary cost of the assets concerned, any further sums necessary to provide for the increased cost of replacement being set aside as reserves.

It will be observed that the Sinking Fund and Endowment Policy Methods aim at accumulating funds outside the business with which to replace the assets in due course, whereas the other methods aim at writing off the original cost of the assets, and retaining as working capital the funds thus kept in the business.

## § 8. The Principal Methods of Providing for Depreciation

### (a) The Fixed Instalment or Straight Line Method

A fixed percentage of the original cost of the asset is written off each year, so as to reduce the asset to nil or break-up value at the end of its life, repairs and small renewals are charged to revenue.

This method is recommended by the Institute of Chartered Accountants as the most suitable in the majority of cases; the full text of the recommendation is quoted on pages 62 to 64 of this work. It is a method commonly used for leases having a comparatively short life, though it is not as accurate as the Annuity method explained in (c) below.

The Reducing Instalment method, explained in (b) below, is frequently used for plant and machinery; but the 'straight line' method is safer to employ as it is more certain in its results and the only difficulty is the calculation of depreciation on additions and the need to keep proper plant registers.

Although the depreciation, charged against profit for an asset, is constant from year to year, there is really a reducing burden when it is considered that the funds retained thereby will themselves earn income. Moreover, fluctuations in the total depreciation charge may be somewhat violent if blocks of assets are wholly written off and not immediately replaced.

In order to calculate the depreciation charge under this system it is necessary to classify the machinery under effective life periods, separate accounts being used for each group having the same expectation of time of utility. The way in which the depreciation charge is ascertained and the asset account kept, is shown in the following illustration:

**Illustration (1)**

Machinery and Plant, Class A, of ten years' effective life, is acquired for £4,000.

Additions are made at the commencement of the second and third years of the value of £400 and £250 respectively.

Show the Asset Account depreciated by 10 per cent. per annum on the original cost, and show how the depreciation is arrived at.

### DEPRECIATION RECORD
### MACHINERY AND PLANT. CLASS A. TEN YEARS' LIFE

| Year | | 1 | 2 | 3 | 4 | 5 | 6 | 7 | 8 | 9 | 10 | Depreciation | Jnl. Fo. | Year |
|---|---|---|---|---|---|---|---|---|---|---|---|---|---|---|
| 1 | Book Value | £ 4,000 | £ | £ | £ | £ | £ | £ | £ | £ | £ | £ | | 1 |
| | Depreciation | 400 | | | | | | | | | | 400 | | |
| 2 | Book Value | 3,600 | 400 | | | | | | | | | | | 2 |
| | Depreciation | 400 | 40 | | | | | | | | | 440 | | |
| 3 | Book Value | 3,200 | 360 | 250 | | | | | | | | | | 3 |
| | Depreciation | 400 | 40 | 25 | | | | | | | | 465 | | |
| 4 etc. | Book Value | 2,800 | 320 | 225 | | | | | | | | | | 4 etc. |

### MACHINERY AND PLANT
### CLASS A. TEN YEARS' LIFE

| | | | | | £ | | | | | | £ |
|---|---|---|---|---|---|---|---|---|---|---|---|
| Year 1 | Cash .. | .. | .. | .. | 4,000 | Year 1 | Depreciation .. | .. | .. | | 400 |
| | | | | | | | Balance c/d. .. | .. | .. | | 3,600 |
| | | | | | £4,000 | | | | | | £4,000 |
| Year 2 | Balance b/d. .. | .. | .. | | 3,600 | Year 2 | Depreciation .. | .. | .. | | 440 |
| | Cash (Additions) | .. | .. | | 400 | | Balance c/d. .. | .. | .. | | 3,560 |
| | | | | | £4,000 | | | | | | £4,000 |
| Year 3 | Balance b/d. .. | .. | .. | | 3,560 | Year 3 | Depreciation .. | .. | .. | | 465 |
| | Cash (Additions) | .. | .. | | 250 | | Balance c/d. .. | .. | .. | | 3,345 |
| | | | | | £3,810 | | | | | | £3,810 |
| Year 4 | Balance b/d. .. | .. | .. | | 3,345 | | | | | | |

*Notes to Illustration:* The Depreciation Record is not a Ledger Account, but a statistical statement, the compilation of which is essential if the depreciation is to be calculated under this system. The annual depreciation figures are totalled in the last column, and this total figure is journalized.

Where the additions are not made at the beginning of the year, the first year's charge may require adjustment, i.e. depreciation may have to be calculated for part of a year. In subsequent years a full year's depreciation must be entered in the appropriate column.

The resulting balances on the statement, when added together, should equal the balance on the Ledger Account concerned.

Since the *Companies Act 1948*, as amended by the 1967 Act, requires the cost of fixed assets and the aggregate amount of the provision made for depreciation thereon to be disclosed in the Balance Sheet, together with details showing the aggregate amount of acquisitions or disposals that have taken place during the period under review, it is expedient to retain the assets in the accounts at original cost, and credit the provision for depreciation to a separate account, instead of to the asset accounts. When an asset is sold or discarded, the original cost is transferred from the Asset Account, and the total provision made for depreciation thereon from the Provision for Depreciation Account, to a Fixed Assets Disposals Account, the balance of which will represent the written down value of the asset at the date on which it is sold or discarded. The proceeds of sale (if any) will be credited to this account, which will then disclose the profit or loss arising from the transaction.

By this method, the balances on the fixed assets accounts will always represent the cost of the fixed assets in use, and the balances of the Provision for Depreciation Accounts the aggregate amount of depreciation thereon to date.

**Illustration (2)**

B & Co commenced manufacturing on January 1st, Year 1. They purchased plant as follows:

|          |          | £     |
|----------|----------|-------|
| Year 1   |          |       |
| Jan.  1  | .. .. .. | .. 4,000 |
| July  1  | .. .. .. | .. 2,000 |
| Year 3   |          |       |
| April 1  | .. .. .. | .. 3,000 |

Depreciation is provided for on the 'straight line' method at the rate of 10 per cent. per annum from the date of purchase, a separate account being opened for the provision made.

On June 30th, Year 2, the machine which had been purchased on July 1st, Year 1 was sold for £1,200.

Write up the Ledger Accounts involved.

### PLANT ACCOUNT

| Year 1 | | £ | Year 1 | | £ |
|--------|--------|-------|--------|--------|-------|
| Jan. 1 | Machine    .. .. .. | 4,000 | Dec. 31 | Balance c/d.   .. .. .. | 6,000 |
| July 1 | ,,          .. .. .. | 2,000 | | | |
| | | £6,000 | | | £6,000 |
| Year 2 | | | Year 2 | | |
| Jan. 1 | Balance b/d.  .. .. .. | 6,000 | June 30 | Plant Disposal Account – Plant Sold | 2,000 |
| | | | Dec. 31 | Balance c/d.   .. .. .. | 4,000 |
| | | £6,000 | | | £6,000 |

## PLANT ACCOUNT (*continued*)

| Year 3 | | £ | Year 3 | | £ |
|---|---|---|---|---|---|
| Jan. 1 | Balance b/d. .. .. .. | 4,000 | Dec. 31 | Balance c/d. .. .. .. | 7,000 |
| Apr. 1 | Machine .. .. .. | 3,000 | | | |
| | | £7,000 | | | £7,000 |
| Year 4 | | | | | |
| Jan. 1 | Balance b/d. .. .. .. | 7,000 | | | |

## PROVISION FOR DEPRECIATION ON PLANT ACCOUNT

| Year 1 | | £ | Year 1 | | £ | £ |
|---|---|---|---|---|---|---|
| Dec. 31 | Balance c/d. .. .. .. | 500 | Dec. 31 | Profit and Loss Account: | | |
| | | | | 12 months on £4,000 .. | 400 | |
| | | | | 6 ,, £2,000 .. | 100 | |
| | | | | | | 500 |
| | | £500 | | | | £500 |
| Year 2 | | | Year 2 | | | |
| June 30 | Plant Disposal Account .. .. | 200 | Jan. 1 | Balance b/d. .. .. | 500 |
| | (on £2,000 for 1 year) | | Dec. 31 | Profit and Loss Account: | | |
| Dec. 31 | Balance c/d. .. .. .. | 800 | | 12 months on £4,000 .. | 400 | |
| | | | | 6 ,, £2,000 .. | 100 | |
| | | | | | | 500 |
| | | £1,000 | | | | £1,000 |
| Year 3 | | | Year 3 | | | |
| Dec. 31 | Balance c/d. .. .. .. | 1,425 | Jan. 1 | Balance b/d. .. .. | 800 |
| | | | Dec. 31 | Profit and Loss Account: | | |
| | | | | 12 months on £4,000 .. | 400 | |
| | | | | 9 ,, £3,000 .. | 225 | |
| | | | | | | 625 |
| | | £1,425 | | | | £1,425 |
| | | | Year 4 | | | |
| | | | Jan. 1 | Balance b/d. .. .. | 1,425 |

## PLANT DISPOSAL ACCOUNT

| Year 2 | | £ | Year 2 | | £ |
|---|---|---|---|---|---|
| June 30 | Plant Account: | | June 30 | Provision for Depreciation Account: | |
| | Cost of Plant sold .. .. | 2,000 | | Depreciation for 1 year on £2,000 | 200 |
| | | | | Cash – Sale .. .. .. | 1,200 |
| | | | | Profit and Loss Account .. .. | 600 |
| | | £2,000 | | | £2,000 |

*Note:* The Plant will appear in the Balance Sheet at December 31st, Year 3, as:

| | | |
|---|---|---|
| Plant at cost .. .. .. .. | £7,000 | |
| *Less* Provision for Depreciation .. | 1,425 | |
| | £5,575 | |

## (b) The Reducing Instalment or Diminishing Balance method

A fixed rate per cent. on the *diminishing* value of the asset is written off each year, so as to reduce the asset to break-up value at the end of its life, repairs and small renewals being charged to revenue. This method is commonly used for plant, fixtures, furniture etc. Among the advantages claimed for this method are the following:

1. The early years are charged with the largest amounts for depreciation, thus reducing the asset in the same proportion as its loss in value for resale accrues, it being recognised that normally a new asset loses its saleable value most rapidly when first put into use. (This introduces into the question a factor which strictly does not affect depreciation, viz. fluctuation in value.)

2. The asset is never completely written off, so that some charge is made to revenue in every year, whereas under the straight line method there will be no charge to revenue in years after the expiration of the basic period adopted for computing the rate of depreciation, even though the asset remains in use.

3. The asset loses efficiency as it gets older and the charge for depreciation should decrease accordingly. (This is not true of all assets.)

4. It is very simple in operation, and the total charge to revenue for depreciation and repairs is more equal each year than under method (*a*), since, while the charge for depreciation is heavy in the early years, that for repairs is lighter, repairs increasing as depreciation decreases; whereas under (*a*) the charge for depreciation is constant, while repairs will tend to increase.

This argument may be sound when applied to an individual asset. In practice, when there are a large number of assets which are renewed at intervals, the total cost of repairs, taking old assets with new, and the total depreciation charge, will not fluctuate much from year to year. When a single asset is considered, however, the objection to the fixed instalment method can be overcome by charging to revenue an equal sum each year for repairs and crediting such sum to a Provision for Repairs Account. The cost of repairs is charged to the Provision for Repairs Account and, if the annual sum has been calculated correctly, the provision will be exhausted at the expiration of the asset's life (*see* § 9 following).

It is desirable, however, under the reducing instalment system, to re-value the asset periodically to ensure the effectiveness of the rate utilized, and it is inadvisable to apply this system to assets whose life is so short as to involve an unduly heavy charge in the earlier years.

Among the disadvantages of this method is the danger that too low a percentage may be adopted, with a result that over the life of the asset full depreciation will not be provided; and owing to its simplicity of operation, assets are grouped in such a way that individual assets are difficult to identify, and the residue of each may be left in the asset account even after the asset has been scrapped. The latter disadvantage can readily be overcome, however, by the maintenance of adequate plant registers. In the later years, the interest earned on the profit retained by writing off the depreciation frequently exceeds the actual charge for those years.

**Illustration (1)**

Balance of Plant Account at January 1st, Year 1, £1,726.
Additions during Year 1, £321, and Year 2, £57.

Depreciation at 10 per cent. per annum on the Reducing Instalment System. Calculate to nearest £.

### PLANT ACCOUNT

| | | | | £ | | | | | £ |
|---|---|---|---|---|---|---|---|---|---|
| Year 1 | | | | | Year 1 | | | | |
| Jan. 1 | Balance b/f. | .. | .. | .. 1,726 | Dec. 31 | Depn. 10% on £1,726 | .. | .. | 173 |
| Dec. 31 | Additions | .. | .. | .. 321 | | Balance c/d. | .. | .. | 1,874 |
| | | | | £2,047 | | | | | £2,047 |
| Year 2 | | | | | Year 2 | | | | |
| Jan. 1 | Balance b/d. | .. | .. | .. 1,874 | Dec. 31 | Depn. 10% on £1,874 | .. | .. | 187 |
| Dec. 31 | Additions | .. | .. | .. 57 | | Balance c/d. | .. | .. | 1,744 |
| | | | | £1,931 | | | | | £1,931 |
| Year 3 | | | | | | | | | |
| Jan. 1 | Balance b/d. | .. | .. | .. 1,744 | | | | | |

On occasions it may be preferable to adopt the reducing instalment system in the early years, and then to change over to the fixed instalment system to ensure that the asset is completely depreciated.

As already explained in connection with the fixed instalment system, the asset may be left in the books at cost, the depreciation being credited to a Provision for Depreciation Account.

### (c) *The Annuity method*

The capital locked up in the asset is regarded as earning interest; a constant annual charge for depreciation is credited to the asset account, so calculated that during the life of the asset it will write off its cost (less any scrap value), plus the interest earned. The interest earned is debited to the asset account; it is calculated at a fixed rate per cent., but on the reducing balance. Actuarily, the cost of the asset is regarded as providing an annuity during its life, the value of the annuity being the annual charge to depreciation.

This is the most scientific system when investment is not desired outside the business, but may be criticized from the viewpoint that it introduces an uncertain element, i.e. the rate of interest, which is bound to be arbitrarily arrived at, and also that it is not sufficiently conservative in the early years, so that if obsolescence supervenes the true depreciation will not have been provided; but the latter objection can be met by shortening the estimated life on which the calculations are based. The annuity system is particularly applicable to long leases, where no additions are made to the asset during its life. It is not generally used for plant, since, when additions are made from time to time, these would at once necessitate further calculations.

### Illustration

Lease costing £6,000 for a term of seven years. Depreciation by the Annuity Method at $6\frac{1}{2}$ per cent. per annum, calculations being taken to the nearest £.

## LEASE ACCOUNT

| | | | | £ | | | | | £ |
|---|---|---|---|---|---|---|---|---|---|
| Year 1 Jan. 1 | Cash .. .. | .. | .. | 6,000 | Year 1 Dec. 31 | Depreciation Account .. | .. | | 1,094 |
| Dec. 31 | Interest Account 6½ % | .. | .. | 390 | | Balance c/d. .. | .. | .. | 5,296 |
| | | | | £6,390 | | | | | £6,390 |
| Year 2 Jan. 1 | Balance b/d. .. | .. | .. | 5,296 | Year 2 Dec. 31 | Depreciation Account .. | .. | | 1,094 |
| Dec. 31 | Interest Account 6½ % | .. | .. | 344 | | Balance c/d. .. | .. | .. | 4,546 |
| | | | | £5,640 | | | | | £5,640 |
| Year 3 Jan. 1 | Balance b/d. .. | .. | .. | 4,546 | Year 3 Dec. 31 | Depreciation Account .. | .. | | 1,094 |
| Dec. 31 | Interest Account 6½ % | .. | .. | 295 | | Balance c/d. .. | .. | .. | 3,747 |
| | | | | £4,841 | | | | | £4,841 |
| Year 4 Jan. 1 | Balance b/d. .. | .. | .. | 3,747 | Year 4 Dec. 31 | Depreciation Account .. | .. | | 1,094 |
| Dec. 31 | Interest Account 6½ % | .. | .. | 244 | | Balance c/d. .. | .. | .. | 2,897 |
| | | | | £3,991 | | | | | £3,991 |
| Year 5 Jan. 1 | Balance b/d. .. | .. | .. | 2,897 | Year 5 Dec. 31 | Depreciation Account .. | .. | | 1,094 |
| Dec. 31 | Interest Account 6½ % | .. | .. | 188 | | Balance c/d. .. | .. | .. | 1,991 |
| | | | | £3,085 | | | | | £3,085 |
| Year 6 Jan. 1 | Balance b/d. .. | .. | .. | 1,991 | Year 6 Dec. 31 | Depreciation Account .. | .. | | 1,094 |
| Dec. 31 | Interest Account 6½ % | .. | .. | 129 | | Balance c/d. .. | .. | .. | 1,026 |
| | | | | £2,120 | | | | | £2,120 |
| Year 7 Jan. 1 | Balance b/d. .. | .. | .. | 1,026 | Year 7 Dec. 31 | Depreciation Account .. | .. | | 1,094 |
| Dec. 31 | Interest Account 6½ % | .. | .. | 68 | | | | | | |
| | | | | £1,094 | | | | | £1,094 |

*Note:* The annual amount of depreciation under this system is calculated from actuarial tables compiled for the purpose employing the formula:

$$\frac{i}{1-(1+i)^{-n}} = \text{Periodic rent of annuity whose present value is 1}$$

where i is the annual rate of interest and $^n$ is the number of years of the term.

Consequently the annual depreciation is:

$$£6,000 \times \frac{\frac{6\cdot5}{100}}{1-(1+\frac{6\cdot5}{100})^{-7}}$$

$$= 6,000 \times \frac{6\cdot5}{100(1-\frac{1}{1\cdot554})}$$

$$= 6,000 \times 0\cdot1823 = £1,094 \text{ to the nearest £.}$$

The interest, which is debited to the asset account, is credited to revenue, it diminishes each year as the balance on the asset account reduces; the depreciation, which is credited to the asset account, is debited to revenue and is a constant figure. There is therefore an increasing net charge each year to revenue as the following illustration shows.

**Illustration (2)**

## DEPRECIATION AND INTEREST ACCOUNT

| | | £ | | | | £ |
|---|---|---|---|---|---|---|
| Year 1 Dec. 31 | Lease Account – Depreciation   .. | 1,094 | Year 1 Dec. 31 | Lease Account – Interest ..    .. <br> Profit and Loss Account ..    .. | | 390 <br> 704 |
| | | £1,094 | | | | £1,094 |
| Year 2 Dec. 31 | Lease Account – Depreciation   .. | 1,094 | Year 2 Dec. 31 | Lease Account – Interest ..    .. <br> Profit and Loss Account ..    .. | | 344 <br> 750 |
| | | £1,094 | | | | £1,094 |
| Year 3 Dec. 31 | Lease Account – Depreciation   .. | 1,094 | Year 3 Dec. 31 | Lease Account – Interest ..    .. <br> Profit and Loss Account ..    .. | | 295 <br> 799 |
| | | £1,094 | | | | £1,094 |
| Year 4 Dec. 31 | Lease Account – Depreciation   .. | 1,094 | Year 4 Dec. 31 | Lease Account – Interest ..    .. <br> Profit and Loss Account ..    .. | | 244 <br> 850 |
| | | £1,094 | | | | £1,094 |
| Year 5 Dec. 31 | Lease Account – Depreciation   .. | 1,094 | Year 5 Dec. 31 | Lease Account – Interest ..    .. <br> Profit and Loss Account ..    .. | | 188 <br> 906 |
| | | £1,094 | | | | £1,094 |
| Year 6 Dec. 31 | Lease Account – Depreciation   .. | 1,094 | Year 6 Dec. 31 | Lease Account – Interest ..    .. <br> Profit and Loss Account ..    .. | | 129 <br> 965 |
| | | £1,094 | | | | £1,094 |
| Year 7 Dec. 31 | Lease Account – Depreciation   .. | 1,094 | Year 7 Dec. 31 | Lease Account – Interest ..    .. <br> Profit and Loss Account ..    .. | | 68 <br> 1,026 |
| | | £1,094 | | | | £1,094 |

*Note:* In practice this account might not be used, depreciation and interest being debited and credited to their separate ledger accounts and thence to Profit and Loss Account.

The increasing charge to revenue each year is more apparent than real. As the profits available for distribution are reduced each year by the charge, they are presumably retained in the business as working capital assets. These assets should themselves earn profits; if these are assumed to be at the rate of no more than $6\frac{1}{2}$ per cent. per annum, the equality of the annual charge to revenue will be seen from the following table:

| Year to Dec. 31st | Charge to Profit and Loss Account as above | Amount of interest deemed to be earned by accumulations of assets retained in business as a result of the charge for depreciation | | Real net charge to Profit and Loss Account |
|---|---|---|---|---|
| | | $6\frac{1}{2}\%$ on | Amount | |
| | £ | £ | £ | £ |
| Year 1 | 704 | — | — | 704 |
| Year 2 | 750 | 704 | 46 | 704 |
| Year 3 | 799 | 1,454 | 95 | 704 |
| Year 4 | 850 | 2,253 | 146 | 704 |
| Year 5 | 906 | 3,103 | 202 | 704 |
| Year 6 | 965 | 4,009 | 261 | 704 |
| Year 7 | 1,026 | 4,974 | 322 | 704 |

### (d) The Depreciation Fund with Investment method

A constant amount is debited to the Profit and Loss Account each year, and credited to a Depreciation Fund Account; an equivalent amount of cash is invested outside the business, in gilt-edged or other securities, and allowed to accumulate at compound interest so as to produce the required amount at the completion of a given number of years.

This system is adopted when money is invested *outside the business* to replace an asset at the end of its life; it avoids the strain on the working capital of the business which might occur if substantial sums had to be withdrawn from the business at any time.

The cash to be invested each year is ascertained by reference to compound interest tables. Such tables show that at $6\frac{1}{2}$ per cent. an annuity of £1, invested at the end of each of seven years, will amount to a sum of £8·523.

To amount to a sum of £6,000, the cash to be so invested each year would need to be:

$$\frac{6,000}{8\cdot523} \times £1 \text{ or } £704$$

**Illustration**

Lease costing £6,000 for term of seven years; depreciated by the Depreciation Fund with Investment method at $6\frac{1}{2}\%$ per annum; replaced at end of term by new lease.

### DEPRECIATION FUND ACCOUNT

| | | £ | | | £ |
|---|---|---|---|---|---|
| Year 2 Dec. 31 | Balance c/d. .. .. .. | 1,454 | Year 1 Dec. 31 | Profit and Loss Account .. .. | 704 |
| | | | Year 2 Dec. 31 | Cash: Interest .. .. .. | 46 |
| | | | ,, | Profit and Loss Account .. .. | 704 |
| | | £1,454 | | | £1,454 |
| Year 3 Dec. 31 | Balance c/d. .. .. .. | 2,253 | Year 3 Jan. 1 | Balance b/d. .. .. .. | 1,454 |
| | | | Dec. 31 | Cash: Interest .. .. .. | 95 |
| | | | ,, | Profit and Loss Account .. .. | 704 |
| | | £2,253 | | | £2,253 |
| Year 4 Dec. 31 | Balance c/d. .. .. .. | 3,103 | Year 4 Jan. 1 | Balance b/d. .. .. .. | 2,253 |
| | | | Dec. 31 | Cash: Interest .. .. .. | 146 |
| | | | ,, | Profit and Loss Account .. .. | 704 |
| | | £3,103 | | | £3,103 |
| Year 5 Dec. 31 | Balance c/d. .. .. .. | 4,009 | Year 5 Jan. 1 | Balance b/d. .. .. .. | 3,103 |
| | | | Dec. 31 | Cash: Interest .. .. .. | 202 |
| | | | ,, | Profit and Loss Account .. .. | 704 |
| | | £4,009 | | | £4,009 |
| Year 6 Dec. 31 | Balance c/d. .. .. .. | 4,974 | Year 6 Jan. 1 | Balance b/d. .. .. .. | 4,009 |
| | | | Dec. 31 | Cash: Interest .. .. .. | 261 |
| | | | ,, | Profit and Loss Account .. .. | 704 |
| | | £4,974 | | | £4,974 |
| Year 7 Dec. 31 | Lease Account .. .. .. | 6,000 | Year 7 Jan. 1 | Balance b/d. .. .. .. | 4,974 |
| | | | Dec. 31 | Cash: Interest .. .. .. | 322 |
| | | | ,, | Profit and Loss Account .. .. | 704 |
| | | £6,000 | | | £6,000 |

## INVESTMENT ACCOUNT

| | | £ | | | £ |
|---|---|---|---|---|---|
| Year 1<br>Dec. 31 | Cash .. .. .. .. | 704 | Year 2 | | |
| Year 2<br>Dec. 31 | ,, .. .. .. .. | 750 | Dec. 31 | Balance c/d. .. .. .. | 1,454 |
| | | £1,454 | | | £1,454 |
| Year 3<br>Jan. 1<br>Dec. 31 | Balance b/d. .. .. ..<br>Cash .. .. .. .. | 1,454<br>799 | Year 3<br>Dec. 31 | Balance c/d. .. .. .. | 2,253 |
| | | £2,253 | | | £2,253 |
| Year 4<br>Jan. 1<br>Dec. 31 | Balance b/d. .. .. ..<br>Cash .. .. .. .. | 2,253<br>850 | Year 4<br>Dec. 31 | Balance c/d. .. .. .. | 3,103 |
| | | £3,103 | | | £3,103 |
| Year 5<br>Jan. 1<br>Dec. 31 | Balance b/d. .. .. ..<br>Cash .. .. .. .. | 3,103<br>906 | Year 5<br>Dec. 31 | Balance c/d. .. .. .. | 4,009 |
| | | £4,009 | | | £4,009 |
| Year 6<br>Jan. 1<br>Dec. 31 | Balance b/d. .. .. ..<br>Cash .. .. .. .. | 4,009<br>965 | Year 6<br>Dec. 31 | Balance c/d. .. .. .. | 4,974 |
| | | £4,974 | | | £4,974 |
| Year 7<br>Jan. 1 | Balance b/d. .. .. .. | £4,974 | Year 7<br>Dec. 31 | Cash .. .. .. .. | £4,974 |

## LEASE ACCOUNT

| | | £ | | | £ |
|---|---|---|---|---|---|
| Year 1<br>Jan. 1 | Cash .. .. .. .. | £6,000 | Year 7<br>Dec. 31 | Depreciation Fund .. .. | £6,000 |

*Notes to Illustration:*

1. For simplicity, interest on the investment has been brought in yearly, without deduction of income tax and invested as received. It has been assumed that the total invested will realize its book value.

2. £322, the interest received during the seventh year, £4,974, the cash received by realizing the investment and £704, the profits due to be set aside at the end of the seventh year, provide £6,000 to purchase a new lease.

3. Often instructions are given to accumulate interest (e.g. interest on building society shares can be added to the principal sum and not be paid out in cash); a book entry must then be made debiting the Investment Account and crediting the Depreciation Fund Account.

4. The fact that in practice the investment will never realize exactly its book value owing to market fluctuations, brokers' commission etc. has been ignored.

5. The Depreciation Fund Account is finally disposed of by transferring the balance to the Lease Account, thus closing both accounts. It represents the total amount of the provision made for depreciation over the life of the asset and is written off to the Asset Account in a lump sum.

6. Various terms are utilized in place of the phrase Depreciation Fund, e.g. Redemption Fund, Amortization Fund, Sinking Fund etc.

At first sight this method has the disadvantage that the gross charge (depreciation plus interest) to Profit and Loss Account increases from year to year, but as already explained the assets representing the fund will be earning income, which increases the profits available.

Where the cost of replacement is estimated to exceed the cost of the original asset, and it is not desired to introduce new capital to meet the excess, but it is the intention to provide it out of profits, the fund must be computed at the amount as is necessary for the acquisition. As already indicated, the excess of the provision over the true depreciation charge should preferably be regarded as an *appropriation* of profits, not a charge against them.

Sometimes the sums set aside are used in the business instead of being invested outside. A charge for interest on the depreciation fund accumulated to date should be debited to Profit and Loss Account and credited to the depreciation fund. Depreciation is provided but there is no certainty that cash, when required, will be available to replace the asset, as the fund may be represented by business assets which cannot be readily realized. With this practice in force, the use of the term 'depreciation fund' will be misleading, as the designation 'fund' should only be applied where the amount is represented by a fund of ready realizable investments, ear-marked for the purpose.

If compound interest tables are not available, ordinary arithmetical calculation will show that at $6\frac{1}{2}$ per cent. an annuity of £100, invested at the end of each of seven years, will amount to a sum of £852·3:

|  | £ |
|---|---|
| Annuity invested at end of year 1 .. | 100·0 |
| Interest thereon for second year @ $6\frac{1}{2}\%$ .. | 6·5 |
| Annuity invested at end of year 2 | 100·0 |
| Amount at beginning of third year | 206·5 |
| Interest thereon for third year @ $6\frac{1}{2}\%$ | 13·4 |
| Annuity invested at end of year 3 | 100·0 |
| Amount at beginning of fourth year | 319·9 |
| Interest thereon for fourth year @ $6\frac{1}{2}\%$ | 20·8 |
| Annuity invested at end of year 4 | 100·0 |
| Amount at beginning of fifth year | 440·7 |
| Interest thereon for fifth year @ $6\frac{1}{2}\%$ | 28·7 |
| Annuity invested at end of year 5 | 100·0 |
| Amount at beginning of sixth year | 569·4 |
| Interest thereon for sixth year @ $6\frac{1}{2}\%$ | 37·0 |
| Annuity invested at end of year 6 | 100·0 |
| Amount at beginning of seventh year | 706·4 |
| Interest thereon for seventh year @ $6\frac{1}{2}\%$ | 45·9 |
| Annuity at end of year 7 | 100·0 |
| Amount at end of seventh year .. | £852·3 |

To amount to a sum of £6,000, the sum to be set aside annually would need to be:

$$\frac{6,000}{852 \cdot 3} \times £100 = £704$$

### (e) The Depreciation Fund with Insurance Policy method

This is similar to the depreciation fund system dealt with in (d) above but, instead of buying securities, a policy is taken out with an insurance company to mature at the end of the life of the asset and to produce the amount required to replace it. The advantage of this method is that, although the interest earned is often lower than could be obtained by investing in securities, the risk of loss on realization, which could arise on the sale of outside investments, is eliminated provided a sound insurance company is chosen.

Some accountants consider that it is advisable for the policy account to be adjusted at the end of each year to the surrender value of the policy; other accountants take the view that, since the policy is for a fixed term and there is no intention of surrendering it, there is no need to write it down to surrender value, but that it can be maintained at cost plus accrued interest, there being the equivalent fund to correspond with it. Of the two methods the surrender value method is the more conservative, since it maintains the policy in the balance sheet at its realizable value.

**Illustration**

Lease costing £10,000 for a term of fifty years. The annual premium on the policy is £100. The surrender value of the policy is the amount of the premiums paid (excluding the first premium) plus 3 per cent. compound interest.

### DEPRECIATION FUND ACCOUNT

| | | £ | | | £ |
|---|---|---|---|---|---|
| 1st year Dec. 31 | Policy Account to adjust to surrender value | 100 | 1st year Dec. 31 | Profit and Loss Account .. | 100 |
| 2nd year Dec. 31 | Balance c/d. | 103 | 2nd year Dec. 31 | Profit and Loss Account .. <br> Policy Account: <br> Adjustment to surrender value .. | 100 <br> <br> 3 |
| | | £103 | | | £103 |
| 3rd year Dec. 31 | Balance c/d. | 209 | 3rd year Jan. 1 <br> Dec. 31 | Balance b/d. <br> Profit and Loss Account .. <br> Policy Account: <br> Adjustment to surrender value .. | 103 <br> 100 <br> <br> 6 |
| | | £209 | | | £209 |
| | | | 4th year Jan. 1 | Balance b/d. .. | 209 |

### POLICY ACCOUNT

| | | £ | | | £ |
|---|---|---|---|---|---|
| 1st year Jan. 1 | Cash .. | 100 | 1st year Dec. 31 | Depreciation Fund Account .. | 100 |
| 2nd year Jan. 1 <br> Dec. 31 | Cash .. <br> Depreciation Fund Account: <br> Interest at 3% on £100 to adjust <br> to surrender value .. | 100 <br> <br> <br> 3 | 2nd year Dec. 31 | Balance c/f. .. | 103 |
| | | £103 | | | £103 |

## POLICY ACCOUNT (continued)

| | | £ | | | £ |
|---|---|---|---|---|---|
| 3rd year Jan. 1 | Balance b/d.    ..         ..         .. | 103 | 3rd year Dec. 31 | Balance c/d.    ..         ..         .. | 209 |
| „ 1 | Cash ..         ..         ..         .. | 100 | | | |
| Dec. 31 | Depreciation Fund Account: Interest at 3 % on £203 to adjust to surrender value    ..         .. | 6 | | | |
| | | £209 | | | £209 |
| 4th year Jan. 1 | Balance b/d.    ..         ..         .. | 209 | | | |

*Notes to Illustration:*

(a) Although the premiums are paid on January 1st of each year, the transfers from Profit and Loss Account to Depreciation Fund Account would be made at the end of the year, when the accounts are closed.

(b) Since the surrender value of the policy is the amount of the premiums paid (excluding the first premium) plus interest, the surrender value at the end of the first year is nil. The whole amount standing to the debit of the Policy Account is therefore written off against the Depreciation Fund Account. In subsequent years the balance on the Policy Account is raised to surrender value by debiting the account with 3 per cent. on the existing balance, the Depreciation Fund Account being credited. The annual charge to Profit and Loss Account is not affected by these transfers between Depreciation Fund Account and Policy Account.

(c) When the policy matures, the Policy Account will be credited and cash debited, any balance remaining on the Policy Account being transferred to the Depreciation Fund Account.

## (f) Revaluation

The amount of depreciation to be written off loose tools, plant which depreciates rapidly, livestock, patents, copyrights and similar assets, should be calculated by revaluation. Should the revaluation disclose any appreciation, created by additions which have been charged to revenue (as additions to plant and loose tools in an engineering business are charged, as materials and wages, to Manufacturing Account), this appreciation should be credited to an appropriate account. Often the depreciation or appreciation of assets revalued is automatically debited or credited in the Profit and Loss Account, by debiting and crediting closing values, in the same way as stock-in-trade is dealt with in the Trading Account.

Where the appreciation has not been brought about by additions from revenue, it will be of a capital nature, and if taken into consideration at all should be placed to the credit of a Special Reserve Account.

## (g) Depletion Unit method

It is a matter of policy whether or not to make provision for depreciation of wasting assets, e.g. mines, quarries. If the business has been floated to work the asset, and to terminate when the asset is exhausted, the proprietors must regard each dividend received by them as being in part a return of their invested capital, and they must make personal provision to replace that capital.

If, however, the concern is floated on the basis of working each asset in succession, acquiring a new asset as each old one is worked out, depreciation should be provided for on the depletion unit basis, such a sum being set aside out of profits each year as represents the expired capital outlay, on the basis of the produce extracted compared with the estimated total contents of the mine, etc.

**Illustration**

A plot of freehold land is acquired at a cost of £1,000 for quarrying. The estimated output of the quarry over its lifetime is 40,000 tons.

For each ton won $\frac{1}{40,000}$ × £1,000 must be written off the book value of the land, i.e. if the tonnage won in a year is 2,000, the sum of £50 should be written off as depreciation.

## (h) Machine Hour method

Where it is possible to keep records of the running hours of each machine, the 'machine hour' plan can be employed. It is necessary to estimate the total effective working hours, during the whole life of the machine, and to divide this total into the cost of the machine, less its scrap value, thus giving an hourly rate of depreciation. Depreciation is then written off at the hourly rate for the number of hours the machine has been engaged during the period.

This method burdens each period with the exact amount of depreciation appropriate to its use of the machine, and can only usefully be employed for large machines. Due consideration must be given to the fact that some depreciation must normally take place even when a machine is not in use.

The labour involved in the maintenance of records renders this method more expedient where a costing system is in operation.

## (i) Sundry methods

In some trades machines are hired on the basis of a royalty payable according to the metered use of the machines, e.g. per 10,000 revolutions. Depreciation can be written off on a similar basis.

Sometimes the original expenditure on small machines with very short lives is capitalized, and all renewals charged to revenue, thus maintaining the original outlay. The renewals system cannot often be recommended, since few assets have a short enough life to give a fair charge to revenue from year to year.

The recommendation of the Council of the Institute of Chartered Accountants on the methods which should be applied in providing for depreciation of fixed assets is set out below.

### RECOMMENDATION

1. Provisions for depreciation, amortization, and depletion of fixed assets should be applied on consistent bases from one period to another. If additional provisions prove to be necessary, they should be stated separately in the Profit and Loss Account. Where practicable, fixed assets *in existence at the Balance Sheet date* should normally be shown in the Balance Sheet at cost, and the aggregate of the provisions for depreciation, amortization and depletion should appear as deductions therefrom. The extent to which these provisions are being kept liquid will then be ascertainable from the Balance Sheet as a whole.

2. Such provisions should be computed on the bases mentioned below as being appropriate to the particular class of asset concerned:

(a) *Goodwill and Freehold Land*

Depreciation does not arise through use in the business, except in the case of freehold land acquired for purposes such as are referred to in (d) below. Amounts set aside to provide for diminution in value do not constitute a normal charge against revenue and should be shown separately in the Profit and Loss Account.

(b) *Freehold Buildings, Plant and Machinery, Tools and Equipment, Ships, Transport Vehicles and similar assets which are subject to depreciation by reason of their employment in the business.*

Provision for depreciation should, in general, be computed on the straight-line method. Assets of very short effective life, such as loose tools, jigs and patterns, may, however, frequently be dealt with more satisfactorily by other methods, such as revaluation, which in no case should exceed cost.

(c) *Leaseholds, Patents and other assets which become exhausted by the effluxion of time.*

Provision for amortization should be made on the straight-line basis, including, in the case of leaseholds, allowance for the estimated cost of dilapidations at the end of the lease or useful life of the asset if shorter. If a leasehold redemption policy is effected with an insurance company, the charge of the annual premiums to Profit and Loss Account provides a satisfactory method of amortization if supplemented in respect of dilapidations.

(d) *Mines, oil wells, quarries and similar assets of a wasting character which are consumed in the form of basic raw material or where the output is sold as such.*

Provision for depreciation and depletion should be made according to the estimated exhaustion of the asset concerned. In the case of an undertaking, formed for the purpose of exploiting this particular class of asset, if the practice is to make no provision, this should be made clear in the accounts so that shareholders may realize that dividends are, in part, a return of capital.

3. Where a method different from that recommended has hitherto been followed, and it is not considered practicable or desirable to make a change in the case of assets already in use, it is suggested that the methods recommended should be followed in cases of assets subsequently acquired.

4. Details of all fixed assets should be kept (preferably in registers specially maintained) to show the cost of each asset, the provisions made for its depreciation and the basis of the provisions made.

5. Amounts set aside out of profits for obsolescence which cannot be foreseen, or for a possible increase in the cost of replacement, are matters of financial prudence. Neither can be estimated with any degree of accuracy. They are in the nature of reserves and should be treated as such in the accounts.

In subsequent memoranda, clarifying the above, the Council of the Institute have reiterated their recommendation that depreciation calculated on historical cost should be the basis on which annual accounts should be prepared and profits computed. Any amount set aside out of profits recognizing the effects which changes in the purchasing power of money have had on the affairs of the business (including any amount to finance the increase in the cost of replacements, whether of fixed or current assets) should be treated as a transfer to reserve and not as a charge in arriving at profits. If such a transfer is shown in the Profit and Loss Account as a deduction in arriving at the balance for the year, that balance should be described appropriately, since it is not the whole of the profits.

For Balance Sheet purposes fixed assets should not, except in special circumstances (e.g. where subscriptions for new capital are invited on the basis of a current valuation of the assets), be written up.

### § 9. The Treatment of Repairs, Renewals and Replacements

When considering depreciation, distinction should be made between the cost of upkeep, e.g. repairs and small renewals, and the cost of large renewals or the entire replacement of an asset.

The cost of upkeep should always be charged to revenue in addition to the provision for depreciation. Depreciation represents the exhaustion of the capital outlay, which cannot be made good by repairs and which must ultimately involve the expenditure of large sums on the replacement of the asset; the annual charge for depreciation spreads this loss fairly over the life of the asset. The current expenditure on repairs is necessary to make the asset last out the period, for which the rate of depreciation has been calculated; consequently it is essential that the cost of current repairs should be charged to revenue, otherwise the rate of depreciation would require to be increased.

When extensive renewals or replacements become necessary it must be considered whether they have the effect of increasing the revenue-earning capacity of the original asset, or merely maintain it. Only expenditure resulting in an increase in earning capacity can properly be capitalized, and this must itself be depreciated, so that it is written off by the same ultimate date as the original asset. This factor renders impracticable the reducing instalment system of depreciation, unless the additional capital outlay is depreciated separately from the original asset and at a higher rate.

If the whole asset is renewed the book value of the original asset will (if the rate of depreciation provided has been sufficient) have been reduced to nil or break up value by the time the expenditure on renewal becomes necessary. This fact determines whether the expenditure on renewal can justifiably be charged to capital. If there remains any book value over and above the break-up value attaching to the asset to be replaced, only such proportion of the cost of replacement as will increase the book value of the asset to the current cost should be capitalized. The balance, which represents accumulated depreciation unprovided for in the past, should be charged to revenue.

It is important to consider whether it is necessary to provide for future expenditure on repairs during the early years of the life of an asset when, although the current expenditure is comparatively light, it is known that the expenditure at a subsequent date will be considerable. Where large sums are involved, the best method is to estimate the total expenditure on repairs during the life of the asset, and to average it over that period. This may be done by raising a Provision for Maintenance Account, to which a credit is made each year from Profit and Loss Account of an amount equal to the average charge so computed. The actual expenditure, as and when it is incurred, will be debited to this account, the balance of which will be carried forward in the Balance Sheet as a reserve.

It may happen that this account will become temporarily in debit owing to excessive expenditure in any one period. If this excess is likely to be recouped during subsequent periods, it can be carried forward, but care should be taken to see that the average annual charge is sufficient. If not recoupable, it must be written off at once, or spread over the remainder of the life of the asset by increasing proportionately the annual charge to revenue.

Dilapidations arising under a lease afford an illustration of expenditure on repairs which arises at some subsequent period, and for which it is advisable to provide during the life of the asset. A convenient method is to estimate the charge for dilapidations, and add it to the cost of the lease, for the purpose of calculating the amount of depreciation which should be written off each year, thus spreading the cost of the dilapidations over the whole period.

### Illustration

A lease was acquired for twenty years, the tenant being liable for all repairs. A premium of £2,000 was paid, and it was estimated that repairs over the twenty years would amount to £1,000. The actual repairs in the first, second and third years were respectively £10, £30 and £25. Write up the Provision for Maintenance Account, bringing down the balance at the beginning of the fourth year.

## PROVISION FOR MAINTENANCE ACCOUNT

| | | | £ | | | | £ |
|---|---|---|---|---|---|---|---|
| 1st year | Repairs .. .. .. | | 10 | 1st year | Profit and Loss Account: | | |
| ,, | Balance c/d. .. .. .. | | 40 | | Annual Charge .. .. | | 50 |
| | | | £50 | | | | £50 |
| 2nd year | Repairs .. .. .. | | 30 | 2nd year | Balance b/d. .. .. .. | | 40 |
| ,, | Balance c/d. .. .. .. | | 60 | ,, | Profit and Loss Account .. .. | | 50 |
| | | | £90 | | | | £90 |
| 3rd year | Repairs .. .. .. | | 25 | 3rd year | Balance b/d. .. .. .. | | 60 |
| ,, | Balance c/d. .. .. .. | | 85 | ,, | Profit and Loss Account .. .. | | 50 |
| | | | £110 | | | | £110 |
| | | | | 4th year | Balance b/d. .. .. .. | | 85 |

If the repairs estimate proves to be exact there will be no balance at the end of the twenty years, but usually there would be some balance to be transferred to Profit and Loss Account. Depreciation would be provided for as usual.

## § 10. The Operation of Sinking Funds for the Repayment of Loans

A sinking fund for the repayment of a loan is created in a manner similar to the depreciation fund for the replacement of an asset, described in § 8 (*d*), except that the annual provision is an appropriation of, and not a charge against, profit. Equal amounts are debited to the Appropriation Account each year and credited to Sinking Fund Account, an equivalent sum is invested outside the business in securities (cash being credited and investments debited) and allowed to accumulate at compound interest, so as to produce the amount required to repay the loan on its due date.

Ultimately, the investments of the fund will be realized and the loan repaid, after which the credit balance remaining on the Sinking Fund Account should be transferred to Reserve Account, since the purpose for which the profits were appropriated has ceased to exist, and whereas the profits were formerly represented by specific investments, they are now represented by general assets of the business which have been acquired out of profits. This emphasizes the fact that the amount set aside to a sinking fund for the repayment of a liability is an appropriation of profit, whereas the amount set aside to a depreciation fund for replacing an asset is a charge against profits (except to the extent that it may exceed the original capital outlay on the asset being depreciated). In the case of a sinking fund for the repayment of a loan, the net assets are *increased* by the amount of the fund; a depreciation fund merely *maintains* the net assets at their original book value.

The amounts allocated to a sinking fund are debited to Profit and Loss Account so that monies may be accumulated and set aside *out of profits* to repay the liability, without having to provide additional capital moneys from external sources. It would be possible to accumulate funds outside the business for the repayment of a liability by making annual investments of cash without debiting the Profit and Loss Account at all, but if this were done the balance of the Profit and Loss Account alone would exceed the amount of profits which are available for distribution, because the cash resources of the business would have been reduced by the amounts invested. The balances on the Profit and Loss Account and the Sinking Fund Account are both reserves which form part of the proprietors' interest in the net assets of the undertaking.

The calculation of the annual amount to be invested is made in the same way as for a depreciation fund, already explained in § 8 (*d*) above.

**Illustration (1)**

On January 1st, Year 1, a loan of £1,000 was raised, repayable at par at the end of five years, and it was decided that a sinking fund should be formed to provide for its repayment.

Show the Ledger Accounts for the five years, assuming that the interest received on the investments representing the sinking fund was at the rate of 5 per cent. on the cost, that income tax was ignored, and that the interest was received yearly and immediately invested.

*Note:* ·180975 of £1 invested at the end of each year, at 5 per cent. compound interest, will produce £1 at the end of five years.

## SINKING FUND ACCOUNT

| | | £ | | | £ |
|---|---|---|---|---|---|
| 1st year Dec. 31 | Balance c/d | 181 | 1st year Dec. 31 | Profit & Loss Account | 181 |
| 2nd year Dec. 31 | Balance c/d | 371 | 2nd year Jan. 1 | Balance b/d | 181 |
| | | | Dec. 31 | Profit & Loss Account | 181 |
| | | | | Cash (Interest) | 9 |
| | | £371 | | | £371 |
| 3rd year Dec. 31 | Balance c/d | 571 | 3rd year Jan. 1 | Balance b/d | 371 |
| | | | Dec. 31 | Profit & Loss Account | 181 |
| | | | | Cash (Interest) | 19 |
| | | £571 | | | £571 |
| 4th year Dec. 31 | Balance c/d | 780 | 4th year Jan. 1 | Balance b/d | 571 |
| | | | Dec. 31 | Profit & Loss Account | 181 |
| | | | | Cash (Interest) | 28 |
| | | £780 | | | £780 |
| 5th year Dec. 31 | Transfer to Reserve Account | 1,000 | 5th year Jan. 1 | Balance b/d | 780 |
| | | | Dec. 31 | Profit & Loss Account | 181 |
| | | | | Cash (Interest) | 39 |
| | | £1,000 | | | £1,000 |

## SINKING FUND INVESTMENT ACCOUNT

| | | £ | | | £ |
|---|---|---|---|---|---|
| 1st year Dec. 31 | Cash | 181 | 1st year Dec. 31 | Balance c/d | 181 |
| 2nd year Jan. 1 | Balance b/d | 181 | 2nd year Dec. 31 | Balance c/d | 371 |
| Dec. 31 | Cash | 190 | | | |
| | | £371 | | | £371 |
| 3rd year Jan. 1 | Balance b/d | 371 | 3rd year Dec. 31 | Balance c/d | 571 |
| Dec. 31 | Cash | 200 | | | |
| | | £571 | | | £571 |
| 4th year Jan. 1 | Balance b/d | 571 | 4th year Dec. 31 | Balance c/d | 780 |
| Dec. 31 | Cash | 209 | | | |
| | | £780 | | | £780 |
| 5th year Jan. 1 | Balance b/d | £780 | 5th year Dec. 31 | Cash | £780 |

## LOAN ACCOUNT

| | | £ | | | £ |
|---|---|---|---|---|---|
| 5th year Dec. 31 | Cash | 1,000 | 1st year Jan. 1 | Cash | 1,000 |

*Note to Illustration:* At the end of the fifth year, no cash will be taken out of the business and invested, since the loan is repayable on that date. Thus the total of £1,000 to repay the loan is made up as follows:

|  | £ |
|---|---|
| Total amount of the Investments .. .. | 780 |
| Final instalment of Sinking Fund uninvested .. | 181 |
| Interest uninvested .. .. .. | 39 |
|  | £1,000 |

The calculation of the amount set aside will be made as follows:

If an annual investment of £·180975 at 5 per cent. compound interest will produce £1 at the end of five years, the amount of the annual investment required to produce £1,000 in the same period will be £·180975 × £1,000 = £181, to the nearest £.

Any profit or loss on the sale of the investments must be credited or debited, to the Sinking Fund Account, as it increases or decreases the amount of the assets by which the fund is represented.

**Illustration (2)**

Assume the same facts as in the previous example, but that the Investments were realized at a loss of £15.

The Accounts for the last year would appear as follows:

### SINKING FUND ACCOUNT

| 5th year Dec. 31 | Sinking Fund Investment Account – loss on realization  ..  .. Transfer to Reserve Account  .. | £ 15 1,000 | 5th year Jan. 1 Dec. 31 | Balance b/d.  ..  ..  .. Profit & Loss Account  ..  .. Cash (Interest) ..  ..  .. Profit & Loss Account – appropriation to meet loss on realization of investments  ..  .. | £ 780 181 39 15 |
|---|---|---|---|---|---|
|  |  | £1,015 |  |  | £1,015 |

### SINKING FUND INVESTMENT ACCOUNT

| 5th year Jan. 1 | Balance b/d.  ..  ..  .. | £ 780 | 5th year Dec. 31 | Cash ..  ..  ..  .. Sinking Fund Account – loss  .. | £ 765 15 |
|---|---|---|---|---|---|
|  |  | £780 |  |  | £780 |

*Note:* Since the investments realized £15 less than their cost price, this amount must be provided out of general assets. In order to maintain working capital, an equivalent amount must be appropriated from Profit and Loss Account.

Had a profit been realized, it could be taken either to Reserve Account or to Profit and Loss Account as the excess cash increases the working capital.

## § 11. Secret Reserves

The term 'secret reserves' is used to denote reserves which exist but are not disclosed on the face of the Balance Sheet.

Secret reserves may arise in two ways, viz. by the deliberate action of creating them, or by unrecorded appreciation in the value of assets. It would normally be unusual to write up assets for an unrealized appreciation in value, hence the appreciation is not as a rule shown on the face of the Balance Sheet.

Secret reserves may be created deliberately by:

1. Writing down assets below their market value by excessive provision for depreciation.

2. Writing off assets altogether, although they are still of value.

3. Creating excessive provisions for bad debts.

4. Charging capital expenditure to revenue.

5. Omitting goodwill from the accounts.

6. Overstating liabilities in the Balance Sheet.

7. Treating reserves for contingencies as provisions for specific liabilities.

8. Grouping free reserves with liabilities, so as to inflate the liabilities on the Balance Sheet.

9. Crediting exceptional or non-recurring profits direct to a contingencies reserve, and including such reserves in the liabilities on the Balance Sheet.

The following objections may be made against the practice of creating and maintaining secret reserves:

1. The resulting Balance Sheet will not disclose a true and fair view as the assets will be under-stated and/or the liabilities over-stated.

2. The Profit and Loss Account, where affected, will not show the correct profit, and consequently the dividend declared may be less than would otherwise have been possible.

3. The practice could lend itself to the manipulation of profits, and to improper dealings in the shares of a company by persons who were aware of the existence of the secret reserves.

4. If the use of secret reserves to pay dividends is not disclosed in the published accounts members will not know that the revenue for the period was insufficient to pay the dividends. The true trading results may thus be obscured.

5. Assets, once depreciated, cannot be written up without attracting attention, whereas reserves for contingencies, being merged with creditors, can be manipulated with little risk of discovery. Hence overstatement of liabilities is open to more objection than undervaluation of assets.

On the other hand the practice of creating secret reserves is often advantageous; banks and insurance companies can maintain the payment of dividends without violent fluctuations, and exceptional losses need not harm their credit, which although alarming to the uninitiated, do not shake their stability.

The *Companies Acts 1948* and *1967*, virtually prohibit the deliberate creation of secret reserves, since they require all reserves and provisions to be disclosed under suitable headings in the Balance Sheet. Where excessive provision is made for diminution in value of assets or for liabilities, the excess must be classified as a reserve.

## § 12. Suspense Accounts

The chief uses of Suspense Accounts are:

1. To provide an account to which one side of the double entry recording a transaction can be posted until its correct destination is known, e.g. if a trader receives a bank note in settlement of an account without a covering letter, he should post the amount from the debit side of the cash book to the credit side of the Suspense Account until he discovers the name of the person from whom the amount is received when he will debit the Suspense Account and credit the personal account of the sender.

2. To provide an account for deferred advertising and other deferred expenses when part of the benefit of the current expenditure will not be received until a subsequent period; it is permissible to carry forward the unexpired proportion of such expenditure, in the same way as a payment in advance, and write it off against the revenue of subsequent periods which benefit from the expenditure.

3. To provide an account to which can be posted any difference on the trial balance pending the discovery of errors; the errors when found are corrected by debiting and crediting, as appropriate, the Suspense Account.

The use of Suspense Accounts should be minimized; care should be taken to see that such accounts opened at the date of the Balance Sheet are correctly shown therein and that they are closed as soon as possible.

**Illustration**

Upon drawing up a Trial Balance a book-keeper finds that the credit total exceeds the debit total by £111 and this amount is posted to a Suspense Account.

Subsequently, the errors are discovered; Journal entries are made to correct the errors, and the Suspense Account can be closed.

(a) Sale of Goods valued at £80 to J. Smith posted to W. Smith's account.

(b) Purchase valued at £20 from W. Adam posted to debit of his account.

(c) Sales Returns Book undercast by £100.

(d) Petty Cash Balance of £10 omitted from Trial Balance.

(e) Cost of Repairing Plant £45 charged to Plant Account as £4.

### JOURNAL

| | | £ | £ |
|---|---|---|---|
| (a) J. Smith | Dr | 80 | |
| To W. Smith | | | 80 |
| Correction of posting made to wrong account. | | | |
| (b) Suspense Account | Dr | 40 | |
| To W. Adam | | | 40 |
| Correction of item of £20 debited instead of credited to W. Adam. | | | |
| (c) Sales Returns Account | Dr | 100 | |
| To Suspense Account | | | 100 |
| Adjustment of error in cast of Sales Returns Book. | | | |
| (d) *Petty Cash | Dr | 10 | |
| To Suspense Account | | | 10 |
| Adjustment of omission of £10 balance. | | | |
| (e) Plant Repairs Account | Dr | 45 | |
| To Plant Account | | | 4 |
| „ Suspense Account | | | 41 |
| Transferring cost of repairing plant erroneously charged to Plant Account as £4. | | | |

*This item will not be posted to the Petty Cash Account as the entry is only necessary to correct the omission from the Trial Balance.

## SUSPENSE ACCOUNT

| | £ | | £ |
|---|---|---|---|
| Difference in Books .. .. .. | 111 | Sales Returns Account .. .. .. | 100 |
| W. Adam .. .. .. .. | 40 | Petty Cash .. .. .. | 10 |
| | | Plant Repairs Account .. .. .. | 41 |
| | £151 | | £151 |

*Notes to Illustration:*

(*a*) This error does not affect the agreement of the Trial Balance, the correct amount having been posted to the correct side of the ledger, although to the wrong account.

(*b*) £20 has been posted to the wrong side of the ledger, thereby causing a difference in the Trial Balance of £40. The incorrect debit must be cancelled and the correct credit made.

(*c*) The undercast in the Sales Returns Book causes the debit in the Sales Returns Account, and consequently the debit side of the Trial Balance, to be £100 short.

(*d*) The omission of the petty cash book balance from the Trial Balance causes the debit side to be £10 short.

(*e*) This involves an error of principle (i.e. the posting of a revenue expense to a real or capital account) as well as an error of commission. The incorrect debit to Plant Account must be cancelled by a *credit* to that account, the correct *debit* must be made to Repairs Account, and the resulting difference credited to Suspense Account.

A Suspense Account raised for a difference in the Trial Balance must be closed before preparing the final accounts, by the adjustment of the differences when they are discovered.

If it proves impossible to discover the whole of the difference, and it is reasonably certain that this does not conceal any serious error, it may be necessary to write the balance off as a loss (if a debit) or to carry it forward as a reserve (if a credit). However, this should be a last resort.

# MANUFACTURING ACCOUNTS; RECEIPTS AND PAYMENTS ACCOUNTS AND INCOME AND EXPENDITURE ACCOUNTS; THE PREPARATION OF ACCOUNTS FROM INCOMPLETE RECORDS

## § 1. Manufacturing Accounts

In a business whose operations include both manufacturing and selling goods it is usual for the Trading Account to be divided into two parts:

1. The Manufacturing (or Production) Account showing the cost of production under normal conditions (any abnormal costs arising from the use of faulty materials etc. should be dealt with in the Profit and Loss Account).

2. The Trading Account showing gross profit realized on goods sold under normal conditions (sales of damaged goods should be dealt with in the Profit and Loss Account).

The Manufacturing Account is designed to show not only the cost of goods manufactured under normal conditions but also an analysis of the elements of cost. The account is debited with the cost of materials consumed (adjustment being made for opening and closing stocks), productive wages (wages that can be identified directly with units of production), and all other expenses attributable to the manufacturing operations classified under appropriate headings.

It is desirable to present the items so that a reconciliation with the Cost Accounts can easily be made. Accordingly, the account should show the *Prime Cost*, i.e. the total cost of the materials, productive wages and other expenses, which are capable of direct identification with production, and the *Works or Factory Cost*, which comprises the prime cost plus the various works indirect expenses, i.e. expenses incurred in production generally, but which cannot be associated directly with particular units of production. All expenses which contribute directly or indirectly to the normal cost of the goods, up to the point at which they are brought into a saleable condition, but excluding expenses of distributing or selling the goods, or of general administration, are debited to the Manufacturing Account. After eliminating the value of work in progress or unfinished goods on hand at the end of the period, the balance of the account represents the cost of the finished goods actually produced during the period, and is carried down to the debit of the Trading Account. The Trading Account is also debited with the opening stock of finished goods, and credited with the sales, and with the closing stock of finished goods (which should preferably be deducted from the sum of the opening stock and finished goods transferred from Manufacturing Account) in order to disclose the cost of, and the gross profit on the goods sold, the amount of which is transferred to the credit of Profit and Loss Account.

Sometimes, instead of transferring finished goods produced from Manufacturing Account to Trading Account at cost price, they are transferred at a price approximating to the market price. When this is done there will be a balance on the Manufacturing Account representing the profit or loss arising from manufacturing the goods instead of purchasing them ready made. This profit or loss must be transferred to Profit and Loss Account.

The items in the Profit and Loss Account should be marshalled in sequence and grouped under appropriate subheadings to show the total amount of the expenditure under each classification. Suitable groupings are Administration, Selling, Distribution, Finance and (possibly) Miscellaneous, but any of these may be subdivided and additional classifications employed to meet the requirements of the particular business. The grouping of items and the disclosure of group totals facilitates comparisons and may be of the greatest assistance to management.

The items in the Balance Sheet should be grouped to show clearly, on the liabilities side, the total amounts of:

(i) the proprietor's capital;

(ii) reserves and other undistributed profits (these being added to the capital to disclose in one sum the amount of the proprietor's interest in the assets);

(iii) loans and other long-term liabilities; and

(iv) current liabilities;

and on the assets side the total amounts of:

(i) the fixed assets; and

(ii) the current assets.

Other classifications may be used, according to the type of business.

**Illustration**

Prepare Manufacturing, Trading and Profit and Loss Account for the year ended December 31st, and Balance Sheet as at that date, of J. Smith, Manufacturer, from the following Trial Balance and information:

TRIAL BALANCE, December 31st

|  | Dr £ | Cr £ |
|---|---|---|
| Advertising.. | 830 | |
| Bad Debts .. | 605 | |
| ,,  ,,  Provision | | 1,000 |
| Bank Charges | 120 | |
| J. Smith, Capital Account, January 1st.. | | 35,000 |
| J. Smith, Current Account, January 1st | | 1,623 |
| J. Smith, Drawings .. | 8,000 | |
| Discount  .. | | 412 |
| Factory Power | 3,614 | |
| Furniture  .. | 900 | |
| Carried forward | £14,069 | £38,035 |

## TRIAL BALANCE (*continued*)

|  | Dr £ | Cr £ |
|---|---|---|
| Brought forward | 14,069 | 38,035 |
| General Expenses – Factory .. .. .. .. | 205 | |
| Office .. .. .. .. | 346 | |
| Insurance .. .. .. .. .. .. | 902 | |
| Light and Heat .. .. .. .. .. | 482 | |
| Plant and Machinery, January 1st .. .. .. | 15,000 | |
| ,, ,, ,, bought June 30th .. .. | 2,000 | |
| Purchases .. .. .. .. .. | 33,668 | |
| Packing and Transport .. .. .. .. | 1,085 | |
| Rent and Rates .. .. .. .. .. | 1,486 | |
| Repairs to Plant .. .. .. .. .. | 785 | |
| Salaries – Office .. .. .. .. .. | 3,690 | |
| Sales .. .. .. .. .. .. | | 79,174 |
| Stocks etc. January 1st – | | |
| Raw Materials .. .. .. .. .. | 5,230 | |
| Finished Goods .. .. .. .. | 7,380 | |
| Work in Progress (at prime cost) .. .. .. | 1,670 | |
| Wages – Factory .. .. .. .. .. | 20,700 | |
| Trading Debtors and Creditors .. .. .. | 10,560 | 6,150 |
| Cash at Bank .. .. .. .. .. | 3,926 | |
| Cash in Hand .. .. .. .. .. | 175 | |
| | £123,359 | £123,359 |

|  | £ |
|---|---|
| Stocks etc. at December 31st, were: | |
| Raw Materials .. .. .. .. .. | 3,560 |
| Work in Progress (at prime cost) .. .. .. | 1,740 |
| Finished Goods .. .. .. .. | 9,650 |
| Packing Materials .. .. .. .. | 125 |
| The following liabilities are to be provided for: | |
| Factory Power .. .. .. .. .. | 562 |
| Rent and Rates .. .. .. .. | 386 |
| Light and Heat .. .. .. .. | 160 |
| General Expenses – Factory .. .. .. | 25 |
| Office .. .. .. | 40 |

Insurance paid in advance is £170.

Five-sixths of Rent and Rates, Light and Heat, and Insurance are to be allocated to the Factory and one-sixth to the Office.

Provide Depreciation at 10 per cent. per annum on Plant and Machinery and 5 per cent. per annum on Furniture.

Increase the Bad Debts Provision by £500.

## MANUFACTURING, TRADING AND PROFIT AND LOSS ACCOUNT
### for the year ended December 31st, 19..

| | £ | £ | | £ |
|---|---|---|---|---|
| RAW MATERIALS CONSUMED: | | | Transfer to Trading Account: | |
| Stock, January 1st .. .. | 5,230 | | Cost of Goods produced .. .. | 65,464 |
| Purchases .. .. .. | 33,668 | | | |
| | 38,898 | | | |
| Less Stock, December 31st .. | 3,560 | | | |
| | | 35,338 | | |
| PRODUCTIVE WAGES .. .. .. | | 20,700 | | |
| | | 56,038 | | |
| Add Work in Progress, January 1st .. | | 1,670 | | |
| | | 57,708 | | |
| Deduct Work in Progress, December 31st | | 1,740 | | |
| PRIME COST OF GOODS PRODUCED .. | | 55,968 | | |
| WORKS INDIRECT EXPENSES: | | | | |
| Factory Power .. .. | 4,176 | | | |
| ,,  Rent and Rates .. | 1,560 | | | |
| ,,  Insurance .. | 610 | | | |
| ,,  Light and Heat .. | 535 | | | |
| General Expenses .. .. | 230 | | | |
| Plant Repairs.. .. .. | 785 | | | |
| ,,  Depreciation .. .. | 1,600 | | | |
| | | 9,496 | | |
| WORKS COST OF GOODS PRODUCED .. | | £65,464 | | £65,464 |
| COST OF FINISHED GOODS SOLD: | | | SALES OF FINISHED GOODS .. .. | 79,174 |
| Stock, January 1st .. .. | 7,380 | | | |
| Cost of Finished Goods produced | 65,464 | | | |
| | 72,844 | | | |
| Less Stock, December 31st .. | 9,650 | | | |
| | | 63,194 | | |
| GROSS PROFIT ON SALES: | | | | |
| Transferred to Profit and Loss Account .. | | 15,980 | | |
| | | £79,174 | | £79,174 |
| ADMINISTRATION: | £ | | GROSS PROFIT FOR YEAR, b/d. .. .. | 15,980 |
| Salaries .. .. .. | 3,690 | | | |
| Rent and Rates .. .. | 312 | | Discounts received .. .. .. | 412 |
| Light and Heat .. .. | 107 | | | |
| Insurance .. .. .. | 122 | | | |
| General Expenses .. .. | 386 | | | |
| Depreciation of Furniture .. | 45 | | | |
| | | 4,662 | | |
| SELLING AND DISTRIBUTION: | | | | |
| Advertising .. .. .. | 830 | | | |
| Packing and Transport .. | 960 | | | |
| | | 1,790 | | |
| FINANCE: | | | | |
| Bank Charges .. .. | 120 | | | |
| Bad Debts .. .. .. | 605 | | | |
| Provision for Doubtful Debts .. | 500 | | | |
| | | 1,225 | | |
| | | 7,677 | | |
| NET PROFIT FOR YEAR | | | | |
| Transferred to Current Account .. | | 8,715 | | |
| | | £16,392 | | £16,392 |

*Note:* In the above illustration, as the work in progress has been valued at prime cost, the adjustment for the values of opening and closing work in progress has been made before arriving at the prime cost of the goods produced. Where the valuation of work in progress includes an amount for works indirect expenses, the adjustment for this part of the valuation should be made in the charge for such expenses in the Manufacturing Account.

## J. SMITH
### BALANCE SHEET as at December 31st, 19..

| | £ | £ | | Cost £ | Depreciation £ | £ |
|---|---|---|---|---|---|---|
| CAPITAL ACCOUNT .. .. | | 35,000 | | | | |
| | | | FIXED ASSETS: | | | |
| | | | Plant and Machinery .. | 17,000 | 1,600 | 15,400 |
| CURRENT ACCOUNT: | | | Furniture .. .. | 900 | 45 | 855 |
| Balance, January 1st .. .. | 1,623 | | | | | |
| Net Profit for year .. .. | 8,715 | | | £17,900 | £1,645 | 16,255 |
| | 10,338 | | | | | |
| *Less* Drawings .. .. | 8,000 | | CURRENT ASSETS: | | | |
| | | 2,338 | Stocks: | | | |
| | | 37,338 | Raw Materials .. .. | | 3,560 | |
| | | | Work in Progress .. .. | | 1,740 | |
| | | | Finished Goods .. | | 9,650 | |
| CURRENT LIABILITIES: | | | Packing Materials .. | | 125 | |
| Trade Creditors .. .. | 6,150 | | | | 15,075 | |
| Expenses .. .. | 1,173 | | | | | |
| | | 7,323 | Book Debts .. .. £10,560 | | | |
| | | | *Less:* Provision for | | | |
| | | | Doubtful Debts 1,500 | | | |
| | | | | | 9,060 | |
| | | | Prepayments .. .. .. | | 170 | |
| | | | Balance at Bank .. .. | | 3,926 | |
| | | | Cash in Hand .. .. | | 175 | |
| | | | | | | 28,406 |
| | | £44,661 | | | | £44,661 |

The following is an alternative form of presentation of the Manufacturing, Trading and Profit and Loss Account, which is sometimes preferred.

## MANUFACTURING, TRADING
## AND PROFIT AND LOSS ACCOUNT
### for the year ended December 31st, 19..

| | | £ | £ |
|---|---|---|---|
| SALES .. .. .. .. .. .. .. .. .. .. | | | 79,174 |
| *Deduct* Cost of Sales: | | | |
| Cost of Materials consumed .. .. .. .. .. .. | | 35,338 | |
| Productive Wages .. .. .. .. .. .. .. | | 20,700 | |
| | | 56,038 | |
| *Add* Work in Progress, January 1st .. .. .. .. .. | | 1,670 | |
| | | 57,708 | |
| *Deduct* Work in Progress, December 31st .. .. .. .. | | 1,740 | |
| PRIME COST OF GOODS PRODUCED .. .. .. .. .. .. | | 55,968 | |
| *Add* WORKS INDIRECT EXPENSES: | £ | | |
| Factory Power .. .. .. .. .. .. .. | 4,176 | | |
| ,, Rent and Rates .. .. .. .. .. .. | 1,560 | | |
| ,, Insurance .. .. .. .. .. .. | 610 | | |
| ,, Light and Heat .. .. .. .. .. .. | 535 | | |
| General Expenses .. .. .. .. .. .. | 230 | | |
| Plant Repairs .. .. .. .. .. .. .. | 785 | | |
| Plant Depreciation .. .. .. .. .. .. | 1,600 | | |
| | | 9,496 | |
| WORKS COST OF GOODS PRODUCED .. .. .. .. .. .. | | 65,464 | |
| *Add* Stock of Finished Goods, January 1st .. .. .. .. .. .. | | 7,380 | |
| | | 72,844 | |
| *Deduct* Stock of Finished Goods, December 31st .. .. .. .. .. | | 9,650 | |
| | | | 63,194 |
| GROSS PROFIT ON SALES .. .. .. .. .. .. .. | | | 15,980 |
| *Add* Discounts received .. .. .. .. .. .. .. | | | 412 |
| Carried forward | | | 16,392 |

| | | | | | | | | £ | £ |
|---|---|---|---|---|---|---|---|---|---|
| | | | | | | Brought forward | | | 16,392 |
| *Deduct:* | | | | | | | | | |
| ADMINISTRATION: | | | | | | | | £ | |
| Salaries | .. | .. | .. | .. | .. | .. | .. | 3,690 | |
| Rent and Rates | .. | .. | .. | .. | .. | .. | .. | 312 | |
| Light and Heat | .. | .. | .. | .. | .. | .. | .. | 107 | |
| Insurance | .. | .. | .. | .. | .. | .. | .. | 122 | |
| General Expenses | .. | .. | .. | .. | .. | .. | .. | 386 | |
| Depreciation of Furniture | .. | .. | .. | .. | .. | .. | .. | 45 | |
| | | | | | | | | | 4,662 |
| SELLING AND DISTRIBUTION: | | | | | | | | | |
| Advertising | .. | .. | .. | .. | .. | .. | .. | 830 | |
| Packing and Transport | .. | .. | .. | .. | .. | .. | 960 | |
| | | | | | | | | | 1,790 |
| FINANCE: | | | | | | | | | |
| Bank Charges | .. | .. | .. | .. | .. | .. | .. | 120 | |
| Bad Debts | .. | .. | .. | .. | .. | .. | .. | 605 | |
| Provision for Doubtful Debts | .. | .. | .. | .. | .. | .. | 500 | |
| | | | | | | | | | 1,225 |
| | | | | | | | | | 7,677 |
| NET PROFIT FOR YEAR | .. | .. | .. | .. | .. | .. | .. | | £8,715 |

When the goods produced are charged out from the factory to the selling department at a price in excess of manufacturing cost, it will be necessary, at the end of each accounting period, in order to arrive at the true profit, to provide in the accounts for the unrealized profit included in the valuation of the stock of finished goods carried forward.

### Illustration

If in the previous illustration goods were charged from the factory to selling department at a price which included a profit of 10 per cent. on the cost, provision would have to be made for the unrealized profit on stock transfers, in respect of stock still unsold at the end of the period, as follows:

### PROVISION FOR UNREALIZED PROFIT ACCOUNT

| 19.. | | £ | 19.. | | £ |
|---|---|---|---|---|---|
| Dec. 31 | Provision carried forward – 10% on Stock at December 31st – 10% on £9,650 .. .. .. | 965 | Jan. 1 | Provision brought forward – 10% on Stock at January 1st – 10% on £7,380 .. .. .. | 738 |
| | | | Dec. 31 | Profit and Loss Account – increase in provision .. .. .. | 227 |
| | | £965 | | | £965 |
| | | | Jan. 1 | Provision brought forward .. | 965 |

*Notes:*

1. A provision for Unrealized Profit Account is prepared in the same way as a Provision for Bad Debts Account.

2. The balance on the Provision for Unrealized Profit Account will be deducted from the closing stock of finished goods at December 31st, 19.., on the Balance Sheet, thus:

| *Current Assets* | £ | £ |
|---|---|---|
| Stock of Finished Goods .. .. .. | 9,650 | |
| *Less* Provision for Unrealized Profit .. .. | 965 | |
| | | 8,685 |

## § 2. Receipts and Payments Account and Income and Expenditure Account

A RECEIPTS AND PAYMENTS ACCOUNT is a summarized cash book (cash and bank) for a given period. It commences with the opening balance of cash in hand and/or at the bank, and is debited with all sums actually received, and credited with all cash paid during the period, whether or not such payments have accrued during that period, or they relate to capital or revenue. The final balance is the balance of cash in hand, and/or the credit or debit balance at the bank at the end of the period.

An INCOME AND EXPENDITURE ACCOUNT is the Profit and Loss Account of a non-trading concern. It contains only revenue items, being debited with all expenditure, and credited with all income of a period, whether or not it has actually been paid or received within that period. The final balance of an Income and Expenditure Account represents the excess of income over expenditure, or the excess of expenditure over income, as the case may be, for the period. This balance is similar to the net profit or loss of a trading concern.

Receipts and Payments Accounts and Income and Expenditure Accounts are used commonly by such non-trading concerns as social clubs, societies etc., for the purpose of presenting their financial position to their members. The Profit and Loss Account of a non-trading business, e.g. a professional firm, or of a property or investment company, is also often called an Income and Expenditure Account.

A Receipts and Payment Account is *no* substitute for an Income and Expenditure Account.

The main differences between the two accounts are:

| *Receipts and Payments* | *Income and Expenditure* |
|---|---|
| Cash transactions only | Includes accruals and prepayments |
| Includes capital receipts and capital payments | Excludes capital receipts and capital payments |
| Balance represents cash in hand, bank balance, or bank overdraft | Balance represents surplus/deficiency of income over expenditure for a given period. |

In order to prepare an Income and Expenditure Account from a Receipts and Payments Account, post all revenue items appearing in the Receipts and Payments Account to the *opposite* sides of the Income and Expenditure Account, and make adjustments for accruals and prepayments at the beginning and the end of the period.

Such items as subscriptions, entrance fees, income from investments etc., which have been received in cash and *debited* to the Receipts and Payments Account, must be *credited* to the Income and Expenditure Account, whilst expenditure such as rent, wages, repairs etc., appearing on the *credit* side of the Receipts and Payments Account must be *debited* to the Income and Expenditure Account. Capital items appearing in the Receipts and Payments Account will be posted to the debit or credit, as the case may be, of the relevant asset or liability accounts, and will not affect the Income and Expenditure Account.

The Balance Sheet of a non-trading concern is prepared in the usual way, and contains particulars of all the assets and liabilities at the date as at which it is made up. The excess of the assets over the liabilities is similar to the capital of a trader, but is usually called the Accumulated Fund, or General Fund, since it is normally made up of the excess of income over expenditure which has been accumulated within the concern.

Separate accounts should be kept for funds raised for special purposes, e.g. Building Appeal Funds and Election Funds.

Two problems on the solutions of which accountants are divided are:

1. Should club entrance fees be credited in the Income and Expenditure Account or be shown on the Balance Sheet of the club as an addition to the accumulated fund?

Provided entrance fees are consistently treated, either method is correct; although it can be argued that revenue might be distorted if there were a large number of entrance fees in any one period, the benefit of which is to be spread over a number of accounting periods.

2. Should club subscriptions in arrear be shown as debtors at the balance sheet date?

In practice a large number of club subscriptions in arrear are never received and the Balance Sheet could be distorted by a fictitious asset of debtors should club subscriptions in arrear be included on the Balance Sheet and never received. Whatever treatment is adopted, it must be consistent; if subscriptions in arrear are brought into account it is essential to bring them in at the beginning as well as at the end of the period. If subscriptions in arrear are ignored, the Income and Expenditure Account could be distorted if a large number of subscription arrears were received in any one period.

A variation of an Income and Expenditure Account is a RECEIPTS AND EXPENDITURE ACCOUNT. This is a revenue account similar in form to an Income and Expenditure Account in which, however, credit is taken only for income actually received. Accrued income which has not been received in cash is ignored, although all expenditure for the period, whether paid or outstanding, is debited. Such an account is occasionally prepared by professional businesses, e.g. solicitors, where it is desired to take no credit for income until it is actually realized, but at the same time to provide for all expenditure, whether paid or not. The balance of the account represents the most conservative estimate of the profit for the period.

**Illustration**

The Westminster Political Association prepared accounts for the year to December 31st.

1. They started the year with £470 in the bank and ended with an overdraft of £615, which was secured by the deposit of investments with the bank.

2. They received subscriptions amounting to £835, of which £25 represented arrears, £760 current subscriptions and £50 in advance.

3. They received £520 donations to the General Fund and £850 to the Election Fund, which had £15 in hand at January 1st, and out of which £720 was paid for election expenses. There was no separate bank account.

4. They held Government securities at January 1st, which cost £2,000. Half were sold for £1,250 and the balance was valued at £1,200 at December 31st. These investments produced interest of £35 during the year.

5. Office premises were purchased during the year for £3,000 and a mortgage was arranged through a building society for £1,500. Legal expenses amounted to £105 and one instalment of £80 was paid to the society of which £45 was interest. Alterations and decorations of the premises cost £570, of which £150 was still owing.

6. Office furniture was valued at £150 at January 1st. £170 was paid for additions during the year and £70 was still owing. Depreciation is estimated at 10 per cent. per annum.

7. The only other receipt was £75 for sale of literature. £60 worth was given away. The total cost of literature amounted to £120, and no stocks were left at the end of the year.

8. Other payments were:

| | | |
|---|---|---|
| Agent's salary and expenses | .. | £700 (of which £50 related to next year) |
| Office salaries.. | .. .. | £350 |
| Rent and rates | .. .. | £170 (£50 owing at January 1st) |
| Meetings and propaganda | .. | £165 (£30 for a meeting to be held in the new year) |
| Stationery, postage and sundries | | £150. |

Prepare a Receipts and Payments Account and an Income and Expenditure Account for the year ended December 31st, and a Balance Sheet as at that date. Subscriptions in arrear are to be brought into account. Ignore taxation.

## THE WESTMINSTER POLITICAL ASSOCIATION
### RECEIPTS AND PAYMENTS ACCOUNT
for the year ended December 31st

| | | £ | | | | £ |
|---|---|---|---|---|---|---|
| Jan. 1 | Balance b/f. .. .. .. | 470 | Dec. 31 | Election Expenses .. .. | | 720 |
| Dec. 31 | Subscriptions .. .. .. | 835 | | Cost of Premises .. £3,000 | | |
| | Donations .. .. .. | 520 | | Legal Expenses .. .. 105 | | |
| | Election Fund .. .. .. | 850 | | | | |
| | Sale of Securities .. .. | 1,250 | | | | 3,105 |
| | Interest Received .. .. | 35 | | *Less* Mortgage .. 1,500 | | |
| | Sale of Literature .. .. | 75 | | | | 1,605 |
| | Balance being Overdraft c/f. .. | 615 | | Building Society Payments .. | | 80 |
| | | | | Alterations and Decorations .. | | 420 |
| | | | | Office Furniture.. .. | | 170 |
| | | | | Agent's Salary .. .. .. | | 700 |
| | | | | Office Salaries .. .. .. | | 350 |
| | | | | Rent and Rates .. .. | | 170 |
| | | | | Meetings etc. .. .. .. | | 165 |
| | | | | Stationery and Postage .. .. | | 150 |
| | | | | Cost of Literature .. .. | | 120 |
| | | £4,650 | | | | £4,650 |

## INCOME AND EXPENDITURE ACCOUNT
for the year ended December 31st

| | | | £ | | £ |
|---|---|---|---|---|---|
| Agent's Salary and Expenses | .. | .. | 650 | Subscriptions Receivable .. .. .. | 760 |
| Office Salaries .. .. | .. | .. | 350 | Interest on Investments .. .. .. | 35 |
| Rent and Rates .. | .. | .. | 120 | Balance, being Excess of Expenditure over In- | |
| Stationery, Postage and Sundries | .. | .. | 150 | come for the year .. .. .. | 739 |
| Meetings and Propaganda .. | .. | .. | 135 | | |
| Cost of Literature distributed | .. | £60 | | | |
| *Less* Profit on Sales | .. | 15 | | | |
| | | | 45 | | |
| Interest on Mortgage | .. | .. | 45 | | |
| Depreciation of Office Furniture | .. | .. | 39 | | |
| | | | £1,534 | | £1,534 |

## BALANCE SHEET

### as at December 31st

| | £ | £ | | £ | £ |
|---|---|---|---|---|---|
| **GENERAL FUND** | | | **FIXED ASSETS** | | |
| Balance at January 1st .. .. | 2,580 | | Office Premises at cost .. . | 3.000 | |
| *Add* Profit on sale of investments .. | 250 | | Legal expenses .. .. | 105 | |
| Donations .. .. .. | 520 | | Alterations and decorations .. | 570 | |
| | 3,350 | | | 3,675 | |
| *Less* Excess of expenditure over income for year .. .. | 739 | | *Less* Mortgage £(1,500-35) .. | 1,465 | |
| | | 2,611 | | | 2,210 |
| | | | Office Furniture: | | |
| **ELECTION FUND** | | | Balance at January 1st .. | 150 | |
| Balance at January 1st .. .. | 15 | | Additions .. .. .. | 240 | |
| *Add* Donations .. .. .. | 850 | | | 390 | |
| | 865 | | *Less* Depreciation written off .. | 39 | |
| *Less* Election expenses .. .. | 720 | | | | 351 |
| | | 145 | Investments at cost (market value £1,200) .. .. .. | | 1,000 |
| **CURRENT LIABILITIES** | | | **CURRENT ASSETS** | | |
| Subscriptions in advance .. .. | 50 | | Payments in advance £(50+30) .. | | 80 |
| Creditors £(150+70) .. .. | 220 | | | | |
| Bank Overdraft .. .. .. | 615 | | | | |
| | | 885 | | | |
| | | £3,641 | | | £3,641 |

*Note:* The balance on the General Fund at January 1st is calculated as follows:

| | | | | | £ |
|---|---|---|---|---|---|
| Bank (excluding Election Fund) | .. | .. | .. | | 455 |
| Subscriptions in arrears | .. | .. | .. | .. | - 25 |
| Investments | .. | .. | .. | .. | 2,000 |
| Office Furniture | .. | .. | .. | .. | 150 |
| | | | | | 2,630 |
| *Less* Rent accrued at January 1st .. | | .. | .. | | 50 |
| | | | | | £2,580 |

## § 3. The Preparation of Accounts from Incomplete Records

For the purpose of this section the expression 'incomplete records' is intended to signify any accounting records which fall short of complete double entry. There are varying degrees of incompleteness, and the procedure to be adopted in order to prepare final accounts must depend upon the nature of the records and data available. In extremes cases it may be found that there are no records whatever of the day to day transactions, owing either to neglect on the part of the trader to keep them, or to the destruction of the books and vouchers by a fire on the trader's premises, or through some other cause. In such circumstances, accounts would have to be built up largely from estimates obtained by exhaustive enquiry and the careful sifting of whatever evidence can be found. In other instances books may have been kept by 'single entry', or data may be available by means of which double entry can be effected in total and a Profit and Loss Account and Balance Sheet extracted when this has been done.

Strict 'SINGLE ENTRY' takes account only of the personal aspect of transactions, and leaves the impersonal aspect entirely unrecorded. It is rarely, if ever, met with in practice, as in almost every case it will be found that some cash records, even though incomplete, have been kept. In any event there will usually be a bank account, and the pass book or statement supplied by the bank will provide details of the operation of that account.

Assuming such to be the case, the following procedure should be followed in order to prepare a Profit and Loss Account and Balance Sheet.

1. A Statement of Affairs at the commencement of the period under review should first be drawn up. In order to prepare this statement, particulars must be obtained of the assets and liabilities of the business at that date. The balance at the bank can be ascertained from the bank statement. The values of any fixed assets can be obtained from such details as the trader is able to supply of their cost and the dates upon which they were acquired, provision for depreciation from the date of acquisition to the commencement of the current period being deducted. The trader must provide an estimate of the value of his stock-in-trade and particulars of any book debts and liabilities. Accounts should be opened, to the debit of which the amounts of the estimated values of the assets should be posted. The total of the book debts should be debited to a Total Debtors Account, and the total of the liabilities credited to a Total Creditors Account. The excess of the aggregate of the assets over the liabilities may be taken to represent the amount of the trader's capital at the commencement of the period, and should be credited to his Capital Account.

2. A careful analysis should now be made of the bank pass book or statement, and a Cash Summary (or Receipts and Payments Account) prepared. For this purpose analysis sheets should be used, in which columns should be provided for each of the principal headings of receipts and payments. For example, the lodgments into the bank may be analysed under the headings of cash takings, income from investments, the sale of assets, new capital paid in and private income of the trader. Payments from bank should be analysed as between payments for goods purchased, rent, rates, insurances and other business expenses, cheques cashed for wages, petty cash and personal expenditure, and cheques drawn for the trader's private purposes. It must be seen that the cross-casts of the analysis columns agree with the total columns.

3. Enquiry should be made as to the amounts of any cash takings which have not been paid into the bank, but have been used by the trader for the payment of business expenses, goods purchased for cash and personal expenses. An estimate should also be obtained of the value of any stock-in-trade which may have been withdrawn by the trader for his own personal use or for that of his family.

4. On completion of the above analysis, postings will be made as follows:

(i) From the debit side of the Cash Summary:

(a) Cash takings to the credit of Total Debtors Account.

(b) Income from investments (if any) to the credit of Income from Investments Account.

(c) Proceeds of sale of assets (if any) to the credit of the appropriate asset accounts.

(*d*) Other items to the credit of the relevant accounts.

If a profit or loss on the sale of assets is disclosed, this should be transferred either to Profit and Loss Account or to the proprietor's Capital Account.

(ii) From the credit of Cash Summary:

(*a*) Payments for goods purchased to the debit of Total Creditors Account.

(*b*) Payments of expenses to the debit of the relevant nominal accounts.

(*c*) Cheques drawn for petty cash to the debit of Petty Cash Account.

(*d*) The proprietor's personal drawings to the debit of his Current Account.

(*e*) The purchase of assets (if any) to the debit of the respective asset accounts.

The amount of any cash takings used for business or private purposes should be journalized, the appropriate nominal accounts or the proprietor's Current Account (as the case may be) being debited and Total Debtors Account credited. The usual adjustments for outstandings and payments in advance may now be made. A schedule should be compiled, from such memoranda as the trader has kept, of the book debts outstanding, the total of which should be credited and carried down in the Total Debtors Account. The balance of this account will now represent the total sales for the period and should be transferred to the credit of Trading Account.

Similarly, a schedule should be made of liabilities outstanding to trade and other creditors, the amounts being checked with the creditors' statements and the total thereof debited and carried down in the Total Creditors Account. The balance of this account will now represent the total purchases for the period, and should be transferred to the debit of Trading Account.

The whole of the transactions will now be recorded in total in double entry form and it will be possible to extract a Trading and Profit and Loss Account and Balance Sheet in the usual way.

The percentage of gross profit revealed by the Trading Account may afford some indication as to the accuracy or otherwise of the data and estimates used in compiling the accounts. If it is found that this percentage is substantially lower than the percentage of gross profit normally earned in the particular trade, doubt would be thrown on the accuracy of the opening or closing stocks, purchases or sales, and further enquiry would be necessary. In particular, information should be elicited as to the style in which the trader lives. It will often be found that the amount of cash takings alleged to be withdrawn for private use is wholly incompatible with the size and character of the trader's domestic establishment and mode of life, and a re-estimation of the amount of the personal drawings might be necessary.

**Illustration (1)**

A is the proprietor of a grocery and general stores. He has not previously engaged an accountant. He informs you that this year the Inspector of Taxes refuses to accept the account A has supplied of his trading results for the year ended March 31st, 1970. That account is as follows:

|  | £ |  |  |  | £ |
|---|---|---|---|---|---|
| Payments for goods | 9,495 | Takings .. | .. | .. | 10,930 |
| Payments for expenses | 1,130 |  |  |  |  |
| Profits .. .. | 305 |  |  |  |  |
|  | £10,930 |  |  |  | £10,930 |

He instructs you to examine his records and prepare accounts.

From your examination of the records and from interviews with your client, you ascertain the following information:

1. The takings are kept in a drawer under the counter; at the end of each day the cash is counted and recorded on a scrap of paper; at irregular intervals Mrs A transcribes the figures into a notebook; a batch of slips of paper was inadvertently destroyed before the figures had been written into the notebook, but Mr and Mrs A carefully estimated their takings for that period, and the estimated figure is included in the total of £10,930.

2. The following balances can be accepted:

|  | March 31st | |
|---|---|---|
|  | *1969* | *1970* |
|  | £ | £ |
| Cash in hand .. .. .. .. .. .. | 45 | 87 |
| Balance at Bank .. .. .. .. .. | 156 | 219 |
| Good debts .. .. .. .. .. .. | 458 | 491 |
| Creditors for purchases of stock .. .. .. .. | 279 | 243 |
| Stock-in-trade at cost .. .. .. .. .. | 1,950 | 1,900 |

3. Debts totalling £356 were abandoned during the year as bad; the takings include £25 recovered in respect of an old debt abandoned in a previous year.

4. A rents the shop and living accommodation on a weekly tenancy for £3 per week including rates; the rent is included in expenses £1,130. The living accommodation may be regarded as one-third of the whole.

5. The expenses total also includes:

 (i) £35 running expenses of A's private car;
 (ii) £60 for exterior decoration of the whole premises, the landlord having refused to have this done;
(iii) £160 for alterations to the premises to enlarge the storage accommodation.

6. A takes £10 per week from the business and hands it over to his wife, who pays all the household and personal expenses except those referred to below.

7. A pays for his own cigarettes and beer with cash taken from the drawer; this is estimated at £1·50 per week.

8. A competed in a football pool for thirty weeks of the year, staking £1 each week, buying a postal order with cash taken from the drawer; his winnings totalled £59.

9. During the year A bought a secondhand car (not used for business) from a friend; the price agreed was £350, but as the friend owed A £67 for goods supplied from the business the matter was settled by a cheque for the difference.

10. An assurance policy on A's life matured and realized £641.

11. A cashed a cheque for £100 for a friend; the cheque was dishonoured and the friend is repaying the £100 by instalments. He had paid £40 by March 31st, 1970.

12. Other private payments by cheque totalled £96 plus a further sum of £110 for income tax.

13. You are to provide £42 for accountancy fees.

You are required to prepare:

(*a*) A Balance Sheet of the business as at March 31st, 1969;
(*b*) A Profit and Loss Account for the year ended March 31st, 1970; and
(*c*) A Balance Sheet for the business as at March 31st, 1970.

A.

## BALANCE SHEET

(a)                          as at March 31st, 1969

| | £ | | £ |
|---|---|---|---|
| A, Capital Account .. .. .. .. | 2,330 | Stock .. .. .. .. .. | 1,950 |
| Creditors .. .. .. .. .. | 279 | Debtors.. .. .. .. .. | 458 |
| | | Balance at Bank .. .. .. .. | 156 |
| | | Cash in Hand .. .. .. .. | 45 |
| | £2,609 | | £2,609 |

## TRADING AND PROFIT AND LOSS ACCOUNT

(b)                   for the year ended March 31st, 1970

| | £ | | £ |
|---|---|---|---|
| Stock, 1/4/69 .. .. .. .. | 1,950 | Sales .. .. .. .. | 11,638 |
| Purchases .. .. .. .. | 9,459 | | |
| | 11,409 | | |
| Less Stock, 31/3/70 .. .. .. | 1,900 | | |
| | 9,509 | | |
| Gross Profit, carried down .. .. .. | 2,129 | | |
| | £11,638 | | £11,638 |
| Rent and Rates (¾ of £3 per week) .. .. | 104 | Gross Profit, brought down .. .. | 2,129 |
| Sundry Expenses .. .. .. .. | 719 | Bad Debts recovered .. .. .. | 25 |
| Cost of enlarging storage accommodation .. | 160 | | |
| Repairs (¾ of £60) .. .. .. .. | 40 | | |
| Bad Debts written off .. .. .. | 356 | | |
| Accountancy Fees .. .. .. .. | 42 | | |
| Net Profit for year .. .. .. .. | 733 | | |
| | £2,154 | | £2,154 |

*Note:* The cost of enlarging storage accommodation could be capitalized, but it has been thought better to write it off.

## BALANCE SHEET

(c)                          as at March 31st, 1970

| | £ | £ | | £ |
|---|---|---|---|---|
| A, Capital Account: | | | Stock, at cost .. .. .. .. | 1,900 |
| Balance at 1/4/69 .. .. | 2,330 | | Sundry Debtors .. .. .. .. | 491 |
| Net Profit for year .. .. | 733 | | Balance at Bank .. .. .. .. | 219 |
| | 3,063 | | Cash in Hand .. .. .. .. | 87 |
| Less Drawings .. .. .. | 651 | | | |
| | | 2,412 | | |
| Liabilities: | | | | |
| Trade Creditors .. .. .. | 243 | | | |
| Accountancy Fees .. .. | 42 | | | |
| | | 285 | | |
| | | £2,697 | | £2,697 |

*Note:* The working accounts would appear as follows:

## CASH SUMMARY

| | £ | | £ |
|---|---|---|---|
| Balances 1/4/69 (Cash £45; Bank £156) .. | 201 | Expenses .. .. .. .. | 1,130 |
| Bad debt recovered.. .. .. .. | 25 | Purchases | 9,495 |
| Football Pool winnings .. .. .. | 59 | Cash Drawings .. .. .. .. | 520 |
| Insurance Policy .. .. .. .. | 641 | Personal Cigarettes etc. .. .. .. | 78 |
| Repaid by Friend .. .. .. .. | 40 | Football Pools .. .. .. .. | 30 |
| Balance=Cash Takings carried to Total Debtors | | Car .. .. .. .. | 283 |
| Account .. .. .. .. | 11,182 | Loan to Friend .. .. .. .. | 100 |
| | | Drawings by cheque .. .. .. | 96 |
| | | Income Tax .. .. .. .. | 110 |
| | | Balance 31/3/70 (Cash £87; Bank £219) .. | 306 |
| | £12,148 | | £12,148 |

## TOTAL DEBTORS

| | £ | | £ |
|---|---|---|---|
| Debtors 1/4/69 .. .. .. .. | 458 | Cash Takings .. .. .. .. | 11,182 |
| Balance=Sales .. .. .. .. | 11,638 | Friend re Car .. .. .. .. | 67 |
| | | Bad Debts w/o .. .. .. .. | 356 |
| | | Debtors 31/3/70 .. .. .. .. | 491 |
| | £12,096 | | £12,096 |

## TOTAL CREDITORS

| | £ | | £ |
|---|---|---|---|
| Cash .. .. .. .. .. | 9,495 | Creditors 1/4/69 .. .. .. .. | 279 |
| Creditors 31/3/70 .. .. .. .. | 243 | Balances=Purchases .. .. .. | 9,459 |
| | £9,738 | | £9,738 |

## EXPENSES

| | £ | | £ |
|---|---|---|---|
| Cash .. .. .. .. .. | 1,130 | Rent .. .. .. .. | 156 |
| | | Car Expenses .. .. .. .. | 35 |
| | | Repairs to premises .. .. .. | 60 |
| | | Alterations .. .. .. .. | 160 |
| | | Balance=Sundry Expenses .. .. | 719 |
| | £1,130 | | £1,130 |

## DRAWINGS

| | £ | | £ |
|---|---|---|---|
| Cash .. .. .. .. | 520 | Football Pool Winnings .. .. .. | 59 |
| Cheques .. .. .. .. | 96 | Life Policy Money .. .. .. | 641 |
| Rent (one-third of £3 per week) .. .. | 52 | Repayments by Friend .. .. .. | 40 |
| Private Car Expenses .. .. .. | 35 | Balance=Net Drawings .. .. .. | 651 |
| Decorations (House) (one-third of £60) .. | 20 | | |
| Purchase of Car .. .. .. | 350 | | |
| Cash paid to Friend .. .. .. | 100 | | |
| Cigarettes etc. .. .. .. .. | 78 | | |
| Football Pools .. .. .. .. | 30 | | |
| Income Tax .. .. .. .. | 110 | | |
| | £1,391 | | £1,391 |

Where the available records are so deficient that it is impossible to compile a reasonably complete cash summary, the only method of estimating the profit or loss for the period is to prepare Statements of Affairs showing the 'net worth' of the business at the beginning and at the end of the period respectively.

A Statement of Affairs for this purpose is a document in the form of a Balance Sheet, showing on one side the estimated amounts of the various assets and on the other the liabilities, the difference beween the two sides representing the proprietor's 'net worth', or capital at the date of the statement.

If a Statement of Affairs has been drawn up at the end of the preceding period, the opening capital for the current period would be shown thereby. It would then be necessary to prepare a similar statement at the end of the current period, and to find the difference between the opening and closing figures of capital, the amount of which, after adding back any sums withdrawn, and deducting any new capital introduced, would represent the profit or loss for the period.

**Illustration (2)**

J's last Statement of Affairs prepared at January 1st, was:

### STATEMENT OF AFFAIRS
#### January 1st

| | £ | | £ |
|---|---|---|---|
| Creditors .. .. .. .. .. | 6,000 | Office Furniture .. .. .. .. | 500 |
| Bills Payable .. .. .. | 500 | Stock .. .. .. .. | 2,000 |
| Capital Account – being excess of assets over lia- | | Debtors.. .. .. .. | 4,500 |
| bilities at this date .. .. .. | 3,000 | Bills Receivable .. .. .. .. | 1,000 |
| | | Cash .. .. .. .. | 1,500 |
| | £9,500 | | £9,500 |

On December 31st, he finds his liabilities to be: Creditors £4,500, Bills Payable £700, and his assets: Office Furniture £450, Stock £1,500, Debtors, £5300, Bills Receivable £700, Cash £800. His drawings during the period have amounted to £450. What profit has he made?

### STATEMENT OF AFFAIRS
#### December 31st

| | £ | | £ |
|---|---|---|---|
| Creditors .. .. .. .. .. | 4,500 | Office Furniture .. .. .. .. | 450 |
| Bills Payable .. .. .. | 700 | Stock .. .. .. .. | 1,500 |
| Capital Account – being excess of assets over lia- | | Debtors.. .. .. .. | 5,300 |
| bilities at this date .. .. .. | 3,550 | Bills Receivable .. .. .. | 700 |
| | | Cash .. .. .. .. | 800 |
| | £8,750 | | £8,750 |

| | | £ |
|---|---|---|
| Capital, December 31st .. .. .. .. | | 3,550 |
| Add Drawings for the year .. .. .. | | 450 |
| | | 4,000 |
| Less Capital, January 1st .. .. .. | | 3,000 |
| Net Profit for year .. .. .. | | £1,000 |

No great difficulty should be experienced in estimating values of the assets and liabilities at the end of the period under review, provided that the work of preparing the statement is undertaken shortly after that date, since the necessary material for the valuation will probably be still accessible. The preparation of earlier statements may present more difficulty, and the most searching enquiries may have to be made. Needless to say this method of ascertaining results is most unsatisfactory, and the trader should be advised to install double entry book-keeping without delay.

CHAPTER V

# GOODS ON SALE OR RETURN, CONSIGNMENT ACCOUNTS ETC.

## § 1. Treatment of Goods sent on Sale or Return

Where goods are sent out on approval, such transactions should not be treated in the books as sales, since the property in the goods does not pass to the buyer until he signifies to the seller his acceptance of them, or does some act by means of which a sale is expressed or implied. If, therefore, these transactions are recorded as sales, profit will be anticipated which may never actually be realized and the Balance Sheet will not exhibit the true state of affairs.

The method of treatment in the books depends upon circumstances and the number of transactions involved, and may be broadly considered under three headings:

*(a) Where the number of Sale or Return transactions is small*

The best way to record these transactions is to have a specially ruled form of day book, such as the following:

### SALE OR RETURN DAY BOOK

| Date | Particulars | Goods sent on Sale or Return | Date | Goods Returned | Goods Sold | Sales Ledger Folio |
|------|-------------|------------------------------|------|----------------|------------|--------------------|
| (1) | (2) | (3) | (4) | (5) | (6) | (7) |
| | | £ | | £ | £ | |
| | | | | | | |

The procedure will be as follows:

1. When goods are sent out they are entered in column 3 at selling price, and no other entry is made until definite information has been obtained as to whether the goods are to be kept by the customer or returned.

2. If the goods are returned, their value is extended into column 5, which like column 3 is simply a memorandum column, and does not affect the double entry.

3. If the goods are sold, their value is extended into column 6, and posted therefrom to the debit of the customer's account in the sales ledger. The total of this column will ultimately be posted to the credit of Sales Account in the impersonal ledger.

4. The difference between the totals of columns 5 and 6 taken together, and that of column 3, will represent the selling price of the goods out on approval at any given date.

89

5. All these transactions will have been entered in the sale or return day book at selling price, but for Balance Sheet purposes the stock of goods out on approval must be valued at cost, and treated in the same way as stock-in-hand.

### (b) Where the number of Sale or Return transactions is considerable

The system outlined above cannot conveniently be applied without some modification where the number of sale or return transactions is considerable, owing to the possibility that a large number of items will be outstanding at the balancing date.

In order to avoid the labour of bringing forward in detail full particulars of these outstanding items to a fresh section of the book, which would be necessary to enable the various columns to be properly balanced off, an extended ruling of the book is suggested.

The following will be found suitable:

### SALE OR RETURN DAY BOOK

| | | | | | | | | | | | |
|---|---|---|---|---|---|---|---|---|---|---|---|
| | | HALF YEAR ENDING.......................................................... | | | | | | HALF YEAR ENDING........................ | | | |
| Date | Particulars | Goods sent on Sale or Return | Date return-ed or sold | Goods return-ed | Goods sold | Sales Ledger Folio | Balance June 30th | Date return-ed or sold | Goods return-ed | Goods sold | Sales Ledger Folio | Remarks |
| | | £ | | £ | £ | | £ | | £ | £ | | |

At the balancing date the selling price of the goods remaining in the hands of customers will be extended into the *Balance* column, and all the columns in the first section cast. The total of the *Balance* column, plus the totals of the *Goods Returned* and *Sold* columns, will equal the total in the *Goods sent out on Sale or Return* column.

In the following period, as these goods are sold or returned, the amounts will be extended into the columns provided, and this should suffice to complete the record, since it is unlikely that any items will remain open beyond the close of the second period. Any such goods still outstanding should be transferred to the next period's records, or called in.

A further section of the book will be utilized to record all goods sent out during each subsequent period, and these in their turn will be completed in a similar manner.

### (c) Where the number of Sale or Return transactions is large, and the goods are of considerable value

In these circumstances it is not wise to rely on a purely memorandum system, which does not readily lend itself to proof. It is preferable to have a separate set of books kept on double entry principles.

These will comprise the following:

1. Sale or Return Ledger.
2. Sale or Return Day Book.
3. Sale or Return Journal.

The procedure will then be as follows:

1. When goods are sent out they are entered in the sale or return day book, and posted therefrom in detail to the debit of the customer's account in the sale or return ledger, and in total at the end of each month or other period to the credit of a Sale or Return Total Account, which can be kept in the sale or return ledger.

2. When the customer intimates his decision to keep the goods, his account in the sale or return ledger must be credited and the Sale or Return Total Account debited. The customer's account in the sales ledger must then be debited (since he is now a debtor) and Sales Account credited. When goods are returned, the customer's account in the sale or return ledger must be credited and the Sale or Return Total Account in the same ledger debited. To record these transactions it is necessary to have a special sale or return journal, which should be ruled as follows:

SALE OR RETURN JOURNAL

| Date (1) | Particulars (2) | S. or R.L. Folio (3) | Sale or Return Ledger (4) | S. L. Folio (5) | Sales Ledger (6) |
|---|---|---|---|---|---|
| | | | £ | | £ |

3. When goods out on sale or return are sold, the customer's name is entered in column 2, and the amount of the sale entered in columns 4 and 6, and posted in detail therefrom to the credit of the customer's account in the sale or return ledger, and to the debit of his account in the sales ledger.

4. When goods are returned they are simply entered in column 4, and posted in detail therefrom to the credit of the customer's account in the sale or return ledger.

5. At the end of each period the total of column 6 is posted to the credit of Sales Account, and that of column 4 to the debit of Sale or Return Total Account in the sale or return ledger.

The main principle of the system above described is to render the sale or return ledger self-balancing, i.e. the total of the debit balances in the ledger should equal the balance of the Sale or Return Total Account. If this is carried out, there is no difficulty in ascertaining the total selling value of goods out on sale or return at any time.

On preparing final accounts, the sale or return ledger, being self-balancing, is outside the double entry, and the actual value of the goods out on sale or return, which should be treated as stock, can be arrived at by reducing the balance of each account in the sale or return ledger to the cost price of the goods.

It sometimes happens that goods sent out on sale or return are erroneously entered in the sales day book as if they were actual sales, and posted therefrom to the debit of the customers' accounts in the sales ledger. They are thus included in the total amount posted to the credit of Sales Account. Where goods sent out on sale or return have been treated in this way it is necessary, when preparing the final accounts, to eliminate the items from the Debtors' Accounts and Sales Account respectively, and include the goods, at cost price or under, in the closing stock figure, in the Trading Account and Balance Sheet; otherwise credit will be taken for a profit which has not yet been realized.

In order to obviate the necessity of making an adjusting entry in each individual debtor's account, the total selling price of all the outstanding items may be debited, in one sum, to Sales Account, and credited to a special account called Sale or Return Suspense Account, the balance of which should be deducted from the total of the book debts for Balance Sheet purposes. These goods will then be valued at or below cost price, and included in the value of the stock in trade which is credited to Trading Account and debited to Stock Account.

**Illustration**

In preparing the final accounts of a company it is found that the amount of the Sundry Debtors, £42,167, includes £4,000 worth of goods sent out on approval, and debited to customers' accounts, in respect of which the time for returning the goods had not yet expired. These goods have been invoiced at $33\frac{1}{3}\%$ above cost.

In preparing the final accounts the following journal entry should be made:

### JOURNAL

| | | £ | £ |
|---|---|---|---|
| Sales Account .. .. .. .. .. .. .. .. .. | Dr | 4,000 | |
| To Sales or Return Suspense Account .. .. .. .. .. .. .. | | | 4,000 |
| Adjusting goods out on Sale or Return treated as Sales. | | | |

The £4,000 debited to Sales Account will reduce the sales figure credited to Trading Account, whilst the £4,000 credited to Sale or Return Suspense Account will be deducted from the figure of Sundry Debtors, which will thus appear in the Balance Sheet as £38,167. The goods will then be valued at cost, viz. £3,000, and included in the stock-in-trade credited to Trading Account and debited to Stock Account.

In subsequent years, if the same procedure is continued, it will only be necessary to increase or decrease (as the case may be) the balance on the Sale or Return Suspense Account to the amount of the outstanding sale or return items as at the date of balancing the accounts, the corresponding entry being a debit or credit to the Sales Account.

## § 2. Consignment Accounts

In some businesses it is the practice to consign goods to agents for sale on commission, the goods remaining the property of the consignors until they are sold. In such cases the agents must not be debited with the value of the goods, since they do not purchase them. When, however, an agent has sold the goods and received the proceeds, he becomes indebted to the consignor for the sums received, less his expenses and commission, and accounts to the consignor by means of an ACCOUNT SALES, which shows particulars of goods sold, the price realized, the agent's charges, brokerage and commission deducted, and the net balance for which he is liable.

**Illustration**

On March 1st, 19. ., the A Mining Company Limited, consigned to B. Jones and Co 160 tons of Chrome Ore per s.s. *Menelaus*, invoiced at £7 per ton. The cost of the ore at the mine was £3 per ton = £480 and Railway Freight to the coast £140, all other expenses being paid by the consignee. On July 1st, B. Jones and Co remitted an Account Sales showing gross weight 160 tons, and tare of bags 10 cwt, the ore being realized at £8 per ton. They deducted for Ocean Freight £2 per ton, for Dock Dues etc. £90, Marine Insurance £15, Brokerage $1\frac{1}{4}$ per cent., and Commission $2\frac{1}{2}$ per cent., remitting a draft for the balance. Make out an Account Sales.

---

ACCOUNT SALES of 160 tons of Chrome Ore *ex* s.s. *Menelaus*, sold by order and for account of the A Mining Company Limited.

By B. JONES & CO.,
5 John Street,
London, July 1st, 19. .

| | | £ |
|---|---|---|
| Discharged | 160 tons 0 cwt. | |
| Tare of Bags | 10 ,, | |
| | 159 ,, 10 ,, @ £8 .. .. .. .. .. .. .. .. | 1,276 |

| CHARGES | | £ | |
|---|---|---|---|
| Ocean Freight at £2 per ton | .. .. .. .. .. .. .. .. | 319 | |
| Dock Dues etc. | .. .. .. .. .. .. .. .. | 90 | |
| Marine Insurance | .. .. .. .. .. .. .. .. | 15 | |
| Brokerage at $1\frac{1}{4}$% on £1,276 | .. .. .. .. .. .. .. .. | 16 | |
| Commission $2\frac{1}{2}$% on £1,276 | .. .. .. .. .. .. .. .. | 32 | |
| | | | 472 |
| Net proceeds as per draft enclosed .. | .. .. .. .. .. | | £804 |

E. & O. E.,
London, July 1st, 19. .
(Signed) B. JONES & CO.

---

Since the consignee sells the goods as agent for the consignor, where sales are made on credit the purchaser becomes the debtor of the consignor, not of the consignee, and if the debtor makes default in payment, it is the consignor who suffers the loss. Sometimes, however, in consideration of an additional commission, called a *del credere* commission, the consignee will indemnify the consignor against loss in respect of any transactions effected by the consignee on the consignor's behalf. Such an agent is called a *del credere* agent. In effect, he guarantees the payment of any debts created by his agency, and undertakes to bear the loss should any of them prove to be irrecoverable.

## § 3. Entries in the Consignor's Books

When the consignor wishes to ascertain the exact profit or loss in respect of each consignment, he should open a separate Consignment Account therefor. Each Consignment Account then constitutes a Profit and Loss Account in respect of the transaction to which it relates.

A personal account must be opened for the consignee. Care must be taken to post to this account only transactions which create or discharge liabilities between the consignor and consignee, e.g. the payment of cash or the charges for expenses and commission. No entry must be made in this account when goods are sent to the consignee, since he does not become a debtor in respect of such goods.

The procedure should be as follows:

1. Debit Consignment Account with the *cost* of the goods, and credit a 'Goods sent on Consignment Account'. (Even though the goods are invoiced *pro forma* to the consignee at an inflated price, only their *cost* price should be debited to Consignment Account, since the function of this account is to show the consignor's profit or loss on the consignment.)

2. Debit Consignment Account with expenses incurred by the consignor, such as insurance, freight etc., crediting cash or the relevant personal accounts.

3. On receipt of the Account Sales from the consignee, debit the Consignee's Account and credit the Consignment Account with the gross proceeds.

4. Debit the Consignment Account with expenses, brokerage and commission deducted by the consignee, crediting the Consignee's Account.

5. When the whole of the goods have been sold, the balance of the Consignment Account will represent the profit or loss on the consignment, and be transferred to Profit and Loss Account.

6. The balance of the Consignee's Account will represent the amount due by or to him. If he remits by bill, Bills Receivable Account will be debited and the Consignee's Account credited, so closing that account. If a draft or cheque is forwarded, cash will be debited.

7. Transfer the balance of the Goods sent on Consignment Account to the credit of Trading Account (or Purchases Account). The total purchases debited to Trading Account include these goods and the cost price of such goods must obviously be eliminated from the Trading Account, since they are fully accounted for in the Consignment Account. If they were not so credited, the cost of sales would be inflated, so that the Trading Account would not show the true gross profit on the ordinary turnover.

Occasionally, by special arrangement, the consignor draws a bill of exchange on the consignee as soon as the goods are forwarded, in which case the amount of the bill will be credited to the Consignee's Account. If the goods are never sold, and therefore returned, the bill will have to be cancelled or the consignee reimbursed. Such an arrangement enables the consignor, if he so desires, to discount the bill and place himself in funds to that extent in anticipation of the sale of the goods. The term of the bill will be such that the consignee can reasonably anticipate that he will have sold sufficient goods to realize the funds to meet the bill by the time it becomes due.

The amount of any such bill will rarely be equal to the full value of the goods, as the consignee will want to retain out of the proceeds, when the goods are sold, a sum to meet expenses and commission. When the consignee sends in his Account Sales, he takes credit for the bill, in whole or proportionately to the goods sold, according to the arrangement.

**Illustration (1)**

From the particulars given in the Account Sales on page 93, make the entries in the consignor's books.

### CONSIGNOR'S BOOKS
### CONSIGNMENT ACCOUNT

| 19.. | | | £ | 19.. | | | £ |
|---|---|---|---|---|---|---|---|
| Mar. 1 | Goods sent on consignment– | | | July 1 | B. Jones & Co. – Sales  ..  .. | | 1,276 |
| | Ore ..  ..  ..  .. | | 480 | | | | |
| | Railway Freight  ..  .. | | 140 | | | | |
| July 1 | B. Jones & Co.– | | | | | | |
| | Ocean Freight  ..  .. | | 319 | | | | |
| | Dock Dues  ..  ..  .. | | 90 | | | | |
| | Marine Insurance  ..  .. | | 15 | | | | |
| | Brokerage  ..  ..  .. | | 16 | | | | |
| | Commission ..  ..  .. | | 32 | | | | |
| Dec. 31 | Profit and Loss Account – | | | | | | |
| | Profit  ..  ..  .. | | 184 | | | | |
| | | | £1,276 | | | | £1,276 |

### B. JONES & CO.

| 19.. | | | £ | 19.. | | | £ |
|---|---|---|---|---|---|---|---|
| July 1 | Consignment Account – Sales  .. | | 1,276 | July 1 | Consignment Account – | | 472 |
| | | | | | Sundry Charges  ..  .. | | |
| | | | | „ 23 | Bank – proceeds of draft ..  .. | | 804 |
| | | | £1,276 | | | | £1,276 |

### GOODS SENT ON CONSIGNMENT ACCOUNT

| 19.. | | | £ | 19.. | | | £ |
|---|---|---|---|---|---|---|---|
| Dec. 31 | Trading Account  ..  .. | | 480 | Mar. 1 | Consignment Account – | | 480 |
| | | | | | Ore ..  ..  ..  .. | | |
| | | | £480 | | | | £480 |

Should the consignor prepare his Balance Sheet and accounts prior to the sale of the goods, the debit balance on the Consignment Account will be carried forward, and treated in the Balance Sheet as stock on consignment. If a loss is anticipated, adequate provision therefor should be made.

Where only part of the goods has been sold at the date upon which the Account Sales is rendered, the unsold stock should be brought down as a balance on the Consignment Account, being valued at the cost price of the goods. A relevant proportion of the expenses already incurred by the consignor and consignee in placing the goods in a saleable condition at the consignee's warehouse (but not of the expenses incurred in selling the goods) may be included in the valuation, and thus carried forward. If the current market value is less than cost, then the stock must be written down accordingly. This procedure discloses the correct profit or loss upon the goods actually sold. On no account should selling expenses be taken into account in valuing stock.

**Illustration (2)**

Applying the same particulars of the consignment as shown in Illustration (1), it is found that the A Mining Co Limited, consigned to B. Jones & Co, 160 tons of Chrome Ore costing £3 per ton at the mine = £480, and the railway freight amounted to £140. The A Mining Co's financial year ended on May 31st, 19.., and at that date only 79 tons, 10 cwts of the ore had been sold, the cost price of ore at the mine-head on May 31st being £2 per ton. At the Mining Co's request B. Jones & Co supplied an Account Sales, dated May 31st, giving the following particulars:

|  | Tons | cwt |  | £ |
|---|---|---|---|---|
| Net landed weight    ..    .. | 159 | 10 |  |  |
| Sold    ..    ..    ..    .. | 79 | 10 | @ £8    .. | 636 |
|  | 80 | 0 |  |  |

| Charges on whole consignment: |  | £ | £ |  |
|---|---|---|---|---|
| Ocean Freight    ..    ..    .. |  | 319 |  |  |
| Dock Dues etc.    ..    ..    .. |  | 90 |  |  |
| Marine Insurance    ..    ..    .. |  | 15 |  |  |
|  |  |  | 424 |  |
| Brokerage $1\frac{1}{4}$% on £636 ..    ..    .. |  |  | 8 |  |
| Commission $2\frac{1}{2}$%    ..    ..    .. |  |  | 16 |  |
|  |  |  |  | 448 |
| Net proceeds    ..    ..    ..    ..    .. |  |  |  | £188 |

Show the Consignment Account and Goods sent on Consignment Account in the consignor's books.

## CONSIGNOR'S BOOKS

### CONSIGNMENT ACCOUNT

| 19.. |  | £ | 19.. |  | £ |
|---|---|---|---|---|---|
| Mar. 1 | Goods sent on consignment – |  | May 31 | B Jones and Co ..    ..    .. | 636 |
|  | Ore ..    ..    ..    .. | 480 |  | Balance carried down – |  |
|  | Railway Freight    ..    .. | 140 |  | 80 tons @ £2 plus shipping and |  |
| May 31 | B. Jones & Co – Charges on whole |  |  | landing charges (see Note)    .. | 443 |
|  | consignment ..    ..    .. | 424 |  |  |  |
|  | B. Jones & Co – |  |  |  |  |
|  | Brokerage on Sales    ..    .. | 8 |  |  |  |
|  | Commission on Sales    ..    .. | 16 |  |  |  |
|  | Profit and Loss Account – |  |  |  |  |
|  | Profit    ..    ..    .. | 11 |  |  |  |
|  |  | £1,079 |  |  | £1,079 |
| June 1 | Balance brought down    ..    .. | 443 |  |  |  |

### GOODS SENT ON CONSIGNMENT ACCOUNT

| 19.. |  | £ | 19.. |  | £ |
|---|---|---|---|---|---|
| May 31 | Trading Account    ..    .. | 480 | Mar. 1 | Consignment Account – |  |
|  |  |  |  | Ore ..    ..    ..    .. | 480 |
|  |  | £480 |  |  | £480 |

*Note:* The balance carried down in the Consignment Account is made up as follows:

|  |  |  |  |  | £ |
|---|---|---|---|---|---|
| 80 tons of Ore @ £2 per ton (current market value) | .. | .. | .. |  | 160 |
| Railway Freight | .. | .. | .. | £140 |  |
| B. Jones & Co's charges on whole consignment | .. | .. | .. | 424 |  |

$$\frac{80}{159\cdot5} \times \quad 564$$

283

£443

The stock on consignment is treated as an asset at the balancing date. The cost price of the whole of the goods sent out on consignment is eliminated from the Trading Account by the transfer from Goods on Consignment Account.

Where the consignee is authorized to sell goods on credit, and at the date of the Account Sales there is an amount outstanding in respect of credit sales, that amount can be recorded as a balance carried down on the Consignment Account, or by crediting Consignment' Account and debiting Consignment Debtors Account. When an Account Sales is subsequently received, showing the receipt of the cash from the debtors, the amount will be transferred to the debit of the Consignee's Personal Account. A consignee, other than a *del credere* agent, should not be debited with the proceeds of sale until he has received them in cash.

### Illustration (3)

On April 1st, Emen & Co had consigned to C. Onsignee, goods costing £4,000, on which they paid freight, insurance etc., amounting to £500. On August 31st, C. Onsignee's first Account Sales was received, showing that he had effected sales of £2,800, of which £2,500 had been received in cash. His expenses to date were £400, and commission, 5 per cent. on gross sales. On receipt of the Account Sales, the Consignment Account was balanced off, stock being valued at £3,000. A further Account Sales was received on December 31st, shewing that the balance of the goods had been sold for £3,450 and the cash collected: debtors had also paid, less a discount of 5 per cent. The expenses of C. Onsignee were £120, commission 5 per cent. Write up the accounts in the books of Emen & Co to December 31st, assuming C. Onsignee remitted the balance due with each Account Sales.

### CONSIGNMENT ACCOUNT

| 19.. |  | £ | 19.. |  | £ |
|---|---|---|---|---|---|
| April 1 | Goods sent on consignment  .. | 4,000 | Aug. 31 | C. Onsignee – |  |
|  | Freight, Insurance etc.  .. | 500 |  | Cash Collected *re* Sales ..  .. | 2,500 |
| Aug. 31 | C. Onsignee – |  |  | Sales on Credit c/d.  ..  .. | 300 |
|  | Expenses  ..  .. | 400 |  | Stock c/d.  ..  ..  .. | 3,000 |
|  | Commission on gross sales at 5% | 140 |  |  |  |
|  | Profit and Loss Account .. | 760 |  |  |  |
|  |  | £5,800 |  |  | £5800 |
| 19.. |  |  | 19.. |  |  |
| Aug. 31 | Balances b/d. – |  | Dec. 31 | C. Onsignee – |  |
|  | Debtors  ..  ..  .. | 300 |  | Cash Collected *re* Sales .. | 3,450 |
|  | Stock  ..  ..  .. | 3,000 |  | From Debtors ..  ..  .. | 285 |
| Dec. 31 | C. Onsignee – |  |  |  |  |
|  | Expenses  ..  .. | 120 |  |  |  |
|  | Commission ..  .. | 173 |  |  |  |
|  | Profit and Loss Account ..  .. | 142 |  |  |  |
|  |  | £3,735 |  |  | £3,735 |

### C. ONSIGNEE

| 19..<br>Aug. 31 | Consignment Account –<br>Cash collected | | £<br>2,500 | 19..<br>Aug. 31 | Consignment Account –<br>Expenses<br>Commission<br>Cash | | | £<br>400<br>140<br>1,960 |
|---|---|---|---|---|---|---|---|---|
| | | | £2,500 | | | | | £2,500 |
| 19..<br>Dec. 31 | Consignment Account –<br>Cash collected | | 3,735 | 19..<br>Dec. 31 | Consignment Account –<br>Expenses<br>Commission<br>Cash | | | 120<br>173<br>3,442 |
| | | | £3,735 | | | | | £3,735 |

*Note:* The discount is automatically recorded by bringing into account only the cash collected. There is no point in shewing it as a debit and a credit in the Consignment Acccount.

### GOODS SENT ON CONSIGNMENT ACCOUNT

| 19..<br>Aug. 31 | Trading Account | | £<br>4,000 | 19..<br>Apl. 1 | Consignment Account | | £<br>4,000 |
|---|---|---|---|---|---|---|---|

Where some of the goods are damaged or lost in transit, the loss, if not material, may be charged to the Consignment Account automatically by crediting that account only with the reduced value of the stock remaining on hand at the date of balancing the accounts. If it is desired to record the loss separately the cost price of the damaged goods can be entered on both sides of the account. Goods lost before they reach the consignees, or if the loss is material, should be credited to the Consignment Account and debited to Profit and Loss Account at cost less any amounts recovered from underwriters. Any goods returned to the consignor will be credited to the Consignment Account and debited to the Goods sent on Consignment Account at cost.

Where the agent is authorized to give goods away for advertising purposes, the cost thereof (including the expenses incurred in connection therewith) should be credited to Consignment Account and debited to Advertising Account, which latter account would in due course be transferred to the debit of Profit and Loss Account. Alternatively, if it is desired that the cost of advertising shall be borne by the consignment, the cost of the goods distributed should be both credited and debited to the Consignment Account, the balance of which will then represent the net profit or loss on the consignment, after all expenses incurred in selling the goods have been deducted.

It is not uncommon for the goods to be invoiced to the consignee at a *pro forma* price in excess of cost, in which case columns should be provided in the Consignment Account for recording the price alongside the ordinary entries. The invoice columns are purely memorandum columns for the purpose of reconciling the invoice price of sales and unsold stock with that of the goods consigned. Entries in the invoice columns form no part of the double entry.

**Illustration (4)**

A, in London, consigns goods to B in Australia, for sale at invoice price or over. B is entitled to a commission of 5 per cent. on invoice prices and 25 per cent. of any surplus prices realized. A draws on B at 90 days sight for 80 per cent. of the invoice price, and upon sale B remits the balance of proceeds, after deducting his commission, by sight draft.

Goods consigned by A to B in the year cost A £10,450, including freight and were invoiced at £14,200. Sales made by B were £13,380, and goods in his hands, unsold at December 31st, represented an invoice value of £3,460 (original cost, including freight £2,610). Sight drafts actually received by A from B up to December 31st, were £3,140; others were in transit.

Prepare accounts in A's books of these transactions and show (by ledger accounts) the manner in which the books would be closed at December 31st.

### CONSIGNMENT TO B (AUSTRALIA) ACCOUNT

| | Invoice Price £ | £ | | Invoice Price £ | £ |
|---|---|---|---|---|---|
| Goods  ..        ..        ..        .. | 14,200 | 10,450 | Sales  ..        ..        ..        .. | 10,740 | 13,380 |
| B. Commission: | | | Stock c/d.        ..        ..        .. | 3,460 | 2,610 |
| 5% on £10,740 ..        ..        .. | | 537 | | | |
| 25% on £2,640 ..        ..        .. | | 660 | | | |
| Profit and Loss Account        .. | | 4,343 | | | |
| | £14,200 | £15,990 | | £14,200 | £15,990 |
| Balance b/d.        ..        ..        .. | 3,460 | 2,610 | | | |

### B

| | £ | | £ |
|---|---|---|---|
| Sales  ..        ..        ..        ..        .. | 13,380 | Bills Receivable ..        ..        ..        .. | 11,360 |
| Balance c/d.        ..        ..        ..        .. | 2,317 | Commission  ..        ..        ..        .. | 1,197 |
| | | Cash  ..        ..        ..        ..        .. | 3,140 |
| | £15,697 | | £15,697 |
| | | Balance b/d.        ..        ..        ..        .. | 2,317 |

*Note:* No account can be taken of drafts in transit which amount to £451.

### GOODS SENT ON CONSIGNMENT ACCOUNT

| | £ | | Invoice Price | £ |
|---|---|---|---|---|
| Trading Account  ..        ..        ..        .. | 10,450 | B  ..        ..        ..        .. £14,200 | | 10,450 |

*Note:* Apparently the arrangement is that on sale of the goods, B shall remit the proceeds, *less* commission and *less* the proportion of the bill of exchange applicable to the goods sold, i.e. he owes A on December 31st.

| | | | | | | £ |
|---|---|---|---|---|---|---|
| Proceeds of Sale | .. | .. | .. | .. | .. | 13,380 |
| *Less* Commission | .. | .. | .. | .. | .. | 1,197 |
| | | | | | | 12,183 |
| *Less* Proportion of Bill applicable to goods sold, 80% of Invoice Price, £10,740 = .. | .. | .. | .. | .. | 8,592 |
| | | | Amount due | .. | .. | 3,591 |
| He has already remitted .. | .. | .. | .. | .. | 3,140 |
| ∴ Drafts in transit amount to | | .. | .. | .. | £451 |

|  |  | £ |
|---|---|---|
| The balance to B's credit is made up of: |  |  |
| Proportion of Bill applicable to goods in Stock, 80% of Invoice |  |  |
| Price, £3,460 = .. .. .. .. .. | | 2,768 |
| *Less* Drafts in transit .. .. .. .. .. | | 451 |
| Balance .. .. .. .. .. .. | | £2,317 |

Where the goods are consigned to an agent abroad whose accounts are rendered in a foreign currency it will be necessary to provide memorandum currency columns in the consignee's personal account, in which the relevant items will be converted into sterling at appropriate rates. As a general rule it will be found convenient to convert sales made by the agent and the agent's expenses and commission at the average rate for the period. Remittances received from the agent should be converted at the actual sums realized, whilst the closing balance of the agent's account should be converted at the rate of exchange prevailing at the date of the Balance Sheet. The resultant sterling balance on the agent's account will represent profit or loss on exchange. This may, if desired, be transferred to the Consignment Account, which will then show the final profit or loss in sterling realized on the consignment. Alternatively, the amount may be transferred to a Difference on Exchange Account which, if in debit, should be written off to Profit and Loss Account, or if in credit carried forward as a provision against future possible losses on exchange.

### Illustration (5)

On January 2nd, B bought for cash 200 machines at £33 each f.o.b. London for shipment to his Agent G in Berne, to sell on a consignment basis. On February 2nd, B paid £500 for freight and £140 for insurance.

G sent B an Account Sales dated May 31st showing that he had sold 100 machines at Fr. 550 each and a further 40 machines at Fr. 570 each. G had paid landing charges Fr. 2,750 and selling expenses on the machines sold Fr. 700. His commission was at the rate of Fr. 20 per machine sold, plus one quarter of the amount by which the gross sale proceeds, less the total commission thereon, exceeded a sum calculated at the rate of Fr. 500 per machine sold. A bank draft dated May 31st was enclosed for the balance due to B, which realized £5,600.

Prepare Consignment Account and G's personal account in B's books as at June 30th, no further machines having been sold by that date.

Sales, expenses and commission are to be converted at the average rate of Fr. 12·5 to £.

### CONSIGNMENT TO G ACCOUNT

|  |  | £ | £ |  |  | £ | £ |
|---|---|---|---|---|---|---|---|
| Jan. 2 | Goods sent on Consignment: | | | May 31 | Sale of 140 Machines as per | | |
| | 200 Machines at £33 each .. | | 6,600 | | Account Sales (*Fr.* 77,800) | | 6,224 |
| Feb. 2 | Freight .. .. .. | | 500 | | Stock on hand: | | |
| | Insurance .. .. .. | | 140 | | 60 Machines at £33 .. | 1,980 | |
| Mar. 31 | General Expenses as per Ac- | | | | Proportion of: | | |
| | count Sales: | | | | Freight .. £500 | | |
| | Landing Charges .. | 220 | | | Insurance .. 140 | | |
| | Selling Expenses .. | 56 | | | Landing Charges 220 | | |
| | Commission .. | 304 | | | $\frac{60}{200} \times £860$ | | |
| | | | 580 | | | 258 | |
| June 30 | Loss on Exchange .. .. | | 44 | | | | 2,238 |
| | Profit and Loss Account– | | | | | | |
| | Profit on consignment .. | | 598 | | | | |
| | | | £8,462 | | | | £8,462 |
| June 1 | Stock on hand b/d. .. | | 2,238 | | | | |

### G – PERSONAL ACCOUNT

| | | | Francs | £ | | | | | Francs | £ |
|---|---|---|---|---|---|---|---|---|---|---|
| May 31 | Consignment Account, Sales: | | | | May 31 | Consignment Account: | | | | |
| | 100 Machines @ Fr. 550 | .. | 55,000 | 4,400 | | Landing Charges | .. | | 2,750 | 220 |
| | 40 „ Fr. 570 | .. | 22,800 | 1,824 | | Selling Expenses | | | 700 | 56 |
| | | | | | | Commission | .. | | 3,800 | 304 |
| | | | | | June 29 | Bank Draft | .. | | 70,550 | 5,600 |
| | | | | | | Consignment Account: | | | | |
| | | | | | | Loss on Exchange | .. | | | 44 |
| | | Fr. | 77,800 | £6,224 | | | | Fr. | 77,800 | £6,224 |

*Note:* Total Commission $= x = Fr. 2,800 + \frac{1}{4}(77,800 - x - 70,000) = Fr. 3,800$.

## § 4. Entries in the Consignee's Books

When the goods are received by the consignee, particulars thereof should be entered in a consignment stock book ruled for marks and quantities, according to the nature of the goods, and having a column for *pro forma* invoice prices. This book, however, is merely a memorandum book, and no entries should be made in the financial books until a sale takes place. The goods, not being the property of the consignee, must be kept entirely distinct from his own stock, and should not be included in his Balance Sheet.

The entries in the consignee's books will be as follows:

1. Debit the Consignor's Account with any expenses incurred in connection with the consignment by the consignee, such as freight, warehousing etc., crediting cash or the relevant personal account.

2. When sales are made, debit the various debtors' accounts with the amounts thereof and credit the Consignor's Account through a consignment sales day book, or, where there are few transactions, through the ordinary journal.

3. When the Account Sales is prepared, debit the Consignor's Account with the brokerage, commission etc., crediting the latter accounts. If any debtors have not yet paid their accounts carry forward a balance to the credit of the Consignor's Account in respect thereof, unless by the terms of the agency the agent has to remit in full.

4. The balance of the Consignor's Account will represent the amount due to him. If a draft is remitted, debit his account and credit Bills Payable or cash, as the case may be, so closing the account.

### Illustration

From the particulars given in the Illustration on page 93 make the entries in the consignee's books.

### CONSIGNEE'S BOOKS
### THE A MINING COMPANY LIMITED

| | | | | | £ | | | | | | £ |
|---|---|---|---|---|---|---|---|---|---|---|---|
| July 1 | Ocean Freight | .. | .. | .. | 319 | July 1 | Sundry Debtors .. | | .. | .. | 1,276 |
| | Dock Dues | .. | .. | .. | 90 | | | | | | |
| | Marine Insurance | .. | .. | .. | 15 | | | | | | |
| | Brokerage | .. | .. | .. | 16 | | | | | | |
| | Commission | .. | .. | .. | 32 | | | | | | |
| | Bank – draft | .. | .. | .. | 804 | | | | | | |
| | | | | | £1,276 | | | | | | £1,276 |

Detailed particulars will also be entered in the consignment stock book by way of memoranda as described above.

An alternative method for recording consignments in the consignee's financial books, is to debit a Consignment Stock Account and credit the Consignor's Account with the invoice value of the goods. When the goods are sold the proceeds are credited to the Consignment Stock Account, and the difference on this account, representing profit, is then transferred to the Consignor's Account. The Consignment Stock Account and the corresponding credits to the Consignor's Account must, of course, be eliminated from the consignee's Balance Sheet. It might be considered preferable to credit a Consignor's Suspense Account with the invoice value, in order to preclude the possibility of a payment inadvertently being made to the consignor before the goods are sold.

This method is not to be recommended, as it takes into the consignee's financial books as assets and liabilities items which are not such from his point of view.

### § 5. Accounts with Agents

In many cases, where agencies are situated in different parts of the world, it is not convenient to treat the goods sent to such agents as consignments, and often, even in cases of consignments proper, it is not desired to show the profit or loss on each shipment. In such cases Consignment Accounts as illustrated in § 3 are not used, but the transactions may be dealt with in the manner described hereunder.

Memorandum quantity stock accounts are kept, showing particulars of goods sent to the agent. No entries are made, otherwise than by way of memoranda, when goods are sent to the agent, except that the proper nominal accounts are debited with any expenses incurred. When the agent's returns are received, Sales Account is credited with the gross sales and the Agent's Account debited. Any expenses incurred by the agent are credited to his account, and debited to the appropriate expense accounts. The Agent's Account is credited with sums remitted by him, and the balance on his account at any time will be the amount due by him for sales effected. In this way the agent will not be debited with the value of any stock unsold, as this will be regarded as stock belonging to the firm and brought into the Balance Sheet at cost plus expenses, or at a lower valuation if necessary.

The agent will forward at regular intervals quantity stock accounts, which will be agreed with the similar accounts kept at the head office, any differences in stock being adjusted.

**Illustration (1)**

The X Manufacturing Company forwarded goods to the value of £3,400 to their agent, incurring the following expenses:

|  |  |  | £ |
|---|---|---|---|
| Carriage and Freight | .. | .. | 140 |
| Insurance | .. | .. | 15 |

Up to the date of balancing the accounts the agent had forwarded returns showing the following transactions:

|  | £ |
|---|---|
| Cash Sales .. .. .. | 1,250 |
| Credit Sales .. .. | 1,575 |
| Cash collected from Debtors .. | 1,300 |
| Sundry expenses .. .. | 130 |
| Cash remitted .. .. | 2,400 |
| Stock on hand at cost .. .. | 1,340 |

Show by Journal entries how these transactions should be recorded in the books of the X Manufacturing Company, and prepare the agent's Personal Account.

## X MANUFACTURING COMPANY
### JOURNAL

|  |  | £ | £ |
|---|---|---|---|
| Carriage and Freight Account .. .. .. .. .. .. .. | Dr | 140 |  |
| Insurance Account .. .. .. .. .. .. .. .. | | 15 | |
| To Cash | | | 155 |
| Expenses incurred in dispatch of goods to agent. | | | |
| Agent's Account .. .. .. .. .. .. .. .. .. | Dr | 2,825 | |
| To Cash Sales Account .. .. .. .. .. .. .. | | | 1,250 |
| Credit Sales Account .. .. .. .. .. .. .. | | | 1,575 |
| Sales effected as per agent's returns. | | | |
| Sundry Expenses Account .. .. .. .. .. .. .. | Dr | 130 | |
| To Agent's Account .. .. .. .. .. .. .. | | | 130 |
| Agent's expenses as per his returns. | | | |
| Cash .. .. .. .. .. .. .. .. .. | Dr | 2,400 | |
| To Agent's Account .. .. .. .. .. .. .. | | | 2,400 |
| Cash remitted by agent. | | | |

### AGENT'S PERSONAL ACCOUNT

|  | £ |  | £ |
|---|---|---|---|
| Sales Account .. .. .. .. | 2,825 | Expenses Account .. .. .. | 130 |
| | | Cash .. .. .. .. .. | 2,400 |
| | | Balance c/d. .. .. .. .. | 295 |
| | £2,825 | | £2,825 |
| Balance b/d. .. .. .. .. | 295 | | |

*Note:* The memorandum Stock Account will be debited with £3,400 stock sent, and credited with the cost of sales. The balance should represent the value of stock in agent's hands and will be included in the company's stock when the Trading Account and Balance Sheet are prepared.

Although not recommended, the Agent's Account is sometimes debited with the cost of the goods sent to him, but care must be taken, if goods are debited at more than cost, to reduce the value of stock in his hands at balancing time to cost price, so that no credit is taken for profit before it is actually realized.

Where the agent is so debited, it is advisable to create a provision of an equal amount. This can readily be done in the following way:

1. Debit the Agent's Account and credit a 'Goods sent to Agent Account' with the invoice price.

2. When sales are notified (*a*) debit Goods sent to Agent Account and credit Sales Account with the amount of the sales; (*b*) debit the Agent's Account and credit Goods sent to Agent Account with the excess of the selling over invoice

price of the goods sold; and (c) debit the various expense accounts and credit Agent's Account with the expenses paid by him.

3. Debit cash and credit the Agent's Account with remittances received from the agent.

4. For the purposes of the Balance Sheet and Profit and Loss Account, the Goods sent to Agent Account will be deducted from the balance on the Agent's Account so that the latter will show only the amount, if any, due from him. Stock will be valued as usual, and included in the accounts as stock in the hands of agents, by debiting a Stock Account and crediting Trading Account. This Stock Account will be closed in due course by transfer to the next period's Trading Account.

### Illustration (2)

Goods costing £1,000 were invoiced to an agent at £1,200. In due course the agent submitted a return showing that he had sold three-fourths of the goods for £1,500, paying expenses amounting to £50, and enclosing a draft for £1,100. The Stock was valued at £240, prices having fallen.

Write up the accounts affected.

### AGENT'S ACCOUNT

| | £ | | £ |
|---|---|---|---|
| Goods at invoice price .. .. .. | 1,200 | Expenses Account .. .. .. | 50 |
| do. excess of selling price over invoice price .. | 600 | Cash .. .. .. .. .. | 1,100 |
| | | Balance c/d. .. .. .. .. | 650 |
| | £1,800 | | £1,800 |
| Balance b/d. .. .. .. .. | 650 | | |

### GOODS SENT TO AGENT ACCOUNT

| | £ | | £ |
|---|---|---|---|
| Sales Account .. .. .. .. | 1,500 | Agent's Account .. .. .. | 1,200 |
| Balance c/d. .. .. .. .. | 300 | „ „ excess of selling price over invoice price .. .. .. .. | 600 |
| | £1,800 | | £1,800 |
| | | Balance b/d. .. .. .. .. | 300 |

### SALES ACCOUNT

| | £ | | £ |
|---|---|---|---|
| Trading Account .. .. .. .. | 1,500 | Goods sent to Agent Account .. .. | 1,500 |

### TRADING ACCOUNT

| | | | £ |
|---|---|---|---|
| | | Sales Account .. .. .. .. | 1,500 |
| | | Stocks in hands of Agent .. .. | 240 |

### EXPENSES ACCOUNT

| | £ | | |
|---|---|---|---|
| Agent's Account .. .. .. .. | 50 | | |

## STOCK IN HANDS OF AGENT ACCOUNT

| | £ | | |
|---|---|---|---|
| Trading Account   ..       ..       ..       .. | 240 | | |

The Balance Sheet will include £350 as due from the agent, viz. the balance of his account, £650, less the provision on Goods sent to Agent Account, £300. This amount is made up of the following:

|  |  | £ | £ |
|---|---|---|---|
| Proceeds of sale of goods | .. |  | 1,500 |
| *Less* Expenses | .. | 50 | |
| Cash remitted | .. | 1,100 | |
|  |  |  | 1,150 |
|  |  |  | £350 |

Where foreign agents are concerned, it may be necessary to record the transactions in currency, in which case currency as well as sterling columns must be utilized, and any difference on exchange dealt with as explained in Chapter X, § 6.

## CHAPTER VI

# BILLS OF EXCHANGE, PROMISSORY NOTES ETC.

## § 1. Definitions

### (a) Bill of Exchange

A *Bill of Exchange* is defined by the *Bills of Exchange Act 1882* as 'an unconditional ORDER in writing, addressed by one person to another, signed by the person giving it, requiring the person to whom it is addressed to pay on demand, or at a fixed or determinable future time, a sum certain in money, to, or to the order of, a specified person or to bearer'.

There are three parties to a bill, viz. – (1) the *drawer*, i.e. the party who draws the bill and signs it; (2) the *drawee*, i.e. the party to whom the bill is addressed; and (3) the *payee*, i.e. the party to whom the bill is expressed to be payable.

A drawee 'accepts' a bill, by signing his name across the face of it, and thereby becomes the *acceptor*. Until the drawee becomes the acceptor he is not liable on the bill. When the bill is negotiated (i.e. transferred from one person to another in such a manner as to constitute the transferee the holder of the bill), each party through whose hands it passes must endorse his name on the back thereof, and thereby becomes an *endorser*, unless the bill is drawn to *bearer*, when it requires no endorsement but is negotiated by delivery only. If a bill drawn to order is endorsed in blank in the first instance it thereby becomes a bearer bill and no further endorsement is legally necessary.

A cheque is the most common form of bill of exchange, being defined by the *Bills of Exchange Act 1882*, as 'a bill of exchange drawn on a banker, payable on demand'.

### (b) Promissory Note

A *Promissory Note* is an unconditional PROMISE in writing made by one person to another, signed by the maker, engaging to pay on demand, or at a fixed or determinable future time, a sum certain in money to, or to the order of, a specified person or to bearer.

The parties to a promissory note are: (1) the *promisor*, i.e. the party who makes the promise and signs the note; and (2) the *promisee*, i.e. the party to whom the promise is made. There may be a single promisor, or two or more promisors. In the latter case the liability of the promisors may be either *joint*, or *joint and several*. If the liability is joint, any judgement without satisfaction against one of the makers of the note is a bar to proceedings against the other joint maker or makers. In the case of a joint and several note an unsatisfied judgement against one can be followed by action against another party.

When a promissory note payable to order is negotiated, each party through whose hands it passes must endorse his name on the back thereof, and thereupon becomes an *endorser*.

A Bank of England Note is the most common form of promissory note. This, however, is payable to bearer, and requires no endorsement.

### (c) Negotiable Instruments

*Negotiable Instruments* are documents representing value in money, such as promissory notes, bills of exchange etc., the property in which passes by mere delivery, or by endorsement and delivery.

As a general rule a party cannot give a better title to property than he himself possesses, but in the case of a negotiable instrument, provided the holder receives it in good faith for valuable consideration, before it is overdue, and without notice of any prior defect in the title, his title will be good, notwithstanding any defect in the title of any prior holder.

### (d) Days of Grace

Three days, termed 'days of grace', are allowed as an addition to the stated term or 'tenor' for the payment of all bills of exchange and promissory notes, except those payable at sight or on demand, or expressed to be payable at a fixed date without days of grace, or for a period *certain*. In calculating the due date, therefore, allowance must be made for the three days of grace. Similarly, three days of grace must be taken into account in calculating interest or discount.

Where a bill is so drawn that the third day of grace falls on a Good Friday, Christmas Day, or other day of public thanksgiving, the bill must be paid upon the *preceding* business day. If the third day of grace is a bank holiday or a Saturday or Sunday the bill is payable on the *succeeding* business day. In a doubtful case the bill is payable on the *nearest* business day.

**Illustration**

If the third day of grace falls on Sunday, November 14th, the bill is payable on Monday, November 15th.

If the third day of grace falls on Saturday, December 25th, Christmas Day, the bill is payable on December 24th.

When the tenor of a bill of exchange is expressed in months the due date is calculated by adding three days to the day of the last month of the tenor which corresponds with the day of the month on which the bill is drawn. Thus by the custom of bankers, a bill of one month drawn on February 28th would fall due on March 31st, i.e. three days after March 28th, not three days after March 31st. No account is, however, taken of missing days, so that if a bill at one month were drawn on January 31st, it would fall due on March 3rd, i.e. three days after February 28th (or, in a leap year, after February 29th).

### § 2. Stamp Duty on Bills of Exchange and Promissory Notes

By Section 33 of the *Finance Act 1961*, the stamp duty payable on any kind of bill of exchange or promissory note (other than a bank note) for any amount drawn or expressed to be payable, or actually paid or endorsed, or in any way negotiated in the United Kingdom is 2*d* (two old pence).

The duty may be denoted by an adhesive stamp, which must be cancelled by the person who signs the bill before it is delivered out of his hands.

This provision applies to all bills and notes drawn or made on or after August

1st, 1961, and up to and including January 31st, 1971. As from February 1st, 1971, the stamp duty payable on any kind of bill of exchange or promissory note was abolished by the *Finance Act 1970* (Seventh Schedule, Section 2 (2)).

### § 3. Specimen Forms of Bills of Exchange and Promisory Notes

The following are specimen forms of bills of exchange:

I.

London, February 1st, 1971

£100          Three months after date pay to my order the sum of One hundred pounds sterling for value received.

To Messrs. BLACK & Co,          F. SMITH.
Glasgow.

In this case the drawer and the payee are one and the same person, viz. F. Smith. Black & Co are the drawees, who, on accepting the bill, become the acceptors.

II.

London, February 1st, 1971

£436          Three months after date pay to F. Blackmore or order the sum of Four hundred and thirty-six pounds for value received.

To Messrs. A. WHITE & Co,          B. WILLIAMS.
London.

In this case the drawer and payee are not the same person.

III.

Calcutta, February 1st, 1971

£5,000          Three months after sight of this first exchange (second and third of even tenor and date unpaid) pay to the order of Mr John Jones the sum of Five thousand pounds for value received.

To Messrs. F. WILKINSON & Co,          R. PHILLIPS & CO.
London.

This is a form of foreign bill drawn in Calcutta payable in this country. Foreign bills are often drawn in duplicate or in sets of three, each part of the set being numbered, and referring to the other parts. The first part coming to hand will be presented for acceptance, and the others destroyed as and when received.

IV.

Bombay, February 1st, 1971

$1,750          Two months after sight of this our second of exchange (first and third of even tenor and date unpaid) pay to the order of Mr F. Brown the sum of One thousand, seven hundred and fifty dollars for value received.

To JOHN L. SMITH,          F. WALL & CO.
New York.

This is an illustration of a bill which is drawn abroad and payable abroad, but assumed to have been negotiated in this country.

––––––––––

The following are some forms of promissory notes:

I.

London, February 1st, 1971

£50        Three months after date I promise to pay A. White & Co or order the sum of Fifty pounds for value received.

JOHN LAKE.

It will be observed that there are only two parties to a promissory note – the promisor and the payee.

II.

London, February 1st, 1971

£1,000     On demand we promise to pay to Messrs. F. White & Co the sum of One thousand pounds for value received.

C. BROWN.
E. GREEN.

This is an instance of a *joint promissory note*. The promisors are jointly liable, i.e. only one action can be brought, and if action is taken and judgement obtained against one of the parties only, and that judgement is unsatisfied, another action cannot subsequently be brought against the other party.

If the note had been worded 'I promise to pay', and had been signed by both parties as above, the liability would have been joint and several.

III.

London, February 1st, 1971

£530       Three months after date we jointly and severally promise to pay to the order of Messrs. F. Wilkins & Co the sum of Five hundred and thirty pounds for value received.

F. T.
W. X.
Y. Z.

This is an instance of a *joint and several promissory note* where the parties are jointly and severally liable. In the event of any one of the parties not contributing his proportion, the holder will have a right of recovery for the full amount of the note against any one of the promisors, who in his turn will have a right of recovery from the remaining promisors of their respective contributions.

## § 4. Forms of Bill Books

Bill books are subsidiary books for recording the history of all bills of exchange handled by the business, and serving the purpose of day books, from which the bills are posted in detail to the personal accounts affected, and in total to the Bills Accounts in the ledger.

### (a) Bills Receivable and Bills Payable Books

The forms of bill books vary considerably in practice, according to the requirements of the business and the class of bills dealt with. The essential point is that the bill book should record a concise history of each bill.

The following is a convenient form of bills receivable book which can be adapted to the majority of cases:

**Illustration (1)**

### BILLS RECEIVABLE BOOK

| No. of Bill | Date received | From whom received | Drawer | Acceptor | Where Payable | Date of Bill | Term | Date due, including Days of Grace | Folio in Ledger | Amount of Bill | How Disposed of |
|---|---|---|---|---|---|---|---|---|---|---|---|
| 1 | 19.. July 2 | H. Marshall | Self | H. Marshall | London | 19.. July 1 | 1 month | 19.. Aug. 4 | 4 | £ 50 | Cash received Aug. 4 |
| 2 | Aug. 1 | J. Wilson | Self | J. Wilson | Lloyds Bank, Ltd | July 31 | 50 days | Sept. 22 | 5 | 70 | Dishonoured Sept. 22 |
| 3 | Sept. 9 | F. Johnson | F. Johnson | L. Taylor | Barclays Bank, Ltd | Sept. 3 | 3 months | Dec. 6 | 6 | 90 | Discounted Sept. 12 |
| | | | | | | | | | | £210 | |
| | | | | | | | | | | Fo. L.1. | |

Each item in the bills receivable book is posted to the credit of the ledger account of the person from whom the bill is received; periodically the total of the bills is posted to the debit of Bills Receivable Account.

The following is a convenient form of bills payable book:

**Illustration (2)**

### BILLS PAYABLE BOOK

| No. of Bill | Date given | To whom given | Drawer | Payee | Where Payable | Date of Bill | Term | Date due, including Days of Grace | Folio in Ledger | Amount of Bill | How Disposed of |
|---|---|---|---|---|---|---|---|---|---|---|---|
| 1 | 19.. July 15 | W. Black | W. Black | W. Black | Lloyds Bank Ltd | 19.. July 14 | 60 days | 19.. Sept. 15 | 7 | £ 90 | Paid Sept. 15 |
| 2 | July 19 | F. White | F. White | F. White | ,, ,, | July 18 | 3 months | Oct. 21 | 8 | 80 | |
| 3 | Aug. 3 | H. Brown | H. Brown | H. Brown | ,, ,, | Aug. 2 | 2 months | Oct. 5 | 9 | 40 | |
| | | | | | | | | | | £210 | |
| | | | | | | | | | | Fo. L.2. | |

Each item in a bills payable book is posted to the debit of the ledger account of the person to whom the bill is given, the total being posted periodically to the credit of Bills Payable Account.

In order to obtain cash before the due date of a bill receivable, the holder may discount it with his banker, i.e. negotiate it to the banker for an immediate cash payment. The banker charges interest on the face value of the bill for the period it still has to run, and pays the balance at its present cash value. This interest is called the 'discount'. It is usual to debit the cash book with the face value of the bill and show the discount as a payment, which will be posted to a Discounting Charges Account.

### (b) Bills Receivable and Bills Payable Ledgers

These books are ruled in a similar way to ordinary bill books, but are provided with additional money columns to show the disposal of the bills.

They may be made to form part of the double entry, in which case it will not be necessary to have ledger accounts for bills receivable and bills payable.

The great advantage of this form of book is that a complete history of each bill is recorded in a manner capable of arithmetical proof. A specimen ruling is given on page 112.

### (c) Bill Diary

Where bill transactions are numerous, it is advisable for all bills, whether receivable or payable, to be entered in special bill diaries, so that the amounts due to be received or paid on any given day can be readily ascertained.

The diaries will be ruled to meet the requirements of the case, a separate space being allotted for each day in the year. The bills are entered under the dates on which they fall due, allowance being made for the three days of grace.

### (d) Discounted Bills

The process of discounting a bill is tantamount to selling the bill for cash, subject to its being met at maturity, the holder thus obtaining the use of the money before the bill falls due.

The consideration for so obtaining the money in advance is termed 'discount', and is based, in the case of good bills, upon the rates ruling at the date of discounting.

This discount has no connection with cash discount or trade discount, and must not be confused therewith, as it is more in the nature of interest.

The entries in the books on discounting a bill are to debit the cash book and credit Bills Receivable Account with the face value of the discounted bill. If the holder's own banker discounts the bill for him, the banker will credit him with the face value of the bill and debit him with the discounting charge, and the entry in the trader's cash book will be made on that basis. Should the holder sell the bill to another bank or to a bill broker, he will receive a cheque for the net amount. He may then debit his cash book with that amount, which will be posted to the credit of Bills Receivable Account, and make a journal entry on

[continued on page 113

The following is a form of bills receivable ledger:

**Illustration**

Dr.                                    BILLS RECEIVABLE LEDGER                                    Cr

| No. of Bill | Date received | From whom received | Drawer | Acceptor | Where Payable | Date of Bill | Term | Date due, including Days of Grace | Folio in Ledger | Discount payable | Amount of Bill | How Disposed of | | | | | |
|---|---|---|---|---|---|---|---|---|---|---|---|---|---|---|---|---|---|
| | | | | | | | | | | | | Date | Fo. | Amount received | Discounting Expenses | Total | Remarks |
| | | | | | | | | | | £ | £ | | | £ | £ | £ | |

*Note to Illustration:* The discount payable column provided in the above form is useful in cases where cash discount is allowed on receipt of an acceptance in the same way as if payment had been made in cash. The detail of each money column on the debit side of this ledger will be posted to the credit of the personal account, the total of the discount payable column being posted to the debit of Discount Payable Account. As already stated, this discount payable must not be confused with the discounting charges on the bill itself.

the same day, debiting Discounting Charges Account and crediting Bills Receivable Account with the discount charged by the buyer of the bill; or he may record it as explained in the first case above mentioned. The latter treatment is recommended.

A contingent liability remains on a discounted bill until it matures and is met, since, if such a bill is dishonoured, the holder has a right of recourse against the drawer and all previous endorsers. A note should be made on the Balance Sheet of the amount of the contingent liability on discounted bills which have not yet matured, except where it is anticipated that a definite liability will materialize, when specific provision therefor should be made in the accounts.

**Illustration**

In the books of T. Atkinson, the following debit balances appear on July 1st, 19..:

|              |    |    | £  |
|--------------|----|----|----|
| H. Marshall  | .. | .. | 50 |
| J. Wilson    | .. | .. | 70 |
| F. Johnson   | .. | .. | 90 |

Also the following credit balances:

|            |    |    |    |
|------------|----|----|----|
| W. Black   | .. | .. | 90 |
| F. White   | .. | .. | 80 |
| H. Brown   | .. | .. | 40 |

Enter these balances in the Ledger, and from the particulars given in the Bills Receivable and Bills Payable books illustrated on page 110, make the necessary entries in T. Atkinson's books.

## CASH BOOK

| 19..      |                  |    | Fo. | £  | 19..      |                |    |    | Fo. | £  |
|-----------|------------------|----|-----|----|-----------|----------------|----|----|-----|----|
| Aug. 4    | Bills Receivable | .. | 1   | 50 | Sept. 12  | Discount       | .. | .. | 3   | 1  |
| Sept. 12  | ,,      ,,        | .. | 1   | 90 | ,, 15     | Bills Payable  | .. |    | 2   | 90 |

## LEDGER
## BILLS RECEIVABLE ACCOUNT

| 19..      |          |    |    | Fo.     | £   | 19..     |                 |    |    | Fo.    | £  |
|-----------|----------|----|----|---------|-----|----------|-----------------|----|----|--------|----|
| Sept. 30  | Sundries | .. | .. | B.R.B. 1| 210 | Aug. 4   | Cash ..         | .. | .. | C.B. 1 | 50 |
|           |          |    |    |         |     | Sept. 12 | Cash ..         | .. | .. | C.B. 1 | 90 |
|           |          |    |    |         |     | ,, 22    | J. Wilson –     |    |    |        |    |
|           |          |    |    |         |     |          | Dishonoured Bill|    |    | J. 1   | 70 |

## BILLS PAYABLE ACCOUNT

| 19..      |      |    |    | Fo.    | £  | 19..      |          |    |    | Fo.     | £   |
|-----------|------|----|----|--------|----|-----------|----------|----|----|---------|-----|
| Sept. 15  | Cash | .. | .. | C.B. 1 | 90 | Sept. 30  | Sundries | .. | .. | B.P.B. 1| 210 |

## DISCOUNTING CHARGES ACCOUNT

| 19..      |          |    |    | Fo.    | £ |  |  |  |  |  |  |
|-----------|----------|----|----|--------|---|--|--|--|--|--|--|
| Sept. 12  | Sundries | .. | .. | C.B. 1 | 1 |  |  |  |  |  |  |

## H. MARSHALL

| 19..   |                         | Fo. | £  | 19..    |                  |    | Fo.     | £  |
|--------|-------------------------|-----|----|---------|------------------|----|---------|----|
| July 1 | Balance brought forward .. .. | | 50 | July 2 | Bills Receivable | .. | B.R.B. 1| 50 |

## J. WILSON

| 19..<br>July 1<br>Sept. 22 | Balance brought forward .. ..<br>Bills Receivable Account – Dishonoured Bill .. .. | Fo.<br><br>J. 1 | £<br>70<br>70 | 19..<br>Aug. 1 | Bills Receivable .. | Fo.<br>B.R.B. 1 | £<br>70 |
|---|---|---|---|---|---|---|---|

## F. JOHNSON

| 19..<br>July 1 | Balance brought forward .. .. | | £<br>90 | 19..<br>Sept. 9 | Bills Receivable .. | Fo.<br>B.R.B. 1 | £<br>90 |
|---|---|---|---|---|---|---|---|

## W. BLACK

| 19..<br>July 15 | Bills Payable .. | Fo.<br>B.P.B. 1 | £<br>90 | 19..<br>July 1 | Balance brought forward | | £<br>90 |
|---|---|---|---|---|---|---|---|

## F. WHITE

| 19..<br>July 19 | Bills Payable .. | Fo.<br>B.P.B. 1 | £<br>80 | 19..<br>July 1 | Balance brought forward | | £<br>80 |
|---|---|---|---|---|---|---|---|

## H. BROWN

| 19..<br>Aug. 3 | Bills Payable .. | Fo.<br>B.P.B. 1 | £<br>40 | 19..<br>July 1 | Balance brought forward | | £<br>40 |
|---|---|---|---|---|---|---|---|

### (e) Advances on the Security of Bills

Sometimes arrangements may be made with the banker for the bills to be deposited with him, and an advance of a proportion of the amount to be made against them.

In these cases, the bills are not discounted, but remain the property of the trader, who deposits them with the bank as security for the advance. In effect, he pledges them with the banker. In the trader's books the bills will accordingly remain as assets in the Bills Receivable Account, an Advances on Bills Account being credited and cash debited with the amounts of the advances received.

When a bill matures, the banker will collect the proceeds and account to the trader for the excess of the amount received over the sum advanced plus the interest charged. The following entries should be made in the trader's books on receiving notification from the bank that a bill deposited as security has been paid:

1. Debit Advances on Bills Account and credit Bills Receivable Account with the full amount of the Bill.

2. Credit Advances on Bills Account and debit Interest on Advances Account with the interest charged by the bank.

3. Debit Cash and credit Advances on Bills Account with the balance of the proceeds of the bill received from the bank.

If notification is received from the bank that a bill deposited as security has been dishonoured, the trader will have to repay the advances made on the bill by the bank, together with the bank's charge for interest and expenses. He should accordingly debit Advances on Bills Account with the amount of the bill, and Interest Account with the bank interest, crediting cash with the total amount so paid.

### Illustration

Amongst the ledger balances of a limited company, carrying on business as shippers, there appeared the following on March 31st:

|  | £ |
|---|---|
| Bills Receivable .. .. .. .. .. | 8,620 |
| Export Bank Ltd: Advances on Bills Account .. .. | 6,535 |
| „ „ „ Special Margins Account .. .. | 816 |

*Note:* The Special Margins Account represents amounts deposited with the Export Bank to provide additional security in respect of the bills against which the bank has made advances.

The undermentioned transactions took place:

April  3   Received from Export Bank Ltd £26, being balance of proceeds of bill No. 308 for £150, a sum of £4 having been charged for interest on the advance.

„  12   Advice from Export Bank Ltd of payment of bill No. 320 for £200, which had been advanced against in full. The bank sent a debit note for interest for £5 and a cheque was sent for this.

„  15   Advice from the company's own bankers of the receipt of £185 being proceeds of bill No. 312 for that amount, sent to them for collection.

„  20   Advice from Export Bank Ltd that XY of Bombay had refused to take delivery of goods relating to bill No. 316 for £125, and that the documents had been handed over to the company's agents. The bank claimed repayment of their advance of £100, plus interest £4, and a remittance was sent to them accordingly. Received from A Y Co an acceptance for £200 (bill No. 330), against which the Export Bank Ltd advanced £160.

„  30   Export Bank Ltd advised having received £350, being payment in full of bill No. 324. They deducted their advance of £280, plus interest £6, and placed the balance to the credit of the company's Special Margins Account.

May 20   Received from the Bombay agent a remittance for £70, being the net proceeds of the sale by him of the goods originally sold to X Y. The agent advised that he had lodged with X Y a claim for the shortfall, plus an amount of £10 for warehousing the goods prior to the sale as this may have to be paid by the company.

„  23   Advice from Export Bank Ltd of the receipt by them of £55, being payment on account, against partial delivery, of bill No. 317 for £165, upon which they had made an advance of 80 per cent.

The company's own bankers were the Empire Bank Ltd. All amounts received were paid to the credit of the company's account there and all payments made by cheque.

Show – by means of ledger accounts – how the foregoing transactions would be entered in the books of the company, and bring down the balances on the various accounts.

## BILLS RECEIVABLE ACCOUNT

| | | £ | | | £ |
|---|---|---|---|---|---|
| Mar. 31 | Balance b/f. | 8,620 | Apr. 3 | Export Bank Ltd, Bill No. 308 .. | 150 |
| Apr. 20 | A. Y. Co. Bill No. 330 .. | 200 | ,, 12 | Export Bank Ltd, Bill No. 320 .. | 200 |
| | | | ,, 15 | Cash, Bill No. 312 .. | 185 |
| | | | ,, 20 | X Y, Bill No. 316 .. | 125 |
| | | | ,, 30 | Export Bank Ltd, Bill No. 324 .. | 350 |
| | | | May 31 | Balance c/d. .. | 7,810 |
| | | £8,820 | | | £8,820 |
| June 1 | Balance b/d. .. | 7,810 | | | |

## SUSPENSE ACCOUNT – RECEIPT ON ACCOUNT OF BILL NO. 317 AGAINST PARTIAL DELIVERY

| | | £ | | | £ |
|---|---|---|---|---|---|
| May 31 | Balance c/d. .. | 55 | May 23 | Export Bank Ltd.. | 55 |
| | | | June 1 | Balance b/d. .. | 55 |

## EXPORT BANK LTD – ADVANCES ON BILLS ACCOUNT

| | | £ | | | £ |
|---|---|---|---|---|---|
| Apr. 3 | Bill No. 308 .. | 150 | Mar. 31 | Balance b/f .. | 6,535 |
| ,, 12 | Bill No. 320 .. | 200 | Apr. 3 | Cash, Bill No. 308 .. | 26 |
| | Cash .. | 5 | | Interest, Bill No. 308 .. | 4 |
| ,, 20 | Cash, repayment of advance on Bill No. 316 .. | 104 | ,, 12 | Interest, Bill No. 320 .. | 5 |
| ,, 30 | Bill No. 324 .. | 350 | ,, 20 | Interest, Bill No. 316 .. | 4 |
| May 23 | Bill No. 317, payment on account .. | 55 | ,, 20 | Cash, advance against Bill No. 330 .. | 160 |
| ,, 31 | Balance c/d. .. | 5,940 | ,, 30 | Interest, Bill No. 324 .. | 6 |
| | | | | Special Margins Account, Balance re Bill No. 324 .. | 64 |
| | | £6,804 | | | £6,804 |
| | | | June 1 | Balance b/d. .. | 5,940 |

## EXPORT BANK LTD – SPECIAL MARGINS ACCOUNT

| | | £ | | | £ |
|---|---|---|---|---|---|
| Mar. 31 | Balance b/f .. | 816 | May 31 | Balance c/d. .. | 880 |
| Apr. 30 | Advances on Bills Account .. | 64 | | | |
| | | £880 | | | £880 |
| June 1 | Balance b/d. .. | 880 | | | |

## XY

| | | £ | | | £ |
|---|---|---|---|---|---|
| Apr. 20 | Bill No. 316, not accepted .. | 125 | May 20 | Cash – Sale of goods covered by Bill No. 316 | 70 |
| May 20 | Warehousing Expenses Account Suspense .. | 10 | ,, 31 | Balance c/d. .. | 65 |
| | | £135 | | | £135 |
| une 1 | Balance b/d. .. | 65 | | | |

## INTEREST ACCOUNT

| | | | | £ | | | | | | £ |
|---|---|---|---|---|---|---|---|---|---|---|
| Apr. 3 | Export Bank Ltd | .. | .. | 4 | May 31 | Balance c/d. | .. | .. | .. | 19 |
| ,, 12 | ,, | .. | .. | 5 | | | | | | |
| ,, 20 | ,, | .. | .. | 4 | | | | | | |
| ,, 30 | ,, | .. | .. | 6 | | | | | | |
| | | | | £19 | | | | | | £19 |
| June 1 | Balance b/d. | .. | .. | .. | 19 | | | | | |

## § 5. Accommodation Bills

An *Accommodation Bill* is one to which a person has put his name, whether as a drawer, acceptor or indorser, without valuable consideration, for the purpose of accommodating some other party who desires to raise money by negotiating it.

Since no consideration has passed between the parties to an accommodation bill, neither party can sue the other on the bill, should it be dishonoured. When once it has been discounted or otherwise negotiated, however, any third person who has given value for the bill may enforce payment by action against the acceptor, the drawer, or any prior indorser of the bill.

There are three common methods of raising money on accommodation bills:

1. Where one party, for the convenience of another, accepts a bill without valuable consideration, to enable the drawer to discount the bill and thus raise money, the drawer repaying the acceptor when the bill becomes due.

### Illustration (1)

For B's accommodation A accepted a bill on January 1st, 19.., for £100 at three months. B discounted the bill forthwith, and paid the proceeds, viz. £98, into his bank.

On the bill falling due A met it and notified B, who had arranged to reimburse A on the due date. B, however, was unable to do this, but arranged to give A immediately a cheque for £50, and a bill at one month for the balance. This bill was duly met at maturity.

Show the entries as they would appear in the books of both A and B, and state at what date the bills fell due.

A's BOOKS
B's ACCOUNT

| 19.. | | | | | £ | 19.. | | | | | | £ |
|---|---|---|---|---|---|---|---|---|---|---|---|---|
| Jan. 1 | Bills Payable | .. | .. | .. | 100 | April 4 | Cash | .. | .. | .. | .. | 50 |
| | | | | | | ,, | Bills Receivable | .. | .. | .. | .. | 50 |
| | | | | | £100 | | | | | | | £100 |

### BILLS PAYABLE ACCOUNT

| 19.. | | | | | £ | 19.. | | | | | | £ |
|---|---|---|---|---|---|---|---|---|---|---|---|---|
| April | Cash | .. | .. | .. | 100 | Jan. 1 | B | .. | .. | .. | .. | 100 |

### CASH BOOK

| 19.. | | | | | £ | 19.. | | | | | £ |
|---|---|---|---|---|---|---|---|---|---|---|---|
| April 4 | B | .. | .. | .. | 50 | April 4 | Bills Payable | .. | .. | .. | 100 |
| May 7 | Bills Receivable | .. | .. | | 50 | | | | | | |
| | | | | | £100 | | | | | | £100 |

### BILLS RECEIVABLE ACCOUNT

| 19..<br>April 4 | B | .. | .. | .. | .. | £<br>50 | 19..<br>May 7 | Cash | .. | .. | .. | .. | £<br>50 |
|---|---|---|---|---|---|---|---|---|---|---|---|---|---|

## B's BOOKS
## A's ACCOUNT

| 19..<br>April 4<br>„ | Cash ..<br>Bills Payable | ..<br>.. | ..<br>.. | ..<br>.. | £<br>50<br>50<br>£100 | 19..<br>Jan. 1 | Bills Receivable .. | .. | .. | £<br>100<br><br>£100 |
|---|---|---|---|---|---|---|---|---|---|---|

### BILLS RECEIVABLE ACCOUNT

| 19..<br>Jan. 1 | A | .. | .. | .. | .. | £<br>100<br>£100 | 19..<br>Jan. 1 | Cash | .. | .. | .. | .. | £<br>100<br>£100 |
|---|---|---|---|---|---|---|---|---|---|---|---|---|---|

## CASH BOOK

| 19..<br>Jan. 1 | Bills Receivable | .. | .. | £<br>100 | 19..<br>Jan. 1<br>April 4<br>May 7 | Discounting Charges<br>A ..<br>Bills Payable | ..<br>..<br>.. | ..<br>..<br>.. | £<br>2<br>50<br>50 |
|---|---|---|---|---|---|---|---|---|---|

### DISCOUNTING CHARGES ACCOUNT

| 19..<br>Jan. 1 | Cash | .. | .. | .. | .. | £<br>2 | | |
|---|---|---|---|---|---|---|---|---|

### BILLS PAYABLE ACCOUNT

| 19..<br>May 7 | Cash | .. | .. | .. | .. | £<br>50 | 19..<br>April 4 | A | .. | .. | .. | .. | £<br>50 |
|---|---|---|---|---|---|---|---|---|---|---|---|---|---|

*Note:* The first bill fell due on April 4th, and the second on May 7th.

2. Where one person draws a bill on another party, who accepts it, without valuable consideration, for their mutual convenience. The bill is discounted by the drawer, who immediately remits half the proceeds to the acceptor, remitting the cash to meet his half share when the bill becomes due, each party sharing the expenses of discount.

**Illustration (2)**

For the mutual accommodation of A and B, A draws a bill on B for £100 at three months on January 1st, 19... B accepts the bill and returns it to A, who discounts it with his bankers on January 4th at 8 per cent., the arrangement breing that A and B shall share the proceeds equally.

On the bill falling due A remits his proportion, and the bill is met in due course by B. Show the entries as they would appear in the books of both A and B, making calculations in months and to the nearest £.

## A's BOOKS
### B's ACCOUNT

| 19..<br>Jan. 4<br><br>April 4 | Cash<br>Discount<br>Cash | .. .. .. | £<br>49<br>1<br>50 | 19..<br>Jan. 1 | Bills Receivable .. .. .. | £<br>100 |
|---|---|---|---|---|---|---|
| | | | £100 | | | £100 |

### BILLS RECEIVABLE ACCOUNT

| 19..<br>Jan. 1 | B .. .. .. .. | £<br>100 | 19..<br>Jan. 4 | Cash .. .. .. .. | £<br>100 |
|---|---|---|---|---|---|

### CASH BOOK

| 19..<br>Jan. 4 | Bills Receivable .. .. .. | £<br>100 | 19..<br>Jan. 4<br>,,<br>April 4 | Discounting Charges .. ..<br>B .. .. .. ..<br>B .. .. .. .. | £<br>2<br>49<br>50 |
|---|---|---|---|---|---|

### DISCOUNTING CHARGES ACCOUNT

| 19..<br>Jan. 4 | Cash .. .. .. .. | £<br>2 | 19..<br>Jan. 4 | B .. .. .. .. | £<br>1 |
|---|---|---|---|---|---|

## B's BOOKS
### A's ACCOUNT

| 19..<br>Jan. 1 | Bills Payable .. .. .. | £<br>100 | 19..<br>Jan. 4<br><br>,,<br>April 4 | Cash .. .. .. ..<br>Discounting Charges .. ..<br>Cash .. .. .. .. | £<br>49<br>1<br>50 |
|---|---|---|---|---|---|
| | | £100 | | | £100 |

### BILLS PAYABLE ACCOUNT

| 19..<br>April 4 | Cash .. .. .. .. | £<br>100 | 19..<br>Jan. 1 | A .. .. .. .. | £<br>100 |
|---|---|---|---|---|---|

### CASH BOOK

| 19..<br>Jan. 4<br>April 4 | A .. .. .. ..<br>A .. .. .. .. | £<br>49<br>50 | 19..<br>April 4 | Bills Payable .. .. .. | £<br>100 |
|---|---|---|---|---|---|

### DISCOUNTING CHARGES ACCOUNT

| 19..<br>Jan. 4 | A .. .. .. .. | £<br>1 | | | |
|---|---|---|---|---|---|

*Note to Illustration:* When it is stated that a bill is discounted at a certain rate per cent., the addition of the words 'per annum' is usually implied, and the calculation of the discount should be made on the unexpired tenor of the bill. In practice, discount is calculated on the number of days, including days of grace, but in these illustrations it has been calculated in months.

3. Where two parties each draw a bill of equal amount on the other, and discount the other's bill, meeting their own bills when they fall due, and paying the expenses of discounting each other's bill.

**Illustration (3)**

On January 1st, 19.., A draws a bill on B at four months for £500, and B draws on A for a similar amount and term. Both bills are accepted and discounted respectively at 5 per cent. At maturity A meets his own acceptance, but B's acceptance is dishonoured, with the result that A, the drawer, is called upon to take it up. The bank charges expenses of £1 on the dishonoured bill. B then accepts a new bill at three months for the amount due by him, plus interest at 5 per cent. per annum, which is duly met at maturity.

Show the entries in the books of both parties, making calculations in months and to the nearest £.

## A's BOOKS
### B's ACCOUNT

| 19.. | | £ | 19.. | | £ |
|---|---|---|---|---|---|
| Jan. 1 | Bills Payable .. .. .. | 500 | Jan. 1 | Bills Receivable .. .. .. | 500 |
| May 4 | Cash: Bill dishonoured and expenses .. .. .. | 501 | May 4 | ,, ,, .. .. .. | 507 |
| | Interest .. .. .. | 6 | | | |
| | | £1,007 | | | £1,007 |

### BILLS RECEIVABLE ACCOUNT

| 19.. | | £ | 19.. | | £ |
|---|---|---|---|---|---|
| Jan. 1 | B .. .. .. | 500 | Jan. 1 | Cash .. .. .. .. | 500 |
| May 4 | B .. .. .. | 507 | Aug. 7 | ,, .. .. .. | 507 |
| | | £1,007 | | | £1,007 |

### BILLS PAYABLE ACCOUNT

| 19.. | | £ | 19.. | | £ |
|---|---|---|---|---|---|
| May 4 | Cash .. .. .. .. | 500 | Jan. 1 | B .. .. .. .. | 500 |

### CASH BOOK

| 19.. | | £ | 19.. | | £ |
|---|---|---|---|---|---|
| Jan. 1 | Bills Receivable.. .. .. | 500 | Jan. 1 | Discounting Charges .. .. | 8 |
| Aug. 7 | ,, ,, .. .. .. | 507 | May 4 | Bills Payable .. .. .. | 500 |
| | | | ,, | B – Bill dishonoured and expenses .. | 501 |

### DISCOUNTING CHARGES AND INTEREST ACCOUNT

| 19.. | | £ | 19.. | | £ |
|---|---|---|---|---|---|
| Jan. 1 | Cash .. .. .. .. | 8 | May 4 | B .. .. .. .. | 6 |

## B's BOOKS
### A's ACCOUNT

| 19.. | | £ | 19.. | | £ |
|---|---|---|---|---|---|
| Jan. 1 | Bills Payable .. .. .. | 500 | Jan. 1 | Bills Receivable .. .. .. | 500 |
| May 4 | ,, ,, .. .. .. | 507 | May 4 | Bills Payable .. .. .. | 500 |
| | | | ,, | Interest and Expenses .. .. | 7 |
| | | £1,007 | | | £1,007 |

## BILLS PAYABLE ACCOUNT

| 19.. | | £ | 19.. | | £ |
|---|---|---|---|---|---|
| May 4 | A – Bill met by him .. .. | 500 | Jan. 1 | A .. .. .. .. | 500 |
| Aug. 7 | Cash .. .. .. .. | 507 | May 4 | A .. .. .. .. | 507 |
| | | £1,007 | | | £1,007 |

## BILLS RECEIVABLE ACCOUNT

| 19.. | | £ | 19.. | | £ |
|---|---|---|---|---|---|
| Jan. 1 | A .. .. .. .. | 500 | Jan. 1 | Cash .. .. .. .. | 500 |

## DISCOUNTING CHARGES, INTEREST AND EXPENSES ACCOUNT

| 19.. | | £ | | | |
|---|---|---|---|---|---|
| Jan. 1 | Cash .. .. .. .. | 8 | | | |
| May 4 | A .. .. .. .. | 7 | | | |

## CASH BOOK

| 19.. | | £ | 19.. | | £ |
|---|---|---|---|---|---|
| Jan. 1 | Bills Receivable .. .. | 500 | Jan. 1 | Discounting Charges .. .. | 8 |
| | | | Aug. 7 | Bills Payable .. .. | 507 |

It should be noted that the interest charged is for the period of the *new* bill, i.e. for the period for which A has to wait for his money.

## § 6. Dishonoured Bills, Retired Bills, Short Bills etc.

### (a) Dishonoured Bills

When a bill is not met at maturity by the acceptor it is said to be 'dishonoured', and the entries in the books of the drawer will be to credit the Bills Receivable Account and debit the account of the person from whom the bill was received.

If a bill which has been discounted by the holder with a bank is dishonoured at maturity, the holder will be required to meet the bill and pay the expenses incurred by the bank in noting it. He will accordingly credit the cash book with the amounts so paid and debit the account of the person from whom he received the bill. The person who discounted the bill will, of course, bear the discounting charge himself, but the expenses incurred by reason of the dishonour of the bill must be charged to the person who dishonoured it. Any cash discount allowed to such person should also be redebited to him, as the condition of allowing such discount was that the bill should be honoured at maturity.

### (b) Retired Bills

Bills may be 'retired' before their due date, either under rebate (*see* (*e*) *below*) or for 'renewal', as in the following circumstances:

It may happen that in order to obtain more time for payment the acceptor of a bill may request the drawer to allow the bill to be withdrawn and a new one maturing at a later date to be given in its place. In such a case interest for the further accommodation would usually be charged.

It may be that the drawer has discounted the bill and is not aware of the identity of the holder, or may be reluctant to approach the holder (e.g. his bank), as such a course may tend to damage his credit. If he wishes to assist the acceptor he may give him a cheque for the amount of the bill to enable it to be met, and draw another bill for an equivalent amount, with possibly the addition of interest, for the agreed new tenor. The drawer would then discount this bill so as to obtain funds to meet the cheque. The charge for interest would compensate him for the discount which he would be called upon to pay in respect of the new bill.

**Illustration**

(a) K & K of New York, on June 8th, consigned goods of the invoice value of £4,375 to J & J, of London, drawing by arrangement on the F. T. Bank Ltd, in London, a three months draft for 80 per cent. of the invoice value.

(b) J & J, whose bankers are Barclays, drew a cheque on September 11th to meet the draft.

(c) In order to finance the transaction, on September 10th, J & J drew a three months' bill on the F. T. Bank for £3,500, discounting this bill with the F. T. Bank, who held the documents of the consignment as security. The F. T. Bank charged £18 commission; discount was £49. The balance was passed by cheque to J & J, who paid the cheque into their bank.

(d) On December 13th, the bill in (c) was returned, J & J giving a cheque to meet it. J & J drew a fresh bill at three months for £4,000 on the F. T. Bank, depositing further security. The bill was discounted by the F. T. Bank, commission being £20 and discount £49. The balance was passed by cheque to J & J, who paid in the cheque to their bankers.

Record the transactions in J & J's ledger.

## J & J's LEDGER

### K & K

| 19..<br>June 8 | F. T. Bank – Bill at 3 months drawn<br>on F. T. Bank .. .. | £<br>3,500 | 19..<br>June 8 | Goods .. .. .. .. | £<br>4,375 |
|---|---|---|---|---|---|

### F. T. BANK

| 19..<br>Sept. 10<br>„ 11<br>Dec. 13<br><br>Dec. 13 | Bills Receivable – Bill dated Sept.<br>10th discounted .. ..<br>Cash – Discharge of Bill dated June<br>8th .. .. .. ..<br>Cash – Discharge of Bill dated Sept.<br>10th .. .. ..<br><br>Bills Receivable – Bill dated Dec.<br>13th discounted .. .. | £<br>3,500<br><br>3,500<br><br>3,500<br><br><br>4,000 | 19..<br>June 8<br>Sept. 10<br><br><br><br><br>Dec. 13 | K & K, Bill at 3 months accepted this<br>day .. .. .. ..<br>Bills Receivable – Bill at 3 months ac-<br>cepted this day .. ..<br>Cash for Bill dated Sept. 10th dis-<br>counted .. .. ..<br>Commission .. .. ..<br>Discounting charge .. ..<br>Bills Receivable, bill at 3 months ..<br>Cash for bill dated Dec. 13th discoun-<br>ted .. .. ..<br>Commission .. .. ..<br>Discounting charge .. .. | £<br>3,500<br><br>3,500<br><br>3,433<br>18<br>49<br>4,000<br><br>3,931<br>20<br>49 |
|---|---|---|---|---|---|

### CASH BOOK

| 19..<br>Sept. 10<br>Dec. 13 | F. T. Bank – Bill discounted ..<br>F. T. Bank – Bill discounted .. | £<br>3,433<br>3,931 | 19..<br>Sept. 11<br>Dec. 13 | F. T. Bank – Discharge of Bill dated<br>June 8th .. .. ..<br>F. T. Bank – Discharge of Bill dated<br>Sept. 10th .. .. .. | £<br>3,500<br>3,500 |
|---|---|---|---|---|---|

## BILLS RECEIVABLE ACCOUNT

| 19.. | | | £ | 19.. | | | £ |
|------|---|---|---|------|---|---|---|
| Sept. 10 | F. T. Bank – Bill at 3 months | .. | 3,500 | Sept. 10 | F. T. Bank, bill discounted .. | .. | 3,500 |
| Dec. 13 | F. T. Bank – Bill at 3 months | .. | 4,000 | Dec. 13 | F. T. Bank, bill discounted | .. | 4,000 |

## COMMISSION AND DISCOUNTING CHARGES ACCOUNT

| 19.. | | | | £ | | |
|------|---|---|---|---|---|---|
| Sept. 10 | F. T. Bank – | | | | | |
| | Commission .. | .. | .. | 18 | | |
| | Discounting | .. | .. | 49 | | |
| Dec. 13 | F. T. Bank – | | | | | |
| | Commission .. | .. | .. | 20 | | |
| | Discounting .. | .. | .. | 49 | | |

### (c) Short Bills

This is a term applied to bills which have been paid into the bank for collection to await maturity. They must not be confused with discounted bills, and no entry whatever need be made in the books when they are lodged with the bank, except by way of memorandum. Sometimes, however, for the sake of convenience, separate bills accounts are kept for the collecting banks, which are debited with all bills paid in for collection and credited when the bills are met or dishonoured. It should be remembered, however, that the banks are not debtors for these bills, but only hold them as agents for collection.

### (d) Documentary Bills

When the seller of goods which are to be exported wishes to obtain payment therefor, or acceptance of a bill, before the goods are actually delivered, he may, by arrangement with the consignee, draw a bill upon him for the value of the goods, and attach to the draft a copy of the invoice and the bill of lading. Such a draft is termed a *documentary bill*. The *bill of lading* is the receipt of the master of the ship for the goods, and the document of title thereto. It also provides evidence of the contract of affreightment. These documents are handed by the consignor to his banker, who in turn forwards them to his own correspondent in the place where the consignee carries on business. To obtain the bill of lading, without which he cannot get possession of the goods, the consignee must either meet or accept the bill, according to the instructions given to the bankers.

As a general rule the consignee is notified of the fact that a bill has been drawn upon him and if he accepts the bill before the arrival of the goods he does so conditionally 'against documents'.

The English banker, upon receiving notification from his correspondent that the bill has been accepted or met as the case may be, credits the seller of the goods with an equivalent amount, less his collecting charges.

Alternatively the bill may be discounted in the first instance, the same procedure being followed.

Where goods are imported, payment is usually effected in a similar manner.

### (e) Rebated Bills

Sometimes a bill may be met before its due date, i.e. retired under rebate, usually for the purpose of obtaining possession of goods or documents against which the bill was drawn and which cannot be released until the bill is discharged. Where this is done a rebate is allowed, representing interest on the amount of the bill for the period unexpired.

On retiring a bill under rebate the cash book is credited and Bills Payable Account debited with the net amount paid in discharge of the bill, while the amount of the rebate is credited to Interest Account (or to Discounting Charges Account), and debited to Bills Payable Account.

## CHAPTER VII

# PARTNERSHIP ACCOUNTS

N.B. Section references in this Chapter are to the *Partnership Act 1890*, unless otherwise stated

## § 1. The Nature of Partnership

The law of partnership is contained in the *Partnership Act 1890*, and in the *Limited Partnerships Act 1907*, the former consolidating the law then existing into the form of a code, and the latter amending it to permit limited liability under certain conditions.

Partnership is defined by the *Partnership Act 1890* as 'the relation which subsists between persons carrying on a business in common with a view of profit'. The participation in profits is not, however, of itself alone conclusive evidence of the existence of a partnership, the relationship resting upon mutual intention. Section 2 of the *Partnership Act 1890* sets forth circumstances where a person so participating would not necessarily be deemed to be a partner; e.g. the receipt of remuneration by a servant on the basis of a share of profits, or the payment to the widow of a deceased partner of an annuity consisting of a portion of the profits. It is a matter of considerable importance to the persons interested, since where a partnership exists, each partner incurs unlimited liability for all the debts and obligations of the firm.

In the event of any person advancing money to the firm on loan, and receiving a rate of interest varying with the profits, or an actual share of profits, it is essential for him to see that the agreement is in writing and signed by, or on behalf of, all the parties, in order that he may not be held liable as a partner, with consequent risk of being called upon to meet the liabilities of the firm (*Partnership Act 1890*, Section 2). The lender in the circumstances mentioned would be subject to a further disability, inasmuch as in the event of the bankruptcy of the firm, his claim would rank after those of the other unsecured creditors (s. 3).

Persons may be co-owners of property, and may derive a profit from the use of such property, without being partners. The true test in such cases is whether a business is being carried on and whether every co-owner is empowered to act as agent for the other or others. Partnership entails the mutual agency of the partners. Each partner, while himself a principal, is also an agent for the other partners within the scope of the business carried on, and the other partners are bound by his acts so performed. The mere co-ownership of property does not imply such a condition.

In the case of a partnership, the number of partners is limited to twenty, with the exception that members within each of the undermentioned groups may form partnerships of more than twenty persons:

(*a*) practising solicitors provided each partner is a solicitor of the Supreme Court;

(*b*) practising accountants where each of the partners is qualified under s. 161 of the *Companies Act 1948* for appointment as auditor of a company;

(*c*) members of a recognized Stock Exchange provided each partner is a member of that exchange;

(*d*) other groups who obtain approval under regulations made by the Board of Trade.

In the case of private banking concerns the number is limited to twenty.

If associations with more than this number carry on business they are illegal bodies and are unable to enforce any rights under contracts into which they may have entered, unless they are registered under the Companies Acts or under some other Act of Parliament, or are formed under a Royal Charter.

Partners are entitled to rely upon the utmost good faith of their co-partners, both in the inception of the partnership agreement and in the carrying out of its terms. The partnership agreement is therefore of the class *uberrimæ fidei*, as between the partners, and all material information which could influence their decision to enter into the agreement must be given to each other by the partners.

A partnership may be formed for a specified term or for an indefinite period. When no period is fixed, it is termed a 'partnership at will', and any partner is entitled to retire upon giving reasonable notice to his co-partners. Where the partnership has been formed for a fixed term it may be dissolved when that term has expired, but if the partnership continues beyond that term it becomes a partnership at will, unless an agreement is entered into for a new term.

Persons in partnership may, in the same way as persons carrying on business as sole traders, select whatever name they choose as the firm name. If, however, a name is selected which is similar to that under which another business is carried on, so that people may be induced to deal with the firm in the belief that they are dealing with the other business of that name, the Court will afford protection to the proprietors of the other firm by granting an injunction restraining the new firm from using the name.

Where the name selected does not consist of the true surnames of *all* the partners with no addition thereto other than christian names or initials, registration is necessary under the *Registration of Business Names Act 1916*. The information which must be supplied to the registrar consists of:

1. the business name;

2. the general nature of the business;

3. the principal place of business;

4. the present christian name and surname, any former christian name or surname, the nationality, the usual residence, and the other occupations (if any) of each of the partners and the corporate name and registered or principal office of every corporation which is a partner;

5. the date of commencement of the business.

Any changes in these particulars must be notified. The register is open to inspection, so that anyone may discover who the partners are. Firms which come within the operation of the Act must disclose, in legible characters, the full names and any former names of the partners on all trade catalogues, trade circulars, showcards and business letters (initials may be used instead of the full christian names).

## § 2. The Partnership Agreement

Since the essence of partnership is mutual agreement, it is desirable for the partners to come to some understanding before entering into partnership as to the conditions upon which the business is to be carried on, and as to their respective rights and powers.

The Act lays down certain rules to be observed in the absence of agreement. The circumstances must determine whether these rules are applicable in the particular case, and since many matters should be decided which are not included in these rules, it is desirable that a formal agreement be entered into with a view to preventing disputes in the future. The advantages of a written agreement need no emphasis, and it is preferable that it should be under seal, since the character of a deed precludes contradiction by any party of the terms which have been agreed.

Even though a formal agreement be made, this does not preclude subsequent variation where changing circumstances demand it; such variation can always be effected with the consent of all the partners, which may be evidenced by an amending agreement, or inferred from a course of dealing (s. 19).

### (a) Clauses relating to Accounts in Partnership Agreements

The general provisions affecting questions of accounts that should be contained in all partnership agreements, apart from any special circumstances, are as follows:

1. As to capital; whether each partner should contribute a fixed amount or otherwise.

2. As to the division of profits and losses between the partners, including capital profits and losses.

3. Whether the capitals are to be fixed, drawings and profits being adjusted on current accounts, or whether they are to be adjusted on the capital accounts.

4. Whether interest on capital or on drawings, or both, is to be allowed or charged before arriving at the profits divisible in the agreed proportions, and if so, at what rate.

5. Whether current accounts (if any) are to bear interest, and if so, at what rate.

6. Whether partners' drawings are to be limited in amount.

7. Whether partners are to be allowed remuneration for their services before arriving at divisible profits, and if so, the amounts thereof.

8. That proper accounts shall be prepared at least once a year and that these shall be audited by a professional accountant, and signed by all the partners.

9. That such accounts when duly signed shall be binding on the partners, but shall be capable of being reopened within a specified period on an error being discovered.

10. The method by which the value of goodwill shall be determined in the event of the retirement or death of any of the partners.

11. The method of determining the amount due to a deceased partner and the manner in which the liability to his personal representatives is to be settled, e.g. by a lump sum payment within a specified period, by instalments of certain proportions etc., and the rate of interest to be allowed on outstanding balances.

12. In the event of there being any partnership insurance policies, the method of treating the premiums thereon and the division of the policy money.

### (b) Rules as to the Rights and Duties of Partners in the absence of Agreement

Section 24 of the *Partnership Act 1890, which applies to all partnerships in so far as there is no agreement to the contrary*, provides as follows:

The interests of partners in the partnership property, and their rights and duties in relation to the partnership shall be determined, subject to any agreement, express or implied, between the partners, by the following rules:

1. All the partners are entitled to share equally in the capital and profits of the business, and must contribute equally towards the losses, whether of capital or otherwise, sustained by the firm.

2. The firm must indemnify every partner in respect of payments made and personal liabilities incurred by him –

(*a*) in the ordinary and proper conduct of the business of the firm; or

(*b*) in or about anything necessarily done for the preservation of the business or property of the firm.

3. A partner making, for the purpose of the partnership, any payment or advance beyond the amount of capital which he has agreed to subscribe, is entitled to interest at the rate of 5 per cent. per annum from the date of the payment or advance.

4. A partner is not entitled, before the ascertainment of profits, to interest on the capital subscribed by him.

5. Every partner may take part in the management of the partnership business.

6. No partner shall be entitled to remuneration for acting in the partnership business.

7. No person may be introduced as a partner without the consent of all existing partners.

8. Any difference arising as to ordinary matters connected with the partnership business may be decided by a majority of the partners, but no change may

be made in the nature of the partnership business without the consent of all existing partners. (In the absence of any agreement to the contrary no majority of partners may expel a partner (s. 25).)

9. The partnership books are to be kept at the place of business of the partnership (or the principal place, if there is more than one), and every partner may, when he thinks fit, have access to and inspect and copy any of them.

The *duties* of a partner are as under:

(*a*) To act with the utmost good faith in his relations with his co-partners.
(*b*) To render true accounts and full information of all things affecting the partnership to any partner or his legal representatives (s. 28).
(*c*) To account to the firm for any benefit derived by him without the consent of the other partners from any transaction concerning the partnership, or from any use by him of the partnership property, name or business connection (s. 29).
(*d*) To refrain from competing with the firm. Where a partner, without the consent of his co-partners, carries on a competing business, he must account for and pay over to the firm all profits made by him in that business (s. 30).

### § 3. The usual Adjustments necessary in Partnership Accounts

Before ascertaining the profits which are divisible in the agreed proportions, adjustments are frequently necessary in respect of all or any of the following matters:

### (*a*) *Interest on Capital*

By charging against profits interest at a fair commercial rate on the capital employed in a business, it can be seen whether the balance of profit remaining is sufficient to justify the continuance of the firm with unlimited liability, since the interest charged may be regarded as approximately the income the partners would have derived from the investment of their capital in securities involving little or no risk. Apart from this, however, where there are two or more partners with unequal capitals, the effect of charging interest on capital is to adjust the rights of the partners *inter se* as regards capital, giving each a reasonable return on his capital before dividing the balance of profit in the agreed proportions. Where the capital is fixed, and the profits are shared in the same proportions as capital, the charging of interest makes no difference to the ultimate amount credited to each partner. Even in such cases, however, it may be desirable to charge interest for the first reason mentioned above.

Interest on capital should be calculated for the period during which the business has had the use of the capital, allowance being made for any additions or withdrawals during the period. The partners' Capital or Current Accounts will be credited with the amount of the interest, and the Profit and Loss Appropriation Account debited.

It may happen that the profits of the business in a particular year are less than the interest on capital credited to the partners. In such circumstances, unless the partnership agreement provides an alternative method, the interest should be charged in full, the resulting 'loss' being borne by the partners in the proportions in which they share profits. In this manner the *real* result of the trading for the period is disclosed.

As already indicated, partners are not entitled to interest on capital unless the payment thereof is expressly authorized by the partnership agreement.

**Illustration**

A, B and C, sharing profits and losses equally, have capitals of £10,000, £5,000 and £2,000 respectively, on which they are entitled to interest at 5 per cent. per annum. The profits for the year, before charging interest on capital, amounted to £550. Show how the profits will be divided between the partners.

### APPROPRIATION ACCOUNT

| | £ | £ | | £ | £ |
|---|---|---|---|---|---|
| Interest on Capitals: | | | Profit for the year .. .. .. | | 550 |
| A .. .. .. .. | 500 | | Balance being 'loss' transferred to Current Accounts: .. .. .. | | |
| B .. .. .. .. | 250 | | A .. .. .. .. | 100 | |
| C .. .. .. .. | 100 | 850 | B .. .. .. .. | 100 | |
| | | | C .. .. .. .. | 100 | |
| | | | | | 300 |
| | | £850 | | | £850 |

### PARTNERS' CURRENT ACCOUNTS

| | A £ | B £ | C £ | | A £ | B £ | C £ |
|---|---|---|---|---|---|---|---|
| Appropriation Account: Loss .. | 100 | 100 | 100 | Interest on Capital .. .. | 500 | 250 | 100 |
| Balance c/d. .. .. | 400 | 150 | — | | | | |
| | £500 | £250 | £100 | | £500 | £250 | £100 |
| | | | | Balances b/d. .. .. .. | 400 | 150 | — |

### (b) Interest on Drawings

Frequently partners make drawings in varying amounts and at irregular intervals, and in such cases if interest is charged the rights of the partners are adjusted. In many cases, however, drawings are made by mutual agreement and no interest is charged at all.

Where interest is charged, it is usually calculated at a fixed rate per cent. per annum from the date of each drawing to the date the accounts are closed, the amount being credited to the Profit and Loss Appropriation Account and debited to the partners' Current Accounts.

### (c) Partners' Salaries

As already stated, in the absence of agreement no partner is entitled, before arriving at the amount of divisible profits, to remuneration for his services to the firm. In the following cases, however, it may be desirable for the partnership agreement to provide for the payment of salaries to the partners:

1. Where some of the partners take a greater or more effective part in the conduct and management of the business than others.

2. Where there are junior partners, whom it is desired to remunerate by way of a fixed salary plus, perhaps, a small percentage of the profits.

3. Where the partnership business is wholly managed by the partners, and it is desired to ascertain the true profit, after such a charge for managerial services has been made as would have been incurred had the business not been managed by the proprietors.

Where the agreement provides for the payment of salaries to partners, it must be realized that such payments, although designated salaries are, like interest on capital, merely in the nature of preferential shares of the divisible profit. The amounts of such salaries should therefore be debited to Profit and Loss Appropriation Account, and credited to the partners' Current or Capital Accounts, the actual payments, when made, being treated as drawings and debited to the partners' Current or Capital Accounts. Alternatively, if the partners' salaries are drawn at regular intervals, they may be debited direct from the Cash Book to the partners' Salaries Accounts, which should ultimately be closed by transfer to the Profit and Loss Appropriation Account.

**Illustration**

Duck, Drake and Cygnet carried on a retail business in partnership. The partnership agreement provides that:

1. The partners are to be credited at the end of each year with salaries of £1,000 to Duck and £500 each to Drake and Cygnet, and with interest at the rate of 5 per cent. per annum on the balances at the credit of their respective capital accounts at the commencement of the year.

2. No interest is to be charged on drawings.

3. After charging partnership salaries and interest on capital, profits and losses are to be divided in the proportion: Duck, 50 per cent., Drake 30 per cent. and Cygnet 20 per cent., with the proviso, however, that Cygnet's share in any year (exclusive of salary and interest) shall not be less than £1,000 any deficiency to be borne in profit sharing ratio by the other two partners.

The Trial Balance of the firm at December 31st, 19.. was as follows:

|  | Dr £ | Cr £ |
|---|---|---|
| Partners' Capital Accounts: |  |  |
|     Duck   – Balance January 1st |  | 8,000 |
|     Drake  –   ,,      ,,      ,, |  | 5,000 |
|     Cygnet –   ,,      ,,      ,, |  | 3,000 |
| Partners' Current Accounts: |  |  |
|     Duck   – Balance January 1st |  | 1,600 |
|     Drake  –   ,,      ,,      ,, |  | 1,200 |
|     Cygnet –   ,,      ,,      ,, |  | 800 |
| Sales |  | 46,500 |
| Trade Creditors |  | 3,700 |
| Shop Fittings at cost | 3,600 |  |
|     ,,      ,,   Provision for Depreciation, January 1st |  | 1,400 |
| Freehold Premises – cost | 6,000 |  |
| Leasehold Premises – purchased during year | 4,500 |  |
|     ,,      ,,   – additions and alterations | 2,500 |  |
| Purchases | 28,000 |  |
| Stock on hand, January 1st | 4,200 |  |
| Salaries and Wages | 6,400 |  |
| Office and Trade Expenses | 4,520 |  |
| Rent, Rates and Insurance | 1,050 |  |
| Professional Charges | 350 |  |
| Debtors | 2,060 |  |
| Provision for Doubtful Debts, January 1st |  | 50 |
| Balance at bank | 4,370 |  |
| Drawings, other than monthly payments: |  |  |
|     Duck | 1,700 |  |
|     Drake | 1,100 |  |
|     Cygnet | 900 |  |
|  | £71,250 | £71,250 |

You are given the following additional information:

1. Stock on December 31st was valued at £3,600.

2. A debt of £60 is to be written off and the provision against the remaining debtors should be 5 per cent.

3. Salaries and Wages include the following monthly drawings by the partners: Duck £50, Drake £30, Cygnet £25.

4. Partners had during the year been supplied with goods from stock and it was agreed that these should be charged to them as follows: Duck £60, Drake £40.

5. On December 31st, rates paid in advance and office and trade expenses owing were £250 and £240 respectively.

6. Depreciation of shop fittings is to be provided at 5 per cent. per annum on cost.

7. Professional charges include £250 fees paid in respect of the acquisition of the leasehold premises, which fees are to be capitalized.

8. The cost of and the additions and alterations to the leasehold premises were to be written off over twenty-five years, commencing on January 1st in the year in which the premises were acquired.

You are required to prepare:

(a) the Trading and Profit and Loss Account for the year ended December 31st, 19..;

(b) the Balance Sheet as on that date; and

(c) Partners' Current Accounts in columnar form for the year ended December 31st, 19...

DUCK, DRAKE AND CYGNET

TRADING AND PROFIT AND LOSS ACCOUNT

(a)                  For the Year Ended December 31st, 19..

| | £ | | | £ |
|---|---|---|---|---|
| Stock, January 1st .. .. .. | 4,200 | Sales .. .. .. .. .. | 46,500 |
| Purchases .. .. .. .. | 28,000 | Goods supplied to partners .. .. | 100 |
| | 32,200 | | |
| Less Stock, December 31st .. | 3,600 | | |
| Cost of Sales .. .. .. | 28,600 | | |
| Gross Profit, carried down .. .. | 18,000 | | |
| | £46,600 | | £46,600 |
| Salaries and Wages .. .. .. | 5,140 | Gross Profit, brought down .. .. | 18,000 |
| Office and Trade Expenses .. .. | 4,760 | | |
| Rent, Rates and Insurance .. .. | 800 | | |
| Professional Charges .. .. | 100 | | |
| Bad Debts .. .. .. | 110 | | |
| Amortization of Leasehold Premises .. | 290 | | |
| Depreciation of Shop Fittings .. | 180 | | |
| Net Profit, carried down .. .. | 6,620 | | |
| | £18,000 | | £18,000 |

| | £ | | | | £ |
|---|---|---|---|---|---|
| Partners' Salaries: | | | Net Profit, brought down .. .. .. | | 6,620 |
| Duck .. .. .. .. | 1,000 | | | | |
| Drake .. .. .. .. | 500 | | | | |
| Cygnet .. .. .. .. | 500 | | | | |
| | | 2,000 | | | |
| Interest on Capital: | | | | | |
| Duck .. .. .. .. | 400 | | | | |
| Drake .. .. .. .. | 250 | | | | |
| Cygnet .. .. .. .. | 150 | | | | |
| | | 800 | | | |
| Shares of Net Profit: | | | | | |
| Duck, 50 per cent. .. .. | 1,910 | | | | |
| Less Transfer to Cygnet .. .. | 147 | | | | |
| | | 1,763 | | | |
| Drake, 30 per cent. .. .. | 1,146 | | | | |
| Less Transfer to Cygnet .. .. | 89 | | | | |
| | | 1,057 | | | |
| Cygnet, 20 per cent. .. .. | 764 | | | | |
| Add Transfer from Duck and Drake | 236 | | | | |
| | | 1,000 | | | |
| | | £6,620 | | | £6,620 |

(b)                    BALANCE SHEET as on December 31st, 19..

| | £ | £ | | £ | £ |
|---|---|---|---|---|---|
| **CAPITAL ACCOUNTS** | | | **FIXED ASSETS** | | |
| Duck .. .. .. .. | 8,000 | | Freehold Premises – cost .. | | 6,000 |
| Drake .. .. .. .. | 5,000 | | Leasehold Premises – cost .. | 7,250 | |
| Cygnet .. .. .. .. | 3,000 | | *Less* Provision for amortization .. | 290 | |
| | | 16,000 | | | 6,960 |
| **CURRENT ACCOUNTS** | | | Shop Fittings – cost .. .. | 3,600 | |
| Duck .. .. .. .. | 2,403 | | *Less* Provision for depreciation .. | 1,580 | |
| Drake .. .. .. .. | 1,507 | | | | 2,020 |
| Cygnet .. .. .. .. | 1,250 | | | | 14,980 |
| | | 5,160 | | | |
| | | 21,160 | **CURRENT ASSETS** | | |
| | | | Stock .. .. .. .. | | 3,600 |
| **CURRENT LIABILITIES** | | | Debtors .. .. £2,000 | | |
| Trade Creditors .. .. .. | 3,700 | | *Less* Provision for Doubt- | | |
| Expense Creditors .. .. | 240 | | ful Debts .. 100 | | |
| | | 3,940 | | | 1,900 |
| | | | Payments in Advance .. .. | | 250 |
| | | | Balance at Bank .. .. | | 4,370 |
| | | | | | 10,120 |
| | | £25,100 | | | £25,100 |

(c)                    PARTNERS' CURRENT ACCOUNTS

| | Duck £ | Drake £ | Cygnet £ | | Duck £ | Drake £ | Cygnet £ |
|---|---|---|---|---|---|---|---|
| Goods .. .. .. | 60 | 40 | — | Balances, brought forward .. | 1,600 | 1,200 | 800 |
| Cash .. .. .. | 2,300 | 1,460 | 1,200 | Salaries .. .. .. | 1,000 | 500 | 500 |
| Balances, carried forward .. | 2,403 | 1,507 | 1,250 | Interest on Capital .. .. | 400 | 250 | 150 |
| | | | | Share of Profit .. .. | 1,763 | 1,057 | 1,000 |
| | £4,763 | £3,007 | £2,450 | | £4,763 | £3,007 | £2,450 |
| | | | | Balances, brought forward .. | 2,403 | 1,507 | 1,250 |

## § 4. Partners' Fixed Capital Accounts; Current Accounts; Loan Accounts

### (a) *Fixed Capital and Current Accounts*

Where, as is usual, the partnership agreement provides for a fixed amount of capital to be contributed by each partner, it is preferable for the amounts thereof to be credited to the respective partners' Capital Accounts, and for partners' drawings, salaries, interest on capital and shares of profit to be dealt with in Current Accounts, as in the above illustration. This enables a clear distinction to be made in the accounts between fixed capital (no part of which should be withdrawn, except by agreement) and undrawn profits. If partners' drawings, salaries, interest and shares of profit are passed through the Capital Accounts, the balances on these accounts will be constantly fluctuating, and there may be a danger of a partner's capital being depleted by drawings in excess of his share of profits etc., without particular attention being drawn to the fact.

### (b) *Partners' Loan Accounts*

Where a partner makes an advance to the firm as distinct from capital, the amount thereof should be credited to a separate Loan Account, and not to the partner's Capital Account. This is important, since under the *Partnership Act 1890*, advances by partners are repayable on dissolution in priority to capital. Moreover, even in the absence of agreement on the point, a partner is entitled, under the *Partnership Act 1890*, to interest at 5 per cent. per annum on advances made to the firm, whereas he is not entitled to interest on capital. Interest on a partner's advance at the agreed rate (or, in the absence of agreement, at 5 per cent. per annum) should be credited to his Current Account, and debited to Profit and Loss Account. In this respect also, an advance by a partner differs from capital contributed by him, since interest on the advance is as much a charge against profit as interest paid on a loan from a person who is not a partner. Interest on capital, on the other hand, is an appropriation of profit, being in the nature of a preferential allocation of divisible profits.

## § 5. Goodwill in Partnership Accounts

### (a) Definition and Valuation of Goodwill

The following are some judicial definitions of goodwill:

'The goodwill of a business is the advantage, whatever it may be, which a person gets by continuing to carry on, and being entitled to represent to the outside world that he is carrying on a business, which has been carried on for some time previously' (Warrington, J., in *Hill* v. *Fearis* (1905), 1 Ch. 466).

'[Goodwill] is a thing very easy to describe, very difficult to define. It is the benefit and advantage of the good name, reputation and connection of a business. It is the attractive force which brings in custom. It is the one thing which distinguishes an old established business from a new business at its first start . . . Goodwill is composed of a variety of elements. It differs in its composition in different trades and in different businesses in the same trade. One element may preponderate here, and another there' (Lord Macnaughten in *Commissioners of Inland Revenue* v. *Muller* (1901), A.C. 217).

From the accountant's viewpoint, goodwill, in the sense of attracting custom, has little significance unless it has a saleable value. To the accountant, therefore, goodwill may be said to be that element arising from the reputation, connection, or other advantages possessed by a business which enables it to earn greater profits than the return normally to be expected on the capital represented by the net tangible assets employed in the business. In considering the return normally to be expected, regard must be had to the nature of the business, the risks involved, fair management remuneration and any other relevant circumstances.

The goodwill possessed by a firm may be due, *inter alia*, to the following:

(a) The location of the business premises.

(b) The nature of the firm's products or the reputation of its service.

(c) The possession of favourable contracts, complete or partial monopoly etc.

(d) The personal reputation of the partners.

(e) The possession of efficient and contented employees.

(f) The possession of trade marks, patents or a well-known business name.

(g) The continuance of advertising campaigns.

(h) The maintenance of the quality of the firm's product, and development of the business with changing conditions.

(i) Freedom from legislative restrictions.

Although a firm may possess goodwill, it is not customary to raise an account for it in the books except to the extent that cash or other assets of the firm have been used to pay for it. It follows, therefore, that when goodwill exists and is unrecorded in the books, the capitals of the partners of the firm are understated to the extent of the value of their respective shares of the goodwill. Even though a Goodwill Account may at some time have been raised in the books, the Goodwill Account would not be adjusted to give effect to every variation in its value, and in most cases, therefore, the partners' capitals are at all times under-stated or over-stated in the books to some extent by their shares of the unrecorded appreciation or depreciation in the value of goodwill.

As the amount by which goodwill is undervalued (or overvalued) in the books is a profit (or a loss) to be shared by the partners in their agreed profit-sharing ratio, any alteration in the proportions in which profits and losses are shared, without first making an adjustment in the book value of goodwill, will result in an advantage to one or more partners and a disadvantage to others.

In each of the following cases a change in the profit-sharing ratio takes place and therefore, unless a Goodwill Account already stands in the books *at its correct value*, some adjustment must be made:

1. upon the introduction of a new partner;

2. upon the retirement or death of a partner;

3. upon an agreed change in profit-sharing ratio between the partners.

Various methods are advocated for the valuation of goodwill. In many cases the method adopted is a purely arbitrary one and is often governed by the custom of the particular trade in which the business is engaged. The more usual bases of valuation are as follows:

(*a*) The average profits of a given number of past years multiplied by an agreed number. Thus, 'three years' purchase of the net profits' is commonly spoken of as the basis upon which goodwill is to be valued.

This method is purely arbitrary and will frequently produce a figure for goodwill out of all proportion to its true value.

### Illustration (1)

The average net profit made by A, B & Co for the past five years has been £1,000 per annum before charging interest on capital and partners' salaries.

The average capital employed in the business has been £10,000.

On the basis of three years' purchase of the net profits £3,000 would be payable for the goodwill of the firm. It is apparent, however, that no goodwill actually exists; in fact, there is a *badwill*, since no one would be prepared to pay £13,000 for a business which produces only £1,000 per annum before making any provision for fair remuneration to the proprietors in respect of their services to the business. Allowing say £500 per annum for the services of the proprietors, only £500 per annum remains for interest on capital invested and, therefore, at 10 per cent. per annum such a business would be worth as an investment only £5,000, irrespective of the fact that £10,000 was invested in it.

(*b*) The average *gross* income of the business for a number of past years multiplied by an agreed number.

This method is frequently adopted by professional firms, but is subject to the same disadvantages as those described above. In many cases the gross income of certain years will have been inflated by business of a non-recurring nature, and therefore the purchaser will be paying for goodwill calculated on income which he himself will not enjoy. Further, it is quite conceivable that the expenses incurred in earning the gross income may be so great that there is actually a loss, in which case a sum will be payable for the 'goodwill' of a business from which a loss is to be expected.

(c) The capital value of an annuity for an agreed number of years of an amount equal to the average *super profits* of the business.

*Super profits* are the profits in excess of the amount necessary to pay a fair return upon the capital invested in the business, having regard to the nature of the business and the risks involved and a reasonable remuneration for the services of the partners who work therein.

**Illustration (2)**

The average net profits expected in the future by A, B & Co are £10,000 per annum.
The average capital employed in the business is £50,000.
The rate of interest expected from capital invested in this class of business, having regard to the risk involved, is 10 per cent.
Fair remuneration to the partners of the firm in respect of their services to the business is estimated to be £2,500 per annum.

*Valuation of Goodwill*

|  | £ | £ |
|---|---|---|
| Average annual profits      ..      ..      .. |  | 10,000 |
| *Less* Interest on capital employed at 10%      .. | 5,000 | |
| Partners' remuneration (say)      .. | 2,500 | |
|  |  | 7,500 |
| Annual super-profit |  | £2,500 |

It is now necessary to ascertain the present value of an annuity of £2,500 per annum for a suitable number of years. Alternatively, '*x* years' purchase' of £2,500 may be taken as the value of goodwill, according to the number of years that could be regarded as necessary to build up such a goodwill, discounted by reference to the fact that any goodwill purchased is a wasting asset, since the influence of the vendor diminishes as that of the purchaser increases.

(d) The value of the business as a going concern is estimated by reference to the expected earnings and the yield required, and from the figure arrived at the value of the net *tangible* assets is deducted, the difference being taken to represent the value of goodwill.

**Illustration (3)**

|  | £ |
|---|---|
| Estimated future annual profit      ..      ..      .. | 10,000 |
| *Less* Partners' remuneration      ..      ..      .. | 2,500 |
| Available for interest on capital employed      ..      .. | £7,500 |

Assuming a yield of 10 per cent. per annum is expected the capital value of the business is £75,000. If the value of the net tangible assets of the business is £50,000 the goodwill is worth a maximum of £25,000. This figure may have to be discounted as the earning of super-profits entails greater risks than the earning of the smaller amount required to provide a fair return on money invested in tangible assets.

### (b) Methods of treating Goodwill in the case of an Incoming Partner

It has already been stated that if the value of goodwill is unrecorded in the books the Capital Accounts of the partners are understated by the value thereof.

Assume that the following is the Balance Sheet of the firm of A and B, who share profits in the proportion of two-thirds and one-third respectively:

### A AND B
### BALANCE SHEET

| | £ | £ | | | | £ | £ |
|---|---|---|---|---|---|---|---|
| Capital Accounts: | | | Land and Buildings | .. | .. | | 5,250 |
| A  ..      ..      ..      .. | 8,500 | | Plant and Machinery | .. | .. | | 3,075 |
| B  ..      ..      ..      .. | 3,500 | | Stock-in-Trade  .. | .. | .. | | 4,500 |
| | | 12,000 | Debtors | .. | .. | 3,000 | |
| | | | *Less* Provision | .. | .. | 150 | |
| Creditors  ..      ..      .. | | 3,975 | | | | | 2,850 |
| | | | Cash at Bank  .. | .. | .. | | 300 |
| | | £15,975 | | | | | £15,975 |

The goodwill of the firm is valued at £6,000 and, therefore, the true capitals of A and B are £4,000 and £2,000 respectively more than the amounts standing to the credit of their Capital Accounts. As these increments arise from the fact that goodwill is not recorded in the books, it is apparent that some adjustment must be made in the event of the introduction of a new partner, in order that he shall not take a share of goodwill without payment.

There are, for all practical purposes, three methods of dealing with the question of goodwill upon the introduction of a new partner.

1. An account is raised in the old firm's books for the full value of goodwill, the old partners' Capital Accounts being credited therewith in the proportions in which they share profits or losses. The new partner may or may not bring in capital according to the agreement. In any event, whatever he brings in will be credited to his Capital Account. The effect of this method is to increase the old partners' Capital Accounts to the extent of the value of goodwill previously unrecorded.

**Illustration (1)**

Assuming the facts given above, A and B agree to admit C into partnership, giving him a one-fifth share of profits; C to bring in capital to the extent of one-quarter of the combined capitals of A and B after adjustment for goodwill. A's and B's proportions of profit in the new firm are to be in the same ratio between themselves as before.

Give journal entries recording these transactions, and prepare the Balance Sheet of the new firm, assuming C to have brought in the requisite cash, stating the proportion in which profits will in future be shared.

## JOURNAL

| | | | £ | £ |
|---|---|---|---:|---:|
| Goodwill .. .. .. .. .. .. .. .. .. | | Dr | 6,000 | |
| To A Capital Account .. .. .. .. .. .. .. .. | | | | 4,000 |
| B ,, ,, .. .. .. .. .. .. .. .. | | | | 2,000 |
| Creation of Goodwill as agreed on admittance of C into partnership. | | | | |
| Cash .. .. .. .. .. .. .. .. .. | | Dr | 4,500 | |
| To C Capital Account .. .. .. .. .. .. | | | | 4,500 |
| Being Capital brought in, one-fourth of £12,000 + £6,000. | | | | |

## A, B AND C
## BALANCE SHEET

| Capital Accounts: | | | | £ | | | | | £ |
|---|---|---|---:|---:|---|---|---|---:|---:|
| A .. .. .. | £8,500 | | | | Goodwill .. .. .. .. | | | | 6,000 |
| Add Goodwill .. .. | 4,000 | | | | Land and Buildings .. .. | | | | 5,250 |
| | | | 12,500 | | Plant and Machinery .. .. | | | | 3,075 |
| B .. .. .. | 3,500 | | | | Stock-in-Trade .. .. .. | | | | 4,500 |
| Add Goodwill .. .. | 2,000 | | | | Debtors .. .. .. | | | £3,000 | |
| | | | 5,500 | | Less Provision .. .. | | | 150 | |
| C .. .. .. .. | | | 4,500 | | | | | | 2,850 |
| Creditors .. .. .. .. | | | 3,975 | | Cash at Bank .. .. .. .. | | | | 4,800 |
| | | | £26,475 | | | | | | £26,475 |

As C is to receive one-fifth of the profits, the remaining four-fifths must be divided— $\frac{4}{5} \times \frac{2}{3}$ to A $= \frac{8}{15}$, $\frac{4}{5} \times \frac{1}{3}$ to B $= \frac{4}{15}$ } $\frac{12}{15}$ leaving $\frac{1}{5}$ C $= \frac{3}{15}$

*Note to Illustration:* Since the goodwill now stands in the books at its full value, and the amounts thereof attributable to A and B are included in the amounts standing to the credit of their Capital Accounts, if the business were sold and the goodwill realized its book value, A and B would automatically receive cash for their shares of the goodwill. If, on the sale of the business, the goodwill realized more or less than its book value, the difference would represent a profit or loss arising *after* the admission of C as a partner, and would be divided between A, B *and* C in their new profit-sharing ratio, viz. 8 : 4 : 3.

It is sometimes agreed on the admission of a new partner that he shall acquire a share of goodwill, without payment, over a period of years. This recognizes the fact that the sources of goodwill of a business are constantly changing and that the goodwill existing at the date of the new partner's admission is gradually replaced by a new goodwill, to the building up of which the new partner has contributed. Effect may be given to such an agreement by writing off the book value of the goodwill over an agreed period of years against the Capital Accounts of the old partners only in the proportions in which the goodwill was originally credited to them. For example, if, in the above illustration, it were agreed that C should acquire his share of the firm's goodwill, without payment, over ten years, in each year £600 should be written off the goodwill account, A's capital account being debited with £400 and B's with £200. By this means goodwill would disappear from the books by the end of the ten years, and would become an undisclosed asset, the proceeds of which, if sold, would be divisible between A, B and C in profit-sharing ratio. C would thus have acquired his share of the goodwill without making any payment to A and B. Alternatively, if it is desired to retain goodwill in the books at £6,000 instead of writing down the goodwill by £600 a year C's Capital account would be credited with one-fifth of that amount, viz. £120, A's Capital Account being debited with £80 and B's with £40. In this way C's Capital Account would be credited over the period of ten years with £1,200, being the value of his one-fifth share of the book value of the goodwill, A's and B's accounts being debited with £800 and £400 respectively.

2. No Goodwill Account is raised in the books, but the proportion of the agreed value of goodwill attributable to the incoming partner's share of profit is paid for by him in cash. The additional cash brought in by the new partner for the acquisition of a share of goodwill is credited to the Capital Accounts of the old partners in the proportions in which they shared profits before the introduction of the new partner if the old partners continue to share profits as between themselves in the same proportions as they did before. The cash brought in by the new partner as his capital will be credited to his Capital Account in the normal manner.

**Illustration (2)**

Assuming the same facts as for the previous example, but that no goodwill account is to be opened in the books on C's admission, the latter introducing £3,300 as his capital and £1,200 for his share of goodwill.

Show by journal entries the adjustments to be made on C's introduction, and the Balance Sheet of the new firm.

JOURNAL

| | | £ | £ |
|---|---|---|---|
| Cash .. .. .. .. .. .. .. .. .. .. Dr | | 1,200 | |
| To Capital Accounts: | | | |
| A two-thirds .. .. .. .. .. .. .. .. .. | | | 800 |
| B one-third .. .. .. .. .. .. .. .. | | | 400 |
| Payment by C for a one-fifth share in the Goodwill. | | | |

| | | £ | £ |
|---|---|---|---|
| Cash .. .. .. .. .. .. .. .. .. .. Dr | | 3,300 | |
| To C Capital Account .. .. .. .. .. .. .. .. | | | 3,300 |
| Capital introduced by C. | | | |

A, B AND C<br>BALANCE SHEET

| | | £ | | | | £ |
|---|---|---|---|---|---|---|
| Capital Accounts: | | | Land and Buildings .. .. .. | | | 5,250 |
| A .. .. .. .. £9,300 | | | Plant and Machinery .. .. .. | | | 3,075 |
| B .. .. .. .. 3,900 | | | Stock-in-Trade .. .. .. | | | 4,500 |
| C .. .. .. .. 3,300 | | | Debtors .. .. .. £3,000 | | | |
| | | 16,500 | Less Provision .. .. 150 | | | |
| Creditors .. .. .. .. | | 3,975 | | | | 2,850 |
| | | | Cash at Bank .. .. .. .. | | | 4,800 |
| | | £20,475 | | | | £20,475 |

The same result can be achieved by opening a Goodwill Account (as per Method 1) but as no Goodwill Account is to be opened it is necessary to credit the Goodwill Account and debit the Capital Accounts of the old and new partners in the *new* profit sharing ratio so that goodwill remains unrecorded.

The ledger accounts would appear as over:

CAPITAL ACCOUNTS

| | A £ | B £ | C £ | | | | A £ | B £ | C £ |
|---|---|---|---|---|---|---|---|---|---|
| Goodwill Account .. | 3,200 | 1,600 | 1,200 | Balances b/f. .. .. | | | 8,500 | 3,500 | |
| Balances c/f. .. | 9,300 | 3,900 | 3,300 | Goodwill Account .. | | | 4,000 | 2,000 | |
| | | | | Cash introduced: | | | | | |
| | | | | for Goodwill .. | .. | | | | 1,200 |
| | | | | for Capital .. | .. | | | | 3,300 |
| | £12,500 | £5,500 | £4,500 | | | | £12,500 | £5,500 | £4,500 |

GOODWILL ACCOUNT

| | | | £ | | | | | £ |
|---|---|---|---|---|---|---|---|---|
| Capital Accounts: | | | | Capital Accounts: | | | | |
| A 2/3rds × £6,000 .. .. .. | | | 4,000 | A 8/15ths × £6,000 .. .. .. | | | | 3,200 |
| B 1/3rd × £6,000 .. | | | 2,000 | B 4/15ths × £6,000 .. .. .. | | | | 1,600 |
| | | | | C 3/15ths × £6,000 .. .. .. | | | | 1,200 |
| | | | £6,000 | | | | | £6,000 |

When, as in the above illustration the old partners continue to share profits as between themselves in the same proportions as before, the amount introduced by the new partner for his share of goodwill if credited to the old partners in the proportions in which they divided profits prior to the introduction of the new partner gives exactly the same result as if a Goodwill Account had been opened and then written down again.

If, however, the profit sharing ratio of the new firm is modified as between the old partners, the amount paid in for goodwill by the new partner should be divided between the old partners according to the share of profit each surrenders.

**Illustration (3)**

Assuming the same facts as for the previous example but that after the admission of C, the profit sharing ratio was to be A 9/15ths, B 3/15ths and C 3/15ths, show by journal entry the apportionment of C's payment for goodwill.

| | A | B | C |
|---|---|---|---|
| Profit sharing ratio (old firm) .. | 10/15ths | 5/15ths | |
| ,, ,, ,, (new firm) .. | —9/15ths | —3/15ths | +3/15ths |
| | —1/15th | —2/15ths | +3/15ths |

Therefore the payment of £1,200 received from C will be apportioned between A and B in the ratio 1 : 2.

JOURNAL

| | | | £ | £ |
|---|---|---|---|---|
| Cash | | Dr | 1,200 | |
| To A .. .. .. .. .. .. | | | | 400 |
| B .. .. .. .. .. .. | | | | 800 |

Payment by C for one-fifth share in Goodwill.

The same result can be achieved by writing up the book value of goodwill to its full value by crediting the old partners' capital accounts in the old profit sharing ratio with the value thereof, crediting the new partner with the cash he introduced for goodwill and capital, and then, as goodwill is to remain unrecorded, crediting Goodwill Account and debiting the old and new partners in the new profit sharing ratio.

### CAPITAL ACCOUNTS

| | A £ | B £ | C £ | | | | A £ | B £ | C £ |
|---|---|---|---|---|---|---|---|---|---|
| Goodwill Account .. | 3,600 | 1,200 | 1,200 | Balances b/f. . .. | | | 8,500 | 3,500 | |
| Balances c/f. .. .. | 8,900 | 4,300 | 3,300 | Goodwill Account .. | | | 4,000 | 2,000 | |
| | | | | Cash introduced: | | | | | |
| | | | | for Goodwill . .. | | | | | 1,200 |
| | | | | for Capital . .. | | | | | 3,300 |
| | £12,500 | £5,500 | £4,500 | | | | £12,500 | £5,500 | £4,500 |

### GOODWILL ACCOUNT

| | £ | | | | | £ |
|---|---|---|---|---|---|---|
| Capital Accounts: | | Capital Accounts: | | | | |
| A 2/3rds × £6,000 .. .. .. | 4,000 | A 9/15ths × £6,000 .. .. .. | | | | 3,600 |
| B 1/3rd × £6,000 .. .. .. .. | 2,000 | B 3/15ths × £6,000 .. .. .. | | | | 1,200 |
| | | C 3/15ths × £6,000 .. .. .. | | | | 1,200 |
| | £6,000 | | | | | £6,000 |

3. The third method is similar to the second, with the exception that the money paid by the incoming partner for goodwill is not left in the business but is paid to the old partners personally in the proportions in which they share profits and losses. In this case there will be no entries in the books, unless the amount is first paid into the firm's account and then withdrawn, in order to keep some record of the transaction. Naturally this method is the least advantageous of all to the incoming partner, as the money which he pays for goodwill is not utilized for the general benefit of the business. It must be appreciated that it is only in the ultimate disposition of the cash that this method differs from the second.

By methods 2 and 3 the old partners, A and B, are compensated in cash for the shares of their existing goodwill which they surrender to C, and the goodwill remains an undisclosed asset, the proceeds of which, if sold, would now be divided between A, B and C in their agreed profit-sharing ratio. C would thus recover the sum paid by him for a share of goodwill, plus or minus his share of any increase or decrease in its value since he became a partner.

4. Where the goodwill stands in the books at less than its true value, on the admission of a new partner either of the following courses may be followed:

(*a*) The book value of the goodwill may be entirely written off against the old partners' capital accounts in their original profit-sharing ratio. Any cash paid by the new partner for a share of goodwill would then be credited to the old partners, as in method 2 or 3 above.

(*b*) The book value of the goodwill may be written up to its full value by crediting the old partners in profit-sharing ratio, with their shares of the amount by which the goodwill is written up. The position would then be as in method 1 and any sum paid in by the new partner would be credited to his Capital Account.

(*c*) If it is desired to retain the goodwill in the books at its existing book value, which is less than its true value, the incoming partner should only be required to pay for a share of the *undisclosed* goodwill. For example, if in Illustration 1 the goodwill stood in the books at £1,000, its true value being

£6,000, and it was desired to retain the asset in the books at £1,000, C should only pay to A and B in respect of his share of goodwill one-fifth of £5,000 = £1,000, which sum should be credited to A and B in profit-sharing ratio. The capital accounts of A and B are already credited with their respective shares of the £1,000 goodwill appearing in the books, and they are therefore entitled to no payment from C in respect thereof.

### (c) Goodwill affecting Outgoing Partners

When a partner retires or dies, it is usual for his share of the goodwill to be determined, either according to the terms of the original agreement or by valuation, and for such an amount to be credited to his Capital Account as represents his proportion of the value of the goodwill so ascertained.

It will be appreciated, however, that such an adjustment would not be necessary if an account for goodwill, at its correct value, already stood in the books of the firm.

The amount to be credited to the retiring or deceased partner's account in respect of goodwill may be debited to Goodwill Account, or if it is preferred that no Goodwill Account shall be raised, or that the balance appearing on an existing Goodwill Account shall not be altered, to the Capital Accounts of the remaining partners in their profit-sharing proportions.

**Illustration**

The following is the Balance Sheet of A, B & C on December 31st, 19.. on which date A retires. Profits and losses have been shared in the ratio of 3 : 2 : 1, and B and C continue the business sharing profits in the ratio of 2 : 1. For the purposes of A's retirement goodwill is valued at £5,000.

BALANCE SHEET, as at December 31st, 19..

| | | | | £ | | | | | | £ |
|---|---|---|---|---|---|---|---|---|---|---|
| Capital Accounts: | | | | | Goodwill | .. | | .. | .. | 1,000 |
| A | .. | .. | .. £16,000 | | Freehold Property | | .. | .. | .. | 13,500 |
| B | .. | .. | .. 5,000 | | Plant and Machinery | .. | .. | .. | .. | 2,493 |
| C | .. | .. | .. 4,000 | | Stock-in-Trade | .. | .. | .. | .. | 6,159 |
| | | | | 25,000 | Debtors | .. | .. | .. | .. | 4,832 |
| Current Accounts: | | | | | Cash at Bank | .. | .. | .. | .. | 1,108 |
| A | .. | .. | .. £400 | | | | | | | |
| C | .. | .. | .. 100 | | | | | | | |
| | | | | 500 | | | | | | |
| Creditors | .. | .. | .. | 3,592 | | | | | | |
| | | | | £29,092 | | | | | | £29,092 |

Show by journal entries the adjustments necessary on A's retirement, having regard to the fact that the partners do not wish to increase the present book value of goodwill.

JOURNAL

| | | | | | | | | | | | £ | £ |
|---|---|---|---|---|---|---|---|---|---|---|---|---|
| Capital Accounts: | | | | | | | | | | Dr | | |
| B two-thirds .. | | | | | | | | | .. | | 1,333 | |
| C one-third .. | .. | .. | .. | .. | .. | .. | .. | .. | .. | | 667 | |
|     To Capital Account A | .. | .. | .. | .. | .. | .. | .. | .. | | | 2,000 |
| Purchase from A of one-half of the unrecorded value of Goodwill. | | | | | | | | | | | | |
| Current Account A | | | | | | .. | | .. | Dr | | 400 | |
|     To Capital Account A | .. | .. | .. | .. | .. | .. | .. | | | | 400 |
| Transfer of balance on retirement. | | | | | | | | | | | | |
| Capital Account A | .. | .. | .. | .. | .. | .. | .. | .. | Dr | | 18,400 | |
|     To Loan Account A .. | .. | .. | .. | .. | .. | .. | .. | .. | | | 18,400 |
| Transfer of balance due to A on his retirement pending settlement. | | | | | | | | | | | | |

*Note to Illustration:* As the value of goodwill has been agreed at £5,000, an increase over its book value is disclosed of £4,000. Of this sum A is entitled to one-half, and as the book value of the goodwill is not to be increased, B and C must be debited therewith in their profit-sharing proportions as they have, in effect, purchased this share of goodwill from A.

It will be appreciated that the same amount would have been credited to A had the Goodwill Account been raised to its real value, thus:

| | | | | | | | | | | £ | £ |
|---|---|---|---|---|---|---|---|---|---|---|---|
| Goodwill Account | .. | .. | .. | .. | .. | .. | .. | Dr | 4,000 | |
| To Capital Accounts: | | | | | | | | | | |
| A one-half | .. | .. | .. | .. | .. | .. | .. | .. | | 2,000 |
| B one-third | .. | .. | .. | .. | .. | .. | .. | .. | | 1,333 |
| C one-sixth | .. | .. | .. | .. | .. | .. | .. | .. | | 667 |
| Adjustment necessary to increase Goodwill Account to its correct value. | | | | | | | | | | |

An alternative arrangement is sometimes made whereby a retiring partner receives, in lieu of an amount representing his share of the goodwill, an annuity or a proportion of the profits, for life or for an agreed number of years. This method is not to be recommended, however, as the ultimate amount which will be paid by the continuing partners for the old partner's share of goodwill will be uncertain and may have little relationship to its true value.

### (d) Treatment of Assets including Goodwill on a change in the ratios in which profits are shared by partners

When partners agree that the proportion in which they share profits and losses shall be changed, it is necessary for all the assets of the firm, including goodwill, to be revalued, in order that each partner may be credited or charged, before the change in the division of profits takes effect, with his proper share of any unrecorded profit or loss in respect of these assets.

**Illustration (1)**

The following is the Balance Sheet of X, Y & Z, at December 31st, 19.... The partners agree that from January 1st, 19.. they will share profits in the ratio of 3 : 2 : 1, instead of in their former ratio of 2 : 2 : 1.

X, Y AND Z
BALANCE SHEET, as at December 31st, 19..

| | | | | | £ | | | | | | £ |
|---|---|---|---|---|---|---|---|---|---|---|---|
| Capital Accounts: | | | | | | Goodwill | .. | .. | .. | .. | 4,000 |
| X | .. | .. | .. | .. £10,000 | | Land and Buildings | .. | .. | .. | | 6,000 |
| Y | .. | .. | .. | .. 5,000 | | Plant and Machinery | .. | .. | .. | | 4,000 |
| Z | .. | .. | .. | .. 3,000 | | Stock .. | .. | .. | .. | | 5,500 |
| | | | | | 18,000 | Debtors | .. | .. | .. | | 3,100 |
| Creditors | .. | .. | .. | | 7,500 | Bills Receivable | .. | .. | .. | | 2,000 |
| | | | | | | Cash at Bank | .. | .. | .. | | 900 |
| | | | | | £25,500 | | | | | | £25,500 |

The assets of the firm are revalued as under:

| | £ |
|---|---|
| Goodwill .. | 6,000 |
| Land and Buildings | 8,500 |
| Plant and Machinery | 3,500 |
| Stock .. | 5,000 |
| Sundry Debtors | 2,600 |
| Bills Receivable | 2,000 |

Show by journal entries the adjustments which must be made on the occasion of the change in the profit-sharing ratios between the partners.

## JOURNAL

| | | | £ | £ |
|---|---|---|---:|---:|
| Goodwill .. .. .. .. .. .. .. .. | Dr | | 2,000 | |
| Land and Buildings .. .. .. .. .. .. | | .. | 2,500 | |
| To Revaluation Account .. .. .. .. .. | | .. | | 4,500 |
| Adjustment to record increase in value of assets as at December 31st, 19.. | | | | |
| Revaluation Account .. .. .. .. .. | Dr | | 1,500 | |
| To Plant and Machinery .. .. .. .. .. | | .. | | 500 |
| Stock .. .. .. .. .. .. | | .. | | 500 |
| Bad Debts Provision .. .. .. .. .. | | .. | | 500 |
| Adjustment to record decrease in value of assets as at December 31st, 19.. | | | | |
| Revaluation Account .. .. .. .. .. | Dr | | 3,000 | |
| To Capital Accounts: | | | | |
| X two-fifths .. .. .. .. .. .. | | .. | | 1,200 |
| Y two-fifths .. .. .. .. .. .. | | .. | | 1,200 |
| Z one-fifth .. .. .. .. .. .. | | .. | | 600 |
| Transfer of balance as at December 31st, 19.., in old profit-sharing ratio, 2:2:1. | | | | |

If it is desired to restore the assets to their original book values the above entries may be reversed, the partners being debited with the differences disclosed in their *new* profit-sharing ratio. Alternatively, to avoid writing up the assets in the first place a *Memorandum* Revaluation Account could be prepared to disclose the net increase in the value of the assets, and the following entry made:

## STATEMENT SHOWING ADJUSTMENT NECESSARY

Net increase in value of assets .. .. .. **£3,000**

| | X | Y | Z |
|---|---:|---:|---:|
| | £ | £ | £ | £ |
| Proportion thereof applicable to each partner in old ratio, 2:2:1 .. .. .. .. .. | 3,000 | 1,200 | 1,200 | 600 |
| Proportion thereof applicable to each partner in new ratio, 3:2:1 .. .. .. .. .. | 3,000 | 1,500 | 1,000 | 500 |
| Adjustment.. .. .. .. .. | — | +£300 | —£200 | —£100 |

## JOURNAL

| | | | £ | £ |
|---|---|---|---:|---:|
| Capital Account X .. .. .. .. .. .. .. .. | Dr | | 300 | |
| To Capital Accounts: | | | | |
| Y .. .. .. .. .. .. .. .. .. | | .. | | 200 |
| Z .. .. .. .. .. .. .. .. .. | | .. | | 100 |
| Adjustment between partners consequent upon a change in the profit-sharing ratios as shown by the statement above. | | | | |

Another alternative is for the net increase in the assets to be credited to the partners' Capital Accounts in their *original* profit-sharing ratio, and then debited to the Capital Accounts in the *new* ratio.

## CAPITAL ACCOUNTS

| | X £ | Y £ | Z £ | | X £ | Y £ | Z £ |
|---|---:|---:|---:|---|---:|---:|---:|
| Revaluation Account – Net increase in value of assets written off in new ratio 3:2:1 .. .. | 1.500 | 1,000 | 500 | Balances b/f. .. .. | 10,000 | 5,000 | 3,000 |
| | | | | Revaluation Account – Net increase in value of assets in old ratio 2:2:1 .. | 1,200 | 1,200 | 600 |
| Balances c/d. .. .. | 9,700 | 5,200 | 3,100 | | | | |
| | £11,200 | £6,200 | £3,600 | | £11,200 | £6,200 | £3,600 |
| | | | | Balances b/d. .. .. | 9,700 | 5,200 | 3,100 |

In effect, X has purchased 3/6ths — 2/5ths=1/10th (or £300) of the net increase and is accordingly debited with that amount, whilst Y has sold 2/5ths — 2/6ths = 1/15th (or £200) and Z 1/5th — 1/6th = 1/30th (or £100) and their accounts are credited with those amounts. If the capitals are to be restored to their original amounts X must pay in £300, Y withdrawing £200 and Z £100.

In more complicated cases it may be desirable to open a special Adjustment Account, in which to record the transactions.

**Illustration (2)**

A, B, C, D and E are partners in A & Co, making up accounts to December 31st each year. The capital of the firm is contributed in proportion to their shares in profits and losses. No Goodwill Account appears in the books.

As from January 1st, 19.., those shares change under the partnership deed as under:

|   | Previous to January 1st | As from January 1st |
|---|---|---|
| A .. .. | 40 per cent. | 30 per cent. |
| B .. .. | 30 ,, ,, | 25 ,, ,, |
| C .. .. | 15 ,, ,, | 20 ,, ,, |
| D .. .. | 10 ,, ,, | 15 ,, ,, |
| E .. .. | 5 ,, ,, | 10 ,, ,, |

The partnership deed further provides that partners whose shares increase shall purchase goodwill from the partners whose shares diminish on the basis of 2½ years' purchase of the average profits for the preceding five years.

The profits for those years were £20,700, £16,250, £17,000, £16,950 and £16,300 respectively.

The following further arrangements are made at March 31st.

1. The capital of the firm, which was £20,000, is to be reduced as from January 1st to £18,000.

2. A agrees to lend E £1,250 towards the sum due by E as a result of the adjustment.

3. B receives C's personal cheque for £2,500 and A receives D's personal cheque for £2,000.

4. E, having regard to the state of his account with the firm, obtains from his wife securities which he sells for £1,750, handing the proceeds over to the firm. D follows his example paying in £1,000.

An additional account, called 'Adjustment Account', is opened for each partner in the firm's ledger, through which the above-mentioned transactions are to be passed.

The entries incidental to the transactions and arrangements indicated above are all made in the firm's books at March 31st, on which date the Adjustment Accounts are closed by the payment in or withdrawal of cash; no record is, however, retained in those books of E's liability to pay and A's right to receive the above-mentioned loan of £1,250.

The accounts will appear as follows:

## CAPITAL ACCOUNTS

|  | A £ | B £ | C £ | D £ | E £ |  | A £ | B £ | C £ | D £ | E £ |
|---|---|---|---|---|---|---|---|---|---|---|---|
| Adjustment Accounts, reduction in capital .. | 2,600 | 1,500 | — | — | — | Balances b/f. .. | 8,000 | 6,000 | 3,000 | 2,000 | 1,000 |
| Balances c/d. .. | 5,400 | 4,500 | 3,600 | 2,700 | 1,800 | Adjustment Accounts, increase in capital .. | — | — | 600 | 700 | 800 |
| £ | 8,000 | 6,000 | 3,600 | 2,700 | 1,800 | £ | 8,000 | 6,000 | 3,600 | 2,700 | 1,800 |
|  |  |  |  |  |  | Balances b/d. .. | 5,400 | 4,500 | 3,600 | 2,700 | 1,800 |

## ADJUSTMENT ACCOUNTS

| | A £ | B £ | C £ | D £ | E £ | | A £ | B £ | C £ | D £ | E £ |
|---|---|---|---|---|---|---|---|---|---|---|---|
| Purchase of goodwill .. | — | — | 2,180 | 2,180 | 2,180 | Sale of goodwill .. | 4,360 | 2,180 | — | — | — |
| Capital Accounts | — | — | 600 | 700 | 800 | Capital Accounts .. | 2,600 | 1,500 | — | — | — |
| C – personal cheque .. | — | 2,500 | — | — | — | B – personal cheque .. | — | — | 2,500 | — | — |
| D – personal cheque .. | 2,000 | — | — | — | — | A – personal cheque .. | — | — | — | 2,000 | — |
| E – personal loan | 1,250 | — | — | — | — | Cash .. | — | — | — | 1,000 | 1,750 |
| Cash – to balance | 3,710 | 1,180 | — | 120 | 20 | A – personal loan .. | — | — | — | — | 1,250 |
| | | | | | | Cash – to balance .. | — | — | 280 | — | — |
| £ | 6,960 | 3,680 | 2,780 | 3,000 | 3,000 | £ | 6,960 | 3,680 | 2,780 | 3,000 | 3,000 |

*Notes to Illustration:*

1. The Adjustment Accounts are personal accounts for the partners, being credited with amounts due *to* them and debited with amounts due *by* them respectively in respect of the adjustments. Payments *by* partners are then credited and payments *to* them debited to their respective Adjustment Accounts.

2. Transfers are made from Capital Accounts to Adjustment Accounts to reduce the total capital to £18,000 and to adjust the holdings of the partners to the new proportions as at January 1st.

3. The value of the goodwill, on the basis stated, is £43,600. Since A's share of the total profit is to be reduced by 10 per cent. and B's by 5 per cent., A and B are, in effect, selling similar shares of goodwill, and their Adjustment Accounts must therefore be credited with £4,360 and £2,180 respectively. C, D, and B are purchasing these shares in equal proportions, since the share of profit of each is to be increased by 5 per cent. The Adjustment Account of each must therefore be debited with £2,180.

4. Since no record is to be retained in the books of E's liability to pay and A's right to receive the loan of £1,250 made by A to E, this loan, so far as the firm is concerned, is tantamount to a payment *to* the firm by E and a withdrawal *by* A of £1,250. A's Adjustment Account is therefore debited, and E's credited, with £1,250. E then owes this £1,250 to A *outside* the business.

### (e) *Life Assurance Policies to provide for repayment of share of a deceased partner*

In some cases partners effect assurance on their lives, either jointly or severally, in order to provide the cash required to pay out the whole or part of the capital and goodwill of a partner who dies. Such an assurance is of particular advantage where the surviving partners have insufficient resources outside the business to purchase a deceased partner's interest in the partnership.

Partnership life assurance may be dealt with in the accounts by any of the following methods:

(i) The premiums paid on the policy are written off to Profit and Loss Account, thereby reducing the profits divisible between, and available to be withdrawn from, the business by the partners. This has the effect of charging the partners with the cost of the assurance in the proportions in which they share profits. No account in respect of the policy appears in the books, so that the value of the policy at any time represents a secret reserve which belongs to the partners in profit-sharing ratio. Accordingly, on the death of a partner each partner's Capital Account must be credited with his proper share of the policy money received. The cash so made available can then be applied in or towards the sum due to the representatives of the deceased partner.

The advantage of this method is that it avoids the danger of the working capital of the firm being depleted by the withdrawal of cash to pay the premiums, the cost of the assurance being borne by the partners out of their shares of profit.

(ii) A Life Policy Account is opened in the books, to which the premiums are debited as and when they are paid. The policy will thus appear in the books as an asset at cost, and the amount receivable on the death of a partner will be credited to this account, any difference between the amount standing to the debit of the account and the sum received being divided between the partners in profit-sharing ratio, and credited to their respective Capital Accounts.

Although this method has the advantage of disclosing the existence of the asset acquired by the payment of the premiums, if (as is usually the case in the early years of the policy) its surrender value is less than the total amount of the premiums paid, the policy will appear in the books at more than its current realizable value. Furthermore, as the profits disclosed by the accounts are not reduced by the premiums, if the whole of the profits are withdrawn the premiums will, in effect, have been paid out of capital, and the liquid resources of the business may become unduly depleted.

(iii) The premiums paid are debited to a Life Policy Account, as in method (ii), but the book value of the policy is adjusted each year to its surrender value by a transfer from Profit and Loss Account. This overcomes the objection, referred to in method (ii), to the policy appearing in the books at more than its realizable value. It does not, however, conserve the working capital by reducing the divisible profits by the premiums paid.

(iv) The premiums paid are debited to a Life Policy Account, and a sum equal to the annual premium is debited each year to Profit and Loss Account and credited to a Life Policy Fund Account. The book value of the policy is then adjusted to surrender value by a transfer from the Life Policy Fund Account instead of from Profit and Loss Account. On the death of a partner the sum received under the policy will be credited to the Life Policy Account, any profit disclosed by the account being transferred to the credit of the Life Policy Fund Account. The final balance on the latter account will now represent a reserve equal to the total sum received under the policy, and will be transferred to the credit of the partners' Capital Accounts in their profit-sharing proportions.

This method has the advantages of disclosing the existence of the asset at its realizable value and also of avoiding the danger of depleting the working capital of the firm.

Each of the above methods is exemplified by the following illustration:

**Illustration**

A, B and C are in partnership, sharing profits in the proportion of two-thirds, one-sixth, and one-sixth respectively, and in order to provide cash for the immediate payment of a portion of the amount due to any one of them in the event of death, in respect of both capital and goodwill, an assurance was effected on their lives jointly for £9,000 without profits, at an annual premium of £350.

A died on June 30th, 19.., three months after the annual accounts had been prepared, and in accordance with the partnership agreement, his share of the profits to the date of death, was estimated on the exact basis of the profits for the preceding year. In addition to this, the agreement provided for interest on capital at 5 per cent. per annum on the balance standing to the credit of the capital account at the date of the last Balance Sheet, and also for goodwill, which was to be brought into account at two years' purchase of the average profits for the last three years, prior to charging the above-mentioned insurance premiums, but after charging interest on capital.

A's capital on March 31st, 19.., stood at £12,000, and his drawings from then to the date of death amounted to £900.

The net profits of the business for the three preceding years amounted to £3,350, £4,150 and £4,050, respectively, after charging interest on capital but before charging insurance premiums, or adjustments of the Policy Account to surrender value (as the case may be).

The total premiums paid on the life policy to March 31st preceding A's death amounted to £4,500, and the surrender value at that date was £4,000. In that year it became necessary to debit Profit and Loss Account with £250 in order to adjust the Policy Account to the surrender value of the policy.

You are instructed to adjust A's capital account as at the date of death, for a settlement with his executors.

METHOD (i)

## A's CAPITAL ACCOUNT

| | £ | | £ |
|---|---|---|---|
| Drawings .. | 900 | Balance b/f. .. .. .. | 12,000 |
| Balance c/d. | 23,000 | Interest on Capital 5% for 3 months .. | 150 |
| | | Profit to date of death .. .. | 617 |
| | | Goodwill .. .. .. | 5,130 |
| | | Insurance Policy, two-thirds of £9,000 .. | 6,003 |
| | £23,900 | | £23,900 |
| | | Balance b/d. .. .. .. | 23,000 |

*Notes:*

1. The value of goodwill is arrived at as follows:          £

| | | | |
|---|---|---|---|
| Profit 1st year .. .. .. .. .. | 3,350 |
| „ 2nd „ .. .. .. .. .. | 4,150 |
| „ 3rd „ .. .. .. .. .. | 4,050 |
| | 3) 11,550 |
| Three years' average profit .. .. .. | £3,850 |
| Total amount of Goodwill .. .. .. | £7,700 |

A's Share = two-thirds of £7,700 = £5,133

2. A's share of profit for the 3 months to the date of death, based on the profit of the previous year is $\frac{1}{4} \times \frac{2}{3}$ £(4,050—350) = £617.

METHOD (ii)

## A's CAPITAL ACCOUNT

| | | £ | | | £ |
|---|---|---|---|---|---|
| Drawings .. .. .. .. .. | | 900 | Balance b/f. .. .. .. .. | | 12,000 |
| Balance c/d. .. .. .. .. | | 20,058 | Interest on Capital – 3 months .. .. | | 150 |
| | | | Profit to date of death .. .. .. | | 675 |
| | | | Goodwill .. .. .. .. | | 5,133 |
| | | | Life Policy Account – share of profit | | 3,000 |
| | | £20,958 | | | £20,958 |
| | | | Balance b/d. .. .. .. .. | | 20,958 |

*Note:* A's share of profit is $\frac{1}{4} \times \frac{2}{3} \times £4,050 = £675$.

## LIFE POLICY ACCOUNT

| | | | £ | | | £ |
|---|---|---|---|---|---|---|
| Balance (Premiums paid to date) b/f. .. | | | 4,500 | Cash .. .. .. .. .. | | 9,000 |
| Profit: | | | | | | |
| A two-thirds .. .. .. | £3,000 | | | | | |
| B one-sixth .. .. .. | 750 | | | | | |
| C one-sixth .. .. .. | 750 | | 4,500 | | | |
| | | | £9,000 | | | £9,000 |

METHOD (iii)

## A's CAPITAL ACCOUNT

| | | £ | | | £ |
|---|---|---|---|---|---|
| Drawings .. .. .. .. .. | | 900 | Balance b/f. .. .. .. .. | | 12,000 |
| Balance c/d. .. .. .. .. | | 20,350 | Interest on Capital .. .. .. | | 150 |
| | | | Profit to date of death .. .. .. | | 633 |
| | | | Goodwill .. .. .. .. | | 5,133 |
| | | | Life Policy Account – share of profit .. | | 3,334 |
| | | £21,250 | | | £21,250 |
| | | | Balance b/d. .. .. .. .. | | 20,350 |

*Note:* The divisible profit for the previous year was £4,050 less £250 charged to Profit and Loss Account and credited to Policy Account to adjust it to surrender value = £3,800. A's share is $\frac{1}{4} \times \frac{2}{3} \times £3,800 = £633$.

## LIFE POLICY ACCOUNT

| | | | £ | | | £ |
|---|---|---|---|---|---|---|
| Balance (surrender value) b/f. .. .. | | | 4,000 | Cash .. .. .. .. .. | | 9,000 |
| Profit: | | | | | | |
| A two-thirds .. .. .. | £3,334 | | | | | |
| B one-sixth .. .. .. | 833 | | | | | |
| C one-sixth .. .. .. | 833 | | 5,000 | | | |
| | | | £9,000 | | | £9,000 |

METHOD (iv)

## A's CAPITAL ACCOUNT

| | | £ | | | £ |
|---|---|---|---|---|---|
| Drawings .. .. .. .. .. | | 900 | Balance b/f. .. .. .. .. | | 12,000 |
| Balance c/d. .. .. .. .. | | 23,000 | Interest on Capital .. .. .. | | 150 |
| | | | Profit to date of death .. .. .. | | 617 |
| | | | Goodwill .. .. .. .. | | 5,133 |
| | | | Life Policy Fund Account .. .. | | 6,000 |
| | | £23,900 | | | £23,900 |
| | | | Balance b/d. .. .. .. .. | | 23,000 |

*Note:* A's share of profit is as in method (i).

## LIFE POLICY ACCOUNT

| | £ | | £ |
|---|---|---|---|
| Balance b/f. .. .. .. .. | 4,000 | Cash .. .. .. .. .. | 9,000 |
| Life Policy Fund – Profit transferred .. .. | 5,000 | | |
| | £9,000 | | £9,000 |

## LIFE POLICY FUND ACCOUNT

| | | £ | | £ |
|---|---|---|---|---|
| Balance transferred to partners: | | | Balance b/f. .. .. .. .. | 4,000 |
| A two-thirds .. .. .. £6,000 | | | Life Policy Account, profit transferred .. | 5,000 |
| B one-sixth .. .. .. 1,500 | | | | |
| C one-sixth .. .. .. 1,500 | | 9,000 | | |
| | | £9,000 | | £9,000 |

### (f) *Readjustment of Partners' Shares of Profit over a period of years*

When a manager or other servant of the firm is admitted into partnership, it is sometimes agreed that retrospective effect shall be given to the new arrangement, as if, from the point of view of sharing profits, he had become a partner at an earlier date. In such a case an entry must be made at the commencement of the new partnership, debiting the original members of the firm and crediting the incoming partner with the amount (if any) found to be due to him in respect of the earlier period.

**Illustration**

A and B have carried on business for four years, and their books show the following results:

| | | | £ |
|---|---|---|---|
| First year .. | .. Loss | | 788 |
| Second year .. | .. Profit | | 3,635 |
| Third year .. | .. „ | | 4,129 |
| Fourth year .. | .. „ | | 5,362 |

The capital (in which no change has been recorded in the books during the four years) is A £30,000, B £20,000, the profits and losses being divisible in these proportions; and in addition to the capital there is a loan from C (the manager) of £5,000 at 5 per cent. The above results are after charging 4½ per cent. interest on capital, 5 per cent. interest on the loan, and C's salary of £500 per annum.

At the end of the fourth year the partners agree to adjust the accounts by treating C as a partner from the commencement, his loan of £5,000 to be regarded as capital, entitling him to one-eleventh of the profits, and carrying 4½ per cent. interest instead of the 5 per cent. paid on the loan, but his salary is reduced to £400 per annum for the whole period of four years.

Make the necessary entries to adjust the accounts to accord with the new arrangement, and show how the loss of the first year and the profits of the second, third and fourth years are divisible between A, B and C. Calculations to be made to the nearest £.

Under the new arrangement the divisions are as follows:

|  |  |  |  |  |  | £ |
|---|---|---|---|---|---|---|
| **First Year:** |  |  |  |  |  |  |
| Loss £788 – Interest £25 and Salary £100 = Loss £663 .. | .. | A | 30/55 | .. | .. | 362 |
|  |  | B | 20/55 | .. | .. | 241 |
|  |  | C | 5/55 | .. | .. | 60 |
|  |  |  | Loss | .. | .. | **£663** |
| **Second Year:** |  |  |  |  |  |  |
| Profit £3,635 + Interest £25 and Salary £100 = Profit £3,760 | .. | A | 30/55 | .. | .. | 2,051 |
|  |  | B | 20/55 | .. | .. | 1,367 |
|  |  | C | 5/55 | .. | .. | 342 |
|  |  |  | Profit | .. | .. | **£3,760** |
| **Third Year:** |  |  |  |  |  |  |
| Profit £4,129 + Interest £25 and Salary £100 = Profit £4,254 | .. | A | 30/55 | .. | .. | 2,320 |
|  |  | B | 20/55 | .. | .. | 1,547 |
|  |  | C | 5/55 | .. | .. | 387 |
|  |  |  | Profit | .. | .. | **£4,254** |
| **Fourth Year:** |  |  |  |  |  |  |
| Profit £5,362 + Interest £25 and Salary £100 = Profit £5,487 | .. | A | 30/55 | .. | .. | 2,993 |
|  |  | B | 20/55 | .. | .. | 1,995 |
|  |  | C | 5/55 | .. | .. | 499 |
|  |  |  | Profit | .. | .. | **£5,487** |

| By the above arrangement C receives the following: |  |  |  | £ |
|---|---|---|---|---|
| Second Year | .. | .. | .. | 342 |
| Third  „ | .. | .. | .. | 387 |
| Fourth  „ | .. | .. | .. | 499 |
|  |  |  |  | 1,228 |
| *Less* First Year Loss | .. | .. | £60 |  |
| £125 per annum for 4 years, viz. £25 interest ($\frac{1}{2}$% on £5,000) and £100 salary to be taken at £400 instead of £500 per annum | .. | .. | 500 |  |
|  |  |  |  | 560 |
| Net Credit for C | .. | .. | .. | £668 |
| Debit to A three-fifths of £668 | .. | .. | .. | 401 |
| „  „  B two-fifths of £668 | .. | .. | .. | 267 |
|  |  |  |  | £668 |

A's Current Account will therefore be debited with £401, and B's with £267, C's being credited with £668.

## (g) *Where a proportion of one Partner's Share of Profit is borne personally by another*

It occasionally happens where a member of the staff of a private firm is taken into partnership, that the difference between the amount of his share in the profits as a partner and the amount which, as an employee he would have received by way of salary, plus possibly a commission varying with the profits, is not shared by all the other partners, but is borne personally by one or more of them.

### Illustration

John Smith, Peter Jones and his son George Jones were partners in the firm of Smith & Jones, solicitors.

On January 1st, Charles Davis, the managing clerk, was admitted as a partner.

Profits and losses in the new partnership were to be shared: John Smith four-tenths, Peter Jones three-tenths, George Jones two-tenths and a salary of £650 per annum, Charles Davis one-tenth.

Davis had previously been paid a salary of £1,200 per annum and a commission of 3 per cent. of the profits, after charging his salary and commission, but before charging any partner's salary.

It was agreed that for the first year of the new partnership, any excess of his share of the profits over the sum he would have earned had he remained managing clerk increased by £1,000, should be charged to John Smith's share of profit.

On considering the draft accounts for the year ended December 31st, the partners agreed to the following adjustments:

1. to provide for a staff bonus of £1,500;

2. that John Smith's son Albert, an employee of the partnership, should receive an additional bonus of £200 chargeable against his father's share of profit;

3. that £300 of Peter Jones's share of profit should be credited to his son George.

The profits for the year before making the above adjustments and before charging George Jones's salary amounted to £33,600.

Prepare a statement showing the division of profits between partners.

### STATEMENT OF DIVISION OF PROFITS
#### For the year ended December 31st

| | £ | John Smith £ | Peter Jones £ | George Jones £ | Charles Davis £ |
|---|---|---|---|---|---|
| Profit for the year .. .. .. .. | 33,600 | | | | |
| *Less* Staff bonus .. .. .. | 1,500 | | | | |
| | 32,100 | | | | |
| *Less* George Jones's salary .. .. | 650 | | | 650 | |
| Divisible in profit-sharing ratio .. .. | £31,450 | 12,580 | 9,435 | 6,290 | 3,145 |
| Bonus payable to Albert Smith .. .. | | —200 | | | |
| Transfer to George Jones .. .. .. | | | —300 | +300 | |
| | | 12,380 | 9,135 | 7240 | 3,145 |
| Excess of Davis's share over previous share | £ | | | | |
| Profit for year .. .. .. .. | 33,600 | | | | |
| *Less* Staff bonus .. .. .. | 1,500 | | | | |
| | 32,100 | | | | |
| *Less* Salary .. .. .. .. | 1,200 | | | | |
| | 30,900 | | | | |
| Commission: $\frac{3}{103} \times$ £30,900 .. .. .. | 900 | | | | |
| | £ | | | | |
| Salary .. .. .. .. .. | 1,200 | | | | |
| Commission .. .. .. .. | 900 | | | | |
| Increase .. .. .. .. | 1,000 | | | | |
| | 3,100 | | | | |
| Share of profits .. .. .. .. | 3,145 | | | | |
| Excess .. .. .. .. | £45 | | | | |
| Adjustment: $\frac{5}{9}$ths of excess charged to John Smith and credited to Peter & George Jones in proportion 3 : 2 .. .. .. | | —25 | +15 | +10 | |
| | | £12,355 | £9,150 | £7,250 | £3,145 |

*Note:* In dividing the profits between the four partners in profit sharing ratio, the excess of Davis's share over £3,100, i.e. £45, has been charged to John Smith, Peter and George Jones 4 : 3 : 2; as a result of this 5/9ths of the excess has been borne by Peter and George Jones. To the extent of 4/9ths, the excess has already been provided out of John Smith's share, and in order to comply with the agreement, it is only necessary to make an adjustment debiting his account with the amount borne by Peter and George Jones, namely 5/9ths of the excess. The shares of Peter and George Jones are therefore the same as if Davis's share of profits had been exactly £3,100, viz:

| | £ | John Smith £ | Peter Jones £ | George Jones £ | Charles Davis £ |
|---|---|---|---|---|---|
| Profit for the year .. .. .. .. | 33,600 | | | | |
| Less Staff bonus .. .. .. | 1,500 | | | | |
| | 32,100 | | | | |
| Less George Jones's salary .. .. | 650 | | | 650 | |
| | 31,450 | | | | |
| Less Davis's salary .. .. .. | 3,100 | | | | 3,100 |
| Divisible 4 : 3 : 2 .. .. .. .. | £28,350 | 12,600 | 9,450 | 6,300 | |
| Bonus payable to Albert Smith .. .. | | —200 | | | |
| Transfer to George Jones .. .. .. | | | —300 | +300 | |
| | | 12,400 | 9,150 | 7,250 | 3,100 |
| Excess of Davis's share borne by Smith .. | | —45 | | | +45 |
| | | £12,355 | £9,150 | £7,250 | £3,145 |

## § 6. Outgoing Partners

In the absence of any agreement or uniform usage to the contrary, a partner, on retirement, or the representative of a deceased partner, is entitled to have the partnership assets, including goodwill, revalued on a proper basis as at the date of the retirement or death, and any appreciation or depreciation so revealed taken into account in computing the sum due to him or them. The total amount so ascertained to be due is normally a debt due by the firm to the retired partner or the representatives of the deceased partner.

An agreement may, however, be made between the partners whereby, in the event of the death or retirement of a partner, the remaining partners shall assume, personally, the liability for the amount due. In such circumstances the debt is no longer due by the firm but by the partners individually in the ratio agreed upon.

In the case of *Elliott* v. *Elliott* (1911), 45 Acct. L.R. 47, the partnership agreement provided that at the death of a partner his share in the assets and goodwill of the business should, as from the time of his death, belong to and be purchased by the remaining partners in proportion to their shares in the business, and that they should execute a joint and several bond for securing the repayment of the amount due, payment being made in eight half-yearly instalments. On the death of one partner his capital was treated as a liability of the firm. On the death of a second partner the latter's executors brought an action to determine *inter alia* whether the debt due to the estate of the first mentioned partner should be treated as a debt of the partnership.

It was held that the amount in question was not a liability of the firm but was to be apportioned between and borne by the remaining partners in the ratio in which they shared profits and losses. In the course of his judgement, Mr Justice Warrington stated that he thought it was a debt due by each partner to the deceased partner's executors as the purchase money for a personal benefit acquired by such partner. The balance remaining due to the deceased partner's executors must, therefore, be transferred to the credit of the capital accounts of the remaining partners. In effect they had paid into the firm as capital their respective shares of the net assets attributable to the deceased partner, and had become personally liable to the estate of the deceased partner for such amounts.

**Illustration**

A, B and C were in partnership, sharing profits in the ratio of 3 : 2 : 1. On December 31st A retired, and it was agreed that an annuity of £900 per annum should be paid to him by the continuing partners, through the firm, and he accepted this undertaking by B and C in full settlement of the balance due to him. The Balance Sheet of the firm before revaluation of assets on December 31st was as follows:

### BALANCE SHEET

| CAPITAL ACCOUNTS | | | | £ | £ | | £ |
|---|---|---|---|---|---|---|---|
| A .. | .. | .. | .. | 9,000 | | Net Assets (excluding goodwill) .. .. | 18,000 |
| B .. | .. | .. | .. | 5,000 | | | |
| C .. | .. | .. | .. | 4,000 | | | |
| | | | | | 18,000 | | |
| | | | | | £18,000 | | £18,000 |

To ascertain the amount due to A, goodwill was valued at £6,000 and the net assets were valued at £3,000 in excess of the amounts at which they stood in the books. No goodwill account was raised, and there was to be no alteration in the book amounts of the net assets.

The Capital Accounts, and the Balance Sheet after A's retirement, would be as under:

### CAPITAL ACCOUNTS

| | A £ | B £ | C £ | | A £ | B £ | C £ |
|---|---|---|---|---|---|---|---|
| Surplus on revaluation of assets *per contra* written off in new profit sharing ratio .. | | 6,000 | 3,000 | Balances, b/f. .. .. | 9,000 | 5,000 | 4,000 |
| B and C – balance of A's capital transferred .. .. | 13,500 | | | Revaluation of Assets:<br>Goodwill .. £6,000<br>Net Assets .. 3,000 | | | |
| Balances c/f. .. .. | | 11,000 | 7,000 | —— 9,000 | 4,500 | 3,000 | 1,500 |
| | | | | A – transfer to B and C *per contra* .. .. | | 9,000 | 4,500 |
| | £13,500 | £17,000 | £10,000 | | £13,500 | £17,000 | £10,000 |

When the annuity is paid, £600 will be charged to B and £300 to C.

### BALANCE SHEET
(after A's retirement)

| CAPITAL ACCOUNTS | | | | £ | £ | | £ |
|---|---|---|---|---|---|---|---|
| B .. | .. | .. | .. | 11,000 | | Net Assets (excluding goodwill) .. .. | 18,000 |
| C .. | .. | .. | .. | 7,000 | | | |
| | | | | | 18,000 | | |
| | | | | | £18,000 | | £18,000 |

It must, however, be appreciated that unless an agreement of this description is entered into, the amount due to the retired partner or to the estate of a deceased partner is, as stated above, a debt due by the firm, and must be shown as such on its balance sheet.

The retired partner, or the estate of the deceased partner, remains liable for the firm's debts at the date of retirement or death, although, as between the partners themselves, he is only responsible for his share of the liabilities. When the amount due to him has been ascertained and either repaid or assumed by the remaining partners, he should in equity be discharged from further liability, and for this reason care should be taken to obtain an undertaking from the remaining partners to indemnify him, or his estate, against any action which may be brought against him by any creditor in respect of any debt incurred prior to his retirement or death. When a new partner is introduced the creditors may, by a contract of substituted liability (novation), agree to look to the new partner in place of the old, in which case the latter will be released from liability to the creditors concerned.

A retired partner may be held liable for debts contracted after his retirement by reason of the persons subsequently dealing with the firm giving credit on the strength of his supposed continued association with the firm. In order to avoid such liability resulting from being 'held out' as a partner, he must give specific notice of his retirement to all existing creditors, and to all those who have been creditors of the firm and may be such again. He should also give notice of his retirement in the appropriate *Gazette*, and this will operate as notice to the world at large, and will preclude the operation of the doctrine of 'holding out' in favour of any person who might be induced to give credit to the firm on the strength of the supposed partner's financial standing.

The estate of a deceased or bankrupt partner cannot be held liable for debts contracted by the firm after the death, or bankruptcy, as the case may be.

It may not be practicable for the firm to discharge the debt due to a retired partner, or to the deceased partner's estate, out of its existing resources, nor may it be possible for the other partners immediately to bring in additional capital. In such circumstances one of the following methods of settlement may be adopted:

(*a*) Repayment may be made by agreed instalments over a period of years, interest being allowed on the diminishing balance of the amount due.

(*b*) The amount due may be regarded as a loan to the firm to carry the right to either a fixed rate of interest or a share of the profits of the firm.

(*c*) An annuity may be paid to a retired partner for life, or for an agreed number of years, or for the life of some dependant of his.

### (*a*) *Repayment of Outgoing Partner's Capital etc. by Instalments*

Upon the retirement or death of a partner the value of his capital and share of the goodwill etc. is ascertained, either in accordance with the provisions of the partnership agreement or by accounts taken at the date of the dissolution, and the amount so ascertained is paid out to him or his representatives forthwith, or credited to a Loan Account, and repaid by instalments, with interest running on the outstanding balance. It is important, where payment is not made at once, that the amount due should be credited to a loan account, and not retained in the books as capital, especially in the case of a retired partner, when retention of the amount due to him as capital might imply that he was still a partner.

**Illustration**

M, a partner in a firm, dies on March 31st, 19.., and his share of capital and goodwill is ascertained to be £7,600. It is arranged that this shall be paid out by annual instalments of £2,000, to include principal and interest on the outstanding balance at 5 per cent. per annum. The first payment is made one month after death, and succeeding payments are made on the anniversary of the date of death. Show the account in the firm's books relating thereto until completion. Ignore income tax, and make calculations to nearest £.

### THE EXECUTORS OF M (DECEASED) ACCOUNT

| | | | | | £ | | | | | | £ |
|---|---|---|---|---|---|---|---|---|---|---|---|
| 19.. April 30 | Cash .. | .. | .. | .. | 2,000 | 19.. Mar. 31 | Capital Account | .. | .. | | 7,600 |
| | Balance c/f. | .. | .. | .. | 5,632 | April 30 | Interest, 1 month | .. | .. | | 32 |
| | | | | | £7,632 | | | | | | £7,632 |
| 19.. Mar. 31 | Cash .. | .. | .. | .. | 2,000 | 19.. May 1 | Balance b/f. | .. | .. | .. | 5,632 |
| | Balance c/f. | .. | .. | .. | 3,890 | 19.. Mar. 31 | Interest, 11 months | .. | .... | | 258 |
| | | | | | £5,890 | | | | | | £5,890 |
| 19.. Mar. 31 | Cash .. | .. | .. | .. | 2,000 | 19.. April 1 | Balance b/f. | .. | .. | .. | 3,890 |
| | Balance c/f. | .. | .. | .. | 2,085 | 19.. Mar. 31 | Interest, 1 year .. | .. | .. | | 195 |
| | | | | | £4,085 | | | | | | £4,085 |
| 19.. Mar. 31 | Cash .. | .. | .. | .. | 2,000 | 19.. April 1 | Balance b/f. | .. | .. | .. | 2,085 |
| | Balance c/f. | .. | .. | .. | 189 | 19.. Mar. 31 | Interest, 1 year .. | .. | .. | | 104 |
| | | | | | £2,189 | | | | | | £2,189 |
| 19.. Mar. 31 | Cash .. | .. | .. | .. | 198 | 19.. April 1 | Balance b/f. | .. | .. | .. | 189 |
| | | | | | | 19.. Mar. 31 | Interest, 1 year | .. | .. | | 9 |
| | | | | | £198 | | | | | | £198 |

### (b) Outgoing Partner's Capital etc. allowed to remain as a Loan to the firm

Where this course is adopted, the retired partner's capital must be transferred to a Loan Account. Usually the rate of interest payable on this loan and the conditions of repayment are laid down in the partnership agreement or by a contract entered into at the date of retirement, but in the absence of agreement it is provided by Section 42 of the *Partnership Act 1890* that the retired partner is entitled to interest at 5 per cent. per annum, or such share of the profits as the court may determine to be attributable to the use of his share of the partnership assets. If a retired partner enforces his right to a share of profit in these circumstances, the court would deduct a reasonable sum for the services of the remaining partners for carrying on the business, before arriving at the profit to be divided.

Where an option is given to the continuing partners to purchase the share of the retired partner, and the option is exercised, the retired partner is not entitled to any further share of the profits. His capital is, therefore, transferred to the capital accounts of the continuing partners, who must pay him according to the terms of the agreement.

When it is agreed that the loan shall carry a rate of interest varying with the profits of the firm, or entitle the retired partner to a share of such profits, such an agreement will not of itself cause the retired partner to continue to be liable as a partner of the firm, *provided that the contract is in writing* and signed by or on behalf of all the parties thereto (s. 2). If, however, the firm should become bankrupt, the retired partner will be a deferred creditor in respect of any loan made in such circumstances (s. 3).

### (c) *Repayment of Outgoing Partner's Capital etc. by way of an Annuity*

Where a partner retires or dies, the liability of the continuing partners for his capital and share of goodwill, is sometimes discharged by an agreement to pay to him or to his widow, dependants or representatives an annuity, either for a certain term of years or for the lifetime of the retired partner, or his widow, or some named dependants.

In such a case the most convenient method of dealing with the matter in the partnership books is to transfer the amount due to an Annuity Suspense Account, which must be credited with interest at a fixed rate per annum on the diminishing balance (Profit and Loss Account being debited), and debited annually with the annuity paid. If the credit balance on the Annuity Suspense Account is exhausted during the lifetime of the annuitant, subsequent instalments of the annuity must be borne by the partners and debited to their Current Accounts (or to Profit and Loss Account before arriving at divisible profits). In the event of the annuitant dying before the credit on the Annuity Suspense Account is exhausted the balance then remaining on the account is a profit to the continuing partners and should be transferred to their Capital Accounts in the proportion in which they share profits. Such a profit will not, normally, be represented by liquid resources available for distribution and, therefore, it might be inadvisable to transfer it to Profit and Loss Account or to the partners' Current Accounts.

The balance of the Annuity Suspense Account at the commencement of the transaction and at the date of each balance sheet should, strictly, represent the present worth of the annuity, subject to variation in the expectation of life. An actuarial valuation for the adjustment of the Suspense Account might be made periodically, say every five years, but as with a single annuity there is no scope for the law of average to apply, it is not usual to do this, the simpler procedure outlined above being adopted.

**Illustration**

A, B and C are partners sharing profits in the ratio of 3, 2 and 1. A retires from the firm as from December 31st, 19. ., the determined amount of his share being £10,000. It is agreed that this should be commuted by an annuity of £1,500, the first payment to be made on the following day, and subsequent payments on January 1st of each year. A dies after the receipt of the fifth annuity payment.

Show the Annuity Suspense Account in the books of the firm, assuming that the amount outstanding is deemed to earn interest at the rate of 6 per cent. Ignore income tax, and make calculations to nearest £.

## ANNUITY SUSPENSE ACCOUNT

| 19.. | | | | | £ | 19.. | | | £ |
|---|---|---|---|---|---|---|---|---|---|
| Jan. 1 | Cash | .. | .. | .. | 1,500 | Jan. 1 | Balance b/f. .. .. .. | | 10,000 |
| | | | | | | Dec. 31 | Profit and Loss Account— | | |
| Dec. 31 | Balance c/f. | .. | .. | .. | 9,010 | | Interest (on £8,500) .. .. | | 510 |
| | | | | | £10,510 | | | | £10,510 |
| 19.. | | | | | | 19.. | | | |
| Jan. 1 | Cash | .. | .. | .. | 1,500 | Jan. 1 | Balance b/f. .. .. .. | | 9,010 |
| | | | | | | Dec. 31 | Profit and Loss Account— | | |
| Dec. 31 | Balance c/f. | .. | .. | .. | 7,961 | | Interest (on £7,510) .. .. | | 451 |
| | | | | | £9,461 | | | | £9,461 |
| 19.. | | | | | | 19.. | | | |
| Jan. 1 | Cash | .. | .. | .. | 1,500 | Jan. 1 | Balance b/f. .. .. .. | | 7,961 |
| | | | | | | Dec. 31 | Profit and Loss Account— | | |
| Dec. 31 | Balance c/f. | .. | .. | .. | 6,849 | | Interest (on £6,461) .. .. | | 388 |
| | | | | | £8,349 | | | | £8,349 |
| 19.. | | | | | | 19.. | | | |
| Jan. 1 | Cash | .. | .. | .. | 1,500 | Jan. 1 | Balance b/f. .. .. .. | | 6,849 |
| | | | | | | Dec. 31 | Profit and Loss Account— | | |
| Dec. 31 | Balance c/f. | .. | .. | .. | 5,670 | | Interest (on £5,349) .. .. | | 321 |
| | | | | | £7,170 | | | | £7,170 |
| 19.. | | | | | | 19.. | | | |
| Jan. 1 | Cash .. .. | .. | .. | | 1,500 | Jan. 1 | Balance b/f. .. .. .. | | 5,670 |
| | Profit transferred to: | | | | | | | | |
| Dec. 31 | B ⅔rds .. | .. | £2,780 | | | | | | |
| | C ⅓rd .. | .. | 1,390 | | | | | | |
| | | | | | 4,170 | | | | |
| | | | | | £5,670 | | | | £5,670 |

It cannot be assumed that the business would be able to pay the amount of
the annuity in all cases out of its liquid resources, as this might result in considerable embarrassment in the course of a few years. The remaining partners
should therefore, if necessary, introduce annually additional capital to the
extent of the amount of the annuity less the amount of interest credited to the
Annuity Suspense Account. As this interest has been charged to Profit and Loss
Account before arriving at the amount of the divisible profits, cash to the extent
thereof has been retained in the business and it is therefore only necessary for
B and C to introduce the balance.

Alternatively, B and C could restrict their drawings each year by the amount
required. For example, at the end of the first year the following entry could be
made:

## JOURNAL

| | | | £ | £ |
|---|---|---|---|---|
| Current Accounts: .. .. .. .. .. .. .. .. .. | | Dr | | |
| B .. .. .. .. .. .. .. .. .. .. | | | 660 | |
| C .. .. .. .. .. .. .. .. .. .. | | | 330 | |
| To Capital Accounts: | | | | |
| B .. .. .. .. .. .. .. .. .. .. | | | | 660 |
| C .. .. .. .. .. .. .. .. .. .. | | | | 330 |
| Transfer from Current Accounts to Capital Accounts of amount necessary to restore the firm's working | | | | |
| capital after the payment of annuity of £1,500 to A. | | | | |
| B ⅔rds of £(1,500—510)=£660. | | | | |
| C ⅓rd of £(1,500—510)=£330. | | | | |

The position is somewhat complicated by the introduction of a new partner.
As the business has the benefit of the capital represented by the Annuity Suspense Account, the new partner should bear his share of the interest, which

should therefore continue to be debited to Profit and Loss Account. Should the annuitant die before the balance on the Annuity Suspense Account is exhausted, the credit balance should be divided between the remaining old partners in the proportions in which they shared profits and losses in the old partnership. If, however, the Annuity Suspense Account is exhausted before the annuitant dies, the subsequent payments should be debited to the Current Accounts of the remaining members of the old partnership in the proportions in which they shared profits and losses in the old firm.

## (d) Adjustment of values of assets upon change of personnel

When a partner retires it does not follow that the balance of his Capital Account represents his true interest in the partnership, apart from the question of goodwill, to which reference has already been made, since some assets may have appreciated in value without any adjustment having been made in the books, whilst others may have been insufficiently depreciated, over-depreciated, or entirely written off. It will be necessary, therefore, to correct these values, in order that the outgoing partner shall receive his true share. A Revaluation Account should be opened, to which all differences in values should be debited or credited, as the case may be, the resultant balance being divided among the partners according to the ratio in which they share profits and losses.

### Illustration

Brown, Jones and Robinson, sharing profits and losses equally, had been trading for many years, and Robinson decided to retire as at December 31st, 19.. on which date the Balance Sheet of the firm was as under:

| | | | | £ | £ | | | | | £ |
|---|---|---|---|---|---|---|---|---|---|---|
| Capitals: | | | | | | Freehold Premises | .. | .. | .. | 8,000 |
| Brown .. | .. | .. | .. | 10,000 | | Plant | .. | .. | .. | 4,000 |
| Jones .. | .. | .. | .. | 8,000 | . | Patents | .. | .. | .. | 6,000 |
| Robinson | .. | .. | .. | 6,000 | | Stock .. | .. | .. | .. | 5,000 |
| | | | | | 24,000 | Debtors | .. | .. | .. | 6,000 |
| Creditors | .. | .. | .. | | 8,000 | Cash .. | .. | .. | .. | 3,000 |
| | | | | | £32,000 | | | | | £32,000 |

The value of the goodwill was agreed at £8,000.

The freehold premises had increased in value as a result of general economic conditions, the value being agreed at £11,000. Plant and patents were respectively revalued at £3,600 and £5,300, and it was also agreed to provide 5 per cent. in respect of debtors, it having been the practice in the past only to write off bad debts actually incurred.

Show the adjusted Balance Sheet of the firm, and the amount to which Robinson would be entitled.

### REVALUATION ACCOUNT

| | | | | £ | £ | | | | | £ |
|---|---|---|---|---|---|---|---|---|---|---|
| Plant .. | .. | .. | .. | | 400 | Goodwill | .. | .. | .. | 8,000 |
| Patents .. | .. | .. | .. | | 700 | Freehold Premises | .. | .. | .. | 3,000 |
| Provision for Bad Debts | .. | .. | | 300 | | | | | |
| Balance transferred to Capital Accounts: | | | | | | | | | | |
| Brown .. | .. | .. | .. | 3,200 | | | | | | |
| Jones .. | .. | .. | .. | 3,200 | | | | | | |
| Robinson | .. | .. | .. | 3,200 | | | | | | |
| | | | | | 9,600 | | | | | |
| | | | | | £11,000 | | | | | £11,000 |

### BALANCE SHEET (AFTER ADJUSTMENT)

| | £ | £ | | | £ | £ |
|---|---|---|---|---|---|---|
| Capitals: | | | Goodwill .. .. .. | | | 8,000 |
| Brown .. .. .. .. | 13,200 | | Freehold Premises .. .. | | | 11,000 |
| Jones .. .. .. .. | 11,200 | | Plant .. .. .. .. | | | 3,600 |
| Robinson .. .. .. | 9,200 | | Patents .. .. .. | | | 5,300 |
| | | 33,600 | Stock .. .. .. | | | 5,000 |
| Creditors .. .. .. | | 8,000 | Debtors .. .. | | 6,000 | |
| | | | *Less* Provision for Bad Debts .. | | 300 | |
| | | | | | | 5,700 |
| | | | Cash .. .. .. .. | | | 3,000 |
| | | £41,600 | | | | £41,600 |

Although the above adjustments have been made in order to ascertain the amount due to Robinson, the remaining partners may not desire to disturb the existing book values, in which case the difference on revaluation (£9,600) would be written back to the Capital Accounts of Brown and Jones, in the proportions in which they will share profits and losses in future, the position then being:

| | £ | £ | | | £ |
|---|---|---|---|---|---|
| Capital Accounts: | | | Freehold Premises .. .. .. | | 8,000 |
| Brown £(13,200—4,800) .. .. | 8,400 | | Plant .. .. .. .. .. | | 4,000 |
| Jones £(11,200—4,800) .. .. | 6,400 | | Patents .. .. .. .. .. | | 6,000 |
| | | 14,800 | Stock .. .. .. .. .. | | 5,000 |
| Robinson, Loan Account .. .. | | 9,200 | Debtors .. .. .. .. .. | | 6,000 |
| Creditors .. .. .. | | 8,000 | Cash .. .. .. .. .. | | 3,000 |
| | | £32,000 | | | £32,000 |

Alternatively, the same position could have been achieved by the preparation of a *memorandum* Revaluation Account for the purpose of ascertaining the amount of the net increase in the values of the assets attributable to Robinson, the following entry then being made in the books:

### JOURNAL

| | | £ | £ |
|---|---|---|---|
| Capital Accounts: | *Dr* | | |
| Brown .. .. .. .. .. .. .. .. .. .. .. | | 1,600 | |
| Jones .. .. .. .. .. .. .. .. .. .. .. | | 1,600 | |
| To Capital Account: | | | |
| Robinson .. .. .. .. .. .. .. .. .. | | | 3,200 |
| Proportion of net increase in value of assets due to Robinson on retirement, acquired by Brown and Jones. | | | |

In effect Brown and Jones have purchased from Robinson his share of the undisclosed profit represented by the net increase in the value of the assets and are debited with the cost thereof.

Should a new partner (Smith) be introduced concurrently with Robinson's retirement, he should come in on the basis of the Balance Sheet as adjusted after the revaluation of the assets, or else pay a premium commensurate with his share of goodwill and other net differences. Assuming that no premium is paid, that he introduces £4,000 as capital and that future profits are to be shared in the ratio of: Brown two-fifths, Jones two-fifths, and Smith one-fifth, the initial Balance Sheet will be:

### BROWN, JONES AND SMITH
### BALANCE SHEET

| | £ | £ | | | £ | £ |
|---|---|---|---|---|---|---|
| Capitals: | | | Goodwill .. .. .. | | | 8,000 |
| Brown .. .. .. .. | 13,200 | | Freehold Premises .. .. | | | 11,000 |
| Jones .. .. .. .. | 11,200 | | Plant .. .. .. .. | | | 3,600 |
| Smith .. .. .. .. | 4,000 | | Patents .. .. .. | | | 5,300 |
| | | 28,400 | Stock .. .. .. | | | 5,000 |
| Robinson, Loan Account .. .. | | 9,200 | Debtors .. .. .. | | 6,000 | |
| Creditors .. .. .. | | 8,000 | *Less* Provision for Bad Debts .. | | 300 | |
| | | | | | | 5,700 |
| | | | Cash .. .. .. .. | | | 7,000 |
| | | £45,600 | | | | £45,600 |

If the partners now agree that the original book values shall be maintained, the difference (£9,600) must be written off to the Partners' Capital Accounts, in the ratio of 2 : 2 : 1, the new partner being required to participate in the adjustment, since he will be entitled to participate in the proceeds of subsequent realization when such occurs.

The following will be the final Balance Sheet in such circumstances:

BROWN, JONES AND SMITH
BALANCE SHEET

| Capitals: | | £ | £ | | | | | £ |
|---|---|---:|---:|---|---|---|---|---:|
| Brown  £(13,200—3,840) .. | .. | 9,360 | | Freehold Premises | .. | .. | .. | 8,000 |
| Jones   £(11,200—3,840) .. | .. | 7,360 | | Plant .. | .. | .. | .. | 4,000 |
| Smith    £(4,000—1,920) .. | .. | 2,080 | | Patents | .. | .. | .. | 6,000 |
| | | | 18,800 | Stock .. | .. | .. | .. | 5,000 |
| Robinson, Loan Account | .. | .. | 9,200 | Debtors | .. | .. | .. | 6,000 |
| Creditors | .. | .. | 8,000 | Cash  .. | .. | .. | .. | 7,000 |
| | | | £36,000 | | | | | £36,000 |

In any case, arrangements must be made to pay to Robinson the amount due to him, which remains undisturbed by any subsequent adjustments which may be made in the accounts.

### (e) Apportionment of Profit or Loss upon change in personnel

In order to apportion the profits or losses between the partners upon a change of personnel, or where the existing partners vary as between themselves the profit sharing ratio, then unless the change takes place at the financial year end of the business, it will be necessary for stock to be taken and work in progress valued, or alternatively for the profits for the year to be apportioned. If the profits are to be apportioned, they will be apportioned either on a time basis, or in proportion to the turnover of the periods prior to and after the change or by a combination of these methods.

The principles of apportionment are dealt with fully in Chapter VIII, §11 (b), in relation to profits or losses prior to incorporation to which reference should be made.

### Illustration

Green and Blue were partners in a retail business sharing profits and losses: Green two-thirds, Blue one-third. Interest on fixed capitals was allowed at the rate of 6 per cent. per annum but no interest was charged or allowed on current accounts. Accounts were made up to March 31st in each year.

The following was the partnership trial balance as on March 31st, 1970:

| | £ | | | £ | £ |
|---|---:|---|---|---:|---:|
| Leasehold premises purchased April 1st, 1969  .. | 6,000 | Fixed Capital Accounts: | | | |
| Purchases    ..        ..        ..        .. | 16,400 | Green    ..        ..        .. | 3,000 | |
| Motor vehicles, at cost    ..        ..        .. | 3,400 | Blue    ..        ..        .. | 2,000 | |
| Balance at bank    ..        ..        .. | 9,280 | | | 5,000 |
| Salaries, including partners' drawings .. | 5,200 | | | |
| Stock, March 31st, 1969    ..        ..        .. | 4,800 | Current Accounts: | | |
| Shop fittings, at cost    ..        ..        .. | 1,200 | Green    ..        ..        .. | 1,600 | |
| Debtors  ..        ..        ..        ..        .. | 900 | Blue    ..        ..        .. | 1,200 | |
| Professional charges    ..        ..        .. | 420 | | | 2,800 |
| Shop  wages    ..        ..        ..        .. | 2,200 | Cash introduced – Black  ..        .. | | 5,000 |
| Rent, rates, lighting and heating    ..        .. | 1,240 | Sales (£14,000 to September 30th, | | |
| General expenses (£1,410 for six months to Sept-ember 30th, 1969)    ..        ..        .. | 2,640 | 1969)    ..        ..        ..        .. | | 35,000 |
| | | Provisions for depreciation on April 1st, 1969: | | |
| | | Motor vehicles    ..        .. | 1,200 | |
| | | Shop fittings ..        ..        .. | 400 | |
| | | | | 1,600 |
| | | Creditors    ..        ..        .. | | 4,280 |
| | £53,680 | | | £53,680 |

You are given the following additional information:

1. On September 30th, 1969, Black was admitted as a partner and from that date, profits and losses were shared: Green two-fifths, Blue two-fifths and Black one-fifth. For the purpose of these changes the value of the goodwill of the firm was agreed at £12,000. No account for goodwill was to be maintained in the books, adjusting entries for transactions between the parties being made in their current accounts. On October 1st, 1969, Black had introduced £5,000 into the firm of which it was agreed £1,500 should comprise his fixed capital and the balance should be credited to his current account.

Any apportionment of gross profit was to be made on the basis of sales; expenses, unless otherwise indicated, were to be apportioned on a time basis.

2. On March 31st, 1970, the stock was valued at £5,100.

3. Provision was to be made for depreciation on the motor vehicles and shop fittings at 20 per cent. and 5 per cent. per annum respectively, calculated on cost.

4. Salaries included the following partners' drawings: Green £600, Blue £480 and Black £250.

5. At March 31st, 1970, rates paid in advance amounted to £260 and a provision of £60 for electricity consumed was required.

6. A difference on the books of £120 had been written off at March 31st, 1970, to general expenses, which was later found to be due to the following errors:

(a) Sales returns of £80 had been debited to Sales but had not been posted to the account of the customer concerned.

(b) The purchase journal had been undercast by £200.

7. Professional charges included £210 paid in respect of the acquisition of the leasehold premises. These fees are to be capitalized as part of the cost of the lease, the total cost of which was to be written off in 25 equal annual instalments. Other premises, owned by Blue were leased by him to the partnership at £600 per annum, but no rent had been paid or credited to him for the year to March 31st, 1970.

8. Doubtful debts (for which full provision was required) as on September 30th, 1969, amounted to £120 and as on March 31st, 1970, to £160.

You are required to prepare:

(a) the Trading and Profit and Loss Accounts for the year ended March 31st, 1970;

(b) the Balance Sheet as on that date; and

(c) partners' current accounts, in columnar form.

### MESSRS GREEN, BLUE AND BLACK
### TRADING, PROFIT AND LOSS ACCOUNTS

(a)                    for the year ended March 31st, 1970

| | £ | | £ | £ |
|---|---|---|---|---|
| Stock, April 1st, 1969 | 4,800 | Sales: | | |
| Purchases £(16,400+200) | 16,600 | April 1st to September 30th, 1969 | 14,000 | |
| | | October 1st, 1969 to March 31st, 1970 | 21,000 | |
| | 21,400 | | | 35,000 |
| Less Stock, March 31st, 1970 | 5,100 | | | |
| | 16,300 | | | |
| Gross profit, carried down | 18,700 | | | |
| | £35,000 | | | £35,000 |

| | April 1st–September 30th, 1969 £ | October 1st, 1969–March 31st, 1970 £ | | April 1st–September 30th, 1969 £ | October 1st, 1969–March 31st 1970 £ |
|---|---|---|---|---|---|
| Salaries £(5,200—1,330) .. | 1,935 | 1,935 | Gross profit, brought down (ratio 14 : 21) .. .. .. .. | 7,480 | 11,220 |
| Rent, rates, lighting and heating £(1,240+600+60—260) .. | 820 | 820 | | | |
| Shop wages .. .. .. | 1,100 | 1,100 | | | |
| Professional charges £(420—210) .. | 105 | 105 | | | |
| General expenses £(2,640—120) .. | 1,410 | 1,110 | | | |
| Depreciation: | | | | | |
|   Motor vehicles .. £680 | | | | | |
|   Shop fittings.. .. 60 | | | | | |
|              £740 | 370 | 370 | | | |
| Amortization of lease– | | | | | |
|   1/25th of £(6,000+210) .. | 124 | 124 | | | |
| Provision for doubtful debts .. | 120 | 40 | | | |
| Net profit carried down .. .. | 1,496 | 5,616 | | | |
| | £7,480 | £11,220 | | £7,480 | £11,220 |
| Interest on capital .. .. | 150 | 195 | Net profit, brought down .. | 1,496 | 5,616 |
| Balance divisible: | | | | | |
|   Green .. .. 2/3rds | 897 | 2/5ths 2,168 | | | |
|   Blue .. .. 1/3rd | 449 | 2/5ths 2,168 | | | |
|   Black .. .. | | 1/5th 1,085 | | | |
| | £1,496 | £5,616 | | £1,496 | £5,616 |

(b)

# BALANCE SHEET
## as at March 31st, 1970

| | | £ | £ | | Cost £ | Depreciation £ | Balance £ |
|---|---|---|---|---|---|---|---|
| **FIXED CAPITAL ACCOUNTS** | | | | **FIXED ASSETS** | | | |
| Green .. .. .. .. | | 3,000 | | Leasehold premises .. | 6,210 | 248 | 5,962 |
| Blue .. .. .. .. | | 2,000 | | Motor vehicles .. | 3,400 | 1,880 | 1,520 |
| Black .. .. .. .. | | 1,500 | | Shop fittings.. .. | 1,200 | 460 | 740 |
| | | | 6,500 | | £10,810 | £2,588 | 8,222 |
| **CURRENT ACCOUNTS** | | | | **CURRENT ASSETS** | | | |
| Green .. .. .. .. | | 7,445 | | Stock .. .. | | 5,100 | |
| Blue .. .. .. .. | | 3,257 | | Debtors £(900—80) .. | 820 | | |
| Black .. .. .. .. | | 1,980 | |   *Less* Provision for | | | |
| | | | 12,682 |     doubtful debts .. | 160 | 660 | |
| | | | 19,182 | Prepaid expenses .. | | 260 | |
| CREDITORS £(4,280+60) .. .. | | | 4,340 | Balance at bank .. | | 9,280 | 15,300 |
| | | | £23,522 | | | | £23,522 |

(c)

# PARTNERS' CURRENT ACCOUNTS

| | Green £ | Blue £ | Black £ | | Green £ | Blue £ | Black £ |
|---|---|---|---|---|---|---|---|
| Goodwill adjustment (*contra*) | | 800 | 2,400 | Balances brought forward | 1,600 | 1,200 | |
| Drawings .. .. | 600 | 480 | 250 | Cash introduced .. | | | 3,500 |
| Balances carried forward .. | 7,445 | 3,257 | 1,980 | Goodwill adjustment | | | |
| | | | |   (*contra*) .. .. | 3,200 | | |
| | | | | Rent .. .. | | 600 | |
| | | | | Interest on capital .. | 180 | 120 | 45 |
| | | | | Share of profit .. .. | 897 | 449 | |
| | | | |   ditto .. .. | 2,168 | 2,168 | 1,085 |
| | £8,045 | £4,537 | £4,630 | | £8,045 | £4,537 | £4,630 |

WORKINGS

| | | | | | | | | Green | Blue | Black | Total |
|---|---|---|---|---|---|---|---|---|---|---|---|
| 1. Interest on capital: | | | | | | | | £ | £ | £ | £ |
| Half-year to September 30th, 1969 | | | .. | | .. | | | 90 | 60 | | 150 |
| ,, ,, March 31st, 1970 | | | .. | | .. | | | 90 | 60 | 45 | 195 |
| | | | | | | | | £180 | £120 | £45 | £345 |

2. Goodwill adjustment:

| | | | | | | | | Profit-sharing rates | | |
|---|---|---|---|---|---|---|---|---|---|---|
| | | | | | | | | Old | New | Difference |
| Green .. | .. | .. | .. | .. | .. | .. | .. | 2/3rds | 2/5ths | 4/15ths less |
| Blue .. | .. | .. | .. | .. | .. | .. | .. | 1/3rd | 2/5ths | 1/15th more |
| Black .. | .. | .. | .. | .. | .. | .. | .. | — | 1/5th | 1/5th (3/15ths) more |

Therefore Green must be credited with 4/15ths × £12,000 = £3,200
while Blue must be debited with 1/15th × £12,000 = £800
and Black must be debited with 3/15ths × £12,000 = £2,400

## § 7. Sleeping, Quasi and Limited Partners

The term *sleeping partner* is applied to a partner who takes no active part in the business or who has retired from active participation in the business, but retains his capital therein and probably a reduced share of the profits. In such a case no change need be made in the books. Such a partner is sometimes called a *dormant* partner. The *Partnership Act* does not distinguish between a sleeping partner and an acting partner; the liability of a partner for the firm's debts is the same whether he is dormant or active.

It is common for a partner to retire and at the same time to take advantage of sub-section (3) (*d*) of Section 2 of the *Partnership Act 1890*, by leaving his capital in the business in the form of a loan, receiving interest thereon at a rate varying with the profits. In such a case the balance standing to the credit of his Capital Account should be transferred to a Loan Account, and the interest, based on a proportion of the profits, should be regarded as an expense of the business and debited to Profit and Loss Account. Such an individual, although sometimes termed a *quasi-partner*, is merely a deferred creditor of the firm, his loan not being repayable until after all the other creditors of the firm are paid in full.

The term *quasi-partner* is normally applied to a person who, although not a partner, becomes liable as such by 'holding out'. Third parties may become liable for the debts and liabilities of a firm under the operation of this doctrine which is contained in Section 14 of the *Partnership Act*. Under that section, where a person has by words spoken or written, or by his conduct represented himself or has knowingly suffered himself to be represented as a partner in a particular firm, and some other person has given credit to the firm on the strength of the supposed association, the person so holding himself out will be liable to the party who has so given credit as if he were actually a partner.

A *limited partnership* is defined by the *Limited Partnerships Act 1907* as one which must consist of one or more persons called *general* partners, who shall be liable for all the debts and obligations of the firm, and one or more persons, to be called *limited* partners, who shall, at the time of entering into such partnership, contribute thereto a sum or sums as capital or property valued at a stated amount, and who shall not be liable for the debts or obligations of the firm beyond the amount so contributed. A body corporate may be either a general or a limited partner.

Every limited partnership must be duly registered (the registrar being the Registrar of Companies), otherwise it will be regarded as an ordinary partnership, in which case the limited partner will not secure the protection which he requires. It is therefore incumbent upon the limited partner, in his own interests, to see that registration is duly effected. Registration involves disclosure of particulars as to the firm's name, the general nature of the business, the principal place of business, the full names of each of the partners, the term of the partnership, a statement that the partnership is limited, and the description of every limited partner and the sum contributed by him, and whether paid in cash or otherwise. Any alteration must similarly be registered. Stamp duty is payable upon the capital of a limited partner at the rate of £0.50 per cent., fractions of £100 being counted as £100 (*Finance Act 1933*). An advertisement must also be inserted in the *Gazette* if a general partner at any time becomes a limited partner, or if a limited partner assigns his share to another person, who will become a limited partner.

Since a limited partner is placed in a privileged position with regard to his liability, it is only reasonable that he should be subject to certain restrictions as to participation in management, and this is provided for in Section 6 of the *Limited Partnerships Act 1907*, as under:

1. A limited partner shall not take part in the management of the partnership business, and shall not have power to bind the firm. A limited partner may, however, by himself or his agent, at any time inspect the books of the firm and examine into the state and prospects of the partnership business, and may advise the partners generally.

If a limited partner takes part in the management of the partnership business, he shall be liable for all debts and obligations of the firm incurred while he so takes part in the management, as though he were a general partner.

2. A limited partnership shall not be dissolved by the death or bankruptcy of a limited partner, and the lunacy of a limited partner shall not be a ground for dissolution of the partnership by the court, unless the lunatic's share cannot be otherwise ascertained and realized.

3. In the event of the dissolution of a limited partnership its affairs shall be wound up by the general partners, unless the court otherwise orders.

4. Subject to any agreement expressed or implied between the partners –

(*a*) any difference arising as to ordinary matters connected with the partnership business may be decided by a majority of the general partners;

(*b*) a limited partner may, with the consent of the general partner, assign his share in the partnership, and upon such an assignment the assignee shall become a limited partner with all the rights of the assignor;

(*c*) the other partners shall not be entitled to dissolve the partnership by reason of any limited partner suffering his share to be charged for his separate debt;

(*d*) a person may be introduced as a partner without the consent of the existing limited partners;

(*e*) a limited partner shall not be entitled to dissolve the partnership by notice.

As regards the books of the limited partnership, the amount of capital contributed by the limited partner should be placed to the credit of his Capital Account, a note being made in the ledger to the effect that he is a limited partner. Any share of profits or interest on capital to which he may be entitled should be placed to the credit of his Current Account, and not to his Capital Account.

It is important to observe that the Act provides that a limited partner shall not, during the continuance of the partnership, either directly or indirectly, draw out or receive back any part of his contribution, and if he does so draw out or receive back any such part he shall be liable for debts and obligations of the firm to the extent of the amount withdrawn.

## § 8. Dissolution of Partnerships

Upon the dissolution of a partnership, Section 44 of the *Partnership Act 1890* provides that the assets of the firm, including the sums (if any) contributed by the partners to make up losses or deficiencies of capital, must be applied in the following manner and order:

1. In paying the debts and liabilities of the firm to persons who are not partners therein.

2. In paying to each partner rateably what is due from the firm to him for advances as distinguished from capital.

3. In paying to each partner the amount due to him in respect of his Capital and Current Account balances.

In the absence of agreement to the contrary the *Partnership Act 1890* provides that the following shall be grounds for the dissolution of a partnership:

(i) The expiration of the term for which the partnership was entered into, if a fixed term was agreed upon.

(ii) The termination of the adventure or undertaking, when a single adventure or undertaking was the purpose of the partnership.

(iii) When one partner gives notice to the others of his intention to dissolve the firm.

(iv) The death of a partner.

(v) The bankruptcy of a partner.

(vi) The happening of an event which causes the partnership to become illegal.

(vii) When a partner allows his share of the partnership to be charged for his separate debt.

In the following cases, dissolution may be obtained on application to the court:

(viii) When a partner is shown to the satisfaction of the court to be of permanently unsound mind.

(ix) When a partner, other than the partner suing, becomes in any other way permanently incapable of performing his part of the partnership contract.

(x) When a partner, other than the partner suing, has been guilty of such conduct, as in the opinion of the court, regard being had to the nature of the business, is calculated prejudicially to affect the carrying on of the business.

(xi) When a partner, other than the partner suing, wilfully or persistently commits a breach of the partnership agreement or otherwise so conducts himself in matters relating to the partnership business that it is not reasonably practicable for the other partner or partners to carry on the business in partnership with him.

(xii) When the business of the partnership can only be carried on at a loss.

(xiii) Whenever in any case circumstances have arisen which, in the opinion of the court, render it just and equitable that the partnership be dissolved.

When the partnership agreement contains an arbitration clause, which is a general submission of all matters in difference between the partners, the arbitrator may dissolve the partnership.

The above rules are applicable to limited partnerships in a modified form as explained in § 7.

### (a) Formula for closing Partnership Books on Dissolution

Apart from special circumstances, the following outline of the steps necessary to close the books of a partnership when the assets are sold *en bloc*, may be found useful:

1. Open a Realization Account, and debit thereto the book value of the assets, crediting the various Asset Accounts. The Realization Account will also be debited with any expenses of realization, and cash credited.

2. Debit cash and credit Realization Account with the amount realized on the sale of the assets.

*Note:* Should any of the assets be taken over at a valuation by any of the partners, debit such partners' Capital Accounts, and credit Realization Account with the agreed price.

3. Pay off the liabilities, crediting cash and debiting sundry creditors. Any discount allowed by creditors on discharging liabilities should be debited to the creditors' accounts and credited to Realization Account.

4. The balance of the Realization Account will be the amount of the profit or loss on realization, which will be divided between the partners in the proportion in which they share profits and losses and transferred to their Capital Accounts.

5. Pay off any partners' advances as distinct from capital, first setting off any *debit* balance on the Capital Account of a partner against his Loan Account.

6. The balance of the cash book will now be exactly equal to the balances on the Capital Accounts, provided they are in credit; credit cash and debit the partners' Capital Accounts with the amounts paid to them to close their accounts.

Should the Capital Account of any partner be in debit after being debited with his share of the loss, or credited with his share of the profit on realization, the cash will be insufficient by the amount of such debit balance to pay the other partners the amounts due to them. If the partner whose account is in debit pays to the firm the amount of his indebtedness, the other partners' Capital Accounts can then be closed by the payment of cash. If, however, he is unable to do so the deficiency must, according to the decision in *Garner* v. *Murray*, be borne by the solvent partners, in proportion to their capitals, and not in the proportion in which they share profits and losses. The application of this rule is illustrated on p. 173.

The following illustrations show the closing of the books on the dissolution of partnerships in varying circumstances:

(1) *Where, on dissolution, there is a profit on the realization of the assets.*

**Illustration**

X and Y are in partnership sharing profits – five-eighths and three-eighths. They agree to dissolve partnership, and their Balance Sheet at the date of dissolution, June 30th, 19.., is as follows:

X AND Y<br>BALANCE SHEET, June 30th, 19..

| | | £ | | | £ |
|---|---|---:|---|---|---:|
| Capital Accounts: | | | Premises .. .. .. .. | | 1,200 |
| X .. .. .. .. £1,500 | | | Stock .. .. .. .. .. | | 1,400 |
| Y .. .. .. .. 1,300 | | | Debtors .. .. .. .. | | 1,100 |
| | | 2,800 | Cash .. .. .. .. .. | | 600 |
| Creditors .. .. .. .. .. | | 1,500 | | | |
| | | £4,300 | | | £4,300 |

The dissolution is completed by December 31st, 19.., the assets, other than cash, being sold *en bloc* and realizing £4,500. Close the books of the firm.

REALIZATION ACCOUNT

| | | £ | | | £ |
|---|---|---:|---|---|---:|
| June 30 | Sundry Assets .. .. .. | 3,700 | Dec. 31 | Cash .. .. .. .. | 4,500 |
| Dec. 31 | Profit transferred to Capital Accounts: | | | | |
| | X five-eighths.. .. £500 | | | | |
| | Y three-eighths .. 300 | | | | |
| | | 800 | | | |
| | | £4,500 | | | £4,500 |

SUNDRY CREDITORS

| | | £ | | | £ |
|---|---|---:|---|---|---:|
| Dec. 31 | Cash .. .. .. .. | 1,500 | June 30 | Balance b/f. .. .. .. | 1,500 |

X CAPITAL ACCOUNT

| | | £ | | | £ |
|---|---|---:|---|---|---:|
| Dec. 31 | Cash .. .. .. .. | 2,000 | June 30 | Balance b/f. .. .. .. | 1,500 |
| | | | Dec. 31 | Realization Account: Profit .. | 500 |
| | | £2,000 | | | £2,000 |

Y CAPITAL ACCOUNT

| | | £ | | | £ |
|---|---|---:|---|---|---:|
| Dec. 31 | Cash .. .. .. .. | 1,600 | June 30 | Balance b/f. .. .. .. | 1,300 |
| | | | Dec. 31 | Realization Account: Profit .. | 300 |
| | | £1,600 | | | £1,600 |

## CASH

| | | £ | | | £ |
|---|---|---|---|---|---|
| June 30 | Balance b/f. .. .. .. | 600 | Dec. 31 | Creditors .. .. .. | 1,500 |
| Dec. 31 | Realization Account .. .. | 4,500 | | Capital Accounts: | |
| | | | | X .. .. .. £2,000 | |
| | | | | Y .. .. .. 1,600 | |
| | | | | | 3,600 |
| | | £5,100 | | | £5,100 |

(2) *Where, on dissolution, the liabilities are paid in full, but there is a loss on the realization of the assets.*

**Illustration**

D, E and F, sharing profits and losses, one-half, one-third, and one-sixth respectively, dissolve partnership. At the date of dissolution their creditors amount to £2,300, and in the course of winding-up a contingent liability of £200, not brought into the accounts, matured and had to be met. The capitals stood at £6,000, £4,000 and £1,500, respectively. D had lent to the firm as distinct from capital £2,000. The assets realized £10,000. Close the books of the firm.

## REALIZATION ACCOUNT

| | £ | | £ |
|---|---|---|---|
| Sundry Assets .. .. .. .. | 15,800 | Cash .. .. .. .. .. | 10,000 |
| Contingent liability matured .. .. | 200 | Loss transferred to Capital Accounts: | |
| | | D one-half .. .. .. £3,000 | |
| | | E one-third .. .. .. 2,000 | |
| | | F one-sixth .. .. .. 1,000 | |
| | | | 6,000 |
| | £16,000 | | £16,000 |

## SUNDRY CREDITORS

| | £ | | £ |
|---|---|---|---|
| Cash .. .. .. .. .. | 2,500 | Balance b/f. .. .. .. .. | 2,300 |
| | | Realization Account: | |
| | | Contingent liability matured .. .. | 200 |
| | £2,500 | | £2,500 |

## D LOAN ACCOUNT

| | £ | | £ |
|---|---|---|---|
| Cash .. .. .. .. .. | 2,000 | Balance b/f. .. .. .. .. | 2,000 |

## D CAPITAL ACCOUNT

| | £ | | £ |
|---|---|---|---|
| Realization Account: Loss .. .. .. | 3,000 | Balance b/f. .. .. .. .. | 6,000 |
| Cash .. .. .. .. .. | 3,000 | | |
| | £6,000 | | £6,000 |

## E CAPITAL ACCOUNT

| | £ | | £ |
|---|---|---|---|
| Realization Account: Loss .. .. .. | 2,000 | Balance b/f. .. .. .. .. | 4,000 |
| Cash .. .. .. .. .. | 2,000 | | |
| | £4,000 | | £4,000 |

## F CAPITAL ACCOUNT

| | £ | | £ |
|---|---|---|---|
| Realization Account: Loss  ..    ..    .. | 1,000 | Balance b/f.   ..    ..    ..    .. | 1,500 |
| Cash   ..    ..    ..    ..    .. | 500 | | |
| | £1,500 | | £1,500 |

## CASH

| | £ | | £ |
|---|---|---|---|
| Realization Account   ..    ..    ..    .. | 10,000 | Creditors   ..    ..    ..    .. | 2,500 |
| | | D Loan Account   ..    ..    .. | 2,000 |
| | | D Capital Account   ..    ..    .. | 3,000 |
| | | E      ,,         ,,     ..    ..    .. | 2,000 |
| | | F      ,,         ,,     ..    ..    .. | 500 |
| | £10,000 | | £10,000 |

*Note:* The book value of the assets is equal to the sum of the capitals plus the creditors, viz.
£6,000+£4,000+£1,500+£2,300+£2,000=£15,800.

(3) *Where, on dissolution, there is a loss on the realization of the assets, placing one partner's Capital Account in debit, which amount he pays into the firm's account in cash.*

**Illustration (1)**

J and P are in partnership, with capitals of £700 and £100. The creditors are £2,300. The assets realize £1,900. Partners share profits and losses equally. Close the books of the firm, P having brought in the amount due by him.

## REALIZATION ACCOUNT

| | £ | | £ |
|---|---|---|---|
| Sundry Assets   ..    ..    ..    .. | 3,100 | Cash  ..    ..    ..    ..    .. | 1,900 |
| | | Loss to Capital Accounts: | |
| | | J one-half   ..    ..    ..    .. | 600 |
| | | P one-half   ..    ..    ..    .. | 600 |
| | £3,100 | | £3,100 |

## J CAPITAL ACCOUNT

| | £ | | £ |
|---|---|---|---|
| Realization Account: Loss  ..    ..    .. | 600 | Balance b/f.   ..    ..    ..    .. | 700 |
| Cash   ..    ..    ..    ..    .. | 100 | | |
| | £700 | | £700 |

## P CAPITAL ACCOUNT

| | £ | | £ |
|---|---|---|---|
| Realization Account: Loss  ..    ..    .. | 600 | Balance b/f.   ..    ..    ..    .. | 100 |
| | | Cash  ..    ..    ..    ..    .. | 500 |
| | £600 | | £600 |

## CREDITORS

| | £ | | £ |
|---|---|---|---|
| Cash   ..    ..    ..    ..    .. | 2,300 | Balance b/f.   ..    ..    ..    .. | 2,300 |

## CASH

| | £ | | | | | £ |
|---|---|---|---|---|---|---|
| Realization Account .. .. .. | 1,900 | Creditors .. .. .. .. | | | | 2,300 |
| P Capital Account .. .. .. .. | 500 | J Capital Account .. .. .. | | | | 100 |
| | £2,400 | | | | | £2,400 |

Where, on dissolution, the assets are not sold *en bloc*, but are realized separately; or certain assets are taken over by partners on account of the sums due to them, it may be preferable, instead of transferring all the assets to a Realization Account and crediting that account with the total proceeds, to credit each separate asset account with the amount at which it is sold or taken over, transferring the resultant profit or loss to a Realization Profit and Loss Account, the ultimate balance of which will represent the net profit or loss on the dissolution.

### Illustration (2)

G and T, having carried on business as drapers and household furnishers at the same premises for a number of years, sharing profits and losses equally, decide to dissolve partnership.

At the date of dissolution their Balance Sheet was as follows:

| | £ | £ | | £ | £ |
|---|---|---|---|---|---|
| Capital Accounts: | | | Goodwill .. .. .. | | 1,000 |
| G .. .. .. .. | 7,000 | | Freehold Premises .. .. | | 8,000 |
| T .. .. .. .. | 8,000 | | Fixtures: | | |
| | | 15,000 | Drapery Department .. .. | 750 | |
| Creditors .. .. .. | | 3,200 | Furnishing Department .. | 400 | |
| | | | | | 1,150 |
| | | | Debtors .. .. .. | | 1,050 |
| | | | Stock: | | |
| | | | Drapery Department .. .. | 1,600 | |
| | | | Furnishing Department .. | 1,400 | |
| | | | | | 3,000 |
| | | | Cash at Bank .. .. .. | | 4,000 |
| | | £18,200 | | | £18,200 |

The agreed terms were:

G was to take over the premises at £7,000, the drapery stock at £1,700, and drapery fixtures at £500.

T, having rented another shop nearby, was to take over the furniture stock at £1,500 and the fixtures of that department at £300.

Goodwill was to be written off.

Any loss on debtors was to be shared as to G three-fifths, and T two-fifths.

The creditors were to be paid by G.

The debtors realized £950, the proceeds being retained by G.

Prepare accounts, showing the final settlement between the partners.

### REALIZATION PROFIT AND LOSS ACCOUNT

| | £ | £ | | £ | £ |
|---|---|---|---|---|---|
| Goodwill written off .. .. | | 1,000 | Profit on transfer of Stock .. | | 200 |
| Bad Debts .. .. .. | | 100 | Loss on Debtors shared by agreement: | | |
| Loss on transfer of: | | | G, three-fifths .. .. | 60 | |
| Freehold Premises .. .. | 1,000 | | T, two-fifths .. .. | 40 | |
| Fixtures .. .. .. | 350 | | | | 100 |
| | | 1,350 | Loss on Realization of other Assets: | | |
| | | | G, Capital Account .. .. | 1,075 | |
| | | | T, „ „ .. | 1,075 | |
| | | | | | 2,150 |
| | | £2,450 | | | £2,450 |

## CASH ACCOUNT

| | £ | | £ |
|---|---|---|---|
| Balance b/f. .. .. .. .. | 4,000 | T, Capital Account .. .. .. | 5,085 |
| G, Capital Account .. .. .. | 1,085 | | |
| | £5,085 | | £5,085 |

## DEBTORS

| | £ | | £ |
|---|---|---|---|
| Balance b/f. .. .. .. .. | 1,050 | G, Proceeds of Realization .. .. | 950 |
| | | Realization Profit and Loss Account .. | 100 |
| | £1,050 | | £1,050 |

## FREEHOLD PREMISES

| | £ | | £ |
|---|---|---|---|
| Balance b/f. .. .. .. .. | 8,000 | G, Capital Account .. .. | 7,000 |
| | | Realization Profit and Loss Account .. | 1,000 |
| | £8,000 | | £8,000 |

## FIXTURES

| | £ | | £ |
|---|---|---|---|
| Balance b/f.: | | G, Capital Account .. .. .. | 500 |
| Drapery .. .. .. .. | 750 | T, ,, .. .. .. | 300 |
| Furnishings .. .. .. .. | 400 | Realization Profit and Loss Account .. | 350 |
| | £1,150 | | £1,150 |

## STOCK

| | £ | | £ |
|---|---|---|---|
| Balance b/f.: | | G, Capital Account .. .. .. | 1,700 |
| Drapery .. .. .. .. | 1,600 | T, ,, ,, .. .. .. | 1,500 |
| Furnishing .. .. .. .. | 1,400 | | |
| Realization Profit and Loss Account .. .. | 200 | | |
| | £3,200 | | £3,200 |

## CAPITAL ACCOUNTS

| | G £ | T £ | | G £ | T £ |
|---|---|---|---|---|---|
| Freehold Premises.. .. .. | 7,000 | | Balances b/f. .. .. .. | 7,000 | 8,000 |
| Stock .. .. .. .. | 1,700 | 1,500 | Creditors taken over .. .. | 3,200 | |
| Fixtures .. .. .. .. | 500 | 300 | Cash .. .. .. .. | 1,085 | |
| Debtors .. .. .. .. | 950 | | | | |
| Bad Debts .. .. .. | 60 | 40 | | | |
| Loss on Realization .. .. | 1,075 | 1,075 | | | |
| Cash .. .. .. .. | | 5,085 | | | |
| | £11,285 | £8,000 | | £11,285 | £8,000 |

(4) *Where, on dissolution, a partner's Capital Account is in debit, and he is unable to discharge his indebtedness, so that the rule in* Garner v. Murray *must be applied.*

Prior to the decision in *Garner* v. *Murray* it was generally supposed that any loss occasioned by one of the partners of a firm being unable to make good a debit balance on his account should be borne by the remaining partners in the proportions in which they shared profits and losses.

In this case, however, it was held that a deficiency of assets occasioned through the default of one of the partners must be distinguished from an ordinary trading loss, and should be regarded as a debt due to the remaining partners individually and not to the firm.

The circumstances of the case, the decision in which gave rise to considerable controversy, were as follows: Garner, Murray and Wilkins were in partnership under a parole agreement by the terms of which capital was to be contributed by them in unequal shares, but profits and losses were to be divided equally. On the dissolution of the partnership, after payment of the creditors and of advances made by two of the partners, there was a deficiency of assets of £635, in addition to which Wilkins' Capital Account was overdrawn by £263, which he was unable to pay. There was thus a total deficiency of £898, and the plaintiff claimed that this should be borne by the solvent partners, Garner and Murray, in their agreed profit-sharing ratio, viz. equally. Mr Justice Joyce held, however, that each of the three partners was liable to make good his share of the £635 deficiency of assets, after which the available assets should be applied in repaying to each partner what was due to him on account of capital. Since, however, one of the 'assets' was the debit balance on Wilkins' account, which was valueless, the remaining assets were to be applied in paying to Garner and Murray rateably what was due to them in respect of capital, with the result that Wilkins' deficiency was borne by them in proportion to their capitals.

The effect of the decision is shown in the following illustration.

### Illustration

A, B and C with unequal capitals, share profits and losses equally. They decide to dissolve partnership, and the following Balance Sheet shows the position of affairs after the assets have been realized and the liabilities discharged.

### BALANCE SHEET

| Capitals: | | | | | | £ | | | | | | £ |
|---|---|---|---|---|---|---|---|---|---|---|---|---|
| A | .. | .. | .. | .. | .. | 600 | Cash .. .. | .. | .. | .. | | 500 |
| B | .. | .. | .. | .. | .. | 400 | Capital C overdrawn | .. | .. | .. | | 200 |
| | | | | | | | Deficiency of Assets | .. | .. | .. | | 300 |
| | | | | | | £1,000 | | | | | | £1,000 |

C is insolvent and is unable to contribute anything towards either his overdraft on capital or his share of the loss on realization.

The loss on realization of £300 should first be debited in profit-sharing ratio to the partners' accounts, thus reducing A's capital to £500 and B's to £300, and increasing C's deficit to £300.

If the ruling in *Garner* v. *Murray* were followed strictly, A and B would introduce cash of £100 each to make good their shares of the deficiency and thus restore their capitals to £600 and £400 respectively. The balances then remaining in the books would be as shown by the reconstructed Balance Sheet given below.

### BALANCE SHEET

| Capitals: | | | | | | £ | | | | | £ |
|---|---|---|---|---|---|---|---|---|---|---|---|
| A | .. | .. | .. | .. | .. | 600 | Cash .. .. | .. | .. | .. | 700 |
| B | .. | .. | .. | .. | .. | 400 | C's Capital overdrawn | .. | .. | .. | 300 |
| | | | | | | £1,000 | | | | | £1,000 |

The only true asset, viz. cash of £700, would now be divided between the solvent partners, A and B, in proportion to their capitals, viz.:

|  |  |  | £ |
|---|---|---|---|
| A 6/10ths of £700 .. | .. | = | 420 |
| B 4/10ths of £700 .. | .. | = | 280 |
|  |  |  | £700 |

The only balances then remaining in the books would be the debit balance on C's Capital Account, £300, and the credit balances on the Capital Accounts of A and B, £180 and £120 respectively. As C is insolvent, the debit balance on his account will be written off against A and B, in the ratio of their respective capitals, viz. £180 to A and £120 to B, thus closing their accounts.

As has been shown the net effect of the above treatment is to cause A and B to bear C's deficiency in proportion to their respective capitals. The introduction of cash by A and B to meet their share of the loss on realization is unnecessary, as the balances on their Capital Account are sufficient to meet this loss. C's deficiency should be written off against the Capital Accounts of A and B in *capital* ratio, viz. 6 : 4, after which the cash in hand will be exactly sufficient to repay to A and B the balances due to them on Capital Account, as shown hereunder.

## CAPITAL ACCOUNTS

|  | A £ | B £ | C £ |  | A £ | B £ | C £ |
|---|---|---|---|---|---|---|---|
| Balance b/f. .. .. .. |  |  | 200 | Balances b/f. .. .. .. | 600 | 400 |  |
| Realization Account – Loss .. | 100 | 100 | 100 | A and B – C's deficiency transferred: |  |  |  |
| C .. .. .. .. | 180 | 120 |  | A six-tenths .. .. |  |  | 180 |
| Cash .. .. .. | 320 | 180 |  | B four-tenths .. .. |  |  | 120 |
|  | £600 | £400 | £300 |  | £600 | £400 | £300 |

## (5) *Piecemeal Realization and Interim Distributions*

When assets are realized piecemeal, the partners may desire, as soon as all liabilities have been discharged, to withdraw immediately such cash as is available for division between them rather than wait until all the assets have been sold. In such circumstances, subject to any contrary agreement between the partners, the interim payments to the partners should be of such amounts that even though the remaining assets prove to be worthless no partner will receive more than the amount to which he is ultimately found to be entitled after being debited with his proper share of the total loss sustained on realization of all the assets. To enable this to be done the proceeds of realization of assets must first be applied in repaying to partners any sums necessary to reduce their capitals to amounts which will bear the same proportion to the total capital as those in which profits and losses are shared. Further realizations will then be shared in that ratio.

**Illustration (1)**

A, B, C and D are in partnership, sharing profits in the ratio 3 : 2 : 1 : 4. It is decided to dissolve the firm on January 1st, 19.., on which date the Balance Sheet was as under:

## BALANCE SHEET as at January 1st, 19..

| Capital Accounts: | | £ | | | | £ |
|---|---|---|---|---|---|---|
| A .. .. .. .. £7,000 | | | Goodwill .. .. .. .. | | | 3,000 |
| B .. .. .. .. 4,000 | | | Land and Buildings .. .. .. | | | 8,500 |
| C .. .. .. .. 3,000 | | | Plant and Machinery .. .. .. | | | 7,921 |
| D .. .. .. .. 4,000 | | | Investments .. .. .. .. | | | 2,000 |
| | | 18,000 | Stock-in-trade .. .. .. .. | | | 6,348 |
| Creditors .. .. .. .. | | 6,923 | Debtors .. .. .. .. | | | 3,841 |
| Leasehold Redemption Fund .. .. | | 2,000 | Cash at Bank .. .. .. .. | | | 313 |
| General Reserve .. .. .. .. | | 5,000 | | | | |
| | | £31,923 | | | | £31,923 |

The assets are realized piecemeal as under:

|  |  |  |  |  |  | £ |
|---|---|---|---|---|---|---|
| January | 10 | Stock (part) .. | .. | .. | .. | 3,500 |
| „ | 14 | Debtors (part) | .. | .. | .. | 2,932 |
| „ | 28 | Investments .. | .. | .. | .. | 2,420 |
| February | 3 | Goodwill .. | .. | .. | .. | 2,000 |
| „ | 21 | Land and Buildings | .. | .. | .. | 7,000 |
| „ | „ | Debtors (part) .. | .. | .. | .. | 500 |
| „ | „ | Stock (balance) | .. | .. | .. | 2,750 |
| March | 15 | Plant and Machinery | .. | .. | .. | 6,560 |
| „ | „ | Debtors (balance) | .. | .. | .. | 351 |

Subject to providing £500 to meet the probable expenses of realization, the partners decide that after the creditors have been paid, all cash received shall be divided between them immediately.

The expenses of realization, which are paid on March 15th, amount to £400.

Prepare a Statement showing how the distributions should be made, and show the Realization Profit and Loss Account, Cash Account and partners' Capital Accounts. Calculations are to be made to the nearest £.

After transferring the General Reserve to the partners' Capital Accounts in profit-sharing ratio the capitals of the partners will be:

|  | . A | B | C | D | Total |
|---|---|---|---|---|---|
|  | £ | £ | £ | £ | £ |
| Balances, January 1st .. .. | 7,000 | 4,000 | 3,000 | 4,000 | 18,000 |
| General Reserve .. .. | 1,500 | 1,000 | 500 | 2,000 | 5,000 |
|  | £8,500 | £5,000 | £3,500 | £6,000 | £23,000 |
| The profit-sharing ratio is .. | 3 | 2 | 1 | 4 | 10 |
| The capital per unit of profit is .. | £2,833 | £2,500 | £3,500 | £1,500 | |

D has the smallest capital in relation to his share of profit, viz. £1,500 capital per unit of profit. If the capitals of the other partners were held on the same basis, A's capital would be £4,500, B's £3,000 and C's £1,500. A, B and C, therefore, have surplus capital over that of D, of £4,000, £2,000 and £2,000 respectively, which surplus must be repaid to them before any payments are made to D.

|  | A | B | C | D | Total |
|---|---|---|---|---|---|
|  | £ | £ | £ | £ | £ |
| Balances as above .. .. | 8,500 | 5,000 | 3,500 | 6,000 | 23,000 |
| Capitals in profit-sharing ratio .. | 4,500 | 3,000 | 1,500 | 6,000 | 15,000 |
| Surplus Capitals .. .. | £4,000 | £2,000 | £2,000 | — | £8,000 |

| | | | | |
|---|---|---|---|---|
| The profit sharing ratio between A, B and C is .. .. | 3 | 2 | 1 | |
| The Surplus Capital per unit of profit is .. .. .. | £1,333 | £1,000 | £2,000 | |

As between A, B and C, B has the smallest surplus capital in relation to his share of profit. If B's surplus capital of £2,000 were in the same proportion to the total surplus capital as his share of profit, the total surplus capital would be £6,000, of which A's share would be £3,000, B's £2,000 and C's £1,000. A and C therefore have surplus capital over B of £1,000 each, which must be repaid to them before any payment is made to B.

| | A | B | C | D | Total |
|---|---|---|---|---|---|
| | £ | £ | £ | £ | £ |
| Surplus Capital as above .. | 4,000 | 2,000 | 2,000 | — | 8,000 |
| Surplus Capitals in profit-sharing ratio (A, 3; B, 2; C, 1) .. | 3,000 | 2,000 | 1,000 | — | 6,000 |
| Further Surplus Capital .. | £1,000 | — | £1,000 | — | £2,000 |

As between A and C the profit-sharing ratio is 3 : 1 so that the further surplus capital per unit of profit is A, £333 and C, £1,000. If A's surplus of £1,000 represented three-fourths of the total surplus, C's share would be £333. C, therefore has a further surplus over A of £667 as shown hereunder.

| | A | B | C | D | Total |
|---|---|---|---|---|---|
| | £ | £ | £ | £ | £ |
| Surplus Capital as above .. | 1,000 | — | 1,000 | — | 2,000 |
| Surplus Capital in profit-sharing ratio (A, 3; C, 1) .. .. | 1,000 | — | 333 | — | 1,333 |
| Ultimate Surplus Capital .. | — | — | £667 | — | £667 |

The amounts becoming available for distribution should accordingly be paid to the partners in the order of priority shown in the following statement.

| | A | B | C | D | Total |
|---|---|---|---|---|---|
| | £ | £ | £ | £ | £ |
| The first £667 .. .. | | | 667 | | 667 |
| The next £1,333 (A, 3; C, 1) .. | 1,000 | | 333 | | 1,333 |
| | 1,000 | | 1,000 | | 2,000 |
| The next £6,000 (A, 3; B, 2; C, 1).. | 3,000 | 2,000 | 1,000 | | 6,000 |
| | £4,000 | £2,000 | £2,000 | — | £8,000 |

After repayment of the above £8,000, the balances remaining on the Capital Accounts will be A £4,500, B £3,000, C £1,500 and D £6,000, these amounts being in the same proportion as that in which profits and losses are shared. By dividing all further realizations in this ratio, therefore, each partner will receive his proper share of the profit or bear his proper share of the loss.

## STATEMENT OF ACTUAL DISTRIBUTIONS

| 19.. | | Cash available £ | A £ | B £ | C £ | D £ | Total £ |
|---|---|---|---|---|---|---|---|
| | Balance b/f. .. .. .. .. | 313 | | | | | |
| Jan. 10 | Realization .. .. .. .. | 3,500 | | | | | |
| 14 | ,, .. .. .. .. | 2,932 | | | | | |
| 28 | ,, .. .. .. .. | 2,420 | | | | | |
| | | 9,165 | | | | | |
| | *Less* Creditors .. .. .. | 6,923 | | | | | |
| | | 2,242 | | | | | |
| Jan. 28 | *Less* Provided for Expenses .. .. | 500 | | | | | |
| | | 1,742 | | | | | |
| | *Less* to C .. .. .. .. | 667 | — | — | 667 | — | 667 |
| | Divisible between A and C in proportion of A, 3 : C, 1 .. .. .. .. | £1,075 | 806 | — | 269 | — | 1,075 |
| | | | £806 | — | £936 | — | £1,742 |
| 19.. Feb. 3 | Realizations .. .. .. .. | 2,000 | | | | | |
| | *Less* Balance of £1,333 to A and C in proportion of A, 3; C, 1 .. .. | 258 | 194 | — | 64 | — | 258 |
| | Divisible between A, B and C in proportion of A, 3; B, 2; C, 1 .. .. .. | £1,742 | 871 | 581 | 290 | — | 1,742 |
| | | | £1,065 | £581 | £354 | — | £2,000 |
| 19.. Feb. 21 | Realizations .. .. .. .. | 10,250 | | | | | |
| | *Less* Balance of £6,000 to A, B and C in proportion of A, 3; B, 2; C, 1 .. | 4,258 | 2,129 | 1,419 | 710 | — | 4,258 |
| | Divisible between A, B, C and D in profit-sharing ratio of A, 3; B, 2 : C, 1; D, 4 .. | £5,992 | 1,798 | 1,198 | 599 | 2,397 | 5,992 |
| | | | £3,927 | £2,617 | £1,309 | £2,397 | £10,250 |
| 19.. Mar. 15 | Realizations .. .. .. .. | 6,911 | | | | | |
| | *Add* Over-provision for expenses .. | 100 | | | | | |
| | Divisible between A, B, C and D in profit-sharing ratio A, 3; B, 2; C, 1; D, 4 .. | £7,011 | £2,103 | £1,403 | £701 | £2,804 | £7,011 |

The accounts will be closed as follows:

## CASH ACCOUNT

| | | £ | | | £ |
|---|---|---|---|---|---|
| Jan. 1 | Balance b/f. .. .. .. | 313 | Jan. 28 | Creditors .. .. .. | 6,923 |
| 10 | Stock Account .. .. .. | 3,500 | | Capital Accounts: | |
| 14 | Debtors .. .. .. | 2,932 | | A .. .. .. .. | 806 |
| 28 | Investments .. .. .. | 2,420 | | C .. .. .. .. | 936 |
| Feb. 3 | Goodwill .. .. .. | 2,000 | Feb. 3 | Capital Accounts: | |
| 21 | Land and Buildings .. .. | 7,000 | | A .. .. .. .. | 1,065 |
| | Debtors .. .. .. | 500 | | B .. .. .. .. | 581 |
| | Stock .. .. .. | 2,750 | | C .. .. .. .. | 354 |
| Mar. 15 | Plant and Machinery .. .. | 6,560 | 21 | Capital Accounts: | |
| | Debtors .. .. .. | 351 | | A .. .. .. .. | 3,927 |
| | | | | B .. .. .. .. | 2,617 |
| | | | | C .. .. .. .. | 1,309 |
| | | | | D .. .. .. .. | 2,397 |
| | | | Mar. 15 | Realization Profit and Loss Account: | |
| | | | | Expenses .. .. .. | 400 |
| | | | | Capital Accounts: | |
| | | | | A .. .. .. .. | 2,103 |
| | | | | B .. .. .. .. | 1,403 |
| | | | | C .. .. .. .. | 701 |
| | | | | D .. .. .. .. | 2,804 |
| | | £28,326 | | | £28,326 |

## REALIZATION PROFIT AND LOSS ACCOUNT

| | | £ | | | £ |
|---|---|---|---|---|---|
| Feb. 3 | Goodwill .. .. .. | 1,000 | Jan. 28 | Investments .. .. .. | 420 |
| 21 | Land and Buildings .. .. | 1,500 | Feb. 21 | Leasehold Redemption Fund .. | 2,000 |
| | Stock .. .. .. | 98 | Mar. 15 | Loss transferred to Capital Accounts: | |
| | Plant and Machinery .. .. | 1,361 | | A 3/10ths .. .. £599 | |
| | Debtors .. .. .. | 58 | | B 2/10ths .. .. 399 | |
| | Cash – Expenses of Realization .. | 400 | | C 1/10th .. .. 200 | |
| | | | | D 4/10ths .. .. 799 | |
| | | | | | 1,997 |
| | | £4,417 | | | £4,417 |

## CAPITAL ACCOUNTS

| | | A £ | B £ | C £ | D £ | | | A £ | B £ | C £ | D £ |
|---|---|---|---|---|---|---|---|---|---|---|---|
| Jan. 28 | Cash .. .. | 806 | — | 936 | — | Jan. 1 | Balances b/f. .. | 7,000 | 4,000 | 3,000 | 4,000 |
| Feb. 3 | ,, .. .. | 1,065 | 581 | 354 | — | | General Reserve .. | 1,500 | 1,000 | 500 | 2,000 |
| 21 | ,, .. .. | 3,927 | 2,617 | 1,309 | 2,397 | | | | | | |
| Mar. 15 | Loss on Realization | 599 | 399 | 200 | 799 | | | | | | |
| | Cash .. | 2,103 | 1,403 | 701 | 2,804 | | | | | | |
| | £ | 8,500 | 5,000 | 3,500 | 6,000 | | £ | 8,500 | 5,000 | 3,500 | 6,000 |

Another, and more cautious method, is to treat the assets remaining unrealized after each realization as completely valueless, and to charge each partner with his share of the notional loss in the agreed profit-sharing ratio. If a partner's capital is thereby thrown into debit, the amount thereof is charged to the other partners in proportion to their capitals, in accordance with the rule in *Garner* v. *Murray*. The aggregate of the balances of the partners' Capital Accounts, after deducting the amounts of any previous distributions, will then equal the sum available for distribution. This process will be repeated on each realization, with the result that after the final distribution, each partner will have borne his proper share of the ultimate loss and in no circumstances will any partner be required to repay anything.

**Illustration (2)**

A, B and C share profits in the proportion of $\frac{1}{2}$, $\frac{1}{3}$ and $\frac{1}{6}$. Their Balance Sheet is as follows:

| | | £ | | £ |
|---|---|---|---|---|
| A Capital Account | .. .. | 3,000 | Assets, *less* liabilities .. .. | 8,000 |
| B Capital Account | .. .. | 3,000 | | |
| C Capital Account | .. .. | 2,000 | | |
| | | £8,000 | | £8,000 |

The partnership is dissolved, and the assets are realized as follows:

| | | £ |
|---|---|---|
| First Realization | .. .. | 1,000 |
| Second Realization | .. .. | 1,500 |
| Third and Final Realization | .. | 2,500 |
| | | £5,000 |

| | £ | A £ | B £ | C £ | Total Distributions £ |
|---|---|---|---|---|---|
| Capitals .. .. .. | | 3,000 | 3,000 | 2,000 | |
| First Realization .. .. | 1,000 | | | | |
| Balance of assets treated as loss .. | 7,000 | ($\frac{1}{2}$) 3,500 | ($\frac{1}{3}$) 2,333 | ($\frac{1}{6}$) 1,167 | |
| | £8,000 | *Dr* £500 | 667 | 833 | |
| A's debit balance divided between B and C in *capital* ratio (*Garner* v. *Murray*) .. .. .. | | | ($\frac{3}{5}$) 300 | ($\frac{2}{5}$) 200 | |
| Distribution of First Realization .. | | | £367 | £633 | 1,000 |

|  | £ | A £ | B £ | C £ | Total Distributions £ |
|---|---|---|---|---|---|
| Capitals .. .. .. |  | 3,000 | 3,000 | 2,000 |  |
| Second Realization .. .. | 1,500 |  |  |  |  |
| Balance of assets treated as loss .. | 5,500 | ($\frac{1}{2}$) 2,750 | ($\frac{1}{3}$) 1,833 | ($\frac{1}{6}$) 917 |  |
|  | £7,000 | 250 | 1,167 | 1,083 |  |
| *Less* First Distribution .. .. |  | — | 367 | 633 |  |
| Distribution of Second Realization.. |  | £250 | £800 | £450 | 1,500 |
|  | £ | £ | £ | £ |  |
| Capitals .. .. .. |  | 3,000 | 3,000 | 2,000 |  |
| Final Realization .. .. | 2,500 |  |  |  |  |
| Balance of assets, being ultimate loss | 3,000 | ($\frac{1}{2}$) 1,500 | ($\frac{1}{3}$) 1,000 | ($\frac{1}{6}$) 500 |  |
|  | £5,500 | 1,500 | 2,000 | 1,500 |  |
| *Less* First and Second Distributions |  | 250 | 1,167 | 1,083 |  |
| Distribution of Final Realization .. |  | £1,250 | £833 | £417 | 2,500 |

The ultimate loss of £3,000 has thus been borne by the partners in the correct proportions.

The accounts will be closed as follows:

### REALIZATION ACCOUNT

| | £ | | | | | £ |
|---|---|---|---|---|---|---|
| Net Assets .. .. .. .. | 8,000 | Cash: | | | | |
| | | 1st Realization .. .. .. | | | | 1,000 |
| | | 2nd　　" .. .. .. | | | | 1,500 |
| | | 3rd　　" .. .. .. | | | | 2,500 |
| | | Loss transferred to Capital Accounts: | | | | |
| | | A $\frac{1}{2}$ .. .. .. | | £1,500 | | |
| | | B $\frac{1}{3}$ .. .. .. | | 1,000 | | |
| | | C $\frac{1}{6}$ .. .. .. | | 500 | | |
| | | | | | | 3,000 |
| | £8,000 | | | | | £8,000 |

### CASH ACCOUNT

| | £ | | | | | £ |
|---|---|---|---|---|---|---|
| 1st Realization .. .. .. .. | 1,000 | Capital Accounts: | | | | |
| | | B .. .. .. .. .. | | | | 367 |
| | | C .. .. .. .. .. | | | | 633 |
| 2nd Realization .. .. .. .. | 1,500 | Capital Accounts: | | | | |
| | | A .. .. .. .. .. | | | | 250 |
| | | B .. .. .. .. .. | | | | 800 |
| | | C .. .. .. .. .. | | | | 450 |
| 3rd Realization .. .. .. .. | 2,500 | Capital Accounts: | | | | |
| | | A .. .. .. .. .. | | | | 1,250 |
| | | B .. .. .. .. .. | | | | 833 |
| | | C .. .. .. .. .. | | | | 417 |

## CAPITAL ACCOUNTS

| | A £ | B £ | C £ | | A £ | B £ | C £ |
|---|---|---|---|---|---|---|---|
| Cash 1st Realization .. | | 367 | 633 | Balances b/f. .. .. | 3,000 | 3,000 | 2,000 |
| ,, 2nd ,, .. | 250 | 800 | 450 | | | | |
| ,, 3rd ,, .. | 1,250 | 833 | 417 | | | | |
| Realization Account: Loss .. | 1,500 | 1,000 | 500 | | | | |
| | £3,000 | £3,000 | £2,000 | | £3,000 | £3,000 | £2,000 |

The partners may, of course, agree between themselves on some other basis of distribution. One or other of the above methods should be used in the absence of agreement.

### (b) Dissolution of Partnership by death or bankruptcy

Under Section 33 of the *Partnership Act 1890* any partnership, except where otherwise agreed, is dissolved as regards all the partners by the death or bankruptcy of any partner.

Section 42 of the Act provides that where any member has died, or otherwise ceased to be a partner, and the surviving or continuing partners carry on the business of the firm with its capital or assets, without any final settlement of accounts as between the firm and the outgoing partner or his estate, the outgoing partner or his estate is, in the absence of agreement, entitled to such share of the profits made since the dissolution as the court may find to be attributable to the use of his share of the partnership assets, or to interest at 5 per cent. per annum on the amount of his share of the partnership assets.

**Illustration**

F, G and H are partners in a manufacturing business. F is entitled to one-fourth of the partnership profits, G to one-eighth, and H to five-eighths. The yearly accounts are made up to Sept. 30th.

F became bankrupt on March 31st, 1970, and G and H continued the business without paying out F's share of the partnership assets, or settling accounts with his trustee, until the close of the year, September 30th, 1970.

The Balance Sheet at September 30th, 1969, showed F's capital to be £4,000.

The partners' drawings during the year to September 30th, 1970, have been as follows: F £250, G £100, and H £700.

There is no agreement for interest on capital, but the partners F and G are each to be credited with a salary at the rate of £100 per annum. Subject to this charge, the profits for the year ended September 30th, 1970, are £1,750, which may be assumed to have accrued evenly throughout the year.

Show the balance of profits and salary due to each partner, and the total amount due by G and H to F's Estate at September 30th, 1970, assuming that F's trustee does not propose to apply to the court for a share of profits.

### F, G AND H PROFIT AND LOSS ACCOUNT
For the six months ended March 31st, 1970

| | £ | £ | | £ |
|---|---|---|---|---|
| Partners' Salaries: | | | Profit for 6 months to date (½ × £1,750) .. | 875 |
| F .. .. .. .. | 50 | | | |
| G .. .. .. .. | 50 | | | |
| | | 100 | | |
| Balance c/d. .. .. .. | | 775 | | |
| | | £875 | | £875 |
| F one-fourth .. .. .. | | 194 | Balance b/d. .. .. .. .. | 775 |
| G one-eighth .. .. .. | | 97 | | |
| H five-eighths .. .. .. | | 484 | | |
| | | £775 | | £775 |

## G AND H PROFIT AND LOSS ACCOUNT
### For the six months ended September 30th, 1970

| | £ | | £ |
|---|---|---|---|
| Partner's Salary: | | Profit for 6 months to date ($\frac{1}{2} \times$ £1,750) .. | 875 |
| G .. .. .. .. .. | 50 | | |
| Interest: F | | | |
| 5% per annum on £3,994, balance of Capital | | | |
| and Current Accounts .. .. .. | 100 | | |
| Balance c/d. .. .. .. .. | 725 | | |
| | £875 | | £875 |
| | | | |
| G one-sixth .. .. .. .. | 121 | Balance b/d. .. .. .. .. | 725 |
| H five-sixths .. .. .. .. | 604 | | |
| | £725 | | £725 |

## F CURRENT ACCOUNT

| | £ | | £ |
|---|---|---|---|
| Drawings .. .. .. .. .. | 250 | Salary to March 31st .. .. .. | 50 |
| | | Profit .. .. .. .. .. | 194 |
| | | Balance to Capital Account .. .. | 6 |
| | £250 | | £250 |

## F CAPITAL ACCOUNT

| | £ | | £ |
|---|---|---|---|
| Current Account .. .. .. .. | 6 | Balance b/f. .. .. .. .. | 4,000 |
| Balance c/d. .. .. .. .. | 4,094 | Interest to 30th September – 6 months at 5% | |
| | | per annum .. .. .. .. | 100 |
| | £4,100 | | £4,100 |
| | | Balance, being total amount due to F's Estate | |
| | | b/d. .. .. .. .. .. | 4,094 |

## G CURRENT ACCOUNT

| | £ | | £ |
|---|---|---|---|
| Drawings .. .. .. .. .. | 100 | Salary – F, G and H .. .. .. | 50 |
| Balance c/d. .. .. .. .. | 218 | Profit .. .. .. .. .. | 97 |
| | | Salary – G and H .. .. .. | 50 |
| | | Profit .. .. .. .. .. | 121 |
| | £318 | | £318 |
| | | Balance b/d. .. .. .. .. | 218 |

## H CURRENT ACCOUNT

| | £ | | £ |
|---|---|---|---|
| Drawings .. .. .. .. .. | 700 | Profit – F, G and H .. .. .. | 484 |
| Balance c/d. .. .. .. .. | 388 | „ G and H .. .. .. | 604 |
| | £1,088 | | £1,088 |
| | | Balance b/d. .. .. .. .. | 388 |

*Note:* If F's trustee applied to the court for a share of the profits, the latter would probably direct that the profits should be charged with reasonable salaries for the services of the continuing partners, before arriving at the balance of which F was entitled to a share.

## (c) Amalgamation of Firms

Where the members of two or more partnerships decide to amalgamate, the transaction resolves itself into the dissolution of the existing partnerships and the formation of a new one. For the purposes of the amalgamation it is probable that the goodwill and other assets of the original firms will be revalued, and the capitals of the respective partners adjusted by reference to the profit or loss arising on such revaluation, before arriving at the amount of capital introduced by each partner into the new firm. Where the capital of the new firm is a fixed amount, to be provided by the partners in specified proportions or sums, it may be necessary, after giving effect to the agreed revaluations of assets, for cash to be withdrawn or paid in by one or more of the partners in order to adjust the capitals to the agreed amounts.

### Illustration

In similar type businesses, R and Y are in partnership as R Y & Co and V and B as V B & Co. It was mutually agreed that as on January 1st, 1970, the partnerships be amalgamated into one firm, Tints Co. The profit sharing ratios in the various firms were and are to be as follows:

|  |  |  | R | Y | V | B |
|---|---|---|---|---|---|---|
| Old firms .. | | .. | 4 | 3 | 3 | 2 |
| New firms .. | | .. | 6 | 5 | 4 | 3 |

As on December 31st, 1969, the Balance Sheets of the firms were as follows:

| | R Y & Co £ | V B & Co £ | | R Y & Co £ | V B & Co £ |
|---|---|---|---|---|---|
| Capital Accounts: | | | Property .. .. .. | 7,400 | 10,000 |
| R .. .. .. .. | 15,300 | — | Fixtures .. .. .. | 1,800 | 1,400 |
| Y .. .. .. .. | 11,000 | — | Vehicles .. .. .. | 3,000 | 1,800 |
| V .. .. .. .. | — | 11,300 | Stock .. .. .. .. | 8,300 | 6,600 |
| B .. .. .. .. | — | 7,400 | Investment .. .. .. | 800 | |
| Creditors .. .. .. | 5,200 | 6,000 | Debtors .. .. .. | 6,800 | 5,800 |
| Bank overdraft .. .. .. | — | 900 | Bank balance .. .. .. | 3,400 | — |
| | £31,500 | £25,600 | | £31,500 | £25,600 |

The agreement to amalgamate contains the following provisions:

1. Provision for doubtful debts at the rate of 5 per cent. be made in respect of debtors, and a provision for discount receivable at the rate of $2\frac{1}{2}$ per cent. be made in respect of creditors.

2. Tints Co to take over the old partnership assets at the following values:

| | | | | R Y & Co £ | V B & Co £ |
|---|---|---|---|---|---|
| Stock | .. | .. | .. | 8,450 | 6,390 |
| Vehicles | .. | .. | .. | 2,800 | 1,300 |
| Fixtures | .. | .. | .. | 1,600 | — |
| Property | .. | .. | .. | 10,000 | — |
| Goodwill | .. | .. | .. | 6,300 | 4,500 |

3. The property and fixtures of V B & Co not to be taken over by Tints Co. (These assets were sold for £13,500 cash on January 1st, 1970.)

4. Y to take over his firm's investment at a value of £760.

5. The capital of Tints Co to be £54,000 and to be contributed by the partners in profit sharing ratios, any adjustments to be made in cash.

Close the books of R Y & Co and of V B & Co and prepare the opening Balance Sheet of Tints Co.

## RY & CO AND VB & CO
## REALIZATION ACCOUNTS

| | RY & Co £ | VB & Co £ | | RY & Co £ | £ | VB & Co £ |
|---|---|---|---|---|---|---|
| Assets (at book values) | | | Creditors | 5,200 | | 6,000 |
| Property | 7,400 | 10,000 | Partners' Capital Account: | | | |
| Fixtures | 1,800 | 1,400 | Y – Investment | 760 | | |
| Vehicles | 3,000 | 1,800 | Tints Co: | | | |
| Stock | 8,300 | 6,600 | Assets taken over (at | | | |
| Investment | 800 | | agreed values) | | | |
| Debtors | 6,800 | 5,800 | Stock .. £8,450 | | 6,390 | |
| | 28,100 | 25,600 | Vehicles .. 2,800 | | 1,300 | |
| | | | Fixtures .. 1,600 | | — | |
| Partners' Capital Accounts: | | | Property .. 10,000 | | — | |
| Profit on realization: | | | Goodwill .. 6,300 | | 4,500 | |
| R (4/7ths) .. £4,800 | | | Debtors .. 6,460 | | 5,510 | |
| Y (3/7ths) .. 3,600 | | | | 35,610 | 17,700 | |
| | 8,400 | | Less Creditors 5,070 | | 5,850 | |
| | | | | 30,540 | | 11,850 |
| V (3/5ths) .. 3,450 | | | Cash – Sale of property and | | | |
| B (2/5ths) .. 2,300 | | | fixtures .. .. | | | 13,500 |
| | | 5,750 | | | | |
| | £36,500 | £31,350 | | £36,500 | | £31,350 |

## PARTNERS' CAPITAL ACCOUNTS

| | R £ | Y £ | V £ | B £ | | R £ | Y £ | V £ | B £ |
|---|---|---|---|---|---|---|---|---|---|
| Realization Account: | | | | | Balances b/f. .. | 15,300 | 11,000 | 11,300 | 7,400 |
| Investment taken over .. | | 760 | | | Realization Account | 4,800 | 3,600 | 3,450 | 2,300 |
| Cash .. .. | 2,100 | | 2,750 | 700 | Cash .. .. | | 1,160 | | |
| Transferred to Tints Co .. | 18,000 | 15,000 | 12,000 | 9,000 | | | | | |
| | £20,100 | £15,760 | £14,750 | £9,700 | | £20,100 | £15,760 | £14,750 | £9,700 |

## CASH ACCOUNTS

| | RY & Co £ | VB & Co £ | | RY & Co £ | VB & Co £ |
|---|---|---|---|---|---|
| Balance brought forward .. .. | 3,400 | | Balances brought forward | | 900 |
| Realization Account – Sale of property | | | Tints Co. .. .. .. | 2,460 | 9,150 |
| and fixtures .. .. .. | | 13,500 | R .. .. .. | 2,100 | |
| Y .. .. .. .. | 1,160 | | V .. .. .. | | 2,750 |
| | | | B .. .. .. | | 700 |
| | £4,560 | £13,500 | | £4,560 | £13,500 |

## TINTS CO

| | RY & Co £ | VB & Co £ | | RY & Co £ | VB & Co £ |
|---|---|---|---|---|---|
| Realization account .. .. | 30,540 | 11,850 | Capital accounts: | | |
| Cash .. .. .. .. | 2,460 | 9,150 | R 6/18ths of £54,000 .. .. | 18,000 | |
| | | | Y 5/18ths of  ,, .. .. | 15,000 | |
| | | | V 4/18ths of  ,, .. .. | | 12,000 |
| | | | B 3/18ths of  ,, .. .. | | 9,000 |
| | £33,000 | £21,000 | | £33,000 | £21,000 |

## TINTS CO
### BALANCE SHEET as at January 1st, 1970

| CAPITAL ACCOUNTS | £ | £ | FIXED ASSETS, at cost | £ | £ |
|---|---|---|---|---|---|
| R .. .. .. .. | 18,000 | | Goodwill .. .. .. | 10,800 | |
| Y .. .. .. .. | 15,000 | | Property .. .. .. | 10,000 | |
| V .. .. .. .. | 12,000 | | Fixtures .. .. .. | 1,600 | |
| B .. .. .. .. | 9,000 | | Vehicles .. .. .. | 4,100 | |
| | | 54,000 | | | 26,500 |
| CURRENT LIABILITIES | | | CURRENT ASSETS | | |
| Creditors .. .. | 11,200 | | Stock .. .. .. | 14,840 | |
| *Less* Provision for discount receiv- | | | Debtors .. .. £12,600 | | |
| able .. .. | 280 | | *Less* Provision for doubt- | | |
| | | 10,920 | ful debts .. .. 630 | | |
| | | | | 11,970 | |
| | | | Balance at bank .. .. | 11,610 | |
| | | | | | 38,420 |
| | | £64,920 | | | £64,920 |

### (d) The Conversion of a Private Firm into a Limited Company

Frequently a private business is 'converted' into a limited company, i.e. transferred to the company in exchange for shares therein. The company may be either a private one, in which case the shares will be held by the families concerned, or a public company, the shares or debentures of which may be offered for subscription to the public.

The advantages of such a 'conversion' are set out in Section 1 of Chapter VIII.

Such a transaction will necessitate the books of the firm being closed, and new books being opened for the company. The following will be the procedure for closing the firm's books:

1. Open a Realization Account, and transfer to the debit thereof the book value of the assets taken over by the purchasing company, crediting the various asset accounts.

2. Transfer to the credit of Realization Account the liabilities assumed by the company, debiting the respective liability accounts.

3. Debit the Purchasing Company's Account, and credit Realization Account with the agreed purchase price of the net assets taken over by the company.

*Note:* The term 'net assets' means the assets less the liabilities.

4. The balance on the Realization Account, after debiting expenses (if any), will represent the profit or loss on realization of the net assets, and will be transferred to the partners' capital accounts in the proportions in which they share profits and losses.

5. Debit the accounts of the assets (e.g. cash, shares, debentures etc.) received as purchase consideration, and credit the Purchasing Company's Account.

6. Pay off any liabilities not taken over by the new company, crediting cash and debiting the liability accounts.

7. Distribute between the partners the shares, debentures etc. received from the company in the proportions agreed between them, debiting their Capital Accounts and crediting the accounts of the shares, debentures etc.

8. Any balances remaining on Capital Accounts must now be cleared by the withdrawal or payment in of cash.

**Illustration**

The firm of J, S and R decide to form a limited company, J, S & R Ltd, and transfer business thereto. Their Balance Sheet is as follows:

**J, S & R**

**BALANCE SHEET, as at June 30th**

| | | | | £ | | | | | £ |
|---|---|---|---|---|---|---|---|---|---|
| Capital Accounts: | | | | | Freehold Property | .. | .. | .. | 30,000 |
| J | .. | .. | .. | .. £25,000 | Plant .. | .. | .. | .. | 10,900 |
| S | .. | .. | .. | 15,000 | Fixtures, Fittings and Furniture | .. | .. | 1,500 |
| R | .. | .. | .. | 10,000 | Stock-in-Trade.. | .. | .. | .. | 19,500 |
| | | | | 50,000 | Debtors | .. | .. | £68,830 | |
| | | | | | *Less* Provision | .. | .. | 2,000 | |
| Creditors | .. | .. | .. | 63,300 | | | | | 66,830 |
| Loan on Mortgage | .. | .. | .. | 20,000 | Cash at Bank .. | .. | .. | 4,500 | |
| | | | | | „   in Hand .. | .. | .. | 70 | |
| | | | | | | | | | 4,570 |
| | | | | £133,300 | | | | | £133,300 |

They share profits – J four-ninths, S three-ninths, R two-ninths. The purchase consideration was £85,000 (the company taking over all the assets and liabilities except the loan on mortgage), and was payable as to £25,000 in cash, £20,000 in 5 per cent. mortgage debentures, and £40,000 in ordinary shares. Expenses amounting to £600 were payable by the firm.

Assuming the transactions to have been carried through, and the loan on mortgage repaid close the books of the firm, the debentures and shares being divided between the partners in the following proportions: J one-half, S one-quarter, R one-quarter.

**REALIZATION ACCOUNT**

| | | | | £ | | | | £ |
|---|---|---|---|---|---|---|---|---|
| Sundry Assets | .. | .. | .. | 135,300 | Provision for Bad Debts | .. | .. | 2,000 |
| Expenses.. | .. | .. | .. | 600 | Creditors | .. | .. | 63,300 |
| Capital Accounts, being profit: | | | | | J, S & R Ltd., purchase consideration | .. | 85,000 |
| J four-ninths | .. | .. | £6,400 | | | | | |
| S three-ninths | .. | .. | 4,800 | | | | | |
| R two-ninths | .. | .. | 3,200 | | | | | |
| | | | | 14,400 | | | | |
| | | | | £150,300 | | | | £150,300 |

**LOAN ON MORTGAGE**

| | | | | | £ | | | | | | £ |
|---|---|---|---|---|---|---|---|---|---|---|---|
| Cash | .. | .. | .. | .. | 20,000 | Balance b/f. | .. | .. | .. | .. | 20,000 |

**J, S & R LTD**

| | £ | | | | | £ |
|---|---|---|---|---|---|---|
| Realization Account, purchase consideration | .. | 85,000 | Cash .. | .. | .. | 25,000 |
| | | | Debentures in J. S. & R. Ltd | .. | .. | 20,000 |
| | | | Ordinary Shares in J, S & R Ltd | .. | 40,000 |
| | | £85,000 | | | | £85,000 |

**DEBENTURES IN J, S & R LTD**

| | | | | £ | | | | | £ |
|---|---|---|---|---|---|---|---|---|---|
| J, S & R Ltd | .. | .. | .. | 20,000 | J Capital Account, one-half | .. | .. | 10,000 |
| | | | | | S „ „ one-quarter | .. | .. | 5,000 |
| | | | | | R „ „ one-quarter | .. | .. | 5,000 |
| | | | | £20,000 | | | | | £20,000 |

## ORDINARY SHARES IN J, S & R LTD

| | £ | | | £ |
|---|---|---|---|---|
| J, S & R Ltd .. .. .. .. | 40,000 | J Capital Account, one-half .. .. | | 20,000 |
| | | S ,, ,, one-quarter .. .. | | 10,000 |
| | | R ,, ,, one-quarter .. .. | | 10,000 |
| | £40,000 | | | £40,000 |

## J CAPITAL ACCOUNT

| | £ | | | £ |
|---|---|---|---|---|
| Debentures in J, S & R Ltd .. .. | 10,000 | Balance b/f. .. .. .. .. | | 25,000 |
| Ordinary Shares in J, S & R Ltd .. .. | 20,000 | Realization Account, profit .. .. | | 6,400 |
| Cash .. .. .. .. .. | 1,400 | | | |
| | £31,400 | | | £31,400 |

## S CAPITAL ACCOUNT

| | £ | | | £ |
|---|---|---|---|---|
| Debentures in J, S & R Ltd .. .. | 5,000 | Balance b/f. .. .. .. .. | | 15,000 |
| Ordinary Shares in J, S & R Ltd .. .. | 10,000 | Realization Account, profit .. .. | | 4,800 |
| Cash .. .. .. .. .. | 4,800 | | | |
| | £19,800 | | | £19,800 |

## R CAPITAL ACCOUNT

| | £ | | | £ |
|---|---|---|---|---|
| Debentures in J, S & R Ltd .. .. | 5,000 | Balance b/f. .. .. .. .. | | 10,000 |
| Ordinary Shares in J, S & R Ltd .. .. | 10,000 | Realization Account, profit .. .. | | 3,200 |
| | | Cash .. .. .. .. .. | | 1,800 |
| | £15,000 | | | £15,000 |

## CASH ACCOUNT

| | £ | | | | £ |
|---|---|---|---|---|---|
| J, S & R Ltd .. .. .. .. | 25,000 | Loan on Mortgage .. .. .. | | | 20,000 |
| Capital Account: R .. .. .. | 1,800 | Expenses .. .. .. | | | 600 |
| | | Capital Accounts: | | | |
| | | J .. .. .. .. | | £1,400 | |
| | | S .. .. .. .. | | 4,800 | |
| | | | | | 6,200 |
| | £26,800 | | | | £26,800 |

Normally, where a partnership is converted into a limited company, the partners of the firm will agree as to the manner in which the shares, debentures etc. of the company, received as purchase consideration, are to be divided between them. Where, however, the partners cannot agree upon such proportions an independent valuation of the shares, debentures etc. should be obtained and the profit or loss disclosed thereby divided between the partners in their profit-sharing ratio. The shares, debentures etc., at their agreed valuation, will then be divided between the partners in proportion to the adjusted balances on their capital accounts. If it is desired by the partners to share the profits of the company in the proportions in which the profits of the partnership were formerly divided, the shares, debentures etc., should be allocated to the partners in their profit-sharing ratio, a cash adjustment being made between the partners in respect of any balances remaining due to or by them individually.

## § 9. Joint Venture Accounts

'Joint venture' is defined in 'Bell's Principles', Art. 392, as follows: 'Joint adventure or joint trade is a partnership confined to a particular adventure, speculation, course of trade or voyage, and in which the partners, either latent or known, use no firm or social name, and incur no responsibility beyond the limits of the adventure.' A joint venture cannot be distinguished in any way from an ordinary partnership, beyond the fact that the agreement is of a specially limited character.

In actual practice joint ventures resolve themselves broadly into two classes:

### (a) Where a separate set of books is opened for the transactions of the Joint Venture

In such a case, a joint banking account may be opened and the transactions recorded in a manner precisely similar to those of ordinary partnerships, each partner's Capital Account being credited with the amount which he pays into the Joint Account. Interest on capital is usually taken into consideration, and the profits or losses are divided according to the shares agreed upon.

### Illustration (1)

A and B were partners in a joint venture in timber, sharing profits – two-thirds and one-third respectively. A banking account in their joint names is opened on January 1st, A paying in £700, and B £850.

The transactions were as follows:

|  |  |  |  |
|---|---|---|---:|
|  |  |  | £ |
| Jan. | 8 | Purchased from F. Daponta Cargo of Timber valued at　..　　..　 | 665 |
|  |  | Accepted draft for same at one month　..　　..　　..　　.. | 665 |
| „ | 11 | Paid Freight and Expenses to Liverpool ..　　..　　..　　.. | 142 |
| Feb. | 20 | Sold T. Stephens & Sons Logs　..　　..　　..　　..　　.. | 180 |
| „ | 21 | Received Cash *less* 5%　　..　　..　　..　　..　　.. | 171 |
| „ | 26 | Bought for Cash from Lehman & Co. Cargo of Timber, net　　.. | 800 |
| Mar. | 17 | Paid Freight and Expenses to Hull　　..　　..　　..　　.. | 125 |
|  |  | Sold M. White & Co Deals, net..　　..　　..　　..　　.. | 300 |
|  |  | Received their acceptance at one month ..　　..　　..　　.. | 300 |
| April | 21 | Sold for Cash to M. Black & Co. Cargo purchased from Lehman & Co　..　　..　　..　　..　　..　　.. | 1,400 |
| „ | 30 | Stock balance of Daponta's Cargo valued at　　..　　..　　.. | 320 |

The venture was closed on April 30th, by B taking over the unsold stock at an agreed valuation of £320, less 10 per cent.

Adjust the accounts as between the partners at April 30th, allowing interest on capital (calculated to the nearest £) at 5 per cent. per annum, and show:

1. The Joint Venture Account.
2. The Partners' Capital Accounts.
3. The Joint Cash Account.
4. The Joint Bills Receivable and Bills Payable Accounts.

## JOINT VENTURE ACCOUNT

| | £ | | £ |
|---|---|---|---|
| Purchases: | | Sales: | |
| F. Daponta .. .. .. £665 | | T. Stephens & Sons .. .. £180 | |
| Lehman & Co .. .. .. 800 | | M. White & Co .. .. 300 | |
| | 1,465 | M. Black & Co .. .. 1,400 | |
| Freight and Expenses: | | | 1,880 |
| Liverpool .. .. .. 142 | | | |
| Hull .. .. .. .. 125 | | B Capital Account: value of stock taken over, | |
| | 267 | £320 *less* 10% .. .. .. .. | 288 |
| Discount .. .. .. .. .. | 9 | | |
| Interest on Capital: | | | |
| A .. .. .. .. 12 | | | |
| B .. .. .. .. 14 | | | |
| | 26 | | |
| Balance, being Profit: | | | |
| A two-thirds .. .. .. 267 | | | |
| B one-third .. .. .. 134 | | | |
| | 401 | | |
| | £2,168 | | £2,168 |

## A CAPITAL ACCOUNT

| | | £ | | | £ |
|---|---|---|---|---|---|
| April 30 | Cash .. .. .. .. | 979 | Jan. 1 | Cash .. .. | 700 |
| | | | April 30 | Interest on Capital .. .. | 12 |
| | | | ,, | Profit .. .. .. .. | 267 |
| | | £979 | | | £979 |

## B CAPITAL ACCOUNT

| | | £ | | | £ |
|---|---|---|---|---|---|
| April 30 | Stock taken over .. .. | 288 | Jan. 1 | Cash .. .. | 850 |
| ,, | Cash .. .. .. .. | 710 | April 30 | Interest on Capital .. .. | 14 |
| | | | ,, | Profit .. .. .. .. | 134 |
| | | £998 | | | £998 |

## CASH BOOK

| | | £ | | | £ |
|---|---|---|---|---|---|
| Jan. 1 | A Capital Account .. .. | 700 | Jan. 11 | Freight and Expenses .. .. | 142 |
| | B ,, ,, .. .. | 850 | Feb. 11 | Bills Payable .. .. | 665 |
| Feb. 21 | T. Stephens & Sons .. .. | 171 | ,, 26 | Cash Purchases: | |
| April 20 | Bills Receivable .. .. .. | 300 | | Lehman & Co. .. .. | 800 |
| ,, | Cash Sales: | | Mar. 17 | Freight and Expenses .. .. | 125 |
| | M. Black & Co. .. .. | 1,400 | April 30 | Balance c/d. .. .. | 1,689 |
| | | £3,421 | | | £3,421 |
| April 30 | Balance b/d. .. .. .. | 1,689 | April 30 | A .. .. .. .. | 979 |
| | | | | B .. .. .. .. | 710 |
| | | £1,689 | | | £1,689 |

## BILLS RECEIVABLE ACCOUNT

| | | £ | | | £ |
|---|---|---|---|---|---|
| Mar. 17 | M. White & Co. .. .. | 300 | April 20 | Cash .. .. .. .. | 300 |

## BILLS PAYABLE ACCOUNT

| | | £ | | | £ |
|---|---|---|---|---|---|
| Feb. 11 | Cash .. .. .. .. | 665 | Jan. 8 | F. Daponta .. .. .. | 665 |

In some cases, although a separate set of books is kept for the joint venture, it is not considered necessary to open a special banking account therefor. In these circumstances each party to the venture will disburse sums on behalf of the joint account from his own banking account, into which he will also pay cash received by him from time to time. In the books of the joint venture the Capital Accounts of the parties concerned will be credited with the sums paid out on behalf of the venture and debited with the cash collected.

### Illustration (2)

A and B are partners in a joint venture in produce, sharing profits in the ratio 2 : 1. A separate set of books is opened for the venture, but all cash transactions are dealt with by the partners through their own banking accounts.

The transactions of the venture were as under:

| | | | £ |
|---|---|---|---|
| Jan. | 1 | Purchased produce from J. Smith .. .. .. .. | 1,000 |
| | | Freight and expenses thereon paid by A .. .. .. .. | 120 |
| Feb. | 1 | J. Smith's account met by A subject to 10% cash discount .. .. | |
| „ | 13 | Sold to A. Brown produce for .. .. .. .. .. | 860 |
| „ | 15 | Sold to T. Jones produce for .. .. .. .. .. | 620 |
| March | 1 | Cash purchase by B for .. .. .. .. .. | 600 |
| April | 1 | Payment to B by A. Brown in settlement of his account .. .. | |
| May | 1 | Payment to A by T. Jones in settlement of his account .. .. | |
| June | 1 | Sundry expenses paid by A .. .. .. .. .. | 61 |
| | | Balance of produce sold by A for £700 cash. | |

The accounts of the venture are to be made up to June 30th, on which date a settlement is effected between the parties. Interest is to be calculated to the nearest £ at 5 per cent. per annum.

### A CAPITAL ACCOUNT

| | | Mos. | Int. £ | £ | | | Mos. | Int. £ | £ |
|---|---|---|---|---|---|---|---|---|---|
| May 1 | Cash from T. Jones .. | 2 | 5 | 620 | Jan. 1 | Freight and Expenses | 6 | 3 | 120 |
| June 1 | Cash Sales .. | 1 | 3 | 700 | Feb. 1 | J. Smith .. .. | 5 | 19 | 900 |
| „ 30 | Balance of Interest to contra .. .. | | 14 | | June 1 | Sundry Expenses .. | 1 | | 61 |
| | | | | | „ 30 | Balance of Interest .. | | | 14 |
| | | | £22 | | | | | £22 | |
| | Cheque from B in settlement .. .. | | | 99 | | Profit .. .. | | | 324 |
| | | | | £1,419 | | | | | £1,419 |

### B CAPITAL ACCOUNT

| | | Mos. | Int. £ | £ | | | Mos. | Int. £ | £ |
|---|---|---|---|---|---|---|---|---|---|
| April 1 | Cash from A. Brown .. | 3 | 11 | 860 | Mar. 1 | Cash Purchase .. | 4 | 10 | 600 |
| June 30 | Balance of Interest .. | | | 1 | June 30 | Balance of Interest to contra .. .. | | | 1 |
| | | | £11 | | | | | £11 | |
| | | | | | | Profit .. .. | | | 162 |
| | | | | | | Cheque to A in settlement .. .. | | | 99 |
| | | | | £861 | | | | | £861 |

## JOINT VENTURE ACCOUNT

| | | | | | £ | | | | | | £ |
|---|---|---|---|---|---|---|---|---|---|---|---|
| Purchases: | | | | | | Sales: | | | | | |
| J. Smith | .. | .. | .. | £1,000 | | A. Brown | .. | .. | .. | £860 | |
| Cash | .. | .. | .. | 600 | | T. Jones | .. | .. | .. | 620 | |
| | | | | —— | 1,600 | Cash | .. | .. | .. | 700 | |
| Freight and Expenses | .. | .. | .. | | 120 | | | | | —— | 2,180 |
| Sundry Expenses | .. | .. | .. | | 61 | Discount | .. | .. | .. | .. | 100 |
| Interest: A | .. | .. | .. | | 14 | Interest: B | .. | .. | .. | .. | 1 |
| Profit: | | | | | | | | | | | |
| A two-thirds | .. | .. | .. | 324 | | | | | | | |
| B one-third | .. | .. | .. | 162 | | | | | | | |
| | | | | —— | 486 | | | | | | |
| | | | | | £2,281 | | | | | | £2,281 |

In their respective books A and B will keep accounts to record the payments made by them on behalf of the venture and the cash received therefrom. These accounts will appear as under:

### A's BOOKS
### JOINT VENTURE WITH B

| | | | | £ | | | | | | £ |
|---|---|---|---|---|---|---|---|---|---|---|
| Jan. 1 | Cash – Freight and Expenses | .. | | 120 | May 1 | Cash – T. Jones.. | .. | .. | | 620 |
| Feb. 1 | ,,    J. Smith | .. | | 900 | June 1 | Cash Sales | .. | .. | | 700 |
| June 1 | ,,    Sundry Expenses .. | | | 61 | ,,   30 | Cheque from B .. | | .. | | 99 |
| ,, 30 | Interest Account | .. | | 14 | | | | | | |
| | Profit and Loss Account – two-thirds | | | | | | | | | |
| |    of profit on venture | .. | | 324 | | | | | | |
| | | | | £1,419 | | | | | | £1,419 |

### B's BOOKS
### JOINT VENTURE WITH A

| | | | | £ | | | | | | £ |
|---|---|---|---|---|---|---|---|---|---|---|
| Mar. 1 | Cash Purchase | .. | .. | 600 | April 1 | Cash – A. Brown | .. | .. | | 860 |
| June 30 | Profit and Loss Account – one-third | | | | June 30 | Interest Account | .. | .. | | 1 |
| |    of profit on venture | .. | .. | 162 | | | | | | |
| | Cheque to A | .. | .. | 99 | | | | | | |
| | | | | £861 | | | | | | £861 |

### (b) Where no separate set of books is opened for the transactions of the joint venture

In such a case each party will record his own transactions on behalf of the joint venture in his own books, and no joint banking account will normally be opened. In order to ascertain the profit or loss, each party must render to the other a complete statement of all transactions entered into by him, and these must then be combined into a *memorandum* Joint Venture Account. This account, which does not appear in the books of either party, but is raised from material supplied by both, is in the nature of a Profit and Loss Account. As soon as the result is ascertained, each partner will debit or credit the account for the joint venture in his own books with his share of the result, and the balance of this account, if the venture has been completed, will then represent the amount due to or by the other party.

**Illustration (1)**

M and R were partners in an underwriting venture, sharing profits and losses M three-fifths and R two-fifths. They agree to guarantee the subscription at par of 100,000 shares of £1 each in a company, and to pay all expenses up to allotment, in consideration of a commission of 6 per cent. in cash and 10 per cent. in fully-paid shares of the company.

M provided cash for the following expenses: Registration Fees £620; Advertising £2,700; Printing and Prospectuses £270. R provided the cash for the remainder, viz. Rent of Offices £45; Petty Cash £20; Stamps £90; Law Costs £250. The whole of the commission was received by M.

The public having subscribed for only 70,000 shares, the underwriters had to take up 30,000, the cash being provided by and shares allotted to them in the proportions of – M three-fifths and R two-fifths.

In due course they sold all the shares except 5,000, including those received for commission, at an average price of 80p, less brokerage of 5p per share, the remaining 5,000 being taken over by M at 65p per share. The sales were effected as to 21,000 by M and 14,000 by R.

Prepare a Joint Venture Account, and the separate accounts of the partners in their own books, showing the final balance payable by the one to the other, the shares taken over by M being brought into account, and no interest being taken into consideration.

## M's BOOKS
### JOINT ACCOUNT WITH R

|  | Shares | £ |  | Shares | £ |
|---|---|---|---|---|---|
| Cash – Expenses .. .. .. |  | 3,590 | Cash – Commission .. .. |  | 6,000 |
| ,,   Shares taken up .. | 18,000 | 18,000 | ,,   Proceeds of Shares sold .. | 21,000 | 15,750 |
| Shares received as Commission .. | 10,000 | — | Own Investment Account – Shares |  |  |
| Profit and Loss Account: |  |  | taken over .. .. .. | 5,000 | 3,250 |
| three-fifths of £1,505 .. .. |  | 903 | Shares sold by R. .. .. | 2,000 | — |
| Balance due to R. c/d. .. .. |  | 2,507 |  |  |  |
|  | 28,000 | £25,000 |  | 28,000 | £25,000 |
|  |  |  | Balance due to R. b/d .. .. |  | 2,457 |

## R's BOOKS
### JOINT ACCOUNT WITH M

|  | Shares | £ |  | Shares | £ |
|---|---|---|---|---|---|
| Cash – Expenses .. .. .. |  | 405 | Cash – Proceeds of Shares sold .. | 14,000 | 10,500 |
| ,,   Shares taken up .. .. | 12,000 | 12,000 | Balance due from M. c/d .. | | 2,507 |
| Shares drawn from M. .. .. | 2,000 | — |  |  |  |
| Profit and Loss Account: |  |  |  |  |  |
| Two-fifths of £1,505 .. .. |  | 602 |  |  |  |
|  | 14,000 | £13,007 |  | 14,000 | £13,007 |
| Balance due from M. b/d .. .. |  | 2,507 |  |  |  |

## MEMORANDUM JOINT VENTURE ACCOUNT

|  |  | £ | £ |  | £ | £ |
|---|---|---|---|---|---|---|
| Expenses paid by M: |  |  |  | Cash – Underwriting Commission .. |  | 6,000 |
| Registration Fees .. .. | 620 |  |  |  |  |  |
| Advertising .. .. .. | 2,700 |  |  | Sale of 35,000 shares at £0·75 net: |  |  |
| Printing etc. .. .. .. | 270 |  |  |  |  |  |
|  |  | 3,590 |  | M .. .. .. .. | 15,750 |  |
| Expenses paid by R: |  |  |  | R .. .. .. .. | 10,500 |  |
| Rent .. .. .. .. | 45 |  |  |  |  | 26,250 |
| Petty Cash .. .. .. | 20 |  |  |  |  |  |
| Stamps .. .. .. .. | 90 |  |  | Shares taken over by M, 5,000 @ £0·65 .. |  | 3,250 |
| Law Costs .. .. .. | 250 |  |  |  |  |  |
|  |  | 405 |  |  |  |  |
| Cost of Shares taken up: |  |  |  |  |  |  |
| M .. .. .. .. | 18,000 |  |  |  |  |  |
| R .. .. .. .. | 12,000 |  |  |  |  |  |
|  |  | 30,000 |  |  |  |  |
| Balance, being Profit: |  |  |  |  |  |  |
| M three-fifths .. .. .. | 903 |  |  |  |  |  |
| R two-fifths .. .. .. | 602 |  |  |  |  |  |
|  |  | 1,505 |  |  |  |  |
|  |  | £35,500 |  |  |  | £35,500 |

*Notes to Illustration*

1. It is preferable to place no value on the shares received as commission until they are sold, when the proceeds are credited to the Joint Account. As these shares were received by M the receipt and sale thereof appear in the Joint Account in his books.

2. The shares allotted to M and R respectively are the property of the partnership, not of the individual partners; they represent the stock-in-trade of the venture, part of which is in the custody of M and part of R. Where it is neccessary for one partner to draw on stock held by the other for the purpose of effecting delivery of shares sold, this involves no payment of cash between the partners, but each partner must account to the venture for the proceeds of the sales effected by him. Thus, R must credit his Joint Account with the proceeds of the 14,000 shares sold by him, although delivery of 2,000 of these shares must be made out of the shares held by M.

3. The 5,000 shares taken over by M represent a purchase by him from the venture, the agreed price being credited to the Joint Account in his books as the proceeds of a sale by the venture, and debited to M's personal Investment Account.

An alternative method is for one (or each) of the partners to record the *whole* of the transactions in his own books, in which, in addition to the Joint Venture Account, a personal account for the other partner will be opened. The Joint Venture Account will be debited with all the payments made, and credited with all the sums received, by *both* partners, the cash book being credited with the payments made and debited with the receipts of the partner in whose books the transactions are being recorded, and the personal account of the other partner credited and debited respectively with the payments and receipts made by him. Any stock taken over by the partners will be credited to the Joint Venture Account, and debited, in the case of the first named partner, to his purchases or other appropriate account, and in the case of the other partner to his personal account.

The profit disclosed by the Joint Venture Account will be divided between the partners according to the agreement between them, the first-named partner's share being credited to his Profit and Loss Account or Capital Account, and the other partner's share to his personal account. A loss will be treated in the converse manner. The balance remaining on the personal account of the other partner will now represent the sum due to or from him to close the venture.

**Illustration (2)**

Bear and Bull agreed to deal in stocks and shares on joint account and to share any profits or losses equally.

The following transactions took place:

1. January 4th. Bear purchased 2,000 £1 shares in Washers Ltd at £1·75 per share, expenses amounting to £34.

2. January 10th. Bull purchased 1,000 £1 Ordinary Stock units in Assurances Ltd at £2·10 cum div., expenses amounting to £32.

3. March 30th. Bull purchased a further 500 £1 Ordinary Stock units in Assurances Ltd at £2 ex div., expenses amounting to £16.

4. April 15th. A dividend, less tax of £83, for the year ended the previous December 31st, on 1,500 Assurances Ltd £1 Ordinary Stock units, was received by Bull, who immediately paid to the broker the amount applicable to the seller, £28.

5. April 30th. A fully-paid allotment letter was received by Bear from Washers Ltd in respect of an issue in the proportion of one new £1 share, credited as fully-paid for every two shares held. These shares ranked for dividend *pari passu* with the old shares as from May 1st Bear sold the new shares for £1·15 each, less a brokerage of 5*p* per share.

6. April 30th. A dividend, less tax of £220, for the year ended the previous December 31st, was received by Bear from Washers Ltd.

7. June 25th. Bull purchased £250 (1,000 units of 25*p*) Ordinary Stock in Showers Ltd at 50*p* per unit, expenses amounting to £25.

8. July 31st. A capital distribution of 5*p* per unit was received by Bull on the Showers Ltd Ordinary Stock.

9. August 30th. Bear sold the shares in Washers Ltd at £1·25 per share, expenses amounting to £32.

On September 30th, it was agreed to terminate the venture, Bull taking over the Assurances Ltd stock at a valuation of £2·50 per £1 unit, and Bear the Showers Ltd stock at a valuation of 75*p* per 25*p* unit, the balance between them being settled by cash.

You are required to prepare:

(*a*) The Joint Venture Account, and

(*b*) Bear's Account,

as they would appear in Bull's books.

### JOINT VENTURE ACCOUNT

| Date | Particulars | £ | Date | Particulars | £ |
|---|---|---|---|---|---|
| Jan. 4 | Bear, purchase 2,000 £1 Shares in Washers Ltd at £1·75 a share plus expenses of £34 | 3,534 | Apr. 15 | Cash, Dividend less tax on 1,500 £1 Ordinary Stock units in Assurances Ltd | 83 |
| „ 10 | Cash, 1,000 £1 Ordinary Stock units in Assurances Ltd at £2·10 each plus expenses of £32 | 2,132 | „ 30 | Bear, sale of 1,000 Shares in Washers Ltd at £1·10 net | 1,100 |
| Mar. 30 | Cash, 500 £1 Ordinary Stock units in Assurances Ltd at £2 ex div. plus expenses of £16 | 1,016 | | Bear, dividend less tax on 2,000 £1 Shares in Washers Ltd | 220 |
| Apr. 15 | Cash, Dividend on 500 £1 Ordinary Stock units in Assurances Ltd paid to seller | 28 | July 31 | Cash, Capital distribution on Showers Ltd Stock | 50 |
| June 25 | Cash, 1,000 Stock units of 25*p* in Showers Ltd at 50*p* a unit plus expenses £25 | 525 | Aug. 30 | Bear, sale of 2,000 £1 Shares in Washers Ltd at £1·25 a Share less expenses £32 | 2,468 |
| Sept. 30 | Bear, half share of profit on venture £593 | | Sept. 30 | Investment Account, 1,500 £1 Ordinary Stock units in Assurances Ltd taken over at £2·50 each | 3,750 |
| | Profit and Loss Account, half share of profit on venture 593 | 1,186 | | Bear, 1,000 Stock units of 25*p* in Showers Ltd taken over at 75*p* each | 750 |
| | | £8,421 | | | £8,421 |

### BEAR's ACCOUNT

| Date | Particulars | £ | Date | Particulars | £ |
|---|---|---|---|---|---|
| Apr. 30 | Joint Venture Account, sale of 1,000 £1 Shares in Washers Ltd received as bonus shares at £1·10 net | 1,100 | Jan. 4 | Joint Venture Account, purchase of Shares in Washers Ltd | 3,534 |
| | Joint Venture Account, dividend less tax on 2,000 Shares in Washers Ltd | 220 | Sept. 30 | Joint Venture Account, half share of profit on Venture | 593 |
| Aug. 30 | Joint Venture Account, sale of 2,000 Shares in Washers Ltd at £1·25 less expenses £32 | 2,468 | | Cash | 411 |
| Sept. 30 | Joint Venture Account, Stock units in Showers Ltd taken over | 750 | | | |
| | | £4,538 | | | £4,538 |

*Note:* Since the £500 stock in Assurances Ltd was purchased on March 30th *ex div.* the dividend received thereon on April 15th belongs to the seller and must be paid over to him.

Where the venture is not completed at the time the accounts of one or both parties are normally closed, and it is desired to ascertain the profit or loss to date, the unsold stock must be valued and brought into account.

It is suggested that the basis of valuation should be similar to that adopted in the case of unsold stock on consignment, viz. cost plus a proportion of the expenses which have been incurred (reducible if necessary to the net realizable value). The proportions in which the parties provided the stock or bore expenses in connection therewith are, at this stage, irrelevant. As already stated, the stock is the property of the partnership, not of the individual partners, and for the purpose of an interim settlement of account, each party should carry forward in his Joint Account his proportion of the value of the stock in the ratio in which he shares profits. By carrying down the unsold stock in the profit-sharing ratio the profit or loss earned to date will automatically be divided between the partners in the correct proportions.

If an immediate settlement between the parties is not required it will be sufficient for each partner to balance his Joint Venture Account, bringing down the balance disclosed thereon and deferring settlement until the completion of the venture.

**Illustration (3)**

On January 1st A and B entered into a joint venture, agreeing to share profits and losses in the ratio of 3 : 2. A supplied goods to the value of £3,000 and incurred expenses amounting to £400. B supplied £1,000 in goods and paid £500 expenses. Their agent sold three-fourths of the goods for £5,500, and remitted the proceeds to B after deducting 5 per cent. commission on sales, on March 31st, on which date accounts were prepared, and an interim settlement was effected between A and B.

On June 30th the agent reported that he had sold the remainder of the goods for £2,000, and remitted the proceeds to B, less 5 per cent. commission. A financial settlement was then effected between the partners.

### A's BOOKS
### JOINT ACCOUNT WITH B

| | | | £ | | | £ |
|---|---|---|---|---|---|---|
| Jan. 1 | Goods.. | | 3,000 | Mar. 31 | Balance c/d. – proportion of unsold | |
| | Cash – Expenses | | 400 | | stock.. | 735 |
| Mar. 31 | Profit to date .. | | 930 | | Cash from B | 3,595 |
| | | | £4,330 | | | £4,330 |
| Apr. 1 | Balance b/d. | | 735 | | | |
| June 30 | Profit .. | | 405 | June 30 | Cash from B in settlement.. | 1,140 |
| | | | £1,140 | | | £1,140 |

### B's BOOKS
### JOINT ACCOUNT WITH A

| | | | £ | | | £ |
|---|---|---|---|---|---|---|
| Jan. 1 | Goods.. | | 1,000 | Mar. 31 | Agent – Sales | 5,500 |
| | Cash – Expenses | | 500 | | Balance c/d. – proportion of unsold | |
| Mar. 31 | Agent's Commission | | 275 | | stock.. | 490 |
| | Profit to date .. | | 620 | | | |
| | Cash to A | | 3,595 | | | |
| | | | £5,990 | | | £5,990 |
| June 30 | Balance b/d. | | 490 | June 30 | Agent – Sales | 2,000 |
| | Agent's Commission | | 100 | | | |
| | Profit .. | | 270 | | | |
| | Cash to A in settlement .. | | 1,140 | | | |
| | | | £2,000 | | | £2,000 |

## MEMORANDUM JOINT VENTURE ACCOUNT

| | | | £ | £ | | | | £ |
|---|---|---|---|---|---|---|---|---|
| Jan. 1 | Goods supplied, A | .. | 3,000 | £ | Mar. 31 | Sales  ..  ..  ..  .. | | 5,500 |
| | „  „  B | .. | 1,000 | | | Balance c/d. – stock unsold  .. | | 1,225 |
| | | | | 4,000 | | | | |
| | Expenses – A  .. | .. | 400 | | | | | |
| | „  B  .. | .. | 500 | | | | | |
| | | | | 900 | | | | |
| Mar. 31 | Agent's Commission | .. | | 275 | | | | |
| | Profit – A three-fifths | .. | 930 | | | | | |
| | „  – B two-fifths | .. | 620 | | | | | |
| | | | | 1,550 | | | | |
| | | | | £6,725 | | | | £6,725 |
| Apr. 1 | Balance – Stock b/d. | .. | | 1,225 | June 30 | Sales  ..  ..  ..  .. | | 2,000 |
| | Agent's Commission | .. | | 100 | | | | |
| | Profit – A three-fifths | .. | 405 | | | | | |
| | „  – B two-fifths | .. | 270 | | | | | |
| | | | | 675 | | | | |
| | | | | £2,000 | | | | £2,000 |

*Note:* The unsold stock at March 31st is valued as follows:

One-fourth of £4,000, cost of goods  ..    £1,000
One-fourth of £900, expenses      ..     225

£1,225 – apportioned A $\frac{3}{5}$ths  ..    £735
           B $\frac{2}{5}$ths  ..     490

£1,225

At the conclusion of the venture, A has received from B a total of £4,735, being the amount of his expenditure on the venture, £3,400, plus his share of the profit, £1,335. B has received back his expenditure of £1,500 plus his share of the profit £890 = £2,390, represented by:

Remittances received from Agent   ..     ..   £7,125
*Less* paid to A    ..     ..     ..     ..    4,735

£2,390

## CHAPTER VIII

# COMPANY ACCOUNTS

### PART I

*General legal considerations and accounting for Share Capital etc.*

### PART II

*Balance Sheet and Accounts – disclosure requirements.*

### PART III

*Interpretation and Accounting Ratios.*

### PART IV

*Amalgamations, Reconstructions and Reduction of Capital.*

N. B. Section References in this Chapter are to the *Companies Act 1948* except where otherwise indicated

## PART I

### § 1. The Distinctions between Partnerships and Limited Companies

Company Law is today embodied in the *Companies Acts 1948* and *1967*. Companies may be registered as limited companies with the liability of their members limited for the company's debts to the amount, on becoming members, they undertake to contribute towards the company's capital. Alternatively companies may be registered as unlimited companies with no restriction at all on the liability of their members for the company's debts.

Companies with limited liability may be limited either by guarantee or by shares. In companies limited by guarantee, each member undertakes to contribute a specified sum towards the liabilities of the company if it is wound-up. In a company limited by shares, the capital is divided into a number of shares, and the liability of each member is limited to the amount for the time being unpaid on the shares which he has agreed to take up.

The main distinctions between an unlimited partnership and unlimited company and a limited company are as follows:

| *Unlimited Partnerships* | *Unlimited Companies* | *Limited Companies* |
|---|---|---|
| 1. No SEPARATE LEGAL ENTITY apart from its members | SEPARATE LEGAL ENTITY which is not affected by changes in its membership. It may contract, sue, and be sued in its own name and capacity. | SEPARATE LEGAL ENTITY which is not affected by changes in its membership. It may contract, sue, and be sued in its own name and capacity. |

| *Unlimited Partnerships* | *Unlimited Companies* | *Limited Companies* |
|---|---|---|
| 2. LIABILITY of each member for debts of the firm is unlimited. | LIABILITY of each shareholder for debts of the firm is unlimited. | If the company is limited by shares LIABILITY of each shareholder is limited to the amount he has agreed to pay to the company for shares allotted. If his shares are fully paid he has no further liability. |
| 3. Numbers limited to twenty except for firms of solicitors, accountants, and stockbrokers and certain other professions approved by the Board of Trade on which no limit is placed. The maximum number of partners in a private banking concern is twenty. | Maximum membership is limited by the number of shares issued and authorized; minimum membership is two. | In a public company membership is limited by the number of shares issued and authorized but there cannot be less than seven members. In a private company maximum membership is fifty exclusive of past and present employees; minimum membership is two. |
| 4. If the maximum number of partners is exceeded the partnership is illegal; legal action for the enforcement of contracts or rights cannot be taken; partners can still be sued and their liability remains unchanged. | Winding-up petitions can be presented if the membership falls below two. | In public and private companies petitions for winding-up can be presented if membership falls below the minimum (seven for a public company, two for a private company); limited liability continues for six months after membership falls below the minimum, thereafter members are severally liable for all new debts contracted by the company. |
| 5. Every partner can normally take part in the *management* of the business; he can legally bind the firm by his action with the outside world within the scope of his real or apparent authority. | Rights of *management* are delegated to directors who alone can act on behalf of and bind the company. | Rights of *management* are delegated to directors who alone can act on behalf of and bind the company. |
| 6. Every partner is entitled to access to the firm's books and accounts. | The Rights of the members to have access to the books depends on the Articles with the exception of the books open to members for inspection by statute. Copy of accounts need not be filed with Registrar of Companies. | The Rights of the members to have access to the books depends on the Articles with the exception of the books open to members for inspection by statute. Copy of accounts must be filed with Registrar of Companies and is open to inspection by the public at Companies House. |

| Unlimited Partnerships | Unlimited Companies | Limited Companies |
|---|---|---|
| 7. The Rights of partners between themselves are governed by agreement which can be varied. | Powers are defined by the Memorandum of Association which can be altered within the limits provided by the *Companies Act 1948*. Powers and duties of directors are defined by the Articles of Association and can be varied by passing a special resolution of the company in general meeting. | Powers are defined by the Memorandum of Association which can be altered within the limits provided by the *Companies Act 1948*. Powers and duties of directors are defined by the Articles of Association and can be varied by passing a special resolution of the company in general meeting. |
| 8. A partnership is subject to the *Partnership Act 1890* which can be varied by mutual agreement as it affects the partners *inter se* (and where appropriate by the provisions of the *Limited Partnerships Act 1907* and the *Registration of Business Names Act 1916*). | An unlimited company is subject to the *Companies Acts 1948 and 1967* which cannot be varied. | A limited company is subject to the *Companies Acts 1948 and 1967* which cannot be varied. |
| 9. The capital is contributed by the partners by agreement; the amount need not be fixed; it is frequently increased by undrawn profits and reduced by losses and withdrawals. | The authorized capital is fixed by the Memorandum of Association; it can be increased by resolution of the company in general meeting; it cannot be reduced except by special resolution sanctioned by the Court. | The authorized capital is fixed by the Memorandum of Association; it can be increased by resolution of the company in general meeting; it cannot be reduced except by special resolution sanctioned by the Court. |
| 10. A share in a partnership cannot be transferred except by the consent of all partners. | Shares are transferable subject to restrictions imposed by the Articles of Association. | In public companies shares are freely transferable; in private companies shares are transferable subject to restrictions imposed by the Articles of Association. |
| 11. There is no statutory obligation to keep books of account. | Books of account are prescribed by the *Companies Act 1948*. | Books of account are prescribed by the *Companies Act 1948*. |
| 12. An audit is NOT compulsory. | Audit is compulsory. | Audit is compulsory. |
| 13. Profits may be withdrawn as and when ascertained; drawings may be made by mutual agreement for accruing profits. | Profits are distributed in the form of dividend calculated at a percentage or rate per share on the authority of a resolution passed by the company in general meeting, although the Articles may provide for interim dividends to be declared by the directors. | Profits are distributed in the form of dividend calculated at a percentage or rate per share on the authority of a resolution passed by the company in general meeting, although the Articles may provide for interim dividends to be declared by the directors. |

| Unlimited Partnerships | Unlimited Companies | Limited Companies |
|---|---|---|
| 14. Death duties are payable on a partner's share based on assets including goodwill. | Death duties are calculated on asset values in accordance with Section 55, *Finance Act 1940*, as amended. | Death duties are payable on the market value of shares held by deceased, but sometimes on asset values calculated in accordance with Section 55, *Finance Act 1940*, as amended. |
| 15. Profits are subject to Schedule 'D' income tax. | Profits are subject to corporation tax. | Profits are subject to corporation tax. |

A company, as compared with a partnership, offers the following additional advantages:

1. The share of a deceased member is more readily ascertainable and transferable. Moreover, the actual carrying on of the business is not liable to be so disturbed by the death of a member as it is in a partnership. Whereas, subject to any agreement to the contrary, the death of a partner dissolves the firm, the death of a member does not affect the legal existence of a company.

2. The control of a company can be secured by one or more members holding the shares (or a majority of them) which carry the voting rights. Additional capital can be obtained by the issue of further shares, e.g. preference shares, without the disturbance of the controlling interest.

3. Family provision is made easy; e.g. a parent can transfer shares to children, whilst retaining control, whereas if he took them into partnership, they would have all the rights and liabilities of partners.

4. In limited companies a larger capitalization of the business is possible, since it is much easier, as a rule, to raise large or small units of capital where the holders will have the protection of limited liability.

5. An interest in the business can be given to employees in the form of shares, without loss of control.

6. By transferring a business to a company the proprietor is able to realize the goodwill, either for a cash consideration or for shares, without relinquishing control of the business.

On the other hand, companies are more subject to statutory and constitutional restrictions, and some publicity is given to their affairs; heavy stamp duties and fees are payable upon incorporation; companies are liable to corporation tax and dividends from companies are unearned income for taxation purposes (this disadvantage can be overcome partially by paying profits out to members in the form of directors' emoluments). Occasionally the credit of a limited company will not be so favourably regarded by creditors as was that of the former partnership because of the limited liability of the shareholders.

To form a company limited by shares, the following documents must be lodged with the Registrar of Companies, and the requisite fees and stamp duties paid:

1. The Memorandum of Association, which must be stamped with a 50*p* stamp, and with a fee stamp on the following graduated scale:

|  | £ |
|---|---|
| Where the authorized share capital does not exceed £2,000    .. | 20 |
| For every further £1,000 or part thereof up to £5,000    ..    .. | 1 |
| For every further £1,000 or part thereof up to £100,000    ..    .. | 0·25 |
| For every further £1,000 or part thereof    ..    ..    .. | 0·05 |

The maximum fee is £68.

2. The Articles of Association, which must be stamped with a 50*p* stamp.

3. A Statement of Nominal Capital giving details of the authorized capital with which the company is to be registered, as stated in the Memorandum of Association; it must be stamped with a capital duty of 50*p* per £100 calculated on the authorized amount.

4. A Declaration of Compliance signed by a solicitor engaged in the formation of the company or by a person named in the Articles as a director or secretary of the company, that all the statutory requirements of the *Companies Act 1948* have been complied with.

The above documents must be filed by all companies, but if the company is to be a public company, there must also be filed—

5. A list of the persons who have consented to act as directors;

6. Their written consent to act; and

7. An undertaking in writing by each person to take up and pay for the minimum number of shares (if any) stated in the Articles as the qualification of a director.

The undertaking to take up the qualification shares needs a 5*p* contract stamp for each director if his nominal qualification exceeds £5.

Notice of the situation of the company's registered office (and of any change) must be given within fourteen days of incorporation (or of the change); usually this notice is filed with the above documents.

The fees to be paid to the Registrar of Companies are contained in Schedule 3 of the *Companies Act 1967*, and came into operation on October 27th, 1967.

### § 2(a). Private Companies

A PRIVATE COMPANY is defined by Section 28, *Companies Act 1948*, as a company which *by its Articles:*

(*a*) restricts the right to transfer its shares; and

(*b*) limits the number of its members to fifty (joint holders being treated as one person), not including persons who are in the employment of the company, and persons who, having been formerly in the employment of the company were, while in such employment, and have continued after the determination of such employment, to be members of the company; and

(*c*) prohibits any invitation to the public to subscribe for any shares or debentures of the company.

Every company which does not contain these clauses in its Articles is a PUBLIC COMPANY.

If a company fails to comply with any of the provisions of its Articles which constitute it a private company, the company will cease to be entitled to the privileges and exemptions conferred on private companies, but the Court may give relief if the default is accidental or on other reasonable cause (s. 29).

If a private company alters its Articles so that they no longer include the above provisions, the company forthwith ceases to be a private company and must, within fourteen days, deliver to the Registrar of Companies a prospectus, or a statement in lieu of prospectus, in the prescribed form (s. 30).

The privileges of a private company are:

1. It may have a minimum of two members (s. 1).

2. It need not issue a prospectus or statement in lieu of prospectus (s. 48).

3. It can commence business immediately on incorporation (s. 109).

4. The minimum number of directors is one instead of two (s. 176).

5. There are no restrictions on the appointment of directors by the Articles (s. 181).

6. The age limit of seventy for directors does not apply (s. 185).

7. A separate resolution is not required for the appointment of each director individually (s. 183).

8. Neither a statutory meeting nor a statutory report is required (s. 130).

9. Proxy holders may speak at meetings.

A certificate signed by a director and the secretary must be given on the annual return of a private company to the effect that no invitation has been issued to the public to subscribe for any shares or debentures, and where it appears from the list of members that the number of members exceeds fifty, a further certificate must be given stating that the excess comprises employees or ex-employees who were members when employed by the company and have continued to be members since ceasing to be so employed (s. 128).

One of the privileges which was accorded to every private company prior to July 1st, 1948, was exemption from the obligation to annex to its Annual Return (which must be filed with the Registrar of Companies) a certified copy of its accounts including every document required by law to be annexed thereto. Between July 1st, 1948, and the introduction of the *Companies Act 1967* it was possible for a private company which satisfied the conditions of s. 129, *Companies Act 1948*, to be termed an Exempt Private Company. As from July 1st, 1948, the exemption to file accounts only applied to Exempt Private Companies. The status of an 'exempt private company' was abolished by s. 2 of the *Companies Act 1967* so that every company except an unlimited company must forward copies of its accounts, its auditors' report and its directors' report to the Registrar of Companies. The first accounts to be filed by companies that were previously 'exempt private companies' were those accompanying annual returns filed on or after January 27th, 1968.

### § 2(b). Unlimited Companies

In an unlimited company the liability of the members for the debts of the company is unlimited.

The Memorandum of Association must conform with Table E of the First Schedule of the *Companies Act 1948* and show:

1. The name of the company excluding the word 'limited'.
2. The situation of the registered office.
3. The objects of the company.

The Articles of Association must state the number of members and the amount of share capital if any; any increase in membership must be notified to the Registrar of Companies within fifteen days of such increase taking place.

The privileges of an unlimited company are:

1. No *ad valorem* stamp duty is payable on its capital.
2. It can return capital to its members without obtaining the permission of the Court.
3. It only need give seven days notice to call a meeting.
4. It can purchase its own shares (*re Borough Commercial Building Society*).
5. It can make loans to its directors.
6. It need not file with its annual return a copy of the balance sheet, the documents required to be annexed thereto, the auditors' report, and the directors' report provided that during the period to which the return relates:

(*a*) It has not to its knowledge been the subsidiary of a limited company.

(*b*) There have not to its knowledge been shares held by, or powers exercisable by, two or more limited companies which, had they been held or exercisable by one of them, would have made the company its subsidiary, or

(*c*) It has not been the holding company of a limited company, or

(*d*) It has not been carrying on business under the *Trading Stamps Act 1964*.

### § 3. The Memorandum and Articles of Association

(*a*) The *Memorandum of Association* is the document forming the constitution of a company, and defining its objects and powers.

The Memorandum of Association of a company limited by shares contains five clauses:

1. The name of the company, followed by the word 'limited', except in an unlimited company or where it is formed for promoting commerce, art, science, religion, charity or other useful object and the licence of the Board of Trade has been obtained (s. 19, *Companies Act 1948*).

2. The domicile of the company, i.e. whether its registered office is to be situated in England (which includes Wales) or Scotland.

3. The objects of the company.

4. In limited companies a declaration that the liability of the members is limited.

5. The amount of capital, and the shares into which it is divided.

The Memorandum must be signed by not less than seven persons, or not less than two in a private company, agreeing to take up not less than one share each.

(b) The *Articles of Association* contain the regulations for running the company, and define the rights of the members and the powers and duties of the directors. The principal clauses deal with:

1. A declaration on how far the provisions of Table A are expressly excluded; Table A applies when not excluded or modified by the Articles.

Table A, *Companies Act 1948*, is a model set of Articles which automatically applies to any company, not having Articles of its own, registered after June 30th, 1948; any company working under an earlier Table A can adopt the present Table A by special resolution.

Many companies register special Articles excluding Table A entirely, but most clauses of Table A, modified where expedient, are reproduced.

2. The regulations for the issue of capital and variation of rights of members, lien on shares, payment of underwriting commission etc.

3. The making of calls on shares.

4. The transfer and transmission of shares.

5. The forfeiture and surrender of shares; conversion of shares into stock, and alteration of capital.

6. The holding, notice of, and procedure at general meetings.

7. The voting rights of members; polls and proxies.

8. The directors – their number, remuneration, qualification, rotation, disqualification and removal.

9. The appointment and powers of managing directors.

10. The proceedings and powers and duties of the board of directors.

11. The borrowing powers of the company.

12. The appointment, remuneration, removal etc., of the secretary.

13. The use of the company's seal.

14. Accounts and audit.

15. Dividends and reserves.

16. The capitalization of profits.

17. Notices to members.

18. The rights of members *inter se*.

## § 4. The Statutory Books and Returns

### (a) *The Register of Members*

Under Section 110 every company must keep a register of its members, and enter therein the following particulars:

(i) The names and addresses of the members, and in a company having a share capital, a statement of the shares held by each member, distinguishing each share by its number if the share has a number, and of the amount paid or agreed to be considered as paid on the shares of each member.

(ii) The date at which each person was entered in the register as a member.

(iii) The date at which any person ceased to be a member.

Where the company has converted any of its shares into stock and given notice of the conversion to the Registrar of Companies, the register must show the amount of stock held by each member instead of the amount of shares and the particulars relating to shares specified above.

The register of members must be kept at the registered office of the company, unless the work of making it up is done at another office of the company or of the person making it up, when it can be kept there, provided that other office is not outside the country of the company's domicile. If the register is not kept at the registered office at all times after July 1st, 1948, the company must file with the Registrar of Companies the address where it is kept and any change in that address (s. 110).

When the company has more than fifty members, and the register does not itself constitute an index, an index must be kept at the same place as the register for facilitating ready reference. Any alteration in the register must be reflected in the index (where necessary) within fourteen days. A loose leaf register kept in alphabetical order therefore appears desirable.

The register and index must be open to the inspection of members of the company without charge, and of other persons at a fee not exceeding 5p, for at least two hours on each business day. Copies of any part of the register can be required by any person on payment (s. 113 as amended by s. 52 (2), *Companies Act 1967*). The company has power on giving notice by newspaper advertisement (s. 115) to close the register for an aggregate of thirty days in each year, thus permitting and facilitating the preparation of the annual return and the dividend warrants to shareholders.

### (b) *The Register of Charges*

Under Section 104 every limited company must keep at its registered office a register of charges, and enter therein all charges specifically affecting property of the company, and all floating charges on the undertaking or any property of the company, giving a short description of the property charged, the amount of the charge, and, except in the case of securities to bearer, the names of the persons entitled thereto.

This book and a copy of every instrument creating any charge must be open for inspection by any creditor or member of the company without charge, and by any other person on payment of a fee not exceeding 5p, for at least two hours on each business day (s. 105).

### (c) *Register of Debenture Holders*

Although a company is under no statutory obligation to keep a separate register of debenture holders, if such a register is kept at an address other than its registered office, notice of the address at which it is kept must be given to the Registrar of Companies, as for the share register. Notice must also be given of the situation of duplicate registers in England (by a Scottish company) or Scotland (by an English company) unless such register has always been kept at the same place (s. 86). Registers of debenture holders must be open to inspection in the same way as registers of members (s. 87), and copies of the register can be required by any person on payment (s. 87 as amended by s. 52 (1), *Companies Act 1967*).

### (d) Annual Return

Every company having a share capital must at least once in every year make a return containing the names and addresses of all persons who, on the fourteenth day after the company's annual general meeting for the year, are members of the company, and of persons who have ceased to be members since the date of the last return, or, in the first return, of the incorporation of the company (s. 124).

The return must state the number of shares held by each of the existing members at the date of the return, specifying shares transferred since the date of the last return (or in the first return, since the incorporation of the company), by persons who are still members and by persons who have ceased to be members respectively, and the dates of registration of the transfers; and if the names therein are not arranged in alphabetical order, must have annexed to it an index sufficient to enable the name of any person in the list to be readily found.

Where, however, the company has converted any of its shares into stock and given notice of the conversion to the Registrar of Companies, the return must state the amount of stock held by each of the existing members instead of the amount of shares and the particulars relating to shares.

In any year, if the return for either of the two immediately preceding years has given the full particulars mentioned above, there need only be included in the return particulars of persons ceasing to be or becoming members since the date of the last return, and to shares transferred or changes in stock held since that date, i.e. a full return of members who do not change their holdings need only be made every third year.

The return must state the address of the registered office of the company and if the register of members or of debenture holders is not kept there, the address at which it is kept, and must contain a summary distinguishing between shares issued for cash and shares issued as fully or partly paid up otherwise than in cash, and specifying the following particulars:

(a) The amount of the share capital of the company, and the number of the shares into which it is divided.

(b) The number of shares taken up from the commencement of the company up to the date of the return.

(c) The amount called up on each share.

(d) The total amount of calls received.

(e) The total amount of calls unpaid.

(*f*) The total amount of the sums, if any, paid by way of commission on any shares or debentures.

(*g*) The discount allowed on the issue of any shares issued at a discount, or of so much of that discount as has not been written off at the date on which the return is made.

(*h*) The total amount of the sums, if any, allowed by way of discount on any debentures, since the date of the last return.

(*i*) The total number of shares forfeited.

(*j*) The total amount of shares for which share warrants are outstanding at the date of the return, and of share warrants issued and surrendered respectively since the date of the last return, and the number of shares comprised in each share warrant.

(*k*) The total amount of the indebtedness of the company for all mortgages and charges which are required (or, in a company registered in Scotland, which, if the company had been registered in England, would be required) to be registered with the Registrar of Companies under the Act, or which would have been required so to be registered if created after July 1st, 1908.

(*l*) Particulars of the persons who at the date of the return are the directors of the company, and any person who at that date is the secretary of the company as are by the Act required to be contained in the register of directors and secretaries of a company.

The return must be in the form set out in the Sixth Schedule to the Act, or as near thereto as circumstances admit.

In a company keeping a dominion register, the particulars of the entries in that register must, so far as they relate to matters which are required to be stated in the return, be included in the return made next after copies of those entries are received at the registered office of the company, and the full particulars (including existing members) must be included.

A company need not make an annual return in the year of its incorporation, and if no annual general meeting is held in the following year (because the first general meeting, which must be held within eighteen months of incorporation, does not fall in that year (s. 131)), it need not file an annual return in that year.

The copy to be filed with the Registrar must be signed by a director and the secretary and delivered within forty-two days after the annual general meeting for the year. Should no meeting be held in any calendar year, the Registrar will require the return to be made up to December 31st.

Except for assurance companies which have complied with the provisions of Section 8 of the *Insurance Companies Act 1958* (i.e. which have submitted a copy of their accounts to the Registrar when depositing copies with the Board of Trade), a copy (certified by a director and the secretary to be a true copy) of every BALANCE SHEET laid before a limited company in general meeting during the period to which the return relates, together with a copy of the AUDITOR'S REPORT, and including every document (e.g. directors' report, Profit and Loss Account and the Group Accounts of a holding company) required by law to be annexed to the Balance Sheet, must be annexed to the annual return. If the Balance Sheet does not comply with statutory requirements as to its form etc. it must be amended accordingly (s. 127). The Act states that a 'written' copy of such Balance Sheet must be filed, but the Registrar will accept a printed or type-written copy if properly certified by a director, or the manager or secretary of the company.

(As to the certificates required from a private company, see § 2(a) above.)

An unlimited company is not required to file with its annual return a copy of its Balance Sheet or the documents required to be annexed thereto, the auditor's report and the directors' report provided that during the period to which the return relates:

1. it has not, to its knowledge, been the subsidiary of a limited company; or

2. there have not to its knowledge been shares held by or powers exercisable by two or more limited companies which, had they been exercisable by one of them, would have made the company its subsidiary; or

3. it has not been the holding company of a limited company; or

4. it has not been carrying on business under the *Trading Stamps Act 1964.*

A fee of £3 is payable for filing the Annual Return with the Registrar.

### (e) Minute Books

Every company must cause minutes of all proceedings of general meetings, all proceedings at meetings of its directors and, where there are managers, all proceedings at meetings of its managers, to be entered in books kept for that purpose.

Any such minute, if purporting to be signed by the chairman of the meeting at which the proceedings were held, or by the chairman of the next succeeding meeting, is evidence of the proceedings.

Where minutes have been kept, until the contrary is proved, the meeting is deemed to have been duly held and convened, and all proceedings to have been duly held, and all appointments of directors, managers or liquidators are deemed to be valid (s. 145).

The minute books containing records of the proceedings at general meetings of the company must be kept at the registered office and for at least two hours on each business day be open to the inspection of any member without charge (copies can be obtained on payment (s. 146)).

There is no provision for inspection by members of the minutes of meetings of directors: such inspection would not normally be desirable.

Any register, index, minute book or book of account may be kept either by making entries in bound books or by recording their contents in any other manner. Adequate measures must be taken for preventing and detecting falsification (s. 436).

### (f) Register of Directors and Secretaries

Every company must keep at its registered office a register of its directors and secretaries containing the following particulars:

(*a*) Every director's present christian name and surname, any former christian name and surname, his usual residential address, his nationality, his business occupation, if any, particulars of any other directorships held by him, and, in a company that is not a private company (or if a private company, is a subsidiary of a company incorporated in the United Kingdom which is neither a private company, nor registered in Northern Ireland with provisions which, if it were registered in Great Britain would make it a private company), the date of his birth; and

(*b*) If a corporation, its corporate name and registered or principal office.

The register need not contain particulars of directorships held in companies of which the company is a wholly-owned subsidiary, or which are the wholly-owned subsidiaries either of the company or of another company of which it is a wholly-owned subsidiary. For this purpose the expression 'company' includes any body corporate incorporated in Great Britain: a body corporate is a wholly-owned subsidiary of another if it has no members except that other and its wholly-owned subsidiaries and its or their nominee(s) (s. 200).

For the secretary or secretaries, the register must contain:

(*a*) if an individual, his present christian name and surname, any former christian name and surname and his usual residential address, and

(*b*) if a corporation or Scottish firm, its corporate or firm name and registered or principal office.

    If all partners in a firm are joint secretaries, the name and principal office of the firm may be stated instead of particulars of each partner.

The company must, within a period of fourteen days from the appointment of the first directors of the company, send to the Registrar of Companies a return in the prescribed form containing the particulars specified in the said register, and within fourteen days from the happening thereof a notification in the prescribed form of any change in its directors or secretary or in any of the particulars contained in the register (s. 200).

The register is to be open to the inspection of any member of the company without charge, and of any other person at a charge not exceeding 5*p*, for at least two hours on each business day.

### (*g*) (*i*) *Register of Directors' Shareholdings, Debenture holdings and Options*

Every company must keep an indexed register showing for itself, its subsidiaries, its holding company or subsidiary of its holding company:

(i) Every director's (including separately those of any spouse and infant children) interest in shares and debentures stating the class of share or debenture and the date acquired and disposed of.

(ii) Details of share and debenture options, showing date of grant, period during which exercisable, extent exercised and amounts payable not only for the shares and debentures, but also for the options.

Directors must notify the company in writing of acquisitions and disposals of shares and debentures. It is illegal for directors (or their spouses or infant children) to buy options in shares and debentures quoted on a recognized stock exchange. Directors may, however, exercise 'rights' given them in a 'rights' issue.

The register of directors' shareholdings shall be kept with the company's register of members if this is kept at the Registered Office. If, however, the register of members is kept elsewhere, the register of directors' shareholdings may be kept either at the Registered Office or at the same place as the register of members. Any member, free of charge, and any other person, on payment of 5p, may inspect the register of directors' shareholdings during business hours, and this must be indexed and written up in chronological order. At the annual general meeting the register must be available for inspection.

### (g) (ii)  Register of Directors' Service Contracts

Every company shall keep either at its registered office, principal place of business, or with its register of members if that is not kept at its registered office, (unless:

(i) The directors' employment is wholly or mainly outside the United Kingdom; or

(ii) The contract has less than twelve months to run; or

(iii) The contract can be terminated by the company within twelve months without payment of compensation).

(a) A copy of every written director's service agreement, and variations thereof; and

(b) A written memorandum of every director's service agreement which is not in writing.

Such agreements and memoranda must be open to inspection by members of the company during normal business hours free of charge, but are not available for inspection by other persons.

### (g) (iii)  Register of Large Shareholdings

Every company quoted on the stock exchange must keep an indexed register of every person who is interested in 10 per cent. or more of the nominal value of shares of any class of capital which carries voting rights at a general meeting.

The register must disclose:

(a) the amount of shares and class in which the holders are interested;

(b) any change in the number of shares in which they are interested.

Persons acquiring and disposing of such holdings must notify the company in writing.

The register is open to inspection by any person.

### (h)  The Directors' Report for the Statutory Meeting

The STATUTORY MEETING of a PUBLIC COMPANY is a general meeting of the members which must be held not less than one month nor more than three months after the company is entitled to commence business. A STATU-

TORY REPORT must be prepared, to be laid before the meeting, and this must, at least fourteen days before the date fixed for the holding of the meeting, be forwarded to every member of the company. If the statutory report is forwarded later than fourteen days before the meeting, it is nevertheless valid if all the members entitled to attend and vote at the meeting so agree. A copy must be filed with the Registrar of Companies forthwith, after being so forwarded.

The report, which must be certified by not less than two directors, must show:

(a) the total number of shares allotted, distinguishing shares allotted as fully or partly paid up otherwise than in cash, and stating on shares partly paid up the extent to which they are so paid up, and in either case the consideration for which they have been allotted;

(b) the total amount of cash received by the company on the shares allotted, distinguished as aforesaid;

(c) an abstract of the receipts and payments of the company and, up to a date within seven days of the date of the report, showing under distinctive headings the receipts of the company from shares and debentures and other sources, the payments made thereout, and particulars concerning the balance remaining in hand, and an account or estimate of the preliminary expenses of the company;

(d) the names, addresses and descriptions of the directors, auditors (if any), managers (if any), and secretary of the company; and

(e) the particulars of any contract, the modification of which is to be submitted to the meeting for its approval, together with particulars of the modification, or proposed modification.

The statutory report, so far as it relates to the shares allotted by the company, and to the cash received on such shares, and to the receipts and payments of the company on capital account, must be certified as correct by the auditors (if any) of the company (s. 130).

The provisions relating to the statutory meeting and the statutory report do not apply to private companies, and since it is nowadays customary for most companies to be formed in the first place as private companies, and later to be converted into public companies, these provisions have little practical application.

### (i) The Books of Account

The provisions of the Act on accounting are dealt with below in § 15.

### § 5. The Various Classes of Share Capital

A share has been defined as 'the interest of a shareholder in the company measured by a sum of money for the purpose of liability in a limited company in the first place, and of interest in the second, but also consisting of a series of mutual covenants entered into by all the shareholders, *inter se*'.

The share capital of a company may be divided into different classes of shares, of which the following are the most usual:

### (a) Preference Shares

Preference shares entitle the holders to a fixed rate of dividend before any dividend is paid on other classes of shares. They may also carry the right in the Articles to repayment of capital, on a winding-up, in priority to other types of shares.

Preference shares may be either *cumulative* or *non-cumulative*. Non-cumulative preference shares only carry a right to a fixed dividend out of the profits of any year, and if there are insufficient profits in that year to pay the full dividend they have no right to have the arrears made up out of future profits. Preference shares may or may not have a right, in a liquidation, to repayment of capital in priority to other classes of shares.

Cumulative preference shares entitle the holders to a fixed rate of dividend in the same way as non-cumulative preference shares, but with the additional right to have any arrears of dividend paid out of future profits before any dividends are paid on other classes of shares.

The rights of preference shareholders are governed by the Memorandum and Articles of Association, and there are varieties other than those enumerated above; for example, a company may have PARTICIPATING PREFERENCE SHARES, which carry a right, in addition to a fixed dividend, to further participation in profits after a dividend of a specified rate has been paid on the ordinary shares. In the absence of express or implied provision in the Articles to the contrary, preference shares are *cumulative* as to dividend, but are only entitled to rank *pari passu* with other classes of shares in repayment of capital on liquidation.

If authorized by its Articles a company may issue REDEEMABLE PREFERENCE SHARES, as to which see below, § 6 (*l*).

Subject to modification by the Memorandum and Articles of Association every share in a company ranks equally: a preference to dividend does not of itself exclude other rights, e.g. to share in surplus assets on a winding-up. It has, however, been held that where the Articles of a company set out the rights attached to a class of shares to participate in profits while the company is a going concern or to share in the property of the company in liquidation, *prima facie* the rights so set out are exhaustive. The burden of proof that preference shareholders have any further rights is on them and depends upon a true construction of the Articles (*Re Isle of Thanet Electricity Supply Co Ltd*).

### (b) Ordinary Shares

Ordinary shares entitle the holders to the divisible profits remaining after prior interests (if any) have been satisfied. They may be divided into PREFERRED and DEFERRED ordinary shares, the preferred carrying a preferential right to a fixed rate of dividend, and the deferred being entitled to the whole, or a proportion, of the surplus profits after provision has been made for dividends on all classes of shares having prior rights. Ordinary shares are commonly referred to as 'equities'.

### (c) Founders, Deferred or Management Shares

These shares are usually limited in number and are sometimes issued fully paid to the vendors or managers of the business or their nominees, in consideration either of part of the purchase price or of services rendered. Generally, they only rank for dividend after other classes of shares have received specified rates of dividend, when they may be entitled to the whole or a portion of the surplus profits and this may make them extremely valuable.

### (d) Voting Rights of Shareholders

The voting rights attaching to shares are governed by the Articles of the company. Under Table A each share carries one vote, but it is quite common for the Articles to concentrate the voting power in the hands of the ordinary or 'equity' shares, and to confer no voting rights on the preference shareholders except when the preference dividend is in arrear. Placing the control of the company in the hands of the ordinary shareholders is reasonable, since the ordinary shareholders carry the major part of the risk.

Some public companies have adopted the practice of issuing two classes of ordinary shares, only one of which (comprising as a rule the minority of the shares) carries voting rights. Only the non-voting shares (or 'A' or 'B' ordinary shares, as they are usually designated) are made available to the public. Strong objection has been taken to the issue of voteless equity shares, because as a matter of public policy ownership of interests in companies should carry with it some responsibility for their control, and that it is wrong for the holders of a minority of the equity shares to have voting control to the exclusion of shares representing a major proportion of the equity. It is also objected that the holders of voteless shares have no redress short of expensive and difficult Court proceedings in the event of misconduct by directors appointed by the voting minority. A further objection is that the descriptions applied to voteless as distinct from voting shares may not be sufficiently clear to ensure that a purchaser knows what he is buying, or that if he knows he is buying voteless shares he may not fully understand the implications.

### (e) The distinction between Stock and Shares

A share in a company is an individual unit of capital and is indivisible. A holding must consist of a number of complete shares, and although there may be two or more joint holders of a share, no fraction of a share can be held or transferred.

Stock consists of capital consolidated into bulk, which can be made divisible in any monetary fractions. It has been aptly termed 'a bundle of shares'. It is customary, where stock has been issued, for the articles of the company to provide for holdings in multiples of one pound sterling only, so as to minimize clerical labour in effecting transfers, calculating dividends etc.

The chief differences between stock and shares are:

(a) Stock must be fully paid up, whereas shares need not be.

(b) Stock may be issued or transferred in fractional parts (subject to provisions in the Articles). A share cannot be divided, but can only be transferred as a complete unit.

(*c*) Each share must be distinguished by a separate number until all the shares of the class in question are fully paid and rank *pari passu* for all purposes (s. 74); stock need possess no distinguishing numbers.

A company cannot issue stock in the first instance; if it wishes to issue stock it must first issue shares, and then convert them into stock when they are fully paid. Many large concerns whose shares are actively dealt in on the Stock Exchange have converted their shares into stock in order to economize in clerical labour when shares are transferred. The saving in labour will readily be seen when it is realized that a sale of, say, 10,000 shares having distinctive numbers, might involve the entry of numbers which, owing to their not running consecutively, would fill the back of the share certificate. These numbers would have to be written on the transfer in the old member's account, in the new member's account, and on the new share certificate etc., whereas in the case of stock only the monetary value would have to be shown.

### (*f*) Shares of no Par Value

As has been seen, the Memorandum of Association of a company must state the amount of the share capital with which the company is registered and the number of shares into which such capital is divided. Each share is of a fixed amount, which is called the 'nominal' or 'par' value, and it has always been a fundamental principle of company law in this country that every share must have a nominal value. In the United States of America and other countries, shares of 'no par value' have been common for many years.

## § 6. The Application and Allotment of Shares

### (*a*) Application Letters

When the directors of a public company decide to issue shares, forms of *application letters* are sent out with a *prospectus* to those persons who are considered most likely to subscribe, or the form may be printed at the foot of the advertisements of the prospectus.

Usually subscribers are required to remit the amount payable on application (which, under the *Companies Act 1948*, must not be less than 5 per cent. of the nominal value of the shares) direct to the company's bankers. (Where permission to deal in the securities on the London Stock Exchange is applied for, the council of the Stock Exchange require not less than 25 per cent. of the nominal value to be paid on application.)

### (*b*) Application and Allotment Sheets

A separate banking account should be opened for each issue; the company will obtain from the bank the statement of receipts and the application letters, and these will be entered up on *application and allotment sheets*, a form of which is given below.

Each application letter will be numbered in consecutive order, as received, and the name, address and description of the applicant, the number of shares applied for, and the amount paid on application, will be entered on the appli-

[continued on page 215

**Illustration**

## APPLICATION AND ALLOTMENT SHEET

| Number of Application | Date Received | NAME | ADDRESS | Description | No. of Shares applied for | ALLOTMENT | | | | | Amount paid on application | AMOUNT DUE AND PAID ON ALLOTMENT | | | | Calls paid in advance | Amount returnable (if any) | Share Ledger Folio | No. of Share Certificate | REMARKS |
|---|---|---|---|---|---|---|---|---|---|---|---|---|---|---|---|---|---|---|---|---|
| | | | | | | Date | No. of Shares allotted | Distinctive No. of Shares | | | | Amount payable | Date paid | Cash Book Folio | Amount paid | | | | | |
| | | | | | | | | From | To | | | | | | | | | | | |

cation and allotment sheet. When the lists are closed (the closing date will be in the prospectus) and it is ascertained that the minimum subscription (where applicable) has been subscribed, the directors will proceed to allot the shares, and minutes of all allotments will appear in the directors' minute book. The application and allotment sheets should also be initialled by one of the directors when the allotments have been made. The number of shares allotted and the distinctive numbers of such shares (if any), together with the amount payable on allotment, will be entered in the columns provided for that purpose.

No allotment of shares or debentures is permissible when a prospectus has been issued, and no proceedings on applications can be made until the third day after the prospectus has been issued, or such later time (if any) as may be specified in the prospectus. This time is referred to in the Act as 'the time of the opening of the subscription lists' (s. 50).

### (c) The Minimum Subscription

In order that prospective applicants for shares may be able to determine whether or not the company is raising enough capital for its immediate purposes, and to prevent the company from going to allotment if such capital is not raised, Section 47 lays down that, *on a first allotment of shares* offered to the public for subscription, no allotment shall be made unless the amount stated in the prospectus as the minimum amount which, in the opinion of the directors, must be raised by the issue of share capital in order to provide for the matters set out below, has been satisfied, and the amount payable on application for the amount so stated has been paid to and received by the company. This amount is called the MINIMUM SUBSCRIPTION.

The minimum subscription must provide for:

1. The purchase price of any property to be acquired which is to be defrayed in whole or in part out of the proceeds of the issue.

2. Any preliminary expenses payable by the company, and any commission so payable to any person in consideration of his agreeing to subscribe for, or of his procuring or agreeing to procure subscriptions for, any shares in the company.

3. The repayment of any moneys borrowed by the company for any of the foregoing expenditure.

4. Working capital.

Other points are:

1. The minimum subscription must be stated in the prospectus and is reckoned exclusive of any amount payable otherwise than in cash.

2. The amount payable on application must not be less than 5 per cent. of the nominal amount of the share.

3. The provisions relating to minimum subscription do not apply to private companies, which are prohibited from making any invitation to the public to subscribe nor to public companies which secure their capital without a public issue.

4. If the minimum subscription is not received within forty days of the issue of the prospectus, the application money must be returned, and if such a return is not made within forty-eight days of the issue of the prospectus, the directors are personally liable to repay the money with interest at the rate of 5 per cent. per annum.

5. Although the details of the minimum subscription must be stated in every prospectus, the restrictions on allotment do not apply to allotments subsequent to the first allotment of shares offered to the public for subscription.

6. Where a prospectus states that application has been or will be made for permission to deal on any stock exchange, any allotment thereunder is void if permission has not been applied for before the third day after the first issue of the prospectus or if permission has been refused before the expiration of three weeks from the date of the closing of the subscription lists or such longer period not exceeding six weeks as may, within the said three weeks, be notified to the applicant for permission by or for the stock exchange.

7. If permission is not so applied for, or is refused, the application money must be repaid. If not repaid within eight days, the directors become personally liable to repay it with interest at 5 per cent. per annum from the expiration of the eighth day.

8. So long as the company may become liable to repay it the money must be kept in a separate banking account (s. 51).

### (d) Letters of Allotment and Regret

If an issue is over-subscribed the directors must decide the basis of allotment – whether by the selection of all applications for over, say, 100 shares, or rateably to all applications; or by a differential allotment, e.g. all under 100 shares in full; from 100 – 1,000 shares, 50 per cent.; over 1,000 shares, 30 per cent. The course adopted will depend upon the business, and the policy of the directors. Where, for example, the issue is for a departmental store, it would be an advantage to secure as large a number of individual shareholders as possible, as each shareholder is a potential customer, whereas in, say, a ship-building company, the preferential allotment to the applicants for the largest number of shares would save clerical labour.

Where allotment is made of less than the number of shares applied for by an applicant the amount overpaid on application would be deducted from the sums payable by him on allotment and call. An applicant who receives no allotment whatever must have his application money refunded to him in full. Because of these possible adjustments, and because the contract to take shares is not complete until the offer has been accepted by notification of allotment, no entry is made in the financial books until the allotment has been made.

Upon allotment a *letter of allotment* is sent to the applicant setting out the number of shares allotted to him and the amount payable. A *letter of regret* is sent to those to whom no shares have been allotted.

### (e) Vendors' and Signatories' Shares

The shares subscribed for by the signatories to the Memorandum and Articles of Association do not require to be specifically allotted, but should be entered on the application and allotment sheets. Shares issued to vendors and others for a consideration other than cash, should be entered on a separate application and allotment sheet to avoid their being confused with shares issued for cash. When shares are issued to nominees of the vendor, a written authority must be obtained from him, authorizing the company to allot to such nominees, and containing particulars of their names, addresses and descriptions, and the number of shares to be allotted to each.

### (f) Calls

Calls are usually made on dates specified in the prospectus, when one is issued. Where dates are not specified, subsequent calls are regulated by the provisions in the Articles. Table 'A' provides that no call shall exceed one-fourth of the nominal value of the share, or be payable at less than one month from the last call, and each member shall have fourteen days' notice specifying the date of payment. Special Articles, however, commonly modify these periods and amounts.

Sometimes, columns are provided in the application and allotment sheets for calls, but it is more usual to have separate *call sheets*, which are provided with columns showing the amount due, and the date and amount of payment. *Call letters* will be issued with forms of bankers' receipts attached, calls being payable direct to the company's bankers, in the same way as amounts due on allotment.

In due course share certificates will be made out and issued to the shareholders in exchange for their allotment letters and bankers' receipts for sums due in respect of application, allotment and calls.

### (g) The Share Certificate

Within two months of allotment (or within two months after the date of lodgment of any transfer), unless the conditions of issue otherwise provide, the company must complete and have ready for delivery share certificates, indicating the number and class of shares held and the distinctive numbers thereof (where relevant) (s. 80). If all the calls have been made, the shares will be certified as being fully paid. Sometimes the date of a call may be some months after allotment and the certificates would then state that the shares are only partly paid and would give particulars of the payments made, provision being made on the back of the certificate for acknowledgment by the company of the payment of the calls subsequently made.

Where calls are to be made shortly after allotment, the conditions of issue usually provide that share certificates shall not be issued until all calls have been paid, the allotment letters and bankers' receipts constituting the title in the meantime.

### (h) Return of Allotments

Under Section 52, whenever a company limited by shares or limited by guarantee and having a share capital, makes any allotment of its shares, the company must, within one month thereafter, file with the Registrar of Companies:

1. A return of the allotments, stating the number and nominal amount of the shares comprised in the allotment, the names, addresses and descriptions of the allottees, and the amount (if any) paid or due and payable on each share; and

2. When shares are allotted as fully or partly paid up otherwise than in cash, a contract in writing constituting the title of the allottee to the allotment, together with any contract of sale, or for services or other consideration for which that allotment was made, such contracts being duly stamped, and a return stating the number and nominal amount of shares so allotted, the extent to which they are to be treated as paid up, and the consideration for which they have been allotted.

Where such a contract is not in writing, the following particulars, stamped with the same stamp duty payable as if the contract were in writing, must be filed with the Registrar:

1. The number and nominal value of shares issued as paid up otherwise than in cash, and the amount so credited on each.

2. The consideration, and a brief description of any property, and how the purchase price is to be satisfied in shares, cash and liabilities assumed.

3. Details of the apportionment of the purchase price over the following headings:

Freehold property and fixed plant and machinery and other fixtures thereon;
Leasehold property;
Fixed plant, and machinery on leasehold property (including tenants' trade and other fixtures);
Equitable interests in freehold or leasehold property;
Loose plant and machinery, stock-in-trade and other chattels (excluding plant and machinery which cannot be moved);
Goodwill and benefit of contracts;
Patents, designs, trade marks, licences, copyrights etc.;
Book debts;
Cash in hand and at bank on current account, bills, notes etc.;
Cash on deposit at bank or elsewhere;
Shares, debentures and other investments;
Other property detailed.

### (i) Journal entries relating to the issue of Shares

Upon each occasion on which an allotment of shares is made, an entry should be made in the journal, debiting an Application and Allotment Account with the amount payable on application and allotment in respect of the shares so allotted, and (assuming the shares are issued at par) crediting Share Capital Account, reference being made to the minutes of allotment and to the pages in the application and allotment book, where the details are shown. If more than one class of capital is being issued, separate accounts must be opened in the ledger for each class.

Similar entries must be made debiting the vendor or other persons, and crediting Share Capital Account, in respect of all shares issued for a consideration other than cash, reference being made to the minutes of allotment and to the contract under which the shares are issued.

When calls are made, an entry must be made debiting Call Account and crediting Share Capital Account with the total amount due in respect of the call.

### (j) Shares issued at a premium

A company may issue shares at a premium, i.e. for an amount in excess of their nominal value. Such an issue might be made by a successful company which has paid high dividends on its existing capital and where shares, as a result, already stand at a premium on the market. When shares are issued at a premium, whether for cash or otherwise, the premium must be credited to an account called 'the Share Premium Account' (s. 56). The amount credited to Share Premium Account can only be applied as follows:

1. Subject to the confirmation of the Court, in a scheme for reduction of capital, as if it were paid up share capital of the company (*see below* § 19).

2. In paying up unissued shares of the company to be issued to the members as fully paid bonus shares.

3. In writing off–

(a) preliminary expenses; or

(b) the expenses of, or commission paid or discount allowed on, any issue of shares or debentures of the company.

4. In providing for the premium payable on the redemption of redeemable preference shares or debentures of the company (s. 56).

The premium is usually payable with the instalment due on allotment, and where this is so the journal entry for allotment must show the amount payable for the premium, which must be credited direct to the Share Premium Account, only the proportion of the amount due representing a payment on account of the nominal value of the shares being credited to Share Capital Account.

#### Illustration

On April 30th, a company goes to allotment, and the following shares are allotted:

    80,000 Ordinary Shares of £1 each issued at £1·13 per share;

    50,000 7 per cent. Preference Shares of £1 each, issued at par.

The ordinary shares are payable 13p on application, 25p (including the premium) on allotment; 25p one month after allotment and 50p three months after allotment. The preference shares are payable 13p on application, 12p on allotment, 25p one month after allotment, and 50p three months after allotment. Make the journal entries to record these transactions, and show the cash book and ledger accounts.

## JOURNAL

| | | | £ | £ |
|---|---|---|---|---|
| April 30 | Application and Allotment Account (Ordinary Shares) .. .. .. Dr | | 30,400 | |
| | To Sundries— | | | |
| | Ordinary Share Capital Account .. .. .. .. .. .. | | | 20,000 |
| | Share Premium Account .. .. .. .. .. .. | | | 10,400 |
| | 13p on application and 25p on allotment (13p thereof being premium) on 80,000 Ordinary Shares of £1 each, allotted as per minute of this date. | | £30,400 | £30,400 |
| April 30 | Application and Allotment Account (Preference Shares) .. .. Dr | | 12,500 | |
| | To Preference Share Capital Account .. .. .. .. | | | 12,500 |
| | 13p on application and 12p on allotment of 50,000 Preference Shares of £1 each allotted as per minute of this date | | | |
| May 31 | First Call Account (Ordinary Shares) .. .. .. .. .. Dr | | 20,000 | |
| | To Ordinary Share Capital Account .. .. .. .. | | | 20,000 |
| | First Call of 25p on 80,000 Ordinary Shares of £1 each. | | | |
| May 31 | First Call Account (Preference Shares) .. .. .. .. Dr | | 12,500 | |
| | To Preference Share Capital Account .. .. .. .. | | | 12,500 |
| | First Call of 25p on 50,000 Preference Shares of £1 each. | | | |
| July 31 | Final Call Account (Ordinary Shares) .. .. .. .. .. Dr | | 40,000 | |
| | To Ordinary Share Capital Account .. .. .. .. | | | 40,000 |
| | Final Call of 50p on 80,000 Ordinary Shares. | | | |
| July 31 | Final Call Account (Preference Shares) .. .. .. .. Dr | | 25,000 | |
| | To Preference Share Capital Account .. .. .. .. | | | 25,000 |
| | Final Call of 50p on 50,000 Preference Shares. | | | |

It will be noted that a single journal entry is made combining the amounts payable on application and allotment. Some accountants prefer to make these entries separately, but the above course is advocated on two grounds, viz. (1) the contract to take shares is not complete until allotment, and the offer may be withdrawn at any time prior to that date, and (2) applications may not be accepted, or accepted only for a portion of the shares applied for.

## APPLICATION AND ALLOTMENT ACCOUNT
### ORDINARY SHARES

| | | £ | | | £ |
|---|---|---|---|---|---|
| April 30 | Ordinary Share Capital Account .. | 20,000 | April 30 | Cash .. .. .. .. | 10,400 |
| | Share Premium Account .. | 10,400 | May 2 | Cash .. .. .. .. | 20,000 |
| | | £30,400 | | | £30,400 |

### FIRST CALL ACCOUNT: ORDINARY SHARES

| | | £ | | | £ |
|---|---|---|---|---|---|
| May 31 | Ordinary Share Capital Account .. | 20,000 | June 2 | Cash .. .. .. .. | 20,000 |

### FINAL CALL ACCOUNT: ORDINARY SHARES

| | | £ | | | £ |
|---|---|---|---|---|---|
| July 31 | Ordinary Share Capital Account .. | 40,000 | Aug. 1 | Cash .. .. .. .. | 40,000 |

### ORDINARY SHARE CAPITAL ACCOUNT

| | | | | | £ |
|---|---|---|---|---|---|
| | | | April 30 | Application and Allotment Account | 20,000 |
| | | | May 31 | First Call Account .. .. | 20,000 |
| | | | July 31 | Final Call Account .. .. | 40,000 |
| | | | | | £80,000 |

## SHARE PREMIUM ACCOUNT

|  |  |  | April 30 | Application and Allotment Account (Ordinary Shares)    ..        .. | £ 10,400 |
|---|---|---|---|---|---|

## APPLICATION AND ALLOTMENT ACCOUNT PREFERENCE SHARES

| April 30 | Preference Share Capital Account | £ 12,500 | April 30 May 2 | Cash ..        ..        ..        .. Cash ..        ..        ..        .. | £ 6,500 6,000 |
|---|---|---|---|---|---|
|  |  | £12,500 |  |  | £12,500 |

## FIRST CALL ACCOUNT: PREFERENCE SHARES

| May 31 | Preference Share Capital Account | £ 12,500 | June 2 | Cash ..        ..        ..        .. | £ 12,500 |
|---|---|---|---|---|---|

## FINAL CALL ACCOUNT: PREFERENCE SHARES

| July 31 | Preference Share Capital Account | £ 25,000 | Aug. 1 | Cash ..        ..        ..        .. | £ 25,000 |
|---|---|---|---|---|---|

## PREFERENCE SHARE CAPITAL ACCOUNT

|  |  |  | April 30 May 31 July 31 | Application and Allotment Account First Call Account    ..        .. Final Call Account    ..        .. | £ 12,500 12,500 25,000 |
|---|---|---|---|---|---|
|  |  |  |  |  | £50,000 |

## CASH BOOK

| April 30 | Application and Allotment Accounts: 13p per share on Application for 80,000 Ordinary Shares    .. 50,000 Preference Shares    .. | £ 10,400 6,500 |  |  | £ |
|---|---|---|---|---|---|
| May 2 | Application and Allotment Accounts: Ordinary Shares – 25p per share due on allotment on 80,000 shares    ..        ..        .. Preference Shares – 12p per share due on allotment on 50,000 shares    ..        ..        .. | 20,000 6,000 |  |  |  |
| June 2 | First Call Accounts: Ordinary Shares – 25p per share on 80,000 shares    ..        .. Preference Shares – 25p per share on 50,000 shares    ..        .. | 20,000 12,500 |  |  |  |
| Aug. 1 | Final Call Accounts: Ordinary Shares – 50p per share on 80,000 shares    ..        .. Preference Shares – 50p per share on 50,000 shares    ..        .. | 40.000 25,000 |  |  |  |

### (k) *Shares issued at a discount*

If its existing shares are quoted below their nominal value on the market, it would be impracticable for a company to obtain subscriptions for an issue of further shares of the same class at the full nominal value, and it may be thought expedient to issue shares at a discount.

The issue of shares at a discount is illegal, however, except under the provisions of Section 57, which are:

1. The shares to be issued at a discount must be of a class already issued.

2. The company must authorize the issue by a resolution passed in general meeting and the sanction of the Court must be obtained. In giving its sanction, the Court may impose such terms and conditions as it thinks fit.

3. The resolution must specify the maximum rate of discount at which the shares are to be issued.

4. Not less than one year must, at the date of the issue, have elapsed since the date on which the company was entitled to commence business.

5. The shares must be issued within one month after the date of sanction of the Court, or within such extended time as the Court permits.

6. Any prospectus issued about the shares must contain particulars of the discount allowed, or of so much of that discount as has not been written off at the date of the issue of the prospectus.

7. Every Balance Sheet subsequently issued must contain particulars of the amount of the discount not written off (8th Schedule, Pt. I, § 3).

When the issue has been made, Share Capital Account must be credited with the full nominal value of the shares, and a Discount on Shares Account debited with the amount of the discount, cash being debited with the amount received. The Discount on Shares Account should be written off out of profits over a period of years, since it is not represented by value. There is, however, no legal obligation on a company to write off the discount.

On the Balance Sheet discount on shares not written off should be deducted from Reserves.

### (l) *Redeemable Preference Shares*

Power is given under s. 58 to a company limited by shares to issue preference shares which are at the option of the company liable to be redeemed provided that:

1. Authority for the issue is contained in the company's Articles.

2. No such shares shall be redeemed except out of profits of the company which would otherwise be available for dividend or out of the proceeds of a fresh issue of shares made for the purposes of redemption.

3. No such shares shall be redeemed unless they are fully paid.

4. The premium, if any, payable on redemption must have been provided for out of the profits of the company or out of the share premium account before the shares are redeemed.

5. Where any such shares are redeemed otherwise than out of the proceeds of a fresh issue, there shall out of profits which would otherwise have been available for dividend be transferred to a 'Capital Redemption Reserve Fund' a sum equal to the nominal amount of the shares redeemed.

*It should be noted that:*

1. Published Balance Sheets must show the earliest and latest dates of redemption, whether redemption is mandatory or at the company's option, and details of any premium payable on redemption. (For the purposes of the *Income and Corporation Taxes Act 1970* the premium is considered as a distribution.)

2. (i) The Capital Redemption Reserve Fund should be shown in the Balance Sheet under the heading Reserves.

   (ii) The provisions of the *Companies Act 1948* for the reduction of paid-up share capital apply to the Capital Redemption Reserve Fund.

   (iii) The Capital Redemption Reserve Fund may be used to pay up unissued shares of the company to be issued to members of the company as fully paid bonus shares, and for no other purpose.

3. The redemption of redeemable preference shares does not reduce the authorized share capital of the company. After redemption former redeemable preference shares should be described as 'unclassified shares'.

4. If the company makes a new issue of shares for the purposes of redemption of preference shares no stamp duty is payable on the new issue provided the old shares are redeemed within one month (otherwise stamp duty is payable in the normal way).

5. Notice of redemption of redeemable preference shares must be given to the Registrar of Companies within one month of the redemption (s. 62).

The purpose of transferring profits to the Capital Redemption Reserve Fund is to prevent a reduction of capital, as will be seen from the following simple statements.

A company issued 10,000 redeemable preference shares of £1 each, redeemable at par, and two ordinary shares of £1 each. On the date for redemption of the shares the company's Balance Sheet was as follows:

| | | | | £ | | | | | £ |
|---|---|---|---|---|---|---|---|---|---|
| Redeemable Preference Shares | .. | .. | | 10,000 | Investments at Cost | .. | .. | .. | 10,002 |
| Ordinary Shares | .. | .. | .. | 2 | Cash .. | .. | .. | .. | 10,000 |
| Profit and Loss Account | .. | .. | .. | 10,000 | | | | | |
| | | | | £20,002 | | | | | £20,002 |

Immediately after redeeming the shares, the Balance Sheet would read—

| | | | | £ | | | | £ |
|---|---|---|---|---|---|---|---|---|
| Ordinary Shares | .. | .. | .. | 2 | Investments at cost | .. | .. | 10,002 |
| Profit and Loss Account | .. | .. | .. | 10,000 | | | | |

£10,000 of the assets was provided by the issue of the preference shares, and if the company could now realize investments and pay a dividend of £10,000, the effect would be to reduce its capital to £2. If there were creditors, they might be severely prejudiced. Accordingly, since £10,000 of the profits have been applied in repaying capital, the profits remaining available for distribution as dividends are reduced by this sum, and the Act requires an equivalent amount of profits to be capitalized. The capital redemption reserve fund so created can be reduced, as if it were share capital, by passing a special resolution and obtaining the sanction of the Court, or can be used to pay up fully paid bonus shares, but it cannot be applied for any other purpose.

### Illustration

The Balance Sheet of a company at December 31st, was as follows:

| | £ | | £ |
|---|---|---|---|
| Authorized and Issued Capital: | | Sundry Assets .. .. .. .. | 84,000 |
| 40,000 6% Redeemable Preference Shares of | | Cash .. .. .. .. | 30,000 |
| £1 each fully paid .. .. | 40,000 | | |
| 20,000 Ordinary Shares of £1 each fully paid .. | 20,000 | | |
| Profit and Loss Account .. .. .. | 33,000 | | |
| Liabilities .. .. .. | 21,000 | | |
| | £114,000 | | £114,000 |

By the terms of their issue the preference shares were redeemable at a premium of 5 per cent. on the following January 1st, and it was decided to arrange this as far as possible out of the company's resources subject to leaving a balance of £10,000 to the credit of the Profit and Loss Account. It was also decided to raise the balance of money required by the issue of a sufficient number of ordinary shares at a premium of 25p per share.

Show the necessary journal entries and ledger accounts giving effect to the transactions and the Balance Sheet thereafter. Ignore taxation.

### JOURNAL

| | | | £ | £ |
|---|---|---|---|---|
| Jan. 1 | 6% Redeemable Preference Share Capital .. .. .. .. .. | Dr | 40,000 | |
| | Premium on Redemption of Preference Shares .. .. .. .. | .. | 2,000 | |
| | To Preference Shares Redemption Account .. .. .. | .. | | 42,000 |
| | Transferring 40,000 £1 redeemable preference shares redeemable at a premium of 5% | .. | | |
| | Application and Allotment (Ordinary Shares) .. .. .. .. | Dr | 21,250 | |
| | To Ordinary Share Capital .. .. .. .. .. | .. | | 17,000 |
| | ,, Share Premium Account .. .. .. .. .. | .. | | 4,250 |
| | Issue of 17,000 ordinary shares at premium of 25p per share .. .. | .. | | |
| | Cash .. .. .. .. .. .. .. .. | Dr | 21,250 | |
| | To Application and Allotment .. .. .. .. | .. | | 21,250 |
| | Cash received on issue of 17,000 ordinary shares | | | |
| | Preference Share Redemption Account .. .. .. .. | Dr | 42,000 | |
| | To Cash .. .. .. .. .. .. | .. | | 42,000 |
| | Redemption of 40,000 6% Redeemable Preference Shares at premium of 5% | | | |
| | Profit and Loss Account .. .. .. .. .. | Dr | 23,000 | |
| | To Capital Redemption Reserve Fund .. .. .. .. | .. | | 23,000 |
| | Transfer out of profits of amount equal to nominal amount of shares redeemed otherwise than out of the proceeds of a new issue | | | |
| | Share Premium Account .. .. .. .. .. | Dr | 2,000 | |
| | To Premium on Redemption of Preference Shares .. .. | .. | | 2,000 |
| | Providing for premium on redemption out of Share Premium Account | | | |

### LEDGER
### 6% REDEEMABLE PREFERENCE SHARE CAPITAL

| | | | £ | | | | £ |
|---|---|---|---|---|---|---|---|
| Jan. 1 | Preference Share Redemption Account .. .. .. | | 40,000 | Dec. 31 | Balance b/f. .. .. .. | | 40,000 |

## PREMIUM ON REDEMPTION OF PREFERENCE SHARES

| | | £ | | | £ |
|---|---|---|---|---|---|
| Jan. 1 | Preference Share Redemption Account .. .. .. | 2,000 | Jan. 1 | Share Premium Account .. .. | 2,000 |

## PREFERENCE SHARE REDEMPTION ACCOUNT

| | | £ | | | £ |
|---|---|---|---|---|---|
| Jan. 1 | Cash .. .. .. .. | 42,000 | Jan. 1 | 6% Redeemable Preference Shares .. | 40,000 |
| | | | | Premium on Redemption .. .. | 2,000 |

## ORDINARY SHARE CAPITAL

| | | £ | | | £ |
|---|---|---|---|---|---|
| Jan. 1 | Balance c/f. .. .. .. | 37,000 | Dec. 31 | Balance b/f. .. .. .. | 20,000 |
| | | | Jan. 1 | Application and Allotment .. | 17,000 |
| | | £37,000 | | | £37,000 |

## SHARE PREMIUM ACCOUNT

| | | £ | | | £ |
|---|---|---|---|---|---|
| Jan. 1 | Premium on Redemption of Preference Shares .. .. .. | 2,000 | Jan. 1 | Application and Allotment .. | 4,250 |
| | Balance c/f. .. .. .. | 2,250 | | | |
| | | £4,250 | | | £4,250 |

## APPLICATION AND ALLOTMENT (ORDINARY SHARES)

| | | £ | | | £ |
|---|---|---|---|---|---|
| Jan. 1 | Share Capital .. .. .. | 17,000 | Jan. 1 | Cash .. .. .. .. | 21,250 |
| | Share Premium .. .. .. | 4,250 | | | |
| | | £21,250 | | | £21,250 |

## PROFIT AND LOSS ACCOUNT

| | | £ | | | £ |
|---|---|---|---|---|---|
| Jan. 1 | Capital Redemption Reserve Fund .. | 23,000 | Dec. 31 | Balance b/f. .. .. .. | 33,000 |
| | Balance c/f. .. .. .. | 10,000 | | | |
| | | £33,000 | | | £33,000 |

## CAPITAL REDEMPTION RESERVE FUND

| | | | | | £ |
|---|---|---|---|---|---|
| | | | Jan. 1 | Profit and Loss Account .. .. | 23,000 |

## CASH BOOK

| | | £ | | | £ |
|---|---|---|---|---|---|
| Dec. 31 | Balance b/f. .. .. .. | 30,000 | Jan. 1 | Preference Share Redemption Account .. .. .. | 42,000 |
| | Application and Allotment: Ordinary Shares .. .. .. | 21,250 | | Balance c/f. .. .. .. | 9,250 |
| | | £51,250 | | | £51,250 |

## BALANCE SHEET, January 1st

| | £ | £ | | | | | | £ |
|---|---|---|---|---|---|---|---|---|
| Authorized Capital: | | | Sundry Assets .. | .. | .. | .. | | 84,000 |
| 37,000 Ordinary Shares of £1 each .. | | 37,000 | Cash .. | .. | .. | .. | .. | 9,250 |
| 23,000 Unclassified Shares of £1 each | | 23,000 | | | | | | |
| | | £60,000 | | | | | | |
| | | | | | | | | |
| Issued and Paid-up Capital: | | | | | | | | |
| 37,000 Ordinary Shares .. .. | | 37,000 | | | | | | |
| Reserves: | | | | | | | | |
| Share Premium Account .. .. | 2,250 | | | | | | | |
| Capital Redemption Reserve Fund .. | 23,000 | | | | | | | |
| Profit and Loss Account .. .. | 10,000 | | | | | | | |
| | | 35,250 | | | | | | |
| | | 72,250 | | | | | | |
| Liabilities .. .. .. | | 21,000 | | | | | | |
| | | £93,250 | | | | | | £93,250 |

*Notes:*

1. Since £10,000 is to be carried forward on Profit and Loss Account, 23,000 of the redeemable preference shares can be redeemed out of profit, leaving 17,000 to be redeemed out of the proceeds of a new issue of ordinary shares.

2. The premium on redemption of the preference shares has been written off against the company's Share Premium Account in accordance with Section 58 (1) (c) of the *Companies Act 1948.*

It has been suggested that where new shares are issued at a premium for the purpose of redeeming preference shares, Section 58 authorizes the whole proceeds of the fresh issue, including the premium to be applied for that purpose. If this view is correct, it would be necessary in the above illustration to issue only 15,200 ordinary shares at a premium of 25p per share to provide the £19,000 required to redeem the preference shares, to the extent that they are not redeemed out of profit. If this were done, the paid up share capital of the company (including the Capital Redemption Reserve Fund and the Share Premium Account, which have to be regarded for this purpose as paid up share capital) would amount to £60,000.

The purpose of Section 58 is to enable a company to redeem its redeemable preference shares without reducing its capital. Although the section permits a Share Premium Account to be applied in providing the premium payable on the redemption of preference shares, it does not authorize that account to be used either for the redemption of the shares themselves or the creation of a capital redemption reserve fund.

Where it is necessary to realize assets to provide the cash for the redemption of preference shares, losses on the realization of the assets should be written off to Profit and Loss Account (or charged to any reserve which exists to meet such capital losses), but profits on such realizations should be regarded as a capital reserve not available for dividend purposes.

## § 7. Forfeiture of Shares

The articles of a company usually give power to the directors to forfeit shares on which calls are unpaid and overdue, proper notice (Table A prescribes fourteen days) having been given to the defaulting shareholder, that unless the calls are paid, his shares will be forfeited. Table A also gives power to forfeit shares for non-payment of any premium on the shares.

Until the shares are re-issued, the balance on Forfeited Shares Account should appear in the Balance Sheet as a separate item under the heading Reserves.

Forfeited shares can be re-issued as fully paid at any price, so long as the sum received on re-issue, plus the amount received from the original allottee before forfeiture, make up together at least the nominal value of the shares forfeited. If, after the re-issue of the shares, there still remains a credit balance on the Forfeited Shares Account, this would represent an amount received by the company on those shares in excess of their nominal value which, it is submitted, should be regarded as a premium on the issue of such shares and transferred to Share Premium Account.

If the forfeited shares were originally issued at a premium which had been paid before forfeiture, the Share Premium Account need not be disturbed as the premium is not a payment for the shares themselves, but is a payment for the right to acquire the shares. Where, however, shares are forfeited for non-payment of instalments which include the premium, so that the premium has not been received by the company, Share Premium Account should be debited and Forfeited Shares Account credited.

The book-keeping entries can be summarized as follows:

| DEBIT | CREDIT | REMARKS |
|---|---|---|
| *On forfeiture*<br>Share Capital | Forfeited Shares | Total NOMINAL amount payable to date of forfeiture |
| Forfeited Shares | Calls<br>Application and Allotment | Amounts unpaid on shares |
| Share Premium | Forfeited Shares | Any unpaid premium |
| *On reissue*<br>Forfeited Shares | Share Capital | Nominal amount called up to date of reissue |
| Cash | Forfeited Shares | Cash received on reissue |
| Forfeited Shares | Share Premium | Any balance on forfeited shares account must be transferred to Share Premium Account |

**Illustration (1)**

A company has an issued capital of £20,000 in shares of £1 each, fully paid with the exception of 200 shares on which only 50p has been paid, forfeited for non-payment of calls, and subsequently re-issued as fully paid at the price of 75p per share. Show the entries in the company's journal including cash and ledger recording these transactions.

## JOURNAL

| | | £ | £ |
|---|---|---|---|
| Share Capital Account    ..    ..    ..    ..    ..    ..    .. | Dr | 200 | |
|    To Forfeited Shares Account    ..    ..    ..    ..    .. | | | 200 |
| 200 shares of £1 each forfeited for non-payment of calls as per minute dated............. | | | |
| Forfeited Shares Account    ..    ..    ..    ..    ..    .. | Dr | 100 | |
|    To Call Account    ..    ..    ..    ..    ..    .. | | | 100 |
| Calls in arrear, 50p per share on 200 shares forfeited, now transferred. | | | |
| Forfeited Shares Account    ..    ..    ..    ..    ..    .. | Dr | 200 | |
|    To Share Capital Account    ..    ..    ..    ..    .. | | | 200 |
| Reissue of 200 forfeited shares of £1 each. | | | |
| Cash    ..    ..    ..    ..    ..    ..    .. | Dr | 150 | |
|    To Forfeited Shares Account    ..    ..    ..    ..    .. | | | 150 |
| Cash received: 75p per share on 200 shares reissued. | | | |
| Forfeited Shares Account    ..    ..    ..    ..    ..    .. | Dr | 50 | |
|    To Share Premium Account    ..    ..    ..    ..    .. | | | 50 |
| Transfer of balance. | | | |

## LEDGER
## SHARE CAPITAL ACCOUNT

| | £ | | £ |
|---|---|---|---|
| Forfeited Shares Account    ..    ..    .. | 200 | Balance b/f.    ..    ..    ..    .. | 20,000 |
| Balance c/d.    ..    ..    ..    .. | 20,000 | Forfeited Shares Account    ..    .. | 200 |
| | £20,200 | | £20,200 |
| | | Balance b/d.    ..    ..    ..    .. | 20,000 |

## CALL ACCOUNT

| | £ | | £ |
|---|---|---|---|
| Balance b/f.    ..    ..    ..    .. | 100 | Forfeited Shares Account    ..    .. | 100 |

## FORFEITED SHARES ACCOUNT

| | £ | | £ |
|---|---|---|---|
| Call Account    ..    ..    ..    .. | 100 | Share Capital Account    ..    .. | 200 |
| Share Capital Account    ..    ..    .. | 200 | Cash    ..    ..    ..    .. | 150 |
| Share Premium Account    ..    ..    .. | 50 | | |
| | £350 | | £350 |

## SHARE PREMIUM ACCOUNT

| | | | £ |
|---|---|---|---|
| | | Forfeited Shares Account    ..    .. | 50 |

*Note:*

As all the shares have been re-issued, the balance of the Forfeited Shares Account, after transferring 25p per share (the amount necessary to make the price of re-issue up to par), is a premium on the issue of the shares and should be transferred to the Share Premium Account.

It may happen that forfeiture takes place upon failure of the allottee to pay the amount due upon allotment, subsequent calls being due prior to the re-issue of the shares.

### Illustration (2)

A company invites applications for 20,000 shares of £1 each, payable 13p per share on application 37p on allotment, 25p per share two months after allotment, and 25p four months after allotment. An applicant for 200 shares fails to pay the allotment money, and the shares are forfeited prior to the first call becoming due. After all calls have been made, the forfeited shares are re-issued at par. Show the entries in the company's journal including cash and ledger recording these transactions. Ignore taxation.

### JOURNAL

| | | £ | £ |
|---|---|---:|---:|
| Cash ..    ..    ..    ..    .. | Dr | 2,600 | |
| To Application and Allotment Account    ..    ..    ..    ..    ..    .. | | | 2,600 |
| Application money: 13p per share on 20,000 shares. | | | |
| Application and Allotment Account    ..    ..    ..    ..    .. | Dr | 10,000 | |
| To Share Capital Account    ..    ..    ..    ..    ..    .. | | | 10,000 |
| Allotment of 20,000 shares of £1 each payable 13p on application and 37p on allotment as per minute. | | | |
| Cash    ..    ..    ..    ..    ..    ..    .. | Dr | 7,326 | |
| To Application and Allotment Account    ..    ..    ..    ..    .. | | | 7,326 |
| Cash received on allotment: 37p per share on 19,800 shares. | | | |
| Share Capital Account    ..    ..    ..    ..    ..    .. | Dr | 100 | |
| To Forfeited Shares Account    ..    ..    ..    ..    .. | | | 100 |
| 200 shares forfeited 50p per share called up per minute........ | | | |
| Forfeited Shares Account    ..    ..    ..    ..    .. | Dr | 74 | |
| To Application and Allotment Account    ..    ..    ..    .. | | | 74 |
| Allotment money of 37p per share on 200 shares forfeited transferred. | | | |
| First Call Account    ..    ..    ..    ..    ..    .. | Dr | 4,950 | |
| To Share Capital Account    ..    ..    ..    ..    .. | | | 4,950 |
| First call of 25p per share on 19,800 shares per minute........ | | | |
| Cash    ..    ..    ..    ..    ..    ..    .. | Dr | 4,950 | |
| To First Call Account    ..    ..    ..    ..    .. | | | 4,950 |
| Cash received of 25p per share on 19,800 shares. | | | |
| Second Call Account    ..    ..    ..    ..    ..    .. | Dr | 4,950 | |
| To Share Capital Account    ..    ..    ..    ..    .. | | | 4,950 |
| Second call of 25p per share on 19,800 shares. | | | |
| Cash    ..    ..    ..    ..    ..    ..    .. | Dr | 4,950 | |
| To Second Call Account    ..    ..    ..    ..    .. | | | 4,950 |
| Cash received of 25p per share on 19,800 shares. | | | |
| Forfeited Shares Account ..    ..    ..    ..    ..    .. | Dr | 200 | |
| To Share Capital    ..    ..    ..    ..    .. | | | 200 |
| Reissue of 200 forfeited shares of £1 each fully paid. | | | |
| Cash    ..    ..    ..    ..    ..    ..    .. | Dr | 200 | |
| To Forfeited Shares Account    ..    ..    ..    ..    .. | | | 200 |
| Cash received of £1 per share on 200 forfeited shares reissued. | | | |
| Forfeited Shares Account ..    ..    ..    ..    ..    .. | Dr | 26 | |
| To Share Premium Account    ..    ..    ..    ..    .. | | | 26 |
| Transfer of balance. | | | |

### LEDGER
### SHARE CAPITAL ACCOUNT

| | £ | | | £ |
|---|---:|---|---|---:|
| Forfeited Shares Account    ..    ..    .. | 100 | Application and Allotment Account    .. | | 10,000 |
| Balance c/d.    ..    ..    ..    .. | 20,000 | First Call Account    ..    ..    .. | | 4,950 |
| | | Second Call Account    ..    .. | | 4,950 |
| | | Forfeited Shares Account    ..    .. | | 200 |
| | £20,100 | | | £20,100 |
| | | Balance b/d.    ..    ..    ..    .. | | 20,000 |

### APPLICATION AND ALLOTMENT ACCOUNT

| | £ | | £ |
|---|---|---|---|
| Share Capital Account .. .. .. | 10,000 | Cash on application .. .. .. | 2,600 |
| | | ,,   on allotment .. .. .. | 7,326 |
| | | Forfeited Shares Account .. .. | 74 |
| | £10,000 | | £10,000 |

### FIRST CALL ACCOUNT

| | £ | | £ |
|---|---|---|---|
| Share Capital Account .. .. .. | 4,950 | Cash .. .. .. .. .. | 4,950 |

### SECOND CALL ACCOUNT

| | £ | | £ |
|---|---|---|---|
| Share Capital Account .. .. .. | 4,950 | Cash .. .. .. .. .. | 4,950 |

### FORFEITED SHARES ACCOUNT

| | £ | | £ |
|---|---|---|---|
| Application and Allotment Account .. .. | 74 | Share Capital Account .. .. .. | 100 |
| Share Capital Account .. .. .. | 200 | Cash .. .. .. .. .. | 200 |
| Share Premium Account .. .. .. | 26 | | |
| | £300 | | £300 |

**Illustration (3)**

A company issued a prospectus inviting applications for 200,000 shares of 25p each at a premium of 8p, payable as follows:

On application    5p per share.

,, allotment    13p ,,   ,,    (including premium).

,, first call    10p ,,   ,,

,, second call    5p ,,   ,,

Applications were received for 300,000 shares, and allotments made *pro rata* to the applicants for 240,000 shares, the remaining applications being refused. Money overpaid on application was employed on account of sums due on allotment.

X, to whom 400 shares were allotted, failed to pay the allotment money, and on his subsequent failure to pay the first call, his shares were forfeited. Y, the holder of 600 shares, failed to pay the two calls, and his shares were forfeited after the second call had been made.

Of the shares forfeited, 800 were re-issued to Z, credited as fully paid, for 23p per share, the whole of X's shares being included. Show the journal entries required to record the above forfeitures and re-issue. Ignore taxation.

JOURNAL

| | | £ | £ |
|---|---|---|---|
| Share Capital Account .. .. .. .. .. .. .. .. | Dr | 80 | |
| To Forfeited Shares Account.. | | | 80 |
| Forfeiture of 400 shares allotted to X, 20p per share called up, for non-payment of balance due on allotment and first call, per minute of this day. | | | |
| | | | |
| Forfeited Shares Account .. .. .. .. .. .. .. .. | Dr | 56 | |
| Share Premium Account .. .. .. .. .. .. .. .. | | 32 | |
| To Application and Allotment Account .. .. .. .. .. | | | 48 |
| First Call Account .. .. .. .. .. .. .. | | | 40 |
| Amounts unpaid by X on shares forfeited, viz. – | | | |
| Due on application and allotment – 400 shares – 10p each .. .. .. .. £40 | | | |
| Less paid on application for 480 shares – 5p each .. .. .. .. .. 24 | | | |
|                                  16 | | | |
| Add Premium on 400 shares – 8p each .. .. .. .. .. .. 32 | | | |
| First Call on 400 shares – 10p each .. .. .. .. .. .. 40 | | | |
|                                £88 | | | |
| | | | |
| Share Capital Account .. .. .. .. .. .. .. .. | Dr | 150 | |
| To Forfeited Shares Account .. .. .. .. .. .. .. | | | 150 |
| Forfeiture of 600 shares allotted to Y for non-payment of 1st and 2nd calls, per minute of this day. | | | |
| | | | |
| Forfeited Shares Account .. .. .. .. .. .. .. .. | Dr | 90 | |
| To First Call Account .. .. .. .. .. .. .. .. | | | 60 |
| Second ,, ,, .. .. .. .. .. .. .. .. | | | 30 |
| Amounts not paid by Y on 600 shares forfeited. | | | |
| | | | |
| Z .. .. .. .. .. .. .. .. .. .. | Dr | 184 | |
| Forfeited Shares Account .. .. .. .. .. .. .. .. | | 16 | |
| To ShareCapital Account .. .. .. .. .. .. .. | | | 200 |
| Re-issue of 800 forfeited shares for 23p each, credited as fully paid as per minute of this day. | | | |
| | | | |
| Forfeited Shares Account .. .. .. .. .. .. .. .. | Dr | 48 | |
| To Share Premium Account .. .. .. .. .. .. .. | | | 48 |
| Transfer of capital profit on re-issue of shares, viz,– | | | |
| 400 shares formerly held by X: | | | |
| Amounts received from X .. .. .. .. .. ..£24 | | | |
| ,, ,, ,, Z .. .. .. .. .. .. .. 92 | | | |
|                       116 | | | |
| Less credited as paid .. .. .. .. .. ..100 | | | |
|                     —  16 | | | |
| 400 shares formerly held by Y: | | | |
| Amount received from Y 18p per share .. .. .. .. .. ..£72 | | | |
| ,, ,, Z .. .. .. .. .. .. .. 92 | | | |
|                     164 | | | |
| Less Premium included in allotment money .. .. .. .. 32 | | | |
|                     132 | | | |
| Less credited as paid .. .. .. .. .. ..100 | | | |
|                     —  32 | | | |
|                     £48 | | | |

Notes:

1. The balance remaining on Forefeited Shares Account, £20, is the amount paid by Y on application and allotment for the balance of 200 shares, ignoring the premium paid thereon (which is in the Share Premium Account).

2. 200,000 shares were allotted *pro rata* to applicants for 240,000 shares; therefore X's allotment of 400 shares referred to an application for 480 shares; applications for 60,000 shares were refused outright.

## § 8. The Share Books

### (a) The Share Ledger

This book, often arranged for use as the register of members, contains an account for each shareholder, showing the number of shares he has acquired, the number he has transferred, and the balance standing in his name. If shares are issued as partly paid up, cash columns can be provided to record the payment of calls, As soon as the shares become fully paid, the cash columns will no longer be necessary. Where there are different classes of shares, there must either be separate share ledgers for each class, or separate columns must be provided to distinguish between the various classes of shares held by each member.

### (b) Transfer Procedure

The selling broker prepares a transfer deed, abstracting the necessary particulars from his client's share certificate and the 'Ticket' received from the jobber to whom he has sold. He gets his client (the transferor) to sign the deed. He then has the deed stamped and passes it together with the share certificate, to the buying broker, who sends both documents to the company for the transfer to be registered. It is not necessary for the transferee to sign the transfer deed. The company cancels the old certificate, records the transfer in its share books and issues a new certificate in the name of the buyer, which is sent to the buying broker, who delivers it to his client.

*Certified Transfers:* The above procedure operates where a person sells the whole of the shares or stock represented by a certificate. Where only part of the holding is disposed of, or where the total holding is split between more than one purchaser, the seller will hand his certificate to his broker, who will either (*a*) deposit it with the Secretary of the Share and Loan Department of the Stock Exchange, who will forward it to the company concerned and certify on the transfer deed that this has been done, or (*b*) send the transfer and the certificate direct to the company. It should be noted that the Share and Loan Department will only undertake to certify transfers of securities which are quoted on the Stock Exchange.

The certification is effected by impressing on the transfer, with a rubber stamp, a certificate that a share certificate covering the shares referred to in the transfer has been lodged with the company. Such a certified transfer constitutes good delivery of the shares transferred.

Sometimes where a transfer covers only part of a holding, the company will issue a Balance Ticket for the remainder as a temporary certificate, against which, if necessary, a transfer can be certified if the transferor wishes to deal with the balance of his holding before a new certificate is obtained. In due course the balance ticket must be surrendered to the company in exchange for the new certificate.

### (c) The Register of Transfers

This book records particulars of all share transfers registered by the company, and it is usual for the directors, after passing the transfers, to initial the register accordingly. Often, however, the register is dispensed with to save clerical labour and reduce error, the postings into the share ledger being made direct from the share transfers, which are then filed.

The following is a convenient form for general use:

**Illustration**

### REGISTER OF TRANSFERS

| No. of Deed | Date of Registration | No. of Old Certificate | Share Ledger Folio | Transferor | | | Number of Shares Transferred | Transferee | | | No. of New Certificate | Share Ledger Folio | Remarks |
|---|---|---|---|---|---|---|---|---|---|---|---|---|---|
| | | | | Name | Address | De-scrip'n | | Name | Address | De-scrip'n | | | |
| | | | | | | | | | | | | | |
| | | | | | | | | | | | | | |
| | | | | | | | | | | | | | |

## § 9. Preliminary and Formation Expenses

Preliminary and formation expenses which arise on the flotation of a company usually include:

1. Stamp duties and fees on the nominal capital, and on the registration of the company (see p. 200).

2. The law costs of preparing the prospectus, Memorandum and Articles of Association, and contracts etc.

3. Accountants' and valuers' fees for reports, certificates etc.

4. Cost of printing Memorandum and Articles of Association.

5. Cost of the company's seal, statutory books etc.

6. Stamp duties payable on the conveyance or transfer of assets.

Normally duty is payable on consideration for the transfer of assets (other than those which are capable of manual delivery, such as plant and machinery, stock-in-trade, bills receivable, cash etc.) but there are certain exemptions and abatements.

The preliminary and formation expenses are sometimes borne entirely by the company, and sometimes by the vendors of the business to the company, or apportioned between these parties, the expenses up to allotment being payable by the vendors, and the expenses afterwards by the company.

Preliminary expenses are capital expenditure, but as they are not represented by value, it is usual to write them off as soon as possible out of revenue. The balance not written off must be carried forward and shown under a separate heading in the Balance Sheet.

In addition to preliminary expenses, the following expenses incurred in issuing shares and debentures, so far as they are not written off, must each be stated separately in the Balance Sheet of the company (8th Schedule, Pt. I, § 3):

(i) Any expenses incurred in issuing share capital or debentures;

(ii) Any commission on issuing shares or debentures;

(iii) Any discount on debentures;

(iv) Any discount on shares.

## (a) Underwriting Commission

Underwriting commission is payable to persons who undertake to subscribe for shares in a public issue, to the extent that the shares are not subscribed for by the public. An underwriting contract is therefore a speculation. If the public apply for the whole of the shares, the underwriters receive their commission, and do not have to take up any shares. If the public apply for only part of the shares, the underwriters receive their commission but have to take up the shares not subscribed for in proportion to their contracts. It is usual for the underwriters to make formal application for the shares they underwrite, on the understanding that allotment will be made only to the extent to which the public do not apply for shares.

The provisions mentioned in § 6 (c) *above* regarding repayment of application money where a stock exchange quotation is refused, apply also to shares underwritten; the allotment is void (s. 51 (6)).

### Illustration (1)

The Andorra Engineering Company Ltd issued a prospectus inviting applications for 100,000 shares. A underwrote 40% of the total, B 30% and C 30%, in consideration of a commission of 5%. The public made applications for 40,000 shares. There were thus 60,000 shares to be taken up by A, B and C in the ratio in which they had underwritten the issue. A taking 24,000, B 18,000, and C 18,000. The commission received would be on the total amount underwritten, viz. A £2,000, B £1,500, and C £1,500.

The underwriters may enter into subsidiary agreements with sub-underwriters in order to spread the risk; the principal underwriters are frequently paid an additional commission, termed an 'over-riding' commission, since they would generally have to pay to the sub-underwriters underwriting commission at the same rate as they themselves have received.

The payment of an over-riding commission by the company enables it to deal with one or two underwriters instead of a number; the underwriters usually remain responsible for the obligations entered into in the subsidiary agreements.

### Illustration (2)

X Ltd issues a prospectus inviting applications for 100,000 shares of 50p each at £1 per share, enters into a contract with M, who undertakes to underwrite the whole issue at an underwriting commission of 4 per cent., and an over-riding commission of 1 per cent. M makes underwriting contracts with sub-underwriters as follows:

A 40,000 shares, B 30,000 shares, C 20,000 shares.

The underwriting and over-riding commissions are apportioned as follows:

A 4% on £40,000 = £1,600; B 4% on £30,000 = £1,200; C 4% on £20,000 = £800; and M 4% on the balance of £10,000, plus 1% on £100,000 = £1,400.

Sometimes underwriters apply 'firm' for a number of shares; that is, they request the shares so applied for to be allotted to them, whatever the response of the public to the issue may be. If the issue is under-subscribed, each underwriter may still be called upon to fulfil his obligations under the underwriting contract, irrespective of 'firm' applications, unless the contract provides for relief to be given for 'firm' applications, when the number of shares to be taken up under the contract by each underwriter is reduced by the number of shares taken 'firm'.

It is common for an underwriter to lodge a cheque with the company for the application money for all the shares he has underwritten; the sub-underwriters lodge cheques with the underwriter for the application monies on the shares they have sub-underwritten. The cheques will not, however, be presented unless all the shares are left with the underwriters; when the outcome of an issue is known the underwriter will send the company a cheque for the application money on the shares he must take up and the company will return the original cheque; a similar procedure is adopted with the sub-underwriters. Procedure is by no means uniform; often where underwriters are of the highest standing no cheques are written out until the result of the issue is known.

Underwriters often sell shares and loan stock for which they become liable, in partly paid form. They usually stipulate that at least 25 per cent. of the total issue price is payable on application so that even if the issue is a major flop they can sell the shares, the buyers becoming liable for the calls. In current issues it is rare for money to be payable on allotment.

Underwriters sometimes deal in options; e.g. call options (options to buy shares at a given price on a given date), or double options, sometimes described as put and call options (options to either sell or buy).

The book-keeping procedure is as follows:

(*a*) Open a separate account for each underwriting contract.

(*b*) Provide separate columns for shares and cash.

(*c*) (i) Debit the Underwriting Account with the cost of shares taken up, sub-underwriting commission paid, options paid for, incidental expenses (printing costs, postage etc. are usually paid for by the company). If shares are received for remuneration – (very rare these days), debit the shares column only, no other entry is necessary unless calls have to be paid.

(ii) Credit the account with commission, 'over-riding' commission, option money received, and shares sold.

(*d*) Value unsold shares at the end of the accounting period at the lower of cost or market value. Cost is the amount paid on the shares plus commissions etc. paid, less commissions, option money etc. received.

### Illustration (3)

Stock Ltd, a finance company, underwrote 45% of an issue to the public of 280,000 shares of £1 each by Manufacturers Ltd. The issue price was £1·12 payable as to 87p on application and 25p on May 31st. The underwriting contract provided for a commission of 2p per share and an over-riding commission of 1p per share. Stock Ltd arranged a sub-under-writing contract with Jones who sub-underwrote 5% of the whole issue at a commission of 2p per share.

The public applied for, and were allotted, 200,000 shares. The application monies on the shares underwritten by Stock Ltd were paid by them to Manufacturers Ltd and Jones paid Stock Ltd the application monies on the shares sub-underwritten.

These transactions, including payment of all the commissions, were completed by March 31st, except for the final call which was paid on the due date.

Stock Ltd had the following further transactions in the shares of Manufacturers Ltd:

April    Granted a call option on 30,000 shares to Wide Ltd at £1·05 per share exercisable on or before September 30th, in consideration of an immediate payment of 1p per share.

June    Bought and paid for 18,000 shares at 83p per share. Sold and received payment for 20,000 shares at 85p per share.

Stock Ltd closed its books on June 30th, and valued the shares in Manufacturers Ltd at the lower of cost or market value (90p) for which purpose the results of all the transactions in the shares (which were recorded in one account) were taken into account.

Show the account in the books of Stock Ltd recording the foregoing transactions.

Ignore costs.

## MANUFACTURERS LTD
## UNDERWRITING AND INVESTMENT ACCOUNT

| | | Shares | £ | | | Shares | £ |
|---|---|---|---|---|---|---|---|
| Mar. 31 | Cash:<br>87p per share on application and allotment for 36,000 shares underwritten | 36,000 | 31,320 | Mar. 31 | Cash:<br>Jones – 87p per share on 4,000 shares sub-underwritten | 4,000 | 3,480 |
| | Cash:<br>Jones – Underwriting commission on 14,000 at 2p per share | | 280 | | Cash:<br>Underwriting commission on 126,000 shares at 2p per share | | 2,520 |
| | | | | | Cash:<br>Overriding commission on 126,000 shares at 1p per share | | 1,260 |
| | | | | | Balance c/d. | 32,000 | 24,340 |
| | | 36,000 | £31,600 | | | 36,000 | £31,600 |
| Apr. 1 | Balance b/d. | 32,000 | 24,340 | Apr. | Cash:<br>Wide Ltd –Call option on 30,000 shares at £1·05 on payment of 1p per share | | 300 |
| May 31 | Cash:<br>Call of 25p per share on 32,000 shares (36,000-4,000) | | 8,000 | June | | | |
| June | Cash:<br>Shares bought at 83p per share | 18,000 | 14,940 | June 30 | Cash:<br>Sale of 20,000 shares at 85p per share | 20,000 | 17,000 |
| | | | | | Profit and Loss on underwriting account – loss | | 2,980 |
| | | | | | Balance c/f. (at 90p per share) subject to option until September 30th | 30,000 | 27,000 |
| | | 50,000 | £47,280 | | | 50,000 | £47,280 |

*Notes:*

1. The shares underwritten are:                                    £

         Stock Ltd – 45 per cent. of 280,000    ..    ..    ..    .. 126,000

         Jones – 5 per cent. of 280,000    ..    ..    ..    ..    .. 14,000

Of the 80,000 shares not taken up by the public, Stock Ltd must take up 45 per cent. = 36,000, of which Jones is responsible for 5 per cent. of 80,000 = 4,000 under his sub-underwriting contract.

2. The shares on hand at June 30th have been carried forward at market price, which is less than the net cost to the company.

3. Proof of loss, transferred to Profit and Loss on Underwriting Account:

         Investment losses–                                               £

                 Sales 20,000 shares at a loss of 27p each ..    ..    ..    .. 5,400

                 Depreciation 12,000 shares at 22p per share    ..    ..    .. 2,640

                                                               8,040

         *Less* Profit on purchases 18,000 at 7p    ..    ..    ..    .. 1,260

                                                    Carried forward    £6,780

| | | £ | £6,780 |
|---|---|---|---|
| | Brought forward | | £6,780 |
| Underwriting Profits: | | £ | |
| Commission 2p per share on 126,000 shares .. .. .. | | 2,520 | |
| Less Commission payable to Jones 2p per share on 14,000 shares .. | | 280 | |
| | | 2,240 | |
| Add Overriding Commission 1p per share on 126,000 shares .. | | 1,260 | |
| | | 3,500 | |
| Add Share Option – Wide Ltd .. .. .. .. | | 300 | |
| | | | 3,800 |
| | Loss | | £2,980 |

### (b) Commission on placing Shares

This is an amount payable to parties who introduce to the company persons willing to become members, and to take up shares.

The *Companies Act 1948* states that commission on placing shares is only permissible if:

1. Authorized by the Articles of Association.

2. The amount, or rate per cent., of the commission (which must not exceed 10 per cent. of the price at which the shares are issued or the rate stated in the Articles of Association) is stated in the prospectus or statement in lieu.

This commission is usually payable in cash, but is sometimes satisfied by the issue of fully-paid shares, or partly in one form and partly in the other.

Under the Eighth Schedule to the *Companies Act 1948*, Part I, paragraph 3, the total amount of commission paid on any shares or debentures, or the amount not written off, must be stated under a separate heading in every Balance Sheet of the company until the whole amount has been written off.

### § 10. Mortgages and Debentures

### (a) Definition of Mortgage

A mortgage of freehold property is theoretically a long lease (3,000 years) granted by one person (the mortgagor) to another (the mortgagee) as a security for money lent, on condition that if the money is repaid on a certain day with interest at an agreed rate, the lease made in favour of the mortgagee shall automatically terminate. The right of the mortgagor to have the mortgage terminated is called the 'equity of redemption'.

For leasehold property, the term of the lease to the mortgagee is for the unexpired portion of the mortgagor's lease less ten days.

A second mortgage may be given for one day longer than the first mortgage.

In a mortgage both the lender and the borrower have a legal estate: the lender's legal estate is an assignable leasehold; and the borrower's legal estate is either a freehold or leasehold interest upon which he can sue subject to mortgage.

A company can raise money by mortgaging land or other assets. A mortgage is, therefore, briefly a conditional transfer of property to secure the repayment of a loan with interest. Until the terms of the mortgage are contravened (e.g. by failure to pay interest or repay principal) the borrower (mortgagor) retains use and possession of the property, although his title is encumbered and he cannot convey (sell) it without the consent of the lender (mortgagee).

The entries in a company's books when money is borrowed on mortgage will be to debit cash and credit a Loan on Mortgage Account. A note should be made in the Ledger Account of the asset charged under the mortgage; and the appropriate entry must be made in the register of charges. In the Balance Sheet the loan must be shown as a secured liability (*see* Eighth Schedule, Part I, paragraph 9).

### (b) Definition of a Debenture

A debenture is a written acknowledgement of a debt by a company, usually under seal and generally containing provisions for payment of interest and repayment of capital; a simple or naked debenture carries no charge on assets; a secured debenture carries either a fixed charge on a specific asset or a floating charge on all or some of the assets. All forms of loan stock are debentures.

A fixed charge is a mortgage on specific assets, under which the company loses the right to deal with the assets charged, except with the consent of the mortgagee. A floating charge is not a mortgage at all, since the charge is such that so long as the company continues to carry on its business and observe the terms of the charge, the directors are entitled to deal in any way they please in the ordinary course of business with the assets of the company, and may even make specific charges on property which, subject to the terms of the floating charge given, will have priority to the floating charge. The floating charge is a charge on a class of assets, present and future, which in the ordinary course of business is changing from time to time, and attaches to the property included therein in priority to the general liabilities of the company. The floating charge hovers over or 'floats' with the assets, until some event happens (e.g. default in repaying principal or interest) which crystallizes or fixes the charge.

Under Section 95, all mortgages and charges affecting the property of a company must be registered with the Registrar of Companies within twenty-one days after the creation, otherwise the security will be void against the liquidator and any creditor of the company, and the principal monies will immediately become repayable.

Debentures may take the form of (1) bonds to bearer, or (2) they may be registered in the names of the holders, transmission being by transfer. A debenture ledger should be kept, similar in form to the share ledger previously described, in order to record the necessary particulars. Debenture stock may be issued; the distinction between debenture stock and registered bonds being similar to the distinction between stock and shares mentioned earlier in this chapter. Unlike capital stock, debenture stock can be issued in the form of stock immediately without first being issued in some other form, and may be issued at a discount.

Charges should be in the names of trustees who may issue debenture stock for multiples of the amount of the indebtedness. Trustees, often insurance companies, are usually appointed to safeguard the interests of debenture holders; it is much easier for trustees to bring an action against a company which fails to carry out the terms of a mortgage than for individual debenture-holders, scattered over a wide geographical area often holding small amounts and totally ignorant of the law. The stock exchange insists on the appointment of trustees for debenture holders for quoted debentures. Trustees are usually paid fees which are chargeable in the Profit and Loss Account.

A company may make more than one issue of debentures; issues subsequent to the first may rank *pari passu* (i.e. on an equal footing) with the original issue, or may confer a charge, subject to and following the first, according to whether the original debentures contained clauses allowing or forbidding subsequent *pari passu* issues. Where the debentures carry different priorities, they are usually designated first debentures, second debentures etc. – a higher rate of interest usually being payable on those of lower rank to compensate for the lower degree of security.

A company can issue debentures within the limits of its borrowing powers, as set out in its Memorandum and/or Articles of Association. A trading company's borrowing powers are implied unless there are provisions to the contrary in the Memorandum or Articles. Debentures attract a stamp duty of 25p per cent. on the par or redemption price, whichever is higher.

Interest at the agreed rate is payable on the debentures whether the company makes profits or not, since the charge given covers both principal and interest. Income tax is deductible from the interest payable.

In a liquidation the debenture holders are entitled to the proceeds of their securities, if any, otherwise they rank equally with the unsecured creditors; if the proceeds of a security are insufficient to repay the debentures, the debenture holders rank as unsecured creditors for the balance still due to them.

The entries in the books of a company for an issue of debentures are similar to those on an issue of shares, Instalment Accounts being debited with the various instalments as they become due, and Debentures Account credited. If debentures are issued to the vendor as part of the consideration for a business acquired by the company, the Vendor's Account is debited and the Debentures Account credited. The appropriate entry must also be made in the register of charges kept by the company.

### (c) Debentures issued at a Premium

When debentures are issued at a premium, Debenture Account is credited with the nominal amount and Debenture Premium Account with the premium. Debenture Premium Account can be shown in the Balance Sheet as a (revenue) reserve. The Companies Acts do not specify the uses of the Debenture Premium Account; but common uses are:

(a) to form the nucleus of a debenture redemption fund;

(b) to write off fictitious assets;

(c) to write off debenture issue expenses.

## (d) Debentures issued at a Discount

Debentures can be issued at a discount, but must be redeemed at par or a premium; since a capital profit (which is subject to tax) is made on redemption a lower rate of interest can be paid than if the debentures were issued at their redeemable price.

The effect of issuing debentures at a discount can be seen from the following example:

### Illustration (1)

A company issued debentures of £100 at 95, interest at 5 per cent. repayable at the end of twenty years at par.

Over the twenty years, ignoring tax, the holder receives £100 as interest, and at the end of that period is repaid £100 for £95 advanced. The average return is therefore $\frac{£200 - 95}{20} =$ £5·25 on his investment of £95, or 5·5 per cent. (This rate is not accurate, as it ignores compound interest, but it is sufficiently accurate to show the effect.)

Where debentures are issued at a discount, cash is debited with the net sum received and Discount on Debentures Account with the amount of the discount, Debentures Account being credited with the full nominal value of the debentures, at which value they must appear as a liability in the Balance Sheet. The discount on debentures, or so much as has not been written off, must be shown separately in the Balance Sheet (Eighth Schedule, Part I) (preferably as a deduction from Revenue Reserves).

The discount on the issue is, in effect, deferred interest, and should accordingly be written off over the period having the use of the money raised by the debentures, unless a sinking fund is created to accumulate the full redemption price, including the discount. Where the debentures are redeemable at the end of a specified period, the discount should be written off by equal annual instalments over that period. If, however, the debentures are to be redeemed by annual drawings, the discount should be written off by proportionately reducing instalments, since each succeeding year has the use of a reducing amount of principal.

### Illustration (2)

A company issued on January 1st, 19..., £3,000 debentures at 90 per cent. repayable by instalments of £1,000 at the end of the first, second, and third years respectively. Show the Discount Account, assuming the discount to be written off over the period proportionately.

### DISCOUNT ON ISSUE OF DEBENTURES ACCOUNT

| | | £ | | | £ |
|---|---|---|---|---|---|
| 1st year Jan. 1 | Debenture Account .. .. | 300 | 1st year Dec. 31 | Profit and Loss Account: three-sixths of £300 .. .. Balance c/d. .. .. .. | 150 150 |
| | | £300 | | | £300 |
| 2nd year Jan. 1 | Balance b/d. .. .. .. | 150 | 2nd year Dec. 31 | Profit and Loss Account: two-sixths of £300 .. .. Balance c/d. .. .. | 100 50 |
| | | £150 | | | £150 |
| 3rd year Jan. 1 | Balance b/d .. .. .. | 50 | 3rd year Dec. 31 | Profit and Loss Account: one-sixth of £300 .. .. | 50 |
| | | £50 | | | £50 |

*Note:*

The discount has been written off against the profits of the respective years in the proportions of 3:2:1, since the first year has the use of £3,000, the second year £2,000 and the third year £1,000 of the capital provided by the debentures.

Where the redemption of the nominal amount of the debentures repayable is provided for by charges against Profit and Loss Account, the charges should include the provision for discount, so that the discount can be written off against the credit balance on the Redemption Account.

## (e) Debentures repayable at a Premium

These debentures will stand in the Balance Sheet as a liability at their nominal amount, with a note of the amount at which they are repayable, any discount or premium on issue being treated as described above.

If a sinking fund is raised to provide for repayment, it should include provision for the payment of the premium on redemption. If no sinking fund is created, the premium should be provided for out of profits over the period of the debentures.

Debentures may even be issued at a discount and repayable at a premium.

**Illustration**

A company issued £10,000 debentures, at a discount of 5 per cent., repayable at 102 per cent. at the end of ten years.

Over the ten years, in addition to the interest payable, Profit and Loss Account must be charged with £7 per £100 debenture, i.e. £700 in all, by yearly amounts of £70. Of this £50 is credited to Discount on Debentures Account, and £20 to a Provision for Premium on the Redemption of Debentures Account.

If the debentures were repayable by equal annual drawings, the £700 would be charged in the ratio of 10, 9, 8, 7, 6, 5, 4, 3, 2, 1, i.e. $\frac{10}{55}$ths of £700 = £127·27 would be charged to Profit and Loss Account in the first year, $\frac{9}{55}$ths of £700 = £114·55 in the second year, and so on. The premium paid on redemption would be debited to the Provision Account, and the balance carried forward until the last year, when it would be closed by the last redemption.

## (f) Redemption of Debentures

Debentures may be irredeemable (i.e. the company may be under no obligation to repay the debentures at any specified date); but this is unusual except in companies formed under special Act of Parliament.

Debentures may either be redeemed at the end of a given period or by annual drawings. The trust deed, or if there is no trust deed, then the debentures themselves, will contain provision for redemption and will usually stipulate the establishment of a sinking fund for repayment out of profits – see illustration given below.

Alternatively a company may take out a sinking fund policy with an insurance company for the amount of the debentures.

Section 90 empowers a company which has redeemed debentures to re-issue them, either by re-issuing the same debentures, or by issuing other debentures in lieu; unless provision, express or implied, is contained in the Articles or the conditions of issue, or unless the company has, by passing a resolution, or by some other act, shown its intention that the debentures shall be cancelled. Where a company has redeemed debentures every Balance Sheet must show particulars of debentures that may be redeemed. On re-issue, the debentures must be stamped as an original issue; they retain, however, the same priorities as the original debentures.

The company can purchase its own debentures; when debentures are purchased at below the issued price a capital profit will result from the purchase. Strict accounting demands appropriate adjustments for accrued interest included in the purchase price. In practice this would frequently be ignored.

**Illustration (1)**

A company issued £100,000 8 per cent. debenture stock at 98 per cent. on January 1st, Year I, the interest is payable half-yearly on June 30th and December 31st. The stock is redeemable at the end of twenty years, at $102\frac{1}{2}$, but the company has power to redeem at any time after the first year at 105, if it gives six months written notice. Provision is made for the establishment of a sinking fund, and the annual contribution of £2,000, together with the interest received during the preceding year, is invested on January 1st in each year, the first investment being made at the beginning of the second year. The trustees are empowered to purchase debentures in the open market should they be below par with the proceeds of the sinking fund investments. Investments were realized as follows to purchase debenture stock:

| | *Original Cost* | *Produced* | *Nominal value of Debenture Stock Purchased* |
|---|---|---|---|
| April 30th, Year 2 .. .. .. | £1,050 | £1,060 | £1,100 |
| September 30th, Year 3 .. .. | 2,000 | 2,100 | 2,150 |

Interest received on the sinking fund investments was for Year 2, Year 3 and Year 4, £40, £80 and £120, respectively.

Prepare accounts showing the transactions up to December 31st, Year 4. Ignore taxation and calculate to the nearest £.

### DEBENTURE STOCK ACCOUNT

| | | £ | | | £ |
|---|---|---|---|---|---|
| Year 2 Dec. 31 | Debenture Redemption Account, cancellation of £1,100 Debenture Stock .. .. .. | 1,100 | Year 1 Jan. 1 | Cash .. .. .. .. | 98,000 |
| | Balance c/d. .. .. .. | 98,900 | | Debenture Discount Account .. | 2,000 |
| | | £100,000 | | | £100,000 |
| Year 3 Dec. 31 | Debenture Redemption Account, cancellation of £2,150 Debenture Stock .. .. .. | 2,150 | Year 3 Jan. 1 | Balance b/d. .. .. .. | 98,900 |
| | Balance c/d. .. .. .. | 96,750 | | | |
| | | £98,900 | | | £98,900 |
| | | | Year 4 Jan. 1 | Balance b/d. .. .. .. | 96,750 |

### DISCOUNT ON DEBENTURES ACCOUNT

| | | £ | | | £ |
|---|---|---|---|---|---|
| Year 1 Jan. 1 | Debenture Stock Account .. | 2,000 | Year 2 Dec. 31 | General Reserve Account (see note 4) | 1,100 |
| | | | | Balance c/d. .. .. .. | 900 |
| | | £2,000 | | | £2,000 |
| Year 2 Jan. 1 | Balance b/d. .. .. .. | 900 | Year 3 Dec. 31 | General Reserve Account (see note 4) | 900 |

## SINKING FUND ACCOUNT

| Date | Particulars | £ | Date | Particulars | £ |
|---|---|---|---|---|---|
| Year 2<br>Dec. 31 | General Reserve Account<br>Balance c/d. | 1,100<br>3,019 | Year 1<br>Dec. 31 | Profit and Loss Account .. | 2,000 |
| | | | Year 2<br>Dec. 31 | Sinking Fund Investments Account –<br>   Profit on sale<br>Debenture Redemption Account –<br>   Profit on purchase<br>Interest on Investments ..<br>Profit and Loss Account .. | 10<br><br>69<br>40<br>2,000 |
| | | £4,119 | | | £4,119 |
| Year 3<br>Dec. 31 | General Reserve Account<br>Balance c/d. | 2,150<br>3,142 | Year 3<br>Jan. 1<br>Dec. 31 | Balance b/d.<br>Sinking Fund Investments Account –<br>   Profit on sale<br>Debenture Redemption Account –<br>   Profit on purchase<br>Interest on Investments ..<br>Profit and Loss Account | 3,019<br><br>100<br><br>93<br>80<br>2,000 |
| | | £5,292 | | | £5,292 |
| Year 4<br>Dec. 31 | Balance c/d. | 5,262 | Year 4<br>Jan. 1<br>Dec. 31 | Balance b/d.<br>Interest on Investments ..<br>Profit and Loss Account .. | 3,142<br>120<br>2,000 |
| | | £5,262 | | | £5,262 |
| | | | Year 5<br>Jan. 1 | Balance b/d. | 5,262 |

## SINKING FUND INVESTMENTS ACCOUNT

| Date | Particulars | £ | Date | Particulars | £ |
|---|---|---|---|---|---|
| Year 2<br>Jan. 1<br>Dec. 31 | Cash ..<br>Sinking Fund Account – Profit on<br>   sale of investments .. | 2,000<br><br>10 | Year 2<br>Apr. 30<br>Dec. 31 | Cash ..<br>Balance c/d. | 1,060<br>950 |
| | | £2,010 | | | £2,010 |
| Year 3<br>Jan. 1<br>Dec. 31 | Balance b/d.<br>Cash ..<br>Sinking Fund Account – Profit on<br>   sale of investments .. | 950<br>2,069<br><br>100 | Year 3<br>Sept. 30<br>Dec. 31 | Cash ..<br>Balance c/d. | 2,100<br>1,019 |
| | | £3,119 | | | £3,119 |
| Year 4<br>Jan. 1 | Balance b/d.<br>Cash .. | 1,019<br>2,123 | Year 4<br>Dec. 31 | Balance c/d. | 3,142 |
| | | £3,142 | | | £3,142 |
| Year 5<br>Jan. 1 | Balance b/d. | 3,142 | | | |

## DEBENTURE REDEMPTION ACCOUNT

| Date | Particulars | £ | Date | Particulars | £ |
|---|---|---|---|---|---|
| Year 2<br>Apr. 30<br>Dec. 31 | Cash, Purchase of £1,100 Debentures *cum. div.*<br>Sinking Fund Account – Profit on<br>   Debentures purchased for cancellation | 1,060<br><br>69 | Year 2<br>Apr. 30<br>Dec. 31 | Debenture Interest Account, 4 months<br>   accrued interest on £1,100 Debentures purchased *cum. div.*<br>Debentures Account, Debentures cancelled | 29<br><br>1,100 |
| | | £1,129 | | | £1,129 |
| Year 3<br>Sept. 30<br>Dec. 31 | Cash, Purchase of £2,150 Debentures *cum. div.*<br>Sinking Fund Account – Profit on<br>   Debentures purchased for cancellation | 2,100<br><br>93 | Year 3<br>Sept. 30<br>Dec. 31 | Debenture Interest Account, 3 months<br>   accrued interest on £2,150 Debentures purchased *cum. div.*<br>Debentures Account, Debentures cancelled | 43<br><br>2,150 |
| | | £2,193 | | | £2,193 |

## DEBENTURE INTEREST ACCOUNT

| | | £ | | | £ |
|---|---|---|---|---|---|
| Year 1 June 30 | Cash: ½ year's Interest on £100,000 .. | 4,000 | Year 1 Dec. 31 | Profit and Loss Account .. .. | 8,000 |
| Dec. 31 | " " " " .. | 4,000 | | | |
| | | £8,000 | | | £8,000 |
| Year 2 Apr. 30 | Debenture Redemption Account – 4 months' Interest on £1,100 Debentures purchased *cum. div.* | 29 | Year 2 Dec. 31 | Profit and Loss Account .. | 7,941 |
| June 30 | Cash: ½ year's Interest on £98,900 .. | 3,956 | | | |
| | " " " " .. | 3,956 | | | |
| | | £7,941 | | | £7,941 |
| Year 3 June 30 | Cash: ½ year's Interest on £98,900 .. | 3,956 | Year 3 Dec. 31 | Profit and Loss Account .. .. | 7,869 |
| Sept. 30 | Debenture Redemption Account – 3 months' Interest on £2,150 Debentures purchased *cum. div.* | 43 | | | |
| Dec. 31 | Cash: ½ year's Interest on £96,750 .. | 3,870 | | | |
| | | £7,869 | | | £7,869 |
| Year 4 June 30 | Cash: ½ year's Interest on £96,750 .. | 3,870 | Year 4 Dec. 31 | Profit and Loss Account .. .. | 7,740 |
| Dec. 31 | " " " " .. | 3,870 | | | |
| | | £7,740 | | | £7,740 |

## SINKING FUND CASH ACCOUNT

| | | £ | | | £ |
|---|---|---|---|---|---|
| Year 1 Dec. 31 | General Cash – Annual Instalment | 2,000 | Year 2 Jan. 1 | Sinking Fund Investments Account | 2,000 |
| Year 2 Apr. 30 | Sinking Fund Investments Account, Proceeds of sale .. .. | 1,060 | Apr. 30 | Debenture Redemption Account, Debentures purchased .. .. | 1,060 |
| Dec. 31 | Interest on Investments .. | 40 | Dec. 31 | Balance c/d. .. .. .. | 2,069 |
| | General Cash – Annual Instalment | 2,000 | | | |
| | General Cash – Refund of Interest on Debentures cancelled .. | 29 | | | |
| | | £5,129 | | | £5,129 |
| Year 3 Jan. 1 | Balance b/d. .. .. .. | 2,069 | Year 3 Jan. 1 | Sinking Fund Investments Account | 2,069 |
| Sept. 30 | Sinking Fund Investments Account, Proceeds of sale .. .. | 2,100 | Sept. 30 | Debenture Redemption Account, Debentures purchased .. .. | 2,100 |
| Dec. 31 | Interest on Investments .. | 80 | Dec. 31 | Balance c/d. .. .. .. | 2,123 |
| | General Cash – Annual Instalment | 2,000 | | | |
| | General Cash – Refund of Interest on Debentures cancelled .. | 43 | | | |
| | | £6,292 | | | £6,292 |
| Year 4 Jan. 1 | Balance b/d. .. .. .. | 2,123 | Year 4 Jan. 1 | Sinking Fund Investments Account | 2,123 |
| Dec. 31 | Interest on Investments .. .. | 120 | Dec. 31 | Balance c/d. .. .. .. | 2,120 |
| | General Cash – Annual Instalment | 2,000 | | | |
| | | £4,243 | | | £4,243 |
| Year 5 Jan. 1 | Balance b/d. .. .. .. | 2,120 | | | |

## GENERAL RESERVE ACCOUNT

| | | £ | | | £ |
|---|---|---|---|---|---|
| Year 2 Dec. 31 | Discount on Debentures Account.. | 1,100 | Year 2 Dec. 31 | Sinking Fund Account .. .. | 1,100 |
| Year 3 Dec. 31 | Discount on Debentures Account | 900 | Year 3 Dec. 31 | Sinking Fund Account .. .. | 2,150 |
| | Balance c/d. .. .. .. | 1,250 | | | |
| | | £2,150 | | | £2,150 |
| | | | Year 4 Jan. 1 | Balance b/d. .. .. .. | 1,250 |

*Notes:*

1. The profit or loss on redemption of debentures, disclosed in the Debenture Redemption Account, is the difference between the price paid on redemption and the nominal value. As the price paid on redemption includes accrued debenture interest, an adjustment has been made debiting Debenture Interest Account and crediting Debenture Redemption Account with the accrued interest. The amount of such interest, having been paid out of sinking fund cash, must be reimbursed thereto out of general cash, and re-invested.

If debentures are purchased or redeemed when they are *ex*-interest, the price paid will exclude interest from the date of purchase to the interest payment date; an adjustment can be made debiting Debenture Redemption Account and crediting Debenture Interest Account with interest on the debentures purchased or redeemed from the date of purchase to the interest payment date; general cash will be debited and sinking fund cash credited.

2. No purpose is served by apportioning the proceeds of sale of the investments between capital and income, as both the interest earned and any profit or loss on realization of the investments must be transferred to the Sinking Fund Account.

3. An amount equal to the nominal amount of the debenture stock cancelled has been transferred from the Sinking Fund Account to General Reserve, as the assets representing it are now part of the general assets and are not included in the Sinking Fund Investment Account.

4. The discount allowed on the issue should be written off as soon as possible. The discount allowed on the issue of cancelled stock *must* be written off, as the debentures are no longer outstanding. As, however, the general reserve is available, it has been thought advisable to write off the whole discount against it immediately.

If the terms of issue of the debenture stock require a sinking fund to be set up with trustees, the company may be regarded as holding the investments of the sinking fund in trust for the debenture stockholders. In such a case the income from investments is liable to income tax at the standard rate but not to corporation tax. Investment income is therefore brought into account net and no further entries are necessary for taxation.

If *no* trust is created in favour of the debenture stockholders any unfranked investment income will be liable to corporation tax, but the income tax suffered, in so far as it exceeds income tax recouped on charges paid, will be treated as a payment on account of the corporation tax liability. The income credited to the Redemption or Sinking Fund Account would then be net of corporation tax instead of net of income tax. If, however, the investment income consists of dividends from United Kingdom companies it will be franked investment income (exempt from corporation tax) and the company will be able to offset the income tax deducted against its own Schedule 'F' liability. In that event the gross dividends received would be credited to the sinking fund.

Alternatively, the debentures purchased on the open market can be kept alive and treated as Sinking Fund Investments. The annual appropriation of profits is credited to Sinking Fund Account, and the amount expended on the purchase of debentures debited to Sinking Fund Investment Account. Interest on such debentures is credited to the Sinking Fund Account and invested as if it were an 'outside' investment of the fund.

The sinking fund instalments are computed on the basis that they will accumulate at compound interest over the term of the debentures. Where, therefore, investments are realized and debentures purchased at an earlier date, the sinking fund is deprived of interest, and its basis vitiated. On each purchase of debentures, therefore, the sinking fund should be compensated for the loss of interest. This can be done by:

(a) recomputing the annual instalments, having regard to the nucleus available and the remainder of the term of the debentures; or

(b) computing the interest on the debentures purchased, and adding this amount to the annual instalment to be set aside and invested; or

(c) charging as an addition to the annual instalment the interest lost to the sinking fund by the sale of investments.

Methods (b) and (c) are inaccurate expedients. Method (b) involves an increasing annual appropriation of profits; method (c) may fail to provide adequate funds. Accordingly, method (a) is strongly advised.

Where no sinking fund is created, an amount equal to the cash applied in purchasing or redeeming debentures should be transferred from Profit and Loss Account to reserve (unless the necessary funds are already in that account) in order to conserve working capital, since the cash so utilized consists of profits withheld from distribution. This automatically adjusts for any premium or discount.

**Illustration (2)**

On January 1st, 19.. a company had outstanding £50,000 5 per cent. debentures. On the following December 31st, the company purchased for cancellation £20,000 debentures at 98, the expenses being £100. The profits for the year amounted to £34,000.

Show journal entries (including cash).

JOURNAL

| | | £ | £ |
|---|---|---|---|
| 5% Debentures Account .. .. .. .. .. .. .. | Dr | 20,000 | |
| To Debenture Redemption Account .. .. .. .. .. | | | 20,000 |
| Transfer of £20,000 Debentures for cancellation as per minute dated........ | | | |
| Debenture Redemption Account .. .. .. .. .. .. .. | Dr | 20,000 | |
| To Cash .. .. .. .. .. .. .. .. | | | 19,700 |
| General Reserve .. .. .. .. .. .. .. .. | | | 300 |
| Purchase and cancellation of £20,000 Debentures at 98, Expenses £100, and transfer of profit. | | | |
| Profit and Loss Account .. .. .. .. .. .. .. .. | Dr | 19,700 | |
| To General Reserve .. .. .. .. .. .. .. | | | 19,700 |
| Transfer of amount equal to cost of Debentures purchased. | | | |

*Note:* As the company's liquid resources had been reduced, £19,700 should be transferred to General Reserve from Profit and Loss Account so that the balance on Profit and Loss Account will not overstate the amount available for distribution. This entry reflects that the purchase of the debentures has been effected out of profits, and to the extent that profits have been used for this purpose they cannot be distributed as dividend without seriously depleting the company's working capital.

If debentures are redeemed by annual drawings, an amount equal to the cash applied each year in redemption should be transferred to reserve (unless already therein), for the reasons already stated, any premium or discount being debited or credited to General Reserve as in the purchase of debentures on the open market.

If a company has no sinking fund it does not usually invest in its own debentures unless the rate of interest payable is higher than the market rate, or the market price is favourable, or the issue terms forbid cancellation. When a purchase is made, an adjustment may be necessary for accrued debenture interest; Debenture Interest Receivable Account should be debited and Profit and Loss Account credited with the accrued debenture interest included in the purchase price. If debentures are bought *ex*-interest Interest Account may be debited and Debenture Interest Receivable Account credited with the interest appropriate to the period starting on the date of debenture purchase and ending on the interest payment date. The principle is that Debenture Interest Receivable Account must be credited with income only for the period during which the investment is held, although as previously stated these adjustments would frequently be ignored.

In the illustration below, the debenture interest receivable has been shown in a separate column in the Investment Account so that the exact position has been disclosed.

### Illustration (3)

Wyezed Ltd had outstanding £60,000 5 per cent. debentures at the beginning of the year 19.., interest payable March 31st and September 30th. During the year, debentures were purchased in the open market as follows:

March 15th,  £10,000 nominal, *ex* interest, cost £9,890.

August 1st,    £8,000   „    *cum* „    „   £8,050.

The debentures were retained as an investment.

The debentures were cancelled on the following March 31st. Write up the accounts to that date, making calculations to the nearest £. Ignore taxation.

#### DEBENTURE ACCOUNT

| | | £ | | | | £ |
|---|---|---|---|---|---|---|
| Mar. 31 | Own Debenture Investment Account – cancellation of Debentures purchased .. .. | 18,000 | Jan. 1 | Balance b/f. .. .. .. | | 60,000 |
| | Balance c/f. .. .. .. | 42,000 | | | | |
| | | £60,000 | | | | £60,000 |

#### DEBENTURE INTEREST ACCOUNT

| | | £ | | | | £ |
|---|---|---|---|---|---|---|
| Mar. 31 | Cash .. .. .. .. | 1,500 | Jan. 1 | Balance, accrued interest b/f. .. | | 750 |
| Sept. 30 | Own Debenture Investment Account | 450 | Dec. 31 | Profit and Loss Account .. | | 3,000 |
| | Cash .. .. .. .. | 1,050 | | | | |
| Dec. 31 | Balance, accrued interest c/d. .. | 750 | | | | |
| | | £3,750 | | | | £3,750 |
| Mar. 31 | Own Debenture Investment Account | 450 | Jan. 1 | Balance b/d. .. .. .. | | 750 |
| | Cash .. .. .. .. | 1,050 | Mar. 31 | Profit and Loss Account .. .. | | 750 |
| | | £1,500 | | | | £1,500 |

## OWN DEBENTURES INVESTMENT ACCOUNT

**Dr.**

| | | Nominal | Interest Receivable | Principal |
|---|---|---|---|---|
| | | £ | £ | £ |
| Mar. 15 | Cash – purchase *ex*-interest .. | 10,000 | | 9,890 |
| | Interest – contra, ½ month to March 31st .. | | | 21 |
| Aug. 1 | Cash – purchase *cum.* interest .. | 8,000 | | |
| | Cost .. .. .. £8,050 | | | |
| | *Less* accrued interest 4 months .. .. 133 | | 133 | 7,917 |
| Dec. 31 | Profit and Loss Account .. | | 563 | |
| | | £18,000 | £696 | £17,828 |
| Jan. 1 | Balance b/d .. .. | 18,000 | 225 | 17,828 |
| Mar. 31 | Reserve – Profit on cancellation .. .. | | | 172 |
| | Profit and Loss Account .. .. | | 225 | |
| | | £18,000 | £450 | £18,000 |

**Cr.**

| | | Nominal | Interest Receivable | Principal |
|---|---|---|---|---|
| | | £ | £ | £ |
| Mar. 15 | Principal – contra .. | | 21 | |
| Sept. 30 | Debenture Interest Account, ½ year's interest .. | | 450 | |
| | Balance, interest accrued, c/d. .. | | 225 | |
| Dec. 31 | Balance c/d .. .. | 18,000 | | 17,828 |
| | | £18,000 | £696 | £17,828 |
| Mar. 31 | Debenture Interest Account .. | 18,000 | 450 | 18,000 |
| | Debentures Account – cancellation | | | |
| | | £18,000 | £450 | £18,000 |

RESERVE ACCOUNT

| | | | Mar. 31 | Own Debenture Investment Account | £ 172 |
| | | | | Profit and Loss Account .. .. | 17,828 |
| | | | | | 18,000 |

*Notes:*

1. The interest on own debentures credited to Profit and Loss Account at December 31st, 19.. is made up as follows:

$$9\tfrac{1}{2} \text{ months at } 5\% \text{ on } £10,000 = £395\cdot83$$
$$5 \quad ,, \quad ,, \quad ,, \quad ,, \quad £8,000 = \quad 166\cdot67$$

$$£562\cdot50 \text{ (say £563)}$$

2. To maintain working capital, a transfer has been made from Profit and Loss Account of the amount required to increase the reserve to a sum equal to the nominal value of the debentures redeemed.

### (g) *Debentures issued as Security for a Loan*

Companies often issue their own debentures as security for a loan, or a bank overdraft; Section 90 (4) provides that debentures are not automatically redeemed by the repayment of the loan or overdraft.

Such security is termed 'collateral' or additional security; the amount of the debentures will not appear in the company's accounts as a liability in addition to the loan or overdraft.

Debentures thus issued should be shown 'in short' in the Balance Sheet, and stated as having been issued as security. The loan against which they are issued will be extended as a liability in the usual way. A note of the issue should be made at the head of the Debenture Account in the ledger. The debentures require registration in the ordinary way.

No interest is payable on such debentures; the interest on the bank loan or overdraft is paid in the usual way, and the bank will only resort to the debentures if it becomes necessary to protect their security, e.g. in a liquidation or when a receiver is appointed. The word 'secured' should appear after any liability appearing on the Balance Sheet so secured.

### (h) *Debenture Interest in the Final Accounts*

Interest on debentures is a liability payable whether or not the company earns profits. In preparing final accounts provision must be made for interest accrued to Balance Sheet date so that the Profit and Loss Account will be charged with interest for the whole accounting period, and any accrued liability will appear in the Balance Sheet. Debenture interest is paid net, i.e. after deduction of income tax; the tax deducted will be debited to Debenture Interest Account and credited to Income Tax Account and accounted for to the Inland Revenue under Schedule F. In the Profit and Loss Account debenture interest must appear gross, i.e. before deduction of income tax.

### (i) *Conversion of Debentures into new Debentures carrying a lower rate of interest*

Occasionally the market rates of interest require companies to review their debentures. Where the debentures permit the company to redeem on six months' notice, the company gives notice and offers new debentures carrying a lower rate of interest in exchange. Where the holders of the old debentures do not take up the new debentures in full, the balance is offered to the public for subscription or placed privately. The entries are simple, viz. Old Debentures Account is debited and New Debentures Account credited with the debentures exchanged, in so far as the holders accept; Old Debentures Account is debited, and cash credited when the holders desire repayment; the usual entries are made when the new debentures are issued to the public or to private subscribers.

Sometimes there is no power of redemption available at the date when the company wishes to alter the terms of its debentures, an arrangement must therefore be made with the debenture holders whereby some consideration is given for their agreeing to accept a lower rate of interest in future, e.g. a cash payment or an issue of new debentures repayable at a premium.

**Illustration (4)**

A company arranged with holders of £100,000 $5\frac{1}{2}$% debentures that their debentures could either be redeemed at a 103% or converted into $4\frac{1}{2}$% debentures repayable at 104% by annual drawings over twenty years. Holders of £60,000 $5\frac{1}{2}$% debentures opted to take the $4\frac{1}{2}$% debentures; the company then offered the public £40,000 $4\frac{1}{2}$% debentures at 101% payable: on application £20, on allotment £31, and at intervals of one month thereafter £25 per instalment. Applications for £90,000 debentures were received including applications for £25,000 from existing debenture holders. Allotment was made in full to existing holders; no allotments were made to other applicants for less than £500 stock (amounting to £20,000 nominal); *pro rata* allotments were made to other applicants.

Show the journal entries including cash necessary to record these transactions.

JOURNAL

| | | £ | £ |
|---|---|---|---|
| $5\frac{1}{2}$% Debentures Account .. .. .. .. .. .. .. Dr | | 100,000 | |
| To $4\frac{1}{2}$% Debentures Account .. .. .. .. .. .. .. | | | 60,000 |
| Sundry Debenture Holders .. .. .. .. .. .. | | | 40,000 |
| Conversion by holders of £60,000 $5\frac{1}{2}$% debentures into $4\frac{1}{2}$% debentures, and transfer of balance for repayment. | | | |
| Profit and Loss Account .. .. .. .. .. .. .. .. Dr | | 1,200 | |
| To Sundry Debenture Holders .. .. .. .. .. .. | | | 1,200 |
| Premium of 3% on repayment of £40,000 $5\frac{1}{2}$% debentures. | | | |
| Cash .. .. .. .. .. .. .. .. Dr | | 18,000 | |
| To $4\frac{1}{2}$% Debentures Application and Allotment Account .. .. .. .. | | | 18,000 |
| £20 per debenture on £90,000 debentures applied for. | | | |
| $4\frac{1}{2}$% Debentures Application and Allotment Account .. .. .. .. .. Dr | | 24,400 | |
| To $4\frac{1}{2}$% Debentures Account .. .. .. .. .. .. | | | 20,000 |
| Premium on Issue of Debentures Account .. .. .. .. .. | | | 400 |
| Cash .. .. .. .. .. .. .. | | | 4,000 |
| Allotment per minute of this day of £25,000 debentures to existing holders in full; £15,000 debentures to applicants for £45,000, *pro rata*; £51 being due on application and allotment on each £100 debenture and refund of application money on applications for £20,000 debentures. | | | |
| Cash .. .. .. .. .. .. .. .. Dr | | 7,750 | |
| To $4\frac{1}{2}$% Debentures Application and Allotment Account .. .. .. .. | | | 7,750 |
| Allotment monies received on £25,000 debentures allotted in full, £31 per £100 debenture. | | | |

## JOURNAL (*continued*)

| | | | | | | | £ | £ |
|---|---|---|---|---|---|---|---:|---:|
| 4¼% Debentures Application and Allotment Account | .. | .. | .. | .. | Dr | | 1,350 | |
| To 4½% Debentures First Instalment Account | .. | .. | .. | .. | .. | | | 1,350 |
| Transfer of amounts overpaid on application towards amount payable on instalments on £15,000 allotted *pro rata* to applicants for £45,000 debentures, made up as follows: | | | | | | | | |
| £31 per £100 on £15,000 Debentures now due | .. | .. | .. | .. | £4,650 | | | |
| £20 „ „ „ £30,000 „ not allotted | .. | .. | .. | .. | 6,000 | | | |
| Overpayment carried forward | .. | .. | .. | .. | £1,350 | | | |
| 4½% Debentures First Instalment Account .. | .. | .. | .. | .. | Dr | | 10,000 | |
| To 4½% Debentures Account | .. | .. | .. | .. | .. | | | 10,000 |
| £25 per £100 debenture due on £40,000 debentures. | | | | | | | | |
| Cash | .. | .. | .. | .. | Dr | | 8,650 | |
| To 4½% Debentures First Instalment Account | .. | .. | .. | .. | .. | | | 8,650 |
| Balance due now received. | | | | | | | | |
| 4½% Debentures Second Instalment Account | .. | .. | .. | .. | Dr | | 10,000 | |
| To 4½% Debentures Account | .. | .. | .. | .. | .. | | | 10,000 |
| Final instalment of £25 per debenture now due. | | | | | | | | |
| Cash .. | .. | .. | .. | .. | Dr | | 10,000 | |
| To 4½% Debentures Second Instalment Account | .. | .. | .. | .. | .. | | | 10,000 |
| Balance due now received. | | | | | | | | |
| Sundry Debenture Holders | .. | .. | .. | .. | Dr | | 41,200 | |
| To Cash | .. | .. | .. | .. | .. | | | 41,200 |
| Redemption of £40,000 debentures at 103. | | | | | | | | |

*Note:* The premium on the new issue could be applied towards writing off the premium payable on the debentures redeemed, the balance of the premium being written off to Profit and Loss Account.

## § 11. The Purchase of a Business by a Limited Company

As explained in § 1 of this chapter, some advantages may stem from the 'conversion' of a private business into a limited company, e.g. perpetual succession, whereby a member of a company can transfer his shares, or bequeath them by will at death, without disturbing the constitution of the company or its financial resources.

The 'conversion' may take the form of the transfer to a private company of the assets and goodwill of the business in consideration of the allotment of shares in the company, which the sellers of the business will continue to hold, and through which they will retain the control of the business. Alternatively, a public company may be formed to acquire the business; a promoter or syndicate purchases the business from the original owners, and resells it to the company at a profit, the capital of the company being raised by public subscriptions. Or a public company may be formed to take over the business of a private company, the shareholders of the private company receiving shares or other interests in the public company in exchange for their existing holdings.

In the purchasing company's books the assets acquired must be debited at acquisition values, which are often different from the book values shown in the vendor business's books; when a business is sold assets are frequently revalued. Sometimes the purchasing company assumes trade liabilities as part of the purchase consideration; sometimes the company discharges the trade liabilities and collects the book debts as agent for the sellers; interest may be allowed or charged until final settlement between the purchasing company and the sellers is effected. Book debts are usually acquired at book values less an agreed provision for bad or doubtful debts; any excess received over the book values less the provision for doubtful debts is a capital profit in the purchasing company's books.

In addition to the purchase price of the tangible assets, a further sum is usually payable for goodwill. A company making a public issue for the purpose of acquiring a business must state in the prospectus the amount of the purchase consideration attributable to goodwill.

Goodwill is the excess of the total purchase consideration over the value of the other assets acquired, less the amount of any liabilities assumed by the company.

### (a) Entries in the purchasing company's books

The entries in the company's books necessary to record the purchase of the business are as follows:

| DEBIT | CREDIT | NOTES |
|---|---|---|
| Assets | Vendor's Account | Assets acquired at acquisition values |
| Vendor's Account | Liabilities | Liabilities acquired at acquisition values |
| Vendor's Account | Share Capital<br>Share Premium<br>Debentures<br>Cash | Purchase consideration |
| Goodwill | Vendor's Account | Excess of purchase consideration over net assets acquired |
| Vendor's Account | Capital Reserve | Excess of net assets acquired over purchase consideration. |

*Note:* Any debtors taken over should be debited at book values and any provision for doubtful or bad debts should be credited to a Provision for Bad Debts Account.

Some accountants prefer to pass the purchase of a business through a Purchase of Business Account, which replaces the Vendor's Account, being credited with the assets acquired and debited with the liabilities taken over and with the purchase consideration.

**Illustration (1)**

A company takes over the following assets and liabilities of a private business:

|  |  |  |  |  |  |  |  |  |  | £ |
|---|---|---|---|---|---|---|---|---|---|---|
| Leasehold Property | .. | .. | .. | .. | .. | .. | .. | .. | .. | 7,000 |
| Plant and Machinery | .. | .. | .. | .. | .. | .. | .. | .. | .. | 3,000 |
| Stock-in-Trade | .. | .. | .. | .. | .. | .. | .. | .. | .. | 4,600 |
| Sundry Debtors | .. | .. | .. | .. | .. | .. | .. | .. | .. | 3,000 |
| Cash .. | .. | .. | .. | .. | .. | .. | .. | .. | .. | 1,500 |
|  |  |  |  |  |  |  |  |  |  | 19,100 |
| *Less* Trade Creditors .. | .. | .. | .. | .. | .. | .. | .. | .. | .. | 2,100 |
|  |  |  |  |  |  |  |  |  |  | £17,000 |

The purchase consideration is £20,000, payable to the vendor as follows: £10,000 in ordinary shares of £1 each fully paid, £5,000 in 5 per cent. preference shares of £1 each fully paid, all issued at par, and the balance in cash. Show the opening journal entries in the books of the company.

## JOURNAL

| | | | |
|---|---|---|---|
| | | £ | £ |
| Leasehold Property .. .. .. .. .. .. .. .. Dr | | 7,000 | |
| Plant and Machinery .. .. .. .. .. .. .. .. | | 3,000 | |
| Stock-in-Trade .. .. .. .. .. .. .. .. .. | | 3,000 | |
| Sundry Debtors .. .. .. .. .. .. .. .. | | 4,600 | |
| Cash .. .. .. .. .. .. .. .. .. | | 3,000 | |
| Goodwill .. .. .. .. .. .. .. .. | | 1,500 | |
| To Sundry Creditors .. .. .. .. .. .. | | 3,000 | |
| Vendor (or Purchase of Business Account) .. .. .. .. .. | | | 2,100 |
| | | | 20,000 |
| Sundry assets and liabilities taken over as per contract dated........ | | £22,100 | £22,100 |
| | | £ | £ |
| Vendor (or Purchase of Business Account) .. .. .. .. Dr | | 20,000 | |
| To Ordinary Share Capital – 10,000 Shares of £1 each fully paid .. .. .. | | | 10,000 |
| Preference Share Capital – 5,000 Shares of £1 each fully paid .. .. .. | | | 5,000 |
| Cash .. .. .. .. .. .. .. .. .. | | | 5,000 |
| Discharge of purchase consideration as per contract dated........ | | £20,000 | £20,000 |

*Note:* The amount debited to Goodwill Account is the excess of the amount of the purchase consideration, £20,000, over the total amount of the assets acquired, less the amount of the liabilities assumed, £17,000.

Where the purchase consideration is less than the value at which the net assets stood in the books of the vendor, but the values of the assets taken over are correctly stated (as ascertained by revaluation), the surplus, instead of being treated in the company's books as a capital reserve, may be applied in writing down fixed assets to the level of the consideration. The surplus is not available for distribution to shareholders and cannot be credited to a Revenue Reserve Account.

The absence of a Goodwill Account indicates that no payment has been made for goodwill; it does not indicate that it is non-existent.

Where a partnership business is transferred to a limited company some difficulty may be experienced in capitalizing the company so as to ensure that the rights of the partners are preserved. If the capitals of the partners are in the same ratio as that in which profits are shared, the problem is simplified, as the allotment to the partners of ordinary shares in that ratio will preserve the relationship as nearly as possible. Often, where the capitals are not held in profit-sharing ratio, the problem is complicated, particularly when taxation is considered.

The following illustration shows the effect on the books of a firm of the conversion of a private firm into a limited company, and also the entries in the books of the company:

**Illustration (2)**

The X Company, Limited, was formed to purchase the business of A and B, who share profits, two-thirds and one-third respectively, and whose Balance Sheet was as follows:

## BALANCE SHEET A and B

| | | | | | £ | | | | | | £ |
|---|---|---|---|---|---|---|---|---|---|---|---|
| Creditors .. | .. | .. | .. | .. | 2,700 | Goodwill .. | .. | .. | .. | | 1,000 |
| Bills Payable | .. | .. | .. | | 900 | Freehold Property | .. | .. | .. | | 5,000 |
| Loan Account | .. | .. | .. | | 400 | Plant and Machinery | .. | .. | .. | | 2,500 |
| Capitals– | | | | | | Stock .. | .. | .. | .. | | 3,000 |
| A | .. | .. | .. | £8,000 | | Debtors | .. | .. | .. | £3,100 | |
| B | .. | .. | .. | 5,000 | | *Less* Provision for Bad Debts | .. | | 200 | | |
| | | | | | 13,000 | | | | | | 2,900 |
| | | | | | | Bills Receivable .. | .. | .. | .. | | 800 |
| | | | | | | Investments | .. | .. | .. | | 600 |
| | | | | | | Cash .. | .. | .. | .. | | 1,200 |
| | | | | | £17,000 | | | | | | £17,000 |

The company takes over the assets at book value, with the exception of the freehold property, which is taken over at £6,000. The investments are retained by the firm, and sold by them for £450. They also discharge the loan of £400, but the company takes over the remaining liabilities.

The purchase consideration for the net assets taken over is fixed at £18,950, payable as follows: £9,500 5 per cent. debentures, 7,600 fully paid ordinary shares of £1 each, both at par, and the balance in cash. A and B agree to divide the assets forming the purchase consideration in proportion to the balances standing to the credit of their respective capital accounts, after the adjustments caused by the sale of the business and investments have been completed.

Show the ledger accounts closing the firm's books, and the journal entries opening the company's books.

## FIRM'S BOOKS REALIZATION ACCOUNT

| | | | | £ | | | | | | £ |
|---|---|---|---|---|---|---|---|---|---|---|
| Freehold Property .. | .. | .. | .. | 5,000 | Creditors | .. | .. | .. | .. | 2,700 |
| Plant and Machinery | .. | .. | .. | 2,500 | Bills Payable | .. | .. | .. | .. | 900 |
| Goodwill .. | .. | .. | .. | 1,000 | Provision for Bad Debts .. | .. | .. | 200 |
| Stock .. | .. | .. | .. | .. | 3,000 | X Co Ltd | .. | .. | .. | .. | 18,950 |
| Debtors .. | .. | .. | .. | 3,100 | | | | | | |
| Bills Receivable | .. | .. | .. | 800 | | | | | | |
| Cash .. | .. | .. | .. | .. | 1,200 | | | | | |
| Loss on Investments | .. | .. | .. | 150 | | | | | | |
| Balance, being profit on realization c/d. | .. | 6,000 | | | | | | |
| | | | | £22,750 | | | | | | £22,750 |

| | | | | £ | | | | | | £ |
|---|---|---|---|---|---|---|---|---|---|---|
| Capital Accounts: | | | | | Balance b/d. | .. | .. | .. | .. | 6,000 |
| A two-thirds | .. | .. | .. | 4,000 | | | | | | |
| B one-third | .. | .. | .. | 2,000 | | | | | | |
| | | | | £6,000 | | | | | | £6,000 |

## X COMPANY LTD

| | | | | £ | | | | | | £ |
|---|---|---|---|---|---|---|---|---|---|---|
| Realization Account | .. | .. | .. | 18,950 | Debentures | .. | .. | .. | .. | 9,500 |
| | | | | | Ordinary Shares | .. | .. | .. | 7,600 |
| | | | | | Cash .. | .. | .. | .. | .. | 1,850 |
| | | | | £18,950 | | | | | | £18,950 |

## DEBENTURES IN X CO LTD

| | | | | £ | | | £ |
|---|---|---|---|---|---|---|---|
| X Co Ltd | .. | .. | .. | .. | 9,500 | A Capital Account $\frac{12}{19} \times £9,500$ .. | 6,000 |
| | | | | | | B ,, ,, $\frac{7}{19} \times £9,500$ .. | 3,500 |
| | | | | | £9,500 | | £9,500 |

## ORDINARY SHARES IN X CO LTD

| | £ | | | £ |
|---|---|---|---|---|
| X Co Ltd  ..  ..  ..  .. | 7,600 | A Capital Account $\frac{12}{19} \times$ £7,600  ..  .. | | 4,800 |
| | | B  „  „  $\frac{7}{19} \times$ £7,600  ..  .. | | 2,800 |
| | £7,600 | | | £7,600 |

## CAPITAL ACCOUNTS

| | A £ | B £ | | A £ | B £ |
|---|---|---|---|---|---|
| Balances c/d.  ..  ..  .. | 12,000 | 7,000 | Balances b/f.  ..  ..  .. | 8,000 | 5,000 |
| | | | Profit on realization  ..  .. | 4,000 | 2,000 |
| | £12,000 | £7,000 | | £12,000 | £7,000 |
| Debentures in X Co Ltd  ..  .. | 6,000 | 3,500 | Balances b/d.  .. | 12,000 | 7,000 |
| Shares in X Co Ltd  ..  .. | 4,800 | 2,800 | | | |
| Cash  ..  ..  .. | 1,200 | 700 | | | |
| | £12,000 | £7,000 | | £12,000 | £7,000 |

## CASH BOOK

| | £ | | | £ |
|---|---|---|---|---|
| X Co Ltd..  ..  ..  ..  .. | 1,850 | Loan Account  ..  ..  ..  .. | | 400 |
| Investments  ..  ..  ..  .. | 450 | Balance c/d.  ..  ..  ..  .. | | 1,900 |
| | £2,300 | | | £2,300 |
| Balance b/d.  ..  ..  ..  .. | 1,900 | A Capital Account $\frac{12}{19} \times$ £1,900  ..  .. | | 1,200 |
| | | B  „  „  $\frac{7}{19} \times$ £1,900  ..  .. | | 700 |
| | £1,900 | | | £1,900 |

## INVESTMENTS

| | £ | | | £ |
|---|---|---|---|---|
| Balance c/f.  ..  ..  ..  .. | 600 | Cash  ..  ..  ..  ..  .. | | 450 |
| | | Realization Account – loss  ..  .. | | 150 |
| | £600 | | | £600 |

## LOAN

| | £ | | | £ |
|---|---|---|---|---|
| Cash  ..  ..  ..  ..  .. | 400 | Balance b/f.  ..  ..  ..  .. | | 400 |

## X COMPANY LTD'S BOOKS:  JOURNAL

| | | | | | | | | | £ | £ |
|---|---|---|---|---|---|---|---|---|---|---|
| Freehold Property  ..  .. | .. | .. | .. | .. | .. | .. | .. | Dr | 6,000 | |
| Plant and Machinery  ..  .. | .. | .. | .. | .. | .. | .. | .. | | 2,500 | |
| Stock ..  ..  .. | .. | .. | .. | .. | .. | .. | .. | | 3,000 | |
| Debtors  ..  .. | .. | .. | .. | .. | .. | .. | .. | | 3,100 | |
| Bills Receivable..  .. | .. | .. | .. | .. | .. | .. | .. | | 800 | |
| Cash  ..  .. | .. | .. | .. | .. | .. | .. | .. | | 1,200 | |
| Goodwill  ..  .. | .. | .. | .. | .. | .. | .. | .. | | 6,150 | |
| To Creditors ..  .. | .. | .. | .. | .. | .. | .. | .. | | | 2,700 |
| Bills Payable  ..  .. | .. | .. | .. | .. | .. | .. | .. | | | 900 |
| Provision for Bad Debts  ..  .. | .. | .. | .. | .. | .. | .. | .. | | | 200 |
| Vendors (or Purchase of Business Account)  .. | .. | .. | .. | .. | .. | .. | .. | | | 18,950 |
| | | | | | | | | | £22,750 | £22,750 |

Assets and liabilities taken over as per contract dated...........................

*Note:* The amount debited to Goodwill Account is the difference between the total of the assets, less the liabilities taken over, and the purchase consideration payable to the vendors.

| | | | £ | £ |
|---|---|---|---|---|
| Vendors (or Purchase of Business Account) .. | .. | .. | .. | .. | .. | Dr | 18,950 | |
| To Ordinary Share Capital | .. | .. | .. | .. | .. | .. | .. | | 7,600 |
| Debentures | .. | .. | .. | .. | .. | .. | .. | | 9,500 |
| Cash | .. | .. | .. | .. | .. | .. | .. | | 1,850 |
| | | | £18,950 | £18,950 |

7,600 ordinary shares of £1 each, and £9,500 5% debentures issued fully paid, and cash paid in settlement of purchase consideration as per contract dated...............................

Sometimes a company on acquiring a business does not take over the book debts and liabilities of the vendor, but collects as agent the book debts and pays the liabilities out of the proceeds, accounting to the vendor for the balance; the company should provide special columns in its cash book, into which receipts from debtors and payments to creditors made on behalf of the vendor are entered, and from which they are posted to the personal accounts of the vendor's debtors and creditors. These postings, however, form no part of the double entry from the point of view of the company, since the accounts to which the amounts are posted are not in the company's ledgers. The double entry in the company's books for these transactions is completed by posting periodically the *totals* of the receipts and payments made on behalf of the vendor to the credit and debit respectively of the Vendor's Account. If the company wishes to continue to use the old debtors' and creditors' accounts, a line should be ruled across each account some distance below the last entry prior to the transfer, and the company's own transactions should be entered below this line, in order that the debts owing to and by the company may not be confused with those owing to and by the vendor.

If the company carries on the old debtors and old creditors accounts without a break, it has acquired debtors which it has debited to Total Debtors Account. These must be credited to Debtors Suspense Account since from the company's standpoint they are valueless. Similarly creditors are credited to Total Creditors Account and debited to Creditors Suspense Account. In the illustration below, by continuing to operate upon the vendor's Debtors and Creditors Accounts the ledger contains assets £5,400, and liabilities £3,700, which do not belong to the company, Debtors Suspense Account is credited with £5,400 and Creditors Suspense Account debited with £3,700. At the end of the accounting period all transactions relating to these debtors and creditors are transferred in total from the sales ledger to the Debtors Suspense Account and from the bought ledger to the Creditors Suspense Account. Payments made to the vendor for debts collected or receipts from the vendor for liabilities met are passed through the Current Account with the vendor in the normal way.

Any balances remaining on the Suspense Accounts when the company prepares its Balance Sheet represent the amounts of the debtors and creditors of the vendor still appearing in the company's books, and must be deducted from the totals of the debtors and creditors respectively to arrive at the figures to be shown in the company's Balance Sheet.

**Illustration (3)**

On January 1st YZ Ltd acquired the business of X, taking over all the assets with the exception of the book debts, which it undertook to collect on behalf of X, and out of the proceeds pay the liabilities owing at the date of the transfer. At that date the book debts amounted to £5,400 and the liabilities to £3,700.

The company continued to operate on the old Debtors and Creditors Accounts without a break, and at the following December 31st the total of the book debts amounted to £6,200, of which £400 represented debts owing to X, whilst the total creditors were £5,300, the whole of X's liabilities having been discharged. During the year the company had written off £700 debts as bad, of which £300 was for X's debtors. Discounts allowed by the company during the year amounted to £680, of which £185 was allowed to X's debtors. Discounts allowed to the company amounted to £1,400 of which £104 was for pre-transfer liabilities.

Show the relevant Ledger Accounts in the company's books.

### TOTAL DEBTORS ACCOUNT

| | | £ | | | |
|---|---|---|---|---|---|
| Dec. 31 | Balance    ..    ..    .. | 6,200 | | | |

### TOTAL CREDITORS ACCOUNT

| | | | | | £ |
|---|---|---|---|---|---|
| | | | Dec. 31 | Balance    ..    ..    .. | 5,300 |

### X's DEBTORS SUSPENSE ACCOUNT

| | | £ | | | £ |
|---|---|---|---|---|---|
| Dec. 31 | Bad Debts Account    ..    .. | 300 | Jan.  1 | Total Debtors Account – Debts not taken over from X    .. | 5,400 |
| | Discounts Allowed Account    .. | 185 | | | |
| | X's Account – Cash collected    .. | 4,515 | | | |
| | Balance c/d.    ..    ..    .. | 400 | | | |
| | | £5,400 | | | £5,400 |
| | | | Jan.  1 | Balance b/d.    ..    ..    .. | 400 |

### X's CREDITORS SUSPENSE ACCOUNT

| | | £ | | | £ |
|---|---|---|---|---|---|
| Jan.  1 | Total Creditors Account – Liabilities not taken over from X | 3,700 | Dec. 31 | Discounts Received Account    .. | 104 |
| | | | | X's Account – Cash paid    .. | 3,596 |
| | | £3,700 | | | £3,700 |

### X's ACCOUNT

| | | £ | | | £ |
|---|---|---|---|---|---|
| Dec. 31 | X's Creditors Suspense Account – Cash paid to Creditors..    .. | 3,596 | Dec. 31 | X's Debtors Suspense Account – Cash received from Debtors    .. | 4,515 |
| | Balance c/d.    ..    ..    .. | 919 | | | |
| | | £4,515 | | | £4,515 |
| | | | Jan.  1 | Balance b/d.    ..    ..    .. | 919 |

### BAD DEBTS ACCOUNTS

| | | £ | | | £ |
|---|---|---|---|---|---|
| Dec. 31 | Sundry Debtors – Debts written off | 700 | Dec. 31 | X's Debtors Suspense Account – Amounts applicable to X's debtors | 300 |
| | | | | Profit and Loss Account    ..    .. | 400 |
| | | £700 | | | £700 |

## DISCOUNTS ALLOWED ACCOUNT

| | | £ | | | £ |
|---|---|---|---|---|---|
| Dec. 31 | Sundry Debtors – Discounts Allowed .. .. | 680 | Dec. 31 | X's Debtors Suspense Account – Discounts allowed to X's debtors Profit and Loss Account .. .. | 185 495 |
| | | £680 | | | £680 |

## DISCOUNTS RECEIVED ACCOUNT

| | | £ | | | £ |
|---|---|---|---|---|---|
| Dec. 31 | X's Creditors Suspense Account – Discounts received in respect of X's liabilities .. .. Profit and Loss Account .. .. | 104 1,296 | Dec. 31 | Sundry Creditors Accounts – Discounts Received .. .. | 1,400 |
| | | £1,400 | | | £1,400 |

*Note:* As a result of the above entries there will appear in the company's Balance Sheet a liability to X of £919, whilst the sundry debtors will be £5,800, viz. £6,200, less the credit balance of £400 carried down in the Debtors Suspense Account. The bad debts and discounts transferred to the company's Profit and Loss Account are reduced by the amounts transferred to the Suspense Accounts, and thus borne by the vendor.

### (b) *Apportionment of Profit or Loss prior to Incorporation*

In view of the inconvenience that would be caused by an additional stock-taking and the balancing off of the books when a company is formed to take over an existing business, it is common to ante-date the purchase to the date of the last Balance Sheet, i.e. for the company to take over the business as from a date prior to its incorporation. Profits earned prior to the date of incorporation are not available for dividend, since the company cannot earn profits before it comes into existence. The profits increase the net assets on formation and are capital, not revenue. When the vendor is not entitled to take such profits himself, he is usually paid interest on the purchase consideration from the date as from which the business was taken over to the date on which the purchase consideration is discharged. The interest payable to the vendor for the period from the date of taking over the business to the date of incorporation of the company should be charged against the profits earned during that period, any interest payable for any period after the date of incorporation being charged to Profit and Loss Account. The remaining balance of profits earned prior to incorporation (if any) should either be credited to Goodwill Account, or, if there is no Goodwill Account, applied in writing-down an over-valued asset, or carried forward as a capital reserve not available for distribution.

If stock is not taken at the date of incorporation, and consequently the profits prior to that date cannot be ascertained exactly, it is usual to arrive at the profits applicable to the period either by apportioning the profits for the whole accounting period on a time basis, or in proportion to the turnover of the periods prior to and after incorporation respectively, or by a combination of these methods.

Since a business cannot be expected to earn its profits evenly over the accounting period neither the time nor the turnover method may be satisfactory; it is normal to apportion gross profit on the basis of turnover and the expenses on their merits; those varying with turnover will be apportioned on a turnover basis while other expenses will be apportioned on a time basis.

In apportioning the profits any expenditure which relates solely to the company must be charged against the profits applicable to the period subsequent to the date of incorporation, e.g. directors' fees, debenture interest etc. On the other hand, any expense wholly applicable to the period prior to incorporation, e.g. vendors' salaries, should be charged against pre-incorporation profits.

Any contracts entered into by a public company prior to the issue of the certificate entitling it to commence business are provisional only, but on the issue of that certificate they become binding according to their terms (s. 109 (4)), i.e. they are ratified; the date of division would therefore still be the date of incorporation.

If it is found that a loss has been sustained during the accounting period the following alternative courses are open:

1. To make no apportionment at all, but to carry forward the total loss for the whole period to be written off out of subsequent profits. This is the most conservative course.

2. To debit the amount of the pre-incorporation loss to Goodwill Account. The justification for this treatment is that a loss incurred between the date as from which the business is taken over and the date of incorporation of the company reduces the net assets acquired at the date of incorporation, and thus increases the price paid for goodwill.

3. To debit the loss prior to incorporation to a suspense account, which can be subsequently written off in the same way as other fictitious assets.

**Illustration (1)**

The A B Co Ltd was formed on April 1st to take over the business formerly carried on by Brown & Smith as from January 1st. It was agreed that all profits made after January 1st should belong to the company, but that interest on the purchase consideration (£50,000), at the rate of 6 per cent. per annum, should be paid to the vendors until the final settlement, which took place on June 1st.

The following was the Profit and Loss Account as prepared at December 31st, for the year ending on that date:

| | £ | | £ |
|---|---|---|---|
| Expenses of Management .. .. .. | 3,050 | Gross Trading Profit .. .. .. | 20,000 |
| Bad Debts .. .. .. .. | 200 | | |
| Directors' Fees .. .. .. .. | 1,000 | | |
| Interest to Vendors.. .. .. .. | 1,250 | | |
| Preliminary Expenses, amount written off .. | 500 | | |
| Depreciation .. .. .. .. | 1,000 | | |
| Balance being net Profit .. .. .. | 13,000 | | |
| | £20,000 | | £20,000 |

Bad debts written off, £100, related to debts taken over by the company.

Apportion the profit earned between the periods before and after the date of incorporation, assuming the turnover to be spread evenly over the year.

|  |  | £ |
|---|---|---|
| Net Profits | .. .. .. | 13,000 |
| *Add:* |  |  |
| Bad Debts .. | .. .. | 200 |
| Directors' Fees | .. .. | 1,000 |
| Interest to Vendors .. | .. | 1,250 |
| Preliminary Expenses | .. | 500 |
|  |  | £15,950 |

| | £ | Before Incorporation £ | £ | After Incorporation £ |
|---|---|---|---|---|
| Share of Profits one-quarter of £15,950 .. .. .. .. | | 3,987 | | |
| three-quarters of £15,950 .. .. .. .. | | | | 11,963 |
| *Less* Bad Debts .. .. .. .. .. | 100 | | 100 | |
| Directors' Fees .. .. .. .. .. | | | 1,000 | |
| Interest to Vendors .. .. .. .. .. | 750 | | 500 | |
| Preliminary Expenses .. .. .. .. .. | | | 500 | |
| | | 850 | | 2,100 |
| | | £3,137 | | £9,863 |

*Note:* £3,137 should be treated as a capital profit not available for dividend. It has been arrived at after charging the loss of £100 on the diminished value of the book debts taken over. The preliminary expenses have been written off against the profits after incorporation, but it would have been quite in order to have charged them against the capital reserve represented by the profit prior to incorporation.

### Illustration (2)

A company was formed to take over a business as from January 1st, but was not incorporated until April 30th. The turnover for the year to December 31st was £20,000, of which £4,000 was prior to April 30th.

## PROFIT AND LOSS ACCOUNT
### For the Year ended December 31st

| | Ratio | Prior to Incorporation £ | Subsequent to Incorporation £ | | Ratio | Prior to Incorporation £ | Subsequent to Incorporation £ |
|---|---|---|---|---|---|---|---|
| Rent, Rates and other standing charges .. .. | 1 : 2 | 1,200 | 2,400 | Gross Profit b/d. .. | 1 : 4 | 1,500 | 6,000 |
| Travellers' Commission .. | 1 : 4 | 40 | 160 | | | | |
| Discounts .. .. | 1 : 4 | 30 | 120 | | | | |
| Directors' Fees .. .. | — | — | 250 | | | | |
| Interest on Purchase consideration . .. | — | 200 | 50 | | | | |
| Net Profit to Capital Reserve | — | 30 | — | | | | |
| Appropriation Account .. | — | — | 3,020 | | | | |
| | | £1,500 | £6,000 | | | £1,500 | £6,000 |

*Notes:*

1. The ratio of turnover is 4,000 : 16,000 = 4 : 16 or 1 : 4. The time ratio is four months to eight months = 1 : 2.

2. Standing charges continue irrespective of turnover, and are apportioned on a time basis.

3. Travellers' commission and discounts vary with turnover. Strictly, they may vary with the turnover of a period ending earlier than December 31st, owing to the lag in payment, but the turnover of the period is sufficiently accurate for practical purposes unless the amounts are very large.

4. Directors' fees do not require apportionment.

5. Interest on the purchase consideration is apportioned according to the time during which it accrued.

When a company is formed to acquire a private business sometimes the old firm carries on the books until the new or usual accounting date without recording the change. In order to prepare the final accounts adjustments are necessary.

**Illustration (3)**

The following is the Trial Balance of A Ltd on December 31st:

|  | £ | £ |
|---|---:|---:|
| A – Capital Account | | 20,000 |
| Sundry Fixed Assets | 8,000 | |
| Debtors | 10,000 | |
| Stock | 12,000 | |
| Cash | 2,000 | |
| Sundry Liabilities | | 8,000 |
| Profit and Loss Account | | 4,000 |
| | £32,000 | £32,000 |

On the preceding March 1st the business had been transferred to a limited company as from January 1st in consideration of £6,000 cash and £24,000 shares, the company taking over all the assets and liabilities at their book value. No entries relating to the transfer had been made in the books, nor had any entries been made in A's Capital Account since January 1st, except that he had been debited with the £6,000 cash paid to him as part of the purchase consideration.

A's Capital Account at the end of the year stands at £20,000, after having been debited with the £6,000 cash forming part of the purchase consideration, hence his capital at the beginning of the year was £26,000 and this was the amount of the assets, less liabilities, as at January 1st, taken over by the company. If the company had opened a new set of books at that date, the opening journal entries would have been:

### COMPANY'S JOURNAL

|  |  | £ | £ |
|---|---|---:|---:|
| Sundry Net Assets | Dr | 26,000 | |
| Goodwill Account | | 4,000 | |
| To Vendor – A | | | 30,000 |
| Vendor – A | Dr | 30,000 | |
| To Cash | | | 6,000 |
| „ Share Capital Account | | | 24,000 |

Since, instead of opening a new set of books, the company has continued to operate upon the existing asset and liability accounts, A's Capital Account can be treated as the Vendor's Account, the balance on which at the commencement of the year, £26,000, represents the credit for the net assets taken over from him. A has already received, and been debited with, £6,000 of the purchase consideration and the only entries now necessary to put the books in order are as follows:

| | | | | | | | | | | £ | £ |
|---|---|---|---|---|---|---|---|---|---|---|---|
| Goodwill Account | .. | .. | .. | .. | .. | .. | .. | .. | Dr | 4,000 | |
|   To A | .. | .. | .. | .. | .. | .. | .. | .. | .. | | 4,000 |
| A | .. | .. | .. | .. | .. | .. | .. | .. | Dr | 24,000 | |
|   To Share Capital Account | .. | .. | .. | .. | .. | .. | .. | .. | | 24,000 |

Purchase of goodwill and discharge of balance of purchase consideration.

If any adjustment in the book value of the assets is to be made, the amount of each such adjustment will be debited or credited to the particular asset account, and credited or debited to A's Capital Account. The effect will merely be to increase or decrease the balance of A's Account to be transferred to Goodwill Account.

As mentioned, on the sale of a private business to a company, the vendor often retains the book debts and pays off the creditors, thus saving stamp duty on the transfer; the company usually collects the book debts and discharges the creditors as the vendor's agent. Where the book debts and liabilities of the vendor are not taken over by the company, the balance of the Vendor's Capital Account at the date as from which the business is transferred does not represent the net assets taken over by the company under the agreement until the debtors and creditors at that date have been eliminated. Strictly, the vendor's account should be debited and the various debtors' accounts credited with the amount of the sundry debtors at the date of the transfer of the business; and the sundry creditors' accounts debited and the vendor's account credited with the liabilities not taken over by the company, in order to eliminate from the company's books assets and liabilities not taken over. As the amounts are collected from debtors and paid to creditors, they would be debited and credited respectively to the cash book, and credited and debited respectively to the vendor's account, the balance of which would then represent the balance to be accounted for by the company to the vendor, or vice versa. Possibly, in practice, only differences would be adjusted, but great care must be taken, if such a short cut is adopted, to ensure that the final result is accurate.

If the company has continued to post to the old debtors' and creditors' accounts as if no change had taken place, the actual personal accounts of debtors and creditors will have been credited and debited during the period following the transfer with the cash received and paid by the company respectively, and the above entries will not be practicable. It is then necessary to create suspense accounts.

### Illustration (4)

Assume that in Illustration (3) the debtors and creditors amounting on January 1st to £8,000 and £6,000 respectively, were not taken over by the company, but were collected and paid by them as agent for the vendor, and that the old accounts were continued by the company without a break, the debts being collected during the year, subject to discounts of £400, and the creditors paid, subject to discounts of £150.

### COMPANY'S JOURNAL

| | | | | | | | | | £ | £ |
|---|---|---|---|---|---|---|---|---|---|---|
| A's Account | .. | .. | .. | .. | .. | .. | .. | Dr | 8,000 | |
|   To Debtors Suspense Account | .. | .. | .. | .. | .. | .. | .. | | 8,000 |
| Creditors Suspense Account | .. | .. | .. | .. | .. | .. | .. | Dr | 6,000 | |
|   To A's Account | .. | .. | .. | .. | .. | .. | .. | | 6,000 |

Adjusting debtors and creditors not taken over.

The credit on A's account is reduced to £18,000 and the price paid for goodwill increases to £6,000.

At the end of the period, when the amounts collected from debtors and paid to creditors have been ascertained, the following further entries will be necessary:

| | | | | | | | | | £ | £ |
|---|---|---|---|---|---|---|---|---|---|---|
| Debtors Suspense Account | .. | .. | .. | .. | .. | .. | .. | Dr | 8,000 | |
| To A's Account | .. | .. | .. | .. | .. | .. | .. | | | 7,600 |
| Discount Allowed Account | | .. | .. | .. | .. | .. | .. | | | 400 |
| Debts collected and discounts allowed on behalf of vendor. | | | | | | | | | | |
| A's Account | .. | .. | .. | .. | .. | .. | .. | Dr | 5,850 | |
| Discount Received Account | .. | .. | .. | .. | .. | .. | .. | | 150 | |
| To Creditors Suspense Account | .. | .. | .. | .. | .. | .. | .. | | | 6,000 |
| Liabilities paid and discounts received on behalf of vendor. | | | | | | | | | | |

A's Account will then be closed by the payment to him of £1,750 cash, being the excess of receipts over payments; the discounts allowed and received respectively on behalf of the vendor have been eliminated from the company's discount accounts, but the personal accounts of the debtors and creditors are not affected.

### Illustration (5)

XY, the proprietor of a business, wishing to realize part of his capital, decided to convert his business into a limited company as from January 1st, and invite his friends to take up shares.

The company was duly incorporated on February 1st, on which date 9,000 shares of £1 each were issued for cash, XY retaining the remaining 1,000 shares as part consideration.

Out of the proceeds of the issue, XY was paid £7,000 as the balance of the purchase price and £750 for the company's incorporation expenses incurred by him.

XY agreed to be manager of the company, as from January 1st, at a salary of £500 per annum.

A new set of books and accounts was not opened.

The Trial Balance, before adjustment, at December 31st is as follows:

| | | | | | | | | | £ | £ |
|---|---|---|---|---|---|---|---|---|---|---|
| Capital Account (XY) | .. | .. | .. | .. | .. | .. | .. | .. | 1,250 | |
| New Company Account (XY & Co Ltd) | .. | .. | .. | .. | .. | .. | .. | | 9,000 |
| Sales | .. | .. | .. | .. | .. | .. | .. | .. | .. | | 30,000 |
| Stock Account | .. | .. | .. | .. | .. | .. | .. | .. | 22,900 | |
| Wages and Salaries | .. | .. | .. | .. | .. | .. | .. | .. | 2,750 | |
| Other Expenses | .. | .. | .. | .. | .. | .. | .. | .. | 2,500 | |
| Bad Debts written off during year | .. | .. | .. | .. | .. | .. | .. | 175 | |
| Sundry Creditors | .. | .. | .. | .. | .. | .. | .. | .. | | 3,325 |
| Sundry Debtors | .. | .. | .. | .. | .. | .. | .. | .. | 5,000 | |
| Property | .. | .. | .. | .. | .. | .. | .. | .. | 6,000 | |
| Cash on hand and in Bank | .. | .. | .. | .. | .. | .. | .. | 1,750 | |
| | | | | | | | | | £42,325 | £42,325 |

XY has not been credited with salary to date nor has he received payments on account. Interest on the purchase price at 5 per cent. falls to be credited to him as from January 1st to the date of settlement. The Stock at December 31st is valued at £400.

A revaluation at January 1st showed that the property was worth £6,500. It was agreed to provide £200 for doubtful debts; of these doubtful debts £100 proved bad and the rest were collected during the year.

On January 1st XY's capital was £6,500.

Turnover was constant throughout the year.

Prepare Trading Profit and Loss Account for the year ended December 31st and Balance Sheet as at that date.

Ignore taxation.

## TRADING AND PROFIT AND LOSS ACCOUNT
### For the Year ended December 31st, 19..

| | £ | £ | | £ |
|---|---|---|---|---|
| Stock Account .. .. .. £22,900 | | | Sales .. .. .. .. .. | 30,000 |
| *Less* Stock in Hand .. .. 400 | | | | |
| | | 22,500 | | |
| Gross Profit c/d. .. .. .. .. | | 7,500 | | |
| | | £30,000 | | £30,000 |

| | £ | | £ |
|---|---|---|---|
| Wages and Salaries.. .. .. .. | 2,750 | Gross Profit b/d. .. .. .. | 7,500 |
| Manager's Salary .. .. .. .. | 500 | | |
| Other Expenses .. .. .. .. | 2,500 | | |
| Bad Debts .. .. .. .. | 75 | | |
| Net Profit c/d. .. .. .. .. | 1,675 | | |
| | £7,500 | | £7,500 |

| | £ | | £ |
|---|---|---|---|
| Interest on purchase price at 5% on £8,000 prior to incorporation, 1 month .. .. | 34 | Net Profit b/d. – | |
| | | Prior to Incorporation, 1 month .. .. | 140 |
| Net Profit prior to incorporation carried to Capital Reserve .. .. .. .. | 106 | After Incorporation, 11 months .. .. | 1,535 |
| Net Profit carried forward .. .. .. | 1,535 | | |
| | £1,675 | | £1,675 |

## XY LTD
### BALANCE SHEET as at December 31st, 19..

| | £ | | | £ | £ |
|---|---|---|---|---|---|
| SHARE CAPITAL, authorized, issued and fully paid. .. .. .. .. | 10,000 | FIXED ASSETS | | | |
| | | Goodwill .. .. £1,200 | | | |
| | | *Less* Capital Reserve *per contra* .. .. 206 | | | |
| RESERVES | | | | 994 | |
| Capital Reserve – | | Property at cost .. .. .. | | 6,500 | |
| Profits prior to Incorporation .. £106 | | | | | 7,494 |
| Balance of Bad Debt Provision on debts taken over .. .. 100 | | CURRENT ASSETS | | | |
| Deducted *contra* from Goodwill .. £206 | | Stock .. .. .. | | 400 | |
| | | Debtors .. .. .. | | 5,000 | |
| | | Cash on hand and in Bank .. | | 1,750 | |
| Profit and Loss Account .. .. .. | 1,535 | | | | 7,150 |
| | 11,535 | Preliminary Expenses .. .. | | | 750 |
| CURRENT LIABILITIES | | | | | |
| Creditors .. .. .. .. | 3,325 | | | | |
| XY - Salary and Interest .. .. .. | 534 | | | | |
| | £15,394 | | | | £15,394 |

*Notes:*

1. The account of XY will be adjusted as follows:

### XY (Vendor)

| | | £ | | | £ |
|---|---|---|---|---|---|
| Feb. 1 | Cash .. . .. .. | 7,750 | Jan. 1 | Balance (capital) .. .. | 6,500 |
| | | | Dec. 31 | Balance c/d. (as per Trial Balance) .. | 1,250 |
| | | £7,750 | | | £7,750 |
| Jan. 1 | Balance b/d. .. .. .. | 1,250 | Dec. 31 | Property Account – Increase in value | 500 |
| | Share Capital Account – Shares issued as part consideration .. | 1,000 | | Preliminary Expenses Account – amounts paid by XY .. .. | 750 |
| | Bad Debt Provision .. .. | 200 | | Balance, being cost of Goodwill debited to Goodwill Account .. | 1,200 |
| | | £2,450 | . | | £2,450 |

2.                    PROVISION FOR BAD DEBTS ACCOUNT

| | £ | | £ |
|---|---|---|---|
| Bad Debts written off       ..       ..       .. | 100 | XY – Provision created at acquisition of busi- | |
| Balance – excessive Provision transferred to Capi-<br>tal Reserve       ..       ..       ..       .. | 100 | ness       ..       ..       ..       .. | 200 |

By debiting £100 of the bad debts written off against the provision for bad debts, only £75 remains to be debited to Profit and Loss Account as representing bad debts incurred by the company. The balance of the provision for bad debts taken over from the vendor may now be treated as a capital reserve and deducted from the cost of goodwill.

### Illustration (6)

E. Dundas and A. Banbury were in partnership as Ernest Dundas & Co sharing profits and losses: 20 to 17.

Accounts were prepared and the books closed off as at December 31st, 19..

On the following May 1st, Dundas & Banbury Ltd was registered to acquire the business of Ernest Dundas & Co as from January 1st.

The sale and purchase agreement provides:

(a) Purchase consideration 6,000 Preference shares £1 each fully paid.
         6,000 Ordinary shares 10p each fully paid.

(b) Vendors to retain cash and debtors and to pay off liabilities.

(c) Each of the vendors to subscribe in cash for one-half of the balance of authorized capital, 850 Preference shares and 500 Ordinary shares.

The Articles of Association appoint E. Dundas and A. Banbury sole directors with fees of £100 per month each.

You are requested to assist the directors in the preparation of accounts to September 30th. You find that the books have been carried on without a break since January 1st, and that no entries arising from the formation of the company or its acquisition of the business have been made.

The Trial Balance at September 30th was as follows:

| | £ | £ |
|---|---|---|
| A. Banbury – Capital at January 1st       ..       ..       ..       ..       ..       ..       .. | | 2,860 |
| Drawings during period       ..       ..       ..       ..       ..       ..       .. | 250 | |
| E. Dundas  – Capital at January 1st       ..       ..       ..       ..       ..       ..       .. | | 3,000 |
| Drawings during period       ..       ..       ..       ..       ..       ..       .. | 300 | |
| E. Dundas and A. Banbury for shares       ..       ..       ..       ..       ..       .. | | 900 |
| Buildings       ..       ..       ..       ..       ..       ..       ..       ..       ..       .. | 3,800 | |
| Creditors (£1,500 owing at January 1st, having been paid)       ..       ..       ..       .. | | 700 |
| Debtors (£1,000 due at January 1st, having been received)       ..       ..       ..       .. | 950 | |
| Formation of Company Expenses       ..       ..       ..       ..       ..       .. | 150 | |
| Furniture and Fittings (Balance at January 1st, £360)       ..       ..       ..       .. | 460 | |
| Office Expenses..       ..       ..       ..       ..       ..       ..       ..       .. | 350 | |
| Plant and Machinery (Balance January 1st, £1,200)       ..       ..       ..       .. | 1,500 | |
| Purchases       ..       ..       ..       ..       ..       ..       ..       ..       .. | 2,000 | |
| Sales  ..       ..       ..       ..       ..       ..       ..       ..       ..       .. | | 8,200 |
| Salaries       ..       ..       ..       ..       ..       ..       ..       ..       .. | 400 | |
| Selling Expenses       ..       ..       ..       ..       ..       ..       ..       .. | 600 | |
| Stock January 1st       ..       ..       ..       ..       ..       ..       ..       .. | 500 | |
| Wages       ..       ..       ..       ..       ..       ..       ..       ..       .. | 800 | |
| Cash (Balance at Bank at January 1st, £500)       ..       ..       ..       ..       .. | 3,600 | |
| | £15,660 | £15,660 |

The following is additional information:

E. Dundas and A. Banbury have agreed between themselves to take preference shares for the amount of their capital at January 1st.

The average of the monthly sales (which are of one commodity at a fixed price) for the first four months was one-half that of the remainder of the period.

The expenditure each month on items in the Profit and Loss Account was equal.

The stock at September 30th is valued at £700.

Plant and machinery is to be depreciated at 5 per cent. per annum, and furniture and fittings at 10 per cent. per annum, in both cases on commencing figures.

Preliminary expenses are to be written off.

You are required –

(i) To prepare the journal entries necessary to put the books in order.

(ii) To show the shareholdings acquired by the partners.

(iii) To prepare the company's Trading and Profit and Loss Account, and Balance Sheet as at September 30th.

Ignore taxation.

(i)                         JOURNAL

| | | Dr | £ | £ |
|---|---|---|---|---|
| Capital Accounts: | | | | |
| A. Banbury | | | 2,860 | |
| E. Dundas | | | 3,000 | |
| To Vendors | | | | 5,860 |
| Transfer of Capital at January 1st. | | | | |
| Goodwill | | Dr | 740 | |
| To Vendors | | | | 740 |
| Excess of purchase consideration over value of net assets. | | | | |
| Vendors | | Dr | 6,600 | |
| To Preference Share Capital Account | | | | 6,000 |
| Ordinary Share Capital Account | | | | 600 |
| Issue of 6,000 Preference Shares of £1 each, fully paid, and 6,000 Ordinary Shares of 10p each, fully paid, in satisfaction of purchase consideration. | | | | |
| E. Dundas and A. Banbury | | Dr | 900 | |
| To Preference Share Capital Account | | | | 850 |
| Ordinary Share Capital Account | | | | 50 |
| Issue of 850 Preference Shares of £1 each, fully paid and 500 Ordinary Shares of 10p each, fully paid, as per application received. | | | | |

*Note:* The cash at bank on January 1st has been applied in settlement of the difference between the debtors and creditors outstanding at that date, and which have subsequently been received and discharged.

(ii)          SHAREHOLDINGS OF PARTNERS

| | Total | E. Dundas | A. Banbury |
|---|---|---|---|
| | £ | £ | £ |
| Capital Accounts, January 1st | 5,860 | 3,000 | 2,860 |
| Profit on sale of firm | 740 | 400 | 340 |
| Cash subscribed for shares | 900 | 450 | 450 |
| Amount to be discharged | £7,500 | £3,850 | £3,650 |
| | Shares | Shares | Shares |
| Preference shares for capital | 5,860 | 3,000 | 2,860 |
| Preference shares subscribed | 850 | 425 | 425 |
| Balance of preference shares allotted in profit-sharing ratio | 140 | 76 | 64 |
| Total Preference Shares | 6,850 | 3,501 | 3,349 |
| Ordinary shares subscribed | 500 | 250 | 250 |
| Balance of ordinary shares allotted in profit-sharing ratio | 6,000 | 3,243 | 2,757 |
| Total Ordinary Shares | 6,500 | 3,493 | 3,007 |

SUMMARY

| | E. Dundas | | A. Banbury | |
|---|---|---|---|---|
| | Shares | £ | Shares | £ |
| Ordinary | 3,493 | 349·30 | 3,007 | 300·70 |
| Preference | 3,501 | 3,501·00 | 3,349 | 3,349·00 |
| | | £3,850·30 | | £3,649·70 |

A cash payment of 30p must be made by Dundas to Banbury.

## TRADING AND PROFIT AND LOSS ACCOUNT

(iii)

### For the 9 Months ended September 30th, 19..

| | £ | £ | | | £ |
|---|---|---|---|---|---|
| Stock, January 1st .. | | 500 | Sales .. .. | | 8,200 |
| Purchases .. | | 2,000 | Stock, September 30th .. | | 700 |
| Wages .. .. | | 800 | | | |
| Gross Profit. | | | | | |
| Prior to Incorporation | | | | | |
| (two-sevenths) .. | 1,600 | | | | |
| Subsequent to Incorpora- | | | | | |
| tion (five-sevenths) .. | 4,000 | | | | |
| | | 5,600 | | | |
| | | £8,900 | | | £8,900 |

| | | Before Incorporation (4 months) | After Incorporation (5 months) | | Before Incorporation | After Incorporation |
|---|---|---|---|---|---|---|
| | £ | £ | £ | | £ | £ |
| Salaries .. | 400 | | | Gross Profit b/d. .. | 1,600 | 4,000 |
| Office Expenses .. | 350 | | | | | |
| Selling Expenses | 600 | | | | | |
| Depreciation: | | | | | | |
| Plant .. | 45 | | | | | |
| Furniture .. | 27 | | | | | |
| | £1,422 | 632 | 790 | | | |
| Directors' Fees .. .. | | | 1 000 | | | |
| Formation Expenses .. | | | 150 | | | |
| Capital Reserve .. .. | | 968 | | | | |
| Balance c/f. .. .. | | | 2 060 | | | |
| | | £1,600 | £4,000 | | £1,600 | £4,000 |

### BALANCE SHEET

#### As at September 30th, 19..

| | | £ | | | £ | £ |
|---|---|---|---|---|---|---|
| SHARE CAPITAL | | | FIXED ASSETS | | | |
| Authorized and Issued. | | | Goodwill at cost .. .. | | 740 | |
| 6,850 Preference Shares of £1 each, | | | Buildings at cost .. .. | | 3,800 | |
| fully paid .. .. .. | £6,850 | | Plant and Machinery, at | | | |
| 6,500 Ordinary Shares of 10p each, | | | cost .. .. | £1 500 | | |
| fully paid .. .. .. | 650 | | Less Depreciation .. | 45 | | |
| | | 7,500 | | | 1,455 | |
| RESERVES | | | Furniture and Fittings at | | | |
| Capital Reserve .. .. .. | | 968 | cost .. .. | 460 | | |
| Profit and Loss Account .. .. | | 2,060 | Less Depreciation .. | 27 | | |
| | | | | | 433 | |
| | | | | | | 6,428 |
| CURRENT LIABILITIES | | 10,528 | CURRENT ASSETS | | | |
| Creditors: | | | Stock .. .. .. .. | | 700 | |
| Trade .. .. .. .. | £700 | | Debtors .. .. .. | | 950 | |
| Directors' Fees .. .. .. | 450 | | Cash at Bank .. .. | | 3,600 | |
| | | 1,150 | | | | 5,250 |
| | | £11,678 | | | | £11,678 |

*Notes:*

1. The drawings made by the partners since January 1st, have been applied in part payment of the directors' fees accruing to them since May 1st, leaving £450 directors' fees still outstanding.

2. The formation expenses may, alternatively, be written off against the profits before incorporation.

3. Since the average of the monthly sales for the first four months was one-half that of the remainder of the period, the proportion of turnover is 2 : 5.

**Illustration (7)**

A and B, trading in partnership shared profits and losses 3 : 2. On June 1st they sold the business to AB Ltd, as on the previous April 1st, for £120,000 allocated as follows: Goodwill £25,000, Freehold Land and Buildings £60,000, Plant and Machinery, £30,000, Stocks £5,000.

The company was incorporated on June 1st, with an authorized capital of £250,000 in shares of £1 each, of which 120,000 were issued forthwith in satisfaction of the purchase consideration. A and B carried on the business for AB Ltd from April 1st; A and B made up their accounts to March 31st each year, and continued to write up the books until June 30th ignoring the sale of the assets, although during June sales were invoiced and purchases ordered in the name of AB Ltd.

The following Trial Balance was drawn up from the books of A and B as on June 30th:

| DEBITS | £ | CREDITS | £ |
|---|---:|---|---:|
| Goodwill | 9,000 | Creditors (including £3,000 for June pur- | |
| Freehold Land and Buildings | 25,000 | chases) | 5,500 |
| Plant and Machinery (including £2,000 pur- | | Sales | 50,000 |
| chased since March 31st) | 22,000 | Discounts | 300 |
| Stock as on March 31st | 5,000 | Capital Account – A | 35,000 |
| Debtors (including £4,000 for June sales) | 6,000 | B | 25,000 |
| Wages and Salaries (including Directors' Fees, | | Current Account – A | 300 |
| £200) | 20,000 | | |
| Rent | 200 | | |
| Purchases | 18,000 | | |
| AB Ltd Account | 7,000 | | |
| Discounts | 600 | | |
| Expenses | 2,000 | | |
| Current Account. B | 800 | | |
| Balance at Bankers | 500 | | |
| | £116,100 | | £116,100 |

Stocks were valued by the company's officials on June 30th at £4,000.

The balance of £7,000 on AB Ltd account represented cash paid for 7,000 shares of £1 each allotted to A & B on June 1st, which was paid by them into a banking account in the name of AB Ltd on that date. Cheques were drawn on this account on June 28th to pay for Preliminary and Formation Expenses, £1,500, and for Office Furniture, £500. On June 30th the account was credited with £10 for interest allowed by the Bank.

A & B were to pay for purchases made prior to June 1st, and debtors for sales before that date were paid to A & B. There were no purchases or sales for cash. Trading profits accrued regularly over the period.

You are required:

(a) to show the account of AB Ltd in the books of A & B, ignoring interest;

(b) to prepare the Balance Sheet of A & B as on June 30th; and

(c) to prepare the Profit and Loss Account of AB Ltd for the three months ended June 30th, and the Balance Sheet as on that date, ignoring depreciation and taxation.

In this case, although the business was sold to the company on April 1st, the books of the partnership were not closed, and A & B carried on the business for the company, recording the transactions through its own accounts. At June 30th the balances of all accounts representing payments and expenses incurred and sales made for the company must be transferred to the company's account in the firm's books. This account must also be debited with the transfer price of the assets sold to the company, the balances on the asset accounts, representing profit on realization, being divided between the partners in profit-sharing ratio and credited to their capital accounts. The balance of the company's account will represent the amount due by the firm to the company as a result of all these transactions.

## BOOKS OF A AND B

(a)                **AB LTD**

| | £ | | £ |
|---|---|---|---|
| Cash for 7,000 Shares in AB Ltd | 7,000 | Shares in AB Ltd | 127,000 |
| Goodwill | 25,000 | Creditors (for June Purchases) | 3,000 |
| Freehold Land and Buildings | 60,000 | Sales | 50,000 |
| Plant and Machinery | 32,000 | Discounts received | 300 |
| Stocks | 5,000 | | |
| Debtors (June Sales) | 4,000 | | |
| Wages and Salaries | 20,000 | | |
| Rent | 200 | | |
| Purchases | 18,000 | | |
| Discounts allowed | 600 | | |
| Expenses | 2,000 | | |
| Balance c/f. | 6,500 | | |
| | £180,300 | | £180,300 |

*Note:* The company is debited with all purchases and credited with all sales to date, but since A and B are only to pay for purchases, and receive payments from debtors for sales prior to June 1st, the creditors for purchases and debtors for sales after June 1st are transferred to the company. A and B will themselves pay the creditors for purchases, and receive the amounts due from debtors for sales prior to June 1st, having charged the company with these purchases and credited it with these sales.

## A AND B

(b)        **BALANCE SHEET** as at June 30th

| | | £ | £ | | | £ |
|---|---|---|---|---|---|---|
| A – Capital Account | | 71,600 | | Shares in AB Ltd | | 127,000 |
|     Current Account | | 300 | | Debtors | | 2,000 |
| | | | 71,900 | Balance at Bank | | 500 |
| B – Capital Account | | 49,400 | | | | |
|     Current Account | Dr | 800 | | | | |
| | | | 48,600 | | | |
| | | | 120,500 | | | |
| AB Ltd | | | 6,500 | | | |
| Trade Creditors | | | 2,500 | | | |
| | | | £129,500 | | | £129,500 |

*Note:* The partners' Capital Accounts are as follows:

| | A £ | B £ | | | A £ | B £ |
|---|---|---|---|---|---|---|
| Balance c/d. | 71,600 | 49,400 | Balance b/f. | | 35,000 | 25,000 |
| | | | Profit on realization | | 36,600 | 24,400 |
| | £71,600 | £49,400 | | | £71,600 | £49,400 |
| | | | Balance b/d. | | 71,600 | 49,400 |

The profit on realization is:

|  | | | £ |
|---|---|---|---|
| Consideration for assets – | | | |
| Goodwill | | | 25,000 |
| Land and Buildings | | | 60,000 |
| Plant and Machinery | | | 30,000 |
| Stocks | | | 5,000 |
| Carried forward | | | 120,000 |

Brought forward £120,000

|  |  | £ |
|---|---|---|
| *Less* Book Values – | Goodwill .. .. | 9,000 |
|  | Land and Buildings .. | 25,000 |
|  | Plant and Machinery .. | 20,000 |
|  | Stock .. .. .. | 5,000 |
|  |  | 59,000 |
| Profit – divisible A 3/5ths, B 2/5ths .. .. .. .. .. | | £61,000 |

## AB LTD
## TRADING AND PROFIT AND LOSS ACCOUNT

(c)      For 3 Months ended June 30th

|  | £ |  | £ |
|---|---|---|---|
| Stock April 1st .. .. .. | 5,000 | Sales .. .. .. .. | 50,000 |
| Purchases .. .. .. | 18,000 | Stock, June 30th .. .. | 4,000 |
| Gross Profit c/d. .. .. | 31,000 |  |  |
|  | £54,000 |  | £54 000 |

|  | Before Incorporation £ | Since Incorporation £ |  | Before Incorporation £ | Since Incorporation £ |
|---|---|---|---|---|---|
| Wages and Salaries .. .. | 13,200 | 6,600 | Gross Profit b/d. .. .. | 20,667 | 10,333 |
| Directors' Fees .. .. .. |  | 200 | Discounts .. .. .. | 200 | 100 |
| Rent .. .. .. .. | 133 | 67 | Bank Interest .. .. .. |  | 10 |
| Discounts .. .. .. | 400 | 200 |  |  |  |
| Expenses .. .. .. | 1,334 | 666 |  |  |  |
| Profit prior to Incorporation transferred to Capita Reserve .. .. | 5,800 |  |  |  |  |
| Net Profit since Incorporation c/f. .. |  | 2,710 |  |  |  |
|  | £20,867 | £10,443 |  | £20,867 | £10,443 |

*Note:* Gross profit and expenses which move with turnover should more correctly be apportioned on the basis of sales.

## BALANCE SHEET as at June 30th

|  | Authorized £ | Issued and fully paid £ |  | £ | £ |
|---|---|---|---|---|---|
| Share Capital .. .. | | | FIXED ASSETS, at cost | | |
| Shares of £1 each .. | 250,000 | 127,000 | Goodwill .. .. | 25,000 | |
| | | | Freehold Land and Buildings .. .. | 60,000 | |
| RESERVES | | | Plant and Machinery .. | 32,000 | |
| Capital Reserve.. .. | 5,800 | | Office Furniture .. | 500 | |
| *Less* Preliminary Expenses written off .. | 1,500 | | | | 117,500 |
| | 4,300 | | CURRENT ASSETS | | |
| Profit and Loss Account .. | 2,710 | 7,010 | A & B .. .. | 6,500 | |
| | | 134,010 | Stocks .. .. | 4,000 | |
| CURRENT LIABILITIES | | | Trade Debtors .. | 4,000 | |
| Creditors .. .. | | 3,000 | Cash at Bank .. | 5,010 | |
| | | | | | 19,510 |
| | | £137,010 | | | £137,010 |

*Notes:*

1. The following journal entries will be necessary to open the company's books:

JOURNAL

| | | | | | | | | | | £ | £ |
|---|---|---|---|---|---|---|---|---|---|---|---|
| Cash | .. | .. | .. | .. | .. | .. | .. | .. | Dr | 7,000 | |
| Goodwill | .. | .. | .. | .. | .. | .. | .. | .. | | 25,000 | |
| Freehold Land and Buildings.. | | | .. | .. | .. | .. | .. | .. | | 60,000 | |
| Plant and Machinery .. | .. | | .. | .. | .. | .. | .. | .. | | 30,000 | |
| do. | Additions | | .. | .. | .. | .. | .. | .. | | 2,000 | |
| Stock | .. | .. | .. | .. | .. | .. | .. | .. | | 5,000 | |
| Debtors (for June Sales) | .. | | .. | .. | .. | .. | .. | .. | | 4,000 | |
| Wages and Salaries .. | | .. | .. | .. | .. | .. | .. | .. | | 19,800 | |
| Directors' Fees | .. | .. | .. | .. | .. | .. | .. | .. | | 200 | |
| Rent | .. | .. | .. | .. | .. | .. | .. | .. | | 200 | |
| Purchases .. | .. | .. | .. | .. | .. | .. | .. | .. | | 18,000 | |
| Discounts allowable .. | | .. | .. | .. | .. | .. | .. | .. | | 600 | |
| Expenses | .. | .. | .. | .. | .. | .. | .. | .. | | 2,000 | |
| To A & B | .. | .. | .. | .. | .. | .. | .. | .. | | | 173,800 |
| | | | | | | | | | | £173,800 | £173,800 |

Assets taken over from, and expenses paid and incurred by A & B on behalf of the company.

| | | | | | | | | | | | |
|---|---|---|---|---|---|---|---|---|---|---|---|
| A & B | .. | .. | .. | .. | .. | .. | .. | .. | Dr | 180,300 | |
| To Share Capital .. | | .. | .. | .. | .. | .. | .. | .. | | | 127,000 |
| Creditors (for June Purchases) | .. | | .. | .. | .. | .. | .. | .. | | | 3,000 |
| Sales .. | .. | .. | .. | .. | .. | .. | .. | .. | | | 50,000 |
| Discounts receivable | .. | .. | .. | .. | .. | .. | .. | .. | | | 300 |
| | | | | | | | | | | £180,300 | £180,300 |

120,000 Shares issued to A & B as purchase consideration and 7,000 for cash, liabilities assumed from and sales made by A & B on behalf of the company.

2. The company's bank balance is made up as follows:

| | | | | | | |
|---|---|---|---|---|---|---|
| Paid in by A & B | .. | .. | .. | .. | .. | £7,000 |
| Bank Interest | .. | .. | .. | .. | .. | 10 |
| | | | | | | 7,010 |
| Less Preliminary Expenses | .. | .. | .. | £1,500 | | |
| Furniture | .. | .. | .. | .. | 500 | |
| | | | | | | 2,000 |
| | | | | | | £5,010 |

## § 12. Bonus Shares

### (a) Issue of Bonus Shares

When a company has substantial undistributed profits, either on Reserve Account or on Profit and Loss Account, the total capital employed in the business tends to be obscured. Such accumulations are usually represented by fixed assets or permanent working capital.

To bring the issued share capital into correct relationship with the capital employed in the business, the accumulations can be capitalized and applied in paying up the amounts due on shares to be issued to the members as bonus shares.

Cash is not involved in a bonus issue; the resolution authorizes the company to apply the bonus in paying up the shares.

A bonus issue of shares adds nothing to the net assets of the company; it divides the capital employed in the business into a larger number of shares. This can be explained by an illustration.

**Illustration (1)**

A company's summarized Balance Sheet is as follows:

| SHARE CAPITAL in £1 Shares.. | £100,000 | SUNDRY ASSETS, *less* Creditors | £150,000 |
| RESERVES ..      ..      .. | 50,000 | | |

If the assets and goodwill are fully valued, each £1 share is worth £1·50 *cum* dividend. On the profits being capitalized, if the bonus shares are issued at par, the share capital becomes £150,000 in £1 shares. Each share is now worth £1, but each shareholder has 50 per cent. more shares. The shareholders are no better off.

On the Stock Exchange a bonus issue is often considered a bull point and it is common for a bonus issue to be followed by an increased dividend. A bonus issue attracts attention to the company's shares and often increases dealings in the shares which forces up the market value and enables shareholders who wish to do so to realize an immediate profit.

Seldom will the net assets as shown in the Balance Sheet reflect the true market value of the shares, which will depend primarily on the income they yield and growth prospects. The company may have paid a dividend of 12 per cent. and if a reasonable yield were 6 per cent. the shares would be quoted round about £2 each, and the total value of the capital would be £200,000. The real value of the shares after the bonus issues would still be £200,000, or £1·33 each, if it is anticipated that the company will only distribute the same amount of profits as before and will reduce the rate of dividend proportionately, i.e. to 8 per cent. The market, however, will usually gamble on the dividend not being reduced so much, and may quote the shares at, say, £1·50 or £1·75 in the expectation of 9 per cent. or more being paid. A member who shares in this expectation might then sell part of his shares, while retaining the anticipation of the same income.

The distribution of bonus shares usually gives rise to share fractions; the distribution may be on the basis of, say, one bonus share for every five held, therefore the holder of twenty-four shares would be entitled to four complete shares and four-fifths of a share, which must be made up to a complete share by the acquisition of the title to a further one-fifth of a share before registration can finally be effected. This difficulty is normally overcome by the Articles and the resolution voting the bonus issue providing for each shareholder to be allotted the whole number of shares appropriate to his holding. The shares representing the sum of the fractions are then sold, and the proceeds paid to the shareholders entitled to the fractions.

**Illustration (2)**

A company having a reserve of £25,000 and a paid-up capital of £100,000 in £1 shares, resolves to pay a bonus of 20 per cent. out of its reserve by the issue of one fully-paid share for each five shares held. Show the journal entries recording the transaction.

### JOURNAL

| | | £ | £ |
|---|---|---|---|
| Reserve Account          ..          ..          ..          ..          ..          ..          ..          .. | Dr | 20,000 | |
| To Bonus Account          ..          ..          ..          ..          ..          ..          .. | | | 20,000 |
| Bonus of 20 % payable out of the Reserve Account in fully-paid shares as per Resolution dated............... | | | |
| Bonus Account          ..          ..          ..          ..          ..          ..          ..          .. | Dr | 20,000 | |
| To Share Capital Account          ..          ..          ..          ..          ..          ..          .. | | | 20,000 |
| Issue of 20,000 shares of £1 each fully paid in satisfaction of Bonus at the rate of one share for every five held. | | | |

### (b) Application of Bonus to payment of calls

Another method, when the existing shares are only partly called up, is to apply the bonus to the payment of a call on the shares.

**Illustration (3)**

A company having a nominal and issued capital of £100,000 in shares of £1 each, 75p per share called up, declares a bonus out of the reserve account at the rate of $33\frac{1}{3}$ per cent. on the paid-up capital, to be applied for the purpose of making the shares fully paid.

Show the journal entries necessary to record these transactions.

### JOURNAL

| | | £ | £ |
|---|---|---|---|
| Call Account   ..          ..          ..          ..          ..          ..          ..          ..          .. | Dr | 25,000 | |
| To Share Capital Account          ..          ..          ..          ..          ..          ..          .. | | | 25,000 |
| Final call of 25p per share on 100,000 shares as per Resolution of the Board dated............... | | | |
| Reserve Account          ..          ..          ..          ..          ..          ..          ..          .. | Dr | 25,000 | |
| To Bonus Account          ..          ..          ..          ..          ..          ..          .. | | | 25,000 |
| Bonus of 25p per Share on 100,000 shares payable out of the Reserve Account as per Resolution of shareholders dated............... | | | |
| Bonus Account          ..          ..          ..          ..          ..          ..          ..          .. | Dr | 25,000 | |
| To Call Account          ..          ..          ..          ..          ..          ..          .. | | | 25,000 |
| Application of Bonus of 25p per share on 100,000 shares to payment of Call as per Resolution dated....... | | | |

## § 13. Payment of Interest out of Capital

Although a company can, indeed must, pay interest out of capital, where there are no profits out of which to pay it, to meet its obligations on debentures and loans, it is a rule of law that no interest can be paid to members on the share capital of the company (except interest on moneys paid in advance of calls). The only exception to this rule is that provided by Section 65, whereby, to enable companies to construct works or buildings or provide plant with money raised as share capital, interest may be paid to members out of capital in the following circumstances:

Where any shares of a company are issued to raise money to defray the expenses of the construction of any works or buildings, or the provision of any plant which cannot be made profitable for a long period, the company may pay interest on so much of that share capital as is for the time being paid up for the period and subject to the conditions and restrictions mentioned below, and may charge such interest to capital as part of the cost of construction of the work or buildings, or the provision of plant.

The conditions and restrictions are that:

1. No payment shall be made unless authorized by the Articles, or by special resolution.

2. No payment, whether authorized by the Articles or by special resolution, shall be made without the previous sanction of the Board of Trade.

3. Before sanctioning any payment the Board of Trade may, at the expense of the company, appoint a person to enquire and report to them as to the circumstances of the case, and may, before making the appointment, require the company to give security for the payment of the costs of the enquiry.

4. The payment shall be made only for such period as may be determined by the Board of Trade, and that period shall never extend beyond the close of the half year next after the half year during which the works or buildings have been actually completed or the plant provided.

5. The rate of interest shall not exceed 4 per cent. per annum, or such other rate as may for the time being be prescribed by statutory instrument*.

6. The payment of interest shall not operate as a reduction of the amount paid up on the shares for which it is paid.

7. The accounts of the company shall show the share capital on which, and the rate at which, interest has been paid out of capital during the period to which the accounts relate (8th Sch., Pt. I, § 2).

It should be observed that the payment of 'interest' is not a dividend; it is definitely interest on the shares pending the completion of the work which is designed to earn profits out of which dividends will thereafter be payable. The interest is to be treated as capital expenditure and debited to the asset account for which it is paid. The debit will be the gross amount, since the income tax deductible must be accounted for to the Inland Revenue. Interest is only payable on the paid-up amount of the shares.

### § 14. The Preparation of a Company's Books and Accounts for Audit

Arrangements should be made to help the auditor examine the books and accounts with the minimum inconvenience to himself and to the company's staff.

A proper accounting system is essential. Balancing the books is not part of the auditor's legal duties; he may, however, balance them in his separate capacity as accountant.

Subsidiary books should be cast in ink or biro, and the totals posted to the accounts in the impersonal ledger. The various bought and sales ledgers should be proved individually by Total (or Control) Accounts, and their balances brought down in ink, or, if it is inconvenient to rule off and bring down such balances, a note of the amount of the balance should be made on each ledger account in red ink at the side. (In machine accounting the balance will be extended into the balance column of the accounts after each entry.)

The cash book should be balanced off and a reconciliation of the balance with the pass book or bank statement prepared. Vouchers should be numbered consecutively, and the numbers entered in the cash book, the vouchers themselves being filed by a proper system, care being taken to see that, if a voucher is missing,

* The rate at present allowable is 6 per cent.

a note is inserted in the file, giving a reference to any other evidence available. Purchases invoices should either be attached to the statements when filed as vouchers, or should be numbered and filed consecutively, the corresponding numbers being entered in the purchases day book.

When the Trial Balance has been extracted, proper provision must be made for bad debts, depreciation etc. and all other necessary adjustments must be made. The Balance Sheet and Profit and Loss Account can then be drafted, and, after having been passed by the directors, presented to the auditor; it is common for the auditor to prepare the accounts himself, in his capacity of accountant.

Any important provisions and reserves, e.g. for contingent liabilities, revaluations of fixed assets etc. should be supported by directors' minutes.

In the final accounts, ledger folios should be inserted against each item which refers to a single ledger account, schedules being attached showing folios and details of all items composed of several balances taken collectively. In this manner a full and clear record is obtained of the way in which the various totals, particularly of Balance Sheet items, are arrived at.

## PART II

### § 15. The Balance Sheet and Accounts of a Company

#### (a) The Books of Account

By Section 147 (1) of the *Companies Act 1948*, every company must keep proper books of account with respect to:

(a) all sums of money received and expended by the company, and the matters in respect of which the receipt and expenditure takes place;

(b) all sales and purchases of goods by the company;

(c) the assets and liabilities of the company.

A company will not be deemed to have kept proper books of account unless it has kept such books as are necessary to give a true and fair view of the state of the company's affairs and to explain its transactions.

The books of account are to be kept at such office as the directors think fit, and are to be always open for their inspection. If books are kept at a place outside Great Britain there must be sent to and kept at a place in Great Britain, and be at all times open to the inspection of the directors, such accounts and returns with respect to the business dealt with in those books as will disclose with reasonable accuracy the financial position of that business, at intervals not exceeding six months, and will enable to be prepared in accordance with the Acts the company's Balance Sheet and Profit and Loss Account or Income and Expenditure Account and any documents required to be annexed thereto (s. 147 (3)).

If any director of the company fails to take all reasonable steps to secure compliance with the above provisions, or has by his own wilful default been the cause of any default by the company thereunder, he may, for each offence, be liable, on summary conviction, to imprisonment for a term not exceeding six months, or to a fine not exceeding £200. It will be a defence, however, for the director to prove that he had reasonable ground to believe, and did believe, that a competent and reliable person was charged with the duty of seeing that the requirements were complied with and was in a position to discharge that duty; and a person shall not be sentenced to imprisonment for such an offence unless in the opinion of the Court the offence was committed wilfully (s. 147 (4)).

If when a company is wound up it is shown that proper books of account have not been kept throughout the two years immediately preceding the commencement of the winding-up, every officer of the company who is in default shall, unless he shows that he acted honestly and that in the circumstances in which the business was carried on the default was excusable, be liable on conviction on indictment to imprisonment for not more than one year, or on summary conviction, for not more than six months. For this purpose, proper books of account include, in addition to the books already mentioned, books containing entries from day to day in sufficient detail of all cash received and paid, and, where the business involves dealing in goods, statements of the annual stock-takings, and (except in the case of retail sales) of all goods sold and purchased, showing the goods and the buyers and sellers thereof in sufficient detail to enable the goods and the buyers and sellers to be identified (s. 331).

### (b) The Profit and Loss Account and Balance Sheet

By Section 148 the directors of every company shall at some date not later than eighteen months after the incorporation of the company, and subsequently once at least in every calendar year, lay before the company in general meeting:

1. A Profit and Loss Account, or, for a company not trading for profit, an Income and Expenditure Account; and

2. A Balance Sheet as at the date to which the Profit and Loss Account or the Income and Expenditure Account, as the case may be, is made up.

This date must be not more than nine months, or in the case of a company carrying on business or having interests abroad, not more than twelve months earlier than the date of the meeting.

The Profit and Loss Account, or Income and Expenditure Account, must be for the period:

1. In the case of the first account, since the incorporation of the company; and

2. In any other case, since the preceding account.

These periods may be extended by the Board of Trade if for any special reason they think fit so to do.

The penalties for failure to comply with these provisions, and the defences available for an offence under this section are similar to those referred to in s. 147 (4) for the failure to keep proper books of account (see above).

Every Balance Sheet of a company must give a true and fair view of the state of affairs of the company as at the end of its financial year, and every Profit and Loss Account must give a true and fair view of the profit or loss for the financial year (s. 149 (1)).

The contents of the Balance Sheet and Profit and Loss Account must be such as will comply with the requirements of the Eighth Schedule of the Act, as amended by the *Companies Act 1967* so far as applicable thereto, but the Board of Trade may, on the application or with the consent of a company's directors, modify any of the requirements of the Act, as to the matters to be stated in the Balance Sheet and Profit and Loss Account, for the purpose of adapting them to the circumstances of the company (s. 149 (2) and (4)).

Subject to the requirements of the Act, the amount of detailed information disclosed in the published accounts must be carefully considered, but it should not injure the company by affording valuable information to trade rivals.

The provisions of Section 149 (1) and (2) on the *contents* of the Profit and Loss Account do not apply if:

(*a*) the company has subsidiaries; and

(*b*) the Profit and Loss Account is framed as a consolidated Profit and Loss Account, dealing with all or any of the company's subsidiaries as well as the company, and:

(i) complies with the requirements of the Act relating to consolidated Profit and Loss Accounts; and

(ii) shows how much of the consolidated profit or loss for the financial year is dealt with in the accounts of the company (s. 149 (5)).

The following definitions are given in Part IV of the Eighth Schedule as amended by the *Companies Act 1967* for use in relation to matters required by that Schedule to be disclosed in the Balance Sheet and Profit and Loss Account:

1. (*a*) the expression 'provision' shall, subject to 2 below, mean any amount written off or retained by way of providing for depreciation, renewals or diminution in value of assets or retained by way of providing for any known liability of which the amount cannot be determined with substantial accuracy;

　(*b*) the expression 'reserve' shall not, subject to 2 below, include any amount written off or retained by way of providing for depreciation, renewals or diminution in value of assets or retained by way of providing for any known liability, or any sum set aside for the purpose of its being used to prevent undue fluctuations in charges for taxation.

2. Where:

　(*a*) any amount written off or retained by way of providing for depreciation, renewals or diminution in value of assets, not being an amount written off in relation to fixed assets before July 1st, 1948; or

　(*b*) any amount retained by way of providing for any known liability;

is in excess of that which in the opinion of the directors is reasonably necessary for the purpose, the excess shall be treated as a reserve and not as a provision.

3. The expression 'quoted investment' means an investment for which there has been granted a quotation or permission to deal on a recognised stock exchange, or on any stock exchange of repute outside Great Britain, and the expression 'unquoted investment' shall be construed accordingly.

It will be recognized from the above definitions that the meaning given to the expression 'provision' is much narrower than that usually attributed to it in framing accounts. For the purposes of the *Companies Acts* the word 'provision' must not be used, as it commonly is used in practice, to describe amounts set aside to provide for prospective or even potential losses or liabilities; it must only be employed to indicate *known* depreciation or diminution in the value of assets, and *known* liabilities, the amount of which, however, cannot be estimated with reasonable accuracy. If the amount of a known liability *can* be estimated with substantial precision, it must be classified as a liability, and not as a provision.

### (c) *Contents of the Profit and Loss Account*

Greater disclosure of information in the accounts of companies is required by the *Companies Act 1967*, and the following is a summary of what is required to be disclosed under the *Companies Acts* of 1948 and 1967, either in the Profit and Loss Account or in a statement annexed thereto.

### (1) TURNOVER

Turnover for the financial year and the method by which it is arrived at. If some or all of the turnover is omitted by reason of it being attributable to the business of banking or discounting or to such other class as may be prescribed, the fact that it is omitted. A company which is neither a subsidiary nor a holding company is exempted from showing in its accounts particulars of turnover where it does not exceed £50,000.

'Turnover' is not defined by the Act but the Jenkins Report stated that 'generally speaking turnover might be described as the total amount receivable by a company in the ordinary course of its business for goods sold or supplied by it as a principal and for services provided by it. Each company should be free to state the figure which, in the opinion of the directors, gave a true and fair view of its turnover, and an explanation of the basis adopted in the computation should be given in the first accounts after the requirement was enacted.' Therefore, what would be regarded as turnover and the method by which it is arrived at must depend upon the exact nature of the business activity carried on by the company.

### (2) INCOME

(*a*)  The amounts of income respectively from quoted and unquoted investments;

(*b*)  the amount of net revenue of rents from land if this forms a substantial part of the company's revenue.

### (3) EXPENDITURE

(i) Amount of interest on bank loans, overdrafts, and on other loans repayable within five years whether by instalments or not, and loans of other kinds. The interest charged in the Profit and Loss Account will require sub-division as follows:

(*a*)  Interest on bank loans and overdrafts and loans repayable in full within five years from the Balance Sheet date;

(*b*) Interest on all other loans, i.e. those repayable wholly or partly more than five years from the balance sheet date.

(ii) The amount charged to revenue in respect of the hire of plant and machinery, if material.

(iii) Remuneration of the auditors (including expenses). This applies whether or not the remuneration is fixed by the members in A.G.M.

(iv) *Depreciation:*

(*a*) The amount charged to revenue by way of provision for depreciation, renewals or diminution in value of fixed assets;

(*b*) the amount charged to revenue for provision for renewal of assets for which there has also been a depreciation charge (to be shown separately from the depreciation charge);

(*c*) where the amount charged for depreciation has been based otherwise than by reference to the value of those assets as shown in the Balance Sheet, this fact must be stated;

(*d*) if depreciation or replacement of fixed assets is provided for by some method other than a depreciation charge or provision for renewals, or is not provided for, the method by which it is provided for or the fact that it is not provided for as the case may be.

(v) *Reserves and Provisions:*

(*a*) The amounts respectively provided for redemption of share capital and for redemption of loans;

(*b*) the amount, if material, set aside or proposed to be set aside to, or withdrawn from reserves;

(*c*) the amount, if material, set aside to provisions other than provisions for depreciation, renewals or diminution in value of assets or, as the case may be, the amount, if material, withdrawn from such provisions and not applied for the purposes thereof. (The Board of Trade may direct that a company shall not be obliged to show an amount so set aside to provisions if the Board is satisfied that that is not required in the public interest and would prejudice the company, but subject to the condition that any heading stating an amount arrived at after taking into account the amount set aside as aforesaid shall be so framed or marked as to indicate that fact.)

(vi) *Taxation:*

(*a*) The amount of the charge for U.K. corporation tax with a note of the amount it would have been but for relief from double taxation relief, the amount of the charge for U.K. income tax and the amount of the charge for taxation imposed outside the U.K. on profits, income and (so far as charged to revenue) capital gains;

(*b*) the basis on which the charge for U.K. corporation tax and U.K. income tax is computed;

(c) any special circumstances which affect liability in respect of taxation of profits, income or capital gains for the financial year or which will affect liability for succeeding financial years.

(vii) *Dividends:*

The aggregate amount (before deduction of income tax) of the dividends paid and proposed.

(4) MISCELLANEOUS

(a) The number of employees (other than directors) whose emoluments (a) are over £10,000 and not more than £12,500, (b) are over £12,500 and not more than £15,000 and so on in successive multiples of £2,500, unless the duties of the employee were wholly or mainly performed outside the U.K.

(As with directors' emoluments, employees working wholly or mainly outside the United Kingdom are excluded, as are pension contributions, in determining the total emoluments for this purpose. Salaries receivable from a subsidiary company, whether as a director of that company or otherwise, and benefits in kind are to be included.)

(b) any charge or credit arising from an event that took place in a preceding financial year unless included in a heading relating to other matters;

(c) the corresponding amounts for the preceding financial year;

(d) any material amounts in which any items shown in the Profit and Loss Account are affected –

(i) by transactions of a sort not usually undertaken by the company or otherwise by circumstances of an exceptional or non-recurrent nature; or

(ii) by any change in the basis of accounting.

### (d) Payments to Directors

By Section 196, of the *Companies Act 1948* in any accounts laid before a general meeting, or in a statement annexed thereto, there must be shown, so far as the information is contained in the company's books and papers or the company has the right to obtain it from the persons concerned:

(a) the aggregate amount of the directors' emoluments;

(b) the aggregate amount of directors' and past directors' pensions; and

(c) the aggregate amount of directors' or past directors' compensation for loss of office.

The amounts to be shown must include all relevant sums paid by or receivable from:

(i) the company; and

(ii) the company's subsidiaries; and

(iii) any other person;

except sums to be accounted for to the company or any of its subsidiaries, or undisclosed compensation for loss of office etc. for which Section 193 requires the director(s) to account to the vendors of shares (see p. 282).

Where necessary, the directors may apportion any payments between the matters for which they have been paid or are receivable in such manner as they think appropriate.

The amount to be shown under (a) must include any emoluments paid to or receivable by any person for his services as director of the company, or for his services, *while a director of the company*, as director of any subsidiary company (or of any company of which he was a director on the nomination of the principal company while a director of the latter) or otherwise in the management of the affairs of the company or any subsidiary thereof, and must distinguish between emoluments for services as director, whether of the company or its subsidiary, and other emoluments. (It will be observed that payments by subsidiary companies to their directors need only be included in the directors' emoluments disclosed in the holding company's accounts to the extent that they are made to persons who are also directors of the holding company.)

'Emoluments' include fees and percentages, any sums paid by way of expense allowances in so far as chargeable to United Kingdom income tax (i.e. expenses which are not allowed as deductions from emoluments under Section 189 of the *Income and Corporation Taxes Act 1970*, or which are disregarded under Section 199 of that Act), any contribution paid in respect of a director under any pension scheme and the estimated money value of any other benefits received by him otherwise than in cash.

The amount in (b) is not to include any pension paid or receivable under a pension scheme if the scheme is such that the contributions are substantially adequate for the maintenance of the scheme. Otherwise it must include any pension for services of a director or past director of the company, whether paid to or receivable by him or, on his nomination, or by virtue of dependence on or other connection with him, paid to or receivable by any other person. The amount must distinguish between pensions for services as a director and other pensions. 'Pension' includes any superannuation allowance, superannuation annuity or similar payment. 'Contribution' does not include any payment for two or more persons if the amount paid for each of them is not ascertainable.

In (a) and (b) the references to subsidiary companies are to those subsidiaries which were such when the services were rendered.

The amount to be shown under (c) must include compensation for loss of office as a director, or for loss of any other office *while a director*, or on ceasing to be a director either of the company or its subsidiary. It must also include sums paid in consideration of retirement from office. The amount must distinguish between compensation for the office of a director and of other offices and between amounts paid by or receivable from the company, its subsidiaries, and other persons.

It is pointed out that the payment to a *director* of compensation for loss of office is illegal unless previously disclosed to the members and approved by the company (ss. 191 and 192). When on transfer of any shares in a company, resulting from:

(*a*) an offer to the general body of shareholders; or

(*b*) any offer made by another body corporate with a view to the company becoming its subsidiary; or

(*c*) an offer by an individual with a view to his being able to control not less than one-third of the voting power of the company; or

(*d*) any other offer which is conditional on acceptance to a given extent,

a payment is to be made to a director as compensation for loss of or retirement from office, he must take all reasonable steps to see that particulars of the payment are sent to the shareholders with the offer for their shares. If these requirements are not complied with, or the making of the proposed payment is not first approved by a meeting called for that purpose of the holders of the class of shares affected, any sum received by the director shall be deemed to have been received by him in trust for any persons who have sold their shares as a result of the offer (s. 193).

The provisions of ss. 191, 192 and 193, as set out above, do not, however, apply to a *bona fide* payment to a director by way of damages for breach of contract, or by way of pension, superannuation allowance, superannuation gratuity or similar payment for past services (s. 194).

The amounts to be shown for any financial year for payments to directors are the sums receivable for that year, whenever paid, or, if the sums are not paid for any period, the sums paid during that year. If, however, sums are not shown in the accounts for the relevant financial year because they represent amounts to be accounted for to the company, its subsidiaries or past or present members of the company by virtue of Section 193, but the liability is released or not enforced within two years, they must be shown separately in the first accounts in which it is practicable to show them, or in a statement annexed to such accounts. The same applies to expenses allowances charged to United Kingdom income tax after the end of the financial year.

If the accounts do not comply with these provisions, the auditors must include in their report, so far as they are reasonably able to do so, a statement giving the required particulars (s. 196).

Every director of the company and every person who has been an officer of the company within the preceding five years, must give notice to the company of the requisite particulars relating to himself (s. 198).

After June 30th, 1948, it is illegal to pay directors' remuneration (whether as director or otherwise) 'free of tax' or in any way varying with rates of tax; any provision for payment free of tax, is regarded as providing for a payment, as a gross sum subject to income tax and surtax, of the net sum provided (s. 189).

ADDITIONAL DISCLOSURE

If, however,

(*a*) the company is either a holding or subsidiary company, or

(*b*) where the directors' emoluments as defined by s. 196 (1) (*a*) of the *Companies Act 1948* exceed £7,500 per annum, then additional details must be given as required by Sections 6 and 7 of the *Companies Act 1967*.

Section 196 (1) (*a*) of the 1948 Act requires disclosure of 'the aggregate amount of directors' emoluments', and it should be noted that for the purposes of disclosure as required by Sections 6 and 7 of the *Companies Act 1967*, Section 196 (1) (*b*) and (*c*) of the *Companies Act 1948*, namely, the aggregate amount of directors' and past directors' pensions; and the aggregate amount of directors' or past directors' compensation for loss of office are excluded. In ascertaining whether or not the directors' emoluments charged in the accounts exceed £7,500 per annum, contributions paid in respect of a director under any pension scheme must be included, but when making the analysis as required by Section 6 of the *Companies Act 1967* (see below) contributions paid under a pension scheme are excluded.

There must be disclosed under the 1967 Act:

(*a*) Emoluments of the chairman during his period as chairman unless his duties as chairman were wholly or mainly discharged outside the U.K.;

(*b*) The number of directors if any who received:

1. Nil up to and including £2,500 per annum;

2. Over £2,500 and up to and including £5,000 per annum and so on in successive multiples of £2,500

unless their duties as directors were wholly or mainly performed outside the U.K.;

(*c*) the emoluments of the highest paid director if his emoluments exceed those of the chairman unless his duties as director were wholly or mainly performed outside the U.K.;

(*d*) the number of directors who have waived their rights to receive emoluments and the aggregate amount so waived.

**Illustration**

The directors of A Ltd, which is neither a holding nor a subsidiary company, received the following emoluments:

|  | Salaries £ | Fees £ | Pension contributions £ | Benefits in kind £ |
|---|---|---|---|---|
| Chairman A (retired) (3 months) .. .. | — | 250 | — | 50 |
| Chairman B (9 months) .. .. .. | — | 750 | — | 150 |
| Director B (prior to appointment as Chairman) | — | 75 | — | — |
| Director C (Managing Director) .. .. | 3,000 | 300 | 330 | 100 |
| Director D .. .. .. .. | 2,000 | 300 | 220 | 100 |
| Director E .. .. .. .. | — | 300 | — | — |
|  | £5,000 | £1,975 | £550 | £400 |

Pension to Widow of deceased director £500

*Disclosure for Profit and Loss Account*

|  | £ | £ | £* |
|---|---|---|---|
| Directors' remuneration: |  |  |  |
| Fees .. .. .. .. .. | 1,975 | — | — |
| Other emoluments .. .. .. | 5,950 |  |  |
|  |  | 7,925 |  |
| Pension .. .. .. .. |  | £500 |  |

* Comparative figures have been ignored.

To comply with s. 6, *Companies Act 1967*, the following information must be given either in the accounts or in a statement annexed thereto:

*Emoluments of directors*

| | £ | £* |
|---|---|---|
| Emoluments of Chairmen: | | |
|   Mr A (3 months) .. .. .. .. .. | 300 | |
|   Mr B (9 months) .. .. .. .. .. | 900 | |
| Emoluments of highest paid director (in excess of combined Chairmen's emoluments) .. .. .. .. .. | 3,400 | |
| Other directors including B prior to appointment as Chairman: .. | | |
| £0–£2,500 .. .. .. .. .. .. | 3 Directors | |

### (e) Contents of the Balance Sheet

Schedule 1 of the *Companies Act 1967* has substantially extended the disclosure requirements for the Balance Sheet as laid down in the 8th Schedule to the 1948 Act. The following information must be given in the Balance Sheet or statements annexed thereto:

(1) The authorized share capital, issued share capital, liabilities and assets must be summarized, with such particulars as are necessary to disclose the general nature of the assets and liabilities, and there must be specified –

(*a*) any part of the issued share capital that consists of redeemable preference shares, the earliest and latest dates on which the company has power to redeem those shares and whether those shares must be redeemed in any event or are liable to be redeemed at the option of the company and whether any (and, if so, what) premium is payable on redemption;

(*b*) so far as the information is not given in the Profit and Loss Account, any share capital on which interest has been paid out of capital during the financial year, and the rate at which interest has been so paid;

(*c*) the amount of the Share Premium Account and Capital Redemption Reserve Fund;

(*d*) particulars of any redeemed debentures which the company has power to re-issue.

(2) RESERVES AND PROVISIONS

(*a*) The aggregate amounts respectively of reserves and provisions (other than provision for depreciation, renewals or diminution in value of assets) shall be stated under separate headings,
    Provided that –
  (i) a separate statement is not required if either of the said amounts is not material;
  (ii) the Board of Trade may direct that it shall not require a separate statement of the amount of a provision where they are satisfied that it is not required in the public interest and would prejudice the company, but subject to the condition that any heading stating an amount arrived at after taking into account a provision (other than as aforesaid) shall be so framed or marked to indicate that fact.

* Comparative figures have been ignored.

(b) Where the replacement of fixed assets is provided for wholly or partly by charging the cost of replacement against a provision previously made for that purpose or by charging the cost of replacement direct to revenue there shall be stated:

   (i) the means by which their replacement is provided for; and

   (ii) the aggregate amount of the provision (if any) made for renewals and not used.

(c) There must also be shown (unless it is shown in the Profit and Loss Account or a statement or report annexed thereto, or the amount involved is not material),

> where the amount of the reserves or of the provisions (other than provisions for depreciation, renewals or diminution in value of assets) shows an increase, or where the amount of the reserves or of the provisions shows a decrease, it is necessary to disclose the source from which the amount of the increase has been derived and the application in the case of a decrease.

Where the heading showing the reserves or provision is divided into sub-headings, these requirements apply to each of the separate amounts shown in the sub-headings instead of applying to the aggregate amount thereof.

## (3) LIABILITIES

(a) If an amount is set aside for the purpose of being used to prevent undue fluctuations in charges for taxation, it shall be stated.

If this amount has been used during the financial year for another purpose, the amount thereof and the fact that it has been so used shall be stated.

(Note that paragraph 23 of Schedule 1 has caused the definitions of capital and revenue reserves (Schedule 8, Para. 27, 1948 Act) to be deleted. The definition of 'reserve' has been extended so that a reserve shall not include any sum set aside for the purpose of its being used to prevent undue fluctuations in charges for taxation.)

(b) The aggregate amount of bank loans and overdrafts.

(c) The aggregate amount of loans (other than bank loans and overdrafts) which are repayable either wholly or in part more than five years from the date of the Balance Sheet, showing the terms of repayment and the rate of interest in respect of each loan. If this information will result in a statement of excessive length it shall be sufficient to give a general indication of the terms on which the loans are repayable and the rates at which interest is payable thereon.

(d) The aggregate amount (before deduction of income tax) which is recommended for distribution by way of dividend.

(e) Where any liability of the company is secured otherwise than by operation of law on any assets of the company, the fact that that liability is so secured shall be stated, but it shall not be necessary to specify the assets on which the liability is secured.

(*f*) Where any of the company's debentures are held by a nominee of or trustee for the company, the nominal amount of the debentures and the amount at which they are stated in the books of the company must be stated.

(*g*) The amount of any arrears of fixed cumulative dividends on the company's shares and the period for which the dividends or, if there is more than one class, each class of them are in arrear, the amount to be stated before deduction of income tax, except that, in the case of tax-free dividends, the amount shall be shown free of tax and the fact that it is so shown shall also be stated.

(*h*) The general nature of any other contingent liability provided for and, where practicable, the aggregate amount or estimated amount of those liabilities, if it is material.

(*i*) Where practicable the aggregate amount or estimated amount, if it is material, of contracts for capital expenditure, so far as not provided for and, where practicable, the aggregate amount or estimated amount, if it is material, of capital expenditure authorized by the directors which has not been contracted for.

(*j*) The basis on which the amount, if any, set aside for U.K. corporation tax is computed.

(*k*) The number, description and amount of any shares in the company for which any person has an option to subscribe, together with a note of the period in which exercisable and the price to be paid.

### (4) ASSETS EXCEPT INVESTMENTS

(*a*) The fixed assets, current assets and assets which are neither fixed nor current shall be separately identified.

(*b*) The method or methods used to arrive at the amount of assets under each heading shall be stated.

(*c*) The amount of goodwill, patents and trade marks (in so far as they have not been previously written off).

(*d*) The aggregate amount of any outstanding loans for the purchase of the company's own shares by employees of the company under the authority of provisos (*b*) and (*c*) of sub-section 1 of Section 54 of the *Companies Act 1948*.

(*e*) Particulars of any charge on the assets of the company to secure the liabilities of any other person, including, where practicable, the amounts secured.

(*f*) In the case of fixed assets shown at a valuation (other than unquoted investments) the years (so far as they are known to the directors), in which the assets were severally valued and the several values, and, in the case of assets that have been valued during the current financial year, the names of the persons who valued them or particulars of their qualifications for doing so and the bases of valuation used by them.

(*g*) The aggregate amount of fixed assets under any heading acquired during the financial year under review, and the aggregate amount of assets disposed of or destroyed during that year.

(*h*) Of the amount of fixed assets consisting of land, how much is ascribable to land of freehold tenure and how much to land of leasehold tenure and of the latter, how much to land held on long lease and how much to land held on short lease.
(Interests in land are regarded as including any buildings thereon.)
(*Hansard*, Standing Committee E, April 6th, 1967, col. 458.)
   A long lease is defined as one having more than fifty years unexpired at the end of the financial year. The expression 'short lease' means a lease which is not a long lease and the expression 'lease' includes an agreement for a lease.

(*i*) If in the opinion of the directors any of the current assets have not a value on realization in the ordinary course of the company's business, at least equal to the amount at which they are stated, the fact that the directors are of that opinion.

(*j*) If the amount carried forward for stock-in-trade or work-in-progress is material for the appreciation by its members of the company's state of affairs, or of its profit or loss for the financial year, the manner in which that amount has been computed.

(*k*) The amount of loans made to officers showing:
   (i) the amounts advanced during the period;
   (ii) amounts repaid during the period;
   (iii) amounts advanced prior to the period and still outstanding at the expiration thereof.

(5) INVESTMENTS

(*a*) For unquoted investments (other than those whose values, as estimated by the directors, are separately shown) where the holding is in equity share capital of a company:
   (i) the aggregate amount of the income received for the year from the investments during the year under review;
   (ii) the amount of the company's share of the aggregate profits (less losses) before and after taxation in the accounts sent by companies in which the investments are held during the financial year;
   (iii) the shares of the aggregate undistributed profits (less losses) of the companies in which the investments are held, accumulated since the investments were acquired; and
   (iv) the manner in which any losses incurred by those companies in which the investments are held have been dealt with in the company's accounts.

(*b*) The aggregate amounts respectively of the company's quoted and unquoted investments.

(*c*) The heading showing the amount of the quoted investments shall be subdivided where necessary, to distinguish the investments as respects which there has and those as respects which there has not been granted a quotation or permission to deal on a recognized Stock Exchange.

(d) The aggregate market value of the company's quoted investments where it differs from the amount of the investments as stated, and the Stock Exchange value of any investments of which the market value is shown and is taken as being higher than the Stock Exchange value.

(e) If at the end of its financial year a company holds –

(i) more than one-tenth in nominal value of any class of equity shares of another company not being its subsidiary company; or

(ii) shares in another company (not being its subsidiary) which exceeds one-tenth of the total assets, there shall be stated:

(a) the name of the company and the country (if other than Great Britain) of its incorporation; and

(b) each class of shares held and the proportion of nominal value of the issued shares of that class represented by the shares held.

(The Act specifies certain exemptions for companies incorporated or trading outside the U.K. if the Board of Trade agrees that disclosure could be harmful to the business. For the definition of Equity Share Capital see Chapter IX, § 2.)

### (6) SUBSIDIARY COMPANIES

(a) Holding companies are obliged to disclose each subsidiary company's name and specify details in relation to the country of incorporation, the classes of shares held in the subsidiary and the proportion of the nominal value of the issued shares of each class held, distinguishing between subsidiary company shares held directly by the parent company and shares held in one subsidiary through another.

(Subject to Board of Trade agreement the Act specifies certain exemptions for subsidiaries incorporated or trading outside the U.K. if disclosure is considered by the directors of the holding company to be harmful.)

(b) A subsidiary company is required to state the name of the company regarded by the directors as being the subsidiary company's ultimate holding company at the end of the financial year, and the country of the holding company's incorporation, unless the subsidiary company carries on business outside the U.K. and the disclosure is considered by the directors to be harmful to any company in the group and the Board of Trade agrees to the non-disclosure.

(c) The aggregate amount of the assets consisting of shares in or amounts owing (whether on account of loan or otherwise) from the company's subsidiaries, distinguishing shares from indebtedness, shall be set out in the Balance Sheet separately from all the other assets of the company, and the aggregate amount of indebtedness (whether on account of a loan or otherwise) to the company's subsidiaries shall be so set out separately from all its other liabilities.

(d) There shall be shown by way of note on the Balance Sheet or in a statement or report annexed thereto the number, description and amount of the shares in and debentures of the company held by its subsidiaries or their nominees. The Balance Sheet of a company which is a subsidiary of another body corporate, whether or not it is itself a holding company, shall show the aggregate of the amount of its indebtedness to all bodies corporate of which it is a subsidiary or a fellow subsidiary, and the aggregate amount of indebtedness of all such bodies corporate to it, distinguishing in each case between indebtedness in respect of debentures and otherwise and the aggregate amount of assets consisting of shares in fellow subsidiaries.

(e) Where group accounts are not submitted, there must be annexed to the Balance Sheet a statement stating:

  (i) the reasons why subsidiaries are not dealt with in group accounts;

  (ii) the net aggregate amount so far as it concerns members of the holding company of subsidiaries profits (less losses) for the respective financial years of the subsidiaries ending with or during the financial year of the company, together with similar information for the previous financial years since acquisition.

  (iii) any qualifications contained in the auditor's reports on the accounts of subsidiaries or notes on the accounts which, if not made, would have been the subject of a qualification, in so far as the matter which is the subject of the qualification or note is not covered by the company's own accounts and is material from the point of view of its members. Where group accounts are not submitted and the financial years of any subsidiaries are not co-terminus with that of the holding company, a statement must be annexed to the holding company's Balance Sheet showing –

    (a) the reasons why the company's directors consider that subsidiaries' financial years should not end with that of the holding company; and

    (b) the dates on which the subsidiaries' years ending last before that of the company respectively or the earliest and latest of those dates.

(7) PRELIMINARY EXPENSES ETC.

So far as not already written off, the undermentioned must be disclosed separately:

(a) preliminary expenses;

(b) expenses incurred in connection with the issue of share capital or debentures;

(c) commission paid in respect of shares or debentures;

(d) discount allowed in respect of debentures;

(e) discount allowed on the issue of shares at a discount.

(8) MISCELLANEOUS

(a) The basis on which foreign currencies have been converted into sterling must be disclosed by way of a note or statement or report annexed thereto where the amount of the assets or liabilities affected is material.

(*b*) The corresponding figures for the preceding financial year of all items.

EXEMPTIONS FOR SPECIAL CLASSES OF COMPANIES:

Part 3 of the Second Schedule to the *Companies Act 1967* states certain exceptions to the disclosure requirements appropriate to banking, discount, insurance and shipping companies. These have not been dealt with in the main body of the text but have been reproduced in Appendix II at the end of this book. In addition Parts 1 and 2 of the Second Schedule have been reproduced in detail.

### (*f*) *Fixed Assets*

The additional disclosure requirements where fixed assets are shown at a valuation should be noted carefully. Where fixed assets are included in the accounts at a valuation, it is necessary to disclose the years of the valuation and 'the several values', i.e. the values applicable to each year. These requirements, however, are subject to the qualification 'so far as they are known to the directors'. In the year in which fixed assets are revalued, the accounts must give details of the valuers or their qualifications and of the basis of the valuation used by them. Movements of fixed assets, i.e. acquisitions and disposals, are now required to be disclosed in aggregate. It should be noted, however, that movements on depreciation are not required by the *Companies Act 1967*.

**Illustration**

Movements in Fixed Assets:

| Plant | | | | Cost £ | Depreciation £ | Net £ |
|---|---|---|---|---|---|---|
| Balance January 1st, 1969 | .. | .. | .. | 20,000 | 4,000 | 16,000 |
| *Less* Disposals | .. | .. | .. | 3,000 | 300 | 2,700 |
| | | | | 17,000 | 3,700 | 13,300 |
| *Add* Purchases | .. | .. | .. | 3,000 | | 3,000 |
| | | | | 20,000 | | 16,300 |
| Depreciation for the year | .. | .. | .. | | +2,300 | —2,300 |
| | | | | £20,000 | £6,000 | £14,000 |

*Note:* Movements are shown on book values; profits and losses on sale will be credited and debited to Profit and Loss Account in the usual way.

### (*g*) *Loans to Officers*

By Section 197 the accounts which are required by the Act to be laid before the company in general meeting must also contain particulars showing:

The amount of any loans made during the company's financial year to –

    (i) any officer of the company; or

    (ii) any person who, after the making of the loan, became during that year an officer of the company;

        by the company or a subsidiary thereof (i.e. a company which was a subsidiary at the end of the company's financial year (whether or not a subsidiary at the date of the loan) ) or by any other person under a guarantee from or on a security provided by the company or a subsidiary thereof (including any such loans which were repaid during that year).

It should be noted that as a result of the abolition of the status of exempt private companies (Sec. 2) former exempt private companies will no longer be permitted to make loans to their directors or to the directors of their holding companies (Sec. 190, *Companies Act 1948*). This prohibition only affects future loans and the Act neither invalidates nor requires repayment of loans made prior to 27th July, 1967. No legislation has been introduced to prevent the making of loans to members of a director's family, his associates, or to other companies in which he is a controlling shareholder.

### (h) The Directors' Report

The *Companies Act 1948* required that there should be attached to every Balance Sheet laid before a company in general meeting a report by the directors with respect to the state of the company's affairs, the amount, if any, which they recommend should be paid by way of dividend and the amount, if any, which they proposed to carry to Reserves.

Copies of the Directors' Report must be sent to every member of the company, holders of debentures and any other person so entitled, together with copies of every Balance Sheet and Auditors' Report.

The *Companies Act 1967* requires the following information to be contained in the Directors' Report and the full requirements are set out below:

(i) The state of the company's affairs;

(ii) The amount, if any, which they recommend to be paid by way of dividend;

(iii) The amount, if any, they propose to carry to Reserves;

(iv) Names of persons who were at any time during the financial year directors of the company;

(v) The principal activities of the company during the year and of its subsidiaries and any changes therein;

(vi) Significant changes in the company's or its subsidiaries' fixed assets and the market value of land, if the value differs substantially from the book value;

(vii) If any shares or debentures had been issued the number, class and consideration received and the reason for the issue;

(viii) If at the end of the year there subsists a significant contract with the company in which a director has or at any time during the year had a material interest, a statement of the fact with the names of the parties to the contract, the name of the director, and an indication of the nature of the contract and of the director's interest therein;
(It is for the directors of the company to determine whether or not the contract is significant and the director's interest material.)

(ix) Details of any arrangements whereby the company enables directors to acquire benefits by means of acquisition of shares or debentures of the company or of any other body corporate, explaining the effect of the arrangements and giving the names of the directors who at any time during the year were directors and held, or whose nominees held, shares or debentures acquired as a result of the arrangements;

(x) A statement for each director whether or not he had an interest in any shares or debentures of the company or of any other body corporate within the group, specifying the number and amount of shares and debentures held at the beginning and end of each financial year (or if he was not a director at the beginning of the year, the details when he became a director).

(xi) Particulars of any other matters so far as they are material for the appreciation of the state of the company's affairs the disclosure of which will not, in the opinion of the directors, be harmful to the business of the company or of its subsidiaries;

(xii) If turnover is attributable to two or more substantially differing classes of business, the proportions in which the turnover is divided among these classes and in monetary terms the profit or loss before taxation of each class of business;

(A company which is neither a holding nor a subsidiary company is exempted from showing this information where total turnover does not exceed £50,000.)

(xiii) The average number of employees and their aggregate remuneration, including bonuses;

(A company is exempted from giving this information in its Directors' Report if the employees number less than 100 persons or if the company is a wholly owned subsidiary of another company in Great Britain.)

(xiv) The amount of political and charitable contributions made by the company for the year showing separate totals of each if, taken together, they exceed £50 in total;

(It is considered that the phrase used in Section 19 of the Act 'each of the purposes' means that disclosure is required in total only for (a) charitable and (b) for political, and not for each of the charitable and each of the political purposes. For political contributions that exceed £50 individually the Report must specify the recipient and the party supported. It should be noted that similar detail is not required for individual charitable donations.)

(xv) The amount of turnover during the financial year arising from the export of goods by the company (if its turnover exceeds £50,000) or by the group (if the total group turnover exceeds £50,000). If no goods were exported there shall be a statement of that fact.

Where items are shown in the Directors' Report instead of in the accounts of the company, the corresponding amounts for the immediately preceding year must also be shown.

Banking, discount, insurance and shipping companies do not have to comply with paragraph *h* (vi) above, and banking and discount companies only do not have to comply with paragraphs *h* (xii) and *h* (xv).

### (*i*) *Presentation of Balance Sheet and Profit and Loss Account*

While the form in which accounts are submitted to shareholders is (subject to compliance with the Companies Acts) a matter within the discretion of the directors, the following recommendations made by the Council of the Institute of Chartered Accountants in England and Wales are designed to indicate what is regarded as the best practice. These recommendations were all issued prior to the *Companies Act 1967*, and the following is a précis of important recommendations as amended in respect of taxation and other changes since the *Finance Act 1965* and the *Companies Act 1967*.

**Balance Sheet**

1. *Sub-total of share capital and reserves*

A sub-total of share capital and reserves, including any credit balance carried forward on Profit and Loss Account, should be shown and any description should be factual, such as 'share capital and reserves'. Descriptions such as net worth, which lend themselves to being misunderstood as tending to suggest that a balance sheet purports to be a statement of values or to show the value of the undertaking, should be avoided.

2. *Adverse balance on Profit and Loss Account*

Available reserves should be appropriated to extinguish an adverse balance on Profit and Loss Account. Where this practice is not adopted, the adverse balance should be grouped with and be a deduction in arriving at the sub-total of share capital and reserves.

3. *Amounts set aside for Corporation Tax*

Corporation tax payable on the profits made during the year ending on the balance sheet date can either be shown as a current liability, or be shown immediately before the current liabilities in a horizontal balance sheet, and shown as a current liability or deducted from net current assets before ascertaining working capital in a vertical balance sheet; the date when due for payment should be shown. Unpaid corporation tax for earlier periods should be shown as a current liability.

4. *Provisions*

Where the replacement of fixed assets is dealt with by making provision for renewals and charging the cost of replacement against the provision so made, the accumulated amount of provision for renewals, so far as not used, should be shown separately. Such a provision should not be shown as a deduction from the assets.

Where depreciation is provided on fixed assets, an amount set aside in recognition of the increased cost expected to be incurred in replacing fixed assets, as compared with the amount at which they are carried in books, is not a 'provision'; it is a reserve and should be shown as such.

5. *Grouping of liabilities and proposed dividends*

Current liabilities and proposed dividends should normally be shown in one group classified under appropriate descriptions and will include *inter alia:*

(*a*) trade liabilities, bills payable, accrued charges, income tax;

(*b*) short-term loans;

(c) bank loans and overdraft;

(d) corporation tax, showing date when due for payment;

(e) provision for any current liability of which the amount cannot be determined with substantial accuracy;

(f) aggregate proposed dividends, before deduction of tax.

In respect of all liabilities other than current liabilities, a specific description, such as debenture stock, mortgages, or unsecured notes, should be given. The dates and material conditions of redemption or conversion should be indicated.

### 6. *Bank overdrafts*

To comply with paragraph 8 (1) (d) of the Second Schedule the aggregate amount of bank loans and overdrafts must be shown under a separate heading. Where there are debit and credit bank balances with no legal right of set-off the full amounts of bank loans and overdrafts and of bank balances should be shown.

### 7. *Assets*

Paragraph 4 (2) of the Second Schedule requires that fixed assets, current assets and assets that are neither fixed nor current shall be separately identified.

8. *Fixed Assets* will normally include such assets as goodwill, patents and trademarks, land and buildings; plant, machinery and equipment; and investments intended to be held continuously by the business.

Items classified as *Current Assets* should include stock-in-trade and work-in-progress; trade and other debtors, bills receivable and prepayments (other than those on capital expenditure or of a long-term nature); quoted and other realizable investments (other than investments in subsidiaries and fellow subsidiaries and other investments intended to be held continuously even though they may happen to be quoted or otherwise readily realizable); tax reserve certificates; and bank balances and cash.

Items that are neither fixed nor current assets would include, for example, the current account with a subsidiary company, the preliminary and formation expenses, discounts on the issue of shares or debentures etc, in so far as they have not been written off to profit and loss account.

### Treatment of Investments in the Balance Sheet of Trading Companies

*Classification*

Investments which it is intended to hold continuously should be classified as *Fixed Assets*. Investments which are fixed assets may be distinguished from other fixed assets by showing them under a separate heading if desired. In many cases these comprise:

(a) Investments acquired and held primarily in order to protect the company's goodwill, or to facilitate or further its own existing business, rather than for income or appreciation in value;

(b) Investments representing a substantial but not a controlling interest in another company, particularly where the company has the right to appoint its own representatives to take part in the arrangement.

Quoted and other readily realizable investments (other than the above and investments in subsidiaries and fellow subsidiaries) should be classified as *Current Assets*.

When calculating the market value of a quoted investment by reference to a stock exchange quotation, it is usual to use the mean of the two quotations shown in the Stock Exchange Official List. If any other basis is used it may be desirable to indicate its nature.

*Valuation*

Provision should be made for diminution in value of investments:

(*a*) where the market value at the date of the Balance Sheet of investments treated as current assets is lower than cost, and

(*b*) where the value of investments treated as fixed assets appears to have decreased permanently below cost.

## Profit and Loss Account

### 1. *Profit or loss for the year*

Where the turnover is not disclosed in the Profit and Loss Account it should commence with the trading surplus or deficit of the year computed *after* charging depreciation and all other trading expenses. Depreciation and other items which have been charged or brought to credit in arriving at the trading surplus or deficit, but which are disclosed to comply with the Companies Acts, or because the directors consider that they should be disclosed, should be shown by notes on the account or by an unextended inset or in a 'box' immediately after the trading surplus or deficit for the year.

The trading surplus may be described as 'profit before taxation' and against this amount there should be charged the taxation based on this profit. The balance arrived at is the 'profit after taxation'.

Items of an exceptional or non-recurrent nature should be dealt with in such a way as to show in the particular circumstances a true and fair view of the results of the year. Such items, other than tax adjustments of earlier years, may be dealt with as follows:

(*a*) where the items arise from the trading operations of the company, they may be dealt with in arriving at the trading surplus or deficit and disclosed separately;

(*b*) they may be shown separately after the 'profit after taxation';

(*c*) they may in appropriate circumstances be omitted from the profit and loss account and taken direct to reserve.

Where exceptional or non-recurrent items have been taken into account before arriving at 'profit before taxation' any tax charges or relief arising because of the items should be included with the tax charge on such profit.

Where exceptional or non-recurrent items are not taken into account before arriving at 'profit before taxation' the effect of these items on the amount shown in respect of tax should be considered: where appropriate the relevant tax charges or reliefs should be shown as separate adjustments to the respective items.

Whether brought into the account with the tax charge for the year or shown after 'profit after taxation' any adjustment of the tax charge of previous years should be separately disclosed, if material.

### 2. *Depreciation of fixed assets*

The requirements in paragraph 14 (2) of the Second Schedule should be applied to each class of fixed assets and not to fixed assets as a whole: this requirement is that, if depreciation or replacement of fixed assets is provided for by some method other than a depreciation charge or provision for renewals, or is not provided for, the Profit and Loss Account must state the method by which it is provided for or the fact that it is not provided for, as the case may be.

### 3. *Income from subsidiaries*

Although paragraph 12 (1) (*g*) of the Second Schedule requires the amount of income from investments to be shown, paragraph 15 (2) (*a*) excludes income from investments in subsidiaries from this requirement. The Institute of Chartered Accountants, however, recommended that it should be shown (gross) if the amount is material.

4. *Dividends paid and proposed*

In addition to the statutory requirement that the aggregate amount of dividends paid or proposed shall be shown in the Profit and Loss Account, the dividends on *each class* of shares should be shown, distinguishing between dividends already paid and dividends recommended. The rates (per cent. or per share) at which dividends have been declared or are proposed should preferably be stated. It may be helpful to shareholders to state the dates of the payment of the dividends.

**Profit and Loss Account and Balance Sheet**

Schedule 2 of the *Companies Act 1967* contains the word 'material' no fewer than twelve times. In 1968 the Institute of Chartered Accountants in England and Wales issued a recommendation on 'The Interpretation of "Material"' in relation to Accounts and the following is a summary of the factors that should be considered:

1. In an accounting sense, an item is material if its 'non-disclosure, mis-statement or omission would be likely to distort the view given by the accounts or other statements under consideration'.

2. The principle of materiality arises in relation to the preparation and presentation of *any* type of accounts, both statutory and non-statutory, where the object is to present a true and fair view of the results for a period, and a position at a particular date.

3. The question of materiality can arise in relation to:
   (i) disclosure (including manner of disclosure, e.g. inclusion in a conglomerate total, separately, or specific mention with appropriate emphasis);
   (ii) correction or errors or omissions;
   (iii) methods of computation, i.e. whether the particular method gives due regard to all relevant factors.

4. Once an item is adjudged material, consideration will be presumed to have been given to:
   (i) its amount in relation to the overall view of the accounts; the total of which it forms a part; associated items in the final accounts; and the corresponding amount in the previous year;
   (ii) description, emphasis, presentation and context, and statutory requirements for disclosure.

5. Materiality is essentially a relative factor, and those responsible for preparing and auditing accounts must decide which facts of the many available to them have a real bearing on the true and fair view. Percentage differences are useful (if properly used) guides to materiality, but should never be applied indiscriminately.

6. In assessing the latitude permitted in arriving at the amount of a particular item, regard must be had to its nature, distinguishing between those items capable of precise and accurate determination, and those whose amount is determined by assumption and the exercise of informed judgment. In the latter category, the charge for depreciation is a prime example whereas the charge for directors' fees and the audit fee, for example, are items which may be of particular interest to shareholders, and no latitude is permissible, especially as they are normally capable of precise expression.

7. Miscellaneous factors affecting considerations as to materiality, are as follows:
 (i) The degree of approximation which is implicit in ascertaining the amount of an item may be a factor in deciding its materiality.
 (ii) Losses or low profits tend to vitiate the use of the profit figure as a point of comparison.

(iii) Inaccuracies or omissions not normally considered to be material, may affect the view given by the accounts, inasmuch as the *trends* of profit, turnover, or certain expense items may be especially significant in certain circumstances.

(iv) Items of small amount are not necessarily insignificant, especially where they might have been expected to be larger.

(v) Care should be exercised before offsetting items of opposite effect where each on its own might have been regarded as material, e.g. a non-recurring loss against a profit arising from a change in the basis of accounting; moreover, several individually insignificant items might represent a material amount in total.

### Comparative figures

Where an item appears in a note on the accounts or in a document annexed thereto the corresponding amount for the immediately preceding year should be shown.

Where the accounts do not include an item corresponding to an item which appeared in the accounts for the preceding year, the amount for that earlier year should nevertheless be shown, except that where the item appeared in a note on or document annexed to the accounts for the immediately preceding year it may not be necessary to repeat the item unless its omission could cause the comparison of the two years' accounts to be misleading.

If items in the accounts have been re-grouped, subdivided or otherwise rearranged as compared with the accounts for the immediately preceding year, then the items for that year should be similarly rearranged for the purpose of showing the comparative figures.

Where a change in the basis of accounting affects materially the comparability of the Profit and Loss Account of the year with that of the preceding year appropriate information should be included in the accounts by way of a note or otherwise. This information should explain the nature of the change and should indicate either the extent to which the account of the preceding year would have been affected had the revised basis been in use in that year, or, as may be appropriate, the extent to which the account of the current year would have been affected had no change been made.

## (*j*) *Valuation of Stock-in-Trade and Work-in-Progress for purpose of Accounts*

The following are extracts from the recommendations made by The Institute of Chartered Accountants in England and Wales on the value at which stock-in-trade and work-in-progress should be included in financial accounts.

### RECOMMENDATION

The amount carried forward for stock and work in progress should be computed on a basis which, having regard to the nature and circumstances of the business, will enable the accounts to show a true and fair view of the trading results and the financial position. In most businesses the basis should be the cost of the stock held, less any part thereof which properly needs to be written off at the balance sheet date.

The circumstances of each business should determine the basis which is appropriate and the method of computation which should be adopted in determining cost and the part thereof, if any, which should be written off. In most businesses the choice lies between writing off any excess of cost over either (*a*) the net realizable value of the stock, or (*b*) the lower of net realizable value and replacement price, these terms having the meanings attributed to them below. In some businesses it may be appropriate to use special bases, including some which depart from the rule that profit should not be anticipated.

The basis adopted and the methods of computation should be used consistently from period to period. A change of basis or method should not normally be made unless the circumstances have changed in such a way that its continued use would prevent the accounts from showing a true and fair view of the position and results. When a change is made the effect, if material, should be disclosed as an exceptional item in the profit and loss account or by way of note.

The following are the meanings attributed to 'cost', 'net realizable value' and 'replacement price' in this recommendation:

(a) 'cost' means all expenditure incurred directly in the purchase or manufacture of the stock and the bringing of it to its existing condition and location, together with such part, if any, of the overhead expenditure as is appropriately carried forward in the circumstances of the business instead of being charged against the revenue of the period in which it was incurred.

(b) 'net realizable value' means the amount which it is estimated, as on the balance sheet date, will be realized from disposal of the stock in the ordinary course of business, either in its existing condition or as incorporated in the product normally sold, after allowing for all expenditure to be incurred on or before disposal.

(c) 'replacement price' means an estimate of the amount for which in the ordinary course of business the stock could have been acquired or produced either at the balance sheet date or in the latest period up to and including that date. In a manufacturing business this estimate would be based on the replacement price of the raw material content plus other costs of the undertaking which are relevant to the condition of the stock on the balance sheet date.

The comparison between cost and net realizable value or replacement price may be made by considering each article separately, or by grouping articles in categories having regard to their similarity or inter-changeability, or by considering the aggregate cost of the total stock in relation to its aggregate net realizable value or, as the case may be, aggregate replacement price. The aggregate method involves setting foreseeable losses against unrealized profits on stock and may not be suitable for businesses which carry stocks which are large in relation to turnover.

Where the amount carried forward for stock is material in relation to either the trading results or the financial position, the accounts should indicate concisely the manner in which the amount has been computed. If this is not practicable the accounts should contain a note to the effect that a concise statement of the bases and methods used is not practicable but that the amount has been determined for the whole of the stock at the Balance Sheet date on bases and by methods of computation which are considered appropriate in the circumstances of the business and have been used consistently. The use of the term 'market value' should be discontinued.

METHODS OF CALCULATING COST

Apart from the variations which occur in calculating the amount to be attributed to each of the elements of cost there are various methods of computing cost.

In a small business one method only will normally be used but in a large composite business carrying on a variety of activities different methods may be used for different activities; once selected, however, the methods should be applied consistently to those activities from period to period. The following are the principal methods:

(a) 'Unit' cost

The total cost of stock is computed by aggregating the individual costs of each article, batch, parcel or other unit. The method is not always capable of application, either because the individual units lose their identity (notably where stocks are bulked or pass through a number of processes) or because it would involve undue expense or complexity to keep individual records of cost particularly where these necessitate allocations of expense.

(b) 'First in, first out'

Cost is computed on the assumption that goods sold or consumed are those which have been longest on hand and that those remaining in stock represent the latest purchases or production.

(c) 'Average' cost

Cost is computed by averaging the amount at which stock is brought forward at the beginning of a period with the cost of stock acquired during the period; consumption in the period is then deducted at the average cost thus ascertained. The periodical rests for calculating the average are as frequent as the circumstances and nature of the business require and permit. In times of rising price levels this method tends to give a lower amount than the cost of unsold stock ascertained on a 'first in, first out' basis and in times of falling prices a higher amount.

### (d) 'Standard' cost

A predetermined or budgeted cost per unit is used. The method is particularly convenient where goods pass through a number of processes or are manufactured on mass production lines; but it will not result in a fair approximation to actual cost unless there is a regular review of the standards with appropriate adjustment and revision where necessary.

### (e) 'Adjusted selling price'

This method is used widely in retail businesses. The cost of stock is estimated by calculating it in the first instance at selling prices and then deducting an amount equal to the normal margin of gross profit on such stocks. It should be appreciated that where the selling prices have been reduced the calculation will bring out cost only if appropriate allowance for price reductions is included in fixing the margin to be deducted; if no such allowance is made it may bring out amounts which approximate to replacement price. The calculations under this method may be made for individual items or groups of items or by departments.

#### TREATMENT OF OVERHEAD EXPENDITURE

Before deciding upon the method by which to compute 'cost' it is necessary to consider to what extent, if at all, the inclusion of overhead expenditure is appropriate to the particular business.

Overhead expenditure may be divided into:

(a) production expenses such as factory rent, rates, depreciation, insurance and supervision, and other indirect expenses of acquiring and producing stock;

(b) administration expenses not attributable directly to the acquisition or production of stock or the bringing of it to a saleable condition and location;

(c) selling expenses;

(d) finance charges.

Another classification (which can be applied also to each of the foregoing divisions) is to distinguish between 'fixed overheads', that is to say standing charges such as rent and rates which accrue and expire wholly or largely on a time basis, and 'variable overheads', which vary in a greater or lesser degree with the level of activity of the undertaking or of the department concerned but are not so closely associated with production or the volume of production as to be classed as direct expenditure.

Opinions differ on the extent to which overhead expenditure should be included in computing the cost of stock, though it is generally agreed that it cannot properly include selling and finance and other expenses which do not relate to the bringing of stock to its existing condition and location. The following are some practices which reflect the differing views on this matter:

(a) in some businesses no overhead expenditure is included as an element determining the cost of stock which is to be carried forward;

(b) in others only the 'marginal' cost of unsold stock is included, that is to say, that part of the cost of production of the period which has been incurred only because the stock remaining on hand was acquired or produced; all other expenses, including depreciation, are dealt with as revenue charges of the period for which they are incurred, the ground being that they arise irrespective of the quantity of stock which remains on hand at the end of the period and therefore are not an element in its cost;

(c) in other businesses an appropriate proportion of the overhead expenditure relevant to the period of production is included on the ground that for the purpose of financial accounting any expense, whatever its characteristics, which is related even though indirectly to the acquisition or production of goods ought to be included in the cost of those goods and ought not to be charged against revenue until they are sold; an 'appropriate proportion' is determined by reference to a normal level of activity.

These differing views about the inclusion of overhead expenditure may be very important in their effect upon the amounts carried forward for stock and upon the profits disclosed in the accounts. No one method of dealing with overhead expenditure is suitable for all businesses. The method selected by the management needs to be clearly defined and must have regard to the nature and circumstances of the business so as to ensure that the trend of the trading results will be shown fairly. Once the method has been selected it needs to be used consistently from period to period regardless of the amount of profits available or losses sustained. A change of method is appropriate only if there is a change in the relevant circumstances of the business. If material, the effect of a change of method would need to be disclosed in the accounts.

SPECIAL BASES USED IN SOME BUSINESSES

*Stocks at selling prices*

In some types of businesses, such as tea and rubber producing companies and some mining companies, it is a recognized practice to bring stocks of products into account at the prices realized subsequent to the Balance Sheet date, less only selling costs. By this means the whole of the profit is shown in the period in which the crop is reaped or the minerals won. This basis has come to be accepted as customary in the industries concerned.

In manufacturing businesses which carry stocks of by-products the separate cost of which is not ascertainable these stocks are normally included at current selling price (or contract sale price where applicable) less any expenses to be incurred before disposal; the cost of the main product is reduced accordingly.

*Long-term contracts*

In businesses which involve the acceptance and completion of long-term contracts it is often appropriate to spread over the period of the contracts, on a properly determined basis, the profits which are expected to be earned when the contracts are completed. This procedure takes up in each period during the performance of the contract a reasonable amount as representing the contribution of that period towards the eventual profit; it thus recognizes to a prudent extent the value of the work done in each period and restricts the distortion which would result from bringing in the whole of the profit in the period of completion. The principles which determine whether an element of profit is to be included are:

(a) profit should not be included until it is reasonably clear from the state of the work that a profit will ultimately be earned; it is therefore inappropriate to include any profit element where at the balance sheet date the contract has been in progress for a comparatively short time or to include an amount in excess of the profit element properly attributable to the work actually done;

(b) provision should be made for foreseeable losses and allowance should be made as far as practicable for penalties, guarantees and other contingencies;

(c) a clear basis for including a profit element should be established and adhered to consistently.

*'Base stock'*

In some businesses the minimum quantity of raw materials or other goods, without which they cannot operate their plant or conduct their operations, is treated as being a fixed asset which is under constant renewal by charges to revenue; that part of their stock (the base stock) is therefore carried forward not at its cost at the date of the accounts but at the cost of the original quantity of stock with which the business commenced operation. In old established businesses the amount will be based on prices paid for stocks acquired many years previously and many times replaced.

### 'Last in, first out'

The 'last in, first out' basis, which is in use in some overseas countries, assumes that the stocks sold or consumed in any period are those which were most recently acquired or made and therefore that the stocks whose cost is to be carried forward are those which were acquired, or made, earliest. The result is to charge consumption at prices approximating to current replacement prices and to carry forward stocks held at the close of the period at prices at which goods were purchased, or made, in earlier periods. When prices are falling this basis may result in showing the stock at an amount in excess of current prices in which event provision is made for the excess. During periods of rising prices, except in those instances where the physical movement of goods corresponds with the assumption that 'last in' is 'first out', the effect is to state the stock at less than its cost. The amount carried forward for stock may represent prices at which goods were acquired or produced several years earlier.

### DESCRIPTION IN THE ANNUAL ACCOUNTS

In most businesses the amounts carried forward for stock from one period to another are material in their effect upon the presentation of the trading results and financial position. The differences which exist among the methods which are recognized as proper for the computation of those amounts are also so important that, unless an indication is given of the way in which the amounts are computed, the significance of the results and of the financial position shown by the accounts may be obscured. The following are illustrations of how such an indication might be given concisely where the circumstances make this appropriate:

*(a) Normal basis*

'at cost';
'at the lower of cost and net realizable value';
'at the lowest of cost, net realizable value and replacement price';
'at cost less provision to reduce to net realizable value' (or 'to the lower of net realizable value and replacement price').

The expression 'market value' does not indicate whether it implies net realizable value or replacement price and is therefore not regarded as an appropriate description. Such terms as 'at or under cost' or 'as valued by the company's officials' are also not regarded as suitable.

*(b) Special bases*

If one of the special bases mentioned above is used an appropriate description would be required.

## (k) Contingent Liabilities

This expression implies that there are certain transactions the result of which is not yet known, which may or may not involve the payment of money at some subsequent date, or that the amount of a liability is dependent upon some factor not yet decided. The *Companies Act 1948* requires a note to be made on the Balance Sheet of contingent liabilities not provided for in the accounts and, where practicable, of the aggregate amount or estimated amount of these liabilities, if it is material.

The most familiar example of a contingent liability is bills receivable which have been discounted but have not yet matured at the date of the Balance Sheet. If any such bills are dishonoured by the acceptors the holders will have a right of recourse against the drawers or prior endorsers. Since it is not known at the date of the Balance Sheet if outstanding bills will be met in due course, a note should be inserted stating that: 'There is a contingent liability for bills under discount, amounting to £      .' When, however, there is a definite expectation that certain bills will not be met, provision should be made for the anticipated loss. To the extent that provision is made in the accounts, it will be unnecessary to refer to the contingent liability in a note on the Balance Sheet.

Other contingent liabilities are the uncalled liability on partly paid shares held in other companies, liabilities under guarantees, or pending actions at law etc. Contingent liabilities may also exist on contracts for work only partly performed, trade contracts etc., but it is usual only to note on the Balance Sheet the existence of those contingent liabilities which, should they accrue, might involve loss to the business. Other contingent liabilities which, when they accrue, will result in the acquisition of an asset of corresponding value, are sometimes omitted; though a note should be made where the amount is material.

A note of dividend arrears (before deduction of income tax) on cumulative preference shares must be made on the Balance Sheet, dividend arrears, since the payment of dividends is at the discretion of the company are not liabilities but are of interest to shareholders in ascertaining their interests in the company.

### (*l*) *Dividends*

The profits of a limited company may be distributed among the members in the form of dividends on the recommendation of the directors and in accordance with the Articles of the company.

The Articles usually provide that the dividend shall be calculated on the amount for the time being paid up on the shares, so that no dividend would be payable on any calls in arrear. Quite commonly, however, interest is chargeable on calls in arrear, and the dividend may then be made payable on the amount called up, if permitted by the Articles. Where Table A applies, dividends can only be paid on the amounts paid up. Where calls have been paid in advance, Table A (1948) provides that such payments shall *not* be treated as amounts paid up on the shares. No dividend can therefore be paid on calls paid in advance, unless Table A is excluded and the company's special Articles permit a payment.

A dividend is not due to members until declared by the company in general meeting, so that even preference dividends, though usually payable at fixed dates, are not recoverable against the company before declaration. The directors are usually empowered by the Articles to pay interim dividends, but although directors may *pay* such dividends, they do not become debts enforceable against the company until they have been *declared* by the company in general meeting.

Dividends proposed by the directors are debited to the Profit and Loss Appropriation Account and credited to Dividend Account *gross*, proposed dividends being shown as a current liability on the Balance Sheet; the *Companies Act 1967* gives statutory authority to this procedure even though the liability might not materialize if the company meeting either refuses to declare, or reduces, the dividend.

When a dividend is paid the net amount is debited to Dividend Account and cash is credited, at the same time, Dividend Account is debited and Income Tax Account credited with the income tax deducted from the gross dividend. Unless set off is available (see para. (*m*) below) the income tax must be paid over to the

Inland Revenue by the nineteenth of the month following the fifth of the month after the distribution is made.

The usual procedure in large businesses is to transfer the amount of cash payable for any dividend declared to a special Dividend Bank Account, against which the dividend warrants are drawn.

In the financial books, an account is raised for each dividend declared, details of the amounts due to each shareholder being recorded in dividend books or on dividend sheets. Dividends unclaimed are revealed by the balances appearing from time to time on the Dividend Accounts, and these are periodically transferred to an Unclaimed Dividends Account, which will appear as a liability in the Balance Sheet.

Where a company has issued share warrants to bearer, dividend coupons are usually attached thereto, and upon the notification by advertisement of the declaration of a dividend, the appropriate coupon should be detached by the holder of a warrant and paid into his bank for collection in the same manner as a cheque. If no coupons are attached to the warrants, the warrants must be deposited with the secretary of the company who, after verification, will return them together with a cheque for the amount of the dividend.

Unless dividends are declared 'free of tax', income tax at the standard rate must be deducted and only the net amount of the dividend paid. The dividend warrant must state the gross amount or its equivalent, the rate and amount of tax deducted, and the net amount payable, even where the payment is 'free of tax' (Section 242, *Income and Corporation Taxes Act 1970*).

Periodically, the total amount of the dividend warrants which have been presented for payment will be ascertained from the dividend pass book, credited to the dividend cash book, and debited to the appropriate Dividend Account, the balance of which at any time will represent the amount of dividends unclaimed. These should be treated as a liability in the Balance Sheet, the balance of cash as per the dividend pass book appearing as an asset of an equal amount.

The dividends payable are listed on dividend sheets, of which a specimen appears in the illustration given below. These sheets, which provide the data from which the dividend warrants are prepared, are written up from the share register, after all transfers have been recorded therein. The total of the *Net Dividend* column is the amount to be transferred from the general bank account to the dividend bank account. The warrants presented and paid through this account are ticked up on the dividend sheets, and any unticked items at any time represent dividends unclaimed, the total of which should agree with the balance on the Dividend Account.

**Illustration**

W Ltd has an issued capital of £100,000, all in ordinary shares of £1 each, and prepares accounts annually to March 31st.

In December the company declared a dividend of 10 per cent., gross for the year ended March 31st, payable on December 20th, and instructed the company's bankers on the same day to transfer the sum required to pay the dividend to a special Dividend Account. Income tax was paid to the Inland Revenue on January 17th.

On March 31st, the dividend warrants had all been presented for payment, with the exception of two, for £6 and £24 respectively.

You are required:

(a) To give a ruling, with two specimen entries, of a dividend sheet suitable for use in recording the dividend; and

(b) To set out the ledger entries involved, including the Dividend Bank Account, bringing down the balances as on March 31st. Income tax is to be taken into account at 50p in the £.

## DIVIDEND SHEET

Dividend for Year ending March 31st

No. of Dividend . . . . 40 . . . .     Rate: 10 per cent.     Payable December 20th

| Members' Names and Addresses | Share Register Folio | Number of Shares | Dividend | | | Warrant No. | Special Instructions and Remarks |
| | | | Gross | Tax at 50p | Net | | |
| | | | £ | £ | £ | | |
| A. Jones, 14 High Street, Manxton | 1 | 1,000 | 100 | 50 | 50 | 681 | |
| B. Robinson, The Hollies, Wroxton. | 2 | 660 | 66 | 33 | 33 | 482 | Payable to Barclays Bank Ltd Head Office. |

## DIVIDEND No. 40 ACCOUNT

| | | | £ | | | | £ |
| Dec. 20 | Income Tax Account .. .. | | 5,000 | Mar. 31 | Profit and Loss Appropriation Account .. .. .. | | 10,000 |
| Mar. 31 | Dividend No. 40 Bank Account .. | | 4,970 | | | | |
| | Unclaimed Dividends Account .. | | 30 | | | | |
| | | | £10 000 | | | | £10,000 |

## DIVIDEND No. 40 BANK ACCOUNT

| | | | £ | | | | £ |
| Dec. 20 | General Bank Account .. .. | | 5,000 | Mar. 31 | Dividend No. 40 Account – Dividends paid .. .. .. | | 4,970 |
| | | | | | Balance c/d. .. .. .. | | 30 |
| | | | £5,000 | | | | £5,000 |
| Apl. 1 | Balance b/d. .. .. .. | | 30 | | | | |

## INCOME TAX ACCOUNT 19../19..

| | | | £ | | | | £ |
| Jan. 17 | General Bank Account .. .. | | 5,000 | Dec. 20 | Dividend No. 40 Account.. .. | | 5,000 |

## UNCLAIMED DIVIDENDS ACCOUNT

| | | | £ | | | | £ |
| Mar. 31 | Balance c/d. .. .. .. | | 30 | Mar. 31 | Dividend No. 40 – Warrants not presented: | | |
| | | | | | A .. .. .. .. | | 6 |
| | | | | | B .. .. .. .. | | 24 |
| | | | £30 | | | | £30 |
| | | | | Apr. 1 | Balance b/d. .. .. | | 30 |

### PROFIT AND LOSS APPROPRIATION ACCOUNT

| | | £ | | | |
|---|---|---|---|---|---|
| Mar. 31 | Dividend of 10 per cent. gross on 100,000 Ordinary Shares of £1 each paid December 20th .. | 10,000 | | | |

## (*m*) *Treatment of taxation in the accounts of companies*

The amount of the charge for United Kingdom corporation tax (together with a note of the amount it would have been but for double taxation relief), the amount of the charge for United Kingdom income tax, and the amount of overseas taxation on profits, income and (so far as charged to revenue) capital gains, must be respectively disclosed in the Profit and Loss Account. It is also necessary to disclose by way of note (if not otherwise shown) the basis on which these charges (other than in respect of capital gains) are computed, and any special circumstances which affect liability in respect of taxation of profits, income or capital gains for the financial year, or which will affect it in succeeding years (Schedule 8 to *Companies Act 1948*, as amended, paragraphs 12 (*c*), 14 (3) and (3A)).

In the Balance Sheet or by way of note or report annexed thereto:

(*a*) If a sum set aside for the purpose of its being used to prevent undue fluctuations in charges for taxation has been used during the financial year for another purpose the amount thereof and the fact that it has been so used (para. 11 (8A)).

(*b*) If an amount is set aside for the purpose of its being used to prevent undue fluctuations in charges for taxation, it shall be stated (para. 7A).

Corporation tax and income tax are the two principal taxes affecting company records: company profits are subject to corporation tax; companies must deduct, and account to the Inland Revenue for income tax at the standard rate when paying dividends and annual charges; companies normally receive their investment income after income tax has been deducted.

### CORPORATION TAX

The charge for corporation tax shown in the Profit and Loss Account is based on profits for the year; the rate of tax, e.g. 45 per cent. at which the charge has been computed must be shown inset. If the rate of corporation tax is not known for the whole or part of the period covered by the accounts, the latest known rate should be used and disclosed. Overprovisions and underprovisions for corporation tax in previous years will be added to, or subtracted from, as appropriate, the profits brought forward from previous years in the Profit and Loss Appropriation Account.

In the horizontal Balance Sheet corporation tax based on profits for the year will be shown immediately before current liabilities or as a current liability; the date of payment should be shown. In the vertical Balance Sheet corporation tax based on profits for the year will either be shown as a current liability or will be deducted from current assets less current liabilities before ascertaining working capital. In all Balance Sheets corporation tax due for previous accounting periods will be shown as a current liability preferably as a separate item, the date of payment also being shown.

Corporation tax is imposed for 'financial years' which run from April 1st in one year to March 31st in the following year; the 'financial year' 1969 started on April 1st, 1969, and ended on March 31st, 1970. The rate of tax is fixed retrospectively; the rate for 1969 was announced in the Budget, in April 1970; the rate for 1968 was fixed by the *Finance Act 1969* at 45 per cent.

### DATE OF PAYMENT

1. For companies trading before April 1st, 1965 (which were assessed to income tax for 1965–66 on the profits of a year ended not later than March 31st, 1965, and which have not subsequently changed their accounting date), corporation tax will be payable on January 1st, following April 5th, after the company's accounting date, e.g.:

(*a*) Company's year ends February 28th, 1969; corporation tax will be payable on January 1st, 1970.

(*b*) Company's year ends April 30th, 1969; corporation tax will be payable on January 1st, 1971.

2. For new companies, corporation tax will be payable nine months after the end of the accounting period or one month after the making of the assessment, if later.

### INCOME TAX

The law requires companies to deduct income tax at the standard rate at source when paying dividends, debenture interest, royalties etc.; the company acts as agent for the Inland Revenue to prevent tax evasion and to speed collection. Investment income is normally received after deduction of income tax. Familiarity with the following terms is essential to understand the treatment of income tax in accounts:

1. *Distributions*, i.e. dividends paid, capital dividends, payments *in specie* of company assets, bonus issues of redeemable preference shares and debentures, the premium on redemption of redeemable preference shares. The *Finance Act 1965* gives a full list (now Section 233 of the *Income and Corporation Taxes Act 1970*).

2. *Charges*, i.e. payments from which income tax must be deducted at source, e.g. debenture interest, mortgage interest, royalties.

3. *Franked investment income received*, i.e. distributions (as defined in (1) above), received from U.K. companies, e.g. preference and ordinary dividends.

4. *Unfranked investment income received*, i.e. annual charges and income received from Government securities, local authority loans, and building society interest received.

5. *Profits*, i.e. trading profits and other income received without deduction of income tax at source, e.g. rents, $3\frac{1}{2}$ per cent. War Loan Interest, Bank Deposit Interest, British Savings Bond Interest.

The charge for dividends, royalties, debenture interest, and annual charges in the Profit and Loss Account is shown **gross**; the investment income received is also shown **gross**; total franked investment income if material is shown either inset or by way of note. If desired, the net amount of dividend paid or proposed and the income tax appropriate thereto may be shown inset. The double entry recording the payment of a distribution or annual charge is: (*a*) *debit* dividend or debenture interest etc. account with the **gross** amount and *credit* cash with the cash paid to the shareholder or debenture-holder etc. **and** *credit* Income Tax Account with the income tax deducted. When investment income is received, *debit* cash with the cash received, *debit* Income Tax Account with the income tax deducted by the payer at source and *credit* Investment Income Account with the gross amount.

In the Balance Sheet an Income Tax Account credit balance will be included in creditors; a debit balance on Income Tax Account may be included in debtors, or if material:

(*a*) in respect of tax on franked investment income deducted from the gross dividend payable, or

(*b*) in respect of tax on unfranked investment income deducted from the corporation tax payable on profits for the year.

Accrued debenture and loan interest will be included in creditors, gross, and need not be disclosed separately on the Balance Sheet. Aggregate proposed dividends *gross*, must appear separately, preferably as the last item of current liabilities.

SET-OFF

1. *Temporary:* In the Income Tax Account, during the income tax year which runs from April 6th in one year to April 5th in the next, debit entries can be set off against credit entries; no distinction is necessary between income tax on franked investment income received and income tax on unfranked investment income received, or between income tax on distributions made and income tax on annual charges paid. Companies must balance off their income tax accounts on the fifth of every month; credit balances will be paid to the Inland Revenue by the nineteenth of the month; companies can reclaim debit balances to the extent that they have previously paid cash to the Inland Revenue but they cannot reclaim income tax deducted by other persons.

2. *Permanent:* On April 5th in each year permanent set-off must be applied as follows:

(*a*) Income tax on franked investment income received must be set off against income tax on distributions made. Any excess of income tax on franked investment income received over income tax on distributions made should be written off to Profit and Loss Account; it is, however, available for set-off in subsequent income tax years; and should be credited to Profit and Loss Account in the accounting period during which set-off occurs. The excess of income tax deducted from distributions over income tax deducted from franked investment income received will be paid to the Inland Revenue.

(b) Income tax deducted from unfranked investment income received must be set off against:

   (i) income tax deducted from annual charges paid;

   (ii) corporation tax based on profits for the year. Any excess remaining will be repaid by the Inland Revenue. Income tax deducted from annual charges paid which has not been set off against income tax on unfranked investment income received will be paid to the Inland Revenue.

   It is normal procedure to open separate accounts for:

(a) Corporation tax.

(b) Each income tax year, e.g. Income Tax Account 1969-70 and Income Tax Account 1970-71.

**Illustration (1)**

At September 30th, 1968, the Balance Sheet of Fox Ltd showed a provision for corporation tax payable January 1st, 1969, of £5,000 and a provision for corporation tax payable January 1st, 1970, of £6,500.

During the year ended September 30th, 1969:

   (i) Corporation tax on profits for the year ended September 30th, 1967, was finally agreed at £5,250, and paid. Corporation tax on profits for the year ended September 30th, 1968, was finally agreed at £6,100.

   (ii) Interest on debentures repayable January 1st, 1990, £300 (net), was paid on both March 31st, 1969 and September 30th, 1969.

   (iii) Royalties, £2,500 (net), were received on April 1st, 1969.

   (iv) Dividends on ordinary shares (quoted investments) in U.K. companies of £700 (net) and £600 (net), were received on December 1st, 1968 and August 1st, 1969, respectively.

   (v) An interim ordinary dividend of £3,000 (net) was paid on March 15th, 1969.

   (vi) Income tax, Schedule F, £2,300, was paid on April 19th, 1969.

   Corporation tax, assuming a rate of 45 per cent, based on profits for the year, is estimated at £8,000. The directors propose a final ordinary dividend of £4,000 (net), payable November 30th, 1969.

Assume income tax at 50p in the £.

### INCOME TAX ACCOUNT 1968-69

| 1968 | | £ | 1969 | | £ |
|---|---|---|---|---|---|
| Dec. 1 | Investment Income Account – tax deducted from franked investment income received .. .. | 700 | Mar. 31 | Debenture Interest Account – income tax deducted from debenture interest paid .. .. .. | 300 |
| 1969 April 1 | Royalties – income tax deducted from unfranked investment income received .. .. | 2,500 | Mar. 15 | Dividends Payable Account – income tax deducted from distributions paid .. .. .. .. | 3,000 |
| April 19 | Bank – excess of income tax on distributions over franked investment income £(3,000—700) .. .. | 2,300 | April 5 | Corporation Tax Account – income tax on unfranked investment income not set off against charges £(2,500—300).. .. .. | 2,200 |
| | | £5,500 | | | £5,500 |

### INCOME TAX ACCOUNT 1969-70

| 1969 | | £ | 1969 | | £ |
|---|---|---|---|---|---|
| Aug. 1 | Investment Income Account – tax deducted from franked investment income received .. .. | 600 | Sept. 30 | Debenture Interest Account – income tax deducted from debenture interest paid .. .. .. | 300 |
| | | | Sept, 30 | Balance carried forward .. .. | 300 |
| | | £600 | | | £600 |

## CORPORATION TAX ACCOUNT

| 1969 | | £ | 1968 | | £ |
|---|---|---|---|---|---|
| Jan. 1 | Bank .. .. .. .. | 5,250 | Sept. 30 | Balances brought forward: | |
| Sept. 30 | Profit and Loss Account – overpro- | | | 1967 Accounts .. .. | 5,000 |
| | visions £(400—250) .. .. | 150 | | 1968 Accounts .. .. | 6,500 |
| | Balances carried forward: | | | Profit and Loss Account: | |
| | 1969 accounts £(8,000—2,200) .. | 5,800 | | 1969 accounts charge .. .. | 8,000 |
| | 1968 accounts.. .. .. | 6,100 | | | |
| April 5 | Income Tax Account, 1968/69 – in- | | | | |
| | come tax on royalties not set off .. | 2,200 | | | |
| | | £19,500 | | | £19,500 |

## DIVIDENDS PAYABLE ACCOUNT

| 1969 | | £ | 1969 | | £ |
|---|---|---|---|---|---|
| Mar. 15 | Bank – interim .. .. .. | 3,000 | Sept. 30 | Profit and Loss Account: | |
| | Income Tax Account 1968/69 – in- | | | Interim (gross) .. .. | 6,000 |
| | come tax on interim dividend .. | 3,000 | | Final (gross) .. .. .. | 8,000 |
| Sept. 30 | Proposed final dividend (gross) car- | | | | |
| | ried forward .. .. .. | 8,000 | | | |
| | | £14,000 | | | £14,000 |

*Note:* The following extracts from the final accounts are relevant.

### PROFIT AND LOSS ACCOUNT for the year ended September 30th, 1969

| | £ | £ |
|---|---|---|
| PROFIT BEFORE TAXATION .. .. .. .. .. | | X |
| After accounting for: | | |
| Interest on loans repayable after more than 5 years .. .. | 1,200 | |
| | | |
| Income from: | | |
| Quoted investments (all franked) .. .. .. .. | 2,600 | |
| Royalties (see note) .. .. .. .. .. | 5,000 | |
| | | |
| United Kingdom taxation based on profit for the year: | | |
| Corporation tax (45 per cent.) .. .. .. .. .. | | 8,000 |
| | | |
| PROFIT AFTER TAXATION .. .. .. .. .. | | X |
| *Deduct* appropriations: | | |
| Dividends (gross) | | |
| Paid – March 15th, 1969 .. .. .. .. .. | 6,000 | |
| Proposed – payable November 30th, 1969 .. .. .. | 8,000 | |
| | | 14,000 |
| | | |
| UNAPPROPRIATED PROFIT FOR THE YEAR .. .. .. | | X |
| Unappropriated profits brought forward .. .. .. .. | X | |
| *Add* Overprovision for taxation in previous years .. .. .. | 150 | |
| | | X |
| | | |
| UNAPPROPRIATED PROFITS CARRIED FORWARD .. .. | | X |

(The Companies Acts do not require the disclosure of royalties.)

BALANCE SHEET as at September 30th, 1969 (extracts)

| | £ | £ | £ |
|---|---|---|---|
| Corporation tax payable January 1st, 1971 .. .. .. | | — | 5,800 |
| Current liabilities: | | | |
| Corporation tax payable January 1st, 1970 .. .. .. | | 6,100 | — |
| Proposed dividends (gross) .. .. .. .. | 8,000 | | |
| Less Income tax .. .. .. .. .. .. | 300 | | |
| | | 7,700 | X |

Where tax reserve certificates are surrendered in payment of tax, the amount of the certificates surrendered must be debited to Taxation Account and credited to the Tax Reserve Certificates Account, the interest allowed (which is not subject to tax) being debited to Taxation Account and credited to Profit and Loss Account. The face value of the certificates plus the interest together make up the amount of tax discharged.

*Overseas Taxation*

The amount of United Kingdom corporation tax should be shown and from it deducted the relief for overseas taxation to which should be added the amount of overseas taxation both relieved and unrelieved.

*Losses*

If a loss is set against other income of the same accounting period, corporation tax should be provided on the net income. If a loss is set against the profits of the preceding accounting period, the corporation tax recoverable, if material, should be disclosed separately. If a loss is available for set-off against profits to be earned in future accounting periods, a note should be appended to the accounts. If the corporation tax charged for a particular period has been eliminated or materially reduced by losses brought forward the amount of the relief should be indicated.

*Deferred Taxation Account*

The Institute of Chartered Accountants recommend that the charge for corporation tax should be based on the accounting profits for the year. The charge based on the accounting profits may differ from the charge based on the taxable profits because of:

(*a*) expenses disallowable in the tax computation;

(*b*) income (e.g. on tax reserve certificates) excluded in the tax computation;

(*c*) the difference between depreciation charged in the accounts and capital allowances computed for tax purposes;

(*d*) the difference arising from allocating items to different periods for accounting and tax purposes.

The difference between the corporation tax chargeable on the accounting profit and the taxable profit should be transferred to a Deferred Taxation Account; for balance sheet purposes the balance on this account should be treated as a deferred liability rather than a reserve and shown above current liabilities. Debit balances on the account should be written off to Profit and Loss Account unless recovery against the profits of the next succeeding period is reasonably certain, and, if the amount is material, shown annually by way of note.

Whenever the rate of corporation tax is altered the balance on the account should be adjusted.

Whenever trading losses are carried forward, Deferred Taxation Account should be debited and Profit and Loss Account credited with an amount equal to the notional tax relief attributable to the loss.

**Realizations and Revaluation of Assets**

(*a*) *Realized capital surpluses*

Corporation tax payable on realized capital surpluses should be charged to the account to which the surplus is credited:

**Illustration (2)**

|  | £ | £ |
|---|---|---|
| Profit and Loss Account: | | |
| Surplus on sale of freehold property    ..    ..    ..    .. | 20,000 | |
| *Less* Corporation tax on chargeable gain  ..    ..    ..    .. | 2,000 | |
|  | | 18,000 |
| Or alternatively: | | |
| Balance Sheet | | |
| Reserves | | |
| Surplus on sale of freehold property arising during the year    .. | 20,000 | |
| *Less* Corporation tax on chargeable gain    ..    ..    .. | 2,000 | |
|  | | 18,000 |

(*b*) *Surpluses on business assets replaced*

If an election is made that the replacement cost of an asset is to be reduced for tax purposes by the amount of the chargeable gain arising on the disposal of the previous asset corporation tax on the gain should be charged against the surplus and credited to the Deferred Taxation Account.

**Illustration (3)**

A Ltd acquired a shop for £10,000 on January 1st and sold it on July 1st for £12,500 acquiring another shop for £15,000. Expenses of sale (allowable) were £500.

### BALANCE SHEET (EXTRACTS) SEPTEMBER 30th

| | £ | £ | | £ |
|---|---|---|---|---|
| **RESERVES** | | | **FIXED ASSETS** | |
| Surplus on sale of shop during the year  ..    .. | 2,000 | | Shop at cost    ..    .. | 15,000 |
| *Less* Corporation tax due thereon transferred to Deferred Taxation Account    ..    .. | 850 | | | |
| | | 1,150 | | |
| Deferred Taxation Account.. | | 850 | | |

(*c*) *Unrealized capital surpluses*

When assets are written-up on revaluation, attention should be drawn to the corporation tax which would be payable should the assets be sold at revaluation figures. Two methods are recommended:

either  (i) charge the corporation tax payable against the surplus on revaluation and credit Deferred Taxation Account;

or (ii) append a note annually to the accounts that no provision has been made out of the surplus for this potential liability to tax.

If subsequently the assets are sold below revaluation figures corporation tax on the difference between selling price and revaluation figures should be debited to Deferred Taxation Account and credited to surplus on revaluation, if method (i) has been adopted.

### (d) Investments

Where the market value of investments, shown by way of note, exceeds the book value, an estimate should be given of any potential corporation tax liability which would arise on disposal at the value noted. If, because of practical difficulties, no estimate is made, the note of market value should state that had the asset been sold a liability to tax on the chargeable gain would have arisen.

### (e) Realized capital deficits

A note should be appended to the accounts stating that an allowable loss is available for set-off against chargeable gains in future accounting periods.

## Close Companies

A note should be appended to the accounts, stating whether or not a company is a 'close' company. If the status is in doubt, this should be stated together with the basis upon which the tax provision has been made.

In the accounts of a 'close' company a note must appear clarifying the company's position in relation to 'shortfalls'. The Institute of Chartered Accountants recommend the following notes, as appropriate:

### (a) If there is no material shortfall

'The company is a close company. No *material*\* shortfall can arise and no provision for income tax under Section 77 of the *Finance Act 1965*† is therefore necessary.'

### (b) In other circumstances

'The company is a close company and is therefore potentially liable to income tax on any shortfall of distributions below the required standard. It has not yet been established that the *dividends paid and proposed and other distributions*\* for the period satisfy this standard.'

Income tax deducted from a loan to a participator should be shown separately and grouped with the loan to which it relates.

A note should be appended to the accounts, if the relationship between the corporation tax charge and the accounting profits is distorted, because of disallowable expenses, e.g. directors' remuneration, stating the cause.

## The treatment of Income Tax on Surplus Franked Income over Distributions

Income tax on any surplus franked investment income over distributions should be written-off to Profit and Loss Account unless it can be set off against income tax on distributions (including distributions arising in a new fiscal year) of the succeeding accounting period. The amount to be written off is based on the surplus arising when permanent set-off is applied at April 5th before the Balance Sheet date.

The amount of income tax written-off may be disclosed in one of the following ways:

(a) shown as an element of the total taxation charge; or

(b) shown in the same section as the dividends (being dependent on their amount). When this method is adopted a balance should be struck on the Profit and Loss Account after charging corporation tax and overseas taxation (if any), and described as 'profit after corporation tax (and overseas taxation)'.

If income tax written-off but available for set-off in future years is material, the gross equivalent (i.e. the surplus franked investment income) should be shown by way of note, since it is a hidden reserve.

\*Delete words inapplicable.

†Now Section 289 of the *Income and Corporation Taxes Act 1970*.

**Illustration (4)**

A company's accounting year ends on September 30th. During the year ended April 5th, 1969, franked investment income received amounted to £20,000, while dividends of £10,000 were paid. Dividends (normally paid once a year) proposed at September 30th, 1969, payable November 30th, 1969, amounted to £8,000 (gross). Assuming income tax to be 50p in the £, show the amount to be written off at September 30th, 1969, (i) adopting method (a) and (ii) method (b).

Surplus of income tax on franked investment income after permanent set-off at April 5th, 1969:

### INCOME TAX ACCOUNT 1968/69

| | £ | | £ |
|---|---|---|---|
| Investment Income Account – tax deducted from franked investment income*  ..          .. | 10,000 | Dividends Payable Account – tax deducted from distributions paid*    ..          .. | 5,000 |
| | | Balance carried down    ..          ..          .. | 5,000 |
| | £10,000 | | £10,000 |
| Balance brought down      ..          ..          .. | 5,000 | Income Tax Account 1969/70 – income tax to be set off against distributions..      ... | 4,000 |
| | | Profit and Loss Account – income tax on surplus franked investment income  ..      .. | 1,000 |
| | £5,000 | | £5,000 |

*For the year April 6th, 1968, to April 5th, 1969.

(i) *Method (a)*

### PROFIT AND LOSS ACCOUNT
for the year ended September 30th, 1969

| | £ | £ |
|---|---|---|
| PROFIT BEFORE TAXATION    ..      ..      ..      ..      .. | | x |
| After accounting for: | | |
| Depreciation etc.    ..      ..      ..      ..      ..      .. | x | |
| United Kingdom taxation based on the profits for the year | | |
| Corporation tax (45 per cent.)      ..      ..      ..      .. | x | |
| Income tax on surplus franked investment income      ..      .. | 1,000 | x |
| PROFIT AFTER TAXATION    ..      ..      ..      .. | | x |
| *Deduct* appropriations: | | |
| General reserve    ..      ..      ..      ..      ..      .. | x | |
| Proposed dividends (gross) – payable November 30th, 1969      .. | 8,000 | x |
| UNAPPROPRIATED PROFIT FOR THE YEAR      ..      ..      .. | | x |

(ii) *Method (b)*

### PROFIT AND LOSS ACCOUNT
for the year ended September 30th, 1969

| | £ | £ |
|---|---|---|
| PROFIT BEFORE TAXATION    ..      ..      ..      ..      .. | | x |
| After accounting for: | | |
| Depreciation etc.    ..      ..      ..      ..      ..      .. | x | |
| United Kingdom taxation based on the profits for the year | | |
| Corporation tax (45 per cent.)  ..      ..      ..      ..      .. | | x |
| PROFIT AFTER CORPORATION TAX    ..      ..      ..      .. | | x |
| *Deduct* appropriations: | | |
| Proposed dividends (gross) – payable November 30th, 1969      .. | 8,000 | |
| Income tax on surplus franked investment income      ..      .. | 1,000 | 9,000 |
| UNAPPROPRIATED PROFIT FOR THE YEAR      ..      ..      .. | | x |

*Notes:*

(*a*) The remaining balance of £4,000 on Income Tax Account 1968/69 will be deducted from proposed dividends (gross) in the Balance Sheet as on September 30th, 1969.

(*b*) Method (*a*) presupposes that proposed dividends are known. Since, however, the income tax written off is dependent on the amount of the proposed dividends, 'profit after taxation' under this method, does not, theoretically, represent divisible profit.

(*c*) Method (*b*) is based on the view that profits of the company do not attract income tax and that for computing dividend cover and maintaining comparability of profits it is the figure after corporation tax, but before income tax, which is significant.

**The Accounting Treatment of Investment Grants**

Investment grants payable in cash, replace investment allowances; they are principally confined to manufacturing and extractive industries, and are equal to 40 per cent. of asset cost in development areas and 20 per cent. elsewhere, for expenditure between January 17th, 1966, and December 31st, 1966. For the two years ended December 31st, 1968, the rates were increased to 45 per cent. and 25 per cent. respectively, subsequently the rates reverted to 40 per cent. and 20 per cent. respectively.

The methods recommended by The Institute of Chartered Accountants in England and Wales for recording investment grants are:

1. The grant should be credited to the asset account with a consequential reduction in the depreciation charge (based on net cost) in the Profit and Loss Account; or

2. The asset should be shown in the Balance Sheet at cost before deduction of the grant; the grant should be credited to an Investment Grant Account (in the Balance Sheet the investment grant account will appear under the heading 'Reserves'); the balance on the Investment Grant Account should be transferred to Profit and Loss Account at a rate consistent with that at which the relevant depreciation charge is computed.

Grants should be brought into account in the accounting period in which the corresponding assets are brought into the books, and the accounting treatment adopted should be clearly disclosed and followed consistently.

[Investment grants were abolished in respect of expenditure incurred after October 26th, 1970, unless the contract was entered into on or before that date.]

**Illustration (5)**

At June 30th, 1970, the books of Veneering Manufacturers Ltd showed the following balances:

| | £ | £ |
|---|---:|---:|
| 10,000 8 per cent. cumulative preference shares of £1 each fully paid, redeemable at the Company's option on January 1st, 2,000 at a premium of 25*p* per share (Authorized £10,000)    ..    .. | | 10,000 |
| £40,000 Ordinary Stock (Authorized £50,000)    ..    ..    .. | | 40,000 |
| Freehold property July 1st, 1969, at cost    ..    ..    .. | 20,420 | |
| Additions during the year    ..    ..    ..    ..    .. | 2,000 | |
| Plant and equipment (cost £24,000) see note    ..    .. | 12,000 | |
| Office furniture (cost £3,000)    ..    ..    ..    .. | 2,200 | |
| Goodwill (cost £20,000) written down value    ..    .. | 10,000 | |
| Stock of raw materials July 1st, 1969    ..    ..    .. | 9,320 | |
| Stock of finished goods July 1st, 1969    ..    ..    .. | 1,270 | |
| Work-in-progress July 1st, 1969    ..    ..    .. | 920 | |
| Debtors    ..    ..    ..    ..    ..    .. | 10,700 | |
| 4 per cent. Debentures (repayable at par January 1st, 1992) (secured by a floating charge)    ..    ..    ..    .. | | 15,000 |
| Debenture interest, half year to December, 1969 (gross) paid on January 1st, 1970    ..    ..    ..    ..    .. | 300 | |
| Carried forward | 69,130 | 65,000 |

|                                                                                                                        | £       | £       |
| ---------------------------------------------------------------------------------------------------------------------- | ------- | ------- |
| Brought forward                                                                                                        | 69,130  | 65,000  |
| Shares in U.K. subsidiary company at cost (80 per cent. holding in Bye Ltd – 16,000 ordinary shares of £1 each of a total of 20,000 issued ordinary shares)  ..       ..        ..        ..        .. | 18,750  |         |
| Tax Reserve Certificates       ..        ..        ..        ..        ..                                               | 8,000   |         |
| Interest on Tax Reserve Certificates      ..        ..        ..        ..                                              |         | 30      |
| Dividends and interest (gross):                                                                                        |         |         |
| From unquoted investments received December 10th, 1969        ..                                                       |         | 100     |
| From quoted investments received June 20th, 1970       ..        ..                                                    |         | 300     |
| From subsidiary company received June 25th, 1970       ..        ..                                                    |         | 3,800   |
| Share Premium Account       ..        ..        ..        ..        ..                                                  |         | 3,640   |
| General Reserve       ..        ..        ..        ..        ..        ..                                              |         | 10,000  |
| Unquoted Investments at cost (directors' valuation £4,000) (see note)                                                  | 3,200   |         |
| Quoted Investments at cost (British Government securities) (market value £8,680)       ..        ..        ..        ..        ..        .. | 8,020   |         |
| Profit and Loss Account – balance July 1st, 1969        ..        ..                                                   |         | 3,090   |
| Amount owing to subsidiary company  ..        ..        ..        ..                                                    |         | 7,680   |
| Cash at bank and in hand        ..        ..        ..        ..        ..                                              | 8,292   |         |
| Creditors   ..        ..        ..        ..        ..        ..        ..                                              |         | 7,858   |
| Sales   ..        ..        ..        ..        ..        ..        ..                                                  |         | 69,100  |
| Purchases       ..        ..        ..        ..        ..        ..                                                    | 31,960  |         |
| Carriage inwards       ..        ..        ..        ..        ..        ..                                             | 1,600   |         |
| Bank interest       ..        ..        ..        ..        ..        ..                                                | 290     |         |
| Wages and national insurance (factory) ..        ..        ..        ..                                                 | 13,790  |         |
| Plant Hire (internal telephone system)   ..        ..        ..        ..                                              | 130     |         |
| Rates   ..        ..        ..        ..        ..        ..        ..                                                  | 500     |         |
| Repairs to premises  ..        ..        ..        ..        ..        ..                                               | 60      |         |
| Salaries (including Directors' salaries £3,000)       ..        ..        ..                                            | 6,130   |         |
| Postages and Telephone       ..        ..        ..        ..        ..                                                 | 180     |         |
| Printing and Stationery       ..        ..        ..        ..        ..                                                | 40      |         |
| Legal and Professional charges       ..        ..        ..        ..                                                   | 80      |         |
| Trade expenses       ..        ..        ..        ..        ..        ..                                               | 50      |         |
| Directors' fees       ..        ..        ..        ..        ..        ..                                              | 60      |         |
| Bank charges       ..        ..        ..        ..        ..        ..                                                 | 10      |         |
| Commissions       ..        ..        ..        ..        ..        ..                                                  | 520     |         |
| Power and Lighting (factory)  ..        ..        ..        ..        ..                                                | 670     |         |
| Insurances – Factory       ..        ..        ..        ..        ..                                                   | 720     |         |
| Office   ..        ..        ..        ..        ..        ..                                                           | 40      |         |
| Repairs to plant       ..        ..        ..        ..        ..        ..                                             | 850     |         |
| Preference Share Dividend for half year due and paid on January 1st, 1970 (gross)       ..        ..        ..        ..        ..        .. | 400     |         |
| Income Tax Account, 1970/71       ..        ..        ..        ..                                                      | 150     |         |
| Provision for corporation tax payable January 1st, 1971       ..        ..                                             |         | 3,024   |
|                                                                                                                        | £173,622 | £173,622 |

*Provide for:*

1. Accrued charges: power and lighting £240; commissions £160; audit fee (fixed by directors) £85; auditors' travelling expenses £15.

2. Doubtful debts £250.

3. Depreciation on plant and equipment at 10 per cent. on cost, and on office furniture at 10 per cent. on net book values.

4. Corporation tax based on profits for the year at 45 per cent. estimated at £5,600.

5. Half year's preference dividend payable July 1st, 1970.

6. An ordinary dividend of 5 per cent. less tax payable July 31st, 1970.

*The following information is relevant:*

1. Stocks etc. at cost, on June 30th, 1970, were:

|  |  |  |  |  |  |  | £ |
|---|---|---|---|---|---|---|---|
| Raw materials .. | .. | .. | .. | .. | .. | .. | 7,640 |
| Work-in-progress | .. | .. | .. | .. | .. | .. | 1,280 |
| Finished goods .. | .. | .. | .. | .. | .. | .. | 4,010 |

2. Factory insurances prepaid totalled £110, and rates paid for the half year ended September 30th, 1970, amounted to £240.

3. At June 30th, 1970, the company had placed contracts for heavy machinery for £8,000, and the Board had authorized, but not yet placed, a contract for a new storeroom for £3,000.

4. Directors' total emoluments were: S. Hudson (Chairman) £1,000, Mrs Hudson £2,000, J. Hudson £60 plus £1,500 from Bye Ltd.

5. During the year the company acquired new plant for £1,000 and sold obsolete plant at written-down value (cost £500 accumulated depreciation £400). There were no acquisitions or disposals of office furniture.

6. Unquoted investments consisted of ordinary shares in two private associated companies, neither holding consisted of more than 10 per cent. in nominal value of the issued ordinary share capital of either company.

7. Dividends were received from the subsidiary company gross.

8. The income tax position is:

### INCOME TAX ACCOUNT 1969/70

| 1969 |  | £ | 1970 |  | £ |
|---|---|---|---|---|---|
| Dec. 10 | Unquoted Investment Income Account – tax deducted from franked investment income    ..    .. | 50 | Jan. 1<br>,, | Debenture Interest – tax deducted  ..<br>Preference Dividend Account – tax deducted    ..    ..    .. | 150<br><br>200 |
| 1970<br>Jan. 19 | Bank  ..    ..    ..    .. | 300 |  |  |  |
|  |  | £350 |  |  | £350 |

### INCOME TAX ACCOUNT 1970/71

| 1970 |  | £ |  |  |  |
|---|---|---|---|---|---|
| June 20 | Quoted Investment Income Account – tax deducted from unfranked investment income    ..    .. | 150 |  |  |  |

9. Corporation tax payable January 1st, 1971, has been agreed at £2,884.

*Prepare:*

(*a*) Manufacturing, Trading and Profit and Loss Account for the year ended June 30th, 1970, for presentation to the directors.

(*b*) Profit and Loss Account for the year ended June 30th, 1970, and Balance Sheet as at that date in vertical form suitable for presentation to the members, embodying the requirements of the Companies Acts. Take income tax at 50 per cent. (Comparative figures are given for the purposes of Part III of this Chapter.)

## VENEERING MANUFACTURERS LTD
### MANUFACTURING, TRADING AND PROFIT & LOSS ACCOUNT
(a)　　　for the year ended June 30th, 1970 (for presentation to the Directors)

**Debit side**

| 1969 £ | | £ | £ |
|---|---|---|---|
| | Materials: | | |
| 5,700 | Stock July 1st, 1969 .. | 9,320 | |
| 18,500 | Purchases .. .. | 31,960 | |
| 960 | Carriage inwards .. | 1,600 | |
| 25,160 | | 42,880 | |
| 9,320 | *Less* Stock June 30th, 1970.. | 7,640 | |
| 15,840 | | | 35,240 |
| 7,560 | Wages and national insurance .. .. | | 13,790 |
| 23,400 | PRIME COST | | 49,030 |
| | Factory Overheads: | | |
| 680 | Power and lighting .. | 910 | |
| 570 | Insurance .. | 610 | |
| 650 | Repairs to plant .. | 850 | |
| 2,350 | Depreciation of plant etc... | 2,400 | |
| 4,250 | | | 4,770 |
| 27,650 | | | 53,800 |
| 920 | Work-in-Progress — June 30th, 1970 .. .. | 1,280 | |
| 600 | *Less* Work-in-Progress — July 1st, 1969 .. .. | 920 | |
| —320 | | | —360 |
| £27,330 | COST OF PRODUCTION | | £53,440 |
| | Finished Goods: | | |
| 2,040 | Stock July 1st, 1969 .. | | 1,270 |
| 27,330 | Cost of goods produced .. | | 53,440 |
| 29,370 | | | 54,710 |
| 1,270 | *Less* Stock June 30th, 1970.. | | 4,010 |
| 28,100 | Cost of Sales .. .. | | 50,700 |
| 11,100 | Gross profit carried down.. | | 18,400 |
| £39,200 | | | £69,100 |
| | Establishment: | | |
| 370 | Rates .. .. .. | 380 | |
| 130 | Plant Hire (internal telephone) .. | 130 | |
| 50 | Repairs to premises .. | 60 | |
| 36 | Insurances .. .. | 40 | |
| 244 | Depreciation of office furniture .. .. | 220 | |
| 830 | | | 830 |
| | Administration: | | |
| 2,560 | Directors' emoluments .. | 3,060 | |
| 2,870 | Salaries .. .. | 3,130 | |
| 380 | Commissions .. | 680 | |
| 100 | Auditors' remuneration .. | 100 | |
| 150 | Postage and Telephone .. | 180 | |
| 50 | Printing and Stationery .. | 40 | |
| – | Legal and Professional Charges .. .. | 80 | |
| 40 | Trade expenses .. .. | 50 | |
| 10 | Bank charges .. .. | 10 | |
| 6,160 | | | 7,330 |
| | Finance: | | |
| 600 | Interest on debentures .. | 600 | |
| 200 | Bank Interest .. .. | 290 | |
| 150 | Provision for doubtful debts | 250 | |
| 950 | | | 1,140 |
| 7,180 | Net profit carried down .. | | 13,330 |
| £15,120 | | | £22,630 |

**Credit side**

| 1969 £ | | £ | £ |
|---|---|---|---|
| 27,330 | Cost of goods produced transferred to Trading Account.. | | 53,440 |
| £27,330 | | | £53,440 |
| 39,200 | Sales .. .. .. | | 69,100 |
| £39,200 | | | £69,100 |
| 11,100 | Gross profit brought down .. | | 18,400 |
| 20 | Interest on Tax Reserve Certificates.. .. | | 30 |
| 3,600 | Dividend from Subsidiary Company .. .. | | 3,800 |
| | Income from Investments: | | |
| 300 | Quoted .. .. .. | 300 | |
| 100 | Unquoted .. .. | 100 | 400 |
| £15,120 | | | £22,630 |

### VENEERING MANUFACTURERS LTD
### MANUFACTURING, TRADING AND PROFIT & LOSS ACCOUNT
*(continued)*

| £ | | £ | £ | £ | | £ | £ |
|---|---|---|---|---|---|---|---|
| | Taxation on profits for the year: | | | 7,180 | Net Profit brought down .. | | 13,330 |
| 3,024 | Corporation tax (45%) .. | | 5,600 | | | | |
| 4,156 | Balance carried down .. | | 7,730 | | | | |
| £7,180 | | | £13,330 | £7,180 | | | £13,330 |
| | Dividends: | | | 4,156 | Balance brought down .. | | 7,730 |
| | Paid: Half year's preference dividend (4%) on January | | | 1,134 | Balance brought forward from last year .. .. | 3,090 | |
| 400 | 1st, 1970 .. .. | | 400 | 100 | *Add* Overprovision for taxation in previous year ... | 140 | |
| | Proposed: Half year's preference dividend (4%) payable July 1st, 1970 | | 400 | | | | 3,230 |
| 400 | | | | | | | |
| | Ordinary dividend (5%) | | | | | | |
| 1,500 | payable July 31st, 1970 .. | | 2,000 | | | | |
| | | | 2,800 | | | | |
| 3,090 | Balance carried forward .. | | 8,160 | | | | |
| £5,390 | | | £10,960 | £5,390 | | | £10,960 |

### VENEERING MANUFACTURERS LTD – PROFIT AND LOSS ACCOUNT
(b)     for the year ended June 30th, 1970 (for presentation to members)

| 1969 £ | £ | | £ | £ | £ |
|---|---|---|---|---|---|
| | 7,180 | PROFIT BEFORE TAXATION | | | 13,330 |
| | | after accounting for: | | | |
| 2,594 | | Depreciation .. | | 2,620 | |
| 200 | | Bank Interest .. | | 290 | |
| 600 | | Interest on loans repayable after more than five years | | 600 | |
| 100 | | Auditors' remuneration .. | | 100 | |
| | | Directors' emoluments: | | | |
| 60 | | Fees .. | 60 | | |
| 4,000 | | Other emoluments .. | 4,500 | | |
| | | | | 4,560 | |
| | | Income from investments: | | | |
| 300 | | Quoted .. | | 300 | |
| 100 | | Unquoted (all franked) .. | | 100 | |
| | | United Kingdom Taxation based on profits for the year: | | | |
| 3,024 | | Corporation Tax (45%) .. | | | 5,600 |
| 4,156 | | PROFIT AFTER TAXATION | | | 7,730 |
| | | Deduct appropriations: | | | |
| | | Dividends: | | | |
| 400 | | Paid: Preference (4%) on January 1st, 1970 (gross) .. | | 400 | |
| 400 | | Proposed: Preference (4%) on July 1st, 1970 (gross) | | 400 | |
| 1,500 | | Ordinary (5%) on July 31st, 1970 (gross).. | | 2,000 | |
| | 2,300 | | | | 2,800 |
| | 1,856 | UNAPPROPRIATED PROFIT FOR THE YEAR | | | 4,930 |
| 1,134 | | Unappropriated profits brought forward | | 3,090 | |
| 100 | | *Add* Overprovision for taxation in previous year | | 140 | |
| | 1,234 | | | | 3,230 |
| | £3,090 | UNAPPROPRIATED PROFITS CARRIED FORWARD | | | £8,160 |

*Notes:*

1. Turnover based on sales for the year was £69,100.
2. Directors' emoluments:

| | | | | | | | £ |
|---|---|---|---|---|---|---|---|
| Chairman .. | .. | .. | .. | .. | .. | .. | 1,000 |
| Highest paid director | | .. | .. | .. | .. | .. | 2,000 |
| | | | | | | | Other directors |
| Earnings: 0–£2,500 | | | | | | | 1 |

3. No depreciation has been provided for on land and buildings.

## VENEERING MANUFACTURERS LTD
### BALANCE SHEET as at June 30th, 1970

| 1969 £ | CAPITAL EMPLOYED | | Authorized | Issued and fully paid |
|---|---|---|---|---|
| | SHARE CAPITAL | | £ | £ |
| 10,000 | 8% Cumulative Preference Shares of £1 each (redeemable at the company's option at a premium of 25p per share on January 1st, 2000) .. | | 10,000 | 10,000 |
| 30,000 | Ordinary Stock .. .. .. .. .. .. | | 50,000 | 40,000 |
| 40,000 | | | 60,000 | 50,000 |
| | RESERVES | | £ | |
| 2,640 | Share Premium Account .. .. .. .. .. | | 3,640 | |
| 10,000 | General Reserve .. .. .. .. .. .. | | 10,000 | |
| 3,090 | Profit and Loss Account .. .. .. .. .. | | 8,160 | |
| 15,730 | | | | 21,800 |
| | | | | 71,800 |
| 15,000 | 4% DEBENTURES (secured) (repayable at par January 1st, 1992) .. | | | 15,000 |
| £70,730 | | | | £86,800 |

| 1969 £ | Represented by | Cost £ | Depreciation £ | £ |
|---|---|---|---|---|
| | FIXED ASSETS | | | |
| 20,420 | Freehold Property .. .. .. .. .. | 22,420 | — | 22,420 |
| 11,100 | Plant and Equipment .. .. .. .. .. | 24,000 | 14,400 | 9,600 |
| 2,200 | Office Furniture .. .. .. .. .. .. | 3,000 | 1,020 | 1,980 |
| 33,720 | | £49,420 | £15,420 | 34,000 |
| 3,200 | Unquoted Investments at cost (directors' valuation £4,000) .. .. | | | 3,200 |
| 10,000 | Goodwill at written-down value .. .. .. .. | | | 10 000 |
| 46,920 | | | | 47,200 |
| | SUBSIDIARY COMPANY | | | |
| 18,750 | Shares at cost .. .. .. .. | | | 18,750 |
| | CURRENT ASSETS | | £ | |
| 11,510 | Stocks and Work-in-Progress at cost .. .. .. .. | | 12,930 | |
| 9,126 | Debtors .. .. .. .. .. .. | | 10,830 | |
| 8,020 | Quoted Investments at cost (market value £8,680) .. .. | | 8,020 | |
| 6,000 | Tax Reserve Certificates .. .. .. .. | | 8,000 | |
| 4,444 | Cash at Bank and in Hand .. .. .. .. | | 8,292 | |
| 39,100 | | | 48,072 | |
| | Less CURRENT LIABILITIES | £ | | |
| 15,096 | Creditors .. .. .. .. .. .. | 8,658 | | |
| 11 220 | Subsidiary Company .. .. .. .. .. | 7,680 | | |
| 2,800 | Corporation tax payable January 1st, 1971 .. .. .. | 2,884 | | |
| 1,900 | Proposed dividends (gross) .. .. .. .. | 2,400 | | |
| 31,016 | | | 21,622 | |
| 8,084 | | | 26,450 | |
| 3,024 | Less CORPORATION TAX payable January 1st, 1972 .. | | 5,600 | |
| 5,060 | | | | 20,850 |
| £70,730 | | | | £86,800 |

*Notes;*

1. Capital commitments:

| | £ |
|---|---|
| Contracts placed .. .. .. .. .. .. | 8,000 |
| Contracts authorized but not placed .. .. .. .. | 3,000 |
| | £11,000 |

2. Movements in Fixed Assets:

(*a*) Freehold property was acquired during the year for £2,000.

(*b*) Plant and equipment:

| | | | | | Cost £ | Depreciation £ | Net £ |
|---|---|---|---|---|---|---|---|
| Balance 1/7/69 | .. | .. | .. | .. | 23,500 | 12,400 | 11,100 |
| Disposals | .. | .. | .. | .. | 500 | 400 | 100 |
| | | | | | 23,000 | 12,000 | 11,000 |
| Purchases | .. | .. | .. | .. | 1,000 | — | 1,000 |
| | | | | | | | 12,000 |
| Depreciation for year | .. | .. | .. | .. | | +2,400 | −2,400 |
| | | | | | £24,000 | £14,400 | £9,600 |

(*c*) There were no acquisitions or disposals of office furniture during the year.

3. The Company owns 80 per cent. of the nominal value of the issued Ordinary Share Capital of Bye Ltd, its subsidiary.

.................................................................  
.................................................................  } Directors

Specimens of recently published accounts of well-known public companies are given in the Appendix. The accounts of the National and Commercial Banking Group Ltd are of particular interest due to the fact that its financial year ended on September 30th, 1969, and they subsequently revised their accounts in accordance with the decision of the London Clearing Banks and the Scottish Banks to cease to take advantage of the exemptions available under the *Companies Acts 1948* and *1967*. The accounts have therefore been presented showing the position before and after disclosure.

The other accounts reproduced are those of Imperial Chemical Industries Ltd and Bestobell Ltd. These companies were presented with *The Accountant* Annual Awards for 1970.

## PART III

### § 16. Interpretation and Accounting Ratios

*Introduction*

Interpretation of Accounts may be defined as the art and science of translating the figures therein in such a way as to reveal the financial strength and weaknesses of a business and the causes which have contributed thereto. Needless to say, interpretation must be undertaken by those conversant with the language, while the accounts must be drawn up in a form which enables a full appreciation of the facts to be deduced.

Although interpretation is to be considered in relation to the conventional final accounts of a business, the art is equally applicable to subsidiary statements (whether financial or costing), interim accounts, or statements projected in time. Considerable skill and judgement is required to appreciate and unveil the realities underlying a set of final accounts, but the accountant has at his disposal three techniques, which will be discussed in some detail, viz. (*a*) straightforward criticism; (*b*) ratio analysis; and (*c*) movement of funds statements.

Accounts will be perused or scrutinized by the following interested persons:

(a) The owners or, in the case of a limited company, the shareholders.

(b) Debenture holders, or the holders of any other form of long-term loan capital.

(c) Bank managers, financial institutions etc.

(d) Investors and their professional advisers.

(e) Financial journalists and commentators.

(f) Creditors.

(g) H.M. Inspectors of Taxes.

The interpreter must consider and form conclusions on the following matters:

1. *Profitability:* Are the profits adequate in relation to the capital employed, or could a better return be received from another firm or company, or from another industry? Is the capital employed in the right way and in the right place? Can profits be increased by improved management consequent upon a take-over?

2. *Solvency:* Can the business pay its creditors, should they demand payment simultaneously? Is the business operating with sufficient working capital? How liquid are its current assets? Is it over or under-trading? Can its profitable activities be thwarted or halted by a shortage of working capital?

3. *Ownership:* Who owns the business, i.e. does one person or group of persons have control? How is ownership divided between the ordinary and preference shareholders and what voting rights do the holders of various classes of share capital possess? What are their rights as to dividend and repayment of capital in a winding-up? What proportion of the assets are held as security for loans by debenture holders and to what extent is the business financed by its creditors?

4. *Financial strength:* What is the credit position of the company; has it reached the limit of its borrowing powers, if any; has it sufficient resources to finance expansion? Is it the policy of the business to retain a proportion of its profits each year?

5. *Trend:* Are profits rising or falling? How will this reflect on future performance and is the business on the threshold of a breakthrough to higher profits, based on recent planning and investments?

6. *Gearing and cover:* How safe are dividends and/or principal invested, in the form of share capital or a loan? What effect will a given fluctuation of profit have on the ability of the company either to meet its liability for interest on loan capital, or to recommend a dividend?

It will be appreciated that some persons will attach more significance to some factors than to others.

### The criticism of a Trading, Profit and Loss Account

(i) Turnover should be compared with the previous year, or years, and variations investigated. When a budget is available, comparison should also be made therewith. Sales will be influenced by the following factors:

  (*a*) variations in volume;
  (*b*) variations in price;
  (*c*) the opening or closing of branches or departments;
  (*d*) marketing techniques;
  (*e*) variations in the composition of sales at varying prices, e.g. a larger proportion of sales of higher-priced goods;
  (*f*) the inclusion of goods sent out on sale or return.

 (ii) The ratio of gross profit should be ascertained and enquiries made as to the reasons for any variation thereof. Gross profit will be affected both by sales and the cost of purchases; plus factory costs in the case of a manufacturing concern; if it is not possible to ascribe the whole of any variation to these factors, then errors or inconsistencies may have arisen in the valuation of stock, or the stock figures may include goods which have not been debited to purchases.

(iii) The ratios of purchases and sales to creditors and debtors respectively should be computed in order to see whether these approximate to the periods of credit allowed by suppliers and extended to customers. Adverse differences should be investigated, e.g. a considerable amount of book debts may be overdue, producing a high ratio of debtors to sales.

(iv) The ratios of stocks of raw materials (including components) to purchases and finished stocks to sales should be calculated, in order to ascertain the availability of supplies (i.e. the number of days' or weeks' stock in hand) and the length of time finished stocks are held in store, respectively, while the ratio of work-in-progress (if any) to cost of production will indicate the length of the production cycle. These ratios are dealt with exhaustively under stock ratios on page 334.

 (v) Fluctuations in the constituent elements of the Profit and Loss Account, viz. cost of administration, selling and distribution, finance, research and development, should be gauged, whenever possible, both in absolute terms and on a percentage basis, against the movement of related figures in the Trading and Profit and Loss Account and Balance Sheet. Some examples, to illustrate the point, are given below:

  (*a*) Increased discounts allowed, advertising, travellers' expenses and commission will normally stem from increased turnover.
  (*b*) A reduced charge for depreciation will arise where the reducing balance method is employed. An increase in this item may signify increased purchases of plant.
  (*c*) It should be possible to relate interest charges to debentures in issue and bank overdraft.
  (*d*) Most items will probably tend to increase consequent upon a programme of expansion, which should be evident from a perusal of the Balance Sheet.

The above presupposes comparison of items with those for the previous year(s). If a budget is available, deviations therefrom should also be studied. Note also production or cost ratios, discussed on page 335.

(vi) In a manufacturing business, movements in items comprising factory overheads will need to be scrutinized in conjunction with related items.

### The criticism of a Balance Sheet

A summary is given below of the various points to which attention should be paid in examining a Balance Sheet with a view to forming an opinion as to the financial strength of the concern in question. Although the following remarks apply particularly to the Balance Sheet of a limited company, many of the principles will hold good in any other case.

(i) The amounts of the authorized and issued share capital; and the amount of the latter not called up, since this represents a potential source of liquid resources with which to discharge current liabilities or meet the cost of an expansion programme. Calls in arrear should be noted and enquiries made as to why the shares have not been forfeited and reissued where such calls have been outstanding for an undue length of time.

(ii) If debentures have been issued it should be ascertained whether these are secured by a fixed charge on specific assets or a floating charge on the undertaking; also whether the charge covers uncalled capital. If necessary, reference may be made to the Register of Charges. Provision for redemption, if any, should be noted; if a redemption fund has been created this should be represented by specific investments outside the business rather than by assets in general, when the security of such investments will need to be considered. In the absence of a redemption fund represented by investments, the proximity of the redemption date will determine when an outflow of cash will take place, and when steps to replace the capital may have to be taken.

(iii) The amount of working capital (i.e. excess of current assets over current liabilities) should be noted. If expansion is taking place, or envisaged, steps should be taken to ensure that this is matched by an adequate cash flow or additional external finance. While, in the short term, it may be possible to finance expansion by a bank overdraft, this should not be regarded as a permanent source of finance, steps being taken to raise additional long-term capital at the earliest opportunity. Fixed assets should be financed by long-term capital, e.g. share capital or debentures, because, unlike stock-in-trade, these are not acquired for subsequent conversion into cash and payment therefor from current resources may place a company in a precarious financial position. If cash and investments form a significant proportion of the current assets this may be indicative of management's failure to employ the resources at their disposal to the full in the business. Such a situation may, moreover, prompt a take-over bid. Working capital is considered at some length in the section dealing with accounting ratios on page 328.

(iv) The Balance Sheet of a limited company will generally contain reserves; where these are represented by specific investments and are, in effect, reserve funds, the market value, or directors' valuation of the investments should be noted to see whether they approximate to the amount of the reserve(s). Most reserves, however, e.g. capital redemption reserve fund, general reserve, raw material price fluctuation reserve etc., are merely represented by assets in general, so that the extent to which they actually exist depends entirely upon whether the values placed upon the assets, notably the fixed assets, correctly reflect their present value. It will be difficult to discover by mere perusal of the Balance Sheet whether any of the fixed assets have been over or under-stated, but some guidance may be obtained from the aggregate amount written off, or retained by way of provision for depreciation, since the assets were acquired.

(v) *Fixed assets:*

   (*a*) Land and buildings – these may be either freehold or leasehold and, if they are held on lease, the terms of the lease should be enquired into to determine whether amortization has been excessive, thus deflating the net book value, or vice versa. If renewal of the lease is imminent, the company may be faced with the prospect of increased rental and the cost of dilapidations, while it may even be forced to move to new premises with the consequential upheaval and cost thereof.

   (*b*) Plant and machinery (including motor vehicles) – if this item is well written down this may denote that the equipment is old-fashioned and, possibly, inefficient, so that the cost of renewal may arise in the near future. If a sinking fund, represented by secure investments, is in existence the cash will be readily to hand; if, however, no such fund has been raised, then consideration will need to be given to the manner in which replacement is to be financed. Plant may, alternatively, be held under a leasing agreement, when the terms thereof should be fully investigated.

(vi) So far as stock is concerned, the Balance Sheet of a limited company must now give the basis of valuation. If the report of the auditors is unqualified it may be taken for granted that they have done all they can to verify this item and are satisfied with the valuation.

(vii) If the provision for bad and doubtful debts is shown, it should be seen whether this is reasonable, having regard both to the total amount of debtors and the nature of the business.

(viii) If goodwill appears on the Balance Sheet this should be treated as a deduction from reserves, i.e. disregarded, since it is an intangible asset of no realizable value except on sale of the business as a going concern, in which event it could be a vastly different sum to that shown.

(ix) A debit balance on Profit and Loss Account represents capital that has been lost and until it has been made good it is inadvisable, although not illegal, for dividends to be paid out of current profits.

(x) Preliminary expenses, expenses of issue of shares and debentures and similar fictitious assets have no realizable value and should, therefore, be disregarded in the same manner as goodwill, in assessing the financial position from the Balance Sheet. Past Balance Sheets should be examined to ascertain whether, and to what extent, these items are being written off, since failure to do so may have been due to inadequate profits.

(xi) From a creditor's, or prospective creditor's, viewpoint the object of the criticism should be to see whether the credit given or to be given is justified. Attention should be paid to the liquid position, prior claims (e.g. debenture holders' rights) and the position of the company in the event of a winding-up.

(xii) From a shareholder's viewpoint, attention should be paid to the earnings of the company, to ensure that these are sufficient to provide a reasonable return on the capital invested, either in the form of dividends or capital growth, while the capital should be adequately represented by assets, after provision has been made for all external liabilities; consideration should be given to alternative uses to which fixed assets could be put, and a valuation, assuming such use, substituted for the Balance Sheet values in computing capital employed. Capital gearing is another important factor. Conclusions on all these matters are probably best based upon consideration of the relevant accounting ratios, which are dealt with at length below.

(xiii) The existence of contingent liabilities and their significance should be investigated.

### Accounting ratios

By the use of this technique it is possible to facilitate comparision of significant figures, by expressing their relationship in the form of ratios or percentages, thus enabling the accounts of a business to be interpreted by bringing into focus salient features thereof. Ratios are of use principally to the higher levels of management, who are responsible for maximizing profits and planning for the future. It should be stressed that accounting ratios are only a guide and cannot form the basis of definitive statements; rather they should be used to support other information and, in some instances, other ratios. Comparison may be made with ratios for earlier periods in the same business in order to disclose trends, while they may be employed for purposes of inter-firm comparison; however, great caution should be exercised since information appertaining to other concerns will normally be restricted to that embodied in their published accounts, which may contain an element of 'window-dressing', while subtleties may be present which are not immediately apparent, e.g. maximum liquidity may exist at the terminal date of the accounts. Needless to say, such comparisons are only valid if the company or business is engaged in similar activities, and should be made against its general financial background, which may be totally different as regards scale and capital structure.

Accounting ratios should be computed and acted upon, if need be, albeit with caution, while the calculation of superfluous or too many ratios is to be avoided, lest they should lose their interpretive value and become as difficult to assimilate as a conglomeration of absolute figures. A precise definition of the figures used to compute a particular ratio must be given if a proper appreciation of its significance is to result. As a ratio relates one figure to another, it is advantageous if one figure remains constant, so that changes in the ratio reflect changes in the other figure; however, both figures can alter the ratio and cause some confusion as to the reason for the change, besides producing compensating changes which may go unnoticed.

Ratios employed to denote past trends may give an indication as to future trends and thus act as signposts for plans and policies. A full appreciation of the factors which can cause a ratio to change will lead to the ability to make plans and to take action which will produce the desired change in a certain ratio. Properly understood and used, target ratios may, therefore, be computed as a concomitant to budgetary control.

### (1) THE PRIMARY RATIO

*The ratio of net profit to capital employed* is termed the primary ratio because by its use the ultimate object of a business can be assessed. It comments on the efficiency of the management by contrasting the profit made by the business with the funds utilized to make that profit. It may be used to show the relative efficiency of the business as compared with the return on capital employed in other companies in the same industry, or in different industries, or in another country, or for the same concern in earlier years. The maintenance of the same ratio of net profit to capital employed should be the lowest aim of every board of directors or proprietor: its improvement is probably a necessity in the face of mounting competition at home and abroad.

Considerable controversy exists concerning the definition of capital employed but those generally accepted are as follows:

(a) The proprietors' or shareholders' interest in the business, i.e. share capital and reserves in the latter case. Comparison would be with net profit, before adjustment, in this case.

(b) The proprietors' or shareholders' interest plus long-term loans or debentures. When loans are included, it is necessary to add back debenture or loan interest to net profit in order to compare gross earnings with capital employed. If long-term loans form a significant part of the funds employed it seems logical to include these since they are in effect loan capital. It will be noted that capital, as defined here, is tantamount to net assets.

(c) As (b) above *less* the value of investments, where these are additional to the main activities of the business, with a view to assessing the return achieved by management in their particular field. Supporters of this basis argue that inclusion of investments, and the income therefrom, vitiates the result by reflecting the ability of the management as investors. It may be further argued that only speculative investments should be excluded, since trade investments and shares in subsidiary companies (held primarily to protect the goodwill of the concern or further its main business) form a legitimate part of the capital employed. Opponents of this basis argue that management should utilize all the funds at its disposal to maximize profits, including the selection of investments yielding a high return, as an outlet for surplus funds.

In any event, this basis would only appear to be warranted where speculative investments form a significant proportion of total assets, when the income therefrom would need to be deducted from net profit.

It may also be argued that non-speculative investments should be excluded from capital employed where the return on these is minimal (e.g. certain British Funds) compared with the earnings of the business in its chosen trade, since their inclusion in capital employed will depress the primary ratio, thus understating the earnings of the concern which result from its principal activities.

Funds not retained in the business, e.g. a staff pension fund, when appropriations thereto are represented by outside investments should be excluded from capital employed.

(d) Gross assets, i.e. before deduction of current liabilities, on the grounds that these provide capital for use in the business, some of which incur interest payments, e.g. a bank overdraft, and some of which, notably creditors, are provided interest-free; however, over-reliance upon finance from creditors may result in lost discounts and interpreted as a sign of weakness. Where interest has been incurred this should, strictly speaking, be added back to net profit in order that gross earnings may be compared with gross capital employed. Investments may be excluded for reasons already propounded. It should be noted that use of this basis conforms to the accounting convention of conservatism by employing a higher denominator, thus producing a lower ratio.

(e) In considering the foregoing bases, the book values and true worth of assets have been regarded as being identical. Since, however, balance sheets generally show fixed assets at historic cost less depreciation and omit to show other assets at their current 'going concern' value, a clearer picture may emerge if all the assets, including goodwill, are revalued at their current going concern value. Net profit, measured each year at current value, can then be set against the current value of the assets, thereby enabling a truer comparison to be made. In the current economic climate of inflation, this method would produce a more conservative ratio, where, as is usual, a large proportion of capital has been sunk in fixed assets. However, revaluation of a concern's assets year by year is no easy matter, whilst inter-firm comparisons would generally be invalidated. Provided Balance Sheet, i.e. largely historical, values are consistently used as a basis, favourable and adverse movements in this ratio may be adequately discerned, and comparison with other businesses facilitated, despite the fact that the return, in absolute terms, will tend to be overstated.

Some differences of opinion centre around the definition of net profit, viz.

whether this should be before or after tax. The argument for using the former is that as some businesses are more successful than others in minimizing the tax burden, comparisons may be vitiated by using net profit after tax. Furthermore, changes in the rate of corporation tax each year can obscure the ratio of net profit after tax to capital employed over a number of years. On the other hand it may be argued that as tax is a legitimate charge, it is incumbent on management to minimize the burden as part of their normal role. In so far, however, as taxation is now being increasingly handled by specialists in this field, strong counter-arguments could be propounded for basing calculations upon net profit after tax.

Gains or losses of an abnormal, exceptional or non-recurring nature should be excluded from net profit in order to produce a realistic ratio: such items may arise, *inter alia*, from the sale of fixed assets or foreign exchange transactions.

## (2) THE SECONDARY RATIOS

Closely allied to the primary ratio are (a) the profitability of sales disclosed by the ratio or percentage of net profit to sales, and (b) the intensity with which the capital is employed in the business as shown by the ratio of sales to capital employed. These ratios will support any conclusions drawn from the primary ratio and may indicate the reason for an unsatisfactory return on capital employed.

## (3) THE SOLVENCY RATIOS

(a) *The working capital ratio* is ascertained by comparing current assets with current liabilities and shows whether there is an adequate amount of working capital to meet running expenses and service fixed assets. Movements will indicate how much of the concern's own resources are being utilized to finance current assets, as opposed to funds raised from current liabilities, e.g. an upward movement in stocks may be accompanied by a corresponding increase in creditors, rather than a decrease in cash. It should be remembered that the level of debtors and creditors represents the extent to which the business is financing, or is being financed by, respectively, outsiders. The extent of any unused overdraft facilities is important for, if the company has reached the limit of its short-term borrowing powers, difficulties will arise in times of emergency and expansion inhibited unless further long-term capital is raised.

Although it is desirable that current assets should exceed current liabilities, if only to provide ample coverage in the event of a liquidation, no two businesses are alike, and indeed it may be perfectly healthy for many businesses to work on a negative ratio. General criteria, such as the 'two to one' ratio should, therefore, be viewed with some scepticism. Again, due to seasonal idiosyncrasies the working capital position at the date of a Balance Sheet may represent maximum or minimum liquidity, not to mention 'window dressing', when an average over the year may provide a truer picture.

The principal factors which determine the optimum level of working capital may be summarized as follows:

(i) The extent to which the business is subject to seasonal fluctuations and the vagaries of taste and fashion.

(ii) The amount of working capital required to finance any plans for expansion.

(iii) Terms of trade extended by suppliers and allowed to customers.

(iv) Bank overdraft facilities.

(v) The length of the business cycle, i.e. the finance tied up in production, or a specific order, from the time work commences until the receipt of cash. Much will obviously depend upon the nature of the product, e.g. ocean-going liners or safety pins, while the level of work-in-progress will indicate the length of the cycle.

(vi) The amount of working capital required to service fixed assets, which will be governed largely by the amount of capital sunk in these.

(vii) The extent to which speculative activities are undertaken in the purchase of stock.

Attempts to expand turnover to a point when the working capital becomes inadequate to finance day-to-day operations produces a malady known as 'over-trading'. Symptoms of over-trading may take the following forms:

(i) Creditors will tend to increase in relation to debtors.

(ii) A growth in the rate of long and/or short-term borrowing.

(iii) Minimal cash resources.

(iv) An increase in stocks unaccompanied by an increase in turnover.

(v) A diminution of gross and/or net profit.

(vi) Heavy expenditure on fixed assets.

A long production cycle will inevitably aggravate the shortage of liquid resources where this situation prevails.

An inadequate volume of business leads, on the other hand, to 'under-trading'. When trade diminishes beyond a certain point, a business will suffer the embarrassment of meeting its fixed and reduced variable costs from current assets which remain relatively static. The situation will be aggravated when the amount of fixed assets is large, since these will still have to be serviced, probably to a greater extent, due to under-employment.

(b) *The quick assets ratio*, often termed the 'acid test ratio', is computed by comparing quick assets with total current liabilities, with a view to gauging the ability of a business to meet all its creditors from liquid resources, should they demand payment simultaneously. Although a useful guide to the solvency position of a business, it is somewhat unreal since many of the creditors are unlikely to demand payment at once. Quick assets comprise cash, quoted investments and bills receivable (as these may be discounted); in addition an analysis of debtors may warrant the inclusion of some, considered to be readily realizable, but this is, however, a refinement. Businesses may be loath to realize investments where such action would result in a loss, while corporation tax payable on a chargeable gain may inhibit the realization of investments where the reverse applies.

**(4) THE CAPITAL RATIOS**

(a) *The ratio of capital employed to total indebtedness* indicates the significance and power of persons, other than the shareholders, or proprietors, who have a financial interest in the business and may be computed by setting gross assets against capital provided by outside sources, viz. in the form of debentures and current liabilities. Alternatively, this ratio may be based on the comparison of the total interest of shareholders (i.e. share capital plus reserves), sometimes referred to as 'net worth' with total indebtedness. Although over-reliance on outside capitalization is frequently regarded as a sign of weakness, in times of prosperity a larger volume of borrowing may be regarded as normal. In a period of recession, however, net worth would be expected to be much higher than total indebtedness. It is advisable, in this context, to distinguish between current and long-term liabilities, in order to consider the incidence of repayment against the background of the trade cycle.

(b) *The ratio of capital employed to fixed assets* may be used as an adjunct to (a) in order to reveal the ownership of the fixed assets. Capital employed for purposes of this ratio will again represent the total interest of the shareholders. If fixed assets exceed capital employed it will be apparent that part of these are owned by the debenture holders (if any), or the creditors, which may be interpreted as a sign of weakness.

(c) *The capital gearing ratio* discloses the relationship between the ordinary share capital of a company and fixed interest capital, in the form of preference shares and debentures. A company with a preponderance of ordinary share (or equity) capital is said to be 'low-geared', while a company with a capital structure in which fixed interest capital is the higher, is said to be 'high-geared'. Gearing is neutral when ordinary and fixed interest capital are equal, resulting in a ratio of 1 to 1. Where substantial reserves exist, it may be advisable to include these as part of the equity of the company, thus showing it to be lower-geared than it would otherwise appear; inclusion of reserves would indicate a greater degree of security for prior charge capital, since greater losses would have to be sustained before their security was jeopardized. Where a company's capital structure is low-geared, preference shareholders and debenture holders enjoy greater security, while the potential dividends payable to ordinary shareholders will not be subject to violent fluctuation with variations in profit. On the other hand, in a highly-geared company variations in profit will tend to produce disproportionate changes in equity earnings, due to the burden of interest payable on fixed interest capital; in fact if profits fall too low, no dividend may be payable on the ordinary shares. Furthermore, where the structure is highly-geared a higher rate of interest would probably be offered to holders of prior charge capital to compensate for the greater risk attaching to their investment, both as regards security and income thereon.

(d) *The ratio of fixed assets to capital employed* reveals the disposition of funds between fixed and working capital: for purposes of this ratio, fixed assets should be restricted to those of a tangible nature, while capital employed may be based on either gross or net assets, provided either basis is used consistently. Used in conjunction with the working capital ratio, this ratio may indicate the adequacy or otherwise of working capital to service fixed assets or an excess or deficiency of fixed assets, from which earnings can be generated. Comparison of the ratio for the current year with earlier years, against the background of the ratios of sales to working capital and sales to fixed capital, may indicate the optimum disposition of available funds. Comparison with ratios disclosed by the accounts of other businesses of a comparable type and scale may serve to support any conclusions drawn from a study of internal ratios.

## (5) THE EARNINGS RATIOS

These relate to earnings on shares as opposed to earnings of the company itself and provide valuable information to actual or potential shareholders: they are also of great interest to higher management since a company depends upon its shareholders and would-be shareholders for its capital, and further funds for expansion. The following ratios are, therefore, closely associated with the capital ratios, in particular (a) to (c) above.

(a) *The ratio of net profit after Corporation tax and preference dividend to equity capital* (ordinary shares plus reserves) shows the return on capital invested in the business by the ordinary shareholders regardless of the dividends paid or proposed on these shares. A more realistic and, invariably, conservative rate of earnings may be obtained by employing the real value of equity capital employed (i.e. the current value of the assets, less preference shares and liabilities) as the denominator. However, as mentioned earlier, assessment of the current value of the assets of a concern is no easy matter, and for this reason will not generally be available.

(b) *The ratio of profit available for dividend to dividend paid*, or dividend cover, reveals the distribution and 'plough-back' policies of the directors. The ratio of retained earnings to net profit, i.e. the complementary ratio, may also be computed to show the potential of an ordinary share for capital growth, while the margin of profit above that which is required to pay the expected dividend can be used to estimate the security of the share so far as dividend payments are concerned. Investors and would-be investors may use these ratios as criteria for decisions, so that they may have a direct effect on the demand for, and market price (in the case of a quoted company) of, the shares.

The board of directors of a company should, therefore, always endeavour to maintain a careful balance between their dividend and 'plough-back' policies, for if dividends are too restricted, the market price of the shares may fall and a take-over bid ensue. On the other hand distribution of dividends on too generous a scale may inhibit the ability of a company to expand without resort to fresh capital or loans, besides depleting its current liquid resources.

Care should be taken to deduct preference dividends from net profit when computing the cover on ordinary shares.

(c) *The ratio of profit available for dividend to preference dividend* will reveal the number of times the preference dividend is covered by earnings and thus indicate the preference shareholders' security, so far as income is concerned.

(d) *The yield ratio* is the ratio of dividend received to the price paid for a share, or the current market price thereof. The yield acceptable to an investor will depend upon the risk attaching to the investment and the potential for capital growth; generally speaking, the greater the yield the greater the risk. Investors may be induced to accept a low yield where the market price of shares has fallen and the company is ripe for a take-over bid, or where the prospects are outstanding.

(e) *The Price/Earnings ratio* from an individual investor's viewpoint is ascertained by comparing the market price of an ordinary share with the earnings, or net profit per share, after deduction of corporation tax and gross preference dividends; this may be expressed as so many years' purchase of the profits: in other words, assuming stability of market price and ignoring the incidence of taxation of dividends, an investor's capital outlay will, at the present level of earnings, be recouped after so many years, either in the form of dividends received, or capital growth by virtue of retained profits. This ratio may provide a collateral check upon conclusions drawn from other earnings ratios, while calculations may be based upon forecast profits to provide a prospective price/earnings ratio.

This ratio may also be computed by comparing the stock exchange value of the ordinary shares of a company, i.e. price per ordinary share times the number of ordinary shares, with net profit after corporation tax and gross preference dividends, thus enabling the larger investor and board of directors alike to compare the overall efficiency of a particular company with similar, or indeed, dissimilar companies (if the company in question is potentially adaptable): such comparisons will, however, only be valid if a reasonable degree of parity prevails between market prices, bearing in mind that these are subject to external influences, e.g. Government measures or the world economic climate, and/or domestic influences, e.g. restrictive or over-generous dividend policies.

Mention may be made, in passing, that the stock exchange value of a company is, in itself, of immense interest to financiers in connection with prospective take-over bids and mergers.

(6) THE SALES RATIOS

Ratios in which turnover figures are of great significance, since it is from turnover that profits are derived.

(a) *The ratio of gross profit to sales* serves as an overall guide to the efficiency of production in a manufacturing business while, in non-manufacturing businesses it should correspond with the trade mark-up, which may be constant in respect of the whole of the sales, or variable in respect of known proportions of total turnover; in this type of business this ratio also serves as a valuable check upon the accuracy of the closing stock figure. Its limitations lie in the fact that as no account is taken of selling and distribution expenses it may be misleading; a product which is costly to produce, or purchase (in the case of a non-manufacturing concern), may incur very little in the way of selling and distribution expenses and vice versa.

(b) *The ratio of net profit to sales* discloses the ultimate proportion of sales and miscellaneous revenue accruing to the proprietors, or available for appropriation in the case of a limited company. Probably the most widely used ratio of all, this does not suffer from the disadvantages inherent in the ratio of gross profit to sales since it takes all expenditure into account and can serve as a guide to overall performance, when compared with previous years and the ratios for other businesses, e.g. H.M. Inspectors of Taxes may, *inter alia*, employ this ratio when considering the accuracy of accounts submitted to them in respect of sole traders or firms. Where miscellaneous income from investments, rents etc. forms a significant proportion of total revenue, appropriate adjustments should be made to expenditure and net profit to determine the net profit attributable to sales.

(c) *The ratio of sales to capital employed* discloses the 'rate of turnover' of the capital employed in the business. Unless over-trading is prevalent (dealt with above) a high ratio is a healthy sign, for the more times capital is turned over, the greater will be the opportunities for making profits. A low ratio, on the other hand, may be indicative of unused capacity, or under-trading, especially if this is accompanied by a high ratio of fixed factory overhead expenditure to sales. It may be advantageous to subdivide this ratio between fixed and working capital to discover whether fixed capital is over-employed, whilst the working capital ratio remains dormant, or vice versa, for this reason capital employed should, in this context, be taken to mean net assets. However, it will be necessary to study the behaviour of the constituent elements of working capital before reaching a decision, for a constant ratio may merely mask fluctuations of cash, stock, debtors and creditors. Attempts should be made to minimize the level of working capital by, for example, reducing the period of credit extended to debtors as sales increase.

Quoted investments and tax reserve certificates should be excluded from working capital since sales will not be directly influenced by these. Similarly, it may be advisable to exclude trade investments and shares in subsidiary companies from fixed capital, where the return on these is competitive, on the grounds that sales may have been unaffected by the employment of such funds. Much, however, will depend upon the circumstances in each case, which will need to be treated on its merits, for connections with associated and subsidiary companies will often provide outlets for additional sales. A more realistic picture may emerge by basing this ratio upon the average of fixed and working capital employed throughout the year, derived from interim accounts (if any) prepared at monthly or quarterly intervals.

(d) *The ratio of credit sales to debtors* shows the rate at which customers are paying for credit sales. This ratio should approximate to the credit terms allowed by the business and is, therefore, a comment on the efficiency of credit control. If three months' credit is extended to customers, then the normal ratio should be 4 to 1 (365 divided by 91). Thus, if annual turnover is £24,000, debtors should be approximately £6,000. This will, however, only apply if sales in terms of sterling, are spread evenly over the year, since seasonal sales will give rise to variations, e.g. if the above turnover comprised sales of £5,000 for the first three quarters of the year and £9,000 for the last quarter, then debtors at the year end should be in the region of £9,000. The higher the ratio the more favourable the effect upon working capital, because outsiders are being financed to a lesser extent while liquid resources will, other things being equal, increase.

(e) *The ratio of bad debts to sales* discloses whether sales are being made to credit-worthy customers. A high ratio may indicate reckless selling and/or the need for more efficient credit control, by checking the credit-worthiness of new and existing customers and by the collection of outstanding debts before the affairs of customers get out of hand.

### (7) THE STOCK RATIOS

These ratios indicate efficiency in the control of stocks of raw materials, work-in-progress and finished goods. Excessive stocks are to be avoided since, apart from incidental costs, e.g. storage, insurance etc., working capital will be tied up which could perhaps be invested in securities or otherwise profitably employed. Where, moreover, superfluous stocks are in effect financed by an overdraft, the cost of such facilities is wasteful.

The ratios computed will be governed by the type of business; where, for instance, goods are produced for stock, there may be little or no work-in-progress, ratios being confined to raw materials and finished stock; where, however, the business is engaged upon job production, there should be no stocks of finished goods, but levels of raw material stocks and work-in-progress will need to be controlled.

It should be stressed that calculation of ratios is no substitute for efficient storekeeping, a perpetual inventory system and the objective calculation of minimum and maximum stocks for each item of raw material and components.

(a) *Raw material stock to purchases* shows the rate of stock turnover. The ratio of closing stock to purchases indicates the number of days' (weeks' or months') purchases held in stock and can act as a guide to excessive stockholdings. A high ratio may signify the presence of obsolescent stocks, or inefficiency on the part of the buying department by purchasing too far in advance of requirements: if, however, such purchases were made at favourable prices prior to impending price increases, this may, on the contrary, denote efficiency on the part of the buyer. The ratio may be analysed between raw materials and components, and indeed different classes of raw materials, in order to pinpoint obsolescent items and forward purchases.

(b) *Work-in-progress to cost of production* indicates the length of the production
cycle where a uniform product is manufactured. Comparison with earlier
periods can provide a measure of efficiency or otherwise of the production
department. In a medium-sized or large plant, figures should be available
for each direct department, thus enabling the ratio for each department to
be ascertained; bottlenecks indicated by these ratios can result in action
being taken to expedite the production cycle in particular departments,
resulting in a quicker overall production cycle, since this is clearly dependent upon the weakest link in the chain. Ratios based upon monthly figures
may be even more enlightening since seasonal variations due, e.g. to
holidays and sickness, may come to light, both on a global and departmental
basis which, if capable of remedial action, may speed the production cycle
still further. Where production is carried out in accordance with customers'
specifications (i.e. job production) the production cycle will vary widely from
one job to another, when the time taken to complete each job, and the level
of work-in-progress, will need to be considered on its merits.

(c) *Finished stock to total turnover* shows how long finished goods are kept in
store before being sold. Needless to say, stock should be held for as short
a time as possible if profits are to be maximized. This ratio is best calculated
by dividing annual turnover by the average of the stock figures at the close
of each month, as ratios based upon opening or closing stock for the year,
or the average of these, may be misleading, unless stocks are constant
throughout the year. The question arises as to whether turnover and stock
should be at selling price or cost price; however, provided both elements
are either at cost or selling price, a realistic ratio should emerge. When the
ratio increases steps should be taken either to increase sales or to curtail
output, if over-production has occurred. In any event, sales and production
will need to be co-ordinated. Care should be taken to ensure that turnover
of stock does not increase too much, signified by a very low ratio, otherwise
it may prove difficult to meet customers' demands promptly. It should be
noted that this ratio is sometimes expressed as a single figure, turnover
being divided by stock.

## (8) THE PRODUCTION RATIOS

The important cost or expenses ratios may be summarized as follows:
 (i) Factory costs to sales.
 (ii) Administration costs to sales.
(iii) Selling costs to sales.
(iv) Distribution costs to sales.
 (v) Research and development costs to sales.
(vi) Capital expenditure to sales.

Although the above could be expressed as ratios of total cost (being an equally
important factor) it is considered that it is more advantageous to use sales since
these ratios, with the exception of capital expenditure, are probably best ex-

pressed as percentages, when the residual percentage will, after taking into account miscellaneous income, represent net profit: the relative effect upon net profits of trends or proposals will then be readily seen. To enhance their value, each of these would need to be broken down under the main items contained in each category, e.g. it would be vital to analyse factory costs into materials, direct labour and factory overheads. Trends in the ratios over a number of years or periods would need to be studied, while the relative size of each heading and/or item should govern the extent of the investigations undertaken. It will be immediately apparent that if one item amounts to one per cent. of sales, while another accounts for forty per cent. greater potential savings are likely to result from a close scrutiny of the latter item. Some effort should be made by the analyst to distinguish between controllable costs and uncontrollable costs, which are due to external factors, such as a general increase in the price of certain raw materials, while it should be possible to correlate the behaviour of various costs, with a view to reducing total costs. This might apply where, for example, a reduction in direct labour has been achieved, or is proposed, by purchasing components and/or increasing the degree of mechanization. The degree of correlation found from experience, or from one budget may provide a collateral check upon a number of flexible budgets.

The use of historical costs is implicit in the foregoing; however, trends based upon past performance are of limited value only in assessing efficiency due to the absence of an absolute or realistic yardstick. Comparison with carefully prepared budgeted or standard costs can, on the other hand, enhance the value of production and cost ratios immensely.

### Movement of Funds Statements

Another technique used by accountants to interpret the accounts of a business is to compare the Balance Sheet at the beginning of an accounting period with the Balance Sheet at the end of the period, and to express their findings in a statement which discloses the movements which have taken place during the period in respect of each asset and liability. Such a statement may be termed a 'Movement of Funds Statement', or a 'Statement of Sources and Application of Funds'. Although the period covered is normally an accounting year, a statement may be prepared covering a quarter, month or other period. Again, while such statements are normally historical, they may be employed for budgetary purposes to indicate the pattern of changes expected during a forthcoming period. In so far as such statements are purely arithmetical, they may be used to explain the change in any asset or liability, e.g. an increase in fixed assets in terms of the remaining items. However, such statements are more meaningful, especially to laymen, e.g. shareholders, if they reconcile opening and closing bank and cash balances, as this is the only homogeneous element. Moreover, the closing cash balance is, in itself, of some significance, since it indicates whether there is sufficient cash to meet imminent commitments, e.g. dividends and taxation, and/or adequate funds to provide working capital to support any expansion of activities portrayed by the statement. Conversely, an unduly high balance may signify that funds are lying dormant which could otherwise be profitably invested.

It should be stated at this point that this topic should be approached with some caution and flexibility since considerable controversy exists amongst accountants, both as to the form which such statements should take and the precise definition of certain terms. However, the method of preparing a comprehensive Movement of Funds Statement for the use of executives of a business, rather than for publication, is outlined below, followed by an illustration, based on the final accounts of Veneering Manufacturers Ltd, for the year ended June 30th, 1970, on pages 317 to 320.

The statement commences with the opening cash position, i.e. cash and bank balances. Some accountants prefer to include any bank overdraft in this figure, but since this is a source of working capital it is probably best dealt with in that part of the statement. The second part of the statement shows the 'Cash Flow', or the value of fresh funds generated by, and retained in, the business: this will consist of the net profit for the year *plus* any expenses charged before arriving at the net profit, such as depreciation or preliminary expenses, together with overprovision for taxation in the previous year (under-provisions should be deducted) etc., which have not resulted in a flow of cash out of the business; taxation on the profits for the year in question and dividends paid and proposed must then be deducted to disclose the funds which have been ploughed back, or retained in the business, as opposed to 'external' sources of finance, such as funds arising from the issue of shares or debentures. It must be stressed at this juncture that this figure will rarely represent physical cash injected into the business during the year, as part of the purchases and sales are most likely to be represented by creditors and debtors respectively, while corporation tax may not be payable until eighteen months or more later; again, proposed dividends will not become payable until after the end of the accounting year. Nevertheless, the amount of the cash flow will *ultimately* be received as an inflow of cash. Meantime, the extent to which the cash flow is not represented by actual cash is reflected in the section dealing with changes in the form of working capital, which is explained below.

The third part of the statement discloses the amount received from 'external' sources on a long-term basis (as opposed to funds generated by the business), whether from loans, fresh capital or the sale of fixed assets. So far as the latter is concerned, this may be dealt with in one of two ways, viz:

(i) The actual amount received may be included in the third section of the statement, since as the sale of fixed assets is extraneous to the activities of most businesses, inclusion in net profit of profits or losses on sales of these would tend to distort the cash flow, which, it may be argued, should be restricted to amounts retained from normal trading activities each year in order to facilitate comparison with earlier years.

(ii) The profits or losses on sales of fixed assets may be included in net profit, where they form a constituent element of the Profit and Loss Account (i.e. not capitalized), on the grounds that they represent part of total profits from which dividends are appropriated and retained profits derived. If this basis is adopted it is necessary to distinguish between the book value of assets and the profit or loss on sale, the book value only being included as a source in the third section of the statement.

The fourth section shows the manner in which the funds raised have been applied on a long-term basis in the form of purchases of fixed assets, repayment of debentures and the repayment of redeemable preference shares; investments intended to be held permanently, e.g. trade investments, and loans to subsidiary or associated companies would also appear in this section.

The fifth part of the statement reveals any changes in the form of working capital. A comparison of the opening and closing Balance Sheet figures for stocks, debtors, creditors, taxation, overdraft, proposed dividends etc. (excluding, of course, cash itself) must be undertaken and the differences listed as sources or applications, as appropriate, in order to ascertain the net source or application. While it may be immediately apparent that, for instance, an increase in stock is an application and an increase in bank overdraft represents a source, some confusion may arise over the treatment of changes in debtors and creditors: it should, therefore, be stated that an increase in debtors is an application, that an increase in creditors is a source, and vice versa, the reasons being that in the first case the business is financing others to a larger extent while, in the second case, the business is being financed by outsiders to an increasing degree. The statement concludes with the closing cash balance, which must operate as a balancing figure, since the whole statement is merely an analysis of the differences between two Balance Sheets.

Abridged versions of Movement of Funds Statements are frequently appended to the published accounts of public companies, and Illustration (2) shows the form in which the statement for Veneering Manufacturers Ltd might be prepared for the benefit of its members and other interested parties.

It should be noted that the cash flow may be verified by *totalling* the differences in the reserves (including the Profit and Loss Account) and intangible assets between the Balance Sheet figures at the beginning and end of the period and adding to this figure aggregate depreciation. This is because accretions to reserves normally arise from appropriation of profit, while intangible assets, such as goodwill or preliminary expenses, are usually written off to Profit and Loss Account and, in common with depreciation, do not result in an outflow of cash. Care should be taken to watch for intangible assets which have arisen during the year from an outflow of cash, since such amounts should be shown as applications in the fourth section of the statement. Such a situation may arise where goodwill has been acquired on the purchase of a business, or commission or expenses are incurred consequent upon an issue of shares or debentures. A negative cash flow may be verified by deducting from the amount by which the Profit and Loss Account has diminished, depreciation plus the amount, if any, written off intangible assets. Exceptionally, goodwill may be written off direct to capital or general reserve, or an increase in fixed assets, consequent upon revaluation, credited to capital reserve; in neither case will cash flow be affected since the entries will not have passed through the Profit and Loss Account; however, adjustments such as these should be readily apparent from a perusal of a Balance Sheet embodying comparative figures.

**Illustration (1)**

## VENEERING MANUFACTURERS LTD
## MOVEMENT OF FUNDS STATEMENT
for the year ended June 30th, 1970

|  | £ | £ | £ |
|---|---|---|---|
| Opening cash  .. .. .. .. .. |  |  | 4,444 |
| Cash flow: |  |  |  |
| Net profit for the year £(13,330+140)  .. .. |  | 13,470 |  |
| Depreciation  .. .. .. .. .. |  | 2,620 |  |
|  |  | 16,090 |  |
| *Less* Tax payable  .. .. .. .. | 5,600 |  |  |
| Dividends paid and payable  .. .. .. | 2,800 |  |  |
|  |  | 8,400 |  |
|  |  |  | 7,690 |
| Sources of funds: |  |  |  |
| Share capital – Ordinary Stock  .. .. .. .. | | 10,000 |  |
| Share premium  .. .. .. .. .. .. | | 1,000 |  |
| Sale of plant  .. .. .. .. .. .. | | 100 |  |
|  |  | 11,100 |  |
|  |  |  | 23,234 |
| Application of funds: |  |  |  |
| Purchase of freehold property  .. .. .. .. | | 2,000 |  |
| Purchase of plant ..  .. .. .. .. .. | | 1,000 |  |
|  |  | 3,000 |  |
|  |  |  | 20,234 |

| Change in form of working capital | Source | Application |  |
|---|---|---|---|
|  | £ | £ |  |
| Stocks and work-in-progress  .. .. |  | 1,420 |  |
| Debtors ..  .. .. .. .. .. |  | 1,704 |  |
| Tax Reserve Certificates  .. .. .. .. |  | 2,000 |  |
| Creditors  .. .. .. .. .. |  | 6,438 |  |
| Subsidiary company  .. .. .. .. |  | 3,540 |  |
| Dividends  .. .. .. .. .. | 500 |  |  |
| Taxation £(84+2,576)  .. .. .. .. | 2,660 |  |  |
|  | 3,160 | 15,102 |  |
|  |  | Net application | 11,942 |
| Closing cash  .. .. .. .. .. .. .. |  |  | £8,292 |

| Cash flow: |  | £ |
|---|---|---|
| Profit and Loss Account balance 30/6/70  .. .. .. | | 8,160 |
| *Less* Profit and Loss Account balance 30/6/69..  .. .. | | 3,090 |
|  |  | 5,070 |
| *Add* Depreciation ..  .. .. .. .. .. | | 2,620 |
|  |  | £7,690 |

## VENEERING MANUFACTURERS LTD
## MOVEMENT OF FUNDS STATEMENT
*(continued)*

|  | | | | | | £ | £ |
|---|---|---|---|---|---|---:|---:|
| Opening cash | .. | .. | .. | .. | .. | | 4,444 |
| Cash flow | .. | .. | .. | .. | .. | 7,690 | |
| Sources of funds | .. | .. | .. | .. | .. | 11,100 | |
| | | | | | | 18,790 | |
| Application of funds | .. | .. | .. | .. | | 3,000 | |
| | | | | | | | 15,790 |
| Increase in working capital | .. | .. | .. | .. | | | 20,234 |
| Changes in form of working capital: net application | | .. | | .. | | | 11,942 |
| Closing cash | .. | .. | .. | .. | .. | | £8,292 |

---

**Illustration (2)**

### SOURCE AND USE OF FUNDS

| | | | | | £000's |
|---|---|---|---|---|---:|
| Source of funds: | | | | | |
| Profits retained (13·5—8·4) | .. | .. | .. | .. | 5·1 |
| Depreciation | .. | .. | .. | .. | 2·6 |
| Increase in share capital | .. | .. | .. | .. | 10·0 |
| Share premium | .. | .. | .. | .. | 1·0 |
| | | | | | 18·7 |
| Use of funds: | | | | | |
| Expenditure on fixed assets (net) | .. | .. | .. | 2·9 |
| Change in working capital | .. | .. | .. | .. | 11·9 |
| | | | | | 14·8 |
| Increase in cash resources | .. | .. | .. | .. | 3·9 |

---

Illustration (1) reveals that funds generated during the year and retained in the business amounted to £7,690, while £11,100 was received from external sources. After purchase of fixed assets, the balance of £15,790 was utilized to increase working capital, including cash. Consequently, the working capital position of the company has been strengthened considerably by reducing creditors. It will be observed that ample cash is available at June 30th, 1970, to meet proposed dividends and any day-to-day commitments arising from increased activity, which increases in stocks and debtors, coupled with the purchase of property and plant, would seem to indicate. Purchase of further Tax Reserve Certificates seems a prudent move in view of the increasing tax burden.

*Ratios for Veneering Manufacturers Ltd*

The accounting ratios considered above may be exemplified by computing those derived from the final accounts of Veneering Manufacturers Ltd for the year ended June 30th, 1970. These are set out in the same sequence as in the foregoing text with notes, as appropriate. Ratios are given for the previous year in italics where these are considered to be pertinent.

(1) THE PRIMARY RATIO (based upon net profit before tax):

(*a*)  £13,330 : £71,800                    =1 : 5·4 or 18·6 per cent.

*Note:*

This percentage is probably unrealistic, i.e. inflated, since a significant part of the profit is undoubtedly attributable to the use of funds of £15,000 provided by the debenture holders.

(*b*)  £(13,330+600)=£13,930 : £86,800        =1 : 6·2 or 16·0 per cent.

(*c*)  £(13,930—300) : £(86,800—8,020)

    £13,630           : £78,780                =1 : 5·8 or 17·3 per cent.

    *£7,480*           : *£62,710*                =*1 : 8·4 or 11·9 per cent.*

*Note:*

In so far as the quoted investments are represented by holdings in British Funds, they could not really be deemed to be speculative. However, this ratio is important since it eliminates the disparity between the earnings of the company in its chosen trade and the return on the investments, which was minimal, and, therefore, depressed the the rate at (*b*). If security is of paramount importance the company would, it seems, be well advised to re-invest the amount of £8,020, in, say, Local Authority loans, on which a higher return would currently be received.

(*d*)  £13,930 : £(86,800+21,622+5,600)

    £13,930 : £114,022                        =1 : 8·2 or 12·2 per cent.

    *£7,780  : £104,770*                        =*1 : 13·5 or 7·4 per cent.*

*Notes:*

(i) Quoted investments have been included in gross assets, although these could have been excluded.

(ii) Gross assets may be verified as follows:

|  | £ | £ |
|---|---|---|
| Fixed assets          ..          ..          .. | 47,200 | *46,920* |
| Shares in subsidiary company..          .. | 18,750 | *18,750* |
| Current assets          ..          ..          .. | 48,072 | *39,100* |
|  | £114,022 | *£104,770* |

(In the original calculation current liabilities were added to capital employed).

(iii) The ratios at (*c*) and (*d*) reveal a marked improvement in earnings for the latest year.

(*e*)  In the absence of figures based upon a revaluation of the company's assets it is not possible to calculate the primary ratio on this basis.

(2) THE SECONDARY RATIOS

(a)  *Net profit to sales:*

£13,330 : £69,100                              =1 : 5·2 or 19·3 per cent.

(b)  *Sales to capital employed:*

£69,100 : £86,800                              =0·8 : 1

*£39,200 : £70,730*                             *=0·6 : 1*

*Notes:*

(i)  Capital employed represents net assets, as at 1(b) above. This basis has been adopted because of the desirability of comparing sales with both fixed and working capital, as shown at 6(c) below.

(ii)  The above ratios do not suggest an intensive use of capital employed, but much would depend upon the nature of the business and the intensity of use in other companies in the same industry with similar resources at their disposal (assuming that the accounts of such other companies are published).

(3) THE SOLVENCY RATIOS

(a)  *The working capital ratio:*

£48,072 : £21,622                              =2·2 : 1

*£39,100 : £31,016*                             *=1·3 : 1*

*Notes:*

(i)  It would be permissible to include quoted investments at market value.

(ii)  The above ratios show a marked improvement in the current year and less dependence on short term capital from current liabilities for the working capital of the business in that year.

(b)  *The quick assets ratio:*

£24,312 : £21,622                              =1·1 : 1

*£18,464 : £31,016*                             *=0·6 : 1*

*Notes:*

(i)  This ratio demonstrates that, for the current year, should all the creditors demand immediate payment, their demands could be met from readily-realizable assets; however, only proposed dividends call for imminent payment. A marked improvement is again disclosed for the current year since an ostensibly insolvent position existed at June 30th, 1969, nevertheless, it should be noted that ample resources existed to meet proposed dividends at that date.

(ii)  Tax Reserve Certificates have been included as a quick asset, as these are encashable; in view of the loss of interest which would arise on realization, though, the company would be loath to do this.

(iii)  Again, quoted investments could be included at market value.

(4) THE CAPITAL RATIOS

(a)  *The ratio of capital employed to total indebtedness:*

£114,022 : £(15,000+27,222)

£114,022 : £42,222                             =1 : 0·37

*£104,770 : £49,040*                            *=1 : 0·47*

*Notes:*

(i) See 1(*d*) above for calculation of gross assets.

(ii) Total indebtedness, for the current year, comprises debentures (£15,000), current liabilities (£21,622) and corporation tax payable January 1st, 1972 (£5,600). Although the latter is not, strictly speaking, a current liability, it is important to include all creditors when calculating total indebtedness since this represents capital provided by outside sources.

(iii) From the above ratios it is evident that outsiders effectively own rather more than one-third of the gross assets for the current year, while their financial strength has diminished compared with the previous year. The company may thus be considered to be in a stronger financial position at June 30th, 1970, in so far as it relies less on capital provided by persons other than the shareholders.

(iv) This ratio may, alternatively, be expressed as follows:
$$£71,800 : £42,222 = 1.7:1$$

(*b*) *The ratio of capital employed to fixed assets:*

| | |
|---|---|
| £71,800 : £47,200 | =1·5 : 1 |
| *£55,730 : £46,920* | *=1·2 : 1* |

*Note:*

It is clear that for both years, the fixed assets were wholly-owned by the shareholders. It should be noted that, for the current year, they also owned the shares in the subsidiary company and a small proportion of the current assets, thus supporting the conclusions based on the ratios at (*a*).

(*c*) *The capital gearing ratio:*

| | | | |
|---|---|---|---|
| £(40,000+21,800) | : | £(10,000+15,000) | |
| £61,800 | : | £25,000 | =2·5 : 1 |
| *£45,730* | : | *£25,000* | *=1·8 : 1* |

*Notes:*

(i) The company is 'low-geared', the gearing being lower in the current year.

(ii) Although gearing may be readily apparent from a mere perusal of the figures, ratios would (in common with many other relationships so expressed) facilitate appraisal when comparing a number of past periods or years for the same company, or when comparison is made with a number of similar companies. It would, for instance, be easier to assimilate five hundred ratios than one thousand absolute figures.

(iii) Reserves have been included as part of the equity for reasons given in the text.

(*d*) *The ratio of fixed assets to capital employed:*

| | |
|---|---|
| £34,000 : £114,022 | =1 : 3·4 |
| *£33,720 : £104,770* | *=1 : 3·1* |

*Note:*

It appears that a comparatively small amount of capital is sunk in tangible fixed assets. It is considered advisable in this context, to regard capital employed as the gross assets of the company.

(5) THE EARNINGS RATIOS

(a) *The ratio of net profit after corporation tax and preference dividend to equity capital:*

£(7,730—800) : £(40,000+21,800)
£6,930          : £61,800                                  =11·2 per cent.
*£3,356          : £45,730                                  =  7·3 per cent.*

Notes:

(i) The increased return in the current year arises from a more intensive use of capital employed as shown at 2(*b*) above together with a reduction in total costs in relation to increased sales.

(ii) A more realistic and, probably, conservative rate may be obtained by employing the real value of equity capital employed (i.e. the current value of the assets, less preference shares and liabilities) as the denominator. However, the true value of the assets of Veneering Manufacturers Ltd is not known.

(iii) Overprovision for taxation in the previous year has been ignored as this would tend to distort the earnings percentage for the year.

(b) *The ratio of profit available for dividend to dividend paid (often called the 'payout' ratio):*

£(7,730+140—800)       :          £2,000
£7,070                 :          £2,000        =          3·5 : 1
*£3,456                 :          £1,500        =          2·3 : 1*

Notes:

(i) Ordinary dividends were thus covered three-and-a-half times by available profits for the current year, denoting a high rate of cover. For the previous year, the cover was somewhat less at 2·3.

(ii) Overprovision for taxation has been treated as an accretion to available profits for the year.

(iii) From the above it will be apparent that a large proportion of the profit for the current year was retained.

(c) *The ratio of profit available for dividend to preference dividend:*

£(7,730+140)=£7,870  :          £800        =          9·8 : 1
*£4,256  :          £800        =          5·3 : 1*

Note:

In the current year the preference dividend was covered nearly ten times, signifying considerable security of income. Coupled with the fact that the company is low geared, preference shareholders seem to be in a strong position, both as regards security of capital and income.

(d) *The yield ratio:*

Assuming the market price of £1 unit of stock to be £1·50 at June 30th, 1970, the gross yield would be as follows:

$$\frac{\text{Ordinary dividend (gross)}}{\text{Issued Ordinary stock} \times £1\cdot50} \times 100$$

$$\frac{£2,000 \times 100}{£60,000}$$

Gross yield=3·3 per cent.

(*e*) *The price/earnings ratio:*

Assuming the same facts as at (*d*) above, the P/E ratio would be calculated as follows:

$$\frac{\text{Issued Ordinary stock} \times £1\cdot50}{\text{Net profit} - \text{Corporation tax} - \text{Gross Preference dividend}}$$

$$= \frac{£60,000}{£(7,730\text{—}800)=6,930}$$

$$\text{P/E ratio}=8\cdot7$$

(6) THE SALES RATIOS

(*a*) *The ratio of gross profit to sales:*
£18,400 : £69,100 = 26·6 per cent.
*£11,100 : £39,200 = 28·3 per cent.*

(*b*) *The ratio of net profit to sales:*
£13,330 : £69,100 = 19·3 per cent.
*£7,180 : £39,200 = 18·3 per cent.*

(*c*) *The ratio of sales to capital employed:*
(i) *Fixed capital:*
£69,100 : £47,200 = 1·47 : 1
*£39,200 : £46,920 = 0·84 : 1*

*Notes:*
(i) A more intensive use was made of fixed capital during the current year.
(ii) Shares in the subsidiary company have been excluded as the earnings on these, at approximately 20 per cent., appear to be competitive.

(ii) *Working capital:*
£69,100 : £(26,450—8,020—8,000)=£10,430=6·6 : 1
*£39,200 : £(8,084—8,020—6,000)=(£5,936) (see Note iv below)*

*Notes:*
(i) Quoted investments and tax reserve certificates have been excluded for reasons given in the text.
(ii) Corporation tax payable January 1st, 1972, has been excluded from working capital since this is not, strictly speaking, a current liability.
(iii) Ostensibly the above ratios indicate a more intensive use of working capital than fixed assets for the current year.
(iv) The importance of comparing average fixed and working capital employed *throughout the year* with sales *effected during the year* cannot be over-emphasised. By basing the above ratios on the position at the close of the year, one is assuming that this position is representative of the average funds employed throughout the year, which may or may not be true. An average based upon opening and closing fixed and working capitals for the year would be a very poor substitute for an average derived from interim accounts drawn up, on say, a monthly or quarterly basis. This is demonstrated above in respect of the previous year where, after deduction of quoted investments and tax reserve certificates, working capital was negative at the end of the accounting year.

(*d*) *The ratio of credit sales to debtors:*

$$\frac{£10,830}{£69,100} \times 365 \quad = 57 \text{ days or 8 weeks}$$

$$\frac{£\ 9,126}{£39,200} \times 365 \quad = 85 \text{ days or 12 weeks}$$

*Notes:*

(i) All sales are assumed to have been on credit and spread evenly, in terms of sterling, over the year.

(ii) The resultant ratio should approximate to the period of credit extended to customers, i.e. two months for the current year. It is not known whether the improvement in the later year stems from more stringent credit control or a reduction in the period of credit allowed from three to two months. In any event, provided the level of sales and bad debts is unaffected, the current position is the more favourable.

(*e*) *The ratio of bad debts to sales:*

£250 : £69,100 = 0·36 per cent.

*Note:*

This percentage is negligible, especially since it merely represents a provision. Credit control therefore seems to be satisfactory in so far as sales are being made to credit-worthy customers.

(7) THE STOCK RATIOS

(*a*) *Raw material stock to purchases:*

$$\frac{£\ 7,640}{£31,960} \times 365 \quad = 87 \text{ days or 12 weeks stock}$$

$$\frac{£\ 9,320}{£18,500} \times 365 \quad = 184 \text{ days or 6 months stock}$$

*Notes:*

(i) In the absence of monthly stock figures, closing stock has been taken to be representative of average stockholdings.

(ii) *Prima facie*, a stock of raw materials equivalent to three months' purchases, for the current year, seems excessive and may indicate the presence of obsolescent stocks. The level for the previous year, on the other hand, seems somewhat alarming and may indicate either (*a*) obsolete stockholdings; (*b*) advance buying pending price increases; (*c*) manufacture of a product necessitating large stockholdings; or (*d*) a switch (shortly before the close of the year) to manufacture of a product calling for stocks of expensive raw materials or components.

(iii) Ratios should be calculated for each type of raw material and component and compared with minima levels, fixed objectively, to indicate the incidence of excessive holdings.

(*b*) *Work-in-progress to cost of production:*

$$\frac{£\ 1,280}{£53,440} \times 365 = \quad 9 \text{ days}$$

$$\frac{£\ \ \ 920}{£27,330} \times 365 = \quad 12 \text{ days}$$

*Notes:*

(i) Closing work-in-progress has again been assumed to be representative of the average throughout the year.

(ii) Assuming that a uniform product is manufactured and that the closing figure is unaffected by seasonal fluctuations (e.g. the incidence of summer holidays in this instance) the production cycle for the current year is nine days.

(iii) The variation between the two years may be the result of attempts to speed up the cycle of production, or attributable to a change in the type of goods produced.

(c) *Finished stock to cost of total turnover:*

$$\frac{£\ 4,010}{£50,700} \times 365 = 29 \text{ days or 1 month (approx.)}$$

$$\frac{£\ 1,270}{£28,100} \times 365 = 16 \text{ days}$$

*Notes:*

(i) Increased stockholding in the current year corresponds with the increase in turnover, and may be prudent in order to ensure that customers' demands may be met without delay.

(ii) This ratio could, alternatively, have been based on turnover, in which case, however, the selling prices of stocks would need to be known. By basing it upon cost of sales both the numerator and denominator are at cost.

(8) THE PRODUCTION RATIOS

*Factory cost:*

£50,700 : £69,100 = 73·4 per cent.
£28,100 : £39,200 = 71·7 per cent.

*Establishment expenses:*

£830      : £69,100 = 1·2 per cent.
£830      : £39,200 = 2·1 per cent.

*Administration expenses:*

£7,330    : £69,100 = 10·6 per cent.
£6,160    : £39,200 = 15·7 per cent.

*Finance:*

£1,140    : £69,100 = 1·6 per cent.
£950      : £39,200 = 2·4 per cent.

*Notes:*

(i) Factory costs would, of course, need to be analysed between material, labour and overheads while, of the other items, greatest economies are likely to result from a critical examination of administration expenses.

(ii) Since factory costs are mainly variable the percentage is much the same for both years, whereas it has decreased in the current year in the case of other expenses, which are largely fixed.

## PART IV

*Amalgamations, Reconstructions and Reduction of Capital*

### § 17. The Amalgamation of Companies

The term 'AMALGAMATION' in its business sense means the merger of two or more businesses or undertakings, or of interests in business or undertakings. Mergers may be either *Partial* or *Complete*.

A *Partial Merger* may consist of an arrangement for pooling sales or orders, or for the sharing of net profits. Such mergers, however, tend to be temporary rather than permanent.

A *Complete Amalgamation* usually entails the absorption of one or more businesses either by an existing company or by a new company formed specially for the purpose; or it may be effected under a holding company scheme.

Where two or more concerns which occupy different stages in the chain of production and distribution, e.g. the supplier of raw material, the manufacturer, the wholesaler and the retailer of a commodity amalgamate their interests, the merger is said to be a *Vertical* one.

A *Horizontal* merger is one between concerns carrying on the same kind of business, e.g. the amalgamation of a number of retail stores.

A complete amalgamation may be effected by one of the following methods:

(*a*) *A Consolidation.* Two or more companies are completely wound up and their businesses transferred to a new company formed for the purpose.

(*b*) *An Absorption.* The business of one of the merging companies is transferred to another and the transferor company wound up.

(*c*) *The formation of a Holding Company*, which acquires a controlling interest in all the merging companies. Alternatively, one of the merging companies may acquire a controlling interest in the others. By this method, the existing companies retain their individual names and entities, and continue to operate as separate concerns, subject to the direction and control of the holding company. Holding companies are considered in Chapter IX.

The matters to be considered in the preliminary stages, i.e. the legal formalities to be complied with and the taxation considerations, are outside the scope of this work. However, in connection with taxation considerations for the purposes of corporation tax under methods (*a*) and (*b*) above, unless there is common ownership to the extent of 75 per cent. both before and after the amalgamation, the businesses will be considered as discontinued and any unrelieved losses of the companies which cease to trade will not be available to be carried forward against future profits of the acquiring company but will only be available for relief under the terminal loss provisions. If, as in method (*c*) above, the company is not wound up, the losses may be carried forward against the future profits of the same trade of the same company.

For the purposes of capital gains tax, under methods (*a*) and (*b*) above the transfer of assets will be a disposal for capital gains tax purposes and liability may arise. In addition, when the company is wound up, personal capital gains tax liabilities may arise on the deemed disposal of the shares. Under method (c), however, liability to capital gains tax will arise only once on disposal of the shares to the holding company and this liability may be postponed if the new holding can be regarded as taking the place of the old holding for capital gains tax purposes.

In deciding which method to adopt, consideration will have to be given to the effect of the change on capital allowances and capital gains computations and relief for past trading losses of the company, bearing in mind that under methods (a) and (b) above the business or businesses will be treated as discontinued, while under (c) above the same companies will continue to trade and there will be no disposal of the assets. It should be borne in mind, however, that since April 5th, 1966, all company profits are assessable on an actual basis and it is therefore unnecessary to consider the effect of the new and discontinued business rules.

Where a new company is formed to take over the businesses of two or more existing companies, it becomes necessary to revalue the assets (including goodwill) of each of those companies in order to ascertain the total value of its issued share capital and to determine the amount of the consideration which the acquiring company should pay for each of the businesses acquired. It is usual for the consideration to be satisfied by the issue of fully paid shares in the new company to be allotted to the shareholders of the old companies in proportion to their respective holdings and to the relative values of their shares.

Two methods of computing the consideration for the acquisition of a business are:

1. Valuing individual assets, including goodwill.
2. Valuing the business as a whole on its earning capacity.

Often both methods are used and the results compared.

Stock Exchange prices are an unreliable basis; the price on a particular day reflects supply and demand on that day influenced by factors outside the business, e.g. the state of Wall Street. Different considerations may apply to the acquisition of majority and minority holdings; majority holdings give the owner the right to alter policy and fix the rate of dividend; minority holdings give the owner the right to a dividend fixed by the owner of the majority holding. Majority holdings are often valued on an 'asset' basis while minority holdings on an 'earnings' basis.

Preference shares are normally valued on a yield (or earnings) basis. The rate of preference dividend is usually permanently fixed on issue. Their capital value will depend largely upon what the public is willing to pay for the right to receive that rate of dividend. The following is a simple formula for calculating the capital value:

$$\frac{\text{rate of preference dividend}}{\text{rate of yield expected}} \times \text{par value} = \text{value per share.}$$

**Illustration**

A 10 per cent. preference share of £1 would be worth £1·25 if the expected yield on similar shares was 8 per cent.

$$\frac{10}{8} \times £1 = £1·25$$

Where there are arrears of cumulative preference dividend the amount, after deducting income tax at the standard rate, of the arrears per share must be added to the value of the share as computed above.

### Asset Basis

If ordinary shares are valued on the 'assets' basis it will be necessary for a professional valuer to revalue the assets on a 'going concern' basis, i.e. on the basis that the company is making a reasonable profit. Fixed assets are shown in a Balance Sheet at cost less accumulated depreciation which is unlikely to reflect their current value; they should be valued at the price a buyer would pay for them hoping to make a reasonable profit out of their use.

Current Assets should be valued at their realizable value. Stock-in-trade should be valued at *replacement* cost, regardless of actual cost; work-in-progress should be valued at actual cost (after adjusting the raw materials to current replacement value) and should include labour and a fair proportion of overhead expenses (excluding selling expenses). Adequate provision should be made for doubtful debts when valuing the debtors. Investments quoted on the Stock Exchange are usually valued at the mean quoted price at the date of valuation. Where, however, the holding is very large, and the market is restricted a lower value can be taken.

Minority shareholdings in companies not quoted on the Stock Exchange will normally be valued on an earnings basis, i.e. the price which a prudent investor would pay taking into account the income receivable and:

(*a*) The adequacy or otherwise of the 'cover' for the capital, in the form of net tangible assets. A higher yield will be expected on an investment where the underlying security, as represented by net assets, is unsatisfactory, than where there is an ample margin of cover.

(*b*) The amount of the average maintainable profits of the company, as disclosed by past accounts, adjusted where necessary to give effect to any known facts or contingencies which may cause the future profits to diverge from the past average.

(*c*) The dividends payable by the company on shares possessing dividend rights in priority to those in question.

(*d*) The amounts which it is considered desirable to withhold from distribution as dividend each year in order to create and maintain necessary reserves.

(*e*) By deducting (*c*) and (*d*) from (*b*), the amount of the average profits available for distribution to the holders of shares of the class held will be ascertained.

(*f*) The average yield to be expected on shares of the same class in similar undertakings quoted on the Stock Exchange. In this connection, the extent to which the capital is 'covered' by tangible assets as indicated in (*a*) above, and the consistency with which dividends have been paid, would be taken into account.

In determining the expected yield, it must be borne in mind that a higher yield would be looked for on shares in a private company, for which only a restricted market exists, than on shares which are readily realizable on the Stock Exchange. Possibly the expected yield on unquoted shares would be at least 25 per cent. higher than that on quoted shares. In exceptional cases the difference may be even more.

The value of the shares will then be ascertained by the following formula:

$$\frac{\text{Average rate of dividend payable}}{\text{Rate of yield expected}} \times \text{par value}$$

Thus, if the average rate of dividend payable on £1 shares in a company is, say, 10 per cent., and the expected yield is 6 per cent., the value of the shares, apart from other considerations, would be 10/6ths of £1 – £1·67 per share.

Other factors which may affect the valuation are:

1. The prospect of a continuance of the revenue-earning capacity, demand for the output etc.

2. The state of the investment market, and the general rate of interest on loanable capital.

3. The effect of the vendor's severance of his connection with the business (particularly where he was, in fact, the brains of the company), and the value of any office of profit attaching to the holder of the shares.

4. Rights of prior classes of members, extent of bond indebtedness etc.

5. Any anticipated legislation, e.g. safeguarding, prohibition, tariffs etc.

6. Continuance of the existing management.

7. The voting power carried by the particular class of shares.

A minority holder's price is normally dependent on the dividends actually paid on the shares. Where, however, there is a wide discrepancy between the amount of the profits and the amount distributed as dividends, a valuation based on dividends alone might be illusory, and regard should be had to the earnings, as well as the dividends, in valuing the shares. Thus, if the capital of a company consists of 100,000 7 per cent. Preference Shares of £1 each and 100,000 £1 Ordinary Shares, on which 12 per cent. dividend has been regularly paid, a minority holding might be valued as follows:

Preference Shares (assuming 6 per cent. to be a fair market yield)
    7/6ths × £1 = £1·17 per share.

Ordinary Shares (assuming 8 per cent. to be a fair market yield)
    12/8ths × £1 = £1·50 per share.

If, however, the profits of the company had been, say, £30,000, the following method might be adopted:

|  |  |  | £ |
|---|---|---|---:|
| Average adjusted profits .. .. .. .. .. | | | 30,000 |
| *Deduct:* Reasonable transfer to reserves etc. .. .. | | | 10,000 |
| | | | 20,000 |
| *Deduct:* Amount required for Preference Dividend .. .. | | | 7,000 |
| Amount available for Ordinary Shareholders .. .. .. | | | £13,000 |

Capital Value of 100,000 Ordinary Shares on basis of expected yield of 8 per cent. $= \dfrac{13,000 \times 100}{8} = $ £162,500

$$\text{Price per share} = \dfrac{£162,500}{100,000} = £1{\cdot}63$$

A Controlling Interest, which carries the power to appoint the directors and determine the policy of the company, would normally be valued on an *assets* basis (i.e. by reference to the value of the assets, including goodwill, and less liabilities).

### Goodwill

Intangible assets must be valued, of which goodwill is the most important. Goodwill can be defined as the capital value of future super-profits computed on the basis of past super-profits.

In arriving at a value to be placed on goodwill on the sale of a business, it is necessary to determine what is a fair rate of interest to be expected on the capital employed in the business, and for this purpose consideration must be given to the following:

(*a*) The return required on capital invested in an old-established concern of an inherently stable character would naturally be lower than that expected from a newly-established business of a more speculative character, because the 'risk' element is so much greater in the latter (although if successful, it may return larger profits).

(*b*) A lower return would normally be expected from a business producing a necessity than from one dealing in luxuries, because the former would be less subject to fluctuations than the latter.

(*c*) When the market for the products of a concern is in this country or the Dominions, it must be regarded as a more stable undertaking than one dependent for its customers upon some foreign country in which economic or political conditions are uncertain, and where restrictions on business may be imposed.

(*d*) When competition is acute, greater risks are run and a larger return on capital is therefore to be expected.

(*e*) When the demand for the products of an undertaking is dependent upon fashion or the popular taste of the public, considerable fluctuations in turnover may be experienced, and demand may in fact cease entirely. In such a case, there is a very considerable element of speculation in the investment of capital in that business, and a larger return thereon is to be expected.

(*f*) Where the assets employed in a business are of such an unusual nature that they cannot easily be adapted to any other purpose, this fact would warrant a higher return on capital than would be expected when the capital was invested in assets of a more realizable character. (This fact, also, of course, affects the values of the assets themselves.)

In determining the profits upon the basis of which goodwill is to be valued the following matters must be the subject of adjustment:

(i) Income from investments should be excluded, as the capital value of these investments will be arrived at separately and the return therefrom will not normally be that expected from the use of the other assets.

(ii) The charges for depreciation should be reviewed, and where these are deemed to have been excessive the excess written back or, where inadequate, a further charge made.

(iii) Income from any assets not required for the purpose of the business, e.g. surplus properties, should be excluded from profits for the same reason as income from investments.

(iv) Abnormal profits and losses should be eliminated from the profits of the years in which they occurred. By 'abnormal profits and losses' is meant profits and losses due to abnormal circumstances. The results of a particular year would not be excluded merely because the profit or loss is unusually high or low. The experience of many firms is that during a cycle of years certain particularly good or bad years are experienced, and these fluctuations form part of the normal experience of the business. It is only where the results of a particular year are vitiated by abnormal or non-recurring circumstances, e.g. a strike, that such results should be excluded.

(v) When remuneration has been paid to the proprietors or directors on too liberal or too meagre a scale, the charges should be added back and replaced by fair remuneration.

(vi) Any exceptional expenditure on advertising must be adjusted so that each year is charged with the average normal expenditure. Similarly, when during the last year or two advertising has been curtailed, regard must be had to the probable effect thereof on the profits of future years, and if it is thought necessary, a normal charge for advertising should be made against the years in which the smaller expenditure was incurred.

In arriving at the profits, it must be borne in mind that the basis of past profits is taken, not as the measure of goodwill, but as an indication of what the profits can be expected to be in the future. The adjustments mentioned above are necessary to bring past profits into line with future expectations. Goodwill is the price paid for the right to the excess earnings of the *future*, not of the past.

Various bases are advocated for the valuation of goodwill, and the method to be adopted is frequently governed by the custom of the trade in which the business is engaged, and often gives results which could not be justified on any logical grounds.

The usual bases are summarized hereunder:

(i) The average profits of past years multiplied by an agreed number. – Thus '3 years' purchase of the net profits' is often spoken of as the basis upon which goodwill is to be valued. This method, however, is purely arbitrary and does not, except by accident, bear any relation to the true value of goodwill.

(ii) The gross income multiplied by an agreed number. – This method is frequently adopted in professional businesses, but it suffers from most of the disadvantages of the preceding one, and from the further defect that it disregards altogether the working expenses, which may be excessive in relation to the turnover.

(iii) The capital value of an annuity for an agreed number of years of an amount equal to the average 'super-profits'. – For this purpose, 'super-profits' may be defined as the profits which can be expected in the future in excess of the sum required to pay a fair return upon the capital invested, having regard to the risk involved in the particular business, and a fair remuneration for the services of the proprietors who work in the business.

**Illustration**

The average net profits expected in the future are £20,000 per annum.
The average capital employed in the business is £100,000.
The rate of interest to be expected from capital invested in this class of business, having regard to the risk involved etc., is 10 per cent.
Fair remuneration to the proprietors for their services in the business is £5,000 per annum.

|  | £ | £ |
|---|---|---|
| Average annual profits .. .. .. |  | 20,000 |
| *Less* Interest on capital employed at 10 per cent. | 10,000 |  |
| Proprietors' remuneration .. .. | 5,000 |  |
|  |  | 15,000 |
| Annual Super-profits .. .. |  | £5,000 |

The goodwill may now be valued either at 'x years' purchase' of £5,000 or at the present value of an annuity of £5,000 per annum for an agreed number of years.

It may be well to emphasize at this point that in calculating the super-profits the amount deducted in respect of proprietors' remuneration should be a fair commercial return for their services, i.e. such a sum as they could command if they were managing the business for others.

(iv) The business as a whole is valued on a going-concern basis and the value attributed to the net tangible assets is deducted therefrom.

**Illustration**

|  | £ |
|---|---|
| Estimated annual future net profit .. .. .. | 20,000 |
| *Less* Proprietors' remuneration .. .. .. | 5,000 |
| Profit available for interest on capital employed.. | £15,000 |

On a 10 per cent. basis the value of the business is £150,000. If the value of the net assets (apart from goodwill) is £100,000, the goodwill is thus worth a maximum of £50,000.

This is, perhaps, the most satisfactory basis, since goodwill is really only a balancing figure, representing the difference between the price which a purchaser would be prepared to pay for an undertaking and the proportion of such price which is attributable to the net *tangible* assets acquired. In determining the rate of interest to be expected on capital invested in a business which is subject to competition, it is advisable to have regard to the return required to keep a good ordinary share in such a business at par. If there is no such guide, a fair figure can be arrived at by ascertaining what return would have to be offered to get an issue of ordinary shares underwritten.

(v) Trend of profits. – In all cases regard must be had to the trend of past profits. It will be realized that the same average profits are shown by both of the undermentioned businesses, although it is likely that A will continue to show a decrease in profits and B an increase.

|  |  |  |  | £ A | £ B |
|---|---|---|---|---|---|
| Year 1 | .. | .. | .. | 30,000 | 10,000 |
| Year 2 | .. | .. | .. | 20,000 | 20,000 |
| Year 3 | .. | .. | .. | 10,000 | 30,000 |
|  |  |  |  | £60,000 | £60,000 |
| Average | .. | .. | .. | £20,000 | £20,000 |

In such a case it might be more equitable to value the goodwill by reference to a 'weighted' average, in which the greater importance of the more recent results will be reflected.

**Illustration**

|  |  |  |  | A £ | £ | B £ | £ |
|---|---|---|---|---|---|---|---|
| Year 1 | .. | .. | .. | 30,000 × 1 = | 30,000 | 10,000 × 1 = | 10,000 |
| Year 2 | .. | .. | .. | 20,000 × 2 = | 40,000 | 20,000 × 2 = | 40,000 |
| Year 3 | .. | .. | .. | 10,000 × 3 = | 30,000 | 30,000 × 3 = | 90,000 |
|  |  |  |  | 6 | £100,000 | 6 | £140,000 |

| Weighted average | .. | .. | $\dfrac{£100,000}{6} = £16,666$ | $\dfrac{£140,000}{6} = £23,333$ |
|---|---|---|---|---|

The above method of 'weighting' is merely intended as an illustration of the principle, and is not necessarily the method that should be employed in every case. Other and more suitable 'weights' may be devised for particular circumstances.

## Earnings Basis

The alternative method of share valuation is the 'earnings' basis. The capital value of the profits earned is computed. The great difficulty is selecting a rate of return, which satisfactorily reflects the business risks involved, by which to gross up the profits to arrive at the capital sum which an investor would pay to receive those profits. In arriving at the rate of return the same factors as in calculating goodwill must be considered, namely points (a) to (f) above, and in arriving at the profits which are to be grossed up the profit adjustments mentioned in (i) to (vi) above in the valuation of goodwill must be considered.

A variation of the 'earnings' basis is to value the shares on the price earnings ratio. If the equity earnings after tax of a company are divided into its stock exchange value a figure (called the price earnings ratio) of so many years' purchase of the profits of the business can be computed. To value a business whose shares are unquoted on this basis the price earnings ratio of a business similar to the bidding company, quoted on the stock exchange, must be taken and the profits after tax of the business, under valuation, are multiplied by the price earnings ratio, and the product is the capital value. The P/E ratio of the bidding company is used, unless the assets of the selling company have a greater profit potential than those of the bidding company, otherwise there is a danger of paying too much and of over-capitalization and dilution of earning capacity in the amalgamated business.

**Illustration**

The XYZ Co Ltd is a manufacturing business whose Balance Sheet is as follows:

### XYZ CO LTD BALANCE SHEET
as at December 31st, 1969

| 1968 £ | | | | | | | | 1969 £ |
|---|---|---|---|---|---|---|---|---|
| | *Share Capital* | | | | | | | |
| 2,000,000 | 4,000,000 Ordinary Shares of 50p each | .. | .. | .. | .. | .. | .. | 2,000,000 |
| 500,000 | 150,000 7 per cent. Redeemable Preference Shares of £1 each | | | .. | .. | .. | | 150,000 |
| | | | | | | | | 2,150,000 |
| | *Reserves* | | | | | | £ | |
| — | Capital Redemption Reserve Fund | .. | .. | .. | .. | .. | 350,000 | |
| 580,500 | General Reserve | .. | .. | .. | .. | .. | 250,000 | |
| 140,000 | Profit and Loss Account | .. | .. | .. | .. | .. | 150,000 | |
| | | | | | | | | 750,000 |
| | *Long Term Liabilities* | | | | | | | |
| — | 8 per cent. Debentures .. | .. | .. | .. | .. | .. | .. | 400,000 |
| £3,220,500 | | | | | NET CAPITAL EMPLOYED | | | £3,300,000 |

Represented by:

| | | | | | | £ Cost | £ Depreciation | £ Net |
|---|---|---|---|---|---|---|---|---|
| | *Fixed Assets* | | | | | | | |
| 1,630,000 | Freehold Buildings | .. | .. | .. | .. | 1,630,000 | — | 1,630,000 |
| 1,190,000 | Plant | .. | .. | .. | .. | 2,000,000 | 680,000 | 1,320,000 |
| 40,000 | Transport Equipment | .. | .. | .. | .. | 100,000 | 80,000 | 20,000 |
| 2,860,000 | | | | | | £3,730,000 | £760,000 | 2,970,000 |
| 120,000 | Unquoted Investments (at cost) .. | .. | .. | .. | | | | 120,000 |
| | *Current Assets* | | | | | | £ | |
| 217,000 | Stock | .. | .. | .. | .. | | 330,000 | |
| 600,000 | Debtors | .. | .. | .. | .. | | 520,000 | |
| — | Quoted Investments (at cost) | .. | .. | .. | | | 7,000 | |
| 109,000 | Bills Receivable | .. | .. | .. | .. | | 150,000 | |
| 1,400 | Cash | .. | .. | .. | .. | | 500 | |
| 927,400 | | | | | | | 1,007,500 | |
| | *Current Liabilities* | | | | | | | |
| 162,400 | Taxation | .. | .. | .. | .. | 200,000 | | |
| 229,500 | Bank Overdraft .. | .. | .. | .. | | 226,000 | | |
| 110,000 | Trade Creditors .. | .. | .. | .. | | 161,000 | | |
| 185,000 | Dividends (gross) | .. | .. | .. | .. | 210,500 | | |
| | | | | | | | 797,500 | 210,000 |
| (686,900) | | | | | | | | |
| £3,220,500 | | | | | NET ASSETS | | | £3,300,000 |

You visit the offices of the XYZ Co Ltd, and make enquiries which reveal the following facts:

(i) A professional valuer has been consulted, and has set a value of £1,000,000 on the plant. He has re-valued the buildings at £2,000,000. The transport equipment could be sold for £10,000.

(ii) The unquoted investments, acquired in 1968, yield a return of 5 per cent. gross on cost whereas the risk involved in them should be compensated by a return of 10 per cent. The quoted investments have a current market value of £6,000 and yield 5 per cent. gross on cost.

(iii) It is deemed advisable for the purpose of asset valuation only to make a provision of 5 per cent. against the possibility that bills receivable will not all be met on the due date, and a further 5 per cent. provision for doubtful debts. These provisions will not affect the balance on the Profit and Loss Account.

(iv) Stock has been taken and is shown by the stock sheets to be worth £270,000.

(v) Net profit in recent years has been as follows:

$$1966 - £180,000 \qquad 1968 - £406,000$$
$$1967 - £310,000 \qquad 1969 - £400,000$$

The figure for 1969 is net profit before charging debenture interest. Goodwill is to be valued at eight years' purchase of the super-profits.

(vi) In 1967 the cost of marketing a new product totalling £60,000 was written off to the Profit and Loss Account. It is considered, however, that this expenditure will confer an equal benefit on the years 1967 to 1969 inclusive.

(vii) Directors' fees totalling £45,000 have been paid each year from 1967 onwards. It is clear that the work done by the directors could be performed just as well by two newly qualified accountants at a combined salary of £5,000 per annum.

(viii) A fire in 1967 is estimated to have cost the company £50,000.

(ix) The return on similar preference shares to those issued by the XYZ Co Ltd is at present $7\frac{1}{2}$ per cent. The risks of the undertaking of the XYZ Co Ltd are such that a return of 11 per cent. is required from the capital employed. During the year an issue of 8 per cent. debentures was made at par.

(x) Investors have discounted the possibility of capital growth in the future to the extent that the shares of the company now show a P/E ratio of 17.

(xi) Depreciation on the company's assets for the year is equivalent to the capital allowances in the tax computation. Corporation tax is at 45 per cent.

You are required to suggest a value for the shares in XYZ Co Ltd.

### THE XYZ CO LTD – VALUATION OF SHARES

*The Assets Value Method:*

| | £ |
|---|---:|
| Freehold buildings | 2,000,000 |
| Plant | 1,000,000 |
| Transport Equipment | 10,000 |
| Stock | 270,000 |
| Debtors | 494,000 |
| Bills Receivable | 142,500 |
| Cash | 500 |
| | 3,917,000 |
| *Less* current liabilities | 797,500 |
| Capital Employed other than Investments and Goodwill | £3,119,500 |

| | | | | ADJUSTMENTS TO PROFIT | | | |
| GOODWILL | | | | | | | |
| Year | Net Profit | Investment Income | Fire Loss | Directors' Fees | New Product Cost Re-Allocated | Adjusted Profit | Weight | Product |
|---|---|---|---|---|---|---|---|---|
| | £ | £ | £ | £ | £ | £ | | £ |
| 1966 | 180,000 | — | — | — 5,000 | — | 175,000 | 1 | 175,000 |
| 1967 | 310,000 | — | + 50,000 | + 40,000 | + 40,000 | 440,000 | 2 | 880,000 |
| 1968 | 406,000 | —6,000 | — | + 40,000 | —20,000 | 420,000 | 3 | 1,260,000 |
| 1969 | 400,000 | —6,350 | — | + 40,000 | —20,000 | 413,650 | 4 | 1,654,600 |
| | | | | | | | 10 | £3,969,600 |

£3,969,600 ÷ 10 = £396,960 as Part Adjusted Weighted Average Profit.

|  |  | £ |
|---|---|---|
| Part Adjusted Weighted Average Profits | .. .. | 396,960 |
| *Less* 11% Return on Capital Employed of £3,119,500 .. | | 343,145 |
| | | |
| Super-Profit .. .. .. .. .. | | £53,815 |

Goodwill at 8 years' purchase of the super-profits = £430,520.

*Note:* Net profit for 1969 before charging debenture interest has been used on grounds of comparability, since capital employed includes debentures. The gross earnings derived from the use of share *and loan capital* are thus used as the basis for adjusted profits, i.e. before deduction of the cost of servicing loan capital which, in this context, is analogous to dividends.

|  |  | £ |
|---|---|---|
| Capital Employed except investments and goodwill | .. | 3,119,500 |
| Goodwill .. .. .. .. .. .. .. | | 430,520 |
| Investments: Unquoted .. .. .. .. | | 60,000 |
| „ Quoted .. .. .. .. | | 6,000 |
| | | |
| Value of the business .. .. .. .. | | 3,616,020 |
| *Less* Debentures valued at par (because they were recently issued at par) .. .. .. .. | | 400,000 |
| | | |
| | | 3,216,020 |
| *Less* Preference Shares valued as to yield | | |
| $\frac{14}{15} \times$ £150,000 or 93p each .. .. .. | | 140,000 |
| | | |
| Value of 4,000,000 ordinary shares .. .. .. | | £3,076,020 |

Say 77p each

*Note:* The unquoted investments have a book value of £120,000, but as they yield only 5 per cent. as opposed to a return of 10 per cent. necessary with regard to the risk involved, their value is £120,000 $\times \dfrac{5}{10}$ = £60,000.

*The Earnings Method:*

|  |  | £ |
|---|---|---|
| The Average Annual Profits net of investment income but after charging debenture interest (£396,960—£32,000) .. | | 364,960 |
| *Less* Preference Dividend .. .. .. .. | | 10,500 |
| | | |
| Profits belonging to ordinary shareholders net of investment income .. .. .. .. .. .. | | £354,460 |

A return of 11% is deemed necessary.

Capitalized value of equity interest $= \dfrac{\pounds354{,}460 \times 100}{11} = $ 3,222,363

*Add* Value of investments – unquoted and quoted
£(60,000+6,000)    ..        ..        ..        ..        66,000

Value of 4,000,000 ordinary shares    ..    ..    ..    £3,288,363

Say 82*p* each

*The Price Earnings Method:*

| | £ |
|---|---|
| Average annual profits after charging debenture interest .. | 364,960 |
| *Add* Investment income, gross    ..    ..    .. | 6,350 |
| | 371,310 |
| *Less* Corporation tax at 45 per cent., say    ..    .. | 166,310 |
| | 205,000 |
| *Less* Preference dividend    ..    ..    ..    .. | 10,500 |
| Earnings after tax and preference dividend    ..    .. | £194,500 |

Earnings after tax and preference dividend × P/E ratio of 17
= £3,306,500 as the value of 4 million ordinary shares.

Value per ordinary share say 83*p*

## Stamp Duty Considerations

Where a new company as in Illustration (1) below is formed for the purpose of acquiring the undertakings of other companies and the consideration for the acquisition consists as to not less than 90 per cent. thereof of shares in the new company, relief from the payment of the *ad valorem* duty can be claimed under Section 55, *Finance Act 1927* (as amended by Section 31, *Finance Act 1928*, and Section 41, *Finance Act 1930*).

These provisions cover the following cases:

1. Where a new limited company is formed, or the capital of an existing limited company is increased, for the purpose of *acquiring the undertaking or part of the undertaking of another company*, and *at least 90 per cent. of the consideration for the acquisition* (other than any arrangements for taking over or paying off creditors) *consists of the allotment of shares in the transferee company* to the transferor company or to the transferor company's members.

2. Where a new limited company is formed, or an existing limited company increases its capital, for the purpose of *acquiring at least 90 per cent. of the issued share capital of another company*. In this case, the buying company becomes a holding company, and if *at least 90 per cent. of the consideration consists of the allotment of shares in the holding company to the shareholders of the existing company* in exchange for their shareholdings, the scheme comes within the relief provisions.

In either of the above cases, for the purposes of charging capital duty on the nominal capital or increased capital, as the case may be, that capital is deemed to be reduced by an amount equal to the share capital of the vending or subsidiary company.

When the above provisions apply, capital stamp duty must be considered *separately* for each company; relief is available up to the amount of the capital of each vendor company to the extent that share capital in the new company is issued therefor.

### Illustration (1)

Two companies, whose businesses are similar, and whose tangible assets are properly valued, agree to amalgamate, and a new company is formed with an authorized capital of £200,000 to take over their respective assets and liabilities. The following are their Balance Sheets:

### JONES & JOHNSON LIMITED
#### Balance Sheet as at December 31st

| | £ | | £ |
|---|---|---|---|
| Share Capital – Authorized and Issued: | | Goodwill    ..    ..    ..    .. | 30,000 |
| 75,000 Shares of £1 each fully paid    .. | 75,000 | Freehold Premises    ..    ..    .. | 10,000 |
| Revenue Reserve Account    ..    ..    .. | 4,200 | Plant and Machinery    ..    ..    .. | 18,300 |
| Profit and Loss Account    ..    ..    .. | 800 | Stock    ..    ..    ..    .. | 16,000 |
| Liabilities    ..    ..    ..    .. | 3,300 | Debtors    ..    ..    .. | 7,500 |
| | | Cash    ..    ..    ..    .. | 1,500 |
| | £83,300 | | £83,300 |

### BLACK AND SONS LIMITED
#### Balance Sheet as at December 31st

| | £ | | £ |
|---|---|---|---|
| Share Capital – Authorized    ..    .. | 50,000 | Goodwill    ..    ..    ..    .. | 24,500 |
| | | Plant and Machinery    ..    ..    .. | 13,450 |
| Issued – 50,000 Shares of £1 each fully paid    .. | 50,000 | Stock    ..    ..    ..    .. | 11,550 |
| Profit and Loss Account    ..    .. | 4,500 | Debtors    ..    ..    .. | 6,000 |
| Liabilities    ..    ..    ..    .. | 2,000 | Cash    ..    ..    .. | 1,000 |
| | £56,500 | | £56,500 |

The book value of the net assets of Jones & Johnson Limited is arrived at as follows:

| | | £ | £ |
|---|---|---|---|
| Gross Assets    ..    ..    ..    ..    ..    ..    ..    ..    .. | | 83,300 | |
| *Less* Liabilities    ..    ..    ..    ..    ..    ..    ..    ..    .. | | 3,300 | |
| | | | £80,000 |

From the shareholders' point of view, this amount is represented by:

| | | £ | £ |
|---|---|---|---|
| Share Capital    ..    ..    ..    ..    ..    ..    ..    .. | | 75,000 | |
| Revenue Reserve Account    ..    ..    ..    ..    ..    .. | | 4,200 | |
| Profit and Loss Account    ..    ..    ..    ..    ..    .. | | 800 | |
| | | | £80,000 |

Similarly the book value of the net assets of Black & Sons Limited is £54,500, represented as follows:

| | £ | £ |
|---|---|---|
| Share Capital .. .. .. .. .. .. .. .. .. .. .. | 50,000 | |
| Profit and Loss Account .. .. .. .. .. .. .. .. .. | 4,500 | |
| | | £54,500 |

The consideration was:

1. To the shareholders of Jones and Johnson Ltd 80,000 shares of £1 each fully paid, being at the rate of sixteen new shares for every fifteen old, i.e. $\frac{80,000}{75,000} = \frac{16}{15}$

2. To the shareholders of Black & Sons Limited 40,000 shares of £1 each fully paid, being at the rate of four new shares for every five old, i.e. $\frac{40,000}{50,000} = \frac{4}{5}$

Fractions of shares are usually allotted to the liquidator of each company who sells the shares and distributes the proceeds to the parties entitled.

(Sometimes, it is possible to avoid fractions by altering the denomination of the shares, e.g. instead of allotting six new £1 shares for each five old, allotting twelve new 10p shares for each £1 old share.)

The Balance Sheet of the new company will then be as follows:

### NEW COMPANY'S BALANCE SHEET

| | £ | | | | | £ |
|---|---|---|---|---|---|---|
| Share Capital: | | Goodwill .. | .. | .. | .. | 40,000 |
| Authorized 200,000 shares of £1 each .. | 200,000 | Freehold Premises | .. | .. | .. | 10,000 |
| | | Plant and Machinery | .. | .. | .. | 31,750 |
| Issued 120,000 shares of £1 each fully paid .. | 120,000 | Stock .. | .. | .. | .. | 27,550 |
| Liabilities .. .. .. .. | 5,300 | Debtors .. | .. | .. | .. | 13,500 |
| | | Cash .. | .. | .. | .. | 2,500 |
| | £125,300 | | | | | £125,300 |

*Notes:*

1. Since the net assets of Black & Sons Limited were valued at £40,000 for the purposes of the amalgamation £14,500 has in effect been written off the goodwill of that company, the remaining assets being taken over at book value.

2. The Reserve and Profit and Loss Account balances of the transferor companies do not appear in the books of the acquiring company, as they are not available for revenue purposes in the hands of the new company, being represented by net assets purchased and paid for out of capital.

3. Any dividends paid by the new company must be paid out of profits earned after the amalgamation. If Jones & Johnson Ltd had either acquired all the shares of Black & Sons Limited, keeping that company in existence as a subsidiary, or acquired all the assets and liabilities, putting Black & Sons Limited into liquidation, the pre-amalgamation reserves of Jones & Johnson Ltd, £5,000, would have been available for payment of dividend to the shareholders of Jones & Johnson Ltd after the amalgamation (including persons receiving shares in compensation for their holdings in Black & Sons Limited).

In the above illustration relief is obtainable on £75,000 for Jones and Johnson Limited, and on £40,000 for Black & Sons Ltd; the new company will therefore pay capital stamp duty on £85,000 (£200,000 − £115,000).

If only part of the undertaking is acquired the reduction in capital stamp duty is *pro rata* to the part of the undertaking acquired. If the shares issued as consideration are partly paid only the amounts credited as paid-up (including the amount credited in shares issued to creditors for the release or assignment of debts) is available for relief if this is less than the *pro rata* proportion of share capital mentioned above.

**Illustration (2)**

The X Company with a nominal capital of £100,000, of which £90,000 is issued and fully paid, increases its nominal capital by £50,000 for the purpose of acquiring one-half of the undertaking of Y Ltd, whose nominal capital is £50,000. The purchase consideration is £30,000, payable as to £3,000 in cash and 54,000 £1 shares in the X Company Ltd, credited as 50*p* per share paid up.

| | |
|---|---:|
| For the purposes of stamp duty, the increase in the nominal capital of X Ltd of is reduced by the lower of (*a*) one-half the nominal capital of Y Ltd, £25,000, or (*b*) the amount credited as paid up on the shares issued as consideration, viz. 50*p* per share on 54,000 shares = £27,000     ..          ..          ..          ..          .. | £50,000 <br><br><br> 25,000 |
| Stamp duty will therefore be payable on ..          ..          ..          ..          .. | £25,000 |

No stamp duty is chargeable on any contract, transfer or assignment made for the purpose of transferring to the buying or holding company the undertaking or shares or debts due to creditors of the vending company, provided the contract etc. is duly stamped with a 'denoting stamp' showing that it is not chargeable with duty, and is executed within twelve months from the date of registration of the new company or increase of capital, or is made to give effect to an agreement (or particulars thereof) filed with the Registrar of Companies within such twelve months. (The agreement here referred to is that required on an allotment of shares for a consideration other than cash.) The debts due to creditors other than banks or trade creditors must have been incurred more than two years prior to the time of claiming exemption. For the purpose of exemption from stamp duty on any contract, transfer or assignment a company which issues any of its unissued share capital for the purpose of a reconstruction or amalgamation, is included in the relief (although no relief from stamp duty on nominal capital is available).

For the purposes of relief from *any* of the duties, the newly formed buying company's Memorandum of Association must include as one of its objects the acquisition of the undertaking of or shares in the vendor company. If an existing company increases its capital the resolution must state the purpose of the increase.

If two or more companies are involved as vending companies, the relief is to be computed separately for each company.

The relief will be disallowed, and the appropriate duties, with interest at 5 per cent. per annum, charged where:

(*a*) it is subsequently found that any material particular in the claim was untrue; or

(*b*) the conditions are not fulfilled; or

(c) within two years the vending company parts with the shares issued to it, otherwise than on reconstruction, amalgamation or liquidation; or

(d) within two years the holding company parts with the shares acquired otherwise than on reconstruction etc.

The Commissioners may allow relief from capital duty to a holding company, where all the other conditions are satisfied, if the acquisition of 90 per cent. or more of the shares in the vending company is completed within six months from the issue of the invitation to the members of the vending company to exchange their shares or seven months from the first allotment of shares for the purposes of the acquisition, if earlier. Duty already paid will be repaid.

It has been held that for the purposes of Section 55, *Finance Act 1927*, the legal as well as the equitable title must pass in order to constitute an 'issue' of shares. Where the transferee company sent out allotment letters, with forms of renunciation attached, to the shareholders of the transferor company, and so many of them renounced that of the first registered shareholders in the transferee company, those who had been shareholders in the transferor company held less than 90 per cent. of the shares in the new company, this did not constitute an issue of shares to the old shareholders entitling the company to relief (*Oswald Tillotson Ltd* v. *Commissioners of Inland Revenue* (1932), 48 T.L.R. 582).

### Illustration (3)

Three companies, A, B and C, propose to sell their undertakings for shares in a company to be formed, and supply you with the following figures:

|  | A £ | B £ | C £ | Total £ |
|---|---|---|---|---|
| Fixed Assets, *less* depreciation | 34,500 | 9,400 | 11,900 | 55,800 |
| **Current Assets:** |  |  |  |  |
| Stocks | 1,500 | 3,750 | 3,400 | 8,650 |
| Investments (Government Securities) at market values | 5,000 | 2,200 | — | 7,200 |
| Debtors, *less* Provision | 6,300 | 3,050 | 2,900 | 12,250 |
| Cash at Bank and in Hand | 5,400 | 2,400 | 165 | 7,965 |
|  | 18,200 | 11,400 | 6,465 | 36,065 |
| Total Assets | £52,700 | £20,800 | £18,365 | £91,865 |
| Authorized and Issued Capital (fully paid-up) | 27,000 | 10,000 | 16,000 | 53,000 |
| Creditors | 1,500 | 2,200 | 400 | 4,100 |
| Reserves | 24,200 | 8,600 | 1,965 | 34,765 |
|  | £52,700 | £20,800 | £18,365 | £91,865 |
| Trading Profit for last year | 8,100 | 4,000 | 3,600 | 15,700 |

The investments have been held for three years and yield approximately 5 per cent. on their present market values.

The trading profits for the previous two years were:

|  | A £ | B £ | C £ | Total £ |
|---|---|---|---|---|
| First year | 6,750 | 3,500 | 4,000 | 14,250 |
| Second year | 7,425 | 3,750 | 4,400 | 15,575 |

Report on the basis upon which the transfer should be effected and on the capitalization of the new company.

## REPORT

1. Assuming all necessary adjustments have been made in the valuation of the assets of the respective companies as disclosed by the Balance Sheets the net capital employed in the businesses is as follows:

|  | A £ | B £ | C £ |
|---|---|---|---|
| Fixed Assets | 34,500 | 9,400 | 11,900 |
| Current Assets (exclusive of Investments) | 13,200 | 9,200 | 6,465 |
|  | 47,700 | 18,600 | 18,365 |
| *Less* Liabilities | 1,500 | 2,200 | 400 |
| Net Capital employed | £46,200 | £16,400 | £17,965 |

2. The average trading profits for the past three years weighted to give more bias to the results of the later years, are as follows:

|  | A | | B | | C | |
|---|---|---|---|---|---|---|
| Year | £ | £ | £ | £ | £ | £ |
| 1 | 6,750 × 1 | 6,750 | 3,500 × 1 | 3,500 | 4,000 × 1 | 4,000 |
| 2 | 7,425 × 2 | 14,850 | 3,750 × 2 | 7,500 | 4,400 × 2 | 8,800 |
| 3 | 8,100 × 3 | 24,300 | 4,000 × 3 | 12,000 | 3,600 × 3 | 10,800 |
|  | 6 | )45,900 | 6 | )23,000 | 6 | )23,600 |
|  |  | 7,650 |  | 3,833 |  | 3,933 |
| *Less* Income from Investments |  | 250 |  | 110 |  | — |
| Average trading profits |  | £7,400 |  | £3,723 |  | £3,933 |

3. On the basis of an earnings yield of 10 per cent., which it is assumed ought to be provided on capital employed in businesses of the type carried on by the three companies, the values of the undertakings are as under:

|  | A | £ | B | £ | C | £ |
|---|---|---|---|---|---|---|
| Net trading assets | $£7,400 \times \dfrac{100}{10}$ | 74,000 | $£3,723 \times \dfrac{100}{10}$ | 37,230 | $£3,933 \times \dfrac{100}{10}$ | 39,330 |
| Investments at market value |  | 5,000 |  | 2,200 |  | — |
| Value of shares |  | £79,000 |  | £39,430 |  | £39,330 |
| Say |  | £80,000 |  | £40,000 |  | £40,000 |

4. To issue shares in the new company at par in exchange for the above values would involve a capitalization of £160,000, as compared with the aggregate existing paid-up capital of £53,000. If it is desired to take advantage of Section 55 of the *Finance Act 1927*, and obtain the maximum relief from capital duty, the new company should be capitalized with a capital of 40,000 shares of £1, which should be issued at a premium of £3 (approx.) per share and allotted in the following proportions:

To the shareholders of A $-\dfrac{80}{160} \times 40,000 = 20,000$ shares (being 20 new shares for every 27 old).

,, ,, ,, ,, B $-\dfrac{40}{160} \times 40,000 = 10,000$ shares (being 1 new share for every 1 old).

,, ,, ,, ,, C $-\dfrac{40}{160} \times 40,000 = 10,000$ shares (being 5 new shares for every 8 old).

*Notes:*

1. In order to decide how much nominal capital to issue to obtain maximum relief from capital stamp duty find the company with the largest amount of assets in relation to its authorized capital. Company B's assets are worth £40,000 while its authorized capital is £10,000. Allot £10,000 nominal capital to the shareholders of company B and calculate the nominal capitals to issue to the shareholders of companies A and C on this basis. The premium (which does not attract capital stamp duty) at which the shares are to be issued is the difference between the nominal capital and the net assets of each company (Company B net assets £40,000, nominal capital allotted £10,000 share premium therefore £30,000).

2. In the above computation, the values attributable to goodwill are:

|  | A £ | B £ | C £ |
|---|---|---|---|
| Value of net trading assets .. .. | 74,000 | 37,230 | 39,330 |
| *Less* Tangible assets, less liabilities .. | 46,200 | 16,400 | 17,965 |
|  | £27,800 | £20,830 | £21,365 |

Alternatively, the undertakings could be valued by computing the value of the goodwill of each company at so many years' purchase of its super-profits, and adding the value so found to that of the tangible assets less liabilities.

The book-keeping entries involved in an amalgamation are similar to those on an absorption of one company by another, and are described and illustrated in the next paragraph.

## § 18. The Absorption of one Limited Company by another

Where the constitution and capitalization of the merging companies make it possible and practicable, the amalgamation may be carried out by one of the companies absorbing the others, thus avoiding the expense and trouble of forming a new company.

The companies to be absorbed will go into voluntary liquidation, and the purchasing company will usually take over the whole of the assets and assume the ordinary trade liabilities of the others, any debentures being either paid off in cash or exchanged for debentures or other interests in the purchasing company.

### (a) *Book-keeping entries for closing the Vendor Company's books*

The entries in the books will be similar to those required for the purpose of closing the books of a partnership on dissolution, viz.

| Debit | Credit | With |
|---|---|---|
| Realization Account | Asset Accounts | Book values of assets taken over by the purchasing company |
| Cash | Asset Accounts | Proceeds of assets not taken over by purchasing company |

| Debit | Credit | With |
|---|---|---|
| Asset Accounts | Realization Account | Profit on disposal of assets *not* taken over by the purchasing company |
| | *OR* | |
| Realization Account | Asset Accounts | Loss on disposal of assets *not* taken over by the purchasing company |
| Liability Accounts | Cash | Settlement of liabilities not taken over by the purchasing company |
| Liability Accounts | Realization Account | Profit on settlement of liabilities, e.g. cash discounts received |
| | *OR* | |
| Realization Account | Liability Accounts | Loss on settlement of liabilities, e.g. under-provision for taxation |
| Share Capital. Reserve. (Capital and Revenue) Profit and Loss Account. Debenture Sinking Fund. Working Men's Compensation Fund. Staff Welfare Fund | Sundry Members Account | Balances attributable to Sundry Members. Sinking Funds, Working men's compensation funds etc. will be transferred to Sundry Members Account, provided no liability to pay working men's compensation remains in the vendor company they are similar to provisions no longer required |
| Sundry Members Account | Profit and Loss Account. Preliminary Expenses etc. | Debit balances and fictitious assets attributable to Sundry Members |
| Purchasing Company | Realization Account | Total purchase consideration. (including agreed amounts payable to creditors, debenture-holders etc. taken over) |
| Sundry Members Account Sundry Debenture Holders etc. Cash Creditors | Purchasing Company | Allocation of purchase consideration (e.g. shares, debentures, cash). Discharge of creditors etc. taken over |
| Sundry Debenture Holders | Realization Account | Remaining credit balance |
| | *OR* | |
| Realization Account | Sundry Debenture Holders | Remaining debit balance |

| Debit | Credit | With |
|---|---|---|
| Realization Account | Cash | Realization expenses |
| Realization Account | Sundry Members Account | Balance on Realization Account |
|  | *OR* |  |
| Sundry Members Account. Liability Accounts | Cash | Closure of cash book by payment to members of residual cash and/or cash element of purchase consideration and/or settlement of liabilities deferred until receipt of cash from the purchasing company. |

*Note:* In some examples, liabilities taken over by the purchasing company are credited to Realization Account and the purchase consideration excludes the amounts the purchasing company has agreed to pay in settlement of the liabilities. It is, however, considered easier to adopt the above method because no difficulties will arise when the liabilities are not taken over at book values.

Separate Provision for Depreciation Accounts should be closed by transfer to the credit of Realization Account since they represent reductions in the book values of the assets transferred.

A provision for bad and doubtful debts must be dealt with on its merits. If the debts are taken over by the absorbing company at their book value, the Provision for Doubtful Debts Account should be transferred to the credit of Realization Account; if the debts are taken over at their full value, the provision, since it is being ignored, must be transferred to the credit of Sundry Members Account. If book debts are not taken over, any bad debts incurred can be charged to the Provision Account, and the balance, if a debit, taken to Realization Account, or if a credit, to Sundry Members Account.

**(b) Book-keeping entries for opening the Purchasing Company's books**

| Debit | Credit | Notes |
|---|---|---|
| 1. Asset Accounts Goodwiil | Liabilities Vendor Account Capital Reserve | Assets and liabilities at acquisition values; the vendor account is credited with the purchase consideration. Goodwill is debited with the excess of the purchase consideration over the net assets acquired; capital reserve is credited if the net assets acquired exceed the purchase consideration (net assets=all assets less all liabilities) |

| Debit | Credit | Notes |
|---|---|---|
| 2. Vendor Account | Share Capital<br>Cash etc. | Discharge of purchase consideration by issue of shares, paying cash etc. |

### (c) Shares issued at a Premium Valuation

When the purchasing company's shares are issued to the members of the vendor company at a premium, the shares should be brought into the vendor company's books *at their full value* (i.e. including the premium) since the transaction is tantamount to the sale of the undertaking for cash, represented by shares in the purchasing company at the price at which they are issued. In the purchasing company's books the transaction is equivalent to the issue of shares at a premium for cash, and the purchase with the proceeds of the undertaking of the vendor company. As is usual when shares are issued at a premium, only the nominal value of the shares must be credited to Share Capital Account, the premium being credited to a Share Premium Account, which can only be utilized for the purposes stated in Section 56 of the *Companies Act 1948* (*see* p. 219).

### (d) Treatment of Revenue Balances and Reserves

The accumulated revenue balances and reserves of the vendor company should not be brought into the purchasing company's books, since they are not profits of the purchasing company, but are represented by assets which the company purchases and pays for. The purchasing company cannot distribute them as dividend.

Sinking funds for the redemption of liabilities are reserves, the assets representing them being taken over. In the vendor company's books all such balances should be transferred to the Sundry Members Account; they will not enter into the purchasing company's books at all. Sinking funds for depreciation of assets, however, are created by *charges* against profits for diminution in the value of the assets, and, as already explained, must be credited to the Realization Account, or preferably to the relevant asset accounts, before transferring them to Realization Account. A Capital Redemption Reserve Fund is capital, and must be credited to the Sundry Members Account.

**Illustration (1)**

The Associated Engineering Company Limited is absorbed by the United Engineering Company Limited, the consideration being the assumption of the liabilities, the discharge of the debentures at a premium of 5 per cent., by the issue of 5 per cent. debentures in the United Company, a payment in cash of £3 per share, and the exchange of three £1 shares in the United Company, at an agreed value of £1·50 per share, for every share in the Associated Company.

Close off the books of the Associated Company, giving both Journal Entries and Ledger Accounts, and show the opening Journal Entries in the books of the United Company.

The following is the Balance Sheet of the Associated Company at the date of transfer:

## ASSOCIATED ENGINEERING COMPANY LIMITED
### BALANCE SHEET

| | £ | | £ |
|---|---|---|---|
| Share Capital – 60,000 £5 Shares fully paid .. | 300,000 | Goodwill .. .. .. .. | 25,000 |
| General Reserve Account .. .. .. | 32,000 | Land and Buildings .. .. .. | 76,500 |
| Profit and Loss Account .. .. .. | 3,000 | Plant and Machinery .. .. .. | 220,000 |
| Accident Insurance Fund .. .. .. | 5,000 | Patents .. .. .. .. | 5,000 |
| 5% Debentures .. .. .. .. | 150,000 | Patterns and Drawings .. .. | 2,500 |
| Creditors .. .. .. .. | 30,000 | Work-in-Progress and Stocks-on-Hand .. | 106,000 |
| | | Debtors .. .. .. .. | 45,000 |
| | | Investments on Compensation Fund Account | 5,000 |
| | | Cash at Bank and in Hand .. .. | 35,000 |
| | £520,000 | | £520,000 |

## ASSOCIATED ENGINEERING COMPANY'S JOURNAL

| | | £ | £ |
|---|---|---|---|
| Realization Account .. .. .. .. .. .. .. .. Dr | | 520,000 | |
| To Sundry Assets .. .. .. .. .. .. .. .. | | | 520,000 |
| Assets sold to the United Engineering Co as per Balance Sheet. | | | |
| Creditors .. .. .. .. .. .. .. .. Dr | | 30,000 | |
| To Realization Account .. .. .. .. .. .. .. | | | 30,000 |
| Liabilities taken over by the United Engineering Co. | | | |
| Realization Account .. .. .. .. .. .. .. .. Dr | | 7,500 | |
| To Debentures Account .. .. .. .. .. .. .. | | | 7,500 |
| Premium of 5% now provided for. | | | |
| United Engineering Co Limited .. .. .. .. .. .. .. Dr | | 607,500 | |
| To Realization Account .. .. .. .. .. .. .. | | | 607,500 |
| Purchase price as per Agreement. | | | |
| Cash .. .. .. .. .. .. .. .. Dr | | 180,000 | |
| Shares (United Engineering Co) .. .. .. .. .. .. | | 270,000 | |
| 180,000 Shares of £1 each, fully paid, at £1·50 per share. | | | |
| Debentures Account – 5% Debentures exchanged. .. .. .. .. | | 157,500 | |
| To United Engineering Co Ltd .. .. .. .. .. | | | 607,500 |
| Discharge of Purchase Consideration. | | | |
| Accident Insurance Fund .. .. .. .. .. .. .. Dr | | 5,000 | |
| General Reserve Account .. .. .. .. .. .. | | 32,000 | |
| Profit and Loss Account .. .. .. .. .. .. | | 3,000 | |
| Realization Account – Profit on Transfer .. .. .. .. .. | | 110,000 | |
| Share Capital Account .. .. .. .. .. .. .. | | 300,000 | |
| To Sundry Members Account .. .. .. .. .. .. | | | 450,000 |
| Balances transferred. | | | |
| Sundry Members Account .. .. .. .. .. .. .. Dr | | 450,000 | |
| To Cash .. .. .. .. .. .. .. | | | 180,000 |
| United Engineering Co Shares Account .. .. .. .. .. | | | 270,000 |
| 3 shares of £1 each valued at £1·50 per share, and £3 per share in cash for each of 60,000 shares distributed to Shareholders. | | | |

## ASSOCIATED ENGINEERING COMPANY'S LEDGER
### REALIZATION ACCOUNT

| | £ | | £ |
|---|---|---|---|
| Sundry Assets .. .. .. .. | 520,000 | Creditors .. .. .. .. | 30,000 |
| Premium on Debentures .. .. .. | 7,500 | United Engineering Co Limited – Purchase | |
| Sundry Members Account, Profit on absorption | 110,000 | consideration .. .. .. | 607,500 |
| | £637,500 | | £637,500 |

### SUNDRY LIABILITIES

| | £ | | £ |
|---|---|---|---|
| Realization Account .. .. .. | 30,000 | Creditors .. .. .. .. | 30,000 |
| | £30,000 | | £30,000 |

## DEBENTURES

| | £ | | | £ |
|---|---|---|---|---|
| United Engineering Co Ltd .. .. | 157,500 | Balance b/f. .. .. .. .. | | 150,000 |
| | | Realization Account – Premium .. .. | | 7,500 |
| | £157,500 | | | £157,500 |

## SUNDRY MEMBERS

| | £ | | | £ |
|---|---|---|---|---|
| Cash .. .. .. .. .. | 180,000 | Share Capital .. .. .. .. | | 300,000 |
| Shares in United Engineering Co Ltd .. | 270,000 | Accident Insurance Fund .. .. | | 5,000 |
| | | General Reserve .. .. .. | | 32,000 |
| | | Profit and Loss Account .. .. .. | | 3,000 |
| | | Realization Account – Profit .. .. | | 110,000 |
| | £450,000 | | | £450,000 |

## SHARES IN UNITED ENGI·NEERING CO LTD

| | £ | | | £ |
|---|---|---|---|---|
| United Engineering Co Limited .. .. | 270,000 | Sundry Members Account .. .. | | 270,000 |

## ACCIDENT INSURANCE FUND

| | £ | | | £ |
|---|---|---|---|---|
| Sundry Members .. .. .. .. | 5,000 | Balance b/f. .. .. .. .. | | 5,000 |

## GENERAL RESERVE

| | £ | | | £ |
|---|---|---|---|---|
| Sundry Members .. .. .. .. | 32,000 | Balance b/f. .. .. .. .. | | 32,000 |

## PROFIT AND LOSS ACCOUNT

| | £ | | | £ |
|---|---|---|---|---|
| Sundry Members .. .. .. .. | 3,000 | Balance b/f. .. .. .. .. | | 3,000 |

## UNITED ENGINEERING COMPANY LIMITED

| | £ | | | £ |
|---|---|---|---|---|
| Realization Account – Purchase consideration | 607,500 | Cash .. .. .. .. .. | | 180,000 |
| | | Shares .. .. .. .. | | 270,000 |
| | | Debentures .. .. .. .. | | 157,500 |
| | £607,500 | | | £607,500 |

## UNITED ENGINEERING COMPANY'S JOURNAL

| | | £ | £ |
|---|---|---|---|
| Land and Buildings .. .. .. .. .. .. .. .. | Dr | 76,500 | |
| Plant and Machinery .. .. .. .. .. .. .. | | 220,000 | |
| Patents .. .. .. .. .. .. .. .. | | 5,000 | |
| Patterns and Drawings .. .. .. .. .. .. .. | | 2,500 | |
| Work-in-Progress and Stocks-on-Hand .. .. .. .. | | 106,000 | |
| Debtors .. .. .. .. .. .. .. .. | | 45,000 | |
| Investments .. .. .. .. .. .. .. | | 5,000 | |
| Cash at Bank and in Hand .. .. .. .. .. | | 35,000 | |
| Goodwill .. .. .. .. .. .. .. | | 142,500 | |
| To Associated Engineering Company Limited .. .. .. .. | | | 607,500 |
| Creditors .. .. .. .. .. .. .. | | | 30,000 |
| Assets and Liabilities taken over as per Purchase Agreement. | | | |
| | | £637,500 | £637,500 |

| | | £ | £ |
|---|---|---|---|
| Associated Engineering Company Limited .. .. .. .. .. | | 607,500 | |
| To Cash .. .. .. .. .. .. .. .. | | | 180 000 |
| 5% Debentures Account .. .. .. .. .. .. | | | 157,500 |
| Share Capital Account— | | | |
| 180,000 Shares of £1 each .. .. .. .. .. | | | 180,000 |
| Share Premium Account .. .. .. .. .. | | | 90,000 |
| Discharge of Purchase Consideration, the shares being taken as issued at £1·50 per share. | | | |
| | | £607,500 | £607,500 |

### Notes to Illustration:

#### 1. ACCIDENT INSURANCE FUND

This fund has been raised by the Associated Company out of profits and is represented by specific investments. Since there remains a credit balance on the Fund Account at the date of the sale of the undertaking, the Associated Company has made a profit of £5,000 by undertaking their own risks instead of insuring outside. Therefore, although the United Company takes over the investments representing such insurance profits, it only buys them as investments, and should not bring the Fund Account into its books. In the vendor company's books the balance of this Fund Account will be transferred to the Sundry Members Account in common with the other accumulated profit balances.

#### 2. GOODWILL

The final figure of goodwill, £142,500, shown in the United Company's books, is arrived at by taking the difference between the valuation of the assets acquired and the purchase consideration plus liabilities taken over.

The amount can be proved as follows:

| | £ |
|---|---|
| Goodwill as per vendor company's books .. .. .. .. | 25,000 |
| Profit on absorption .. .. .. .. .. .. | 110,000 |
| Premium on Debentures unrepresented by assets .. .. .. .. | 7,500 |
| | £142,500 |

#### 3. PREMIUM ON SHARES

In the vendor company's books the premium forms part of the cost of the shares in the purchasing company acquired; it forms part of the price received for goodwill, since it increases the profit on realization disclosed by the Realization Account. In the purchasing company's books, the share premium increases the cost of goodwill; it must be credited to Share Premium Account and can only be dealt with in accordance with the provisions of Section 56 of the *Companies Act 1948*.

### (e) *Where Debtors and Creditors are not taken over*

If relief from stamp duty is available under Section 55, *Finance Act 1927*, there is no reason why the debtors and creditors should not be taken over by the purchasing company, but where such relief is not available, a considerable saving may result from leaving the debtors to be collected by the new company and the creditors paid by them as agents for the vending company. Where this is done, the liquidation of the vending company cannot be completed until the debts are discharged.

**Illustration (2)**

Done Ltd's summarized Balance Sheet at December 31st was as follows:

| | £ | | £ |
|---|---|---|---|
| Issued Capital: | | Goodwill .. .. .. .. | 3,000 |
| 10,000 6% Preference Shares .. .. | 10,000 | Fixed Assets .. .. .. .. | 22,300 |
| 8,000 Ordinary Shares .. .. .. | 8,000 | Stock .. .. .. .. .. | 4,000 |
| Reserve .. .. .. .. .. | 2,000 | Debtors .. .. .. .. | 7,000 |
| Profit and Loss Account .. .. .. | 1,000 | Preliminary Expenses .. .. .. | 500 |
| 5% Debentures .. .. .. .. | 12,000 | Cash .. .. .. .. .. | 1,200 |
| Creditors .. .. .. .. | 5,000 | | |
| | £38,000 | | £38,000 |

A new company, Start Ltd, was formed to acquire (as part of an amalgamation scheme) the business of Done Ltd, which was to be wound up.

Start Ltd acquired the assets of Done Ltd, with the exception of book debts and cash, but took over no liabilities, agreeing, however, to collect the debts and pay the creditors as agent for Done Ltd.

The purchase consideration was to be satisfied as follows:

1. To the preference shareholders of Done Ltd were to be allotted six 7% preference shares of £1 each in Start Ltd for every five held, and to the ordinary shareholders of Done Ltd, five £1 ordinary shares credited as 90p paid for every four held.

2. Sufficient 6 per cent. debentures in Start Ltd to enable the liquidator of Done Ltd to satisfy the existing debenture holders by new debentures at a premium of 15 per cent.

The expenses of liquidation were £585.

The Articles of Association of Done Ltd gave to the preference shares a cumulative preference dividend, any arrears of which were payable on winding-up in priority to return of capital, and a preferential return of capital in a winding-up. Six months' dividend was payable.

Of the debtors, £200 proved bad, and a discount of 2½ per cent. had to be allowed on settlement. Creditors were paid, subject to 4 per cent. discount on £2,500. The purchasing company was allowed a commission of ½ per cent. on sums collected and ¼ per cent. on sums disbursed.

Show the Ledger Accounts necessary to close Done Ltd's books, making any necessary calculations to the nearest £. Ignore taxation.

## REALIZATION ACCOUNT

| | £ | | £ |
|---|---|---|---|
| Goodwill .. .. .. .. .. | 3,000 | Start Ltd, Purchase consideration .. .. | 34,800 |
| Fixed Assets .. .. .. .. | 22,300 | Discounts received .. .. .. | 100 |
| Stock .. .. .. .. | 4,000 | | |
| Premium on Debentures – 15% on £12,000 .. | 1,800 | | |
| Cash, expenses of liquidation.. .. .. | 585 | | |
| Bad Debts .. .. .. .. | 200 | | |
| Discounts allowed .. .. .. .. | 170 | | |
| Start Ltd – Commission on collection of debts and | | | |
| payment of creditors .. .. .. | 45 | | |
| Preference Members Account– | | | |
| Arrears of Dividends .. .. .. | 300 | | |
| Sundry Members Account– | | | |
| Profit on realization: | | | |
| Preference .. .. .. .. | 2,000 | | |
| Ordinary .. .. .. .. | 500 | | |
| | £34,900 | | £34,900 |

## SUNDRY MEMBERS

|  | Preference | Ordinary |  | Preference | Ordinary |
|---|---|---|---|---|---|
|  | £ | £ |  | £ | £ |
| Preliminary Expenses .. .. |  | 500 | Capital .. .. .. | 10,000 | 8,000 |
| Shares in Start Ltd .. .. | 12,000 | 9,000 | Reserve .. .. .. |  | 2,000 |
| Cash .. .. .. | 300 | 2,000 | Profit and Loss Account .. |  | 1,000 |
|  |  |  | Profit on Realization .. | 2,000 | 500 |
|  |  |  | Arrears of Dividend .. | 300 |  |
|  | £12,300 | £11,500 |  | £12,300 | £11,500 |

## SUNDRY DEBENTURE HOLDERS

|  | £ |  | £ |
|---|---|---|---|
| 6% Debentures in Start Ltd .. .. | 13,800 | 5% Debentures .. .. .. .. | 12,000 |
|  |  | Realization Account, premium .. .. | 1,800 |
|  | £13,800 |  | £13,800 |

## CASH

|  | £ |  | £ |
|---|---|---|---|
| Balance b/f. .. .. .. .. | 1,200 | Expenses of Liquidation .. .. .. | 585 |
| Start Ltd. .. .. .. .. | 1,685 | Preference Shareholders – Arrears of Dividend | 300 |
|  |  | Ordinary Shareholders .. .. .. | 2,000 |
|  | £2,885 |  | £2,885 |

## START LTD

|  | £ |  | £ |
|---|---|---|---|
| Realization Account, purchase consideration .. | 34,800 | 12,000 7% £1 Preference Shares in Start Ltd fully paid .. .. .. .. | 12,000 |
|  |  | 10,000 £1 Ordinary Shares in Start Ltd 90p paid .. .. .. .. .. | 9,000 |
|  |  | 6% Debentures in Start Ltd .. .. | 13 800 |
| Sundry Debts collected .. .. .. | 6,630 | Creditors paid .. .. .. .. | 4,900 |
|  |  | Realization Account, Commission– |  |
|  |  | ½% on £6,630 = £33 |  |
|  |  | ¼% on £4,900 = 12 |  |
|  |  | — .. .. .. | 45 |
|  |  | Cash .. .. .. .. .. | 1,685 |
|  | £6,630 |  | £6,630 |

## SUNDRY DEBTORS

|  | £ |  | £ |
|---|---|---|---|
| Balance b/f. .. .. .. .. | 7,000 | Realization Account: |  |
|  |  | Bad Debts .. .. .. .. | 200 |
|  |  | Discounts, 2½% on £6,800 .. .. | 170 |
|  |  | Start Ltd – cash collected .. .. | 6,630 |
|  | £7,000 |  | £7,000 |

## SUNDRY CREDITORS

|  | £ |  | £ |
|---|---|---|---|
| Realization Account– |  | Balance b/f. .. .. .. .. | 5,000 |
| Discounts, 4% on £2,500 .. .. .. | 100 |  |  |
| Start Ltd – amount paid .. .. .. | 4,900 |  |  |
|  | £5,000 |  | £5,000 |

*Note:* Since the Articles define the rights of the preference shareholders in a winding-up, they are entitled to no further share in the assets of the company, and the surplus, after the preference shareholders have received their agreed share of the sale consideration and their arrears of dividend, goes to the ordinary shareholders (*Scottish Insurance Corporation* v. *Wilsons and Clyde Coal Co Ltd* (1949), A.C. 462).

## § 19. Reduction of Capital

Section 66 makes provision for the reduction of the share capital of a company as follows:

1. Subject to confirmation by the court, a company limited by shares, or a company limited by guarantee and having a share capital may, if so authorized by its Articles, by special resolution reduce its share capital in any way, and in particular, without prejudice to the generality of the foregoing power, may:

(*a*) extinguish or reduce the liability on any of its shares in respect of share capital not paid up; or

(*b*) either with or without extinguishing or reducing liability on any of its shares, cancel any paid-up share capital which is lost or unrepresented by available assets; or

(*c*) either with or without extinguishing or reducing liability on any of its shares, pay off any paid-up share capital which is in excess of the wants of the company, and may, if and so far as is necessary, alter its Memorandum by reducing the amount of its share capital, and of its shares accordingly.

2. A special resolution under this section is in this Act referred to as 'a resolution for reducing share capital'.

Where the proposed reduction of share capital involves either diminution of liability on unpaid share capital, or the payment to any shareholder of any paid-up share capital, and in any other case if the court so directs, creditors are entitled to object, and those so objecting must be either paid off or secured.

In assenting to a scheme, the principal points the court takes into consideration are the protection of the rights of creditors, and the equitable adjustment of the loss between the various classes of shareholders, according to their capital and dividend rights.

Schemes acceptable to all parties and the court are difficult to arrange; a detailed discussion of the subject is beyond the scope of this book.

The reduction does not take effect until a copy of the court order and a minute approved by the court have been registered with the Registrar of Companies. The court may, at its discretion, order the words 'and reduced' to be added to the company's name for a period.

In formulating a scheme of reduction of capital, it is desirable simultaneously to pass a resolution to increase the capital to its original figure by the creation of unissued shares, otherwise, if it becomes necessary to issue further shares, capital stamp duty will be payable.

It must be borne in mind that by Section 22 of the *Companies Act 1948* no member of a company can be bound by an alteration made in the Memorandum or Articles after the date on which he became a member, which, without his consent in writing, seeks to increase his liability to contribute to the share capital of, or otherwise pay money to, the company.

A resolution for the reduction of share capital under Section 66, when confirmed by the Court, is, however, binding on all the members; there is no provision, as there is under Section 287, whereby a member who did not vote in favour of the resolution may demand to be bought out. It follows that a scheme could not be carried through under Section 66 which provides for the reduction of fully paid shares to partly paid shares and for a further call to be made on the shareholders, unless the consent in writing of every member could be obtained. A reduction or reconstruction of capital which entails a further call upon the shareholders could, however, be effected under Section 287, under which the company could be wound up voluntarily and its business or property transferred to another company in exchange for partly paid shares therein, see § 20 (p. 382).

## (a) Writing off Capital unrepresented by available Assets

The following illustration shows the entries in a company's books to give effect to a reduction of capital where capital has been lost or is unrepresented by available assets.

It is first necessary to create the fund for the reduction by debiting the various Share Capital Accounts and crediting Capital Reduction Account with the amounts by which the capital is to be reduced, and then applying the fund in writing off the items decided upon. Where drastic alterations in capital are involved, it is preferable to close the old Capital Accounts by crediting all the capital to the Capital Reduction Account and then debiting the Capital Reduction Account and crediting the new Share Capital Accounts with the new shares issued.

### Illustration

The summarized Balance Sheet of P. Ltd at March 31st, 19.., was:

| | £ | | £ |
|---|---|---|---|
| Authorized and Issued Capital: | | Goodwill | 25,000 |
| 100,000 6 per cent. Cumulative Preference Shares of £1 each | 100,000 | Patents and Trade Marks | 10,000 |
| 200,000 Ordinary Shares of £1 each | 200,000 | Land and Buildings | 88,000 |
| | | Plant and Machinery | 86,000 |
| | 300,000 | Shares in Subsidiary Ltd .. | 30,000 |
| 5 per cent. Debenture (secured on Land and Buildings)  £50,000 | | Stock .. | 73,000 |
| Add Accrued Interest  £2,500 | | Debtors | 98,500 |
| | 52,500 | Deferred Expenditure – Advertising | 25,000 |
| Bank Overdraft | 60,000 | Profit and Loss Account .. | 85,000 |
| Creditors | 85,000 | | |
| Directors' Loans | 23,000 | | |
| | £520,500 | | £520,500 |

Notes:

1. Dividends on the Preference Shares are three years in arrear.

2. There is a contingent liability for damages of £10,000.

A Capital Reduction Scheme, duly approved, settled the following terms:

1. The Preference Shares to be reduced to 80p each and the Ordinary Shares to 25p each and the resulting shares then to be converted into Preference and Ordinary Stock respec-

tively and consolidated into units of £1. The authorized capital to be restored to £100,000 6 per cent. Cumulative Preference Stock and £200,000 Ordinary Stock. The Preference shareholders waive two-thirds of the dividend arrears and receive Ordinary Stock for the balance.

2. All intangible assets to be eliminated, and bad debts of £7,500 and obsolete stock of £10,000 to be written off.

3. The shares in Subsidiary Ltd are sold to an outside interest for £60,000.

4. The Debenture-holder agreed to take over one of the company's properties (book value £18,000) at a price of £25,000 in part satisfaction of the Debenture and to provide further cash of £15,000 on a floating charge. The arrears of interest are paid.

5. The contingent liability materialized but the company recovered £5,000 of these damages in an action against one of its directors. This was debited to his loan account of £8,000, the balance of which was repaid in cash on his resignation.

6. The remaining directors agreed to take Ordinary Stock in satisfaction of their loans.

You are required to:

(a) Give the necessary Journal entries to record the above, including the cash transactions.

(b) Set out the revised Balance Sheet after giving effect to the entries in (a).

(Ignore taxation.)

P. LTD

JOURNAL

(a)

| | | £ | £ |
|---|---|---:|---:|
| Preference Share Capital Account .. .. .. .. .. .. Dr | | 20,000 | |
| Ordinary Share Capital Account .. .. .. .. .. .. .. | | 150,000 | |
| To Capital Reduction Account .. .. .. .. .. .. | | | 170,000 |
| 20p per share written off 100,000 6 per cent. Cumulative Preference Shares of £1 each and 75p per share written off 200,000 Ordinary Shares of £1 each, in accordance with Capital Reduction Scheme. | | | |
| Preference Share Capital Account .. .. .. .. .. .. Dr | | 80,000 | |
| Ordinary Share Capital Account .. .. .. .. .. .. .. | | 50,000 | |
| To 6 per cent. Cumulative Preference Stock Account .. .. .. .. .. | | | 80,000 |
| ,, Ordinary Stock Account .. .. .. .. .. .. | | | 50,000 |
| Conversion of 100,000 Preference Shares of 80p each and 200,000 Ordinary Shares of 25p each into stock and consolidation into 80,000 £1 units of 6 per cent. Cumulative Preference Stock and 50,000 £1 units of Ordinary Stock respectively. | | | |
| Capital Reduction Account .. .. .. .. .. .. .. Dr | | 6,000 | |
| To Ordinary Stock Account .. .. .. .. .. .. | | | 6,000 |
| Allotment of 6,000 £1 Ordinary Stock units in satisfaction of one-third of the arrears of Preference dividend, the other two-thirds being waived. | | | |
| Capital Reduction Account .. .. .. .. .. .. .. Dr | | 162,500 | |
| To Goodwill .. .. .. .. .. .. .. .. | | | 25,000 |
| ,, Patents and Trade Marks .. .. .. .. .. .. | | | 10,000 |
| ,, Deferred Expenditure – Advertising .. .. .. .. | | | 25,000 |
| ,, Profit and Loss Account .. .. .. .. .. .. | | | 85,000 |
| ,, Debtors .. .. .. .. .. .. .. | | | 7,500 |
| ,, Stock .. .. .. .. .. .. .. | | | 10,000 |
| Writing off of intangible assets, bad debts and obsolete stock. | | | |
| Cash .. .. .. .. .. .. .. .. Dr | | 60,000 | |
| To Shares in Subsidiary Ltd .. .. .. .. .. .. | | | 30,000 |
| ,, Capital Reduction Account .. .. .. .. .. .. | | | 30,000 |
| Sale of shares in Subsidiary Ltd for £60,000 and transfer of profit (£30,000) to Capital Reduction Account. | | | |
| 5 per cent. Debenture .. .. .. .. .. .. .. Dr | | 25,000 | |
| To Land and Buildings .. .. .. .. .. .. .. | | | 18,000 |
| ,, Capital Reduction Account .. .. .. .. .. .. | | | 7,000 |
| Transfer to debenture-holder at a valuation of £25,000 in part satisfaction of Debenture for £50,000 of property of book value of £18,000 and transfer of profit to Capital Reduction Account. | | | |
| Debenture Interest .. .. .. .. .. .. .. Dr | | 2,500 | |
| To Cash .. .. .. .. .. .. .. .. | | | 2,500 |
| Payment of accrued interest on £50,000 5 per cent. Debenture. | | | |
| Cash .. .. .. .. .. .. .. .. Dr | | 15,000 | |
| To Second Debenture .. .. .. .. .. .. .. | | | 15,000 |
| Cash received for a new debenture carrying a floating charge over the assets of the company. | | | |
| Capital Reduction Account .. .. .. .. .. .. .. Dr | | 5,000 | |
| Directors' Loan Account .. .. .. .. .. .. .. | | 5,000 | |
| To Cash .. .. .. .. .. .. .. .. | | | 10,000 |
| Payment of £10,000 in settlement of contingent liability and recovery of £5,000 thereof by set-off against director's loan. | | | |

## P. LTD

(a)                          JOURNAL
                          (*continued*)

| | | £ | £ |
|---|---|---:|---:|
| Directors' Loans .. .. .. .. .. .. .. .. Dr | | 18,000 | |
| To Cash .. .. .. .. .. .. .. .. .. | | | 3,000 |
| „ Ordinary Stock Account.. .. .. .. .. .. .. .. | | | 15,000 |
| Repayment to former director of balance of loan and allotment of Ordinary Stock in satisfaction of other directors' loans. | | | |
| Capital Reduction Account .. .. .. .. .. .. .. Dr | | 33,500 | |
| To Capital Reserve Account .. .. .. .. .. .. .. | | | 33,500 |
| Balance on Capital Reduction Account transferred to Capital Reserve. | | | |

## P. LTD

(b)        BALANCE SHEET AFTER REDUCTION OF CAPITAL

| | £ | | | £ | £ |
|---|---:|---|---|---:|---:|
| AUTHORIZED CAPITAL | | FIXED ASSETS | | | |
| £100,000 6 per cent. Cumulative Preference | | Land and Buildings .. .. | | 70,000 | |
| Stock (£1 units) .. .. .. | 100,000 | Plant and Machinery .. | | 86,000 | |
| £200,000 Ordinary Stock (£1 units) .. | 200,000 | | | | 156,000 |
| | £300,000 | CURRENT ASSETS | | | |
| | | Stock .. .. .. | | 63,000 | |
| | | Debtors .. .. .. | | 91,000 | |
| ISSUED CAPITAL | | | | | 154,000 |
| 80,000 6 per cent. Cumulative Preference | | | | | |
| Stock (£1 units) .. .. .. | 80,000 | | | | |
| 71,000 Ordinary Stock (£1 units) .. .. | 71,000 | | | | |
| | 151,000 | | | | |
| CAPITAL RESERVE .. .. .. | 33,500 | | | | |
| DEBENTURES | | | | | |
| 5 per cent. Debenture (secured) .. £25,000 | | | | | |
| Second Debenture (secured) .. 15,000 | | | | | |
| | 40,000 | | | | |
| CURRENT LIABILITIES | | | | | |
| Creditors .. .. .. £85,000 | | | | | |
| Bank Overdraft.. .. .. 500 | | | | | |
| | 85,500 | | | | |
| | £310,000 | | | | £310,000 |

*Note:* The Capital Reduction Account will appear as under:

| | £ | | £ |
|---|---:|---|---:|
| Ordinary Stock Account Allotment of £6,000 | | Preference Share Capital – Reduction of 20p | |
| Ordinary Stock in satisfaction of arrears of | | per share on 100,000 shares .. .. | 20,000 |
| preference dividend .. .. .. | 6,000 | Ordinary Share Capital – Reduction of 75p per | |
| Cash – Discharge of contingent liability .. | 10,000 | share on 200,000 shares .. .. | 150,000 |
| Amounts written off: | | Shares in Subsidiary Company: | |
| Goodwill .. .. .. .. | 25,000 | Profit on sale .. .. .. | 30,000 |
| Patents and Trade Marks .. .. | 10,000 | Property – profit on sale .. .. | 7,000 |
| Deferred Expenditure .. .. .. | 25,000 | Cash – Recovery of damages from director | 5,000 |
| Profit and Loss Account .. .. | 85,000 | | |
| Debtors .. .. .. .. | 7,500 | | |
| Stock .. .. .. .. | 10,000 | | |
| Capital Reserve – Balance transferred .. | 33,500 | | |
| | £212,000 | | £212,000 |

## (b) Other modes of Reduction of Capital

Share capital is reduced by share forfeiture. Reissue of forfeited shares does not require sanction of the court, the forfeiture being carried out under the terms of the Articles for non-payment of calls or premiums on shares.

Shares cannot be surrendered unless they have already been forfeited. A company cannot buy its own shares; redeemable preference shares can be repaid but the capital repaid must be replaced either by a fresh issue or by a Capital Redemption Reserve Fund.

### (c) *Schemes for Capital Reduction*

Capital reduction schemes are only worth considering if the company has recovery prospects; the rights of the various classes of persons interested must be considered. The object of the scheme is the resumption of dividend payments.

The first step is to determine the amount required to eliminate any fictitious assets, and write down over-valued assets; over-valuation of assets may result in excessive charges to Profit and Loss Account for depreciation, causing profits to be understated or losses overstated.

**Illustration (1)**

Plant standing in the books at £100,000 is depreciated at the rate of 10 per cent. per annum; a current valuation on a going concern basis shows that the plant is worth £40,000. The reduction of £60,000 is a loss of capital and the decrease in the charge for depreciation from £10,000 to £4,000 might make all the difference between a profit and a loss or the payment or non-payment of dividends.

Debit balances on Profit and Loss Account and fictitious assets, e.g. preliminary expenses should be written off; goodwill, patents, trade marks, patterns etc. should be written down to their book values.

Having determined the total amount to be written off the rights of the debenture holders, creditors and various classes of shareholders must be considered. The following factors are relevant:

1. *Debenture holders* can sometimes be persuaded to make sacrifices to give the company a new lease of life. If it can be proved that on a forced realization of assets such as would ensue if the company were driven into liquidation, the assets, after providing for preferential creditors and the costs, would not realize sufficient to repay the debentures in full, but that there is every prospect of the security being enhanced in the future if the company is reorganized, then the debenture holders may consent to co-operate by sacrificing some of their capital. Some recompense is usually required, e.g. an increased rate of interest, and/or an interest in the equity by the issue to them of fully-paid ordinary shares for a proportion of their capital contribution to the amount required for writing off assets.

2. *Creditors*, other than preferential creditors in a winding-up, may agree to share in a reduction particularly if the debenture holders have agreed to a sacrifice, since in a liquidation they would obtain little or nothing. It must be proved to creditors that they will obtain more by accepting a reduction than by forcing the company into liquidation.

Usually, neither debenture holders nor creditors can be expected to share in the reduction, the amount required being provided by writing down share capital alone.

3. *Shareholders.* The bulk of the loss, usually the whole of it, must fall upon the shareholders. If creditors are to come into the scheme, the shareholders must surrender something to them, e.g. a share in the equity that will enable the creditors to reap some reward in future years for their immediate sacrifice.

It is now necessary to consider the position of the various classes of share-holders.

Where capital has been lost, the brunt of the loss must fall on the ordinary shareholders, but if this meant the loss of their whole interest in the company they would not agree to the scheme. The company may have retained in the past profits which could have been distributed as dividends, but which the share-holders allowed to remain in order to strengthen the company's finances. As the company fell on lean times such reserves may have been drawn upon to pay preference dividends, with the result that the ordinary shareholders have already made a sacrifice for the benefit of the preference shareholders.

It is essential to appreciate the effect of writing down capital, for example, the capital of a company is £100,000, divided into 60,000 6 per cent. preference shares of £1 each and 40,000 £1 ordinary shares. Profits, after the preference dividend of £3,600 has been paid, are divisible among the ordinary shareholders. It does not matter to what nominal value the ordinary shares are written down; the *amount* of the dividend per share remains the same, and the market value of the shares will not be affected by the reduction in nominal value. Writing down ordinary shares therefore entails no real sacrifice so long as the shareholders' interest in the divisible profits is not reduced. A reduction in the nominal value of the preference shares, however, or in their rate of dividend, will reduce the preference shareholders' participation in profits and, consequently, the market value of their shares. Again, if the preference shares have the right to preferential repayment of capital, but are entitled to no right to share in a surplus on a winding-up, the ordinary shareholders will receive all the assets remaining after repaying the preference capital, no matter what the nominal value of the ordinary shares may be. Writing down ordinary shares imposes only a nominal sacrifice upon the holders of such shares.

Where preference shareholders are entitled to share in a surplus the writing down of the ordinary shares does involve a sacrifice of rights, since a bigger pro-portion of any surplus would then go to the preference shareholders. The ulti-mate winding-up rights, however, are not so immediately important as the dividend, i.e. going concern rights, and, therefore, where preference share-holders are called upon to share in a reduction of capital it is only equitable that ordinary shareholders should surrender part of their rights to the preference shareholders.

Preference shareholders should only be asked to share in a reduction if the amount to be written off exceeds the ordinary share capital; either their capital and/or their rate of dividend may be reduced; they should be compensated by a share in the equity so that they may recoup their losses should the company's fortunes improve.

Arrears of cumulative preference dividends must be dealt with on their merits. If they are cancelled, the preference shareholders should be compensated by the issue of shares or income certificates (to be paid off out of future profits in priority to dividends) for the whole or part of the arrears, the cancellation of which will benefit the ordinary shareholders.

The test of whether the scheme is reasonably equitable is to compute how the estimated future income will be divisible under the new share capital holdings compared with the old, bearing in mind that all classes of shares can anticipate immediate dividends instead of waiting until the debit balance on Profit and Loss Account is eliminated by profits. The benefit of immediate dividends is greater, the lower the priority the class of shares has. Deferred shares, as a rule, will have to be cancelled, or given a very minute interest in the reorganized company. If, however, they hold valuable rights *pari passu* with the ordinary shares, they will have to rank equitably with the latter.

### Illustration (2)

The following is the Balance Sheet of Mills Ltd as on December 31st:

| | £ | | | | £ |
|---|---|---|---|---|---|
| Capital Authorized and Issued: | | Goodwill .. .. | .. | .. | 100,000 |
| 250,000 6 per cent. Cumulative Preference | | Patents and Trade Marks | .. | .. | 80,000 |
| Shares of £1 each .. .. .. | 250,000 | Freehold Land and Buildings | .. | | 135,000 |
| 250,000 Ordinary Shares of £1 each .. | 250,000 | Plant and Machinery | .. | .. | 85,000 |
| 6 per cent. Debentures secured by a floating | | Stock-in-Trade .. .. | .. | .. | 79,900 |
| charge on the assets .. .. .. | 100,000 | Debtors .. .. | .. | .. | 110,000 |
| Arrears of Interest thereon .. .. | 12,000 | Cash in Hand .. .. | .. | .. | 100 |
| Creditors .. .. .. .. | 64,000 | Profit and Loss Account .. | .. | .. | 110,000 |
| Bank Overdraft .. .. .. .. | 24,000 | | | | |
| | £700,000 | | | | £700,000 |

The dividends on the preference shares are five years in arrear.

The directors state that the current trading results show a marked improvement, and that they anticipate a net profit of £20,000 per annum will be maintained in future years.

They desire to resume the payment of dividends as soon as possible and are accordingly considering the reduction of the company's capital.

The debenture holders, to assist in the revival of the company, have expressed their willingness to exchange their arrears of interest for an interest in the equity of the business of one-half of the nominal value of the arrears, and to provide £25,000 further cash (on a floating charge) to repay the bank overdraft and to provide working capital of £1,000.

The preference shares are described by the Articles as not preferential to capital, but any arrears of dividends are to form a first charge upon any surplus on winding-up. The preference shareholders have expressed their willingness to a reduction in the rate of dividend to 5 per cent. and to forego two-thirds of their arrears, provided that they receive an interest in the equity equal in nominal value to the remaining third.

You are required:

(a) To draft a suggested scheme for the reduction of capital which should include the elimination of goodwill (acquired from James Mill on the formation of the company in exchange for 100,000 ordinary shares which he still holds) and the Profit and Loss Account balance, the reduction of the value of patents and trade marks by £50,000, and the provision of a capital reserve through which any adjustments arising out of the capital rearrangements etc. may be dealt with. After reduction, the ordinary shares are to be converted into 5p shares.

(b) To re-draft the Balance Sheet, giving effect to the scheme you suggest.

*Scheme for Reduction of Capital*

The capital must be reduced by £285,000, made up as follows:

| | £ |
|---|---|
| To eliminate Goodwill.. .. .. .. .. | 100,000 |
| ,,     ,,     Profit and Loss Account balance .. .. | 110,000 |
| ,, write down Patents and Trade Marks .. .. | 50,000 |
| ,, provide for one-third of arrears of Preference Dividend .. | 25,000 |
| | £285,000 |

Since the preference shares are not entitled to a prior return of capital at first sight the loss of capital should be borne equally between the ordinary and preference shareholders. It makes no difference that the preference shareholders are to receive a share in the equity of £25,000 for the cancellation of £75,000 dividend arrears. But since the preference shareholders have consented to a reduction in their rate of cumulative dividend to 5 per cent., which, of itself, will reduce the value of their shares, they should be required to suffer a correspondingly smaller reduction in their nominal capital.

The capital should be reorganized as follows:

1. The 250,000 6 per cent. cumulative preference shares of £1 each to be reduced to shares of £0·675 each, and subdivided into:

|  |  | £ |
|---|---|---|
| 250,000 5 per cent. cumulative preference shares of 50p each | . . £125,000 | |
| 875,000 ordinary shares of 5p each     . .        . .        . . | . . 43,750 | |
| | £168,750 | |

This represents a reduction in capital of    . .    . .    . .    . .    81,250

In addition, the preference shareholders to receive 500,000 ordinary shares of 5p each=£25,000, in satisfaction of one-third of their arrears of dividend, the balance to be cancelled.

2. The 250,000 ordinary shares of £1 each to be reduced to shares of 20p each, and converted into 1,000,000 ordinary shares of 5p each

This represents a reduction in capital of    . .    . .    . .    . .    200,000

3. The debenture holders to be allotted 120,000 ordinary shares of 5p each in satisfaction of half their arrears of interest, the balance to be cancelled.

This represents a reduction of    . .    . .    . .    . .    . .    6,000

Total reduction    . .    . .    . .    . .    £287,250

Of this amount, £285,000 will be applied in writing down the assets and providing for the £25,000 arrears of preference dividend, as shown above. The balance of £2,250 may be applied in meeting the costs of the reduction scheme and any adjustments arising out of it, and in reducing the book value of such other of the assets as may be determined by the directors.

The paid-up capital of the company will now consist of:

| 250,000 5 per cent. cumulative preference shares of 50p each | . . | £125,000 |
|---|---|---|
| 2,495,000 ordinary shares of 5p each    . .    . .    . . | . . | . . 124,750 |
| | | £249,750 |

The resolution for reduction of capital should at the same time provide for the restoration of the authorized capital to £500,000, leaving £250,250 unissued capital, which would be available for issue at some future date, if required.

The effect of the above reorganization of capital, assuming an annual profit of £20,000 to be maintained, will be to cause the profits to be divided between the existing preference and ordinary shareholders in approximately the following proportions. Although on a profit of £20,000, the preference shareholders will receive a little less than previously, their holding of ordinary shares will give them the control of the company, and they will take a major share in any increase in distributable profits over £20,000.

|  | £ | £ |
|---|---|---|
| Existing preference shareholders will receive: | | |
| Dividend of 5 per cent. on £125,000 new preference shares . . | . . 6,250 | |
| Dividend of, say, 10 per cent. on £68,750 new ordinary shares | . . 6,875 | |
| Carried forward | | 13,125 |

| | Brought forward | £13,125 |
|---|---|---|
| Existing ordinary shareholders will receive: | | |
| Dividend of, say, 10 per cent. on £50,000 new ordinary shares | .. | 5,000 |
| Debenture holders will receive: | | |
| Dividend of, say, 10 per cent. on £6,000 new ordinary shares | .. | 600 |
| | | 18,725 |
| Carry forward    ..    ..    ..    ..    ..    .. | .. | 1,275 |
| | | £20,000 |

*Note:* It is assumed that the debenture interest would already have been provided for before arriving at the profit of £20,000.

### MILLS LTD
### RE-DRAFTED BALANCE SHEET

| | £ | £ | | £ | £ |
|---|---|---|---|---|---|
| **CAPITAL** | | | **FIXED ASSETS** | | |
| Authorized   ..   ..   .. | 500,000 | | Patents and Trade Marks    .. | 30,000 | |
| | | | Freehold Land and Buildings   .. | 135,000 | |
| Issued | | | Plant and Machinery   ..   .. | 85,000 | |
| 250,000 5 per cent. Cumulative | | | | | 250,000 |
| Preference Shares of 50p each | 125,000 | | **CURRENT ASSETS** | | |
| 2,495,000 Ordinary Shares of 5p | | | Stock-in-Trade   ..   ..   .. | 79,900 | |
| each   ..   ..   .. | 124,750 | | Debtors   ..   ..   .. | 110,000 | |
| | | 249,750 | Cash   ..   ..   .. | 1,100 | |
| Capital Reserve ..   ..   .. | | 2,250 | | | 191,000 |
| 6 per cent. Debentures secured by a | | | | | |
| floating charge on the assets   .. | | 125,000 | | | |
| Creditors   ..   ..   .. | | 64,000 | | | |
| | | £441 000 | | | £441,000 |

## § 20. Reconstructions and Reorganizations

The sale of the undertaking of an existing company to a new company specially formed for that purpose is termed a reconstruction, and may be resorted to for any of the following objects:

1. For the purpose of raising fresh capital by issuing partly paid shares in the new company in exchange for fully paid shares in the old company, and calling up the balance of such new shares as and when required.

2. For amalgamating two or more companies.

3. For taking new powers in the Memorandum, or changing the domicil of the company.

4. For rearranging the capital and the rights of members as between themselves.

5. For effecting a compromise with creditors, or the allotment to them of shares or debentures in settlement of their claims.

The amalgamation and absorption of one company by another has already been dealt with.

Where it is proposed to wind-up a company voluntarily, and to dispose of the whole or part of its undertaking to another company in consideration for shares in that company, to be distributed rateably amongst the shareholders of the vendor company, the scheme must be approved by the members by special resolution (in a creditors' winding-up, with the sanction of the committee of inspection or of the court). Any dissentient member may call upon the liquidator by notice in writing within seven days of the date of the resolution, either to abandon the scheme, or purchase the dissentient's interest at a price to be agreed or settled by arbitration. This course might be adopted where the shares of the new company are to be allotted as only partly paid.

If the liquidator elects to purchase the member's interest, the purchase money must be paid before the company is dissolved, and be raised by the liquidator in such manner as may be determined by special resolution (s. 287).

Shares not taken up by shareholders can be allotted to the nominee of the liquidator, who will sell them for the best price he can obtain, and divide the proceeds among the shareholders who dissent from the scheme.

Where a company has sustained a considerable loss of capital and is unable to satisfy its creditors in full, the reconstruction scheme commonly provides for a reduction of the original capital, a compromise with the creditors either for cash or for the issue of fully paid shares or debentures and the provision of new working capital by the issue to the existing shareholders of partly paid up shares, in exchange for the shares held in the old company.

**Illustration**

The final Trial Balance of the Patent Bottle Company Limited was as follows:

| Share Capital: | | | | | | £ | £ |
|---|---|---|---|---|---|---|---|
| 50,000 Shares of £1 each fully paid | .. | .. | .. | .. | | | 50,000 |
| Creditors .. | .. | .. | .. | .. | .. | .. | 26,500 |
| Patent Rights | .. | .. | .. | .. | .. | 48,000 | |
| Debtors .. | .. | .. | .. | .. | .. | 4,500 | |
| Stock .. | .. | .. | .. | .. | .. | 10,000 | |
| Preliminary Expenses .. | .. | .. | .. | .. | .. | 1,800 | |
| Profit and Loss Account | .. | .. | .. | .. | .. | 12,050 | |
| Cash .. | .. | .. | .. | .. | .. | 150 | |
| | | | | | | £76,500 | £76,500 |

Efforts to secure sufficient new capital to pay off the liabilities and place the concern on a sound basis having proved unsuccessful, it was decided to reconstruct, and the following scheme was submitted to, and approved by, the shareholders and creditors:

1. The company to go into voluntary liquidation, and a new company having a nominal capital of £100,000 to be formed, called the New Patent Bottle Company Limited, to take over the assets and liabilities of the old company.

2. The assets to be taken over at book value, with the exception of the patent rights, which were to be subject to adjustment.

3. The creditors to be discharged by the new company on the following basis:        £

| | £ |
|---|---|
| Preferential creditors to be paid in full .. .. .. .. | 500 |
| Unsecured creditors to be discharged by cash composition of 50p in the £ .. | 13,400 |
| Unsecured creditors to be discharged by issue of 6 per cent. debentures fully paid at a bonus of 10 per cent. .. .. .. .. .. .. | 12,600 |
| | £26,500 |

4. 50,000 shares of £1 each, 50p paid up, to be issued to the shareholders in the old company, payable 25p on application and 25p on allotment.

5. The costs of liquidation amounting to £250 to be paid by the new company as part of the purchase consideration.

Close the books of the old company, and show the opening entries in the new company's books, preparing therefrom a Balance Sheet, assuming all the shares and debentures have been allotted, and all the cash for the shares has been received.

### OLD COMPANY'S BOOKS
### JOURNAL

| | | £ | £ |
|---|---|---:|---:|
| Realization Account .. .. .. .. .. .. .. .. | Dr | 62,650 | |
| To Patent Rights .. .. .. .. .. .. .. .. | | | 48,000 |
| ,, Debtors .. .. .. .. .. .. .. .. | | | 4,500 |
| ,, Stock .. .. .. .. .. .. .. .. | | | 10 000 |
| ,, Cash .. .. .. .. .. .. .. .. | | | 150 |
| Sundry Assets transferred. | | | |
| | | | |
| Realization Account .. .. .. .. .. .. .. .. | Dr | 1,260 | |
| To Creditors | | | 1,260 |
| Bonus of 10 per cent. on £12,600, payable in 6 per cent. Debentures fully paid, as per agreement. | | | |
| | | | |
| Purchasing Company .. .. .. .. .. .. .. .. | Dr | 46,310 | |
| To Realization Account .. .. .. .. .. .. .. | | | 46,310 |
| Purchase consideration payable under scheme as follows: | | | |
| 50,000 Shares of £1 each, 50p paid up, to be issued to Shareholders ..   £25,000 | | | |
| £13,860 6 per cent. Debentures fully paid, to be issued to Creditors in part payment   13,860 | | | |
| Cash to Creditors in part payment of Unsecured Creditors and in full discharge of | | | |
| Preferential Creditors .. .. .. .. .. .. ..   7,200 | | | |
| Cash for Liquidation Expenses ..   250 | | | |
|   £46,310 | | | |
| | | | |
| Realization Account .. .. .. .. .. .. .. .. | Dr | 250 | |
| To Cash .. .. .. .. .. .. .. .. | | | 250 |
| Payment of Liquidation Expenses. | | | |
| | | | |
| Shares Account – 50,000 shares of £1 each, 50p paid up .. .. .. .. | Dr | 25 000 | |
| Debentures Account – £13,860 6 per cent. Debentures .. .. .. .. | | 13,860 | |
| Cash .. .. .. .. .. .. | | 7,450 | |
| To Purchasing Company | | | 46,310 |
| Assets handed over by New Company to liquidator in settlement of purchase consideration. | | | |
| | | | |
| Creditors .. .. .. .. .. .. .. .. | Dr | 27,760 | |
| To Debentures .. .. .. .. .. .. .. .. | | | 13,860 |
| ,, Cash .. .. .. .. .. .. .. .. | | | 7,200 |
| ,, Realization Account .. .. .. .. .. .. .. | | | 6,700 |
| Discharge of amounts due to Creditors as per agreement, and transfer of balance to Realization Account. | | | |
| | | | |
| Sundry Members .. .. .. .. .. .. .. .. | Dr | 11,150 | |
| To Realization Account .. .. .. .. .. .. .. | | | 11,150 |
| Loss on Realization. | | | |
| | | | |
| Sundry Members .. .. .. .. .. .. .. .. | Dr | 13,850 | |
| To Profit and Loss Account .. .. .. .. .. .. | | | 12,050 |
| ,, Preliminary Expenses .. .. .. .. .. .. .. | | | 1,800 |
| Balances transferred. | | | |
| | | | |
| Share Capital .. .. .. .. .. .. .. .. | Dr | 50,000 | |
| To Sundry Members Account .. .. .. .. .. .. | | | 50,000 |
| Share Capital transferred. | | | |
| | | | |
| Sundry Members .. .. .. .. .. .. .. .. | Dr | 25,000 | |
| To Shares in New Company | | | 25,000 |
| Issue of 50,000 Shares £1 each, 50p paid up in New Company in exchange for Shares in Old Company. | | | |

### LEDGER
### REALIZATION ACCOUNT

| | £ | | £ |
|---|---:|---|---:|
| Patent Rights .. .. .. .. | 48,000 | Purchasing Company – Purchase consideration | 46,310 |
| Debtors .. .. .. .. .. | 4,500 | Creditors. Rebate allowed .. .. | 6,700 |
| Stock .. .. .. .. .. | 10,000 | Sundry Members Account, Loss .. .. | 11,150 |
| Cash .. .. .. .. .. | 150 | | |
| Creditors 10 per cent. Bonus .. .. | 1,260 | | |
| Cash – Expenses .. .. .. .. | 250 | | |
| | £64,160 | | £64,160 |

### PURCHASING COMPANY

| | £ | | £ |
|---|---|---|---|
| Realization Account – Purchase consideration | 46,310 | Shares in Purchasing Company .. | 25,000 |
| | | Debentures in Purchasing Company .. | 13,860 |
| | | Cash ..  ..  ..  .. | 7,450 |
| | £46,310 | | £46,310 |

### SUNDRY CREDITORS

| | £ | | £ |
|---|---|---|---|
| Debentures in New Company .. .. | 13,860 | Balance b/f. ..  ..  .. | 26,500 |
| Cash .. .. .. .. .. | 7,200 | Realization Account .. .. .. | 1,260 |
| Realization Account .. .. .. | 6,700 | | |
| | £27,760 | | £27,760 |

### SUNDRY MEMBERS

| | £ | | £ |
|---|---|---|---|
| Realization Account, Loss .. .. .. | 11,150 | Share Capital Account .. .. .. | 50,000 |
| Profit and Loss Account .. .. .. | 12,050 | | |
| Preliminary Expenses .. .. .. | 1,800 | | |
| Shares in New Company .. .. .. | 25,000 | | |
| | £50,000 | | £50,000 |

### CASH BOOK

| | £ | | £ |
|---|---|---|---|
| Purchasing Company .. .. .. | 7,450 | Creditors .. .. .. | 7,200 |
| | | Liquidation Expenses .. .. .. | 250 |
| | £7,450 | | £7,450 |

## NEW COMPANY'S BOOKS
### JOURNAL

| | | £ | £ |
|---|---|---|---|
| Patent Rights .. .. .. .. .. .. .. .. .. | Dr | 31,660 | |
| Debtors .. .. .. .. .. .. .. .. | | 4,500 | |
| Stock .. .. .. .. .. .. .. .. | | 10,000 | |
| Cash .. .. .. .. .. .. .. .. | | 150 | |
|  To Vendor .. .. .. .. .. .. .. | | | 46,310 |
| Assets taken over per scheme of reconstruction. | | | |
| Vendor .. .. .. .. .. .. | Dr | 46,310 | |
|  To Share Capital Account – 50,000 Shares of £1 each, 50p paid up .. .. | | | 25,000 |
|  ,, 6 per cent. Debentures .. .. .. .. .. | | | 13,860 |
|  ,, Cash .. .. .. .. .. .. | | | 7,450 |
| Shares and Debentures issued and Cash paid in settlement of purchase consideration. | | | |
| Application and Allotment Account .. .. .. .. .. | Dr | 25,000 | |
|  To Share Capital .. .. .. .. .. | | | 25,000 |
| 25p per Share payable on application and 25p on allotment of 50,000 Shares issued. | | | |

### CASH BOOK

| | £ | | £ |
|---|---|---|---|
| Vendor .. .. .. .. .. | 150 | Vendor .. .. .. .. | 7,450 |
| Application .. .. .. .. | 12,500 | Balance c/f. .. .. .. .. | 17,700 |
| Allotment .. .. .. .. | 12,500 | | |
| | £25,150 | | £25,150 |

## BALANCE SHEET
### as at................................

| | £ | | | | | | £ |
|---|---|---|---|---|---|---|---|
| Authorized Capital: | | Patent Rights at cost | .. | .. | .. | | 31,660 |
| 100,000 Shares £1 each .. | .. .. | 100,000 | Debtors | .. | .. | .. | 4,500 |
| | | Stock .. | .. | .. | .. | .. | 10 000 |
| Issued Capital: | | Cash .. | .. | .. | .. | .. | 17,700 |
| 50,000 Shares £1 each, fully paid .. | .. | 50,000 | | | | | |
| 6 per cent. Debentures .. | .. .. | 13,860 | | | | | |
| | | £63,860 | | | | | £63,860 |

*Notes:*

(*a*) PAYMENT OF CREDITORS

As the liquidator is responsible to the creditors of the old company to see that the conditions of the scheme of reconstruction are carried out, the liabilities will be discharged through him, and the transactions will consequently be recorded in the books of the old company.

(*b*) THE ADJUSTED VALUE OF THE PATENT RIGHTS

The value placed upon the patent rights is the difference between the purchase price payable to the vendor and the assets taken over upon which an agreed value was placed.

## CHAPTER IX

# THE ACCOUNTS OF HOLDING COMPANIES

## § 1. Holding Companies

In addition to trading, many companies invest substantial capital in the purchase of shares in subsidiary companies in order to control their operations. Sometimes the whole of the share capital of the holding company is employed in this way and no trading operations are carried on direct. Control of the subsidiary companies is secured by acquiring a majority of the shares carrying voting rights, which empowers the holding company to control the composition of the board of directors of the subsidiary.

The more important advantages of the holding company system are:

1. A number of businesses can be amalgamated but yet their separate entities and connections are preserved.

2. Where it is desired to decentralize an existing business, subsidiary companies may be formed to take over certain of its branches or activities.

3. The retention of the separate entities of the members of the group will enable any unrelieved losses or writing down allowances to continue to be carried forward and set off against future profits.

4. If it is desired to discontinue certain of the operations, only the subsidiary company or companies carrying on those operations need be closed down or the interest therein sold, whereas if all the businesses are merged into one, the discontinuance of part might be much more difficult and disturbing.

5. Since each company must prepare separate accounts, the separate results of each business are available, whereas in a single concern there might be a temptation to dispense with the necessary analysis required to ascertain departmental results.

6. Most of the advantages of complete amalgamation apply equally to the holding company type of merger.

7. The capital structure of the subsidiary companies can be retained, e.g. the subsidiary companies' preference shares can continue to carry the rate of interest at which they were issued; debentures in subsidiaries can continue to carry the rate of interest at which they were issued and the terms on which any security given for them can remain unchanged.

Where one company desires to obtain a controlling interest in another company, shares can either be acquired by purchase in the open market, or an offer can be made to its shareholders through its directors. Often the purchasing company may not be able to acquire the whole of the shares, and the acquisition of a majority of the shares carrying the voting rights is all that is considered necessary. Sometimes it may be desired to obtain a complete interest, and this is rendered possible under Section 209 of the *Companies Act 1948*, which provides that where a scheme or contract involving the transfer of shares has, within four months after the making of the offer, been approved by the holders of not less than nine-tenths in value of the shares affected (other than shares already held by the transferee company or its nominee), the transferee company may, at any time within two months after the expiration of the said four months, give notice in the prescribed manner to any dissentient shareholder that it desires to acquire his shares. It is then entitled and bound to acquire those shares on the same terms as those on which the other shares are to be transferred, unless the court, upon the application of the dissentient shareholder, within one month of the date of the notice orders otherwise.

Where the transferee company already holds more than one-tenth of the aggregate value of the class (or classes) of shares under consideration (i.e. *excluding* shares already held), the foregoing provisions shall not apply, unless:

(*a*) the transferee company offers the same terms to all holders of the shares whose transfer is involved; and

(*b*) the holders who approve the scheme or contract, besides holding not less than nine-tenths in value of the said shares (other than those already held) represent not less than 75 per cent. of the holders of those shares (s. 209 (1)).

Where in any such scheme or contract, shares in a company are transferred to another company or its nominee, and those shares, together with any other such shares already held by the transferee company or its subsidiary, comprise or include nine-tenths in value of the shares in the transferor company, or of any class thereof, the transferee company must, within one month from the date of the transfer, give notice of that fact in the prescribed manner to the holders of the remaining shares who have not assented to the scheme. Any such holder may then, within three months, require the transferee company to acquire his shares, and the transferee company shall then be entitled and bound to acquire those shares on the same terms as those under which the shares of the approving shareholders were transferred to it, or on such other terms as may be agreed or as the court thinks fit to order (s. 209 (2)).

Where a notice has been given under Section 209 (1), and the court has not, upon application, seen fit to interfere, the transferee company shall at the expiration of one month from the date of the notice, or upon the disposal of the application to the court, transmit a copy of the notice to the transferor company together with an instrument of transfer duly executed, and pay the amount of the consideration for the shares to be acquired, and the transferee company shall then be registered as the holder of the shares in question.

The consideration shall be paid into a separate bank account, to be held on trust for the shareholders entitled thereto, who can presumably obtain it upon surrender of their share certificates (s. 209 (3)).

Apart from the statutory requirements the boards of companies involved in take-over and merger arrangements have, since early 1968, had to comply with the requirements of the City Code on Take-overs and Mergers. The latter is implemented by a specially appointed Take-over Panel. The intention behind the City Code was to lay down principles to be followed by all parties engaged in take-over, merger and similar proceedings, and the whole text of the Code was revised in April, 1969 in the light of the experience gained by the panel during their first year of office (when they investigated some 300–400 individual cases). The decisions of the panel are not supported by statutory sanctions, but they have the powerful support of:

(*a*) the Board of Trade, and

(*b*) members of the major long-established city institutions, e.g. the Issuing Houses Association, with the result that any delinquent member bears the risk of exclusion from his appropriate parent body.

Findings of the panel which are felt to have a bearing on the contemporary conduct of procedings within this sphere, are given expression by the issue of 'Practice Notes' whenever appropriate.

## § 2. Definition of Subsidiary Company

Section 154 of the *Companies Act 1948* defines a subsidiary. The following is a précis of the provisions:

A company is considered to be the subsidiary of another if:

(*a*) that other company either:

 (i) is a member of and controls the composition of its Board of directors; or

 (ii) holds more than half in nominal value of its 'equity' share capital; or

(*b*) the first mentioned company is a subsidiary of any company which is that other's subsidiary.

A person or a company is considered to control the composition of the Board of directors if without the consent or concurrence of anybody else he can appoint or remove the holders of all or a majority of directorships, and, if he can veto the appointment of directors, or if his appointment necessarily follows his appointment to the Board of the other company, or if the directorship is held by the other company itself or by one of its subsidiaries.

In determining whether a company is a holding company, shares held in a fiduciary capacity or as security for a loan are ignored.

The expression 'equity share capital' means issued share capital, except any part which, *neither* as respects dividend *nor* as respects capital carries any right to participate beyond a specified amount in a distribution. Preference shares carrying the right to a fixed rate of dividend, but which are entitled to participate beyond a fixed amount in a winding-up would appear, however, to be part of the equity share capital for this purpose.

For A Ltd to be a subsidiary of B Ltd:

(*a*) B Ltd must *both* hold shares in, *and* control the composition of the board of directors of A Ltd in the manner defined in the Act; or

(*b*) B Ltd or other subsidiaries or nominees of B Ltd must together hold more than half in nominal value of the equity share capital of A Ltd; or

(*c*) A Ltd must be a subsidiary of another company which itself is a subsidiary of B Ltd.

In determining whether B Ltd holds more than half of the equity share capital of A Ltd, any shares in A Ltd held by a nominee or subsidiary of B Ltd will be considered to be held by B Ltd.

A body corporate or its nominee cannot be a member of a company which is its holding company, and any allotment or transfer of shares in a company to its subsidiary is void, except as follows:

(a) Where the subsidiary is concerned as personal representative or as trustee (unless the holding company or a subsidiary thereof is beneficially interested under the trust and is not so interested merely by way of security for money lent in the ordinary course of a business which includes lending money);

(b) Where a subsidiary was a member of its holding company at July 1st, 1948, it may continue to be a member, but shall have no right to vote at any meeting of the holding company or any class of members thereof (s. 27).

A subsidiary company must be distinguished from an associated company. An associated company engages in similar business, but is not a subsidiary; share-holdings in an associated company should be classified as quoted or unquoted investments; it is possible for the directors of the associated company to be the same as those of the company who owns its shares.

## § 3. Group Accounts

Where at the end of its financial year a company has subsidiaries, accounts or statements (referred to as 'group accounts') dealing with the state of affairs and profit or loss of the company and the subsidiaries must be laid before the company in general meeting when the company's own Balance Sheet and Profit and Loss Account are so laid, except that:

(a) group accounts are not required where the company is at the end of its financial year the wholly owned subsidiary of another body corporate incorporated in Great Britain. A wholly owned subsidiary is one which has no members other than its holding company and that holding company's wholly owned subsidiaries and its or their nominees; and

(b) group accounts need not deal with a subsidiary of the company if the company's directors are of opinion that:

　(i) it is impracticable, or would be of no real value to members of the company, in view of the insignificant amounts involved, or would involve expense or delay out of proportion to the value to members of the company; or

　(ii) the result would be misleading, or harmful to the business of the company or any of its subsidiaries; or

　(iii) the business of the holding company and that of the subsidiary are so different that they cannot reasonably be treated as a single undertaking;

and, if the directors are of such an opinion about each of the company's subsidiaries, group accounts shall not be required.

It is, however, provided that the approval of the Board of Trade shall be required for not dealing in group accounts with a subsidiary on the ground that the result would be harmful, or on the ground of the difference between the business of the holding company and that of the subsidiary (s. 150).

The group accounts laid before a holding company must be consolidated accounts comprising:

(a) a Consolidated Balance Sheet dealing with the state of affairs of the company and all the subsidiaries to be dealt with in group accounts;

(b) a Consolidated Profit and Loss Account dealing with the profit or loss of the company and those subsidiaries.

If, however, the company's directors are of opinion that it is better for the purpose of presenting the same or equivalent information about the state of affairs and profit or loss of the company and those subsidiaries, so that it may be readily appreciated by the company's members, the group accounts may be prepared in some other form. In particular they may consist of more than one set of consolidated accounts, dealing respectively with the company and one group of subsidiaries, and with other groups of subsidiaries, or of separate accounts dealing with each of the subsidiaries, or of statements expanding the information about the subsidiaries in the company's own accounts, or any combination of those forms.

The group accounts may be wholly or partly incorporated in the company's own Balance Sheet and Profit and Loss Account (s. 151).

The following are some of the forms of group accounts, other than the conventional Consolidated Balance Sheet and Profit and Loss Account, which are met with in practice:

(i) Consolidated statements of assets and earnings of some or all of the subsidiaries. Sometimes the earnings of all the companies in the group are consolidated, but separate statements are submitted with regard to the net assets of some or all of the subsidiaries. This method may be useful where the parent company has substantial interests in foreign companies and exchange restrictions operate.

(ii) The separate Balance Sheets and Profit and Loss Accounts of subsidiaries, amplified by such notes as are necessary, are submitted as exhibits to the holding company's own accounts. This method may be useful where a company has only one or two subsidiaries, or has a subsidiary whose business is entirely different from that of the holding company and its other subsidiaries.

(iii) The insertion of notes in the separate accounts of the holding company, or in the consolidated accounts.

Sometimes the consolidated figures are shown in columns provided in the holding company's own accounts, any necessary additional information being given by way of notes.

The group accounts must give a true and fair view of the state of affairs and profit or loss of the company and the subsidiaries dealt with thereby as a whole, so far as concerns members of the holding company.

Where the financial year of a subsidiary does not coincide with that of the holding company, the group accounts must, unless the Board of Trade, on the application or with the consent of the holding company's directors, otherwise directs, deal with the subsidiary's state of affairs as at the end of its financial year ending with or last before that of the holding company, and with the subsidiary's profit or loss for that financial year.

If prepared as consolidated accounts, the group accounts must comply with the requirements of the Eighth Schedule to the 1948 Act as amended by the Second Schedule to the 1967 Act (*see below and Appendix II*), so far as applicable thereto, and if not so prepared must give the same or equivalent information. The Board of Trade may, however, on the application or with the consent of a company's directors, modify the requirements for the purpose of adapting them to the circumstances of the company (s. 152).

A holding company's directors must secure that except where, in their opinion, there are good reasons against it, the financial year of each of its subsidiaries shall coincide with the company's own financial year (s. 153 (1)).

Where it appears to the Board of Trade desirable for a holding company or a holding company's subsidiary to extend its financial year so that the subsidiary's financial year may end with that of the holding company, and for that purpose to postpone the submission of the relevant accounts to a general meeting from one calendar year to the next, the Board may on the application, or with the consent, of the directors of the company whose financial year is to be extended direct that, for that company, the submission of accounts to a general meeting, the holding of an annual general meeting or the making of an annual return shall not be required in the earlier of the said calendar years (s. 153 (2)).

The Second Schedule of the *Companies Act 1967*, Part II, contains the accounting provisions for holding and subsidiary companies which can be summarized as follows:

1. The holding company's Balance Sheet must show *separately:*

(*a*) the aggregate amount of assets consisting of shares in subsidiaries;

(*b*) the aggregate amount of indebtedness of subsidiaries to the holding company;

(*c*) the aggregate amount of indebtedness of the holding company to the subsidiaries.

2. The accounting requirements for investments do not apply to investments in subsidiaries;

3. The holding company's Balance Sheet must show by way of note the amount of its shares and debentures held by subsidiaries, other than in a fiduciary capacity.

4. WHERE GROUP ACCOUNTS ARE NOT SUBMITTED, there shall be annexed to the Balance Sheet a statement showing –

(*a*) the reasons why subsidiaries are not dealt with in group accounts;

(*b*) the net aggregate amount, so far as it concerns members of the holding company and is not dealt with in the company's accounts, of the subsidiaries' profits after deducting the subsidiaries' losses (or vice versa) *since acquisition*:

   (i) for the respective financial years of the subsidiaries ending with or during the financial year of the company; and

   (ii) for their previous financial years since they respectively became the holding company's subsidiary;

(c) the net aggregate amount of the subsidiaries' profits after deducting the subsidiaries' losses (or vice versa) *since acquisition*:

   (i) for the respective financial years of the subsidiaries ending with or during the financial year of the company; and

   (ii) for their other financial years since they respectively became the holding company's subsidiary;

so far as those profits are dealt with, or provision is made for those losses, in the company's accounts;

(d) qualifications contained in the reports of the auditors of subsidiaries.

5. WHERE GROUP ACCOUNTS ARE NOT SUBMITTED, there shall be annexed to the Balance Sheet a statement showing, in relation to the subsidiaries (if any) whose financial years did not end with that of the company:

(a) the reasons why the company's directors consider that the subsidiaries' financial years should not end with that of the company; and

(b) the dates on which the subsidiaries' financial years ending last before that of the company respectively ended or the earliest and latest of those dates.

6. A subsidiary's Balance Sheet must show:

(i) The aggregate amount of its indebtedness to its holding company and fellow subsidiaries;

(ii) The aggregate amount of indebtedness of the holding company and fellow subsidiaries to the subsidiary. (Distinction must be made between debentures and other indebtedness.)

7. The provisions of Sections 196 (directors' remuneration) and 197 (loans to officers) of the *Companies Act 1948*, and Sections 6 and 7 (particulars of chairman's and other directors' emoluments) and Section 8 (particulars of employees receiving more than £10,000 per annum) of the *Companies Act 1967* do *not* apply to consolidated accounts. Similarly, consolidated accounts do not need to show movements on reserves.

In the statement on profits and losses of subsidiary companies required by the 1948 Act to be annexed to the Balance Sheet of the holding company where group accounts are not submitted, in the opinion of counsel obtained by the Institute of Chartered Accountants the term 'profits' in paragraph (4) (b) and (c) only includes profits of a subsidiary which are or might have been distributed so as to become revenue profits in the hands of the holding company *in the year to which the holding company's accounts relate*; they do not include profits which have been distributed in past years, which to the extent that they had been received by the holding company would have been dealt with in the previous accounts of that company. In view of the above opinion the Council of the Institute of Chartered Accountants communicated with the Board of Trade, who authorized it to state that no exception will be taken by the Board to the following information being disclosed in the statement:

(*a*) the amount of the profits less losses (or vice versa) of subsidiaries which has neither been dealt with in the holding company's accounts of the year, nor in the accounts of any prior year; and

(*b*) the amount of profits less losses (or vice versa) dealt with in the holding company's accounts of the year, subdivided to distinguish the amounts derived respectively from current and other results of the subsidiaries dealt with.

Where, for example, two wholly owned subsidiaries acquired by a company on January 1st, 1968, made a net aggregate profit (after charging Corporation Tax) of £20,000 in each of the years 1968, 1969 and 1970 and distributed £10,000 (gross) in each year between them, and retained as a revenue reserve £10,000 in each year, the statement recommended by the Council of the Institute would be in the following form:

### PROFITS FOR FINANCIAL YEARS OF SUBSIDIARIES

|  | Ending in 1970 | Other years | Total |
|---|---|---|---|
|  | £ | £ | £ |
| The net aggregate amount of the profits *less* losses of the subsidiaries *so far as it concerns the members of this company:* |  |  |  |
| (i) dealt with in this company's accounts for the year 1970 amounted to (gross) .. .. | 10,000 | — | 10,000 |
| (ii) not dealt with in this company's accounts for the year 1970 or in prior years amounted, after charging taxation, to .. .. .. .. .. .. .. | 10,000 | 20,000 | 30,000 |

Alternatively, the necessary information may be given by means of the following entry and note in the holding company's Profit and Loss Account:

|  | £ | £ |
|---|---|---|
| Dividend (gross) (*less* provisions for losses) from subsidiaries not consolidated: |  |  |
| For their financial years ending in 1970 .. .. .. .. .. .. .. | 10 000 |  |
| For other years .. .. .. .. .. .. .. .. | nil |  |
|  |  | 10,000 |

*Note:* This company's proportion of the undistributed profits, less losses, of these companies not taken into this company's accounts after deducting corporation tax were:

|  | £ |
|---|---|
| For their financial years ending in 1970 .. .. .. .. | 10,000 |
| For prior years since acquisition .. .. .. .. .. | 20,000 |
|  | £30,000 |

It is assumed that the group has elected to pay inter-company dividends gross, which is the general practice.

Where shares are held by a subsidiary in a fellow subsidiary, these must be shown separately in the Balance Sheet of the subsidiary.

## § 4. Consolidated Balance Sheet

### (a) General Principles

A Consolidated Balance Sheet is really a 'Consolidated Statement of Assets and Liabilities', but the more usual title has much to commend it, as it is, in fact, a consolidation of Balance Sheets.

In order to consolidate Balance Sheets it is desirable for them all to be made up to the same date, otherwise adjustments must be made to enable the exact position at the date of the consolidation to be ascertained. All assets and liabilities should be classified in the same manner, and valuations should be made upon the same basis. If this is not done, adjustments should be made to bring them into line.

It is provided by Section 152 of the 1948 Act that where the financial year of a subsidiary does not coincide with that of its holding company, the group accounts must deal with the subsidiary's accounts for its financial year ending with or last before that of the holding company.

Adjustments may be necessary to meet the following circumstances:

1. To provide for any material trading loss known to have been sustained by the subsidiary between the end of its financial year and the date of the consolidated accounts.

2. Where large transfers of cash between one company and another have taken place, or a subsidiary has incurred substantial capital expenditure in the interval between the two Balance Sheet dates, so that the liquid position of the group is materially affected.

3. For the purpose of reconciling the balances on inter-company accounts for cash and other assets in transit at the date of the consolidated accounts.

Where, owing to differences in accounting dates, inter-company balances do not cancel out, it is usual to show the net difference in the Consolidated Balance Sheet under an appropriate heading, such as 'Difference on consolidation between companies with different accounting dates'.

### (b) Problems Involved

The problems involved in consolidating the accounts of several undertakings into one are:

(i) Elimination of inter-company indebtedness, e.g. current accounts, inter-company bills of exchange.

(ii) Calculation of cost of control of subsidiaries.

(iii) Minority interests.

(iv) Pre-acquisition profits and losses; dividends paid out of pre-acquisition profits.

(v) Preference shares in subsidiaries.

(vi) Unrealized inter-company profits.

(vii) Revaluation of assets of subsidiary companies and depreciation thereon.

(viii) Subsidiaries holding shares in other subsidiaries.

### (c) Method of Working

The double-entry method is strongly advocated and in practice a 'Memorandum Ledger' is opened to record the consolidating entries; no adjustments being made in the individual company's books.

Memoranda Ledger Accounts should be opened for:

(i) Every component account of shareholders' funds ,including the holding company's; experienced accountants sometimes omit the Share Capital Account.

(ii) Cost of Control (or Goodwill) for each subsidiary.

(iii) Minority Interests. State at the head of the account the fractional interest, e.g. one-fifth, for quick reference.

(iv) Assets containing inter-company profit loading.

(v) Assets revalued at the time of acquisition by the group if no adjustment has been made to the assets concerned in the books in which they appear.

After writing up these Memoranda Ledger Accounts their closing balances will be transferred to the Consolidated Balance Sheet and the assets and liabilities on the individual companies' balance sheets to which no alteration has been made will be added together and shown on the Consolidated Balance Sheet.

### (d) Inter-Company Balances

As in branch accounts (where each branch maintains separate records) the first step is to eliminate inter-company balances.

Any inter-company indebtedness, in the form of trade debts, loans or Current Account balances, which appears as a liability in the Balance Sheet of one member of the group and as an asset in the Balance Sheet of another, will cancel out in the Consolidated Balance Sheet.

Any difference between the balance on an inter-company Current Account in one company's books and that of the corresponding Current Account in the books of the other company will usually be occasioned by cash or goods in transit, or some other transaction which has been recorded in one set of books but not in the other. The amount of such difference must be transferred out of the 'Memorandum' Current Account affected to the appropriate Value in Transit Account and shown in the Consolidated Balance Sheet as an asset. The Current Accounts in the respective books will then cancel out.

Bills of exchange drawn by one company and accepted by another member of the group are shown in the separate Balance Sheets as bills receivable and bills payable respectively. In the Consolidated Balance Sheet they will cancel each other out, since they represent inter-company indebtedness, and are not assets or liabilities of the group. If, however, a member of the group has discounted any bills drawn by it on, and accepted by, other members of the group, the discounted bills will not appear as assets in the first company's Balance Sheet, but a contingent liability will be noted thereon. In the Consolidated Balance Sheet, however, the discounted bills will appear as an actual, not a contingent, liability, since they are held by persons outside the group, to whom the amounts of the bills will have to be paid on maturity. Only the inter-company bills actually held within the group at the date of the Consolidated Balance Sheet will cancel out.

The following are extracts from the Balance Sheets as at December 31st of a holding company and its subsidiary company. The holding company has a 90 per cent. interest in the subsidiary company. Show how the items would appear in the Consolidated Balance Sheet.

### HOLDING COMPANY

| | £ | | £ |
|---|---|---|---|
| *Note:* There is a contingent liability on Bills Discounted – £1,500　.. 　　.. 　　.. 　　.. | | Bills Receivable (accepted by Subsidiary Company) .. 　　.. 　　.. 　　.. 　　.. | 2,000 |

### SUBSIDIARY COMPANY

| | £ | | £ |
|---|---|---|---|
| Bills payable (drawn by Holding Company)　　.. | 3,500 | | |

### CONSOLIDATED BALANCE SHEET

| | £ | £ | | £ |
|---|---|---|---|---|
| Bills payable　　.. 　　.. 　　.. | 3,500 | | | |
| *Less* held by Holding Company.. 　　.. | 2,000 | 1,500 | | |

### (e) Wholly owned Subsidiaries

Where a company acquires the whole of the share capital of another company, the Consolidated Balance Sheet will consist of the Balance Sheet of the holding company in which 'Shares in Subsidiary Company' is replaced by the actual assets and liabilities of the subsidiary grouped, under their appropriate headings, with those of the holding company. If the price paid for the shares exceeds the book value of the net assets of the subsidiary, the excess is a premium paid for the right to exercise control over the subsidiary, and must appear in the Consolidated Balance Sheet as goodwill, cost of control, or under some other suitable designation.

Since the value of the net assets of a company is represented in its Balance Sheet by the amount of its paid-up capital, plus any reserves and other undistributed profits, the amount to be shown in the Consolidated Balance Sheet under the heading of goodwill can be ascertained by deducting from the cost of the shares held the nominal amount of the paid-up share capital of the subsidiary plus all reserves and profits existing at the date on which the shares were acquired. The consolidation is then completed by combining the remaining items appearing in the Balance Sheets of both companies.

**Illustration (1)**

The Balance Sheets of H Ltd, and S Ltd, immediately after the whole of the share capital of S Ltd had been acquired by H Ltd, were as follows:

| | H Ltd £ | S Ltd £ | | | | | H Ltd £ | S Ltd £ |
|---|---|---|---|---|---|---|---|---|
| Share Capital (in £1 shares) .. | 12,000 | 5,000 | Fixed Assets .. | .. | .. | | 11,000 | 7,000 |
| Reserves .. .. .. .. | 5,000 | 2,000 | Current Assets .. | .. | .. | | 6,000 | 4,000 |
| Profit and Loss Account .. .. | 6,000 | 1,000 | 5,000 Shares in S Ltd | .. | .. | | 10,000 | |
| | 23,000 | 8,000 | | | | | | |
| Liabilities .. .. .. | 4,000 | 3,000 | | | | | | |
| | £27,000 | £11,000 | | | | | £27,000 | £11,000 |

*Note:* The net assets of S Ltd amount to £8,000, viz. total assets £11,000 less liabilities £3,000 (represented by the Share Capital of £5,000, Reserves £2,000 and Profit and Loss Account £1,000). The excess of the cost of the shares to H Ltd over the net assets of S Ltd is the amount attributable to goodwill.

Open Memoranda Ledger Accounts for the share capital, reserves and Profit and Loss Account for the subsidiary company; then apply the following double entry procedure to ascertain the amount to be shown in the Consolidated Balance Sheet under the heading 'goodwill'.

1. Transfer to the *debit* of Goodwill Account the cost of the shares in the subsidiary company held by the holding company.

2. Transfer to the *credit* of Goodwill Account from the Share Capital Account of the subsidiary the nominal value of the shares so held.

3. Transfer to the *credit* of Goodwill Account the proportion attributable to the holding company of any Reserves, Profit and Loss Account credit balance, or other account representing surplus assets of the subsidiary at the date on which the shares were acquired. (Where there are a number of accounts representing reserves or other surpluses, it may be more convenient to transfer the pre-acquisition amounts first to a Capital Reserve Account and thence to Goodwill Account.)

4. If, at the date on which the shares were acquired, the Profit and Loss Account of the subsidiary was in debit, transfer to the *debit* of Goodwill Account the proportion of such debit balance applicable to the shares in the subsidiary held by the holding company.

The following are the relevant Memoranda Accounts:

### S LTD
### SHARE CAPITAL

| | £ | | | | | £ |
|---|---|---|---|---|---|---|
| Goodwill .. .. .. .. .. | 5,000 | Balance .. .. .. .. | | | | 5,000 |

### RESERVES

| | £ | | | | | £ |
|---|---|---|---|---|---|---|
| Goodwill .. .. .. .. .. | 2,000 | Balance .. .. .. .. | | | | 2,000 |

## PROFIT AND LOSS ACCOUNT

| | £ | | £ |
|---|---|---|---|
| Goodwill .. .. .. .. .. | 1,000 | Balance .. .. .. .. | 1,000 |

## H LTD
## GOODWILL

| | £ | | £ |
|---|---|---|---|
| Cost of 5,000 shares in S Ltd .. .. .. | 10,000 | Share Capital, S Ltd, nominal value of 5,000 shares .. .. .. .. | 5,000 |
| | | Reserves .. .. .. | 2,000 |
| | | Profit and Loss Account .. .. .. | 1,000 |
| | | Balance = Goodwill .. .. .. | 2,000 |
| | £10,000 | | £10,000 |

## CONSOLIDATED BALANCE SHEET

| | £ | £ | | £ | £ |
|---|---|---|---|---|---|
| Share Capital .. .. .. | | 12,000 | Fixed Assets: | | |
| Consolidated Reserve .. .. | | 5,000 | H Ltd .. .. .. | 11,000 | |
| Consolidated Profit and Loss Account | | 6,000 | S Ltd .. .. .. | 7,000 | |
| | | 23,000 | | | 18,000 |
| Liabilities: | | | Current Assets: | | |
| H Ltd .. .. .. .. | 4,000 | | H Ltd .. .. .. | 6,000 | |
| S Ltd .. .. .. .. | 3,000 | | S Ltd .. .. .. | 4,000 | |
| | | 7,000 | Goodwill .. .. .. | | 10,000 |
| | | | | | 2,000 |
| | | £30,000 | | | £30,000 |

Where, at the date of the acquisition of the controlling interest by the holding company, a subsidiary has a *debit* balance on Profit and Loss Account, its net assets are reduced thereby, and the cost of goodwill is correspondingly increased. For example, if in the above illustration, instead of pre-acquisition profits of £3,000, S Ltd had a *debit* balance on Profit and Loss Account of £3,000, its net assets would be represented by Share Capital £5,000 *less* Profit and Loss Account debit balance £3,000 = £2,000, and the sum attributable to goodwill in the Consolidated Balance Sheet would be ascertained as follows:

## GOODWILL

| | £ | | £ |
|---|---|---|---|
| Cost of 5,000 shares .. .. .. | 10,000 | Share Capital, S Ltd .. .. .. | 8,000 |
| Profit and Loss Account – pre-acquisition loss .. | 3,000 | Balance = Goodwill .. .. .. | 5,000 |
| | £13,000 | | £13,000 |

It will be seen that, for consolidation, the amount of any pre-acquisition surplus, i.e. of any *credit* balances on Reserves or Profit and Loss Account, is transferred to the *credit* of the Goodwill Account, whereas the amount of any pre-acquisition *loss* is transferred to the *debit* of that account. The procedure is, in fact, merely a simple double entry operation – the transfer of a sum from one account to the *same side* of another account.

Where the cost of the shares in the subsidiary is less than the net assets attributable thereto, the balance should appear in the Consolidated Balance Sheet under the heading of capital reserve. For example, if in the above illustration the pre-acquisition reserves etc. of S Ltd amounted to £7,000, the net assets of S Ltd would amount to £12,000, and the difference between this sum and the cost of the shares, viz. £2,000, would appear in the Consolidated Balance Sheet as a capital reserve.

## COST OF CONTROL

| | | | £ | | £ |
|---|---|---|---|---|---|
| Cost of 5,000 shares in S Ltd | .. | .. | 10,000 | Share Capital, S Ltd, nominal value of 5,000 shares acquired    ..    ..    .. | 5,000 |
| Balance = Capital Reserve  .. | .. | .. | 2,000 | Pre-acquisition profits    ..    ..    .. | 7,000 |
| | | | £12,000 | | £12,000 |

Where shares have been issued at a premium by one member of the group to another, the credit to Share Premium Account in the Balance Sheet of the issuing company should be treated in the same way as any other capital reserve. Any premium on the issue of preference shares belongs to the ordinary shareholders.

Profits earned by a subsidiary company after it becomes a subsidiary are revenue of the group, and are included in the Consolidated Balance Sheet as part of the Consolidated Revenue Reserves or Profit and Loss Account balance. When preparing a Consolidated Balance Sheet at a date subsequent to that on which the controlling interest was acquired, therefore, it is first necessary to transfer from the Reserves and Profit and Loss Account of the subsidiary to Goodwill Account, the amounts of the pre-acquisition surpluses of the subsidiary, leaving any balances of such surpluses to be treated as revenue reserves of the group.

### Illustration (2)

The Balance Sheets of the companies referred to in Illustration (1) one year later than the Balance Sheet therein, are as under:

| | | | | H Ltd £ | S Ltd £ | | | | | H Ltd £ | S Ltd £ |
|---|---|---|---|---|---|---|---|---|---|---|---|
| Share Capital | .. | .. | .. | 12,000 | 5,000 | Fixed Assets  .. | .. | .. | 12,000 | 7,000 |
| Reserves .. | .. | .. | .. | 7,000 | 3,000 | Current Assets .. | .. | .. | 10,000 | 7,500 |
| Profit and Loss Account | .. | .. | 8,000 | 2,500 | 5,000 Shares in S Ltd | .. | .. | 10,000 | |
| | | | | 27,000 | 10,500 | | | | | | |
| Liabilities | .. | .. | .. | 5,000 | 4,000 | | | | | | |
| | | | | £32,000 | £14,500 | | | | | £32,000 | £14,500 |

Assuming no dividends to have been paid by S Ltd, and no inter-company adjustments to be necessary, the increase of £1,000 in the Reserves and £1,500 in the Profit and Loss Account balance of S Ltd, being post-acquisition profits, would be credited to Consolidated Reserves and Profit and Loss Account respectively. The Consolidated Balance Sheet at this date will then appear as under:

## CONSOLIDATED BALANCE SHEET

| | £ | £ | | £ | £ |
|---|---|---|---|---|---|
| Share Capital .. .. .. | | 12,000 | Fixed Assets: | | |
| | | | H Ltd .. .. .. | 12,000 | |
| Consolidated Reserves: | | | S Ltd .. .. .. | 7,000 | |
| H Ltd .. .. .. .. | 7,000 | | | | 19,000 |
| S Ltd .. .. .. .. | 1,000 | | Current Assets: | | |
| | | 8,000 | H Ltd .. .. .. | 10,000 | |
| Consolidated Profit and Loss Account: | | | S Ltd .. .. .. | 7,500 | |
| H Ltd .. .. .. .. | 8,000 | | | | 17,500 |
| S Ltd .. .. .. .. | 1,500 | | Goodwill .. .. .. | | 2,000 |
| | | 9,500 | | | |
| | | 29,500 | | | |
| Liabilities: | | | | | |
| H Ltd .. .. .. .. | 5,000 | | | | |
| S Ltd .. .. .. .. | 4,000 | | | | |
| | | 9,000 | | | |
| | | £38,500 | | | £38,500 |

## S LTD
## SHARE CAPITAL

WORKINGS

| | £ | | £ |
|---|---|---|---|
| Goodwill .. .. .. .. .. | 5,000 | Balance .. .. .. .. | 5,000 |

## RESERVES

| | £ | | £ |
|---|---|---|---|
| Goodwill – pre-acquisition reserves .. .. | 2,000 | Balance .. .. .. .. | 3,000 |
| H Ltd Revenue Reserves .. .. .. | 1,000 | | |
| | £3,000 | | £3,000 |

## PROFIT AND LOSS ACCOUNT

| | £ | | £ |
|---|---|---|---|
| Goodwill – pre-acquisition reserves .. .. | 1,000 | Balance .. .. .. .. | 2,500 |
| H Ltd Profit and Loss Account .. .. | 1,500 | | |
| | £2,500 | | £2,500 |

## H LTD
## REVENUE RESERVES

| | £ | | £ |
|---|---|---|---|
| Balance to Consolidated Balance Sheet .. | 8,000 | Balance .. | 7,000 |
| | | S Ltd transferred .. .. .. | 1,000 |
| | £8,000 | | £8,000 |

## PROFIT AND LOSS ACCOUNT

| | £ | | £ |
|---|---|---|---|
| Balance to Consolidated Balance Sheet .. | 9,500 | Balance .. | 8,000 |
| | | S Ltd transferred .. .. .. | 1,500 |
| | £9,500 | | £9,500 |

## (f) *Partly owned Subsidiaries*

Where the holding company does not own the whole of the share capital of the subsidiary, if credit is taken in the Consolidated Balance Sheet for the whole of the net assets of the subsidiary, the amount of the minority interest, i.e. the proportion of the net assets applicable to the shares held outside the group, must be shown as a liability. Such liability will comprise the nominal amount of the shares held by the outside shareholders, plus the proportion appropriate thereto of all reserves and undistributed profits of the subsidiary, or less the appropriate proportion of any debit balance on its Profit and Loss Account.

### Illustration (3)

Assume the same circumstances as those appearing in Illustrations (1) and (2), except that H Ltd's holding in S Ltd consists of only 4,000 shares, acquired at a cost of £10,000.

As will be seen from the Balance Sheet in Illustration (2), the net assets of S Ltd amount to £10,500 of which one-fifth=£2,100 is attributable to the 1,000 shares held outside the group. This sum is represented by:

| | |
|---|---:|
| Share Capital      ..         ..          ..         ..         .. | £1,000 |
| One-fifth of Reserve (£3,000)         ..         ..         .. | 600 |
| ,,   ,,   ,,   Profit and Loss Account Balance (£2,500) .. | 500 |
| | £2,100 |

Since only four-fifths of the share capital of S Ltd is held by the holding company, only four-fifths of that company's Reserves and Profit and Loss Account balance will be treated as applicable to the group.

S LTD
SHARE CAPITAL

WORKINGS

| | £ | | £ |
|---|---:|---|---:|
| Goodwill (4/5)   ..      ..      ..      .. | 4,000 | Balance   ..      ..      ..      .. | 5,000 |
| Minority Interest (1/5)      ..      ..      .. | 1,000 | | |
| | £5,000 | | £5,000 |

RESERVES

| | £ | | £ |
|---|---:|---|---:|
| Goodwill – *pre*-acquisition reserves (4/5 × £2,000) | 1,600 | Balance   ..      ..      ..      .. | 3,000 |
| H Ltd – *post*-acquisition reserves (4/5 × £1,000) .. | 800 | | |
| Minority Interest (1/5 × £3,000)      ..      .. | 600 | | |
| | £3,000 | | £3,000 |

PROFIT AND LOSS ACCOUNT

| | £ | | £ |
|---|---:|---|---:|
| Goodwill – pre-acquisition reserves (4/5 × £1,000) | 800 | Balance   ..      ..      ..      .. | 2,500 |
| H Ltd Profit and Loss Account (4/5 × £1,500)   .. | 1,200 | | |
| Minority Interest (1/5 × £2,500)      ..      .. | 500 | | |
| | £2,500 | | £2,500 |

## H LTD
### RESERVES

| | £ | | | | | | £ |
|---|---|---|---|---|---|---|---|
| | | Balance .. | .. | .. | .. | | 7,000 |
| | | S Ltd transferred | .. | .. | .. | | 800 |
| | | | | | | | £7,800 |

### PROFIT AND LOSS ACCOUNT

| | £ | | | | | | £ |
|---|---|---|---|---|---|---|---|
| | | Balance .. | .. | .. | .. | | 8,000 |
| | | S Ltd transferred | .. | .. | .. | | 1,200 |
| | | | | | | | £9,200 |

### GOODWILL

| | £ | | | £ | |
|---|---|---|---|---|---|
| Cost of 4,000 Shares in S Ltd .. .. | 10,000 | Share Capital, S Ltd Nominal value of 4,000 Shares .. .. | | | 4,000 |
| | | Pre-acquisition surplus. | | | |
| | | Reserve, 4/5ths of £2,000 .. | £1,600 | | |
| | | Profit and Loss, 4/5ths of £1,000 .. | 800 | | |
| | | | | | 2,400 |
| | | Balance = Goodwill .. .. | | | 3,600 |
| | £10,000 | | | | £10,000 |

### MINORITY INTEREST (1/5th)

| | £ | | | | £ |
|---|---|---|---|---|---|
| | | Share Capital, S Ltd .. .. | .. | | 1,000 |
| | | Reserves, S Ltd 1/5th of £3,000 .. | .. | | 600 |
| | | Profit and Loss, S Ltd 1/5th of £2,500 | .. | | 500 |
| | | | | | £2,100 |

### CONSOLIDATED BALANCE SHEET

| | £ | £ | | £ |
|---|---|---|---|---|
| Share Capital .. .. .. | | 12,000 | Fixed Assets .. .. .. .. | 19,000 |
| Consolidated Reserve: | | | Current Assets .. .. .. .. | 17,500 |
| H Ltd .. .. .. .. | 7,000 | | Goodwill .. .. .. .. | 3,600 |
| S Ltd (4/5 × £1,000) .. .. | 800 | | | |
| | | 7,800 | | |
| Consolidated Profit and Loss Account: | | | | |
| H Ltd .. .. .. .. | 8,000 | | | |
| S Ltd (4/5 × £1,500) .. .. | 1,200 | | | |
| | | 9,200 | | |
| | | 29,000 | | |
| Minority Interests .. .. .. | | 2,100 | | |
| Liabilities .. .. .. | | 9,000 | | |
| | | £40,100 | | £40,100 |

Minority interest can be checked by calculating the minority fraction of the total subsidiary company's shareholders' funds (in this example 1/5 × £10,500 = £2,100). This proof will not be effective if there have been unrecorded asset revaluations for the purposes of consolidation.

It might be argued that as the holding company paid a premium of £3,600 for a four-fifths interest in the capital of the subsidiary, the true value of the 'goodwill' is £3,600 × ¼ = £4,500, and that it should appear in the Consolidated Balance Sheet at £4,500, the balance of £900 being credited to the minority interest. The objection to such a procedure is that the purpose of the Consolidated Balance Sheet is to show the state of affairs of the group *so far as it affects the members of the holding company*, and that the price paid by the holding company for a controlling interest may not reflect the value of the shares held by outside shareholders nor the goodwill element included therein. The Consolidated Balance Sheet is, in reality, the holding company's own Balance Sheet presented in a different form. It must, therefore, include only assets and liabilities which arise from the expenditure of funds belonging to the group. These will comprise the assets and liabilities of the holding company itself, plus the proportion of the assets and liabilities of the subsidiaries attributable to the holding company's interest therein, and this proportion is, in effect, so included by bringing into the Consolidated Balance Sheet the whole of the assets and liabilities of the subsidiaries, and showing as a separate liability therein an amount representing the interest of the outside shareholders in the net assets of the subsidiaries. The amount which should appear in the Consolidated Balance Sheet as goodwill of the group should not exceed the amount actually expended by the group in the acquisition of that asset.

A Consolidated Balance Sheet is of little value to minority interests since the individual assets upon which their interests are based are not disclosed.

**Illustration (4)**

### SUMMARIZED BALANCE SHEETS

| | H Ltd £ | S Ltd £ | | | H Ltd £ | S Ltd £ |
|---|---|---|---|---|---|---|
| Share Capital, £1 shares    ..    .. | 3,600 | 2,000 | 1,600 shares in S Ltd, at cost    .. | | 1,100 | 1,600 |
| Creditors    ..    ..    .. | 1,600 | 600 | Sundry Assets    ..    ..    .. | | 4,800 | 2,100 |
| Profit and Loss Account    .. | 700 | — | Profit and Loss Account ..    .. | | — | 500 |
| | £5,900 | £2,600 | | | £5,900 | £2,600 |

H Ltd acquired the shares in S Ltd when S Ltd had a *debit* balance on Profit and Loss Account of £800. On that date, therefore, the net assets of S Ltd were £1,200 (equal to the net interest of the shareholders, viz. capital £2,000, *less* loss £800). H Ltd acquired in effect net assets of 80 per cent. of £1,200 = £960 at a cost of £1,100, and therefore paid £1,100—£960 = £140 for goodwill. Moreover, the debit balance on Profit and Loss Account having been reduced since the acquisition to £500, S Ltd must have made a post-acquisition profit of £300.

WORKINGS            GOODWILL

| | £ | | £ |
|---|---|---|---|
| Cost of 1,600 Shares in S Ltd    ..    .. | 1,100 | Share Capital, S Ltd, Nominal value of 1,600 | |
| Profit and Loss Account, S Ltd proportion of pre-acquisition loss of S Ltd applicable to H Ltd – 4/5ths of £800    ..    ..    ..    .. | 640 | Shares    ..    ..    ..    ..    .. <br> Balance= Goodwill    ..    ..    .. | 1,600 <br> 140 |
| | £1,740 | | £1,740 |

## MINORITY INTEREST (1/5th)

| | £ | | £ |
|---|---|---|---|
| Profit and Loss Account, S Ltd – 1/5th of debit balance of £500 .. .. .. .. | 100 | Share Capital, S Ltd .. .. .. | 400 |
| Balance to Consolidated Balance Sheet .. | 300 | | |
| | £400 | | £400 |

## PROFIT AND LOSS ACCOUNT – S LTD

| | £ | | £ |
|---|---|---|---|
| Balance .. .. .. .. .. | 500 | Transfer to Goodwill – 4/5ths of £800 .. | 640 |
| Consolidated Profit and Loss Account, being post-acquisition profit applicable to H Ltd – 4/5ths of £300 .. .. .. .. .. | 240 | ,, ,, Minority Interest – 1/5th of £500 | 100 |
| | £740 | | £740 |

## PROFIT AND LOSS ACCOUNT – H LTD

| | £ | | £ |
|---|---|---|---|
| | | Balance .. .. .. .. | 700 |
| | | S Ltd transferred .. .. .. | 240 |
| | | | £940 |

## CONSOLIDATED BALANCE SHEET

| | £ | £ | | £ | £ |
|---|---|---|---|---|---|
| Share Capital .. .. .. | | 3,600 | Goodwill .. .. .. | | 140 |
| Consolidated Profit and Loss Account: | | | Sundry Assets: H Ltd .. .. | 4,800 | |
| H Ltd .. .. .. .. | 700 | | S Ltd .. .. | 2,100 | |
| S Ltd .. .. .. .. | 240 | | | | 6,900 |
| | | 940 | | | |
| Minority Interests .. .. .. | | 300 | | | |
| Creditors: H Ltd .. .. .. | 1,600 | | | | |
| S Ltd .. .. .. | 600 | | | | |
| | | 2,200 | | | |
| | | £7,040 | | | £7,040 |

It should be noted that the £240 credited to the Consolidated Profit and Loss Account for post-acquisition profits of S Ltd is not available for distribution, since S Ltd still has a debit balance on its Profit and Loss Account.

**Illustration (5)**

The following are the Balance Sheets of a holding company and its subsidiary company:

| | H Ltd £ | S Ltd £ | | H Ltd £ | S Ltd £ |
|---|---|---|---|---|---|
| Share Capital, £1 shares .. .. | 1,600 | 900 | 720 Shares in S Ltd at cost .. | 800 | — |
| Creditors .. .. .. | 300 | 550 | Sundry Assets .. .. .. | 1,500 | 1,250 |
| Profit and Loss Account .. .. | 400 | — | Profit and Loss Account .. | — | 200 |
| | £2,300 | £1,450 | | £2,300 | £1,450 |

When H Ltd acquired the shares in S Ltd, S Ltd had a *credit* balance on Profit and Loss Account of £150. No dividends have been declared by S Ltd. Prepare a Consolidated Balance Sheet.

WORKINGS

## COST OF CONTROL

| | £ | | £ |
|---|---|---|---|
| Cost of 720 Shares in S Ltd .. .. .. | 800 | Share Capital, S Ltd, Nominal value of 720 Shares .. .. .. .. | 720 |
| Transfer to Capital Reserve .. .. .. | 40 | Profit and Loss, S Ltd, pre-acquisition profit 4/5ths of £150.. .. .. .. | 120 |
| | £840 | | £840 |

## CAPITAL RESERVE

| | £ | | £ |
|---|---|---|---|
| | | Transfer from Goodwill .. .. .. | 40 |

## PROFIT AND LOSS ACCOUNT – S LTD

| | £ | | £ |
|---|---|---|---|
| Balance .. .. .. .. .. | 200 | Minority Interest – 1/5th of £200 .. .. | 40 |
| Goodwill – Transfer of pre-acquisition *credit* balance applicable to H Ltd – 4/5ths of £150 .. | 120 | Balance to Consolidated Profit and Loss Account .. .. .. .. | 280 |
| | £320 | | £320 |

## MINORITY INTEREST (1/5th)

| | £ | | £ |
|---|---|---|---|
| Profit and Loss, S Ltd, Share of *debit* balance – 1/5th of £200 .. .. .. .. | 40 | Share Capital, S Ltd .. .. .. | 180 |
| Balance to Consolidated Balance Sheet .. | 140 | | |
| | £180 | | £180 |

## CONSOLIDATED PROFIT AND LOSS ACCOUNT

| | £ | | £ |
|---|---|---|---|
| S Ltd Profit and Loss Account .. .. | 280 | Balance – H Ltd .. .. .. | 400 |
| Balance to Consolidated Balance Sheet .. | 120 | | |
| | £400 | | £400 |

The net assets of S Ltd at the date of acquisition of the 720 shares therein by H Ltd were represented by:

| | | | | | £ |
|---|---|---|---|---|---|
| Share Capital | .. | .. | .. | .. | 900 |
| Profit and Loss Account | .. | .. | .. | .. | 150 |
| | | | | | £1,050 |

of which four-fifths = £840 is attributable to H Ltd's holding. Since H Ltd only paid £800 for the shares, it paid, in fact, nothing for goodwill, but acquired a capital reserve of £40, which is shown in the Consolidated Balance Sheet. The 'goodwill' entries in the above solution are not therefore strictly necessary, but have been shown in order to preserve consistency of treatment, the balance of Goodwill Account being transferred to capital reserve.

As S Ltd had a *credit* balance of £150 on Profit and Loss Account at the date of acquisition of the shares therein by H Ltd, but now has a *debit* balance of £200, it has made a post-acquisition loss of £350, of which four-fifths = £280 is applicable to H Ltd's holding. This amount is *debited* to Consolidated Profit and Loss Account.

## CONSOLIDATED BALANCE SHEET

| | £ | £ | | | £ | £ |
|---|---|---|---|---|---|---|
| Share Capital .. .. .. | | 1,600 | Sundry Assets – H Ltd .. .. | | 1,500 | |
| Consolidated Profit and Loss Account – H Ltd .. .. .. .. | 400 | | S Ltd .. .. | | 1,250 | 2,750 |
| *Less* Proportion of post-acquisition loss of S Ltd .. .. | 280 | | | | | |
| | | 120 | | | | |
| Capital Reserve .. .. .. | | 40 | | | | |
| Minority Interests .. .. .. | | 140 | | | | |
| Creditors – H Ltd .. .. | 300 | | | | | |
| S Ltd .. .. | 550 | | | | | |
| | | 850 | | | | |
| | | £2,750 | | | | £2,750 |

The proportion applicable to the holding company of ALL undivided profits and reserves (both revenue and capital) of the subsidiary at the date of acquisition of control by the holding company must be transferred to goodwill for the purpose of the consolidation. Where the shares are acquired at a date falling between two Balance Sheet dates of the subsidiary, the pre-acquisition profits will usually comprise the balances on reserves and Profit and Loss Account at the commencement of the year plus the proportion of the current year's profits accruing before the date of acquisition, less any dividends paid during the same period. The apportionment of the profits will normally be made on a time basis although some other basis may occasionally be more correct, e.g. where the subsidiary's trade is seasonal. The minority interests must be credited with their relevant proportion of all undivided profits of the subsidiary of which they are members, regardless of whether such profits arose before or after that company became a subsidiary of the holding company.

### Illustration (6)

The summarized Balance Sheet of Minor Ltd at December 31st, 1970, was as follows:

| | £ | £ | | £ |
|---|---|---|---|---|
| Share Capital, 100,000 Shares of £1 each .. .. .. .. | | 100,000 | Fixed Assets .. .. .. .. | 160,000 |
| Share Premium Account (as at January 1st, 1970) .. .. .. | | 20,000 | Sinking Fund Investments .. .. | 15,000 |
| Sinking Fund for Redemption of Debentures: | | | Current Assets .. .. .. | 116,000 |
| Balance, January 1st, 1970 .. | 12,000 | | | |
| Transfer from Profit and Loss Account, December 31st 1970 | 3,000 | | | |
| | | 15,000 | | |
| General Reserve: | | | | |
| Balance, January 1st, 1970 .. | 50,000 | | | |
| Transfer from Profit and Loss Account, December 31st, 1970 | 10,000 | | | |
| | | 60,000 | | |
| Profit and Loss Account: | | | | |
| Balance January 1st, 1970 .. | 8,000 | | | |
| Profit for year 1970 .. .. | 22,000 | | | |
| | 30,000 | | | |
| *Less* Transfers to Reserve and Sinking Fund Accounts at December 31st, 1970 .. 13,000 | | | | |
| Dividend paid March 31st 1970 out of 1969 profits .. .. 3,000 | | | | |
| Proposed Dividend 10,000 | | | | |
| | 26,000 | | | |
| | | 4,000 | | |
| 4% Debentures .. .. .. | | 40,000 | | |
| Current Liabilities (including proposed dividend) .. .. | | 52,000 | | |
| | | £291,000 | | £291,000 |

Assume that the profit for the year has accrued evenly throughout the period.

Major Ltd acquired 75,000 of the shares in Minor Ltd at a cost of £2·50 per share on June 30th, 1970. Ignore taxation.

For the purposes of the Consolidated Balance Sheet prepared as at 31st December, 1970, the sum attributable to goodwill and minority interests may be computed as follows:

## GOODWILL

| | £ | | | £ |
|---|---|---|---|---|
| Cost of 75,000 shares in Minor Ltd  ..        .. | 187,500 | Share Capital, Minor Ltd – Nominal value of 75,000 shares  ..         ..         .. | | 75,000 |
| | | Pre-acquisition profits of Minor Ltd, applicable to Major Ltd: | | |
| | | Share Premium, Jan 1st, 1970 (¾ × £20,000)  ..         ..         .. | | 15,000 |
| | | Sinking Fund, Jan. 1st, 1970 (¾ × £12,000)  ..         ..         .. | | 9,000 |
| | | General Reserve, Jan. 1st, 1970 (¾ × £50,000)  ..         ..         .. | | 37,500 |
| | | Profit and Loss Account: | | |
| | | Balance, Jan. 1st, 1970  ..  | £8,000 | |
| | | Less Dividend paid March 31st, 1970  ..         ..         .. | 3,000 | |
| | | | 5,000 | |
| | | Profit for half year to June 30th, 1970 (½ × £22,000) ..  ..  | 11,000 | |
| | | | ¾ × £16,000 | 12,000 |
| | | Balance - Goodwill  ..         ..         .. | | 39,000 |
| | £187,500 | | | £187,500 |

## MINORITY INTERESTS (1/4th)

| | £ | | | £ |
|---|---|---|---|---|
| Balance (shown separately in Consolidated Balance Sheet)  ..         ..         ..         .. | 49,750 | Share Capital – 25,000 shares  ..         .. | | 25,000 |
| | | Share Premium (¼ × £20,000)  ..         .. | | 5,000 |
| Proposed dividend (shown separately in Consolidated Balance Sheet under the heading Current Liabilities)  ..         ..         ..         .. | 2,500 | Sinking Fund (¼ × £15,000)  ..         .. | | 3,750 |
| | | General Reserve (¼ × £60,000)  ..  | | 15,000 |
| | | Profit and Loss Account (¼ × £4,000)  ..  | | 1,000 |
| | | Proposed Dividend (¼ × £10,000)  ..  | | 2,500 |
| | £52,250 | | | £52,250 |

### SHARES IN SUBSIDIARIES ACQUIRED OVER A PERIOD OF TIME

Often a company buys shares in another company over a period of time; it may be months or years before a controlling interest is obtained. Should pre-acquisition profits be calculated each time shares are purchased or only when control is obtained? Legally it is not necessary to calculate pre-acquisition profits until control is gained; it would be tiresome to have to make calculations every time a small number of shares were purchased. The Institute of Chartered Accountants, however, recommend that calculations of pre-acquisition profits should be made every time a substantial purchase is made and the investing company's objective is to gain a controlling interest.

### Illustration (7)

B Ltd's issued share capital was £320,000 ordinary shares of £1. On April 1st, 1967, when B Ltd had revenue reserves of £64,000, A Ltd acquired 80,000 ordinary shares. On April 1st, 1970, when B Ltd had revenue reserves of £96,000, A Ltd acquired 200,000 more ordinary shares. Calculate the pre-acquisition profits arising on consolidating A Ltd and B Ltd, assuming B Ltd paid no dividends.

1. On the basis of calculating pre-acquisition profits at April 1st, 1970, the date A Ltd obtained control of B Ltd:

| | |
|---|---|
| Revenue reserves April 1st, 1970 .. .. .. | £96,000 |
| Proportion of pre-acquisition reserves appropriate to a holding of 280,000 out of 320,000 shares (7/8 × £96,000) .. .. .. .. .. | £84,000 |

2. On the basis of calculating pre-acquisition profits each time shares are purchased:

| | |
|---|---|
| Revenue reserves April 1st, 1967 .. .. .. | £64,000 |
| Proportion of pre-acquisition reserves appropriate to a holding of 80,000 out of 320,000 shares (1/4 × £64,000) | £16,000 |
| Revenue reserves April 1st, 1970 .: .. .. | £96,000 |
| Proportion of pre-acquisition reserves appropriate to a holding of 200,000 out of 320,000 shares (5/8 × £96,000) .. .. .. .. .. | £60,000 |
| TOTAL PRE-ACQUISITION PROFITS arising on consolidation £(16,000 + 60,000) .. .. .. | £76,000 |

## (g) Losses incurred by Subsidiary

Where a subsidiary has incurred losses these should be charged to the holding company and the minority holders of ordinary shares (if any) in proportion to their holdings, as has been done in Illustrations (4) and (5) above. If, however, a subsidiary continues to incur losses after all its previously earned reserves and profits have been exhausted, the minority shareholders should not be charged with any part of such losses in excess of the nominal value of the shares held by them, which is the limit of their liability; if it is not proposed to wind up the subsidiary, the holding company should make provision in its own accounts for the excess losses. If, however, the holding company intends to abandon the subsidiary and allow it to be wound up, the amount of the investment in the subsidiary would be written off in the holding company's books without providing for such excess losses. In these circumstances no good purpose would be served in including the subsidiary in group accounts.

## (h) Dividends paid by a Subsidiary out of Pre-acquisition Profits

Since profits of a subsidiary earned before (and remaining undistributed at) the date on which the parent company acquires its shares therein, are represented by assets which are, in effect, paid for by the holding company as part of the purchase price of the shares, any dividends paid by a subsidiary out of such pre-acquisition profits must be treated as capital receipts not available for distribution by the holding company. Such dividends represent a realization of part of the price paid for the shares, and must be credited to the Shares in Subsidiary Account, thus reducing the cost of the shares to the holding company, and, in consequence, the amount applicable to goodwill.

**Illustration (8)**

The Balance Sheets of H Ltd and S Ltd at the date on which H Ltd acquired 75 per cent. of the ordinary share capital of S Ltd were as follows:

### BALANCE SHEETS

| | H Ltd £ | S Ltd £ | | | H Ltd £ | S Ltd £ |
|---|---|---|---|---|---|---|
| Share Capital, £1 shares .. .. | 200,000 | 40,000 | 30,000 Shares in S L.d .. .. | | 60,000 | |
| Reserves .. .. .. | 40,000 | 10,000 | Sundry Assets, *less* liabilities .. | | 205,000 | 64,000 |
| Profit and Loss Account .. .. | 25,000 | 14,000 | | | | |
| | £265,000 | £64,000 | | | £265,000 | £64,000 |

Since the net assets of S Ltd amount ot £64,000, and H Ltd has become the owner of three-fourths of the share capital of S Ltd, the net assets of S Ltd, attributable to H Ltd's holding amount to £48,000, and the price paid by H Ltd for goodwill is £60,000—£48,000 =£12,000.

If, immediately after the purchase of the shares by H Ltd, S Ltd paid a 'gross' dividend of 20 per cent., the effect would be to reduce the net assets of S Ltd by £8,000 to £56,000, and the proportion applicable to H Ltd's holding to $\frac{3}{4} \times$ £56,000 = £42,000. If the cost of the shares remained in H Ltd's books at £60,000, the amount appearing as goodwill in the Consolidated Balance Sheet would be increased to £18,000, and the £6,000 dividend received by H Ltd would be incorrectly credited to its Profit and Loss Account, causing the divisible profits of that company to appear to be £6,000 more than the amount legally distributable.

The dividend should therefore be credited to Shares in Subsidiary Account, and the Balance Sheets of H Ltd and S Ltd would then be as follows:

| | H Ltd £ | S Ltd £ | | £ | H Ltd £ | S Ltd £ |
|---|---|---|---|---|---|---|
| Share Capital, £1 shares .. .. | 200,000 | 40,000 | 30,000 shares in S Ltd at cost .. .. | 60,000 | | |
| Reserves .. .. .. | 40,000 | 10,000 | *Less* Dividend received out of pre-acquisition profits .. .. | 6,000 | | |
| Profit and Loss Account .. | 25,000 | 6,000 | | | 54,000 | |
| | | | Sundry Assets, *less* liabilities .. .. | | 205,000 | 56,000 |
| | | | Cash .. .. | | 6,000 | |
| | £265,000 | £56,000 | | | £265,000 | £56,000 |

The following Memorandum Ledger Accounts would then be necessary in order to prepare the Consolidated Balance Sheet.

### GOODWILL (H LTD in S LTD)

| | £ | £ | | £ |
|---|---|---|---|---|
| Cost of 30,000 shares .. .. | 60,000 | | Share Capital S Ltd .. .. .. | 30,000 |
| *Less* dividend out of pre-acquisition profits .. .. .. | 6,000 | | S Ltd Reserve – pre-acquisition profits ($\frac{3}{4} \times$ £10,000) .. | 7,500 |
| | | 54,000 | S Ltd Profit and Loss Account pre-acquisition profits ($\frac{3}{4} \times$ £6,000) .. .. .. | 4 500 |
| | | | Balance to Consolidated Balance Sheet .. | 12,000 |
| | | £54,000 | | £54,000 |

## MINORITY INTEREST (1/4th)

| | £ | | £ |
|---|---|---|---|
| Balance to Consolidated Balance Sheet    .. | 14,000 | Share Capital – S Ltd    ..          ..          .. | 10,000 |
| | | S Ltd Reserves ($\frac{1}{4}$ × £10,000)          ..          .. | 2,500 |
| | | S Ltd Profit and Loss Account ($\frac{1}{4}$ × £6,000)    .. | 1,500 |
| | £14,000 | | £14,000 |

## RESERVES – S LTD

| | £ | | £ |
|---|---|---|---|
| Goodwill($\frac{3}{4}$ × £10,000)    ..          ..          .. | 7,500 | Balance          ..          ..          ..          .. | 10,000 |
| Minority Interest ($\frac{1}{4}$ × £10,000)          ..          .. | 2,500 | | |
| | £10,000 | | £10,000 |

## PROFIT AND LOSS ACCOUNT – S LTD

| | £ | | £ |
|---|---|---|---|
| Goodwill – pre-acquisition profits ($\frac{3}{4}$ × £6,000)    .. | 4,500 | Balance          ..          ..          ..          .. | 6,000 |
| Minority Interests ($\frac{1}{4}$ × £6,000)          ..          .. | 1,500 | | |
| | £6,000 | | £6,000 |

## CONSOLIDATED BALANCE SHEET OF H LTD
## AND ITS SUBSIDIARY S LTD

| | £ | | £ |
|---|---|---|---|
| Share Capital, £1 shares    ..          ..          .. | 200,000 | Goodwill arising on consolidation          .. | 12,000 |
| Reserves          ..          ..          ..          .. | 40,000 | Sundry Assets (including cash) *less* liabil- | |
| Profit and Loss Account    ..          ..          .. | 25,000 | ities          ..          ..          ..          .. | 267,000 |
| Minority Interests          ..          ..          .. | 14,000 | | |
| | £279,000 | | £279,000 |

### (i) Corporation Tax

Amounts due for corporation tax will be aggregated. Corporation tax due on profits for the accounting period will be shown immediately before current liabilities in the horizontal Balance Sheet; in the vertical Balance Sheet as a deduction from current assets less current liabilities in calculating working capital.

Corporation tax due for previous accounting periods will be shown as a separate item under the heading current liabilities and the due date of payment stated.

### (j) Bonus Shares received by Holding Company from Subsidiary

Where a subsidiary company capitalizes profits by the issue of bonus shares, the treatment in the group accounts of the bonus shares received by the holding company will depend upon whether the bonus is paid out of pre-acquisition or post-acquisition profits of the subsidiary. Capitalized profits are not available for distribution. If, therefore, the bonus is declared out of post-acquisition profits included in the Consolidated Revenue Reserves a sum equal to the amount capitalized should be transferred therefrom to Capital Reserve Account. If this is not done, the aggregate of the revenue reserves appearing in the Consolidated Balance Sheet will exceed the maximum sum which could be distributed as dividend to the members of the holding company were all the subsidiaries to pay to the holding company as dividends the whole of their profits available for distribution. If, however, the bonus is declared out of pre-acquisition profits, no adjustment is necessary, since these profits have already been treated as capital in the consolidated accounts in computing goodwill, and no longer appear therein as revenue reserves.

**Illustration (9)**

H Ltd acquired 75 per cent. of the ordinary share capital of S Ltd. The following are Balance Sheet extracts at the date of acquisition:

### BALANCE SHEETS

|  | H Ltd | S Ltd |  | H Ltd | S Ltd |
|---|---|---|---|---|---|
|  | £ | £ |  | £ | £ |
| Share Capital – shares of £1    .. | 250,000 | 100,000 | Cost of 75,000 shares         .. | 125,000 | — |
| Reserves     ..         ..         .. | 125,000 | 50,000 |  |  |  |

During the first year after acquisition S Ltd made a profit of £200,000 and made a one for one bonus issue using as far as possible reserves earned before H Ltd acquired its shareholding. Show the Cost of Control Account (a) at the date of acquisition and (b) one year later.

(a)            COST OF CONTROL ACCOUNT (at date of acquisition)

|  | £ |  | £ |
|---|---|---|---|
| Cost of 75,000 shares    ..       ..       .. | 125,000 | Share Capital – nominal value    ..         .. | 75,000 |
|  |  | Reserves – ¾ of pre-acquisition reserves    .. | 37,500 |
|  |  | Balance = Goodwill    ..         ..         .. | 12,500 |
|  | £125,000 |  | £125,000 |

(b)            COST OF CONTROL ACCOUNT (one year later)

|  | £ |  | £ |
|---|---|---|---|
| Cost of 150,000 shares    ..       ..       .. | 125,000 | Share capital – nominal value    ..         .. | 150,000 |
| Balance = CAPITAL RESERVE    ..       .. | 25,000 |  |  |
|  | £150,000 |  | £150,000 |

WORKINGS            RESERVES – S LTD

|  | £ |  | £ |
|---|---|---|---|
| Share Capital – one-for-one bonus  ..       .. | 100,000 | Balance at date of H Ltd's acquisition of |  |
| Transfer to Consolidated Profit and Loss |  | shares    ..       ..       ..       .. | 50,000 |
|   Account    ..       ..       ..       .. | 112,500 | Profit since H Ltd acquired shares    .. | 200,000 |
| Minority Interests (¼ × £150,000)    ..       .. | 37,500 |  |  |
|  | £250,000 |  | £250,000 |

### (k) *Preference Shares in Subsidiaries*

It has been assumed in the preceding examples that the shares held by the outside members are ordinary shares, so that the minority interest in the net assets is represented by the nominal value of the capital held by them plus the proportion of all reserves and undistributed profits or less the proportion of losses attributable to such holding. Where the shares held by outside members are preference shares, which do not participate in the surplus profits or assets, the minority interest will normally consist of the nominal value of the preference shares held by the outside shareholders plus *only the fixed dividend accrued* on the shares to the date of the Consolidated Balance Sheet.

Where preference shareholders are entitled to share in a surplus on a winding-up it might be contended that they should be credited also with a share of the surplus assets proportionate to their capital. Since, however, the Consolidated Balance Sheet is intended to show the position of the group as a going concern as at a given date, it is considered that such a contention cannot be upheld. If it were proposed to wind up the subsidiary, its accounts would probably not be consolidated with those of the holding company. Until liquidation supervenes, the ordinary shareholders (subject to any special rights given to other classes) are entitled to all undivided profits, and the preference shareholders only to their fixed dividends. Any rights of the preference shareholders to participate in a possible surplus can, if thought fit, be mentioned in a footnote. Redeemable preference shares which are redeemable at a premium are in a different category, and prudence would seem to dictate that the premium should be provided for by annual instalments over the period between the date of the Balance Sheet and the redemption date.

If the holding company itself holds preference shares in the subsidiary, the nominal value will be deducted from their cost to the holding company, in the same way as ordinary shares, any premium or discount on the purchase being deducted from, or added to, goodwill. The fixed dividend thereon accrued to the date of acquisition will be transferred to goodwill as being the proportion of the pre-acquisition profits of the subsidiary applicable to the preference shares.

Participating preference shares in a subsidiary present a special problem, the solution to which must depend upon the rights of the holders of such shares as laid down in the company's Articles. For example, the shares may be cumulative in respect of the fixed dividend, but non-cumulative as regards the further partici-pation up to a specified maximum. Where such shares are held by outside share-holders it is usually desirable to allocate the profits of the subsidiary between them and the holding company on the assumption that the whole of the profits are to be distributed. The minority shareholders of the participating preference shares would thus be credited with the maximum sum they could expect to receive. If this is not done a note should be appended to the accounts indicating the rights attaching to such shares and the amount of their maximum possible participation.

Where the profits of a subsidiary have been insufficient to pay, in whole or in part, the cumulative dividend on preference shares, there would be no obligation to provide for arrears of dividend out of the consolidated profits except to the extent that the existing reserves of the subsidiary in question are sufficient to meet them, but a note should be made on the Consolidated Balance Sheet of the amount of such arrears not provided for.

Where the subsidiary has a debit balance on Profit and Loss Account, this should normally be charged against the ordinary shareholders only, as the holders of the cumulative preference shares are entitled to have arrears of dividend paid out of future profits, and thus the debit balance on Profit and Loss Account would be borne by the ordinary shareholders. Exceptionally, where the winding-up of the subsidiary is imminent, if the preference shares carry no right to priority of repayment of capital the debit balance should quite properly be apportioned between the holders of the ordinary and the preference capital; however, it is improbable that the subsidiary would be included in the group accounts.

### (*l*) *Unrealized Inter-Company Profits*

Where goods which have been sold by one company in the group to another at a profit and have not been resold by the recipient company at the date of its Balance Sheet, but are included in its stock at the price at which they were invoiced by the selling company, the profit on the transaction (which, from the point of view of the group is unrealized) must be deducted from the stock and from the consolidated profit in the consolidated accounts. Where, however, any part of the capital of a subsidiary is held by members outside the group, only the proportion of the inter-company profit on the transaction which is attributable to the members of the group must be regarded as unrealized and deleted. From the point of view of the outside shareholders, there is a realized profit arising from a purchase or sale of goods by the company of which they are members from or to another company, and no adjustment is necessary for their interest in such profit. Where, for example, only four-fifths of the capital of the subsidiary is held by the holding company, only four-fifths of the inter-company profit on the unsold stock will be deducted from the figures of stock and profit in the consolidated accounts. This adjustment is illustrated in § 5 of this chapter in describing the preparation of a Consolidated Profit and Loss Account.

A similar position arises where one company in the group undertakes capital expenditure for another company in the group, e.g. where a subsidiary manufactures plant and machinery that is acquired by the holding company or another subsidiary as a fixed asset. Here again any unrealized profit must be eliminated from the consolidated accounts by being deducted from the book value of the plant and from the profit.

Where there is a chain of companies the minority interest in each of the companies affected by the transaction must be taken into account in making the necessary adjustment. For example, if X holds 90 per cent. of the capital of Y, and Y holds 80 per cent. of the capital of Z, in respect of any profit included in the invoiced price of assets sold by X or Y to Z, or by Z to X or Y, 90 per cent. of 80 per cent. = 72 per cent. ($\frac{90}{100} \times \frac{80}{100}$ = 72 per cent.) is applicable to the group, and must be eliminated from the consolidated profit and consolidated assets. The minority interest consists of:

| | |
|---|---|
| Outside shareholders of Z .. .. .. .. | 20% |
| Outside shareholders of Y – 10 per cent. of 80 per cent. $\left(\frac{10}{100} \times \frac{80}{100}\right)$ .. .. .. .. .. .. | 8% |
| | 28% |

The effect of the above adjustments is to include the stock or other relevant assets in the Consolidated Balance Sheet at more than their actual cost to the group, the excess being included on the opposite side of the Balance Sheet as part of the liability to outside shareholders.

Not all accountants agree with the argument that only the proportion of the inter-company profit attributable to the members of the group must be eliminated. They argue that the assets transferred from one company to another in the group have not been acquired or sold by the minority, and therefore all profit should be eliminated either by debiting reserves with the group proportion and debiting minority interests with their proportion, or by debiting reserves with the whole unrealized profit and making no adjustment to minority interests. If minority interests are debited with their proportion of unrealized profit the consolidated accounts will understate the potential liability to minority interests. These alternative methods are valid but are not used in this textbook.

In order to simplify the preparation of the group accounts it is desirable for the parent company to carry in its own accounts a provision for unrealized profits on inter-company transactions.

### (m) Revaluation of Assets of Subsidiary Company

Where any of the assets of a subsidiary company have been revalued to arrive at the price paid for the shares by the holding company, although no adjustment has been made in the books of the subsidiary company, it is preferable to include in the Consolidated Balance Sheet the difference in value as a specific addition to, or deduction from, the assets affected, increasing or decreasing the pre-acquisition surplus and the liability to minority interests accordingly.

Any such increase or decrease in value will necessitate an adjustment of the charge for depreciation in the Consolidated Profit and Loss Account and such adjustment must be made *before* arriving at the proportion of the profits attributable to outside shareholders.

**Illustration (10)**

If plant and machinery standing in the books of the subsidiary company at £10,000 had been revalued for the purpose of fixing the price of the shares purchased, at £15,000, and depreciation had been written off in the books of the subsidiary company at the rate of 10 per cent., on the book value of £10,000 only, the subsidiary company's plant and machinery would be shown in the Consolidated Balance Sheet one year later, as:

|  | £ | £ | £ |
|---|---|---|---|
| Plant at cost, per books .. .. .. .. .. |  | 10,000 |  |
| *Less* Depreciation written off .. .. .. .. |  | 1,000 |  |
|  |  | 9,000 |  |
| *Add* Excess of valuation over book value.. .. .. | 5,000 |  |  |
| *Less* Depreciation on such excess .. .. .. | 500 |  |  |
|  |  | 4,500 |  |
|  |  |  | 13,500 |

The charge for depreciation in the Consolidated Profit and Loss Account will be increased by £500.

In the consolidated accounts the outside shareholders will have been credited with their share of the £5,000 appreciation in value, and will automatically be charged with their proportion of the increased depreciation since their share of profit will be a proportion of the reduced amount.

### Illustration (11)

The following are the Balance Sheets of H Ltd and its subsidiary S Ltd.

Prepare a Consolidated Balance Sheet having regard to the following:

(a) On the date when H Ltd acquired the shares in S Ltd, S Ltd had a reserve of £500 and a credit balance on Profit and Loss Account of £100. The shares in H Ltd, allotted in exchange for those of S Ltd, were issued at a premium of 50p per £1 share.

(b) In arriving at the value of the S Ltd shares, the plant, which then stood in the books at £4,500, was revalued at £5,400; and the furniture etc. then standing in the books at £600, was revalued at £360. The new values were not incorporated in the books of S Ltd. No changes in these assets have been made since that date.

(c) S Ltd has purchased goods from H Ltd, of which goods invoiced at £1,400 are still in stock. H Ltd adds 25 per cent. to cost in arriving at the invoice price to S Ltd.

### BALANCE SHEETS

| | H Ltd £ | S Ltd £ | | H Ltd £ | S Ltd £ |
|---|---|---|---|---|---|
| Share Capital .. .. .. | 22,000 | 8,000 | Goodwill .. .. .. | 3,500 | 2,500 |
| Premium on 5,200 shares .. | 2,600 | — | Plant .. .. .. | 7,000 | 3,900 |
| Revenue Reserve .. | — | 2,000 | Furniture .. .. .. | 1,200 | 500 |
| Profit and Loss Account .. | 2,800 | 600 | Stock .. .. .. | 4,000 | 2,700 |
| Creditors .. .. | 1,900 | 2,300 | Debtors .. .. | 5,000 | 3,100 |
| Current Account, H Ltd .. .. | | 700 | Current Account, S Ltd .. .. | 700 | |
| | | | Bank Balance .. .. | 100 | 900 |
| | | | Shares in S Ltd, 7,200 at cost .. | 7,800 | |
| | £29,300 | £13,600 | | £29,300 | £13,600 |

### PROCEDURE

First eliminate the current accounts; an asset of £700 in the books of H Ltd and a liability of £700 in the books of S Ltd. Then prepare memoranda ledger accounts.

### PLANT – S LTD

| | £ | £ | | £ |
|---|---|---|---|---|
| Balance per illustration .. .. | | 3,900 | Depreciation per contra .. .. .. | 600 |
| Depreciation per contra .. .. | | 600 | S Ltd – Profit and Loss Account: | |
| | | 4,500 | Additional depreciation (600/4,500 × £900) | 120 |
| | | | Balance to Consolidated Balance Sheet .. | 4,680 |
| Revaluation: Goodwill .. .. | 810 | | | |
| Minority (1/10) .. .. | 90 | | | |
| | | 900 | | |
| Revised value .. .. .. | | 5,400 | | |
| | | £5,400 | | £5,400 |

### FURNITURE – S LTD

| | £ | | £ |
|---|---|---|---|
| Balance per illustration .. .. .. | 500 | Depreciation per contra .. .. | 100 |
| Depreciation per contra .. .. .. | 100 | Revaluation: | |
| | 600 | Goodwill .. .. .. | 216 |
| | | Minority (1/10) .. .. .. | 24 |
| | | | 240 |
| S Ltd – Profit and Loss Account – depreciation over-provided (100/600 × £240) .. .. | 40 | Balance to Consolidated Balance Sheet | 300 |
| | £640 | | £640 |

## STOCK – S LTD

| | £ | | £ |
|---|---|---|---|
| Balance per illustration .. .. .. | 2,700 | Consolidated Profit and Loss Account – 9/10 × 25/125 × £1,400 .. .. .. | 252 |
| | | Balance to Consolidated Balance Sheet .. | 2,448 |
| | £2,700 | | £2,700 |

## GOODWILL

| | £ | | £ |
|---|---|---|---|
| Goodwill H Ltd .. .. .. .. | 3,500 | S Ltd – share capital .. .. .. | 7,200 |
| S Ltd .. .. .. .. | 2,500 | S Ltd – revenue reserves (9/10 × £600) .. | 540 |
| | 6,000 | Plant – increase on revaluation .. .. | 810 |
| Cost of Shares in S Ltd .. .. | 7,800 | Balance = Goodwill to Consolidated Balance | |
| Furniture – decrease on revaluation .. | 216 | Sheet .. .. .. .. | 5,466 |
| | £14,016 | | £14,016 |

## S LTD REVENUE RESERVES

| | £ | | £ |
|---|---|---|---|
| Goodwill – pre-acquisition reserves – 9/10 × 600 £(500 + 100) .. .. .. | 540 | Reserves .. .. .. .. | 2,000 |
| S Ltd plant – additional depreciation .. .. | 120 | Profit and Loss Account .. .. .. | 600 |
| Minority interest – 1/10 × £(2,000 + 600 + 40—120) | 252 | S Ltd – furniture – depreciation over-provided | 40 |
| Balance transferred to Consolidated Revenue Reserves £(2,600—252—540 + 40—120) .. | 1,728 | | |
| | £2,640 | | £2,640 |

## CONSOLIDATED REVENUE RESERVES

| | £ | | £ |
|---|---|---|---|
| Provision for unrealized stock profit .. .. | 252 | H Ltd – Profit and Loss Account balance .. | 2,800 |
| Balance to Consolidated Balance Sheet .. | 4,276 | S Ltd – transferred .. .. .. | 1,728 |
| | £4,528 | | £4,528 |

## MINORITY INTEREST (1/10th)

| | £ | | £ |
|---|---|---|---|
| S Ltd – furniture revaluation .. .. | 24 | S Ltd – share capital (1/10 × £8,000) .. | 800 |
| Balance to Consolidated Balance Sheet .. | 1,118 | S Ltd – revenue reserves 1/10 × £(2,000 + 600 + 40—120) .. .. | 252 |
| | | S Ltd – plant revaluation .. .. .. | 90 |
| | £1,142 | | £1,142 |

## CONSOLIDATED BALANCE SHEET

| | £ | £ | | £ | £ | £ |
|---|---|---|---|---|---|---|
| Share Capital | | 22,000 | Goodwill | | | 5,466 |
| Share Premium Account | | 2,600 | Plant etc, H Ltd | | 7,000 | |
| Revenue Reserves: | | |      S Ltd | 3,900 | | |
|   H Ltd | 2,548 | |   *Add* Increase on | | | |
|   S Ltd | 1,728 | |     revaluation   £900 | | | |
| | | 4,276 |   *Less* Depreciation thereon 120 | | | |
| | | | | 780 | | |
| | | 28,876 | | | 4,680 | |
| | | | | | | 11,680 |
| Minority Interest in subsidiary | | 1,118 | Furniture etc. H Ltd | | 1,200 | |
| | | |      S Ltd | 500 | | |
| Creditors: | | |   *Deduct* Reduction in value £240 | | | |
|   H Ltd | 1,900 | |   *Less* Depreciation thereon 40 | | | |
|   S Ltd | 2,300 | | | 200 | | |
| | | 4,200 | | | 300 | |
| | | | | | | 1,500 |
| | | | Stock H Ltd | | 4,000 | |
| | | |      S Ltd | 2,700 | | |
| | | |   *Less* Provision for unrealized | | | |
| | | |     profit | 252 | | |
| | | | | | 2,448 | |
| | | | | | | 6,448 |
| | | | Debtors H Ltd | | 5,000 | |
| | | |      S Ltd | | 3,100 | |
| | | | | | | 8,100 |
| | | | Bank Balance H Ltd | | 100 | |
| | | |      S Ltd | | 900 | |
| | | | | | | 1,000 |
| | | £34,194 | | | | £34,194 |

*Notes:*

1. The Revenue Reserves have been grouped under one heading in accordance with the recommendations of the Council of the Institute of Chartered Accountants.

2. Some authorities prefer to show the consolidation of the goodwill figures actually appearing in the holding company's and subsidiary company's Balance Sheets separately from the sum attributable to cost of control. If this were done, Goodwill would appear in the Consolidated Balance Sheet at £6,000, and £534, £(6,000—5,466) being the excess of the book value of the net assets of S Ltd applicable to H Ltd's holding over the cost of such holding, would appear on the opposite side of the Balance Sheet as a Capital Reserve.

3. When H Ltd acquired the shares in S Ltd the double entry in H Ltd's books was debit Shares in S Ltd and credit Share Capital and Share Premium. In the consolidated accounts the balances on H Ltd's Share Capital and Share Premium Accounts will be shown. No special adjustments are needed.

### (n) Subsidiaries holding shares in other subsidiaries

Where subsidiaries hold shares in other subsidiaries, and possibly the parent company holds shares in more than one subsidiary, consolidation should start with the company which does *not* hold shares in any other company. If this procedure is not adopted errors in the calculation of indirect minority interests are likely to occur. If the parent company holds shares in two or more companies but subsidiaries do not hold shares in other subsidiaries it does not matter which subsidiary is consolidated first.

An indirect minority interest arises when one subsidiary with outside shareholders holds shares in another subsidiary, e.g. P Ltd the holding company holds 60 per cent. of the shares in A Ltd and A Ltd holds 70 per cent. of the shares in B Ltd. The indirect minority interest is A Ltd's outside shareholders' interest in B Ltd's *post-acquisition* profit; their minority interest is 40 per cent. of 70 per cent. of B Ltd's post-acquisition profits (i.e. 28 per cent.).

**Illustration (12)**

The following is an abstract of the Balance Sheets of Holding Ltd and its subsidiaries A Ltd and B Ltd as on December 31st. Prepare a Consolidated Balance Sheet.

| | Holding Ltd £ | £ | A Ltd £ | £ | B Ltd £ | £ |
|---|---|---|---|---|---|---|
| Share Capital Authorized and Issued: | | | | | | |
| Ordinary Shares of £1 each, fully paid .. .. | | 100,000 | | 40,000 | | 30,000 |
| Share Premium Account: | | | | | | |
| (Premium on issue of 20,000 Shares issued in payment for 30,000 Shares in A Ltd) .. .. .. .. | | 10,000 | | | | |
| Profit and Loss Account: | | | | | | |
| Balance brought forward .. .. .. .. | 3,000 | | | | 6,000 | |
| Add Profit for year .. .. .. .. | 20,000 | | | | 3,000 | |
| | | 23,000 | | | | 9,000 |
| Creditors .. .. .. .. .. | | 19,000 | | 20,000 | | 3,000 |
| Bills Payable (all issued to Holding Ltd) .. .. | | | | 18,000 | | |
| | | £152,000 | | £78,000 | | £42,000 |

*Note:* Holding Ltd had a contingent liability on Bills discounted, £10,000. Creditors of A Ltd, £20,000, includes £15,000 owed to Holding Ltd.

| | Holding Ltd £ | £ | A Ltd £ | £ | B Ltd £ | £ |
|---|---|---|---|---|---|---|
| Goodwill at cost .. .. .. .. | | | | 6,000 | | |
| Land, Buildings, Plant and Machinery, at cost .. .. | | 25,000 | | 30,000 | | 20,000 |
| Investments, at cost: | | | | | | |
| 30,000 Ordinary Shares in A Ltd .. .. .. | 30,000 | | | | | |
| 20,000 ,,     ,,   ,, B Ltd .. .. .. | 40,000 | | | | | |
| | | 70,000 | | | | |
| 10,000 ,,     ,,   ,, B Ltd .. .. .. | | | | 20,000 | | |
| Stocks, as valued by Companies' officials .. .. | | 10,000 | | 3,000 | | 8,000 |
| Debtors .. .. .. .. .. | 10,000 | | | 2,000 | | 7,000 |
| Advance to A Ltd .. .. .. .. | 15,000 | | | | | |
| | | 25,000 | | | | |
| Bills Receivable (accepted by A Ltd) .. .. | 8,000 | | | | | |
| Balances at Bankers .. .. .. | | 14,000 | | 6,000 | | 7,000 |
| Profit and Loss Account: | | | | | | |
| Balance brought forward .. .. .. | | | 5,000 | | | |
| Add Loss for year .. .. .. | | | 6,000 | | | |
| | | | | 11,000 | | |
| | | £152,000 | | £78,000 | | £42,000 |

On January 1st of the previous year, the date when Holding Ltd purchased the 30,000 Shares in A Ltd, the debit balance on the A Ltd's Profit and Loss Account was £1,000. Holding Ltd and A Ltd both purchased their shares in B Ltd on January 1st in the current year.

METHOD OF WORKING

First eliminate the inter-company balances. £8,000 bills payable in A Ltd – will cancel out with £8,000 bills receivable in Holding Ltd, creditors of A Ltd – £15,000, will cancel out with the £15,000 advance to A Ltd shown in Holding Ltd.

Secondly prepare memoranda ledger accounts to consolidate B Ltd, the sub-subsidiary company.

## GOODWILL

| | £ | | £ |
|---|---|---|---|
| Shares in A Ltd | 30,000 | Share Capital A Ltd, Nominal Value | 30,000 |
| Profit and Loss Account: A Ltd Pre-acquisition loss | 750 | Balance = Goodwill | 750 |
| | £30,750 | | £30,750 |
| Shares in B Ltd held by Holding Ltd | 40,000 | Share Capital B Ltd, Nominal Value | 20,000 |
| | | Profit and Loss Account – B Ltd, Pre-acquisition profit | 4,000 |
| | | Balance = Goodwill | 16,000 |
| | £40,000 | | £40,000 |
| Shares in B Ltd held by A Ltd | 20,000 | Share Capital B Ltd, Nominal Value | 10,000 |
| | | Profit and Loss Account – B Ltd, Pre-acquisition profit | 2,000 |
| | | Balance = Goodwill | 8,000 |
| | £20,000 | | £20,000 |

## B LTD, PROFIT AND LOSS ACCOUNT

| | £ | | £ |
|---|---|---|---|
| Goodwill – Pre-acquisition profits applicable to: | | Balance | 9,000 |
|   Holding Ltd | 4,000 | | |
|   A Ltd | 2,000 | | |
| A Ltd: Profit and Loss Account – Share of post-acquisition profit applicable to A Ltd | 1,000 | | |
| Consolidated Profit and Loss Account – Share of post-acquisition profit applicable to Holding Ltd | 2,000 | | |
| | £9,000 | | £9,000 |

## A LTD, PROFIT AND LOSS ACCOUNT

| | £ | | £ |
|---|---|---|---|
| Balance | 11,000 | Goodwill – Pre-acquisition loss applicable to Holding Ltd | 750 |
| | | B Ltd Profit and Loss Account – Share of post-acquisition profit applicable to A Ltd | 1,000 |
| | | Minority Interest – ¼ £(11,000—1,000) | 2,500 |
| | | Balance to Consolidated Profit and Loss Account | 6,750 |
| | £11,000 | | £11,000 |

## CONSOLIDATED PROFIT AND LOSS ACCOUNT

| | £ | | £ |
|---|---|---|---|
| A Ltd's Profit and Loss Account – Share of post-acquisition loss applicable to Holding Ltd | 6,750 | Holding Ltd's Profit and Loss Account: Balance | 23,000 |
| Balance to Consolidated Balance Sheet | 18,250 | B Ltd's Profit and Loss Account – Share of post-acquisition profit applicable to Holding Ltd | 2,000 |
| | £25,000 | | £25,000 |

## MINORITY INTEREST (1/4th of A Ltd)

| | £ | | £ |
|---|---|---|---|
| Profit and Loss Account – A Ltd Share of Loss | 2,500 | Share Capital, A Ltd | 10,000 |
| Balance to Consolidated Balance Sheet | 7,500 | | |
| | £10,000 | | £10,000 |

The goodwill appearing in the Consolidated Balance Sheet will be:

| | £ |
|---|---:|
| Balance per A Ltd's Balance Sheet .. .. .. .. .. | 6,000 |
| Holding Company's Goodwill in A Ltd (as above) .. .. .. | 750 |
| ,, ,, ,, B Ltd ,, ,, .. .. .. | 16,000 |
| A Ltd's ,, ,, ,, B Ltd ,, ,, .. .. .. | 8,000 |
| | £30,750 |

### CONSOLIDATED BALANCE SHEET OF HOLDING LTD AND ITS SUBSIDIARY COMPANIES – as at December 31st

| | £ | £ | | | £ | £ |
|---|---:|---:|---|---|---:|---:|
| SHARE CAPITAL | | | FIXED ASSETS | | | |
| Authorized and Issued .. .. | | 100,000 | Goodwill .. .. | | | 30,750 |
| | | | Land, Buildings, Plant and Machinery, at cost: | | | |
| RESERVES | | | H Ltd .. .. | | 25,000 | |
| Share Premium Account .. | | 10,000 | A Ltd .. .. | | 30,000 | |
| | | | B Ltd .. .. | | 20,000 | |
| CONSOLIDATED PROFIT AND LOSS ACCOUNT | | | | | | 75,000 |
| Holding Ltd .. .. | 23,000 | | | | | 105,750 |
| Less Subsidiaries – Loss .. | 4,750 | | | | | |
| | | 18,250 | CURRENT ASSETS | | | |
| | | 128,250 | Stocks– | | | |
| | | | H Ltd .. .. | 10,000 | | |
| MINORITY INTERESTS .. .. | | 7,500 | A Ltd .. .. | 3,000 | | |
| | | | B Ltd .. .. | 8,000 | | |
| CREDITORS | | | | | 21,000 | |
| H Ltd .. .. .. | 19,000 | | Debtors– | | | |
| A Ltd .. .. £20,000 | | | H Ltd .. .. | 10,000 | | |
| Less due to H Ltd .. 15,000 | | | A Ltd .. .. | 2,000 | | |
| | 5,000 | | B Ltd .. .. | 7,000 | | |
| B Ltd .. .. .. | 3,000 | | | | 19,000 | |
| | | 27,000 | Balances at Bankers– | | | |
| BILLS PAYABLE | | | H Ltd .. .. | 14,000 | | |
| A Ltd .. .. | 18,000 | | A Ltd .. .. | 6,000 | | |
| Less held by H Ltd .. .. | 8,000 | | B Ltd .. .. | 7,000 | | |
| | | 10,000 | | | 27,000 | 67,000 |
| | | £172,750 | | | | £172,750 |

Observe that in computing the goodwill of £8,000 in A Ltd's holding in B Ltd no part of the pre-acquisition profits of B Ltd applicable to A Ltd is credited to the outside shareholders of A Ltd because such pre-acquisition profits are represented by part of the assets of B Ltd which A Ltd has, in effect, purchased and paid for out of its capital funds, and are not revenue available for distribution by A Ltd among its shareholders. The excess of the price paid by A Ltd for these shares over the net assets by which they are represented at the date of their acquisition is the sum paid by A Ltd for goodwill, and would appear as an asset in the Consolidated Balance Sheet of A Ltd and B Ltd, were the Balance Sheets of these two companies consolidated separately, as shown hereunder.

### CONSOLIDATED BALANCE SHEET OF A LTD AND B LTD

| | £ | £ | | | £ | £ |
|---|---:|---:|---|---|---:|---:|
| Share Capital A Ltd .. .. | | 40,000 | Goodwill – A Ltd .. .. | | | 6,000 |
| Minority Interests .. .. | | 26,000 | Goodwill re A's holding in B Ltd (see Goodwill Account on p. 420) .. | | | 8,000 |
| | | | | | | 14,000 |
| Creditors: | | | | | | |
| A Ltd .. .. .. | 20,000 | | Land etc. | | | |
| B Ltd .. .. .. | 3,000 | | A Ltd .. .. .. | 30,000 | | |
| | | 23,000 | B Ltd .. .. .. | 20,000 | | |
| Bills Payable, A Ltd .. .. | | 18,000 | | | | 50,000 |
| | | | Stocks: | | | |
| | | | A Ltd .. .. .. | 3,000 | | |
| | | | B Ltd .. .. .. | 8,000 | | |
| | | | | | | 11,000 |
| | | | Debtors: | | | |
| | | | A Ltd .. .. .. | 2,000 | | |
| | | | B Ltd .. .. .. | 7,000 | | |
| | | | | | | 9,000 |
| | | | Bank Balances: | | | |
| | | | A Ltd .. .. .. | 6,000 | | |
| | | | B Ltd .. .. .. | 7,000 | | |
| | | | | | | 13,000 |
| | | | Profit and Loss Account .. .. | | | 10,000 |
| | | £107,000 | | | | £107,000 |

### PROFIT AND LOSS ACCOUNT – B LTD

| | £ | | £ |
|---|---|---|---|
| Goodwill – Pre-acquisition profits (1/3 × £6,000) | 2,000 | Balance    ..    ..    ..    .. | 9,000 |
| Minority Interest (2/3 × £9,000)    ..    .. | 6,000 | | |
| Consolidated – Profit and Loss Account (1/3 × £3,000)    ..    ..    .. | 1,000 | | |
| | £9,000 | | £9,000 |

### MINORITY INTEREST

| | £ | | £ |
|---|---|---|---|
| | | B Ltd Share Capital    ..    ..    .. | 20,000 |
| | | B Ltd – Profit and Loss Account ..    .. | 6,000 |
| | | | £26,000 |

### CONSOLIDATED PROFIT AND LOSS ACCOUNT

| | £ | | £ |
|---|---|---|---|
| Balance per Balance Sheet ..    ..    .. | 11,000 | A Ltd's share of B Ltd's post-acquisition profit | 1,000 |
| | | Balance    ..    ..    ..    .. | 10,000 |
| | £11,000 | | £11,000 |

*Note:* A Ltd's goodwill in B Ltd is one of the assets of A Ltd, which will enter into the Consolidated Balance Sheet of Holding Ltd in the same way as the other assets of A Ltd when the above Balance Sheet is incorporated therein.

Some accountants take the view that only the proportion of this goodwill which is attributable to the members of the holding company should appear in the Consolidated Balance Sheet of the group and accordingly that the proportion of the goodwill applicable to the outside members should be eliminated. If this were done in the above illustration, one-fourth of the £8,000 paid by A Ltd for goodwill for its holding in B Ltd would be written off against the outside shareholders, thereby reducing the goodwill figure in the Consolidated Balance Sheet of Holding Ltd to £28,750 and the minority interest to £5,500. There would seem to be no logical justification for this procedure; the goodwill is in no different category from the other assets of A Ltd and if part of the goodwill is written off against outside shareholders of A Ltd it would be logical to write off part of the other assets also, and thereby eliminate the minority interest from the consolidated accounts altogether.

If the price paid by A Ltd for the shares in B Ltd were *less* than the value of the net assets attributable to the holding, so that instead of 'goodwill' there was a 'capital reserve', the proportion thereof applicable to the outside shareholders of A Ltd *should* be credited to minority interest, as it represents part of the value of the net assets shown in the consolidated accounts which is attributable to their holdings. Thus, in the above example, if the price paid by A Ltd for the shares in B Ltd had been only £10,000, there would have been a 'capital reserve' of £2,000, of which £500 would be credited to the minority interest in A Ltd, and the balance of £1,500 deducted from the consolidated goodwill. Alternatively the 'capital reserve' could be applied in writing down the assets of B Ltd for the purpose of the consolidated accounts.

If in the above illustration the price paid by Holding Ltd for the shares in A Ltd were less than the value of the net assets attributable to the holding so that there was a capital reserve arising on consolidation it would be illogical to show goodwill as an asset acquired on the other side of the Balance Sheet at its book value; enough should be written off goodwill in the proportions three-quarters to capital reserve, one-quarter to minority interests, to eliminate the capital reserve. If the capital reserve arising on consolidation is larger than goodwill in A Ltd's books the whole of goodwill should be written off.

### Illustration (13)

Assume facts as in Illustration (12) except that H Ltd has paid £25,650 for the shares in A Ltd instead of £30,000, all the balances in A Ltd's books being the same. The Goodwill Account would have been:

### GOODWILL

| | £ | | £ |
|---|---|---|---|
| Shares in A Ltd .. .. .. .. | 25,650 | Share Capital nominal value .. .. | 30,000 |
| Profit and Loss Account: | | | |
| A Ltd – Pre-acquisition loss (¾) .. .. | 750 | | |
| Balance carried down .. .. .. | 3,600 | | |
| | £30,000 | | £30,000 |
| | £ | | £ |
| Goodwill per A Ltd's books .. .. | 6,000 | Balance brought down .. .. .. | 3,600 |
| | | Minority Interest: | |
| | | Goodwill written off (¼ × 4/3 × £3,600) .. | 1,200 |
| | | Balance = Goodwill .. .. .. | 1,200 |
| | £6,000 | | £6,000 |

*Note:* Only capital reserve arising on consolidation of £3,600 is to be written off against Goodwill of £6,000. £3,600 will therefore represent three-quarters of the goodwill to be written off, total goodwill to be written off will therefore be 4/3 × £3,600.

In the preceding illustration the shares in B Ltd were acquired by Holding Ltd and A Ltd on the same date.

Where shares in a subsidiary have been acquired by different members of the group at different dates, the 'goodwill' element in each holding will be represented by the excess of the cost thereof over the proportion of the net assets of the subsidiary attributable thereto *at the date of the particular acquisition.* Any undivided profits of such subsidiary which have accrued *after* the acquisition will be revenue profits from the viewpoint of that holding member. If, however, such holding member later becomes a subsidiary of the parent company, the proportion of the post-acquisition profits of the first mentioned subsidiary attributable to that holding member will constitute part of its net assets at the date on which it, in turn, became a subsidiary of the parent company, and must be treated as a pre-acquisition profit in computing the 'goodwill' ingredient of the parent company's holding.

### Illustration (14)

The following schedules summarize the Balance Sheets, as on December 31st, of a group of companies:

| | X Ltd | Y Ltd | Z Ltd |
|---|---|---|---|
| | £ | £ | £ |
| Land and Buildings .. .. .. .. | 125,000 | 71,700 | 16,000 |
| Plant and Machinery .. .. .. .. | 175,000 | | 16,500 |
| Fixtures and Fittings .. .. .. .. | 15,000 | 6,000 | 2,500 |
| Carried forward | 315,000 | 77,700 | 35,000 |

|  | X Ltd £ | Y Ltd £ | Z Ltd £ |
|---|---|---|---|
| Brought forward | 315,000 | 77,700 | 35,000 |
| Investments: |  |  |  |
| Y Ltd 120,000 shares .. .. .. .. | 105,000 |  |  |
| Z Ltd 20,000 shares .. .. .. .. | 14,000 |  |  |
| „ 10,000 shares .. .. .. .. |  | 7,000 |  |
| Stock-in-trade .. .. .. .. .. | 150,460 | 46,655 | 24,500 |
| Sundry Debtors: |  |  |  |
| General .. .. .. .. .. | 37,450 | 28,300 | 8,500 |
| Y Ltd .. .. .. .. .. .. | 15,685 |  |  |
| Z Ltd .. .. .. .. .. .. | 15,985 | 8,750 |  |
| Cash and Bank Balances .. .. .. .. | 25,200 | 1,350 | 2,315 |
| Profit and Loss Account balance .. .. .. |  |  | 5,000 |
|  | £678,780 | £169,755 | £75,315 |

|  | X Ltd £ | Y Ltd £ | Z Ltd £ |
|---|---|---|---|
| Capital, issued in shares of £1 each: |  |  |  |
| Fully paid up .. .. .. .. .. | 500,000 |  | 50,000 |
| 75p paid up (160,000 shares) .. .. .. |  | 120,000 |  |
| General Reserves .. .. .. .. | 100,000 | 20,000 |  |
| Profit and Loss Account balances .. .. .. | 51,500 | 5,000 |  |
| Sundry Creditors: |  |  |  |
| General .. .. .. .. .. | 27,280 | 12,070 | 1,830 |
| X Ltd .. .. .. .. .. .. |  | 12,685 | 15,985 |
| Y Ltd .. .. .. .. .. .. |  |  | 7,500 |
|  | £678,780 | £169,755 | £75,315 |

On December 31st, goods to the value of £3,000 were in transit from X Ltd to Y Ltd and a remittance of £1,250 from Z Ltd to Y Ltd was not recorded by Y Ltd until after the books had been closed.

Y Ltd had a credit balance on Profit and Loss Account of £10,000, and no General Reserve, when it became a subsidiary of X Ltd, but has since paid dividends of £20,000, of which £10,000 was paid out of pre-acquisition profits. X Ltd has taken credit for its share of these dividends in its Profit and Loss Account.

Z Ltd had a debit balance on Profit and Loss Account of £15,000 when Y Ltd purchased 10,000 shares, and of £10,000 when, later, X Ltd purchased 20,000 shares in Z Ltd. X Ltd purchased its holdings in Y Ltd and Z Ltd on the same date.

Prepare a Consolidated Balance Sheet for the group as at December 31st. Ignore Taxation.

PROCEDURE

1. Eliminate inter-company balances. In Y's books Z Ltd is a debtor for £8,750; in Z's books Y Ltd is a creditor for £7,500, the difference is cash in transit which must be included in the cash balances in the Consolidated Balance Sheet.

In X Ltd's books Z Ltd is shown as a debtor for £15,985 which cancels out with the credit balance of £15,985 in Z Ltd's books. In X Ltd's books Y Ltd is a debtor for £15,685 while in Y Ltd's books X Ltd is a creditor for £12,685, the difference is goods in transit which must be included in stock in the Consolidated Balance Sheet.

2. Prepare Memoranda Ledger Accounts for Z Ltd showing Goodwill for Y in Z and X in Z, Profit and Loss Account Z Ltd, and minority interests in Z Ltd.

3. The pre-acquisition losses of Z Ltd which must be transferred from Z Ltd's Profit and Loss Account to the debit of Goodwill are:                                                £

$re$ Y Ltd's holding: $1/5 \times £15,000$     ..        ..        ..     3,000
$re$ X Ltd's holding: $2/5 \times £10,000$     ..        ..        ..     4,000
                                                                                    £7,000

4. Since Z Ltd had a debit balance of £15,000 when Y Ltd acquired its holding and now has a debit balance of £5,000 on Profit and Loss Account, Z Ltd must have earned £10,000 profit since Y Ltd acquired its shares. Y Ltd is therefore entitled to $1/5 \times £10,000 = £2,000$.

5. Since Z Ltd had a debit balance of £10,000 when X Ltd acquired its shares and now has a debit balance on Profit and Loss Account of £5,000, Z Ltd must have earned £5,000 profit since X Ltd acquired its shares, X Ltd is therefore entitled to $2/5 \times £5,000 = £2,000$.

6. Z Ltd's outside shareholders are entitled to 2/5ths of the share capital and 2/5ths of the debit balance on Profit and Loss Account, i.e. $2/5 \times £5,000 = £2,000$.

7. Prepare Memoranda Ledger Accounts for Y Ltd: Goodwill, Profit and Loss Account and Minority Interest Account. Pick up balance from Y Ltd's Balance Sheet and appropriate balances from the Memoranda Ledger Accounts for Z Ltd.

8. The dividends received by X Ltd from Y Ltd amount to 3/4ths of £20,000 = £15,000, of which £7,500 was paid out of pre-acquisition profits and must be transferred from X Ltd's Profit and Loss Account to the credit of Goodwill Account. The dividends are capital receipts reducing the cost of the shares. Open Profit and Loss Account X Ltd.

9. When X Ltd bought shares in Y Ltd, X Ltd bought not only a share in the disclosed reserves of Y Ltd but also in the undisclosed reserves of Y Ltd.
Since X Ltd acquired its shares in Y Ltd when the debit balance on Z Ltd's Profit and Loss Account was £10,000, Z Ltd must have earned £5,000 since Y Ltd acquired its holding in Z Ltd. (£15,000 Dr – less £10,000 Dr) Y Ltd is entitled to $1/5 \times £5,000 = £1,000$ and since X Ltd acquired 3/4ths of Y Ltd's share capital, X Ltd must therefore have acquired $3/4 \times £1,000 = £750$ pre-acquisition profits of Z Ltd, which must be credited to goodwill.

10. Y Ltd's minority shareholders must be credited with one-fourth of Y Ltd's profits including Y Ltd's share of the post-acquisition profits of Z Ltd.

11. Complete Profit and Loss Account X Ltd: pick up balance from X Ltd's Balance Sheet and appropriate balances from the Memoranda Ledger Accounts of Y Ltd and Z Ltd.

12. Complete Memoranda Ledger Accounts, aggregate other assets and liabilities and prepare Consolidated Balance Sheet.

The Consolidating Ledger Accounts will appear as follows:

## GOODWILL

| | £ | | £ |
|---|---|---|---|
| Shares in Y Ltd held by X Ltd     ..        .. | 105,000 | Y Ltd Share Capital, nominal value     .. | 90,000 |
| *Less* Dividend paid out of pre-acquisition | | Profit and Loss Account, Y Ltd | |
| profits ..        ..        ..        .. | 7,500 | Pre-acquisition profit ..        ..        .. | 750 |
| | 97,500 | Balance = Goodwill     ..        ..        .. | 6,750 |
| | £97,500 | | £97,500 |
| Shares in Z Ltd held by X Ltd     ..        .. | 14,000 | Z Ltd, Share Capital, nominal value     .. | 20,000 |
| Z Ltd, Profit and Loss Account: | | | |
| Pre-acquisition loss     ..        ..        .. | 4,000 | | |
| Balance = Capital Reserve   ..        ..        .. | 2,000 | | |
| | £20,000 | | £20,000 |
| Shares in Z Ltd, held by Y Ltd     ..        .. | 7,000 | Z Ltd, Share Capital, nominal value     .. | 10,000 |
| Z Ltd, Profit and Loss Account: | | | |
| Pre-acquisition Loss     ..        ..        .. | 3,000 | | |
| | £10,000 | | £10,000 |

### PROFIT AND LOSS ACCOUNT – Z LTD

| | £ | | £ |
|---|---|---|---|
| Balance .. .. .. .. .. | 5,000 | Minority Interest (2/5ths of £5,000) .. | 2,000 |
| Y Ltd Profit and Loss Account – Share of profit | | Goodwill (see Note 3) .. .. | |
| attributable to Y Ltd since acquisition (1/5th | | re Y Ltd's holding (1/5 × £15,000) .. | 3,000 |
| of £10,000). (see Note 4) .. .. | 2,000 | re X Ltd's holding (2/5 × £10,000) .. | 4,000 |
| X Ltd Profit and Loss Account – Share of profit | | | |
| attributable to X Ltd since acquisition (2/5ths | | | |
| of £5,000) (see Note 5) .. .. .. | 2,000 | | |
| | £9,000 | | £9,000 |

### MINORITY INTERESTS

| | (1/4th) Y Ltd £ | (2/5ths) Z Ltd £ | | (1/4th) Y Ltd £ | (2/5ths) Z Ltd £ |
|---|---|---|---|---|---|
| Profit and Loss Account (2/5 × £5,000) .. .. .. .. | | 2,000 | Share Capital .. .. .. | 30,000 | 20,000 |
| Balances to Consolidated Balance Sheet .. .. .. | 36,750 | 18,000 | General Reserve (1/4 × £20,000) .. | 5,000 | |
| | | | Profit and Loss Account (1/4 × £7,000) .. .. .. | 1,750 | |
| | £36,750 | £20,000 | | £36,750 | £20,000 |

### PROFIT AND LOSS ACCOUNT – X LTD

| | £ | | £ |
|---|---|---|---|
| Goodwill – Dividend from Y Ltd paid out of | | X Ltd – Balance .. .. .. | 51,500 |
| pre-acquisition profit .. .. .. | 7,500 | Y Ltd – Post-acquisition profit .. .. | 4,500 |
| Balance to Consolidated Profit and Loss Account .. .. .. .. .. | 50,500 | Z Ltd – Post-acquisition profit .. .. | 2,000 |
| | £58,000 | | £58,000 |

### PROFIT AND LOSS ACCOUNT – Y LTD

| | £ | | £ |
|---|---|---|---|
| Minority Interest (1/4 × £7,000) .. .. | 1,750 | Balance .. .. .. .. .. | 5,000 |
| Goodwill (3/4 × £1,000) being Y Ltd's share | | Share of post-acquisition profit of Z Ltd (1/5 × | |
| of Z Ltd's profit earned between date of ac- | | £10,000) (see Note 4) .. | 2,000 |
| quisition by Y Ltd of shares in Z Ltd and date | | | |
| on which Y Ltd became a subsidiary of X Ltd | | | |
| (see Note 9) .. .. .. .. | 750 | | |
| Balance to Consolidated Profit and Loss Ac- | | | |
| count .. .. .. .. .. | 4,500 | | |
| | £7,000 | | £7,000 |

*Note:* It is preferable to set off the 'capital reserve' arising from the purchase by X Ltd of shares in Z Ltd against the goodwill purchased in Y Ltd. The goodwill appearing in the Consolidated Balance Sheet will thus be:

| | | | | £ |
|---|---|---|---|---|
| Goodwill in Y Ltd (as above).. | .. | .. | .. | 6,750 |
| *Less* Capital Reserve in Z Ltd | .. | .. | .. | 2,000 |
| | | | | £4,750 |

Since the price paid by Y Ltd for its holding in Z Ltd (£7,000) is exactly equal to the net assets of Z Ltd attributable thereto (share capital £10,000 less pre-acquisition loss £3,000) no goodwill or capital reserve arises on this holding.

## CONSOLIDATED BALANCE SHEET

| | £ | £ | | £ | £ |
|---|--:|--:|---|--:|--:|
| Share Capital | | 500,000 | Goodwill | | 4,750 |
| General Reserve: | | | Land and Buildings: | | |
| X Ltd | 100,000 | | X Ltd | 125,000 | |
| Y Ltd (3/4 × £20,000) | 15,000 | | Y Ltd | 71,700 | |
| | | 115,000 | Z Ltd | 16,000 | |
| Consolidated Profit and Loss Account: | | | | | 212,700 |
| X Ltd | 44,000 | | Plant and Machinery: | | |
| Subsidiaries | 6,500 | | X Ltd | 175,000 | |
| | | 50,500 | Z Ltd | 16,500 | |
| | | 665,500 | | | 191,500 |
| | | | Fixtures and Fittings: | | |
| Minority Interests | | 54,750 | X Ltd | 15,000 | |
| | | | Y Ltd | 6,000 | |
| | | | Z Ltd | 2,500 | |
| Creditors: | | | | | 23,500 |
| X Ltd | 27,280 | | Stock-in-Trade: | | |
| Y Ltd | 12,070 | | X Ltd | 150,460 | |
| Z Ltd | 1,830 | | Y Ltd | 46,655 | |
| | | 41,180 | Z Ltd | 24,500 | |
| | | | In transit | 3,000 | |
| | | | | | 224,615 |
| | | | Debtors: | | |
| | | | X Ltd | 37,450 | |
| | | | Y Ltd | 28,300 | |
| | | | Z Ltd | 8,500 | |
| | | | | | 74,250 |
| | | | Cash and Bank Balances: | | |
| | | | X Ltd | 25,200 | |
| | | | Y Ltd | 1,350 | |
| | | | Z Ltd | 2,315 | |
| | | | In transit | 1,250 | |
| | | | | | 30,115 |
| | | £761,430 | | | £761,430 |

### (o) Foreign Subsidiaries

Foreign subsidiaries raise special problems, particularly where exchange restrictions prevent the remittance of money to the United Kingdom. If current and liquid assets of the subsidiary company are included in the Consolidated Balance Sheet, not only is it difficult to decide upon a rate of exchange for their conversion into sterling, but, since no use of the funds can be made here, a misleading statement may result. Where subsidiaries operate in many foreign countries, the problem is magnified, and it is suggested that, in general terms, it is better to keep separate from the other assets and liabilities the balances applicable to subsidiary companies operating in countries with 'frozen' exchanges, or even to exclude such companies from consolidation.

Great care must be taken with foreign subsidiary companies to ensure that any unrealized profits are eliminated in the Consolidated Balance Sheet, e.g. where the holding company in this country has sold goods to the foreign subsidiary, the 'sale' will have been credited, normally, at the usual selling price, and taken in by the subsidiary at the currency equivalent on the date of delivery. In valuing its stock for its Balance Sheet, the subsidiary will have valued any such goods at cost or realizable value, whichever is lower, and, according to the rules normally adopted for conversion, this value will be converted into sterling at the rate ruling at the date of the Balance Sheet. Not only therefore is there an unrealized profit (from the viewpoint of the group) in the stock-in-hand which emanated from the holding company, but there may be a fictitious profit or loss on exchange arising through the difference between the rates of exchange on the dates of delivery and of the Balance Sheet respectively. Adjusting entries must therefore be made in the process of preparing the Consolidated Balance Sheet, to ensure that the stock does not appear in the Consolidated Balance Sheet at more than its cost to the group.

In other respects, the conversion of currency into sterling follows generally the same rules as in Branch Accounts (*see* Chapter X).

Fixed assets of foreign subsidiaries should appear in the Consolidated Balance Sheet at their sterling cost, which must, therefore, be recorded as and when each asset is acquired. In regard to any new fixed assets acquired during an accounting period these should be converted at the rates in force at the dates when the remittances from the holding company were made, or, if the assets were purchased out of the subsidiary's own resources, at the rates in force at the dates of purchase. Where, however, the rates of exchange have not fluctuated materially during the year, the cost of additions may be converted at the average rate for the period.

An adjustment may be necessary for depreciation of fixed assets. The depreciation will be converted at the rate ruling at the date that the expenditure on the asset was incurred, which may differ greatly from current rates. If the effect is that the aggregate depreciation on all subsidiary companies' assets, as converted into sterling on this basis, is considerably less than it would be on a current rate basis, there may be a serious paper inflation of profits, since the apparent profit may exceed the sterling equivalent of the money which would be remitted in payment of a dividend equal to the whole currency profit. A special provision should be created, or it may be considered whether consolidation should be made at all in the circumstances.

Exchange differences on conversion may never be realized; they may be wholly on capital items etc., and until realized on remittance should, if profits, be credited to reserve or, if losses, be written off.

### (*p*) *Bank Overdrafts*

Balances at the bank in hand cannot be set off in consolidated accounts against bank overdrafts unless there is a legal arrangement giving the bank the right of set off.

### § 5. Consolidated Profit and Loss Account

As already stated, the group accounts laid before a holding company will normally comprise a Consolidated Profit and Loss Account and a Consolidated Balance Sheet. The information given must comply with the requirements of the Second Schedule to the *Companies Act 1967* as if they were the accounts of an actual company. Sections 196 and 197 of the 1948 Act and Sections 6, 7 and 8 of the 1967 Act (which relate to the disclosure in the accounts laid before the members of emoluments etc. paid to directors and employees and loans to officers etc.), do not, however, apply to the consolidated accounts.

The preparation of a Consolidated Profit and Loss Account follows similar lines to a Consolidated Balance Sheet, all the information contained in the separate Profit and Loss Accounts of the respective companies being combined together and set out under appropriate headings, after eliminating inter-company transactions, e.g. inter-company debenture interest, directors' fees paid by a subsidiary to its parent company, inter-company dividends.

The Consolidated Profit and Loss Account shows total profits after tax and after eliminating inter-company transactions for the accounting period giving the information shown in published accounts. It then divides the total profit after tax between minority interests and group shareholders. For the benefit of the group shareholders a group Profit and Loss Appropriation Account is shown, disclosing appropriations only as far as group shareholders are concerned, e.g. dividends, transfers to reserves, and amounts brought forward from previous accounting periods so far as these are available for group shareholders (pre-acquisition profits and losses and balances brought forward belonging to minority interests being strictly excluded). The balance carried forward represents undistributed profits belonging to group shareholders only. No details are given in the appropriations and balances brought forward of amounts appertaining to minority interests.

### CONSOLIDATED PROFIT AND LOSS ACCOUNT
for the year ended ............

|  | £ | £ |
|---|---|---|
| Total profit before taxation .. .. .. .. .. .. |  | X |
| after accounting for: |  |  |
| Depreciation etc. .. .. .. .. .. .. | X |  |
| *Less* United Kingdom Taxation based on profits for the accounting period |  | X |
| Total profit after tax .. .. .. .. .. .. |  | X |
| *Deduct* Minority Interests .. .. .. .. .. .. |  | X |
| Profit applicable to group shareholders .. .. .. .. |  | X |
| *Deduct* appropriations (applicable to group shareholders) |  |  |
| Transfer to General Reserve .. .. .. .. .. | X |  |
| Dividends – paid and proposed .. .. .. .. .. | X |  |
|  |  | X |
| Unappropriated profit attributable to group shareholders.. .. .. |  | X |
| *Add* Unappropriated profits brought forward (attributable to group shareholders only) .. .. .. .. .. .. |  | X |
| Balance carried forward (unappropriated profits attributable to group shareholders) .. .. .. .. .. .. .. .. |  | £ X |

In consolidating the Profit and Loss Accounts, particular attention must be paid to the following matters:

### (a) Pre-acquisition profits or losses

Where the balance brought forward in a subsidiary's Profit and Loss Account includes any profit or loss which arose before the date on or as from which the shares therein were acquired by the holding company, the amount thereof applicable to the holding company must be transferred to Goodwill Account, as already explained, and will be taken into account in computing the sum attributable to goodwill in the Consolidated Balance Sheet.

Similarly, if the shares in the subsidiary were acquired during the year to which the Profit and Loss Account relates, the profit for the year must be apportioned to the date of acquisition, and the pre-acquisition profit transferred to goodwill.

**Illustration (1)**

### A LTD AND ITS SUBSIDIARY B LTD
Extracts from PROFIT AND LOSS ACCOUNT

|  | £ | £ |
|---|---|---|
| Total PROFITS AFTER TAX ..    ..    ..    ..    ..    .. |  | X |
| *Deduct* Minority Interests ..    ..    ..    ..    ..    .. |  | X |
| PROFITS ATTRIBUTABLE TO GROUP SHAREHOLDERS    ..    .. |  | X |
| *Deduct* Transfer to Goodwill (or Capital reserve): |  |  |
|        Pre-acquisition profits    ..    ..    ..    ..    .. | X |  |
|        Proposed dividends (gross)    ..    ..    ..    .. | X |  |
|  |  | X |
| UNAPPROPRIATED PROFITS attributable to group shareholders ..    .. |  | X |
| *Add* Unappropriated profits brought forward ..    ..    ..    .. |  | X |
| BALANCE CARRIED TO CONSOLIDATED BALANCE SHEET    ..    .. |  | £ X |

*Notes:*

1. The amount deducted for minority interests includes their share of pre-acquisition profits.

2. The unappropriated profits brought forward will be those of A Ltd only if B Ltd was acquired during the year.

3. Where a dividend has been paid out of pre-acquisition profits it will have been credited to goodwill (or capital reserve) reducing the cost of the shares. In the Consolidated Profit and Loss Account no additional entry is required; the amount is merely an analysis of the transfer to goodwill (or capital reserve) shown in the above illustration.

### (b) Inter-company unrealized profits

The profit included in the price at which any stock-in-hand at the date of the accounts has been transferred from one company to another, in so far as it affects the members of the holding company, must be deducted from the trading profit in the Consolidated Profit and Loss Account, and from the stock valuation in the Consolidated Balance Sheet. Similarly, any unrealized profit included in the price at which any fixed assets have been transferred from one company in the group to another must be deleted from the profit and from the value of the asset.

It has already been seen that from the point of view of minority shareholders in a subsidiary, the inter-company profit may be regarded as realized, whether it operates for or against the particular subsidiary. Thus, if H Ltd holds 90 per cent. of the ordinary capital of S Ltd, of any profit included in the invoice price of goods sold by S Ltd to H Ltd, and which are still held by H Ltd, only 90 per cent. will be deleted; the remaining 10 per cent. is a realized profit from the viewpoint of the minority shareholders and may be treated as part of the cost of the goods to the group. Similarly, if H Ltd has sold goods to S Ltd, which are still in stock, only 90 per cent. of the profit thereon will be eliminated; the other 10 per cent. is tantamount to a profit earned by H Ltd on a sale to the outside members of S Ltd.

### (c) Inter-company dividends

A dividend paid by a subsidiary to its holding company will appear as a debit in the subsidiary's Profit and Loss Account and as a credit in the holding company's Profit and Loss Account; for purposes of consolidation they cancel out. Proposed dividends payable to the holding company shown as a current liability in the subsidiary company's Balance Sheet will cancel out with 'Dividends receivable' shown as a current asset in the holding company's Balance Sheet. If no entry has been made in the holding company's books the proposed dividend should be re-credited in the subsidiary company's books and debited against creditors for proposed dividends.

Dividends paid to minority interests should be debited to Minority Interests Account and thus be eliminated from Profit and Loss Account. Proposed dividends to minority interests should be re-credited in the Profit and Loss Account and creditors for proposed dividends (to minority interests) debited. They will be included in the amount of profit attributable to minority interests, but not shown separately.

Under the provisions of the *Income and Corporation Taxes Act 1970* companies may elect that debenture interest and dividends paid by subsidiary companies to the holding company be paid without deduction of income tax. If an election is made the holding company will receive the gross amount of dividend and debenture interest and no entries will have been made in its Income Tax Account. In consolidating the accounts, the dividends and interest received from subsidiaries in the holding company's Profit and Loss Account will cancel out the dividends and interest paid shown in the subsidiaries' Profit and Loss Account. If no group election has been made, then the subsidiary company will pay its dividends after deduction of income tax and it must account to the Revenue for income tax at the standard rate on the gross equivalent of the actual dividend paid. The holding company may therefore use the gross dividend received to partly or wholly 'frank' its own dividends. In this event, the income tax on such dividends payable will cancel out against the income tax debited in respect of dividends received. If the income tax deducted from dividends paid is greater than the income tax deducted from dividends received, the net income tax payable will appear under the heading of Current Taxation amongst the current liabilities. If the income tax deducted from dividends paid is less than the income tax deducted from dividends received, the excess may appear in the Consolidated Profit and Loss Account as 'Income tax borne on surplus franked investment income', whilst the amount provided by the subsidiary will appear as current taxation in the Consolidated Balance Sheet. The income tax borne on surplus franked investment income written off as mentioned above, is available for set-off in future years and if material the gross equivalent (i.e. the surplus franked investment income) should show by way of a note to the accounts.

If a dividend received by the holding company, and credited to its Profit and Loss Account, is found to have been paid by the subsidiary out of pre-acquisition profits, the amount thereof must be transferred from the Profit and Loss Account to the credit of the Shares in the Subsidiary Company Account. Any such dividend should not have been treated as revenue by the holding company, as it is paid out of assets which are included in the property forming the underlying security for the shares acquired by the holding company, and must be regarded as reducing the price of the shares. In effect, the shares were purchased *cum div.*, and the dividend included in the price must, when received, be treated as capital.

### (d) Transfers to reserves etc.

Only such proportion of any sum transferred to reserve by a subsidiary, as is attributable to the holding company's interest in that subsidiary will be added to any sums transferred to reserve by the holding company and debited to the Consolidated Profit and Loss Account. The proportion of any such transfer attributable to minority interests will be included in their share of the undistributed profits of subsidiaries.

### (e) Depreciation Adjustments

As explained in § 4 (*m*) of this chapter, where any fixed assets of a subsidiary have been revalued for the purpose of the consolidated accounts, the charge for depreciation in the Consolidated Profit and Loss Account may require adjustment. Where, for example, the value of a fixed asset has been written up to a higher figure than that at which it appears in the subsidiary's books, the charge for depreciation to the Consolidated Profit and Loss Account must be increased by depreciation at the appropriate rate on the increase in value; where the value of the asset has been written down, the charge for depreciation must be proportionately reduced. Similarly, if plant has been purchased by one company from another at a profit, the profit must be eliminated and the charge for depreciation reduced by the amount applicable to the amount by which the value of the asset has been reduced.

### (f) Minority Interests

The share of a subsidiary's profit or loss attributable to minority interests will be made up of –
(*a*) the appropriate proportion of the balance brought forward from the previous year;
(*b*) the appropriate proportion of the profit or loss for the year, before debiting dividends, and transfers to reserve.

The minority interest in current profits is calculated on profits after tax as shown by the subsidiary's own Profit and Loss Account, no adjustment being made for unrealized inter-company profits on stock etc. Adjustments, however, will be necessary where for the purposes of consolidation, assets in the subsidiary have been revalued and depreciation requires increasing or decreasing. Inter-company dividends received should be excluded, since the profit after tax of each subsidiary is apportioned to minority interests; by including inter-company dividends received the same profits would be included twice. Where the subsidiary has preference shares the total gross preference dividend must be deducted from the profits after tax before arriving at the amount due to ordinary minority shareholders; the preference dividends belonging to any minority preference shareholders will be credited to the minority interests.

### Illustration (2)

P Ltd owns 80 per cent. of A Ltd's and 60 per cent. of B Ltd's share capitals which are all in ordinary shares. A Ltd owns 20 per cent. of the capital of B Ltd. A Ltd's profit after tax and after crediting £2,100 gross dividend received from B Ltd was £63,000. B Ltd's profit after tax was £48,000. Compute minority interests.

|  |  | £ | | Minority £ |
|---|---|---|---|---|
| A Ltd: Profit after tax | .. .. .. .. .. | 63,000 | | |
| Less Inter-company dividends | .. .. .. | 2,100 | | |
| Minority 1/5th of | .. .. .. .. | £60,900 | = | 12,180 |
| B Ltd: Profit after tax | .. .. .. .. | £48,000 | | |
| Direct minority 1/5th of | .. .. .. .. | £48,000 | = | 9,600 |
| Indirect minority 1/5th of 1/5th (1/25th) | .. .. | £48,000 | = | 1,920 |
| | | | | £23,700 |

In the Consolidated Balance Sheet the liability to the minority interests will be the aggregate of the nominal amounts of their shareholdings and the proportion of the reserves and Profit and Loss Account balance attributable thereto. Proposed dividends payable to outside shareholders should be shown separately and grouped with the current liabilities.

### (g) Balance carried forward

In the Consolidated Balance Sheet the Revenue Reserves and Profit and Loss Account balances should be divided to show the amount of the holding company's undistributed profits separately from those of the subsidiaries, so as to facilitate reconciliation with the figures shown in the holding company's own Balance Sheet.

### (h) Directors' Emoluments

Although the provisions of Section 196 of the 1948 Act (as to the disclosure of directors' emoluments) do not apply to consolidated accounts, since the requisite information must be given by the holding company in its own accounts or in a note attached thereto, it may be given in the consolidated accounts which are laid before the members at the same time as the company's own accounts and are normally attached thereto. The amounts disclosed must include payments to the directors of the holding company by its subsidiaries, as well as payments by the company itself, but not payments to directors of subsidiaries who are not also directors of the holding company. Any such payments may be treated as salaries to executives other than directors in combining the relevant figures for the purposes of the consolidated accounts.

### Illustration (3)

The summarized Profit and Loss Accounts of A Ltd and its subsidiary B Ltd for the year ended December 31st, 19...... are as follows:

## PROFIT AND LOSS ACCOUNT

| | A | B | | A | B |
|---|---|---|---|---|---|
| | £ | £ | | £ | £ |
| Depreciation | 20,000 | 15,000 | Trading profit | 127,817 | 45,460 |
| Directors' emoluments | 10,000 | 5,000 | Interest on government securities (gross) | 3,000 | 450 |
| Interest on loans repayable within 5 years (gross) | 5,000 | 3,000 | Dividend from B Ltd (gross) | 4,200 | |
| Corporation Tax | 49,000 | 13,110 | | | |
| Profit after tax c/d | 51,017 | 9,800 | | | |
| | £135,017 | £45,910 | | £135,017 | £45,910 |
| Transfer to Reserve | 10,000 | 2,000 | Balances b/d | 15,500 | 7,000 |
| Transfer to Debenture Redemption Reserve Fund | 3,000 | 1,000 | Profit for year after tax | 51,017 | 9,800 |
| Dividends (gross): | | | | | |
| Interim (paid) | | | | | |
| Preference | 700 | 700 | | | |
| Ordinary (5%) | 5,000 | (4%) 1,600 | | | |
| Final (proposed): | | | | | |
| Preference | 700 | 700 | | | |
| Ordinary (20%) | 20,000 | (10%) 4,000 | | | |
| Balance carried forward | 27,117 | 6,800 | | | |
| | £66,517 | £16,800 | | £66,517 | £16,800 |

You are given the following information:

1. The paid-up share capital of the companies consist of:

| | A Ltd £ | B Ltd £ |
|---|---|---|
| £1 seven per cent. Cumulative Preference Shares | 40,000 | 20,000 |
| £1 Ordinary Shares | 100,000 | 40,000 |

2. A Ltd holds 30,000 of the ordinary shares of B Ltd. The whole of the preference shares of B Ltd are held outside the group.

3. At the date on which A Ltd acquired its holding in B Ltd the credit balance on B Ltd's Profit and Loss Account was £5,000. All subsequent dividends have been paid out of current earnings.

4. A Ltd's stock includes goods purchased from B Ltd during the year for £5,200, invoiced by B Ltd at cost plus 33⅓ per cent. There were no similar transactions in the previous year.

5. For the purpose of the Consolidated Balance Sheet, B Ltd's plant was revalued at £10,000 above its book value. Depreciation for the year had been provided for by B Ltd at 10 per cent. per annum on the book value.

6. The directors of B Ltd are also directors of A Ltd.

7. Inter-company dividends are paid gross.

Prepare a Consolidated Profit and Loss Account for the year ended December 31st, 19......
Income tax is to be taken into account at 50p in the £.

The figures for inclusion in the Consolidated Profit and Loss Account are computed as follows:

| | A Ltd £ | £ | B Ltd £ | £ | Total £ |
|---|---|---|---|---|---|
| (1) Trading profit: | | | | | |
| As per Profit and Loss Account | 127,817 | | 45,460 | | |
| Unrealized profit on sale of goods to A Ltd: | | | | | |
| *Deduct* 25 per cent. on £5,200 | | 1,300 | | | |
| *Less* Minority Interest (1/4th) | | 325 | 975* | | |
| | £127,817 | | £44,485 | | 172,302 |
| (2) Depreciation: | | | | | |
| As per Profit and Loss Account | 20,000 | | 15,000 | | |
| *Add* 10 per cent. on £10,000 | | | | | |
| increase in valuation  .. | | | 1,000 | | |
| | £20,000 | | £16,000 | 36,000 | |
| (3) Directors' emoluments..        .. | £10,000 | | £5,000 | 15,000 | |
| (4) Interest on loans repayable within 5 years      ..        ..        .. | £5,000 | | £3,000 | 8,000 | |
| | | | | | 59,000 |
| | | | | | 113,302 |
| (5) Income from quoted investments | £3,000 | | £450 | | 3,450 |
| Per Consolidated Profit and Loss Account   ..        ..        .. | | | | | £116,752 |
| (6) Corporation Tax        ..        .. | £49,000 | | £13,110 | | £62,110 |
| (7) Transfers to Reserve: | | | | | |
| As per Profit and Loss Account | 10,000 | | 2,000 | | |
| *Deduct* Minority interest (1/4th) | | | 500 | | |
| | £10,000 | | £1,500 | | £11,500 |
| (8) Transfer to Debenture Redemption Fund  ..        ..        .. | 3,000 | | 1,000 | | |
| *Less* Minority interest (1/4th) | | | 250 | | |
| | £3,000 | | £750 | | £3,750 |

* See page 436.

| | A Ltd | | B Ltd | | Total |
|---|---|---|---|---|---|
| | £ | £ | £ | £ | £ |
| (9) Proportion of profit for year attributable to minority interest in B Ltd: | | | | | |
| Trading profit .. .. | | | 45,460 | | |
| Interest on government securities .. .. .. | | | 450 | | |
| | | | 45,910 | | |
| *Deduct* Depreciation .. | | 16,000 | | | |
| Directors' emoluments | | 5,000 | | | |
| Interest on loans repayable within 5 years .. .. | | 3,000 | | | |
| Corporation tax .. | | 13,110 | | | |
| Preference dividend.. | | 1,400 | | | |
| | | | 38,510 | | |
| | | | £7,400 | | |
| Attributable to ordinary shareholders (1/4 × £7,400) .. | | | 1,850 | | |
| Preference dividends .. .. | | | 1,400 | | |
| | | | | | £3,250 |
| (10) Balance brought forward: | | | | | |
| Per Profit and Loss Account .. | 15,500 | | 7,000 | | |
| *Less* Minority interest (1/4) .. | | | 1,750 | | |
| | | | 5,250 | | |
| *Deduct* Pre-acquisition profit transferred to good will | | 5,000 | | | |
| *Less* Minority interest (1/4) | | 1,250 | | | |
| | | | 3,750 | | |
| | £15,500 | | £1,500 | | £17,000 |

*If there had been any similar goods at the beginning of the accounting period this provision would be adjusted to £975 by setting off against it the provision brought forward.

## CONSOLIDATED PROFIT AND LOSS ACCOUNT
### for the year ended December 31st, 19......

| | £ | £ | £ |
|---|---:|---:|---:|
| PROFIT BEFORE TAXATION .. .. .. .. .. .. .. | | | 116,752 |
| after accounting for; | | | |
| Depreciation .. .. .. .. .. .. .. .. | | 36,000 | |
| Directors' emoluments .. .. .. .. .. .. | | 15,000 | |
| Interest on loans repayable within 5 years .. .. .. .. | | 8,000 | |
| Income from quoted investments .. .. .. .. | | £3,450 | |
| United Kingdom taxation based on profits for the year – Corporation Tax (45%) .. .. | | | 62,110 |
| PROFIT AFTER TAXATION .. .. .. .. .. .. | | | 54,642 |
| Deduct Minority interest .. .. .. .. .. .. | | | 3,250 |
| PROFIT FOR YEAR APPLICABLE TO GROUP .. .. .. .. | | | 51,392 |
| *Deduct* Appropriations: .. .. .. .. .. | | | |
| Transfers to: Reserve .. .. .. .. .. | | 11,500 | |
| Debenture Redemption Fund .. .. .. .. | | 3,750 | |
| Dividends paid (gross): .. | | | |
| Preference .. .. .. .. .. .. .. | 700 | | |
| Ordinary (interim) .. .. .. .. .. .. | 5,000 | | |
| Dividends proposed (gross): | | | |
| Preference .. .. .. .. .. .. | 700 | | |
| Ordinary .. .. .. .. .. .. .. | 20,000 | | |
| | | 26,400 | |
| | | | 41,650 |
| UNAPPROPRIATED PROFIT FOR THE YEAR .. .. .. .. | | | 9,742 |
| *Add* Balance brought forward .. .. .. .. .. .. | | | 17,000 |
| BALANCE CARRIED TO BALANCE SHEET .. .. .. .. | | | £26,742 |

*Note:* In the Consolidated Balance Sheet the liability to minority interests for undistributed profits will be made up as follows:

| | £ | £ |
|---|---:|---:|
| Balance brought forward (¼ × £7,000) .. .. .. | | 1,750 |
| Share of profit for year (per Consolidated Profit and Loss Account) .. .. .. .. | | 3,250 |
| | | 5,000 |
| *Less* Interim dividends paid: | | |
| Preference .. .. .. .. .. .. .. .. | 700 | |
| Ordinary (¼ × £1,600) .. .. .. .. .. .. .. | 400 | |
| | | 1,100 |
| | | £3,900 |

Of the £3,900, £1,700 proposed preference and ordinary dividends payable to outside shareholders will be shown under the heading current liabilities and the balance will be aggregated with the relevent proportion of the nominal share capital and reserves of B Ltd, to arrive at the liability to minority interests.

## § 6. Holding Company's Profit and Loss Account framed as a Consolidated Profit and Loss Account

By Section 149, *Companies Act 1948*, a holding company which publishes a Consolidated Profit and Loss Account need not also publish a separate Profit and Loss Account, provided that the Consolidated Profit and Loss Account:

(i) complies with the requirements of the Act relating to Consolidated Profit and Loss Accounts; and

(ii) shows how much of the consolidated profit or loss *for the financial year* is dealt with in the accounts of the company.

Since a holding company normally takes credit in its own accounts only for dividends paid and proposed by its subsidiaries, and not for its full share of the profits earned by them, in order to satisfy the second of the above requirements there must be deducted from the consolidated profit appropriate to the holding company such amount thereof as is retained and carried forward in the accounts of the subsidiaries.

The resulting balance will be transferred to the holding company's Appropriation Account, in which that company's own balance of Profit and Loss Account brought forward, and dividends paid and proposed and other appropriations will be entered. The final balance is that which will appear in the holding company's *own* Balance Sheet (not in the Consolidated Balance Sheet), to which is added the total profit retained by subsidiaries attributable to the group to give the balance carried forward to the Consolidated Balance Sheet.

### Illustration

The Profit and Loss Accounts of A Ltd and its subsidiaries B Ltd and C Ltd for the year ended March 31st, 19.. are as follows:

| | A Ltd | B Ltd | C Ltd | | A Ltd | B Ltd | C Ltd |
|---|---|---|---|---|---|---|---|
| | £ | £ | £ | | £ | £ | £ |
| Depreciation | 8,000 | 3,000 | 4,000 | Trading Profit | 50,000 | 20,000 | 25,000 |
| Directors' Emoluments | 10,000 | 5,000 | 3,000 | Income from Govt. Securities (gross) | 5,000 | 1,000 | 1,500 |
| Corporation Tax | 18,000 | 6,000 | 9,000 | Dividend from B Ltd (gross) | 3,000 | | |
| Profit for year c/d. | 26,000 | 7,000 | 10,500 | Dividend from C Ltd (gross) | 4,000 | | |
| | £62,000 | £21,000 | £26,500 | | £62,000 | £21,000 | £26,500 |
| Dividends (gross) | 12,000 | 4,000 | 5,000 | Profit for year b/d. | 26,000 | 7,000 | 10,500 |
| Balances c/f. | 36,000 | 9,000 | 13,500 | Balance from last year | 22,000 | 6,000 | 8,000 |
| | £48,000 | £13,000 | £18,500 | | £48,000 | £13,000 | £18,500 |

All three companies had the same directors.

A Ltd holds 75% of the Share capital of B Ltd and 80% of that of C Ltd, each of whom had paid a dividend of 10 per cent. during the year, out of the current year's profit, for which credit had been taken by A Ltd in its accounts. There were no other inter-company transactions and no pre-acquisition profits.

Prepare A Ltd's Profit and Loss Account framed as a Consolidated Profit and Loss Account to comply with Section 149, *Companies Act 1948*.

Assume income tax at 50p in the £ and that a group election has been made.

## CONSOLIDATED PROFIT AND LOSS ACCOUNT
### for the year ended March 31st, 19......

| | £ | £ |
|---|---|---|
| PROFIT FOR YEAR BEFORE TAXATION | | 69,500 |
| after accounting for: Depreciation | 15,000 | |
|      Directors' emoluments | 18,000 | |
| Income from Quoted investments | 7,500 | |
| U.K. taxation based on profits for the year.. | | |
|      Corporation Tax (45%) | | 33,000 |
| PROFIT AFTER TAXATION | | 36,500 |
| *Less* proportion attributable to minority interests | | 3,850 |
| Group profit for the year | | 32,650 |
| *Less* profit for year retained by subsidiaries attributable to the group | | 6,650 |
| Group profit for year dealt with in the accounts of A Ltd | | 26,000 |
| *Deduct* appropriations: Dividends (gross) | | 12,000 |
| Unappropriated Profits A Ltd | | 14,000 |
| *Add* Balance brought forward by A Ltd | | 22,000 |
| Balance carried forward by A Ltd.. | | 36,000 |
| *Add* total profit retained by subsidiaries attributable to the group | | 17,550 |
| BALANCE CARRIED TO CONSOLIDATED BALANCE SHEET | | £53,550 |

## WORKING SCHEDULES

|  | A Ltd | (75%) B Ltd | (80%) C Ltd | Total |
|---|---|---|---|---|
|  | £ | £ | £ | £ |
| Trading Profit | 50,000 | 20,000 | 25,000 | 95,000 |
| Income from government securities | 5,000 | 1,000 | 1,500 | 7,500 |
|  | 55,000 | 21,000 | 26,500 | 102,500 |
| Depreciation | 8,000 | 3,000 | 4,000 | 15,000 |
| Directors' emoluments | 10,000 | 5,000 | 3,000 | 18,000 |
|  | 18,000 | 8,000 | 7,000 | 33,000 |
| Profit before taxation | £37,000 | £13,000 | £19,500 | £69,500 |
| Corporation Tax | 18,000 | 6,000 | 9,000 | 33,000 |
| Profit after taxation | £19,000 | £7,000 | £10,500 | £36,500 |
| Minority Interests: |  |  |  |  |
| B Ltd 25% of £ 7,000 |  |  |  | 1,750 |
| C Ltd 20% of £10,500 |  |  |  | 2,100 |
|  |  |  |  | £3,850 |

Profits retained by subsidiaries attributable to the Group:

|  | B Ltd | C Ltd | Total |
|---|---|---|---|
|  | £ | £ | £ |
| Profit for year | 7,000 | 10,500 |  |
| Less Dividends paid and proposed (gross) | 4,000 | 5,000 |  |
|  | £3,000 | £5,500 |  |
| Attributable to A Ltd | (75%) 2,250 | (80%) 4,400 | 6,650 |
| Balances brought forward – amounts attributable to A Ltd | 4,500 | 6,400 | 10,900 |
| Balances carried forward | £6,750 | £10,800 | £17,550 |

By deducting the retained profit £6,650 from the group profit for the year, the Consolidated Profit and Loss Account discloses how much of the consolidated profit for the financial year has been dealt with in the accounts of A Ltd, viz. £26,000. After deducting A Ltd's appropriations (dividends) and adding the balance brought forward, the balance £36,000 represents the balance on Profit and Loss Account appearing in A Ltd's Balance Sheet. By adding to this amount the *total* profits retained by subsidiaries (including the balances brought forward) the Profit and Loss Account balance appearing in the *Consolidated* Balance Sheet is revealed.

Alternatively the requirements of Section 149 on disclosure would be satisfied if the Consolidated Profit and Loss Account were presented in the following form:

## CONSOLIDATED PROFIT AND LOSS ACCOUNT
### for the year ended March 31st, 19......

| | £ | £ |
|---|---:|---:|
| PROFIT BEFORE TAXATION | | 69,500 |
| after accounting for: Depreciation .. .. .. .. .. .. | 15,000 | |
| Directors' emoluments .. .. .. .. .. .. | 18,000 | |
| Income from quoted investments .. .. .. .. .. | 7,500 | |
| U.K. taxation based on profits for the year: | | |
| Corporation Tax (45%) .. .. .. .. .. .. | | 33,000 |
| PROFIT AFTER TAXATION .. .. .. .. .. .. .. | | 36,500 |
| *Less* Proportion attributable to minority interests .. .. .. .. | | 3,850 |
| GROUP PROFIT FOR YEAR | | |
| Retained by subsidiaries .. .. .. .. .. .. | 6,650 | |
| Dealt with in the Holding Company's Accounts .. .. .. .. .. | 26,000 | |
| | | 32,650 |
| *Deduct* dividends (gross) .. .. .. .. .. .. | | 12,000 |
| UNAPPROPRIATED PROFIT FOR YEAR .. .. .. .. .. | | 20,650 |
| *Add* Balance brought forward from previous year .. .. .. .. | | 32,900 |
| BALANCE CARRIED FORWARD | | |
| Retained by subsidiaries .. .. .. .. .. .. | 17,550 | |
| Dealt with in Holding Company's Accounts .. .. .. .. .. | 36,000 | |
| | | £53,550 |

## § 7. General Illustration

The following are the draft Profit and Loss Accounts for the year ended March 31st, 19.. and Balance Sheets at that date of A Ltd, and its two subsidiaries B Ltd and C Ltd.

### PROFIT AND LOSS ACCOUNTS

| | A Ltd | B Ltd | C Ltd | | A Ltd | B Ltd | C Ltd |
|---|---:|---:|---:|---|---:|---:|---:|
| | £ | £ | £ | | £ | £ | £ |
| Directors' emoluments .. | 5,500 | 750 | 500 | Trading profit .. | 24,340 | 10,560 | 6,580 |
| Debenture interest .. | | 600 | | Dividends on U.K. Or- | | | |
| Depreciation .. .. | 6,000 | 1,500 | 1,500 | dinary shares .. | 1,440 | 800 | 700 |
| Corporation Tax .. | 12,332 | 4,490 | 3,084 | Interest on Debentures in | | | |
| Profit for year after tax | | | | B Ltd .. .. | 400 | | |
| c/d .. .. | 7,023 | 4,060 | 2,213 | Dividends on Ordinary | | | |
| | | | | shares in B Ltd .. | 2,400 | | |
| | | | | Dividends on shares in C | | | |
| | | | | Ltd: | | | |
| | | | | Preference .. | 360 | | |
| | | | | Ordinary .. | 1,800 | | |
| | | | | Interest on Tax Reserve | | | |
| | | | | Certificates .. | 115 | 40 | 17 |
| | £30,855 | £11,400 | £7,297 | | £30,855 | £11,400 | £7,297 |
| Dividends (gross): | | | | Profit for year b/d. .. | 7,023 | 4,060 | 2,213 |
| Preference paid .. | | | 600 | Balance brought forward | 12,000 | 4,500 | 5,000 |
| Ordinary proposed .. | 15,000 | 4,000 | 1,800 | | | | |
| Balance carried forward | 4,023 | 4,560 | 4,813 | | | | |
| | £19,023 | £8,560 | £7,213 | | £19,023 | £8,560 | £7,213 |

## BALANCE SHEETS

| | A Ltd £ | A Ltd £ | B Ltd £ | B Ltd £ | C Ltd £ | C Ltd £ |
|---|---|---|---|---|---|---|
| SHARE CAPITAL – Authorized, issued and fully paid (£1 shares) | | | | | | |
| 6% Preference | | | | | 10,000 | |
| Ordinary | | 150,000 | | 20,000 | 6,000 | 16,000 |
| RESERVES | | | | | | |
| General | 24,000 | | 8,000 | | 8,000 | |
| Profit & Loss Account | 4,023 | 178,023 | 4,560 | 32,560 | 4,813 | 28,813 |
| 4% DEBENTURES repayable January 1st, 2000 | | | | 15,000 | | |
| CORPORATION TAX | | 12,332 | | 4,490 | | 3,084 |
| CURRENT LIABILITIES | | | | | | |
| Creditors | 6,076 | | 4,170 | | 3,424 | |
| Dividends (gross) | 15,000 | 21,076 | 4,000 | 8,170 | 1,800 | 5,224 |
| | | £211,431 | | £60,220 | | £37,121 |

| | A Ltd £ | A Ltd £ | B Ltd £ | B Ltd £ | C Ltd £ | C Ltd £ |
|---|---|---|---|---|---|---|
| FIXED ASSETS | | | | | | |
| Goodwill | | 15,000 | | | | |
| Freehold Premises, at cost | | 25,000 | | 11,000 | | |
| Plant, at cost | 41,000 | | 22,000 | | 14,000 | |
| Less Depreciation | 26,000 | 15,000 | 10,500 | 11,500 | 6,500 | 7,500 |
| | | 55,000 | | 22,500 | | 7,500 |
| SUBSIDIARY COMPANIES | | | | | | |
| 12,000 Ordinary Shares in B Ltd at cost less dividend paid out of pre-acquisition profits | 32,125 | | | | | |
| 4% Debentures £10,000 in B Ltd | 10,000 | | | | | |
| 6,000 Preference Shares in C Ltd | 8,000 | | | | | |
| 6,000 Ordinary Shares in C Ltd | 16,000 | 66,125 | | | | |
| CURRENT ASSETS | | | | | | |
| Stock | 18,295 | | 12,700 | | 6,465 | |
| Debtors | 20,000 | | 8,110 | | 7,725 | |
| Quoted investments | 18,000 | | 7,500 | | 10,000 | |
| Tax Reserve Certificates | 10,000 | | 4,000 | | 1,875 | |
| Dividends receivable (gross): B Ltd | 2,400 | | | | | |
| C Ltd | 1,800 | | | | | |
| Bank | 19,811 | 90,306 | 5,410 | 37,720 | 3,556 | 29,621 |
| | | £211,431 | | £60,220 | | £37,121 |

*Notes:*

1. Assume income tax at 50*p* in the £. The group paid inter-company dividends gross.

2. The shares in B Ltd were acquired on April 1st (the first day of the accounting period) when B Ltd had a credit balance on Profit and Loss Account (after charging the final dividends for the previous year) of £4,500 and a general reserve of £8,000.

3. The shares in C Ltd were purchased many years ago when C Ltd had a credit balance on Profit and Loss Account of £2,000 and a general reserve of £3,000. All subsequent dividends have been paid out of post-acquisition profits.

4. Inter-company indebtedness (included in debtors and creditors) at Balance Sheet date was: A Ltd to C Ltd £700, B Ltd to A Ltd £1,240.

5. A Ltd's stock includes goods purchased from B Ltd for £15,000 of which the cost to B Ltd was £10,000. A provision for unrealized profit of £3,000 has been made by A Ltd and deducted from the value of the stock and the trading profit.

6. Proposed dividends are (gross): A Ltd – 10%; B Ltd – 20%; C Ltd – ordinary 30%.

7. All the directors of the subsidiaries are also directors of A Ltd.

Prepare Consolidated Profit and Loss Account for the year ended March 31st, 19.. and Consolidated Balance Sheet as at that date.

The Goodwill Account will appear as follows:

## GOODWILL

|  | £ |  | £ |
|---|---|---|---|
| Ordinary Shares in B Ltd | 32,125 | Share Capital, B Ltd | 12,000 |
| Debentures in B Ltd | 10,000 | Debentures, B Ltd | 10,000 |
|  |  | Pre-acquisition profits (12/20 × £12,500) | 7,500 |
|  |  | Balance = Goodwill in B Ltd | 12,625 |
|  | £42,125 |  | £42,125 |
| Preference Shares in C Ltd | 8,000 | Preference Share. Capital C Ltd | 6,000 |
| Ordinary Shares in C Ltd | 16,000 | Ordinary Share. Capital C Ltd | 6,000 |
|  |  | Pre-acquisition profits £(3,000+2,000) | 5,000 |
|  |  | Balance = Goodwill in C Ltd | 7,000 |
|  | £24,000 |  | £24,000 |

Goodwill = £(12,625 + 7,000) = £19,625.

The figures appearing in the Consolidated Profit and Loss Account and Consolidated Balance Sheet are the combined figures appearing in the separate accounts, after effect has been given to the consolidating adjustments. Detailed workings are given hereunder.

## WORKINGS
### PROFIT AND LOSS ACCOUNT

|  | A | B |  | C | Total |
|---|---|---|---|---|---|
|  | £ | £ | £ | £ | £ |
| (i) PROFIT BEFORE TAXATION |  |  |  |  |  |
| Trading Profit | 24,340 |  | 10,560 | 6,580 |  |
| *Add* Interest on Tax Reserve Certificates | 115 |  | 40 | 17 |  |
|  | £24,455 |  | £10,600 | £6,597 | 41,652 |
| *Less* Expenses: |  |  |  |  |  |
| Directors' Emoluments | 5,500 |  | 750 | 500 |  |
| Depreciation | 6,000 |  | 1,500 | 1,500 |  |
| Debenture Interest | | 600 | | | |
| *Less* Paid to A | | 400 | | | |
|  |  |  | 200 |  |  |
|  | £11,500 |  | £2,450 | £2,000 | 15,950 |
|  |  |  |  |  | 25,702 |
| Income from Quoted Investments | £1,440 |  | £800 | £700 | 2,940 |
|  |  |  |  |  | £28,642 |

| | A | B | C | Total |
|---|---|---|---|---|
| | £ | £ | £ | £ |
| (ii) Corporation Tax .. .. .. .. | 12,332 | 4,490 | 3,084 | 19,906 |
| (iii) Profit for year applicable to minority interests: | | | | |
| B Ltd (8/20 × £4,060) .. .. .. | | 1,624 | | |
| C Ltd – Preference dividend (6% on £4,000) | | | 240 | |
| | | | | £1,864 |
| (iv) Group profit/loss for year retained by subsidiaries: | | | | |
| Profit per Profit and Loss Accounts .. | | 4,060 | 2,213 | |
| *Less* dividends paid thereout .. .. | | 4,000 | 2,400 | |
| | | £60 | | |
| Applicable to group .. .. .. .. | | Profit 12/20ths 36 | | |
| | | | Loss 187 | |
| | | | | Loss 151 |
| Dealt with in A's accounts (per Profit and Loss Account) .. .. .. .. | 7,023 | | | Profit 7,023 |
| | | | | £6,872 |
| (v) Balance brought forward: | | | | |
| Per Profit and Loss Accounts .. .. | 12,000 | £ 4,500 | 5,000 | |
| *Less* Minority Interests .. .. | | (8/20) 1,800 | | |
| Pre-acquisition profits .. .. .. | | (12/20) 2,700 | 2,000 | |
| | | 4,500 | | |
| | £12,000 | — | £3,000 | £15,000 |
| (vi) Proposed dividend .. .. .. .. | £15,000 | | | £15,000 |
| (vii) Balance carried forward: | | | | |
| Retained by subsidiaries– | | | | |
| Profit/loss for year per (iv) above .. .. | | Profit 36 | Loss 187 | |
| Brought forward per (v) above .. .. | | | Profit 3,000 | |
| | | 36 | 2,813 | |
| | | | | 2,849 |
| A Ltd per Profit and Loss Account .. .. | 4,023 | | | 4,023 |
| | | | | £6,872 |

## BALANCE SHEET

| | A | | B | | C | | Total |
|---|---|---|---|---|---|---|---|
| | £ | £ | £ | £ | £ | £ | £ |
| (viii) Fixed Assets: | | | | | | | |
| Goodwill – per Balance Sheet .. | | 15,000 | | | | | 15,000 |
| re B .. .. | | 12,625 | | | | | |
| re C .. .. | | 7,000 | | | | | 19,625 |
| (See Goodwill Account on p.442) | | 34,625 | | | | | 34,625 |
| Freehold Premises .. .. | | 25,000 | | 11,000 | | — | 36,000 |
| Plant and Machinery (*less* Depreciation) .. .. .. | | 15,000 | | 11,500 | | 7,500 | 34,000 |
| | | £74,625 | | £22,500 | | £7,500 | £104,625 |
| (ix) Current Assets: | | | | | | | |
| Stock .. .. .. .. | | 18,295 | | 12,700 | | 6,465 | 37,460 |
| Debtors .. .. .. | 20,000 | | | 8,110 | 7,725 | | |
| *Less* Inter-company debts .. | 1,240 | | | | 700 | | |
| | | 18,760 | | | | 7,025 | 33,895 |
| Quoted Investments .. .. | | 18,000 | | 7,500 | | 10,000 | 35,500 |
| Tax Reserve Certificates .. | | 10,000 | | 4,000 | | 1,875 | 15,875 |
| Bank balances .. .. .. | | 19,811 | | 5,410 | | 3,556 | 28,777 |
| | | £84,866 | | £37,720 | | £28,921 | £151,507 |
| (x) Reserves: | | | | | | | |
| General Reserves (per Balance Sheet) | | 24,000 | | 8,000 | | 8,000 | |
| *Less* Minority Interests .. | | | 3,200 | | | | |
| Pre-acquisition reserves .. | | | 4,800 | | | 3,000 | |
| | | | | 8,000 | | | |
| | | | | | | 5,000 | 29,000 |
| Profit and Loss Accounts (see (vii) above) | | 4,023 | | 36 | | 2,813 | 6,872 |
| | | £28,023 | | £36 | | £7,813 | £35,872 |

## BALANCE SHEET (*continued*)

| | A | B | C | Total |
|---|---|---|---|---|
| | £ | £ | £ | £ |
| (xi) Corporation Tax .. .. .. | £12,332 | £4,490 | £3,084 | £19,906 |
| (xii) 4% Debentures, B Ltd .. .. | | 15,000 | | |
| *Less* held by A Ltd .. .. | | 10,000 | | |
| | | £5,000 | | £5,000 |
| (xiii) Minority Interests: | | | | |
| Share Capital .. .. | (8/20) | 8,000 | 4,000 | |
| General Reserve (8/20 × £8,000) .. | | 3,200 | | |
| Profit and Loss Account: | | | | |
| Balance b/forward (8/20 × £4,500) | | 1,800 | | |
| Profit for year (8/20 × £4,060) .. | | 1,624 | (6% on £4,000) 240 | |
| | | 14,624 | 4,240 | |
| *Less* dividends paid and (8/20) proposed .. .. .. | | 1,600 | 240 | |
| | | £13,024 | £4,000 | £17,024 |
| (xiv) Trade Creditors .. .. .. | 6,076 | 4,170 | 3,424 | |
| *Less* Inter-company debts .. | 700 | 1,240 | | |
| | £5,376 | £2,930 | £3,424 | £11,730 |
| (xv) Proposed dividend: | | | | |
| Holding company .. .. | 15,000 | | | |
| Minority .. .. .. | | 1,600 | | £16,600 |

*Note:* The amount of the unrealized profit included in the value of the stock purchased by A Ltd from B Ltd is 12/20ths × £5,000 = £3,000. Provision for this amount has already been made by A Ltd in its own accounts, before arriving at the trading profit and stock figures appearing therein.

## A LTD AND SUBSIDIARIES
## CONSOLIDATED PROFIT AND LOSS ACCOUNT
### for the year ended March 31st, 19......

| | £ | £ |
|---|---|---|
| PROFIT BEFORE TAXATION .. .. .. .. .. .. .. .. | | 28,642 |
| after accounting for: | | |
| Directors' emoluments .. .. .. .. .. .. .. .. | 6,750 | |
| Interest on loans repayable after more than 5 years .. .. .. .. .. | 200 | |
| Depreciation .. .. .. .. .. .. .. .. | 9,000 | |
| Income from Quoted investments .. .. .. .. .. .. | £2,940 | |
| U.K. taxation based on profits for the year: | | |
| Corporation Tax (45%) .. .. .. .. .. .. .. .. | | 19,906 |
| PROFIT AFTER TAXATION .. .. .. .. .. .. .. .. | | 8,736 |
| *Deduct* profit for year applicable to minority interests .. .. .. .. .. | | 1,864 |
| GROUP PROFIT FOR YEAR | | |
| Retained by subsidiaries (*loss*) .. .. .. .. .. .. | 151 | |
| Dealt with in the Accounts of A Ltd .. .. .. .. .. .. | 7,023 | |
| | | 6,872 |
| Balance brought forward from previous year: | | |
| A Ltd .. .. .. .. .. .. .. .. | 12,000 | |
| Subsidiaries .. .. .. .. .. .. .. | 3,000 | |
| | | 15,000 |
| PROFITS AVAILABLE FOR APPROPRIATION .. .. .. .. .. | | 21,872 |
| *Deduct* proposed dividend payable to A's shareholders .. .. .. .. | | 15,000 |
| BALANCE CARRIED FORWARD | | |
| Retained profits of subsidiaries .. .. .. .. .. .. | 2,849 | |
| Dealt with in the Accounts of A Ltd .. .. .. .. .. | 4,023 | |
| | | £6,872 |

Alternatively if A Ltd published its own Profit and Loss Account the following would be appropriate:

## A LTD AND SUBSIDIARIES
## CONSOLIDATED PROFIT AND LOSS ACCOUNT
### for the year ending March 31st, 19......

|  |  | £ | £ |
|---|---|---:|---:|
| PROFIT BEFORE TAXATION | | | 28,642 |
| after accounting for: | | | |
| Directors' emoluments | | 6,750 | |
| Interest on loans repayable after more than 5 years | | 200 | |
| Depreciation | | 9,000 | |
| Income from quoted investments | | £2,940 | |
| U.K. taxation based on profits for the year: | | | |
| Corporation Tax (45%) | | | 19,906 |
| PROFIT AFTER TAXATION | | | 8,736 |
| *Deduct* profit applicable to minority interests | | | 1,864 |
| Profit applicable to group shareholders | | | 6,872 |
| *Add* Balance brought forward from previous year applicable to A Ltd's shareholders | | | 15,000 |
| | | | 21,872 |
| *Deduct* appropriation: Proposed dividends payable to group shareholders | | | 15,000 |
| BALANCE CARRIED FORWARD TO CONSOLIDATED BALANCE SHEET | | | £6,872 |

## A LTD AND SUBSIDIARIES
## CONSOLIDATED BALANCE SHEET
### as at March 31st, 19......

| | £ | £ | | £ | £ |
|---|---:|---:|---|---:|---:|
| SHARE CAPITAL | | | FIXED ASSETS | | |
| Authorized, issued and fully paid. | | | Goodwill A Ltd | | 15,000 |
| 150,000 ordinary shares of £1 | | | *Add* Excess of cost of Shares and | | |
| each. | | 150,000 | Debentures in subsidiaries | | |
| | | | over net assets attributable | | |
| RESERVES | | | thereto | | 19,625 |
| General Reserve | 29,000 | | | | 34,625 |
| Profit and Loss Account | 6,872 | | | | 36,000 |
| | | 35,872 | Freehold Premises at cost | | |
| | | 185,872 | Plant at cost.. | 77,000 | |
| MINORITY INTERESTS | | 17,024 | *Less* Depreciation | 43,000 | |
| | | | | | 34,000 |
| 4 per cent. DEBENTURES.. | | 5,000 | | | 104,625 |
| CORPORATION TAX | | 19,906 | CURRENT ASSETS | | |
| | | | Stock | 37,460 | |
| CURRENT LIABILITIES | | | Debtors | 33,895 | |
| Creditors | | 11,730 | Quoted investments | 35,500 | |
| Proposed Dividends: | | | Tax Reserve Certificates | 15,875 | |
| A Ltd's shareholders.. | 15,000 | | Bank | 28,777 | |
| Minority | 1,600 | | | | 151,507 |
| | | 16,600 | | | |
| | | 28,330 | | | |
| | | £256,132 | | | £256,132 |

....................................................  }
....................................................  } *Directors*

## § 8. Accounting for the Results of Associated Companies

The Institute of Chartered Accountants, in January 1971, issued the first statement of 'Standard Accounting Practice'. In view of its importance it is reproduced as Appendix IV in its entirety. The statement was published too late for it to be considered in further detail in this chapter.

## CHAPTER X

# DEPARTMENTAL ACCOUNTS; BRANCH ACCOUNTS

## § 1. Departmental Accounts

In a business where there are two or more departments, it may be important for the accounting system to be so devised as to enable the trading results of each department to be accurately ascertained for turnover and expenses, as well as profits.

In order to obtain the desired particulars, separate records must be kept of the purchases and sales of each department. Stock of each department must be taken separately, and the expenses that can be allocated directly to any department must be charged thereto, other expenses being apportioned on some reasonable basis; for example, either in proportion to the turnover of each department, or (as for rent) to the amount of floor space occupied, or in any other way which may be expedient in the circumstances. In order to allocate the purchases and sales correctly, either separate day books must be kept for each department, or columnar day books with a column for each department; otherwise the day books must be analysed. The first method is not always convenient, as it frequently involves a large number of duplicate entries, especially for purchases.

Where the number of departments is small, it is convenient to use columnar forms of bought and sold day books, return books etc. having a total column from which the posting is made to the personal accounts, and detail columns, the totals of which at the end of each month or other period are posted to their respective accounts in the impersonal ledger.

It is important to note that stock must be taken for each department separately, and proper records kept of all transfers from one department to another.

Where a mechanized accounting system has been installed the necessary analysis would be effected by the machines, as explained in Chapter XI.

**Illustration (1)**

The following is the trial balance of the Excelsior Trading Company Limited, on December 31st.

| | | | | | | | | | £ | £ |
|---|---|---|---|---|---|---|---|---|---|---|
| Ordinary Share Capital | .. | .. | .. | .. | .. | .. | .. | .. | | 10,000 |
| Preference ,, ,, .. | .. | .. | .. | .. | .. | .. | .. | .. | | 5,000 |
| 8 % Debentures .. | .. | .. | .. | .. | .. | .. | .. | .. | | 2,500 |
| Stock January 1st, Dept. A | .. | .. | .. | .. | .. | .. | .. | .. | 8,000 | |
| ,, ,, ,, ,, B | .. | .. | .. | .. | .. | .. | .. | .. | 3,000 | |
| Purchases, Dept. A | .. | .. | .. | .. | .. | .. | .. | .. | 23,000 | |
| ,, ,, B | .. | .. | .. | .. | .. | .. | .. | .. | 15,000 | |
| | | | | | | | Carried forward | .. | £49,000 | £17,500 |

| | | | | | | | | | | £ | £ |
|---|---|---|---|---|---|---|---|---|---|---|---|
| | | | | | Brought forward | | | .. | 49,000 | 17,500 |
| Wages, Dept. A | .. | .. | .. | .. | .. | .. | .. | .. | 1,000 | |
| ,,    ,,    B | | | | | | | | | 500 | |
| Carriage and Freight | .. | .. | .. | .. | .. | .. | .. | .. | 1,500 | |
| Salaries | .. | .. | .. | .. | .. | .. | .. | .. | 750 | |
| Travelling Expenses | .. | .. | .. | .. | .. | .. | .. | .. | 900 | |
| Incidental   ,, | .. | .. | .. | .. | .. | .. | .. | .. | 150 | |
| Rates and Taxes | .. | .. | .. | .. | .. | .. | .. | .. | 300 | |
| Fuel, Light and Water | .. | .. | .. | .. | .. | .. | .. | .. | 120 | |
| Insurance | .. | .. | .. | .. | .. | .. | .. | .. | 60 | |
| Sales Dept. A .. | .. | .. | .. | .. | .. | .. | .. | .. | | 30,000 |
| ,,    ,,    B .. | | | | | | | | | | 20,000 |
| Debtors | .. | .. | .. | .. | .. | .. | .. | .. | 9,000 | |
| Bills Receivable | .. | .. | .. | .. | .. | .. | .. | .. | 1,500 | |
| Creditors | .. | .. | .. | .. | .. | .. | .. | .. | | 6,500 |
| Freehold Premises at cost | .. | .. | .. | .. | .. | .. | .. | .. | 4,200 | |
| Managing Director's Salary | .. | .. | .. | .. | .. | .. | .. | .. | 1,000 | |
| Directors' Fees | .. | .. | .. | .. | .. | .. | .. | .. | 500 | |
| Stationery and Stamps | .. | .. | .. | .. | .. | .. | .. | .. | 170 | |
| Discounts | .. | .. | .. | .. | .. | .. | .. | .. | 600 | |
| Preference Dividend half-year to June 30th | | .. | .. | .. | .. | .. | .. | 150 | |
| Debenture Interest half-year to June 30th .. | | | .. | .. | .. | .. | .. | 100 | |
| Cash in Hand .. | .. | .. | .. | .. | .. | .. | .. | .. | 100 | |
| Balance at Bank | .. | .. | .. | .. | .. | .. | .. | .. | 3,000 | |
| Profit and Loss Account – Balance at January 1st | .. | | .. | .. | .. | .. | .. | | 600 |
| | | | | | | | | | £74,600 | £74,600 |

Provide £500 for doubtful debts, and prepare departmental Trading and Profit and Loss Accounts (dividing the expenses between the departments in proprtion to the sales), and Balance Sheet at December 31st. The stock at December 31st was – Department A, £6,000; Department B, £2,800. The nominal capital of the company is £25,000, divided into 15,000 ordinary shares of £1 each, and 10,000 6 per cent. cumulative preference shares of £1 each. All the shares issued are fully paid. Ignore taxation.

## THE EXCELSIOR TRADING COMPANY, LIMITED
### DEPARTMENTAL TRADING AND PROFIT AND LOSS ACCOUNTS
#### for the year ended December 31st

| | Dept. A | Dept. B | Total | | | | Dept. A | Dept. B | Total |
|---|---|---|---|---|---|---|---|---|---|
| | £ | £ | £ | | | | £ | £ | £ |
| Stock .. | 8,000 | 3,000 | 11,000 | Sales | .. | .. | 30,000 | 20,000 | 50,000 |
| Purchases | 23,000 | 15,000 | 38,000 | Stock | .. | .. | 6,000 | 2,800 | 8,800 |
| Wages .. | 1,000 | 500 | 1,500 | | | | | | |
| Balance being Gross Profit c/d. .. | 4,000 | 4,300 | 8,300 | | | | | | |
| | £36,000 | £22,800 | £58,800 | | | | £36,000 | £22,800 | £58,800 |
| Managing Director's Salary | 600 | 400 | 1,000 | Gross Profit b/d. .. | | | 4,000 | 4,300 | 8,300 |
| Directors' Fees .. | 300 | 200 | 500 | Balance, being Net Loss | | | 50 | — | — |
| Carriage and Freight .. | 900 | 600 | 1,500 | | | | | | |
| Salaries .. | 450 | 300 | 750 | | | | | | |
| Travelling Expenses .. | 540 | 360 | 900 | | | | | | |
| Incidental Expenses .. | 90 | 60 | 150 | | | | | | |
| Rates and Taxes .. | 180 | 120 | 300 | | | | | | |
| Fuel, Light and Water .. | 72 | 48 | 120 | | | | | | |
| Insurance .. | 36 | 24 | 60 | | | | | | |
| Stationery and Stamps .. | 102 | 68 | 170 | | | | | | |
| Discounts .. | 360 | 240 | 600 | | | | | | |
| Doubtful Debts Provision | 300 | 200 | 500 | | | | | | |
| Debenture Interest .. | 120 | 80 | 200 | | | | | | |
| Balance, being Net Profit carried forward .. | — | 1,600 | 1,550 | | | | | | |
| | £ 4,050 | £4,300 | £8,300 | | | | £4,050 | £4,300 | £8,300 |

## THE EXCELSIOR TRADING COMPANY, LIMITED
### BALANCE SHEET as at December 31st

| | £ | £ | | | £ | £ |
|---|---:|---:|---|---:|---:|---:|
| Share Capital: | | | Fixed Assets: | | | |
| Authorized— | | | Freehold Premises at cost .. | | | 4,200 |
| 15,000 Ordinary Shares of £1 each .. .. .. | 15,000 | | | | | |
| 10,000 6% Cumulative Preference Shares of £1 each .. | 10,000 | | Current Assets: | | | |
| | | £25,000 | Stock .. .. .. | | 8,800 | |
| | | | Debtors .. .. £9,000 | | | |
| | | | *Less* Provision for doubtful Debts .. 500 | | | |
| Issued and Fully Paid Capital: | | | | | 8,500 | |
| 10,000 Ordinary Shares of £1 each .. | 10,000 | | Bills Receivable .. | | 1,500 | |
| 5,0000 6% Cumulative Preference Shares of £1 each .. .. | 5,000 | | Balance at Bank .. £3,000 | | | |
| | 15,000 | | Cash in Hand .. 100 | | | |
| Profit and Loss Account: £ | | | | | 3,100 | |
| Balance at January 1st 600 | | | | | | 21,900 |
| *Add* Profit for year .. 1,550 | | | | | | |
| 2,150 | | | | | | |
| *Less* Preference Share Dividends paid and payable .. .. 300 | | | | | | |
| | 1,850 | | | | | |
| | | 16,850 | | | | |
| 8% Debentures .. .. | | 2,500 | | | | |
| Current Liabilities: | | | | | | |
| Creditors .. .. .. | 6,500 | | | | | |
| Debenture Interest .. .. | 100 | | | | | |
| Provision for Final Dividend on Preference Shares .. .. | 150 | | | | | |
| | | 6,750 | | | | |
| | | £26,100 | | | | £26,100 |

In order to keep an adequate check on departmental stocks, and to ensure that all are fully accounted for, it is common for goods to be charged to the departments at selling prices, ascertained by adding a fixed percentage to cost price. For this purpose the following accounts are required in respect of each department:

(*a*) Stock Account;

(*b*) 'Mark-up' Account.

Goods entering a department are debited to the Stock Account at selling prices, Purchases Account being credited with the cost price and the Mark-up Account with the percentage added thereto. The proceeds of all sales are credited to the Stock Account, the balance of which, if the full selling price has been realized on all sales, will represent the selling price of the unsold stock. At the balancing date the Mark-up Account is debited with the percentage added to cost in respect of such stock, and the balance will then be the actual gross profit realized, while the balance carried forward on the Stock Account, less the balance carried forward on the Mark-up Account will be the cost price of the stock.

Where it becomes necessary to reduce selling prices, the amount by which the mark-up is written down must be credited to Stock Account and debited to the Mark-up Account, and the reduced mark-up must be allowed for in carrying forward the mark-up on unsold stock at the balancing date.

These accounts may be in memorandum form, or may, if desired, be incorporated in the system of double entry.

**Illustration (2)**

Service Stores Ltd has a number of departments for each of which a Memorandum Stock Account and a Memorandum Mark-up Account are kept.

The following figures relate to department X:

|  |  | £ |
|---|---|---|
| Stock on January 1st, at cost .. .. .. .. .. .. | | 16,800 |
| Purchases for year .. .. .. .. .. .. .. | | 92,100 |
| Sales .. .. .. .. .. .. .. .. | | 125,000 |

Mark-up – $33\frac{1}{3}$ per cent. of cost.

The stock on January 1st included goods which cost £4,500, the selling price of which had been marked down by £700. These goods were sold during the year at the reduced prices. During the year the selling price of goods which had cost £27,000 was reduced to £35,100. Two-thirds of these goods were sold at the reduced prices and the remainder were in stock on December 31st.

At the stocktaking on December 31st, it was found that goods which had cost £270 were missing from department X and it was decided to regard this amount as irrecoverable.

The Stock Account and Mark-up Account for the year ended December 31st will appear as under:

## MEMORANDUM STOCK ACCOUNT
### (at Mark-up prices)

| Date | Particulars | £ | £ | Date | Particulars | £ | £ |
|---|---|---|---|---|---|---|---|
| Jan. 1 | Balance brought forward: | | | Dec. 31 | Sales .. .. .. | | 125,000 |
| | Cost .. .. | 16,800 | | | Mark-down (4/3 × £27,000) | 36,000 | |
| | Mark-up (1/3 × £16,800) .. £5,600 | | | | *Less* Reduced selling price | 35,100 | |
| | *Less* Mark-down 700 | | | | | | 900 |
| | | 4,900 | | | Missing goods: | | |
| | | | 21,700 | | Cost – Profit and Loss Account .. .. | 270 | |
| Dec. 31 | Purchases – Cost .. | 92,100 | | | Mark-up .. | 90 | |
| | Mark-up .. .. | 30,700 | | | | | 360 |
| | | | 122,800 | | Stock carried forward: .. | | |
| | | | | | Cost (See Note 1) .. | 13,905 | |
| | | | | | Mark-up (See Note 3) .. | 4,335 | |
| | | | | | | | 18,240 |
| | | | £144,500 | | | | £144,500 |
| Jan. 1 | Balance brought forward | | 18,240 | | | | |

## MEMORANDUM MARK-UP ACCOUNT

| Date | Particulars | £ | Date | Particulars | £ |
|---|---|---|---|---|---|
| Dec. 31 | Stock Account – Mark-down .. | 900 | Jan. 1 | Balance brought forward .. | 4,900 |
| | „ „ – Mark-up on missing goods .. | 90 | Dec. 31 | Stock Account .. .. .. | 30,700 |
| | Balance – Mark-up on closing stock carried forward .. .. | 4,335 | | | |
| | Gross Profit realized .. .. | 30,275 | | | |
| | | £35,600 | | | £35,600 |
| | | | Jan. 1 | Balance brought forward .. | 4,335 |

*Notes:*

|  |  |  | £ | £ |
|---|---|---|---|---|
| (1) Stock on January 1st .. .. .. .. .. | | | | 16,800 |
| Purchases .. .. .. .. .. .. | | | | 92,100 |
| | | | | 108,900 |
| *Less* Cost of Sales (see Note (2)) .. .. .. .. | | | 94,725 | |
| Cost of missing goods .. .. .. .. | | | 270 | |
| | | | | 94,995 |
| Stock on December 31st, at cost .. .. | | | | £13,905 |

| | | | | Selling Price | Cost Price | Gross Profit |
|---|---|---|---|---|---|---|
| (2) Analysis of Sales: | | | | | | |
| (i) In opening stock at mark-down prices: | | | | £ | £ | £ | £ |
| Cost | .. | .. | .. | .. | 4,500 | | |
| Plus $33\frac{1}{3}$ per cent. | .. | .. | .. | 1,500 | | |
| | | | | 6,000 | | |
| Less Mark-down | .. | .. | .. | 700 | | |
| | | | | 5,300 | 4,500 | 800 |
| (ii) From goods marked-down during the year: | | | | | | |
| Selling price– $\frac{2}{3} \times$ £35,100 | .. | ... | .. | 23,400 | | |
| Cost price thereof – $\frac{2}{3} \times$ £27,000 | .. | .. | | | 18,000 | 5,400 |
| (iii) Balance at full mark-up prices | .. | .. | .. | 96,300 | 72,225 | 24,075 |
| (Cost=75 per cent. of sales) | .. | .. | .. | | | |
| | | | | £125,000 | £94,725 | £30,275 |

|  | £ |
|---|---|
| (3) Mark-up on £13,905 at normal rate, $33\frac{1}{3}$ per cent. .. .. .. | 4,635 |
| Less Mark-down on unsold goods: $\frac{1}{3}(\frac{4}{3} \times$ £27,000—£35,100)$=\frac{1}{3} \times$ £900 .. | 300 |
| Effective mark-up on Stock at December 31st.. .. | £4,335 |

There are two methods of charging goods to a branch or department, other than at cost. These are:

(a) *Cost plus a percentage;*

(b) *Selling Price less a percentage.*

There are many methods of making these calculations but the following formulae may be found useful:

*Method (a):*

Where the goods are invoiced to the branch or department at cost plus a percentage, cost should be taken to be 100 and adjustments made using this figure as the base.

### Example (1)

What is the unrealized profit if:

(i) Goods are invoiced at cost plus 10 per cent.; and

(ii) ,,       ,,       ,,       ,,  ,,     ,,   20   ,,     ,,

and

closing stock at cost to the department/branch is £1,320?

SOLUTION:

| | Cost | | Loading | | Invoice price to Branch |
|---|---|---|---|---|---|
| (i) | 100 | + | 10 | = | 110 |
| (ii) | 100 | + | 20 | = | 120 |

Unrealized profit:

$$(i) \qquad \frac{10}{110} \times £1,320 = £120$$

$$(ii) \qquad \frac{20}{120} \times £1,320 = £220$$

### Example (2)

What is the unrealized profit if:

Goods are invoiced at cost plus 20 per cent., the branch incurring warehouse costs averaging 5 per cent. of invoice price and closing stock at cost to branch is £2,520?

WORKING:

| Cost | | Loading | | Invoice price to Branch | | Warehousing cost | | Cost to Branch |
|------|---|---------|---|------------------------|---|------------------|---|----------------|
| 100 | + | 20 | = | 120 | + | 6 | = | 126 |

(note: 5 per cent. of 120 is 6).

Unrealized profit: $\dfrac{20}{126} \times £2{,}520 = £400$

*Method (b):*

Where the goods are invoiced at selling price less a percentage and all sales are made at a fixed selling price.

Selling price should be taken as 100 and adjustments made using this figure as the base:

**Example (3)**

What is the unrealized profit if:

Goods are invoiced at selling price less 10 per cent., all sales being made at the fixed selling price, yielding 25 per cent. gross profit on selling price. The closing stock at cost to branch is £2,700?

| Cost | | Head Office Loading | | Invoice price to Branch | | Branch gross profit | | Selling price |
|------|---|---------------------|---|------------------------|---|---------------------|---|---------------|
| 75 | + | 15 | = | 90 | + | 10 | = | 100 |

Unrealized profit: $\dfrac{15}{90} \times £2{,}700 = £450$

## § 2. Branch Accounts

For accounting purposes there is no clear distinction between a department and a branch; the method of accounting outlined in the previous section could be applied to a branch. Branches are usually situated at a distance from the head office. The objects of branch accounting generally include:

(*a*) the ascertainment of the profit or loss of the branch;

(*b*) proper control over the branch. The degree of control which the head office will wish to exercise will vary from business to business.

The system of accounts to be employed by a concern having branch establishments must depend to a large extent upon the nature of the trade carried on and the form of organization of the business, the principal aim being to impose an effective control over the branches and to ensure that all goods and cash passing through their hands are fully accounted for.

For accounting purposes, branches may be divided into three classes, viz.:

1. Branches for which the whole of the accounting records are kept at the head office.

2. Branches which maintain separate accounting records.

3. Foreign Branches.

## § 3. Branches for which the whole of the accounting records are kept at head office

This system is recommended for use where the branches are, in effect, merely sales departments, receiving all the goods they deal in from the head office, to whom the branch managers must account therefor. The system is particularly suitable for retail branches, the whole or the bulk of whose sales are for cash. Where credit sales are permitted a personal ledger may be kept at the branch for credit customers, the head office maintaining a Total (or Control) Account for branch debtors which is written up in total from the branch manager's returns. Wherever practicable, the whole of the cash takings and cash received by the branch from debtors should be remitted intact to the head office daily by being paid into a local branch of the bank for the credit of Head Office Account. The expenses of the branch should be paid, as far as possible, by cheque from the head office, in whose books they will be debited to appropriate branch Expenses Accounts. Incidental expenses which have to be paid locally, in cash, may be dealt with through an imprest provided by head office, and replenished at regular intervals by a cheque for the actual amount of such expenditure, as shown by the branch manager's returns.

Where credit sales at the branch are considerable, it is sometimes expedient for the debtors' accounts to be kept in the head office books, and for statements to be rendered by, and remittances made direct to, the head office. In such a case, each sale will be recorded at the branch in triplicate, one copy going to the customer as an invoice, the second being sent to the head office to be used as the posting medium, and the third being retained by the branch for reference.

With regard to stock, where the nature of the goods renders it possible, quantity stock accounts should be maintained at the head office of all goods sent to, and sales made by the branch. These accounts will operate as a perpetual inventory by means of which the quantity of each of the various lines of goods in hand at the branch can be checked and discrepancies enquired into. Where, owing to the nature of the goods, it is not possible to maintain quantity stock accounts, goods should, if practicable, be charged out to the branch either at actual selling price, or at cost price plus a fixed percentage. This will enable a check to be imposed on the branch dealings, as will be shown hereunder.

All goods should be purchased through a central buying department at the head office, from which they should be issued to the branches on requisitions from the managers, or in accordance with directions given by the sales manager. Where it is expedient to empower a branch manager to requisition supplies of goods direct from manufactureres or wholesalers, copies of the orders given should be sent by the manager to the head office, and the goods should be invoiced by the suppliers to the head office, by whom they should then be charged out to the branch.

Analysis books or loose leaf records must be maintained in which the day-to-day transactions of the branches will be entered and from which the periodical totals to be posted to the ledger accounts relating to each branch will be obtained.

Preferably, all cash received by the branch, both for cash sales and from debtors, should be paid intact into a local branch of the bank for the credit of head office, the branch expenses being discharged by head office, either by cheque direct, or through a branch cash float provided by head office and maintained on the imprest system.

The branch manager should be required to forward to head office at weekly or other intervals returns giving particulars of goods received from and returned to head office, cash and credit sales, cash received from debtors, expenses, cash banked etc. and showing the figures of stock, debtors and cash in hand at the end of the period. From these particulars the necessary entries can be made in the statistical records relating to the branch, from which postings to the ledger accounts can be made periodically.

The following is a form of a branch manager's weekly return suitable for use by a concern operating a chain of retail shops:

**BRANCH RETURN FOR WEEK ENDED** ............... 19......   **BRANCH REF.** ...............

| | Allowances to Customers £ | CASH RECEIVED — Credit Sales £ | CASH RECEIVED — Cash Sales £ | CASH RECEIVED — Total £ | CASH PAYMENTS — Expenses £ | CASH PAYMENTS — Bankings £ | GOODS RECEIVED — Advice Numbers | GOODS RECEIVED — Amount £ | SALES CONTROL: |
|---|---|---|---|---|---|---|---|---|---|
| MONDAY .. | | | | | | | | | Debtors at end .. ___ £ |
| TUESDAY .. | | | | | | | | | Allowances to Customers |
| WEDNESDAY | | | | | | | | | Cash from Credit Sales |
| THURSDAY | | | | | | | | | *Less* Debtors at start .. |
| FRIDAY .. | | | | | | | | | Credit Sales for Week .. |
| SATURDAY | | | | | | | | | Cash Sales .. .. |
| | | | | | | | | | TOTAL SALES .. |

Cash Float at start ___   At end ___

Stock at start ___ £
*Less* Total Sales
    Returns ___ £
Stock at end .. ___

On reverse of this Return:
(i) List the names and addresses of customers and amount of each debt where more than 4 weeks in arrear.
(ii) Give details of all allowances to customers in excess of £1.
Attach vouchers for all cash expenses.

Remarks: ....................................................

............................................ *Signature of Manager.*

## Method (1) Cost Price

The cost price method is often used either because the stock is of a perishable nature, or by reason of the fact that selling prices are subject to considerable fluctuation. In such cases the goods will normally be charged out at cost. As a result, it will not be possible, in the head office books, to keep a Branch Stock Account which can be reconciled by including the closing stock, but, on the other hand, all the necessary material will be provided for the preparation of a proper Trading Account for the branch, the opening and closing stocks being taken at cost price, and the goods sent to the branch being charged out at cost price. The cash and credit sales will be ascertained in a similar manner to that described under the first described system, as also will all the other items.

Although, when goods are charged out at cost, the exact result of the trading can be ascertained, it is apparent that the check imposed by the selling price system (*see below*) is not available, and consequently it may be advantageous to maintain stock records for each branch compiled monthly in the following manner.

The opening stock will be taken, and to it will be added the purchases. From the total thus obtained, the sales will be deducted. The gross profit, estimated at the average rate, will then be added, and the result will represent the estimated cost price of the stock on hand. By a comparison of these monthly figures it can be seen whether the stock fluctuates, and if there is reason to suspect any irregularity the actual stock can be taken without previous notice to the manager. It must be remembered, however, that this arrangement forms no part of the double entry book-keeping, and is merely in the nature of a periodical test check.

## Illustration (1)

### BRANCH A. MONTHLY STOCK ACCOUNTS
January to June

|  | Jan. | Feb. | March | April | May | June |
|---|---|---|---|---|---|---|
|  | £ | £ | £ |  |  |  |
| Opening Stock | 1,400 | 1,225 | 1,175 |  |  |  |
| *Add* Purchases | 200 | 250 | 350 |  |  |  |
|  | 1,600 | 1,475 | 1,525 |  |  |  |
| *Less* Sales | 500 | 400 | 420 |  |  |  |
|  | 1,100 | 1,075 | 1,105 |  |  |  |
| *Add* Gross Profit 25% on Sales | 125 | 100 | 105 |  |  |  |
| Estimated Closing Stock | £1,225 | £1,175 | £1,210 |  |  |  |

## Illustration (2)

West opened a new branch in Hove on January 1st. Head office maintains all records and charges goods to branch at cost. From the information given prepare appropriate ledger accounts for the branch for the year ended December 31st and show the Trading and Profit and Loss Account.

|  | £ |
|---|---|
| Goods sent to branch at cost by head office | 90,000 |
| Returns from branch at cost | 4,000 |
| Branch credit sales | 75,000 |

|  | £ |
|---|---|
| Cash takings remitted to head office . . . . . . . . . . | 21,000 |
| Cash takings stolen (uninsured) . . . . . . . . . . | 300 |
| Goods stolen (uninsured) . . . . . . . . . . . . | 100 |
| Branch expenses paid by head office . . . . . . . . . . | 3,200 |
| Closing stock at branch at cost . . . . . . . . . . . . | 25,000 |

There was no cash in hand at the branch on December 31st

|  | £ |
|---|---|
| Cash received from branch debtors . . . . . . . . . . | 58,000 |
| Discounts allowed to branch debtors . . . . . . . . . . | 3,000 |

Head office:

|  | £ |
|---|---|
| opening stock January 1st . . . . . . . . . . . . | 120,000 |
| purchases . . . . . . . . . . . . . . . . | 700,000 |
| sales . . . . . . . . . . . . . . . . | 900,000 |
| closing stock December 31st . . . . . . . . . . . . | 70,000 |
| expenses . . . . . . . . . . . . . . . . | 40,000 |

## WEST
## HOVE BRANCH STOCK ACCOUNT (TRADING ACCOUNT)

|  | £ |  | £ |
|---|---|---|---|
| Goods sent to Branch Account: |  | Goods sent to Branch Account: |  |
| Goods from head office . . . . | 90,000 | Returns . . . . . . . . | 4,000 |
| Profit and Loss Account – Gross Profit . . | 35,400 | Debtors – Credit Sales . . . . | 75,000 |
|  |  | General Cash – Cash Sales . . . . | 21,000 |
|  |  | Defalcations – Cash sales stolen . . | 300 |
|  |  | Defalcations – Goods stolen . . . . | 100 |
|  |  | Closing Stock at cost carried forward . . | 25,000 |
|  | £125,400 |  | £125,400 |

## GOODS SENT TO BRANCH ACCOUNT

|  | £ |  | £ |
|---|---|---|---|
| Hove Branch Stock Account – Returns . . | 4,000 | Hove Branch Stock Account . . . . | 90,000 |
| H.O. Trading Account – Purchases . . | 86,000 |  |  |
|  | £90,000 |  | £90,000 |

## HOVE BRANCH DEBTORS

|  | £ |  | £ |
|---|---|---|---|
| Branch Stock Account – Credit Sales . . | 75,000 | Cash Received . . . . . . . . | 58,000 |
|  |  | Discount Allowed . . . . . . | 3,000 |
|  |  | Balance carried forward . . . . . . | 14,000 |
|  | £75,000 |  | £75,000 |

## DEFALCATIONS ACCOUNT

|  | £ |  | £ |
|---|---|---|---|
| Hove Branch Stock Account – Cash Sales stolen | 300 | General Profit and Loss Account . . . . | 400 |
| ,,  ,,  ,,  ,, – Goods stolen . . | 100 |  |  |
|  | £400 |  | £400 |

## BRANCH EXPENSES

|  | £ |  | £ |
|---|---|---|---|
| General Cash . . . . . . . . | 3,200 | General Profit and Loss Account . . . . | 3,200 |

## H.O. TRADING ACCOUNT
### for the year ended December 31st

| | £ | | £ |
|---|---|---|---|
| Opening Stock .. .. .. .. | 120,000 | Sales .. .. .. .. .. | 900,000 |
| Purchases .. .. .. £700,000 | | | |
| *Less* Transfers to Hove Branch .. 86,000 | 614,000 | | |
| | 734,000 | | |
| *Less* Closing Stock .. .. .. | 70,000 | | |
| Cost of Goods Sold .. .. .. | 664,000 | | |
| Gross Profit transferred to General Profit and Loss Account .. .. .. .. | 236,000 | | |
| | £900,000 | | £900,000 |

## GENERAL PROFIT AND LOSS ACCOUNT

| | £ | | £ |
|---|---|---|---|
| Branch Discounts Allowed .. .. | 3,000 | H.O. Gross Profit transferred from Trading Account .. .. .. .. | 236,000 |
| Defalcations .. .. .. .. | 400 | Hove Branch Gross Profit .. .. | 35,400 |
| Branch Expenses .. .. .. | 3,200 | | |
| Head Office Expenses .. .. .. | 40,000 | | |

*Notes to Illustration.* PILFERAGES: Goods have been stolen at the branch before they were sold. Since the Branch Stock Account shows gross profit on sales it should not be distorted by non-trading account items. If no entry were made in the Branch Stock Account gross profit would be reduced by the pilferage. Therefore, Branch Stock Account must be credited with the amount of the pilferage and Defalcations Account debited; Defalcations Account would be credited with insurance money received (if any) and closed off to Profit and Loss Account.

As cash takings have been stolen, the gross profit on these goods sold has been realized, and in order not to distort the gross profit, the amount thereof must be credited to Branch Stock Account (thus forming part of the total sales credited) and debited to Profit and Loss Account.

## Method (2) Cost plus a percentage

Where practicable cost plus a percentage is the most effective method of charging goods to the branch; the head office keeps accounts which disclose the gross profit or loss of the branch and in circumstances where cost plus a percentage is equivalent to selling price the head office also possesses stock control (i.e. goods received from head office must equal sales plus returns plus closing stock).

Where it is not practicable to adopt a fixed gross profit percentage for all goods, the selling price method (described below) should be used. In some cases, however, the nature of the business is such that the selling prices of all goods can be fixed by adding the same percentage to cost. In others, although the selling prices of particular lines of goods may be subject to fluctuation, experience may show that on the turnover as a whole a certain average percentage of gross profit may be expected. In such cases, it may be practicable to charge out all goods to branches at cost price plus a fixed percentage. The advantages of such a system are that in addition to providing a reasonably reliable check upon the stock and cash at the branch, since a record is available of the cost as well as the selling price of the goods, the gross profit earned by each branch is disclosed by the accounts.

Under this system, in addition to the Branch Stock Account and the Goods sent to Branch Account, a Branch Stock Adjustment Account is maintained for each branch, to which account the amount of the 'loading' added to the cost of the goods sent to the branch is credited, and from which the actual gross profit of the branch can be ascertained. The entries in the accounts are as follows:

1. Goods sent to branches are debited to the Branch Stock Account at the full *invoiced price*, Goods sent to Branch Account being credited with the *cost price* and Branch Stock Adjustment Account (or 'Mark-up Account') with the *profit percentage* added to cost. These entries are reversed in respect of goods returned by the branch to head office.

2. Cash and credit sales are credited to Branch Stock Account, Cash and Total Debtors Account respectively being debited.

3. At the close of the accounting period the stock on hand at the branch, valued at the price at which it was invoiced, is credited to the Branch Stock Account and carried forward to form the opening entry in that account in the new period. At the same time, the amount of the profit loading (or 'mark-up') included in such value is *debited* to the Branch Stock Adjustment Account and carried down to the *credit* of that account to form the opening entry in the new period.

4. Assuming no difference to be disclosed in the Branch Stock Account after the invoiced price of the closing stock has been credited thereto, the balance remaining on the Branch Stock Adjustment Account should now represent the actual gross profit realized by the branch, since this account has been credited with the profit percentage added to cost on all goods sent to the branch, and debited with the profit percentage on such of those goods as have not been sold. This balance should be transferred from the Branch Stock Adjustment Account to the credit of the Branch Profit and Loss Account.

5. For Balance Sheet purposes, the credit balance carried forward in the Branch Stock Adjustment Account will be set off against the debit balance carried forward in the Branch Stock Account to give the cost price of the stock on hand at the branch.

6. The Goods sent to Branch Account, which has been credited with the *cost* price of the goods issued to the branch, will be closed by transfer to head office Purchases Account, thus relieving the Head Office Trading Account of the charge for these goods, which have been fully accounted for in the Branch Stock Account and the Adjustment Account.

7. Any difference disclosed in the Branch Stock Account after the closing stock has been credited thereto, if reasonable in amount, may be regarded as the margin of error in computing the percentage to be added to cost, and should be transferred to the Adjustment Account before transferring the balance thereof to Profit and Loss Account. Differences beyond a reasonable limit should be investigated.

The following additional problems may be encountered under this method:

### (i) *Stock differences*

Physical stock-taking may reveal a difference between book stock per the Branch Stock Account and actual stock. The figure of physical stock should be substituted for the actual stock in the Branch Stock Account; the difference, if normal, e.g. arising from breaking bulk, or the margin of error in computing the loading should be debited or credited, as appropriate, to Branch Stock Account and Branch Adjustment Account before arriving at the gross profit to be transferred to Profit and Loss Account.

If the difference on the Stock Account is abnormal a thorough investigation should be made; management must make use of information supplied to it. The book-keeping will depend upon the result of the investigation.

If the reason for the difference is goods stolen the double entry will be: credit Branch Stock Account at *full invoiced price*, and debit defalcations account with the *cost price* of the goods and debit Branch Adjustment Account with the loading. The goods were never sold so that the profit was never earned. Defalcations Account is written off to Profit and Loss Account after being credited with any insurance receipts.

If the reason for the difference is cash stolen, i.e. cash sales stolen before banking, the gross profit on the sale has been earned, therefore no entry should be made in the Branch Adjustment Account. The double entry will be: credit Branch Stock and debit Defalcations Account (which is written off to Profit and Loss Account).

### (ii) *Allowances off selling prices* (*or cost plus the percentage*)

Sometimes owing to market conditions or, for example, in the clothing trade at seasonal sales, the prices of goods are reduced below the cost plus the original percentage. Branch Adjustment Account, which is credited with the loading, or potential gross profit, must therefore be debited, and Branch Stock Account credited with the allowances off selling prices. Unless Branch Stock Account is credited, either the account will show a non-existent stock discrepancy or, if the goods reduced in price are still in stock, stock will be over-valued.

### (iii) *Goods in transit*

Head office will debit Branch Stock Account at the time goods are invoiced to the branch; it may be that the goods have not arrived at the branch by the accounting date. When book stock is compared with physical stock there will be discrepancies and goods in transit must be included in closing stock and the necessary provision made for unrealized profit.

If goods are lost in transit between head office and the branch, the loss is suffered by the head office. Branch Stock Account will be credited with goods in transit at cost plus the percentage, Branch Adjustment Account will be debited with the loading, and a Goods Lost in Transit Account debited with the cost; Goods Lost in Transit Account will be credited with any insurance recoveries, the balance being written off to Profit and Loss Account.

### (iv) *Goods transferred by one branch to another*

Since the object of the Branch Adjustment Account is to show branch gross profit and no profit will be earned by the transferor branch, goods transferred should be treated by the transferor branch as a return direct to head office; therefore the transferor branch will debit Goods sent to Branch Account with the cost and debit the Branch Adjustment Account with the loading and it will credit Branch Stock Account with the invoiced price.

In the records kept for the transferee branch the transaction will appear as goods received from head office.

### (v) *Goods returned by credit customers direct to head office*

Since no sale has been made by the branch the loading on the goods returned must be eliminated from the Branch Adjustment Account. The double entry will be: credit Branch Debtors at invoiced price, debit Branch Adjustment Account with the loading and debit Goods sent to Branch Account with the cost. Some accountants also like to record the transaction in the Branch Stock Account and create a 'contra' entry; the double entry is: credit Branch debtors and debit Branch Stock Account at invoiced price, and then credit Branch Stock Account at invoiced price debiting Branch Adjustment Account with the loading and debiting Goods sent to Branch Account with cost.

### Illustration (1)

A company charges out goods to its branches at cost, plus 25 per cent. From the following particulars show the accounts of the branch in the head office books, indicating the actual profit made by the branch.

|  | £ |
|---|---|
| Goods sent to branch | 12,000 |
| Goods returned to head office | 1,000 |
| Sales | 10,400 |
| Stock at commencement | 1,500 |
| Stock at close | 2,120 |

### BRANCH STOCK ACCOUNT

| | £ | | £ |
|---|---|---|---|
| Stock b/f. | 1,500 | Sales | 10,400 |
| Goods from Head Office | 12,000 | Returns to Head Office | 1,000 |
| Adjustment Account, apparent profit | 20 | Stock c/d. | 2,120 |
| | £13,520 | | £13,520 |
| Balance – Stock b/d. | 2,120 | | |

### BRANCH STOCK ADJUSTMENT ACCOUNT

| | £ | | £ |
|---|---|---|---|
| 25% on cost of Returns | 200 | Balance 25% on cost price of stock, b/f. | 300 |
| 25% on cost price of Stock c/d. | 424 | 25% on cost of goods transferred | 2,400 |
| Profit and Loss Account, gross profit | 2,096 | Branch Stock Account – apparent profit | 20 |
| | £2,720 | | £2,720 |
| | | Balance b/d. | 424 |

### GOODS SENT TO BRANCH ACCOUNT

| | £ | | £ |
|---|---|---|---|
| Branch Stock Account – Cost of Returns | 800 | Branch Stock Account, cost of goods sent to branch | 9,600 |
| Trading Account – Purchases | 8,800 | | |
| | £9,600 | | £9,600 |

*Notes:*

1. The credit balance carried down on the Branch Stock Adjustment Account of £424 will be deducted from the debit balance of £2,120 on the Branch Stock Account, to give the cost price of the stock for Balance Sheet purposes, viz. £1,696.

2. The gross profit of £2,096 is the balancing item on the Branch Stock Adjustment Account, after debiting the gross profit not earned, viz. the addition to cost price on the goods returned to head office and the unsold stock.

3. Proof of gross profit:

|  |  |  |  | £ |
|---|---|---|---|---:|
| $\frac{1}{5} \times$ £10,400 (profit on sales).. | .. | .. | .. | 2,080 |
| $\frac{4}{5} \times$ £20 (profit on surplus in stock account) | .. | .. | | 16 |
| | | | | £2,096 |

The remaining one-fifth of £20 of the stock account surplus represents loading on the surplus and should be ignored.

As already stated, if a difference of unreasonable dimensions is disclosed in the Branch Stock Account, the cause must be investigated, and suitable adjusting entries made to give effect to it. Where, for example, the difference is found to be caused by the loss of goods (e.g. by destruction or theft), since the goods were never sold the gross profit on them has never been earned; the profit percentage added to the cost must therefore be debited to the Branch Stock Adjustment Account, and the cost price, being the amount of the loss actually sustained, to Profit and Loss Account (or, if the risk is covered by insurance, to the Insurance Claim Account). Where, however, the difference is attributable to misappropriation of the cash proceeds of goods sold, no debit should be made to Branch Stock Adjustment Account, since the gross profit *has* been earned, and both the cost of the goods and the realized profit have been lost. The full invoice price of the goods should be written off to Profit and Loss Account.

### Illustration (2)

Goods are charged to branch at cost plus 20 per cent., and a shortage of £748 on the Branch Stock Account is found to be due to:

1. Theft of Goods, £348.
2. Theft of Cash, £400.

#### BRANCH STOCK ACCOUNT

| | £ | | | £ |
|---|---:|---|---|---:|
| Sundries (invoice price of goods = cost plus 20 per cent.) .. .. .. .. | 12,000 | Sales .. .. .. .. .. | | 8,852 |
| | | Goods stolen: | | |
| | |   Profit and Loss Account .. £290 | | |
| | |   Branch Adjustment Account .. 58 | | |
| | | | | 348 |
| | | Cash sales stolen – Profit and Loss Account | | 400 |
| | | Stock c/d. .. .. .. .. | | 2,400 |
| | £12,000 | | | £12,000 |
| Balance b/d. .. .. .. .. | 2,400 | | | |

#### BRANCH ADJUSTMENT ACCOUNT

| | £ | | £ |
|---|---:|---|---:|
| Branch Stock Account 16⅔ per cent. on £348 Goods stolen .. .. .. .. | 58 | Branch Stock Account (20 per cent. on £10,000) | 2,000 |
| Profit and Loss Account – Gross Profit | 1,542 | | |
| Balance c/d. – being 16⅔ per cent. on £2,400 Stock | 400 | | |
| | £2,000 | | £2,000 |
| | | Balance b/d. .. .. .. .. | 400 |

## GOODS SENT TO BRANCHES ACCOUNT

| | £ | | £ |
|---|---|---|---|
| Trading Account – Purchases .. .. | 10,000 | Branch Stock Account (cost of goods invoiced at £12,000) .. .. .. .. | 10,000 |

## BRANCH PROFIT AND LOSS ACCOUNT

| | £ | | £ |
|---|---|---|---|
| Branch Stock Account:<br>*Cost* of goods stolen .. .. .. | 290 | Branch Adjustment Account:<br>Gross Profit of Branch.. .. .. | 1,542 |
| Cash stolen .. .. .. .. | 400 | | |

*Note:* Proof of gross profit:

| | £ |
|---|---|
| Sales .. .. .. .. .. | 8,852 |
| Cash sales stolen .. .. .. .. .. | 400 |
| | £9,252 |
| $\frac{1}{6} \times £9,252$ .. .. .. .. = | £1,542 |

An alternative method of dealing with the position where goods are charged out at cost plus a fixed percentage, is to rule the Branch Stock Account with two columns, one to record the invoice price of the goods, and the other their cost price. The entries in the invoice price columns form no part of the double entry, but are 'memoranda' only, their purpose being to provide a check upon the stock. Where this system is adopted a Branch Stock Adjustment Account is not required, but the Branch Stock Account is maintained as if the goods were charged out at cost.

**Illustration (3)**

A Ltd invoices its branch at cost, plus $33\frac{1}{3}\%$. From the following particulars prepare the Branch Stock Account as it would appear in the head office books:

| | £ |
|---|---|
| Stock at commencement, at invoice price .. .. | 3,000 |
| Stock at close, at invoice price .. .. .. | 2,400 |
| Goods sent to branch during the year, at invoice price .. | 20,000 |
| Credit sales .. .. .. .. .. | 1,000 |
| Returns to head office, at invoice price .. .. | 1,000 |
| Cash sales .. .. .. .. .. | 18,000 |
| Invoice value of goods pilfered .. .. .. | 200 |
| Normal loss due to wastage and deterioration of stock .. | 300 |

### BRANCH STOCK ACCOUNT

| | Invoice Price (memo) £ | £ | | Invoice Price (memo) £ | £ |
|---|---|---|---|---|---|
| Stock b/f. .. .. .. | 3,000 | 2,250 | Branch Total Debtors Account: | | |
| Goods from Head Office .. | 20,000 | 15,000 | Credit Sales .. .. .. | 1,000 | 1,000 |
| Gross Profit transferred to Profit and | | | Returns to Head Office .. .. | 1,000 | 750 |
| Loss Account.. .. .. | | 4,450 | Cash Sales .. .. .. | 18,000 | 18,000 |
| | | | Pilferage Account – Loss by theft | 200 | 150 |
| | | | Wastage and Deterioration (normal) | 300 | — |
| | | | Apparent Loss (normal) .. | 100 | — |
| | | | Stock c/d. .. .. .. | 2,400 | 1,800 |
| | £23,000 | £21,700 | | £23,000 | £21,700 |
| Stock b/d. .. .. .. | 2,400 | 1,800 | | | |

*Notes:*

1. Note that no amount is extended into the outer column for the normal wastage and the further small difference on the invoice columns; the loss on these items is automatically reflected in the gross profit, the amount of which has been arrived at after crediting the account with the cost price of the actual stock on hand, in which these items are not included. Where, however, a difference on the invoice columns is found to be due to 'irregularities', adjusting entries will be necessary. If, for example, the £300 represented the invoice price of goods lost or destroyed, the cost price, viz. £225, should be credited in the outer column of the Branch Stock Account and debited to Profit and Loss Account. If the whole of the £300 represented loss of cash, the full amount should be extended into the outer column and debited to Profit and Loss Account, as this would be the measure of the loss sustained.

2. Proof of gross profit:

|  |  | £ |
|---|---|---:|
| Cash sales | .. .. .. .. .. | 18,000 |
| Credit sales | .. .. .. .. .. | 1,000 |
|  |  | £19,000 |
| $\frac{1}{4} \times £19,000$ | .. .. .. .. .. | 4,750 |
| *Less* wastage and deterioration | .. .. .. | 300 |
|  |  | £4,450 |

**Illustration (4)**

R Ltd own two retail shops, all goods being supplied from a main store at head office at cost plus 50 per cent. which is the selling price.

Cash takings are paid in daily to the bank to the credit of head office and all payments are made by head office. Only a small credit trade is done at the branches.

The following information is extracted from the books at head office and the branch returns for the year ended December 31st, 19......

|  | Head Office £ | Branch A £ | Branch B £ |
|---|---:|---:|---:|
| Stock, December 31st .. .. .. .. | 6,040 | | |
| Stock at selling price, January 1st .. .. .. | | 3,000 | 6,000 |
| Goods sent to branches at selling price .. .. .. | | 10,800 | 19,500 |
| Purchases .. .. .. .. .. .. | 21,240 | | |
| Cash Sales paid into Bank .. .. .. | | 9,960 | 20,610 |
| Credit Sales .. .. .. .. .. | | 750 | 600 |
| Debtors, January 1st .. .. .. .. | | 500 | 400 |
| Cash received from Debtors (paid into Bank) .. | | 850 | 700 |
| Trade Creditors, January 1st .. .. .. .. | 4,000 | | |
| ,, ,, December 31st .. .. .. | 4,500 | | |
| Bank Balance, January 1st .. .. .. .. | 3,500 | | |
| Expenses paid .. .. .. .. .. | 1,500 | 1,870 | 4,190 |
| Sundry Assets, January 1st .. .. .. .. | 10,000 | 8,000 | 7,000 |
| Capital .. .. .. .. .. .. | 32,500 | | |
| Profit and Loss Account, January 1st – Credit Balance .. | 3,900 | | |

During the year Branch A had sent to Branch B goods to the value of £720 at selling price.

On stocktaking at December 31st, the Stock Account of Branch A showed a deficiency of £150, and that of Branch B a surplus of £90 at selling prices.

The head office expenses are to be apportioned equally between the two branches.

You are required to prepare:

1. Cash Account for the year.
2. Stock Account of each branch (in columnar form) in the head office books.
3. Total Debtors Account for each branch.
4. Profit and Loss Account for each branch.
5. Balance Sheet as at December 31st.

(1)                                        CASH ACCOUNT

| | | £ | | | | £ |
|---|---|---|---|---|---|---|
| Jan. 1 | Balance b/f. .. .. .. | 3,500 | Dec. 31 | Expenses: | | |
| Dec. 31 | Branch A: | | | Head Office .. .. .. | | 1,500 |
| | Cash Sales .. .. .. | 9,960 | | Branch A .. .. .. | | 1,870 |
| | Debtors .. .. .. | 850 | | „ B .. .. .. | | 4,190 |
| | Branch B: | | | Creditors .. .. .. | | 20,740 |
| | Cash Sales .. .. .. | 20,610 | | Balance c/d. .. .. .. | | 7,320 |
| | Debtors .. .. .. | 700 | | | | |
| | | £35,620 | | | | £35,620 |
| Jan. 1 | Balance b/d. .. .. .. | 7,320 | | | | |

(2)                            BRANCH STOCK ACCOUNTS

| | | Branch A Invoice Price | Dr | Branch B Invoice Price | Dr | | | Branch A Invoice Price | Cr | Branch B Invoice Price | Cr |
|---|---|---|---|---|---|---|---|---|---|---|---|
| | | £ | £ | £ | £ | | | £ | £ | £ | £ |
| Jan. 1 | Balances b/f. .. | 3,000 | 2,000 | 6,000 | 4,000 | Dec. 31 | Cash Sales .. | 9,960 | 9,960 | 20,610 | 20,610 |
| Dec. 31 | Goods from H.O. .. | 10,800 | 7,200 | 19,500 | 13,000 | | Credit Sales | 750 | 750 | 600 | 600 |
| | Transfers .. | — | — | 720 | 480 | | Transfers .. | 720 | 480 | — | — |
| | Surplus .. | — | — | 90 | — | | Deficiency .. | 150 | — | — | — |
| | Gross Profit carried to Profit and Loss Account .. | — | 3,470 | — | 7,130 | | Stock c/f. .. | 2,220 | 1,480 | 5,100 | 3,400 |
| | £ | 13,800 | 12,670 | 26,310 | 24,610 | | £ | 13,800 | 12,670 | 26,310 | 24,610 |

(3)                            TOTAL DEBTORS ACCOUNTS

| | | Branch A | Branch B | | | Branch A | Branch B |
|---|---|---|---|---|---|---|---|
| | | £ | £ | | | £ | £ |
| Jan. 1 | Balances b/f. .. .. | 500 | 400 | Dec. 31 | Cash .. .. .. | 850 | 700 |
| Dec. 31 | Credit Sales .. .. | 750 | 600 | | Balances c/d. .. .. | 400 | 300 |
| | | £1,250 | £1,000 | | | £1,250 | £1,000 |
| Jan. 1 | Balances b/d. .. | 400 | 300 | | | | |

                          PROFIT AND LOSS ACCOUNTS
(4)                        for the year ended December 31st

| | Branch A | Branch B | | Branch A | Branch B |
|---|---|---|---|---|---|
| | £ | £ | | £ | £ |
| Expenses .. .. .. | 1,870 | 4,190 | Gross Profit from Stock Accounts | 3,470 | 7,130 |
| Head Office Expenses .. .. | 750 | 750 | | | |
| Net Profit, to General Profit and Loss Account .. .. .. | 850 | 2,190 | | | |
| | £3,470 | £7,130 | | £3,470 | £7,130 |

## BALANCE SHEET
(5)      as at December 31st

| | £ | £ | | H.O. | A | B | Total |
|---|---|---|---|---|---|---|---|
| | | | | £ | £ | £ | £ |
| Capital .. .. .. .. | | 32,500 | Sundry Assets .. | 10,000 | 8,000 | 7,000 | 25,000 |
| Profit and Loss Account: | | | Stock .. .. | 6,040 | 1,480 | 3,400 | 10,920 |
| Balance July 1st .. .. | 3,900 | | Debtors .. | — | 400 | 300 | 700 |
| Net Profit for year: | | | Bank Balance .. | 7,320 | — | — | 7,320 |
| Branch A .. .. .. | 850 | | | | | | |
| ,, B .. .. .. | 2,190 | | | | | | |
| | | 6,940 | | | | | |
| Trade Creditors .. .. .. | | 4,500 | | | | | |
| | | £43,940 | | £23,360 | £9,880 | £10,700 | £43,940 |

*Workings:*

(1)      **TOTAL CREDITORS ACCOUNT**

| | | £ | | | | | | | £ |
|---|---|---|---|---|---|---|---|---|---|
| Dec. 31 | Cash paid .. .. .. | 20,740 | Jan. 1 | Balance b/f. .. .. .. | | | | | 4,000 |
| | Balance c/f. .. .. .. | 4,500 | Dec. 31 | Purchases .. .. .. | | | | | 21,240 |
| | | £25,240 | | | | | | | £25,240 |

(2) Proof of profit:                             £

     Branch A:

         Cash sales    ..    ..    ..    ..    ..      9,960

         Credit sales    ..    ..    ..    ..    ..      750

                                        £10,710

         $\frac{1}{3} \times £10,710$                        =      3,570

            *Less* deficiency reduced to cost $\frac{2}{3} \times £150$    =      100

                                         £3,470

     Branch B:

         Cash sales    ..    ..    ..    ..    ..      20,610

         Credit sales    ..    ..    ..    ..    ..      600

                                         £21,210

         $\frac{1}{3} \times £21,210$                        =      7,070

            *Add* surplus reduced to cost $\frac{2}{3} \times £90$    =      60

                                         £7,130

*Notes:*

(1) The entries in the 'Invoice Price' columns are memoranda. The profit and loss on the surplus and deficiency in the closing stocks at the branches are automatically reflected in the gross profit, as the amounts entered in the 'credit' columns for closing stock are the adjusted stock figures, reduced to cost.

(2) The Head Office Trading Account is not asked for but could be prepared as follows; the opening stock is the balancing figure.

### HEAD OFFICE TRADING ACCOUNT

| | | | | | | £ | | | | | £ |
|---|---|---|---|---|---|---|---|---|---|---|---|
| Purchases | .. | .. | .. | .. | | 21,240 | Goods sent to Branches at cost | .. | | .. | 20,200 |
| Balancing figure = Opening Stock | .. | | .. | | | 5,000 | Closing Stock | .... | .. | .. | 6,040 |
| | | | | | | £26,240 | | | | | £26,240 |

## Method (3) Selling Price

The principal aim in formulating a system of accounts for a concern having a number of branches, such as retail shops, all of which sell the same lines of goods at fixed selling prices, is to provide an adequate check on the branch managers and staffs, to ensure that all goods and cash passing through their hands are fully accounted for. This can most effectively be done, where the nature of the business permits it, by charging out all goods at the actual prices at which they are to be sold by the branches. In cases where the selling prices of all goods are ascertained by adding the same percentage to cost price, the system described in Method 2 above should be employed. Where, however, it is not possible to adopt a fixed gross profit percentage for all goods (e.g. where they consist of proprietary lines, the selling prices of which are fixed by the manufacturers; or where the market conditions in relation to certain lines of goods render it necessary to offer them at more competitive prices than others) a system analogous to that now to be described should be adopted.

All goods charged by head office to a branch should be invoiced at the selling prices fixed by head office.

In the head office books the following accounts should be kept in respect of each branch:

(1) Branch Stock Account; (2) Goods sent to Branch Account;

(3) Expense Accounts; (4) Total Debtors Account;

the last account being required only where the branch is permitted to sell goods on credit.

Branch Stock Account will be debited and Goods sent to Branch Account credited with the total selling price of all goods sent to the branch. Goods returned by the branch to head office will be credited to Branch Stock Account and debited to Goods sent to Branch Account. Any transfers of goods from one branch to another should be credited to the Branch Stock Account of the transferor branch and debited to the Branch Stock Account of the transferee branch. (Alternatively they may be recorded as having been returned to head office by the transferor branch and reissued by head office to the transferee branch.) All these transactions would be recorded at selling price.

The total amount received by the branch in respect of cash sales, and the total of the credit sales at the branch will be credited to the Branch Stock Account, Cash and Total Debtors Accounts respectively being debited. The Total Debtors Account will be credited with cash received from and discounts allowed to debtors during the period, and with bad debts written off, so that the balance of this account will represent the amount of the book debts at the end of the period. Branch expenses will be debited to the appropriate nominal accounts.

Having been debited with the total of the goods sent to the branch and credited with sales and goods returned to head office, all at selling prices, the Branch Stock Account should disclose a balance representing the closing stock of the branch at selling prices, and this should be credited to the account and carried forward to the debit of the account for the next period. The stock figure must be reconciled with the actual stock taken, any difference being traced to its origin and the requisite adjustment made or, if immaterial in amount, written off to Goods sent to Branch Account.

Where the above system is adopted, it will not be possible to ascertain from the books, without special calculation, the exact profit or loss of the branch, owing to the fact that the goods are charged out at selling prices which do not include a fixed percentage of profit, but this disadvantage is more than counter-balanced by the very material benefit obtained from being able to prove the correctness of the stock, and consequently also of the cash. Moreover, in businesses of this nature the rate of gross profit earned by each branch may usually be taken to be the same as that earned by the business as a whole, as re-vealed by the Trading Account, and consequently, so long as the turnover of the branch is known, a reliable estimate of the result of trading can easily be made.

The issue of goods by the head office to the branch does not constitute a sale, but is merely a change of location of stock within the business. The goods are accordingly credited, in the first instance, not to Sales Account, but to a Goods sent to Branch Account. If the whole of the goods were sold by the branch at the prices at which they were invoiced, the amount credited to this account could, at the end of the accounting period, be transferred to the credit of Sales Account. If, however, as will usually be the case, some of the goods remain unsold, the selling price of such unsold stock must be deleted from the Goods sent to Branch Account, by being debited thereto and carried down to the credit of the account to form an opening balance in the new period. The balance of the Goods sent to Branch Account will then represent the sales actually effected by the branch, and may be transferred to Sales Account. The amount of the unsold stock carried forward to the credit of that account is in the nature of a reserve for the amount of stock brought down as a debit in the Branch Stock Account. When preparing the final accounts, therefore, the balances carried forward on the Branch Stock Account and the Goods sent to Branch Account will cancel each other out, and can thus be eliminated from the accounts as a whole. (In effect, these entries are the same as if the unsold stock had been returned to the head office on the last day of the accounting period, and re-issued by the head office to the branch on the first day of the new period.) The branch stock may then be valued at cost, or under, and included in the stock figure which is credited to Trading Account and debited to General Stock Account.

**Illustration**

Messrs. J. Foster & Co have a head office which acts as a distributing centre to their two branches, where all sales are made. All purchases are made by the head office, and goods are charged out to the branches at selling price. All expenses (except petty expenses which are provided for by imprest from head office) are paid by the head office, where the books are kept, except the sales ledgers, which are kept at the branches. The head office, however, keeps Total Debtors Accounts in respect of these. On taking stock at Branch A at selling price, it was found that the actual stock was short by £12 compared with the balance of the Stock Account. In the same way the actual stock at Branch B was greater by £7 than the balance on their Stock Account. It was decided to write off these differences.

From the particulars given, write up the Branch Accounts in the head office books, and prepare Trading and Profit and Loss Account for the year ended December 31st, and Balance Sheet as at that date.

|  | Head Office | Branch A | Branch B |
|---|---|---|---|
|  | £ | £ | £ |
| Stock at January 1st at Selling Price .. .. .. .. .. |  | 2,000 | 1,400 |
| Goods sent to Branches .. .. .. .. .. .. |  | 15,000 | 10,000 |
| Net Credit Sales .. .. .. .. .. .. .. |  | 9,820 | 6,390 |
| Cash Sales.. .. .. .. .. .. .. .. |  | 5,150 | 3,321 |
| Goods Returned to Head Office .. .. .. .. .. |  | 200 | 120 |
| Allowances off Selling Price .. .. .. .. .. |  | 118 | 76 |
| Debtors at January 1st .. .. .. .. .. |  | 750 | 540 |
| Cash received from Debtors .. .. .. .. .. |  | 9,615 | 6,192 |
| Discounts allowed to Debtors .. .. .. .. .. |  | 160 | 107 |
| Bad Debts .. .. .. .. .. .. .. |  | 105 | 41 |
| Stock at January 1st, at Cost, at Head Office and Branches .. .. | 7,600 |  |  |
| ,,         December 31st .. .. .. .. .. | 6,900 |  |  |
| Purchases .. .. .. .. .. .. .. | 13,621 |  |  |
| Salaries .. .. .. .. .. .. .. | 1,020 | 620 | 490 |
| Trade Expenses .. .. .. .. .. .. | 420 | 115 | 76 |
| Rent and Rates .. .. .. .. .. .. | 349 | 325 | 190 |
| Depreciation .. .. .. .. .. .. | 650 |  |  |
| Discounts Received.. .. .. .. .. .. | 264 |  |  |
| Creditors .. .. .. .. .. .. .. | 2,432 |  |  |
| J. Foster, Capital Account .. .. .. .. .. | 14,942 |  |  |
| ,,         Drawings Account.. .. .. .. .. | 5,140 |  |  |
| Leasehold Premises .. .. .. .. .. .. | 5,200 |  |  |
| Fixtures and Fittings .. .. .. .. .. | 3,120 |  |  |
| Cash at Bank .. .. .. .. .. .. | 1,640 |  |  |
| Petty Cash .. .. .. .. .. .. .. | 22 | 18 | 10 |

## STOCK ACCOUNT, BRANCH A

| | | £ | | | £ |
|---|---|---|---|---|---|
| Jan. 1 | Balance – Stock b/f. .. .. | 2,000 | Dec. 31 | Net Credit Sales .. .. | 9,820 |
| Dec. 31 | Goods from Head Office .. | 15,000 | | Cash Sales .. .. | 5,150 |
| | | | | Returns to Head Office .. | 200 |
| | | | | Allowances off Selling Price .. | 118 |
| | | | | Difference in Stock .. | 12 |
| | | | | Balance – Stock c/d. .. | 1,700 |
| | | £17,000 | | | £17,000 |
| Jan. 1 | Balance – Stock b/d. .. .. | 1,700 | | | |

## STOCK ACCOUNT, BRANCH B

| | | £ | | | £ |
|---|---|---|---|---|---|
| Jan. 1 | Balance – Stock b/f. .. .. | 1,400 | Dec. 31 | Net Credit Sales .. .. | 6,390 |
| Dec. 31 | Goods from Head Office .. | 10,000 | | Cash Sales .. .. | 3,321 |
| | Difference in Stock .. .. | 7 | | Returns to Head Office .. | 120 |
| | | | | Allowance off Selling Price .. | 76 |
| | | | | Balance – Stock c/d. .. | 1,500 |
| | | £11,407 | | | £11,407 |
| Jan. 1 | Balance – Stock b/d. .. .. | 1,500 | | | |

## TOTAL DEBTORS ACCOUNT, BRANCH A

| | | £ | | | £ |
|---|---|---|---|---|---|
| Jan. 1 | Balance b/f. .. .. .. | 750 | Dec. 31 | Cash .. .. .. .. | 9,615 |
| Dec. 31 | Net Credit Sales .. .. | 9,820 | | Discounts .. .. .. | 160 |
| | | | | Bad Debts .. .. .. | 105 |
| | | | | Balance c/d. .. .. | 690 |
| | | £10,570 | | | £10,570 |
| Jan. 1 | Balance b/d. .. .. .. | 690 | | | |

## TOTAL DEBTORS ACCOUNT, BRANCH B

| | | £ | | | £ |
|---|---|---:|---|---|---:|
| Jan. 1 | Balance b/f. .. .. .. | 540 | Dec. 31 | Cash .. .. .. .. | 6,192 |
| Dec. 31 | Net Credit Sales .. .. | 6,390 | | Discounts .. .. .. | 107 |
| | | | | Bad Debts .. .. .. | 41 |
| | | | | Balance c/d. .. .. | 590 |
| | | £6,930 | | | £6,930 |
| Jan. 1 | Balance b/d. .. .. .. | 590 | | | |

## GOODS SENT TO BRANCH A ACCOUNT

| | | £ | | | £ |
|---|---|---:|---|---|---:|
| Dec. 31 | Returns from Branch .. .. | 200 | Jan. 1 | Balance – Stock Suspense b/f. .. | 2,000 |
| | Allowances off Selling Price .. | 118 | Dec. 31 | Goods to Branch .. .. | 15,000 |
| | Difference in Stock .. | 12 | | | |
| | Transfer to Sales Account .. | 14,970 | | | |
| | Balance – Stock Suspense c/d. .. | 1,700 | | | |
| | | £17,000 | | | £17,000 |
| | | | Jan. 1 | Balance – Stock Suspense b/d. .. | 1,700 |

## GOODS SENT TO BRANCH B ACCOUNT

| | | £ | | | £ |
|---|---|---:|---|---|---:|
| Dec. 31 | Returns from Branch .. .. | 120 | Jan. 1 | Balance – Stock Suspense b/f. .. | 1,400 |
| | Allowances off Selling Price .. | 76 | Dec. 31 | Goods to Branch .. .. | 10,000 |
| | Transfer to Sales Account .. | 9,711 | | Difference in Stock .. .. | 7 |
| | Balance – Stock Suspense c/d. .. | 1,500 | | | |
| | | £11,407 | | | £11,407 |
| | | | Jan. 1 | Balance – Stock Suspense b/d .. | 1,500 |

## TRADING AND PROFIT AND LOSS ACCOUNT
### for the year ended December 31st

| | £ | £ | | £ | £ |
|---|---:|---:|---|---:|---:|
| Stock .. .. .. .. | | 7,600 | Sales: | | |
| Purchases .. .. | | 13,621 |  Branch A .. .. .. | 14,970 | |
| Gross Profit c/d. .. .. | | 10,360 |  Branch B .. .. .. | 9,711 | |
| | | | | | 24,681 |
| | | | Stock .. .. .. .. | | 6,900 |
| | | £31,581 | | | £31,581 |
| Salaries: | | | Gross Profit b/d. .. .. | | 10,360 |
|  Head Office .. .. .. | 1,020 | | Discounts Received .. .. | | 264 |
|  Branch A .. .. .. | 620 | | | | |
|  Branch B .. .. .. | 490 | | | | |
| | | 2,130 | | | |
| Trade Expenses: | | | | | |
|  Head Office .. .. .. | 420 | | | | |
|  Branch A .. .. .. | 115 | | | | |
|  Branch B .. .. .. | 76 | | | | |
| | | 611 | | | |
| Rent and Rates: | | | | | |
|  Head Office .. .. .. | 349 | | | | |
|  Branch A .. .. .. | 325 | | | | |
|  Branch B .. .. .. | 190 | | | | |
| | | 864 | | | |
| Discounts Allowed: | | | | | |
|  Branch A .. .. .. | 160 | | | | |
|  Branch B .. .. .. | 107 | | | | |
| | | 267 | | | |
| Bad Debts: | | | | | |
|  Branch A .. .. .. | 105 | | | | |
|  Branch B .. .. .. | 41 | | | | |
| | | 146 | | | |
| Depreciation .. .. .. | | 650 | | | |
| Balance, being Net Profit carried to | | | | | |
|  Capital Account .. .. | | 5,956 | | | |
| | | £10,624 | | | £10,624 |

## BALANCE SHEET
### as at December 31st

| | £ | £ | | | £ | £ | £ |
|---|---|---|---|---|---|---|---|
| J. Foster, Capital Account: | | | Fixed Assets: | | | | |
| Balance at January 1st .. .. | 14,942 | | Leasehold Premises .. | | | 5,200 | |
| *Add* Profit .. .. .. | 5,956 | | Fixtures and Fittings .. | | | 3,120 | |
| | 20,898 | | | | | | 8,320 |
| *Less* Drawings .. .. | 5,140 | | Current Assets: | | | | |
| | | 15,758 | Stock .. .. | | | 6,900 | |
| Creditors .. .. .. | | 2,432 | Debtors: | | | | |
| | | | Branch A .. .. | | 690 | | |
| | | | Branch B .. .. | | 590 | | |
| | | | | | | 1,280 | |
| | | | Cash: | | | | |
| | | | At Bank .. .. | | 1,640 | | |
| | | | In Hand: | | | | |
| | | | Head Office | £22 | | | |
| | | | Branch A .. | 18 | | | |
| | | | Branch B .. | 10 | | | |
| | | | | | 50 | | |
| | | | | | | 1,690 | |
| | | | | | | | 9,870 |
| | | £18,190 | | | | | £18,190 |

If desired, the gross profit of each branch can be approximately ascertained by apportioning the gross profit disclosed by the Trading Account between the branches on the basis of their respective turnovers. Thus, in the above illustration, the gross profit of £10,360 would be apportioned as to $\frac{14,970}{24,681} = £6,284$ to Branch A, and $\frac{9,711}{24,681} = £4,076$ to Branch B. The net profit of each branch could then be found by deducting the expenses relating to that branch from its gross profit.

In the above illustration, the shortages in the branch stocks are immaterial, and can probably be attributed to normal causes, such as evaporation, loss in weight, breaking bulk, clerical errors etc. In such circumstances the differences would be written off by crediting the Branch Stock Account and debiting the Goods sent to Branch Account, thereby reducing the figure of branch sales. Where, however, the difference is large, and irregularities are suspected, their origin must be investigated and appropriate adjustments made. If, for example, a shortage is found to be due to the misappropriation of cash takings, the full amount of the difference should be credited to the Branch Stock Account and debited to Profit and Loss Account. The goods having been sold, the gross profit thereon has been earned, and the amount of the gross profit disclosed by the Trading Account should not, therefore, be reduced. The misappropriation of cash, however, represents a loss *after* the earning of the gross profit, and must be debited to Profit and Loss Account.

If the difference on the Branch Stock Account is found to be due to the pilferage or destruction of stock, the correct adjustment is to eliminate the selling price of the goods from the accounts by crediting the Branch Stock Account and debiting the Goods sent to Branch Account therewith, as if the goods had been returned by the branch to the head office. The *cost* price of the goods lost must then be credited to Trading Account (or Purchases Account) and debited to Profit and Loss Account. In this case, since the goods were never sold the gross profit has not been earned, and the true measure of the loss to the business is the *cost* of the goods, which must accordingly be taken out of the Trading Account and debited to Profit and Loss Account.

**General Illustration** (showing the use of all three methods)

Lemon Ltd opened a new branch on January 1st. The head office is to maintain all records. The managing director wishes to assess the relative merits of the three systems of charging goods to branch:

(i) Cost;

(ii) Cost plus a percentage; and

(iii) Selling price.

He requests you to prepare the appropriate ledger accounts under all three systems. He gives you the following information for the year ended December 31st:

| | £ |
|---|---|
| Goods sent to branch at cost .. .. .. | 50,000 |
| Returns from branch at cost .. .. .. | 500 |
| Branch credit sales .. .. .. .. | 35,000 |
| Cash takings remitted to head office .. .. | 10,000 |
| Branch expenses paid out of takings .. .. | 950 |
| Cash takings stolen (insured) .. .. .. | 150 |
| Closing stock at branch (at cost) .. .. .. | 12,500 |
| There was no cash in hand on December 31st | |
| Goods are invoiced to branch at cost plus 25% which is selling price | |
| Goods pilfered (at cost) .. .. .. .. | 40 |
| Allowances off selling prices .. .. .. | 100 |

(i) *Cost method*

## LEMON LIMITED
### BRANCH STOCK ACCOUNT (Trading Account)

| | £ | | £ |
|---|---|---|---|
| Goods sent to Branch Account .. .. | 50,000 | Goods sent to Branch Account (goods returned) .. .. .. .. | 500 |
| Profit and Loss Account – gross profit .. | 9,140 | Branch Debtors – credit sales .. .. | 35,000 |
| | | Cash Sales .. .. .. .. | 10,000 |
| | | Expenses paid out of takings .. .. | 950 |
| | | Insurance Claim – cash stolen .. .. | 150 |
| | | Goods pilfered – Profit and Loss Account .. | 40 |
| | | Stock c/f. .. .. .. .. | 12,500 |
| | £59,140 | | £59,140 |

### GOODS SENT TO BRANCH ACCOUNT

| | £ | | £ |
|---|---|---|---|
| Branch Stock Account (returns) .. .. | 500 | Branch Stock Account .. .. .. | 50,000 |
| Trading Account – purchases .. .. | 49,500 | | |
| | £50,000 | | £50,000 |

(ii) *Cost plus a percentage method:*

### BRANCH STOCK ACCOUNT

| | Memo (Cost plus) £ | £ | | Memo (Cost plus) £ | £ |
|---|---|---|---|---|---|
| Goods sent to Branch .. .. | 62,500 | 50,000 | Goods sent to Branch Account – returns .. .. .. | 625 | 500 |
| Profit and Loss Account – gross profit .. .. .. | — | 9,140 | Branch Debtors – credit sales .. | 35,000 | 35,000 |
| | | | Cash Sales .. .. .. | 10,000 | 10,000 |
| | | | Expenses paid out of takings .. | 950 | 950 |
| | | | Insurance Claim – cash stolen .. | 150 | 150 |
| | | | Goods pilfered .. | 50 | 40 |
| | | | Allowances off selling prices .. | 100 | — |
| | | | Stock c/f. .. .. .. | 15,625 | 12,500 |
| | £62,500 | £59,140 | | £62,500 | £59,140 |

## GOODS SENT TO BRANCH ACCOUNT

| | £ | | £ |
|---|---|---|---|
| Branch Stock Account (returns) .. .. | 500 | Branch Stock Account .. .. .. | 50,000 |
| Trading Account – purchases .. .. | 49,500 | | |
| | £50,000 | | £50,000 |

*Alternatively:*

## BRANCH STOCK ACCOUNT

| | £ | | £ |
|---|---|---|---|
| Goods sent to Branch Account .. .. | 50,000 | Goods sent to Branch Account (returns) .. | 500 |
| Branch Stock Adjustment Account .. .. | 12,500 | Branch Stock Adjustment Account .. | 125 |
| Invoice price to Branch .. .. .. | 62,500 | Returns at invoice price to Branch .. | 625 |
| | | Branch Debtors – credit sales .. .. | 35,000 |
| | | Cash Sales .. .. .. .. | 10,000 |
| | | Expenses paid out of takings .. .. | 950 |
| | | Insurance Claim – cash stolen .. .. | 150 |
| | | Goods pilfered – Profit and Loss Account .. | 40 |
| | | ,, ,, – Branch Stock Adjustment .. | 10 |
| | | Allowances off selling prices – Branch Stock Adjustment Account .. .. .. | 100 |
| | | Stock c/f. .. .. .. .. | 15,625 |
| | £62,500 | | £62,500 |

## BRANCH STOCK ADJUSTMENT ACCOUNT

| | £ | | £ |
|---|---|---|---|
| Branch Stock Account (returns) .. .. | 125 | Branch Stock Account .. .. .. | 12,500 |
| ,, ,, ,, (pilferages) .. .. | 10 | | |
| ,, ,, ,, (allowances) .. .. | 100 | | |
| Provision c/f. (unrealized stock profit) .. | 3,125 | | |
| Profit and Loss Account – gross profit .. | 9,140 | | |
| | £12,500 | | £12,500 |

## GOODS SENT TO BRANCH ACCOUNT

| | £ | | £ |
|---|---|---|---|
| Branch Stock Account (returns) .. .. | 500 | Branch Stock Account .. .. .. | 50,000 |
| Trading Account – purchases .. .. | 49,500 | | |
| | £50,000 | | £50,000 |

(iii) *Selling price method:*

## BRANCH STOCK ACCOUNT

| | £ | | £ |
|---|---|---|---|
| Goods sent to Branch Account .. .. | 62,500 | Goods sent to Branch Account (returns) .. | 625 |
| | | Branch Debtors – credit sales .. .. | 35,000 |
| | | Cash Sales .. .. .. .. | 10,000 |
| | | Expenses paid out of takings .. .. | 950 |
| | | Insurance Claim .. .. .. | 150 |
| | | Goods sent to Branch Account: | |
| | | – Allowances off selling prices .. .. | 100 |
| | | – Goods pilfered .. .. .. | 50 |
| | | Stock c/f. .. .. .. .. | 15,625 |
| | £62,500 | | £62,500 |

## GOODS SENT TO BRANCH ACCOUNT

| | £ | | £ |
|---|---|---|---|
| Branch Stock Account (returns) .. .. | 625 | Branch Stock Account .. .. .. | 62,500 |
| ,, ,, ,, (pilferages) .. .. | 50 | | |
| ,, ,, ,, (authorized reduction in selling prices) .. .. .. .. | 100 | | |
| Trading Account – Sales .. .. .. | 46,100 | | |
| Balance c/f. .. .. .. .. | 15,625 | | |
| | £62,500 | | £62,500 |

*Notes to Illustration:*

1. Goods pilfered –

    (*a*) Under the cost method:

    Since the Branch Stock Account shows the gross profit on trading and goods pilfered are an overhead expense and not a trading loss, Branch Stock Account must be credited and Profit and Loss Account debited.

    (*b*) Under the cost plus a percentage method:

    Since the goods were stolen before sale a gross profit on them was never earned, therefore credit Branch Stock Account at cost plus a percentage and debit Branch Adjustment with the loading and Profit and Loss Account with the cost.

    If the memo column method is used, the goods pilfered will be credited in the memo column at cost plus a percentage, otherwise the entries will be the same as in the cost method.

    (*c*) Under the selling price method:

    Since the goods were never sold, credit Branch Stock Account and debit Goods sent to Branch Account at selling price. In the whole business accounts, credit Trading Account and debit Profit and Loss Account at cost price since pilferage is not a trading loss, but an overhead expense.

2. Allowances off selling prices –

    (*a*) Under the cost method no entries are necessary.

    (*b*) Under the cost plus a percentage method credit Branch Stock Account and debit Branch Adjustment Account. Allowances off selling price are a reduction in gross profit.

    If the memo column method is used the only entry necessary is to credit the memo column in the Branch Stock Account.

    (*c*) Under the selling price method credit Branch Stock Account and debit goods sent to Branch Account. Allowances off selling prices are a reduction in sales values.

3. Cash takings stolen (insured) –

    (*a*) Under the cost method:

    Since the goods have been sold and subsequently the cash received for them has been stolen, gross profit must not be affected. Therefore credit Branch Stock Account and debit the Insurance Claim Account with the amount stolen. If the claim is not met in full, write off the balance on the Insurance Claim Account to Profit and Loss Account.

    (*b*) Under the cost plus a percentage method:

    Since the gross profit has been earned, credit Branch Stock Account and debit Insurance Claim Account. If the memo column method is used, the amount stolen will also be entered in the memo column.

    (*c*) Under the selling price method:

    Since total sales are unaffected, credit Branch Stock Account and debit Insurance Claim Account.

## Semi-Autonomous Branches

The above examples have dealt with branches where the double-entry records are kept at head office. In some cases it may be inexpedient for the branch expenses to be paid by the head office, and the branch manager may be permitted to pay expenses incurred locally out of his cash takings, and to make periodical remittances to the head office of the balance of cash remaining in his hands, or of round sums, instead of paying the whole of his takings into the bank for the credit of head office. Where this is done, instead of being credited with the total sales, the Branch Account will be credited with the remittances made to the head office and the expenses paid by the branch. The balance of the Branch Stock Account will then represent the unsold stock at the branch, valued at selling price, plus any balance of cash takings not yet remitted to the head office. Where credit sales are small, and it is not considered necessary to maintain a Total Debtors Account for the branch in the head office books, the balance of the Branch Stock Account may also include the total of any outstanding debts owing by branch customers at the date of balancing the accounts.

**Illustration**

Biddington & Co carry on a retail business in London, and have a suburban branch to which all goods are supplied by head office and invoiced at selling prices. The branch manager pays all the branch expenses out of takings and makes remittances periodically to the head office.

From the following information, show the accounts in the head office books recording the branch transactions, and prepare a Trading and Profit and Loss Account of the business for the year ended December 31st.

| Extracts from branch returns to head office: | £ | £ |
|---|---|---|
| Goods invoiced from head office | | 6,696 |
| Remittances to head office | | 5,250 |
| Sales: | | |
|     Cash sales | | 4,700 |
|     Credit sales | | 1,786 |
| Expenses paid: | | |
|     Rent | 400 | |
|     Rates and Insurance | 120 | |
|     Wages | 650 | |
|     Lighting and Heating | 50 | |
|     General Expenses | 72 | |
| | | 1,292 |
| Cash in hand (December 31st) | | 64 |
| Debtors (December 31st) | | 130 |
| Stock (December 31st) | | 750 (cost £508) |
| Cash collected from debtors | | 1,813 |
| Extracts from head office books: | £ | £ |
| Rent | | 1,000 |
| Rates and Insurance | | 320 |
| Salaries and Wages | | 5,400 |
| Heating and Lighting | | 120 |
| General Expenses | | 742 |
| Carriage Outwards | | 563 |
| Travelling Expenses | | 748 |
| Discounts | | 450 |
| Stock at cost (January 1st) | | 3,247 |
| Purchases | | 36,214 |
| Sales | | 45,402 |
| Branch Account (January 1st): | | |
|     Cash | 93 | |
|     Debtors | 157 | |
|     Stock | 540 | |

Head office stock at December 31st was valued at £3,625.

The following provisions are to be made:

        Depreciation: Head office £100  Branch £20

        Bad debts      ,,     ,,   £250   ,,    £10

The branch is to be charged with £400 for management expenses.

## BRANCH STOCK ACCOUNT

| | | £ | | | £ |
|---|---|---|---|---|---|
| Jan. 1 | Balance b/f. .. .. | 540 | Dec. 31 | Debtors – credit sales .. .. | 1,786 |
| Dec. 31 | Goods from Head Office .. | 6,696 | | Cash Control Account – cash sales | 4,700 |
| | | | | Balance c/f. .. .. .. | 750 |
| | | £7,236 | | | £7,236 |

## GOODS SENT TO BRANCH ACCOUNT

| | | £ | | | | £ |
|---|---|---|---|---|---|---|
| Dec. 31 | Trading Account: | | Jan. 1 | Stock b/f. .. .. .. | | 540 |
| | Sales .. .. .. | 6,486 | Dec. 31 | Branch Account: | | |
| | Balance c/f.: | | | Goods to Branch .. | | 6,696 |
| | Stock .. .. .. | 750 | | | | |
| | | £7,236 | | | | £7,236 |

## BRANCH CASH CONTROL ACCOUNT

| | £ | | £ |
|---|---|---|---|
| Balance b/f. ... .. .. | 93 | Remittances to Head Office .. .. | 5,250 |
| Branch Stock Account – cash sales .. | 4,700 | Expenses .. .. .. .. | 1,292 |
| Debtors – cash received .. .. | 1,813 | Balance c/f. .. .. .. | 64 |
| | £6,606 | | £6,606 |

## BRANCH TOTAL DEBTORS CONTROL

| | £ | | £ |
|---|---|---|---|
| Balance b/f. .. .. .. .. | 157 | Cash Control – cash received .. .. | 1,813 |
| Branch Stock Account – credit sales .. | 1,786 | Balance c/f. .. .. .. | 130 |
| | £1,943 | | £1,943 |

## TRADING AND PROFIT AND LOSS ACCOUNT
### for the year ended December 31st

| | £ | £ | | | £ | £ |
|---|---|---|---|---|---|---|
| Stock, January 1st .. .. | | 3,247 | Sales – Head Office .. .. | | 45,402 | |
| Purchases .. .. | | 36,214 | – Branch .. .. | | 6,486 | |
| Gross Profit (apportioned on basis of | | | | | | 51,888 |
| Sales): | | | Stock, December 31st: | | | |
| Head Office .. .. .. | 14,490 | | Head Office .. .. | | 3,625 | |
| Branch .. .. .. | 2,070 | | Branch .. .. | | 508 | |
| | | 16,560 | | | | 4,133 |
| | | £56,021 | | | | £56,021 |

| | Head Office £ | Branch £ | Total £ | | Head Office £ | Branch £ | Total £ |
|---|---|---|---|---|---|---|---|
| Rent .. .. .. | 1,000 | 400 | 1,400 | Gross Profit b/d. .. | 14,490 | 2,070 | 16,560 |
| Rates and Insurance .. | 320 | 120 | 440 | Management Expenses | | | |
| Salaries and Wages .. | 5,400 | 650 | 6,050 | charged to Branch .. | 400 | | |
| Heating and Lighting .. | 120 | 50 | 170 | | | | |
| General Expenses .. | 742 | 72 | 814 | | | | |
| Carriage Outwards .. | 563 | | 563 | | | | |
| Travelling Expenses .. | 748 | | 748 | | | | |
| Discounts .. .. | 450 | | 450 | | | | |
| Provision for Bad Debts .. | 250 | 10 | 260 | | | | |
| Depreciation .. | 100 | 20 | 120 | | | | |
| Management Expenses .. | | 400 | | | | | |
| Net Profit .. .. | 5,197 | 348 | 5,545 | | | | |
| | £14,890 | £2,070 | £16,560 | | £14,890 | £2,070 | £16,560 |

*Note:*

The branch cash and debtors carried forward appear in the Balance Sheet under their appropriate headings. The branch stock, however, is brought down in the Branch Account at selling price. This is cancelled out against the credit balance of a similar amount carried down in the Goods sent to Branch Account. The *cost* of the branch stock, viz. £508, is then credited to Trading Account and debited to General Stock Account as part of which it appears in the Balance Sheet.

Instead of opening three control accounts as in the above illustration, i.e. Branch Stock Account, Branch Cash Control and Branch Total Debtors, some accountants prefer to use only one Branch Account, which controls stock, cash and debtors. By eliminating all the inter-control account entries the figures remaining will form the basis of the Stock Control Account.

**Illustration**

Using the information given in the previous illustration prepare one Control Account covering stock, cash and debtors.

### BRANCH CONTROL ACCOUNT

| | | £ | £ | | | | £ | £ |
|---|---|---|---|---|---|---|---|---|
| Jan. 1 | Balance b/f.: | | | Dec. 31 | Cash from Branch .. | | | 5,250 |
| | Cash .. .. .. | 93 | | | Expenses: | | | |
| | Debtors .. .. | 157 | | | Rent .. .. .. | 400 | | |
| | Stock .. .. | 540 | | | Rates and Insurance .. | 120 | | |
| | | | 790 | | Wages .. .. | 650 | | |
| Dec. 31 | Goods from Head Office .. | | 6,696 | | Lighting and Heating .. | 50 | | |
| | | | | | General Expenses .. | 72 | | |
| | | | | | | | | 1,292 |
| | | | | | Balance c/f.: | | | |
| | | | | | Cash .. .. .. | 64 | | |
| | | | | | Debtors .. .. | 130 | | |
| | | | | | Stock .. .. .. | 750 | | |
| | | | | | | | | 944 |
| | | | £7,486 | | | | | £7,486 |

## § 4. Branches which maintain separate accounting records

In the case of branches where, on account of their distance from the head office, or for some other good reason, it is considered expedient to keep complete financial records at the branch, the following system should be employed whether the goods are invoiced to the branch at *cost* price or at a loaded price. Special considerations apply when the head office invoice goods at a loaded price, and these are considered fully later.

An account will be opened in the branch books called 'Head Office Current Account' (or 'Head Office Account') and in the head office books there will be a corresponding account opened called 'Branch Current Account' (or 'Branch Account'). All remittances of cash and transfers of goods etc. to or from the head office, or other transactions between the head office and the branch will be passed through these accounts, either in detail or in total, at convenient intervals. In the branch books the Head Office Account can be regarded as the Capital Account of the branch and, consequently, if the assets in the branch books exceed the liabilities, the Head Office Account will show a credit balance. In the head office books the Branch Account will, in the same way, reveal a debit balance representing the excess of assets over liabilities at the branch.

At the end of each accounting period, the balance of the Profit and Loss Account in the books of the branch will be transferred to the Head Office Account, and the Branch Balance Sheet will then disclose the assets and the liabilities at the branch, and the balance due to or from the head office.

The head office, on receiving these accounts, will incorporate the profit at the branch in its own books by debiting the Branch Account and crediting Profit and Loss Account with the amount thereof. Assuming no other adjustments to be necessary, it will then be found that the balance on the Branch Account in the head office books agrees with the balance on the Head Office Account in the branch books. The head office and branch Balance Sheets can now be amalgamated, the various assets and liabilities being aggregated together under their respective headings, while the Current Account balances, being contra items, are eliminated.

### Illustration (1)

The following are the trial balances of the head office and Leeds branch, respectively, of a business at December 31st. Prepare summarized amalgamated Balance Sheet and show the Leeds Current Account in the head office books, and the Head Office Current Account in the Leeds branch books.

| DEBIT BALANCES | Head Office | Leeds |
|---|---|---|
| | £ | £ |
| Goodwill | 5,000 | |
| Stock | 6,500 | 3,200 |
| Debtors | 7,300 | 4,100 |
| Cash at Bank | 2,100 | 520 |
| Plant and Machinery | 4,300 | 1,700 |
| Leeds Current Account January 1st | 6,380 | |
| Goods sent to Leeds | 1,500 | |
| Cash sent to London | | 2,000 |
| | £33,080 | £11,520 |

| CREDIT BALANCES | | |
|---|---|---|
| Share Capital – Authorized and Issued 21,000 Shares of £1 each, fully paid | 21,000 | |
| Profit and Loss Account – Balance at January 1st | 530 | |
|     ,,    ,,    ,,    – Profit for year | 6,200 | 1,900 |
| Creditors | 3,100 | 1,600 |
| Provision for Bad Debts | 250 | 140 |
| Goods received from London | | 1,500 |
| Cash received from Leeds | 2,000 | |
| Head Office Current Account January 1st | | 6,380 |
| | £33,080 | £11,520 |

## LEEDS CURRENT ACCOUNT IN HEAD OFFICE BOOKS

| | | £ | | | | £ |
|---|---|---|---|---|---|---|
| Jan. 1 | Balance b/f. | 6,380 | Dec. 31 | Cash | | 2,000 |
| Dec. 31 | Goods | 1,500 | | Balance c/f. | | 7,780 |
| | Profit and Loss Account: Profit for year | 1,900 | | | | |
| | | £9,780 | | | | £9,780 |

## HEAD OFFICE CURRENT ACCOUNT IN LEEDS BOOKS

| | | £ | | | | £ |
|---|---|---|---|---|---|---|
| Dec. 31 | Cash | 2,000 | Jan. 1 | Balance b/f. | | 6,380 |
| | Balance c/f. | 7,780 | Dec. 31 | Goods received from London | | 1,500 |
| | | | | Profit for year | | 1,900 |
| | | £9,780 | | | | £9,780 |

## BALANCE SHEET
### as at December 31st

| | H.O. | Branch | Combined | | H.O. | Branch | Combined |
|---|---|---|---|---|---|---|---|
| | £ | £ | £ | | £ | £ | £ |
| Share Capital, Authorized and Issued: | | | | FIXED ASSETS | | | |
| 21,000 Shares of £1 each fully paid .. | 21,000 | | 21,000 | Goodwill .. .. | 5,000 | | 5,000 |
| Profit and Loss Account .. .. | 8,630 | — | 8,630 | Plant .. .. | 4,300 | 1,700 | 6,000 |
| Creditors .. .. | 3,100 | 1,600 | 4,700 | CURRENT ASSETS | | | |
| H.O. Current Account | | 7,780 | — | Stock .. .. | 6,500 | 3,200 | 9,700 |
| | | | | Debtors, less provision .. | 7,050 | 3,960 | 11,010 |
| | | | | Cash .. .. | 2,100 | 520 | 2,620 |
| | | | | Leeds Current Account .. .. | 7,780 | | — |
| | £32,730 | £9,380 | £34,330 | | £32,730 | £9,380 | £34,330 |

It will be seen that the Leeds Current Account is represented in the Balance Sheet by the net assets of the branch, viz.:

| | | | | | | £ |
|---|---|---|---|---|---|---|
| Plant and Machinery | .. | .. | .. | .. | | 1,700 |
| Stock .. | .. | .. | .. | .. | | 3,200 |
| Debtors .. | .. | .. | .. | .. | | 3,960 |
| Cash .. | .. | .. | .. | .. | | 520 |
| | | | | | | 9,380 |
| *Less* Creditors .. | .. | .. | .. | .. | | 1,600 |
| | | | | | | £7,780 |

Where, as frequently happens, cash or goods are in transit between the head office and the branches, or between one branch and another, at the date of the Balance Sheet, the balances of the relative Current Accounts will not agree, since the entries relating to the value in transit will have been made in one set of books, and not in the other. Before preparing the final accounts, therefore, adjustments are necessary in respect of these items. Where the cash or goods are in transit between a branch and its head office (i.e. either from or to the head office), the adjustment in respect thereof will normally be made in the books of the head office, by crediting the Branch Account and debiting Cash or Goods in Transit Account with the amount in transit. Alternatively, the amount can be carried down as a separate balance in the Branch Account to form an opening entry in the new period. In this manner the balance of the Branch Account in the head office books is reconciled with that appearing on the Head Office Account in the branch books, and no adjusting entries in the latter books are required.

Where the value in transit is between one branch and another, it is advisable for the adjustment to be made in the books of the transferor branch by crediting the account of the transferee branch and debiting a Cash or Goods in Transit Account, or carrying the amount down as a separate balance.

**Illustration (2)**

A company has its head office in London, and branches at Liverpool and Sheffield. The following are the separate Balance Sheets on December 31st:

## LONDON

| | £ | | £ |
|---|---|---|---|
| Share Capital: | | Stock .. .. .. .. .. | 36,250 |
| 100,000 Shares of £1 each fully paid .. | 100,000 | Debtors .. .. .. .. .. | 42,500 |
| Creditors .. .. .. .. | 6,000 | Sheffield Current Account (after debiting £300 | |
| Liverpool Current Account (after debiting £100 | | Stock returned to Sheffield on December | |
| Cash remitted on December 31st, and received | | 31st, and received at Sheffield on January | |
| at Liverpool on January 1st) .. .. | 390 | 3rd) .. .. .. .. .. | 27,140 |
| Profit and Loss Account: | | Cash at Bank .. .. .. .. | 11,500 |
| Balance at January 1st .. .. £1,750 | | | |
| *Add* Profit for year .. .. 9,250 | | | |
| | 11,000 | | |
| | £117,390 | | £117,390 |

## LIVERPOOL

| | £ | | £ |
|---|---|---|---|
| Creditors .. .. .. .. | 1,750 | Stock .. .. .. .. .. | 3,505 |
| Bank Overdraft .. .. .. .. | 4,000 | Debtors .. .. .. .. .. | 1,750 |
| Sheffield Current Account (after debiting £150 | | Head Office Current Account (after debiting | |
| Stock sent to Sheffield December 31st, and | | £75 Stock sent to London December 31st | |
| received at Sheffield on January 3rd) .. | 70 | and received at London on January 2nd) | 565 |
| | £5,820 | | £5,820 |

## SHEFFIELD

| | £ | | £ |
|---|---|---|---|
| Creditors .. .. .. .. | 5,050 | Plant and Machinery .. .. .. | 20,470 |
| Head Office Current Account (after debiting | | Stock .. .. .. .. .. | 5,200 |
| £500 Cash sent to Head Office December 31st | | Debtors .. .. .. .. | 3,250 |
| and received at London January 1st) .. | 26,340 | Liverpool Current Account .. .. | 220 |
| | | Cash at Bank .. .. .. .. | 2,250 |
| | £31,390 | | £31,390 |

The profit and loss balances at the branches have been adjusted.

Make the further adjustments necessary, and prepare aggregate Balance Sheet as at December 31st.

## HEAD OFFICE BOOKS
### LIVERPOOL CURRENT ACCOUNT

| | £ | | £ |
|---|---|---|---|
| Balance c/d. .. .. .. .. | 565 | Balance b/f. .. .. .. .. | 390 |
| | | Stock in transit .. .. .. .. | 75 |
| | | Cash in transit .. .. .. .. | 100 |
| | £565 | | £565 |
| | | Balance b/d. .. .. .. | 565 |

### SHEFFIELD CURRENT ACCOUNT

| | £ | | £ |
|---|---|---|---|
| Balance b/f. .. .. .. .. | 27,140 | Cash in transit .. .. .. .. | 500 |
| | | Stock in transit .. .. .. .. | 300 |
| | | Balance c/d. .. .. .. .. | 26,340 |
| | £27,140 | | £27,140 |
| Balance b/d. .. .. .. .. | 26,340 | | |

## CASH IN TRANSIT

| | £ | | |
|---|---|---|---|
| Liverpool Current Account.. .. .. | 100 | | |
| Sheffield Current Account .. .. .. | 500 | | |

## STOCK IN TRANSIT

| | £ | | |
|---|---|---|---|
| Liverpool Current Account .. .. | 75 | | |
| Sheffield Current Account .. .. .. | 300 | | |

## LIVERPOOL BOOKS
## SHEFFIELD CURRENT ACCOUNT

| | | | £ |
|---|---|---|---|
| | Balance b/f. .. .. .. .. | | 70 |
| | Stock in transit .. .. .. .. | | 150 |

## STOCK IN TRANSIT

| | £ | | |
|---|---|---|---|
| Sheffield Current Account .. .. .. | 150 | | |

## HEAD OFFICE CURRENT ACCOUNT

| | £ | | |
|---|---|---|---|
| Balance b/f. .. .. .. .. | 565 | | |

## SHEFFIELD BOOKS
## HEAD OFFICE CURRENT ACCOUNT

| | | | £ |
|---|---|---|---|
| | Balance b/f. .. .. .. .. | | 26,340 |

## LIVERPOOL CURRENT ACCOUNT

| | £ | | |
|---|---|---|---|
| Balance b/f. .. .. .. .. | 220 | | |

## BALANCE SHEET
### as at December 31st

| | £ | £ | | £ | £ | £ |
|---|---|---|---|---|---|---|
| | | | Fixed Assets: | | | |
| | | | Plant and Machinery .. | | | 20,470 |
| Authorized and Issued Share Capital: | | | | | | |
| 100,000 Shares of £1 each fully paid | | 100,000 | Current Assets: | | | |
| | | | Stock: | | | |
| Profit and Loss Account: | | | London .. .. | 36,250 | | |
| Balance at January 1st .. .. | 1,750 | | Liverpool .. .. | 3,505 | | |
| Add Profit for year .. .. | 9,250 | | Sheffield .. .. | 5,200 | | |
| | | 11,000 | Stock in transit .. | 525 | | |
| | | | | | 45,480 | |
| | | 111,000 | Debtors: | | | |
| Creditors: | | | London .. .. | 42,500 | | |
| London .. .. .. | 6,000 | | Liverpool .. .. | 1,750 | | |
| Liverpool .. .. .. | 1,750 | | Sheffield .. .. | 3,250 | | |
| Sheffield .. .. .. | 5,050 | | | | 47,500 | |
| | | 12,800 | Cash at Bank: | | | |
| Bank Overdraft: | | | London .. .. | 11,500 | | |
| Liverpool .. .. .. | | 4,000 | Sheffield .. .. | 2,250 | | |
| | | | Cash in transit .. | 600 | | |
| | | | | | 14,350 | |
| | | | | | | 107,330 |
| | | £127,800 | | | | £127,800 |

In some cases it is more convenient to keep the accounts for fixed assets of the branch, such as land, buildings, plant and machinery etc., in the head office books rather than in the branch books. If this is done, the branch should be charged with depreciation on these assets, the Head Office Account in the branch books being credited, and Depreciation Account debited with the amount thereof. In the head office books the Provision for Depreciation Account will be credited and the Branch Current Account debited with the amount of the depreciation. The transaction is equivalent to a transfer of value from the head office to the branch, which, in the head office books, must be charged to the branch and credited to the account giving the value, and in the branch books must be credited to the head office and debited to the account receiving the value.

In combining the final accounts of a business where there are only one or two branches, it is frequently found convenient to show the accounts in columnar form, columns being provided for the head office, for each branch, and for the total figures. When this is done, care should be taken to see that the amount of sales from the head office to branches, and the amount of purchases by branches from head office, together with any similar transactions as between the branches themselves, are not extended into the total column, otherwise the total figures will be unduly swollen by the inclusion of transactions which merely represent internal transfers and have no relation to the actual turnover. If the Balance Sheet is in columnar form, it will be necessary to include the balances of the Current Accounts between the head office and branches in the columns to which they relate, in order that the totals of these columns shall agree, but these Current Account balances must not be extended, since they represent the net assets or liabilities at the branches, which have already been included in the total columns.

When inter-branch transactions occur, each branch must have a Current Account for the branch with which the transactions are effected, and these accounts must be agreed at the end of each period in the same manner as the Current Accounts between the head office and branches.

**Illustration (3)**

A, B and C are partners in a firm having separate businesses in London, Edinburgh and Dublin. A manages in London, and receives two-thirds of the profits there, the balance being shared equally between B and C. B manages in Edinburgh, and receives half of the profits there, the balance being shared equally between A and C. C manages in Dublin, and receives one-third of the profits there, the balance being shared equally between A and B. The Capital Account of each partner is kept in the books of his branch. Each branch from time to time buys from and sells to the other branches at agreed rates sufficient to give the selling branch a reasonable profit on the handling of the goods, and such transactions have been adjusted through the Current Accounts.

From the following Trial Balances of the respective branches, prepare Columnar Trading and Profit and Loss Account for the year ended December 31st, and Columnar Balance Sheet as at that date. It is agreed that the special legal expenses incurred in London shall be borne by the three branches equally. Show the Current Accounts and Partners' Capital Accounts in the books of each branch. Interest on capital to be charged at 5 per cent. per annum, but no interest on drawings. Provide depreciation on plant and machinery at 10 per cent. per annum. Closing stocks: London, £14,000; Edinburgh, £11,500; Dublin, £7,500.

## TRIAL BALANCES – December 31st

| Debit Balances | London | Edinburgh | Dublin | Credit Balances | London | Edinburgh | Dublin |
|---|---|---|---|---|---|---|---|
| | £ | £ | £ | | £ | £ | £ |
| Stock January 1st .. | 15,000 | 10,000 | 7,000 | Sales .. .. | 57,000 | 39,000 | 25,000 |
| Purchases .. .. | 40,000 | 25,000 | 12,000 | Do.  Internal  .. | 7,000 | 2,500 | 1,500 |
| Do.   Internal .. | 1,000 | 4,000 | 6,000 | Creditors   .. | 16,800 | 7,000 | 7,600 |
| Wages   .. .. | 5,000 | 3,500 | 2,500 | Current Accounts: | | | |
| Trade Expenses  .. | 4,900 | 2,900 | 1,550 | London  .. | | 3,000 | 2,000 |
| Special Legal Expenses | 600 | | | Dublin  .. | | 1,000 | |
| Plant  .. .. | 7,000 | 4,000 | 3,000 | Capital Accounts: | | | |
| Debtors  .. .. | 17,800 | 8,600 | 6,550 | A  .. .. | 20,000 | | |
| Current Accounts: | | | | B  .. .. | | 8,000 | |
| Edinburgh  .. | 3,000 | | 1,000 | C  .. .. | | | 5,000 |
| Dublin ..  .. | 2,000 | | | | | | |
| Cash   .. .. | 2,500 | 1,500 | 500 | | | | |
| Drawings Accounts: | | | | | | | |
| A  .. .. | 2,000 | | | | | | |
| B  .. .. | | 1,000 | | | | | |
| C  .. .. | | | 1,000 | | | | |
| | £100,800 | £60,500 | £41,100 | | £100,800 | £60,500 | £41,100 |

## GENERAL TRADING AND PROFIT AND LOSS ACCOUNT
### for the year ended December 31st

| | London | Edinburgh | Dublin | TOTAL | | London | Edinburgh | Dublin | TOTAL |
|---|---|---|---|---|---|---|---|---|---|
| | £ | £ | £ | £ | | £ | £ | £ | £ |
| Stock January 1st | 15,000 | 10,000 | 7,000 | 32,000 | Sales .. .. | 57,000 | 39,000 | 25,000 | 121,000 |
| Purchases    .. | 40,000 | 25,000 | 12,000 | 77,000 | Do. Internal  .. | 7,000 | 2,500 | 1,500 | — |
| Do.    Internal  .. | 1,000 | 4,000 | 6,000 | — | Stock, Dec. 31st | 14,000 | 11,500 | 7,500 | 33,000 |
| Wages ..    .. | 5,000 | 3,500 | 2,500 | 11,000 | | | | | |
| Gross  Profit c/d. | 17,000 | 10,500 | 6,500 | 34,000 | | | | | |
| | £78,000 | £53,000 | £34,000 | £154,000 | | £78,000 | £53,000 | £34,000 | £154,000 |
| Trade Expenses .. | 4,900 | 2,900 | 1,550 | 9,350 | Gross Profit b/d. | 17,000 | 10,500 | 6,500 | 34,000 |
| Special  Legal  Expenses   .. | 200 | 200 | 200 | 600 | | | | | |
| Depreciation  .. | 700 | 400 | 300 | 1,400 | | | | | |
| Interest on Capital | 1,000 | 400 | 250 | 1,650 | | | | | |
| Net Profit c/d.  .. | 10,200 | 6,600 | 4,200 | 21,000 | | | | | |
| | £17,000 | £10,500 | £6,500 | £34,000 | | £17,000 | £10,500 | £6,500 | £34,000 |
| A  ..   .. | 6,800 | 1,650 | 1,400 | 9,850 | Balance b/d.  .. | 10,200 | 6,600 | 4,200 | 21,000 |
| B  ..   .. | 1,700 | 3,300 | 1,400 | 6,400 | | | | | |
| C  ..   .. | 1,700 | 1,650 | 1,400 | 4,750 | | | | | |
| | £10,200 | £6,600 | £4,200 | £21,000 | | £10,200 | £6,600 | £4,200 | £21,000 |

## LONDON BOOKS – A CAPITAL ACCOUNT

| | | | | | £ | | | | | £ |
|---|---|---|---|---|---|---|---|---|---|---|
| Drawings  .. | .. | .. | .. | | 2,000 | Balance b/f.  .. | .. | .. | .. | 20,000 |
| Balance c/d.  .. | .. | .. | .. | | 28,850 | Interest on Capital | .. | .. | .. | 1,000 |
| | | | | | | Profit and Loss Account: | | | | |
| | | | | | | London Profit | .. | .. | .. | 6,800 |
| | | | | | | Edinburgh Profit | .. | .. | .. | 1,650 |
| | | | | | | Dublin Profit | .. | .. | .. | 1,400 |
| | | | | | £30,850 | | | | | £30,850 |
| | | | | | | Balance b/d.  .. | .. | .. | .. | 28,850 |

## EDINBURGH CURRENT ACCOUNT

| | | | | | £ | | | | | £ |
|---|---|---|---|---|---|---|---|---|---|---|
| Balance b/f.  .. | .. | .. | .. | | 3,000 | Profit and Loss Account: | | | | |
| A, Edinburgh Profit | .. | .. | .. | | 1,650 | London Profit, B | .. | .. | .. | 1,700 |
| Law Charges  .. | .. | .. | .. | | 200 | Balance c/d.  .. | .. | .. | .. | 3,150 |
| | | | | | £4,850 | | | | | £4,850 |
| Balance b/d.  .. | .. | .. | .. | | 3,150 | | | | | |

## DUBLIN CURRENT ACCOUNT

| | £ | | £ |
|---|---|---|---|
| Balance b/f. .. .. .. .. | 2,000 | Profit and Loss Account: | |
| A, Dublin Profit .. .. .. .. | 1,400 | London Profit, C .. .. .. | 1,700 |
| Law Charges .. .. .. .. | 200 | Balance c/d. .. .. .. .. | 1,900 |
| | £3,600 | | £3,600 |
| Balance b/d. .. .. .. .. | 1,900 | | |

## EDINBURGH BOOKS
## B CAPITAL ACCOUNT

| | £ | | £ |
|---|---|---|---|
| Drawings .. .. .. .. | 1,000 | Balance b/f. ... .. .. .. | 8,000 |
| Balance c/d. .. .. .. .. | 13,800 | Interest on Capital .. .. .. | 400 |
| | | Profit and Loss Account: | |
| | | Edinburgh Profit .. .. .. | 3,300 |
| | | London Profit .. .. .. | 1,700 |
| | | Dublin Profit .. .. .. | 1,400 |
| | £14,800 | | £14,800 |
| | | Balance b/d. .. .. .. .. | 13,800 |

## LONDON CURRENT ACCOUNT

| | £ | | £ |
|---|---|---|---|
| B, London Profit .. .. .. .. | 1,700 | Balance b/f. .. .. .. .. | 3,000 |
| Balance c/d. .. .. .. .. | 3,150 | Law Charges .. .. .. .. | 200 |
| | | Profit and Loss Account: | |
| | | Edinburgh Profit, A .. .. .. | 1,650 |
| | £4,850 | | £4,850 |
| | | Balance b/d. .. .. .. .. | 3,150 |

## DUBLIN CURRENT ACCOUNT

| | £ | | £ |
|---|---|---|---|
| B, Dublin Profit .. .. .. .. | 1,400 | Balance b/f. .. .. .. .. | 1,000 |
| Balance c/d. .. .. .. .. | 1,250 | Profit and Loss Account: | |
| | | Edinburgh Profit, C .. .. .. | 1,650 |
| | £2,650 | | £2,650 |
| | | Balance b/d. .. .. .. .. | 1,250 |

## DUBLIN BOOKS
## C CAPITAL ACCOUNT

| | £ | | £ |
|---|---|---|---|
| Drawings .. .. .. .. | 1,000 | Balance b/f. .. .. .. .. | 5,000 |
| Balance c/d. .. .. .. .. | 9,000 | Interest on Capital .. .. .. | 250 |
| | | Profit and Loss Account: | |
| | | Dublin Profit .. .. .. | 1,400 |
| | | London Profit .. .. .. | 1,700 |
| | | Edinburgh Profit .. .. .. | 1,650 |
| | £10,000 | | £10,000 |
| | | Balance b/d. .. .. .. .. | 9,000 |

## LONDON CURRENT ACCOUNT

| | £ | | £ |
|---|---|---|---|
| C, London Profit .. .. .. .. | 1,700 | Balance b/f. .. .. .. .. | 2,000 |
| Balance c/d. .. .. .. .. | 1,900 | Law Charges .. .. .. .. | 200 |
| | | Profit and Loss Account: | |
| | | Dublin Profit, A .. .. .. | 1,400 |
| | £3,600 | | £3,600 |
| | | Balance b/d. .. .. .. .. | 1,900 |

## EDINBURGH CURRENT ACCOUNT

| | £ | | £ |
|---|---|---|---|
| Balance b/f. .. .. .. .. | 1,000 | Profit and Loss Account: | |
| C, Edinburgh Profit .. .. .. | 1,650 | Dublin Profit, B .. .. .. | 1,400 |
| | | Balance c/d. .. .. .. | 1,250 |
| | £2,650 | | £2,650 |
| Balance b/d. .. .. .. .. | 1,250 | | |

## A, B and C BALANCE SHEET
### as at December 31st

| | London | Edin-burgh | Dublin | TOTAL | | London | Edin-burgh | Dublin | TOTAL |
|---|---|---|---|---|---|---|---|---|---|
| | £ | £ | £ | £ | | £ | £ | £ | £ |
| Creditors .. | 16,800 | 7,000 | 7,600 | 31,400 | Plant .. .. | 6,300 | 3,600 | 2,700 | 12,600 |
| Current Accounts: | | | | | Stock .. .. | 14,000 | 11,500 | 7,500 | 33,000 |
| London .. | | 3,150 | 1,900 | | Debtors .. | 17,800 | 8,600 | 6,550 | 32,950 |
| Dublin .. | | 1,250 | | | Current Accounts: | | | | |
| Capital Accounts: | | | | | Edinburgh .. | 3,150 | | 1,250 | |
| A .. .. | 28,850 | | | 28,850 | Dublin .. | 1,900 | | | |
| B .. .. | | 13,800 | | 13,800 | Cash .. .. | 2,500 | 1,500 | 500 | 4,500 |
| C .. .. | | | 9,000 | 9,000 | | | | | |
| | £45,650 | £25,200 | £18,500 | £83,050 | | £45,650 | £25,200 | £18,500 | £83,050 |

*Note:*

It will be observed that A's Capital Account, which appears in the London books, is credited with A's share of the Edinburgh and the Dublin profits, the Edinburgh and Dublin Current Accounts in the London books being debited. By these entries, the Edinburgh and Dublin branches become indebted to London for the London partner's share of their profits. The corresponding entries in the branch books are a credit to the London Current Account and a debit to Profit and Loss Account.

Similar entries are made in the respective books to record the fact that each of the branch partners is entitled to a share of the profits of the head office and of the other branch.

It will sometimes be found that although the branch keeps a complete set of books, the Capital and Current Accounts of the resident partner, as well as the fixed asset accounts of the branch, are kept in the head office books. Since no entries can be made direct from one set of books to another, all payments by the branch which have to be debited to accounts in the head office books, and vice versa, must be passed through the Current Accounts.

**Illustration (4)**

P and Q carry on a retail business in partnership. The business comprises two shops, one at London managed by P, and the other at Birmingham managed by Q. Each shop keeps complete double-entry books working up to a Profit and Loss Account, but accounts relating to capital and fixed assets are all kept in the London books.

Each partner takes half the net working profit of the shop he manages and the balance of revenue is divided between P and Q in the ratio of 3 to 2. No interest is allowed on the partners' capital drawings or current accounts, but each shop is charged by way of rent with an amount equal to 5 per cent. on the book value of the shop buildings, this amount being credited to General Profit and Loss Account as interest.

The following were the trial balances extracted from the two sets of books as on December 31st.

|  | London Dr £ | London Cr £ | Birmingham Dr £ | Birmingham Cr £ |
|---|---|---|---|---|
| P – Capital Account |  | 35,000 |  |  |
| Current Account, January 1st |  | 1,351 |  |  |
| Drawings | 4,200 |  |  |  |
| Q – Capital Account |  | 19,000 |  |  |
| Current Account, January 1st |  | 708 |  |  |
| Drawings |  |  | 2,700 |  |
| Freehold Buildings: |  |  |  |  |
| London | 16,000 |  |  |  |
| Birmingham | 10,500 |  |  |  |
| Fixtures and Fittings, January 1st: |  |  |  |  |
| London | 1,660 |  |  |  |
| Birmingham | 1,380 |  |  |  |
| Fixtures and Fittings added during year |  |  | 70 |  |
| Stock-in-Trade, January 1st | 10,510 |  | 8,305 |  |
| Purchases, less Returns | 25,251 |  | 6,028 |  |
| Sales, less Returns |  | 25,480 |  | 18,310 |
| Bought Ledger Balances | 12 | 615 |  | 261 |
| Sales Ledger Balances | 4,070 | 48 | 2,862 | 17 |
| Salaries and Wages | 1,806 |  | 1,266 |  |
| Trade Expenses | 1,533 |  | 1,146 |  |
| Expenses accrued |  | 107 |  | 62 |
| Birmingham Current Account, January 1st | 11,997 |  |  |  |
| London Current Account, January 1st |  |  |  | 11,997 |
| Remittances during year |  | 7,850 | 7,950 |  |
| Cash at Bank and in Hand | 1,240 |  | 320 |  |
|  | £90,159 | £90,159 | £30,647 | £30,647 |

Stocks on hand on December 31st were valued as follows: London, £12,330, Birmingham £6,720.

During the year goods valued in all at £5,350 (at cost) had been forwarded by London to Birmingham, no entry in respect of these having been made in the books.

The discrepancy between the Remittances Accounts arose through a cheque for £100 being in the post at the end of the year.

£100 is to be provided for depreciation of the fixtures and fittings at London and £80 at Birmingham.

You are required to set out:

1. Final Accounts of the business to December 31st, and

2. The Birmingham Current Account in the London books.

3. The London Current Account in the Birmingham books.

## TRADING AND PROFIT AND LOSS ACCOUNTS
### for the year ended December 31st

| | London £ | B'ham £ | Total £ | | London £ | B'ham £ | Total £ |
|---|---|---|---|---|---|---|---|
| Stocks, January 1st .. | 10,510 | 8,305 | 18,815 | Sales, *less* Returns .. | 25,480 | 18,310 | 43,790 |
| Purchases, *less* Returns .. | 25,251 | 6,028 | 31,279 | Transfer to Birmingham .. | 5,350 | — | — |
| Transfer from London .. | — | 5,350 | — | Stocks, December 31st .. | 12,330 | 6,720 | 19,050 |
| Gross Profit, c/d. .. | 7,399 | 5,347 | 12,746 | | | | |
| | £43,160 | £25,030 | £62,840 | | £43,160 | £25,030 | £62,840 |
| Rent .. | 800 | 525 | 1,325 | Gross Profit, b/d. .. | 7,399 | 5,347 | 12,746 |
| Salaries and Wages .. | 1,806 | 1,266 | 3,072 | | | | |
| Trade Expenses .. | 1,533 | 1,146 | 2,679 | | | | |
| Depreciation of Fixtures and Fittings .. | 100 | 80 | 180 | | | | |
| Net Profit, c/d. .. | 3,160 | 2,330 | 5,490 | | | | |
| | £7,399 | £5,347 | £12,746 | | £7,399 | £5,347 | £12,746 |

| Division of Profit: | | | | Net Profit b/d: | | |
|---|---|---|---|---|---|---|
| P ½ × £3,160 .. .. | 1,580 | | | London .. .. | | 3,160 |
| Q ½ × £2,330 .. .. | 1,165 | | | Birmingham .. .. | | 2,330 |
| | | | 2,745 | Charges in lieu of rent .. | | |
| P ⅗ × £4,070 .. .. | 2,442 | | | London .. .. | | 800 |
| Q ⅖ × £4,070 .. .. | 1,628 | | | Birmingham .. .. | | 525 |
| | | | 4,070 | | | |
| | | | £6,815 | | | £6,815 |

## P AND Q
## BALANCE SHEET
### as at December 31st

| | | £ | £ |
|---|---|---|---|
| Capital Accounts: | | | |
| P .. .. .. | | 35,000 | |
| Q .. .. .. | | 19,000 | |
| | | | 54,000 |
| | P £ | Q £ | |
| Current Accounts: | | | |
| Balance January 1st .. | 1,351 | 708 | |
| Share of Profit .. | 4,022 | 2,793 | |
| | 5,373 | 3,501 | |
| *Less* Drawings.. .. | 4,200 | 2,700 | |
| | £1,173 | £801 | 1,974 |
| Creditors: | | | |
| London .. .. | | 770 | |
| Birmingham .. .. | | 340 | |
| | | | 1,110 |
| | | | £57,084 |

| | £ | £ | £ | £ |
|---|---|---|---|---|
| Fixed Assets: | | | | |
| Freehold Buildings: | | | | |
| London .. | | 16,000 | | |
| Birmingham .. | | 10,500 | | |
| | | | 26,500 | |
| Fixtures and Fittings as at January 1st: | | | | |
| London .. | 1,660 | | | |
| *Less* Depreciation | 100 | | | |
| | | 1,560 | | |
| Birmingham .. | 1,380 | | | |
| Additions .. | 70 | | | |
| | 1,450 | | | |
| *Less* Depreciation | 80 | | | |
| | | 1,370 | | |
| | | | 2,930 | |
| | | | | 29,430 |
| Current Assets: | | | | |
| Stock in Trade: | | | | |
| London .. | | 12,330 | | |
| Birmingham .. | | 6,720 | | |
| | | | 19,050 | |
| Debtors: | | | | |
| London .. | | 4,082 | | |
| Birmingham .. | | 2,862 | | |
| | | | 6,944 | |
| Cash at Bank and in Hand: | | | | |
| London .. | | 1,240 | | |
| Birmingham .. | | 320 | | |
| | | 1,560 | | |
| In transit .. | | 100 | | |
| | | | 1,660 | |
| | | | | 27,654 |
| | | | | £57,084 |

## BIRMINGHAM CURRENT ACCOUNT IN LONDON BOOKS

| | | £ | | | £ |
|---|---|---|---|---|---|
| Jan. 1 | Balance b/f. .. .. .. | 11,997 | Dec. 31 | Q, Current Account, Drawings .. | 2.700 |
| Dec. 31 | Trading Account: | | | Fixtures and Fittings Account: | |
| | Goods to Birmingham .. | 5,350 | | Additions during year .. .. | 70 |
| | Fixtures Account – Depreciation | 80 | | Cash .. .. .. | 7,850 |
| | Profit and Loss Account – Charge in | | | Cash in transit c/f. .. .. | 100 |
| | lieu of Rent .. .. .. | 525 | | Balance c/f. .. .. | 9,562 |
| | Net Profit .. .. .. | 2,330 | | | |
| | | £20,282 | | | £20,282 |

## LONDON CURRENT ACCOUNT IN BIRMINGHAM BOOKS

| | | £ | | | £ |
|---|---|---|---|---|---|
| Dec. 31 | Cash – Remittances .. | 7,950 | Jan. 1 | Balance b/f. .. .. .. | 11,997 |
| | „ Q's Drawings .. | 2,700 | Dec. 31 | Trading Account: .. .. | |
| | „ Purchase of Fixtures .. | 70 | | Goods from London .. .. | 5,350 |
| | Balance c/f. .. .. .. | 9,562 | | Profit and Loss Account: .. | |
| | | | | Depreciation of Fixtures .. | 80 |
| | | | | Charge in lieu of Rent .. | 525 |
| | | | | Net Profit .. .. | 2,330 |
| | | £20,282 | | | £20,282 |

*Notes:*

1. In this case, although the Birmingham branch keeps complete double-entry books and prepares its own Profit and Loss Account, the fixed asset accounts of the branch and the resident partner's Capital and Current Accounts are kept in the London books. Payments made at the branch in respect of Q's drawings and the purchase of fixed assets are therefore analogous to remittances to head office and must be debited to the London Current Account in the branch books. In the London books these amounts are credited to the Branch Current Account, and debited to Q's Current Account and Fixtures Account respectively.

Depreciation of the fixed assets is debited to Profit and Loss Account and credited to London Current Account in the Birmingham books, whilst in the London books it is debited to the Birmingham Current Account and credited to the fixed asset accounts.

The charge in lieu of rent is similarly treated in the branch books, as it represents the cost of a service received from the head office. In the London books it is debited to the Birmingham Current Account and credited to Profit and Loss Account.

2. The balance on the Current Accounts represents the Birmingham capital, i.e. the assets, *less* liabilities, appearing in the Birmingham books, and included in the firm's Balance Sheet, viz.:

| | | | | | | £ |
|---|---|---|---|---|---|---|
| Stock-in-Trade | .. | .. | .. | .. | .. | 6,720 |
| Sundry Debtors | .. | .. | .. | .. | .. | 2,862 |
| Cash | .. | .. | .. | .. | .. | 320 |
| | | | | | | 9,902 |
| *Less* Creditors | .. | .. | .. | .. | .. | 340 |
| | | | | | | £9,562 |

It may be desired to record in the head office books at the end of each accounting period the whole of the revenue balances of the branch instead of merely the final balance of the Branch Profit and Loss Account. In this manner the head office revenue accounts will reveal the position of the business as a whole, and by extracting a Trial Balance from the head office books, a combined Trading and Profit and Loss Account of the head office and branch can be prepared.

**Illustration (5)**

The undermentioned trial balance, extracted from the books of its branch, is received by the X Trading Co Ltd.

Show by journal entries the incorporation of the revenue balances in the books of the head office.

## TRIAL BALANCE
### December 31st

|  | £ | £ |
|---|---:|---:|
| Head Office Account | | 10,192 |
| Freehold Premises | 15,000 | |
| Stock, January 1st | 10,164 | |
| Purchases | 35,649 | |
| Goods from Head Office | 10,500 | |
| Bank Interest | | 20 |
| Wages | 5,642 | |
| Rates, Insurance etc. | 1,520 | |
| Salaries and Office Expenses | 3,192 | |
| Advertising | 3,429 | |
| Debtors | 4,439 | |
| Rents Receivable | | 200 |
| Creditors | | 5,684 |
| Sales | | 75,326 |
| Cash at Bank and in Hand | 1,887 | |
|  | £91,422 | £91,422 |
| Stock, December 31st | £8,392 | |

## JOURNAL

|  |  | £ | £ |
|---|---|---:|---:|
| Stock | Dr | 10,164 | |
| Purchases | | 35,649 | |
| Goods sent to Branch Account | | 10,500 | |
| Wages | | 5,642 | |
| Rates, Insurance etc. | | 1,520 | |
| Salaries and Office Expenses | | 3,192 | |
| Advertising | | 3,429 | |
| Branch Account | | 5,450 | |
| To Sales | | | 75,326 |
| Bank Interest | | | 20 |
| Rents Receivable | | | 200 |
|  | | £75,546 | £75,546 |

Incorporation of branch trading transactions for the year ended December 31st

|  |  | £ | £ |
|---|---|---:|---:|
| Branch Account | Dr | 8,392 | |
| To Trading Account | | | 8,392 |

Branch Stock at December 31st

The Branch Account in the head office books will now appear as under:

## BRANCH ACCOUNT

| Dec. 31 | | £ | Dec. 31 | | £ |
|---|---|---:|---|---|---:|
| | Balance b/f. | 10,192 | | Balance c/f. | 24,034 |
| | Sundries | 5,450 | | | |
| | Trading Account – Stock | 8,392 | | | |
| | | £24,034 | | | £24,034 |

The above balance will be represented by the branch assets and liabilities, as under:

|  | £ |
|---|---|
| Freehold Premises.. .. .. .. .. | 15,000 |
| Stock .. .. .. .. .. .. | 8,392 |
| Cash at Bank and in hand .. .. .. .. | 1,887 |
| Debtors .. .. .. .. .. | 4,439 |
|  | 29,718 |
| *Less* Creditors .. .. .. .. .. | 5,684 |
|  | £24,034 |

Note that the effect of the above entries is to debit the Branch Account with the net profit made by the branch for the year. The separate Branch Trading and Profit and Loss Account would have appeared as under:

### BRANCH TRADING AND PROFIT AND LOSS ACCOUNT
for the year ended December 31st

|  | £ |  | £ |
|---|---|---|---|
| Stock, January 1st .. .. .. | 10,164 | Sales .. .. .. .. .. | 75,326 |
| Purchases .. .. .. .. | 35,649 | Stock, December 31st .. .. .. | 8,392 |
| Goods from Head Office .. .. .. | 10,500 |  |  |
| Gross Profit c/d. .. .. .. .. | 27,405 |  |  |
|  | £83,718 |  | £83,718 |
| Wages .. .. .. .. .. | 5,642 | Gross Profit b/d. .. .. .. | 27,405 |
| Salaries and Office Expenses .. .. | 3,192 | Bank Interest .. .. .. .. | 20 |
| Rates, Insurance etc. .. .. .. | 1,520 | Rents Receivable .. .. .. | 200 |
| Advertising .. .. .. .. | 3,429 |  |  |
| Net Profit .. .. .. .. | 13,842 |  |  |
|  | £27,625 |  | £27,625 |

The closing balance on the Branch Account shown above is reconciled as under:

|  | £ |
|---|---|
| Balance brought forward .. .. .. .. | 10,192 |
| Profit as per above account.. .. .. .. | 13,842 |
| Closing balance .. .. .. | £24,034 |

As the branch revenue balances are amalgamated with those of the head office, the goods from head office must be debited to Goods sent to Branch Account in the head office books in order to eliminate the internal transfer. It will be appreciated that these goods are already included in the head office purchases.

### *Where goods are invoiced at a loaded price*

Sometimes, as a check on branch profitability, goods are invoiced to branch either at cost plus a percentage or at selling price less a percentage.

The Head Office Trading Account then shows gross profit on sales to the outside world plus profit on goods transferred to the branches. To the extent that goods transferred to branch are unsold at the accounting date, the head office has taken a profit which has not been realized; provision should be made in the head office books for unrealized profit; and the provision will be made not only on unsold stocks at the branch but also on goods in transit. On the Head Office Balance Sheet, the provision for unrealized profit is best shown as a current liability; increases and decreases in the provision will be shown in the Head Office Profit and Loss Account.

The Branch Trading Account shows the gross profit that the branch has earned over and above the loaded price at which the branch has received the goods from head office. Opening and closing stocks and goods received from head office are shown at loaded price.

The whole business Trading and Profit and Loss Accounts are the final accounts that are prepared, treating the business as one entity, i.e. normal final accounts for a business. All internal transactions must be eliminated; in particular profit loading and provision for unrealized profit must be eliminated. Whole business stock will consist of head office stock at cost plus branch stock reduced to cost, plus goods in transit reduced to cost. Sales will be total sales to the outside world.

It is only at the net profit level that head office and branch net profit can be cross-added to give total net profit.

### Damage

Where goods are lost or damaged, they will either be excluded from closing stocks or included at a price below cost. If no adjustment is made in the Trading Account, gross profit will be reduced by a non-trading loss. In order that the gross profit on sales may be truly reflected an adjustment is necessary: Trading Account must be credited and Profit and Loss Account debited with the amount by which goods are reduced below cost. If the loss or damage occurs at the branch, the amount to credit to Branch Trading Account and debit to Branch Profit and Loss Account is the reduction below invoiced price to branch. In the whole business accounts Trading Account will be credited and Profit and Loss Account debited with the reduction below cost.

### Allowances (or credits)

Sometimes the head office gives the branch an allowance for damage, or a credit for some other reason; from the standpoint of the branch these allowances are miscellaneous income and should be credited to branch Profit and Loss Account, Head Office Current Account being debited. In the head office books the allowances (overhead expenses) will be debited to Profit and Loss Account and credited to Branch Account.

### Administration Charges

Sometimes the head office makes a separate charge to the branch for administration charges, clerical assistance, managerial services etc.; in the head office books, Profit and Loss Account will be credited and Branch Account debited; in the branch books, Profit and Loss Account (overhead expenses) will be debited and Head Office Account credited.

#### Illustration (6)

Eyre commenced a merchanting business on January 1st, with a head office and one branch. All goods are purchased by head office and are normally packed immediately, but on December 31st, at the end of the first year, goods costing £1,501 remained unpacked. The cost of packing materials amounted to 1 per cent. of the selling price and there was no loss or wastage.

Only packed goods are sent to the branch and are charged at selling price less 10 per cent. The branch buys no goods elsewhere.

The following Trial Balances as on December 31st were extracted from the books before adjusting any of the matters referred to below:

| | Head Office | | Branch | |
|---|---|---|---|---|
| | Dr £ | Cr £ | Dr £ | Cr £ |
| Capital – Eyre .. | | 20,000 | | |
| Drawings .. | 5,000 | | | |
| Purchases .. | 159,501 | | 46,350 | |
| Packing Materials .. | 2,035 | | | |
| Sales .. | | 120,000 | | 45,000 |
| Packed goods sent to branch .. | | 47,700 | | |
| Selling and administrative expenses | 18,001 | | 1,980 | |
| Debtors .. | 14,000 | | 2,100 | |
| Creditors .. | | 20,536 | | 325 |
| Current Account: | | | | |
|   Head Office .. | | | | 5,550 |
|   Branch .. | 7,700 | | | |
| Balance at Bank .. | 1,999 | | 445 | |
| | £208,236 | £208,236 | £50,875 | £50,875 |

You ascertain that:

1. Sales by head office were at a uniform gross profit, after charging packing materials, of 20 per cent. on a fixed selling price and all branch sales were at the fixed selling price.

2. Goods invoiced and despatched by head office to the branch in December for £1,350 were not received until after the accounting date, and a remittance of £800 from the branch in December to head office was not received at head office until after the accounting date.

3. The branch stocktaking disclosed a shortage of goods of a selling value of £250 and that other goods of a selling value of £1,000 had been damaged, necessitating their value, for stock purposes, being reduced by £545 below invoiced price to the branch. Head office agreed to allow the branch a credit of £160 against these goods. Apart from the foregoing, all stocks on December 31st are to be valued at cost.

Prepare in columnar form for (i) head office, (ii) the branch, and (iii) the business as a whole:

(a) Balance Sheets as on December 31st; and

(b) Trading and Profit and Loss Accounts for the year ended on that date. Ignore taxation.

### EYRE
### BALANCE SHEET
#### as at December 31st

(a)

| | Head Office | Branch | Whole Business | | Head Office | Branch | Whole Business |
|---|---|---|---|---|---|---|---|
| | £ | £ | £ | | £ | £ | £ |
| Capital Account .. | 20,000 | | 20,000 | CURRENT ASSETS: | | | |
| Current Account: | | | | Stocks at cost, less | | | |
|   Net Profit .. 12,374 | | | |   amount written off .. | 23,136 | | 28,891 |
|   Less Drawings 5,000 | | | | Stock at invoiced price, | | | |
| | 7,374 | | 7,374 |   less amounts written | | | |
| | | | |   off .. .. | | 5,080 | |
| | 27,374 | | 27,374 | Goods in transit, at in- | | | |
| CURRENT LIABILITIES: | | | |   voiced price .. | 1,350 | | |
| Provision in Head Office | | | | Debtors .. .. | 14,000 | 2,100 | 16,100 |
|   Books for unrealized | | | | Branch Current Account | 7,300 | | |
|   profit on Branch Stock | | | | Balance at Bank .. | 1,999 | 445 | 2,444 |
|   and goods in transit .. | 675 | | | Cash in transit .. | 800 | | 800 |
| Creditors .. .. | 20,536 | 325 | 20,861 | | | | |
| Head Office Current Ac- | | | | | | | |
|   count .. .. | | 7,300 | | | | | |
| | £48,585 | £7,625 | £48,235 | | £48,585 | £7,625 | £48,235 |

(b)     TRADING AND PROFIT AND LOSS ACCOUNTS

for the year ended December 31st

| | Head Office | Branch | Whole Business | | Head Office | Branch | Whole Business |
|---|---|---|---|---|---|---|---|
| | £ | £ | £ | | £ | £ | £ |
| Goods purchased .. | 159,501 | | | Sales .. .. | 120,000 | 45,000 | 165,000 |
| *Less* Stock of unpacked goods .. .. | 1,501 | | | Goods to Branch .. | 47,700 | | |
| | | | | Amount written off Branch Stocks .. | | 770 | 645 |
| | 158,000 | | | | | | |
| Packing Materials used | 2,000 | | | | | | |
| | 160,000 | | 160,000 | | | | |
| Goods from Head Office (at invoiced price) .. | | 46,350 | | | | | |
| *Less* closing stock .. | 21,600 | 5,080 | 27,355 | | | | |
| | 138,400 | 41,270 | 132,645 | | | | |
| Gross Profit c/d. .. | 29,300 | 4,500 | 33,000 | | | | |
| | £167,700 | £45,770 | £165,645 | | £167,700 | £45,770 | £165,645 |
| Selling and Administrative expenses .. | 18,001 | 1,980 | 19,981 | Gross Profit b/d. .. | 29,300 | 4,500 | 33,000 |
| Amount written off Branch Stocks .. | | 770 | 645 | Allowance for damage | | 160 | |
| Allowance to Branch .. | 160 | | | | | | |
| Provision for unrealized profit on Branch Stocks and goods in transit .. | 675 | | | | | | |
| Net profit for the year .. | 10,464 | 1,910 | 12,374 | | | | |
| | £29,300 | £4,660 | £33,000 | | £29,300 | £4,660 | £33,000 |

*Notes to Illustration:*

1. Since the cost of packing is 1 per cent., and the cost of packed goods is 80 per cent. of selling price, the cost of unpacked goods is 79 per cent. of selling price, and the ratio of cost of packing to goods is 1 : 79. The cost of packing material used is therefore 1/79th × £158,000 = £2,000. As there was no loss or wastage, and the purchases of packing materials amounted to £2,035, the stock of packing materials at December 31st was £35.

2. Gross profits:

| | | | | | | £ |
|---|---|---|---|---|---|---|
| Head Office: | | | | | | |
| 1/5th × £120,000 | .. | .. | .. | .. | .. | 24,000 |
| 1/9th × £47,700 | .. | .. | .. | .. | .. | 5,300 |
| | | | | | | £29,300 |
| Branch: | | | | | | |
| 1/10th × £45,000 | .. | .. | .. | .. | .. | £4,500 |
| Whole Business: | | | | | | |
| 1/5th × £165,000 | .. | .. | .. | .. | .. | £33,000 |

Having included the above figures for gross profit in the trading accounts, the balancing items will be the closing stocks of packed goods.

3. Amounts written off branch stocks:

| | | | | | | | Sale Price | Invoice Price | Cost to whole business |
|---|---|---|---|---|---|---|---|---|---|
| | | | | | | | £ | £ | £ |
| Shortage .. | .. | .. | .. | .. | .. | .. | 250 | (9/10) 225 | (8/10) 200 |
| Damaged goods | .. | .. | .. | .. | .. | .. | 1,000 | ( ,, ) 900 | ( ,, ) 800 |
| | | | | | | | | 1,125 | 1,000 |
| Deduct value for stock purposes | | .. | .. | .. | .. | | | 355 | 355 |
| Write off .. | .. | .. | .. | .. | .. | .. | | £770 | £645 |

Trading Accounts must be credited and Profit and Loss Accounts debited with the write-off relevant to damaged goods so that gross profits are not distorted by non-trading items.

4. In the head office books provision must be made for the unrealized profit on branch stock and goods in transit as follows:

|  |  |  |
|---|---:|---:|
|  |  | £ |
| Branch Stock (as above) .. .. .. .. .. |  | 5,080 |
| *Less* Damaged Goods: |  |  |
| Invoiced price, 90 per cent. of £1,000 .. .. | £900 |  |
| *Less* Amount written off .. .. .. | 545 |  |
|  |  | 355 |
| Invoiced value of other goods .. .. .. .. | | 4,725 |
| Invoiced value of goods in transit .. .. .. .. | | 1,350 |
| Unrealized profit, 1/9th of .. .. .. .. | | £6,075 = £675 |

5. Whole business stocks:

|  | Trading Account | Balance Sheet |
|---|---:|---:|
|  | £ | £ |
| Head Office .. .. .. .. .. | 21,600 | 21,600 |
| Branch .. .. .. .. .. .. | 5,080 | 5,080 |
| Goods in transit .. .. .. .. .. | 1,350 | 1,350 |
| Unpacked goods .. .. .. .. .. |  | 1,501 |
| Packing material .. .. .. .. .. |  | 35 |
|  | 28,030 | 29,566 |
| *Less* Provision for unrealized profit.. .. .. | 675 | 675 |
|  | £27,355 | £28,891 |

6. The Current Accounts will appear as follows:

## BRANCH ACCOUNTS
### (Head office books)

|  | £ |  | £ |
|---|---:|---|---:|
| Balance (per Trial Balance) .. .. .. | 7,700 | Cash in transit .. .. .. .. | 800 |
| Branch Profit and Loss Account, Net Profit .. | 1,910 | Goods in transit .. .. .. .. | 1,350 |
|  |  | Profit and Loss Account, Allowance to Branch |  |
|  |  | re damaged goods .. .. .. | 160 |
|  |  | Balance carried forward .. .. .. | 7,300 |
|  | £9,610 |  | £9,610 |

## HEAD OFFICE ACCOUNT
### (Branch books)

|  | £ |  | £ |
|---|---:|---|---:|
| Profit and Loss Account – Allowance re damaged |  | Balance (per Trial Balance) .. .. | 5,550 |
| goods .. .. .. .. .. | 160 | Profit and Loss Account, Net Profit .. | 1,910 |
| Balance carried forward .. .. .. | 7,300 |  |  |
|  | £7,460 |  | £7,460 |

## § 5. Foreign Exchanges

Foreign exchange is a term which denotes:

1. The exchange of the currency of one country for the currency of another country;

*and*

2. The means whereby such exchange is effected.

If the list of foreign exchange quotations set out in any newspaper is examined it will be seen that:

1. Certain quotations are in terms of the number of units of foreign currency which are equivalent to the £. These quotations are usually called 'Currency' or 'Movable'. Examples are Italy (lire to the £), Belgium (francs to the £), and the United States (dollars to the £).

2. Other quotations are in terms of the amount of sterling which is equivalent to one unit of foreign currency. These quotations are usually called 'Pence' or 'Fixed'. Examples are India (pence to the rupee), Japan (pence to the yen), and China (pence to the dollar).

The terms 'Currency or Movable' and 'Pence or Fixed' refer only to the method of quoting which is employed, and do not refer in any way to the presence or absence of fluctuation in the quoted rates. They are alternative methods of expressing the same fact.

The distinction between these two methods of quoting must be kept clearly in mind, as a rise in a 'Fixed' quotation has the same effect as a fall in a 'Movable' quotation, and a fall in a 'Fixed' quotation has the same effect as a rise in a 'Movable' quotation.

The pound sterling is legal tender in this country only and not elsewhere. Similarly, the Belgian franc is legal tender in Belgium but is not generally acceptable in discharge of a debt payable in this country in terms of sterling.

It is apparent, therefore, that where transactions are entered into between persons or firms in different countries, certain complications may arise by reason of exchange fluctuations. If, for example, A buys goods from B in France at an agreed sterling price, any fluctuation in the franc rate will not concern A, but it will affect the franc value of the sterling received by B. Where, therefore, a trader purchases or sells goods in a currency other than his own, unless the transaction is left unrecorded until the sterling figure is known, some adjustment will be required when payment is actually made or received. This adjustment will be for the difference between the figures recorded in sterling at the time the transaction is entered into and the actual sterling figures which result when the transaction is completed, and will represent a profit or loss on exchange.

### Illustration

A in London purchases goods from B & Company in Ruritania, for 130,000 crowns. B & Company's accounts in A's ledger shows a credit balance of £1,000, A having converted the crowns into sterling at the rate of 130,000. A desires to pay B & Company, and for that purpose purchases in London a draft on Ruritania for 130,000 crowns, at the rate of 131·00.

Make the entries in A's Books, posting up and balancing off B & Company's Account.

**A's BOOKS**
**B & COMPANY'S ACCOUNT**

| | | | Crowns | Sterling £ | | | | Crowns | Sterling £ |
|---|---|---|---|---|---|---|---|---|---|
| Cash for Draft.. | .. | .. | 130,000 | 992·37 | Balance b/f. .. | .. | .. | 130,000 | 1,000·00 |
| Profit on Exchange | .. | .. | | 7·63 | | | | | |
| | | | 130,000 | £1,000·00 | | | | 130,000 | £1,000·00 |

## § 6. Foreign Branches

Where trading and manufacturing branches of a business are situated abroad separate accounting records will normally be kept at the branch and the accounting system described in § 4 will be applied.

The Branch Account in the head office books should be ruled with two columns, one for the foreign currency and the other for sterling. The entries in the currency columns will be memoranda only, but are necessary to facilitate reconciliation with the Head Office Account in the branch books which will record the transactions in the currency of the country in which the branch is situated.

At the conclusion of an accounting period the branch will forward to its head office a copy of its Trading and Profit and Loss Account, and of its Balance Sheet, together with a detailed copy of its Head Office Account. It will be necessary to incorporate the results shown by the Branch Accounts in the accounts of the head office in the same manner as that described in § 4, but before this can be done the branch figures, which are in local currency, must be converted into sterling.

The rate or rates of exchange at which the branch assets, liabilities, and revenue items are converted into sterling will depend upon whether the rate of exchange between the countries of the branch and head office is reasonably stable, or is subject to material fluctuation. It will be apparent that a method suitable where little or no fluctuation in the rate of exchange takes place would yield most unsatisfactory results where exchange fluctuations are considerable.

### (a) Branches working on a fixed rate of exchange

Where the rate of exchange between the countries of the head office and branch is so stable that fluctuations can be disregarded, it is usual to convert all branch balances, except remittances of cash, into sterling at a fixed rate of exchange, and as a result a difference on exchange will only arise on the remittances of cash to and from the branch, which will be converted at their actual cost or at the amount of sterling realized.

The currency balance on the Head Office Account will be automatically converted by inserting in its place in the converted Trial Balance the sterling balance appearing on the Branch Account in the head office books. The difference between the conversion of remittances at the actual and fixed rates respectively will represent profit or loss on exchange, and will be debited or credited to the Branch Account in the head office books, and credited or debited to Difference on Exchange Account.

### Illustration (1)

The following are the final balances of a branch in Illyria at December 31st. Convert at the fixed rate of exchange of $4·90 to the £. The cash remitted from Illyria appeared in the London books as £98·32. Make the necessary adjustments in the London books by journal entry, and show the Branch Account in the London books, and the London Account in the branch books.

## FINAL BALANCES
### December 31st

| | $ | $ |
|---|---:|---:|
| Cash at Bank | 1,161·25 | |
| Cash in Hand | 109·59 | |
| Stock, December 31st | 5,387·02 | |
| Plant | 4,931·94 | |
| Office Furniture | 470·59 | |
| Provision for Bad Debt | | 810·82 |
| Land and Premises | 11,524·75 | |
| Debtors | 8,389·49 | |
| Profit and Loss Account – Profit for year | | 991·04 |
| Creditors | | 10,935·45 |
| Remittances to London | 480·19 | |
| Head Office Account – Balance at January 1st | | 19,717·51 |
| | $32,454·82 | $32,454·82 |

*Rule for converting currency into sterling when the rate is per £:*

Divide the currency figure by the rate of exchange, and the quotient will be £ sterling.

## FINAL BALANCES
### December 31st, converted at $4·90 per £

| | £ | £ |
|---|---:|---:|
| Cash at Bank | 236·99 | |
| Cash in Hand | 22·37 | |
| Stock, December 31st | 1,099·39 | |
| Plant | 1,006·52 | |
| Office Furniture | 96·04 | |
| Provision for Bad Debts | | 165·48 |
| Land and Premises | 2,351·99 | |
| Debtors | 1,712·14 | |
| Profit and Loss Account – Profit for year | | 202·26 |
| Creditors | | 2,231·72 |
| Remittances to London (actual rate) | 98·32 | |
| Head Office Account – Balance at January 1st | | 4,023·98 |
| Difference in Exchange (Profit) | | 0·32 |
| | £6,623·76 | £6,623·76 |

## LONDON JOURNAL

| | | | | | | | | | £ | £ |
|---|---|---|---|---|---|---|---|---|---:|---:|
| Dec. 31 | Illyria Current Account | | | | | | | Dr | 0·32 | |
| | To Difference on Exchange Account | | | | | | | | | 0·32 |
| | Difference in exchange on remittances. | | | | | | | | | |
| Dec. 31 | Illyria Current Account | | | | | | | Dr | 202·26 | |
| | To Profit and Loss Account | | | | | | | | | 202·26 |
| | $991·04 profit for year @ $4·90 per £. | | | | | | | | | |

## LONDON LEDGER
### ILLYRIA ACCOUNT

| | | Dollars | Sterling | | | | Dollars | Sterling |
|---|---|---:|---:|---|---|---|---:|---:|
| | | $ | £ | | | | $ | £ |
| Jan. 1 | Balance b/f. | 19,717·51 | 4,023·98 | Dec. 31 | Remittances | | 480·19 | 98·32 |
| Dec. 31 | Difference on exchange | | ·32 | | Balance c/d. | | 20,228·36 | 4,128·24 |
| | Profit and Loss Account: | | | | | | | |
| | Profit for year | 991·04 | 202·26 | | | | | |
| | | $20,708·55 | £4,226·56 | | | | $20,708·55 | £4,226·56 |
| Jan. 1 | Balance b/d. | 20,228·36 | 4,128·24 | | | | | |

## ILLYRIA LEDGER
### LONDON ACCOUNT

|         |                          |    |    | Dollars   |        |        |                                              |    |    | Dollars   |
|---------|--------------------------|----|----|-----------|--------|--------|----------------------------------------------|----|----|-----------|
| Dec. 31 | Remittances              | .. | .. | 480·19    | Jan. 1 | Balance b/f. ..                  | .. | .. | 19,717·51 |
|         | Balance c/d. ..          | .. | .. | 20,228·36 | Dec. 31 | Profit and Loss Account:        |    |    |           |
|         |                          |    |    |           |        |        | Profit for year                     | .. | .. | 991·04    |
|         |                          |    |    | $20,708·55 |       |        |                                              |    |    | $20,708·55 |
|         |                          |    |    |           | Jan. 1 | Balance b/d. ..                  | .. | .. | 20,228·36 |

*Note:* It is not usual to provide memoranda sterling columns in the branch books, though this can be done if desired.

### (b) Branches working on a fluctuating rate of exchange

Where the exchange rate fluctuates so much that to work on a fixed basis would give a misleading result, the branch balances are usually converted on the following principles:

1. *Fixed assets* at the rate prevailing when purchased (if they were purchased from currency funds) or at the actual cost of a remittance sent by head office for the purpose of the purchase. Renewals of, and additions to, fixed assets will be converted on the same principle, but where small additions are made throughout the year the average rate for the year could be used therefor. It may also be necessary to take an average for a period where major additions are paid for by instalments.

The charge for depreciation of fixed assets must be converted at the same rate as the assets concerned. If a fixed asset is converted at the same rate each year depreciation must be converted at that same rate, if the asset is to be written off or reduced to scrap value over a specific period. Where exchanges have fluctuated greatly, however, it may be necessary, in order to avoid misleading results, to charge the depreciation to Profit and Loss Account at the average rate for the period. Any difference between the amount so charged and the amount credited to the Provision for Depreciation Account is then credited to Reserve (if a profit) or debited to Profit and Loss Account (if a loss).

### Illustration (2)

Fixed plant purchased for 750,000 bancos when the banco was at 75, stands in the branch books at 450,000 bancos. During the year under review, the branch wrote off 90,000 bancos depreciation. The average rate for the year was 106. How should the depreciation be converted into sterling?

For the purposes of the Asset Account, the depreciation must be converted at 75, giving a sterling figure of £1,200. For the purposes of the Profit and Loss Account, however, it would preferably be converted at 106, giving a sterling figure (approx.) of £849. Profit and Loss Account should be debited with the difference of £351.

It will be seen that the above treatment is accurate when it is considered that by writing off depreciation, the branch is setting aside current revenue (converted at the average rate), and if the head office does not provide an equivalent amount, the two sets of books may show grossly misleading results.

2. *Long-term liabilities* on the same basis as fixed assets.

3. *Current assets and liabilities* at the rate ruling at the date of the Balance Sheet, i.e. at the rate which would give the amount of sterling that would be received or paid if the assets were realized and the liabilities paid on that date.

4. *Revenue* balances at the average rate for the period to which they relate.

5. *Remittances* at their actual cost or realized sterling.

6. *Stocks* should be converted at the rate ruling at the date of acquisition or at the actual sterling cost if purchased out of sterling funds. When such rates cannot be identified, stocks should be converted at average rate in the Revenue Account and at the rate ruling at Balance Sheet date on the Balance Sheet. Where stocks are included at a value above cost on the Balance Sheet, a balance sheet note should be appended. By converting stocks in the Revenue Account at average rate, gross profit on trading is distorted as little as possible by exchange rates. It may also be necessary to 'weight' the average where an unduly large number of transactions, or transactions greatly varying in amount, have taken place during a particular period.

7. *Bad Debts* at the same rate as the debts, if known, otherwise at average rate. Increases and decreases in provisions for bad debts should be shown in the Revenue Account at average rate. The provision for bad debts itself should be shown on the Balance Sheet at the rate ruling at balance sheet date.

8. *Head Office Account* at the figure shown in the head office books for the Branch Account after adjusting for items in transit.

The reason why fixed assets continue to be converted at the same rate from year to year, although the exchange may vary, is that such assets remain in the country itself, and are not, in the ordinary way, subject to conversion into cash in the same manner as current assets. Even though the rate of exchange depreciates permanently, it may not be essential to make a special provision for any loss on exchange on fixed assets, if the rate at which such assets are depreciated is satisfactory and will reduce their sterling cost to nil or scrap value at the end of their effective life.

Where, however, the asset must be replaced at the end of its effective life, a provision is desirable. This may be created by the expedient already mentioned, of charging depreciation at current rates to Profit and Loss Account. Then, when the fixed asset is replaced out of current assets, any additional cost will be met by the provision.

### Illustration (3)

Plant was purchased for 500,000 dinars when the dinar stood at 200 to the £, and has been depreciated over 10 years by 50,000 dinars per annum. Today the plant is replaced at a cost of 530,000 dinars, the dinar being quoted at 106 to the £.

In the branch books, the depreciation written off has provided 500,000 dinars, leaving only 30,000 dinars to be found out of capital. In the head office books, however, expenditure of 530,000 dinars, included therein as current assets converted at 106=£5,000 has been capitalized, although only 500,000 dinars, converted at 200=£2,500, has been provided over the lifetime of the plant. If the depreciation had been provided as suggested above, at the current rates year by year, there would be a provision to meet the difference, e.g. if the average rate for ten years has been 100, the amounts set aside would have accumulated to a sum sufficient to replace the plant.

Where long-term liabilities have to be repaid out of current assets, it is essential to provide out of revenue over a period of years for any permanent depreciation in sterling exchange.

### Illustration (4)

A loan of 2,000,000 dinars was contracted when the dinar was quoted at 200 and therefore appears in the head office accounts at £10,000. The dinar appreciated to 75, and later depreciated to 130. The loan is repayable shortly.

On repayment, there will be disbursed out of the branch currency 2,000,000 dinars, which, as current assets with the dinar at 130, stand in the head office books at £15,385. If no provision has been made, there will remain a 'loss' of £5,385 in the head office books. Obviously, therefore, provision should have been made year by year as the dinar appreciated (i.e. sterling depreciated), to ensure that this loss does not fall in any one year. Obviously, the loss cannot be forecast exactly, but must be provided for as accurately as possible.

The average rate for the conversion of revenue balances will be obtained either from the average of the rates published at regular intervals, or by taking the rate at a given day of each month during the period, adding such rates together and dividing the total by the number of months.

The branch Trial Balance will be ruled with two additional sterling columns, a further column being provided for the appropriate rate of exchange, and each item will be converted at its proper rate, with the exception of the opening balance on the Head Office Account, for which the sterling figure shown in the last accounts will be taken. It is convenient to show the remittances and other items relating to the head office separately in the branch Trial Balance, and to leave the Head Office Current Account at its opening figure until the conversions have been made, owing to the different rates of exchange at which the various classes of item must be converted.

The difference on the sterling columns of the Trial Balance will represent the difference on exchange, which will be adjusted through the Branch Account in the head office books. If the difference is a profit, it is advisable to carry the amount forward on Exchange Provision Account, since the fluctuations of the exchange may possibly result in a loss during succeeding periods; if the difference is a loss, it should be written off to the Exchange Provision Account (if any) or to Profit and Loss Account.

Whilst in practice foreign branches would most probably prepare their own Profit and Loss Accounts locally, details of income and expenditure must be supplied to the head office to enable the conversion into sterling at the appropriate rates to be made.

### Illustration (5)

The following is the London trial balance of the Ruritania Trading Co Ltd, at December 31st:

| | £ | £ |
|---|---:|---:|
| Share Capital: | | |
| Authorized, 50,000 Shares of £1 each | | |
| Issued, 33,000 Shares fully paid  ..  ..  .. | | 33,000 |
| Office Expenses  ..  ..  ..  ..  .. | 250 | |
| Director's Fees  ..  ..  ..  ..  .. | 500 | |
| Creditors ..  ..  ..  ..  ..  .. | | 100 |
| Salaries  ..  ..  ..  ..  ..  .. | 300 | |
| Profit and Loss Account – Balance brought forward  .. | | 887 |
| Cash at Bank  ..  ..  ..  ..  .. | 2,000 | |
| Remittances from Ruritania ..  ..  ..  .. | | 2,750 |
| Ruritania Branch Account  ..  ..  ..  .. | 33,915 | |
| Difference on Exchange Account – Balance at January 1st | | 228 |
| | £36,965 | £36,965 |

The following is the trial balance as at December 31st, sent to the head office by the Ruritania Branch:

| | Crowns | Crowns |
|---|---:|---:|
| Stock as at January 1st  ..  ..  .. | 65,000 | |
| Purchases  ..  ..  ..  ..  .. | 120,000 | |
| „  Returns  ..  ..  ..  .. | | 6,000 |
| Sales  ..  ..  ..  ..  .. | | 190,000 |
| Wages and Salaries  ..  ..  ..  .. | 18,000 | |
| Office Expenses  ..  ..  ..  .. | 15,000 | |
| Carriage and Insurance  ..  ..  .. | 5,000 | |
| Bad Debts  ..  ..  ..  ..  .. | 3,000 | |
| Depreciation, Leasehold Premises  ..  .. | 4,000 | |
| „  Furniture and Fittings  ..  .. | 500 | |
| Cash at Bank  ..  ..  ..  .. | 12,000 | |
| Sundry Creditors  ..  ..  ..  .. | | 32,000 |
| Sundry Debtors  ..  ..  ..  .. | 35,500 | |
| Leasehold Premises  ..  ..  ..  .. | 66,000 | |
| Furniture and Fittings  ..  ..  .. | 2,000 | |
| Remittances to Head Office  ..  ..  .. | 11,200 | |
| Head Office Account  ..  ..  ..  .. | | 129,200 |
| | Cr. 357,200 | Cr. 357,200 |

Stock on hand at December 31st was valued at 60,000 Crowns.

The leasehold premises were acquired when the rate of exchange was £·240 per crown, and furniture and fittings at an average rate of £·245. The rate ruling on January 1st was £·265, on December 31st, £·235, and the average rate during the year was £·250.

Convert the foreign trial balance, showing the difference on exchange. Prepare Profit and Loss Account and Balance Sheet of the company, and show the Branch Account in the head office books, and the Head Office Account in the branch books.

## CONVERSION OF RURITANIA TRIAL BALANCE

| | Rate of Exchange | Dr Crowns | Cr Crowns | Dr Sterling | Cr Sterling |
|---|---:|---:|---:|---:|---:|
| | | | | £ | £ |
| Stock as at January 1st  ..  ..  ..  .. | ·265 | 65,000 | | 17,225 | |
| Purchases  ..  ..  ..  ..  ..  .. | ·250 | 120,000 | | 30,000 | |
| „  Returns  ..  ..  ..  ..  .. | ·250 | | 6,000 | | 1,500 |
| Sales  ..  ..  ..  ..  ..  .. | ·250 | . | 190,000 | | 47,500 |
| Wages and Salaries  ..  ..  ..  .. | ·250 | 18,000 | | 4,500 | |
| Office Expenses  ..  ..  ..  ..  .. | ·250 | 15,000 | | 3,750 | |
| Carriage and Insurance  ..  ..  .. | ·250 | 5,000 | | 1,250 | |
| Bad Debts  ..  ..  ..  ..  .. | ·250 | 3,000 | | 750 | |
| Depreciation, Leasehold Premises  ..  .. | ·240 | 4,000 | | 960 | |
| „  Furniture and Fittings..  ..  .. | ·245 | 500 | | 123 | |
| Cash at Bank  ..  ..  ..  ..  .. | ·235 | 12,000 | | 2,820 | |
| Creditors  ..  ..  ..  ..  .. | ·235 | | 32,000 | | 7,520 |
| Debtors ..  ..  ..  ..  ..  .. | ·235 | 35,500 | | 8,343 | |
| Leasehold Premises  ..  ..  ..  .. | ·240 | 66,000 | | 15,840 | |
| Furniture and Fittings  ..  ..  .. | ·245 | 2,000 | | 490 | |
| Remittances to Head Office  ..  ..  .. | | 11,200 | | 2,750 | |
| Head Office Account  ..  ..  ..  .. | | | 129,200 | | 33,915 |
| Difference on Exchange  ..  ..  .. | | | | 1,634 | |
| | | 357,200 | 357,200 | £90,435 | £90,435 |
| Stock on Hand at December 31st  ..  ..  .. | ·235 | | 60,000 | | 14,100 |

## RURITANIA BRANCH PROFIT AND LOSS ACCOUNT
### for the year ended December 31st

| | £ | | £ |
|---|---|---|---|
| Stock | 17,225 | Sales | 47,500 |
| Purchases £30,000 | | Stock | 14.100 |
| *Less* Returns 1,500 | | | |
| | 28,500 | | |
| Balance, being Gross Profit c/d. | 15,875 | | |
| | £61,600 | | £61,600 |
| | | | |
| Wages and Salaries | 4,500 | Balance b/d. | 15,875 |
| Office Expenses | 3,750 | | |
| Carriage and Insurance | 1,250 | | |
| Bad Debts | 750 | | |
| Depreciation, Leasehold Premises £960 | | | |
|     ,,     Furniture and Fittings 123 | | | |
| | 1,083 | | |
| Balance, Net Profit at Branch c/d. | 4,542 | | |
| | £15,875 | | £15,875 |
| | | | |
| London Office Expenses: | | Balance b/d. | 4,542 |
|   Office Expenses | 250 | | |
|   Directors' Fees | 500 | | |
|   Salaries | 300 | | |
| Difference on Exchange £(1,634 – 228) | 1,406 | | |
| Balance, being Net Profit carried forward | 2,086 | | |
| | £4,542 | | £4,542 |

## HEAD OFFICE BOOKS
## RURITANIA BRANCH ACCOUNT

| | | Crowns | Sterling £ | | | Crowns | Sterling £ |
|---|---|---|---|---|---|---|---|
| Jan. 1 | Balance b/f. | 129,200 | 33,915 | Dec. 31 | Remittances | 11,200 | 2,750 |
| Dec. 31 | Profit and Loss Account: | | | | Difference on Exchange | | 1,634 |
| |   Profit for year | 25,500 | 4,542 | | Balance c/f. | 143,500 | 34,073 |
| | | 154,700 | £38,457 | | | 154,700 | £38,457 |

## RURITANIA BRANCH BOOKS
## HEAD OFFICE ACCOUNT

| | | Crowns | | | Crowns |
|---|---|---|---|---|---|
| Dec. 31 | Remittances | 11,200 | Jan. 1 | Balance b/f. | 129,200 |
| | Balance c/f. | 143,500 | Dec. 31 | Profit and Loss Account | 25,500 |
| | | 154,700 | | | 154,700 |

## BALANCE SHEET
### as at December 31st

| | £ | £ | | £ | £ |
|---|---|---|---|---|---|
| AUTHORIZED SHARE CAPITAL | | | FIXED ASSETS | | |
|   50,000 Shares of £1 each | 50,000 | |   Leasehold Premises | 16,800 | |
| | | |   *Less* Depreciation | 960 | |
| ISSUED SHARE CAPITAL | | | | | 15,840 |
|   33,000 Shares of £1 each fully paid | | 33,000 |   Furniture and Fittings | 613 | |
| | | |   *Less* Depreciation | 123 | |
| RESERVES | | | | | 490 |
|   Profit and Loss Account: | | | | | |
|     Balance at January 1st | 887 | | CURRENT ASSETS | | |
|     Profit for year | 2,086 | |   Stock on hand | | 14,100 |
| | | 2,973 |   Debtors | | 8,343 |
| | | 35,973 |   Cash at Bank: | | |
| | | |     Ruritania | 2,820 | |
| CURRENT LIABILITIES | | |     London | 2,000 | |
|   Creditors: | | | | | 4,820 |
|     Ruritania | 7,520 | | | | |
|     London | 100 | | | | |
| | | 7,620 | | | |
| | | £43,593 | | | £43,593 |

*Notes:*

1. The loss on exchange during the year has been written off, after taking into account the credit balance on Difference on Exchange Account brought forward.

2. The currency figure representing profit for the year inserted in the Branch Account at the head office is ascertained by extracting the profit and loss items from the branch trial balance.

3. The final sterling balance of the Ruritania Branch Account does not represent the conversion of the currency balance at any of the rates given, since it is composed of a number of items converted at different rates. The sterling balance of the Branch Account must always agree with the sterling figures of the net assets at the branch.

4. Bad debts incurred during the year were converted into sterling at the average rate.

In the preceding illustration the opening and closing stocks have been converted at the opening and closing rates of exchange respectively, while the purchases and sales have been converted at the average rate for the period. The effect of converting Trading Account figures at different rates is to cause the gross profit in terms of sterling to be distorted by the intrusion of exchange variations, and thereby to render the accounts less effective as a means of comparison with other periods, and of control. The practice is frequently adopted, therefore, of converting all items entering into the Trading Account either at a fixed rate, or at the average rate for the period, at the same time converting the closing stock *for the purposes of the Balance Sheet* at the rate ruling at the date of the Balance Sheet. By this means, the gross profit is not distorted by exchange fluctuations, but any difference on exchange affecting stock valuations is reflected in the Profit and Loss Account, and the correct basis of valuation of the stock is employed for the purpose of the Balance Sheet.

### Illustration (6)

During the year ended March 31st, P Ltd opened a foreign branch. The branch converts head office invoices for goods at a fixed exchange rate of 80 unitas to the £.

The branch trial balance at March 31st was as follows:

|  | Dr<br>Unitas | Cr<br>Unitas |
|---|---|---|
| Balance at Bank | 366,400 | |
| Creditors | | 235,800 |
| Debtors | 777,600 | |
| Local Expenses | 754,200 | |
| Head Office Account (for goods) | | 3,524,800 |
| Remittances to head office | 2,690,000 | |
| Purchases | 3,524,800 | |
| Sales | | 4,352,400 |
|  | U.8,113,000 | U.8,113,000 |

Stocks at March 31st, U.1,045,600.

The average rate of exchange during the period was 90, and the closing rate 100. The remittances realized £35,000.

You are required to:

(*a*) prepare the converted trial balance of the branch for incorporation in the head office books;

(b) to show the Trading and Profit and Loss Account of the branch; and

(c) to show the Branch Account in the head office books.

(a)

### BRANCH TRIAL BALANCE

|  | Dr Unitas | Cr Unitas | Rate | Dr £ | Cr £ |
|---|---|---|---|---|---|
| Balance at Bank .. .. .. .. .. | 366,400 |  | 100 | 3,664 |  |
| Creditors .. .. .. .. .. .. | | 235,800 | 100 | | 2,358 |
| Debtors .. .. .. .. .. .. | 777,600 | | 100 | 7,776 | |
| Local Expenses .. .. .. .. | 754,200 | | 90 | 8,380 | |
| Head Office Account .. .. .. .. | | 3,524,800 | 80 | | 44,060 |
| Remittances to Head Office .. .. | 2,690,000 | | Actual | 35,000 | |
| Goods from Head Office .. .. .. | 3,524,800 | | 80 | 44,060 | |
| Sales .. .. .. .. .. | | 4,352,400 | 80 | | 54,405 |
| Stocks March 31st: | | | | | |
|     For Trading Account .. .. .. | | 1,045,600 | 80 | | 13,070 |
|     „ Balance Sheet .. .. .. | 1,045,600 | | 100 | 10,456 | |
| | U.9,158,600 | U.9,158,600 | | 109,336 | 113,893 |
| Loss on Exchange .. .. | | | | 4,557 | |
| | | | | £113,893 | £113,893 |

(b)    BRANCH TRADING AND PROFIT AND LOSS ACCOUNT
### for the year ended March 31st

|  | Unitas | £ |  | Unitas | £ |
|---|---|---|---|---|---|
| Purchases .. .. .. | 3,524,800 | 44,060 | Sales .. .. .. | 4,352,400 | 54,405 |
| Gross Profit c/d. .. .. | 1,873,200 | 23,415 | Stock .. .. .. | 1,045,600 | 13,070 |
| | 5,398,000 | £67,475 | | 5,398,000 | £67,475 |
| Local Expenses .. .. | 754,200 | 8,380 | Gross Profit b/d. .. .. | 1,873,200 | 23,415 |
| Net Profit .. .. | 1,119,000 | 15,035 | | | |
| | U.1,873,200 | £23,415 | | U.1,873,200 | £23,415 |

(c)            BRANCH ACCOUNT

|  | Unitas | £ |  | Unitas | £ |
|---|---|---|---|---|---|
| Goods .. .. .. | 3,524,800 | 44,060 | Remittances .. .. | 2,690,000 | 35,000 |
| Net Profit .. .. | 1,119,000 | 15,035 | Loss on Exchange .. .. | | 4,557 |
| | | | Balance c/d. .. .. | 1,953,800 | 19,538 |
| | U.4,643,800 | £59,095 | | U.4,643,800 | £59,095 |
| Balance b/d. .. .. | 1,953,800 | 19,538 | | | |

*Notes:*

1. The balance brought down in the Branch Account is represented by the net assets of the branch as follows:

|  | Unitas | £ |
|---|---|---|
| Balance at Bank .. .. .. .. .. | 366,400 | 3,664 |
| Debtors .. .. .. .. .. .. | 777,600 | 7,776 |
| Stock .. .. .. .. .. .. | 1,045,600 | 10,456 |
| | 2,189,600 | 21,896 |
| *Less* Creditors .. .. .. .. .. | 235,800 | 2,358 |
| | U.1,953,800 | £19,538 |

2. The loss on exchange is credited to Branch Account and debited to the General Profit and Loss Account.

3. All the items in the Trading Account are converted at the fixed rate of 80, so that the gross profit is not affected by exchange fluctuations. For the purpose of the Balance Sheet, however, the closing stock is converted at the rate prevailing at the date of the Balance Sheet, in the same way as the other current assets, and the Balance Sheet position is therefore not misrepresented.

### (c) *The treatment of major changes in sterling exchange rates*

So far, only normal exchange fluctuations have been discussed; major changes in sterling exchange rates, however, require special treatment. The devaluation of sterling on November 18th, 1967, is an example of a major change. Accounts which showed profit or loss on exchange arising from a major change in sterling exchange rates in the normal way would be misleading.

The exceptional profit or loss arising on a major change is the difference between the sterling equivalent of the net assets at the old and new rates of exchange on the date the rate of exchange is altered.

Net assets means assets less liabilities, i.e. fixed and current assets less long-term and current liabilities. Problems may arise because it is inconvenient to prepare accurate accounts on the date the rate of exchange is altered, e.g. it may not be possible to take stock on that date. A possible solution is to add or subtract the estimated profit or loss from the last accounting date to the date of change to the net assets at the last accounting date, and then convert the new figure of net assets at both the old and new rates of exchange. Where a fluctuating rate of exchange, see para. (*b*) above, is used, revenue account items will be converted (apart from special items discussed in para. (*b*)) at the average rate ruling between the last accounting date and the date of change. Where a fixed rate of exchange is used, see para. (*a*) above, revenue items will be converted at the old fixed rate up to the date of change.

Where a fluctuating rate of exchange, para. (*b*) above, is used, fixed assets and long-term liabilities are normally converted at their original sterling equivalents. In order that proper provision may be made for depreciation and the repayment of long-term liabilities, fixed assets and long-term liabilities should either be revalued or converted in future at the new rate ruling on the date the rate of exchange is altered. The term 'cost' can still be applied to fixed assets converted on the new basis because a balance sheet note as required by Schedule 2 of the *Companies Act 1967* will show the basis upon which foreign currencies have been converted.

Where accounts have been, or are being prepared, for an accounting date before a major change occurs, no adjustment should be made, although it may be appropriate for the directors to mention the effect of the change in the directors' report or elsewhere.

Where group accounts are prepared for an accounting date after a major change has occurred but include the accounts of overseas subsidiaries whose accounting date is before the change, the new rates should be applied to give as true and fair a view of group affairs as possible.

The Institute of Chartered Accountants in England and Wales recommends that the exceptional gain or loss arising from a major change in rates of exchange should be shown separately in one of the following ways:

(i) as an item entering into the computation of the profit or loss for the period;

(ii) below 'profit after taxation'; any taxation charge or relief arising should be shown as a separate adjustment;

(iii) as a direct transfer to or from reserve when it is considered to be a capital gain or loss.

### Illustration (7)

Apple Ltd, a United Kingdom company, was a partner sharing profits and losses equally with Lemon in a trading venture operating in Ruritania.

Apple Ltd supplied and invoiced goods to the Ruritanian partnership in that country's currency, namely ducats (d's). The goods were invoiced at cost of production and the currency accounts of the partners on trading transactions were agreed at three monthly intervals in accordance with the exchange rates operating at the end of each quarterly accounting period.

The initial capital investment made by Apple Ltd in 1965 had remained unaltered in the books of Apple Ltd at £10,000.

The quarterly statements prepared by Lemon from the partnership's books showed:

| | 31st December 1969 | 31st March 1970 | 30th June 1970 | | | 31st December 1969 | 31st March 1970 | 30th June 1970 |
|---|---|---|---|---|---|---|---|---|
| | d's | d's | d's | | | d's | d's | d's |
| Proprietors' Capital (equal shares) | 180,000 | 180,000 | 180,000 | | Fixed assets at cost less depreciation | 120,000 | 116,000 | 132,000 |
| Current Account: Apple Ltd | 135,000 | 138,000 | 126,000 | | Stock | 150,000 | 140,000 | 120,000 |
| Bill Payable | — | 60,000 | — | | Trade Debtors | 280 000 | 330 000 | 350 000 |
| Creditors (including Lemon's Current Account) | 140,000 | 168,000 | 226,000 | | | | | |
| Bank Overdraft | 95,000 | 40,000 | 70,000 | | | | | |
| | 550,000 | 586,000 | 602,000 | | | 550,000 | 586,000 | 602,000 |

An analysis of Apple Ltd's current account in the partnership's books showed:

| Three months ended | March 31st, 1970 | | June 30th, 1970 | |
|---|---|---|---|---|
| | d's | d's | d's | d's |
| Opening balance | | 135,000 | | 138,000 |
| Share of profit for quarter to date | | 68,000 | | 33,000 |
| Goods supplied, at cost | | 80,000 | | 60,000 |
| | | 283,000 | | 231,000 |
| Payments to Apple Ltd | 85,000 | | 105,000 | |
| Bill of exchange drawn in ducats, and paid as agreed on May 1st, 1970. | 60,000 | 145,000 | — | 105,000 |
| Closing balance | | 138,000 | | 126,000 |

After receipt of the June quarterly statement, Apple Ltd agreed to determine the partnership and to sell its half share therein to Lemon. The sale was deemed to have been effected as on June 30th, 1970. Owing to the trade depression it was further agreed to revalue stock at 99,000 ducats. Goodwill and trade marks were to be introduced at 240,000 ducats and fixed assets revalued at 120,000 ducats. All of these adjustments were to be reflected in the books of account as on June 30th, 1970.

The rate of exchange had remained constant at 9 ducats to £1 until December 1st, 1969, when it was altered to 10 ducats to £1. On April 1st, 1970, following the assassination of the grand duke, the ducat was devalued to 15 ducats to £1.

You are required to write up in the books of Apple Ltd for the half year ended June 30th, 1970:

(*a*) the Investment Account;

(*b*) the Current Account (including a memorandum column in ducats);

(*c*) the Bill Receivable Account; and

(*d*) the Profit and Loss on Exchange Account.

## APPLE LTD
## JOINT VENTURE WITH LEMON

(*a*)

### INVESTMENT ACCOUNT

| | d's | £ | | d's | £ |
|---|---|---|---|---|---|
| Balance | 90,000 | 10,000 | Profit and Loss on exchange – devaluation | | 4,000 |
| | | | Balance carried down | 90,000 | 6,000 |
| | d's90,000 | £10,000 | | d's90,000 | £10,000 |
| Balance brought down | 90,000 | 6,000 | Cash | 319,500 | 21,300 |
| Share of profit on revaluation – June 30th: | | | | | |
| Goodwill and trademarks  d's 240,000 | | | | | |
| *Less* Stock .. 21,000 | | | | | |
| Fixed assets .. 12,000  33,000 | | | | | |
| 207,000 | | | | | |
| ½ × 207,000 .. | 103,500 | 6,900 | | | |
| Transfer current Account | 126,000 | 8,400 | | | |
| | d's319,500 | £21,300 | | d's319,500 | £21,300 |

(*b*)

### CURRENT ACCOUNT

| | d's | £ | | d's | £ |
|---|---|---|---|---|---|
| Balance, December 31st | 135,000 | 13,500 | Remittances to March 31st, 1970 | 85,000 | 8,500 |
| Share of profit, quarter to March 31st, 1970 .. | 68,000 | 6,800 | Bill receivable | 60,000 | 6,000 |
| Goods supplied | 80,000 | 8,000 | Balance carried down | 138,000 | 13,800 |
| | d's283,000 | £28,300 | | d's283,000 | £28,300 |
| Balance brought down .. | 138,000 | 13,800 | Profit and Loss on exchange – devaluation | | 4,600 |
| | | | Balance carried down | 138,000 | 9,200 |
| | d's138,000 | £13,800 | | d's138,000 | £13,800 |
| Balance brought down .. | 138,000 | 9,200 | Remittances to June 30th, 1970 | 105,000 | 7,000 |
| Share of profit – quarter to June 30th, 1970 .. | 33,000 | 2,200 | Balance carried down .. | 126,000 | 8,400 |
| Goods supplied | 60,000 | 4,000 | | | |
| | d's231,000 | £15,400 | | d's231,000 | £15,400 |
| Balance brought down .. | d's126,000 | £8,400 | Transfer to investment account | d's126,000 | £8,400 |

(*c*)

### BILL RECEIVABLE

| | £ | | £ |
|---|---|---|---|
| Current Account .. | 6,000 | Cash | 4,000 |
| | | Profit and Loss on exchange | 2,000 |
| | £6,000 | | £6,000 |

(d)       PROFIT AND LOSS ON EXCHANGE ACCOUNT

| | £ | | £ |
|---|---|---|---|
| Current Account – loss on devaluation    .. | 4,600 | Profit and Loss Account ..    ..    .. | 10,600 |
| Bill Receivable Account    ..    ..    .. | 2,000 | | |
| Investment Account    ..    ..    .. | 4,000 | | |
| | £10,600 | | £10,600 |

### Illustration (8)

P Ltd is a trading company operating an overseas branch in Patagonia.

The branch maintains local accounting records and sends a trial balance, expressed in Patagonian currency, to the head office of P Ltd at the end of each year and head office incorporates these branch operations into its annual accounts.

The unit of currency of Patagonia is the Q and the rate of exchange prior to September 30th, 1969 had always been 2 Q's to one pound sterling. On September 30th, 1969 the Patagonian currency was devalued and the rate altered to $2\frac{1}{2}$ Q's to one pound sterling. The new rate applied for the remainder of the calendar year.

The trial balance submitted by the branch for the year ended December 31st, 1969 showed:

| | Q's | Q's |
|---|---|---|
| Head Office Account: | | |
|     Capital    ..    ..    ..    .. | | 20,000 |
|     Current    ..    ..    ..    .. | | 4,500 |
| Fixed assets: | | |
|     Cost as on January 1st, 1969    ..    .. | 8,000 | |
|     Additions on October 1st, 1969    .. | 2,000 | |
| Depreciation as on January 1st, 1969    .. | | 2,500 |
| Net Current Assets    ..    ..    .. | 28,000 | |
| Profit for year, before depreciation    .. | | 11,000 |
| | 38,000 | 38,000 |

You are informed that:

1. The profit, before depreciation, has been earned evenly throughout the year.

2. Depreciation is calculated from the date of purchase of the asset at the rate of 10 per cent. per annum on a straight line basis; and

3. There have been no movements in the head office accounts subsequent to September 30th, 1969.

The company's practice, in relation to its foreign branches, is to convert the figures representing the head office capital account and the fixed assets at the rates of exchange ruling at the time of each transaction. Any differences in exchange resulting from these conversions are credited or charged to Capital Reserve Account. The net current assets are converted at the rate of exchange operative at the end of the year and the trading results are converted at the rates of exchange applicable to the periods in which they are earned.

You are required to show:

(a) the adjusted branch trial balance expressed in sterling suitable for aggregation with the head office accounts;

(b) an extract of the Profit and Loss Account of P Ltd showing the branch trading results for the year and any profit or loss arising from devaluation; and

(c) the movement in the Capital Reserve Account.

**P LTD**

(a)  PATAGONIA ADJUSTED TRIAL BALANCE

as on December 31st, 1969

| | Dr Q's | Cr Q's | Conversion rate | Dr £ | Cr £ |
|---|---|---|---|---|---|
| Head Office Account: | | | | | |
| Capital Account .. .. .. .. .. | | 20,000 | Actual in head office books | | 10,000 |
| Capital reserve/capital account, loss on devaluation (Note (1)) | | | | 2,000 | |
| Current Account .. .. .. .. .. | | 4,500 | Actual in head office books | | 2,250 |
| Profit and Loss Account/Current Account, loss on devaluation (Note (1)) .. .. .. .. .. | | | | 450 | |
| Profit for year, after depreciation (Note (2)): | | | | | |
| Nine months to September 30th, 1969 .. .. .. | | 7,650 | 2 | | 3,825 |
| Loss on devaluation .. .. .. | | | | 765 | |
| Three months to December 31st, 1969 .. .. | | 2,500 | 2½ | | 1,000 |
| Fixed Assets: | | | | | |
| Cost on January 1st, 1969 .. .. .. | 8,000 | | 2½ | 3,200 | |
| Additions on October 1st, 1969 .. .. .. | 2,000 | | 2½ | 800 | |
| Depreciation: | | | | | |
| As on January 1st, 1969 .. .. .. .. | | 2,500 | 2½ | | 1,000 |
| 1969 provision re fixed assets owned January 1st, 1969 .. | | 800 | 2½ | | 320 |
| 1969 provision re fixed assets bought October 1st, 1969 .. | | 50 | 2½ | | 20 |
| Net current assets .. .. .. .. .. | 28,000 | | 2½ | 11,200 | |
| | 38,000 | 38,000 | | £18,415 | £18,415 |

*Notes:*

1. The net assets of the branch as on the date of devaluation are represented by Branch Capital and Current Account balances (already recorded in the head office books) plus net profit for the nine months to September 30th, 1969.

Head office will necessarily reduce the branch account balances in its books by charging such loss against capital reserve (in respect of the capital account balance) or the Profit and Loss Account of the whole business (in respect of current trading balances).

The amount of the loss on devaluation is, in each case, the difference between the conversion of the relevant balances (above) at the exchange rate prevailing on September 30th, 1969, and that prevailing immediately after September 30th, 1969. In each case, this amounts to one-fifth of the predevaluation value.

2. Profit for year:

| | Pre-devaluation Q's | Post-devaluation Q's |
|---|---|---|
| Profit before depreciation .. .. .. .. .. | (9/12ths) 8,250 | (3/12ths) 2,750 |
| *Less* Depreciation for year: | | |
| On assets held January 1st, 1969 .. .. .. .. | (9/12ths) (600) | (3/12ths) (200) |
| On assets bought October 1st, 1969 .. .. .. .. | | (50) |
| Profit after depreciation .. .. .. .. .. .. | 7,650 Q's | 2,500 Q's |

(b)  EXTRACT FROM PROFIT AND LOSS ACCOUNT

for the year ended December 31st, 1969

| | £ | £ | | £ |
|---|---|---|---|---|
| Losses on exchange arising from devaluation of foreign currency .. .. | 3,215 | | Branch trading profits .. .. .. | 4,825 |
| *Less* Amount attributable to capital written off capital reserve .. | 2,000 | 1,215 | | |

(c)  MOVEMENT IN CAPITAL RESERVE ACCOUNT

| | £ | £ |
|---|---|---|
| Capital reserve: | | |
| As on January 1st, 1969 .. .. .. .. .. .. .. .. | × | × |
| *Less* Loss arising on devaluation attributable to capital invested in Patagonia .. .. .. | 2,000 | |

## CHAPTER XI

# MECHANIZED AND ELECTRONIC ACCOUNTING SYSTEMS

## § 1. Principles

The aims and limitations of mechanized systems of accounting are well described in the following extract from the Report of the Mechanized Accounting Sub-Committee of the Taxation and Research Committee of the Institute of Chartered Accountants.

The use of machines for accounting is not different in principle from the use of machines in a factory. The objects are to reduce the man-power required and time taken for a given process and to reduce the possibility of error; in other words, to increase efficiency. To achieve these objects machines tended by trained operators are used to carry out work which would otherwise require manual labour and mental exertion. Specialization of function is developed extensively and emphasis is transferred from the skill of individual book-keepers to the control exercised over the feeding of material to machines and over their output. Ultimately, the purpose of accounting is to present information for the benefit of interested persons – whether shareholders, directors, managers or others – and for this purpose the personal skill of the accountant is essential. Mechanization can be applied only to the accounting processes involved in preparing the material from which the final information can be presented. Accounting skill and effective control are vital.

In deciding whether or not to mechanize it is necessary to consider what are the products of the existing system, in the form of accounting documents and records for internal and external use, and to ask the following questions:

(a) Are those products actually used or necessary and, if so, do they satisfactorily fulfil their purpose?

(b) Would other documents and information be of value and, if so, could they be obtained from the existing system?

(c) Is the existing system capable of producing the essential records and documents at the time when they are required and at reasonable cost?

(d) What are the possibilities of material variations in the load on the existing system and will that system enable substantial expansion of activity to be dealt with?

If the answers to those questions are satisfactory, further consideration of mechanization is unlikely to serve any useful purpose. If the answers indicate that an improvement may be possible it is then necessary to analyse the accounting operations of the business and to consider whether mechanization could effect the improvement.

Accounting operations comprise four main processes carried out within a framework of accepted principles:

(a) Recording transactions (for example, cash receipts and payments, purchases and sales).

(b) Adding and calculating.

(c) Sorting or analysing, including ledger posting.

(d) Reproducing records (for example, copying of documents, preparation of sales ledger statements, trial balance).

Machines are capable of carrying out all these processes, but it is not necessarily advantageous to use machines in all cases because, *inter alia*, it may not be possible to utilize time

508

saved on manual operations in other profitable ways. Where the number of transactions is small, or where there are few entries of uniform type, mechanization to any great extent is generally unsuitable. Mechanization depends for its success on the grouping of transactions so that each group contains a large number of transactions requiring similar entries. Given a sufficiently large number of entries of uniform type, accounting processes can be mechanized extensively. Each process should be examined and divided into its component operations, involving a review of peak loads and the collation of different operations which may consist in part of similar accounting processes. Care is necessary to distinguish between transactions that are genuinely identical and those that are only superficially so, and it should be borne in mind that abnormal items must usually be treated separately, probably by manual methods.

From an examination in the foregoing manner it will be possible to decide whether or not mechanization would be beneficial. Frequently it is found that whilst mechanization would be helpful in certain directions, it is unnecessary or even undesirable in others and an endeavour must be made to weigh impartially the advantages and disadvantages. Moreover, machines may be introduced for special purposes only, or for general convenience, without causing any major change in the accounting system. Examples of 'special purpose' machines are cash registers for use in shops, postal franking machines, cheque-writing machines, time-recording clocks (attendance and job) for use in connection with the payment and analysis of wages. Examples of 'general convenience' machines are calculating, adding and listing machines, some of which require trained operators while others can be operated easily without special training. Even in the smallest of businesses the use of one (or more) 'general' or 'special purposes' machine(s) has come to be regarded almost as a normal part of the clerical arrangements.

In a limited sense mechanized accounting means the use of machines designed to carry out the routine processes of double-entry book-keeping. Of such processes those most amenable to mechanization are the posting and balancing of the personal ledgers, the writing up of cash received and cash paid books coincidently with the preparation of official receipt forms (if used) and the drawing of cheques respectively, and the analysis and tabulation of data.

The work of the book-keeper is, however, dependent upon many subsidiary processes which, in many cases, are carried out in the same office and to a certain extent (and subject to the limitations imposed by an adequate system of internal check) by the same clerks. These auxiliary processes include the preparation of advice notes and invoices for goods sold, the checking of invoices for goods and services purchased, the preparation of pay rolls (including the necessary P.A.Y.E. calculations), the maintenance of stock records, the evaluation of stock inventories and many others which are all susceptible to mechanization in some degree. In the fullest sense, therefore, the study of mechanized accounting includes a consideration of many different office machines and appliances.

## § 2. Writing and Copying Devices

In modern offices the use of the typewriter extends far beyond its original purpose of writing letters. The following developments and improvements of the original form of typewriter afford examples of the mechanization of office routines:

(a) The use of *continuous or 'fan-fold' stationery* in a machine adapted for the purpose facilitates such repetitive processes as invoicing. Much the same result is achieved by the use of forms fastened together in sets. A set of forms designed for invoicing might comprise the following:

(i) Invoice (top copy, with suitable printed heading).

(ii) Customer's advice or delivery note (first carbon copy also with suitably printed heading).

(iii) Warehouse advice note (the second and subsequent carbon copies are flimsies on which a minimum of printed matter appears).

(iv) Posting slips.

(v) Sales office copy (this may also constitute a form of sales day book).

Each form in a set bears the same serial number as its fellows. The use of different coloured paper helps to distinguish the various parts of the set and facilitates their subsequent distribution to the departments concerned.

(b) *Carbon smearing* ('carback') on the back of all forms except the last of a set, makes the use of loose carbon papers unnecessary. This facilitates selective copying, as it is not always necessary to reproduce all the original data on every copy. For example, advice notes prepared as copies of invoices may omit the price of the goods and the amount of the invoices, dealing only with the quantity and description of the goods to be delivered.

The method also results in a substantial saving of operator's time that would otherwise be occupied by inserting and removing loose carbon papers. As an alternative to the use of carbacked forms, chemically treated paper is obtainable, such as N.C.R. (No Carbon Required) paper, which provides a copy of handwriting or typescript when brought under pressure.

(c) *Stencil copying.* When more than a relatively small number of copies of an original document is required the matter to be duplicated may be typed on a waxed sheet, or stencil. The stencil may be fixed on a flat printing frame and reproduced by passing an inked roller over it or, more commonly, a Rotary Duplicator may be employed when the stencil is mounted on the drum of a rotary copier and the ink is fed automatically behind it. At each turn of the handle, a blank sheet of paper is picked up, passed round the drum and delivered printed into a tray. More up-to-date models are operated electrically, enabling hundreds of copies to be taken at a speed of 100 per minute. Sometimes a cyclometer is attached, recording the number of copies taken.

(d) *Photographic copying.* The *photostat* is a machine which can be used for copying, by photographic method, any sort of document. It consists of a large camera with compartments for developing and fixing, and contains a device for focussing mechanically to any desired size. The document is photographed through a lens, and the copies are made, cut, developed and fixed in the machine itself. No intermediate negative is required and when the copies are washed and dried, they can be used immediately.

Microfilm copies of original documents may be made where an office handles a large volume of records and storage space is limited. Documents are photographed on film and when it is desired to refer to a particular document, the appropriate roll of film is placed in a 'reader' which projects a magnified image on to a screen, the film being turned until the required frame appears. It is, of course, essential to maintain a register to facilitate the location of particular documents on the film(s). This practice may be applied equally to documents received from outside sources (e.g. suppliers' invoices) and those which originate internally (e.g. copies of sales invoices). Carbon or other copies of documents produced in the office will be prepared in the usual way but can be destroyed after they have fulfilled their normal functions of providing posting media etc. Microfilming may be extended to embrace old costing and statistical records, where these are voluminous.

(e) 'Collating Carriage' typewriters are provided with a 'front-feed' in addition to the normal means of inserting forms at the rear of the roller platen. This enables one form or set of forms to be retained in the machine and thus to record a series of transactions while other forms are inserted before and withdrawn after each single entry. With the addition of suitable adding mechanism such a typewriter becomes a book-keeping machine; without this facility it can nevertheless be used for many subsidiary book-keeping processes, e.g. receipt writing combined with the preparation of a cash received sheet, cheque writing combined with the preparation of a cash paid sheet etc.

The application of such a method to the recording of cash receipts can produce at one operation four distinct records, if required, as follows:

(i) *Receipts.* These are printed either in sheets of twenty or more or as a continuous roll or fan-fold. As part of the system of internal check, the serial numbers are printed on the receipts but are typed on the control sheet (cash received book) by the operator.

(ii) *Posting Slip.* This, like the receipt form, is perforated between each entry so that the slips can be sorted into account order and distributed to the various ledger clerks.

(iii) *Cash Received Book.* This is the 'control sheet' since it receives the full record. The entries here are in single spacing, although on the receipt forms they are about one inch apart. Each receipt and posting slip may be detached after completion but the control sheet remains in the machine and is spaced up to receive the next entry.

(iv) *Bank Pay In – Advice.* This is used only where the customers pay by cheque. Where there are also many cash items for which receipts have to be given, they will preferably be dealt with separately, possibly by a form of cash register.

If the machine is fitted with suitable 'adding boxes' or incorporates sufficient registers, the 'amount' and 'discount' columns in the cash received book will be totalled automatically.

A book-keeping machine that is provided with a typewriter keyboard may be used for receipt-writing or cheque-writing and on the more comprehensive accounting machines these functions may be combined with ledger posting. Thus two more documents are added to the list of those created; these are a ledger account (perhaps together with a statement or remittance advice) and also a ledger posting summary. The ledger card is set up beside the receipt (or cheque) and collated stationery, and the figures are transferred mechanically across to the ledger card. This automatically ensures agreement between the amount shown in the cash book and the amount posted to the ledger. The posting slip, that would otherwise have been produced as a carbon copy of the receipt or cheque, is then unnecessary.

(*f*) '*Split Platen*' typewriters and accounting machines enable two forms to be inserted side by side in the machine so that they can be spaced up either independently or in unison. This is not to be confused with the front feed or collating carriage; in certain types of apparatus the two features are found in the same machine.

(*g*) *Controlled Typewriters.* These are operated electrically from the record roll, enabling any number of stock letters to be typed automatically. Such machines may be operated manually, enabling special paragraphs to be inserted, together with the name and address and other individual details.

*The Magnetic Card/Tape Typewriter* consists of two units: a typewriter which may be operated manually or automatically and a small magnetic card/tape recording unit.

Letters and other small documents which are originally typewritten manually would normally be recorded on the magnetic cards, which consist of pieces of magnetically coated plastic ($7'' \times 3''$) accommodating 50 tracks, each of which corresponds to a line of typed text: a maximum of 100 characters can be recorded on each track, thus giving a total capacity of 5,000 characters per card. A standard letter is reproduced automatically at 180 w.p.m. upon insertion of the appropriate card into the recording unit and depression of the relevant key, while additions or amendments are facilitated since the operator is able to locate a particular line (or lines) of text by means of a control, situated on the recording unit, and substitute or delete matter by operating the typewriter manually. Old matter is automatically obliterated when amendments are typed.

While this machine is particularly advantageous in reproducing letters of a standard or semi-standard nature automatically, in *an individual style*, it may also be employed for special letters, since these will not need to be re-typed entirely or disfigured where errors have arisen, the operator needing only to delete one track, word or figure and substitute the correction(s) by overtyping these manually, having set the machine to 'record'. (In this connection the machine is set to produce the matter preceding and superseding the error automatically.)

The machine is extremely versatile in so far as the typing element may be changed, at minimal expense, to alter the typestyle or produce work in a number of foreign languages.

Whereas the production of individually styled, but standard, letters is conveniently achieved by the use of the magnetic card application, other situations would suggest the use of magnetic tape in conjunction with the typewriter. Examples of such applications are:

(i) Lengthy documents such as price catalogues, reports etc., which involve the continuous flow of voluminous material;

(ii) Preparation of material in accordance with special format requirements for use in conjunction with other forms of electronic data processing, such as standard documentation, pre-printed stationery, optical character reading etc. (although magnetic cards might equally prove suitable for such purposes).

(iii) Use as an input device in computer applications. The verification of input data is achieved visually by the typist creating the tape, since a print-out is produced simultaneously. In this connection the machine is ideal for computer bureau applications where input data has to be transmitted in a form convenient for processing, and entering the data on tape eliminates the more cumbersome methods of using punched cards or punched paper tape.

Mechanically, there is little difference in the functioning of the magnetic card and tape devices respectively, and the tape application possesses the same advantages as described above in connection with error correction, typestyle changes, and foreign language usage.

'Peg Board' methods enable many of the principles of mechanized accounting to be applied manually. The peg board is a comparatively simple device which enables forms to be superimposed on each other in the position required by the operator and to retain their relative positions while each entry is made. The method may be explained in relation to a process for which it has proved particularly suitable – the preparation of pay sheets and income tax (P.A.Y.E.) records:

Three forms are normally used:

(i) Employee's personal record which, by arrangement with the Inland Revenue, is an approved alternative to the tax deduction card normally used. Each sheet contains a complete record for one fiscal year of the pay and tax deductions of the employee to whom it relates.

(ii) Pay roll, recording the pay and tax deductions of all employees for one week.

(iii) A carbon copy of the pay roll perforated between each line of entries so that the details applicable to each individual employee can be detached and inserted in his pay packet for that week.

Documents (ii) and (iii), interleaved with carbon paper, are placed on the board and remain in the same position until the whole page or the entries for the week have been completed. The personal record (i) for the first employee on the pay roll is then placed over (ii) so that the spaces in which the entry is to be made come into alignment. A sheet of carbon paper has, of course, previously been inserted between (i) and (ii). After the appropriate entry has been made, this personal record sheet is removed and the next one inserted one space lower on the board, the tax calculations and entry for the second employee are completed, and so on.

The advantages of such a method are not restricted to time saving. Errors that might be involved in the normal process of entering gross wages on tax deduction cards and then transferring the tax deduction back to the pay roll are eliminated. Automatic agreement of the tax deduction for the year as shown by the individual records and in the financial books should be secured.

Further examples of the mechanization of those processes which involve writing or some similar record are:

1. *Cheque writing machines*, which by the use of special pin-point type and/or acid proof ribbons cause the wording to be impregnated into the body of the paper on which the cheque form is printed. An unauthorized alteration of a cheque already drawn is thus made impossible.

The system of internal check must be such that the stock of unused cheque forms is in responsible custody and the use of the machine is strictly controlled.

2. *Cheque signing machines* which enable a facsimile signature or signatures to be applied to batches of cheques and other documents. A very strict system of control is of course essential, and the bank on which the cheques are drawn will normally require an indemnity against losses arising from the unauthorized use of such a device. It may be possible to provide for the paying bank to be given lists of all the cheques signed in this way before they are issued, so that they can be checked by the bank against such lists before they are paid.

3. *Addressing machines* designed primarily to facilitate the rapid addressing of correspondence, circulars etc. (and providing at the same time a convenient permanent record of names and addresses) but having uses that go far beyond that original purpose. The data are recorded on a stencil or metal plate of convenient size and the stencils thus prepared provide a form of 'card index'. In company share registration work where this system is used, the stencils will provide the master record of shareholders' names and addresses; on receipt of a notice of change of address the old stencil is withdrawn and a new one prepared. They can be used for writing up the first column of dividend lists, as a basis for the annual return, for inserting names and addresses in the two parts of dividend warrants and for many other purposes, in addition to the routine task of addressing envelopes either to individual members or to the shareholders (or one class of them) as a whole.

### § 3. Adding and Calculating Machines

Machines which add or subtract figures, giving a result which can be read from the machine but do not produce a permanent record of the amounts or the result constitute the first type of adding machine to be considered.

These machines normally have a full keyboard, as illustrated on page 515, and the result appears in a row of small 'windows' at the foot of the machine. The simplest models have no operating keys other than the number keys shown in the diagram plus a lever for 'clearing' the machine at the end of each operation. The depression of a key or a group of keys operates the mechanism directly and the result (i.e. the sum of all the numbers or amounts recorded since the machine was last cleared) appears at once in the windows.

With such a machine subtraction has to be effected by adding the 'complement' of the number to be subtracted, this being the difference between 9 for each digit and the number itself. Thus the subtraction of 231 from 698 is obtained, in effect, by adding 768 (i.e. 999—231) to 698. The result (1,466) given by the machine has to be corrected by discarding the first digit, 1, and adding 1 to the final digit, giving the correct result, 467.

Other machines may be provided with several operating keys in addition to the number keys, as shown in the diagram. With these a number is first 'set up' by depressing the number keys and is then added to the existing total by pulling a lever in a hand operated machine or depressing a motor bar in one provided with an electric motor. With such machines direct subtraction is usually possible, a 'subtract' operating key being provided.

**Illustration (1)**

The number and position of the operating keys vary according to the make and purpose of the machine. The keyboard illustrated here is suitable for an adding-listing machine.

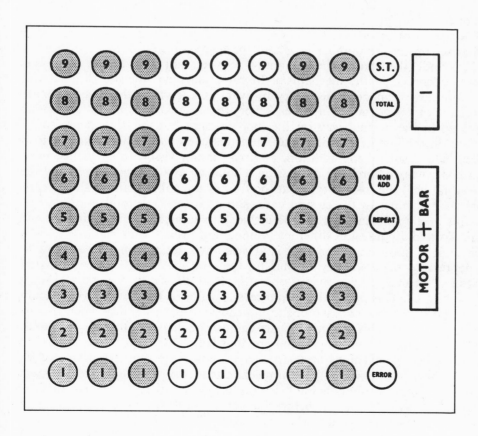

Adding machines with a full keyboard (and particularly those with a direct action, such as the comptometer) can be used for multiplication and division by the process of repeated addition or subtraction, as explained below.

### Half Keyboard Machines

A type of adding machine that is becoming increasingly used in auditing practice because of its lightness and compactness (it fits into a very small attaché case) has a keyboard on which five rows of numbers appear instead of nine, the highest digit being 5. Amounts containing higher digits than 5 are obtained by successive depression of the appropriate keys (e.g. 7 by recording 4 and then 3, and so on).

### Adding-Listing Machines

For many office routines a machine which produces a typewritten record (usually on a roll of paper which can be torn off at the conclusion of each operation) is much more useful than a simple adding machine. Such a machine normally records amounts only, but sometimes has a 'split keyboard' which, in combination with a 'non-add' control enables, say, the first three columns of figures to be recorded as reference numbers, which are not added, while the remaining columns deal with the amounts in the usual way. The machine may also have a platen, like a typewriter, so that forms can be inserted instead of the roll of machine 'tape'.

The action of an adding-listing machine is always two-fold, i.e. the amount is first set up on the number keys and the depression of a separate operating key or handle then causes the amount to be typed and to be added to the total already recorded in the mechanism. In some machines the use of a separate operating key is made unnecessary by what is known as the 'live keyboard' feature. Every key on the number keyboard has two pressures; the amount is set up in the normal way on the first pressure but the second pressure is exerted on the last key to be set up, and this causes the whole amount to be added. The result of the addition, however, is not visible at this stage but is obtained when required by depressing a total or a sub-total key. In the first case (total key) the total is typed at the foot of the column and is then cleared from the machine. In the second case (sub-total key) the total is printed but remains in the machine and will be included in some subsequent total or sub-total. To avoid confusion different symbols are printed automatically against each total or sub-total. Even so it is always advisable to commence a new list by depressing the total key. Assuming that the machine has been properly cleared at the end of the previous operation a 0 followed by the 'Total' symbol will be printed. This precaution is unnecessary if, as is more usual, the machine is equipped with a 'clear' symbol to indicate that it was empty when the first item was entered. This symbol appears against the first item to be listed following the totalling and clearing of the previous list.

Adding-listing machines are particularly useful for the operation of 'prelisting' which is an essential part of mechanized ledger posting systems (q.v.).

Although many adding-listing machines have the full keyboard, the fact that an amount has to be set up before the actual operation is effected has made possible the ten-key keyboard shown in the following illustration.

**Illustration (2)**

The keys appropriate to a number are depressed in their natural order, e.g. to set up £1,023·67 the keys 1, 0, 2, 3, 6, 7, are depressed in that order. When the machine is used for currency purposes the decimal point appears automatically, and it will be printed in front of the last two numbers in every case. In adding invoices, for example, there may be some in whole £'s and the decimal point will still appear, e.g. if £25 was required then the sequence for depressing the keys would be 2, 5, 0, 0, and 25·00 would be printed. With electronic calculating machines it is necessary to depress a decimal key when decimals are involved. Depression of the + bar on an electric model or the pulling of a handle on a manual machine will cause the amount to be typed and recorded in the adding mechanism. The next amount set up will be typed and either added to or deducted from the existing total according to whether the + or − key is depressed. In fact, apart from the routine of setting up an amount, the operation of the machine is similar to that of the full keyboard type.

Other operating keys, in addition to + and − provide either a total or a sub-total; 'non-add' (e.g. an amount is typed but not added to the existing total, which remains undisturbed); 'whole number' which cuts out the pence and which in conjunction with the non-add mechanism also enables reference numbers to be recorded; and 'correction' which enables a number which is known to have been wrongly set up to be deleted before the adding mechanism is operated. Where an error is discovered after an amount has been added in it can only be corrected by subtracting the same wrong amount or by clearing the machine and starting again.

A disadvantage of this keyboard as compared with the full keyboard is the fact that all ciphers have to be recorded, whereas on a full keyboard model they are ignored. It has the advantage of compactness and an unskilled operator can use it with ease and speed.

### FORM OF TEN-KEY KEYBOARD

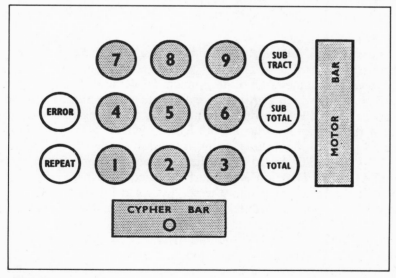

*Duplex Machines*

A machine with two distinct adding mechanisms or 'registers' is known as a duplex machine. It has many advantages as compared with a simplex or single register machine. For example, a simple analysis may be made of amounts under two headings, with their respective totals or amounts which commonly go in pairs, such as cash and discount or goods and purchase tax, may be listed in two columns at the same operation. Alternatively, by automatic transfer of totals from one register to the other, the machine may be used to list items in a number of different batches and to give a grand total automatically.

*Splits*

As an alternative (or in addition) to the provision of two or more distinct adding mechanisms, it may be possible to 'split' one mechanism into two or more sections. Most adding machines have a capacity far in excess of the amounts normally listed on them, e.g. the capacity of a machine may be £9,999,999·99 in the amount keys, with one or two additional columns in the 'total' register, whereas the amounts listed may rarely exceed £100. It is possible by a 'split' mechanism (which may be either fixed or variable) to secure that, say, the four left-hand columns do not receive any carry over from the columns to their right. The left-hand group of figures may then be used to record a reference number or quantity while the remaining columns to the right of the split deal with the amounts in the usual way.

A 'cipher split' has the effect of eliminating all pence columns. This enables the 'pounds' columns of the machine to be used for listing and adding whole numbers.

When the adding mechanism is incorporated in an accounting machine the process of splitting may be varied according to the position of the carriage of the machine at any given time. In some columns the machine will then record whole numbers only and in others full amounts in pounds and pence. The mechanical device which secures this result is known as hammer blocking.

*Calculating Machines*

Calculating machines fall into two main groups, the full keyboard type and the barrel type.

A *full keyboard* machine is an adding machine of the direct operation type (e.g. comptometer) on which a group of keys constituting a number (or amount) can be depressed rapidly from one to nine times, according to the multiplier. Movement of the operator's fingers from left to right or vice versa reflects, as it were, the positions of the decimal point in relation to the various digits in the multiples (1234 multiplied by 56 being the same as 12340 multipled by 5 plus 1234 multiplied by 6). Division is similarly effected by a process of repeated subtraction. For satisfactory results the services of a highly trained operator are required; given this, all ordinary commercial calculations can be carried out with extreme speed and accuracy.

Machines of the *barrel type* also operate by succesive addition (which is, of course, the basis of all multiplication), but this is effected in a different way. In the first place the multiplicand is set up in the machine by moving levers or depressing number keys, which causes a row of cogs to emerge to a greater or less degree from a cylinder. This mechanism is, of course, under cover and cannot be seen during the ordinary operation of a machine; a brief account of the mechanism is necessary, however, to explain the method.

The cylinder can be rotated either by turning a handle or by depressing one of a second set of number keys which causes an electric motor to rotate it the required number of times. At each rotation the cogs that have emerged from the cylinder engage with the teeth of what is, in effect, an ordinary row of adding wheels which can be observed through the result windows of the machine. This part of the mechanism slides from left to right according to the position in the multiplier of whatever digit is being dealt with. Thus to multiply 7654 by 32, the multiplicand 7654 is first set up on the machine, the barrel is rotated twice in the units position and the slide is then moved one place to the right before the barrel is again rotated three times. Rotation in the reverse direction subtracts.

The number of turns of the barrel in successive positions of the slide is recorded in a further row of dials which for multiplication show the number of positive turns but for division can be altered to record positively the number of negative turns. Thus at any given time the machine shows, in relation to multiplication:

(i) The multiplicand that was set up in the machine;

(ii) The multiplier (i.e. the number of rotations of the barrel);

(iii) The result;

and in relation to division:

(i) The dividend that was set up in the machine;

(ii) The divider (i.e. the number of negative or subtractive rotations of the barrel);

(iii) The result.

All these dials must be cleared before the next operation is commenced, unless the multiplicand (or dividend) is common to more than one set of products, when it is possible to pass from one multiplier to the next without clearing.

For example, suppose it is desired to calculate a dividend of $21\frac{1}{4}$ per cent. on holdings of 125, 140, 150 and 175 shares. $21\frac{1}{4}$ per cent. is expressed as a decimal ·2125 and set up as the multiplicand. The first result is obtained by multiplying by 125. Without clearing the machine, five additional turns in the units position plus one in the tens position show the result for 140 shares; one more turn in the tens position converts this into 150 and so on. For repetitive calculations of this sort or for calculations involving large numbers (the capacity is often $999,999,999 \times 999,999,999$) these machines are unrivalled.

Mechanical calculating machines are rapidly being superseded by electronic desk calculating machines. These employ miniature solid-state circuitry and are in effect miniaturized specialized computers. Those which do not print out results of calculations show the products of calculations by means of a lighted display window and are general purpose calculators with full or simplified keyboards. The electronic counterparts to the mechanical add-lister produce their results on a continuous roll of paper similar to that used by the former machines. These calculators perform their calculations far faster than the mechanical and electromechanical models and, due to the elimination of mechanical parts, with far less risk of breakdown.

## § 4. Ledger Posting Machines

Machines of this kind usually combine some of the characteristics of typewriters and adding machines. In early models an ordinary type-writing mechanism was provided with 'adding boxes' which added or subtracted amounts as they were typed. The operator had to read the result from the dials of the adding box and type it on to the form or account. Modern machines perform the mathematical processes, tabulate to the correct positions for the successive operations and type the results (i.e. the new balances on the accounts) automatically. They also provide a control sheet or record of all the postings in a batch and total and 'prove' this automatically.

Where a full typewriter keyboard is provided the figuring is usually done by a row of number keys (one for each digit) operating in the same way as the ten-figure keyboard. Alternatively a full number keyboard may be provided in conjunction with a limited number of keys which use a few standard abbreviations such as CSH, DIS, GDS to record the narration. Some machines have full keyboard and typewriter.

Any form of mechanical ledger posting is based on the principle of the 'slip system', i.e. the ledger is 'posted' from the original documents or copies (posting slips) while the control sheet, which is a carbon copy of the whole of a batch of postings, takes the place of the day book and provides the necessary totals for completing Control Accounts and impersonal ledger postings. Where two copies of the ledger account are made, one serves the purpose of a monthly statement (sales ledger) or payment advice note (bought ledger). Different machines and systems vary in some respects, but the following may be regarded as typical.

A machine-posted ledger differs from the usual form of handwritten ledger in that it shows the balance on each account after each posting (or batch of postings to the same account on the same occasion). The first operation, therefore, is the 'picking up' of the existing balance; the amount being posted is then added or, where appropriate, subtracted.

Another method is the use of magnetic stripe backing to ledger cards for use on machines which have the capability to utilize them. The successive balances are recorded magnetically and are automatically picked up by the machine, eliminating the conventional pick-up procedure.

In the case of a sales ledger, the existing balance is normally a debit balance, which is increased by debit postings for goods sold and reduced by credit postings for cash received and discount allowed. An adding mechanism, known as a 'crossfooter' receives the amount of the 'pick up' (i.e. the old balance) adds to it any amount now recorded in the debit column, deducts from it any credit posting, and causes the result to be recorded in the balance column, where it represents the new balance of the account. A special routine may be necessary to pick up old 'credit balances' on a Sales Ledger Account.

It must be borne in mind that the terms 'debit' and 'credit' have no meaning, in themselves, in relation to adding mechanism; amounts are either positive or negative, and are added or subtracted accordingly. A Bought Ledger Account normally has a credit balance to which credit postings have to be added while debit postings are, in this case, negative. Where the same machine is used for bought and sales ledger postings it is often found, therefore, that the bought ledger cards are printed in reverse, in the following form:

| Date | Narrative | Credit | Debit | Balance |
|------|-----------|--------|-------|---------|
|      |           |        |       |         |
|      |           |        |       |         |

This avoids frequent alteration of the set-up of the machine.

### Sources of Error

So far from eliminating all possibility of error, a machine system may introduce some new ones (e.g. in the pick-up of the existing balance, which does not arise when ledgers are posted by hand). Any well designed system, however, is provided with a number of checks, which enable errors to be detected and rectified almost as soon as they have been made, and the reduction in the physical and mental burden of writing and arithmetic reduces the chances of errors being made. The following are the more important sources of error and the steps which should be taken to prevent or detect them.

1. The operator may select the wrong ledger card and then post to the wrong account. This risk can be minimized by:

(a) Sorting the posting media into account order before a batch of postings is commenced and either 'stuffing' them into the appropriate places in the racks of cards or 'pulling' all the cards required in advance.

(b) Providing suitable racks or trays which facilitate the handling and selection of the ledger cards.

(c) By giving each account a number, which is made part of the typed record of each posting. If the wrong card is used a 'wrong number' will show up in the account number column of the ledger card. The operator must, of course, be trained to type the account number from the posting medium and not from the card itself unless the machine is of the type in which the card, after insertion, is not visible to the operator.

It may be noted that unless the account name (only possible with full typewriter keyboard machines) or number is made an integral part of each posting, the control sheet will only constitute an imperfect day book, for the amounts appearing on it will not be identified with the accounts to which they relate.

(d) Provision may be made for the production of 'hash' totals on the backing sheet. These control totals, much use of which is made in E.D.P., are totals of account numbers and other descriptive numbers, and apart from their control uses are meaningless, hence the word 'hash'.

2. The existing balance may be picked up incorrectly, giving rise to a corresponding error in the amount of the new balance.

Different systems overcome this in different ways but most depend on the 'double pick-up', i.e. after the posting has been completed, but before the card is withdrawn from the machine, the old balance is picked up again. In some systems the machine has two crossfooters, one of which receives the first pick-up and the other the second (as a negative amount); the other operations (i.e. the postings themselves) are received by both, but one records negatively what the other records positively and vice versa. Thus, provided the same old balance was picked up on each occasion, the new balances recorded by the two crossfooters will be equal in amount but opposite in sign. In the clearing of the machine when the card is withdrawn the one balance is added into the other, cancelling it and causing an 'O' (or 'OT') to be printed on the control sheet; this is therefore known as the 'cipher proof'. If the two pick-ups were not of the same amount the final balances would differ and some amount other than 'O' would be printed. Of course, if the operator were to take the second pick-up from the entry just made for the 'old balance' there would be a compensating error and the check would be valueless. It is, therefore, usual to find that the record of the first pick-up is not visible when the second pick-up is made, and whereas the first pick-up comes at the beginning of the sequence, the second is made to come at the end.

3. The amount to be posted (say of a sales invoice) may be copied incorrectly from the posting medium.

This is detected by the process of 'pre-listing' – i.e. the amounts only of the batch of posting media are run off and totalled independently on an adding-listing machine. The system of internal check is strengthened if the pre-list is prepared by someone other than the ledger posting machine operator.

In addition to the crossfooter the machine may be provided with one or more 'registers', each of which totals all the amounts entered in one particular column of the control sheet. When the invoices have been posted the total of the sales ledger debit column postings can be compared with the pre-list and unless compensating errors have been made any error in posting will be revealed.

*Control Accounts*

An overall check on the accuracy of the ledger postings is obtained by maintaining Control Accounts which follow the ordinary principles of self-balancing ledgers. The control sheet totals for each batch of postings provide the amounts to be posted to the Control Accounts.

Where large numbers of accounts are concerned they should be controlled sectionally; otherwise the time spent in looking for a difference may outweigh the advantage of keeping Control Accounts.

It must be remembered that while each control sheet shows the new balance on the accounts affected by that batch of postings, it does not give a complete list of all balances on accounts in that ledger or section. The ledgers are therefore 'balanced' against the Control Account by running out the balances on an adding-listing machine. This cannot usually be done more than once a month so that a Control Account does *not* provide a day by day check on the accuracy of the entries.

*Double Run*

Instead of taking a carbon copy of the ledger card as a statement (or vice versa), the statement can be prepared independently by a second operator using the same posting media. This strengthens the system of internal check. With such a system the double pick-up of old balances and the pre-listing of posting media become unnecessary, and an effective check against posting to the wrong account is obtained.

## § 5. Punched Card Systems

Accounting machines can be divided broadly into two main categories: firstly, there is that group comprising machines which are usually key-operated and which simulate the manual book-keeping processes but relieve the operator of the mental arithmetic; and secondly, there is the punched card group. In the latter class the basic data is first recorded in the form of perforations in cards which, subsequently, are manipulated entirely mechanically and automatically.

In punched card systems one card is normally used to record the basic data relating to one transaction and it is the location of the perforations that gives them a corresponding numerical or alphabetical significance.

The cards can be mechanically sorted into any desired grouping and subsequently passed through a tabulator which 'reads' the perforations and prints the information on to the usual accounting forms, invoices, statements, ledger sheets etc. Addition or subtraction can be carried out simultaneously with the printing operation.

The great advantage of the punched card technique is that once the card is punched and verified an accurate and unalterable record is established from which any accounting or statistical statement can be rapidly obtained. The automatic machines used for processing the punched cards eliminate the human element almost entirely and function at very high speeds.

*The Cards*

The recording capacity of the cards is expressed in columns and the 'standard' size card ($7.325'' \times 3.25''$) is capable of holding 80 columns of information. From top to bottom each column – on each card – has twelve punching positions. They are usually designated A, B, C, 1, 2, 3, 4, 5, 6, 7, 8 and 9, and can be used singly to record twelve base numbers such as the months of the year.

Alternatively, the 1–9 positions are used to record 10 base numbers (it is not essential to punch zeros in some systems) and the upper A, B, C, positions can be allocated values of 10, 20, or 30, so in conjunction with a lower hole any value from 1 to 39 can be accommodated in one column. The days of the month are frequently recorded in this manner.

Perforations to represent the letters of the alphabet and special signs are made in the same way, Z for example (the 26th letter), being punched as a combination of the B and 6 positions.

Cards known as 'dual purpose' cards are frequently used as original documents (stores requisitions for example). They are first written out and later the same information is punched in the same card form.

*Punching the Cards*

Perforating the cards to correspond with the original data is accomplished in a variety of machines which are described in later paragraphs, but it is simpler first to describe the one machine which is essential in most installations but which is used to a lesser degree in those which are highly mechanized. This is the Universal Automatic Key Punch, which is operated much in the same way as a typewriter but it punches holes instead of writing characters. Also, it is power-driven and this enables the operator to repeat such items as the date into any number of cards.

There is also a manually driven Hand Punch, but this is only used for very short runs or for making corrections.

The punching of cards by means of these machines is the only operation in the entire system which is dependent on manual dexterity. It is, however, extremely rapid and provided the information is presented in suitable form and order, can be faster than any other means of original recording. It is customary therefore to have such items as account number, commodity number etc. already coded and recorded on the original document ready for the Punch operator.

*Verifying*

Since the original cards will be used to produce mechanically all subsequent records it is essential for the accuracy of the initial punching to be ensured. There are several ways of achieving this, but for checking original punching the usual principle that two operators will not repeat the same mistake is followed.

In one system the first punching produces round holes. A second passage through the punching machine with a control lever set to 'verify' causes the original holes to be 'ovalized' if the second operator depresses the same keys as the first. If there are any differences in the two sets of depressions some round holes will remain.

The batch of cards is then passed through an Automatic Verifier which detects cards with errors and inserts a signal card to indicate their location so that they can be easily extracted and corrected.

There is also a Hand Verifier, a very simple machine, which locks if the key depressions made by a second operator do not correspond with the holes made by the first. Such machines are only used for small quantities of work.

*Sorting*

Having been punched and verified the cards form a medium which can be processed physically rather than by the mental processes usually associated with book-keeping. They can be mechanically sorted and re-grouped as often as may be required and it is this facility of automatic sorting that provides the great advantage of punched card systems.

Thus, after tabulating invoices when the cards may be in no particular order, they can be sorted at speeds of up to 60,000 per hour into, say, Commodity or Salesman's order for the preparation of statistics.

Sorting is done column by column, so if account numbers run to four digits (9999) it is necessary to run the cards through the machine four times. In each run, the machine groups all cards with a common number in the column being sorted and at the same time puts all groups into numerical sequence.

### Tabulating

After the punched cards have been sorted into the required sequence and grouping they are ready for the third (and usually final) operation known as 'tabulating', a term which covers the mechanical production of the various accounting records from the punched cards.

The cards are fed into the Tabulator, which automatically senses the perforations in the cards and prints, in normal characters, all the information punched in each card on continuous forms, loose-leaf sheets or, in fact, any orthodox business stationery. Simultaneously the Tabulator accumulates quantities and amounts (both debit and credit) and automatically prints totals and balances where required.

The punching in all the columns of each card is sensed simultaneously and one complete line of type representing all the information punched in a card is printed at one stroke as compared with the step by step methods of manual or other machine methods.

In one system the wide flexibility of application of the Tabular is achieved by the 'Connection Box' which controls the location of the printed result in relation to the perforations in the cards. By means of the Connection Box the order in which the printed information appears may be varied from the sequence in which it is punched; for example, the information punched in column 1 of the card may be printed in, say, column 4 of the tabulation. In some installations a number of different tabulations such as invoices, statements or payroll may be produced with one Connection Box; in others there may be several. In any case the boxes provide a means of changing the set up of the tabulator which can be carried out in a few seconds and which cannot be done incorrectly.

### Ancillary Machines

The machines already described, i.e. the Punches, the Sorter and the Tabulator, are the basic machines in all punched card installations and comprise the essentials. The punches described, and to a lesser degree the sorters, are now largely supplemented by other ancillary machines which make the processing even more automatic.

### The Reproducing Punch

This machine reproduces punched data from one set of cards into a new set. Thus unchanging data in, say, payroll cards, employee's number, name, department, rate of pay etc., can be reproduced from last week's cards into those of the current week without manual effort.

### Electronic Calculator

This machine, which works at very high speed, replaces an earlier mechanical model and is used for extensions and cross-adding or deduction. It will, for example, sense from a punched card an employee's rate per hour and hours worked, multiply the two and punch the product into the same card. Simultaneously, bonus items could be added and tax deducted to arrive at the net wage.

### Summary Card Punch

This is an entirely automatic slave machine which is coupled to a Tabulator. As the latter machine lists out and adds information from groups comprising maybe hundreds or thousands of detail cards, every time it strikes a total or balance, the Summary Card Punch punches a card to correspond. This greatly reduces the number of cards to be subsequently tabulated for further summaries or analyses.

### The Interpreter

The Interpreter prints, on the face of a punched card, an interpretation, in ordinary characters, of the perforations in the card. Special models of the Interpreter provide for 'posting' the interpretation of the punched card on to another card immediately following. It can thus be used, for example, for the posting of periodical payments to card records.

### The Interpolator

This machine is designed to save sorting time and will accomplish in one passage of the cards what a Sorter may require several to do. It will, for example, in one passage interpolate opening balance cards into another pack comprising account movement cards, and should there be cards for unmoved balances they will be ejected. It is used for any work where matching (or marrying) is involved or for the segregation of unmatched cards.

### Applications

The punched card machine installations differ from those with key operated machines in one important respect, namely, that it is unusual to find one installation devoted to one class of work. Except in very large organizations, therefore, one installation will be found to be doing quite a number of jobs such as invoicing, ledger posting, stores, payroll, and so on. The punched card lends itself to this way of working as once it has been punched it can be re-analysed for any number of tabulations and so it is quite usual to find invoicing and stores accounts, for example, produced from the same initial cards.

### Invoicing

There are various methods of preparing invoices with punched card machines and naturally the procedure will vary according to the nature of the business but all, broadly, involve the use of:

(a) Name and Address cards, one card for each line and one set for each customer.

(b) Item cards, i.e. one card which will print one line, for every item to be included on the invoice.

The Item cards can be prepared in a number of ways, the simplest being to use a pre-printed salesman's order for the original data and to punch the cards on an Automatic Key punch.

If an electronic calculator is available it can be used to extend the price by quantity automatically. Similarly, discounts can be calculated and deducted from the gross value.

It may be possible to assemble the Name and Address and Item cards as the work proceeds or they may be sorted together mechanically. In any case, the grouped cards are then passed through the Tabulator to print out the invoice. The machine adds the values and prints out the totals automatically.

Simultaneously, a coupled Summary Card Punch will perforate a summary card which will contain all the identifying matter, Account No. etc., and the total amount to be debited to the customer's account. This summary card is filed until the appropriate time when it will be used for the preparation of the ledger account and statements.

The Item cards, after segregation from the Name and Address cards, are available for arriving at the credits to stock accounts, sales statistics and such allied work.

An alternative method of obtaining the Item cards is known as 'pre-punching' and this involves setting up files of pre-punched cards which physically represent the actual stock in hand. The cards are punched as the stock is received and a white card might represent a single item, a green card one dozen and a yellow card one gross.

If a sale of thirty-nine items is made, three green cards and three white cards would be extracted from the file to tabulate the invoice and the balance of cards left in the file represents the balance of goods left in stock. This method eliminates manual pricing and extending as well as punching at invoicing time, and where it can be applied is very economical.

*Ledger Posting and Statements*

The following is a comparatively simple example of a card which records the balance brought forward on a ledger account on July 1st:

**Illustration (1)**

The vertical lines divide the card into the appropriate 'fields'– in this case Account No., Date, Name or Description, Reference and Amount. The number of columns provided in each field is determined by the size of the organization and the nature of the transactions that must be recorded. Thus, this card can record transactions concerning up to 999,999 different accounts in amounts not exceeding £99,999·99 for any one transaction. In addition to the field of alphabetical or numerical data, the two top horizontal rows can be used as controls in those columns in which they would otherwise be ignored. A good example of this is afforded by the DR. and CR. in columns 35 and 37 of the above card. The hole in the top row of column 35 not only records that the balance brought forward was a debit but in the subsequent operations of ledger posting for which this card will be used will activate the adding mechanism accordingly.

For ledger posting work a card similar to the above must be prepared for each entry to be made in the account. The principal debit cards, i.e. those for goods supplied, will be available as a by-product of the invoicing process, as mentioned above. Other cards for Cash, Discount Allowed, Journal etc., are usually punched on the Automatic Key Punch. For the time being these cards, which are stored in convenient trays, constitute the current ledger. The actual work of reproducing the ledger in written form is normally a monthly routine which is made to coincide with the preparation of customers' statements in the case of the sales ledger or payment advice sheets in the case of the bought ledger. There are two procedures in common use – the 'open item' method and the 'balance card' method.

*Open Item Method*

All the cards relating to each account are filed together in trays until a remittance is received (or, in the case of the bought ledger, a payment is made) which relates to specific items in the account. The cards for these specific items are then withdrawn or 'pulled' from the 'unpaid' tray and tabulated with the cash (and discount if applicable) card to prove by revealing 'nil' balances that the correct cards have been pulled and that the correct amount has been received or paid. The cards that have been pulled are then filed away in a 'paid' tray.

Where a payment 'on account' is received so that it does not clear specific items, the cash card itself is filed in customer and date order in the 'unpaid' tray.

At the end of the month, the cards in the 'unpaid' tray are merged with the name and address cards, this process being carried out most efficiently by the use of an 'interpolator' particularly where many of the accounts may not be 'active' each month. Name and address cards, arranged strictly in account number order, are inserted in the machine at one end while the pack of ledger cards, also in account number order, is inserted at the other end. The machine senses the account number holes in the first (i.e. bottom) card of both packs. If they agree all the name and address cards followed by all the account cards relating to that one account are directed into one 'box', while if they do not agree (because the first name and address card is for an account for which there are no cards in the 'unpaid' ledger pack) the name and address cards only are discarded into a second box. The same machine is later used to separate the name and address cards from the account cards.

When all the 'unpaid' cards have been merged with name and address cards they are tabulated to produce a separate statement in duplicate for each customer. The tabulator automatically calculates and prints the balances and accumulates them to provide at the end of the run a grand total for agreement with the Ledger Control Accounts.

After the statements have been tabulated, and the name and address cards have been sorted out of the pack, the other cards are returned to the 'unpaid' tray and these constitute, in effect, the opening balances ready to recommence the cycle of operations next month. The carbon copies of the statements are filed in a sales ledger binder but these copies only show outstanding items on each customer's account and do not give any record of cash payments and completed transactions. To provide this information the cards from the 'paid' tray are posted by the tabulator on to individual customers' History Sheets, which are, in effect, the sales ledger record of all past and settled transactions. After this posting has been completed all the 'paid' cards are filed away and are available for providing any statistics which may subsequently be required.

When the open-item method is used 'balance' cards such as the one illustrated above will be prepared only in exceptional cases.

### Balance Card Method

All the cards relating to each sales ledger account for the current month, including those recording cash settlements and a balance card recording the opening balance, are filed in the current ledger tray in account number order. At the end of the month they are merged with name and address cards and tabulated to produce a statement in duplicate, the total of the balances also being accumulated in the tabulator and agreed with the Control Account. The top copies of the statements are despatched to the customers while the carbon copies are filed to provide the permanent sales ledger.

New balance cards having been prepared (if a Summary Card Punch is connected to the tabulator they will be prepared automatically; if not they must be punched by hand) and filed in the current trays as a starting point in the next month's routine, and the name and address cards having been withdrawn and returned to their file, the item cards for the past month are filed away.

### Other applications

It would be quite beyond the scope of this work to attempt to describe in detail the large number of office routines that have been adapted to the punched card technique, many of them having only a remote connection with book-keeping in the ordinary sense. The following may, however, be noted:

The maintenance of stock methods.

The evaluation of stock in total by the method of 'digiting'.

Wages, including P.A.Y.E. routines.

Costing systems.

Dividend and share transfer work.

*Flow Charts*

A flow chart illustrating the analysis of the flow of documents through an organization, or the sequence of operations in a system, facilitates the mechanization of an accounting process. Such a chart sets out, step by step, the procedures in a system. A number of symbols have been evolved to represent the common features of a flow chart, but it is not vital to use these in order to produce a workable chart.

**Illustration (2)**

An example of a Flow Chart to illustrate the Punched Card System of a Builder to produce Purchases Ledger, Job Cost Tabulation and Remittance Advices is given below:

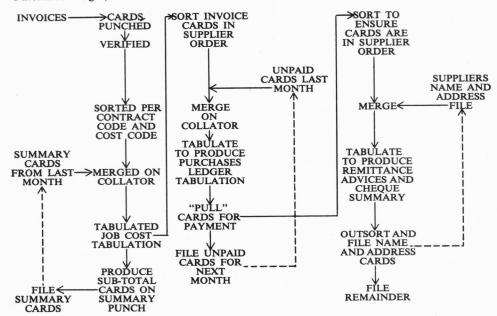

## § 6. Electronic Computers

The Institute of Chartered Accountants in England and Wales has issued recommendation T2 entitled 'Accounting by Electronic Methods', and the Association of Certified and Corporate Accountants has issued a series of five Electronic Data Processing booklets.

Computer techniques naturally follow on from punched cards and differ therefrom mainly in that more operations are carried on within one machine and consequently there is less physical handling of the media (punched cards or tapes) and corresponding savings in time. The electronic computer can also make certain decisions on its own and so needs less manual attention on the part of the operator.

Electronic computers are of two main types; analogue computers, which are used mainly for scientific and engineering purposes; and digital computers, which are used for commercial purposes. As analogue computers are not commonly used for commercial applications we shall not consider them further.

A digital computer represents a complex of equipment which is able to store information and process it, together with new input, in accordance with a program of instructions, which itself is stored in the machine.

The electronic digital computer employs the binary system of arithmetic as opposed to the commonly used denary system (0 to 9). This is due to the method of operation which involves comparison between opposites, e.g. between a condition of no charge and charge. Information entering a computer and its associated storage equipment must be in some code capable of being translated into binary arithmetic, which is an expression of the data, in terms of powers of 2.

Example:
$$0 = 0$$
$$1 = 1$$
$$2 = 10 \quad \text{i.e. } 2^1 + 0$$
$$3 = 11 \quad \text{i.e. } 2^1 + 2^0$$
$$4 = 100 \quad \text{i.e. } 2^2$$
$$7 = 111 \quad \text{i.e. } 2^2 + 2^1 + 2^0$$
$$111 = 1101111 \quad \text{i.e. } 2^6 + 2^5 + 2^3 + 2^2 + 2^1 + 2^0$$

Originally all programs had to be written in binary form, but improvements in programming methods have eliminated much time-consuming effort.

These can be illustrated in the form of a Flow Chart:

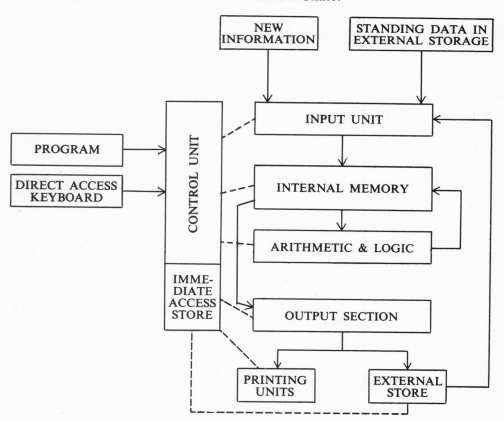

A computer operates by means of electronic impulses passing through complicated circuits, which have been specially designed to achieve addition, subtraction, comparison etc. It has five basic component parts:

(i) the input unit;

(ii) the storage (or 'memory') unit;

(iii) the arithmetic and logic unit;

(iv) the output unit;

(v) the control unit.

### (i) The Input Unit

As the computer operates by means of electronic impulses it is necessary to present information to the equipment in a manner which it will be able to interpret. The main methods of achieving this at present in use are:

(a) by punched cards, which are passed through a punched card reader;

(b) by punched paper tape, which is passed through a paper tape reader;

(c) by magnetic tape, which is passed through a magnetic tape reader;

(d) by magnetic discs, which are read by read/write arms suspended above and below the respective recording surfaces;

(e) by optical scanning devices.

A computer will usually have more than one of these alternative methods of input.

The speeds of the different methods of input vary greatly and as computers calculate at electronic speeds, the speed at which data are fed into the machines is a factor to be taken into account, especially in commercial applications, where the quantity of data to be dealt with is very great.

### (ii) The Storage Unit

This unit has several functions:

(a) to store the program of instructions covering the processing operations to be performed;

(b) to store any reference data which are required during processing, such as tax tables, price lists etc.

(c) to receive the data read from the input section prior to their use in the operations;

(d) to retain temporarily results of sub-calculations pending further processing; and

(e) to receive final results of calculations before passing them to the output unit.

This ability to store information and programs is one of the basic characteristics of the computer. The storage is achieved normally by magnetizing positions on a tape or drum or setting up a magnetic field in wires. The details of this process need not concern us; all that is necessary is a knowledge of the various types of storage device used. These are:

### (a) Core storage

This consists of a network of wires with tiny ferrite rings at the intersections. Each ring holds one binary digit of information. This type of store has a very quick access time, i.e. information can be read from it in a millionth part of a second. Core storage is expensive and therefore is only used for working stores, i.e. the storage in which the processing operations are performed.

### (b) Magnetic drum

This consists of a drum coated with a magnetic material. It revolves inside a container which holds many reading and writing heads, which can magnetize a position on the drum or detect a magnetized position. Information is stored on the drum by means of magnetized spots. The drum itself is divided into parallel channels each of which has its own reading and writing head. Within each channel there are again various positions. Each position on the drum is referenced, or has an 'address'. The addresses to be used are specified in the program which controls the processing.

Access time on the magnetic drum storage systems is fairly fast, of the order of five thousandths of a second, and again this system is widely used for working stores.

### (c) Magnetic tape

This consists of a tape similar to that used in tape recorders, on which the data are stored by means of magnetized spots. As information is stored in sequential order, the computer has to scan the tape to find the particular item of information required; average access time is therefore the time taken to scan half the tape. Magnetic tape is fairly cheap and of relatively slow access time and so is commonly used as an external store of information. The tape is kept on reels which are inserted into peripheral units termed 'tape decks' when the store is required for operation. Tape tends to be of most use where sequential processing is required as with sales ledger operations.

### (d) Magnetic Discs

These are discs similar in appearance to gramophone records mounted on a spindle and rotated at high speed. The face of each disc is divided into 'tracks' each of which has a read/write head that can read off or write on the track as it rotates.

The magnetic stores referred to in (b), (c) and (d) above are called permanent, because if the electric current failed the information in the 'memory' would remain.

### (e) Punched Cards and Punched Paper Tape

These can also be used as a store. The output from the computer may be punched into cards or tape, which are retained for further processing. Such 'memories' are, however, slow and are not used when alternatives are available.

### (f) Buffer Stores

Because of the difference in speed between the electronic sections of the computer and the mechanical sections, e.g. input readers and output devices, a buffer store is required. For example, the speed of feeding and reading the information on a punched card is limited by mechanical factors to about 800 digits per second. As the electronic section is much faster the computer would be held up whilst the next portion of data was read. To avoid this a buffer store, frequently a drum store, is utilized. The information on the card is first read into the buffer store and the computer can then process this information whilst the next card is being read. Again, as the speed of computer output is greater than that of available printing devices the output is first entered on a magnetic tape which is then used to feed a printer. Thus the computer is not held up through the printer's comparative lack of speed.

### (iii) The Arithmetic and Logic Unit

This unit is composed of miniature printed circuits, transistors etc., which can perform their operations at speeds measured in millionths of seconds. The arithmetic unit is able to carry out all the ordinary operations of addition, subtraction, multiplication and division. Multiplication is carried out by repeated addition at great speed.

The logic sections of the computer are used to make decisions where the program requires a decision to be made. Such decisions are invariably of a 'yes' or 'no' type.

The computer compares the results of a computation and is programmed to act in differing ways dependent on the result. For example, in hire-purchase accounting, if the result of deducting the expected balance at a certain date from the actual balance is a positive amount the account is in arrear, and the computer could be programmed to print out an arrears notice.

### (iv) The Output Unit

The output of the computer can be in one of a number of forms, punched cards, punched paper tape, magnetic tape or magnetic film. Output in these forms may be used:

(a) as input for a further process; or

(b) to operate printing or tabulating machines.

Output required in printed form is dealt with in one of two ways:

(a) on-line, which means that the printers are operated directly from the computer so that the results are printed as they become available;

(b) off-line, which means that the output is first recorded on punched cards, paper tape or magnetic tape, which is then used to operate separate printing machines not connected directly to the computer.

### (v) The Control Unit

The control unit interprets the program of instructions and directs its operation. All the other sections of the computing system are co-ordinated and brought into operation in their correct sequence by this section. The control section usually has a control console which enables the human operator to monitor the various sections of the computer and communicate directly with the computing systems. In this way instructions can be fed into the computer manually. This has certain disadvantages from the audit viewpoint inasmuch as the program can be altered, but sound internal control systems should obviate the possibility of error or fraud.

The console normally has illuminated dials which give a continuous display of information regarding the computing process. If the machine stops or errors arise the dials may give some indication of the cause.

## THE PROGRAM

The program is the means by which the whole computing process is directed and controlled; each process to be performed being broken down into its smallest constituent steps, and each operation coded numerically, e.g. in job costing 'take direct wages for the week and add it to the direct wages to date' might be programmed as follows:

| 1211 | : | 30 | : | 922 |
|---|---|---|---|---|
| Location in memory of direct wages to date | | Operation | | Location of next step |

This means that the item in location 1211 (the direct wages to date) is to be acted upon in accordance with function 30 (move to arithmetic section and add to the figure already there). This having been done the computer must know the next operation; 922 instructs it to go to that location in the memory and read the next instruction.

The program thus tells the computer in detail the steps to be performed. This may be to transfer a figure out of a specific location to the arithmetic section and add it to or subtract it from a figure already there, or multiply it or divide it and place the result back in memory. Moreover, comparison with another figure may be made and acted upon. In taking a figure out of memory, a computer acts rather like a tape recorder, in so far as it does not eradicate the data but merely reads it. However, when placing information in memory, anything previously contained at that location is supplanted by the new information.

Computer programming is an extremely intricate operation, calling for the exercise of a great deal of analytical thought, patience and time. Various short-cut methods termed 'auto codes' have, however, been developed in recent years which can simplify and expedite the programming of the less complicated and more routine applications.

Both the information to be acted upon and the program of instructions must be fed into the computer. Since the advantages of high speed working would be lost if the data had to be fed into the machine by the ordinary process of indexing keys, faster methods of input have evolved, the information being converted into a form suitable for high speed input. This may be achieved by the use of:

(*a*) punched paper tape;
(*b*) punched cards;
(*c*) magnetic tape or film.

In the first two methods holes in the tape or cards provide the means of communication with the computer; whereas in the case of magnetic film, the data is contained in small magnetized spots which take the place of holes in the punched paper tape.

It is imperative that all input data is accurate. Although computers are capable of performing built-in checks on the information fed into them, should an error be detected, waste of processing time will arise, while some errors are incapable of detection by the computer when an error in the input data will result in incorrect output.

Computers are able to compare quantitative information and take separate courses of action, depending on the result of the comparison; because of this they are able to perform extremely complicated routines at great speed, without human intervention. All that is required is that a complete program of instructions of 'steps' be fed into the control section.

A number of 'languages' have been evolved in which instructions can be given to the computer.

### 1. R.P.G. – Report Program Generator

    (i) This is the lowest of high level languages.

    (ii) Not very complex; good for quick straight-forward answers.

### 2. FORTRAN – Formula Translation

    Usually for highly scientific use.

### 3. COBOL – Common Business Orientated Language

    (i) Commercial equivalent of Fortran.

    (ii) In theory, it can be read as English.

### 4. P.L./1 – Programming Language 1

    (i) All purpose language which combines Fortran and Cobol, so that it is ideal for intricate commercial application, and almost any other application.

    (ii) It can deal with programs written in Cobol.

On very simple computers a number of symbols can be used as a program language.

The following is an example of the application of a computer to a Building Society interest calculation.

*INPUT* (*a*) Mortgage Account Number     } From Memory – Magnetic Tape.
        (*b*) Opening Balance on the Account }
        (*c*) Rate of Interest         – Enter via Console.
        (*d*) Amount Paid during the month   – Punched Card.

*Program* 1. **Start**
        2. **Loop – Get List**   ..   Pick up account number and old balance from memory, rate from console and amount paid from input.

3. **Check** .. .. Check account number agrees with account for which payment has been made.

4. **No** .. .. Does not agree – Stop.

5. **Yes** .. .. Does agree – Continue.

6. **Int.** .. .. Calculate interest by applying the rate to the old balance.

7. **If** .. .. Does amount paid exceed amount of interest required?

8. **No** .. .. Not enough interest paid. Exception Report. Proceed to next account.

9. **Yes** .. .. Proceed with run.

10. **Princ.** .. .. Calculate repayment of principal by deducting interest required from amount paid.

11. **N.B.** .. .. Find principal carried forward by deducting principal paid from old balance.

12. **Prepare List** .. Set figures aside in memory so that a list of account numbers, amounts of principal paid and new balances can be produced at the end of the run.

13. **Print Out – Loop** .. Print out the individual mortgage account, and file the updated information on magnetic tape for use as input next time – Father and Son technique.

14. **End** .. .. Proceed to next instruction.

*OUTPUT*   (i) Mortgage Ledger Account with copy for customer to show account number, name and address, old balance, interest paid, principal paid and new balance.

(ii) List of account numbers, old balances and amounts of principal and interest paid and new balances, all totalled.

(iii) Exception Report on cases where interest has fallen behind.

## THE INSTALLATION

Computer installations are expensive in terms of capital cost and necessitate changes in the organization and flow of paper work within an organization. A thorough review of accounting and reporting procedures is therefore essential before the decision to install a computer is made.

Management must decide what advantages are likely to accrue to the organization by the installation of a computer and should appoint a committee to investigate the matter. The possible advantages in any particular instance are:

(*a*) electronic speed of processing means that information can be made available more quickly;

(*b*) additional control information can be obtained;

(*c*) records can be integrated, e.g. stores and ordering can be combined with production control;

(*d*) because electronic records are so compact, additional information may be kept;

(*e*) the speed of processing may enable records of outlying branches or divisions to be processed centrally, with corresponding advantages of increased control;

(*f*) savings in clerical labour may also be made and staff is freed from monotonous calculation and routine processing work for more important tasks.

The advantages expected to be obtained must be considered carefully, bearing in mind the difficulties of arranging for the installation and the essential requirements of the computer. These are:

(*a*) adequate electric power;

(*b*) constant temperature and humidity, necessitating specific ventilation and heating etc;

(*c*) large floor space;

(*d*) sound foundation to floor to take the weight of the installation;

(*e*) extreme cleanliness, e.g. it is essential that dust be reduced to an absolute minimum to prevent interference with electronic circuits, switches, magnetic tape etc.

There are certain disadvantages to computer installations which must also be borne in mind, although they may not be sufficiently serious to outweigh the advantages. The disadvantages most commonly experienced are:

(*a*) lack of visible records of the intermediate processes;

(*b*) difficulty sometimes experienced in answering random queries without disturbing the current processing;

(*c*) the effect on staff of the new routines through lack of adequate consultation;

(*d*) difficulty of obtaining staff of the right calibre both to run the computer installation and to provide the input data at outlying sources;

(*e*) if the installation centralizes processing data for outlying areas, the absence of records at those areas;

(*f*) the problem of ensuring that input is accurate and of solving queries arising on input data from outlying sources.

On completion of the investigation the committee should report to the management on:

(*a*) the feasibility of a computer installation in the organization;

(*b*) estimated costs and savings;

(*c*) additional information to be provided;

(*d*) changes required in organization;

(*e*) recommendations on:

    (i) the type of equipment required;

    (ii) the transitional period.

Computers can be used for all business routines provided that the application is sufficiently voluminous, either alone or in conjunction with other applications, to justify their use. However, good commercial returns can be obtained from the use of computers in planning, e.g. linear programming calculations to determine siting of warehouses, vehicle routing and product mix etc.

Many firms now use computers to process Payroll, Stock Records, Production Control, Invoicing, Costing Analysis, Debtors Accounting and Purchasing.

By the use of computers these applications – performed separately under manual methods – can be integrated. Thus stock records and purchasing may be combined, as may payroll preparation and costing analysis.

Smaller firms which cannot justify their own computer installations, are able to take advantage of service bureaux which hire out computer time, and so are able to use electronic methods to perform difficult calculations or analyses quickly and economically.

*Desk-top Computers*

Since 1967 a large number of compact miniature computers have come on to the market. These machines possess the capability of producing visible ledger-card records, while capable of carrying out complicated analyses and computations, controlled by programs of the type associated with larger computers. The ledger cards have magnetic stripe backing eliminating the traditional balance pick-up. Programs are usually supplied by the manufacturers, though some machines can be programmed by the user.

*Direct Access Devices*

Recent developments in computer technology include the development of systems allowing users to interrogate the computer by direct access usually by means of a typewriter keyboard. In the more complicated systems a number of access points are made available. The replies to queries are usually shown in video form on screens. Such systems require a high-speed access device which is either a disc file or a fast drum. The video terminals are linked to the computer by cable or telephone line.

It is outside the scope of this book to describe the changeover from one type of accounting system to another. Considerable effort must be employed both in systems analysis and system design. Further, the timing of the change requires careful planning. Students will find additional information in the booklets published by the accountancy bodies.

Readers requiring further material on this complex and ever-growing topic are advised to consult the following books:

*Computers for Management* by Sanderson, published by Pan Piper.

*Electronic Computers* by Hollingdale and Tootill, published by Pelican.

*The Impact of Computers on Accounting* by McRae, published by Wiley.

*Fundamentals of Data Processing* by Lytel, published by Foulsham.

### Glossary of Computer Terms

*Access Time* – The interval in time taken to communicate with the memory of a digital computer.

*Address* – The means, whether by name or number, used to describe the location of data in storage or memory device.

*Arithmetic Unit* – That component of a digital computer which, acting upon information, performs logical and arithmetic operations.

*Automatic Coding* – The automatic preparation in code of a program of computer operations to solve particular problems.

*Binary* – A numbering system involving the integer 2 as its base of notation.

*Binary Digit or Bit* – A digit in the binary scale of notation. It is either zero or one.

*Branch* – This is one of the two alternative paths that a computer may follow at a given point in its program.

*Capacity* – (1) The capacity in numbers of bits of a store; or (2) the total number of characters which are regularly processed by a digital computer.

*Central Processor* – That part of the computer which contains the arithmetic and control circuits.

*Check Digit* – One or more digits added to a machine word which permit checking for errors (parity digit).

*Control Circuits* – Those circuits in a digital computer which control the carrying out of the program instructions in the correct sequence.

*Data* – Information.

*Erasable Storage* – Media of storage, such as magnetic tapes or discs, which can be erased and re-used.

*Flow Chart or Flow Diagram* – The representation of the program of operations for a computer by graphical means using specific symbols to describe operations.

*Input Equipment* – The various types of equipment employed for the introduction of data into a computer.

*Library* – A collection of programs and data files usually stored under fire-proof conditions under the control of a librarian.

*Line Printer* – A modern high-speed mechanical printing device which prints a line at a time under the control of the computer or from off-line storage.

*Location* – A storage register or position which permits storing one computer word.

*Machine Language* – Information submitted to the computer in the code appropriate to the machine's requirements.

*Microsecond* – a millionth of a second.

*Millisecond* – a thousandth of a second.

*Nanosecond* – a billionth of a second.

*Output Equipment* – employed for the transfer of data out of a computer, in an acceptable form and language.

*Parallel Operation* – The passage of data through a computer or part of it, using two or more channels simultaneously.

*Program* – The plan for solving a problem with a computer which reaches the computer as a precise sequence of coded instructions.

*Random Access* – Where the sequence of access to stored information is in no way dependent upon the position of the previous register examined.

*Simulation* – The representation of a physical or business problem by means of a mathematical model capable of solution by a computer.

*Store* – A device associated with a computer employed for holding items of information.

*Zone* – One of the three top positions, 12, 11 and 0 on punched cards which, in combination with a punch in one of the positions 1 to 9, is employed to represent an alphabetic or special character.

## CHAPTER XII

# BANKRUPTCY, LIQUIDATION
# AND RECEIVERSHIP ACCOUNTS

### § 1. General Principles

Proceedings in bankruptcy or liquidation (except as regards a *members'* voluntary liquidation) or the appointment of a Receiver for debenture holders indicate a condition of actual or suspected insolvency, i.e. a condition in which a person (individual, partner or company) is unable to meet financial obligations as they become due. If bankruptcy or liquidation follows, any business carried on will usually be terminated and the assets will have to be sold on the best terms possible. Realizable values, under these circumstances, may be very much less than book values or 'going concern' values.

A Balance Sheet prepared according to accepted accountancy principles very rarely reflects the value of assets on a forced sale basis and it does not normally distinguish creditors in accordance with the securities and preferences enjoyed by them. It is therefore necessary to prepare, at the outset of insolvency proceedings, a Statement of Affairs in the prescribed form. In essence this statement shows:

(i) assets at their estimated realizable value;

(ii) liabilities grouped according to the status of the creditors as preferential, secured, contingent etc.; and

(iii) the excess of (ii) over (i) which is the deficiency of assets to meet all claims of creditors.

The statement is accompanied by a Deficiency Account which attempts to give some explanation of the way in which the deficiency has arisen.

The prescribed forms in which Statements of Affairs must be presented are laid down in the *Bankruptcy Rules 1952* and the *Companies (Winding-up) Rules 1949*. They are supported by detailed schedules and in cases of bankruptcy and compulsory winding-up must be verified by affidavit. Nevertheless it must be stressed that any statement of affairs in insolvency is necessarily an estimate of the position made by an interested party (the debtor or officers of an insolvent company) at the commencement of the proceedings. In particular no provision is made for the expenses, costs and remuneration that will be incurred in realizing the assets.

The actual results of the bankruptcy are reflected in accounts submitted by the trustee or the liquidator. These are accounts of his stewardship in the form of Receipts and Payments Accounts and they show the amounts actually realized by disposal of the assets, the costs and expenses, including the remuneration of the trustee or liquidator, incurred in doing so and the amounts actually distributed to the various classes of creditors.

## § 2. The Preparation of a Statement of Affairs in Bankruptcy

Within three days of the making of the receiving order, if made on the debtor's own petition, or within seven days if made on a creditor's petition, the debtor must lodge with the Official Receiver his Statement of Affairs. This must be compiled in the official form, be accompanied by detailed schedules of particulars and verified by affidavit. It is made up as on the date of the Receiving Order.

The method of preparation of a Statement of Affairs and its accompanying Deficiency Account will depend upon the information available. Where books of account have been kept on a double-entry system they should be written up to date and a trial balance taken out as at the date of the Receiving Order. The Deficiency Account is required to commence on a date twelve months before the date of the Receiving Order or 'such other time as the Official Receiver may have fixed'. Where annual accounts have been prepared by a trader it is usually possible to agree with the Official Receiver that the Deficiency Account may commence on a Balance Sheet date. This will be of considerable assistance in establishing the opening excess of assets over liabilities or of liabilities over assets, as the case may be.

The Statement of Affairs and Deficiency Account should be completed simultaneously. Then, starting from the trial balance it will be easy to preserve the arithmetical accuracy of the figures and ensure that the deficiency exhibited by the Statement of Affairs agrees with that explained in the Deficiency Account. For example, if the debtor estimates that fixtures which appear as an asset in his books valued at £500 will realize £300, the latter figure should be entered in the Statement of Affairs and £200 should immediately be credited in the Deficiency Account as 'Other losses and expenses – Fixtures £200'.

In the bankruptcy of a sole trader there is no distinction between his business assets and liabilities and any other assets and liabilities. The Statement of Affairs must therefore reflect his position as a whole and when working from a trial balance or Balance Sheet extracted from the business books it is therefore necessary to make suitable adjustments for any non-business assets and liabilities that are known. For example, if a debtor in addition to his business assets has an investment which cost him £400 three years ago and which now has a saleable value of £700, the latter figure should be entered in the Statement of Affairs, £400 should be added to the opening surplus (or deducted from the opening deficiency) and £300 should be debited in the Deficiency Account as 'estimated surplus on realization of investment'.

Where no books have been kept or they are incomplete, it will usually be advisable to prepare initially lists of assets and liabilities on the opening and closing dates of the Deficiency Account. In these lists assets will normally be included at cost. This will enable the opening deficiency or surplus to be calculated. The assets at the date of the Receiving Order will then be revalued at realizable values, the liabilities will be sorted out according to their preferences and securities, if any, and the differences between cost and realizable values will be written off to the Deficiency Account in the usual way.

In the illustration that follows, a *pro forma* example of the front sheet of a

Statement of Affairs and the Deficiency Account is given. The lists referred to are the detailed schedules as follows.

### (A) Unsecured Creditors

A schedule of these creditors must be prepared in the prescribed form, containing in respect of each item, the name, address and occupation of the creditor, the amount of the debt, the date when contracted, and the consideration given. All liabilities, whether in respect of trading operations or otherwise, which cannot be listed in any of the other schedules, must be included here, particularly bills payable on which the debtor is liable as acceptor for value, the necessary particulars of each bill being inserted; bank overdraft if unsecured; balances of rent etc. not recoverable by distress; and of wages etc. in excess of the limit allowed as a preferential payment. Where there is a contra account against a creditor, only the net balance must be included, the debt being reduced to the extent of the contra.

The following classes of debts do not rank for dividend until all other unsecured creditors have been paid in full:

1. Money lent by a married woman to her husband for the purpose of his trade or business, or by a husband to his wife in similar circumstances.

2. Money lent to a firm, the lender to receive a share in the profits instead of interest, or a rate of interest varying with the profits; or money due to the vendor of goodwill (where he is being paid by way of an annuity or share of profits).

3. Beneficiaries under an ante-nuptial agreement to settle after-acquired property, if the agreement becomes void against the trustee on the settlor becoming bankrupt.

4. Interest on debts in excess of 5 per cent. In bankruptcy (but not in liquidation), this is not payable until all creditors have been paid in full. 4 per cent. interest is also payable on all debts from the date of the receiving order to the final payment when all the debts are paid in full and all other claims for interest have been met.

Deferred debts must, nevertheless, be included in the list of unsecured creditors, since the question of postponement is dealt with when proofs of debts are scrutinized for voting and dividend purposes, and not at this early stage. The deferred debts are therefore not distinguished as such in the Statement of Affairs.

In all cases, the gross liabilities must be entered in the 'gross liabilities' column, whether secured or not, and even though part may be met by third parties.

### (B) Creditors fully secured

The schedule of these creditors, in addition to containing the same information as is necessary in respect of unsecured creditors, must also contain particulars of the security held, the date when the security was given, the estimated value of the security, and the estimated surplus. On the liabilities side of the Statement of Affairs these creditors will be entered in short, the security being shown as a deduction, and the surplus carried to the assets side. If, however, partly secured creditors have a second charge on any or all of such surplus, the amount so charged is deducted from the surplus (only the balance of which (if any) is carried to the assets side), and added to the securities of the partly secured creditors (*see* (*C*) below).

Interest due but unpaid and interest accrued up to the date of the Receiving Order should be added to the principal outstanding. To the extent that the security is sufficient to cover all interest due and accrued the limit of 5 per cent. does not apply. Where a debt is fully secured, therefore, interest should be provided for at the rate at which the debtor has contracted to pay it.

Where the creditor holds security of a third party for the liability of the debtor, such security must be ignored; the asset forming the security does not belong to the debtor, and the creditor, so far as the bankrupt's estate is concerned, is unsecured.

If the debtor has given security for the debt of a third party, the creditor of that third party is a fully secured creditor of the debtor giving the security. In such a case, the creditor should be included here, but his claim must be reduced by the amount expected to be paid by such third party, i.e. if the third party is solvent, there will be no debt to rank here. Full details will, of course, appear in the schedule of liabilities.

### (C) Creditors partly secured

Similar particulars must be afforded in this schedule, and the unsecured balance shown. In the Statement of Affairs these creditors are shown in short on the liabilities side, the security being deducted, together with any surplus from fully secured creditors over which the partly secured creditors have a second charge, and the balance unsecured, which ranks against the estate, extended.

### (D) Liabilities on Bills Discounted other than Debtor's own Acceptances for value

The schedule of these bills must contain in respect of each bill particulars of the acceptor's name, address and occupation, whether the debtor is liable as drawer or endorser, the date when the bill falls due, the amount of the bill (accommodation bills being separated from other bills), the name, address and occupation of the holder (if known), and the amount expected to rank against the estate for dividend.

Bills receivable discounted by the debtor with his bank or other parties will be included here, since the debtor will be liable on the bills as drawer or endorser. If, however, it is expected that the acceptor will meet these bills in due course, nothing will be extended to rank against the estate for dividend. If any amount is expected to rank it must be extended here and also shown in the Deficiency Account as an expected loss.

The case of accommodation bills is more complicated, especially where there have been cross-transactions between the debtor and another party. Briefly, the whole of the accommodation bills must be inserted, whether the debtor is liable as drawer, acceptor, or endorser. Each accommodation bill must be examined, to ascertain the precise nature of the liability attaching to it as regards the estate. Where the accommodation bill was accepted by the debtor, the amount ranking for dividend will be the face value less the amount expected to be recovered from any person who shared in the proceeds of discounting it. If there is no such estimated recovery, the full face value will rank for dividend, unless the bill has not been negotiated. If the debtor is only liable as drawer or endorser, it will depend on the financial position of those primarily liable on the bill how much (if any) of the amount should be extended as ranking for dividend. If the party primarily liable dishonours the bill and becomes bankrupt, the holder will have a right of proof to the full extent of the bill against the estates of both parties, though he will not be entitled to receive dividends exceeding the total face value of the bill, together with interest and expenses.

As previously stated, liabilities on bills payable accepted by the debtor for value will be included in the list of unsecured creditors, and not in this schedule.

### (E) Contingent or other liabilities

The chief claims under this heading will be under contracts of guarantee or suretyship, claims for dilapidations under leases, uncalled capital on partly-paid shares etc. In these cases the gross amount is inset and only the amount expected to rank for dividend extended. Any amount recoverable from other persons will be considered when arriving at the amount expected to rank. The amounts expected to rank will also appear in the Deficiency Account as losses.

### (F) Creditors for Rent etc. recoverable by distress, and (G) Preferential Creditors

The schedules of these items must contain full particulars, and disclose the difference between the gross amounts of the claims and the amounts recoverable by distress, or payable in full under the *Bankruptcy Act*. The amounts not so recoverable or payable in full will be included in the list of unsecured creditors. In the Statement of Affairs the amount recoverable or payable in full will be shown in short on the liabilities side, and deducted from the gross assets on the assets side.

The landlord is entitled to recover by distress any rent in arrear, up to a maximum of six months' rent, accrued due up to the date of the adjudication order, and since the Statement of Affairs is usually prepared prior to this date, if any rent is accrued due, such amount, but not exceeding six months' rent, should be included. Any balance should be included with the amounts due to unsecured creditors.

If the landlord distrains within three months of the receiving order, preferential debts are a first charge upon the goods or proceeds of sale, the landlord having the same rights of priority in place of the persons preferred. If, therefore, there are insufficient assets to cover the preferential debts and the rent accrued within the six months, the landlord's claim will be restricted to the excess of the available assets over the preferential debts.

The *Bankruptcy Act 1914*, as amended by s. 115, *Companies Act 1947*, provides for certain classes of liabilities to be paid in priority to others, and these should be treated as indicated above. The preferential debts are similar to those in the winding-up of a company, which are fully set out on pages 557-61. The following is a summary:

1. Parochial and local rates which became due and payable within the twelve months next before the receiving order. If the rates are payable by instalments, only the instalments *due* should be entered. If the premises have been vacated prior to the receiving order, only the apportioned rates to the date of vacating the premises should be included, since no rates are payable when the premises are not occupied.

2. All land tax, income tax, surtax, or other assessed taxes assessed on the debtor up to April 5th next before the receiving order, not exceeding one year's assessment. Where more than one year's assessment is in arrear, the highest amount will be treated as preferential, the balance being unsecured.

The expression 'assessed up to April 5th next before the receiving order' includes tax due for the period up to the previous April 5th, even though not actually assessed before that date (*Gowers* v. *Walker* [1930], 1 Ch. 262).

3. Any tax deducted from emoluments under P.A.Y.E. for the twelve months next before the receiving order (*Finance Act 1952*, s. 30).

4. Any unpaid purchase tax which became due to the Crown in the twelve months preceding the date of the receiving order.

5. Wages or salary of any clerk, servant, labourer or workman in respect of services rendered during the four months before the receiving order, with a maximum of £200 for each individual. Holiday or sick pay ranks as payment in respect of services.

6. All accrued holiday remuneration becoming payable to any clerk, servant, workman or labourer (or in case of his death to any other person in his right) on the termination of his employment before or by reason of the receiving order.

7. All National Insurance contributions payable during the twelve months prior to the receiving order by the debtor as an employer of any person or as a self-employed or non-employed person.

The following claims rank even before the above:

1. Funds belonging to a friendly society or trustee savings bank, which are in the hands of the debtor as an officer of the society.

2. The proportion of an articled clerk's premium, as the trustee shall decide, where the employer becomes bankrupt, and the trustee does not transfer the Articles to some other person.

3. Reasonable funeral and testamentary expenses in the case of a deceased insolvent debtor.

4. The expenses properly incurred by the trustee under a deed of arrangement which was avoided by the bankruptcy of the debtor.

### (H) Valuation of Assets

All assets should be brought into the Statement of Affairs at a fair estimate of their realizable value. Care must be taken to see that the debtor does not overestimate the break-up value. Stock must be valued with particular reference to the conditions under which a forced realization might have to be made. Similar considerations apply to the valuation of other assets, such as freehold and leasehold properties, machinery and plant, fixtures, furniture etc. Private assets, such as furniture and investments, must be included, as these are available to satisfy *any* liability of the debtor.

Property held in trust for others must be excluded, also the tools and necessary wearing apparel and bedding of the debtor, his wife and children, to an inclusive value of £20.

No account can be taken of any property which the trustee may be expected to recover under the 'doctrine of relation back' or the 'reputed ownership' clause.

A full description of every kind of property must be made in the specified form, together with the statement of the amount it is expected to proddce.

Assets which are mortgaged or charged in favour of fully or partly secured creditors are included in the appropriate Lists (B or C) and do not appear in List H. However, the same principles of valuation apply to them.

### (I) Book Debts

A schedule of debts due to the estate must be prepared, showing the name, address and occupation of the debtor, the amount of the debt, distinguishing between good, doubtful and bad; the date of contraction, the amount each debt is estimated to produce, and particulars of any securities given for debts. In the Statement of Affairs the amount of the good debts is extended into the outer column; the doubtful and bad debts are shown in short at their gross figure, and the amount they are estimated to produce extended.

### (J) Bills of Exchange etc. on hand

Bills deposited with bankers for collection (not discounted) must be included.

### (K) The Deficiency Account

The excess of liabilities expected to rank against the estate over the net assets available to meet those liabilities is termed the 'deficiency', or in the event of the assets exceeding the liabilities, the 'surplus'. A Deficiency Account is prepared in order to disclose how the deficiency or surplus has arisen.

On the debit side of the Deficiency Account will be found the various items which go to make up the total amount to be accounted for. These are as follows:

1. Excess of assets over liabilities (if any) at the commencement of the period under review. Care must be taken to bring in private as well as business capital.

2. Net profits (if any) from the business during the period under review, before charging interest on capital or proprietor's salary.

3. Any other receipts. These will include any gifts, e.g. legacies received during the period and any expected surpluses on realization of assets.

4. Deficiency (if any), as per Statement of Affairs.

The total of these will be accounted for on the credit side of the Deficiency Account as follows:

1. Excess of liabilities over assets (if any) at the commencement of the period under review.

2. Net loss (if any) from carrying on business during the period.

3. Bad debts. These are the amounts written off in arriving at the amount estimated to be produced from debtors in the Statement of Affairs.

4. Expenses incurred during the period, other than usual trade expenses, viz. household expenses and personal expenses of self, wife and children.

5. Other losses and expenses, including estimated losses on realization of assets.

6. Surplus (if any).

Just as a Statement of Affairs is in some respects similar to a Balance Sheet, so a Deficiency Account fulfils some of the functions of a Profit and Loss Account. Thus it relates to a period of time and reflects profits and losses. However, whereas a trader's drawings or personal living expenses would not appear in a Profit and Loss Account, they are a necessary ingredient of a Deficiency Account because they reduce the assets that would otherwise be available for creditors.

It will be observed that the official form differs from a Profit and Loss Account in having its sides reversed. Thus losses and expenditure appear on the *credit* side while profits and other accretions are shown as *debits*. This no doubt reflects the tendency of lawyers to regard all accounts in terms of receipts and payments.

**Illustration**

A filed his own petition on December 10th, 19...... and a Receiving Order was made on the same day. A Trial Balance of his business books taken out as on that date showed the following position:

| | £ | £ |
|---|---:|---:|
| Capital Account (balance at January 1st, 19......) | | 20,000 |
| Drawings Account (after crediting Interest on Capital £1,200) .. .. .. | 2,400 | |
| Bought Ledger .. .. .. .. | | 93,600 |
| Sales Ledger .. .. .. .. | 30,000 | |
| Freehold premises .. .. .. | 11,000 | |
| Machinery .. .. .. .. | 15,000 | |
| Fixtures .. .. .. .. | 3,000 | |
| Stock at January 1st, 19...... .. .. | 50,000 | |
| Stock on Consignment .. .. .. | 5,000 | |
| Bills Receivable .. .. .. .. | 1,300 | |
| Bank overdraft .. .. .. | | 5,000 |
| Cash in hand .. .. .. .. | 200 | |
| Mortgage .. .. .. .. | | 10,000 |
| Sales .. .. .. .. .. | | 300,000 |
| Purchases .. .. .. .. | 120,000 | |
| Wages and Expenses .. .. .. | 189,500 | |
| Interest on Capital .. .. .. | 1,200 | |
| | £428,600 | £428,600 |

The stock on December 10th, 19......, is valued for Balance Sheet purposes at £60,000; it is expected to realize £40,000 on a forced sale. Some Sales Ledger balances totalling £6,000 are bad and others totalling £4,000 are expected to produce one-half of the amount due. There is no provision for bad debts in the books. The freehold premises, machinery and fixtures are estimated to realize £13,000, £12,000 and £1,500 respectively. The mortgage is secured on the freehold premises; accrued interest amounting to £400 has not been provided for. One creditor for £100 has a lien on stock valued at and estimated to produce £150. Bills of exchange for £9,000 have been drawn by A on customers, accepted by them and discounted by A. One of these for £3,500 is expected to be dishonoured and to prove worthless. The creditors in the Bought Ledger include liabilities for wages, rates and purchase tax payable preferentially and amounting to £3,000. The only security for the bank overdraft is a second charge on the freehold premises.

In addition to the above, A owns the house in which he lives, valued at £6,500 and has investments worth £13,000 which he has pledged as security for an interest-free loan of £20,000 from a relative. These have not varied during the past year.

The Official Receiver has supplied A with the appropriate forms and agreed that the Deficiency Account may commence on January 1st, 19......

WORKINGS

The following preliminary calculations are necessary:

## PROFIT AND LOSS ACCOUNT

| | £ | | £ |
|---|---|---|---|
| Opening Stock    ..    ..    ..    .. | 50,000 | Sales    ..    ..    ..    .. | 300,000 |
| Purchases    ..    ..    ..    .. | 120,000 | Closing Stock    ..    ..    .. | 60,000 |
| Wages and Expenses    ..    ..    .. | 189,500 | | |
| Net Profit    ..    ..    ..    .. | 500 | | |
| | £360,000 | | £360,000 |

Interest on A's own capital is not charged as it does not reduce his available assets. His drawings are therefore adjusted to £2,400 + £1,200 = £3,600 and in the absence of information to the contrary it is assumed that this amount represents personal household expenditure for the period.

## SURPLUS
at January 1st, 19......

| | £ | | £ |
|---|---|---|---|
| Loan from relative    ..    ..    .. | 20,000 | Business Capital representing net assets of    .. | 20,000 |
| Balance ..    ..    ..    ..    .. | 19,500 | Residence    ..    ..    ..    .. | 6,500 |
| | | Investments    ..    ..    .. | 13,000 |
| | £39,500 | | £39,500 |

| | £ | Security £ | Surplus £ |
|---|---|---|---|
| Fully secured Credidtors: | | | |
| Mortgage (incluing accrued Interest)    ..    ..    ..    .. | 10,400 | 13,000 | 2,600 |
| Creditor with lien    ..    ..    ..    ..    ..    .. | 100 | 150 | 50 |
| | £10,500 | £13,150 | £2,650 |

| | £ | £ | Deficiency £ |
|---|---|---|---|
| Partly secured Creditors: | | | |
| Bank    ..    ..    ..    ..    ..    ..    ..    .. | 5,000 | 2,600 | 2,400 |
| Relative    ..    ..    ..    ..    ..    ..    .. | 20,000 | 13,000 | 7,000 |
| | £25,000 | £15,600 | £9,400 |

## K.     DEFICIENCY (OR SURPLUS) ACCOUNT

| | £ | £ |
|---|---:|---:|
| Excess of Assets over Liabilities on the (¹) 1st day of January 19.... (if any) | | 19,500 |
| Net Profit (if any) arising from carrying on business from the (¹) 1st day of January, 19...., to date of Receiving Order, after deducting usual trade expenses | | 100 |
| Income or profit from other sources (if any) since the (¹) 1st day of January, 19.... | | |
| Gifts from relations and others | | 2,000 |
| Estimated surplus on realization of freehold premises | | 18,000 |
| (⁶) Deficiency as per Statement of Affairs | | |
| Total amount to be accounted for | | (⁶) £39,600 |

| | £ | £ |
|---|---:|---:|
| Excess of Liabilities over Assets on the (¹) .... day of 19.... (if any) | | |
| Net loss (if any) arising from carrying on business from the (¹) .... day of .... 19...., to date of Receiving Order, after charging against Profits the usual trade expenses | | 8,000 |
| Bad Debts (if any) as per Schedule 'I' (²) | 20,000 | |
| Depreciation of stock-in-trade | 3,000 | |
|        " machinery | 1,500 | |
|        " trade fixtures, fittings etc. | | 24,500 |
| Expenses incurred since the (¹) 1st day of January 19...., other than usual trade expenses, viz. household and personal expenses of self and (³) | | 3,600 |
| (⁴) Other losses and expenses (if any): Liability on Bills discounted | | 3,500 |
| (⁵) Surplus as per Statement of Affairs | | |
| Total amount accounted for | | (⁶) £39,600 |

Signature.................................     Dated.................19.........

*Notes:*

(1) This date should be twelve months before date of Receiving Order, or such other time as Official Receiver may have fixed.

(2) This Schedule must show when debts were contracted.

(3) Add 'wife and children' (if any), stating number of latter.

(4) Here add particulars of other losses or expenses (if any), including liabilities (if any) for which no consideration received.

(5) Strike out words which do not apply.

(6) These figures should agree.

## STATEMENT OF AFFAIRS  No.  of 19

### IN BANKRUPTCY

RE A ...............

TO THE DEBTOR: You are required to fill up, carefully and accurately, this sheet, and such of the several sheets A, B, C, D, E, F G, H, I, J, and K,* as are applicable showing the state of your affairs on the day on which the Receiving Order was made against you, viz. the tenth day of December 19...... Such sheets, when filled up, will constitute your Statement of Affairs, and must be verified by oath or declaration.

| Gross Liabilities | Liabilities (as stated and estimated by Debtor) | | Expected to Rank |
|---|---|---|---|
| £ | | £ | £ |
| 90,500 | Unsecured Creditors a per List (A) .. .. | | 90,500 |
| 10,500 | Creditors fully secured, as per List (B) .. | 10,500 | |
| | Estimated value of securities .. | 13,150 | |
| | Surplus .. .. .. | 2,650 | |
| | Less amount thereof carried to Sheet (C) .. | 2,600 | |
| | Balance thereof to contra .. .. | 50 | |
| 25,000 | Creditors partly secured, as per List (C) .. | 25,000 | 9,400 |
| | Less estimated value of securities .. | 15,600 | |
| | Liabilities on Bills discounted other than Debtor's own acceptances for value, as per List (D), viz.: | | |
| | On Accommodation Bills as Drawer, Acceptor, or Endorser £ | | |
| | On other Bills as Drawer or Endorser £ 9,000 | | |
| | £9,000 | | |
| 3,500 | Of which it is expected will rank against the estate for dividend | | 3,500 |
| | Contingent or other Liabilities as per List (E) .. .. .. | | |
| | Of which it is expected will rank against the estate for dividend | | |

| Assets (as stated and estimated by Debtor) | | Estimated to Produce |
|---|---|---|
| Property as per List (H), viz.: | | £ |
| (a) Cash at Bankers | .. .. | |
| (b) Cash in hand | .. .. | 200 |
| (c) Cash deposited with Solicitor for Costs of Petition | | |
| (d) Stock-in-trade (cost £59,850) | .. | 39,850 |
| (e) Machinery | .. .. | 12,000 |
| (f) Trade fixtures, fittings, utensils etc. | | 1,500 |
| (g) Farming Stock | | |
| (h) Growing crops and tenant right | | |
| (i) Furniture | .. | |
| (j) Life policies | .. | |
| (k) Stocks and Shares | .. | |
| (l) Reversionary or other interests under Wills | | |
| (m) Other property, viz.: | | |
| Freehold residence | .. | 6,500 |
| Goods out on Consignment | | 5,000 |
| Total as per List (H) .. | | 65,050 |
| Book Debts as per List (I), viz.: | £ | |
| Good .. .. .. | 4,000 | 20,000 |
| Doubtful .. .. | 6,000 | |
| Bad .. .. | | |
| | £10,000 | |

| | £ | |
|---|---|---|
| Creditors for rent etc. recoverable by distress, as per List (F) | | |
| Creditors for rates, taxes, wages etc. payable in full, as per List (G) | 3,000 | |
| Sheriff's charges payable under Sec. 41 of the Act estimated at | | |
| Deducted *contra* | £3,000 | |
| 3,000 | | |
| † Surplus explained in Statement (K) | | |
| £132,500 | | |

| | £ | |
|---|---|---|
| Estimated to produce | | 2,000 |
| Bills of Exchange or other similar securities on hand, as per List (J) | £1,300 | |
| Estimated to produce | | 1,300 |
| Surplus from securities in the hands of Creditors fully secured (per *contra*) | | 50 |
| | | 88,400 |
| *Deduct* Creditors for distrainable rent, and preferential rates, taxes wages, sheriff's charges, etc. (per *contra*) | | 3,000 |
| | | 85,400 |
| † Deficiency explained in Statement (K) | | 18,000 |
| | | £103,400 |

£103,400

\* Sheet 'L' should be substituted for any one or more of such of the sheets named as will have to be returned blank.  † Strike out words which do not apply.

I, A

of

in the County of        make oath and say that the above Statement and the several lists hereunto annexed, marked A, B, C, D, G, H, I, J, K, and L are, to the best of my knowledge and belief, a full, true, and complete statement of my affairs on the date of the above-mentioned Receiving Order made against me.

*Sworn at*  ...................................

*in the County of*  ...................................

*this* ........... *day of* ............ *19* ......      Signature  ...................................

*Before me*

...................................

## § 3. Bankruptcy of Partnerships

When a partnership is made bankrupt, the trustee of the joint estate becomes also the trustee of the separate estate of each partner. A Statement of Affairs, with Deficiency Account, must be prepared for the firm, and separate Statements of Affairs and Deficiency Accounts for each partner. Distinct accounts must be kept of the joint and separate estates, the separate creditors of each estate being first paid out of the assets of that estate. In the event of there being a surplus on any of the separate estates, this will form an asset of the joint estate, but the joint creditors cannot receive more than the full amount of their debts, together with 4 per cent. per annum interest from the date of the order. Any surplus on the joint estate will be divided between the partners, according to their rights under the partnership agreement and each partner's share will be included as an asset of his separate estate.

Where a partner has given personal security as collateral to his personal guarantee of a debt due from the firm, the creditor can prove in the joint estate for the full amount of the debt, deducting only the value of any security provided out of the joint estate. The creditor may also prove in the separate estate of the partner for the full amount guaranteed by him, deducting only the value of any security given by that partner out of his separate estate. (*Re Turner; ex parte West Riding Bank* [1881], 19 Ch.D. 105). This might appear to give the creditor a right of double proof; however, the rule against double proof applies only to claims against the same estate. Where two or more partners have personally guaranteed a debt of the firm the creditor may prove in the joint estate and each separate estate. However, he may not receive in all more than 100 per cent. of the amount of the debt.

In a case where a partner had charged his own property as security for a partnership overdraft and had also guaranteed it (but the security given was not collateral to his guarantee) it was held in *re Dutton, Massey & Co; ex parte Manchester & Liverpool District Banking Co* [1924], 2 Ch.199, that the bank was entitled to prove in the separate estate of the partner for the full amount of his liability under the guarantee, without deducting the value of the securities held.

**Illustration**

X and Y are in partnership and file their petition in bankruptcy. From the following particulars, prepare the Statements of Affairs and Deficiency Accounts of the joint estate and the separate estates of the partners.

### BALANCE SHEETS

|  | | Firm | X | Y |  | | Firm | X | Y |
|---|---|---|---|---|---|---|---|---|---|
|  | | £ | £ | £ |  | | £ | £ | £ |
| Mortgage of Leasehold | .. | 3,000 | | | Leasehold Premises | .. | 6,000 | | |
| Bank Overdraft | .. | 3,000 | | | Plant | .. | 6,500 | | |
| Sundry Creditors | .. | 12,400 | 1,500 | 2,900 | Furniture | .. | 400 | 1,000 | 1,200 |
| Preferential Creditors | .. | 100 | | | Stock | .. | 5,500 | | |
| Capital X | .. | 3,000 | | | Debtors.. | .. | 5,000 | | |
| ,,       Y | .. | 2,000 | | | Investments (cost) | .. | | 2,500 | 1,000 |
| Surplus .. | .. | | 5,000 | 1,300 | Cash | .. | 100 | 3,000 | 2,000 |
|  | | | | | Capital in X and Y | .. | | | |
|  | | £23,500 | £6,500 | £4,200 |  | | £23,500 | £6,500 | £4,200 |

The bank overdraft of the firm was secured by a second mortgage on the firm's premises, and by Y's personal guarantee, supported by the deposit of Y's investments as collateral security.

The firm's assets are estimated to realize the following: Lease, £4,500; Plant, £3,000; Furniture, £150; Stock, £3,100; Debtors, good, £2,575; doubtful (£1,000) 50 per cent.; bad (£1,425) nil. X's assets: Furniture, £600; Investments, £2,000. Y's assets: Furniture, £800; Investments, £300

X and Y shared profits and losses equally. In the year preceding the date of the Receiving Order the firm incurred a trading loss of £1,500 and the partners' drawings had been X £2,000, Y £2,500 (including cost of a personal investment £500).

## STATEMENTS OF AFFAIRS

(*Note:* In practice each would be on a separate form)

| | Firm | X | Y | | | Firm | X | Y |
|---|---|---|---|---|---|---|---|---|
| | £ | £ | £ | £      £ | | £ | £ | £ |
| Unsecured Creditors .. | | 12,400 | 1,500 | 2,900 | Cash | 100 | | |
| Fully Secured Creditor .. 3,000 | | | | | Stock | 3,100 | | |
| Estimated value of security 4,500 | | | | | Plant | 3,000 | | |
| | | | | | Furniture | 150 | 600 | 800 |
| | | | | | Investments | | 2,000 | |
| Surplus to partly secured Creditor .. 1,500 | | | | | Surplus from X's Estate .. | 1,100 | | |
| | | | | | | 7,450 | 2,600 | 800 |
| Partly Secured Creditor .. 3,000 | | | | | Debtors Good .. | 2,575 | | |
| Estimated value of security 1,500 | | | | 3,000 | ,, Doubtful £1,000 | | | |
| | | | | | ,, Bad .. 1,425 | | | |
| | | 1,500 | | 300 | | £2,425 | | |
| | | | | 2,700 | Estimated to produce .. | 500 | | |
| Preferential Creditors deducted contra .. 100 | | | | | *Less* Preferential debts .. | 10,525 100 | 2,600 | 800 |
| | | | | | | 10,425 | 2,600 | 800 |
| Surplus carried to Joint Estate .. | | | 1,100 | | Deficiency .. .. | 3,475 | | 4,800 |
| | £13,900 | £2,600 | £5,600 | | | £13,900 | £2,600 | £5,600 |

*Note:* As the joint estate will only be sufficient to pay at the most 75 per cent. of unsecured claims, the bank will retain the whole of Y's investments towards the balance of the overdraft remaining (£375). The proof would be made in the joint estate for £1,500, the value of the investments not being deducted, as they were lodged by and belonged to Y, and did not form part of the assets of the firm. The bank will also be entitled to prove in Y's estate for the full amount of £3,000, less £300, the value of the investments which were lodged as collateral security for his guarantee. It cannot, however, receive, in the aggregate, more than £3,000.

## DEFICIENCY ACCOUNTS

| | Firm | X | Y | | | Firm | X | Y |
|---|---|---|---|---|---|---|---|---|
| | £ | £ | £ | | | £ | £ | £ |
| Surplus 1 year ago .. .. | 11,000 | 2,000 | | Deficiency 1 year ago .. | | | 1,200 |
| Surplus from X's estate .. | 1,100 | | | Trading Loss .. .. | 1,500 | | |
| Drawings from firm .. | | 2,000 | 2,500 | Partners' Drawings from firm .. .. | 4,500 | | |
| Deficiency per Statement of Affairs.. .. .. | 3,475 | | 4,800 | Partners' personal expenditure .. .. | | 2,000 | 2,000 |
| | | | | Losses on: Stock .. | 2,400 | | |
| | | | | Plant .. | 3,500 | | |
| | | | | Furniture .. | 250 | 400 | 400 |
| | | | | Lease .. | 1,500 | | |
| | | | | Investments .. | | 500 | 700 |
| | | | | Bad Debts .. | 1,925 | | |
| | | | | Liability on guarantee .. | | | 3,000 |
| | | | | Surplus per Statement of Affairs .. .. | | 1,100 | |
| | £15,575 | £4,000 | £7,300 | | | £15,575 | £4,000 | £7,300 |

*Notes:*

1. The opening surplus of X and deficiency of Y relate only to the assets and liabilities of their separate estates. In the absence of information to the contrary (e.g. the investments known to have been purchased by Y at a cost of £500) the net assets of their separate estates are assumed to have been the same at the beginning of the period as at the end.

2. It is assumed that the partners' drawings have been used entirely for the personal expenditure of themselves and their households except as regards the £500 invested by Y.

3. As the bank has the right to prove in Y's separate estate for £2,700 in addition to realizing his investments worth £300 his personal deficiency is increased by the full £3,000 which has to be shown in the Deficiency Account as a loss of his separate estate.

### § 4. The Accounts of a Trustee in Bankruptcy

Detailed accounts must be kept by the trustee in a cash book of all his receipts and payments. This book must be in the prescribed form (see Appendix III A), and contain columns for every class of receipt and payment.

At the expiration of six months from the date of the receiving order, and every succeeding six months until his release, the trustee must send to the Board of Trade a duplicate copy of the cash book for such period, together with the necessary vouchers and copies of the certificate of audit by the committee of inspection. The first accounts so submitted must be accompanied by a summary of the debtor's Statement of Affairs, showing in red ink the amounts realized, and explaining the cause of the non-realization of any assets not realized.

If the trustee carries on the business of the debtor, he must keep a Trading Account recording simply the cash receipts and payments. This account must be kept in the prescribed form, and only the weekly total of the receipts and payments need be inserted in the general cash book.

Not less than once in every year, and, in practice, upon the occasion of each Board of Trade audit, the trustee must submit to the Board a statement containing the prescribed particulars and on the prescribed form (see Appendix III B) showing the proceedings in the bankruptcy up to date.

At the date of declaring the first and each subsequent dividend, and at the date of application by the trustee for release, he must prepare a summarized Statement of Receipts and Payments in the prescribed form (see Appendix III C), showing the position of the estate at the date in question. A copy of this statement must be sent to each creditor who has proved, and to the debtor.

The trustee's final account is similar in principle to that of a liquidator except that it is not concerned with payments (if any) to debenture holders or shareholders. The remuneration of the trustee must be in two parts of which the first is a percentage on the amount realized by him after deducting any sums paid to secured creditors out of the proceeds of their securities, and the other a percentage on the amount distributed in dividend.

### § 5. Deeds of Arrangement

Where a trustee is appointed under a private deed of arrangement, it is usual for a Statement of Affairs to be presented to the creditors, drawn up more or less on the lines of a Statement of Affairs in bankruptcy, but disclosing considerably less detail. A list of creditors is also usually furnished.

The trustee under a deed of arrangement is not compelled to keep a columnar cash book similar to that required to be kept by a trustee in bankruptcy; but he must, within thirty days after the expiration of twelve months from the date of the registration of the deed, and again on finally ceasing to act, transmit to the Board of Trade an account of his receipts and payments as trustee, sufficient indication being given of each receipt and payment to explain its nature.

Where trading is carried on, a separate Trading Account must be kept, and the totals entered in the cash account.

By Section 14 of the *Deeds of Arrangement Act 1914*, it is provided that every trustee under a deed of arrangement must send, every six months from the registration of the deed, to each creditor who has assented to the deed, a statement in the prescribed form (see Appendix III D), of the trustee's accounts and of the proceedings under the deed to the date of the statement. This is in addition to the Statement of Accounts sent annually to the Board of Trade, or (as provided by Section 13 of the *Deeds of Arrangement Act 1914*), at such times as may be prescribed.

## § 6. The Preparation of a Statement of Affairs of a Company in Compulsory Liquidation

Within fourteen days from the date of the winding-up order, or of the appointment of a provisional liquidator, a Statement of Affairs in the prescribed form must be submitted by the directors or secretary, or one of the chief officers of the company. If necessary, the official receiver may require some other employee of the company competent to do so, to prepare the statement, or even an employee of a company which is an officer, e.g. secretary, of the company in liquidation.

The form of this statement is prescribed by the Companies (Winding-up) Rules 1949, and differs substantially from that used in bankruptcy. It is designed to show not only the estimated surplus or deficiency as regards creditors of the company, but also the estimated surplus or deficiency so far as the members are concerned, while the adoption of a more modern vertical form enables the various claims against the available assets to be shown as successive deductions in order of priority which is:

(*a*) secured creditors to the extent that their claims are covered by the assets charged (gross liabilities column only);

(*b*) preferential creditors;

(*c*) debenture holders with a floating charge over the assets;

(*d*) unsecured creditors; and

(*e*) shareholders.

The statement must be accompanied by detailed schedules of assets and liabilities.

In the case of a winding-up where the relevant date is after June 30th, 1948, the following debts are preferential (*Companies Act 1948*, s. 319). For this purpose the expression 'the relevant date' means:

(i) in the case of a company ordered to be wound up compulsorily, the date of the appointment (or first appointment) of a provisional liquidator, or, if no such appointment was made, the date of the winding-up order, unless in either case the company had commenced to be wound up voluntarily before that date; and

(ii) in any other case the date of the passing of the resolution for the winding-up of the company.

Where, however, either a receiver is appointed on behalf of the holders of debentures secured by a floating charge on assets of the company, or possession is taken by or on behalf of those debenture holders of any property comprised in the charge, the 'relevant date' is the date of the appointment of the receiver, or of possession being taken, as the case may be (s. 94 (3)).

(*a*) The following rates and taxes:

(i) all local rates due from the company at the relevant date, and having become due and payable within twelve months next before that date;

(ii) all land tax, income tax, profits tax, excess profits tax or other assessed taxes assessed on the company up to April 5th next before that date (including tax *due* for the period to April 5th although not yet assessed (*Gowers* v. *Walker* [1930], 1 Ch. 262)), and not exceeding in the whole one year's assessment.

The scope of this provision has been substantially amended by subsequent taxation legislation. Thus land tax was abolished by the *Finance Act 1963* while excess profits tax and profits tax terminated in 1946 and 1966 respectively. A few outstanding liabilities, particularly in back duty cases, may still arise, however. New taxes which have been given similar preferential rights by the *Finance Acts 1965* and *1966* are capital gains tax and corporation tax. A company does not normally pay capital gains tax as such but is liable to pay corporation tax on its capital gains. Although since 1965-66 a company has not been liable to income tax on its own profits or income, income tax liabilities still arise in respect of tax deducted from dividends and interest paid.

Where income tax liabilities are outstanding for more than one year of assessment (ending not later than April 5th preceding the relevant date) the Crown is entitled to select the largest liability as preferential (*Re Pratt, I.R.C.* v. *Phillips*, 31 T.C. 27). Outstanding liabilities to corporation tax (and, possibly, profits tax) will not relate to years of assessment ending on April 5th, but to the accounting periods of the company which are usually but not necessarily of twelve months. The Crown can claim preference for the liability for any one accounting period ending not later than April 5th preceding the relevant date (*Re Pratt* (above)). It is not necessary that the accounting year chosen should coincide with or end in the year of assessment for which a preferential claim for income tax is made. Where more than one tax is outstanding the Crown can therefore select the largest liability under each heading always subject to the rule that the year of assessment or accounting period chosen in each case must end not later than April 5th immediately preceding the relevant date (*I.R.C.* v. *Purvis Industries*, 38 T.C. 155);

(iii) the amount of any purchase tax due from the company at the relevant date, and having become due within twelve months next before that date;

(iv) any sums due at the relevant date by the company on account of tax deductions under P.A.Y.E. for the twelve months next before that date (*Finance Act 1952*, s. 30);

(v) any estate duty payable by a company in respect of assets of a company deemed to pass on a death by virtue of Section 46, *Finance Act 1940*.

(b) All wages or salary (whether or not earned wholly or in part by way of commission) of any clerk or servant in respect of services rendered to the company during four months next before the relevant date and all wages (whether payable for time or for piece work) of any workman or labourer in respect of services so rendered. Any remuneration in respect of a period of holiday or of absence from work through sickness or other good cause is deemed to be wages in respect of services rendered to the company during that period.

The sum to which priority is to be given is not, in the case of any one claimant, to exceed £200. Where, however, a claimant is a labourer in husbandry who has entered into a contract for the payment of a portion of his wages in a lump sum at the end of the year of hiring, he has priority in respect of the whole of such sum, or a part thereof, as the court may decide to be due under the contract, proportionate to the time of service up to the relevant date.

(c) Any sum ordered under the *Reinstatement in Civil Employment Act 1944*, to be paid by way of compensation where the default by reason of which the order for compensation was made occurred before the relevant date, whether or not the order was made before that date. The limit for any one claimant, taking (b) and (c) together is £200. However, liabilities under the *Reinstatement in Civil Employment Act 1944* are not now likely to arise.

It would appear that payments due to former employees under the *Redundancy Payments Act 1965* are not entitled to preference. The individual entitled to a redundancy payment will in any event be paid by the Minister if he does not receive the amount due to him. The Minister will then claim from the employer the net amount due from him but there is no provision in the Act requiring this to be treated as a preferential claim. The contributions of employers to the redundancy fund are included in their National Insurance Contributions and therefore enjoy the preference accorded to those contributions (see (e) below).

(d) All accrued holiday remuneration becoming payable to any clerk, servant, workman or labourer (or in the case of his death to any other person in his right) on the termination of his employment before or by the effect of the winding-up order or resolution.

The expression 'accrued holiday remuneration' includes all sums which, by virtue either of his contract of employment or of any enactment (including any order made or direction given under any Act), are payable to any person on account of the remuneration which would, in the ordinary course, have become payable to him in respect of a period of holiday had his employment with the company continued until he became entitled to be allowed the holiday.

References to remuneration in respect of a period of holiday include any sums which, if they had been paid, would have been treated for the purposes of the *National Insurance Act 1946*, or any enactment repealed by that Act as remuneration in respect of that period.

(*e*) Unless the company is being wound up voluntarily merely for the purposes of reconstruction or of amalgamation with another company, all amounts due in respect of contributions payable during the twelve months next before the relevant date by the company as the employer of any person under the National Insurance Acts. This includes amounts such as selective employment tax and payments under the *Redundancy Payments Act 1965* which are combined with contributions under the National Insurance Acts for the purpose of payment.

(*f*) Unless the company is being wound up voluntarily merely for the purposes of reconstruction or of amalgamation with another company, or unless the company has, at the commencement of the winding-up, under such a contract with insurers as is mentioned in Section 7 of the *Workmen's Compensation Act 1925*, rights capable of being transferred to and vested in the workman, all amounts due in respect of any compensation under the said Act, which have accrued before the relevant date in satisfaction of a right which arises or has arisen in respect of employment before the fifth day of July, 1948.

Where any payment has been made:

(*a*) to any clerk, servant, workman or labourer in the employment of a company, on account of wages or salary; or

(*b*) to any such clerk, servant, workman or labourer, or, in the case of his death, to any other person in his right, on account of accrued holiday remuneration;

out of money advanced by some person for that purpose, the person by whom the money was advanced has a right of priority in respect of the money so advanced and paid up to the amount by which the sum in respect of which the clerk, servant, workman or labourer, or other person in his right, would have been entitled to priority in the winding-up has been diminished by reason of the payment having been made.

This important right of subrogation which is expressed to apply as regards payments made to an employee of a company and has no application in bankruptcy proceedings may be reflected by the existence of a bank loan or overdraft which has been negotiated by the company for the express purpose of paying wages or salaries.

The foregoing debts:

(*a*) rank equally among themselves and are to be paid in full, unless the assets are insufficient to meet them, in which case they are to abate in equal proportions; and

(*b*) in the case of a company registered in England, so far as the assets of the company available for payment of general creditors are insufficient to meet them, have priority over the claims of holders of debentures under any floating charge created by the company, and be paid accordingly out of any property comprised in or subject to that charge.

Subject to the retention of such sums as may be necessary for the costs and expenses of the winding-up, the foregoing debts are to be discharged forthwith so far as the assets are sufficient to meet them, and in the case of the debts to which priority is given by paragraph (*e*) formal proof thereof is not required except in so far as is otherwise provided by general rules.

In the event of a landlord or other person distraining or having distrained on any goods or effects of the company within three months next before the date of a winding-up order, the debts to which priority is given by this section are a first charge on the goods or effects so distrained on, or the proceeds of the sale thereof; but, in respect of any money paid under any such charge, the landlord or other person has the same rights of priority as the person to whom the payment is made.

Unpaid calls on shares are treated in the Statement of Affairs as an asset at the amount they are expected to realize, the balance being entered as a loss in the Deficiency Account. The nominal amount of unpaid capital liable to be called up is not shown as an asset, but is given as a note at the foot of the Statement of Affairs.

The Deficiency Account covers a period commencing on a date not less than three years before the date of the winding-up order, or, if the company was formed within the three years, the date of formation of the company. It sets out in detail all items contributing to the deficiency (or reducing the surplus) commencing with the excess (if any) of capital and liabilities over assets (i.e. any debit balance on Profit and Loss Account) three years previously. From the total of these items is deducted the total of all items reducing the deficiency (or contributing to the surplus), and the balance represents the deficiency or surplus disclosed by the Statement of Affairs. A note is appended of the items taken into account in arriving at the amount of the net trading profits or losses shown in the account.

**Illustration**

From the following particulars prepare Statement of Affairs of the General Trading Company Limited, as at December 31st, 1970, the date of the Winding-up Order:

| | £ |
|---|---|
| Land and Premises (book value £13,000) valued at | 11,210 |
| Secured Creditors holding First Mortgage on Land and Premises | 8,090 |
| Partly Secured Creditors holding Second Mortgage on Land and Premises | 4,510 |
| Unsecured Creditors | 10,160 |
| 100 6% Mortgage Debentures of £100 each, carrying a floating charge on the assets and uncalled capital, interest payable June 30th and December 31st, paid to June 30th, 1970 | |
| Liabilities on Bills discounted | 1,400 |
| Of which it is expected to rank | 420 |
| Managing Director's Salary, owing for five months | 200 |
| Weekly Wages unpaid (4 weeks) | 140 |
| Debtors: Good | 9,265 |
| „    Doubtful, estimated to produce £980 | 2,940 |
| „    Bad | 1,750 |
| Bills Receivable: Good | 320 |
| Bank Overdraft | 26 |
| Cash in Hand | 3 |
| Stock (cost £15,000) valued at | 11,000 |
| Issued Capital: | |
| 100 Founders' Shares of £1 each, 50p called up. | |
| 15,000 Ordinary Shares of £1 each, issued as fully paid. | |
| 5,000 Preference Shares of £1 each, fully called up, on which there are Calls in arrear of £150, estimated to produce £100. | |

The debit balance on Profit and Loss Account on December 31st, 1967, was £2,200. Net losses for the three years ended December 31st, 1970, after charging £600 depreciation, £1,800 interest on debentures and £6,000 directors' fees, and crediting £50 transfer fees and profit on sale of investments £120, were £8,848.

STATEMENT AS TO THE AFFAIRS OF

### GENERAL TRADING COMPANY LIMITED

On December 31st, 1970, the Date of the Winding-up Order
showing Assets at Estimated Realizable Values and Liabilities
expected to rank

| | Estimated Realizable Values |
|---|---|
| ASSETS NOT SPECIFICALLY PLEDGED (as per List 'A') | £ |
| Balance at Bank | |
| Cash in Hand | 3 |
| Marketable Securities | |
| Bills Receivable | 320 |
| Trade Debtors | 10,245 |
| Loans and Advances | |
| Unpaid Calls | 100 |
| Stock in Trade | 11,000 |
| Work in Progress | |
| ............................... | |
| ............................... | |
| Freehold Property | |
| Leasehold Property | |
| Plant and Machinery | |
| Furniture, Fittings, Utensils etc. | |
| Patents, Trade Marks etc. | |
| Investments other than marketable securities | |
| Other property, viz.: | |
| ............................... | |
| ............................... | |
| Carried forward | £21,668 |

## GENERAL TRADING COMPANY LIMITED (*continued*)    £

Brought forward    21,668

| ASSETS SPECIFICALLY PLEDGED (as per List 'B') | (a) Estimated Realizable Values | (b) Due to Secured Creditors | (c) Deficiency ranking as Unsecured (see next page) | Surplus carried to last column |
|---|---|---|---|---|
| | £ | £ | £ | £ |
| Freehold Property    .. | 11,210 | 12,600 | 1,390 | — |
| ......................... ..    .. | | | | |
| ......................... ..    .. | | | | |
| | £11,210 | £12,600 | £1,390 | £— |

Estimated surplus from Assets specifically pledged    ..        ..        ..        —

ESTIMATED TOTAL ASSETS AVAILABLE FOR PREFERENTIAL CREDITORS, DEBENTURE HOLDERS SECURED BY A FLOATING CHARGE, AND UNSECURED CREDITORS*    21,668

| SUMMARY OF GROSS ASSETS | (d) £ |
|---|---|
| Gross realizable value of assets specifically pledged    .. | 11,210 |
| Other Assets    ..        ..        ..        ..        .. | 21,668 |
| GROSS ASSETS ..        ..        ..        ..        .. £ | 32,878 |

| (e) Gross Liabilities £ | LIABILITIES (to be deducted from surplus or added to deficiency as the case may be) | |
|---|---|---|
| 11,210 | SECURED CREDITORS (as per List 'B') to extent to which claims are estimated to be covered by Assets specifically pledged (item (a) or (b) on preceding page, whichever is the less)    ..        .. (Insert in 'Gross Liabilities' column only.) | — |
| 140 | PREFERENTIAL CREDITORS (as per List 'C')..        ..        .. | 140 |
| | Estimated balance of assets available for Debenture Holders secured by a floating charge, and Unsecured Creditors*        ..        .. £ | 21,528 |
| 10,300 | DEBENTURE HOLDERS secured by a floating charge (as per List 'D') | 10,300 |
| | Estimated SURPLUS as regards Debenture Holders* c/f ..        .. £ | 11,228 |
| 21,650 | Carried forward | |

## GENERAL TRADING COMPANY LIMITED (*continued*)

|  | | £ | £ |
|---|---|---|---|
| | Estimated Surplus as regards Debenture holders* b/f | | 11,228 |
| £21,650 | Brought forward | | |
| | UNSECURED CREDITORS (as per List 'E'): | | |
| 1,390 | Estimated unsecured balance of claims of Creditors partly secured on specific assets, brought from preceding page (*c*) .. .. .. .. | 1,390 | |
| 10,160 | Trade Accounts.. .. .. .. .. | 10,160 | |
| | Bills Payable .. .. .. .. .. | | |
| 200 | Outstanding Expenses .. .. .. .. | 200 | |
| 26 | Bank Overdraft .. .. .. .. | 26 | |
| | .. .. .. .. | | |
| | Contingent Liabilities (State nature): | | |
| 420 | Bills Discounted .. .. .. .. | 420 | |
| | | | 12,196 |
| | ESTIMATED DEFICIENCY AS REGARDS CREDITORS* | £ | |
| | being difference between: | | |
| | GROSS ASSETS brought from preceding page (*d*) .. | 32,878 | |
| | and GROSS LIABILITIES as per column (*e*) .. | 33,846 | |
| £33,846 | | | 968 |
| | ISSUED AND CALLED-UP CAPITAL | £ | |
| | 5,000 preference shares of £1 each.. .. .. | 5,000 | |
| | £1 called-up (as per List 'F') .. .. .. | | |
| | 15,000 ordinary shares of £1 each .. .. .. | 15,000 | |
| | £1 called-up (as per List 'G') .. .. .. | | |
| | 100 founders' shares of £1 each .. .. .. | | |
| | 50*p* called-up .. .. .. .. .. | 50 | |
| | | | 20,050 |
| | ESTIMATED DEFICIENCY AS REGARDS MEMBERS* | | |
| | (as per List 'H').. .. .. .. .. | £ | 21,018 |

*These figures must be read subject to the following notes:

1. (*f*) There is no unpaid capital liable to be called up *or*

   (*g*) The nominal amount of unpaid capital liable to be called-up is £50, estimated to produce £50, which is charged in favour of Debenture Holders.     Strike out (*f*) *or* (*g*)

2. The estimates are subject to costs of the winding-up and to any surplus or deficiency on trading pending realization of the Assets.

## LIST 'H' – DEFICIENCY OR SURPLUS ACCOUNT

The period covered by this Account must commence on a date not less than three years before the date of the winding-up order (or the date directed by the official receiver) or, if the company has not been incorporated for the whole of that period, the date of formation of the company, unless the official receiver otherwise agrees.

## LIST 'H' – DEFICIENCY OR SURPLUS ACCOUNT (*continued*)

| ITEMS CONTRIBUTING TO DEFICIENCY (OR REDUCING SURPLUS): | | £ |
|---|---|---|
| 1. Excess (if any) of Capital and Liabilities over Assets on December 31st, 1967, as shown by Balance Sheet (copy annexed) .. .. .. | | 2,200 |
| 2. Net dividends and bonuses declared during the period from December 31st, 1967, to the date of the Statement .. .. .. | | — |
| 3. Net trading losses (after charging items shown in note below) for the same period .. .. .. .. .. .. .. | | 9,018 |
| 4. Losses other than trading losses written off or for which provision has been made in the books during the same period (give particulars or annex schedule) .. .. .. .. .. .. | | — |
| 5. Estimated losses now written off or for which provision has been made for the purpose of preparing the Statement (give particulars or annex schedule) [see page 566] .. .. .. .. .. | | 9,970 |
| 6. Other items contributing to Deficiency or reducing Surplus: ..................................................... .. .. | | — |
| | | 21,188 |
| ITEMS REDUCING DEFICIENCY (OR CONTRIBUTING TO SURPLUS): | £ | |
| 7. Excess (if any) of Assets over Capital and Liabilities on December 31st, 1967, as shown on the Balance Sheet (copy annexed) | — | |
| 8. Net trading profits (after charging items shown in note below) for the period from December 31st, 1967, to the date of the Statement .. .. .. .. .. .. | — | |
| 9. Profits and income other than trading profits during the same period – Transfer Fees .. .. .. .. | 50 | |
| Profit on Sales of Investments .. .. | 120 | |
| 10. Other items reducing Deficiency or contributing to Surplus........... | — 170 | 170 |
| | — | — |
| DEFICIENCY as shown by Statement .. .. .. | | £21,018 |

NOTE AS TO NET TRADING PROFITS AND LOSSES:

Particulars are to be inserted here (so far as applicable) of the items mentioned below, which are to be taken into account in arriving at the amount of net trading profits or losses shown in this Account:

| | £ |
|---|---|
| Provisions for depreciation, renewals, or diminution in value of fixed assets .. .. .. .. .. | 600 |
| Charges for United Kingdom income tax and other United Kingdom taxation on profits .. .. .. .. .. | — |
| Interest on debentures and other fixed loans .. .. .. | 1,800 |
| Payments to directors made by the company and required by law to be disclosed in the accounts .. .. .. .. | 6,000 |
| Exceptional or non-recurring expenditure: ............................................ .. | — |
| *Less* Exceptional or non-recurring receipts: ........................................ .. | 8,400 |
| | — |
| | 8,400 |
| Balance, being other trading profits or losses .. .. .. | 618 |
| Net trading profits or losses as shown in Deficiency or Surplus Account above .. .. .. .. .. .. | £9,018 |

Signature                              Dated January 14th, 1971

*Schedule of Losses now written off*

| | | | | |
|---|---|---|---|---|
| Land and Buildings | .. | .. | £1,790 |
| Stock .. | .. | .. | .. | 4,000 |
| Book Debts | .. | .. | .. | 3,710 |
| Calls .. | .. | .. | .. | 50 |
| Bills discounted .. | .. | .. | 420 |
| | | | £9,970 |

## § 7. The Accounts of a Liquidator in Compulsory Liquidation

These accounts are similar to those of a trustee in bankruptcy. The liquidator must keep a cash book in the prescribed form (see Appendix III E), containing columns for every class of receipt and payment.

At the expiration of six months from the date of the winding-up order, and every succeeding six months until his release, the liquidator must send to the Board of Trade a copy of the cash book for such period in duplicate, together with the necessary vouchers, and copies of the certificate of audit of the committee of inspection.

If the liquidator carries on business for the company, he must keep a Trading Account, recording simply the cash receipts and payments. This account must be kept in the prescribed form, and the weekly totals of receipts and payments on Trading Account must be incorporated in the cash book.

The liquidator must transmit to the Board of Trade with his accounts a summary thereof in the prescribed form, copies of which are sent out to creditors and contributories.

At the date of application by the liquidator for release, he must prepare a summarized statement of receipts and payments in the prescribed form, showing the position of the company at that date.

## § 8. The Accounts of a Liquidator in Voluntary Liquidation

Where it is proposed to wind-up a company voluntarily, the directors (or a majority if there are more than two) may make a statutory declaration that they have made a full enquiry into the affairs of the company and have formed the opinion that the company will be able to pay its debts in full within such period, not exceeding twelve months, from the commencement of the winding-up as is stated in the declaration. Such a statement, to be effective, must be made within the five weeks preceding the date of the passing of the resolution for winding-up and be filed with the Registrar of Companies before that date, and must embody a statement of the company's assets and liabilities at the latest practicable date prior to the declaration. The winding-up will then be a 'members' voluntary winding-up'; if the declaration is not made, it will be 'a creditors' voluntary winding-up'. There are heavy penalties for making such a declaration without reasonable grounds; if the company does not pay or provide for its debts in full within the period stated in the declaration, it will be presumed that the directors did not have reasonable grounds for that opinion, unless the contrary is shown (s. 283, *Companies Act 1948*).

The statement of assets and liabilities must be in the following form:

Statement as at...................................................................19................ showing Assets at estimated realizable values and Liabilities expected to rank

| Assets and Liabilities | Estimated to realize or to rank for payment (to nearest £) |
|---|---|
| ASSETS: | £ |
| Balance at Bank .. .. .. .. .. .. .. | |
| Cash at Bank .. .. .. .. .. .. .. | |
| Cash in Hand .. .. .. .. .. .. | |
| Marketable Securities .. .. .. .. .. .. | |
| Bills Receivable .. .. .. .. .. .. .. | |
| Trade Debtors .. .. .. .. .. .. .. | |
| Loans and Advances .. .. .. .. .. .. | |
| Unpaid Calls .. .. .. .. .. .. .. | |
| Stock in Trade .. .. .. .. .. .. | |
| Work in Progress.. .. .. .. .. .. | |
| .......................................... .. .. .. .. .. | |
| Freehold Property .. .. .. .. .. .. | |
| Leasehold Property .. .. .. .. .. .. | |
| Plant and Machinery .. .. .. .. .. | |
| Furniture, Fittings, Utensils etc. .. .. .. .. .. | |
| Patents, Trade Marks etc. .. .. .. .. .. | |
| Investments other than marketable securities .. .. | |
| Other property, viz.: | |
| .......................................... .. .. .. .. | |
| Estimated realizable value of Assets.. .. .. | £ |
| LIABILITIES: | |
| Secured on specific assets, viz.: £ | |
| .......................................... .. .. .. .. | |
| Secured by Floating Charge(s) .. .. .. | |
| Estimated Costs of Liquidation and other expenses including interest accruing until payment of debts in full .. .. .. .. .. | |
| Unsecured Creditors (amounts estimated to rank for payment): £ | |
|   Trade Accounts .. .. .. | |
|   Bills Payable .. .. .. | |
|   Accrued Expenses .. .. .. | |
|   Other Liabilities: | |
|   .......................................... .. .. .. | |
|   Contingent Liabilities: | |
|   .......................................... .. .. .. | |
| Estimated Surplus after paying Debts in full .. .. .. .. £ | |
| *Remarks:* | |

It will be noted that it is not necessary to show preferential creditors separately because where all creditors are to be paid in full no question of preference arises. The statement also differs in principle from other forms of Statements of Affairs in that it is necessary to provide in it for the costs and expenses that are expected to be incurred.

If the liquidator is at any time of opinion that the company will not be able to pay its debts in full within the period stated in the above mentioned declaration, he must forthwith summon a meeting of creditors and lay before it a statement of the assets and liabilities in a form identical to that of the Statement of Affairs shown on pages 562-66 except that the date as at which the assets and liabilities are stated is left open, since the liquidator may have been continuing the company's business and have fresh assets and liabilities to disclose (*Companies Act 1948*, Section 288).

In a creditors' voluntary winding-up, the company must summon a meeting of creditors for the day, or the day next following the day on which the resolution for winding-up is proposed to be passed. The directors must lay before that meeting a full statement of the company's affairs and a list of the creditors and their estimated claims (Section 293, *Companies Act 1948*). No form of statement is laid down, but it can conveniently follow that shown on pages 562-66.

In any voluntary winding-up, the liquidator is required to keep an account of his receipts and payments.

If the liquidation continues for more than one year, the liquidator must summon a general meeting of the company at the end of the first year (unless a meeting under Section 288 of the *Companies Act 1948* was held within three months before the end of that year), and of each succeeding year from the commencement of the winding-up, or as soon thereafter as may be convenient, and lay before the meeting an account of his receipts and payments.

When the liquidation is finally completed, a general meeting must be summoned by the liquidator, and an account laid before it showing the way in which the property of the company has been disposed of.

The account must be in the prescribed form (see Appendix III F).

Returns to the Registrar under Section 342, *Companies Act 1948*, in the prescribed form (see Appendix III G) must be made by the liquidator if the winding-up is not completed within one year.

**Illustration**

The X Company Limited went into voluntary liquidation on December 31st, 1969, with preferential creditors £408, other unsecured creditors £3,750, and 6 per cent. debentures £4,000, secured by a floating charge on the undertaking, the interest on which was paid to June 30th, 1969.

The assets realized £7,255, being £4,200 from sale of stock, £3,030 from books debts and £25 cash in hand at the commencement of liquidation. The debentures were paid off on June 30th, 1970, and a first and final dividend distributed to creditors. Cost of liquidation amounted to £95.

Prepare the liquidator's final Statement of Account for presentation to the shareholders, his remuneration being at the rate of 3 per cent. on the amount realized and 2 per cent. on the amount distributed to unsecured creditors. Ignore income tax.

## THE X COMPANY, LIMITED (IN LIQUIDATION)
## LIQUIDATOR'S STATEMENT OF ACCOUNT

| RECEIPTS | | | | £ | £ | PAYMENTS | | £ | £ |
|---|---|---|---|---|---|---|---|---|---|
| Realization of Assets: | | | | | | Costs .. .. .. .. | | | 95 |
| Cash .. | .. | .. | .. | 25 | | Liquidator's Remuneration: | | | |
| Stock .. | .. | .. | .. | 4,200 | | 3% on £7,230 realized .. | .. | 217 | |
| Book Debts | .. | .. | .. | 3,030 | | 2% on £2,250 distributed | .. | 45 | |
| | | | | | 7,255 | | | | 262 |
| | | | | | | Preferential Creditors | .. | | 408 |
| | | | | | | Debenture-holders | .. | 4,000 | |
| | | | | | | Interest to date of payment | .. | 240 | |
| | | | | | | | | | 4,240 |
| | | | | | | Unsecured Creditors: | | | |
| | | | | | | First and Final Dividend of 60p | | | |
| | | | | | | in the £ on £3,750 .. | .. | | 2,250 |
| | | | | | £7,255 | | | | £7,255 |

*Note:* The first part of the liquidator's remuneration will be calculated on the amounts *realized* by him. He will not, therefore, be entitled to any percentage on the cash in hand at the commencement of the liquidation. His remuneration will, however, be calculated on the *gross* amounts realized before deducting expenses.

Rule 159 of the Winding-Up Rules, which applies only to a winding-up by the court, provides that this percentage shall be on the amount realized 'after deducting the sums (if any) paid to secured creditors (other than debenture holders) out of the proceeds of their securities'.

Applying this principle to this example, the liquidator will be entitled to remuneration on the full £7,230, before deducting the amounts paid to the debenture holders.

The second portion of the liquidator's remuneration is computed on the amount distributed to unsecured creditors.

The cash to be divided between the liquidator and the unsecured creditors amounts to £2,295. Since the commission is to be 2 per cent. on the amount distributed (i.e. *after* deducting such commission), it will be equal to $\frac{2}{102}$ of £2,295, viz. £45, leaving £2,250 (equivalent to a dividend of 60p in the £) available for the unsecured creditors.

## § 9. Return to Shareholders

In the event of some shares being fully paid up and others only partly paid up, it will become necessary for the liquidator to adjust the rights of the contributories between themselves, and this may involve the making of a call on those shareholders whose shares are only partly paid up. It is essential that the amounts finally contributed by shareholders in any one class should be equal as between themselves.

If a surplus remains after all costs and liabilities have been discharged, this must be distributed between the shareholders according to their rights under the Memorandum and Articles of Association.

Shares which are entitled to priority as to repayment of capital should be paid off first (if necessary out of the proceeds of a call made on shares of an inferior degree); if a surplus remains after all the shareholders have received the nominal amount of their shares, it would appear from the decision of the House of Lords in *Scottish Insurance Corporation Ltd* v. *Wilsons and Clyde Coal Co Ltd* (1949), which overruled the previous decision in *Re William Metcalfe & Sons Ltd* that unless, on a true construction of the Articles, the preference shareholders are entitled to share in such surplus, it belongs to the ordinary shareholders. If the Articles give the preference shareholders the right to priority as to the return of capital, the presumption is that they are not entitled to any further share in the assets.

In regard to any arrears of preference dividend, the basic rule is that in the absence of some provision in the Articles to the contrary preference share-holders have no right to arrears of dividend unless declared before the commence-ment of the winding-up (*Re Crichton's Oil Co Ltd* (1902), 2 Ch. 86). It would seem, however, that any indication that the shares are to be preferential as to dividend on a winding-up may be sufficient to exclude this rule. In *Re E. W. Savory Ltd* (1951), 2 All E.R. 1036, where the Articles stated that the preference shares '. . . shall confer on the holders the right to a fixed cumulative preference dividend at the rate of 6 per cent. per annum on the capital paid up thereon and shall rank both as regards dividends and capital in priority to all other shares, both present and future' it was held that the preference shareholders were entitled to arrears of dividend on winding-up although no dividends had been declared. The arrears are calculated up to the commencement of the winding-up and not to the date of repayment of capital. Income tax is not deductible from arrears of preference dividends payable in a winding-up (*Re Dominion Tar and Chemical Co Ltd* (1929), 2 Ch. 387).

**Illustration (1)**

The capital of The Motor Company Limited (in voluntary liquidation), consists of:

2,000 Preference Shares of £5 each, fully paid up.

8,000 Ordinary Shares of £5 each, fully paid up.

6,000 Ordinary Shares of £5 each, £4 per share paid up.

2,000 Deferred Shares of £5 each, £4 per share paid up.

Under the Articles of Association, the preference shares have priority as to repayment of capital over the ordinary shares, and the ordinary shares priority over the deferred shares.

The costs of liquidation, including the liquidator's remuneration, amounted to £700, and the creditors to £8,900.

The assets realized £18,700. The call made by the liquidator on the deferred shareholders for the adjustment of the rights of shareholders *inter se* was fully paid. A call of 50p per share was made on the partly-paid ordinary shareholders, which was duly paid, with the exception of that on 200 Shares, which was irrecoverable.

Prepare the liquidator's final Statement of Account.

### THE MOTOR COMPANY, LIMITED (IN LIQUIDATION)
### LIQUIDATOR'S FINAL STATEMENT OF ACCOUNT

| | £ | £ | | £ | £ |
|---|---|---|---|---|---|
| Realization of Assets .. .. | | 18,700 | Costs of Liquidation .. .. | | 700 |
| Proceeds of Call of £1 per Share on 2,000 Deferred Shares of £5 each .. | | 2,000 | Creditors paid in full .. .. | | 8,900 |
| Call of 50p per Share on 6,000 Ordinary Shares of £5 each, to make them £4·50 paid .. .. | 3,000 | | Return to Shareholders: £5 per Share on 2,000 Preference Shares of £5 each, being return in full .. .. | 10,000 | |
| *Less* Call unpaid on 200 Shares .. | 100 | | 50p per Share on 8,000 Ordinary Shares of £5 each, leaving £4·50 per Share paid .. .. | 4,000 | |
| | | 2,900 | | | 14,000 |
| | | £23,600 | | | £23,600 |

*Notes:*

1. The 200 shares in respect of which the call is irrecoverable will be forfeited.

2. The call from the holders of the partly paid ordinary shares makes the partly paid shares £4·50 paid, and the proceeds must be applied in payment of 50p per share to holders of fully-paid ordinary shares, which leaves all the ordinary shares £4·50 paid.

There would be no point in calling up 75p per share on the partly paid shares and then repaying 25p. The effect is obtained by merely calling up 50p per share.

### Illustration (2)

A company having the following issued share capital went into voluntary liquidation:

   40,000 6 per cent. preference shares of £1 each, 75p paid.
   500,000 ordinary shares of 40p each, 15p paid.

The Articles gave the preference shareholders a preferential right to dividends, but were silent as to repayment of capital.

The assets were realized, and the liquidator's expenses and remuneration and the preferential creditors paid. It was then found that the remaining balance was insufficient by the sum of £3,000 to pay the unsecured creditors.

Advise the liquidator as to his procedure in raising calls on the members.

---

The liquidator should be advised as follows:

The shareholders will all rank *pari passu*, and it will therefore be necessary to call up on some and repay on others. Care must be taken to compute the exact amounts in each case, since it would be inexpedient to make unnecessary calls on members entitled to a repayment.

Ascertain first what would be available if all the uncalled capital were called up. This would produce:

|  | £ |
|---|---|
| 25p per share on 40,000 £1 preference shares .. .. .. .. | 10,000 |
| 25p ,, ,, ,, 500,000 40p ordinary shares .. .. .. .. | 125,000 |
|  | 135,000 |
| Deduct amount to meet balance of creditors .. .. .. | 3,000 |
| Leaving available for repayment to members .. .. .. | £132,000 |

The paid-up capital would then be:

|  | £ |
|---|---|
| 40,000 £1 preference shares .. .. .. .. .. .. | 40,000 |
| 500,000 40p ordinary shares .. .. .. .. .. .. | 200,000 |
|  | £240,000 |

The amount available would make possible a repayment of $\frac{132,000}{240,000}$ in the £ on the whole capital, or 55 per cent.

This amounts to 55p per preference share, and 22p per ordinary share.

There would be no point, however, in calling up 25p per preference share and repaying 55p per share, so no call would be made on these shares, the net balance of 30p being repaid. Similarly, instead of calling up 25p per ordinary share, and repaying 22p per share, a net call of 3p per share would be made.

The final advice therefore would be:

|  |  | £ |
|---|---|---|
| Call up 3p per share on 500,000 ordinary shares, producing .. .. | | £15,000 |
| Pay balance of liabilities .. .. .. .. .. | 3,000 | |
| Repay 30p per share on 40,000 preference shares .. .. | 12,000 | |
|  |  | £15,000 |

In practice, of course, provision would have to be made for any calls not expected to be received. An adjustment of the call can be made on this account.

## § 10. The Accounts of a Receiver

Where a receiver or manager of the whole or substantially the whole of the property of a company is appointed on behalf of any debentures secured by a floating charge, he must forthwith send notice to the company of his appointment, and there shall, within fourteen days after receipt of the notice, or such longer period as may be allowed by the court or by the receiver, be made out and submitted to the receiver a statement in the prescribed form as to the affairs of the company. The prescribed form is similar in all respects to that used in a compulsory winding-up, and shown on pages 562-66 except that the relevant date is the date of the appointment of the receiver (s. 372 (1)).

The accounts of a receiver appointed by the court take the form of a record of his receipts and payments, supported by vouchers, and made out in the prescribed manner. The accounts must be verified by affidavit, and will be passed periodically as directed by the order appointing the receiver.

A receiver of the whole of a company's property appointed on behalf of debenture holders secured by a floating charge must within two months, or such longer period as the court may allow after the expiration of twelve months from the date of his appointment, and of every subsequent twelve months, and within two months or such longer period as the court may allow after he ceases to act as receiver or manager of the property of the company, send to the Registrar of Companies, to any trustees of the debenture holders on whose behalf he was appointed, to the company and (so far as he is aware of their addresses) to all such debenture holders, an abstract in the prescribed form of his receipts and payments during the period of twelve months or, where he ceases to act, during the period from the end of the period to which the last preceding abstract related up to the date of his so ceasing, and the aggregate amounts of his receipts and payments during all preceding periods since his appointment.

Where the receiver is appointed under the powers contained in any instrument, for references in the preceding paragraph to the court, references to the Board of Trade should be substituted.

Where the receiver is appointed under the powers contained in any instrument and is not a receiver of the whole or substantially the whole of the property of the company under a floating charge, the only requirement is that abstracts must be sent to the Registrar within one month of the receiver's appointment, and thereafter at intervals of six months, and within one month after the receiver ceases to act. This applies to receivers appointed out of court under a fixed charge.

Every receiver or manager who makes default in complying with the provisions of this section is liable to a fine not exceeding £5 for every day during which the default continues.

### Illustration

On March 31st, 1970, a receiver was appointed by the debenture-holders of X Ltd under powers in the instrument, which gave a floating charge.

A resolution to wind up the company voluntarily was passed on April 30th, 1970, when a liquidator was appointed.

The following is a summary of the company's position as on March 31st, 1970:

| | £ | £ | | | | | | £ |
|---|---|---|---|---|---|---|---|---|
| 20,000 6 per cent. Cumulative Preference shares of £1 each, fully paid .. | | 20,000 | Fixed assets .. .. .. .. | | | | | 77,500 |
| 100,000 Ordinary shares of £1 each, 80p called up .. .. .. | 80,000 | | Stocks.. .. .. .. .. | | | | | 61,230 |
| Less Call in arrear – 20p a share on 5,000 shares.. .. .. | 1,000 | | Debtors .. .. .. | | | | | 21,365 |
| | | 79,000 | Profit and Loss Account .. | | | | | 59,150 |
| Capital reserve .. .. .. | | 8,000 | | | | | | |
| 5 per cent. Debentures .. .. | 20,000 | | | | | | | |
| Interest accrued – net .. .. | 375 | | | | | | | |
| | | 20,375 | | | | | | |
| Bank loan, at 10 per cent. per annum including interest to date .. | | 8,725 | | | | | | |
| (£10,000 Debentures ranking with the above were deposited with the bank as collateral security) | | | | | | | | |
| Creditors .. .. .. | | 83,145 | | | | | | |
| | | £219,245 | | | | | | £219,245 |

| | £ | £ |
|---|---|---|
| Creditors comprised the following: | | |
| 1. Local rates due and payable on April 1st, 1969, £150 and on October 1st, 1969, £150 .. .. .. | | 300 |
| 2. Purchase tax due on March 31st, 1969, £230; due for year to date, £130 .. .. .. | | 360 |
| 3. Managing director's remuneration for three months to date .. .. .. .. .. | | 1,200 |
| 4. Directors' fees for year to date .. .. .. .. .. .. | | 3,000 |
| 5. Commissioners of Inland Revenue: | | |
| Income tax deducted from payments not made out of taxed profits: | | |
| 1968-69 .. .. .. .. .. .. .. .. | 500 | |
| 1969-70 .. .. .. .. .. .. .. .. | 500 | |
| In respect of tax deductible from debenture interest accrued for nine months to March 31st, 1970 | 375 | |
| | | 1,375 |
| 6. Loan by director to enable salaries for the month of March, 1970 to be paid .. .. .. | | 2,600 |
| 7. Trade creditors .. .. .. .. .. .. .. .. .. | | 74,310 |
| | | £83,145 |

The receiver collected £12,490 from debtors and sold for £30,792 stock which had been valued at £36,253. His expenses and remuneration amounted to £2,778. On June 30th, 1970, he made all his obligatory payments and transferred to the liquidator the balance of cash in his hands.

The liquidator realized £42,886 from the fixed assets and £22,339 from the remaining stocks and collected the rest of the book debts which were all good.

He called up the uncalled capital and the call was met by all the members except the one who owed £1,000 for calls in arrear and could not be traced.

The liquidator made his distribution on August 31st, 1970. His expenses amounted to £299 and his remuneration was fixed at a sum equal to 2 per cent. on the amount realized by him (excluding the cash transferred to him by the receiver) and 1 per cent. on the amount he distributed to unsecured creditors and contributories.

The company's Articles provided that the preference capital, together with any arrears of dividend to the date of winding-up, should rank in priority to the ordinary capital. No preference dividend had been paid since that in respect of the year ended June 30th, 1968.

Prepare the Receipts and Payments Accounts of the Receiver and Liquidator respectively, showing the payments in order of priority.

For the purposes of this illustration, the standard rate of income tax is to be assumed to be 50p in the £.

## RECEIVER'S RECEIPTS AND PAYMENTS ACCOUNT

| | £ | | £ | £ |
|---|---|---|---|---|
| Realizations: | | Receiver's expenses and remuneration | | 2,778 |
| Debtors | 12,490 | Preferential creditors: | | |
| Stock | 30,792 | Rates | 300 | |
| | | Purchase tax (due for year to date) | 130 | |
| | | Income tax, 1968-69 | 500 | |
| | | Loan by director for payment of wages | 2,600 | |
| | | | | 3,530 |
| | | 5 per cent. Debentures | 20,000 | |
| | | Interest thereon for 1 year to June 30th, 1970 | 1,000 | |
| | | | | 21,000 |
| | | 10 per cent. Bank Loan | 8,725 | |
| | | Interest thereon for 3 months to June 30th, 1970 | 218 | |
| | | | | 8,943 |
| | | Balance transferred to liquidator | | 7,031 |
| | £43,282 | | | £43,282 |

## LIQUIDATOR'S RECEIPTS AND PAYMENTS ACCOUNT

| | £ | £ | | £ | £ |
|---|---|---|---|---|---|
| Transfer from Receiver | | 7,031 | Liquidator's Expenses | | 299 |
| Realizations: | | | Liquidator's Remuneration: | | |
| Fixed Assets | 42,886 | | 2 per cent. on £93,100 | 1,862 | |
| Stock | 22,339 | | 1 per cent. on £97,000 | 970 | |
| Debtors | 8,875 | | | | 2,832 |
| Calls – 20p a share on 95,000 Ordinary Shares | 19,000 | | Unsecured Creditors: | | |
| | | 93,100 | Purchase tax (due March 31st, 1969) | 230 | |
| | | | Directors' Remuneration | 3,000 | |
| | | | Managing Director's Remuneration | 1,200 | |
| | | | Income tax, 1969-70 | 500 | |
| | | | Trade Creditors | 74,310 | |
| | | | | | 79,240 |
| | | | Preference Shareholders (80 per cent. on £22,200) | | 17,760 |
| | | £100,131 | | | £100,131 |

*Notes:*

1. The preferential creditors payable in priority to debentures carrying a floating charge are:

(*a*) local rates which have become due and payable within one year before the relevant date;

(*b*) income tax assessed on the company for a year ending not later than April 5th, next, before the relevant date;

(*c*) purchase tax due within the twelve months prior to the relevant date;

(*d*) salaries for one month. (The director who has advanced money for the payment of salaries is entitled to the same priority as the employees to whom the payments are made.)

The relevant date is the date of the appointment of the Receiver, March 31st, 1970.

2. The Receiver will pay the interest on the debentures under deduction of tax and account to the Revenue for the tax deducted. The Revenue is not a creditor of the company for tax deductible from interest until the interest is paid and the tax deducted.

3. The amount due to the preference shareholders is:

| | £ |
|---|---|
| Share capital | 20,000 |
| Arrears of dividend – 6 per cent. per annum for 22 months (gross) | 2,200 |
| | £22,200 |

Arrears of preference dividend are payable up to the commencement of the winding-up (April 30th, 1970). Income tax is not deductible from arrears of preference dividend paid in a winding-up (*Re Dominion Tar and Chemical Co Ltd*).

## CHAPTER XIII

# MISCELLANEOUS ACCOUNTS

## § 1. Hire-purchase Agreements, Agreements to pay by Instalments and Rental Agreements

Under a hire-purchase agreement the owner of goods leases them to a person, called the hirer, on the terms that the hirer shall pay to the owner a number of instalments, until a price has been paid, when the ownership of the goods will either pass automatically to the hirer, or he may exercise an option to purchase them by the payment of a stated small sum. Thus the property in the goods does not pass to the hirer until he has paid the last instalment or exercised his option to purchase. The *Hire-Purchase Act 1965* applies to such an agreement where the total purchase price does not exceed £2,000. Under that Act the owner cannot obtain repossession of the goods, after one-third of the hire-purchase price has been paid, unless he obtains a Court Order. Otherwise the owner may repossess himself of the goods if the hirer fails to pay an instalment.

The *Hire-Purchase Act 1965* does not apply where the hirer or buyer is a body corporate. Subject to this, certain provisions of the Act also apply to credit-sale agreements.

In a credit-sale agreement, i.e. an agreement for sale under which the price is to be paid by five or more instalments, the property in the goods passes to the buyer immediately on delivery, and, in the event of default by the buyer, the seller's only remedy is to sue for the unpaid instalments; he cannot recover the goods. Even if the contract forbids the buyer to sell the goods until the price has been paid, a purchaser in good faith from the original buyer gets a good title to the goods and is not liable to the original seller (*Sale of Goods Act 1893*, Section 25).

By a rental agreement, a customer agrees to hire goods for a period of time. The goods remain the property of the supplier, unless, during or at the end of the period of hire, he negotiates their sale. The *Hire-Purchase Act 1965* does not apply.

### (a) Hire-purchase Agreements

There is no universal method of recording hire-purchase transactions. Although legally, since the goods should be treated as continuing to belong to the vendor until all the instalments have been paid, until that time the buyer should treat the instalments paid as payments for the option to purchase, except that the portion of each payment, representing the interest or finance charge, would be written off to Profit and Loss Account in the period to which it relates.

However, this strictly legal position is seldom maintained; goods on hire-purchase are usually treated as assets as soon as delivery is taken.

From the point of view of the vendor, it might be considered that no profit

575

on the transaction has been earned until all the instalments have been paid, or alternatively that credit should only be taken in each accounting period for the profit included in the instalments that have been received, the instalments not yet due being treated as stock-in-trade and brought into account at a proportionate part of the cost of the goods.

Some hire-purchase vendors make no distinction between hire-purchase and ordinary trade sales, but take credit for the whole profit in the period in which delivery is made, treating the outstanding instalments as 'debtors'.

Again, there are various ways of fixing the hire-purchase price. In some cases a stated rate of interest is added to that reducing balance of the cash price, which has been outstanding since an instalment was last paid; the instalments discharge the interest and part of the principal, until the whole debt is cleared.

In others no specific rate of interest is charged, but a fixed sum, called a 'finance charge' or 'credit charge' is added to the cash price of the goods at the outset, and the total amount is then discharged by an agreed number of instalments.

Set out below are various methods any of which can be adapted to fit the circumstances of the case.

BUYER'S BOOKS

*Method 1:*

(a) Debit the Asset Account and credit the Vendor with the cash price.

(b) (i) Debit the Vendor and credit Cash, with any deposit paid.

　　(ii) On an instalment being paid, debit the Vendor and credit Cash with the payment.

(c) At the end of the accounting period, apportion the hire-purchase interest by one of the recommended methods (see page 582); debit Interest Payable Account and credit the Vendor, with interest for the period.

(d) Debit Profit and Loss Account and credit Interest Payable Account, with balance on the latter account.

In the Balance Sheet, the asset will appear at full cash price, less any provision for depreciation; from the start, depreciation must be computed on the full amount of the cash price, not just on the payments made.

The balance on the Vendor's Account will represent the instalments not yet paid, less any interest apportioned to later accounting periods. This balance can either be deducted from the cost price of the asset or, preferably, included under current liabilities.

If any instalments which are not yet paid are overdue, they must appear in the balance sheet as current liabilities, being distinguished by an appropriate description from the remainder of the Vendor's Account.

To summarize:

The double entry for Method 1 is:

| Debit | Credit | With |
|-------|--------|------|
| (a) Asset | Hire Vendor | The cash purchase price (excluding interest) |
| (b) Hire Vendor | Cash | Deposits and Instalments paid. |
| (c) Interest Payable | Hire Vendor | Hire-purchase interest apportioned to the accounting period |
| (d) Profit and Loss Account | Interest Payable | Balance on Interest Payable Account |

**Illustration (1)**

On January 1st, 1968, Hawkins acquired a car under a two year hire-purchase agreement requiring an immediate deposit of £400, and four half-yearly instalments of £400 commencing July 1st, 1968, the cash price was £1,886; Hawkins prepared his accounts annually on September 30th and apportioned the finance charge of £114 to the years ended September 30th, 1968, £62; 1969, £46; 1970, £6.

### MOTOR CAR ACCOUNT

| 1968 | | £ | | | |
|------|--|---|--|--|--|
| Jan. 1 | Hire Vendor .. .. .. | 1,886 | | | |

### HIRE VENDOR ACCOUNT

| 1968 | | £ | 1968 | | £ |
|------|--|---|------|--|---|
| Jan. 1 | Cash .. .. .. .. | 400 | Jan. 1 | Motor Car .. .. .. | 1,886 |
| July 1 | Cash .. .. .. .. | 400 | Sept. 30 | Hire-purchase Interest .. .. | 62 |
| Sept. 30 | Balance carried down .. .. | 1,148 | | | |
| | | £1,948 | | | £1,948 |
| 1969 | | | 1968 | | |
| Jan. 1 | Cash .. .. .. .. | 400 | Oct. 1 | Balance brought down .. .. | 1,148 |
| July 1 | Cash .. .. .. .. | 400 | 1969 | | |
| Sept. 30 | Balance carried down .. .. | 394 | Sept. 30 | Hire-purchase Interest .. .. | 46 |
| | | £1,194 | | | £1,194 |
| 1970 | | | 1969 | | |
| 1 Jan. | Cash .. .. .. .. | 400 | Oct. 1 | Balance brought down .. .. | 394 |
| | | | 1970 | | |
| | | | Sept. 30 | Hire-purchase Interest .. .. | 6 |
| | | £400 | | | £400 |

## INTEREST PAYABLE ACCOUNT

| 1968 Sept. 30 | Hire-purchase Interest | .. | .. | £ 62 | 1968 Sept. 30 | Profit and Loss Account .. | .. | £ 62 |
|---|---|---|---|---|---|---|---|---|
| 1969 Sept. 30 | Hire-purchase Interest | .. | .. | 46 | 1969 Sept. 30 | Profit and Loss Account .. | .. | 46 |
| 1970 Sept. 30 | Hire-purchase Interest | .. | .. | 6 | 1970 Sept. 30 | Profit and Loss Account .. | .. | 6 |

*Method 2:*

An alternative method of recording the transactions is to credit the Vendor at the outset with the full hire-purchase price, debiting the cash price to the Asset Account and the finance charge to a Hire-purchase Interest Suspense Account; this is an Expense Account, but not all the expense is chargeable in the current accounting period. At the end of each accounting period the interest apportioned to that period is transferred from the Interest Suspense Account to the Profit and Loss Account.

The balance on the Vendor's Account will represent all the instalments not yet paid; the balance on the Hire-purchase Interest Suspense Account will represent the interest apportioned to later accounting periods; this must be deducted from the balance on the Vendor's Account, to show the current liability.

The double entry for Method 2 is:

| *Debit* | *Credit* | *With* |
|---|---|---|
| Asset | Hire Vendor | The cash purchase price (excluding interest) |
| Hire Vendor | Cash | Deposits and Instalments paid |
| Hire-purchase Interest Suspense | Hire Vendor | Total finance charge |
| Profit and Loss Account | Hire-purchase Interest Suspense | Hire-purchase interest apportioned to the accounting period |

**Illustration (2)**

Facts as in Illustration (1):

### MOTOR CAR ACCOUNT

| 1968 Jan. 1 | Hire Vendor | .. | .. | .. | £ 1,886 | | |
|---|---|---|---|---|---|---|---|

## HIRE VENDOR ACCOUNT

| 1968 | | £ | 1968 | | £ |
|---|---|---|---|---|---|
| Jan. 1 | Cash .. .. .. .. | 400 | Jan. 1 | Motor Car .. .. .. | 1,886 |
| July 1 | Cash .. .. .. .. | 400 | ,, | Hire-purchase Interest Suspense .. | 114 |
| Sept. 30 | Balance carried down .. .. | 1,200 | | | |
| | | £2,000 | | | £2,000 |
| 1969 | | | 1968 | | |
| Jan. 1 | Cash .. .. .. .. | 400 | Oct. 1 | Balance brought down .. .. | 1,200 |
| July 1 | Cash .. .. .. .. | 400 | | | |
| Sept. 30 | Balance carried down .. .. | 400 | | | |
| | | £1,200 | | | £1,200 |
| 1970 | | | 1969 | | |
| Jan. 1 | Cash .. .. .. .. | £400 | Oct. 1 | Balance brought down .. .. | £400 |

## HIRE-PURCHASE INTEREST SUSPENSE ACCOUNT

| 1968 | | £ | 1968 | | £ |
|---|---|---|---|---|---|
| Jan. 1 | Hire Vendor .. .. .. | 114 | Sept. 30 | Profit and Loss Account .. .. | 62 |
| | | | ,, | Balance carried down .. .. | 52 |
| | | £114 | | | £114 |
| Oct. 1 | Balance brought down .. .. | 52 | 1969 | | |
| | | | Sept. 30 | Profit and Loss Account .. .. | 46 |
| | | | ,, | Balance carried down .. .. | 6 |
| | | £52 | | | £52 |
| 1969 | | | 1970 | | |
| Oct. 1 | Balance brought down .. .. | £6 | Sept. 30 | Profit and Loss Account .. .. | £6 |

## BALANCE SHEET EXTRACT as at September 30th, 1968

| CURRENT LIABILITIES | | £ | FIXED ASSETS | | Cost £ | Depn. £ | Balance £ |
|---|---|---|---|---|---|---|---|
| Amount outstanding on Hire-purchase agreement £(1,200—52) .. .. .. | | 1,148 | Motor Car .. .. | | 1,886 | x | x |

*Hire-purchase Agreements terminated prematurely*

Agreements may be terminated prematurely, when the hirer

(a) with the consent of the hire-purchase vendor

    (i) wishes to complete the purchase; he pays the remainder of the cash purchase price, and so much of the finance charge still outstanding, as the vendor may require, as consideration for his consent and as compensation for his loss of future interest; or

    (ii) sells or assigns the asset to a second hirer, who undertakes to pay the instalments as they fall due; or

(b) fails to pay an instalment which falls due.

In the case of (a) (i), if, under Method 1 above, the Vendor's Account was credited with the cash purchase price only, it must now be credited with the amount of the finance charge still required by the vendor. This will be debited to Interest Payable Account and eventually written off to Profit and Loss Account. Alternatively if, under Method 2 above, the Vendor's Account was credited with the finance charge as well, the amount of the finance charge which the vendor has *foregone* must be *debited* to the Vendor's Account and credited to Hire-purchase Interest Suspense Account; the balance on the latter will eventually be written off to Profit and Loss Account. When the agreed amount is paid, a debit closes the Vendor's Account, the credit being made to Cash.

### Illustration (3) (a)

Facts as in Illustration (1), to Method 1, but Hawkins wished to complete the purchase on September 30th, 1968, and the Vendor agreed to allow a rebate of 30 per cent. of the finance charge.

#### HIRE VENDOR ACCOUNT

| 1968 | | £ | 1968 | | £ |
|---|---|---|---|---|---|
| Sept. 30 | Cash  ..  ..  ..  .. | 1,166 | Oct. 1 | Balance brought down  ..  .. | 1,148 |
| | | | | Hire-purchase Interest Account  .. | 18 |
| | | £1,166 | | | £1,166 |

Alternatively, see Illustration (2) to Method 2:

#### HIRE VENDOR ACCOUNT

| 1968 | | £ | 1968 | | £ |
|---|---|---|---|---|---|
| Sept. 30 | Hire-purchase Interest Suspense Account  ..  ..  .. | 34 | Oct. 1 | Balance brought down  ..  .. | 1,200 |
| | Cash  ..  ..  ..  .. | 1,166 | | | |
| | | £1,200 | | | £1,200 |

The calculation of the final payment is as follows:

| | £ |
|---|---|
| Cash purchase price  ..  ..  ..  ..  ..  ..  .. | 1,886 |
| Finance charge  ..  ..  ..  ..  ..  ..  .. | 114 |
| Hire-purchase price  ..  ..  ..  ..  ..  ..  .. | 2,000 |
| *Less* 30 per cent. rebate of £114  ..  ..  ..  ..  .. | 34 |
| Adjusted hire-purchase price  ..  ..  ..  ..  ..  .. | 1,966 |
| *Less* Payments to date  ..  ..  ..  ..  ..  .. | 800 |
| Final payment  ..  ..  ..  ..  ..  ..  .. | £1,166 |

In the case of a termination under (*a*) (ii), the Vendor's Account is closed by a debit for the whole balance; the credit is made to an Asset Disposal Account. Any balance on the Hire-purchase Interest Suspense Account under Method 2, above, is debited to the Asset Disposal Account; the ultimate balance of the latter is written-off to Profit and Loss Account.

When under (b) an agreement is terminated prematurely, by the failure to pay an instalment and the owner repossesses the goods, the hirer is still liable under the agreement for all the unpaid instalments, though he may obtain some relief under the *Hire-Purchase Act 1965*. Whatever the hirer has to pay to the owner is debited to the Vendor's Account; the balance on this account is then credited to the Asset Disposal Account, any balance on a Hire-purchase Interest Suspense Account is debited to the Asset Disposal Account and the ultimate balance on the latter is written off to Profit and Loss Account.

**Illustration (3) (b)**

Facts as in Illustration (1) to Method 1, but Hawkins is unable to pay the instalment of £400 due on January 1st, 1969. The owner repossesses the car and the agreement is terminated by Hawkins paying £200 on April 1st, 1969. Hawkins had made a Provision for Depreciation of £600.

### MOTOR CAR ACCOUNT

| 1968 Jan. 1 | Hire Vendor Account .. .. | £ 1,886 | 1969 April 1 | Motor Car on Hire-purchase Disposal Account .. .. .. | £ 1,886 |
|---|---|---|---|---|---|

### HIRE VENDOR ACCOUNT

| 1969 Apr. 1 | Cash, to terminate agreement .. Motor Car on Hire-purchase Disposal Account .. .. .. | £ 200 948 ——— £1,148 | 1968 Oct. 1 | Balance brought down .. .. | £ 1,148 ——— £1,148 |
|---|---|---|---|---|---|

### MOTOR CAR ON HIRE-PURCHASE DISPOSAL ACCOUNT

| 1969 Apr. 1 | Motor Car Account .. .. | £ 1,886 ——— £1,886 | 1969 Apr. 1  Sept. 30 | Provision for Depreciation Account Hire Vendor Account .. .. Profit and Loss Account – Loss on disposal .. .. | £ 600 948 338 ——— £1,886 |
|---|---|---|---|---|---|

APPORTIONMENT OF HIRE-PURCHASE INTEREST

In every hire-purchase agreement, the cash purchase price must be given; the hire-purchase price can be computed by adding the total of the instalments to any deposit required; the finance charge is the difference between these two prices.

**Illustration (4)**

An asset with a cash purchase price of £1,274 is to be bought on hire-purchase by a deposit of £200 and twelve instalments of £100.

|  |  |  |  |  | £ |
|---|---|---|---|---|---|
| Deposit paid | .. | .. | .. | .. | 200 |
| Twelve Instalments of £100 |  | .. | .. | .. | 1,200 |
|  |  |  |  |  | —— |
| Hire-purchase price | .. | .. | .. | .. | 1,400 |
| Cash purchase price | .. | .. | .. | .. | 1,274 |
|  |  |  |  |  | —— |
| Finance charge | .. | .. | .. | .. | £126 |

The BUYER may want to know the rate of interest charged. This can be found from actuarial tables and is the rate of interest at which the 'present value' of the instalments payable is equal to the net cash purchase price (after deduction of any deposit paid).

**Illustration (5)**

Twelve monthly instalments of £100 are to be paid; the net cash purchase price is £1,074.

From actuarial tables, the present value of 12 instalments of £1 is £10·74 at $1\frac{3}{4}$ per cent. At this rate of interest, the present value of twelve instalments of £100 is £1,074. The monthly rate of interest is $1\frac{3}{4}$ per cent; the annual rate is therefore 21 per cent.

The SELLER, having decided what rate of interest to charge and the number of instalments to allow, needs to know how much each instalment should be.

**Illustration (6)**

Current rate of interest is 21 per cent. p.a; a net cash purchase price of £1,074 is to be settled by twelve monthly instalments.

Monthly rate of interest is $1\frac{3}{4}$ per cent. From actuarial tables, the present value of twelve instalments of £1 at this rate of interest is £10·74; each instalment should therefore be £100.

The rate of interest having been determined, as well as the finance charge, the latter has to be apportioned to the accounting periods during which the asset is on hire-purchase, so as to debit expenditure in the books of the BUYER or to credit income in the books of the SELLER. Three methods are in common use and are recommended by the Institute of Chartered Accountants:

*Method 1:* INTEREST ON THE REDUCING BALANCE

Simple interest is calculated on the outstanding debt, and added to that debt, at the time each instalment becomes payable. The interest added during each accounting period is apportioned to that period.

**Illustration (7)**

Under a hire-purchase agreement, an asset with a cash purchase price of £1,274 is to be paid for by a deposit of £200 and twelve monthly instalments of £100, the deposit to be paid on November 30th and the first instalment on December 31st. Accounts are taken out quarterly. How should the finance charge be apportioned?

The finance charge is £126. From actuarial tables, the rate of interest is $1\frac{3}{4}$ per cent. per month.

| Date | Outstanding hire-purchase debt | Simple interest for 1 month, added | Instalment paid, deducted | Balance c/f. |
|---|---|---|---|---|
| | £ | £ | £ | £ |
| November 30th | 1,274 | | | |
| Less deposit | 200 | | | |
| December 31st | $1,074 \times 1\frac{3}{4}\%$ = | 19 | 100 | 993 |
| Interest for December quarter = | | £19 | | |
| January 31st | $993 \times 1\frac{3}{4}\%$ = | 17 | 100 | 910 |
| February 28th | $910 \times 1\frac{3}{4}\%$ = | 16 | 100 | 826 |
| March 31st | $826 \times 1\frac{3}{4}\%$ = | 15 | 100 | 741 |
| Interest for March quarter = | | £48 | | |
| April 30th | $741 \times 1\frac{3}{4}\%$ = | 13 | 100 | 654 |
| May 31st | $654 \times 1\frac{3}{4}\%$ = | 11 | 100 | 565 |
| June 30th | $565 \times 1\frac{3}{4}\%$ = | 10 | 100 | 475 |
| Interest for June quarter = | | £34 | | |
| July 31st | $475 \times 1\frac{3}{4}\%$ = | 8 | 100 | 383 |
| August 31st | $383 \times 1\frac{3}{4}\%$ = | 7 | 100 | 290 |
| September 30th | $290 \times 1\frac{3}{4}\%$ = | 5 | 100 | 195 |
| Interest for September quarter = | | £20 | | |
| October 31st | $195 \times 1\frac{3}{4}\%$ = | 3 | 100 | 98 |
| November 30th | $98 \times 1\frac{3}{4}\%$ = | 2 | 100 | NIL |
| Interest for December quarter = | | £5 | | |
| Total interest = | | £126 | = Finance charge | |

A BUYER would use this method to determine accurately the cost to him, in each quarter, of the capital which, effectively, he borrowed when he entered into the hire-purchase agreement.

A SELLER has high initial expenses, which may include status investigations, introductory commissions and documentation; he charges a rate of interest to cover these, together with the cost to him of borrowing money, which is greatest while most instalments are outstanding; there are also the possibilities of the interest, which he is charged on his own borrowing, increasing at a later date or of the hirer defaulting. He would use this method, with its emphasis on crediting income in the earlier periods, to offset the known initial expenses, rather than those possible later.

*Method 2:* SUM OF THE DIGITS

(*a*) Number the instalments, giving the highest digit to the first instalment and the digit 1 to the last instalment;

(*b*) add all these digits together.

Apportion to each accounting period, as interest, a fraction of the finance charge, for each instalment paid in that period. The fraction is (*a*) the digit given to the instalment, divided by (*b*) the sum of the digits.

**Illustration (8)**

Facts as in Illustration (7). The sum of the digits is 78.

| Quarter | Digit(s) given to instalment(s) paid during quarter | Fraction | Interest apportioned to quarter |
|---|---|---|---|
| | | | £ |
| December | 12 | 12/78 | 19 |
| March | 11, 10, 9 | 30/78 | 48 |
| June | 8,  7, 6 | 21/78 | 34 |
| September | 5,  4, 3 | 12/78 | 20 |
| December | 2, 1 | 3/78 | 5 |
| Sum of the digits | 78 | | Finance charge £126 |

This method gives a very close approximation to the accurate results given by the interest on the reducing balance method. It would be used by both a BUYER or a SELLER instead of that method.

As well as its simplicity (in the illustration only three fractions need be calculated), the sum of the digits method has the advantage that the interest apportioned to an accounting period, or to any period in which an instalment is paid, can be calculated directly; there is no need to compute the opening balances of previous periods and the interest apportioned to them.

**Illustration (9)**

Under a hire-purchase agreement, the finance charge is £126. How much of this should be apportioned to an accounting period during which the 5th, 6th and 7th of 12 instalments were paid?

The sum of the digits for 12 instalments is $(12+11+10+9+8+7+6+5+4+3+2+1=)78$. The digits for the 5th, 6th and 7th instalments to be paid are 8, 7 and 6. The fraction of the finance charge is $\left(\dfrac{8+7+6}{78}=\ \right)\dfrac{21}{78}\times£126=\underline{\underline{£34}}$

*Method 3:* STRAIGHT LINE

Interest is deemed to accrue evenly over the life of the hire-purchase agreement. The interest to be apportioned to an accounting period is computed from the formula:

$$\frac{\text{Number of instalments payable during the period}}{\text{Total number of instalments payable over the whole agreement}} \times \text{Finance charge} = \text{Interest for period}$$

**Illustration (10)**

Facts as in Illustration (7).

| Quarter | Number of instalments payable during quarter | Fraction | Interest apportioned to quarter |
|---|---|---|---|
| | | | £ |
| December | 1 | 1/12 | 11 |
| March | 3 | 3/12 | 31 |
| June | 3 | 3/12 | 32 |
| September | 3 | 3/12 | 31 |
| December | 2 | 2/12 | 21 |
| Number of instalments | 12 | | Finance charge £126 |

This method gives results very different from those given by the interest on the reducing balance and the sum of the digits methods; it apportions much larger fractions of the interest to the later periods. However, like the sum of the digits method, it is simple and the interest apportioned to any period, in which an instalment is paid, can be calculated directly.

Although this method gives insufficient weight to the cost, in the earlier periods of hire-purchasing, a BUYER might use it for its simplicity, particularly when the finance charge is only a minor part of his expenses.

As well as for its simplicity, a SELLER might use this method, because he considers that it is prudent to delay taking credit for income and because the larger fractions of interest, which it apportions to the later periods, give some provision against bad debts and the increased costs of financing, should interest rates rise.

There are many formulae for obtaining an approximate value of the rate of interest being charged on hire-purchases, when actuarial tables are not available. Perhaps the simplest is:

$$\text{Rate per cent. per annum} = 100 \times \frac{F}{L} \times 2 \times \frac{M}{N}$$

Here one hundred times F, the finance charge, is divided by L, the actual debt (the cash price, less any deposit paid), multiplied by two (since on average only half of the debt is outstanding during the period); this is adjusted by M, the number of instalments in a full year, divided by N, the total number of instalments (to allow for the period, during which the instalments are paid, being more or less than twelve months).

This formula overstates the true rate of interest by about one-ninth.


SELLER'S BOOKS

In normal circumstances, the majority of hire-purchase transactions are financed by hire-purchase finance companies, formed for the purpose; many of these are owned in whole or in part by the Clearing or Merchant Banks.

Such companies earn their profits out of the hire-purchase interest they charge. The usual procedure is for the finance company to buy the goods from the dealer, after the hirer has paid his initial deposit, and then lease them to the hirer; the goods become the finance company's property, until the hirer has exercised his option to purchase. In order to attract business, many finance companies pay the dealers an introductory commission; to minimize bad debts a 'recourse plan' is sometimes resorted to, whereby the dealer guarantees the hire-purchase contracts and the finance company agrees to return to the dealer any repossessed goods. Finance companies will usually rebate the hire charges to hirers who wish to exercise their option to purchase earlier than is stipulated in the hire-purchase agreement. Hire-purchase finance companies apportion their income (i.e. the hire-purchase interest charges) over their accounting periods by one or other of the methods discussed previously.

Where the dealer or hire-purchase vendor finances his own hire-purchase sales, he has two sources of profit, namely, the normal gross profit, as if the goods had been sold for cash, plus the interest paid by the hirers in respect of the financial accommodation given.

Basically there are two different methods of accounting in the vendor's books. These are:

*Method 1:*

Credit is taken, for the normal gross profit on the whole transaction, in the accounting period in which the agreement is entered into; only the interest is deferred until it is earned, being credited to a Hire-purchase Interest Suspense Account; in this case, this is an Income Account, but not all the income is due in the current accounting period.

In the Trading Account, goods sent out on hire-purchase are treated as sales at cash price. In the Profit and Loss Account, hire-purchase interest receivable is credited, having been apportioned to the accounting period by one of the recommended methods (see page 582).

In the Balance Sheet, goods out on hire-purchase, being treated as sold, will not appear; the debit balance on the Hire-purchaser's Account will represent all the instalments not yet paid; a balance on the Hire-purchase Interest Suspense Account will represent the income apportioned to later accounting periods and must be deducted from the balance on the Hire-purchaser's Account to show the current asset.

*Method 1 (a):* The double entry is:

| Debit | Credit | With |
|---|---|---|
| Hire-purchase Trading Account | General Trading Account | Cash selling price of goods sent out on hire-purchase |
| Hire-purchase Debtors | Hire-purchase Trading Account | Cash selling price of goods sent out on hire-purchase |
| Hire-purchase Debtors | Hire-purchase Interest Suspense Account | Total hire-purchase interest charges |
| Hire-purchase Interest Suspense Account | Profit and Loss Account | Hire-purchase interest apportioned to the accounting period |

**Illustration (11) (a)**

On January 1st, 1968, a dealer sold a car under a two year hire-purchase agreement requiring an immediate deposit of £400, with four half-yearly instalments of £400 commencing on July 1st, 1968; his selling price for cash would have been £1,886. He prepared his accounts annually and apportioned his finance charge of £114 to the years ended September 30th, 1968, £28; 1969, £57; 1970, £29; that is, according to the number of instalments receivable in each accounting year.

### HIRE-PURCHASE TRADING ACCOUNT

| | | £ | | | £ |
|---|---|---|---|---|---|
| 1968 Sept. 30 | General Trading Account.. .. | 1,886 | 1968 Jan. 1 | Hire-purchaser Account .. .. | 1,886 |

### HIRE-PURCHASER ACCOUNT

| | | £ | | | £ |
|---|---|---|---|---|---|
| 1968 Jan. 1 „ | Hire-purchase Trading Account .. <br> Hire-purchase Interest Suspense Account .. .. .. | 1,886 <br> 114 | 1968 Jan. 1 <br> July 1 <br> Sept. 30 | Cash – Deposit .. .. .. <br> Cash .. .. .. .. <br> Balance carried down .. .. | 400 <br> 400 <br> 1,200 |
| | | £2,000 | | | £2,000 |
| 1968 Oct. 1 | Balance brought down .. .. | 1,200 | 1969 Jan. 1 <br> July 1 <br> Sept. 30 | Cash .. .. .. .. <br> Cash .. .. .. .. <br> Balance carried down .. .. | 400 <br> 400 <br> 400 |
| | | £1,200 | | | £1,200 |
| 1969 Oct. 1 | Balance brought down .. .. | £400 | 1970 Jan. 1 | Cash .. .. .. .. | £400 |

## HIRE-PURCHASE INTEREST SUSPENSE ACCOUNT

| | | £ | | | £ |
|---|---|---|---|---|---|
| 1968 Sept. 30 | Profit and Loss Account .. .. | 28 | 1968 Jan. 1 | Hire-purchaser Account .. .. | 114 |
| ,, | Balance carried down .. .. | 86 | | | |
| | | £114 | | | £114 |
| 1969 Sept. 30 | Profit and Loss Account .. .. | 57 | Oct. 1 | Balance brought down .. .. | 86 |
| ,, | Balance carried down .. .. | 29 | | | |
| | | £86 | | | £86 |
| 1970 Sept. 30 | Profit and Loss Account .. | £29 | 1969 Oct. 1 | Balance brought down .. .. | £29 |

Alternatively, the Hire-purchase Trading Account may be debited with the cost price of the car, which will be deducted from Purchases in the General Trading Account; the normal gross profit on the transaction will then appear in the Hire-purchase Trading Account. The need for a Hire-purchase Interest Suspense Account may be avoided, if there is a reliable memorandum system in force for charging the hire-purchaser with the interest, which has been apportioned to the accounting period.

*Method 1 (b):* The double entry is:

| *Debit* | *Credit* | *With* |
|---|---|---|
| Hire-purchase Trading Account | Purchases or General Trading Account | Cost of goods sent out on hire-purchase |
| Hire-purchase Debtors | Hire-purchase Trading Account | Cash selling price of goods sent out on hire-purchase |
| Hire-purchase Debtors | Interest Receivable | Interest apportioned to the accounting period |
| Interest Receivable | Profit and Loss Account | Balance on Interest Receivable Account |
| Hire-purchase Trading Account | Profit and Loss Account | Gross profit earned in the accounting period |

**Illustration (11) (b)**

Facts as in Illustration (11) (*a*). Assume the car cost the seller £1,500.

### HIRE-PURCHASE TRADING ACCOUNT

| 1968 Sept. 30 | | £ | 1968 Jan. 1 | | £ |
|---|---|---|---|---|---|
| | General Trading Account– purchases .. .. .. | 1,500 | | Hire-purchaser Account .. .. | 1,886 |
| ,, | Gross Profit carried to Profit and Loss Account .. .. | 386 | | | |
| | | £1,886 | | | £1,886 |

### HIRE-PURCHASER ACCOUNT

| 1968 | | £ | 1968 | | £ |
|---|---|---|---|---|---|
| Jan. 1 | Hire-purchase Trading Account .. | 1,886 | Jan. 1 | Cash – Deposit .. .. .. | 400 |
| Sept. 30 | Hire-purchase interest receivable .. | 28 | July 1 | Cash .. .. .. .. | 400 |
| | | | Sept. 30 | Balance carried down .. .. | 1,114 |
| | | £1,914 | | | £1,914 |
| Oct. 1 1969 | Balance brought down .. .. | 1,114 | 1969 Jan. 1 | Cash .. .. .. .. | 400 |
| | | | July 1 | Cash .. .. .. .. | 400 |
| Sept. 30 | Hire-purchase interest receivable .. | 57 | Sept. 30 | Balance carried down .. .. | 371 |
| | | £1,171 | | | £1,171 |
| Oct. 1 | Balance brought down .. .. | 371 | 1970 Jan. 1 | Cash .. .. .. .. | 400 |
| 1970 Sept. 30 | Hire-purchase interest receivable .. | 29 | | | |
| | | £400 | | | £400 |

### ANNUAL PROFIT

| Year ended | Hire-purchase Trading | Hire-purchase Interest | Total |
|---|---|---|---|
| | £ | £ | £ |
| 30.9.68 | 386 | 28 | 414 |
| 30.9.69 | — | 57 | 57 |
| 30.9.70 | — | 29 | 29 |
| | £386 | £114 | £500 |

*Method 2:*

Where there are numerous hire-purchase transactions for small amounts, Method 1 would require an 'army of clerks' apportioning the finance charges for all the different transactions. A system has therefore been devised which greatly reduces the arithmetical calculations. No distinction is made in the Hire-purchase Ledger Accounts between retail gross profit and hire-purchase interest. In the Trading Account, sales are replaced by cash receivable (deposits and instalments receivable during the accounting period). The unpaid instalments not yet due are *not*, as in Method 1, considered as debtors but as stock which must be reduced to cost. The only hire-purchase debtors are instalments in arrear.

**Illustration (12)**

A dealer starts a new business, including hire-purchase vending. During his first accounting period he sells on hire-purchase to:

A, a piano costing £80, sold for £120, payable by a deposit of £12 and 36 instalments of £3 each;

B, a suite costing £50, sold for £100, payable by a deposit of £10 and 45 instalments of £2 each, and

C, a radiogram, costing £60, sold for £80 payable by a deposit of £8 and 9 instalments of £8 each.

A paid the deposit and 7 instalments; B paid the deposit and 9 instalments; and C paid the deposit and 2 instalments, a further instalment from C being overdue.

The dealer's total Purchases were £6,690, his ordinary Sales were £8,000 and his closing Stock in hand was £500.

Write up the hire-purchase day book, the Hire-purchase Ledger Accounts and the General Trading Account.

*Procedure (a):*

Stage (i): The hire-purchase day book is ruled with columns showing number and date of agreement, name and address of hire-purchaser, cost and hire-purchase price of the goods, deposit payable, number of instalments and amount of each instalment. Hire-purchase Debtors' Accounts are debited with the hire-purchase price of goods in their agreements; they are credited with the instalments they pay. A Hire-purchase Sales Account is credited with the hire-purchase price of goods sold.

### HIRE-PURCHASE DAY BOOK

| No. | Date | Name and address | Article | Folio | Cost Price | Hire-purchase Price | Amount of deposit | No. of Instalments | Amount of each Instalment | Remarks |
|---|---|---|---|---|---|---|---|---|---|---|
| | | | | | £ | £ | £ | | | |
| 1 | | A ........... | Piano | | 80 | 120 | 12 | 36 | £3 | |
| 2 | | B ........... | Suite | | 50 | 100 | 10 | 45 | £2 | |
| 3 | | C ........... | Radio-gram | | 60 | 80 | 8 | 9 | £8 | |
| | | | | | £190 | £300 | £30 | | | |

### HIRE-PURCHASE PERSONAL LEDGER

**A**

| | | | £ | | | | | £ |
|---|---|---|---|---|---|---|---|---|
| 1st qr | Hire-purchase Sales Account – Piano .. | | 120 | 1st qr | Cash – Deposit .. | .. | .. | 12 |
| | | | | | Cash – 1 instalment .. | .. | .. | 3 |
| | | | | 2nd qr | Cash – 2 instalments | .. | .. | 6 |
| | | | | 3rd qr | Cash – 2 instalments | .. | .. | 6 |
| | | | | 4th qr | Cash – 2 instalments | .. | .. | 6 |
| | | | | | Balance carried down | .. | .. | 87 |
| | | | £120 | | | | | £120 |
| | Balance brought down .. .. | | 87 | | | | | |

**B**

| | | | £ | | | | | £ |
|---|---|---|---|---|---|---|---|---|
| 1st qr | Hire-purchase Sales Account – Suite .. | | 100 | 1st qr | Cash – Deposit .. | .. | .. | 10 |
| | | | | 2nd qr | Cash – 3 instalments | .. | .. | 6 |
| | | | | 3rd qr | Cash – 3 instalments | .. | .. | 6 |
| | | | | 4th qr | Cash – 3 instalments | .. | .. | 6 |
| | | | | | Balance carried down | .. | .. | 72 |
| | | | £100 | | | | | £100 |
| | Balance brought down .. .. | | 72 | | | | | |

**C**

| | | | £ | | | | | £ |
|---|---|---|---|---|---|---|---|---|
| 1st qr | Hire-purchase Sales Account – Radiogram | | 80 | 1st qr | Cash – Deposit .. | .. | .. | 8 |
| | | | | 2nd qr | Cash – 1 instalment .. | .. | .. | 8 |
| | | | | 3rd qr | Cash – 1 instalment .. | .. | .. | 8 |
| | | | | 4th qr | Balance carried down | .. | .. | 56 |
| | | | £80 | | | | | £80 |
| | Balance brought down .. .. | | 56 | | | | | |

Stage (ii): Balances are carried down on the Hire-purchase Debtors Accounts, showing the instalments still owing. A schedule of these closing balances is prepared, distinguishing any overdue instalments from instalments not yet due; this schedule is used to calculate the value of the stock out on hire, under each agreement, from the formula:

$$\frac{\text{Instalments not yet due}}{\text{Total hire-purchase price}} \times \text{Cost} = \text{Value of stock out on hire.}$$

From a column in the cash book, totalled to show all deposits and instalments received, and from any instalments shown overdue in the schedule of closing balances, a debit is made to the Hire-purchase Sales Account for the amount due for the period; the balance of this account is carried down.

### SCHEDULE OF CLOSING BALANCES

|   | Instalments overdue | Instalments not yet due | Sale Price | Cost Price | Proportion not due | Cost Price of Instalments not due |
|---|---|---|---|---|---|---|
|   | £ | £ | £ | £ |  | £ |
| A |  | 87 | 120 | 80 | 87/120 | 58 |
| B |  | 72 | 100 | 50 | 72/100 | 36 |
| C | 8 | 48 | 80 | 60 | 48/80 | 36 |
|   | £8 | £207 | £300 |  |  | £130 |

### HIRE-PURCHASE SALES ACCOUNT

|  | £ |  |  |  | £ |
|---|---|---|---|---|---|
| Hire-purchase Trading Account, Amount due for period .. .. .. .. | 93 | Sundry Hire-purchasers A | .. | .. | 120 |
|  |  | B | .. | .. | 100 |
| Balance, being instalments not due, carried down | 207 | C | .. | .. | 80 |
|  | £300 |  |  |  | £300 |
|  |  | Balance brought down .. | .. | .. | £207 |

Stage (iii): The amount due for the period, which was debited to the Hire-purchase Sales Account, is credited to the Hire-purchase Trading Account. The cost price of instalments not due, from the schedule of closing balances, is also credited to the Hire-purchase Trading Account and carried down as the value of stock out on Hire-purchase. The cost price, taken from the hire-purchase day book, of articles sold on hire-purchase during the period, is debited to the Hire-purchase Trading Account and deducted from Purchases in the General Trading Account. The gross profit shown by the Hire-purchase Trading Account is carried to the Profit and Loss Account.

The percentage of this gross profit to the cost price of articles sold on hire-purchase during a period, adjusted for opening and closing stocks at cost, should remain constant or reflect changes intended by the dealer; it is for this reason that overdue instalments are credited to the Hire-purchase Trading Account, as well as those which have been paid, since irregularities in paying instalments around the accounting date would otherwise distort the percentage. A system of credit control, the description of overdue instalments as Hire-purchase Debtors in the Balance Sheet and the need to make repossessions and to write off bad debts are sufficient indications of any inefficiency in hire-purchase trading.

### HIRE-PURCHASE TRADING ACCOUNT

| | £ | | £ |
|---|---|---|---|
| General Trading Account— | | Hire-purchase Deposits and instalments for period .. .. .. .. | 93 |
| Cost price of articles sold on hire-purchase during period .. .. .. .. | 190 | Instalments not yet due, reduced to cost, being stock out on hire-purchase carried down .. | 130 |
| Gross Profit carried to Profit and Loss Account .. .. .. .. | 33 | | |
| | £223 | | £223 |
| Stock out on hire-purchase brought down .. | 130 | | |

### GENERAL TRADING ACCOUNT

| | £ | | £ |
|---|---|---|---|
| Purchases .. .. .. .. | 6,690 | Sales .. .. .. .. .. | 8,000 |
| Less Transferred to Hire-purchase Trading Account.. .. .. .. | 190 | Stock .. .. .. .. .. | 500 |
| | 6,500 | | |
| Gross Profit .. .. .. .. | 2,000 | | |
| | £8,500 | | £8,500 |

The goods sold on hire-purchase having been eliminated from the General Trading Account, this account shows the true gross profit on ordinary sales. The Stock out on hire-purchase appears as an asset on the Balance Sheet. The provision carried forward on the Hire-purchase Sales Account is equal to the debtors for instalments not due; it is deducted from the total of the debit balances in the Hire-purchase Personal Ledger, leaving only £8, the overdue instalment, to appear as a debtor on the Balance Sheet.

*Procedure (b):*

In an alternative to Method 2, but giving the same figure for gross profit on hire-purchase trading, the whole of stages (i) and (ii) are treated as memoranda. The same entries must be made to show the state of each Hire-purchase Personal Ledger Account, but these Accounts need not be kept in ordinary ledger form; for instance they can be on conveniently-ruled cards, attached to correspondence and removed for as long as required, for the process of credit verification and debt collection.

Stage (iii) of this procedure entails regular credits, taken from the column in the cash book which is totalled at convenient intervals to show deposits and instalments received, direct to the Hire-purchase Trading Account. At the end of the period, another credit is made to Hire-purchase Trading Account, for any overdue instalments (as shown by the Schedule of Closing Balances) and these are debited to a Hire-purchase Debtors Account and appear on the Balance Sheet. The other entries are the same as for stage (iii) of procedure (a).

Facts as in Illustration (12). Stages (i) and (ii) are completed as memoranda.

Stage (iii):

## HIRE-PURCHASE TRADING ACCOUNT

| | | £ | | | | | | | £ |
|---|---|---|---|---|---|---|---|---|---|
| 4th qr | General Trading Account—<br>Cost price of articles sold on hire-pur-<br>chase during period | | 1st qr | Cash | .. | .. | .. | .. | 33 |
| | | | 2nd qr | Cash | .. | .. | .. | .. | 20 |
| | | 190 | 3rd qr | Cash | .. | .. | .. | .. | 20 |
| | Gross Profit carried to Profit and Loss<br>Account .. | | 4th qr | Cash | .. | .. | .. | .. | 12 |
| | | 33 | | Hire-purchase Debtors Account | .. | | | .. | 8 |
| | | | | Instalments not yet due, reduced to cost<br>being stock out on hire-purchase carried<br>down | .. | .. | .. | .. | 130 |
| | | £223 | | | | | | | £223 |
| | Stock out on hire-purchase brought down | 130 | | | | | | | |

## HIRE-PURCHASE DEBTORS ACCOUNT

| | | £ | | |
|---|---|---|---|---|
| 4th qr | Hire-purchase Trading Account—<br>Instalment overdue .. .. | 8 | | |

When the balance on the Memorandum Hire-purchase Sales Account is deducted from the total of the balances on the Memorandum Hire-purchase Personal Ledger Accounts, a check should be obtained of this figure for hire-purchase debtors.

### Provision for Unrealized Profit

· When the Seller uses Method 1 he takes credit in the first accounting period for the whole of the retail gross profit in the cash price; only the hire-purchase interest is deferred. If it is considered prudent to defer taking credit for some of the retail gross profit, either Method 2 should be used, since it does not distinguish between retail gross profit and hire-purchase interest but apportions both over the accounting periods in which instalments are received, or a Provision for Unrealized Profit Account should be opened and used in conjunction with Method 1.

At the end of the accounting period, in which the hire-purchase agreement is entered into, Profit and Loss Account is debited and Provision for Unrealized Profit Account credited, with the part of the retail gross profit which is deemed not yet to have been earned; the provision for unrealized profit is deducted from the figure for debtors on the Balance Sheet. This provision will be reduced in subsequent accounting periods, by a debit to Provision for Unrealized Profit and a credit to Profit and Loss Account, for the amount of the retail gross-profit now deemed to be earned in the period. The unrealized profit can be calculated on a time basis or according to the number of instalments not yet paid.

### Illustration (13)

Facts as in Illustrations (11) (*a*) and (11) (*b*). The gross profit, £386, is to be apportioned according to the number of instalments receivable in each accounting year.

### PROVISION FOR UNREALIZED PROFIT

| | | £ | | | £ |
|---|---|---|---|---|---|
| 1968 Sept. 30 | Provision carried down (¾ × £386) .. | 290 | 1968 Sept. 30 | Profit and Loss Account (£386—£96) | 290 |
| 1969 Sept. 30 | Provision carried down (¼ × £386) .. | 96 | 1968 Oct. 1 | Provision brought down .. .. | 290 |
| ,, | Profit and Loss Account .. .. | 194 | | | |
| | | £290 | | | £290 |
| 1970 Sept. 30 | Profit and Loss Account .. .. | £96 | 1969 Oct. 1 | Provision brought down .. .. | £96 |

### ANNUAL PROFIT

| Year ended | Instalments receivable | Hire-purchase Trading | Hire-purchase Interest | Total |
|---|---|---|---|---|
| | | £ | £ | £ |
| 30.9.68 | 1 | 96 | 28 | 124 |
| 30.9.69 | 2 | 194 | 57 | 251 |
| 30.9.70 | 1 | 96 | 29 | 125 |
| | | £386 | £114 | £500 |

The ordinary gross profit, on the goods sold by hire-purchase trading, has been apportioned on the same basis, as the finance charge, for hire-purchase interest; that is, according to the number of instalments receivable in each accounting period.

Other methods of apportionment may be used, but, if the same method is suitable for both the gross profit and the finance charge, the computation for apportioning the finance charge may also be used to calculate the provision for unrealized profit.

**Illustration (14)**

A Vendor, whose accounting year ends on December 31st, makes hire-purchase sales over three years. Monthly instalments are receivable, beginning in the month following that of purchase.

### HIRE-PURCHASE SALES

| | | | | | | A | B | C | D |
|---|---|---|---|---|---|---|---|---|---|
| Asset sold: Year: | | | | | | 1 | 2 | 2 | 3 |
| Month of sale: | | | | | | August | March | November | July |
| | | | | | | £ | £ | £ | £ |
| Cost .. .. | .. | .. | .. | .. | .. | 963 | 467 | 242 | 72 |
| Gross Profit 50% on cost | .. | .. | .. | .. | .. | 482 | 233 | 121 | 36 |
| Cash Price .. .. | .. | .. | .. | .. | .. | 1,445 | 700 | 363 | 108 |
| Finance Charge .. | .. | .. | .. | .. | .. | 555 | 180 | 57 | 12 |
| Hire-purchase Price .. | .. | .. | .. | .. | .. | 2,000 | 880 | 420 | 120 |
| Deposit .. | .. | .. | .. | .. | .. | 200 | 88 | 42 | 12 |
| Payable by monthly instalments | .. | .. | .. | .. | .. | 1,800 | 792 | 378 | 108 |
| Payment .. .. | .. | .. | .. | .. | .. | 50 | 33 | 21 | 9 |
| Number of instalments .. | .. | .. | .. | .. | .. | 36 | 24 | 18 | 12 |

The Vendor apportions his hire-purchase interest by the sum of the digits method and decides to provide for unrealized profit by the same method.

## GROSS PROFIT, FINANCE CHARGE, SUM OF DIGITS

| Asset | A | B | C | D |
|---|---|---|---|---|
| | £ | £ | £ | £ |
| Gross Profit .. | 482 | 233 | 121 | 36 |
| *Less* one-third Deposit .. | 67 | 29 | 14 | 4 |
| Gross Profit received in instalments = G | 415 | 204 | 107 | 32 |
| Finance charge = F | 555 | 180 | 57 | 12 |
| Number of instalments = N | 36 | 24 | 18 | 12 |
| Sum of digits $\frac{N}{2}(N+1) = S$ | 666 | 300 | 171 | 78 |

The apportionment is computed for each Asset in turn, using the following code:

M = number of instalments during year.

A = digit of month of first instalment in year.

L = digit of month of last instalment in year.

T = sum of the digits of the months in which instalments are payable $= \frac{M}{2}(A+L)$.

F (i) = Credit to be taken during the year for hire-purchase interest.

F (ii) = Hire-purchase interest carried forward in suspense.

G (i) = Gross profit for which credit is taken during year.

G (ii) = Provision for unrealized profit carried forward.

for example: *Asset A* Year 1 T = 4/2 (36+33) = 138

T/S × F = 138/666 × £555 = £115 = F(i)

T/S × G = 138/666 × £415 = £86 = G (i)

G (ii) = G—G (i) = £329

## COMPUTATIONS

| Year | 1 | 2 | 3 | 4 |
|---|---|---|---|---|
| *Asset A* | | | | |
| M | 4 | 12 | 12 | 8 |
| A | 36 | 32 | 20 | 8 |
| L | 33 | 21 | 9 | 1 |
| T | 138 | 318 | 174 | 36 |
| Apportionment to year = T/S | | | | |
| | £ | £ | £ | £ |
| × F = (i) | 115 | 265 | 145 | 30 |
| (ii) | 440 | 175 | 30 | |
| × G = (i) | 86 | 198 | 108 | 23 |
| (ii) | 329 | 131 | 23 | — |
| *Asset B* | | | | |
| M | — | 9 | 12 | 3 |
| A | — | 24 | 15 | 3 |
| L | — | 16 | 4 | 1 |
| T | — | 180 | 114 | 6 |
| Apportionment to year = T/S | | | | |
| | | £ | £ | £ |
| × F = (i) | — | 108 | 68 | 4 |
| (ii) | — | 72 | 4 | |
| × G = (i) | — | 122 | 78 | 4 |
| (ii) | — | 82 | 4 | — |
| *Asset C* | | | | |
| M | — | 1 | 12 | 5 |
| A | — | 18 | 17 | 5 |
| L | — | 18 | 6 | 1 |
| T | — | 18 | 138 | 15 |
| Apportionment to year = T/S | | | | |
| | | £ | £ | £ |
| × F = (i) | — | 6 | 46 | 5 |
| (ii) | — | 51 | 5 | |
| × G = (i) | — | 11 | 87 | 9 |
| (ii) | — | 96 | 9 | — |
| *Asset D* | | | | |
| M | — | — | 5 | 7 |
| A | — | — | 12 | 7 |
| L | — | — | 8 | 1 |
| T | — | — | 50 | 28 |
| Apportionment to year = T/S | | | | |
| | | | £ | £ |
| × F = (i) | — | — | 8 | 4 |
| (ii) | — | — | 4 | |
| × G = (i) | — | — | 21 | 11 |
| (ii) | — | — | 11 | — |

At the end of the first accounting period, whether the finance charge has been (a) credited to a Hire-purchase Interest Suspense Account or (b) recorded by memorandum to be charged to the Hire-purchaser Account, the credit to Profit and Loss Account will be the amount shown by F (i). The gross profit, however, has been taken in full in the Trading Account and, at the end of the first accounting period, a debit to Profit and Loss Account is required, which will be the amount shown by G (ii).

Thereafter, if it is unnecessary to distinguish between hire-purchase interest in suspense and the provision for unrealized profit, F can be added to G to obtain (F+G) (i) and (F+G) (ii).

When several hire-purchase sales are made on the same date and are payable by the same number of instalments, they can be totalled and treated as one transaction for the purposes of computation.

When identical hire-purchase sales are made on a number of different dates in one year, each being payable by the same number of instalments, an average date can be taken and computations made as if the total of the sales took place on the average date.

### Goods Repossessed

If default occurs in the payment of instalments and the seller repossesses the goods, he will open a Repossessions Account. This account will be charged with all losses and expenses and credited with the value of any recoveries, the net balance being taken to Profit and Loss Account. The double entry will depend on the method of accounting used in the seller's books for hire-purchase sales.

### Method 1 (a):

Where the seller takes immediate credit for gross profit but spreads the interest:

| Debit | Credit | With |
|---|---|---|
| Repossessions Account | Hire-purchase Debtors | Outstanding hire-purchase price of goods repossessed |
| Hire-purchase Interest Suspense Account | Repossessions Account | Hire-purchase interest apportioned to later periods |

### Method 1 (b):

The hire-purchase interest being apportioned by memorandum to each accounting period, only the first of the above entries is required.

### Method 2 (a):

Where the seller apportions both the gross profit and the finance charge to the accounting period in proportion to the instalments for the period:

| Debit | Credit | With |
|-------|--------|------|
| Repossessions Account | Hire-purchase Trading Account | Instalments unpaid, for current and all later accounting periods, reduced to cost |
| Hire-purchase Sales Account | Hire-purchase Trading Account | Any instalments paid for current accounting period |
| Hire-purchase Sales Account | Defaulter's Account in Hire-purchase Personal Ledger | Instalments not yet due |
| Repossessions Account | Defaulter's Account in Hire-purchase Personal Ledger | Balance of Defaulter's Account after crediting to him any cash or damages paid. |

*Method 2 (b):*

The Hire-purchase Sales and Hire-purchasers' Ledger Accounts being memoranda, only the first of the above entries is required, but any hire-purchase debts for the goods being repossessed, brought forward from a previous accounting period but now considered irrecoverable, are written off to Repossessions Account. The credit to the Hire-purchase Trading Account for any instalments paid will be transferred from the Cash Account.

All methods:

| Debit | Credit | With |
|-------|--------|------|
| Repossessions Account | Cash | Expenses and costs of reconditioning |
| General Trading Account | Repossessions Account | Value of goods when taken back into general stock |
| Profit and Loss Account | Repossessions Account | Loss on repossession |

### (b) Agreement to pay by Instalments

A contract for the sale of goods, the price of which is to be paid by instalments, resembles a hire-purchase agreement, but differs in that the property in the goods passes to the buyer on delivery and the seller becomes the creditor for the price. A transaction may be recorded in the buyer's or the seller's books in the same way as an ordinary purchase or sale, but, when interest is charged, it will be found that the accounting methods used for hire-purchase transactions are, in fact, those applicable to credit sale agreements, although the legal position is different.

BUYER'S BOOKS

1. Always debit the Asset Account with the whole cash price (excluding interest) and provide for depreciation on this price.

2. Either (a) Credit the Vendor Account with the purchase price (cash price and interest) and debit the interest to an Interest Suspense Account;

Or (b) Credit the Vendor Account with only the cash price at first; but keep a memorandum of the interest, apportioning it to each accounting period, and, at the end of the current period, credit it to the Vendor Account and debit it to an Interest Payable Account.

3. Debit the Vendor Account with deposit and instalments paid.

4. Debit Profit and Loss Account with the interest apportioned to the accounting period and credit

(a) Interest Suspense Account;

or (b) Interest Payable Account

according to which account has been opened.

In the Balance Sheet, the asset appears at full cash price, less provision for depreciation, and the Vendor Account, less any balance on an Interest Suspense Account, is a liability.

APPORTIONMENT OF INTEREST

Three Methods are available, as for the apportionment of hire-purchase interest:

(1) Interest on the reducing balance.

(2) Sum of the digits.

(3) Straight line.

Agreements to pay by instalments may require apportionment by Method 1, instead of by the simpler Methods 2 and 3, if some latitude is permitted in the early or late payment of instalments and interest is charged at a fixed percentage rate on the balances which result.

1. (i) Debit an Instalment Trading Account and credit General Trading Account, with

   (*a*) the ordinary cash selling price, excluding interest; or

   (*b*) the original cost price of the goods sold by instalments.

   (ii) Credit the Instalment Trading Account with the cash price (excluding interest).

2. Either (*a*) debit the Buyer Account with the purchase price (cash price and interest) and credit the interest to an Interest Suspense Account; or (*b*) debit the Buyer Account with only the cash price at first; but keep a memorandum of the interest, apportioning it to each accounting period, and, at the end of the current period, debit it to the Buyer Account and credit it to an Interest Receivable Account.

3. Credit the Buyer Account with cash received.

4. Credit Profit and Loss Account with the interest apportioned to the accounting period and debit

   (*a*) Interest Suspense Account;

   or (*b*) Interest Receivable Account;

according to which account has been opened.

In the Balance Sheet, the Buyer Account, less any balance on an Interest Suspense Account, is an asset.

### (c) *Rental Agreements*

Under a rental agreement a customer hires goods from a supplier for a period of time. A simple agreement will provide for a comparatively short period of hire at a steady rent; the customer may have the right to renew his lease, but there will be no intention that the goods should cease to be the property of the supplier.

In the customer's books, the rent is charged to revenue; it will usually be payable in advance and a prepayment at balance sheet date is treated as an asset. No other asset or personal account is opened.

In the supplier's books, the rent is treated as income, but provision must be made for depreciation on the assets out on rental. If rental payments fall into arrear, taking credit for them must be deferred or further provisions must be made for bad debts and the costs of repossession. The values of the assets out on rental, less depreciation, appear in the Balance Sheet and rent received in advance is a liability.

Some rental agreements provide for a long period of hire, during which the customer must continue to pay a comparatively high rent, but also provide that at the end of the period the rent shall be reduced drastically – to one-twelfth or less. If a sale is then negotiated for a nominal sum, the effect is that of a hire-purchase transaction; but if no option to purchase is given by the agreement, the Act does not apply and the accounting methods are as for any other rental agreement.

Such rental agreements are usually for assets the economic limit to whose lives is well known or which are likely to be rendered obsolete by new inventions. If a sale is negotiated the buyer will show the value of the asset in his Balance Sheet. The supplier, in view of the nominal sum or low rent which he will eventually receive, should make ample provision for depreciation.

### § 2. Mine etc. Rents and Royalties

The rent of a mine or quarry is rarely fixed in amount, but is generally a royalty based on the output; there is usually a clause in the lease fixing a minimum or dead rent, which must be paid, whatever the output may be. This minimum rent merges into a royalty rent, so that the actual rent paid is either the minimum rent or the royalty rent, whichever is the greater. Another clause frequently found in leases deals with short workings, providing that where the royalty rent based on the output is less than the minimum rent, the difference may be recouped subsequently when the royalty rent exceeds the minimum rent. A fixed limit of time is usually prescribed within which to recoup these short workings, or as they are sometimes called, redeemable dead rents.

In any period the landlord must receive in cash at least the amount of the minimum rent. Income tax is deductible from royalties of this nature, including any amount paid as minimum rent.

The double entry is:

(a) *Where the minimum rent for any period exceeds the royalty rent*

| Debit | Credit | With |
|---|---|---|
| Royalties (Payable) Account | Landlord | Royalty rent for the period |
| Short Workings Account | Landlord | Amount by which the royalties fall short of the minimum rent |
| Landlord | Cash Income Tax Account | Cash paid and Income tax thereon |
| Profit and Loss Account | Royalties (Payable) Account | Royalties Account written off to Profit and Loss Account |

*(b) Where the royalty rent exceeds the minimum rent*

| Debit | Credit | With |
|---|---|---|
| Royalties (Payable) Account | Landlord | Royalties for the period |
| Landlord | Short Workings Account | Short workings, if any recoverable in the period |
| Landlord | Cash Income Tax Account | Cash paid and Income tax thereon |
| Profit and Loss Account | Royalties (Payable) Account | Royalties Account written off to Profit and Loss Account |
| Profit and Loss Account | Short Workings Account | Short workings which cannot be recouped |

The balance on Short Workings Account if it is likely to be recouped should be included in sundry debtors, if it is unlikely to be recouped within the specified period it should be written off to Profit and Loss Account. In published accounts it need not be shown separately.

**Illustration (1)**

A company leased a mine at a minimum rent of £1,500 per annum, merging into a royalty of £0·025 per ton. The short workings were recoverable during the first five years of the lease only. The output for the first six years was 36,000, 52,000, 72,000, 76,000 and 96,000 tons of mineral, respectively. Show the accounts recording those transactions, ignoring income tax.

### ROYALTIES PAYABLE ACCOUNT

| | | | £ | | | | £ |
|---|---|---|---|---|---|---|---|
| 1st Year | Landlord's Account .. .. | | 900 | 1st Year | Profit and Loss Account .. .. | | 900 |
| 2nd „ | „ „ .. | .. | 1,300 | 2nd „ | „ „ „ .. | .. | 1,300 |
| 3rd „ | „ „ .. | .. | 1,450 | 3rd „ | „ „ „ .. | .. | 1,450 |
| 4th „ | „ „ .. | .. | 1,800 | 4th „ | „ „ „ .. | .. | 1,800 |
| 5th „ | „ „ .. | .. | 1,900 | 5th „ | „ „ „ .. | .. | 1,900 |
| 6th „ | „ „ .. | .. | 2,400 | 6th „ | „ „ „ .. | .. | 2,400 |

## LANDLORD'S ACCOUNT

| | | £ | | | £ |
|---|---|---|---|---|---|
| 1st Year | Cash .. .. .. .. | 1,500 | 1st Year | Royalties Account .. .. | 900 |
| | | | | Short Workings Account.. .. | 600 |
| | | £1,500 | | | £1,500 |
| 2nd ,, | ,, .. .. .. .. | 1,500 | 2nd ,, | Royalties Account .. .. | 1,300 |
| | | | | Short Workings Account.. .. | 200 |
| | | £1,500 | | | £1,500 |
| 3rd ,, | ,, .. .. .. .. | 1,500 | 3rd ,, | Royalties Account .. .. | 1,450 |
| | | | | Short Workings Account.. .. | 50 |
| | | £1,500 | | | £1,500 |
| 4th ,, | Cash .. .. .. .. | 1,500 | 4th ,, | Royalties Account .. .. | 1,800 |
| | Short Workings Account.. .. | 300 | | | |
| | | £1,800 | | | £1,800 |
| 5th ,, | Cash .. .. .. .. | 1,500 | 5th ,, | ,, ,, .. .. | 1,900 |
| | Short Workings Account.. .. | 400 | | | |
| | | £1,900 | | | £1,900 |
| 6th ,, | Cash .. .. .. .. | £2,400 | 6th ,, | ,, ,, .. .. | £2,400 |

## SHORT WORKINGS ACCOUNT

| | | £ | | | £ |
|---|---|---|---|---|---|
| 1st Year | Landlord's Account .. .. | 600 | 4th Year | Landlord's Account .. .. | 300 |
| 2nd ,, | ,, ,, .. .. | 200 | 5th ,, | ,, ,, .. .. | 400 |
| 3rd ,, | ,, ,, .. .. | 50 | | Profit and Loss Account .. .. | 150 |
| | | £850 | | | £850 |

Sometimes mining rights held on lease are sublet, in whole or in part, often at an increased royalty; the first lessee is liable to the head lessor (or landlord) for the agreed royalty on the full output irrespective of the arrangements made between the first lessee and the sub-lessee. The lessee must make provision for short workings allowable where the sub-lessee is entitled to recoup short workings, otherwise he may find himself liable for paying royalties on the output of the sub-lessee from whom he has received royalties (minimum rent) in an earlier accounting period, e.g.

B leases land from the landlord A for mining at a minimum rent of £200 merging into a royalty of £0·025 per ton, and B sub-leases half the land to C at a minimum rent of £120 merging into a royalty of £0·030 per ton with the right to recoup shortworkings. In the first year C produced 3,000 tons. C must pay B the minimum rent of £120 (3,000 tons at £0·030 equals only £90), B must pay A £75 (3,000 tons at £0·025 per ton) on account of C's production (subject to his own output plus the output of C exceeding his (B's) minimum rent). In subsequent years C may recoup his shortworkings of £30 (the difference in year 1 between £120 minimum rent and the actual royalties payable £90) but B will have to pay A royalties on 1,000 tons at £0·025=£25 for which he will receive nothing from C. At the end of year 1 it is normal for B to make a provision for Shortworkings Allowable of £30, although strictly a provision for £25 is adequate, i.e. the amount of royalty payable to A on the production by which C's royalties fall short of the minimum rent. The difference between £30 and £25 represents B's profit on 1,000 tons at £0·005 per ton; he receives royalties at £0·030 per ton and pays the landlord at £0·025 per ton.

**Illustration (2)**

On January 1st, 1968, Fir Ltd, patentees of a new type of electric razor, issued a licence to Non-nick Ltd for the manufacture and sale of razors. On the same date, Non-nick Ltd issued to Shave Ltd a sub-licence for the same purpose.

The licence issued by Fir Ltd provided for a royalty of £1 per razor sold, subject to a minimum sum of £7,500 per annum, and the sub-licence issued by Non-nick Ltd provided for a royalty of £1·50 per finished razor manufactured, subject to a minimum sum of £3,000 per annum. Both the licence and the sub-licence provided that, should the royalties for any calendar year be less than the specified minimum, the deficiency could be recouped out of royalties, in excess of the minimum, for either of the two immediately following calendar years.

You are given the following information:

| | Sales by Non-nick Ltd | Sales by Shave Ltd | Stock held by Shave Ltd at December 31st |
|---|---|---|---|
| 1968 | 4,520 razors | 1,220 razors | 340 razors |
| 1969 | 6,180 ,, | 2,790 ,, | 60 ,, |
| 1970 | 5,675 ,, | 1,940 ,, | 400 ,, |

All payments under both licence and sub-licence have been made annually on December 31st.

Show the accounts in the books of Non-nick Ltd necessary to record these transactions for the years 1968, 1969 and 1970, closing the accounts on December 31st in each year. Ignore taxation.

### ROYALTIES PAYABLE ACCOUNT

| | | £ | | | £ |
|---|---|---|---|---|---|
| 1968 Dec. 31 | Fir Ltd | 4,520 | 1968 Dec. 31 | Profit and Loss Account | 4,520 |
| 1969 Dec. 31 | ,, | 6,180 | 1969 Dec. 31 | ,, ,, ,, ,, | 6,180 |
| 1970 Dec. 31 | ,, | 5,675 | 1970 Dec. 31 | ,, ,, ,, ,, | 5,675 |

### (PROFIT ON) ROYALTIES RECEIVABLE

| | | £ | | | £ |
|---|---|---|---|---|---|
| 1968 Dec. 31 | Fir Ltd | 1,220 | 1968 Dec. 31 | Shave Ltd | 2,340 |
| | Balance c/d. – Provision of £1 on 340 razors | 340 | | | |
| | Profit and Loss Account (i.e. £0·50 per razor on 1,560 manufactured) | 780 | | | |
| | | £2,340 | | | £2,340 |
| 1969 Dec. 31 | Fir Ltd | 2,790 | 1969 Jan. 1 | Balance b/d. | 340 |
| | Balance c/d. – Provision of £1 on 60 razors | 60 | Dec. 31 | Shave Ltd | 3,765 |
| | Profit and Loss Account (i.e. £0·50 per razor on 2,510 manufactured) | 1,255 | | | |
| | | £4,105 | | | £4,105 |
| 1970 Dec. 31 | Fir Ltd | 1,940 | 1970 Jan. 1 | Balance b/d. | 60 |
| | Balance c/f. – Provision of £1 on 400 razors | 400 | Dec. 31 | Shave Ltd | 3,420 |
| | Profit and Loss Account (i.e. £0·50 per razor on 2,280 manufactured) | 1,140 | | | |
| | | £3,480 | | | £3,480 |

## FIR LTD

| 1968 | | £ | 1968 | | £ |
|---|---|---|---|---|---|
| Dec. 31 | Cash  ..  ..  ..  .. | 7,500 | Dec. 31 | Royalties Payable  ..  .. | 4,520 |
| | | | | Royalties Receivable  .. | 1,220 |
| | | | | Short Workings Recoverable  .. | 1,760 |
| | | £7,500 | | | £7,500 |
| 1969 | | | 1969 | | |
| Dec. 31 | Cash  ..  ..  .. | 7,500 | Dec. 31 | Royalties Payable  ..  .. | 6,180 |
| | Short Workings Recoverable  .. | 1,470 | | Royalties Receivable  ..  .. | 2,790 |
| | | £8,970 | | | £8,970 |
| 1970 | | | 1970 | | |
| Dec. 31 | Cash  ..  ..  .. | 7,500 | Dec. 31 | Royalties Payable  ..  .. | 5,675 |
| | Short Workings Recoverable  .. | 115 | | Royalties Receivable  ..  .. | 1,940 |
| | | £7,615 | | | £7,615 |

## SHAVE LTD

| 1968 | | £ | 1968 | | £ |
|---|---|---|---|---|---|
| Dec. 31 | Royalties Receivable  ..  .. | 2,340 | Dec. 31 | Cash  ..  ..  ..  .. | 3,000 |
| | Short Workings Allowable  .. | 660 | | | |
| | | £3,000 | | | £3,000 |
| 1969 | | | 1969 | | |
| Dec. 31 | Royalties Receivable  ..  .. | 3,765 | Dec. 31 | Short Workings Allowable  .. | 660 |
| | | | | Cash  ..  ..  ..  .. | 3,105 |
| | | £3,765 | | | £3,765 |
| 1970 | | | 1970 | | |
| Dec. 31 | Royalties Receivable  ..  .. | £3,420 | Dec. 31 | Cash  ..  ..  ..  .. | £3,420 |

## SHORT WORKINGS RECOVERABLE

| 1968 | | £ | 1969 | | £ |
|---|---|---|---|---|---|
| Dec. 31 | Fir Ltd  ..  ..  .. | 1,760 | Dec. 31 | Fir Ltd  ..  ..  .. | 1,470 |
| | | | | Balance carried down  ..  .. | 290 |
| | | £1,760 | | | £1,760 |
| 1970 | | | 1970 | | |
| Jan. 1 | Balance brought down  ..  .. | 290 | Dec. 31 | Fir Ltd  ..  ..  .. | 115 |
| | | | | Profit and Loss Account – Short Workings irrecoverable  .. | 175 |
| | | £290 | | | £290 |

## SHORT WORKINGS ALLOWABLE

| 1969 | | £ | 1968 | | £ |
|---|---|---|---|---|---|
| Dec. 31 | Shave Ltd  ..  ..  .. | 660 | Dec. 31 | Shave Ltd  ..  ..  .. | 660 |

| | | | | | | | | 1968 | 1969 | 1970 |
|---|---|---|---|---|---|---|---|---|---|---|
| Razors manufactured by Shave Ltd: | | | | | | | | | | |
| Sales.. | .. | .. | .. | .. | .. | .. | .. | 1,220 | 2,790 | 1,940 |
| *Add* Closing stock – December 31st | .. | .. | .. | .. | .. | .. | | 340 | 60 | 400 |
| | | | | | | | | 1,560 | 2,850 | 2,340 |
| *Less* Opening stock – January 1st | .. | .. | .. | .. | .. | .. | | — | 340 | 60 |
| | | | | | | | | 1,560 | 2,510 | 2,280 |
| Royalty payable to Non-nick Ltd at £1·50 | .. | .. | .. | .. | .. | .. | | £2,340 | £3,765 | £3,420 |
| | | | | | | | | 1968 | 1969 | 1970 |
| Royalty payable to Fir Ltd: | | | | | | | | | | |
| Razors sold by Non-nick Ltd | .. | .. | .. | .. | .. | .. | | 4,520 | 6,180 | 5,675 |
| Razors sold by Shave Ltd | .. | .. | .. | .. | .. | .. | | 1,220 | 2,790 | 1,940 |
| | | | | | | | Total sales | 5,740 | 8,970 | 7,615 |
| Royalty of £1 per razor sold | .. | .. | .. | .. | .. | .. | | £5,740 | £8,970 | £7,615 |

*Note:* The licence issued by Fir to Non-nick provided for a royalty of £1 per razor SOLD, whereas the sub-licence issued by Non-nick provided for a royalty of £1·50 per finished razor manufactured. Thus in the accounts of Non-nick provision has been made each year for the royalty payable to Fir when the closing stocks of Shave are ultimately sold, viz.

| | £ |
|---|---|
| Stock of Shave – 31/12/68, 340 razors | |
| Royalty receivable by Non-nick .. .. | 510 |
| „ payable by Non-nick when sold .. | 340 |
| Profit taken by Non-nick on Shave's stock (340 @ £0·50) | 170 |
| „ „ „ „ „ Shave's sales (1,220 @ £0·50) | 610 |
| Total profit taken for the year .. .. | £780 |

It might be contended, however, that the liability of Non-nick to pay Fir does not arise until the stock is in fact sold. In this event no provision would be made in the accounts of Non-nick and the Royalties Receivable credited to Profit and Loss Account each year would be: 1968 £1,120; 1969 £975; 1970 £1,480.

## § 3. Farmers' Accounts

The Ministry of Agriculture and Fisheries has issued booklets explaining, in very simple language, how the farm books should be kept and how the profit or loss arising from the farming operations should be ascertained.

The farmer should make an inventory and valuation of his farm assets such as livestock, growing crops, foodstuffs, manures, seeds etc., at the beginning and end of each year, the basis of valuation being cost or market value, whichever is the lower. In the case of livestock, where the farmer is unable to estimate the actual cost of home-bred cattle, sheep or pigs, they may be brought in at 75 per cent. of the current market value of each animal at the time of the valuation. The cost figure of home grown grain, straw, hay, roots etc. may be taken at market (or controlled) price, less 15 per cent.

At the end of each accounting period accruals and prepayments will be dealt with in the normal way. Assuming it is desired to prepare the accounts in a manner that would be acceptable for taxation purposes, then as a general rule only one-third of the amount of any rent, rates, repairs etc. of the farmhouse should be charged in the farm accounts, two-thirds being attributable to personal use, as this is normally the fraction allowable for tax purposes. There must be credited to Trading Account and debited to the farmer's Current (or Drawings) Account, the estimated value of the farm produce etc. consumed by the farmer and his household. For taxation purposes following the decision in *Sharkey* v. *Wernher* this must be valued at retail selling price.

The decision in *Sharkey* v. *Wernher* does not apply where the farmer incurs expenditure on the construction of a fixed asset, e.g. a barn, this being valued at cost. Depreciation of plant and machinery should be provided for, but in the case of small tools, in respect of which writing down allowances are not given for tax purposes, the cost of replacement should be charged against revenue.

The following illustration shows the form in which the farm Trading and Profit and Loss Account may be prepared.

**Illustration**

### J. SMITH ESQ.
### TRADING AND PROFIT AND LOSS ACCOUNT
for the year ended December 31st, 19..

| | £ | £ | | £ | £ |
|---|---|---|---|---|---|
| Crop expenses: | | | Crop – Gross output: | | |
| Fertilizers (subsidies deducted) .. | 700 | | Wheat .. .. .. | 1,930 | |
| Seeds .. .. .. | 1,600 | | Barley .. .. .. | 540 | |
| Contract work .. .. .. | 2,100 | | Oats.. .. .. .. | 280 | |
| Casual labour .. .. | 50 | | Potatoes .. .. .. | 750 | |
| Other crop expenses .. | 260 | 4,710 | Sugar beet .. .. | 2,300 | |
| | | | Turnips .. .. .. | 140 | |
| Livestock expenses: | | | Hay .. .. .. | 20 | |
| Feed bought .. .. | 2,800 | | Grazing .. .. | 40 | 6,000 |
| Casual labour .. .. | 150 | | | | |
| Veterinary and medicines .. | 400 | | Livestock – Gross output: | | |
| Milk and dairy expenses .. | 100 | | Cattle .. .. | 15,500 | |
| Other livestock expenses .. | 200 | 3,650 | Milk and dairy produce .. | 600 | |
| Gross profit, carried down .. | | 15,600 | Sheep and wool .. | 20 | |
| | | | Pigs .. .. .. | 470 | |
| | | | Poultry and eggs .. .. | 210 | 16,800 |
| | | | Miscellaneous: | | |
| | | | Production grants not allocated .. | 60 | |
| | | | Contracting .. .. .. | 1,100 | 1,160 |
| | | £23,960 | GROSS OUTPUT .. .. | | £23,960 |

| | £ | £ | | £ | £ |
|---|---|---|---|---|---|
| Fixed costs: | | | Gross profit, brought down .. | | 15,600 |
| Regular labour: | | | Way-leaves .. .. .. | | 20 |
| Wages, national insurance etc. .. | | 6,100 | Gain on sale of machinery .. | | 220 |
| Machinery, equipment and farm vehicles: | | | Private share of: | | |
| Repairs .. .. .. | 850 | | Rent and rates of farmhouse .. | 200 | |
| Petrol, oil and lubricants .. | 420 | | Fuel and electricity .. .. | 100 | |
| Electricity .. .. .. | 600 | | Telephone .. .. .. | 20 | 320 |
| Depreciation .. .. .. | 700 | 2,570 | | | |
| General overheads: | | | | | |
| Rent and rates .. .. | 800 | | | | |
| Insurance .. .. .. | 100 | | | | |
| Repairs to property, fencing, draining etc. .. .. | 900 | | | | |
| Telephone .. .. .. | 120 | | | | |
| Bank interest .. .. | 170 | | | | |
| Loan interest .. .. | 1,200 | | | | |
| Other general overheads .. | 300 | 3,590 | | | |
| Net profit for year .. .. | | 3,900 | | | |
| | | £16,160 | | | £16,160 |

## SCHEDULE OF GROSS OUTPUT

| | Wheat | Barley | Oats | Potatoes | Sugar Beet | Turnips | Hay | Grazing | Cattle | Milk and Dairy Produce | Sheep and Wool | Pigs | Poultry and eggs |
|---|---|---|---|---|---|---|---|---|---|---|---|---|---|
| | £ | £ | £ | £ | £ | £ | £ | £ | £ | £ | £ | £ | £ |
| Sales .. | 3,000 | 400 | 300 | 640 | 2,700 | 400 | 120 | 40 | 20,700 | 500 | 600 | 1,600 | 400 |
| Subsidies .. | 200 | 20 | 10 | 50 | 200 | — | — | — | 400 | — | 50 | 200 | — |
| Own consumption | — | — | — | 20 | — | — | 40 | — | 50 | 100 | — | 60 | 130 |
| Closing stock | 300 | 200 | 20 | 80 | 300 | 30 | 50 | — | 3,000 | — | 250 | 230 | 70 |
| | £3,500 | £620 | £330 | £790 | £3,200 | £430 | £210 | £40 | £24,150 | £600 | £900 | £2,090 | £600 |
| Opening stock | 1,570 | 80 | 50 | 40 | 900 | 290 | 190 | — | 2,750 | — | 700 | 260 | 90 |
| Purchases .. | — | — | — | — | — | — | — | — | 5,900 | — | 180 | 1,360 | 300 |
| | £1,570 | £80 | £50 | £40 | £900 | £290 | £190 | — | £8,650 | — | £880 | £1,620 | £390 |
| GROSS OUTPUT .. | £1,930 | £540 | £280 | £750 | £2,300 | £140 | £20 | £40 | £15,500 | £600 | £20 | £470 | £210 |

*Notes:*

1. Details of gross output are relegated to schedules attached to the Trading Account. Gross output is sales, subsidies, and private consumption, less purchases, adjustments being made for opening and closing stocks.

2. The Trading Account shows gross profit less expenses which vary directly with production. The Profit and Loss Account on the debit side shows fixed costs, i.e. those which do *not* vary directly with production. It is considered that normally the cost of regular labour, in contrast with casual labour, does not vary directly with production, e.g. if four extra fields are brought under cultivation it is not necessary to employ another man full time; regular labour has therefore been charged to Profit and Loss Account.

## § 4. Fire Claims for Stock

Where the exact value of stock-in-trade destroyed by fire is unknown, the usual method of ascertaining the amount of the claim is to prepare an estimated Trading Account for the period since the last accounts were drawn up. The average rate of gross profit on turnover for past years will be ascertained, and the percentage so arrived at, calculated on the sales for the period under review, will be considered to represent the estimated gross profit for the period. The balance of the account will then show the estimated value of the stock damaged or destroyed.

Where the books of account have been destroyed, it becomes more difficult to obtain the details necessary to prepare the estimated Trading Account. In order to arrive at the approximate amount of sales, all known customers should be circularized. From the replies and the knowledge of the proportion of cash sales, the approximate sales for the period can be estimated.

Similarly, all suppliers should be circularized, and an estimate of the total purchases obtained. Copies of previous Profit and Loss Accounts and Balance Sheets will usually be available from the auditors or Inspectors of Taxes, so there should be no difficulty in arriving at the opening stock value or the usual percentage of gross profit.

In circularizing the customers and suppliers, care should be taken to ask for the corresponding figures for the previous year, in order that estimates can be made by comparison. The bank statements will assist in building up estimates, particularly for wages, where wages are charged in the Trading Account.

Any partially destroyed stock will be valued, and the amount deducted from the amount of the estimated total stock. The resulting figure will represent the claim to be made against the insurance company. If uninsured, the cost of the stock lost must be charged to Profit and Loss Account.

### Illustration (1)

John Smith carries on business as a timber merchant. On March 31st, a fire occurred at his yard, and the greater portion of his stock was destroyed, the value of the portion salvaged being £600. His books, however, were saved, and from these it appeared that on January 1st, his stock amounted to £3,000. The purchases to March 31st were £5,000, whilst the sales were £7,200. From an examination of his accounts for the previous three years it appears that the gross profit on the sales was 25 per cent. He is fully insured against fire.

Prepare a statement showing what amount he should claim from the insurance company.

## JOHN SMITH
## ESTIMATED TRADING ACCOUNT
for three months ended March 31st

| | £ | | £ |
|---|---|---|---|
| Stock at January 1st .. .. .. | 3,000 | Sales .. .. .. .. .. | 7,200 |
| Purchases .. .. .. .. | 5,000 | Balance=Estimated Stock at March 31st .. | 2,600 |
| Estimated Gross Profit, being 25% on sales of | | | |
| £7,200 .. .. .. .. .. | 1,800 | | |
| | £9,800 | | £9,800 |

### CLAIM

| | £ |
|---|---|
| Estimated stock at March 31st .. .. .. .. .. .. .. .. .. | 2,600 |
| *Less* salvaged stock .. .. .. .. .. .. .. .. .. .. | 600 |
| | £2,000 |

Frequently the salvaged stock can be made saleable after it has been reconditioned. Its value should be credited to the Trading Account and debited to Salvaged Stock Account, any expenses incurred in reconditioning it being charged to the Salvaged Stock Account. Sales should be credited to the Salvaged Stock Account, the ultimate profit or loss on which should be transferred to Profit and Loss Account. If any of the salvaged stock remains on hand at a Balance Sheet date, it must be valued on the usual principles and carried down on the account.

**Illustration (2)**

Taking the facts in the previous illustration, assume that £200 was spent in reconditioning the stock. Sales amounted to £900, and at the Balance Sheet date the stock was valued at £125. Write up the account.

### SALVAGED STOCK ACCOUNT

| | £ | | £ |
|---|---|---|---|
| Trading Account .. .. .. .. | 600 | Sales .. .. .. .. .. | 900 |
| Expenses .. .. .. .. .. | 200 | Stock c/d. .. .. .. .. | 125 |
| Profit and Loss Account – profit .. .. | 225 | | |
| | £1,025 | | £1,025 |
| Stock b/d. .. .. .. .. | 125 | | |

## § 5. Loss of Profits Insurance (Consequential Loss) Policies

These policies provide for indemnification of the insured for losses ensuing from the interruption, wholly or in part, of the normal activities of a business consequent upon a fire or kindred perils. The terms of each policy are framed to meet the requirements of the insured. The normal policy provides for indemnification against the loss of profit due to (*a*) the reduction in turnover during the period of indemnity and (*b*) the increased cost of working incurred in order to avoid or diminish the reduction in turnover.

The contemplated period of disorganization for which the insurance is effected is known as the 'period of indemnity' and its length will vary with the nature of the business and the delay anticipated in obtaining new machinery, equipment etc. The longer the period of indemnity for which cover is required the greater will be the amount of the premium charged; but the premiums for policies for periods of indemnity of a year or less vary little. No adjustments are required to the sum insured when 'averaging' the claim (see below) because the period of indemnity is less than a year.

The normal method of calculating a claim under such a policy is by way of a percentage on loss of turnover, such percentage being either a rate agreed by the terms of the policy or based on certified accounts of the year preceding the year in which the fire occurred. The loss of turnover is the difference between the turnover for the period of indemnity covered by the policy and the turnover for the corresponding period in the preceding financial year. The agreed percentage on this difference represents the loss suffered, to which may be added any specified increased costs of working covered by the policy to arrive at the total claim.

### Illustration (1)

The principles underlying the claim can readily be seen from the following comparative accounts.

## TRADING AND PROFIT AND LOSS ACCOUNTS

| | Year | | | Year | |
|---|---|---|---|---|---|
| | 1 | 2 | | 1 | 2 |
| | £ | £ | | £ | £ |
| Stock ..   ..   ..   .. | 3,000 | 2,000 | Sales ..   ..   ..   .. | 40,000 | 28,000 |
| Purchases   ..   ..   .. | 29,000 | 21,500 | Stock   ..   ..   .. | 2,000 | 2,500 |
| Gross Profit c/d   ..   .. | 10,000 | 7,000 | | | |
| | £42,000 | £30,500 | | £42,000 | £30,500 |
| Expenses fluctuating with turnover | 2,000 | 1,400 | Gross Profit b/d   ..   .. | 10,000 | 7,000 |
| Standing Charges   ..   .. | 6,100 | 6,500 | Net Loss   ..   ..   .. | | 900 |
| Net Profit   ..   ..   .. | 1,900 | | | | |
| | £10,000 | £7,900 | | £10,000 | £7,900 |

The result of the fall in turnover plus the increase in standing charges has been to convert a net profit of £1,900 into a loss of £900, the business thus being worse off to the extent of £2,800. In order to meet the normal standing charges and to make the normal profit, a percentage on turnover must be earned equal to the total of those two items. Assuming Year 1 to be the basic year, the percentage on turnover must be $\dfrac{£(6,100 + 1,900)}{£40,000} \times 100 = 20\%$.

(The amount to be earned is thus equal to gross profit less charges which fluctuate with turnover, viz. £10,000–£2,000 = £8,000. Where there is no turnover, there will be no variable expenses, but many standing charges will continue whilst the business is carried on.)

The effect of the fall in turnover is thus:

*Loss* of 20% on fall in turnover, 20% on (£40,000–£28,000)      =    £2,400
Increase in Standing Charges ..   ..   ..   ..   ..      400

Total ..   ..   ..   ..   ..   ..      £2,800

What is true of a whole year is true of part of a year, provided the same period of each year is taken to ascertain the fall in turnover.

**Illustration (2)**

Date of Fire, June 1st.
  Amount Insured, £12,000.
  Percentage of net profit and standing charges to turnover, 12 per cent.

|  | Turnover prior to fire | Turnover after fire | Decrease |
|---|---|---|---|
|  | £ | £ | £ |
| June    .. .. .. .. | 12,000 | Nil. | 12,000 |
| July    .. .. .. .. | 13,000 | 500 | 12,500 |
| August  .. .. .. .. | 11,500 | 1,500 | 10,000 |
| September .. .. .. | 12,500 | 5,000 | 7,500 |
| October .. .. .. .. | 13,000 | 8,000 | 5,000 |
| November .. .. .. | 12,700 | 10,000 | 2,700 |
| Total decrease    .. |  |  | £49,700 |
| Claim 12% on Total Decrease    .. .. |  |  | £5,964 |

Policies normally require adjustments to be made to claims to take account of:

(*a*) *Changes in turnover.* The turnover of the corresponding period in the previous year is not necessarily an indication of the turnover during the period of disruption. An upward or downward trend in sales may have become apparent since the previous year.

(*b*) *Changes in earning potential of the business.* Past accounts may not reflect current net profit and standing charges; changes in material costs, selling prices, manufacturing operations, products sold may have occurred.

The following terms are commonly found in policies:

(i) *Gross profit:* Net profit plus insured standing charges or, in the case of a net loss, the amount of the insured standing charges *less* such proportion of the net loss as the amount of the insured standing charges bears to all the standing charges of the business.

(ii) *Standing charges:* Expenditure which does not vary directly with production. Insured standing charges are expenses specified in the policy which the insured wishes to recover in the event of damage.

(iii) *Turnover:* The money paid or payable to the insured for goods sold and delivered and for services rendered in the course of the business at the premises.

Net profit and standing charges bear a direct relationship to the turnover of a business. Consequently, turnover as a basis for measuring the loss sustained provides a reliable guide.

(iv) *Indemnity period:* The period beginning with the occurrence of the damage and ending not later than..........months thereafter during which the results of the business shall be affected in consequence of the damage.

The period chosen sets the limit on the time during which compensation is payable under the policy.

(v) *Rate of Gross Profit:* The rate of gross profit earned on the turnover during the financial year immediately before the date of the damage.

(vi) *Annual Turnover:* The turnover during the twelve months immediately before the date of the damage.

(vii) *Standard Turnover:* The turnover during that period in the twelve months immediately before the date of the damage which corresponds with the indemnity period.

(viii) *Average:* The 'average clause' reads: 'provided that if the sum insured by the policy be less than the sum produced by applying the rate of gross profit to the annual turnover the amount payable shall be proportionately reduced'.

This is a simple condition of average. If the company insures for only a proportion of its gross profit, then it can only expect to recover a corresponding proportion of the loss.

(ix) *Special circumstances clause:* A policy usually contains a 'special circumstances clause' to provide for the trend of the business or special circumstances affecting the business either before or after the damage; its scope is wide, having as its object the formulation of a fair claim reflecting the results which, but for the damage, would have been obtained during the period of disruption. It will affect the calculation of (*a*) the rate of gross profit, (*b*) the reduced turnover, and (*c*) the increased cost of working. Note that the increased cost of working is subject, in addition to a restriction on account of any uninsured standing charges, to a further limit represented by the sum produced by applying the calculated (or otherwise agreed) rate of gross profit to the reduction in turnover avoided as in the illustration (*infra.*).

During the continuance of the policy, the insured submits to the insurance company a statement (normally certified by the auditors) showing the amount of the net profit and standing charges for that financial year.

The procedure to be followed and the steps necessary to compute a claim may be summarized as follows:

(*a*) Determine the period of claim, viz. the period during which normal business is interrupted or the period of indemnity laid down in the policy, whichever is the smaller.

(*b*) Ascertain the shortage of turnover by deducting from standard turnover (i.e. the turnover for the corresponding period in the year preceding the fire) the actual turnover during the period of interruption. The special circumstances clause may permit an increase in the turnover for the standard period to allow for the trend of, or special circumstances affecting, the business, thus having the effect of increasing the shortage of turnover. Conversely, the turnover for the standard period may be reduced, thus decreasing the shortage of turnover.

(*c*) Calculate the rate of gross profit for the previous financial year by adding to the net profit the *insured* standing charges and expressing this total as a percentage of the turnover for the previous financial year. Again, under the 'special circumstances clause' the rate of gross profit may be agreed at a different figure to reflect the trend of the trading results of the business.

(*d*) Apply the calculated or agreed rate of gross profit to the shortage of turnover.

(*e*) Add to (*d*) above the increased cost of working, applying the undermentioned restrictions:

    (i) Where all the insurable standing charges are not covered by the policy then a proportion only will be allowed, viz:

$$\frac{\text{Net profit plus insured standing charges}}{\text{Net profit plus all insurable standing charges}}$$

    (ii) In addition, the claim under this heading cannot exceed the sum produced by applying the rate of gross profit, as calculated or agreed at (*c*), to the amount of the reduction in turnover avoided by the increased cost of working.

(*f*) Deduct any savings in insured standing charges.

(*g*) Determine whether the average clause is applicable and apply it accordingly. Such a clause imposes a final limitation to the claim if the sum insured is less than the sum produced by applying the rate of gross profit (as computed at (*c*)) to the annual turnover (i.e. the turnover for the twelve months *immediately* preceding the fire), the amount payable being proportionately reduced. Again, it is imperative to bring into account any agreed variations in the percentage of gross profit or turnover arising from the 'special circumstances clause' as exemplified in the illustration below:

**Illustration (3)**

    From the following information compute a consequential loss claim:

        Financial year ends December 31st.
        Fire occurs September 1st following.
        Period of disruption September 1st to December 31st.
        Period of indemnity six months.
        Net profit for previous financial year £10,000.
        Insured Standing Charges £15,000.
        Uninsured Standing Charges £3,000.
        Increased cost of working £2,100.
        Saving in insured standing charges £600.
        Reduced turnover avoided through increased cost of working £5,000.
        With the insurer's agreement the 'special circumstances clause' provides for:
            (i) increase in turnover (standard and annual) by 20 per cent.
            (ii) increase in rate of gross profit of 5 per cent.
        Sum insured £32,400.
        Turnover for the periods of four months ended April 30th, August 31st and December 31st in each of the years concerned was as follows:

| | | | | | | |
|---|---|---|---|---|---|---|
| Yr. 1 | £20,000 | : | £45,000 | : | £35,000 |
| Yr. 2 | £30,000 | : | £55,000 | : | £10,000 |

*Computation of Claim*

SHORTAGE OF TURNOVER:

| | £ |
|---|---|
| Standard turnover (September 1st – December 31st, Yr. 1) ..     ..     .. | 35,000 |
| *Add* agreed increase of 20 per cent.    ..     ..     ..     ..     .. | 7,000 |
| | 42,000 |
| *Less* actual turnover during period of disruption    ..     ..     .. | 10,000 |
|     (period of indemnity of six months being adequate) | |
| | £32,000 |

RATE OF GROSS PROFIT:

$$\frac{\text{Net profit plus insured standing charges for the preceding financial year}}{\text{Turnover for the preceding financial year}}$$

$$£ \frac{10,000+15,000}{100,000} \times 100 = 25\%$$

Agreed rate of Gross Profit $= (25\%+5\%) = 30\%$

CLAIM:                                                          £          £

Loss through reduction in turnover 30 per cent. of £32,000  ..    ..                9,600

Loss incurred through additional cost of working:

$$\frac{\text{Net profit plus insured standing charges}}{\text{Net profit plus all standing charges}}$$

$$= £ \frac{10,000+15,000}{10,000+18,000} \times £2,100 = \frac{25}{28} \times £2,100 = 1,875$$

Restricted to the sum produced by applying rate of adjusted gross profit to the amount of the reduction in turnover avoided, i.e. £5,000 at 30 per cent.  ..      ..      ..      ..      ..      ..                1,500

                                                                             11,100

*Less* saving in insured standing charges      ..      ..      ..                600

CLAIM SUBJECT TO FULL INSURANCE      ..      ..      ..                £10,500

AVERAGE PROVISO:

The adjusted rate of gross profit applied to the adjusted annual turnover (i.e. for the twelve months immediately preceding the fire) is 30 per cent. of £(120,000+(20%), i.e. £24,000) or £144,000 = £43,200 which is more than the amount insured (£32,400) so that the average clause applies, viz:

$$\frac{\text{Amount insured}}{\text{Rate of gross profit (adjusted)} \times \text{Annual turnover (adjusted)}}$$

$$= \frac{32,400}{43,200} = \tfrac{3}{4} \text{ (or 75 per cent.)}$$

The amount payable under the policy is:

75% of £10,500 = £7,875

## § 6. Contract Accounts

Contract costing is a system of cost accounting employed by contractors, such as builders and constructional engineers, whose business renders it possible to allocate most of the expenditure incurred directly to the individual contracts and so to prepare, within the framework of the financial accounts, a separate account which will disclose the profit or loss on each contract.

It is not within the province of this book to describe in detail the principles of contract cost accounting or the methods by which the various elements of cost are allocated and controlled. All that it is proposed to do here is to give a broad outline of the form and contents of a Contract Account and to indicate some of the more important matters to which consideration should be given in its construction.

Readers wishing to study the subject more deeply should read *Cost Accounts* by W. W. Bigg.

A Contract Account should be debited with all expenditure, directly incurred on the contract, and with such proportion of the indirect expenditure as can appropriately be apportioned to it. Direct expenses will normally consist of the cost of materials and labour, plant and equipment acquired specially for the particular contract, and any other expenditure incurred on the site wholly for the purposes of the contract. Indirect expenditure will include establishment and administrative expenses, office salaries, directors' remuneration, audit fees, postages, telephone and stationery etc. Such expenditure is normally small in relation to the direct charges and will normally be apportioned to the various contracts on some arbitrary basis, e.g. by way of a percentage on prime cost, or labour cost, or by reference to the time occupied on the contract.

On the completion of the contract, the Contract Account will be credited with the contract price (including extras) and the balance of the account will represent the ultimate profit or loss.

Where the execution of a contract extends over more than one accounting period, the question will arise, at the end of each period, to what extent (if at all) credit should be taken for profit estimated to be earned to date on the uncompleted work. In determining this question the following principles should be observed:

1. No profit should be taken unless the contract is reasonably advanced, as it may be impossible to foresee, at an earlier stage, whether a profit will ultimately accrue.

2. Profit should only be taken on work for which architect's or surveyor's certificates have been given. Uncertified work should be valued at cost.

3. Provision should be made for contingencies, such as fines for possible late completion, increases in the costs of labour and materials etc.

A common method of book-keeping is:

(*a*) *Where the contract has just started*

Debit the Contract Account with expenditure to date and credit it with plant at written down value, unused materials on site, and work in progress at cost. No profit should be taken.

(*b*) *Where the contract is fairly well advanced but it is impossible to estimate future expenditure and hence the total cost with reasonable accuracy*

 (i) Debit the Contract Account with all expenditure to date.

(ii) Credit and carry down at the end of each accounting period plant at written down value and unused materials on the site.

(iii) Credit, and carry down, work in progress at cost plus the proportion of profit taken to date.

(iv) Debit the Contract Account and credit Profit and Loss Account with the proportion of profit taken in the accounting year.

There are several methods of calculating the proportion of profit to date, the most common is expressed in the formula:

$$\frac{2}{3} \times \frac{\text{Apparent profit to date}}{} \times \frac{\text{Cash received}}{\text{Value of work certified}}$$

The apparent profit to date is calculated as follows:

|  |  |  |  | £ | £ |
|---|---|---|---|---|---|
| Value of architect's certificates to date | .. | .. | .. |  | x |
| *Less* cost of work to date | .. | .. | .. | x |  |
| *Less* cost of work not yet certified | .. | .. | .. | x |  |
|  |  |  |  | —— | x |
|  |  |  |  |  | x |

(v) Cash received from the customer is credited to his personal account. A memorandum record is kept of certificates received. Only on completion will the contract account be credited with the contract price and the customer debited.

(vi) On balance sheets prepared during the progress of the contract, plant will be shown at cost less depreciation under the heading fixed assets. Work in progress will be shown under current assets at cost, plus proportion of profit, less cash received to date; materials on site are a current asset.

(c) *Where the contract is nearing completion and total cost can be estimated with reasonable accuracy*

1. Debit the Contract Account with expenditure to date. Credit the account with plant at written down value, unused materials, and work in progress at cost plus proportion of profit. Debit the account with the proportion of profit taken in the accounting year.

2. The proportion of profit is calculated by subtracting from the contract price:

  (i) expenditure to date.

  (ii) estimated further expenditure necessary to complete, less any residual value of plant etc.

(iii) any necessary contingency provision.

The profit now arrived at should be further reduced in accordance with the following formula:

$$\frac{\text{Cash received}}{\text{Contract price}} \times \text{Apparent profit}$$

If under methods (a), (b), or (c) after debiting expenditure and crediting plant at written down value, unused materials on site and work in progress at cost, the Contract Account discloses a loss, the whole loss should be charged to Profit and Loss Account immediately. If further losses are anticipated adequate provision should be made forthwith, so that future accounting periods will not be burdened with unprofitable contracts made in the past.

**Illustration**

Barbican Ltd was working on three contracts at its year end on June 30th, 1969. Details were:

| | Contract 41 | Contract 42 | Contract 43 |
|---|---|---|---|
| | £ | £ | £ |
| Contract Price | 450,000 | 300,000 | 630,000 |
| Work certified by architects | 225,000 | 105,000 | 600,000 |
| Cash received | 180,000 | 75,000 | 570,000 |
| Work not yet certified at June 30th, 1969 | 11,100 | 4,500 | 1,500 |
| Work in progress brought forward July 1st, 1968 | — | — | 450,000 |
| Stock of materials brought forward July 1st, 1968 | — | — | 3,000 |
| Profit included in work in progress brought forward | — | — | 15,000 |
| Plant at July 1st, 1968 | — | — | 60,000 |
| Materials charged during year | 120,000 | 75,000 | 27,000 |
| Labour charged during year | 90,000 | 30,000 | 30,000 |
| Overheads charged during year | 7,500 | 3,000 | 15,000 |
| New plant charged | 45,000 | 24,000 | — |
| Plant value June 30th, 1969 | 36,000 | 12,000 | 12,000 |
| Stock of materials June 30th, 1969 | 12,300 | 9,000 | 3,000 |
| Materials returned to stores | 1,500 | — | — |
| Scrap sales | 600 | — | — |
| Estimated additional expenditure necessary to complete contract | Not Known | Not Known | 18,900 |
| Estimated value of plant and materials at completion | Not Known | Not Known | 9,000 |
| Provision to be made for contingencies | — | — | 3,000 |
| Accrued expenses | 3,000 | 1,500 | 3,000 |

(*a*) Prepare Contract Accounts in columnar form; (*b*) show computations of profits or losses to be taken to Profit and Loss Account; and (*c*) show the Balance Sheet entries on the assets side appropriate to the Contracts.

(*a*)

## BARBICAN LTD
### CONTRACT ACCOUNTS

| | 41 | 42 | 43 | | 41 | 42 | 43 |
|---|---|---|---|---|---|---|---|
| | £ | £ | £ | | £ | £ | £ |
| Work in progress brought forward | | | 450,000 | Materials returned to store | 1,500 | | |
| Stock of materials brought forward | | | 3,000 | Scrap sales | 600 | | |
| Plant brought forward | | | 60,000 | Plant carried forward | 36,000 | 12,000 | 12,000 |
| Materials | 120,000 | 75,000 | 27,000 | Stock of materials carried forward | 12,300 | 9,000 | 3,000 |
| Labour | 90,000 | 30,000 | 30,000 | | | | |
| Overheads | 7,500 | 3,000 | 15,000 | | 50,400 | 21,000 | 15,000 |
| New plant | 45,000 | 24,000 | — | Loss to Profit and Loss Account | — | 3,000 | |
| Accruals c/f. | 3,000 | 1,500 | 3,000 | Work in progress c/f. | 226,300 | 109,500 | 597,900 |
| | 265,500 | 133,500 | 588,000 | | | | |
| Profit to Profit and Loss Account | 11,200 | — | 24,900 | | | | |
| | £276,700 | £133,500 | £612,900 | | £276,700 | £133,500 | £612,900 |

(*b*) *Computation of profits and losses to be taken to Profit and Loss Account*

| Contract No. 41: | | | | | | £ |
|---|---|---|---|---|---|---|
| Cost to date £265,500–£50,400 | .. | .. | .. | .. | .. | 215,100 |
| *Less* cost of work not certified | .. | .. | .. | .. | .. | 11,100 |
| Cost of work certified | .. | .. | .. | .. | .. | 204,000 |
| Work certified by architects | .. | .. | .. | .. | .. | 225,000 |
| Profit | .. | .. | .. | .. | .. | £21,000 |

Profit to be taken to Profit and Loss Account:

$$\frac{2}{3} \times \frac{£180,000}{£225,000} \times £21,000 = £11,200$$

Contract No. 42:

| | £ |
|---|---:|
| Cost to date £133,500–£21,000 .. .. .. .. .. | 112,500 |
| *Less* Cost of work not certified .. .. .. .. .. | 4,500 |
| | |
| Cost of work certified .. .. .. .. .. .. | 108,000 |
| Work certified by architects .. .. .. .. .. | 105,000 |
| | |
| Loss .. .. .. .. .. .. .. .. | £3,000 |

Contract No. 43:

| | £ |
|---|---:|
| Expenditure to date *less* profit taken £(588,000—15,000—15,000) .. | 558,000 |
| Expected costs to completion .. .. .. .. | 18,900 |
| Plant and materials costs to completion £(12,000+3,000—9,000) .. | 6,000 |
| Contingencies .. .. .. .. .. .. | 3,000 |
| | |
| Estimated total cost .. .. .. .. .. | 585,900 |
| Contract price .. .. .. .. .. .. | 630,000 |
| | |
| Expected total profit .. .. .. .. .. .. | £44,100 |

Profit to be taken to Profit and Loss Account:      £

$$\frac{\text{Cash received}}{\text{Contract price}} \times \text{Apparent Profit}$$

| | £ |
|---|---:|
| $\dfrac{£570,000}{£630,000} \times £44,100 = $ | 39,900 |
| *Less* profit taken in earlier accounting period .. .. .. .. | 15,000 |
| | |
| Profit to be taken for current period .. .. .. .. .. | £24,900 |

(c) *The Balance Sheet entries are:*

| | £ | £ | £ |
|---|---:|---:|---:|
| FIXED ASSETS | | | |
| Plant at cost *less* depreciation or at valuation .. | | | 60,000 |
| CURRENT ASSETS | | | |
| Stock of raw materials.. .. .. .. | | 24,300 | |
| Work in progress .. .. .. .. | 933,700 | | |
| *Less* cash on account .. .. .. .. | 825,000 | 108,700 | 133,000 |

## § 7. Bankers' Accounts

The principal functions of a joint stock bank are:

1. To receive deposits from customers and collect cheques, bills of exchange and other credit instruments on their behalf; and to pay on demand cheques drawn on current accounts and repay deposit accounts after the required period of notice has expired.

2. To discount bills of exchange and promissory notes on behalf of customers and others.

3. To grant loans and overdrafts. Either a fixed sum is advanced on loan, the amount being credited to the customer's Current Account, or the customer is given an overdraft, i.e. he is allowed to draw cheques up to a specified limit in excess of the amount standing to the credit of his Current Account. The bank charges interest either on the total amount of the fixed loan or on the amount of the overdraft used.

4. Agency services, e.g. the collection of foreign cheques, bills of exchange, dividend warrants and other credit instruments; the payment of 'standing orders' for subscriptions, insurance premiums and other regularly recurring liabilities on behalf of customers; the purchase and sale, through the bank's brokers, of stock exchange securities for customers; the services of the new issue department for raising fresh capital by a limited company (mainly the receipt of the application monies and financial business up to the allotment of the securities); the specialized services of the executor and trustee department; etc.

5. Miscellaneous services, including the transaction of foreign exchange business, issuing traveller's cheques, letters of credit etc.; the receipt for safe custody of plate, jewellery, title deeds to property, stock and share certificates and other valuables on behalf of customers.

Four services which the commercial banks have introduced in recent years are as follows:

1. A cheque card system, whereby a bank's customer can present his card at any branch of the bank and draw up to a stated sum in cash, or pay for goods in a shop by cheque up to the stated sum, with the payment guaranteed by the bank, e.g. Midland Card.

2. A credit card system, whereby the bank's customer makes his payments to selected shops who are in the scheme, by signing the bill and quoting his card number. The shop obtains payment immediately from the bank at a discount, and the customer receives a statement from the bank's computer centre at the end of the month, requesting him to pay a cheque for, or an instalment on account of, his purchases; e.g. Barclaycard. The Barclaycard may also be used as a cheque card.

3. A unit trust for customers. This form of investment has proved popular with savers, and the commercial banks seek to enter this field by encouraging depositors to save a fixed amount each month by bankers order, to be invested by the bank in its own unit trust, e.g. Lloyds Bank Ltd.

4. Cash machines. Banks are open for the withdrawal of deposits from 9.30 a.m. until 3.30 p.m. on five days of the week, and from 4.30 p.m. until 6.30 p.m. one day per week at selected branches. A machine is in use, which if a card is inserted into a slot, will give the owner of the card ten one pound notes neatly packaged. The customer can collect his card from the bank next day, after his account has been charged, or it can be returned to him by post.

Apart from balances with the Bank of England and other British banks, and cheques in the course of collection, the banks' resources are used for the purpose of earning income, in such a way, however, that a sufficient proportion of the assets is in a form in which they can be easily and speedily realized.

As previously mentioned the accounts of the National and Commercial Banking Group Ltd are reproduced in Appendix I. Although a banking company which is incorporated under one of the Companies Acts must comply with the requirements of Part III of the Second Schedule to the *Companies Act 1967* as respects the information to be disclosed in the accounts laid before its members, in accordance with the decision of the London Clearing Banks and the Scottish Banks they have ceased to take advantage of the exemptions available.

In connection with bank accounts reference can also be made to Chapter XV of Spicer & Pegler's *Practical Book-Keeping and Commercial Knowledge.*

## § 8. Voyage Accounts

The owner or charterer of a ship, in addition to ascertaining the profit or loss from carrying on his business for a period, should be in a position to determine the exact result of each voyage made. In order to do this, it is usual to open a separate account for each voyage, the accounts referring to each voyage being numbered consecutively.

The account should be charged with all expenses actually incurred on the particular voyage, and with a proper proportion of all other charges which are attributable to the voyages generally, such as insurance premiums on time policies, manager's remuneration etc. and should be credited with the freight and other income earned. The final balance of the account will represent the profit or loss on the voyage.

The Voyage Account will be in the form of an ordinary Profit and Loss Account.

### Illustration

The 'Glenisla' Steamship Company Limited own one 'tramp steamer', the s.s. *Glenisla*, which was chartered on February 27th, as follows:

(*a*) Cardiff to Genoa with general cargo at £3 per ton. The charter stipulates for an address commission to the charterers of 2 per cent. on the freight, payable on signing bill of lading, together with a brokerage of 5 per cent. to the charterers' agents, of which one-third is repayable to the vessel.

(*b*) Agua Amarga to Barrow with Ore at £1·50 per ton. Address commission of 2 per cent. on freight payable to charterers and a brokerage of one-third of 5 per cent. payable to charterers' agents on signing charter.

The vessel was insured at Lloyd's on April 29th, in the previous year, the inclusive premium for one year being £3,000, and the managing owners' remuneration was fixed by the Articles of Association at 5 per cent. of gross freight charges.

The following are the particulars from which the accounts are to be made up:

| | £ |
|---|---|
| Freight on 3,000 tons general cargo to Genoa, and on 3,500 tons Ore to Barrow  ..  ..  .. | 14,250 |
| Stores Account  ..  ..  ..  ..  ..  ..  ..  ..  .. | 560 |
| Port Charges etc., Cardiff  ......  ..  ..  ..  ..  ..  ..  .. | 350 |
| Captain's Accounts for Harbour Wages etc., Cardiff  ..  ..  ..  ..  ..  ..  .. | 150 |
| Bunker Coals  ..  ..  ..  ..  ..  ..  ..  ..  .. | 1,600 |
| Discharging at Genoa  ..  ..  ..  ..  ..  ..  ..  ..  .. | 145 |
| Agents' Disbursements, Genoa  ..  ..  ..  ..  ..  ..  ..  .. | 75 |
| Captain's Expenses, Genoa  ..  ..  ..  ..  ..  ..  ..  .. | 15 |

*(continued on next page)*

| | £ |
|---|---:|
| Stevedores at Agua Amarga | 420 |
| Provisions | 640 |
| Repairs on voyage | 125 |
| Captain's Expenses, Amarga | 10 |
| Agents' Accounts for Port Charges, Agency etc., exclusive of Address Commission and Brokerage | 150 |
| Wages | 1,750 |
| Port Charges and Discharging at Barrow | 1,150 |
| Captain's Portage Bill | 325 |
| Proportion of annual provision for repairs and replacement | 2,500 |

The voyage terminated on April 28th.

Prepare the Voyage Account, apportioning where necessary in months.

## VOYAGE ACCOUNT
### February 27th to April 28th

| | £ | £ | | £ |
|---|---:|---:|---|---:|
| Stores Account | | 560 | Freight: | |
| Port Charges etc. | | 350 | Outward – 3,000 tons of general cargo from | |
| Captain's Account, Cardiff | | 150 | Cardiff to Genoa at £3 per ton (a) | 9,000 |
| Bunker Coals | | 1,600 | Homeward – 3,500 tons of Ore to Barrow at | |
| Wages | | 1,750 | £1·50 per ton (b) | 5,250 |
| Discharging at Genoa | | 145 | Brokerage refunded on (a): | |
| Agents' Disbursements, Genoa | | 75 | One-third of £450 | 150 |
| Captain's Expenses, Genoa | | 15 | | |
| Stevedores at Agua Amarga | | 420 | | |
| Provisions | | 640 | | |
| Repairs | | 125 | | |
| Captain's Expenses, Amarga | | 10 | | |
| Port Charges, Agency etc. | | 150 | | |
| Port Charges etc. at Barrow | | 1,150 | | |
| Captain's Portage Bill | | 325 | | |
| Address Commissions: | | | | |
|   2% on £9,000 | 180 | | | |
|   2% on £5,250 | 105 | | | |
| | | 285 | | |
| Brokerage: | | | | |
|   (a) 5% on £9,000 | 450 | | | |
|   (b) One-third of 5% on £5,250 | 87 | | | |
| | | 537 | | |
| Insurance Premium for 2 months | | 500 | | |
| Managing Owners' Commission | | 712 | | |
| Provision for Repairs and Replacement | | 2,500 | | |
| Profit on Voyage | | 2,401 | | |
| | | £14,400 | | £14,400 |

## § 9. Marine Insurance Accounts

There are three parties to be considered in dealing with these accounts:

    (1) The person for whom the insurance is effected.

    (2) The marine insurance broker.

    (3) The underwriter.

When a person wishes to insure a ship or cargo, he will instruct an insurance broker, who will negotiate the premium with the underwriter with whom he desires to place the insurance. The underwriter may be a marine syndicate at Lloyd's or an ordinary insurance company with a marine insurance department.

The broker's remuneration takes the form of a brokerage which is deducted from the payment he makes to the underwriter.

When a claim is made under a policy, it is the business of the insurance broker to collect the amount of the loss on behalf of his client, from the various underwriters *pro rata*, receiving for his services a commission calculated at an agreed percentage on the total amount of the claim. Thus the broker will collect the full amount of the loss from the underwriters, and pay this to his client, less the agreed collecting commission.

Owing to the time unavoidably taken in settling marine insurance claims, it is necessary for each year's account to be kept open for three years. There are, therefore, always three accounts open, except at the date of the Balance Sheet, when the first of the three accounts then open will be closed by the passing of a reinsurance premium to the following year's account which in return takes over the liability for further claims.

### Illustration

The following are the balances on December 31st, 1969, in the books of A. Wreck and Others, an underwriting syndicate at Lloyd's.

| | | 1967 Account | 1968 Account | 1969 Account |
|---|---|---|---|---|
| | | £ | £ | £ |
| Premiums (*less* Returns and Reinsurances)  .. | 1967 | 2,018,000 | — | — |
| | 1968 | 723,000 | 2,020,000 | — |
| | 1969 | 61,450 | 684,000 | 2,621,000 |
| Dividends and Interest | 1967 | 11,150 | — | — |
| | 1968 | 12,500 | 13,100 | — |
| | 1969 | 14,400 | 15,450 | 12,150 |
| Claims (*less* Refunds, Salvages and Reinsurance Recoveries) | 1967 | 298,100 | — | — |
| | 1968 | 1,617,400 | 594,900 | — |
| | 1969 | 312,150 | 1,828,300 | 626,200 |
| Expenses | | 153,000 | 191,500 | 181,400 |
| Reinsurance Premium to close 1966 Account .. | | 521,000 | — | — |
| Investments (all accounts) at market value | | | 1,049,250 | |
| Creditors | | | 103,000 | |
| Debtors | | | 424,000 | |
| Balance at Bank .. | | | 2,254,000 | |
| Names Personal Accounts: Balance January 1st, 1969 .. | | | 700,000 | |

It has been calculated that the Reinsurance Premium required to close the 1967 Account amounts to £623,000.

Prepare Underwriting Accounts to December 31st, 1969, and Balance Sheet as on that date. Ignore taxation.

### A. WRECK AND OTHERS
### 1967 UNDERWRITING ACCOUNT
#### Closed at end of Third Year

| | £ | | £ |
|---|---|---|---|
| Claims, *less* Refunds, Salvages and Reinsurance Recoveries | 2,227,650 | Premiums, *less* Returns and Reinsurances | 2,802,450 |
| Reinsurance Premium to close this Account .. | 623,000 | Reinsurance Premium from 1966 Account | 521,000 |
| Expenses | 153,000 | Dividends and Interest  ..       .. | 38,050 |
| Profit transferred to Names Personal Accounts | 357,850 | | |
| | £3,361,500 | | £3,361,500 |

### 1968 UNDERWRITING ACCOUNT
#### at end of Second Year

| | £ | | £ |
|---|---|---|---|
| Claims *less* Refunds, Salvages and Reinsurance Recoveries  ..       ..       .. | 2,423,200 | Premiums, *less* Returns and Reinsurances | 2,704,000 |
| Expenses  ..       ..       ..       .. | 191,500 | Reinsurance Premium from 1967 Account | 623,000 |
| Balance as per Balance Sheet  ..       .. | 740,850 | Dividends and Interest       ..       .. | 28,550 |
| | £3,355,550 | | £3,355,550 |

### 1969 UNDERWRITING ACCOUNT at end of First Year

| | £ | | £ |
|---|---|---|---|
| Claims *less* Refunds, Salvages and Reinsurance Recoveries  .. .. .. | 626,200 | Premiums, *less* Returns and Reinsurances | 2,621,000 |
| Expenses  .. .. | 181,400 | Dividends and Interest  .. .. | 12,150 |
| Balance as per Balance Sheet  .. .. | 1,825,550 | | |
| | £2,633,150 | | £2,633,150 |

### BALANCE SHEET as at December 31st, 1969

| | £ | | £ |
|---|---|---|---|
| Names Personal Accounts  .. .. | 1,057,850 | Balance at Bank  .. .. .. | 2,254,000 |
| Balances on Open Underwriting Accounts. | | Investments at Market value  .. .. | 1,049,250 |
| 1968 Account  .. .. .. | 740,850 | Debtors  .. .. .. .. | 424,000 |
| 1969 Account  .. .. .. | 1,825,550 | | |
| Creditors  .. .. .. .. | 103,000 | | |
| | £3,727,250 | | £3,727,250 |

## § 10. Ledger Accounts for Investments

Where investments are numerous, the interest and dividends arising therefrom should be passed through the Investment Accounts in the ledger, so that it can be seen at a glance whether or not all the income due on each investment has been received.

Investment Accounts should be ruled with two columns on either side, one for income and the other for capital; it is often convenient to have a third column for the nominal value or number of shares or units. The dates when dividends or interest fall due should be noted at the head of the accounts kept for fixed interest bearing stocks or shares or debentures.

When income is received, cash is debited and the income column of the Investment Account credited, and, at the end of the period, the total income received from each investment is transferred to an Income from Investments Account.

### Illustration (1)

An investment company held during the whole of the year, £1,000 4 per cent. debentures costing £987, in the Phoenix Iron Company, the interest being payable on the 30th June and 31st December in each year.

Show in the books of the company the Phoenix Iron Company Investment Account. Ignore income tax.

### THE PHOENIX IRON COMPANY FOUR PER CENT. DEBENTURE ACCOUNT
Interest payable June 30th and December 31st

| Date | Particulars | Fo. | Nominal Value | Income | Capital | Date | Particulars | Fo. | Nominal Value | Income | Capital |
|---|---|---|---|---|---|---|---|---|---|---|---|
| | | | £ | £ | £ | | | | £ | £ | £ |
| Jan. 1 | Balance b/f. .. | | 1,000 | | 987 | June 30 | Cash: .. | | | | |
| Dec. 31 | Interest on Investments Account .. | | | 40 | | | ½ year's interest | | | 20 | |
| | | | | | | Dec. 31 | „ | | | 20 | |
| | | | | | | | Balance c/d. | | 1,000 | | 987 |
| | | | £1,000 | £40 | £987 | | | | £1,000 | £40 | £987 |
| Jan. 1 | Balance b/d. .. | | 1,000 | | 987 | | | | | | |

It is usual in Investment Accounts to carry down the balances at cost, and not adjust them to the current market value of the investments. In the case of companies holding a large number of investments, the practice is for a schedule to be prepared, showing the book value and the market value of each investment at the date of the Balance Sheet, a general provision being made for depreciation, if the total market value is less than the total book value. If the market value exceeds the book value, no credit should be taken for the excess, as this is not a realized profit. Under the *Companies Act 1967* a note of the market value of quoted investments must be made on the Balance Sheet of a company in which investments appear as an asset.

The profit or loss resulting on the sale of investments should be adjusted when the sale takes place. Where only a portion of the investment is sold, the balance remaining should be carried down at the price at which it stands in the books; the difference on the account will then represent profit or loss on the portion of the investment sold, and should be transferred to a Profit and Loss on Investments Account.

If it is desired to take credit for accrued income on loans or fixed interest stocks, this may be done by carrying forward the appropriate gross amount as a debit balance on the income columns of the Investment Account. Where this practice is adopted by a company or other body (e.g. a building society) which is liable to corporation tax, provision should be made for the corporation tax which will be payable for the ensuing accounting period in respect of this income when it is received (see p. 676 for an illustration of this in the Balance Sheet of a building society).

It may be noted that corporation tax liabilities as such are not dealt with in individual Investment Accounts, because corporation tax is not payable by deduction.

Dividends and interest are payable for periods of time, e.g. War Loan Interest is payable on June 1st, 1970, for the half year ended on that date. If stocks or shares are sold on dates other than dividend payment dates the purchase or sale price will normally include accrued income (see exceptions below), therefore, in order that income, due for the period the investment is held, is reflected in the income account some apportionment would appear necessary.

Where investments are sold *cum div.* (which implies that the whole of the next dividend will go to the purchaser), some portion of the amount received will represent the dividend (less income tax) accrued to the date of sale on the stock sold, and, strictly speaking, the amount received should be apportioned accordingly, the amount representing accrued income to date being credited to the income column, and the balance to the capital column of the Investment Account.

Similarly, when stocks are purchased *cum div.*, the purchase price includes the net interest or dividend accrued before the date of purchase. This is also included in the full amount of the periodical interest or dividend when it is subsequently received. The effect of the apportionment is to treat the capital portion as a recoupment of the amount paid for it and included in the *cum div.* price.

The most important application of this principle in the field of company accounts is found in the treatment of dividends received by a holding company out of pre-acquisition profits of a newly acquired subsidiary company.

Most British Government and Municipal Corporation stocks are quoted *ex div.* about one month before the interest is payable. Industrial securities are quoted *ex div.* at the commencement of dealings for the Stock Exchange account preceding the first day on which the company closes its transfer books. It will frequently be found that shares of large companies are quoted *ex div.* many weeks before the dividend is due, as it is necessary for such companies to close their transfer books long before dividends are payable owing to the volume of work involved in preparing and issuing the dividend warrants.

In arriving at the *ex div.* price, the full amount of the forthcoming dividend (less income tax) is deducted from the *cum div.* price. Accordingly, the price paid for the stock is short of the principal value by the amount of the dividend accruing from the date of the transaction to the dividend date.

When stocks are bought *ex div.* therefore, it is permissible to debit the capital column and credit the income column of the Investment Account with dividend accrued from the date of purchase to the next dividend date; and when stocks are sold *ex div.*, correspondingly to debit income and credit capital. In the latter case the adjustment is sometimes effected by apportioning the dividend, when received.

It is unusual to apportion dividends or to take credit for accrued income on portfolio holdings of ordinary shares. Even preference dividends, which are normally paid at fixed rates for periods fixed in advance, are dependent on the availability of profits out of which they can be paid. It is therefore unusual to take credit for accrued preference dividends. Indeed it is unusual in practice for a company other than one which makes investments and receives income from them as a necessary ingredient of its main business to make any adjustments or apportionments of interest and dividends received.

Dealings in British Government securities having five years or less to run to maturity are subject to the gross accrued interest being accounted for between buyer and seller, up to the day for which the bargain is done. The accrued interest is part of the cost, *cum div.* of the investment to the purchaser and of the proceeds of sale to the seller. If a transaction is entered into in the *ex div.* period a *deduction* is made from the *ex div.* price for the gross accrued interest from the date of the bargain to the due date of the next interest payment.

With the exception of $3\frac{1}{2}$ per cent. War Loan and one or two other securities income tax must be deducted at source from interest and dividends so that the investor receives only the net amount. The gross amount, however, must be brought to the credit of Profit and Loss or Revenue Account; Income Tax Account will be debited and the Investment Account, income column, will be credited with the income tax deducted at source. If the standard rate of income tax has changed during the accounting period care must be taken to transfer the tax actually suffered, having regard to the due dates of the various amounts received. Where a company is concerned it may also be desirable to distinguish in Income Tax Account between income tax transfers arising from franked and unfranked investment income respectively. (See Chapter VIII, Section 15 (*m*), treatment of taxation in accounts.)

**Illustration (2)**

On March 1st an investment trust company purchased £20,000 Corporation 3 per cent. Stock (interest payable quarterly, January 1st etc.) at 87½ *cum div.* On August 1st, £4,000 stock was sold at 87 *cum div.*, and on September 1st, £4,000 stock was sold at 88¼ *ex div.*

Show the Ledger Account of the investment for the year ending December 31st ignoring expenses of purchase and sale and making apportionments in months. Take income tax into account at the assumed standard rate of 50p in the £.

### CORPORATION 3 PER CENT. STOCK

Interest payable: January 1st, April 1st, July 1st, October 1st

| Date | | Nominal | Income | Capital | Date | | Nominal | Income | Capital |
|---|---|---|---|---|---|---|---|---|---|
| | | £ | £ | £ | | | £ | £ | £ |
| Mar. 1 | Cash – purchase at 87½ *cum div.* | 20,000 | | 17,500 | Apl. 1 | Cash – 3 months' interest on £20,000 | | 25 | 50 |
| Aug. 1 | Transfer to income – interest accrued for 1 month on £4,000 stock sold *cum div.* | | 5 | | July 1 | Cash – 3 months' interest on £20,000 | | 75 | |
| Dec. 31 | Transfer to Profits and Losses on Sales of Investments Account | | | 50 | Aug. 1 | Cash – sale at 87 *cum div.* | 4,000 | | 3,480 |
| | | | | | | Transfer from capital per contra | | 5 | |
| | Transfer to Income on Investments Account | | 410 | | Sept. 1 | Cash – sale at 88¼ *ex div.* | 4,000 | | 3,530 |
| | | | | | Oct. 1 | Cash – 3 months' interest on £16,000 | | 55 | 5 |
| | | | | | Dec. 31 | Transfer to Income Tax Account | | 160 | 50 |
| | | | | | | Balances c/f | 12,000 | 90 | 10,440 |
| | | £20,000 | £410 | £17,555 | | | £20,000 | £410 | £17,555 |

*Notes*

1. The interest of £75 received on April 1st includes two months' interest, £50 net, that had accrued before the holding was acquired. This is apportioned to capital as representing a recoupment of that amount included in the purchase price. Apportionment of the interest when received rather than of the original purchase is to be preferred as the cost of the investment for taxation purposes (e.g. corporation tax on capital gains) is £17,500 and is not affected by the apportionment.

2. On the sale of £4,000 nominal at 87 *cum div.* the £3,480 received includes one month's interest on the £4,000 for a period of 1 month during which this part of the holding was still owned. This is credited to income, preferably by a transfer from capital to income as shown rather than by apportioning the sum received because for taxation purposes the sale has realized the full amount of £3,480.

3. As a result of the sale of £4,000 nominal at 88¼ *ex div.* the interest received on October 1st, £60 net, includes £5 net interest for 1 month subsequent to the sale of this part of the holding; this is accordingly apportioned to capital.

4. The transfer to income tax could alternatively be made quarterly immediately after each instalment of interest is received. In any case it does not apply to the final balance of accrued income which is calculated gross because it is not in fact taxable until received.

5. The effect of all the foregoing is that the amount transferred to Income on Investments Account represents the interest actually earned before deduction of tax, on the balance of stock held from month to month, viz.

|  |  | £ |
|---|---|---|
| 3 per cent. per annum on £20,000 for 5 months | | 250 |
| ,,      ,,      on £16,000 for 1 month | | 40 |
| ,,      ,,      on £12,000 for 4 months | | 120 |
| | | £410 |

6. Opinions may differ as to the necessity for any transfer to Income Tax Account from the capital columns but by making this transfer as shown (it is calculated by reference to the net figures apportioned to capital, viz. £50+£5—£5) the Income Tax Account is debited with the total amount of tax actually suffered by deduction, viz. April 1st £75, July 1st £75, October 1st £60. The whole of this tax will be available to the company as an offset to its corporation tax liability, if any, or for repayment if there is no corporation tax liability.

7. The combined effect of the apportionment of £50 net interest to capital on April 1st and the subsequent doubling of this amount by the transfer to Income Tax Account is to reduce the book value of the original purchase to £17,400. The unsold balance of £12,000 nominal is valued accordingly, viz. $\frac{12,000}{20,000} \times £17,400 = £10,440$

If there had been more than one acquisition of this investment during the year the remaining balance would normally be valued by reference to the average cost, bearing in mind that any sale made during the year could have been effected only out of the holding as it existed at that date, the profit or loss on sale being calculated accordingly.

## BONUS SHARES

Many companies, having financed their expansion out of profits ploughed back into the business, find that their accumulated reserves represent a very large percentage of their issued share capital; sometimes they may actually exceed their capital. As a result, dividends declared on the issued share capital appear to be at a high percentage rate, whereas in fact the dividend should be compared with the real capital employed in the company, namely, the aggregate of the issued share capital and the accumulated profits. In order to bring the share capital into line with the true capital employed, such companies frequently make bonus issues (more correctly called capitalization issues) of shares to their shareholders. It will be appreciated that the assets underlying the share capital are not in any way changed by a bonus issue and, therefore, in theory, the increased number of shares subsequently held by a shareholder is of the same value as his original holding. In practice, however, it is usually found that the market value of the total holding will have increased because of the anticipation that the company will continue to pay the same rate of dividend on its increased capital as it did on its original capital or that it will at least pay a dividend which represents an increase on the former rate. Another reason why the total market value of the new capital will usually be found to exceed the original value is that the number of shares available for dealing on the Stock Exchange having increased, a more active market is created. From the viewpoint of the recipient of bonus shares, however, they have been acquired without payment and therefore no value should be placed upon them in the books, the only amendment required in the Investment Account being an addition to the number of shares held. If, however, the shareholder sells the bonus shares he receives, it would be permissible to take credit for the profit on the sale, as the price obtained contains some element of the profit which existed on the original holding before the allotment of the bonus shares.

### Illustration (3)

J. Brown purchased 1,000 ordinary shares of £1 each in Wyezed Company Limited for £1,250, inclusive of brokerage and stamp duty. Some years later the company resolved to capitalize profits and to issue to the holders of ordinary shares one new ordinary share for every share held by them. Prior to the capitalization, the shares of Wyezed Company Limited stood in the market at £1·75 per share. After the capitalization the company's shares were dealt in on the market at 93p per share. J. Brown decided to sell the bonus shares he received and the sale was effected at 90p per share net.

### WYEZED CO. LTD £1 ORDINARY SHARES

| Date | | | Nominal | £ | Date | | | Nominal | £ |
|---|---|---|---|---|---|---|---|---|---|
| | Cash .. .. | | 1,000 | 1,250 | | Cash-Sale at 90p .. | | 1,000 | 900 |
| | Bonus .. .. | | 1,000 | — | | Balance c/d... .. | | 1,000 | 625 |
| | Profit transferred .. | | | 275 | | | | | |
| | | | 2,000 | £1,525 | | | | 2,000 | £1,525 |
| | Balance b/d. .. .. | | 1,000 | 625 | | | | | |

*Notes:* (i) As no value is placed on the bonus shares when received the book value of the total holding is reduced from £1·25 to £0·625 per share.

(ii) The shares held after the sale are carried down at cost, viz. $\frac{1,000}{2,000} \times £1,250 = £625$.

Capital gains tax has been ignored in the illustrations as it would not be reflected in the individual Investment Accounts. Provision for capital gains tax (or, in the case of a company, corporation tax on capital gains) would be made in the annual accounts and will have the effect of reducing the balance of profits, less losses, on sale of investments.

Companies sometimes seek to raise additional capital by offering to their shareholders new shares at a price which compares very favourably with the current market price of their existing shares. There is thus an element of bonus given to existing shareholders in that they are able to acquire free of brokerage, stamp duty etc., further shares in the company at less than the current market price or, if they so desire, to sell their 'rights' on the market. Where a share-holder exercises his rights by taking up the shares, the cost of the additional shares he acquires will be recorded in the relevant Investment Account in the same manner as any other purchase. If, however, the shareholder decides to sell his 'rights', it is considered that the proceeds of sale should be credited to the Investment Account in the capital column thus reducing the book value of the original holding, particularly as the immediate effect of a 'rights' issue is normally to depress the market value per share of the increased capital. This may be illustrated as follows:

Market Value of 1,000,000 shares at £2 per share    ..        ..  £2,000,000

Proceeds of 'Rights' issue 1,000,000 shares at £1 per share    ..  £1,000,000

Value of 2,000,000 shares = £1·50 per share  ..        ..        ..  £3,000,000

Nevertheless, if, after the rights issue, the market value of the increased capital has recovered to the original price of £2 or more, no objection could be taken to treating the proceeds of the 'rights' as a profit.

**Illustration (4)**

Included in the investments of Bull Ltd, on January 1st, was a holding of 10,000 ordinary shares of £1 each, fully paid, in Bear Ltd, having a book value of £11,250.

Bull Ltd does not make apportionments of dividends received or receivable.

On February 1st, Bull Ltd sold 2,000 shares in Bear Ltd for £4,300.

At a meeting held on March 31st, Bear Ltd decided:

1. to make a bonus issue of two fully paid shares for every five shares held on March 20th, and

2. to give its members the right to apply for one share for every two shares held on March. 20th, at a price of £1·25 per share of which 75p was payable on application on or before April 30th, and the balance of 50p on or before June 30th,

3. the new shares issued under 1 and 2 were not to rank for dividend for the year ended March 31st.

Bull Ltd duly received the bonus shares and took up the entitlement under the rights issue making the payments on the due dates.

Bear Ltd declared and paid dividends as follows:

July 20th, a final dividend of 10 per cent. for the year ended March 31st, and November 30th, an interim dividend of 5 per cent. for the year ended March 31st following.

Show the Investment Account in the books of Bull Ltd for the year ended December 31st. Ignore expenses of sale and taxation.

## BULL LTD
## BEAR LTD ORDINARY SHARES OF £1 EACH

| | | Nominal Value £ | Income £ | Capital £ | | | Nominal Value £ | Income £ | Capital £ |
|---|---|---|---|---|---|---|---|---|---|
| Jan. 1 | Balance b/f | 10,000 | | 11,250 | Feb. 1 | Bank – Sale | 2,000 | | 4,300 |
| Feb. 1 | Profit and Loss on Sales of Investments Account | | | 2,050 | July 20 | Dividend: 10 per cent. on 8,000 £1 shares for year to March 31st | | 800 | |
| Mar. 31 | Bonus Issue: (two fully paid for every five held) | 3,200 | | | Nov. 30 | Dividend: 5 per cent. on 15,200 £1 shares-interim for year to March 31st following | | 760 | |
| Apr. 30 | Bank: Shares taken up under rights issue 75p paid | 4,000 | | 3,000 | Dec. 31 | Balance, carried forward | 15,200 | | 14,000 |
| June 30 | Bank: Balance due on shares issued 50p per share | | | 2,000 | | | | | |
| Dec. 31 | Transfer to Income on Investments Account | | 1,560 | | | | | | |
| | | £17,200 | £1,560 | £18,300 | | | £17,200 | £1,560 | £18,300 |

*Note:* Profit of sale on investments –

|  |  |  |  | £ |
|---|---|---|---|---|
| Proceeds of sale, 2,000 shares | .. | | .. | 4,300 |
| *Less* Cost $\frac{2,000}{10,000} \times £11,250$ | .. | | .. | 2,250 |
| | | | | £2,050 |

## General Illustration

The Zip Investment Co Ltd was incorporated on January 1st, with an authorized capital of £40,000 in £1 shares, to hold and deal in securities. The following investments were bought and sold during the ensuing year:

*Purchases:*

Jan. 5th  £10,000 3½ per cent. War Loan at 73¾ (interest dates June 1st, December 1st).

Jan. 6th  £8,000 2½ per cent. Consols at 52¾ (interest dates January 5th, April 5th, July 5th, October 5th).

Mar. 31st  2,000 Ordinary Shares of £1 each, fully paid in B. & B. Ltd, at £1·25 per share.

June 8th  £5,600 2½ per cent. Consols at 53 *ex div.*

*Sales:*

May 3rd  £4,000 3½ per cent. War Loan at 72¼ *ex div.*

July 31st  £4,000 2½ per cent. Consols at 54 *cum div.*

All interest on the War Loan and Consols was received on the due dates. The only other dividend was: 10 per cent. for the year to May 31st, from B. and B. Ltd, received on June 30th.

The market values of the investments on December 31st, were: War Loan Stock 71¾, Consols 51, B. & B. Ltd £1·20.

Show the ledger accounts for the investments, for the year ended December 31st. Make apportionments in months. All investments are to be valued at December 31st at 'average cost'.

Ignore taxation.

## 3½ PER CENT. WAR LOAN ACCOUNT
### (June 1st/December 1st)

| | | Nominal | Income | Capital | | | Nominal | Income | Capital |
|---|---|---|---|---|---|---|---|---|---|
| | | £ | £ | £ | | | £ | £ | £ |
| Jan. 5 | Cash – Purchase at 73¾ *cum div.* £7,375 .. | 10,000 | | | May 3 | Cash – Sale at 72¼ *ex div.* .. | 4,000 | | 2,890 |
| | Income – 1 month's Interest .. | | 30 | | June 1 | Cash – ½ year's Interest on £10,000 – £175. Capital 1 month's Interest on £4,000 sold *ex div.* .. | | | |
| | Capital – Balance .. | | | 7,345 | | | | | 12 |
| Dec. 31 | Transfer to Income on Investments A/c | | 255 | | | Income – Balance .. | | 163 | |
| | | | | | Dec. 1 | Cash – ½ year's Interest on £6,000 .. | | 105 | |
| | | | | | Dec. 31 | Profit and Loss on Sale of Investments Account – Loss | | | 36 |
| | | | | | | Balances c/f. Income – 1 month's accrued Interest on £6,000 .. | | 17 | |
| | | | | | | Capital – 6/10 × £7,345 .. | 6,000 | | 4,407 |
| | | £10,000 | £285 | £7,345 | | | £10,000 | £285 | £7,345 |

WORKING:

Proof: Cost of £4,000 3½ per cent. War Loan sold  $\frac{4,000}{10,000} \times 7,345$  ..  £ 2,938

*Less:* Proceeds £(2,890+12)  ..    ..    ..    ..    .. 2,902

Loss  £36

## $2\frac{1}{2}$ PER CENT. CONSOLS ACCOUNT
### (January 5th, April 5th, July 5th and October 5th)

| | | Nominal | Income | Capital | | | Nominal | Income | Capital |
|---|---|---|---|---|---|---|---|---|---|
| | | £ | £ | £ | | | £ | £ | £ |
| Jan. 6 | Cash – Purchase at 52¾ *cum div.* | 8,000 | | 4,220 | Apr. 5 | Cash – ¼ year's Interest on £8,000 .. | | 50 | |
| June 8 | Purchase at 53 *ex div.* .. | 5,600 | | 2,968 | June 8 | Capital, contra 1 month's Interest on £5,600 purchased *ex div.* | | 12 | |
| | Income, contra 1 month's Interest thereon .. | | | 12 | | | | | |
| | | | | 7,200 | July 5 | Cash – ¼ year's Interest on £8,000 .. | | 50 | |
| Dec. 31 | Profit and Loss on Sale of Investments A/c | | | 34 | July 31 | Cash – Sale at 54 *cum div.* £2,160 .. | 4,000 | | |
| | Income from Investments A/c. .. | | 240 | | | Income – 1 month's Interest .. | | 8 | |
| | | | | | | Capital – Balance | | | 2,152 |
| | | | | | Oct. 5 | Cash – ¼ year's Interest on £9,600 .. | | 60 | |
| | | | | | Dec. 31 | Balances c/f: Income 3 months' accrued Interest on £9,600 .. | | 60 | |
| | | | | | | Capital – 96/136 × £7,200 .. | 9,600 | | 5,082 |
| | | £13,600 | £240 | £7,234 | | | £13,600 | £240 | £7,234 |

WORKING:

| | £ |
|---|---|
| Proceeds .. .. .. .. .. .. .. 2,152 | |
| *Less* Cost of proceeds $\frac{4,000}{13,600}$ × £7,200 .. .. .. .. 2,118 | |
| Profit £34 | |

## ORDINARY SHARES OF £1 EACH IN B. & B. LTD

| | | Nominal | Income | Capital | | | Nominal | Income | Capital |
|---|---|---|---|---|---|---|---|---|---|
| | | £ | £ | £ | | | £ | £ | £ |
| Mar. 31 | Cash – Purchase at £1·25 *cum div.* .. | 2,000 | | 2,500 | June 30 | Cash – Dividend for year to May 31st: Capital, 10 months .. | | | 167 |
| Dec. 31 | Income on Investments Account .. | | 33 | | | Income, 2 months .. | | 33 | |
| | | | | | Dec. 31 | Balance c/f. .. | 2,000 | | 2,333 |
| | | £2,000 | £33 | £2,500 | | | £2,000 | £33 | £2,500 |

*Note:* The investments are carried down and taken into the Balance Sheet at average cost, a note of the market value being appended, as required by the Companies Acts. Any permanent provision for fall in market value of investments would normally be made in a Provision for Depreciation of Investments Account.

## § 11. Tabular Ledgers

In certain businesses, considerable labour can be saved by utilizing tabular ledgers, particularly where the transactions concerned are numerous and similar.

The following are some of the more usual forms of tabular ledgers:

### (a) Bought Day Book and Ledger combined

It is sometimes possible, where accounts are settled regularly on a fixed monthly pay-day, to dispense with the bought ledger altogether by having a specially ruled form of bought day book. As invoices are received, they are filed away in alphabetical order. At the end of each month the special bought day book is written up from the invoices in alphabetical order. Under the name of each creditor particulars are inserted of all the invoices relating to his account in order of date, the amounts being enered in the detail column, and the total extended into the total column. Any returns or allowances should be deducted from the invoices to which they relate, and the amounts of the invoices entered in the day book net. When cash is paid, the amount thereof, together with the discount (if any), is posted in one sum from the credit of the cash book to the cash and discount column in the bought day book opposite to the item to which it relates. Each item in the total column is extended into the proper subsidiary column to which it refers, and the totals of these columns are posted monthly to the respective nominal accounts. This procedure has already been described in Chapter I, § 15.

The following is a convenient ruling for the book, with a few specimen entries:

**Illustration**

### BOUGHT DAY BOOK AND LEDGER

| Date | Invoice No. | Creditor | Detail | Total Credit | Date Paid | C.B. Folio | Cash and Discount | Materials | Packages | Freight | Repairs and Renewals | Trade Expenses |
|---|---|---|---|---|---|---|---|---|---|---|---|---|
| | | | £ | £ | | | £ | £ | £ | £ | £ | £ |
| Feb. 3 | 1 | Aldgate & Co Goods .. | 13 | | | | | | | | | |
| " 7 | 2 | " .. | 12 | | | | | | | | | |
| " 21 | 3 | " .. | 5 | | | | | | | | | |
| | | | | 30 | Mar. 4 | 31 | 30 | 30 | | | | |
| " 5 | 4 | Braid & Pierce Goods .. | 16 | | | | | | | | | |
| " 17 | 5 | " .. | 8 | | | | | | | | | |
| | | | | 24 | Mar. 4 | 31 | 24 | | 24 | | | |

### (b) Rental Ledger

Where numerous properties are held a rental ledger should be used, which may be ruled for the purpose of recording half-yearly, quarterly or weekly rentals. An illustration is given below of a quarterly rental ledger.

At the end of each quarter a 'Total' Rent Account can be prepared for the purposes of double entry posting.

The arrears brought forward will be the outstanding rental debtors per the last Balance Sheet or quarter in the rental ledger. The quarterly rent will be credited to Rent Receivable Account (which is closed off to Profit and Loss Account). The arrears brought forward plus the rent receivable give the total debits in the rent ledger.

The cash received will be debited to the cash book. The allowances will be debited to the appropriate account, e.g. to repairs if the tenant has paid for landlord's repairs. The arrears carried forward represent the outstanding debtors for rent and will be shown on the Balance Sheet (if one is prepared) or carried forward to the next quarter in the rent ledger. The cash received plus allowances and arrears carried forward give the total rent ledger credits which will equal the total debits.

### RENT LEDGER

| No. and Street | Name of Tenant | Arrears brought forward | Quarterly Rent | C B folio | Cash | Allowances | Arrears carried forward |
|---|---|---|---|---|---|---|---|
| 1 Hirst | Brown | £ — | £ 70 | 5 | £ 70 | £ — | £ — |
| 2 Hirst | Smith | 5 | 40 | 8 | 15 | 18 | 12 |
| 3 Hirst | Wood | — | 130 | 12 | 110 | — | 20 |
|  |  | £5 | £240 |  | £195 | £18 | £32 |

### TOTAL RENT ACCOUNT

| | £ | | £ |
|---|---|---|---|
| Balance – arrears brought forward  ..  .. | 5 | Cash received  ..  ..  ..  .. | 195 |
| Rents receivable  ..  ..  ..  .. | 240 | Allowance  ..  ..  ..  .. | 18 |
| | | Balance – arrears carried forward  ..  .. | 32 |
| | £245 | | £245 |

## (c) Hotel Visitors' Ledger

The personal accounts for visitors at an hotel can be most conveniently recorded by means of a tabular visitors' ledger, which contains similar particulars to those furnished on the accounts rendered to visitors.

The following is a typical form:

### VISITORS' LEDGER

| DEBITS | Room 1 Name | Room 2 Name | Room 3 Name | Room 4 Name | Room 5 Name | Room 6 Name | Room 7 Name | Room 8 Name | Room 9 Name | Room 10 Name | DEBITS | Total |
|---|---|---|---|---|---|---|---|---|---|---|---|---|
|  | £ | £ | £ | £ | £ | £ | £ | £ | £ | £ |  | £ |
| Brought fd. |  |  | 2·63 |  |  |  |  |  |  |  | Brought fd. |  |
| Apartments .. |  |  | 1·60 |  |  |  |  |  |  |  | Apartments .. |  |
| Board etc. |  |  |  |  |  |  |  |  |  |  | Board etc. |  |
| Fires .. |  |  |  |  |  |  |  |  |  |  | Fires .. |  |
| Breakfasts .. |  |  | ·35 |  |  |  |  |  |  |  | Breakfasts .. |  |
| Luncheons etc. .. |  |  |  | ·40 |  |  |  |  |  |  | Luncheons etc. |  |
| Dinners .. .. |  |  | ·75 | ·50 |  |  |  |  |  |  | Dinners .. |  |
| Tea, Coffee, Milk.. |  |  | ·05 | ·03 |  |  |  |  |  |  | Tea, Coffee, Milk |  |
| Wine .. .. |  |  | 1·25 |  |  |  |  |  |  |  | Wine .. |  |
| Spirits .. |  |  |  | ·12 |  |  |  |  |  |  | Spirits .. |  |
| Beer .. |  |  |  |  |  |  |  |  |  |  | Beer .. |  |
| Minerals .. |  |  |  | ·03 |  |  |  |  |  |  | Minerals .. |  |
| Cigars and Cigarettes .. |  |  |  |  |  |  |  |  |  |  | Cigars and Cigarettes .. |  |
| Laundry.. .. |  |  |  |  |  |  |  |  |  |  | Laundry .. |  |
| Paid out.. .. |  |  |  |  |  |  |  |  |  |  | Paid out .. |  |
| Etc. .. .. |  |  |  |  |  |  |  |  |  |  | Etc. .. |  |
| Total £ |  |  | 6·63 | 1·08 |  |  |  |  |  |  | Total £ |  |

[continued on next page

## VISITORS' LEDGER (continued)

| CREDITS | | | | | | | | | | CREDITS | £ |
|---|---|---|---|---|---|---|---|---|---|---|---|
| Cash   ..    .. | | | 6·63 | | | | | | | Cash ..    .. | |
| Allowance    .. | | | | | | | | | | Allowances   .. | |
| Personal | | | | | | | | | | Personal | |
|    Accounts   .. | | | | | | | | | |    Accounts   .. | |
| Bal. c/f. ..    .. | | | 1·08 | | | | | | | Bal. c/f. ..    .. | |
| Total £ | | | 6·63 | 1·08 | | | | | | Total £ | |

A separate page is opened for each day's transactions, and a column provided for each visitor, headed with the number of his room. The amount brought forward at the commencement of the page in each column represents the balance due at the commencement of the day from the visitor concerned. When an account is settled, as in column (3) of the illustration, the cash received is entered as a credit, and there will be no balance to be carried forward to the next day's page.

Where circumstances render it desirable, the amount due at any date from a visitor can be transferred to a ledger account in the personal ledger, and in this way taken out of the visitors' ledger.

The daily totals for each heading, both debits and credits, are entered in the total column on the right-hand side, and transferred to a summary ledger, from which the monthly, quarterly, or half-yearly totals, can be obtained, or posted to the impersonal accounts.

### (d) Plant Ledger

Where there are numerous items of plant it is essential that a plant ledger be kept in order that the cost and written down value of each item can be ascertained quickly. A separate account will be kept for each machine showing expenditure on repairs. To facilitate computations of writing down allowances etc. for taxation purposes it is advantageous to provide each account with columns showing the allowances received and the written down values carried forward.

The following ruling will be found convenient:

## PLANT LEDGER
### WRAPPING MACHINE NO. 3

Rate of Depreciation 10% (on diminishing balance).     *Purchased* July 1st, 1968
Taxation Writing Down Allowances 15%.         *Cost*      £600

| Date | Particulars | Alterations or Additions | Repairs | Total Capital Cost | Date | Provision for Depreciation | Written Down Value | Taxation Allowances | | | |
|---|---|---|---|---|---|---|---|---|---|---|---|
| | | | | | | | | Year | Initial | Annual | w.d.v. |
| 1968 | | £ | £ | £ | 1968 | £ | £ | | £ | £ | £ |
| July 1 | Cost – Brown & Co | | | 600 | Dec. 31 | 30 | 570 | 1969-70 | 180 | 90 | 330 |
| Nov. 1 | Motor Repairs – X Ltd   ..    .. | | 25 | | 1969 Dec. 31 | 57 | 513 | 1970-71 | | 50 | 280 |

Further columns may be provided to record the cumulative amount of depreciation provided for and the cost of repairs etc. to date, in order that a complete history of the machine may be disclosed at a glance.

## § 12. Stock Exchange Transactions

Only a stockbroker who is a member of one of the recognized Stock Exchanges is permitted to deal in Quoted Stocks and Shares on behalf of a client.

The procedure is for the stockbroker to approach one of the stock jobbers on the Stock Exchange and ask for a price. The jobber will quote two prices, e.g. his buying price and his selling price. If these are acceptable, the broker will then reveal whether he wishes to buy or sell. When the broker has dealt with the jobber he will send his client a contract note.

A contract note is the basic document in stockbrokers' book-keeping. A bought contract note shows the consideration payable for the bargain, also the transfer stamp duty, the contract stamp and the stockbroker's commission and the total amount due. A sold contract note also shows the consideration for the bargain, but from this is deducted the contract stamp and the stockbroker's commission to arrive at the net amount due to the client. The transfer stamp duty (at present at the rate of 1 per cent.) on the amount of the consideration is always charged to and paid by the buyer. The actual stamping of the document, however, is carried out by the selling broker who receives the cost from the buying broker.

It is the Stock Exchange practice to deal in Government securities on a cash basis. Purchases and sales of other Quoted Stocks and Shares are normally dealt in for 'the account'. 'The account' generally covers a period of two weeks but occasionally (about twice a year) it covers three weeks. Settlement between client and broker takes place on the Tuesday week following the last day of the account. Each 'bargain' is recorded in the stockbroker's bought and sold journal, the client being debited with the amount of the contract note, in the case of a purchase, and the jobber's account is credited with the consideration. Impersonal accounts are credited accordingly with the stamp duty, commission etc.

Documents known as 'Tickets' are used as the basis of settlement between broker and jobber. During the period between the last day of dealing for a particular account and the 'settlement' date, tickets are passed by the buying broker to the jobbers in respect of transactions made during the 'account'. The 'ticket' shows the name of the buyer, the number of shares dealt in and the bargain price. The ticket is then passed on to the selling broker whose account is debited by the jobber.

The ticket is attached to the security and delivered to the buying broker who pays the selling broker the consideration plus stamp duty. The office copy of the ticket embodies a Ledger Account. When the ticket is passed to the jobbers his Ledger Account is debited and the relevant Ticket Ledger Account is credited with the bargain price. At the same time Bought Stamp Account is debited and the Ticket Ledger Account credited with the transfer stamp duty. The Ticket Account is closed by the payment to the selling broker.

A summary of the basic double entry is set out below.

*A purchase of shares by a client:*

| Debit | Credit | With |
|---|---|---|
| Client | Jobber<br>Commission Receivable<br>Stamp Account<br>Contract Stamp Account | Price paid for shares<br>Stockbroker's Commission<br>Stamp Duty on purchase<br>Contract stamp |
| Jobber<br>Bought Stamp Account | Bought Ticket Accounts | 'Make-up' price of shares *plus* Stamp duty |
| Jobber or Cash | Cash or Jobber | Difference between price paid for shares and 'make-up' price (plus stamp duty) |
| Cash | Client | Cash received from client |
| Ticket Account | Cash | Cash paid to Stock Exchange for purchases during the account |
| Contract Sold Stamp Account | Cash | Monthly payment to the Inland Revenue |
| Commission Receivable | Profit and Loss Account | Commission earned |

*A sale of shares by a client:*

| Debit | Credit | With |
|---|---|---|
| Jobber | Client<br>Commission Receivable Account<br>Contract Stamp Account | – Net proceeds<br>– Selling commission<br><br>– Contract stamp |

*A sale of shares by a client (continued) :*

| Debit | Credit | With |
|---|---|---|
| Ticket Accounts | Jobber <br> Inland Revenue | 'Make-up' price of shares sold, *plus* buyer's stamp duty |
| Cash or Jobber | Jobber or Cash | Difference between gross proceeds and 'make-up' price |
| Inland Revenue | Cash | Stamp duty paid on behalf of the buyer |
| Contract <br> Stamp Account | Cash | Monthly payment to the Inland Revenue |
| Cash | Ticket Accounts | Cash received from the Stock Exchange for sales during the account |
| Client | Cash | Payment to client of net proceeds |
| Commission Receivable Account | Profit and Loss Account | Commission for accounting period |

If a client does not wish to take up and pay for the shares on the due date the stockbroker may be able to arrange for the transaction to be 'Contangod', on his behalf, so that the bargain is carried over for settlement on the due date for the next Stock Exchange Account. Bargains are carried over at a 'make-up' price and the client then pays or receives the difference between 'make-up' and bargain price.

The old account is thus adjusted with the 'make-up' price plus refund of stamp duty and the new account is debited with the same amount plus interest which is charged by the jobber.

**Illustration**

S. Fuller entered into the following transactions with his stockbrokers:
Purchases –

On July 16th £10,000 L.N. Co Ltd 2nd Preference Stock at 24. Stamp Duty, £48.
On July 20th £12,000 L.N. Co Ltd 8 per cent. Preference Stock at 84. Stamp Duty, £202.
On July 23rd £9,000 S. Co Ltd Deferred Stock at 23. Stamp Duty £42.

Sales –

On July 24th £10,000 L.N. Co Ltd 2nd Preference Stock at 24½.

The brokers charged a commission of one per cent. on the money value of stocks. Only one commission was charged on stocks bought and sold for the same account. At the close of the account, S. Fuller carried over the remaining stocks at 83 and 23½ respectively, contango being charged at 5 per cent. per annum on the amount due, the following account being a 14-day account.

Ignore contract stamps and transfer fees, and make calculations to the nearest £.

### S. FULLER

| Date | Description | £ | £ | Date | Description | £ | £ |
|---|---|---|---|---|---|---|---|
| July 16 | £10,000 L.N. Co 2nd Pref. Stock at 24 .. .. | 2,400 | | July 24 | £10,000 L.N. Co 2nd Pref. Stock at 24½ .. .. | | 2,450 |
| | Commission .. .. | 24 | | | Stamp Duty written back | | 48 |
| | Stamp Duty .. | 48 | | | | | |
| | | | 2,472 | | Stock carried over: | | |
| ,, 20 | £12,000 L.N. Co 8% Pref. Stock at 84 .. .. | 10,080 | | | £12,000 L.N. Co Pref. at 83 .. .. | 9,960 | |
| | Commission .. .. | 101 | | | £9,000 S. Co at 23½ .. | 2,115 | |
| | Stamp Duty .. | 202 | | | | | 12,075 |
| | | | 10,383 | | Stamp Duty on L.N. Co and S. Co Stocks c/d... | | 244 |
| ,, 23 | £9,000 S. Co Deferred Stock at 23 .. .. | 2,070 | | | | | |
| | Commission .. .. | 21 | | | Cash .. .. .. | | 171 |
| | Stamp Duty .. | 42 | | | | | |
| | | | 2,133 | | | | |
| | | | £14,988 | | | | £14,988 |
| | Balance b/d.: £12,000 L.N. Co Pref. at 83.. .. .. | 9,960 | | | | | |
| | £9,000 S. Co Def. at 23½ | 2,115 | | | | | |
| | | | 12,075 | | | | |
| | Contango .. .. | | 23 | | | | |
| | Stamp Duty b/d. .. | | 244 | | | | |

*Note:* As the L.N. Co 2nd Preference Stock was bought and re-sold within the same account, no transfer will be executed by Fuller and the stamp duty charges must therefore be credited back.

The requirements concerning the accounts and balance sheets of members of the Stock Exchange, London, are dealt with in Stock Exchange Rule 79a which is reproduced hereunder, as revised in August 1966:

### RULE 79a

(*Note:* 'Partners' shall include limited partners unless otherwise stated)

1. Every Firm shall maintain records in sufficient detail to show particulars of:

(a) all moneys received or paid by the Firm;

(b) all purchases and sales of securities by the Firm and the charges and credits arising therefrom;

(c) all transactions by the Firm with or for the account of –
    (i) clients, excluding partners in the Firm;
    (ii) partners in the Firm;
    (iii) Firms of The Stock Exchange, London (including bargains to be settled through the Settlement Office);
    (iv) Firms of all other Stock Exchanges in Great Britain and Ireland;
    (v) Associated Members, Attachés and employees;
    (vi) other persons.

(d) all income from commissions, interest and other sources and all expenses, commissions and interest paid;

(*e*) all assets and liabilities, including contingent liabilities, of the Firm;

(*f*) all securities which are the property of the Firm, showing by whom they are held and whether, if held otherwise than by the Firm itself, they are so held as collateral against loans or advances;

(*g*) all securities which are not the property of the Firm but for which the Firm or any nominee company controlled by it is accountable, showing by whom and for whom they are held and:

　　(i) the extent to which they are held for safe custody in which case, with effect on and after January 1st, 1967, they must either be registered in the name of the client or of the Firm's nominee company or be deposited in a specially designated Safe Custody Account with the Firm's bankers;

　　(ii) the extent to which they are deposited with any third party as collateral against loans or advances to the Firm in which case such deposit must be authorized by the client or other person concerned. Such authority must be in writing and must specify the period to which it relates and be renewed annually.

(*h*) all purchases and sales of options by the Firm, fees (option moneys) arising therefrom, any related covering transactions and all declarations to exercise the options.

The provisions of this Clause shall in so far as they are relevant apply not only to records in the United Kingdom, but also to those of any Overseas Branch Office and not only to the Firm itself, but also to any company owned or controlled thereby for the purpose of conducting the business of the Firm.

2. Every Firm shall cause a Balance Sheet to be prepared from time to time showing in accordance with the provisions of this Rule the assets and liabilities of the Firm and the partners' capital therein. The assets and liabilities shall be brought into account in the said Balance Sheet at such amounts and shall be classified and described therein in such manner that the Balance Sheet gives a true and fair view of the state of affairs of the Firm, as at the Balance Sheet date. The said Balance Sheet shall be signed by each and all of the partners in the Firm.

3. Each such Balance Sheet shall be prepared as at a date which is not, without the consent of the Council, more than fifty-four weeks after the date as at which a Balance Sheet was last prepared under the provisions of Rule 79a, or, as the case may be, the date on which the Firm began to trade. A Balance Sheet shall be deemed to comply with this Rule notwithstanding that it does not take into account transactions in securities since the close of dealing for the last preceding Stock Exchange Account.

4. (*a*) Without prior consent of the Council no Firm shall change its practice with regard to the date as at which the said Balance Sheet is prepared.

(*b*) Every new Firm shall within one month from the date of commencement of business, notify the Council of the date as at which its Balance Sheet will be prepared in each year.

5. In addition to all other requirements of this Rule there shall be disclosed in the said Balance Sheet:

(*a*)　(i) the balances at credit on the Capital Account of –
　　　　(*a*) each limited partner;
　　　　(*b*) each general partner;
　　(ii) the balances at debit on the Capital Account of each general partner.

(*b*) the balance due to or from each partner in respect of transactions in securities.

(*c*)　(i) credit balances on current and all other accounts of –
　　　　(*a*) each limited partner;
　　　　(*b*) each general partner;
　　(ii) debit balances on current and all other accounts of each general partner.

(*d*) Amounts due to banker specifying the nature and market value of any security given and the fact, where applicable, that the security given is not the property of the Firm;

(*e*) any other liabilities which are secured, either by the deposit of securities or otherwise, specifying the nature and market value of the security at the date of the Balance Sheet and the fact, where applicable, that the security given is not the property of the Firm;

(*f*) by way of note, full particulars of any transactions in stocks or shares for the account of partners which have been closed at the end of the Stock Exchange Account immediately prior to the date of the Balance Sheet and opened for the immediately following Account. If there were no such transactions such fact must be stated.

6. For the purpose of clause (14) of this Rule and without prejudice to the general requirement of clause (2) the said Balance Sheet:

(*a*) shall distinguish the following classes of assets from one another and from any other assets –

    (i) money receivable in the ordinary course of business from –

        (*a*) clients, excluding partners in the Firm;

        (*b*) Associated Members, Attachés and employees;

        (*c*) Firms of any Stock Exchange in Great Britain and Ireland (including tickets receivable), excluding amounts relating to transactions in securities undertaken for the account of partners in the Firm;

        (*d*) other persons, excluding partners in the Firm.

    (ii) securities in which dealings are permitted under Rule 163 (1), stating by way of note the aggregate market value of such securities;

    (iii) payments for or towards the purchase of securities for which a quotation is pending;

    (iv) treasury bills, defence bonds, national development bonds and tax reserve certificates;

    (v) money on deposit (other than with banks) which is encashable within six months after the Balance Sheet date;

    (vi) cash and stamps in hand and balances on current or deposit account with banks;

    (vii) such other assets as may be agreed with the Council for the purpose of clause (14);

(*b*) shall include among the liabilities a provision for income tax to the extent, whichever is the greater, of –

    (i) the total amount of the income tax (or a fair estimate thereof) outstanding in respect of all years of assessment ended on or before the Balance Sheet date and, where applicable, the accrued proportion for the year of assessment in which the Balance Sheet date falls, or

    (ii) the total amount of the income tax liability (or a fair estimate thereof) which would be outstanding if the Firm had ceased business at the Balance Sheet date;

(*c*) shall distinguish the following liabilities from one another and from all other liabilities –

    (i) credit balances as defined in paragraphs (*a*), (*b*) and (*c*) of clause (5) of partners in the Firm;

    (ii) those liabilities, if any, to Firms of any Stock Exchange in Great Britain and Ireland (including tickets payable) which relate to transactions in securities undertaken for the account of partners in the Firm;

    (iii) any amount set aside for income tax in excess of the provision specified in paragraph (*b*) of this clause;

    (iv) such other liabilities as may be agreed with the Council for the purpose of clause (14).

7. Without prejudice to the general requirements of clause (2) of this Rule, the said Balance Sheet shall include provision for, or a note of:

(*a*) the amount, if any, by which the sum at which securities in which dealings are permitted under Rule 163 (1) owned by the Firm are brought into account exceeds their aggregate market value;

(*b*) the amount, if any, by which bear positions in securities in which dealings are permitted under Rule 163 (1) are brought into account falls short of the aggregate market value of the securities comprised in the bear position;

(*c*) the amount of any loss which the Firm could incur in respect of options granted and outstanding calculated on the basis of market values;

(*d*) the amount of any accumulated losses, so far as they concern the Firm, of any Service Company of which the Firm is owner;

(*e*) the amount of any foreseeable losses from bad or doubtful debts or from any other causes;

and for the purpose of clause (14) the said amounts shall be taken into account as liabilities except to the extent that any provision for them has been applied in the Balance Sheet in reduction of the amounts at which related assets have been included. In relation to securities quoted on The Stock Exchange, London, market value means the market value at the Balance Sheet date as evidenced by the quotations in the Stock Exchange Daily Official List.

8. The said Balance Sheet shall be submitted to an independent qualified Accountant to whom shall be made available all the books and records of the Firm and all such explanations and other information as he may require for the purpose of carrying out under this Rule such examinations as will enable him to meet the requirements of clause (10) of this Rule.

9. For the purpose of this Rule 'independent qualified Accountant' means a person who is:

(*a*) in public practice; and

(*b*) independent of the Firm; and

(*c*) a member, or a firm all of whose partners are members, of one or more of the following professional bodies –

> The Institute of Chartered Accountants in England and Wales
> The Institute of Chartered Accountants of Scotland
> The Association of Certified and Corporate Accountants
> The Institute of Chartered Accountants in Ireland.

10. (*a*) The said independent qualified Accountant shall provide the Firm with three signed copies of a report addressed to the Council of The Stock Exchange stating:

(i) whether, subject to any reservations relating to the scope of his examination or to any other matters, he is of the opinion that –

(*a*) the Firm had at the Balance Sheet date records properly maintained which comply with the requirements of clause (1) of this Rule;

(*b*) the Balance Sheet is in accordance with those records;

(*c*) the Balance Sheet gives a true and fair view of the state of affairs of the Firm at the Balance Sheet date;

(*d*) the Balance Sheet complies with the requirements of clauses (5), (6) and (7) of this Rule;

and whether or not at the Balance Sheet date securities referred to in clause (1) (*g*) (ii) of this Rule were deposited with any third party as collateral for loans or advances to the Firm and, if so, whether he has inspected the written authorizations referred to in the said clause;

(ii) whether, as shown by the Balance Sheet and at the date thereof, the excess of assets over liabilities as defined by clause (14) of this Rule was not less than the minimum amount which that clause requires the Firm to maintain;

(iii) whether, in the case of a limited partnership, as shown by the Balance Sheet and at the date thereof, the aggregate of the balances on capital, current and all other accounts of the limited partners was within the limits prescribed by clause (15) of this Rule.

(*b*) In the case of Broker Firms engaged in Arbitrage business as Arbitrageurs on Joint Account or conducting option business as Option Dealers, the independent qualified Accountant shall also provide the Firm with three signed copies of a Report addressed to the Council of The Stock Exchange stating whether, subject to any reservations regarding the scope of his examination or to any other matter, he is of the opinion that the Firm had properly maintained records in compliance with the undertakings in Appendices 32 or 32c as may be applicable and, that on the basis of his examination, no business had been executed on behalf of any of its clients with the Firm's Arbitrage or Option Accounts.

11. Where the assets of a Firm include the entire share capital of a Service Company operated under the provisions of Rule 30b, the provisions of this Rule may be applied as though a Consolidated Balance Sheet of the Firm and the company were the Balance Sheet of the Firm.

12. (*a*) Where the assets of a Firm include the share capital of an unlimited company which is operating as a Corporate Member under the provisions of Rule 57b, the provisions of clause (14) of this Rule shall be applied as though the Balance Sheet of the Firm and the Balance Sheet of the company were consolidated.

(*b*) Where the assets of a Firm include an interest in any Branch Office whether separately incorporated or not, the Balance Sheet required by this Rule –

   (i) shall include the assets and liabilities of such Branch Office;

   (ii) shall disclose the aggregate amount of such assets included in those classes of asset which are specified in clause (6) (*a*) of this Rule.

13. The Firm shall forthwith submit one copy of the Accountant's Report referred to in sub-clause (10) (*a*) to the Council so as to be received by the Council not later than six months after the Balance Sheet date together with any report pursuant to sub-clause (10) (*b*) and shall at the same time submit a further copy of any such Reports together with the related Balance Sheet to the Exchange Accountant selected under clause (16) (*b*) (i), who shall receive them on behalf of the Council.

14. The partners of the Firm shall at all times maintain collectively a balance on Capital Account of such amount that the assets specified in clause (6) (*a*) of this Rule and such assets of the individual general partners as may be agreed by the Council in the aggregate (but, except as may be agreed otherwise with the Council, excluding the amount specified in clause (12) (*b*) (ii) of this Rule) exceed the liabilities (excluding liabilities specified in clause (6) (*c*) but including the amounts specified in clause (5) (*c*) (i) (*a*) and amounts falling to be treated as liabilities by virtue of clause (7)) by not less than the sum obtained by multiplying £5,000 by the number of partners in the Firm, provided that in the case of any Jobber Firm or in the case of a Broker Firm engaged in Arbitrage business on Joint Account or conducting option business as Option Dealers such sum shall not in any event be less than £15,000 and in the case of any Member continuing to carry on the business of a Broker on his own account pursuant to Rule 86, such sum shall not in any event be less than £10,000.

Where a Firm has Associated Members and/or Attachés and the number of such persons exceeds the number of the general partners in the Firm then for the purposes of this clause the excess number of such persons shall be regarded as partners of the Firm.

15. In the case of a limited partnership the sum of the amounts specified in paragraphs (*a*) (i) (*a*) and (*c*) (i) (*a*) of clause (5) of this Rule shall not at any time exceed one half (or such larger proportion as the Council may agree) of the net aggregate credit balance represented by the sum of the amounts specified in paragraphs (*a*) (i) (*b*) and (*c*) (i) (*b*) of that clause less debit balances as specified in paragraphs (*a*) (ii) and (*c*) (ii) thereof.

16. (*a*) The Council shall from time to time appoint one or more Firms of professional Accountants as Exchange Accountants (in this Rule referred to as Exchange Accountant) and shall notify Member Firms of the name and address of each Exchange Accountant so appointed.

(*b*) (i) Every Firm shall select the Exchange Accountant to which its Balance Sheet is to be submitted and shall inform the Council of its selection and shall not make any change therein without the consent of the Council.

   (ii) An Exchange Accountant shall be deemed to be authorized by the Firm to obtain direct from the Accountants reporting on the Balance Sheet any information or explanation which he may consider necessary for the purpose of carrying out his duties under sub-clause (*c*).

(iii) The Exchange Accountant selected shall not be either the Firm's independent Accountant or the Firm's Tax Adviser.

(c) In any case where a Balance Sheet or the information obtained (under sub-clause (b)) or any other matter arising out of his enquiries leads an Exchange Accountant to consider that further information should be obtained by the Council regarding the Firm's state of affairs, he shall report accordingly to the Council. All such reports shall be deemed to have been authorized by the Member Firm concerned.

(d) All Balance Sheets and other documents lodged for inspection as above provided shall be retained by the Exchange Accountant and shall be regarded as confidential to him and no disclosure of information contained therein or derived therefrom shall be made by him to any body or person except as the Exchange Accountant may consider necessary for the purposes of any report he may make under sub-clause (c) above.

*Note:* Rule 79a (10) (b) refers to the undertakings contained in Appendices 32 and 32c. These undertakings are set out as follows:

APPENDIX 32

### ARBITRAGE
### (Rule 92 (1))
### BROKER MEMBERS
#### (Joint Account)

........................................19.....

*To the Council of the Stock Exchange*

Gentlemen,

We apply under Rule 92 (1) for authority to carry on Arbitrage on Joint Account until March 24th, 19    , with or between the arbitrage correspondent(s) whose name(s), address(es) and description(s) are set out in the Schedule to this form. We have sent a copy of Rule 92 (1) to our correspondent(s) and attach a letter from them intimating their acceptance of the conditions laid down so far as such conditions affect the correspondents.

We hereby undertake –

(a) to exclude from Arbitrage any order received from a non-Member; and that if we execute such an order with a firm which is also our Arbitrage correspondent we will act solely as Broker and Agent and issue a Contract Note containing a charge for commission at a rate not less than that laid down in the Commission Rules.

(b) to maintain separate records for our Broker and Arbitrage business respectively showing for whom and with whom bargains have been transacted in such a manner as readily to demonstrate compliance with this undertaking.

(c) to instruct our Firm's independent qualified Accountant appointed to report on the Balance Sheet also to examine and report on these records as required by Rule 79a (10) (b).

Yours faithfully,

SCHEDULE

| Name of Arbitrage Correspondent | Address | Description of Business* |
|---|---|---|
| .................................................. | .................................................. | .................................................. |
| .................................................. | .................................................. | .................................................. |

*The applicant must state whether the Arbitrage Correspondents are Members or otherwise of the Overseas Stock Exchange.

*Regulation*

Except in special circumstances permission will not be granted to a Broker to carry on Arbitrage on Joint Account with more than one correspondent in the same centre or to more than one Member Firm to carry on Arbitrage on Joint Account with the same correspondent.

APPENDIX 32C

## OPTION DEALING
### (Rule 94)
### BROKER MEMBERS

....................................................19......

*To the Council of the Stock Exchange*

Gentlemen,

We apply under Rule 94 for authority to carry on business as Option Dealers until March 24th, 19.........

We hereby undertake:

(*a*) not to execute any Option business received from our clients with the Option Dealing side of our business.

(*b*) to maintain separate records for our Broker and Option Dealing respectively showing for whom and with whom bargains have been transacted in such a manner as readily to demonstrate compliance with this undertaking.

(*c*) to instruct our Firm's independent qualified Accountant appointed to report on the Balance Sheet also to examine and report on these records as required by Rule 79a (10) (*b*).

Yours faithfully,

The following further memorandum was issued in 1966 by the Council of The Stock Exchange with the approval of the Council of the Institute of Chartered Accountants in England and Wales, the Institute of Chartered Accountants of Scotland and the Association of Certified and Corporate Accountants.

### NOTES FOR THE GUIDANCE OF
### MEMBER FIRMS AND THEIR ACCOUNTANTS

(*Note:* 'Partners' includes limited Partners unless otherwise stated.)

1. *Summary of Provisions*

The Rule provides for the following matters, *inter alia:*

(*a*) The maintenance of a collective balance on Capital Account sufficient to ensure the required Minimum Margin of Solvency (see paragraph 2 below).

(*b*) The extent to which limited Partners may participate in providing finance for the Firm (see paragraph 3 below).

(*c*) The manner in which clients' securities must be held and the authority necessary before such securities can be pledged.

(*d*) The keeping by the Firm of adequate records including records of all securities held whether the property of the Firm or not.

(*e*) The preparation by or on behalf of the Firm of a Balance Sheet (which must be signed by every Partner) showing a true and fair view of its state of affairs as at the date thereof.

(*f*) The classification and disclosure of assets and liabilities included in the Balance Sheet.

(*g*) The appointment by each Firm of an independent Accountant to examine its Balance Sheet and to prepare a report thereon addressed to the Council of The Stock Exchange.

(*h*) The submission by each Firm of a copy of its Balance Sheet and of the Accountant's report to an Exchange Accountant for examination on behalf of the Council of The Stock Exchange. The Exchange Accountant selected shall not be the Firm's independent Accountant.

## 2. *Minimum Margin of Solvency*

The minimum margin of solvency must be maintained at all times and must not be less than £5,000 per Partner with a minimum of £15,000 for a Jobbing Firm and any Broking Firm engaged in arbitrage on joint account or option business. All principals whether full Partners or otherwise and irrespective of whether they receive part or all of their remuneration by share of profits, commission or salary must be regarded as Partners for the purpose of calculating the minimum margin of solvency. Also to be regarded as Partners but only for this purpose is any excess in the number of Associated Members and Attachés over the number of general Partners in a Firm. The inclusion of Attachés will become operative from January 1st, 1967. (Attachés are those people entered on the Register of Attachés kept by the Council under Rule 199 (2) (*c*).)

Clause (14) lays down the manner in which the margin is to be computed. Broadly speaking, only money receivable in the ordinary course of business and those assets which are readily realizable may be taken into account. All balances related to uncompleted transactions in securities undertaken by the Firm for the account of Partners individually are to be ignored, as are securities in which dealings have been suspended, unquoted securities, and amounts receivable otherwise than in the ordinary course of business, e.g. Loans to staff for housing. Apart from the liabilities specified in Clause (6) (*c*), which are excluded for the purpose of this margin, all liabilities must be taken into account. The Council of The Stock Exchange have powers on application by a Firm to approve the inclusion of other assets of the Firm and assets of individual Partners (Clauses (6) (*a*) (vii) and (14)).

## 3. *Limited Partners*

Clause (15) restricts the extent of limited Partners' interests in a Firm. Reference should be made to the *Limited Partnerships Act 1907* for the statutory rights and obligations of such Partners.

## 4. *Brokers acting as Joint Account Arbitrageurs and/or Option Dealers*

Brokers acting as Joint Account Arbitrageurs and/or Option Dealers have to apply annually to the Council of The Stock Exchange for permission under Rules 92 (i) (*f*) and 94 respectively and, when permission is given, it is subject to the condition that there shall be a segregation of the two sides of the business of the Broker Firm. Separate records for each side of the business have to be maintained and an undertaking given that such a Firm will not execute business on behalf of its clients with the other (non-Broker) side of the business (Appendices 32 and 32c). As evidence of compliance with this undertaking, the Firm is required to submit a report from its Accountants addressed to the Council of The Stock Exchange at the same time as the report on the Balance Sheet is provided (Clause (10) (*b*)).

## 5. *Securities*

Particular attention is drawn to sub-clauses (*f*) and (*g*) of Clause (1) regarding securities. All movements of securities should be recorded in such a manner as to enable the security position of the Firm and of any third party for whom securities are held to be readily ascertained as at any particular date.

The provision contained in Clause (1) (*g*) (i) in so far as it relates to the specially designated safe custody account with the Firm's bankers will become operative on January 1st, 1967, and evidence of compliance at the Balance Sheet date with this and the other provisions of Clause (1) will be provided in the Accountant's report (Clause (10) (*a*) (i) (*a*)).

## 6. *Defence Bonds and National Development Bonds*

It is understood that Defence Bonds and National Development Bonds cannot be held in the name of a Firm, but for the purpose of Clause (6) (*a*) (iv) they may be held in the name of a Nominee Company on the Firm's behalf.

### 7. *Other Assets of the Firm*

Clause (6) (*a*) (vii) refers to assets of the Firm as distinct from the assets of individual Partners which are dealt with in Clause (14). Normally the Council of The Stock Exchange will only give permission under the former clause for the inclusion in the margin of solvency calculation of those assets of the Firm which are readily realizable.

### 8. *Assets of Individual Partners*

An application under Clause (14) may be made by a Firm for permission to include securities belonging to individual general Partners (and therefore not appearing as assets in the Firm's Balance Sheet) in the calculation of the margin of solvency. The following conditions will be included in any grant of permission which may be made by the Council of The Stock Exchange:

(*a*) Such assets must be limited to the securities held from time to time by the individual general Partners of the Firm, such securities being registered in the name of the Nominee Company of the Firm's bank and held to the Firm's order. A separate note to the Balance Sheet must disclose the market value of such securities and the manner in which they are held.

(*b*) (i) The Firm must have adequate control over the securities to ensure that they are available at all times for its requirements; the withdrawal from deposit must be adequately controlled to ensure that an individual Partner cannot withdraw securities from deposit on his signature alone.

    (ii) The Firm must have adequate control over the quantum of the securities deposited with the Firm's bank by each individual Partner.

(*c*) These conditions must be notified by the Firm to its Independent Accountant who must confirm that, in his opinion, the measure of control by the Firm over the custody and quantum of such securities is not less than would be required to satisfy him were the securities included in the Balance Sheet as assets of the Firm. Such confirmation must be made at the same time as the report required by Clause (10) and a copy thereof furnished both to the Council of The Stock Exchange and to the Exchange Accountant.

(*d*) The permission of the Council of The Stock Exchange must be renewed annually.

### 9. *The Balance Sheet*

(*a*) The general provisions, including the date as at which a Firm's Balance Sheet must be prepared, are contained in Clauses (2), (3) and (4).

(*b*) It is essential that the Balance Sheet should be prepared as soon as possible after the end of the accounting year in order to give adequate time for the Accountant's examination and the making of his report to the Council of The Stock Exchange who will require strict compliance with the six months' time limit (Clause (13)).

(*c*) To assist Firms to appreciate the matters dealt with in the Rule there follows a *pro forma* Balance Sheet [*not reproduced in this extract*] of a Broker Firm cross-referenced to the relevant Clauses of the Rule. This *pro forma* Balance Sheet is adaptable for a Jobbing Firm, subject to differences in the nature and description of certain assets and liabilities and to the inclusion of any amounts required to be provided under Clause (7) (*b*).

(*d*) It is emphasized that the *pro forma* Balance Sheet is illustrative only, does not form part of the Rule and is not to be regarded as a prescribed form. Each Firm is free to prepare its Balance Sheet in whatever form and showing whatever information the Firm thinks fit, provided it complies with the Rule and in particular with the requirement to give a true and fair view of the state of affairs of the Firm.

(*e*) Where a Corporate Member is owned by a Firm the Rule requires the preparation of a Consolidated Balance Sheet. If, in such a case, the Balance Sheet of the Corporate Member is not made up on the same date as that of the Firm, it will be necessary for one or other to prepare a special Interim Balance Sheet for consolidation to comply with Clause (12) of the Rule.

(*f*) The method of valuing securities is laid down in Clause (7); where the security is not listed in the appropriate Stock Exchange Official List, the accepted practice of valuing such securities will be followed.

(*g*) The adequacy of the provision for any foreseeable losses from bad or doubtful debts or from other causes should be carefully considered by member Firms (see paragraph 10 (*b*) below).

(*h*) In accordance with normal accountancy practice, option money receivable by a Firm in respect of options granted for the put or call should not be included in the Balance Sheet as an asset until the option is exercised or abandoned.

(*i*) In the case of a Firm with many Partners, it may be convenient to show the balances of each Partner's Capital, Current and other Accounts in an annexed schedule transferring the totals (both credit and debit) of each type of account to the Balance Sheet, which should make suitable reference to the schedule. Balances of general Partners must be distinguished from those of limited Partners.

### 10. *The Independent Accountant's Report*

In accordance with Clause (10), which also specifies its contents, the independent Accountant's report is to be addressed to the Council of The Stock Exchange.

While the full extent of the Accountant's examination will be a matter for arrangement between him and the Firm, it must, as a minimum, be sufficient to enable him to discharge his responsibilities to the Council of The Stock Exchange in accordance with Clause (10) and, if the Firm has made an application under Clause (14), to comply with the additional requirements set out in paragraph 8 above.

The Council of The Stock Exchange will place great reliance on the Accountant's report and his verification for that purpose of the assets and liabilities. It follows that he will need to do a considerable amount of auditing work and to base his examination of the books and records (including correspondence files) on a careful and critical review of the system of accounting and internal control.

Particular attention should be paid to:

(*a*) the soundness of the debts due to the Firm;

(*b*) the adequacy of the provisions made for liabilities and losses, including losses on collection of the debts;

(*c*) the system of control over securities held for safe custody;

(*d*) the provision of information called for by the Exchange Accountant under Clause (16) (*b*) (ii) particularly those matters referred to in paragraph 11 below.

It will be for the Accountant to consider in the circumstances of the particular Firm and in the light of his assessment of its system of accounting and internal control whether, and if so to what extent, he needs:

(i) to make spot checks at dates other than that of the Balance Sheet;

(ii) to obtain independent confirmation of debtor or creditor balances;

(iii) to make a test verification of securities held for safe custody.

In making his report the Accountant will, if necessary, include such reservations as he considers appropriate having regard to any limitations the Firm has imposed on the scope of his examination (for example, in relation to the matters set out above) or to any other matters.

In many cases the independent Accountant will also assist in the preparation of the Balance Sheet and there is nothing in the Rule to prohibit the same Accountant acting in this way. Nevertheless the Firm remains responsible for the Balance Sheet.

### 11. *The Exchange Accountant*

Clauses (13) and (16) provide for the examination of the Balance Sheet and Accountant's Report by an Exchange Accountant on behalf of the Council of The Stock Exchange, who will not themselves receive a copy of the Balance Sheet. Clause (16) (*d*) provides for all Balance Sheets and other documents lodged with an Exchange Accountant to be treated as confidential.

In order to assist the Exchange Accountant and to minimize the number of questions which it may be necessary to ask, Firms should arrange for their Accountants to supply the following information in so far as it applies to them in schedules accompanying the Balance Sheet:

(*a*) Particulars, without names, of each client's debit balance in excess of £500, which was outstanding at the date of the Balance Sheet and not fully secured at that date and which had not been paid by 14 days prior to the date of the Accountant's report. The schedule should include against each item, notes as to the reason for non-payment and indicate the extent to which provision against non-recovery has been made.

(*b*) Similar information in respect of money receivable in the ordinary course of business from Associated Members, Attachés, employees and other persons distinguishing between Associated Members, Attachés, employees and other persons (Clause (6) (*a*) (i) (*b*) and (*d*)).

(*c*) The total value of securities lodged as collateral against loans or advances to the Firm distinguishing between those which are the property of the Firm, of the Partners and of clients respectively.

Where an Exchange Accountant has reason to believe that a Broker Firm is conducting 'margin business', he may require the Firm to submit additional information with regard to the adequacy of the cover provided by the individual clients.

## § 13. Professional Accounts

The accounts maintained by professional men present certain special features, the most important of which are dealt with hereunder:

### (*a*) *Separate Banking Accounts for Clients' and Trust Monies*

It is essential for all professional men who handle money belonging to clients to take all possible steps to ensure that there can be no danger of clients' monies becoming confused with their own. This object is best attained by the maintenance of one or more special banking accounts to be used exclusively for clients' money. Although such a system is strongly to be recommended it is not obligatory, except for solicitors.

Section 29 of the *Solicitors Act 1957* provides that the Council of the Law Society shall make rules as to the keeping by solicitors of banking accounts for clients' monies and contains similar provisions regarding rules for banking accounts to be kept by a solicitor for trusts of which he is a sole trustee or where he is co-trustee with his partner, clerk or servant. (In such circumstances the solicitor is deemed a solicitor-trustee.) This section also empowers the Council of the Law Society to take such action as may be necessary to enable them to determine whether or not the rules are being complied with. If a solicitor fails to comply with any of the rules under the above section any person may make a complaint in respect of that failure to the disciplinary committee.

Rules at present in force are the *Solicitors' Accounts Rules 1967* and the *Solicitors' Trust Account Rules 1967*. The following is a synopsis of the Rules and they have been renumbered for the purposes of simplifying this extract.

(i) Every solicitor who holds or receives client's money, or money which under Rule (ii) hereof he is permitted and elects to pay into a Client Account, shall without delay pay such money into a Client Account. Any solicitor may keep one Client Account or as many such accounts as he thinks fit.

(ii) There may be paid into a Client Account –

(*a*) trust money;

(*b*) such money belonging to the solicitor as may be necessary for the purpose of opening or maintaining the account;

(*c*) money to replace any sum which for any reason may have been drawn from the account in contravention of paragraph (2) of Rule (vi) of these Rules; and

(*d*) a cheque or draft received by the solicitor which under paragraph (*b*) of Rule (iii) of these Rules he is entitled to split but which he does not split.

(iii) Where a solicitor holds or receives a cheque or draft which includes client's money or trust money of one or more trusts –

(*a*) he may where practicable split such cheque or draft and, if he does so, he shall deal with each part thereof as if he had received a separate cheque or draft in respect of that part; or

(*b*) if he does not split the cheque or draft, he shall, if any part thereof consists of client's money, and may, in any other case, pay the cheque or draft into a Client Account.

(iv) No money other than money which under the foregoing Rules a solicitor is required or permitted to pay into a Client Account shall be paid into a Client Account, and it shall be the duty of a solicitor into whose Client Account any money has been paid in contravention of this Rule to withdraw the same without delay on discovery.

(v) There may be drawn from a Client Account –

(*a*) in the case of client's money –

(i) money properly required for a payment to or on behalf of the client;

(ii) money properly required for or towards payment of a debt due to the solicitor from the client or in reimbursement of money expended by the solicitor on behalf of the client;

(iii) money drawn on the client's authority;

(iv) money properly required for or towards payment of the solicitor's costs where there has been delivered to the client a bill of costs or other written intimation of the amount of the costs incurred and it has thereby or otherwise in writing been made clear to the client that money held for him is being or will be applied towards or in satisfaction of such costs; and

(v) money which is thereby transferred into another Client Account;

(*b*) in the case of trust money –

(i) money properly required for a payment in the execution of the particular trust; and

(ii) money to be transferred into a separate bank account kept solely for the money of the particular trust;

(*c*) such money as may have been paid into the account under paragraph (*b*) of Rule (ii) or paragraph (*b*) of Rule (iii), or money which may have been paid into the account in contravention of Rule (iv);

provided that in any case under paragraph (*a*) or paragraph (*b*) of this Rule the money so drawn shall not exceed the total of the money held for the time being in such account on account of such client or trust.

(vi) (1) No money drawn from a Client Account under sub-paragraph (ii) or sub-paragraph (iv) of paragraph (*a*) or under paragraph (*c*) of Rule (v) above shall be drawn except by:

(*a*) a cheque drawn in favour of the solicitor; or

(*b*) a transfer to a bank account in the name of the solicitor not being a Client Account.

(2) No money other than money permitted by Rule (v) to be drawn from a Client Account shall be so drawn unless the Council specifically authorize in writing its withdrawal upon application by the solicitor.

(vii) (1) Every solicitor shall at all times keep properly written up such accounts as may be necessary –

(*a*) to show all his dealings with –

(i) clients' money received, held or paid by him; and

(ii) any other money dealt with by him through a Client Account; and

(*b*) (i) to show separately in respect of each client all money of the categories specified in sub-paragraph (*a*) of this paragraph which is received, held or paid by him on account of that client; and

(ii) to distinguish all money of the said categories received, held or paid by him, from any other money received, held or paid by him.

(2) All dealings referred to in sub-paragraph (*a*) of paragraph (1) of this Rule shall be recorded as may be appropriate –

(i) (*a*) either in a clients' cash book, or a clients' column of a cash book; or

(*b*) in a record of sums transferred from the Ledger Account of one client to that of another; and in addition –

(ii) in a clients' ledger, or a clients' column of a ledger;

and no other dealings shall be recorded in such clients' cash book and ledger or, as the case may be, in such clients' columns.

(3) In addition to the books, ledgers and records referred to in paragraph (2) of this Rule, every solicitor shall keep a record of all bills of costs (distinguishing between profit, costs and disbursements) and of all written intimations under Rule (v) (*a*) (iv) of these Rules delivered or made by the solicitor to his clients, which record shall be contained in a bills delivered book or a file of copies of such bills and intimations.

(4) In this Rule the expressions 'accounts', 'books', 'ledgers' and 'records' shall be deemed to include loose-leaf books and such cards or other permanent documents or records as are necessary for the operation of any system of book-keeping, mechanical or otherwise.

(5) Every solicitor shall preserve for at least six years from the date of the last entry therein all accounts, books, ledgers and records kept by him under this Rule.

(viii)      In order to ascertain whether these Rules have been complied with, the Council may require any solicitor to produce at a time and place to be fixed by the Council, his books of account, bank pass books, loose-leaf bank statements, statements of account, vouchers and any other necessary documents for the inspection of any person appointed by the Council and to supply to such person any necessary information and explanations and such person shall be directed to prepare for the information of the Council a report on the result of such inspection. Such report may be used as a basis for proceedings under the *Solicitors Acts 1957* and *1965*.

The following points in connection with these Rules are stated by the Law Society as matters to be noted:

1. *Signature of Cheques* – The signature of cheques on a client bank account by a person other than a solicitor is deprecated by the Council. Only in exceptional circumstances, e.g. illness, or unavoidable absence on business or holiday, should solicitors depart from the practice of themselves signing cheques drawn on client account. The practice of signing cheques in blank and leaving them with an employee is clearly unwise and is also deprecated.

2. *A solicitor must not treat himself as a client* – By virtue of the definition of clients' money contained in the Rules [not reproduced in the previous extract], a solicitor cannot treat himself as his own client for the purposes of the Rules nor can a member of the firm of solicitors be treated as a client of that firm.

3. *Money received by a solicitor as trustee may be paid into a Client Bank Account* – Where a solicitor is a trustee of a trust and receives money subject to that trust, he may receive it

either in the capacity of a solicitor or in the capacity of trustee. To decide in which capacity a solicitor receives the money may, in some cases, present difficulties and to prescribe means whereby the capacity could be determined would involve the introduction of extremely complicated Rules. Accordingly, the Solicitors' Accounts Rules provide that money subject to a trust of which the solicitor is a trustee, whether or not he is a solicitor-trustee in the limited sense used in the Rules, may be dealt with through a Client Account.

4. *The financing of clients out of a solicitor's own money held in a Client Account is forbidden* – If a solicitor wishes to advance money to or on behalf of a client, he must do so out of his office or private account.

5. *A solicitor can only withdraw his own money from a Client Bank Account by transfer to his Office Bank Account or a cheque in his own favour* – Rule (vi) [see extract above] of the Solicitors' Accounts Rules provides that where money is due to the solicitor from his Client Account he can only withdraw it by a cheque in his own favour or by a transfer to his own or Office Bank Account. The Council recommend that withdrawals from Client Account should be only for specific sums which the solicitor is entitled to withdraw and not of round sums generally on account of costs or other money due to the solicitor.

It should be noted that notwithstanding delivery to a client of a bill or other written intimation of costs incurred and notwithstanding that the client has been notified that money held for him will be applied towards or in satisfaction of such costs the money so held will continue to belong to that client until it is withdrawn from Client Account in accordance with Rule (vi) (1).

6. *Recording of cheques or drafts endorsed over in the ordinary course of business* – While a cheque or draft received on behalf of a client and endorsed over in the ordinary course of business would not pass through the solicitor's Client Bank Account, it should nevertheless be recorded in the solicitor's books of account as a transaction conducted on behalf of the client. Similarly cash received and paid out on behalf of the client should also be appropriately recorded.

7. *Drawing against a cheque before it is cleared* – Where a solicitor receives on behalf of a client a cheque or draft which he does not endorse over in the ordinary course of business to a third party or to the client he must deal with that cheque through his Client Account. Ordinarily his bankers will credit the account with the amount of the cheque before it has been cleared and will later debit the account if the cheque is not honoured. A solicitor should therefore use discretion in drawing against the cheque before it has been cleared and should only do so with the clear understanding that if the cheque is not in fact met and if the amount drawn from the Client Account is in excess of the amount held for the particular client, other client's money will have been used to make the payment and the solicitor will have committed a breach of the Rules. Where the solicitor on discovery of the breach at once pays the appropriate amount from his own resources into Client Account, it will be for his own accountant to decide whether to qualify his report.

8. *Money paid to a solicitor for costs which have been agreed or costs incurred in respect of which a bill or other intimation of the amount has been delivered* – When a solicitor receives money on account of costs he must, if the costs have been incurred and an intimation or bill of costs has been delivered, pay the money into his Office Account and not into a Client Account. Moreover, any payment of or on account of an agreed fee must also be paid into Office Account. Money received on account of costs in any other circumstances must be paid into a Client Account.

By Section 30 of the *Solicitors Act 1957*, as amended by Section 9 of the *Solicitors Act 1965*, every solicitor in practice is required to deliver to the Law Society every year a report signed by an accountant, stating whether the solicitor has complied or not with the above rules.

This section does not apply, however, if the solicitor satisfies the Council that owing to the circumstances of his case the delivery of an accountant's report is unnecessary, or that he is a 'public officer' who does not take out a practising certificate.

Columns for clients' money and office money should be provided, not only in the cash book but also in each personal account in the clients' ledger. The following entries should be made:

1. On receipt of money from or on behalf of a client (other than money referred to in paragraph 7 above) debit 'client' column in cash book and credit 'client' column in personal account.

2. On payment of money to or on behalf of a client for whom at least an equivalent amount of money is held, credit 'client' column in cash book and debit 'client' column in personal account.

3. If money is paid away to or on behalf of a client in excess of the amount standing to his credit in a 'client' account, credit 'office' column in cash book and debit 'office' column in personal account.

4. When a bill of costs is rendered to a client, debit 'office' column in personal account and credit Costs Account in impersonal ledger. (This would be done in total from the costs book.)

5. When a transfer of cash is made from a Client Bank Account to Office Bank Account in payment of a bill of costs rendered to a client or other amount due to the solicitor by the client, debit 'office' column and credit 'client' column in cash book.

If the solicitor's transactions are recorded in the above manner, the balance on the Client Bank Account at any time should be equal to the total of the balances of the 'client' columns in the personal accounts in the clients' ledger. At no time can there be a *debit* balance on the 'client' columns in a personal account, since no amount must be paid out of the Client Bank Account to or on behalf of a client in excess of the amount standing to his credit in the Client Bank Account.

**Illustration (1)**

A B & Co. keep all monies of clients in a separate banking account used exclusively for the purpose. At the end of each month they make any necessary transfer from 'Client Account' to 'Office Account'.

On July 1st, the balance at bank on 'Office Account' was £750, and the balance at bank on 'Client Account' was £1,055, made up of the following credit balances, viz.:

|  |  |  |  | £ |
|---|---|---|---|---|
| D & Co | .. | .. | .. | 50 |
| X Trust | .. | .. | .. | 115 |
| Z & Co | .. | .. | .. | 350 |
| J & Co Ltd | .. | .. | .. | 540 |
|  |  |  |  | £1,055 |

The receipts and payments for the month of July were as follows, all receipts being banked at once:

July  2  Received from C & Co, clients, £105 for costs as rendered.
  „   9  Paid £5 for insurance premium for D & Co.
  „   9  Paid £9 for repairs to premises rented by E & Co. under X Trust.
  „  15  Paid £9 for advertisements *re* J & Co Ltd.
  „  15  Authorized to draw £35 on account of costs *re* X trust.
  „  15  Authorized to draw £120 on account of costs *re* J & Co Ltd.
  „  16  Received from E & Co, £44 rent under X Trust.
  „  17  Cashed cheque for £10 for K from petty cash.
  „  18  Received from F & Co £100 in advance on account of professional services to be rendered.
  „  18  At the request of G & Co, paid £1 registration fees.
  „  19  Received £99 debt collected for H & Co.
  „  20  Paid H & Co £84, being amount recovered, less costs as agreed.
  „  21  Received £45 from T & Co, being debt due to J & Co Ltd.
  „  23  Received from D & Co cheque for £34, being balance of costs as rendered (£79), plus out-of-pockets.
  „  31  Agreed costs with F & Co, at £120 and received their cheque for balance, of £20.
  „  31  Paid salaries, £240, and drew petty cash, £20.

You are required:

(*a*) To write up the Cash Book and the Clients' Ledger Accounts.

(*b*) To draw a cheque on 'Client Account' for the amount due to 'Office Account' on July 31st; and

(*c*) To bring down the balances in the Cash Book, showing the agreement of the 'Client Account' bank balance with the credit balances on the Clients' Ledger.

## CASH BOOK

| | | Client | Office | | | Client | Office |
|---|---|---|---|---|---|---|---|
| | | £ | £ | | | £ | £ |
| July 1 | Balances b/f. | 1,055 | 750 | July 9 | D & Co Insurance Premium | | |
| „ 2 | C & Co – Costs | | 105 | | mium | 5 | |
| „ 16 | X Trust – Rent from E & Co | 44 | | | X Trust – Repairs to Premises rented by E & Co | 9 | |
| „ 17 | Petty Cash – Cheque cashed for K | | 10 | „ 15 | J & Co Ltd – Advertisements | 9 | |
| „ 18 | F & Co on A/c. | 100 | | „ 18 | G & Co – registration fees paid | | 1 |
| „ 19 | H & Co Debt collected | 99 | | „ 20 | H & Co – Debt recovered, *less* costs | 84 | |
| „ 21 | J & Co Ltd Debt from T & Co | 45 | | „ 31 | Salaries | | 240 |
| „ 23 | D & Co Balance of costs and out-of-pockets | | 34 | | Petty Cash | | 20 |
| „ 31 | F & Co Balance | | 20 | | Office Account | | 315 |
| | Client Account | | 315 | | Balances c/d. | 921 | 973 |
| | | £1,343 | £1,234 | | | £1,343 | £1,234 |
| Aug. 1 | Balances b/d. | 921 | 973 | | | | |

## CLIENTS LEDGER
### D & CO

| | | Client | Office | | | Client | Office |
|---|---|---|---|---|---|---|---|
| | | £ | £ | | | £ | £ |
| July 9 | Cash Insurance Premium | 5 | | July 1 | Balance b/f. | 50 | |
| „ 23 | Costs | | 79 | „ 23 | Cash | | 34 |
| „ 31 | Office Account | 45 | | „ 31 | Client Account | | 45 |
| | | £50 | £79 | | | £50 | £79 |

## X TRUST

| | | Client | Office | | | | Client | Office |
|---|---|---|---|---|---|---|---|---|
| | | £ | £ | | | | £ | £ |
| July 9 | Cash – Repairs to premises rented by E & Co .. | 9 | 35 | July 1 | Balance b/f. .. .. | 115 | |
| ,, 15 | Costs .. ... .. | | | ,, 16 | Cash – Rent from E & Co | 44 | |
| ,, 31 | Office Account .. .. | 35 | | ,, 31 | Client Account .. | | 35 |
| | Balance c/d. .. .. | 115 | | | | | |
| | | £159 | £35 | | | | £159 | £35 |
| | | | | Aug. 1 | Balance b/d. .. .. | 115 | |

## Z & CO

| | | Client | Office | | | | Client | Office |
|---|---|---|---|---|---|---|---|---|
| | | £ | £ | July 1 | Balance b/f. .. .. | £ 350 | £ |

## J & CO LTD

| | | Client | Office | | | | Client | Office |
|---|---|---|---|---|---|---|---|---|
| | | £ 9 | £ | | | | £ 540 | £ |
| July 15 | Cash – Advertisements .. | | 120 | July 1 | Balance b/f. .. .. | | |
| | Costs .. .. .. | | | ,, 21 | Cash – Debt collected from T & Co | 45 | |
| ,, 31 | Office Account .. .. | 120 | | ,, 31 | Client Account .. | | 120 |
| | Balance c/d. .. .. | 456 | | | | | |
| | | £585 | £120 | | | | £585 | £120 |
| | | | | Aug. 1 | Balance b/d. .. .. | 456 | |

## C & CO LTD

| | | Client | Office | | | | Client | Office |
|---|---|---|---|---|---|---|---|---|
| | | £ | £ 105 | | | | £ | £ 105 |
| July 1 | Balance b/f. .. .. | | | July 2 | Cash .. .. .. | | |

## F & CO LTD

| | | Client | Office | | | | Client | Office |
|---|---|---|---|---|---|---|---|---|
| | | £ | £ 120 | | | | £ | £ |
| July 31 | Costs .. .. .. | 100 | | July 18 | Cash on Account of future services .. .. | 100 | |
| | Office Account .. .. | | | ,, 31 | Client Account .. | | 100 |
| | | | | | Cash .. .. .. | | 20 |
| | | £100 | £120 | | | | £100 | £120 |

## G & CO

| | | Client | Office | | | | Client | Office |
|---|---|---|---|---|---|---|---|---|
| | | | £ 1 | | | | | |
| July 19 | Cash – Registration Fees .. | | | | | | |

## H & CO

| | | Client | Office | | | Client | Office |
|---|---|---|---|---|---|---|---|
| | | £ | £ 15 | | | £ 99 | £ |
| July 20 | Costs | | | July 19 | Cash – debt collected | | |
| | Cash | 84 | | „ 31 | Client Account .. | | 15 |
| „ 31 | Office Account .. | 15 | | | | | |
| | | £99 | £15 | | | £99 | £15 |

| Agreement: Balances on Clients' Accounts: | £ |
|---|---|
| X Trust | 115 |
| Z & Co | 350 |
| J & Co Ltd | 456 |
| | £921 |
| *Dr* Balance, G & Co out of pocket expenses | £1 |

| Amount transferred: | £ |
|---|---|
| Advance Costs, F & Co | 100 |
| „      „     D & Co | 45 |
| Costs, H & Co | 15 |
| „   X Trust | 35 |
| „   J & Co Ltd | 120 |
| | £315 |

*Note:* The out-of-pocket expenses for G & Co must not be taken to reduce the credit balance held on behalf of clients, no money having been received from that firm.

Pursuant to Section 8 of the *Solicitors Act 1965*, Rules have been made by the Council of the Law Society, approved by the Master of the Rolls, designed to deal with the special question of whether in individual circumstances the interest arising on a client's money held by the solicitor on deposit account, should properly be regarded as the property of the solicitor or the client. These Rules are known as The Solicitors' Accounts (Deposit Interest) Rules 1965, and are reproduced hereunder:

1. These Rules may be cited as the Solicitors' Accounts (Deposit Interest) Rules, 1965, and shall come into operation on the 1st day of September, 1965.

2. (1) Subject to Rule 5 of these Rules, when a solicitor holds or receives for or on account of a client money on which, having regard to all the circumstances (including the amount and the length of time for which the money is likely to be held), interest ought in fairness to the client to be earned for him, the solicitor shall either –

(*a*) deposit such money in a separate designated account and account to the client for any interest earned thereon; or

(*b*) pay to the client out of his own money a sum equivalent to the interest which would have accrued for the benefit of the client if the money had been deposited in a separate designated account under this Rule.

(2) In this Rule the expression 'a separate designated account' shall mean a deposit account at a bank in the name of the solicitor or his firm in the title of which the word 'client' appears and which is designated by reference to the identity of the client or matter concerned.

3. Without prejudice to the generality of Rule 2 of these Rules, it shall be deemed that interest ought in fairness to a client to be earned for him where a sum of money is received for or on account of the client which exceeds £500 and at the time of its receipt is unlikely within two months thereafter to be either wholly disbursed or reduced by payments to a sum less than £500.

4. Without prejudice to any other remedy which may be available to him, any client who feels aggrieved that interest or a sum equivalent thereto has not been paid to him under these Rules shall be entitled to require the solicitor to obtain a certificate from The Law Society as to whether or not interest ought to have been earned for him and, if so, the amount of such interest and upon the issue of such a certificate the sum certified to be due shall be payable by the solicitor to the client.

5. Nothing in these Rules shall –

(a) affect any arrangement in writing, whenever made, between a solicitor and his client as to the application of the client's money or interest thereon; or

(b) apply to money received by a solicitor being money subject to a trust of which the solicitor is a trustee.

### (b) *Treatment of Disbursements on behalf of Clients*

Disbursements made on behalf of clients may be (a) charged direct to the accounts of the clients concerned, or (b) debited to a Clients Disbursements Account, pending the rendering of a bill of costs. Whichever method is adopted, the Bills Rendered Book should record the following details in columnar form:

> (i)   Costs chargeable.
>
> (ii)  Disbursements on behalf of clients.
>
> (iii) Total.

If method (a) is adopted Clients Accounts will already have been debited with (ii), and will now be debited with (i) only. The total of column (i) will be credited to Costs Account, the entries in column (ii) being regarded merely as memoranda.

When method (b) is adopted items in both columns (i) and (ii) will be debited to the Clients Accounts. The total of column (ii) will be credited to Clients Disbursements Account, the balance on which will be the amount of debtors for disbursements not yet charged up. At the end of each accounting period the balance on Clients Disbursements Account should be analysed to ensure that no irrecoverable items are included therein.

It is sometimes the practice to credit the total amount of the accounts rendered to clients (i.e. the total of column (iii)) to the Costs Account. In these circumstances the disbursements made on behalf of clients must be debited to the Costs Account so that credit will only be taken for the profit costs earned. When this system is adopted, the Costs Account must also be credited with the amount of disbursements not yet charged up, this amount being carried forward to the debit of the succeeding period. The Costs Account would then appear as under:

### COSTS ACCOUNT

| | | £ | | | £ |
|---|---|---|---|---|---|
| Jan.      1 | Disbursements on behalf of clients b/f... | | Jan./Dec. | Bills Rendered .. | 7,896 |
| | | 362 | Dec.    31 | Disbursements not yet charged out | |
| Jan./Dec. | Disbursements during year | 1,342 | | c/d .. | 192 |
| Dec.   31 | Profit and Loss Account: costs transferred | 6,384 | | | |
| | | £8,088 | | | £8,088 |
| Jan.      1 | Balance b/d. .. | 192 | | | |

### (c) Outstanding Costs at the Balance Sheet Date

At the end of each accounting period there will usually be a certain amount of uncompleted work in hand for which bills have not been rendered to clients.

Before arriving at the profit or loss for the period under review, the value of this outstanding work should be taken into account, as the period in which work has been done should get the benefit of the proportionate part of the costs or at least receive credit for the cost of the work performed. It is unwise, however, to debit the clients' accounts until bills have been rendered, as this may very easily lead to confusion and difficulties.

The value placed upon the uncompleted work should be debited to Work in Progress Account and credited as such to the Profit and Loss Account or to the Costs Account. In estimating the value of outstanding work, full allowance should be made for contingencies and possible reductions in charges.

If a special account for work in progress is not opened the amount thereof will be carried down as a debit balance on the Costs Account. This item will be shown in the Balance Sheet as an asset, under the heading of 'Uncompleted Work', or 'Work in Progress', any cash received on account thereof being shown as a deduction.

#### Illustration (2)

F. Adams started in practice as a professional accountant on July 1st. He decides to prepare accounts half-yearly, on June 30th and December 31st, in each year.

The net fees for the first two half-years ended December 31st, and June 30th, amounted to £487 and £621 respectively, and the uncompleted work was estimated at December 31st, to be worth £126, and at June 30th, £233.

Show the Fees Account for the two periods, bringing down as a debit balance on the account the amount of uncompleted work at the end of each period.

### FEES ACCOUNT

| | | £ | | | £ |
|---|---|---|---|---|---|
| Dec. 31 | Profit and Loss Account .. .. | 613 | Dec. 31 | Sundries .. .. .. | 487 |
| | | | ,, | Work in progress c/d. .. .. | 126 |
| | | £613 | | | £613 |
| Jan. 1 | Balance b/d. .. .. .. | 126 | June 30 | Sundries .. .. .. | 621 |
| June 30 | Profit and Loss Account .. .. | 728 | ,, | Work in progress c/d. .. .. | 233 |
| | | £854 | | | £854 |
| July 1 | Balance b/d. .. .. .. | 233 | | | |

### (d) The ascertainment of profit on a cash basis

In some instances, professional men prefer to prepare their accounts on a *cash receipts basis*, i.e. to ignore fees earned but not yet received in cash, whether an account has been rendered therefor or not. This is the normal accounting practice of barristers owing to their inability to sue for their fees. In the case of professional firms, however, it is essential that accounts be prepared first on a normal basis in order that the true results of the year's working shall be known, adjustments being made subsequently to provide against fees not yet received in cash.

A Profit and Loss Account or Income and Expenditure Account will therefore be prepared in the usual manner, and the balance shown thereby transferred to a Receipts and Expenditure Account through which the necessary adjustments will be made.

In the latter account a provision will be made of a sum equal to the whole amount of the debtors for fees (debtors for disbursements must not be included in this provision as the intention is not to regard the debtors as bad, but merely to ignore all fees until received in cash). A further provision will be created in respect of the value placed upon uncompleted work, or work in progress. By debiting these two provisions to the Receipts and Expenditure Account the income included in the Income and Expenditure Account which has not yet been received in cash is deleted. The provision created at the close of the preceding year will be credited to the Receipts and Expenditure Account. Alternatively, only the net increase or decrease required in the provision, calculated by reference to the increase or decrease in debtors and uncompleted work during the year, may be adjusted through the account.

### Illustration (3)

A, B and C are in partnership as solicitors, sharing profits as 3 : 2 : 1. The following Trial Balance is extracted from their books at December 31st, 19... Prepare accounts for the year ended December 31st, 19.., together with Balance Sheet as at that date. The uncompleted work at December 31st, 19.., was valued at £1,539. Debts amounting to £356 are to be written off as bad.

Profits are to be divided between the partners on a cash basis, each partner being entitled to interest at 5 per cent. per annum on his capital.

### TRIAL BALANCE, December 31st, 19..

|  | £ | £ |
|---|---:|---:|
| Capital Accounts: |  |  |
| A | | 3,000 |
| B | | 4,000 |
| C | | 2,000 |
| Current Accounts – Drawings: |  |  |
| A | 1,560 | |
| B | 1,420 | |
| C | 650 | |
| Disbursements on behalf of clients | 1,329 | |
| (Balance not yet charged to clients.) | | |
| Salaries | 1,852 | |
| Rent and Rates.. | 850 | |
| Printing and Stationery .. | 356 | |
| Postages, Telephones etc.. | 184 | |
| Costs charged to clients .. | | 9,483 |
| Work in Progress, January 1st, 19...... | 1,296 | |
| Work in Progress Provision, January 1st, 19...... | | 1,296 |
| Clients for moneys held on their behalf | | 2,000 |
| Creditors | | 492 |
| Debtors Provision, January 1st, 19...... | | 3,567 |
| Debtors (includes £1,400 for disbursements) | 5,926 | |
| Sundry Office Expenses .. | 1,232 | |
| Furniture, Fittings and Library | 2,800 | |
| Cash at Bank: .. | | |
| Clients' Account | 2,000 | |
| Own Account | 4,283 | |
| | 6,283 | |
| Petty Cash | 100 | |
| | £25,838 | £25,838 |

## INCOME AND EXPENDITURE ACCOUNT
### Year ended December 31st, 19..

| | £ | | £ |
|---|---|---|---|
| Work in Progress, January 1st, 19 .. .. | 1,296 | Costs charged to clients .. .. .. | 9,483 |
| Rent and Rates .. .. .. .. | 850 | Work in Progress, December 31st, 19 .. | 1,539 |
| Salaries .. .. .. .. .. | 1,852 | | |
| Printing and Stationery .. .. .. | 356 | | |
| Postages, Telephones etc. .. .. .. | 184 | | |
| Sundry Office Expenses .. .. .. | 1,232 | | |
| Bad Debts .. .. .. | 356 | | |
| Balance, being excess of income over expenditure for the year, c/d. .. .. .. .. | 4,896 | | |
| | £11,022 | | £11,022 |

## RECEIPTS AND EXPENDITURE ACCOUNT
### Year ended December 31st, 19..

| | £ | | £ |
|---|---|---|---|
| Work in Progress Provision – December 31st, 19 | 1,539 | Balance from Income and Expenditure Account b/d. .. .. .. .. | 4,896 |
| Debtors Provision – December 31st, 19 .. | 4,170 | Work in Progress Provision – January 1st, 19 | 1,296 |
| Balance, being 'cash' profit c/d. .. .. | 4,050 | Debtors Provision – January 1st, 19 .. | 3,567 |
| | £9,759 | | £9,759 |

| | | £ | | £ |
|---|---|---|---|---|
| Interest on Capital: | | | Balance b/d. .. .. .. .. | 4,050 |
| A .. .. .. .. | £150 | | | |
| B .. .. .. .. | 200 | | | |
| C .. .. .. .. | 100 | | | |
| | | 450 | | |
| Balance: | | | | |
| A one-half .. .. .. | £1,800 | | | |
| B one-third .. .. .. | 1,200 | | | |
| C one-sixth .. .. .. | 600 | | | |
| | | 3,600 | | |
| | | £4,050 | | £4,050 |

## A, B AND C
### BALANCE SHEET as at December 31st, 19..

| | £ | £ | | £ | £ |
|---|---|---|---|---|---|
| CAPITAL ACCOUNTS | | | FIXED ASSETS | | |
| A .. .. .. .. | 3,000 | | Furniture, Fittings and Library .. | | 2,800 |
| B .. .. .. .. | 4,000 | | | | |
| C .. .. .. .. | 2,000 | | CURRENT ASSETS | | |
| | | 9,000 | Debtors for Fees .. .. | 4,170 | |
| | | | Less Provision .. .. | 4,170 | |
| CURRENT ACCOUNTS | | | | | — |
| A – Interest on Capital .. .. | 150 | | | | |
| Share of Profit .. .. | 1,800 | | Debtors for Disbursements .. .. | | 2,729 |
| | 1,950 | | £(1,329 + 1,400) | | |
| Less Drawings .. .. | 1,560 | | Work in Progress .. .. | 1,539 | |
| | | 390 | Less Provision .. .. | 1,539 | |
| B – Interest on Capital .. .. | 200 | | | | — |
| Share of Profit .. .. | 1,200 | | | | |
| | 1,400 | | Cash at Bank: | | |
| Less Drawings .. .. | 1,420 | | Own Account .. .. | 4,283 | |
| | | | Clients' Account .. .. | 2,000 | |
| Balance to contra .. .. | £20 | | | | 6,283 |
| | | | Petty Cash in hand .. .. | | 100 |
| C – Interest on Capital .. .. | 100 | | | | |
| Share of Profit .. .. | 600 | | Current Account B – per contra .. | | 20 |
| | 700 | | | | |
| Less Drawings .. .. | 650 | | | | |
| | | 50 | | | |
| CURRENT LIABILITIES | | | | | |
| Creditors: | | | | | |
| General .. .. .. | 492 | | | | |
| Clients for monies held on their behalf .. .. .. | 2,000 | 2,492 | | | |
| | | £11,932 | | | £11,932 |

*Workings:*                                                                      £      £

Debtors provision at December 31st per Receipts and Expenditure
  Account:

Debtors per trial balance　　..　　　　..　　　　..　　　　..　　　　..　　5,926

*Less* Bad Debts　　..　　　..　　　..　　　..　　　..　　　..　　356

　　Disbursements charged to clients not received　　..　　　..　　1,400
　　　　　　　　　　　　　　　　　　　　　　　　　　　　　　　　　　———　1,756
　　　　　　　　　　　　　　　　　　　　　　　　　　　　　　　　　　　　　£4,170

## § 14. Insurance Companies

A contract of insurance is one under which, in consideration for one or more payments called 'premiums' made by the insured person to the insurer (usually a company or a Lloyd's underwriter), the insurer undertakes to pay to the insured a determinable sum of money on the happening of a specified event. If the event is bound to happen (e.g. death or the expiration of a period of time) it is usually termed a contract of 'assurance'; if the event is *not* bound to happen it is termed a contract of 'insurance' or indemnity, i.e. the insured is indemnified against loss should the specified event occur.

The principle of indemnity insurance is entirely different from that of life assurance. In an indemnity insurance the company undertakes, in consideration of a premium, to indemnify the insured if the event happens against the risk of which the policy is taken out. If the policy is for a larger amount than the actual loss, only the loss will be paid, whereas if the policy is for less than the loss only the amount of the policy will be paid, subject to 'average' (see below). There is only one exception, viz. where an agreed value is placed on the subject matter of the insurance, that amount will be paid irrespective of its value at the date of the loss, a higher premium being paid on such insurances.

The principle of averaging is important. In all indemnity policies, other than marine (where the term 'average' has a special meaning) if the value of the property insured exceeds the amount of the policy, the insured is deemed to have insured himself for the excess, and in the event of a loss, only the proportionate amount of the loss is payable by the insurance company, unless there is a clause in the policy to delete average (when the premium will be increased).

The justice of averaging will be seen from the following simple illustration:

**Illustration**

A trader had three shops in each of which he had a maximum stock at any time amounting to £1,000. He took out an insurance policy against loss of stock by fire, but, arguing that the likelihood of all three shops being destroyed together was so remote, insured the whole stock for £1,000 only. Subsequently, one shop was destroyed, together with the stock therein, then worth £900.

Average would operate. The trader tried to cover three risks at the price of one, and must be considered as having himself carried the risk for two-thirds of the stock. The insurance company would therefore pay £300 only.

Insurance companies may be either 'proprietary' or 'mutual'. A proprietary company has a share capital and applies its profits, at least in part, to pay shareholders dividends. A mutual company has no share capital and its profits belong wholly to its policy holders; in its early days it may be financed by loans, and until it has built up an adequate insurance fund part of its liability under policies will be reinsured with other companies.

Fire insurance companies are termed 'tariff offices' if they belong to the Tariff Association; companies which are not members of the Association are called 'non-tariff offices'. The Tariff Association fixes for members rates of premium for different risks and minimum rates below which members agree not to accept business. The distinction between 'tariff' and other offices was abolished for household insurance as from December 1st, 1969.

The following different classes of insurance business cover the main operations in this field, and all are governed by the *Insurance Companies Act 1958*:

(*a*) life assurance;

(*b*) industrial assurance;

(*c*) accident insurance;

(*d*) fire insurance;

(*e*) bond investment business;

(*f*) motor vehicle insurance;

(*g*) marine, aviation and transit insurance.

'Bond investment business' is the business of issuing bonds or endowment certificates by which the company contracts to pay the bondholder a sum on some future date in return for subscriptions payable at intervals of less than six months.

'Industrial assurance business' is the business of effecting assurances upon human life, the premiums in respect of which are collected at intervals of less than two months. Where an assurance company carries on industrial assurance business, the provisions of the principal Act relating to life assurance business also apply to the industrial assurance business.

The list of traditional insurance business was extended, under Section 59 of the *Companies Act 1967*, to include:

(*a*) liability insurance, i.e. third party risks not arising from the use of motor vehicles;

(*b*) pecuniary loss insurance, i.e. bad debts etc.;

(*c*) property insurance.

Other classes of insurance were redefined by the 1967 Act which also increased the scope of the 'principal Act' (*Insurance Act 1958*). The chief object of that part of the 1967 Act relating to insurance business was to establish more rigorous standards of conduct; more demanding financial criteria are combined with provision for Board of Trade supervision and intervention, where necessary. Moreover, qualifications for entry into insurance business were considerably raised.

Under Section 71, *Companies Act 1967*, all insurance companies are required to prepare a Profit and Loss Account as well as an Annual Revenue Account and Balance Sheet. The Profit and Loss Account must contain such information as is prescribed by the Board of Trade and must be accompanied by any further documents, reports and certificates likewise prescribed.

Section 72 provides for such accounts to be audited in the prescribed manner and by a person of prescribed description. Regulations made for the purposes of this section may apply the audit provisions of the *Companies Acts 1948* and *1967* to insurance companies, subject to any necessary modifications or adaptations.

Section 73 provides that the annual statement of business (previously limited to accident insurance companies) is now extendable to any class of business by the Board of Trade. The Board may grant exemption from disclosure of confidential information under Section 76, where such disclosure might prove harmful.

Under Section 78 the maximum interval between statutory actuarial valuations, required under the principal Act, has been reduced from five years to three.

The Act provides that the fund of any particular class of business shall be as absolutely the security of the policy holders of that class as though it belonged to a company carrying on no other business than insurance business of that class, and shall not be applied directly or indirectly for any purposes other than those of the class of business to which the fund is applicable.

Where, however, an insurance company carries on, together with other business, an insurance business of only one of the classes to which the Act applies, or carries on, with or without other business, insurance business of two or more of the said classes, the receipts of that class of business, or of each of those classes of business, as the case may be, must be entered in a separate account and must be carried to and form a separate insurance fund with an appropriate name.

LIFE ASSURANCE

From observation of groups of persons over long periods, statistics have been prepared showing the average expectation of life of members of each group. With this knowledge, it is possible to calculate what sum of money must be invested in each year to accumulate at compound interest (i.e. by investing each year's interest with that year's contribution to the fund), to any stated amount on the average date when a member of the group would die. The share of each member of the group in this annual sum can obviously be computed by simple division. If, therefore, the group were 'assured' for a given amount to be paid to each member on the date of his death, and the contributions payable by each member were invested, year by year, at compound interest, the required sum would become available. Some members would die before the average date and contribute less than their share; others would outlive the average date and the excess contributions of the latter would compensate for the deficiency of the former.

When a person desires to insure his life, the insurers require him to complete a proposal form showing details of his age, health, family history including the ages of his close relatives at the date of their death, serious illnesses etc. from which they can place him in his appropriate group and compute the premium payable for the sum for which he wishes to be assured. The assured person will pay this premium annually (or by instalments at more frequent intervals if so arranged), and on his death the company will pay the sum assured to his estate, on due proof of death and representation.

The premium payable by an individual comprises 'pure premium' to cover the assurance plus 'loading' to cover the company's running expenses and profit. The company invests the 'pure premium' at compound interest to meet the ultimate liability. Unless the company has an adequate number of assured persons in each group considerable reserves will be required to meet contingencies.

If the assured wishes to share in the company's profits he can, by paying an increased premium, take out a 'with profits' assurance policy. The profits made by the company are then allocated partly to policy-holders and declared in the form of 'bonuses', which are normally 'reversionary bonuses', i.e. amounts added to the sums assured, to be paid as an addition to the moneys payable on death. Most companies allow such bonuses to be surrendered for a present cash payment of their present worth, i.e. the sum which, invested at the date of surrender at compound interest would produce the amount of the reversionary bonus on the date of expected death. The cash value of the bonus can be applied in part payment of the premium instead of being drawn in cash.

Reversionary bonuses may be 'simple', i.e. always calculated on the original sum assured, or 'compound', i.e. calculated upon the sum assured, plus the aggregate of all previous bonuses.

When a person dies, or a policy matures between valuation dates, an 'interim bonus' is usually added for the period since the last valuation, at a rate fixed at or slightly lower than the rate declared at the last valuation.

So far, only whole life assurance has been considered. A popular variation is the endowment policy. A pure endowment policy is a simple investment, whereby the assured pays an annual premium for a fixed capital sum payable at the end of a stated period of years, the capital sum amounting to the total of his premiums, plus a small amount of interest. Here again, by paying an increased premium, he can share in profits. The most common type of endowment however, combines a death benefit, the sum assured being payable at the end of the stated number of years or on earlier death. The premium is naturally higher to cover the risk of death.

Pure endowments are commonly in the form of sinking fund or leasehold redemption policies. Many variations of whole life and endowment policies are met with, but the fundamental principles are the same.

It will be appreciated that as each assured person becomes older and pays more premiums, the amount that it is necessary for the company to retain in the assurance fund to meet the liability to the assured correspondingly increases. The fund retained to meet the aggregate liability on all policies outstanding is termed the 'Life Assurance Fund', and until the proper amount thereof and the liability on outstanding policies has been computed, the amount of profit cannot be ascertained.

Accordingly, Section 5 of the *Insurance Companies Act 1958*, as amended by the *Companies Act 1967*, prescribes that every company which carries on life assurance business, industrial insurance business or bond investment business shall at least once in every three years cause an investigation to be made into its financial condition, including a valuation of its liabilities by an actuary and shall cause an abstract of the actuary's report to be made on the prescribed form. Many companies make the valuation more frequently, some every year. At the triennial (or more frequent) valuation, actuaries prepare a Consolidated Revenue Account (in form similar to the annual one), for the period since the last valuation, and compute what sum it would be necessary to invest at compound interest to accumulate the sums insured by their due dates, i.e. the present worth of the sums assured (including reversionary bonuses). From this they deduct the present worth of the pure premiums still remaining to be paid by the assured persons. The balance is the minimum amount that the company should have invested on account of the fund if it is to remain solvent. The rate of interest to be taken into account in valuations is always a conservative estimate of the yield expected from the investment of the funds, and varies from time to time. In the years between valuations, the excess of premiums and other income over claims and expenses is carried forward as an addition to the fund.

From this point onwards all explanations are made on the basis of a triennial valuation; if more frequent valuations are made, readers can readily supply for themselves the differences which arise, the principles being unchanged.

The profit for the triennial is found by means of what is called in the Insurance Companies Act a 'Valuation Balance Sheet'. This title is a misnomer; it is really a statement of affairs similar to that used in ascertaining profits from books kept by single entry.

The following items appearing in the Consolidated Revenue Accounts will now be briefly described (see Appendix I).

*Annuity Considerations*

The capital sum required to produce a given income is more than the capital sum required to produce the same annual return if the capital itself is to be used up, e.g. if a person requires £100 per annum from his capital for three years, he can obtain this by using the money himself in three ways:

1. By setting aside £300 capital, without investment, and spending £100 each year.

2. By investing £2,500 capital at 4 per cent.

3. By investing £277·51 at 4 per cent. realizing each year a sufficient amount of capital to make, with the interest received £100 per annum, i.e.

Year 1. Interest £11·1 capital realized £88·9. Total £100.

Year 2. Interest (on £188·61) £7·54. Capital realized £92·46. Total £100.

Year 3. Interest (on £96·15) £3·85. Capital realized £96·15. Total £100.

By the end of the period £277·51 capital has been used. (Taxation has been ignored for the sake of simplicity.)

If, however, the person approaches an assurance company, the company will be willing to take his capital and employ it according to the third method to pay him an annuity, not for a fixed period, but for life. The company has to consider the possibility of the annuitant outliving the period of their basic calculations and the possibility of his dying earlier. The 'group' principle arises and assurance companies can offer very attractive annuities, e.g. a man aged 60 who has £10,000 capital, and could invest it at 8 per cent. would receive an income of £800 per annum, but by purchasing an annuity would, by the loss of his capital, receive say £1,200 per annum. Where there are no dependants for whom provision must be made, this proposition has its attractions.

The sums received by the assurance company for the purchase of annuities come under this heading in the Revenue Account, and the actual payments of annuities are shown as 'annuities' on the other 'side' of the account. Income tax is deductible only from the income element of an annuity, the capital element is not subject to tax.

In valuing annuity business, unlike life assurance, as the annuitant grows older, the liability of the company on his annuity decreases, just as an annuity to a person produces a higher return for the same cost the older the annuitant is when it is purchased.

### Investment Income – Gross

The amounts to be included are the income from the investments earmarked for Long Term Business only. Income from other investments must be carried to the Revenue Account(s) of the fund(s) to which they belong, or if they are not earmarked for any fund, to Profit and Loss Account. A company carrying on life business only will not have a Profit and Loss Account; it is only where more than one class of business is carried on that this account is necessary. The interest etc. must be stated gross.

### Surrenders

Sometimes through force of circumstances an assured person decides to discontinue his contract and 'surrender' his policy. The surrender value will be less then the premiums paid unless it is a 'with profits' policy which has been in existence for sometime and on which the present worth of reversionary bonuses compensate for other factors. Assurance is based upon the 'group' principle and when a policy holder determines his contract he disturbs the whole group; the company takes into account the potential benefit accruing from the possibility of the assured outliving the average age and for the risk of death it has carried during the existence of the policy. Only 'pure premium' is considered in arriving at the surrender value; the first premium is substantially absorbed by expenses. The surrender value is usually fixed at a percentage of the premiums paid excluding the first, with an addition for the present worth of bonuses.

CONSOLIDATED PROFIT AND LOSS ACCOUNT

As already mentioned, a Profit and Loss Account is required only where more than one class of business is carried on.

Where a Profit and Loss Account is required, the profit or loss on each fund (in life business, the amount appropriated) is transferred from the appropriate Revenue Account to the Profit and Loss Account.

The investment income not earmarked for any particular fund also appears in the Profit and Loss Account. In other respects, this account is an Appropriation Account.

BALANCE SHEET

Since it is most important that the various funds should be represented by realizable assets, the most important assets of an insurance company are its investments, and these are shown on the prescribed Balance Sheet (see Appendix I) in the order of security. In other respects the Balance Sheet requires no particular explanation.

## § 15. (Treatment of Scrip Profits etc.) – Underwriters' Accounts

Finance companies are sometimes remunerated for their services for promoting and floating new companies by the allotment of fully paid shares in the new company; these shares may either be unquoted, or if quoted, the price may bear little relationship to their intrinsic value. There are two common methods of dealing with these shares in the books of the finance company:

*Method 1:*

Regard the cost of shares allotted for remuneration as the excess of promotion expenses incurred over remuneration received in cash. If the remuneration in cash exceeds the promotion expenses the shares allotted should be given a nil value. If the market value is below the figure so arrived at, provision should be made to reduce them to market value. If any shares are sold, the profit or loss should be transferred to Profit and Loss Account; only realized profit should be distributed in dividend; adequate provision should be made against losses on the sale of unsold shares.

*Method 2:*

Bring the shares allotted for remuneration in at par value and have two columns in the Underwriting Account, one for cash transactions, the other for scrip transactions; the two columns will show respectively the cash profit and the scrip profit. This method is particularly suitable where scrip dividends are declared.

**Illustration**

A finance company underwrote part of a new issue of shares, about to be made to the public by Wyezed Ltd. The issue was of 100,000 £1 shares, payable 10p on application, 40p on allotment, and 50p one month later. The finance company underwrote 60 per cent., and applied 'firm' for 20,000 shares which were duly allotted. The public applied for and were allotted 50,000 shares. The finance company had deposited with the underwriting letter a cheque for the application money on the shares underwritten, and this cheque was cleared by Wyezed Ltd on the result of the issue becoming known. The underwriting commission was 1 per cent. on cash and $\frac{1}{2}$ per cent. in shares, credited as fully paid, and was duly discharged.

The finance company sold 500 shares, when 50p paid, for £243·75 and paid the sums due on the balance, afterwards selling 15,000 shares for £14,625. On their Balance Sheet date the shares were quoted at £1. Write up the Underwriting Account in the finance company's books, carrying down as a provision on the account any profit made, or writing off any loss.

### UNDERWRITING WYEZED LTD ACCOUNT

| | Shares | £ | | Shares | £ |
|---|---|---|---|---|---|
| Cash, Application money, 10p per share .. .. .. | 20,000 | 2,000 | Cash, Commission 1% on £60,000 | — | 600·00 |
| Cash, on shares taken up under underwriting agreement (10p per share paid on 60,000) .. . | 18,000 | 6,000 | Contra, $\frac{1}{2}$% Commission received in shares .. .. .. | | |
| Cash, Allotment money: £ £ | | | Cash, 500 shares 50p paid .. | 500 | 243·75 |
| 40p per share on 20,000    8,000 | | | Cash, 15,000 shares fully paid | 15,000 | 14,625·00 |
| 40p per share on 18,000 7,200 | | | Balance c/d. .. .. .. | 22,800 | 22,264·23 |
| Less Overpaid on application 10p per share on 60,000—18,000   4,200 | | | Profit and Loss Account – Loss to date .. .. .. | | 17·02 |
| ——— 3,000 | | 11,000 | | | |
| Contra, shares (fully paid) received as commission .. .. .. | 300 | — | | | |
| Cash, balance due, 50p per share on 37,500 shares .. .. | | 18,750 | | | |
| | 38,300 | £37,750 | | 38,300 | £37,750·00 |
| Balance b/d. .. .. .. | 22,800 | 22,264·23 | | | |

*Notes:*

1. Since no cash was paid for the shares received as commission, they are brought in as part of the total holding by being entered in the shares column on the debit side, without any value being extended.

2. The underwriting and firm application are part of a single transaction. Accordingly, the cash commission goes to reduce the cost of the shares to the underwriters.

3. The underwriters applied firm for 20,000 shares and the public applied for 50,000 making a total of 70,000. Of the 30,000 shares not applied for, the company must take up 60 per cent., or 18,000 shares, under the underwriting contract, as 60 per cent. of the issue was underwritten.

The unsold shares are valued at cost, computed as follows:

| | | | | | | £ |
|---|---|---|---|---|---|---|
| Cost price of 38,000 shares, £1 paid .. | .. | .. | .. | .. | 38,000 | |
| 300 „ received, fully paid, as commission .. | | | | .. | — | |
| 38,300 | | | | | 38,000 | |
| Less Commission received in Cash | .. | .. | | 600 | | |
| Cost price of 38,300 fully paid shares.. | | .. | | £37,400 | | |

Value of shares in hand $\frac{22,800}{38,300}$ of £37,400 .. .. £22,264·23

Showing a loss of .. .. .. .. £17·02

Since the shares are held for resale, the lower of cost or market value may be taken. Market value is £1, i.e. a total of £22,800. Since this exceeds cost, it must be disregarded in this case.

### § 16. Accounts of Containers

The method of recording containers must depend on whether or not they are charged out to customers and, if so, whether or not credit is given for them when they are returned.

When containers are not returnable the charge is included in the sale price of the goods, and any profit made on the containers will automatically be included in the profit on the sale of goods.

Where, however, containers are returnable, the charges made for them should be debited to customers' accounts when they are sent out, and the appropriate amounts credited when they are returned.

The following methods of treatment are suggested:

*Method 1:*

The cost of containers purchased should be debited to a Containers Account (or Containers Stock Account) which should also be debited with the value of any stock of containers brought forward from the previous period, and credited with the stock carried forward at the end of the period.

The sales day book should contain a special column for containers, in which the charges made for containers should be entered. These amounts should be debited to the personal accounts of the customers concerned and credited in total periodically to a Containers Suspense (or Containers Charged-out) Account. Particulars of containers returned by customers should be recorded either in a special column in the returns inwards book or in a separate containers returned book, from which postings should be made to the credit of the personal accounts, and in total to the debit of the Containers Suspense Account.

For Balance Sheet purposes the credit balance remaining on the Containers' Suspense Account after the above entries have been made, will be set off against the total of the debit balances on debtors' accounts, in which the charges for such containers are included. The containers in customers' hands will then be valued at cost, less depreciation, and included in the value of the stock of containers which is credited and carried forward in the Containers Stock Account.

The amount carried down in the Containers Suspense Account should not include the value of any containers which are no longer returnable. These may be regarded as having been sold at the price at which they have been credited to the Containers Suspense Account and this amount should be transferred therefrom to the credit of Containers Stock Account.

Sometimes the credit given on the return of containers is either greater (to induce their return) or less than the price at which they are charged out. Where it is greater, the debits to the Containers Suspense Account in respect of containers returned by customers, and of the containers still in customers' hands at the end of the period, will be greater than the amounts credited to that account when the containers were charged out. The resultant debit balance on the account represents an expense to the business, which should be transferred to the debit of Containers Stock Account.

Conversely, where the credit given for containers returned is less than the amount at which they are charged out, only the amount allowable on their return should be debited and carried forward in the Containers Suspense Account, the profit on the containers sent out being transferred therefrom to the credit of Containers Stock Account.

In either case, the balance remaining on Containers Stock Account, after carrying forward at valuation the closing stocks of containers on hand and in customers' hands, will be transferred to Profit and Loss Account.

### Illustration (1)

A manufacturing company sells goods in cases which it purchases for 50p each. The cases are charged out to customers at 60p each and credited, if returned within six months, at 40p each. All cases are valued at stocktaking at 30p each.

The stock in the warehouse on January 1st was 4,000 cases, and 8,400 cases, for which the return period had not expired, were in the hands of customers at that date. During the year ended December 31st, 6,000 cases were purchased, 12,800 were sent out to customers, 9,200 were returned, 120 were destroyed in the warehouse and 200 were sold as firewood for £10. The return period for 7,600 cases in the hands of customers on December 31st had not expired; the remaining cases sent to customers were retained by them.

Show the Ledger Accounts in the firm's books for cases for the year ended December 31st:

#### CASES STOCK ACCOUNT

| | | Rate p | Quantity | £ | | | Rate p | Quantity | £ |
|---|---|---|---|---|---|---|---|---|---|
| Jan. 1 | Stocks in Warehouse brought forward .. | 30 | 4,000 | 1,200 | Dec. 31 | Cases Destroyed .. | | 120 | |
| | Stocks with Customers brought forward | 30 | 8,400 | 2,520 | | Cases Sold .. | | 200 | 10 |
| Dec. 31 | Purchases .. .. | 50 | 6,000 | 3,000 | | Cases Suspense Account: Profit on 12,800 cases sent to Customers .. | 20 | — | 2,560 |
| | Profit and Loss Account: Net profit on cases | | — | 1,714 | | Cases retained by Customers .. .. | 40 | 4,400 | 1,760 |
| | | | | | | Stocks in Warehouse carried forward .. | 30 | 6,080 | 1,824 |
| | | | | | | Stocks with Customers carried forward | 30 | 7,600 | 2,280 |
| | | | 18,400 | £8,434 | | | | 18,400 | £8,434 |

#### CASES SUSPENSE ACCOUNT

| | | Rate p | Quantity | £ | | | Rate p | Quantity | £ |
|---|---|---|---|---|---|---|---|---|---|
| Dec. 31 | Cases Stock Account: Profit on 12,800 cases issued to Customers | 20 | — | 2,560 | Jan. 1 | Balance b/f.: Cases in Customers' hands .. | 40 | 8,400 | 3,360 |
| | Cases Stock Account: Cases retained by Customers .. | 40 | 4,400 | 1,760 | Dec. 31 | Sundry Debtors: Cases charged to Customers .. .. | 60 | 12,800 | 7,680 |
| | Sundry Debtors: Cases returned by Customers .. .. | 40 | 9,200 | 3,680 | | | | | |
| | Balance c/f. Provision for Cases in Customers' hands .. | 40 | 7,600 | 3,040 | | | | | |
| | | | 21,200 | £11,040 | | | | 21,200 | £11,040 |

### Method 2:

As an alternative to the above method the following accounts should be opened. These are:

1. A Containers Stock Account;

2. Containers Suspense Account;

3. Profit and Loss on Containers Account;

4. Containers sent to Customers Account (this is a total account controlling the Debtors Account in respect of dealings in containers).

The book-keeping entries are as follows:

(i) Purchase of Containers. Debit Containers Stock Account and credit Cash or Sundry Creditors for cost. Debit Profit and Loss on Containers Account and credit Containers Stock Account with any depreciation on containers to adjust their value to stock-taking prices.

(ii) Issue of Containers to customers. Debit Containers sent to Customers Account with the price at which containers are charged out to them. Credit Containers Suspense Account with the firm's liability if the containers are returned and credit Profit and Loss on Containers Account with the excess of the price charged to the customers over the return price due when the containers are returned.

(iii) Containers returned by customers. Debit Containers Suspense Account and credit Containers sent to Customers Account with the allowance on return.

(iv) Containers retained by customers. Debit Containers Suspense Account with the allowance on return; credit Stock Account with the stock-taking valuation and credit Profit and Loss Account with the excess of the allowance on return over the stock-taking value.

(v) Containers scrapped or sold. Debit Profit and Loss on Containers Account with the stock-taking value and credit Containers Stock Account. Any proceeds of sale will be debited to debtors or cash and credited to Profit and Loss on Containers Account.

(vi) At balancing date:
  (a) Carry forward as a debit balance on Containers Stock Account the stock of containers with customers and in the warehouse or factory.
  (b) Carry forward as a debit balance on Containers Sent to Customers Account the returnable cases in customers' hands at invoice price.
  (c) Carry forward as a credit balance on Containers Suspense Account the firm's liability in respect of cases in hands of customers.

The debit balance on (b) above less the credit balance on (c) above represents the handling charge payable by customers irrespective of whether or not the customers subsequently return the containers. For Balance Sheet purposes this credit balance will be deducted from the balance on Containers Sent to Customers Account so that the figure of Debtors will not include the value of returnable containers as these have already been taken into account under (a) above.

The balance on Profit and Loss on Containers Account represents the profit or loss arising from the transactions involving containers and the balance on this account may be transferred to the general Profit and Loss Account.

**Illustration (2)**

H. Ltd sold goods in boxes which are charged out to customers at £3 each. Customers were credited with £2 for each box returned within three months.

In the annual accounts the stock of boxes in factory and all returnable boxes in the hands of customers, invoiced within three months, were valued at £1 each. On December 31st, 1969, the number of such boxes were 2,000 and 7,000 respectively.

During the year ended December 31st, 1970, the following transactions in boxes took place:
1. 8,000 were purchased at £1·50 each;
2. 30,000 were charged to customers;
3. 25,000 were returned by customers;
4. 800 of those returned were useless and sold for £100;
5. On December 31st, 1970, 11,000 boxes invoiced since September 30th, 1970, were in the hands of customers.

You are required to record the above transactions in the books of the company.

## CONTAINERS STOCK ACCOUNT

| | No. | £ | | No. | £ |
|---|---|---|---|---|---|
| Stocks brought forward at £1 per box: | | | Profit and Loss on Containers Account – depreciation on purchases | — | 4,000 |
| In Factory | 2,000 | 2,000 | – boxes destroyed | 800 | 800 |
| With Customers | 7,000 | 7,000 | Containers Suspense Account – boxes retained | 1,000 | 1,000 |
| Purchases at £1·50 per box | 8,000 | 12,000 | Stocks, carried forward: | | |
| | | | In Factory | 4,200 | 4,200 |
| | | | With Customers | 11,000 | 11,000 |
| | 17,000 | £21,000 | | 17,000 | £21,000 |

## CONTAINERS SUSPENSE ACCOUNT

| | No. | £ | | No. | £ |
|---|---|---|---|---|---|
| Containers sent to Customers Account – returns | 25,000 | 50,000 | Balance brought forward | 7,000 | 14,000 |
| Boxes retained: | | | Containers sent to Customers Account – issued | 30,000 | 60,000 |
| Stock Account | 1,000 | 1,000 | | | |
| Profit and Loss on Containers Account | — | 1,000 | | | |
| Balance carried forward | 11,000 | 22,000 | | | |
| | 37,000 | £74,000 | | 37,000 | £74,000 |

## PROFIT AND LOSS ON CONTAINERS ACCOUNT

| | £ | £ | | £ |
|---|---|---|---|---|
| Containers Stock Account – depreciation on purchases | | 4,000 | Containers sent to Customers Account, 30,000 at £1 | 30,000 |
| – boxes scrapped | 800 | | Containers Suspense Account, Profit on boxes retained | 1,000 |
| Less Sale proceeds | 100 | | | |
| | | 700 | | |
| General Profit and Loss Account | | 26,300 | | |
| | | £31,000 | | £31,000 |

## CONTAINERS SENT TO CUSTOMERS ACCOUNT

| | No. | £ | | No. | £ |
|---|---|---|---|---|---|
| Balance brought forward | 7,000 | 21,000 | Containers Suspense Account | 25,000 | 50,000 |
| Containers issued: | 30,000 | | *Cash – handling charge – 25,000 at £1 | | 25,000 |
| Profit and Loss Account, 30,000 at £1 | | 30,000 | *Cash – retentions | 1,000 | 3,000 |
| Containers Suspense Account, 30,000 at £2 | | 60,000 | Balance c/f. at £3 per box | 11,000 | 33,000 |
| | 37,000 | £111,000 | | 37,000 | £111,000 |

*It has been assumed that there were no amounts outstanding in respect of either handling charges or retentions.

## § 17. The Accounts of Building Societies

### (1) Constitution of Building Societies

Building Societies are now governed by the *Building Societies Act 1962*, which consolidated, with certain corrections and improvements, the *Building Societies Acts 1874 to 1960* and certain related enactments.

Section references given hereunder are to the *Building Societies Act 1962*.

Section 1 defines the purpose for which a society may be established under the Act as 'that of raising, by the subscription of the members, a stock or fund for making advances to members out of the funds of the society upon security by way of mortgage of freehold or leasehold estate'.

A society so established may be either:

(*a*) *a permanent society*, i.e. a society which has not by its rules any fixed date at which, or specified result on the attainment of which, it is to terminate, or

(*b*) *a terminating society*, i.e. a society which, by its rules, is to terminate at a fixed date, or when a result specified in the rules is attained.

A society may be established by not less than ten persons agreeing upon rules which comply with the requirements of the Act, and sending two copies of those rules, signed by not less than ten persons and by the intended secretary, to the central office of the Chief Registrar of Friendly Societies. If the rules comply with the requirements of the Act, a certificate of incorporation will be issued.

By s. 4 the rules must set out (*inter alia*):

(*a*) the terms on which unadvanced subscription shares are to be issued, and the manner in which contributions are to be paid to the society and withdrawn by the members;

(*b*) the terms on which paid up shares (if any) are to be issued and withdrawn;

(*c*) whether preferential shares are to be issued, and if so, within what limits;

(*d*) the purposes for which the funds of the society are to be applied;

(*e*) the manner in which advances are to be made and repaid.

### (2) Advances on Mortgage

Arrangements must be made by the directors to ensure that (*a*) the adequacy of any security taken in respect of an advance made by the society will be assessed either by a director or other officer who is competent to make the assessment, and (*b*) that there will be made available to such person an appropriate report by a competent and experienced person as to the value of any freehold or leasehold estate comprised in the security and as to any matter likely to affect the value thereof (s. 25). Records must be kept in respect of every advance made by the society showing (*a*) the value placed upon the property by the above-mentioned report and the name of the person by whom the report was made, and (*b*) particulars of any additional security taken by the society (s. 27).

A building society is not allowed to advance money on second mortgages of property, except land acquired by a local authority under an Act of Parliament, unless the prior mortgage is in favour of the society (s. 32).

*Special Advances* (s. 21)

A 'special advance' on the security of freehold or leasehold estate is an advance of one of the following descriptions:

(*a*) an advance of any amount to a body corporate;

(*b*) an advance of a sum exceeding £10,000* to a person other than a body corporate;

(*c*) an advance of any amount to a person other than a body corporate, being a person who, after the advance is made to him, is indebted to the society in an amount exceeding the limit in force for the purposes of this paragraph.

A person shall be taken to be indebted to the society in an amount exceeding the limit in force if either:

(*a*) the amount of his indebtedness to the society (including all debts of any description) immediately after the making of the advance, exceeds £20,000; or where the advance is one in relation to which a sum is prescribed by the Chief Registrar, exceeds twice the sum so prescribed, or

(*b*) the amount of his indebtedness to the society, ascertained at the end of a period of three months after the date of the advance, or (if sooner) the end of the financial year in which the advance was made, exceeds £10,000; or where the advance is one in relation to which a sum is prescribed by the Chief Registrar under this section, exceeds the amount so prescribed.

Section 22 imposes limits upon the amounts building societies can advance by way of 'special advances' in any year.

At the end of each financial year the society must ascertain:

(*a*) the total amount of advances not repaid, together with arrears of interest thereon, and

(*b*) the proportion of that amount which is in respect of advances made to a body corporate, or to a person who at that time is indebted to the society in an amount exceeding £10,000 (or such other sum as may be prescribed by the Chief Registrar) or made jointly to two or more persons any one of whom is so indebted to the society.

If the proportion ascertained in accordance with (*b*) does not exceed 10 per cent. the special advances made in the next financial year may not exceed 10 per cent. of the total amount of all advances made in that year; if the proportion exceeds 10 per cent. but does not exceed 25 per cent., the special advances made in the next financial year may not exceed $2\frac{1}{2}$ per cent. of the total advances; if the proportion exceeds 25 per cent., no special advances may be made in the next financial year, and no advance may be made in that year unless it can first be ascertained that it will not be a special advance.

No special advances may be made in the calendar year in which the society is established.

*The Chief Registrar may, by an order contained in a statutory instrument, prescribe a sum exceeding £10,000 in relation to advances in any financial year beginning on or after the coming into operation of the order.

N.B. By s. 128 'financial year' means a period of twelve months ending on December 31st. A society whose financial year does not end on December 31st may alter its financial year by making up accounts for one period of more than six months, and not more than eighteen months ending with December 31st.

### (3) *Borrowing Powers*

A building society is empowered to receive deposits or loans at interest, apart from receiving money from investing shareholders to be applied for the purposes of the society.

In a permanent building society the amount of such deposits and loans outstanding shall not at any time exceed two-thirds of the amount for the time being secured to the society by mortgages from its members.

In a terminating building society the limit is the greater of (*a*) two-thirds of the amount secured by mortgages, and (*b*) twelve months' subscriptions on the shares for the time being in force (s. 39).

### (4) *Accounts*

By s. 76 every building society shall:

(*a*) cause to be kept proper books of account with respect to its transactions and its assets and liabilities, and

(*b*) establish and maintain a system of control and inspection of its books of account and a system for supervising its cash holdings and all receipts and remittances.

The books and accounts, for the purposes of (*a*) above must be such as are necessary to give a true and fair view of the state of the affairs of the society and to explain its transactions.

The society must also establish and maintain a system to ensure the safe custody of all documents of title belonging to the society, and of the deeds relating to the property mortgaged to the society. The system must provide that on each occasion on which any document or deed is released from the custody of the officers of the society, the consent is obtained of the board of directors or of a person authorized by the board to give such consent.

There must be laid before the society at its annual general meeting (which must be held in the first four months of the financial year):

(*a*) a Revenue and Appropriation Account for the last financial year ending before the date of the meeting, and

(*b*) a Balance Sheet as at the end of that financial year (s. 77).

The Revenue and Appropriation Account must give a true and fair view of the income and expenditure for the year, and the Balance Sheet a true and fair view of the state of affairs of the society at the end of the year, and each must be in the form prescribed by the Chief Registrar by statutory instrument. The Balance Sheet must be signed by two directors, and by the manager or secretary. The Revenue and Appropriation Account must be annexed to the Balance Sheet and the auditors' report must be attached to it (s. 78).

There must be submitted to the annual general meeting and attached to the Balance Sheet a DIRECTORS' REPORT, setting out:

(*a*) the total amount advanced during the year on the security of freehold or leasehold estate and the total number of mortgages executed in favour of the society during the year;

(*b*) the proportion of the total amount advanced as mentioned in (*a*) which represents special advances, and the number of mortgages executed during the year to secure special advances;

(*c*) the total amount of money received during the year by way of investments in, or loans to, the society from members or depositors, and the total amount of shares and deposits repaid by the society;

(*d*) the number of cases in which at the end of the financial year a mortgagor was in arrears with payments due to the society;

(*e*) the total amount of the arrears at the end of the financial year (s. 82).

A copy of every Balance Sheet, including every document required by law to be annexed to it, together with a copy of the auditors' report and of the directors' report, must within twenty-one days before the date of the meeting be sent to the Chief Registrar and to every member of the society who holds shares to the value of £25 or more. Other members may obtain copies, without charge, on demand (s. 83).

The following are the forms of Revenue and Appropriation Account and Balance Sheet which illustrate the requirements of the *Building Societies (Accounts) Regulations 1962* (S.I. 1962, No. 2042).

## REVENUE AND APPROPRIATION ACCOUNT
### FOR THE YEAR ENDED...

| | £ | £ | | £ | £ |
|---|---|---|---|---|---|
| Management expenses:<br>　Directors' fees and expenses<br>　Remuneration and expenses of staff<br>　Contributions to pension funds | | | Interest charged to borrowers on mortgages<br>Recoverable from H.M. Government under option mortgage scheme<br>Interest and dividends from investments (gross)<br>Bank interest<br>Rents and other income from letting office premises<br>Valuation fees and expenses<br>Other fees and fines<br>Commission (Insurance etc.)<br>Recoveries on mortgages<br>Sundry receipts | | |
| Remuneration of auditors<br>Office accommodation and expenses<br>Printing, stationery, postages and telephones<br>Advertising<br>Commission and agency fees<br>Bank charges<br>Sundry expenses | | | | | |
| Total management expenses<br>Depreciation:<br>　Office premises<br>　Office and other equipment | | | *Note:* Income Tax on deposit and share interest relates to the interest charged in this account. | | |
| Valuation fees and expenses<br>Losses on mortgages | | | | | |
| Interest on Deposits<br>*Add* Income Tax on deposit interest | | | | | |
| Interest to shareholders for year ended<br>*Add* Income Tax on share interest | | | | | |
| Provision for bonus under contractual savings scheme<br>Corporation Tax for year ended (at ... per cent.) excluding tax on capital gains<br>Balance carried down | | | | | |
| | £ | | | | £ |

[*continued on next page*

## REVENUE AND APPROPRIATION ACCOUNT (*continued*)

| | £ | £ | | £ | £ |
|---|---|---|---|---|---|
| Transfer to general reserve  ..  .. | | | Balance brought down  ..  .. | | |
| Balance carried forward  ..  .. | | | Balance brought forward from last | | |
| | | | year ..  ..  ..  .. | | |
| | | | Profit on Realization: | | |
| | | |   Investments  ..  ..  .. | | |
| | | |   Properties  ..  ..  .. | | |
| | | | *Less* Corporation Tax relating | | |
| | | |   thereto  ..  ..  .. | | |
| | £ | | | | £ |

## BALANCE SHEET AS AT . . .

| | £ | £ | | £ | £ |
|---|---|---|---|---|---|
| Due to investing shareholders  .. | | | Balance due or outstanding on mort- | | |
| Deposits ..  ..  ..  .. | | |   gages:  ..  ..  .. | | |
| Other liabilities: | | |   From persons other than bodies | | |
|   Corporation Tax for year ended  .. | | |     corporate where total indebted- | | |
|   Corporation Tax attributable to in- | | |     ness | | |
|     terest accrued..  ..  .. | | |     (*a*) does not exceed £10,000  .. | | |
|   Income Tax  ..  ..  .. | | |     (*b*) exceeds £10,000  ..  .. | | |
|   Creditors..  ..  ..  .. | | |   From housing societies where Sec- | | |
| | | |     tion 8 of the *Housing Act 1964* | | |
| Provision for bonus under contractual | | |     applies to the advance | | |
|   savings scheme ..  ..  .. | | |   From other bodies corporate  .. | | |
| General reserve and balance carried | | | | | |
|   forward:  ..  ..  .. | | | Total ..  ..  ..  .. | | |
|   General reserve  ..  ..  .. | | | *Less* Provision for anticipated losses | | |
|   Balance carried forward  ..  .. | | |   on mortgages ..  ..  .. | | |
| | | | Mortgage assets..  ..  .. | | |
| | | | Investments: | | |
| | | |   Quoted: | | |
| | | |     British Government securities .. | | |
| | | |     Final redemption date in not | | |
| | | |       more than 5 years ..  .. | | |
| | | |     Others: | | |
| | | |       (Market value  )..  .. | | |
| | | |       (Redemption value  )  .. | | |
| | | |   Unquoted: | | |
| | | |     Loans to Local authorities  .. | | |
| | | |     Repayable in not more than 6 | | |
| | | |       months (including £  at | | |
| | | |       not more than 7 days notice) | | |
| | | |     Repayable in more than 6 months | | |
| | | |   Interest accrued (gross)  ..  .. | | |
| | | |   Total Investments  ..  .. | | |
| | | | Cash at banks and in hand  .. | | |
| | | | Debtors  ..  ..  .. | | |
| | | | Office premises at cost *less* depreci- | | |
| | | |   ation:  ..  ..  .. | | |
| | | |   Freehold  ..  ..  .. | | |
| | | |   Leasehold (50 or more years un- | | |
| | | |     expired)  ..  ..  .. | | |
| | | |   Leasehold (less than 50 years un- | | |
| | | |     expired)  ..  ..  .. | | |
| | | | Office and other equipment at cost | | |
| | | |   *less* depreciation  ..  .. | | |
| | | £ | | | £ |

*Notes:*

1. There shall, if not otherwise shown, be stated by way of note to the Revenue and Appropriation Account every material respect in which any items shown therein are affected:

(*a*) by transactions of an exceptional or non-recurrent nature; or

(*b*) by any change in the basis of accounting.

2. The following matters shall be stated by way of note to the Balance Sheet, or in a statement or report annexed thereto, if not otherwise shown:

(*a*) particulars of any moneys owing by the society in respect of deposits, loans and overdrafts which are wholly or partially secured;

(*b*) the general nature of any contingent liability not provided for, and, where practicable, the estimated amount of that contingent liability, if it is material;

(*c*) where practicable, the aggregate amount or estimated amount, if it is material, of contracts for capital expenditure, so far as not provided for;

(*d*) where the amounts of the separate reserves or provisions as compared with the amounts at the end of the immediately preceding financial year show any increases or decreases, the sources from which the increases have been derived and how the amounts of any decreases have been applied;

(*e*) the method of arriving at the amount at which any office premises are shown;

(*f*) the basis on which any item of corporation tax has been computed;

(*g*) acquisition and disposal of fixed assets.

3. Comparative figures for the preceding year must be shown.

Two items in the final accounts of building societies have appeared recently and require further explanation. The term 'Recoverable from H.M. Government under option mortgage scheme' refers to the subsidy paid to building societies under the *Housing Subsidies Act 1967* where mortgages are granted to people with moderate incomes at a rate below that normally charged. For fixed instalment mortgages the subsidy is 2 per cent. and with an endowment mortgage the subsidy has been fixed at $1\frac{3}{4}$ per cent. 'Provision for bonus under contractual savings scheme' represents the amount of interest accrued in relation to the bonus to be paid on maturity for contractual savings schemes. These saving schemes are operated by the building societies as part of the Government's Save-As-You-Earn contractual scheme which commenced on October 1st, 1969.

## (5) *Annual Return*

Every building society must in the first three months of each financial year make to the Chief Registrar of Friendly Societies an annual return relating to the affairs of the society for the previous financial year (s. 88).

The contents and form of the annual return are prescribed by the *Building Societies (Annual Return, etc.) Regulations 1962*.

The return must be signed by two directors and by the manager or secretary.

# APPENDIX I

*Before Additional Disclosure*

[The notes relating to the accounts 'Before Additional Disclosure' have not been reproduced.]

## NATIONAL AND COMMERCIAL BANKING GROUP LIMITED
## AND ITS SUBSIDIARY COMPANIES

### CONSOLIDATED BALANCE SHEET
at September 30th 1969

|  | £ | *1968*<br>*£* |
|---|---:|---:|
| **Share Capital and Reserves** | | |
| Issued share capital | 28,995,000 | *28,995,000* |
| Reserves and retained profits (note 3) | | |
| General reserves | 23,182,931 | *21,547,500* |
| Profit and loss accounts | 2,862,697 | *2,467,212* |
|  | 26,045,628 | *24,014,712* |
|  | **55,040,628** | ***53,009,712*** |
| **Current Liabilities and Other Accounts** | | |
| Current, deposit and other accounts, including provisions and reserves for contingencies | 1,045,474,228 | *932,791,202* |
| Notes in circulation | 74,995,635 | *71,466,870* |
| Dividends payable on December 31st, 1969: | | |
| Preference | 38,500 | *36,750* |
| Proposed ordinary | 2,247,600 | *1,053,562* |
|  | **1,122,755,963** | ***1,005,348,384*** |
| **Acceptances, Guarantees and Other Obligations on account of Customers** | 78,006,341 | *65,051,803* |

J. O. Blair-Cunynghame ⎫
David Alexander　　　　⎬ Directors
T. G. Waterlow　　　　 ⎭

John Renilson　　　　　Secretary

|  | | |
|---|---:|---:|
|  | **£1,255,802,932** | ***£1,123,409,899*** |

# NATIONAL AND COMMERCIAL BANKING GROUP LIMITED
## AND ITS SUBSIDIARY COMPANIES

### CONSOLIDATED BALANCE SHEET
at September 30th 1969

| | £ | *1968*<br>*£* |
|---|---|---|
| **Liquid Assets** | | |
| Coin, bank notes and balances with Bank of England | 117,670,110 | *117,022,216* |
| Balances with, and cheques in course of collection on, other banks in the British Isles | 72,305,708 | *68,225,234* |
| Money at call and short notice | 158,147,608 | *140,351,311* |
| Bills discounted and bankers' certificates of deposit (note 4) | 36,985,889 | *46,308,999* |
| | 385,109,315 | *371,907,760* |
| | | |
| **Other Current Assets** | | |
| Special deposits with Bank of England | 10,900,000 | *10,600,000* |
| Investments (note 5) | 147,537,301 | *136,961,982* |
| Advances to customers and other accounts | 531,590,699 | *444,168,451* |
| Items in transit | 62,223,336 | *58,181,034* |
| | 752,251,336 | *649,911,467* |
| | | |
| **Trade Investments** (note 6) | 16,057,459 | *16,281,077* |
| | | |
| **Investment in Subsidiary Company not consolidated** (note 7) | | |
| Shares at cost | 350,000 | — |
| Amount due | 28,928 | — |
| | 378,928 | — |
| | | |
| **Fixed Assets** | | |
| Bank premises, other properties and equipment (note 8) | 23,999,553 | *20,257,792* |
| | | |
| **Liabilities of Customers for Acceptances, Guarantees and Other Obligations** | 78,006,341 | *65,051,803* |
| | | |
| | **£1,255,802,932** | ***£1,123,409,899*** |

*After Disclosure*

## NATIONAL AND COMMERCIAL BANKING GROUP LIMITED AND ITS SUBSIDIARY COMPANIES

### CONSOLIDATED BALANCE SHEET
at September 30th 1969

|  | Notes | £ |
|---|---|---|
| **Shareholders' Funds** | | |
| Issued share capital | 8 and 9 | 28,995,000 |
| Reserves | 10 | 63,254,936 |
| | | **92,249,936** |
| **Provisions for Pensions** | 11 | **6,876,781** |
| **Liabilities** | | |
| Customers' deposit and current accounts | | 939,438,829 |
| Notes in circulation | | 74,995,635 |
| Creditors and accrued expenses | | 5,442,721 |
| Taxation | 12 | 5,745,721 |
| Dividends | 13 | 2,286,100 |
| | | **1,027,909,006** |

J. O. Blair-Cunynghame ⎫
David Alexander　　　 ⎬ Directors
T. G. Waterlow　　　　⎭

John Renilson　　　　　　 Secretary

**£1,127,035,723**

The notes on pages 684 to 690 form part of these accounts

# NATIONAL AND COMMERCIAL BANKING GROUP LIMITED
## AND ITS SUBSIDIARY COMPANIES

### CONSOLIDATED BALANCE SHEET
at September 30th 1969

| | Notes | £ |
|---|---|---|
| **Liquid Assets** | | |
| Coin, bank notes and balances with Bank of England | | 117,670,110 |
| Balances with, and collections on, other banks in the British Isles | | 46,435,347 |
| Money at call and short notice | | 158,147,608 |
| Bills discounted and bankers' certificates of deposit | 14 | 36,985,889 |
| | | 359,238,954 |
| | | |
| **Special Deposits with Bank of England** | | 10,900,000 |
| **Investments** (other than trade investments) | 15 | 158,068,141 |
| **Advances to Customers,** *less* provisions | | 553,544,766 |
| **Other Debtors and Prepayments** | | 4,968,362 |
| **Trade Investments** | 16 and 17 | 16,057,459 |
| **Investment in Subsidiary Company not Consolidated** | 18 | 378,928 |
| **Fixed Assets** | 19 and 20 | 23,879,113 |
| | | £1,127,035,723 |

*Before Additional Disclosure*

## NATIONAL AND COMMERCIAL BANKING GROUP LIMITED AND ITS SUBSIDIARY COMPANIES

### CONSOLIDATED PROFIT AND LOSS ACCOUNT
for the year ended September 30th 1969

| | £ | 1968 £ |
|---|---:|---:|
| **Group Profit** (note 13) | | |
| As published in the 1968 accounts and appropriated below | | £6,189,643 |
| Group profit for the year after providing for taxation and after making transfers to reserves for contingencies, out of which provision has been made for any diminution in the value of assets | £6,607,210 | £7,235,000 |
| Appropriations: | | |
| **Transfers by Subsidiary Companies** | | |
| Transfers to published reserves | 1,780,000 | 1,950,000 |
| Additional transfers to reserves for contingencies | — | 250,000 |
| | 1,780,000 | 2,200,000 |
| **Dividends** | | |
| Half-yearly and interim dividends paid on May 30th 1969 on: | | |
| 11 per cent. cumulative preference shares at 5½ per cent. | 27,500 | |
| 5½ per cent. cumulative preference shares at 2¾ per cent. | 11,000 | |
| Ordinary shares at 7½ per cent. | 2,107,125 | |
| | 2,145,625 | |
| Interim dividends paid to former members of The Royal Bank of Scotland and National Commercial Bank of Scotland Limited | | 2,613,219 |
| Final dividends payable on December 31st 1969 on: | | |
| 11 per cent. cumulative preference shares at 5½ per cent. | 27,500 | 26,250 |
| 5½ per cent. cumulative preference shares at 2¾ per cent. | 11,000 | 10,500 |
| Ordinary shares at 8 per cent. (proposed) | 2,247,600 | 1,053,562 |
| | 2,286,100 | 1,090,312 |
| | 4,431,725 | 3,703,531 |
| **Retained Profit for the Year** | | |
| National and Commercial Banking Group Limited | 226,631 | 224,411 |
| Subsidiary companies | 168,854 | 61,701 |
| | 395,485 | 286,112 |
| | £6,607,210 | £6,189,643 |

*After Disclosure*

# NATIONAL AND COMMERCIAL BANKING GROUP LIMITED AND ITS SUBSIDIARY COMPANIES

## CONSOLIDATED PROFIT AND LOSS ACCOUNT
for the year ended September 30th 1969

|  | Notes | £ |
|---|---|---|
| **Group Profit before Taxation** after dealing with realized losses *less* profits on dated British Government and local authority securities on the basis set out in note 2 (*c*) and quantified in note 10. | 2 to 6 | **18,393,752** |
| **Taxation** | 7 | **8,618,219** |
| **Group Profit after Taxation** | | **£9,775,533** |

Appropriated as follows:

**Dividends (gross) paid to Shareholders:**

Preference

| | |
|---|---|
| 11 per cent. | 55,000 |
| 5½ per cent. | 22,000 |

Ordinary

| | |
|---|---|
| Interim of 7½ per cent. paid on May 30th 1969 | 2,107,125 |
| Final of 8 per cent. paid on December 31st 1969 | 2,247,600 |
| | **4,431,725** |

**Retained Profit for the Year**

| | |
|---|---|
| National and Commercial Banking Group Limited | 226,631 |
| Subsidiary companies | 5,117,177 |
| | **5,343,808** |
| | **£9,775,533** |

The notes on pages 684 to 690 form part of these accounts

## NOTES ON THE ACCOUNTS

### Corresponding figures

**1.** The Board of Trade has granted exemption from showing the corresponding figures for 1968 in view of the changes in the bases of accounting introduced in 1969. However, corresponding figures have been included in certain notes to the accounts where there has been no change in the bases of accounting.

### Bases of accounting

**2.** The following bases of accounting have been adopted for the purposes of the accounts:

(*a*) The charge against profit in respect of provisions for losses on advances to customers has been calculated by reference to the average experience for the five years ended September 30th, 1969.

(*b*) Premiums and discounts on the acquisition of dated British Government and local authority securities are being amortized over the period from date of purchase to date of maturity and an appropriate proportion thereof included in group profit. Such securities are shown in the Balance Sheet at amortized cost.

(*c*) Realized profits and losses on sales of British Government and local authority securities are taken to an Investment Suspense Account and are subsequently transferred to the Profit and Loss Account in five equal annual instalments, commencing with the year of realization. The balance on the Investment Suspense Account is deducted from reserves in the Balance Sheet (note 10).

(*d*) Balance Sheet presentation has been changed from that previously adopted, resulting in an aggregate reduction of £64·2 millions for collections on other banks and items in transit with a corresponding reduction in liabilities. Items in transit are no longer shown separately and are included in advances.

### Turnover

**3.** As the business of the Group is the provision of banking and other financial services turnover is not shown.

### Group profit

**4.** The group profit before taxation is stated:

| after crediting | Trade Investments £ | Other Investments £ |
|---|---|---|
| Income from investments (including the amortization of dated stocks referred to in note 2 (*b*)): | | |
| Quoted | 740,811 | 10,139,886 |
| Unquoted | 2,317,483 | 553,150 |
| | £3,058,294 | £10,693,036 |

The above totals include £3,040,443, being the gross equivalent (at the current rate of corporation tax) of the franked investment income received of £1,672,244; £1,368,199 being correspondingly included in the taxation charge for the year.

and after charging                                                    £
  Interest payable                                               28,582,903
  Amortization of premises and depreciation of equipment            978,987
  Auditors' remuneration                                             23,391
  Emoluments of directors (comprising fees as directors £42,860 and other
    emoluments including pension contributions £81,623)             124,483
  Exceptional and non-recurring expenditure:
    Capital duty and other expenses relating to the merger of the Group's
      Scottish banks                                                 79,435
    Introduction of new note issue                                  155,892

**5.** The profit after taxation of Lloyds and Scottish Limited for the year ended September 30th, 1969, attributable to the Group's 50 per cent. interest in that company amounted to £1,653,500 of which £937,500 is included by way of dividend income in the group profit after taxation.

**Directors' emoluments**

**6.** Further particulars of directors' emoluments (excluding pension contributions) are:
  Fees amounting to £2,000 (*1968 – nil*) have been waived by a director.
  The emoluments of the chairman were £20,000 (*1968 – £14,029 for nine months*) and those of the highest paid director £24,266 (*1968 – £16,103 for nine months*).

  The numbers of directors, whose annual emoluments fell into the following categories, were:

| £        £      | 1969 | *1968* |
|-----------------|------|--------|
| 0— 2,500        | 1    | —      |
| 2,501— 5,000    | 2    | —      |
| 5,001— 7,500    | 1    | —      |
| 7,501—10,000    | —    | *1*    |
| 10,001—12,500   | 3    | *3*    |
| 15,001—17,500   | 1    | —      |
| 17,501—20,000   | 1    | —      |
| 20,001—22,500   | —    | *3*    |
| 22,501—25,000   | 1    | —      |

**Taxation**

**7.** Taxation based on the profit for the year is:

|                                                                      | £          |
|----------------------------------------------------------------------|------------|
| U.K. corporation tax (at 45 per cent.)                               | 8,471,113  |
| Deduct: Relief for double taxation                                   | (67,784)   |
|                                                                      | 8,403,329  |
| Overseas taxes                                                       | 67,784     |
|                                                                      | 8,471,113  |
| Adjustments for prior years due to increase in rate of corporation tax | 147,106  |
|                                                                      | £8,618,219 |

**Share capital**

**8.** The share capital of the company is:

| | Authorized £ | Issued and fully paid £ |
|---|---|---|
| 11 per cent. cumulative preference shares of £1 each | 500,000 | 500,000 |
| 5½ per cent. cumulative preference shares of £1 each | 400,000 | 400,000 |
| Ordinary shares of 5s each | 29,100,000 | 28,095,000 |
| | £30,000,000 | £28,995,000 |

**9.** The shares issued by the company on July 17th, 1968, as consideration for the acquisition of The Royal Bank of Scotland and National Commercial Bank of Scotland Limited have been treated as having been issued at their nominal value of £28,995,000. The excess amounting to £4,132,500 of such capital over the then combined issued capitals of the two banks has been deducted from reserves in the Consolidated Balance Sheet.

**Reserves**

**10.** Movements in reserves during the year were:

| | Reserves £ | Investment Suspense Account (note 2(c)) £ | Total £ |
|---|---|---|---|
| Balances at October 1st, 1968: | | | |
| Published reserves | 24,014,712 | | 24,014,712 |
| Reserves for contingencies | 34,654,820 | (410,715) | 34,244,105 |
| | 58,669,532 | (410,715) | 58,258,817 |
| Losses *less* profits on investments realized during the year (*less* taxation relief) | | (346,241) | (346,241) |
| Proportion of realized losses *less* profits transferred to Profit and Loss Account in accordance with note 2(c) (£415,344 *less* taxation relief) | | 237,735 | 237,735 |
| Surplus on sales of premises (*less* taxation) | 111,820 | | 111,820 |
| Goodwill arising on acquisition of subsidiary companies | (144,569) | | (144,569) |
| Reorganization costs | (206,434) | | (206,434) |
| Retained profit for the year | 5,343,808 | | 5,343,808 |
| Balances at September 30th, 1969 | £63,774,157 | £(519,221) | £63,254,936 |

**Provisions for pensions**

**11.** The provisions for pensions represent the estimated amounts, *less* taxation relief, required to cover unfunded back service pension obligations based on latest available actuarial valuations principally at October 1964 and December 1965 and taking account of funding payments made subsequent to such valuations. The cost of providing pensions in respect of current service has been charged against profit.

**Taxation**

**12.** Taxation comprises:

|  | £ |
|---|---|
| Corporation tax payable October 1st, 1970 | 2,300,838 |
| Current taxation | 3,444,883 |
|  | £5,745,721 |

**Dividends**

**13.** Dividends paid on December 31st, 1969:

|  | £ | *1968* £ |
|---|---|---|
| Half-yearly preference dividends | 38,500 | *36,750* |
| Final ordinary dividend | 2,247,600 | *1,053,562* |
|  | £2,286,100 | *£1,090,312* |

**Bills discounted and bankers' certificates of deposit**

**14.** Bills discounted and bankers' certificates of deposit comprise:

|  | £ | *1968* £ |
|---|---|---|
| British treasury bills | 15,850,000 | *36,660,000* |
| Other bills and re-financeable credits | 16,951,946 | *9,648,999* |
| Bankers' certificates of deposit | 4,183,943 | *—* |
|  | £36,985,889 | *£46,308,999* |

**Investments**

**15.** Investments (other than trade investments) comprise:

| **Quoted:** | | £ |
|---|---|---|
| At amortized cost referred to in note 2(*b*): | | |
| Securities of, or guaranteed by, the British Government | | 131,997,137 |
| Local authority securities | | 12,959,226 |
| At the lower of cost or market value: | | |
| Other investments quoted in Great Britain | | 2,639,154 |
| Quoted elsewhere | | 315,610 |
| (Market valuation £137,551,148) | | 147,911,127 |
| **Unquoted:** | | |
| Local authority securities at amortized cost referred to in note 2(*b*) | 749,226 | |
| Others, including bullion, at cost *less* amounts written off | 9,407,788 | |
| (Directors' valuation £10,156,210) | | 10,157,014 |
|  | | £158,068,141 |

**Trade investments**

**16.** Trade investments, at cost *less* amounts written off, comprise:

| Quoted | £ |
|---|---|
| In Great Britain | 2,613,951 |
| Elsewhere | 1,500,725 |
| (Market valuation £9,231,982) | 4,114,676 |
| **Unquoted:** | |
| (Directors' valuation £32,375,864) | 11,942,783 |
| | £16,057,459 |

No provision has been made for liability to corporation tax which might arise on disposal of investments at above valuations.

**17.** The Group's principal trade investments are:

| | Capital and reserves per latest accounts £ | Percentage of equity capital held by Group |
|---|---|---|
| Hire Purchase: | | |
| (i) United Kingdom | | |
| Lloyds and Scottish Limited | 20,756,000* | 50·0 |
| St Margaret's Trust Limited | 731,806 | 33·3 |
| United Dominions Trust Limited | 41,050,000 | 8·1 |
| (ii) Australia | | |
| Associated Securities Limited | 10,666,548 | 11·7 |
| Beneficial Finance Corporation Limited | 2,174,828 | 23·0 |
| Other financial interests in the United Kingdom: | | |
| Industrial and Commercial Finance Corporation Limited | 50,612,000 | 8·6 |
| The Scottish Agricultural Securities Corporation Limited | 266,720 | 33·3 |
| Yorkshire Bank Limited | 7,500,000 | 8.0 |

*In accordance with Stock Exchange requirements the following details are given for Lloyds and Scottish Limited:

| | £ |
|---|---|
| Capital – Ordinary shares of £1 each | 15,000,000 |
| Reserves | 5,756,000 |

**Investment in subsidiary company not consolidated**

**18.** The investment in subsidiary company not consolidated represents the wholly owned interest in Loganair Limited which has not made up its accounts since it was acquired in October 1968. This interest comprises:

| | £ |
|---|---|
| Shares at cost | 350,000 |
| Amount due | 28,928 |
| | £378,928 |

**Fixed assets**

**19.** Fixed assets comprise:

| Premises: | Book value or cost £ | Aggregate depreciation £ | Net book value £ |
|---|---|---|---|
| Freehold | 19,137,700 | — | 19,137,700 |
| Long leaseholds | 1,006,647 | — | 1,006,647 |
| Short leaseholds | 1,297,612 | (57,026) | 1,240,586 |
| Computers, office machinery and motor vehicles | 4,605,633 | (2,679,101) | 1,926,532 |
| | £26,047,592 | £(2,736,127) | 23,311,465 |
| Furniture and fittings | | | 567,648 |
| | | | £23,879,113 |

Premises are stated at book value at October 1st, 1968, with additions during the year at cost. No provision is made for depreciation or amortization on freeholds or leaseholds with more than fifty years unexpired. Leaseholds with less than fifty years unexpired are amortized over the period of the lease.

Computers, office machinery and motor vehicles are depreciated on a straight line basis over their estimated useful lives.

Furniture and fittings are stated at book value at October 1st, 1968, with additions during the year at cost. Renewals are charged to Profit and Loss Account.

**20.** Movements in fixed assets during the year:

| | £ |
|---|---|
| Additions (net of investment grants) | 4,188,977 |
| Disposals | 124,890 |

**Capital commitments**

**21.** Contracts for capital expenditure of the Group at September 30th, 1969, totalled £3,894,000 (*1968 – £3,183,000*). Capital expenditure of the Group authorised by the directors at that date, but not contracted for, was estimated to total £495,000 (*1968 – £759,000*).

**Acceptances, guarantees and other obligations**

**22.** Acceptances, guarantees and other obligations on account of customers at September 30th, 1969, totalled £78,006,341 (*1968 – £65,051,803*) and are not included in the Balance Sheet. In addition there are outstanding contracts for the sale and purchase of foreign currencies.

**Contingent liabilities**

**23.** There are contingent liabilities in respect of:

(*a*) subsidiary companies with unlimited liability, and

(*b*) uncalled capital in respect of investments held by subsidiary companies.

**Exchange rates**

**24.** Foreign currency balances have been expressed in sterling at the rates of exchange ruling at September 30th, 1969.

**Principal subsidiary companies**

**25.** The principal subsidiary companies, all of which are wholly owned, are:

| | Country of incorporation or registration |
|---|---|
| Owned by the company: | |
| The Royal Bank of Scotland Limited | Scotland |
| Williams & Glyn's Bank Limited | England |
| Glyn, Mills & Co | England |
| The National Bank Limited | England |
| Williams Deacon's Bank Limited | England |
| Natcomputer Services Limited | Scotland |
| | |
| Owned by The Royal Bank of Scotland Limited: | |
| National Commercial & Glyns Limited | Scotland |
| National & Commercial Development Limited | Scotland |
| Loganair Limited | Scotland |
| | |
| Owned by Glyn, Mills & Co: | |
| Glyn Mills Finance Company | England |
| | |
| Owned by Williams Deacon's Bank Limited: | |
| Williams Deacon's Investment and Finance Limited | Jersey |
| Williams Deacon's Bank (Finance) Limited | England |
| | |
| Owned by Williams Deacon's Investment and Finance Limited: | |
| Williams Deacon's Investment and Finance (Guernsey) Limited | Guernsey |

# BESTOBELL LIMITED
## CONSOLIDATED PROFIT AND LOSS ACCOUNT
for the year ended December 31st, 1968

| | Notes | 1968 | | 1967 |
|---|---|---|---|---|
| | | £ | | £ |
| Turnover | 1 | £23,612,162 | | £20,056,459 |
| Trading Profit | 2 | 2,472,706 | | 1,917,017 |
| *Add:* | | | | |
| Dividend received | 3 | 53,673 | | — |
| Interest received | | 12,613 | | 15,165 |
| Profit on Devaluation (see Note 14) | | 66,628 | | 20,398 |
| | | 2,605,620 | | 1,952,580 |
| *Deduct:* | £ | | £ | |
| Depreciation of Fixed Assets | 4 | 422,483 | 379,736 | |
| Auditors' Remuneration | | 41,237 | 31,847 | |
| Preliminary and Share Issue Expenses | | 1,144 | 9,675 | |
| Trade Marks, Patents etc., written off | | 3,263 | — | |
| Interest on Bank Loans and Overdrafts | | 118,950 | 94,991 | |
| Interest on Debenture Stock | | 101,126 | 84,530 | |
| | | 688,203 | | 600,779 |
| **Group Profit before Taxation** | | 1,917,417 | | 1,351,801 |
| *Deduct:* | | | | |
| Taxation | 5 | 871,937 | | 595,112 |
| **Group Profit after Taxation** | | 1,045,480 | | 756,689 |
| *Deduct:* | | | | |
| Provision for loss by Associated Company | | 1,362 | 6,302 | |
| Minority Interests | | 31,969 | 13,192 | |
| | | 33,331 | | 19,494 |
| **Net Profit attributable to Bestobell Limited** | | 1,012,149 | | 737,195 |
| *Deduct:* | | | | |
| Dividends paid or proposed, gross | | | | |
| First Preference Shares | | 8,250 | 8,250 | |
| Second Preference Shares | | 13,750 | 13,750 | |
| Ordinary Shares– | | | | |
| Interim 10% (*10%*) | | 226,812 | 224,614 | |
| Final 15⅞% (*15%*) | | 358,080 | 336,922 | |
| | | 606,892 | | 583,536 |
| **Retained Profit for the year** | | 405,257 | | 153,659 |
| Balance brought forward from previous year (as adjusted, see Note 8) | | 4,025,325 | | 3,726,222 |
| **Unappropriated Profit and Revenue Reserves carried forward** | | £4,430,582 | | £3,879,881 |

## NOTES ON PROFIT AND LOSS ACCOUNT

**1. Turnover**

This includes both sales and services, the figure for the previous year having been adjusted to include services.

**2. Trading Profit**

The following items have been dealt with in arriving at the Trading Profit for the year:

| | £ |
|---|---|
| *Charged:* | |
| Rents Payable | 231,787 |
| Hire Charges | 58,885 |
| *Credited:* | |
| Rents Receivable | 32,385 |

**3. Dividends Received**

The figure of £53,673 is the amount of the dividend receivable for the year from an unquoted Associated Company, but includes £42,001 in respect of profits earned in previous years.

| **4. Depreciation of Fixed Assets** | 1968 £ | 1967 £ |
|---|---|---|
| Land and Buildings ($2\frac{1}{2}\%$) | 45,023 | 41,009 |
| Plant, Vehicles and Equipment (according to estimated life) | 384,264 | 345,170 |
| | 429,287 | 386,179 |
| *Deduct:* Profit (Net) on Disposals | 6,804 | 6,443 |
| | £422,483 | £379,736 |

| **5. Taxation** (and see Note 11) | | |
|---|---|---|
| United Kingdom Corporation Tax | 703,859 | 457,480 |
| *Deduct:* Double Taxation Relief | 215,116 | 150,357 |
| | 488,743 | 307,123 |
| *Add:* Overseas Taxation | 417,536 | 352,503 |
| | 906,279 | 659,626 |
| *Deduct:* Overspill Relief (third year) | 23,200 | 40,200 |
| | 883,079 | 619,426 |
| *Deduct:* Taxation over-provided in previous year | 11,142 | 24,314 |
| | £871,937 | £595,112 |

Notes on Profit and Loss Account (*continued*)

| 6. Directors' Emoluments | 1968 £ | 1967 £ |
|---|---|---|
| As Directors | 3,208 | 3,750 |
| Other Offices (including contributions to Pension Schemes) | 55,117 | 50,478 |
| Past Directors' Pensions | 9,975 | 8,500 |
| | £68,300 | £62,728 |
| Benefits | £1,121 | £1,571 |
| Chairman's Emoluments (excluding Pension Scheme contributions) | £9,850 | £12,100 |
| Highest paid Director (excluding Pension Scheme contributions) | £10,614 | Chairman |

Number of Directors whose emoluments fall within the following
scales (excluding Pension Scheme contributions)

| | | |
|---|---|---|
| Up to £2,500 | 1 | 2 |
| Over £2,500, up to £5,000 | 1 | 1 |
| Over £5,000, up to £7,500 | 1 | 1 |
| Over £7,500, up to £10,000 | 2 | 3 |
| Over £10,000, up to £12,500 | 2 | 1 |

Two Directors have waived emoluments to which they were entitled
for 1968, to the value of £3,747 (*1967 £4,010*).

There were no employees, other than Directors, whose remuneration in 1968 exceeded £10,000.

## BESTOBELL LIMITED

### BALANCE SHEETS
December 31st, 1968

| | Notes | COMPANY 1968 £ | COMPANY 1967 £ | GROUP 1968 £ | GROUP 1967 £ |
|---|---|---|---|---|---|
| **Fixed Assets** | | | | | |
| Land and Buildings, Plant and Equipment | 1 | 120,894 | 28,044 | 2,736,002 | 2,588,796 |
| Goodwill, Patents and Know-how | 2 | — | — | 910,900 | 917,291 |
| Unquoted Investments | 3 | 2 | 2 | 412 | 352 |
| Interests in: | | | | | |
| Associated Companies | 4 | — | — | 230,021 | 152,346 |
| Subsidiary Companies | 5 | 5,377,225 | 5,337,189 | — | — |
| | | 5,498,121 | 5,365,235 | 3,877,335 | 3,658,785 |
| | | | | | |
| **Current Assets** | | | | | |
| Stock and Work in Progress | 6 | — | — | 5,309,418 | 4,906,189 |
| Debtors and Bills Receivable | 6 | 78,391 | 86,677 | 6,591,244 | 5,843,349 |
| Tax Recoverable | | 213,840 | 186,728 | 119,126 | 145,271 |
| Cash | | 42,761 | 4,850 | 530,409 | 316,301 |
| | | 334,992 | 278,255 | 12,550,197 | 11,211,110 |
| | | | | | |
| **Current Liabilities** | | | | | |
| Creditors | | 34,132 | 26,179 | 3,175,473 | 2,855,849 |
| Overdrafts | | — | 6,031 | 1,489,656 | 1,438,238 |
| Taxation | | 4,858 | 11,188 | 729,854 | 740,319 |
| Dividends (gross) | | 369,080 | 347,922 | 369,080 | 347,922 |
| | | 408,070 | 391,320 | 5,764,063 | 5,382,328 |
| **Net Current Assets** | | (73,078) | (113,065) | 6,786,134 | 5,828,782 |
| *Deduct:* Difference on consolidation due to varying accounting dates | | — | — | 22,902 | 55,535 |
| | | £5,425,043 | £5,252,170 | £10,640,567 | £9,432,032 |
| | | | | | |
| **Issued Share Capital** | 7 | 2,693,121 | 2,671,144 | 2,693,121 | 2,671,144 |
| **Reserves** – Share Premium | 8 | 267,094 | 164,000 | 267,094 | 164,000 |
| Capital | 8 | 81,445 | 79,411 | 794,161 | 499,306 |
| Revenue | 8 | 1,405,133 | 1,337,615 | 4,430,582 | 3,879,881 |
| **Shareholders' Funds** | | 4,446,793 | 4,252,170 | 8,184,958 | 7,214,331 |
| **Minority Interests in Subsidiaries** | 9 | — | — | 480,712 | 516,082 |
| **Loan Capital** | 10 | 978,250 | 1,000,000 | 1,489,545 | 1,438,247 |
| **Deferred Taxation** | | — | — | 485,352 | 263,372 |
| **Capital Employed** | | £5,425,043 | £5,252,170 | £10,640,567 | £9,432,032 |

A. J. M. Miller  
J. D. Taylor  } *Directors*

## BESTOBELL LIMITED

## NOTES ON BALANCE SHEETS

### 1. Land and Buildings, Plant and Equipment

Freehold and leasehold land and buildings show the original cost to Companies in the Group and the cumulative depreciation to date. During the year certain properties were transferred from Subsidiary Companies to the Holding Company.

Other fixed assets are stated at the book value at July 1st, 1948, *less* sales, *plus* additions at cost and the cumulative depreciation since that date.

The movements in the fixed assets accounts during the year were as follows:

| | 1968 Holding Company | | 1968 Group | | 1967 Holding Company | | 1967 Group | |
|---|---|---|---|---|---|---|---|---|
| | Land & Buildings | Other Fixed Assets | Land & Buildings | Other Fixed Assets | Land & Buildings | Other Fixed Assets | Land & Buildings | Other Fixed Assets |
| | £'000 | £'000 | £'000 | £'000 | £'000 | £'000 | £'000 | £'000 |
| Cost (as above) at December 31st, 1967 | 17 | 44 | 1,616 | 3,271 | 15 | 47 | 1,387 | 2,892 |
| *Add:* | | | | | | | | |
| Devaluation adjustments | — | — | 155 | 166 | — | — | 1 | 7 |
| Transfers from Subsidiaries | 131 | — | — | — | — | — | — | — |
| Adjustments | 8 | — | 13 | — | — | — | — | — |
| Subsidiaries acquired | — | — | — | — | — | — | 63 | 188 |
| Additions during year | — | 13 | 84 | 421 | 2 | 6 | 264 | 432 |
| | 156 | 57 | 1,868 | 3,858 | 17 | 53 | 1,715 | 3,519 |
| *Deduct:* Disposals during year | — | 6 | 50 | 276 | — | 9 | 99 | 248 |
| Cost (as above) at December 31st, 1968 | 156 | 51 | 1,818 | 3,582 | 17 | 44 | 1,616 | 3,271 |
| *Deduct:* Cumulative provision for depreciation | 54 | 32 | 478 | 2,186 | 4 | 29 | 391 | 1,908 |
| Written down value at December 31st, 1968 | 102 | 19 | 1,340 | 1,396 | 13 | 15 | 1,225 | 1,363 |
| Per Balance Sheet | £121 | | £2,736 | | £28 | | £2,588 | |

**Land and Buildings**

| | 1968 Holding Company | | 1968 Group | | 1967 Holding Company | | 1967 Group | |
|---|---|---|---|---|---|---|---|---|
| | Cost | Book Value | Cost | Book Value | Cost | Book Value | Cost | Book Value |
| | £'000 | £'000 | £'000 | £'000 | £'000 | £'000 | £'000 | £'000 |
| Freehold | 148 | 99 | 1,547 | 1,126 | 17 | 13 | 1,357 | 1,011 |
| Leasehold: | | | | | | | | |
| Long Leases (over 50 years) | 8 | 3 | 78 | 64 | — | — | 66 | 57 |
| Short Leases (under 50 years) | — | — | 193 | 150 | — | — | 193 | 157 |
| | £156 | £102 | £1,818 | £1,340 | £17 | £13 | £1,616 | £1,225 |

| | £ | | £ | | £ | | £ | |
|---|---|---|---|---|---|---|---|---|
| Investment Grants for the year, deducted from the cost of fixed assets | — | | 33,147 | | — | | 43,652 | |
| Capital Commitments: | | | | | | | | |
| Contracted but not provided | — | | 120,000 | | — | | 68,000 | |
| Authorised by the Directors and not contracted | 15,000 | | 19,000 | | | | | |

**2. Goodwill, Patents and Know-how**

| | Group | |
|---|---|---|
| | 1968 | 1967 |
| | £ | £ |
| Trade Marks, Patents, Know-how, Manufacturing and Selling Rights, at cost, *less* amounts written off | 37,503 | 40,675 |
| Cost of shares in Subsidiary Companies in excess of book value of net tangible assets on acquisition, *less* amount written off | 873,397 | 876,616 |
| | £910,900 | £917,291 |

**3. Unquoted Investments**

| | Company | | Group | |
|---|---|---|---|---|
| | 1968 | 1967 | 1968 | 1967 |
| | £ | £ | £ | £ |
| Trade Investments at cost, December 31st, 1967 | 200 | 200 | 550 | 550 |
| *Add:* Adjustment for devaluation | — | — | 60 | — |
| | 200 | 200 | 610 | 550 |
| *Deduct:* Amounts written off | 198 | 198 | 198 | 198 |
| Book value at December 31st, 1968 | £2 | £2 | £412 | £352 |

In the opinion of the Directors the approximate market value of these investments at December 31st, 1968, was £600, compared with the book value of £412.

**4. Associated Companies**

| | 1968 | 1967 |
|---|---|---|
| | £ | £ |
| Equity shares at cost, December 31st, 1967 | 99,922 | 99,922 |
| *Add:* Adjustment for devaluation | 15,439 | — |
| | 115,361 | 99,922 |
| *Add:* Indebtedness | 160,972 | 92,818 |
| | 276,333 | 192,740 |
| *Deduct:* Provisions for losses | (32,535) | (26,617) |
| Reserves | (13,777) | (13,777) |
| Balance, December 31st, 1968 | £230,021 | £152,346 |

In the opinion of the Directors the value of shares held in Associated Companies at December 31st, 1968, amounted to approximately £111,600, based on the net asset values of those Companies. This compares with a book value of £82,991.

## 5. Subsidiary Companies

|  | 1968 £ | 1967 £ |
|---|---|---|
| Shares at cost | 2,970,421 | 2,569,540 |
| *Add:* Amounts due from Subsidiaries | 3,445,704 | 3,466,215 |
|  | 6,416,125 | 6,035,755 |
| *Deduct:* Amounts due to Subsidiaries | 981,566 | 641,232 |
|  | 5,434,559 | 5,394,523 |
| *Deduct:* Provision for indebtedness | 57,334 | 57,334 |
| Balance, December 31st, 1968 | £5,377,225 | £5,337,189 |

## 6. Stock and Work in Progress

Stock of materials and bought in products are valued at cost, net realisable value and replacement cost, whichever is the lowest.

Stock of manufactured products and work in progress are valued at cost including an appropriate proportion of overheads, or net realisable value, whichever is the lower.

Progress payments have been deducted from the value of work in progress.

The stock and book debts of Bestobell India Private Limited have been charged to Banks as security for overdraft facilities to a maximum of £221,120, the actual overdraft being £152,341.

## 7. Share Capital of Bestobell Limited

|  | Authorised | | Issued and Fully Paid | |
|---|---|---|---|---|
|  | 1968 £ | 1967 £ | 1968 £ | 1967 £ |
| 5½ per cent. Redeemable Cumulative Preference Shares of £1 each | 150,000 | 150,000 | 150,000 | 150,000 |
| 5 per cent. Second Cumulative Preference Shares of £1 each | 275,000 | 275,000 | 275,000 | 275,000 |
| Ordinary Shares of 5s each | 3,000,000 | 3,000,000 | 2,268,121 | 2,246,144 |
|  | £3,425,000 | £3,425,000 | £2,693,121 | £2,671,144 |

The 5½ per cent. Redeemable Cumulative Preference Shares are redeemable as follows:

| Before December 31st, 1987 | @ 21s 0d per share |
|---|---|
| At December 31st, 1987 | @ 20s 6d per share |

## 8. Movements of Reserves

| | Company | | Group | |
|---|---|---|---|---|
| | 1968 £ | 1967 £ | 1968 £ | 1967 £ |
| SHARE PREMIUM at December 31st, 1967 | 164,000 | 142,358 | 164,000 | 142,358 |
| Premium on shares issued to Staff | 18,259 | 21,642 | 18,259 | 21,642 |
| Premium on shares exchanged for Carson-Paripan Limited Shares | 84,835 | — | 84,835 | — |
| Share Premium at December 31st, 1968 | £267,094 | £164,000 | £267,094 | £164,000 |
| | | | | |
| CAPITAL RESERVES at December 31st, 1967 | 79,411 | 79,411 | 499,306 | 192,929 |
| Profit (Loss) on Sale of Land and Buildings | — | — | (8,309) | 75,424 |
| Profit on Disposal of Leases | — | — | — | 24,187 |
| Profit on Sale of Shares in Subsidiary Companies | — | — | — | 124,448 |
| Accumulated profits of Company sold | — | — | — | 2,780 |
| Reserve against indebtedness of Subsidiary Company | — | — | — | 57,334 |
| Adjustment on devaluation | 325 | — | 321,455 | 22,204 |
| Profit on Debenture redemption | 1,709 | — | 1,709 | — |
| Provision for Subsidiary Company | — | — | (20,000) | — |
| Capital Reserves at December 31st, 1968 | £81,445 | £79,411 | £794,161 | £499,306 |
| | | | | |
| REVENUE RESERVES at December 31st, 1967 | 1,337,615 | 1,242,887 | 3,879,881 | 3,753,307 |
| Accumulated profits of Company sold | — | — | — | (2,780) |
| Adjustment on devaluation | — | — | 145,444 | (24,305) |
| Adjusted balance | 1,337,615 | 1,242,887 | 4,025,325 | 3,726,222 |
| Undistributed profit for year | 67,518 | 94,728 | 405,257 | 153,659 |
| Revenue Reserves at December 31st, 1968 | £1,405,133 | £1,337,615 | £4,430,582 | £3,879,881 |

## 9. Minority Interests

| | 1968 £ | 1967 £ |
|---|---|---|
| Ordinary Capital | 288,650 | 315,279 |
| Preference Capital | 158,795 | 154,500 |
| Proportion of Reserves and Profit | 33,267 | 46,303 |
| | £480,712 | £516,082 |

**10. Loan Capital** (Secured)

| | Company | | Group | |
|---|---|---|---|---|
| | 1968 | 1967 | 1968 | 1967 |
| | £ | £ | £ | £ |
| 6¾% Debenture Stock 1986/91 | 1,000,000 | 1,000,000 | 1,000,000 | 1,000,000 |
| *Deduct:* Nominal amount of Stock redeemed during the year | (21,750) | — | (21,750) | — |
| Debenture Stock issued by Bestobell Australia Limited pursuant to a Trust Deed dated February 15th, 1967: | | | | |
| 5½% A$500,000 1973 | — | — | 199,203 | 199,203 |
| 8% A$600,000 1987 | — | — | 239,044 | 239,044 |
| *Add:* Adjustment for devaluation | — | — | 73,048 | — |
| | £978,250 | £1,000,000 | £1,489,545 | £1,438,247 |

The 6¾% Debenture Stock 1986/91 is secured by a first floating charge on the undertaking, property and assets of the Company and by joint and several guarantees of the wholly owned Subsidiary Companies operating in the United Kingdom as at December 31st, 1965, such guarantees being secured by first floating charges on the undertaking, property and assets of those Subsidiaries.

**11. Taxation**

Provision has been made in these Accounts for Corporation Tax at 42½ per cent. on the profits of the resident United Kingdom Companies.

In the case of Subsidiary Companies which are not resident in the United Kingdom the provision made is for Overseas Taxes on profits.

No provision has been made for United Kingdom Taxes which may become payable should retained profits of non-resident Overseas Companies be remitted to this country.

**12. Pension Arrangements**

(*a*) A quinquennial valuation of the United Kingdom Group Pension Scheme was made at April 30th, 1968, which showed that the premiums paid to that date, which were to have continued for a period of twenty years for past service pensions, proved to be sufficient to liquidate the liability. Current service contributions contain an element for additional benefits, which were not included in the original scheme.

In addition to the United Kingdom Scheme there are certain other schemes relating to Overseas Companies where past service contributions are spread over twenty years of the remaining period of service with the Company.

The past service premium payable for the year amounted to £15,117.

(*b*) Pensions for those employees not eligible for admission to the funded schemes are generally charged against profits as they arise, but in certain cases provisions are being made to meet the cost of pensions accruing.

### 13. Contingent Liabilities

(a) The following guarantees have been given by the Holding Company:

(1) The overdrafts of thirteen Subsidiary Companies to a maximum of £662,600. At December 31st, 1968, the total of the overdrafts covered by the guarantees amounted to £423,129.

(2) The dividends on 85,000 5½ per cent. Redeemable Cumulative Preference Shares of 2 Rands each, fully paid, in Bell's Asbestos and Engineering (Africa) Limited. The shares are redeemable:

    Before December 31st, 1984    @ 2·05 Rands per share

    At December 31st, 1984    @ 2 Rands per share

(3) In respect of the capital and interest on Debenture Stock to the equivalent value of £511,295 Sterling issued by Bestobell Australia Limited. Stock is repayable from 1973 to 1987 (see Note 10).

(b) There are contingent liabilities to Bankers in respect of bills discounted, credits opened and houses purchased by employees and to customers in respect of guarantees on completed contracts.

### 14. Rates of Exchange and Devaluation

Overseas Currencies have been converted to Sterling at the rates of exchange ruling at the respective Balance Sheet dates.

The remittance of funds to the United Kingdom from certain overseas countries is subject to Exchange Control restrictions.

The profits of the Overseas Companies whose years ended on June 30th, were converted to Sterling in 1967 at pre-devaluation rates. The profits for 1968 have been enhanced by conversion to Sterling at the new rates of exchange.

| | £ |
|---|---|
| The following changes in the Accounts have resulted from devaluation: | |
| Increase in Capital Reserves, on conversion of Share Capital, Reserves, Loans etc. | 321,455 |
| Increase in Revenue Reserves, on conversion of existing Profit and Loss balances | 145,444 |
| Increase in profits for the year, due to the conversion of Sterling debts, current assets etc., *less* adjustment to stock value | 66,628 |
| | £533,527 |

### 15. Financial Year

The financial year of the Company and of its United Kingdom Subsidiaries ended on December 31st, 1968, and the Overseas Subsidiaries on June 30th, 1968, except that the financial year of certain Subsidiary Companies in Europe ended on December 31st, 1968.

The Directors consider it undesirable to change the financial year of the Overseas Subsidiaries as this would cause undue delay in the publication of the Group Accounts.

### 16. Budget

Corporation Tax has been provided in these Accounts at the rate prevailing prior to the Budget announcement of April 15th, 1969.

# BESTOBELL LIMITED

## FINANCIAL SUMMARY
### For years 1960 to 1968

| | 1960 £'000 | 1961 £'000 | 1962 £'000 | 1963 £'000 | 1964 £'000 | 1965 £'000 | 1966 £'000 | 1967 £'000 | 1968 £'000 |
|---|---|---|---|---|---|---|---|---|---|
| **TURNOVER** to third parties 1967 and 1968 include services | 9,218 | 10,953 | 11,987 | 13,805 | 15,158 | 16,278 | 17,957 | 20,056 | 23,612 |

### GROUP PROFIT AND DIVIDENDS

| | 1960 | 1961 | 1962 | 1963 | 1964 | 1965 | 1966 | 1967 | 1968 |
|---|---|---|---|---|---|---|---|---|---|
| Profit before charging Taxation | 737 | 746 | 805 | 1,158 | 1,506 | 1,702 | 1,601 | 1,352 | 1,917 |
| *Add:* Interest on Loan Capital | 11 | 11 | 11 | 10 | 10 | 12 | 69 | 85 | 011 |
| *Less:* Provision for losses by Associated Companies | — | — | — | — | 4 | 39 | 35 | 6 | 1 |
| | 748 | 757 | 816 | 1,168 | 1,512 | 1,675 | 1,635 | 1,431 | 2,017 |
| Taxation (*after adjustment in respect of previous years*) | 359 | 404 | 446 | 583 | 773 | 675 | 662 | 595 | 872 |
| Interest on Loan Capital | 11 | 11 | 11 | 10 | 10 | 12 | 69 | 85 | 101 |
| Net Profit | 378 | 342 | 359 | 575 | 729 | 988 | 904 | 751 | 1,044 |
| Minority Interests | 6 | 6 | 3 | 1 | 8 | 14 | 4 | 13 | 32 |
| Net Profit attributable to Holding Company | 372 | 336 | 356 | 574 | 721 | 974 | 900 | 738 | 1,012 |
| Preference Dividends | 13 | 13 | 13 | 13 | 13 | 13 | 22 | 22 | 22 |
| Ordinary Dividends | 127 | 151 | 176 | 244 | 294 | 466 | 560 | 562 | 585 |
| Retained in business | 232 | 172 | 167 | 317 | 414 | 495 | 318 | 154 | 405 |

### CAPITAL EMPLOYED

| | 1960 | 1961 | 1962 | 1963 | 1964 | 1965 | 1966 | 1967 | 1968 |
|---|---|---|---|---|---|---|---|---|---|
| Ordinary Share Capital | 1,016 | 1,645 | 1,645 | 2,193 | 2,193 | 2,239 | 2,241 | 2,246 | 2,268 |
| Reserves | 2,729 | 2,693 | 2,860 | 2,653 | 3,086 | 3,722 | 4,088 | 4,543 | 5,492 |
| **Ordinary Shareholders' Funds** | 3,745 | 4,338 | 4,505 | 4,846 | 5,279 | 5,961 | 6,329 | 6,789 | 7,760 |
| Preference Share Capital | 425 | 425 | 425 | 425 | 425 | 425 | 425 | 425 | 425 |
| Loan Capital | 211 | 209 | 208 | 207 | 205 | 724 | 1,199 | 1,438 | 1,490 |
| Minority Interests | 127 | 129 | 278 | 273 | 272 | 273 | 278 | 516 | 481 |
| Deferred Taxation | 242 | 271 | 269 | 349 | 444 | 458 | 396 | 264 | 485 |
| **Total Capital Employed** | 4,750 | 5,372 | 5,685 | 6,100 | 6,625 | 7,841 | 8,627 | 9,432 | 10,641 |
| **Represented by:** | | | | | | | | | |
| Fixed Assets (*including investments*) | 1,212 | 1,532 | 1,689 | 1,724 | 1,782 | 2,117 | 2,266 | 2,589 | 2,736 |
| Goodwill | 234 | 369 | 297 | 281 | 282 | 406 | 489 | 917 | 911 |
| Interests in Associated Companies | — | — | 90 | 54 | 250 | 142 | 287 | 153 | 230 |
| Net Current Assets (*other than cash*) | 2,838 | 3,517 | 3,606 | 3,803 | 4,085 | 5,337 | 6,039 | 6,895 | 7,723 |
| Net Cash Balance or (*Overdraft*) | 466 | (46) | 3 | 238 | 226 | (161) | (454) | (1,122) | (959) |
| | 4,750 | 5,372 | 5,685 | 6,100 | 6,625 | 7,841 | 8,627 | 9,432 | 10,641 |

| | 1960 % | 1961 % | 1962 % | 1963 % | 1964 % | 1965 % | 1966 % | 1967 % | 1968 % |
|---|---|---|---|---|---|---|---|---|---|
| Profit before Tax to Sales | 8·0 | 6·8 | 6·7 | 8·4 | 9·9 | 10·5 | 8·9 | 6·7 | 8·1 |
| Return on Capital Employed (*before charging loan interest*) | 15·7 | 14·1 | 14·4 | 19·2 | 22·8 | 21·4 | 19·0 | 15·2 | 19·0 |
| Return after Tax on Ordinary Shareholders' Funds | 9·6 | 7·4 | 7·6 | 11·6 | 13·4 | 16·1 | 13·9 | 10·5 | 12·8 |
| Earnings on Ordinary Shares (*adjusted for Scrip Issues*) | 28·8 | 24·1 | 25·6 | 41·7 | 53·4 | 51·5 | 39·2 | 31·8 | 43·7 |
| Ordinary Dividend (*adjusted for Scrip Issues*) | 10·2 | 11·3 | 13·1 | 18·1 | 22·5 | 25·0 | 25·0 | 25·0 | 25·9 |

## IMPERIAL CHEMICAL INDUSTRIES LTD AND 342 SUBSIDIARIES
### (318 IN 1967)

### GROUP PROFIT AND LOSS ACCOUNT
for the year ended December 31st, 1968

| | Notes | 1967 £m | | 1968 £m |
|---|---|---|---|---|
| **Sales to external customers** | | 978·8 | | **1,237·3** |
| | | | | |
| **Trading profit** | (1) | 122·4 | | **175·3** |
| Investment income | (2) | 11·0 | | **17·2** |
| | | 133·4 | | **192·5** |
| Interest payable | (3) | 25·6 | | **29·6** |
| | | 107·8 | | **162·9** |
| Employees' profit-sharing bonus | | 7·2 | | **10·2** |
| | | | | |
| **Profit before taxation and investment grants** | | 100·6 | | **152·7** |
| Taxation | (4) | 47·0 | **69·5** | |
| *Less:* Investment grants | (5) | 9·1 | **10·8** | |
| | | 37·9 | | **58·7** |
| | | | | |
| **Profit after taxation** | | 62·7 | | **94·0** |
| Applicable to minorities | | 4·9 | | **8·1** |
| | | | | |
| **Applicable to parent company** | | 57·8 | | **85·9** |
| Dividends paid and proposed | | | | |
| Net dividends | (6) | 33·6 | **34·9** | |
| Income tax on dividends | | 23·6 | **24·5** | |
| | | 57·2 | | **59·4** |
| Retained in the business | (7) | ·6 | | **26·5** |

# IMPERIAL CHEMICAL INDUSTRIES LTD AND 342 SUBSIDIARIES
## (318 IN 1967)
### GROUP BALANCE SHEET
at December 31st, 1968

| | Notes | 1967 £m | | 1968 £m |
|---|---|---|---|---|
| ASSETS EMPLOYED | | | | |
| Fixed assets | (8) | 946·0 | | 972·5 |
| Goodwill | (9) | 38·7 | | 38·7 |
| Interests in associated companies | (11) | 118·0 | | 110·8 |
| Net current assets | (12) | | | |
| Stocks | | 226·4 | 261·6 | |
| Debtors | | 234·4 | 289·3 | |
| Liquid resources | | 109·2 | 155·3 | |
| | | 570·0 | 706·2 | |
| Creditors | | 236·1 | 277·6 | |
| Short-term borrowings | | 62·7 | 63·7 | |
| | | 298·8 | 341·3 | |
| | | 271·2 | | 364·9 |
| | | 1,373·9 | | 1,486·9 |
| FINANCED BY | | | | |
| Capital and reserves | | | | |
| Applicable to parent company | | | | |
| Issued capital | (13) | 478·9 | | 480·8 |
| Reserves employed in the business | (14) | 342·3 | | 372·0 |
| | | 821·2 | | 852·8 |
| Applicable to minorities | | 94·2 | | 105·1 |
| | | 915·4 | | 957·9 |
| Investment grants | (5) | 28·0 | | 48·4 |
| Deferred taxation | | | | |
| UK Corporation tax payable January 1st, 1970 | | 41·6 | 63·5 | |
| Deferments due to accelerated capital allowances | (4) | 44·3 | 43·0 | |
| | | 85·9 | | 106·5 |
| Loans | (15) | 344·6 | | 374·1 |
| | | 1,373·9 | | 1,486·9 |

F. J. K. HILLEBRANDT, Treasurer

P. C. ALLEN  
A. E. FROST  } Directors

## IMPERIAL CHEMICAL INDUSTRIES LTD

### COMPANY BALANCE SHEET
at December 31st, 1968

| | Notes | 1967 £m | | 1968 £m |
|---|---|---|---|---|
| ASSETS EMPLOYED | | | | |
| Fixed assets | (8) | 625·3 | | 630·5 |
| Goodwill | (9) | 38·7 | | 38·7 |
| Interests in subsidiaries | (10) | 216·5 | | 214·1 |
| Interests in associated companies | (11) | 61·5 | | 56·8 |
| Net current assets | (12) | | | |
| Stocks | | 92·2 | 101·1 | |
| Debtors | | 105·5 | 129·2 | |
| Liquid resources | | 92·8 | 139·6 | |
| | | 290·5 | 369·9 | |
| Creditors | | 141·5 | 166·5 | |
| Short-term borrowings | | 13·2 | 16·1 | |
| | | 154·7 | 182·6 | |
| | | 135·8 | | 187·3 |
| | | 1,077·8 | | 1,127·4 |
| | | | | |
| FINANCED BY | | | | |
| Capital and reserves | | | | |
| Issued capital | (13) | 478·9 | | 480·8 |
| Reserves employed in the business | (14) | 281·1 | | 299·9 |
| | | 760·0 | | 780·7 |
| Investment grants | (5) | 27·3 | | 46·3 |
| Deferred taxation | | | | |
| UK Corporation tax payable January 1st, 1970 | | 36·4 | 52·5 | |
| Deferments due to accelerated capital allowances | (4) | 40·7 | 35·4 | |
| | | 77·1 | | 87·9 |
| Loans | (15) | 213·4 | | 212·5 |
| | | 1,077·8 | | 1,127·4 |

F. J. K. HILLEBRANDT, Treasurer      P. C. ALLEN ⎱ Directors
                                     A. E. FROST ⎰

# NOTES RELATING TO THE ACCOUNTS 1968
### (Figures in italics represent deductions)

| | 1967 £m | 1968 £m |
|---|---|---|
| **1. Trading profit** | | |
| The following amounts have been charged in arriving at trading profit: | | |
| Depreciation | 88·0 | 105·3 |
| Pension fund contributions, pensions and gratuities | 14·9 | 17·2 |
| Audit fees and expenses | ·3 | ·4 |
| | | |
| **2. Investment income** | | |
| Dividends and interest from: | | |
| Associated companies – quoted | 3·3 | 2·8 |
| – unquoted | 3·0 | 4·6 |
| Other quoted investments | 2·1 | 2·2 |
| Short-term deposits and sundry loans | 2·6 | 7·6 |
| | 11·0 | 17·2 |
| | | |
| **3. Interest payable** | | |
| Loans– repayable within 5 years | ·6 | 1·4 |
| – not repayable within 5 years | 19·8 | 23·3 |
| Bank overdrafts | 3·1 | 3·7 |
| Other | 2·1 | 1·2 |
| | 25·6 | 29·6 |
| | | |
| **4. Taxation** | | |
| United Kingdom | | |
| Corporation tax | 48·0 | 68·5 |
| Double taxation relief | *6·7* | *8·4* |
| | 41·3 | 60·1 |
| Adjustment of amount deferred due to accelerated capital allowances | *5·7* | *5·2* |
| | 35·6 | 54·9 |
| Overseas | | |
| Overseas taxes | 10·9 | 16·5 |
| Adjustment of amount deferred due to accelerated capital allowances | ·5 | *1·9* |
| | 47·0 | 69·5 |

UK and overseas taxation has been provided on the profits earned for the periods covered by the Group accounts. UK corporation tax has been provided at rates of 40 per cent. up to March 31st, 1967, and 42½ per cent. thereafter.

The amount of United Kingdom tax deferred due to accelerated capital allowances is adjusted each year to bring the UK tax charge to the figure which would have applied had there been no such allowances. Adjustments of a similar nature are made in the accounts of certain overseas subsidiaries and have this year been shown separately above. The Company Balance Sheet shows the sum of the UK adjustments made each year at the tax rates applicable to those years. The amount in the Group Balance Sheet includes the sum of the overseas adjustments of which £3·6m. in respect of past years, was transferred from Group reserves in 1968.

### 5. Investment grants

Investment grants on UK capital expenditure in 1968 are expected to amount to £30·0m in the Group (1967 £28·9m) and £28·3m (£27·3m) in the Company. The grants in respect of each year's capital expenditure are being credited to Profit and Loss Account over a period of ten years, the estimated average life of the relevant fixed assets. The investment grants shown in the Balance Sheets represent the total grants received to date less the amounts so far credited to profits.

### 6. Net dividends

|  | 1967 £m | 1968 £m |
|---|---|---|
| 5 per cent. Cumulative Preference stock | 1·0 | 1·0 |
| Ordinary stock– Interim 1s per £1 unit paid | 13·0 | 13·1 |
| – Final 1s 7·05d (1967 1s 6d) per £1 unit proposed | 19·6 | 20·8 |
|  | 33·6 | 34·9 |

### 7. Retained in the business

|  | 1967 | 1968 |
|---|---|---|
| By parent company | 1·1 | 16·0 |
| By subsidiaries | ·5 | 10·5 |
|  | ·6 | 26·5 |

### 8. Fixed assets

| | Land and buildings | | | Plant etc. | | | Total |
|---|---|---|---|---|---|---|---|
| | Cost or as revalued £m | Depreciation £m | Net book value £m | Cost or as revalued £m | Depreciation £m | Net book value £m | Net book value £m |
| GROUP | | | | | | | |
| At beginning of year | 292·4 | 84·4 | 208·0 | 1,175·0 | 437·0 | 738·0 | 946·0 |
| New subsidiaries | 9·1 | 1·0 | 8·1 | 16·8 | 7·0 | 9·8 | 17·9 |
| Capital expenditure | 12·7 | — | 12·7 | 112·7 | — | 112·7 | 125·4 |
| Sales, demolitions etc. | 2·6 | 1·5 | 1·1 | 27·8 | 17·4 | 10·4 | 11·5 |
| Depreciation for year | — | 12·4 | 12·4 | — | 92·9 | 92·9 | 105·3 |
| At end of year | 311·6 | 96·3 | 215·3 | 1,276·7 | 519·5 | 757·2 | 972·5 |
| COMPANY | | | | | | | |
| At beginning of year | 145·8 | 48·0 | 97·8 | 837·2 | 309·7 | 527·5 | 625·3 |
| Capital expenditure | 5·5 | — | 5·5 | 75·6 | — | 75·6 | 81·1 |
| Sales, demolitions etc. | ·8 | ·4 | ·4 | 12·7 | 7·6 | 5·1 | 5·5 |
| Depreciation for year | — | 6·9 | 6·9 | — | 63·5 | 63·5 | 70·4 |
| At end of year | 150·5 | 54·5 | 96·0 | 900·1 | 365·6 | 534·5 | 630·5 |

The company revalued the major part of its assets in 1950 and again in 1958 and there have also been revaluations by various subsidiaries. At the end of the year the amounts (comprising original cost and revaluation adjustments) relating to such assets included in the 'cost or as revalued' columns of the above table were:

| | Year of revaluation | Land and buildings £m | Plant etc. £m |
|---|---|---|---|
| Company | 1950 | 1·2 | — |
| | 1958 | 66·5 | 199·1 |
| Subsidiaries in: | | | |
| UK | 1958 | 8·3 | 9·2 |
| | 1962 | 4·8 | 5·6 |
| Australia | 1960 | 15·9 | 16·1 |
| Argentina | 1964 | 1·3 | 1·9 |
| Africa | 1961 | ·9 | 1·0 |
| Others | various | 4·3 | 4·3 |
| | | 103·2 | 237·2 |

Land and buildings comprise the following:

| | Group 1967 £m | Group 1968 £m | Company 1967 £m | Company 1968 £m |
|---|---|---|---|---|
| Freeholds | 272·1 | 286·5 | 141·0 | 145·6 |
| Long leases (over 50 years unexpired) | 12.8 | 18·8 | 4·1 | 4·2 |
| Short leases | 7·5 | 6·3 | ·7 | ·7 |
| | 292·4 | 311·6 | 145·8 | 150·5 |

## 9. Goodwill

Except for that arising on the acquisition of British Nylon Spinners Ltd in 1964, all goodwill has been charged against reserves.

## 10. Interests in subsidiaries

| | 1967 £m | 1968 £m |
|---|---|---|
| Shares at cost *less* amounts written off | 153·1 | 157·8 |
| Scrip issues capitalised | 11·5 | 11·7 |
| Book value of shares* | 164·6 | 169·5 |
| Amounts owed by subsidiaries | 87·2 | 84·9 |
| Amounts owed to subsidiaries* | 35·3 | 40·3 |
| | 216·5 | 214·1 |

*The amounts owed to dormant subsidiaries (£86·1m) have been set off against the book value of the corresponding investments.

[Information relating to the principal subsidiaries has not been reproduced.]

### 11. Interests in associated companies

| | Group | | Company | |
|---|---|---|---|---|
| | 1967 | **1968** | 1967 | **1968** |
| | £m | **£m** | £m | **£m** |
| **Quoted investments** | | | | |
| Shares at cost | 32·0 | **23·6** | 11·8 | **12·7** |
| Scrip issues capitalised | 6·8 | **2·4** | — | — |
| Book value | 38·8 | **26·0** | 11·8 | **12·7** |
| (Market value) | (66·8) | **(38·6)** | (10·3) | **(16.4)** |
| **Unquoted investments** | | | | |
| Equity shares at cost *less* amounts written off | 50·4 | **59·6** | 29·9 | **27·8** |
| Scrip issues capitalised | 4·9 | **10·2** | 4·4 | **5·3** |
| Book value | 55·3 | **69·8** | 34·3 | **33·1** |
| **Advances** | 23·9 | **15·0** | 15·4 | **11·0** |
| | 118·0 | **110·8** | 61·5 | **56·8** |

[Information relating to the principal associated companies has not been reproduced.]

The following information is given in respect of the investments in unquoted equity shares:

| | Group 1968 £m | Company 1968 £m |
|---|---|---|
| Income (before taxation) included in ICI accounts for 1968 | **3·9** | **1·6** |
| ICI share of aggregate profits *less* losses per latest accounts received | | |
|     Before taxation | **5·6** | **1·7** |
|     After taxation | **3·6** | **·8** |
| ICI share of aggregate undistributed profits *less* losses since acquisition (including amounts capitalized) | **7·7** | **4·6** |
| Aggregate amounts provided by ICI in respect of losses | **4·1** | **3·5** |

## 12. Net current assets

### Stocks

In general, finished goods are stated at the lower of cost or net sales value, other stocks at the lower of cost or replacement price; in determining cost, depreciation and certain overhead expenses are excluded.

|  | Group | | Company | |
|---|---|---|---|---|
|  | 1967 | **1968** | 1967 | **1968** |
| **Liquid resources** | £m | **£m** | £m | **£m** |
| Quoted investments | 35·5 | **19·6** | 33·4 | **17·9** |
| Short-term deposits | 64·3 | **127·9** | 59·0 | **120·8** |
| Cash | 9·4 | **7·8** | ·4 | **·9** |
|  | 109·2 | **155·3** | 92·8 | **139·6** |

The market value of the quoted investments at Balance Sheet dates was £21·0m in the Group (1967 £35·9m) and £18·2m in the Company (£33·3m).

### Creditors

| Trade and other creditors | 160·6 | **175·5** | 80·7 | **85·7** |
|---|---|---|---|---|
| Gross dividends | 34·2 | **36·3** | 34·2 | **36·3** |
| Current taxation | 41·3 | **65·8** | 26·6 | **44·5** |
|  | 236·1 | **277·6** | 141·5 | **166·5** |

### Short-term borrowings

| Bank overdrafts – secured | 7·6 | **8·9** | — | — |
|---|---|---|---|---|
| – unsecured | 49·0 | **48·3** | 8·5 | **10·9** |
| Other short-term borrowings | 6·1 | **6·5** | 4·7 | **5·2** |
|  | 62·7 | **63·7** | 13·2 | **16·1** |

## 13. Capital of parent company

|  | Issued 1967 | Authorized **1968** | Issued **1968** |
|---|---|---|---|
|  | £m | **£m** | **£m** |
| 5 per cent. Cumulative Preference stock | 34·7 | **34·7** | **34·7** |
| Ordinary stock | 444·2 | **446·1** | **446·1** |
| Unclassified shares of £1 each | — | **41·2** | — |
|  | 478·9 | **522·0** | **480·8** |

### 14. Reserves

Details of movements in Group reserves applicable to the Company and in Company reserves are as follows:

|  | Group £m | Company £m |
|---|---|---|
| At beginning of year | 342·3 | 281·1 |
| Profit of the year retained in the business | 26·5 | 16·0 |
| Share premiums received | 2·7 | 2·7 |
| Losses *less* profits on disposal of investments and fixed assets | 3·6 | 3·3 |
| Miscellaneous capital receipts (*less* tax) | 3·1 | 2·6 |
| Deferred overseas taxation adjustment | 3·6 | — |
| Changes in percentage holdings and other adjustments | 4·6 | ·8 |
| At end of year | **372·0** | **299·9** |

Reserves at end of year include share premiums amounting to £45·8m (1967 £43·1m).

### 15. Loans

|  | Group 1967 £m | Group 1968 £m | Company 1967 £m | Company 1968 £m |
|---|---|---|---|---|
| **Secured loans** | | | | |
| United Kingdom | 3·5 | **8·3** | — | — |
| Overseas | 29·1 | **39·1** | — | — |
|  | 32·6 | **47·4** | — | — |
| **Unsecured loans** | | | | |
| United Kingdom | | | | |
| 4¾ per cent.* stock 1972/74 | 30·0 | **30·0** | 30·0 | **30·0** |
| 6¾ per cent.* stock 1972/77 | 18·9 | **18·9** | 18·9 | **18·9** |
| 7¼ per cent.  stock 1986/91 | 71·1 | **71·1** | 59·2 | **59·2** |
| 7¾ per cent.  stock 1988/93 | — | **10·0** | — | — |
| 8 per cent.  stock 1988/93 | 60·0 | **60·0** | 60·0 | **60·0** |
| Others | 5·7 | **7·6** | 3·7 | **4·3** |
| Overseas | | | | |
| Bank loan | 11·4 | **11·4** | 11·4 | **11·4** |
| Others | 114·9 | **117·7** | 30·2 | **28·7** |
|  | 312·0 | **326·7** | 213·4 | **212·5** |
| **Total** | 344·6 | **374·1** | 213·4 | **212·5** |
| Repayable within 5 years | 14·4 | **16·5** | 4·0 | **2·5** |
| Not repayable within 5 years | 330·2 | **357·6** | 209·4 | **210·0** |

*Rate of interest increased by ¼ per cent. as from May 1st, 1968.

16. **Balance Sheet dates**

Owing to seasonal trade or local conditions and to avoid undue delay in the presentation of the Group accounts, it is impracticable for 207 subsidiaries to make up accounts to December 31st. The accounts of such subsidiaries are made up to dates varying from June 30th to October 31st, 1968; 195 of them are made up to September 30th or later.

17. **Foreign currencies**

Assets and liabilities in foreign currencies have been converted into sterling at the rates of exchange ruling at the dates of the respective Balance Sheets (adjusted in 1967 for devaluation). For subsidiaries in South America special rates to take account of inflation have been used.

Profit and Loss Accounts for 1968 have been converted into sterling at Balance Sheet rates of exchange, whereas in 1967 the rates ruling before sterling devaluation were used (except for the special rates for South America). The effect of the difference in exchange rates has been to increase sales in 1968 by about £60m and trading profit by about £5m.

18. **Commitments and contingent liabilities**

Contracts in respect of future capital expenditure on fixed assets which had been placed at the dates of the respective Balance Sheets were approximately £58m (1967 £48m) for the Group and £34m (£30m) for the Company. Expenditure sanctioned but not yet contracted for amounted to £93m (£109m) for the Group and £69m (£71m) for the Company. Commitments to acquire share and loan capital in subsidiary and associated companies amounted to £5m (£5m) for the Group and £6m (£10m) for the Company. The Company is committed to pay to the Workers' Pension Fund eight future annual instalments of £740,000 and to the Staff Pension Fund seven future annual instalments of £130,000; these relate to initial liabilities for past service and improvements in benefits.

Contingent liabilities existed at December 31st, 1968, in connection with (a) guarantees and uncalled capital relating to subsidiary and associated companies, the maximum liability in respect of which would be £33m (£35m) for the Group and £97m (£83m) for the Company, (b) guarantees relating to the Company Pension Funds and (c) other guarantees arising in the ordinary course of business.

19. **Emoluments of directors and senior employees**

The total emoluments of the directors of the Company for the year comprised fees £43,000 (1967 £47,000) and other emoluments £425,000 (£456,000). Pensions, commutations of pensions and gratuities in respect of executive service of former directors amounted to £643,000 (£494,000).

Two directors served as Chairman during the year and their emoluments whilst serving in that capacity were as follows:

|                   | 1967 £ | 1968 £ |
|-------------------|--------|--------|
| Sir Peter Allen   | —      | 45,750 |
| Sir Paul Chambers | 54,500 | 9,150  |

The table which follows shows the numbers of directors and senior employees of the Company whose emoluments during the year were within the bands stated. The table also shows the total amount of income tax and surtax applicable at the higher end of each band over £10,000 and the corresponding take-home pay; it has been assumed that the recipient is a married man without children and with no other source of income.

| Emoluments | Tax £ | Take-home pay £ | 1967 | 1968 |
|---|---|---|---|---|
| Directors | | | | |
| Up to £2,500 | | | 1 | 1 |
| £ 2,501 – £ 5,000 | | | 1 | — |
| £ 5,001 – £ 7,500 | | | 4 | 5 |
| £ 7,501 – £10,000 | | | 1 | 2 |
| £10,001 – £12,500 | 6,100 | 6,400 | 2 | 1 |
| £15,001 – £17,500 | 10,300 | 7,200 | 1 | — |
| £20,001 – £22,500 | 14,800 | 7,700 | — | 2 |
| £22,501 – £25,000 | 17,100 | 7,900 | 3 | — |
| £25,001 – £27,500 | 19,400 | 8,100 | 1 | 1 |
| £27,501 – £30,000 | 21,700 | 8,300 | 2 | 3 |
| £30,001 – £32,500 | 24,000 | 8,500 | 3 | 2 |
| £32,501 – £35,000 | 26,300 | 8,700 | — | 2 |
| £35,001 – £37,500 | 28,500 | 9,000 | 1 | 1 |
| £37,501 – £40,000 | 30,800 | 9,200 | — | 1 |
| £40,001 – £42,500 | 33,100 | 9,400 | 2 | — |
| £52,501 – £55,000 | 44,500 | 10,500 | 1 | 1 |
| | | | | |
| Employees | | | | |
| £10,001 – £12,500 | 6,100 | 6,400 | 40 | 63 |
| £12,501 – £15,000 | 8,100 | 6,900 | 10 | 23 |
| £15,001 – £17,500 | 10,300 | 7,200 | 5 | 6 |
| £17,501 – £20,000 | 12,500 | 7,500 | — | 4 |
| £20,001 – £22,500 | 14,800 | 7,700 | — | 1 |

# GROUP FINANCIAL RECORD
## For the years ended December 31st

| Assets employed | 1959 £m | 1960 £m | 1961 £m | 1962 £m | 1963 £m | 1964 £m | 1965 £m | 1966 £m | 1967 £m | 1968 £m |
|---|---|---|---|---|---|---|---|---|---|---|
| Fixed assets | 498 | 520 | 544 | 559 | 570 | 646 | 760 | 880 | 946 | 972 |
| Goodwill | — | — | — | — | — | 39 | 39 | 39 | 39 | 39 |
| Interests in associated companies | 44 | 51 | 58 | 130 | 147 | 92 | 108 | 119 | 118 | 111 |
| Net current assets | 118 | 124 | 136 | 154 | 176 | 189 | 160 | 170 | 271 | 365 |
| Total | 660 | 695 | 738 | 843 | 893 | 966 | 1,067 | 1,208 | 1,374 | 1,487 |
| **Financed by** | | | | | | | | | | |
| Ordinary capital of ICI | 246 | 252 | 266 | 269 | 416 | 419 | 438 | 441 | 444 | 446 |
| Group reserves applicable to ICI Ordinary stockholders | 230 | 270 | 307 | 325 | 227 | 262 | 326 | 333 | 342 | 372 |
| Capital and reserves applicable to ICI Ordinary stockholders | 476 | 522 | 573 | 594 | 643 | 681 | 764 | 774 | 786 | 818 |
| Preference capital of ICI | 35 | 35 | 35 | 35 | 35 | 35 | 35 | 35 | 35 | 35 |
| Minority interests | 26 | 36 | 40 | 41 | 42 | 43 | 61 | 74 | 94 | 105 |
| Investment grants | — | — | — | — | — | — | — | — | 28 | 48 |
| Deferred taxation | 37 | 42 | 31 | 33 | 41 | 56 | 49 | 72 | 86 | 107 |
| Loans | 86 | 60 | 59 | 140 | 132 | 151 | 158 | 253 | 345 | 374 |
| Total funds invested | 660 | 695 | 738 | 843 | 893 | 966 | 1,067 | 1,208 | 1,374 | 1,487 |
| **Sales, profits, dividends and retentions** | | | | | | | | | | |
| Sales (external) | 509 | 558 | 550 | 579 | 624 | 720 | 816 | 885 | 979 | 1,237 |
| Trading profit (after depreciation) | 80 | 94 | 66 | 73 | 85 | 113 | 113 | 99 | 122 | 175 |
| Depreciation | 33 | 37 | 41 | 44 | 54 | 61 | 69 | 77 | 88 | 105 |
| Profit before taxation and investment grants | 73 | 88 | 62 | 70 | 85 | 108 | 101 | 86 | 101 | 153 |
| Taxation | 31 | 40 | 28 | 32 | 42 | 47 | 22 | 33 | 47 | 70 |
| Investment grants | — | — | — | — | — | — | — | 4 | 9 | 11 |
| Profit after taxation | 42 | 48 | 34 | 38 | 43 | 61 | 79 | 57 | 63 | 94 |
| Applicable to ICI | 39 | 45 | 32 | 36 | 40 | 58 | 74 | 52 | 58 | 86 |
| Net dividends | 18 | 22 | 23 | 24 | 26 | 33 | 33 | 33 | 33 | 35 |
| Income tax on dividends | — | — | — | — | — | — | — | 17 | 24 | 25 |
| Retained in the business | 21 | 23 | 9 | 12 | 14 | 25 | 41 | 2 | 1 | 26 |
| Rate of ICI gross Ordinary dividend per £1 stock (in shillings and pence) | 1/6* | 1/10* | 1/10* | 1/10* | 2/– | 2/6 | 2/6 | 2/6 | 2/6 | 2/7.05 |
| Group profit before charging loan interest and before taxation and investment grants, as a percentage of total funds invested | 11·7 | 13 2 | 8·7 | 9·1 | 10·4 | 12·0 | 10·3 | 8·1 | 8·8 | 11·9 |

* Adjusted for scrip issue in 1963.

## LEGAL AND GENERAL ASSURANCE SOCIETY LIMITED

### REVENUE ACCOUNTS

for the year ended December 31st, 1969

| 1968 | | LIFE ASSURANCE AND ANNUITY | 1969 | |
|---:|---:|---|---:|---:|
| *£,000* | *£,000* | | £,000 | £,000 |
| 844,131 | | Fund at the beginning of the year .. .. | | 928,545 |
| 98,790 | | Premiums .. .. .. .. | | 105,455 |
| 5,451 | | Consideration for annuities granted .. | | 2,757 |
| 58,120 | | Interest, dividends and rents .. .. | | 63,153 |
| 88 | | Realised profits on Reversions *less* taxation | | 39 |
| 10,415 | | Part of unrealised appreciation of investments (see Note 8, page 725) | | 1,983 |
| 1,016,995 | | | | 1,101,932 |
| | 21,716 | *Less:* Claims paid and outstanding .. | 24,588 | |
| | — | Pension Schemes bonuses .. .. | 13,595 | |
| | 16,983 | Surrenders .. .. .. | 18,170 | |
| | 17,990 | Annuities .. .. .. .. | 20,102 | |
| | 5,374 | Commission .. .. .. | 5,523 | |
| | 559 | Short term interest paid .. .. | 638 | |
| | 5,789 | Taxation (see Note 5, page 725) .. | 4,880 | |
| | 10,470 | Expenses of management .. .. | 11,057 | |
| | 769 | Staff pension contributions .. .. | 837 | |
| 79,650 | | | | 99,390 |
| 937,345 | | | | 1,002,542 |
| 8,800 | | *Less:* Transfer to Profit and Loss Account .. | | 2,965 |
| £928,545 | | Fund at the end of the year .. .. | | £999,577 |

## LEGAL AND GENERAL ASSURANCE SOCIETY LIMITED

| 1968 | | | 1969 | |
|---|---|---|---|---|
| £,000 | £,000 | **SINKING FUND AND CAPITAL REDEMPTION** | £,000 | £,000 |
| 5,943 | | Fund at the beginning of the year .. | | 6,243 |
| 602 | | Premiums .. .. .. .. | | 725 |
| 404 | | Interest, dividends and rents .. .. | | 431 |
| 80 | | Part of unrealised appreciation of investments (see Note 8, page 725) | | 16 |
| 7,029 | | | | 7,415 |
| | 71 | *Less:* Claims paid and outstanding .. | 25 | |
| | 160 | Surrenders .. .. .. | 242 | |
| | 10 | Annuities .. .. .. .. | 8 | |
| | 11 | Commission .. .. .. | 20 | |
| | 4 | Short term interest paid .. .. | 4 | |
| | 190 | Taxation (see Note 5, page 725) .. | 177 | |
| | 15 | Expenses of management .. .. | 18 | |
| 461 | | | | 494 |
| 6,568 | | | | 6,921 |
| 325 | | *Less:* Transfer to Profit and Loss Account .. | | 85 |
| £6,243 | | Fund at the end of the year .. . .. | | £6,836 |

### PERMANENT HEALTH INSURANCE

| | | Fund at the beginning of the year: | | |
|---|---|---|---|---|
| | 5 | Actuarial liability in respect of outstanding claims .. .. .. .. | 15 | |
| | 321 | Accumulated fund .. .. .. | 294 | |
| 326 | | | | 309 |
| 312 | | Premiums .. .. .. .. | | 398 |
| 23 | | Interest, dividends and rents .. .. | | 22 |
| 5 | | Part of unrealised appreciation of investments (see Note 8, page 725) | | 1 |
| 666 | | | | 730 |
| | 253 | *Less:* Claims paid .. .. .. | 312 | |
| | 1 | Commission .. .. .. | 5 | |
| | 12 | Taxation (see Note 5, page 725) .. | 5 | |
| | 16 | Expenses of management .. .. | 26 | |
| 282 | | | | 348 |
| 384 | | | | 382 |
| 75 | | *Less:* Transfer to Profit and Loss Account .. | | 5 |
| 309 | | Fund at the end of the year: | | 377 |
| | 15 | Actuarial liability in respect of outstanding claims .. .. .. .. | 30 | |
| | 294 | Accumulated fund .. .. .. | 347 | |
| £309 | | | | £377 |

**Legal and General Assurance Society Limited**
**Gresham Fire and Accident Insurance Society Limited**
**British Commonwealth Insurance Company Limited**

| 1968 | | | 1969 | |
|---|---|---|---|---|
| *£,000* | *£,000* | **CONSOLIDATED FIRE AND ACCIDENT INSURANCE** | £,000 | £,000 |
| 15,135 | | Premiums  ..  ..  ..  .. | | 15,926 |
| | | *Less:* Increases in provisions: | | |
| | 715 | Unearned premiums  ..  .. | 172 | |
| | 231 | Unexpired risks  ..  ..  .. | 178 | |
| 946 | | | | 350 |
| 14,189 | | Premiums earned  ..  ..  .. | | 15,576 |
| | 7,563 | *Less:* Claims paid and outstanding  .. | 7,659 | |
| | 2,230 | Commission  ..  ..  .. | 2,333 | |
| | 4,035 | Expenses of management  ..  .. | 4,342 | |
| | 52 | Overseas taxes other than on profits  .. | 49 | |
| | — | Transfer to Exchange Account  .. | 18 | |
| | — | Transfer to Claims Equalisation Reserve | 166 | |
| 13,880 | | | | 14,567 |
| £309 | | Transfer to Profit and Loss Account  .. | | £1,009 |
| | | Fund at the end of the year: | | |
| | 6,304 | Provision for unearned premiums  .. | 6,476 | |
| | 2,034 | Provision for unexpired risks  .. | 2,212 | |
| | 734 | Claims Equalisation Reserve  .. | 900 | |
| | £9,072 | | £9,588 | |

**Legal and General Assurance Society Limited**
**British Commonwealth Insurance Company Limited**

| 1968 | | | 1969 | |
|---|---|---|---|---|
| *£,000* | *£,000* | **CONSOLIDATED MARINE INSURANCE** | £,000 | £,000 |
| 2,193 | | Fund at the beginning of the year ..  .. | | 2,455 |
| 2,045 | | Premiums  ..  ..  ..  .. | | 2,158 |
| 60 | | Transfer from Profit and Loss Account  .. | | 100 |
| 4,298 | | | | 4,713 |
| | 1,723 | *Less:* Claims paid  ..  ..  .. | 1,841 | |
| | Cr.  30 | Taxation (see Note 5, page 725)  .. | Cr.  40 | |
| | 150 | Expenses of management  ..  .. | 169 | |
| 1,843 | | | | 1,970 |
| £2,455 | | Fund at the end of the year  ..  .. | | £2,743 |

**Legal and General Assurance Society Limited and its Subsidiary Companies**

(*Excluding Gresham Life Assurance Society Limited*)

## CONSOLIDATED PROFIT AND LOSS ACCOUNT
for the year ended December 31st, 1969

| 1968 | | | 1969 | |
|---|---|---|---|---|
| £,000 | £,000 | | £,000 | £,000 |
| 1,461 | | Interest, dividends and rents .. .. | | 1,909 |
| | | Transfers from: | | |
| | | Revenue Accounts– | | |
| | 8,800 | Life Assurance and Annuity .. .. | 2,965 | |
| | 325 | Sinking Fund and Capital Redemption | 85 | |
| | 75 | Permanent Health .. .. .. | 5 | |
| | 309 | Fire and Accident .. .. .. | 1,009 | |
| | (60) | Marine .. .. .. .. | (100) | |
| 9,449 | | | | 3,964 |
| 10,910 | | | | 5,873 |
| | 217 | *Less:* Staff pension contributions .. .. | 244 | |
| | 33 | Short term interest paid .. .. | 36 | |
| | 57 | Taxation (see Note 5, page 725) .. | 663 | |
| 307 | | | | 943 |
| £10,603 | | | | £4,930 |
| | | | | |
| 10,603 | | Balance from above .. .. .. | | 4,930 |
| 1,691 | | *Add:* Balance from last year's account .. | | 8,875 |
| 12,294 | | | | 13,805 |
| 100 | | *Less:* Transfer to investment reserve .. | | 460 |
| 12,194 | | | | 13,345 |
| | 1,500 | *Less:* Interim ordinary dividend (paid December 1st, 1969) .. .. .. | 1,625 | |
| | 1,819 | Proposed final ordinary dividend .. | 2,375 | |
| | — | Proposed special dividend .. .. | 1,250 | |
| 3,319 | | | | 5,250 |
| £8,875 | | Balance carried forward .. .. .. | | £8,095 |

**Legal and General Assurance Society Limited**

## LIFE DEPARTMENT BALANCE SHEET
on December 31st, 1969

| 1968 | | | 1969 | |
|---|---|---|---|---|
| *£,000* | *£,000* | | £,000 | £,000 |
| | | **Insurance Funds:** | | |
| | *928,545* | Life Assurance and Annuity    ..        .. | 999,577 | |
| | *6,243* | Sinking Fund and Capital Redemption    .. | 6,836 | |
| | *309* | Permanent Health        ..        ..        .. | 377 | |
| *935,097* | | | | 1,006,790 |
| | | **Current Liabilities and Provisions:** | | |
| | *2,520* | Claims admitted or intimated but not paid .. | 3,010 | |
| | *12,978* | Outstanding accounts including taxation and other provisions    ..        ..        .. | 18,388 | |
| | *8,967* | Deposits at interest by trustees of superannuation funds        ..        ..        .. | 9,745 | |
| *24,465* | | | | 31,143 |
| *£959,562* | | | | £1,037,933 |

**Legal and General Assurance Society Limited**

| 1968 | | | 1969 | |
| ---: | ---: | :--- | ---: | ---: |
| £,000 | £,000 | | £,000 | £,000 |
| | | **Mortgages, Loans and Investments (at cost or valuation less reserves and provisions):** | | |
| | 220,677 | Mortgages on property .. .. .. | 227,367 | |
| | 13,780 | Loans on life interests, reversions and other securities .. .. .. .. | 14,498 | |
| | 136,905 | British Government and British Government guaranteed securities .. .. .. | 150,174 | |
| | 189,075 | Other fixed interest securities .. .. | 201,130 | |
| | 119,113 | Ordinary shares .. .. .. | 146,354 | |
| | 217,679 | Freehold and leasehold properties, rent charges and ground rents .. .. .. | 229,880 | |
| | 7,355 | Deposits at interest .. .. .. | 6,280 | |
| | 3,124 | Reversions and life interests purchased .. | 2,960 | |
| 907,708 | | | | 978,643 |
| | | **Subsidiary Companies:** | | |
| | 1,562 | Shares at cost *less* amounts written off .. | 1,562 | |
| | 13,654 | Amounts due on loan accounts .. .. | 16,200 | |
| | 259 | Amounts due on current accounts (including dividends since declared and undistributed profits) .. .. .. .. | 531 | |
| 15,475 | | | | 18,293 |
| | | **Current Assets:** | | |
| | 1,154 | Agents' balances .. .. .. | 1,272 | |
| | 7,245 | Outstanding premiums .. .. .. | 9,506 | |
| | 23,310 | Outstanding accounts including taxation recoverable .. .. .. .. | 17,867 | |
| | 7,723 | Accrued interest and rents .. .. | 8,481 | |
| | 6,147 | Short term deposits, bank balances and cash in hand .. .. .. .. | 6,926 | |
| 45,579 | | | | 44,052 |
| 968,762 | | | | 1,040,988 |
| | | **Deduct:** | | |
| | | **Shareholders' Account –** | | |
| 9,200 | | Transfer of Profit .. .. .. | | 3,055 |
| £959,562 | | | | £1,037,933 |

**Legal and General Assurance Society Limited**

## BALANCE SHEET
on December 31st, 1969

| 1968 | | | 1969 | |
|---|---|---|---|---|
| *£,000* | *£,000* | | *£,000* | *£,000* |
| | | **Capital Authorised and Issued:** | | |
| | | £3,000,000 in 60,000,000 Shares of 1/– each | | |
| *3,000* | | fully paid   ..    ..    ..    .. | | 3,000 |
| | | **Reserves:** | | |
| | *500* | General Reserve   ..    ..    .. | 500 | |
| | *8,875* | Profit and Loss Account    ..    .. | 8,095 | |
| *9,375* | | | | 8,595 |
| *12,375* | | | | 11,595 |
| | | **Insurance Funds (including reserves and provisions):** | | |
| | *7,175* | Fire and Accident   ..    ..    .. | 7,584 | |
| | *1,431* | Marine   ..    ..    ..    .. | 1,601 | |
| *8,606* | | | | 9,185 |
| | | **Current Liabilities and Provisions:** | | |
| | *5,989* | Claims admitted or intimated but not paid .. | 6,617 | |
| | *5,459* | Outstanding accounts including taxation and other provisions   ..    ..    .. | 7,988 | |
| | *1,819* | Proposed final ordinary dividend for the year 1969..   ..    ..    ..    .. | 2,375 | |
| | — | Proposed special dividend for the year 1969 | 1,250 | |
| *13,267* | | | | 18,230 |
| *34,248* | | | | 39,010 |
| *959,562* | | **Life Department Balance Sheet** (see pages 718 and 719)   ..    ..    ..    .. | | 1,037,933 |
| *£993,810* | | | | £1,076,943 |

**Legal and General Assurance Society Limited**

| 1968 | | | 1969 | |
|---|---|---|---|---|
| £,000 | £,000 | | £,000 | £,000 |
| | | **Mortgages, Loans and Investments (at cost or valuation less reserves and provisions):** | | |
| | 1,474 | Mortgages on property .. .. .. | 1,561 | |
| | 3,904 | British Government and British Government guaranteed securities .. .. .. | 7,080 | |
| | 2,915 | Other fixed interest securities .. .. | 3,225 | |
| | 2,285 | Ordinary shares .. .. .. | 4,998 | |
| | 1,586 | Freehold and leasehold properties .. | 1,586 | |
| | 574 | Deposits at interest .. .. .. | 3,198 | |
| 12,738 | | | | 21,648 |
| | | **Subsidiary Companies:** | | |
| | 1,043 | Shares at cost *less* amounts written off .. | 1,043 | |
| | 589 | Amounts due on current accounts (including dividends since declared and undistributed profits) .. .. .. .. | 458 | |
| 1,632 | | | | 1,501 |
| | | **Life Department:** | | |
| 9,200 | | Transfer of Profit .. .. .. | | 3,055 |
| | | **Current Assets:** | | |
| | 3,421 | Agents' balances .. .. .. | 4,292 | |
| | 3,952 | Outstanding accounts .. .. .. | 4,764 | |
| | 139 | Accrued interest and rents .. .. | 309 | |
| | 3,166 | Short term deposits, bank balances and cash in hand .. .. .. .. | 3,441 | |
| 10,678 | | | | 12,806 |
| 34,248 | | | | 39,010 |
| 959,562 | | **Life Department Balance Sheet** (see pages 718 and 719) .. .. .. .. | | 1,037,933 |
| £993,810 | | | | £1,076,943 |

**Legal and General Assurance Society Limited and its Subsidiary Companies**
(*Excluding Gresham Life Assurance Society Limited*)

### CONSOLIDATED BALANCE SHEET
on December 31st, 1969

| 1968 | | | 1969 | |
|---|---|---|---|---|
| *£,000* | *£,000* | | £,000 | £,000 |
| | | **Capital Authorised and Issued:** | | |
| | | £3,000,000 in 60,000,000 Shares of 1/- each | | |
| *3,000* | | fully paid     ..        ..        ..        .. | | 3,000 |
| | | **Reserves:** | | |
| | *500* | General Reserve         ..        ..        .. | 500 | |
| | *8,875* | Profit and Loss Account ..        ..        .. | 8,095 | |
| *9,375* | | | | 8,595 |
| *12,375* | | | | 11,595 |
| | | **Insurance Funds (including reserves and provisions):** | | |
| | *928,545* | Life Assurance and Annuity        ..        .. | 999,577 | |
| | *6,243* | Sinking Fund and Capital Redemption        .. | 6,836 | |
| | *309* | Permanent Health        ..        ..        .. | 377 | |
| | | (See Life Department Balance Sheet, pages | | |
| | *935,097* | 718 and 719) ..        ..        ..        .. | 1,006,790 | |
| | *9,072* | Fire and Accident        ..        ..        .. | 9,588 | |
| | *2,455* | Marine        ..        ..        ..        .. | 2,743 | |
| *946,624* | | | | 1,019,121 |
| | | **Current Liabilities and Provisions:** | | |
| | *10,919* | Claims admitted or intimated but not paid .. | 12,287 | |
| | *20,307* | Outstanding accounts including taxation and other provisions        ..        ..        .. | 28,195 | |
| | *8,967* | Deposits at interest by trustees of superannuation funds        ..        ..        .. | 9,745 | |
| | *1,819* | Proposed final ordinary dividend for the year 1969        ..        ..        ..        .. | 2,375 | |
| | *—* | Proposed special dividend for the year 1969 | 1,250 | |
| *42,012* | | | | 53,852 |
| *£1,001,011* | | | | £1,084,568 |

**Legal and General Assurance Society Limited and its Subsidiary Companies**
(*Excluding Gresham Life Assurance Society Limited*)

| 1968 | | | 1969 | |
|---|---|---|---|---|
| £,000 | £,000 | | £,000 | £,000 |
| | | **Mortgages, Loans and Investments (at cost or valuation less reserves and provisions):** | | |
| | 222,151 | Mortgages on property  ..         ..         .. | 228,929 | |
| | 13,780 | Loans on life interests, reversions and other securities     ..         ..         ..         .. | 14,498 | |
| | 142,220 | British Government and British Government guaranteed securities  ..         ..         .. | 158,401 | |
| | 195,219 | Other fixed interest securities     ..         .. | 207,712 | |
| | 121,886 | Ordinary shares         ..         ..         .. | 151,808 | |
| | 233,911 | Freehold and leasehold properties, rent charges and ground rents         ..         ..         .. | 248,698 | |
| | 8,028 | Deposits at interest     ..         ..         .. | 9,628 | |
| | 3,124 | Reversions and life interests purchased     .. | 2,960 | |
| 940,319 | | | | 1,022,634 |
| | | **Subsidiary Company:** | | |
| | 477 | Shares in Gresham Life Assurance Society Limited (at cost *less* amount written off) (see Note 12, page 726)     ..         .. | 477 | |
| | 51 | Amount due on current account  ..         .. | 100 | |
| 528 | | | | 577 |
| | | **Current Assets:** | | |
| | 5,521 | Agents' balances         ..         ..         .. | 6,236 | |
| | 7,245 | Outstanding premiums  ..         ..         .. | 9,506 | |
| | 29,038 | Outstanding accounts including taxation recoverable     ..         ..         ..         .. | 24,468 | |
| | 7,935 | Accrued interest and rents     ..         .. | 8,880 | |
| | 10,425 | Short term deposits, bank balances and cash in hand     ..         ..         ..         .. | 12,267 | |
| 60,164 | | | | 61,357 |
| £1,001,011 | | | | £1,084,568 |

**Legal and General Assurance Society Limited**

## NOTES TO ACCOUNTS

### Profit and Loss Account and Revenue Accounts

1. Profits and losses on sales of investments have been carried to internal reserve accounts, the balances of which have been applied to reduce the Balance Sheet values of the investments.

2. The aggregate emoluments of Directors of Legal and General Assurance Society Limited, including the amount paid to them as Directors of subsidiary companies, was £151,744 (*1968, £59,350*) of which £63,833 (*1968, £58,000*) was in respect of services as Directors, and £87,911 (*1968, £1,350*) was in respect of other emoluments. Included in the above figures is £12,000 (*1968, £12,000*) paid to the Chairman. The highest paid director received £23,500.

The following shows the number of Directors of Legal and General Assurance Society Limited at December 31st, 1969, classified according to their emoluments, excluding pension contributions.

| Emoluments | Number of Directors | |
|---|---|---|
| | 1969 | *1968* |
| £1 – £2,500 | 7 | *7* |
| £2,501 – £5,000 | 5 | *4* |
| £5,001 – £7,500 | 2 | *3* |
| £7,501 – £10,000 | 4 | – |
| £10,001 – £12,500 | 1 | *1* |
| £12,501 – £15,000 | – | – |
| £15,001 – £17,500 | – | – |
| £17,501 – £20,000 | – | – |
| £20,001 – £22,500 | – | – |
| £22,501 – £25,000 | 1 | – |

Some of the Directors served on the Board for part of the year only.

3. The following shows the number of employees whose emoluments, excluding pension contributions, exceeded £10,000.

| Emoluments | Number of Employees | |
|---|---|---|
| | 1969 | *1968* |
| £10,001 – £12,500 | 2 | *3* |
| £12,501 – £15,000 | 1 | *3* |
| £15,001 – £17,500 | – | – |
| £17,501 – £20,000 | – | – |
| £20,001 – £22,500 | – | *1* |

4. The total amount paid by Legal and General Assurance Society Limited and its subsidiaries (excluding Gresham Life Assurance Society Limited) during 1969 for the remuneration of auditors was £33,381 (*1968, £29,030*). This amount has been included in expenses of management in the Revenue Accounts.

5. In the life and annuity, sinking fund and permanent health accounts the taxation charge is based on the annuity profits and income *less* expenses up to December 31st, 1969; the marine account credit relates to 1966 and 1967. The profit and loss charge is based on the results for the year 1969, *less* income tax retainable on payment of dividends under section 48 and section 85, *Finance Act 1965*.

| | | LIFE AND ANNUITY | | SINKING FUND | | PERMANENT HEALTH | | MARINE | | PROFIT AND LOSS | |
|---|---|---|---|---|---|---|---|---|---|---|---|
| | | *1968* | *1969* | *1968* | *1969* | *1968* | *1969* | *1968* | *1969* | *1968* | *1969* |
| | | *£,000* | *£,000* | *£,000* | *£,000* | *£,000* | *£,000* | *£,000* | *£,000* | *£,000* | *£,000* |
| Corporation Tax | .. | 4,879 | 3,575 | 190 | 177 | 12 | 5 | *Cr 1* | *Cr 40* | 779 | 1,306 |
| Double Taxation Relief | | — | — | — | — | — | — | — | — | *Cr 43* | Cr 16 |
| Income Tax | .. | 909 | 1,256 | — | — | — | — | *Cr 18* | — | 53 | — |
| F.A. 1965 Relief: | | | | | | | | | | | |
| Section 48 | .. | — | — | — | — | — | — | — | — | *Cr 597* | Cr 626 |
| Section 85 | .. | — | — | — | — | — | — | — | — | *Cr 150* | Cr 50 |
| Foreign Tax | .. | *1* | 49 | — | — | — | — | *1* | — | 21 | 49 |
| Profits Tax | .. | — | — | — | — | — | — | *Cr 12* | — | *Cr 6* | — |
| | £ | *5,789* | 4,880 | *190* | 177 | *12* | 5 | *Cr 30* | *Cr 40* | *57* | 663 |

## Balance Sheets

6. Part of the assets are deposited under local laws in countries outside the United Kingdom as security to policy holders in those countries.

7. Assets and liabilities in overseas currencies (with the exception of a limited number of Head Office investments which are included at or under their sterling equivalent at the date of acquisition) have been converted at the rates of exchange ruling on December 31st, 1969.

8. The stock exchange securities and other investments at December 31st, 1969, are included in the Balance Sheets at or under their cost or at directors' valuation and in the aggregate, taking each Balance Sheet separately, were under market value. The amounts shown include part of the unrealised appreciation which existed at December 31st, 1969, in the market value of the investments. The amount dealt with in the Revenue Accounts on pages 714 and 715 is in the aggregate £2,000,000, and appropriate provision for the liability to taxation that would arise in the event of realisation in relation to the above amount has been dealt with in the taxation accounts.

9. There are contingent liabilities for uncalled capital on stock exchange and other investments amounting to £796,000 (*1968, £1,529,000*).

10. There are instalments on stock exchange and other investments, payable after December 31st, 1969, amounting to £2,890,000 (*1968, £2,285,000*).

**Balance Sheet (pages 720 and 721)**

**11.** There are contingent liabilities in respect of contracts of Gresham Fire and Accident Insurance Society Limited guaranteed by the Society.

**Balance Sheet (pages 722 and 723)**

**12.** The accounts of Gresham Life Assurance Society Limited have not been consolidated. They are an integral part of the Society's accounts. (*Not reproduced in this Appendix.*)

**General**

**13.** Under the provisions of the *Companies Acts 1948* and *1967* insurance companies are not required to show separately in their accounts their reserves and provisions, the movements therein or the market value of their investments.

**14.** In our belief the assets set forth in the Balance Sheets are, in the aggregate, fully of the value stated therein, and no part of any fund has been applied, directly or indirectly, for any purposes other than those of the class of business to which the fund is applicable.


P. CAHILL,
*Chief Executive Officer*

R. L. SLEIGHT,
*Secretary*

HARCOURT,
*Chairman*

G. W. BRIDGE,
*Deputy Chairman*

R. E. B. LLOYD,
*Director*

# APPENDIX II

## *Companies Act 1967*

### SCHEDULE 2
FORM OF SCHEDULE 8 TO THE COMPANIES ACT 1948
AS AMENDED BY THIS ACT

ACCOUNTS

*Preliminary*

1. Paragraphs 2 to 11 of this Schedule apply to the Balance Sheet and 12 to 14 to the Profit and Loss Account, and are subject to the exceptions and modifications provided for by Part II of this Schedule in the case of a holding or subsidiary company and by Part III thereof in the case of companies of the classes there mentioned; and this Schedule has effect in addition to the provisions of sections one hundred and ninety-six and one hundred and ninety-seven of this Act.

PART I

GENERAL PROVISIONS AS TO BALANCE SHEET AND PROFIT
AND LOSS ACCOUNT

*Balance Sheet*

2. The authorized share capital, issued share capital, liabilities and assets shall be summarized, with such particulars as are necessary to disclose the general nature of the assets and liabilities, and there shall be specified:

(*a*) any part of the issued capital that consists of redeemable preference shares, the earliest and latest dates on which the company has power to redeem those shares, whether those shares must be redeemed in any event or are liable to be redeemed at the option of the company and whether any (and, if so, what) premium is payable on redemption;

(*b*) so far as the information is not given in the Profit and Loss Account, any share capital on which interest has been paid out of capital during the financial year, and the rate at which interest has been so paid;

(*c*) the amount of the Share Premium Account;

(*d*) particulars of any redeemed debentures which the company has power to reissue.

3. There shall be stated under separate headings, so far as they are not written off:

(*a*) the preliminary expenses;

(*b*) any expenses incurred in connection with any issue of share capital or debentures;

(*c*) any sums paid by way of commission in respect of any shares or debentures;

(*d*) any sums allowed by way of discount in respect of any debentures; and

(*e*) the amount of the discount allowed on any issue of shares at a discount.

4. (1) The reserves, provisions, liabilities and assets shall be classified under headings appropriate to the company's business:

Provided that:

(*a*) where the amount of any class is not material, it may be included under the same heading as some other class; and (*b*) where any assets of one class are not separable from assets of another class, those assets may be included under the same heading.

(2) Fixed assets, current assets and assets that are neither fixed nor current shall be separately identified.

(3) The method or methods used to arrive at the amount of the fixed assets under each heading shall be stated.

5. (1) The method of arriving at the amount of any fixed asset shall, subject to the next following sub-paragraph, be to take the difference between:

(*a*) its cost, or, if it stands in the company's books at a valuation, the amount of the valuation; and

(*b*) the aggregate amount provided or written off since the date of acquisition or valuation, as the case may be, for depreciation or diminution in value;

and for the purposes of this paragraph the net amount at which any assets stand in the company's books at the commencement of this Act (after deduction of the amounts previously provided or written off for depreciation or diminution in value) shall, if the figures relating to the period before the commencement of this Act cannot be obtained without unreasonable expense or delay, be treated as if it were the amount of a valuation of those assets made at the commencement of this Act and, where any of those assets are sold, the said net amount less the amount of the sales shall be treated as if it were the amount of a valuation so made of the remaining assets.

(2) The foregoing sub-paragraph shall not apply:

(*a*) to assets for which the figures relating to the period beginning with the commencement of this Act cannot be obtained without unreasonable expense or delay; or

(*b*) to assets the replacement of which is provided for wholly or partly:

(i) by making provision for renewals and charging the cost of replacement against the provision so made; or

(ii) by charging the cost of replacement direct to revenue; or

(*c*) to any quoted investments or to any unquoted investments of which the value as estimated by the directors is shown either as the amount of the investments or by way of note; or

(*d*) to goodwill, patents or trade marks.

(3) For the assets under each heading whose amount is arrived at in accordance with sub-paragraph (1) of this paragraph, there shall be shown:

(*a*) the aggregate of the amounts referred to in paragraph (*a*) of that sub-paragraph; and

(*b*) the aggregate of the amounts referred to in paragraph (*b*) thereof.

(4) As respects the assets under each heading whose amount is not arrived at in accordance with the said sub-paragraph (1) because their replacement is provided for as mentioned in sub-paragraph (2) (*b*) of this paragraph, there shall be stated:

(*a*) the means by which their replacement is provided for; and

(*b*) the aggregate amount of the provision (if any) made for renewals and not used.

5A. In the case of unquoted investments consisting in equity share capital (as defined by subsection (5) of section 154 of this Act) of other bodies corporate (other than any whose values as estimated by the directors are separately shown, either individually or collectively or as to some individually and as to the rest collectively, and are so shown either as the amount thereof, or by way of note), the matters referred to in the following heads shall, if not otherwise shown, be stated by way of note or in a statement or report annexed:

(*a*) the aggregate amount of the company's income for the financial year that is ascribable to the investments;

(*b*) the amount of the company's share before taxation, and the amount of that share after taxation, of the net aggregate amount of the profits of the bodies in which the investments are held, being profits for the several periods to which accounts sent by them during the financial year to the company related, after deducting those bodies' losses for those periods (or vice versa);

(c) the amount of the company's share of the net aggregate amount of the undistributed profits accumulated by the bodies in which the investments are held since the time when the investments were acquired, after deducting the losses accumulated by them since that time (or vice versa);

(d) the manner in which any losses incurred by the said bodies have been dealt with in the company's accounts.

6. The aggregate amounts respectively of reserves and provisions (other than provisions for depreciation, renewals or diminution in value of assets) shall be stated under separate headings:

Provided that:

(a) this paragraph shall not require a separate statement of either of the said amounts which is not material; and

(b) the Board of Trade may direct that it shall not require a separate statement of the amount of provisions where they are satisfied that that is not required in the public interest and would prejudice the company, but subject to the condition that any heading stating an amount arrived at after taking into account a provision (other than as aforesaid) shall be so framed or marked as to indicate that fact.

7. (1) There shall also be shown (unless it is shown in the Profit and Loss Account or a statement or report annexed thereto, or the amount involved is not material):

(a) where the amount of the reserves or of the provisions (other than provisions for depreciation, renewals or diminution in value of assets) shows an increase as compared with the amount at the end of the immediately preceding financial year, the source from which the amount of the increase has been derived; and

(b) where:

(i) the amount of the reserves shows a decrease as compared with the amount at the end of the immediately preceding financial year; or

(ii) the amount at the end of the immediately preceding financial year of the provisions (other than provisions for depreciation, renewals or diminution in value of assets) exceeded the aggregate of the sums since applied and amounts still retained for the purposes thereof;

the application of the amounts derived from the difference.

(2) Where the heading showing the reserves or any of the provisions aforesaid is divided into sub-headings, this paragraph shall apply to each of the separate amounts shown in the sub-headings instead of applying to the aggregate amount thereof.

7A. If an amount is set aside for the purpose of its being used to prevent undue fluctuations in charges for taxation, it shall be stated.

8. (1) There shall be shown under separate headings:

(a) the aggregate amounts respectively of the company's quoted investments and unquoted investments;

(b) if the amount of the goodwill and of any patents and trade marks or part of that amount is shown as a separate item in or is otherwise ascertainable from the books of the company, or from any contract for the sale or purchase of any property to be acquired by the company, or from any documents in the possession of the company relating to the stamp duty payable in respect of any such contract or the conveyance of any such property, the said amount so shown or ascertained so far as not written off or, as the case may be, the said amount so far as it is so shown or ascertainable and as so shown or ascertained as the case may be;

(c) the aggregate amount of any outstanding loans made under the authority of provisos (b) and (c) of subsection (1) of section fifty-four of this Act;

(d) the aggregate amount of bank loans and overdrafts and the aggregate amount of loans made to the company which:

(i) are repayable otherwise than by instalments and fall due for repayment after the expiration of the period of five years beginning with the day next following the expiration of the financial year; or

(ii) are repayable by instalments any of which fall due for payment after the expiration of that period;

not being, in either case, bank loans or overdrafts;

(e) the aggregate amount (before deduction of income tax) which is recommended for distribution by way of dividend.

(2) Nothing in head (b) of the foregoing sub-paragraph shall be taken as requiring the amount of the goodwill, patents and trade marks to be stated otherwise than as a single item.

(3) The heading showing the amount of the quoted investments shall be subdivided, where necessary, to distinguish the investments as respects which there has, and those as respects which there has not, been granted a quotation or permission to deal on a recognized stock exchange.

(4) In relation to each loan falling within head (d) of sub-paragraph (1) of this paragraph (other than a bank loan or overdraft), there shall be stated by way of note (if not otherwise stated) the terms on which it is repayable and the rate at which interest is payable thereon:

Provided that if the number of loans is such that, in the opinion of the directors, compliance with the foregoing requirement would result in a statement of excessive length, it shall be sufficient to give a general indication of the terms on which the loans are repayable and the rates at which interest is payable thereon.

9. Where any liability of the company is secured otherwise than by operation of law on any assets of the company, the fact that that liability is so secured shall be stated, but it shall not be necessary to specify the assets on which the liability is secured.

10. Where any of the company's debentures are held by a nominee of or trustee for the company, the nominal amount of the debentures and the amount at which they are stated in the books of the company shall be stated.

11. (1) The matters referred to in the following sub-paragraphs shall be stated by way of note, or in a statement or report annexed, if not otherwise shown.

(2) The number, description and amount of any shares in the company which any person has an option to subscribe for, together with the following particulars of the option, that is to say:

(a) the period during which it is exercisable;

(b) the price to be paid for shares subscribed for under it.

(3) The amount of any arrears of fixed cumulative dividends on the company's shares and the period for which the dividends or, if there is more than one class, each class of them are in arrear, the amount to be stated before deduction of income tax, except that, in the case of tax free dividends, the amount shall be shown free of tax and the fact that it is so shown shall also be stated.

(4) Particulars of any charge on the assets of the company to secure the liabilities of any other person, including, where practicable, the amount secured.

(5) The general nature of any other contingent liabilities not provided for and, where practicable, the aggregate amount or estimated amount of those liabilities, if it is material.

(6) Where practicable the aggregate amount or estimated amount, if it is material, of contracts for capital expenditure, so far as not provided for and, where practicable, the

aggregate amount or estimated amount, if it is material, of capital expenditure authorized by the directors which has not been contracted for.

(6A) In the case of fixed assets under any heading whose amount is required to be arrived at in accordance with paragraph 5 (1) of this Schedule (other than unquoted investments) and is so arrived at by reference to a valuation, the years (so far as they are known to the directors) in which the assets were severally valued and the several values, and, in the case of assets that have been valued during the financial year, the names of the persons who valued them or particulars of their qualifications for doing so and (whichever is stated) the bases of valuation used by them.

(6B) If there are included amongst fixed assets under any heading (other than investments) assets that have been acquired during the financial year, the aggregate amount of the assets acquired as determined for the purpose of making up the Balance Sheet, and if during that year any fixed assets included under a heading in the Balance Sheet made up with respect to the immediately preceding financial year (other than investments) have been disposed of or destroyed, the aggregate amount thereof as determined for the purpose of making up that Balance Sheet.

(6C) Of the amount of fixed assets consisting of land, how much is ascribable to land of freehold tenure and how much to land of leasehold tenure, and, of the latter, how much is ascribable to land held on long lease and how much to land held on short lease.

(7) If in the opinion of the directors any of the current assets have not a value, on realization in the ordinary course of the company's business, at least equal to the amount at which they are stated, the fact that the directors are of that opinion.

(8) The aggregate market value of the company's quoted investments where it differs from the amount of the investments as stated, and the stock exchange value of any investments of which the market value is shown (whether separately or not) and is taken as being higher than their stock exchange value.

(8A) If a sum set aside for the purpose of its being used to prevent undue fluctuations in charges for taxation has been used during the financial year for another purpose, the amount thereof and the fact that it has been so used.

(8B) If the amount carried forward for stock-in-trade or work in progress is material for the appreciation by its members of the company's state of affairs or of its profit or loss for the financial year, the manner in which that amount has been computed.

(9) The basis on which foreign currencies have been converted into sterling, where the amount of the assets or liabilities affected is material.

(10) The basis on which the amount, if any, set aside for United Kingdom corporation tax is computed.

(11) Except in the case of the first Balance Sheet laid before the company after the commencement of this Act, the corresponding amounts at the end of the immediately preceding financial year for all items shown in the Balance Sheet.

*Profit and Loss Account*

12. (1) There shall be shown:

(*a*) the amount charged to revenue by way of provision for depreciation, renewals or diminution in value of fixed assets;

(*b*) the amount of the interest on loans of the following kinds made to the company (whether on the security of debentures or not), namely, bank loans, overdrafts and loans which, not being bank loans or overdrafts:

(i) are repayable otherwise than by instalments and fall due for repayment before the expiration of the period of five years beginning with the day next following the expiration of the financial year; or

(ii) are repayable by instalments the last of which falls due for payment before the expiration of that period;

and the amount of the interest on loans of other kinds so made (whether on the security of debentures or not);

(c) the amount of the charge to revenue for United Kingdom corporation tax and, if that amount would have been greater but for relief from double taxation, the amount which it would have been but for such relief, the amount of the charge for United Kingdom income tax and the amount of the charge for taxation imposed outside the United Kingdom of profits, income and (so far as charged to revenue) capital gains;

(d) the amounts respectively provided for redemption of share capital and for redemption of loans;

(e) the amount, if material, set aside or proposed to be set aside to, or withdrawn from, reserves;

(f) subject to sub-paragraph (2) of this paragraph, the amount, if material, set aside to provisions other than provisions for depreciation, renewals or diminution in value of assets or, as the case may be, the amount, if material, withdrawn from such provisions and not applied for the purposes thereof;

(g) the amounts respectively of income from quoted investments and income from unquoted investments;

(ga) if a substantial part of the company's revenue for the financial year consists in rents from land, the amount thereof (after deduction of ground-rents, rates and other outgoings);

(gb) the amount, if material, charged to revenue in respect of sums payable in respect of the hire of plant and machinery;

(h) the aggregate amount (before deduction of income tax) of the dividends paid and proposed.

(2) The Board of Trade may direct that a company shall not be obliged to show an amount set aside to provisions in accordance with sub-paragraph (1) (f) of this paragraph, if the Board is satisfied that that is not required in the public interest and would prejudice the company, but subject to the condition that any heading stating an amount arrived at after taking into account the amount set aside as aforesaid shall be so framed or marked as to indicate that fact.

(3) If, in the case of any assets in whose case an amount is charged to revenue by way of provision for depreciation or diminution in value, an amount is also so charged by way of provision for renewal thereof, the last-mentioned amount shall be shown separately.

(4) If the amount charged to revenue by way of provision for depreciation or diminution in value of any fixed assets (other than investments) has been determined otherwise than by reference to the amount of those assets as determined for the purpose of making up the Balance Sheet, that fact shall be stated.

12A. The amount of any charge arising in consequence of the occurrence of an event in a preceding financial year and of any credit so arising shall, if not included in a heading relating to other matters, be stated under a separate heading.

13. The amount of the remuneration of the auditors shall be shown under a separate heading, and for the purposes of this paragraph, any sums paid by the company in respect of the auditors' expenses shall be deemed to be included in the expression 'remuneration'.

13A. (1) The matters referred to in sub-paragraphs (2) to (4) below shall be stated by way of note, if not otherwise shown.

(2) The turnover for the financial year, except in so far as it is attributable to the business of banking or discounting or to business of such other class as may be prescribed for the purposes of this sub-paragraph.

(3) If some or all of the turnover is omitted by reason of its being attributable as aforesaid, the fact that it is so omitted.

(4) The method by which turnover stated is arrived at.

(5) A company shall not be subject to the requirements of this paragraph if it is neither a holding company nor a subsidiary of another body corporate and the turnover which, apart from this sub-paragraph, would be required to be stated does not exceed £50,000.

14. (1) The matters referred to in the following sub-paragraphs shall be stated by way of note, if not otherwise shown.

(2) If depreciation or replacement of fixed assets is provided for by some method other than a depreciation charge or provision for renewals, or is not provided for, the method by which it is provided for or the fact that it is not provided for, as the case may be.

(3) The basis on which the charge for United Kingdom corporation tax and United Kingdom income tax is computed.

(3A) Any special circumstances which affect liability in respect of taxation of profits, income or capital gains for the financial year or liability in respect of taxation of profits, income or capital gains for succeeding financial years.

(5) Except in the case of the first Profit and Loss Account laid before the company after the commencement of this Act the corresponding amounts for the immediately preceding financial year for all items shown in the Profit and Loss Account.

(6) Any material respects in which any items shown in the Profit and Loss Account are affected:

(*a*) by transactions of a sort not usually undertaken by the company or otherwise by circumstances of an exceptional or non-recurrent nature; or

(*b*) by any change in the basis of accounting.


## PART II

### SPECIAL PROVISIONS WHERE THE COMPANY IS A HOLDING OR SUBSIDIARY COMPANY

*Modifications of and Additions to Requirements as to Company's own Accounts*

15. (1) This paragraph shall apply where the company is a holding company, whether or not it is itself a subsidiary of another body corporate.

(2) The aggregate amount of assets consisting of shares in, or amounts owing (whether on account of a loan or otherwise) from, the company's subsidiaries, distinguishing shares from indebtedness, shall be set out in the Balance Sheet separately from all the other assets of the company, and the aggregate amount of indebtedness (whether on account of a loan or otherwise) to the company's subsidiaries shall be so set out separately from all its other liabilities and:

(*a*) the references in Part I of this Schedule to the company's investments (except those in paragraphs 11 (6B) and 12 (4)) shall not include investments in its subsidiaries required by this paragraph to be separately set out; and

(*b*) paragraph 5, sub-paragraph (1) (*a*) of paragraph 12, and sub-paragraph (2) of paragraph 14 of this Schedule shall not apply in relation to fixed assets consisting of interests in the company's subsidiaries.

(3) There shall be shown by way of note on the Balance Sheet or in a statement or report annexed thereto the number, description and amount of the shares in and debentures of the company held by its subsidiaries or their nominees, but excluding any of those shares or debentures in the case of which the subsidiary is concerned as personal representative or in the case of which it is concerned as trustee and neither the company nor any subsidiary thereof is beneficially interested under the trust, otherwise than by way of security only for the purposes of a transaction entered into by it in the ordinary course of a business which includes the lending of money.

(4) Where group accounts are not submitted, there shall be annexed to the Balance Sheet a statement showing:

(*a*) the reasons why subsidiaries are not dealt with in group accounts;

(*b*) the net aggregate amount, so far as it concerns members of the holding company and is not dealt with in the company's accounts, of the subsidiaries' profits after deducting the subsidiaries' losses (or vice versa):

    (i) for the respective financial years of the subsidiaries ending with or during the financial year of the company; and

    (ii) for their previous financial years since they respectively became the holding company's subsidiary;

(*c*) the net aggregate amount of the subsidiaries' profits after deducting the subsidiaries' losses (or vice versa):

    (i) for the respective financial years of the subsidiaries ending with or during the financial year of the company; and

    (ii) for their other financial years since they respectively became the holding company's subsidiary;

so far as those profits are dealt with, or provision is made for those losses, in the company's accounts;

(*d*) any qualifications contained in the report of the auditors of the subsidiaries on their accounts for their respective financial years ending as aforesaid, and any note or saving contained in those accounts to call attention to a matter which, apart from the note or saving, would properly have been referred to in such a qualification, in so far as the matter which is the subject of the qualification or note is not covered by the company's own accounts and is material from the point of view of its members;

or, in so far as the information required by this sub-paragraph is not obtainable, a statement that it is not obtainable:

Provided that the Board of Trade may, on the application or with the consent of the company's directors, direct that in relation to any subsidiary this sub-paragraph shall not apply or shall apply only to such extent as may be provided by the direction.

(5) Paragraphs (*b*) and (*c*) of the last foregoing sub-paragraph shall apply only to profits and losses of a subsidiary which may properly be treated in the holding company's accounts as revenue profits or losses, and the profits or losses attributable to any shares in a subsidiary for the time being held by the holding company or any other of its subsidiaries shall not (for that or any other purpose) be treated as aforesaid so far as they are profits or losses for the period before the date on or as from which the shares were acquired by the company or any of its subsidiaries, except that they may in a proper case be so treated where:

(*a*) the company is itself the subsidiary of another body corporate; and

(*b*) the shares were acquired from that body corporate or a subsidiary of it;

and for the purpose of determining whether any profits or losses are to be treated as profits or losses for the said period the profit or loss for any financial year of the subsidiary may, if it is not practicable to apportion it with reasonable accuracy by reference to the facts, be treated as accruing from day to day during that year and be apportioned accordingly.

(6) Where group accounts are not submitted, there shall be annexed to the Balance Sheet a statement showing, in relation to the subsidiaries (if any) whose financial years did not end with that of the company:

(*a*) the reasons why the company's directors consider that the subsidiaries' financial years should not end with that of the company; and

(*b*) the dates on which the subsidiaries' financial years ending last before that of the company respectively ended or the earliest and latest of those dates.

16. (1) The Balance Sheet of a company which is a subsidiary of another body corporate, whether or not it is itself a holding company, shall show the aggregate amount of its indebtedness to all bodies corporate of which it is a subsidiary or a fellow subsidiary and the

aggregate amount of indebtedness of all such bodies corporate to it, distinguishing in each case between indebtedness in respect of debentures and otherwise, and the aggregate amount of assets consisting of shares in fellow subsidiaries.

(2) For the purposes of this paragraph a company shall be deemed to be a fellow subsidiary of another body corporate if both are subsidiaries of the same body corporate but neither is the other's.

### Consolidated Accounts of Holding Company and Subsidiaries

17. Subject to the following paragraphs of this Part of this Schedule, the consolidated Balance Sheet and Profit and Loss Account shall combine the information contained in the separate Balance Sheets and Profit and Loss Accounts of the holding company and of the subsidiaries dealt with by the Consolidated Accounts, but with such adjustments (if any) as the directors of the holding company think necessary.

18. Subject as aforesaid and to Part III of this Schedule, the Consolidated Accounts shall, in giving the said information, comply so far as practicable, with the requirements of this Act and the *Companies Act 1967* as if they were the accounts of an actual company.

19. Sections one hundred and ninety-six and one hundred and ninety-seven of this Act and sections four and six to eight of the *Companies Act 1967* shall not, by virtue of the two last foregoing paragraphs, apply for the purpose of the Consolidated Accounts.

20. Paragraph 7 of this Schedule shall not apply for the purpose of any Consolidated Accounts laid before a company with the first Balance Sheet so laid after the commencement of this Act.

21. In relation to any subsidiaries of the holding company not dealt with by the Consolidated Accounts:

(*a*) sub-paragraphs (2) and (3) of paragraph 15 of this Schedule shall apply for the purpose of those accounts as if those accounts were the accounts of an actual company of which they were subsidiaries; and

(*b*) there shall be annexed the like statement as is required by sub-paragraph (4) of that paragraph where there are no group accounts, but as if references therein to the holding company's accounts were references to the Consolidated Accounts.

22. In relation to any subsidiaries (whether or not dealt with by the Consolidated Accounts), whose financial years did not end with that of the company, there shall be annexed the like statement as is required by sub-paragraph (6) of paragraph 15 of this Schedule where there are no Group Accounts.

### PART III
#### EXCEPTIONS FOR SPECIAL CLASSES OF COMPANY

23. (1) A banking or discount company shall not be subject to the requirements of Part I of this Schedule other than:

(*a*) as respects its Balance Sheet, those of paragraphs 2 and 3, paragraph 4 (so far as it relates to assets), paragraph 8 (except sub-paragraphs (1) (*d*) and (4)), paragraphs 9 and 10 and paragraph 11 (except sub-paragraphs (6A), (6B), (6C), (8) and (8A)); and

(*b*) as respects its Profit and Loss Account, those of sub-paragraph (1) (*ga*) and (*h*) of paragraph 12, paragraphs 12A and 13 and sub-paragraphs (1) and (5) of paragraph 14;

but, where in its Balance Sheet reserves or provisions (other than provisions for depreciation, renewals or diminution in value of assets) are not stated separately, any heading stating an amount arrived at after taking into account a reserve or such a provision shall be so framed or marked as to indicate that fact, and its Profit and Loss Account shall indicate by appropriate words the manner in which the amount stated for the company's profit or loss has been arrived at.

(2) The accounts of a banking or discount company shall not be deemed, by reason only of the fact that they do not comply with any requirements of the said Part I from which

the company is exempt by virtue of this paragraph, not to give the true and fair view required by this Act.

(3) In this paragraph the expression 'banking or discount company' means any company which satisfies the Board of Trade that it ought to be treated for the purposes of this Schedule as a banking company or as a discount company.

24. (1) An insurance company to which the *Insurance Companies Act 1958* applies shall not be subject to the following requirements of Part I of this Schedule, that is to say:

(*a*) as respects its Balance Sheet, those of paragraphs 4 to 7 (both inclusive), sub-paragraphs (1) (*a*) and (3) of paragraph 8 and sub-paragraphs (4), (5) and (6A) to (8) (both inclusive) of paragraph 11;

(*b*) as respects its Profit and Loss Account, those of paragraph 12 (except sub-paragraph (1) (*b*), (*c*), (*d*) and (*h*)) and paragraph 14 (2);

but, where in its Balance Sheet reserves or provisions (other than provisions for depreciation, renewals or diminution in value of assets) are not stated separately, any heading stating an amount arrived at after taking into account a reserve or such a provision shall be so framed or marked as to indicate that fact, and its Profit and Loss Account shall indicate by appropriate words the manner in which the amount stated for the company's profit or loss has been arrived at:

Provided that the Board of Trade may direct that any such insurance company whose business includes to a substantial extent business other than insurance business shall comply with all the requirements of the said Part I or such of them as may be specified in the direction and shall comply therewith as respects either the whole of its business or such part thereof as may be so specified.

(2) Where an insurance company is entitled to the benefit of this paragraph, then any wholly owned subsidiary thereof shall also be so entitled if its business consists only of business which is complementary to insurance business of the classes carried on by the insurance company.

(2A) The accounts of a company shall not be deemed, by reason only of the fact that they do not comply with any requirement of Part I of this Schedule from which the company is exempt by virtue of this paragraph, not to give the true and fair view required by this Act.

(3) For the purposes of this paragraph a company shall be deemed to be the wholly owned subsidiary of an insurance company if it has no members except the insurance company and the insurance company's wholly owned subsidiaries and its or their nominees.

25. (1) A shipping company shall not be subject to the following requirements of Part I of this Schedule, that is to say:

(*a*) as respects its Balance Sheet, those of paragraph 4 (except so far as it relates to assets), paragraphs 5, 6 and 7 and sub-paragraphs (6A) and (6B) of paragraph 11;

(*b*) as respects its Profit and Loss Account, those of sub-paragraph (1) (*a*), (*e*) and (*f*) and sub-paragraphs (3) and (4) of paragraph 12 and paragraph 13A.

(2) The accounts of a company shall not be deemed, by reason only of the fact that they do not comply with any requirements of Part I of this Schedule from which the company is exempt by virtue of this paragraph, not to give the true and fair view required by this Act.

(3) In this paragraph the expression 'shipping company' means a company which, or a subsidiary of which, owns ships or includes amongst its activities the management or operation of ships, being a company which satisfies the Board of Trade that, in the national interest, it ought to be treated for the purposes of this paragraph as a shipping company.

26. Where a company entitled to the benefit of any provision contained in this part of this Schedule is a holding company, the reference in Part II of this Schedule to Consolidated Accounts complying with the requirements of this Act shall, in relation to Consolidated Accounts of that company, be construed as referring to those requirements in so far only as they apply to the separate accounts of that company.

# APPENDIX III

## APPENDIX III A

### TRUSTEE'S CASH BOOK

| *Dr* RECEIPTS | | | | | | | | PAYMENTS *Cr* | | | |
|---|---|---|---|---|---|---|---|---|---|---|---|
| Date | Particulars | Total | Drawn from Bank | Debts Collected | Property Realized | Receipts from Securities held by Customers | Other Receipts | Date | Particulars | Voucher Nos. (in red) | Total |
| | | | | | | | | | | | |

PAYMENTS *Cr*

| Paid into Bank | COSTS OF REALIZATION | | | | | | | | Allowance to Debtor | Preferential Creditors and Rent | Payments to Redeem Securities | Dividends Paid | Other Payments |
|---|---|---|---|---|---|---|---|---|---|---|---|---|---|
| | Board of Trade and Court Fees | Law Costs of petition (including stamp) | Law Costs after Receiving Order | Commission on Realization and Distribution: Board of Trade | Commission on Realization and Distribution: Trustee | Charges of Auctioneer, Accountant, Shorthand Writer, etc. as taxed | Notices in *Gazette* and Local Paper | Incidental Expenses, including Possession | | | | | |
| | | | | | | | | | | | | | |

## APPENDIX IIIB

# THE BANKRUPTCY ACTS 1914 AND 1926

No. Tr. 13
No. 46

Reg. No. ...........................

Re.....................................................................................................................

Report of Trustee on position of Estate at the..........................Audit, due.......................including Summary of Accounts now lodged (*see* other side)

| Assets as per Statement | Realized | Estimated value outstanding | Remarks |
|---|---|---|---|
| Property as per List H: <br> (a) Cash at bankers    ..    ..    .. <br> (b) Cash in hand    ..    .. <br> (c) Cash deposited with solicitor for costs of petition    ..    .. <br> (d) Stock-in-trade (cost £    ) ..    .. <br> (e) Machinery    ..    .. <br> (f) Trade fixtures, fittings, utensils etc.    .. <br> (g) Farming stock    ..    .. <br> (h) Growing crops and tenant right    .. <br> (i) Furniture ..    ..    .. <br> (j) Life policies    ..    .. <br> (k) Stocks and shares    ..    .. <br> (l) Reversionary or other interests under wills    ..    .. <br> (m) Other property, viz:    ..    .. <br><br> Book Debts and Bills of Exchange    .. <br> Surplus from securities    ..    .. <br> Trading receipts    ..    .. | | | |
| Totals    ..    ..    ..    .. | | | |

## DIVIDENDS

| When declared | What declared per £ | If not declared, state reason. (If delayed by resolution of Committee, state grounds on which such resolution adopted, and forward copy) | State when declaration will probably be effected |
|---|---|---|---|
| | | | |

## LEGAL PROCEEDINGS AUTHORIZED

| Date of Resolution authorizing employment of Solicitors | Name of Solicitors | Nature of work authorized to be done |
|---|---|---|
| | | |

If application for release not yet made, state when you expect to be in a position to apply.
State shortly any circumstances tending to delay the winding-up of the Estate, or affecting its realized value or the costs of its realization.

.................................................................
*Trustee*

Date ........................................19

## APPENDIX III B (*continued*)

Note. The Official Receiver's receipts and payments should be shewn in red ink

Estate of...............................................................................................................................................................

# SUMMARY OF ACCOUNTS

From.............................................

**RECEIPTS**    To .................................    **PAYMENTS**

| | | | |
|---|---|---|---|
| For Official Use | Balance from previous account (if any) .. .. | | Balance from previous account (if any) .. |
| | (a) Cash at bankers .. | | Board of Trade Fees { Audit duty .. .. .. |
| | Unused cheques .. | | Release do. .. .. .. |
| | (b) Cash in hand.. .. | | Stationery .. .. .. |
| | (c) Cash deposited with solicitor for costs of petition .. .. | | Fee of Supervision .. .. |
| | | | Interim Receiver .. |
| | | | Notices to Creditors .. |
| | (d) Stock-in-trade (cost £ ) | | Room .. .. |
| | (e) Machinery .. .. | | Notices to Debtors .. |
| | (f) Trade fixtures, fittings, utensils etc. .. .. | | Local Bank .. |
| | (g) Farming stock .. | | Petition Stamp .. .. |
| | (h) Growing crops and tenant right .. .. | | High Bailiff and other Court Fees .. |
| | (i) Furniture .. .. | | Possession .. .. |
| | (j) Life policies .. .. | | Law Costs of Petition (exclusive of Deposit on Petition) .. .. .. |
| | (k) Stocks and shares .. | | Less Petition Stamp .. .. |
| | (l) Reversionary or other interests under wills .. | | (Assets certified at £ ) .. |
| | (m) Other property, viz: .. | | |
| | | | Law Costs after Receiving Order .. |
| | Book debts and Bills of Exchange.. .. .. | | Special Manager .. .. |
| | | | Person to assist Debtor Sec. 74 (2) .. |
| | Surplus from securities .. | | Remuneration of Trustee .. |
| | | | .......... % on £ .............................. |
| | Trading receipts .. .. | | .......... % on £ .............................. |
| | | | O.R.'s Commission .. .. .. |
| | Deposit .. .. | | on £ .. .. .. |
| | | | Auctioneer's and Valuer's Charges .. |
| | Gross Receipts .. .. | | Other Taxed Charges, viz.: Shorthand Writer .. .. .. |
| Less PAYMENTS | | | |
| Deposit returned to petitioner .. | | | Notices in Gazette and Local Papers .. |
| Secured creditors.. .. .. | | | Incidental Expenses: |
| Cost of Execution .. .. | | | Printing .. .. .. |
| Trading Payments .. .. | | | Postages, telegrams and telephones .. |
| | | | Stationery and Forms .. |
| Maintenance of estate: .. .. | | | Affidavits .. .. .. |
| | | | Bond .. .. |
| | | | Travelling, O.R. .. .. |
| | | | Trustee .. .. |
| Net realization .. | | | C. of I. .. .. |
| | | | Office copies .. .. |
| | | | Carriage on books and papers .. |
| | | | Miscellaneous .. .. |
| Distrainable & preferential Debts | | | Total Costs .. .. |
| For Official Use | | Paid | Allowance to Debtor .. .. |
| | Rent .. .. .. | | |
| | Other distrainable debts .. | | Dividend declared in the £ on £.............. |
| | Rates .. .. .. | | S/A £.............. |
| | Taxes .. .. .. | | |
| | Salaries and Wages .. | | |
| | State Insurance .. .. | | |
| | Other preferential debts .. | | |
| Net available assets .. .. .. | | | |
| Balance .. .. .. .. | | | Balance .. .. .. |

## APPENDIX III C

STATEMENT TO ACCOMPANY NOTICE OF DIVIDEND

AND APPLICATION FOR RELEASE

(*Title*)

Statement showing position of estate at date of declaring dividend or at date of application for release, or as the case may be.

*Dr*                                                                                                               *Cr*

| | Estimated to produce per Debtor's Statement | Receipts | | Payments |
|---|---|---|---|---|
| | | | By Board of Trade and Court Fees, including stamp on petition .. .. .. | |
| To total receipts from date of receiving order, viz.: .. .. | | | Law costs of petition .. .. | |
| (*State particulars under the several headings specified in the Debtor's Statement of Affairs*) .. | | | Other law costs .. .. | |
| Receipts per trading account .. | | | | |
| Other receipts .. .. .. | | | Trustee's remuneration, as fixed by the (*a*), viz.: .. .. .. | |
| Total.. .. .. | | | per cent. on £   assets realized .. | |
| | | | per cent. on £   assets distributed in dividend .. | |
| *Less* | | | | |
| Deposit returned to petitioner .. | | | Special manager's charges .. .. | |
| Payments to redeem securities .. | | | Persons appointed to assist Debtor under Section 74 of the Act .. .. .. | |
| Costs of execution .. .. | | | Auctioneer's charge as taxed .. .. | |
| Payments per trading account .. | | | Other taxed costs .. .. .. | |
| | | | Costs of possession .. .. .. | |
| | | | Costs of notice in *Gazette* and local papers .. | |
| | £ | | Incidental outlay .. .. .. | |
| Net realization .. | £ | | Total costs of realization   £ | |
| | | | Allowance to debtor .. | |
| | | | *Creditors*, viz.: | |
| | | | Preferential .. .. .. | |
| | | | Unsecured .. .. .. | |
| | | | Dividend (*b*) now declared of p in the £ on £ .. | |
| | | | Dividends previously declared .. | |
| | | | *The debtor's estimate of amount expected to rank for dividend was* £ .. .. .. | |
| | | | Balance .. .. .. | |
| | £ | | £ | |

(*a*) Creditors, *or* committee of inspection, *or* Board of Trade, as the case may be.   (*b*) 1st *or* as the case may be.

By Section 82 (2) of the *Bankruptcy Act 1914*, it is provided that 'If one-fourth in number or value of creditors dissent from the resolution, or the bankrupt satisfies the Board of Trade that the remuneration is unnecessarily large, the Board of Trade shall fix the amount of the remuneration.'

Assets not yet realized estimated to produce £

(*Add here any special remarks trustee thinks desirable.*)

Creditors can obtain any further information by enquiry at the office of the trustee.

Dated this                     day of                          19  .

(*Signature of Trustee*)
(*Address*)

NOTE: *When this statement accompanies a declaration of a second or subsequent dividend, it shall incorporate the figures of the preceding statement or statements under their respective headings.*

**APPENDIX III D**

(D.A.R. 1915)

# THE DEEDS OF ARRANGEMENT ACT 1914

Statement pursuant to Section 14.

In the matter of a Deed of Arrangement, between                    and his

creditors, dated the                    day of                    19

and registered under the *Deeds of Arrangement Act 1914*, on the

day of                    19    as Trustee.

Trustee (A.B.)        of

## STATEMENT OF TRUSTEE'S ACCOUNTS AND OF PROCEEDINGS UNDER THE DEED

FROM THE    DAY OF    19    TO THE    DAY OF    19 .

| RECEIPTS | | | PAYMENTS | | |
|---|---|---|---|---|---|
| Cash deposited by debtor with solicitor for costs of deed .. .. .. | | | Law Costs of preparation and regis-tration of deed .. | | |
| Cash at bank at date of deed .. .. .. | | | Law Costs of solicitor to trustee .. | | |
| Cash in hand at date of deed .. | | | | | |
| Book debts .. .. .. .. | | | Other Law Costs [3] .. .. | | |
| Stock-in-trade realized from sale by [1] .. | | | | | |
| Machinery realized from sale by [1] .. | | | Accountant's charges .. .. | | |
| Trade fixtures, fittings, etc., realized from sale by [1] | | | Auctioneer's and valuer's charges .. | | |
| Furniture realized from sale by [1] .. | | | Trustee's remuneration .. | | |
| Surplus from securities in hands of creditors .. | | | Possession .. .. .. | | |
| Trading receipts .. .. .. | | | Incidental expenses .. .. | | |
| Other property, viz. realized from sale by [1] .. | | | Other costs and charges [3] .. .. | | |
| | | | | | |
| | | | Total costs and charges .. .. .. | | |
| | | | Allowance to debtor .. .. .. | | |
| Gross receipts .. .. .. | | | Payments to creditors, viz.: | | |
| | | | Rent from the day of 19 , .. | | |
| | | | to the day of 19 , .. | | |
| *Less* Trading payments .. .. | | | Rates and taxes .. .. | | |
| Payments to redeem securities, viz., [2] .. .. .. | | | Salaries and wages .. .. | | |
| | | | Other preferential payments. viz. [3] .. | | |
| | | | Dividends of in the £ on £ | | |
| | | | Paid.. .. .. .. | | |
| | | | Unpaid .. .. .. | | |
| Net realizations .. .. | | | | | |
| Balance due to trustee (if any) .. .. | | | | | |
| | | | Other payments (if any) [3] | | Total |
| | | | Balance in hand (if any) .. | | .. |
| | £ | | | £ | |

[1] Insert gross proceeds of sale, and state how goods were sold, e.g. by auction, by valuation or as the case may be.

[2] Here insert to whom payments made, nature of security redeemed, and amount of each payment or annex schedule. giving these particulars.

[3] Insert particulars or annex schedule.

**APPENDIX III D** (*continued*)

The total payments into the [4]                          Bank to the                          day of
                  19      were £                          and the total payments out
of the said Bank to the                          day of                          19      were £          .

The amounts of the assets and liabilities at the time the deed was executed as estimated by the debtor were:

Assets after deducting £                          the value of securities held by creditors and required to cover debts due to them £

Liabilities after deducting £                          , the amount covered by securities £

The nature and value of the assets unrealized are [3]

The causes which delay the termination of the winding-up of the estate are [3]

The estate will probably be completely wound up within

The following special circumstances affect the costs of realization and the administration of the estate, viz. [3]

............................................................................*Trustee*

*Address*............................................................................

............................................................................

*Date*............................................................................

[3] Insert particulars or annex Schedule.
[4] Insert name of Bank.

# APPENDIX III E

## LIQUIDATOR'S CASH BOOK

### RECEIPTS      PAYMENTS

| Date | Particulars | Total | Drawn from Bank | Debts Collected | Property Realized | Receipts from Securities held by Creditors | Calls | Other Receipts | Date | Particulars | Voucher Nos. (in red) | Total |
|---|---|---|---|---|---|---|---|---|---|---|---|---|
|  |  |  |  |  |  |  |  |  |  |  |  |  |
|  |  |  |  |  |  |  |  |  |  |  |  |  |
|  |  |  |  |  |  |  |  |  |  |  |  |  |

*Left-hand side*]

### PAYMENTS

| Paid into Bank | COSTS OF REALIZATION | | | | | | | | Preferential Creditors and Rent | Payments to Redeem Securities | Dividends Paid | Repayments to Contributories | Other Payments |
|---|---|---|---|---|---|---|---|---|---|---|---|---|---|
|  | Board of Trade and Court Fees | Law Costs of Petition | Law Costs after Winding-up Order | Remuneration of Manager and Liquidator | Official Receiver's Com. on Assets realized and amounts distributed in Dividend or paid to Contributories | Charges of Auctioneer, Accountant, Shorthand Writer etc., as taxed | Notices in *Gazette* and Local Paper | Incidental Expenses including Possession |  |  |  |  |  |
|  |  |  |  |  |  |  |  |  |  |  |  |  |  |

[*Right-hand side*

## APPENDIX III F

No. 110 (Rule 182)

*No. of Company*.................. **The Companies Act 1948**

LIQUIDATOR'S STATEMENT OF ACCOUNT
(MEMBERS' OR CREDITORS' VOLUNTARY WINDING-UP)
(Pursuant to Sections 290 and 300)

Statement showing how the winding-up has been conducted and the property of the company has been disposed of

*Name of Company*..............................................*Limited (in liquidation)*

*Presented by* ...............................................................

## LIQUIDATOR'S STATEMENT OF ACCOUNT
## [MEMBERS] *[CREDITORS] VOLUNTARY WINDING-UP

*Statement showing how the winding-up has been conducted and the property of the company has been disposed of*

From................19...... (Commencement of Winding-up) to...................19..... (Close of Winding-up)

\* Delete as necessary.

| | Statement of Assets and Liabilities | Receipts | | | Payments |
|---|---|---|---|---|---|
| | £ | £ | Costs of Solicitor to Liquidator .. .. | | £ |
| Receipts: | | | Other law costs .. .. .. | | |
| Cash at Bank .. .. .. | | | Liquidator's remuneration: | | |
| Cash in Hand .. .. .. | | | ......% on £ realized .. | | |
| Marketable Securities .. .. | | | ......% on £ distributed.. | | |
| Sundry Debtors .. .. | | | By whom fixed | | |
| Stock-in-Trade .. .. | | | Auctioneer's and valuer's charges .. | | |
| Work in Progress .. .. | | | Costs of possession and maintenance of | | |
| Freehold Property .. .. | | | estate .. .. .. | | |
| Leasehold Property .. .. | | | Costs of notices in *Gazette* and local papers | | |
| Plant and Machinery .. .. | | | Incidental Outlay .. .. | | |
| Furniture, fittings, utensils etc. .. | | | | | |
| Patents, trade marks etc. .. | | | Total costs and charges .. .. | | |
| Investments other than marketable | | | | £ | |
| securities .. .. .. | | | (i) Debenture holders: | | |
| Surplus from securities .. | | | Payment of £ | | |
| Unpaid calls at commencement of | | | per £ debenture | | |
| winding-up .. .. .. | | | Payment of £ | | |
| Amounts received from calls on | | | per £ debenture | | |
| contributories made in the wind- | | | Payment of £ | | |
| ing-up .. .. | | | per £ debenture .. | | |
| Receipts per trading account .. | | | | £ | |
| Other property, viz.: | | | | | |
| .. | | | (ii) *Creditors:* | | |
| ............................................ | | | * Preferential .. | | |
| ............................................ .. | | | * Unsecured: | | |
| | £ | | Dividend(s) of ............ *p* in £ | | |
| | | | on £................ .. .. | | |
| *Less* | | | | | |
| Payments to redeem securities .. | | | (The estimate of amount expected to | | |
| Costs of execution .. | | | rank for dividend was £ .) .. | | |
| Payments per trading account .. | | | | | |
| | | | (iii) Returns to contributories: | | |
| | | | | £ | |
| | | | ............ *p* per £..... .. | | |
| Net realizations .. .. .. | £ | | ............† share .. | | |
| | | | ............ *p* per £..... .. | | |
| | | | ............† share .. | | |
| | | | ............ *p* per £..... .. | | |
| | | | ............† share .. | | |
| | | | | Balance | |
| | £ | | | | £ |

*(In the margin by the remuneration section:)* When applicable

## APPENDIX III F (*continued*)

1. Assets, including..........................................shown in the statement of assets and liabilities and estimated to be of the value of £................. have proved to be unrealizable.

2. State amount paid into the Companies Liquidation Account in respect of:
   (*a*) unclaimed dividends payable to creditors in the winding-up  ..        ..        ..        .. £
   (*b*) other unclaimed distributions in the winding-up        ..        ..        ..        .. £
   (*c*) moneys held by the company in trust in respect of dividends or other sums due before the commencement of the winding-up to any person as a member of the company  ..        .. £

3. Add here any special remarks the Liquidator thinks desirable:

          Dated this          day of             19............

                                         (Signature of liquidator(s))
                                              (address)

\* State number. Preferential creditors need not be separately shown if all creditors have been paid in full.

† State nominal value and class of share.

**APPENDIX III G**

## No. 92 (Rules 197, 198 and 201)

*No registration*
*fee payable*

   *[Re*

No. of Company  }........................

This is the Exhibit marked B referred to in the affidivat
of
sworn before me this      day of         19

A Commissioner for Oaths

### Statement of Receipts and Payments and General Directions as to Statements

NAME OF COMPANY ...............................................................................................................................................................................................

................................................................................................................................................................................................................ LIMITED

*Size of Sheets*

1. Every statement must be on sheets 13 inches by 16 inches.

*Form and contents of Statement*

2. Every statement must contain a detailed account of all the liquidator's realizations and disbursements in respect of the Company. The statement of realizations should contain a record of all receipts derived from assets existing at the date of the winding-up resolution and subsequently realized, including balance in Bank, Book Debts and Calls Collected, Property Sold &c.; and the account of disbursements should contain all payments for costs and charges, or to creditors or contributories. Where property has been realized, the gross proceeds of sale must be entered under realizations, and the necessary payments incidental to sales must be entered as disbursements. These accounts should not contain payments into the Companies Liquidation Account (except unclaimed dividends, see paragraph 5) or payments into or out of Bank, or temporary investments by the liquidator, or the proceeds of such investments when realized, which should be shown separately:

   (*a*) by means of the Bank Pass Book;

   (*b*) by a separate detailed statement of moneys invested by the liquidator, and investments realized.

Interest allowed or charged by the Bank, Bank commission &c., and profit or loss upon the realization of temporary investments, should, however, be inserted in the accounts of realizations or disbursements, as the case may be. Each receipt and payment must be entered in the account in such a manner as sufficiently to explain its nature. The receipts and payments must severally be added up at the foot of each sheet, *and the totals carried forward from one account to another without any intermediate balance, so that the gross totals shall represent the total amounts received and paid by the liquidator respectively.*

*Trading Account*

3. When the liquidator carries on a business, a Trading Account must be forwarded as a distinct account, and the totals of receipts and payments on the Trading Account must alone be set out in the statement.

*Dividends &c.*

4. When dividends or instalments of compositions are paid to creditors, or a return of surplus assets is made to contributories, the total amount of each dividend, or instalment of composition, or return to contributories, actually paid, must be entered in the statement

**APPENDIX III G** (*continued*)

of disbursements as one sum; and the liquidator must forward separate accounts showing in lists the amount of the claim of each creditor, and the amount of dividend or composition payable to each creditor, and of surplus assets payable to each contributory, distinguishing in each list the dividends or instalments of composition and shares of surplus assets actually paid and those remaining unclaimed. Each list must be on sheets 13 inches by 8 inches.

5. When unclaimed dividends, instalments of compositions or returns of surplus assets are paid into the Companies Liquidation Account, the total amount so paid in should be entered in the statement of disbursements as one sum.

6. Credit should not be taken in the statement of disbursements for any amount in respect of liquidator's remuneration unless it has been duly allowed by resolution of the Committee of Inspection, or of the creditors, or of the Company in General Meeting, or by order of Court, as the case may require.

---

## LIQUIDATOR'S STATEMENT OF ACCOUNT

*pursuant to section 342 of the Companies Act 1948*

Name of Company ......................................................................................................................

.................................................................................................................................LIMITED

Nature of proceedings (whether a members'
   or creditors' voluntary winding up or a
   winding up under the supervision of the
   Court)

Date of Commencement of winding up ......................................................................................

Date to which Statement is brought down ..............................................................................

Name and Address of Liquidator ............................................................................................

..................................................................................................................................

This Statement is required in duplicate.     [P.T.O.

**APPENDIX III G** (*continued*)

## LIQUIDATOR'S STATEMENT OF ACCOUNT

### REALIZATIONS

| Date | Of whom received | Nature of Assets realized | Amount £ |
|------|------------------|---------------------------|----------|
|      |                  | Brought forward    . .    |          |
|      |                  |                           |          |
|      |                  | *<br>Carried forward    . . |          |

*Note:* No balance should be shown on this Account, but only the total Realizations and pursuant to Section 342 of the Companies Act 1948

## DISBURSEMENTS

| Date | To whom paid | Nature of Disbursements | Amount £ |
|------|--------------|-------------------------|----------|
| | | Brought forward  .. | |
| | | | |
| | | Carried forward  .. * | |

Disbursements, which should be carried forward to the next Account.          [P.T.O.

**APPENDIX III G** (*continued*)

# ANALYSIS OF BALANCE

£

Total Realizations ....    ....    ....    ....    ....    ....    ....
„   Disbursements  ....    ....    ....    ....    ....    ....    ....
                                                                 Balance

The Balance is made up as follows:

1. Cash in hands of Liquidator    ....    ....    ....    ....    ....

£

2. Total payments into Bank, including balance at date of commencement of winding up (*as per Bank Book*)    ....    ....
   Total withdrawals from Bank    ....    ....    ....    ....

                        Balance at Bank

3. Amount in Companies Liquidation Account ..    ....    ....    ....

£

*4. Amounts invested by Liquidator    ....    ....    ....    ....
    *Less* Amounts realized from same    ....    ....    ....
                        Balance    ....

            Total balance as shown above    ....    .. £

*Note:* Full details of stocks purchased for investment and realization thereof should be given in a separate statement.

*The investment or deposit of money by the liquidator does not withdraw it from the operation of Section 343 of the *Companies Act 1948*, and any such investments representing money held for six months or upwards must be realized and paid into the Companies Liquidation Account, except in the case of investments in Government securities, the transfer of which to the control of the Board of Trade will be accepted as a sufficient compliance with the terms of the section.

---

**NOTE: The Liquidator should also state**

1. The amount of the estimated assets and liabilities at the date of the commencement of the winding up

{ Assets (after deducting amounts charged to secured creditors and debenture holders)    .. £
Liabilities: Secured creditors .. £
Debenture holders    £
Unsecured  creditors £

---

**APPENDIX III G** (*continued*)

---

2. The total amount of the capital paid up at the date of the commencement of the winding up }    Paid up in cash        ..   £

Issued as paid up otherwise than for cash    ..   £

---

3. The general description and estimated value of outstanding assets (if any) }

---

4. The causes which delay the termination of the winding up }

---

5. The period within which the winding up may probably be completed }

---

# APPENDIX IV

# STATEMENTS OF STANDARD ACCOUNTING PRACTICE

## 1. *Accounting for the results of associated companies* (*Issued January 1971*)

© The Institute of Chartered Accountants in England and Wales.

*Income from investments in 50 per cent and less than 50 per cent owned companies has in the past normally been included in the investing group or company's accounts only to the extent of dividends received or receivable up to its accounting date. With the spread of trading through joint venture and other companies which are 50 per cent or less than 50 per cent owned there started to emerge the practice of bringing into the accounts of the investing group or company its share of the profits or losses of such companies. The purpose of the Statement which follows is to establish a standard method of accounting for the results of associated companies.*

*The better to appreciate the accounting method proposed, there should be kept in mind the distinction between (a) a company's own accounts as a legal entity and (b) its group accounts in the form of consolidated accounts the objects of which are to show the results and state of affairs of the group so far as concerns members of the parent company.*

*Use of the term 'associated company' should in future be restricted to the meaning defined in this Statement.*

## PART 1 – EXPLANATORY NOTE

1   It is accepted accounting practice for a company not to take credit in its own (i.e., non-consolidated) profit and loss account and balance sheet for its share of the profits of other companies (subsidiary or otherwise) which have not been distributed. The view is taken that the inclusion of undistributed profits would ignore the separate legal entities of the companies concerned and, as regards the investing company, be in breach of the principle that credit should not be taken for investment income until it is received or receivable.

2   However, where a company conducts an important part of its business through the medium of other companies, whether more or less than 50 per cent owned, the mere disclosure of dividend income (or mere inclusion of dividend income alone) is unlikely to be sufficient to give shareholders adequate information regarding the sources of their income and of the manner in which their funds are being employed.

3   At one time such operations were usually carried out through the medium of subsidiary companies. It was for this reason that the Companies Act 1948 required the preparation of group accounts, normally in the form of consolidated accounts. In recent years there have been two important developments. One has been the growing practice of companies to conduct parts of their business through other companies (frequently consortium or joint venture companies) in which they have a substantial but not a controlling interest. The other is the importance which investors have come to attach to earnings (as distinct from dividends), the price/earnings ratio (P/E ratio) and, increasingly, earnings per share. Thus, in order that the investing company's accounts as a whole may give adequate information, and provide a total of earnings from which the most meaningful ratios can be calculated, it is considered necessary that the coverage of consolidated accounts

752

be extended so that they shall include (within the framework of the existing law) the share of earnings or losses of companies which are described in this Statement as associated companies (see paragraph 6).

This approach recognises a difference in principle between the nature of investments in associated companies (as defined in this Statement) and other forms of trade investment. The essence of the distinction is that the investing company actively participates in the commercial and policy decisions of its associated companies; it thus has a measure of direct responsibility for the return on its investment, and should account for its stewardship accordingly, whereas it will not normally seek to exert direct management influence over the operating policy of other companies in which it invests, and should continue to deal with them in accordance with traditional accounting methods.    4

The broad concept underlying the accounting treatment of the results of associated companies here stated is the adoption in modified form of the consolidation procedures used for subsidiary companies. It follows from this that the investing group's share of associated companies' profits and losses will be reflected in its consolidated profit and loss account, and its share of their post-acquisition retained profits or surplus will be reflected in its consolidated balance sheet, though not in its own balance sheet as a legal entity.    5

## PART 2 – DEFINITION OF 'ASSOCIATED COMPANY'

A company (not being a subsidiary of the investing group or company) is an associated company of the investing group or company if:    6

(*a*) the investing group or company's interest in the associated company is effectively that of a partner in a joint venture or consortium

    *or*

(*b*) the investing group or company's interest in the associated company is for the long term and is substantial (i.e., not less than 20 per cent of the equity voting rights), and, having regard to the disposition of the other shareholdings, the investing group or company is in a position to exercise a significant influence over the associated company.

In both cases it is essential that the investing group or company participates (usually through representation on the board) in commercial and financial policy decisions of the associated company, including the distribution of profits.

## PART 3 – PROPOSED STANDARD ACCOUNTING PRACTICE

### Bases of accounting for income of associated companies

Income from investments by a company or its subsidiaries in associated companies (as defined in paragraph 6 above) should be brought into account on the following bases:    7

(*a*) *In the investing company's own accounts*

    (i) Dividends received up to the accounting date of the investing company; and

    (ii) dividends receivable in respect of accounting periods ending on or before that date and declared before the accounts of the investing company are approved by the directors.

(*b*) *In the investing group's consolidated accounts* (*see paragraph 8*)

    The investing group's share of profits less losses of associated companies (see paragraph 12 for exceptions).

8 Where the investing company has no subsidiaries, or otherwise does not prepare consolidated accounts, it will be necessary for it to adapt its profit and loss account, suitably titled, to incorporate the additional information required by this Statement (see Appendix 2). References in this Statement to investing groups and consolidated accounts are to be taken as embracing such additional information in the case of investing companies which do not have subsidiaries or which do not otherwise prepare consolidated accounts.

9 Where an associated company itself has subsidiary or associated companies, the profits or losses to be dealt with in the investing group's consolidated accounts are its attributable proportion of the profits or losses of the group of which the associated company is parent.

### Inclusion of associated companies' results in consolidated accounts of investing group

10 The investing group should include in its consolidated accounts its share of all material associated companies' results (whether profits or losses), subject to the exceptions stated in paragraph 12.

11 The accounts used for the purpose of including associated companies' results should be audited accounts either coterminous with those of the investing company or made up to a date which is not more than six months before, or shortly after, the date of the investing group or company's accounts. In the absence of such audited accounts (for which there should be justifiable cause), unaudited accounts may be used provided the investing group is satisfied as to their reliability. If accounts not coterminous with those of the investing company, or unaudited accounts, are used, the facts and the dates of year-ends should be disclosed.

12 An associated company's results should be omitted from the consolidated accounts only on the same grounds as those which would permit group accounts not to deal with a subsidiary, notably if the inclusion of such results:

(a) would involve expense or delay out of proportion to the value to the members of the investing company

or

(b) would be misleading.

The reason for omission should be stated.

### Accounting adjustments

13 Wherever the effect is material, adjustments similar to those adopted for the purpose of presenting consolidated accounts should be made to exclude from the investing group's consolidated accounts such items as unrealised profits on stocks transferred to or from associated companies and to achieve reasonable consistency with the accounting practices adopted by the investing group.

### Profit and loss account items*

14 *Profits before tax.* The investing group should include in its consolidated accounts the aggregate of its share of before-tax profits less losses of associated companies. The item should be shown separately and suitably described, for example as 'share of profits less losses of associated companies'.

15 *Taxation.* The tax attributed to the share of profits of associated companies should be disclosed separately within the group tax charge in the consolidated accounts.

* Examples of profit and loss accounts drawn up to give the information required are shown in Appendices 1 and 2.

*Extraordinary items.* The investing group's share of aggregate extraordinary items dealt   16
with in associated companies' accounts should be included with the group share of
extraordinary items, unless the amount is material in the context of the group's results
when it should be separately disclosed.

*Net profit retained by associated companies.* There should be shown separately the invest-   17
ing group's share of aggregate net profits less losses retained by associated companies.

*Other items.* The investing group should not include its attributable share of associated   18
companies' items such as turnover and depreciation in the aggregate amounts of these
items disclosed in its consolidated accounts. If the results of one or more associated companies are of such significance in the context of the investing group's accounts that more
detailed information about them would assist in giving a true and fair view, this information should be given by separate disclosure of the total turnover of the associated
companies concerned, their total depreciation charge, their total profits less losses
before taxation, and the amounts of such profits attributable to the investing group.

**Balance sheet items**

Unless shown at a valuation, the amount at which the investing group's interests in   19
associated companies should be shown in the consolidated balance sheet is:

(*a*) the cost of the investments less any amounts written off
   *and*

(*b*) the investing company or group's share of the post-acquisition retained profits
   and reserves of the associated companies.

The investing company which has no subsidiaries, or which does not otherwise prepare
consolidated accounts, should show its share of its associated companies' post-acquisition retained profits and reserves by way of note to its balance sheet.

Information regarding associated companies' tangible and intangible assets and liabilities
should be given, if materially relevant for the appreciation by the members of the investing company of the nature of their investment.

The amount at which the investing group's interests in accumulated reserves is shown   20
in the consolidated accounts should distinguish between profits retained by the group
and profits retained by associated companies. If retained profits of associated companies
overseas would be subject to further tax on distribution, this should be made clear. It
will also be necessary to take account of and disclose movements on associated companies' other reserves, e.g., surplus on revaluation of fixed assets.

**Disclosure of particulars of associated companies**

The investing group or company should give particulars of the names of and its interests   21
in companies treated as associated companies, and of any other companies in which
it holds not less than 20 per cent of the equity voting rights but which are not treated
as associated companies.

**Corresponding amounts**

On first introduction of the standard method of accounting set out in this Statement   22
the corresponding amounts for the preceding period should be appropriately stated on
a comparable basis.

**Date from which effective**

The method of accounting for the results of associated companies set out in this State-   23
ment should be adopted as soon as possible and regarded as standard in respect of
reports relating to accounting periods starting on or after 1st January, 1971.

## PART 4 – NOTE ON LEGAL REQUIREMENTS

24  Paragraph 5 A of Schedule 2 to the Companies Act 1967 requires certain information to be given about unquoted equity investments in the absence of a directors' valuation. The information required to be given by this Statement may not fully satisfy the requirements of the Act. To that extent it will be necessary either to re-arrange the information appropriately or, if this is impracticable, to provide it by way of a separate note.

25  In dealing with the results of associated companies, regard should be had to the provisions of paragraph 12 (1) (g) of Schedule 2 to the Companies Act 1967, which requires the amounts respectively of income from quoted investments and income from unquoted investments to be shown in the profit and loss account.

26  The disclosure requirements of this Statement are not intended to override exemptions from the disclosure requirements of the Companies Acts, available to and utilised by special classes of company under Part III of the Second Schedule to the Companies Act 1967, and applicable to companies incorporated outside the United Kingdom under Section 4 (3) of the Companies Act 1967.

**Appendix 1**

*Note. This Appendix does not form part of the Statement of Standard Accounting Practice. The method of presentation used is illustrative only and in no way prescriptive. Other methods of presentation may equally comply with the accounting standard set out in the Statement.*

## EXAMPLE OF CONSOLIDATED PROFIT AND LOSS ACCOUNT FOR A COMPANY WITH SUBSIDIARIES

**Consolidated profit and loss account of an investing company and subsidiaries, incorporating results of associated companies.**

|  | £ |
|---|---|
| *Turnover* (of the investing company and subsidiaries)  ..    ..    .. | £X |

|  | £ |
|---|---|
| *Operating profit* (after charging depreciation and all other trading expenses of the investing company and subsidiaries)  ..    ..    .. | X |
| Share of profits less losses of associated companies    ..    ..    .. | X |
| *Profit before taxation*    ..    ..    ..    ..    ..    ..    .. | X |

|  | £ |  |
|---|---|---|
| Taxation: Investing company and subsidiaries  ..    ..    .. | X |  |
| Associated companies  ..    ..    ..    ..    .. | X | X |
|  |  | X |
| Minority interests  ..    ..    ..    ..    ..    ..    ..    .. |  | X |
| *Profit after taxation before extraordinary items*  ..    ..    .. |  | X |
| Extraordinary items (group proportion after taxation, after deducting minority interests and including share of associated companies' items) ..    ..    ..    ..    ..    ..    .. |  | X |
| *Profit attributable to members of* (*the investing company*) (See note)  ..    ..    ..    ..    ..    ..    ..    .. |  | X |
| Dividends    ..    ..    ..    ..    ..    ..    ..    .. |  | X |
| *Net profit retained*  ..    ..    ..    ..    ..    ..    .. |  | £X* |

|  | £ |
|---|---|
| By the investing company  ..    ..    .. | X |
| By subsidiaries    ..    ..    ..    .. | X |
| In associated companies    ..    ..    .. | X |
|  | £X* |

*Note.* Of the profit attributable to members of the investing company, £— is dealt with in the accounts of the investing company.

## Appendix 2

*Note. This Appendix does not form part of the Statement of Standard Accounting Practice. The method of presentation used is illustrative only and in no way prescriptive. Other methods of presentation may equally comply with the accounting standard set out in the Statement.*

## EXAMPLE OF PROFIT AND LOSS ACCOUNT FOR A COMPANY WITHOUT SUBSIDIARIES

**Profit and Loss Account of an investing company incorporating results of associated companies**

|  | £ |
|---|---|
| *Turnover* (of the investing company)    ..    ..    ..    ..    .. | £X |

|  | £ |
|---|---|
| *Operating profit* (after charging depreciation and all other trading expenses of the investing company)    ..    ..    ..    ..    .. | X |
| Share of profits less losses of associated companies    ..    ..    .. | X |
| *Profit before taxation*    ..    ..    ..    ..    ..    ..    .. | X |

|  | £ |  |
|---|---|---|
| Taxation: Investing company    ..    ..    ..    ..    .. | X | |
| Associated companies    ..    ..    ..    ..    .. | X | |
|  | — | X |
| *Profit after taxation before extraordinary items* ..    ..    ..    .. | | X |
| Extraordinary items (investing company and share of associated companies' items) after taxation    ..    ..    ..    ..    ..    .. | | X |
| *Profit attributable to members of the investing company comprising:*    .. | | X* |

|  | £ |
|---|---|
| Profit of the investing company ..    ..    ..    ..    .. | X |
| Profits retained in associated companies    ..    ..    .. | X |
|  | £X* |

|  | £ |
|---|---|
| Dividends    ..    ..    ..    ..    ..    ..    ..    .. | X |
| *Net profit retained*    ..    ..    ..    ..    ..    ..    .. | £X** |

|  | £ |
|---|---|
| By the investing company    ..    .. | X |
| In associated companies ..    ..    .. | X |
|  | £X** |

# INDEX

**Absorption,**
of one limited company by another, 365 *et seq.*
shares issued at a premium, 368
treatment of revenue balances, 368
**Accident Insurance Fund,** 371
**Accommodation Bills,** 117 *et seq.*
bankruptcy, in, 545
**Accounting Ratios.** (*See* Ratios)
**Account Sales,** 93
**Accounts, Interpretation of,** 320 *et seq.*
**Adding Machines,** 514 *et seq.*
**Adding-Listing Machines,** 516
**Addressing Machines,** 514
**Advance, Payments in,** 44
**Advances by Partners,**
accounts for, in the books, 133
interest on, in the absence of agreement, 128
repayment on dissolution, 166
**Agents,**
accounts with, 102
consignees as, 93
*del credere,* 93, 97
partners as, 125
**Agreements to Pay by Instalments,** 598
entries in buyer's books, 598
entries in seller's books, 599
**Allotments,**
letter of allotment, 216
return of, 217
**Amalgamation,**
holding company scheme and, 387
of companies, 348
of companies, bases of valuation, 350 *et seq.*
of firms, 182
relief from stamp duty on,, 359 *et seq.*
**Annual Charges,**
deductions of tax from, 306
**Annual Return,** 201, 205
**Annuity,**
life assurance accounts, in, 664
repayment of partner's capital by, 157
**Annuity Method of Depreciation,** 54 *et seq.*
**Application and Allotment of Shares,** 213 *et seq.*
allotment letter, 216
application and allotment sheet, 213, 214
application letters, 213
calls, 217
'firm', 235
journal entries relating to, 218
letters of regret, 216
minimum subscription, 215
prospectus, 213, 215
return of allotments, 217
share certificate, 217
vendors' and signatories' shares, 217
**Appropriation Account,** 19
dividends, proposed, in, 280, 296, 302
taxation, treatment of, in, 305 *et seq.*
**Articles of Association,** 202

**Assets,**
application of, on partnership dissolution, 166
classes of, 3
effect of inflation upon, 47 *et seq.*
in balance sheet, 20
realization and revaluation of, corporation tax payable, 311
valuation (*q.v.*)
**Associated Company,**
distinction between subsidiary company and, 390
statement of the Institute of Chartered Accountants, as to accounting for the results of, Appendix IV
**Assurance Companies Accounts,** 290, 293, 660 *et seq.*
**Audit,**
company and partnership, 198
preparation of company's books, for, 274
report annexed to company's filed balance sheet, 206
statutory report, of, 210
**Auditor's Remuneration,** 279

**Bad Debts,**
provision for, 39
**Balance Sheet,**
annual summary, inclusion in, 201, 205, 206
company, of, 275, 284 *et seq.*, 293, 307
consolidated, 395 *et seq.*
definition of, 19
exemptions for special classes of companies, 290, 293
form of, 20, 319
Institute of Chartered Accountants, recommendations of, 293 *et seq.*
specimens of, Appendix I
valuation, 664
**Bank Balance Sheet,**
form of, Appendix I
secret reserves in, 69
**Bank Loans and Overdrafts, disclosure of,** 294
**Bank Note,** 107
**Bank Reconciliation Statement,** 8
**Bankers' Accounts,** 618, Appendix I
**Banking Company,** 290, 293
**Bankruptcy Accounts,**
bills, 545, 548
book debts, 548
contingent liabilities, 546
creditors, 544 *et seq.*
deferred debts, 544
deficiency accounts, 543, 548, 551, 555
incomplete records, 543
partnerships, 554
statement of affairs, 543, 552, 555
trustee's accounts, 556, Appendices III B & III C
valuation of assets, 542, 547

**Bankruptcy of Partners,**
ascertainment of share of profits, 180
liability of estate for partnership debts, 155
operates as dissolution of partnership, 166,
180
**Bill of Lading,** 123
**Bills of Exchange,**
accommodation bill, 117 *et seq.*
advances on the security of, 114 *et seq.*
bankruptcy, in, 545, 548
bill diary, 111
bills payable book, 110
bills payable ledger, 111
bills receivable book, 110
bills receivable ledger, 111, 112
contingent liability on discounted, 113, 301
days of grace, 107
definition, 106
discounting, 111
dishonoured, 121
documentary, 123
entries in books, for, 113 *et seq.*
forms of, 108
inter-company, in consolidated balance sheet,
396
parties to, 106
rebated, 124
retired and renewed, 121
short, 123
stamp duties, on, 107
**Bonus,**
calls, applied in payment of, 273
capital redemption reserve fund, out of, 224
life assurance, in, 663
shares, 271 *et seq.*, 627
**Books of Account,**
company, of, 274
limited partner, access to, 165
members of company, access to, 197
partnership, of, 129
prime entry, of, 5 *et seq.*
sole trader, of, 21
**Bought Day Book.** (*See* Purchases Journal)
**Branch Accounts,** 451 *et seq.*
assets of branch in head office books, 483
assets in transit, 477
current accounts, 475
fixed rate of exchange, 494
fluctuating rate of exchange, 496
foreign branches, 494
foreign exchanges, 493
goods charged to branch at –
cost price, 454
cost price, plus a percentage, 456
selling price, 465
goods damaged or lost, treatment of, 489
head office, when all records kept at, 451
semi-autonomous branches, 472
sterling exchange rates, major charges in,
treatment of, 503
when all detail is recorded in branch books,
475
**Brokerage,**
marine insurance, 621
**Building Societies,**
accounts of, 672 *et seq.*
borrowing powers, 674
constitution, 672

**Calculating Machines,**
barrel type, 518
full-keyboard type, 518
**Calls on Shares,** 217
bonus applied to payment of, 273
call letters, 217
call sheets, 217
forfeiture for non-payment of, 226
liquidator, by, to adjust shareholders' rights,
569
statement of affairs, in, 561
Table 'A' and, 217
**Capital,**
expenditure, definition of, 4
interest, payment of, out of, 273
reserve, 39
revenue, distinguished from, 4
**Capital, Proprietors',**
advance by partner, distinct from, 128, 133
dissolution of partnership, repayment on, 166
interest on partners', 129
outgoing partner, repayment of, 153 *et seq.*
partners, accounts of, 133
reconstructions, 382
reduction of, 374 *et seq.*
share. (*See* Share Capital)
**Capital Redemption Reserve Fund,** 223, 284
**Capital Reserve,**
definition of, 39
excess of liabilities over assets on purchase of
business, 252, 367
pre-acquisition profits, in consolidated
balance sheet, 400
profit prior to incorporation, 258
**Capital Surpluses,**
arising on realization and revaluation,
corporation tax payable, 311
**Carbon Smearing,** 510
**Card Ledgers,**
advantages and disadvantages of, 16
description of, 16
**Cases Accounts.** (*See* Accounts of Containers)
**Cash Account, Total,** 8
**Cash Book,**
columnar, 6 *et seq.*
forms of, 5, 6 *et seq.*
liquidator's, 566, Appendix III E
reconciliation with bank pass book, 8
trustee in bankruptcy, of, 556, Appendix
III A
**Cash Discount,**
definition of, 6
provision for, 42
**Cash Flow.**
(*See* Movement of Funds Statements)
**Cash Summary,**
preparation from incomplete records, 81
**Certified Transfer,** 232
**Charges,**
definition of, for Income Tax purposes, 306
**Charges, Register of,** 204, 238
**Chartered Accountants, Institute of, Recommen-
dations of,**
accounting by electronic methods, 530
apportionment of hire-purchase interest, 582
depreciation, 62
investment grants, accounting treatment of,
314

**Chartered Accountants, Institute of, Recommendations of,** (*continued*)
investments, treatment of, 294
major changes in sterling exchange rates, treatment of, 503
material, interpretation of, 296
presentation of balance sheet and profit and loss account, 293 *et seq.*
provision for replacement of assets having regard to rising costs, 48
shares in subsidiaries acquired over a period of time, 408
statements of standard accounting practice, *re* the results of associated companies, Appendix IV
stock-in-trade, valuation of, 297 *et seq.*
taxation in accounts, treatment of, 310 *et seq.*
tax reserve certificates, 310
**Cheque,**
definition of, 106
signing machines, 514
writing machines, 514
**Circulating Assets,**
definition of, 3
**City Code on Take-overs and Mergers,** 388
**Claims for Compensation,**
loss of profits, 609
stock destroyed by fire, 608
**Close Companies,** 312
**Collating Carriage Typewriters,** 511
**Columnar Books,**
cash book, 6 *et seq.*, 35
departmental accounts, for, 446
petty cash book, 10
purchases day book, 12, 35
sales day book, 35
sectional balancing, for purposes of, 35
**Commission on Shares,**
balance sheet, in, 237
on placing shares, 237
'over-riding', 234
stock exchange transactions, 635
underwriting, 234
**Company,**
absorption of, 365 *et seq.*
accounts of, 196 *et seq.*, Appendix I
amalgamation of, 348 *et seq.*
balance sheet of, 275, 284
bonus shares, 271
books of account of, 274
capital of, 210 *et seq.*
close, 312
compulsory liquidation, in, 557 *et seq.*
directors of, 280 *et seq.*
distributions by, 306
dividends of, 302 *et seq.*
goodwill, valuation of, 352 *et seq.*
holding, accounts of, 387 *et seq.*
interest paid out of capital, 273
memorandum and articles of, 202
partnership and, 196
private, 200
private firm, purchased by, 184, 251 *et seq.*
profit and loss account of, 275, 276, 278
profit or loss prior to incorporation, treatment of, 258 *et seq.*
realization account, on sale of, 365
reconstruction of, 382
reduction of capital of, 374

**Company** (*continued*)
share capital, classes of, 210
statutory books and returns of, 203 *et seq.*
unlimited, 202
**Computers.**
(*See* Electronic Computers)
**Consequential Loss Insurance,** 609 *et seq.*
**Consignment Accounts,**
account sales, 93
consignee, entries in books of, 101
consignor, entries in books of, 93
*del credere* agent, 93, 97
*pro forma* invoice, 98, 101
unsold goods, treatment of, 95
**Consolidated Balance Sheet,**
bonus shares received by holding company from subsidiary, 411
corporation tax, 411
depreciation in respect of subsidiary's assets, 415, 428
dividends paid out of pre-acquisition profits, 409
financial year of subsidiary ending on different date to that of holding company, adjustments required, 395
foreign subsidiaries, 427
goodwill adjustments, 397, 403, 422, 425, 426
group accounts, part of, 391
inter-company balances, 396
losses incurred by subsidiary, 409
method of working, 396
minority interests, 402 *et seq.*
partly-owned subsidiaries, 402 *et seq.*
preference shares in subsidiaries, 412
principles of, 395
recommendation of Institute of Chartered Accountants, as to shares in subsidiaries acquired over a period of time, 408
revaluation of assets of subsidiary, 415
shares in holding company owned by subsidiary, 390
subsidiary owning shares in another subsidiary, 418 *et seq.*
unrealized inter-company profits, 414, 430
wholly-owned subsidiaries, 397 *et seq.*
**Consolidated Profit and Loss Account,**
balance carried forward, 433
Companies Act, provisions relating to, 428
depreciation adjustments, 415, 428, 432
directors' emoluments, 433
holding company's profit and loss account as, 437
inter-company dividends, 431
minority interests, 432
pre-acquisition profits and losses, 429
transfers to reserve, 432
unrealized inter-company profits, 430
**Containers,**
accounts for, 668
**Contingent Liabilities,**
bankruptcy in, 546
bills discounted, 113, 301
consolidated balance sheet and, 396
definition of, 301
disclosure of, 302
examples of, 302
**Continuous Stationery,** 509

**Contract Accounts,** 614
  profit taken, 615 *et seq.*
**Contributories,**
  return to, 569
  statement of affairs, 557
**Control Accounts.** (*See* Total Accounts)
**Controlled Typewriters,** 512
**Conversion,**
  debentures to those carrying lower rate of in-
    terest, 250
  foreign branch trial balance, 494, 496
  private firm, of, into limited company, 184,
    251 *et seq.*
**Copying Devices in Mechanized Accounting,**
  509 *et seq.*
**Corporation Tax,**
  accounts, treatment of, in, 279, 286, 293, 305
  deferred taxation account, and, 310
  holding companies, of, 411
  losses, and, 310
  overseas taxation, 305, 310
  realizations and revaluation of assets, arising
    on, 311
  set off against tax on unfranked investment
    income, 308
**Creditors,**
  deferred, 125, 157, 544
  fully secured, 544
  novation, on change of partnership person-
    nel, 155
  partly-secured, 545
  preferential, 546
  provision for discount on, 42
  statement of affairs in, 543 *et seq.*
  total account for, 31, 83
  unsecured, 544
**Cumulative Preference Shares,**
  arrears of dividend on, 286, 302
  rights of, 211
**Current Accounts,**
  branches, of, 475
  interest on partners', 127
**Current (Floating) Assets,** 3
  definition, 3
  rate of exchange for converting into sterling,
    497
**Current Liabilities,** 4
  rate of exchange for converting into sterling,
    497

**Day Books,**
  columnar, 12
  description of, 5, 11 *et seq.*
  methods of dispensing with, 26
**Days of Grace,** 107
**Dead Rent** (minimum rent), 600
**Debenture Holders, Register of,** 204
**Debentures,**
  balance sheet, in, 238, 240, 249
  bearer, 238
  carrying a fixed charge, 238
  carrying a floating charge, 238
  collateral security, as, 249
  conversion into debentures of lower rate of
    interest, 250
  definition of, 238
  discount, issued at, 240
  interest on, 239, 244, 245, 247, 249, 279
  investment, held as, 245, 247

**Debentures** (*continued*)
  issue of, 239
  ledger, 239
  mortgage, 237
  premium, issued at, 239
  redemption of, 241 *et seq.*
  reduction of capital scheme, in, 378
  register of holders, of, 204
  registration of, 238
  re-issue, available for, 241
  repayable at a premium, 241
  security for a loan, issued as, 249
  simple or naked, 238
  stamp duty on, 239
**Deceased Partner,**
  liability of estate of, 155
  (*See* Outgoing Partner)
**Deeds of Arrangement,**
  accounts in connection with, 556, Appendix
    III D
  trustee under, 556
**Deferred Creditor,**
  bankruptcy, in, 544
  loan to partnership at rate varying with
    profits, 125, 157
**Deferred Revenue Expenditure,**
  nature of, 4
  suspense account, and, 70
**Deferred Shares,** 211
**Deficiency Account,**
  illustration, 551, 555
  in bankruptcy, 543, 548
  in compulsory liquidation, 564
**Del Credere Agent,** 93, 97
**Departmental Accounts,** 446 *et seq.*
**Depreciation,**
  based on historical or replacement cost, 47
  considerations to determine rate of, 45
  consolidated accounts, in, 415, 428, 432
  definition of, 43
  disclosure of, 279, 295
  external, 45
  fluctuation, distinction between, and, 45
  internal, 45
  necessity of providing for, 45 *et seq.*
  obsolescence, and, 45, 47
  principal methods of providing for:
    annuity method, 54
    depletion unit method, 61
    depreciation fund with investment method,
      57
    depreciation fund with insurance policy, 60
    diminishing balance method, 52
    fixed instalment method, 49
    machine hour method, 62
    reducing instalment method, 52
    revaluation, 61
    sinking fund, 57
    straight line method, 49
  profits, deductible in calculating, 46
  provision for, 44 *et seq.*
  recommendation of Institute of Chartered
    Accountants on, 62
  sundry methods, 62
**Dilapidations,**
  lease, provision for, 63
**Directors,**
  compensation for loss of office, disclosure of,
    281

**Directors** (*continued*)
emoluments of, additional disclosure of, 282
" " definition of, 281
" " disclosure of, 280
loans to, disclosure of, 290
minute book, 207
payments to, 280 *et seq.*
pensions, disclosure of, 281
register of, 207
report of, for annual general meeting, 291
" " exemptions for special classes of
companies, 293
report for statutory meeting, 209
service contracts, register of, 209
shareholdings, debenture holdings and
options, register of, 208
**Disbursements on Behalf of Clients,** 656
**Discount,**
bills of exchange, on, 111 *et seq.*, 118, 119,
120, 123
cash, (*q.v.*), 6, 42
debentures issued at, 240
shares issued at, 222
trade, 6
**Discount Company,** 290, 293
**Dishonoured Bills,** 121
**Dissentient Members,**
purchase of shares of, 383
reconstruction scheme and, 383
**Dissolution of Partnership,**
ascertainment of deceased or bankrupt
partner's profits, 180
assets, order of application, 166
death or bankruptcy, by, 166, 180
formula for closing books, 167, 180, 181
*Garner* v. *Murray,* applied on insolvency of
partner, 172, 178
grounds for, 166
limited partnership, of, 165
piecemeal realization, 174 *et seq.*
(*See* Outgoing Partner)
**Distribution of Assets in Specie,**
on dissolution of partnership, 186
**Distributions by Companies,** 306
**Dividends,** 302 *et seq.*
appropriation account, in, 280, 296, 302
arrears of cumulative preference, 286, 302
deduction of income tax from, 303
interim, 302
method of payment, 302
out of pre-acquisition profit, 409
proposed, inclusion in accounts, 280, 296,
302
purchase of investments, adjustment for, on,
624
unclaimed, 303
**Documentary Bills,** 123
**Dominion Register,** 206
**Double Entry,**
advantages of, over single entry, 2
definition of, 1
fundamental rule of, 2
theory of, 1
**Duplex Machines,** 517

**Electronic Computers,** 530 *et seq.*
arithmetic and logic unit, 534
binary system, 531
control unit, 534

**Electronic Computers** (*continued*)
desk-top, 539
direct access devices, 539
flow chart, 531
glossary of terms, 539
input unit, 532
installation, 537
'languages', 536
miniaturized, 519, 539
output unit, 534
program, 535
recommendation of Institute of Chartered
Accountants, *re* accounting by, 530
storage unit, 532
**Employees' Emoluments, Disclosure of,** 280
**Employees' Loans,**
disclosure of, 290
**Equity Share Capital,** 211, 212
definition of, in group accounts, 389
**Errors,**
balancing, in, 17
compensating, 17
location of, 37
of commission, 17
of omission, 17
of principle, 17
rectification of, through journal, 14
**Exempt Private Company,** 201

**'Fan-Fold' Stationery,** 509
**Farmers' Accounts,** 605
**Fictitious Assets,** 3
**Finance Companies,** 666
**Financial Statements,**
balance sheets in form of, 317, 318
profit and loss accounts in form of, 318
**Fire Claims,**
loss of profits, 609
loss of stock, 608
**Firm Application for Shares,** 234
**Fixed Assets,**
basis of valuation necessary, 286, 290
capital expenditure, 4
definition, 3
rate of exchange for converting into sterling,
496
recommendations of Institute of Chartered
Accountants, 293 *et seq.*
**Fixed Charge,** 238
**Fixed (Long Term) Liabilities,** 4
**Floating Charge,** 238
**Flow Charts,** 530, 531
**Fluctuation,**
distinguished from depreciation, 45
**Foreign Branches,** 494 *et seq.*
fixed rate of exchange, 494
fluctuating rate of exchange, 496 *et seq.*
recommendation of Institute of Chartered
Accountants as to treatment of major
changes in sterling exchange rates, 503
subsidiary company, 427
**Foreign Exchange,** 492
**Forfeiture of Shares,** 226 *et seq.*
reduction of capital, as, 377
re-issue, 227
**Formation Expenses,** 233
**Founders' Shares,** 211
**Franked Investment Income,**
definition of, 306

**Franked Investment Income** (*continued*)
set-off of income tax on, 307
treatment of income tax on, in balance sheet, 307
treatment of income tax on, surplus over distributions, 312
**Funds, Movement of,** 336 *et seq.*

**Garner** *v*. **Murray,**
ruling in, 168, 172, 173
**Goods on Consignment,** 92 *et seq.*
(*See* Consignment Accounts)
**Goods on Sale or Return,** 89 *et seq.*
**Goodwill,**
absorption, on 367
amalgamation of companies on, 352 *et seq.*
balance sheet, in, 286
consolidated balance sheet, adjustments in, 397, 398, 423, 425, 426, 427
definition of, 134
due to, 134
incoming partner, and, 135, 137
outgoing partner and, 135, 142
profit sharing ratio, change in, 135, 143
sale of business to a company, 251 *et seq.*
valuation of, 135
**Group Accounts,**
Companies Acts, special provisions, 392
consolidated balance sheet (*q.v.*), 395 *et seq.*
consolidated balance sheet and profit and loss account, 391
consolidated profit and loss account (*q.v.*), 428 *et seq.*
may be in form other than consolidated accounts, 391
not required, where, 390
statement where group accounts not submitted, 392 *et seq.*

**Hire-purchase Agreements,** 575 *et seq.*
distinction between agreements to pay by instalments and, 575
entries in buyer's books, 576 *et seq.*
entries in seller's books, 586 *et seq.*
recommendation of Institute of Chartered Accountants, as to apportionment of interest, 582
**Hire-purchase Finance,** 586
**Holding Companies,** 387 *et seq.*
advantages of, 387
associated company, distinction between subsidiary company and, 390
balance sheet, disclosures *re* subsidiary companies, 288
consolidated balance sheet (*q.v.*), 395 *et seq.*
consolidated profit and loss account, 428 *et seq.*
controlling interest, securing under Sec. 209, 388
directors' and employees' emoluments, disclosure of, not required, 393
disclosure of particulars *re* subsidiary companies, 288
equity share capital, definition of, 389
foreign subsidiaries, 427
formation of, 348
group accounts (*q.v.*), 390 *et seq.*
shares in, owned by subsidiary, 390
subsidiary company, definition of, 389

**Holding Out,** 155, 164
**Hotel,**
visitors' ledger, 633

**Impersonal Accounts,**
definition of, 2,
**Imprest System,** 11
**Income and Expenditure Account,**
definition of, 19, 78
distinguished from receipts and payments account, 78
form of, 80
**Income Tax,**
accounts, treatment of, in, 305 *et seq.*
close companies, *re*, 312
debenture interest, deduction from, 239, 307
dividends, deduction from, 306, 307
franked and unfranked investment income, on, 307
income received, without deduction of, 306
interest paid out of capital, 274
treatment of, on surplus franked income over distributions, 312
**Incoming Partner,**
goodwill affecting, 135, 137
**Incomplete Records,**
preparation of accounts from, 81 *et seq.*
**Indemnity Insurance,** 660
**Insolvent Partner,**
deficiency borne by solvent ones, 168, 173
**Instalments,**
agreements to pay by (*q.v.*), 598
distinction between hire-purchase agreements and, 575
repayment of outgoing partner's capital by, 157
**Insurance Accounts,** 660 *et seq.*
accident, 661
aviation, 661
bond investment business, 661
fire, 661
form of, Appendix I
marine, 621
motor vehicle, 661
**Insurance Claims,**
averaging, principle of, 660
life assurance accounts, in, 663
loss of profits, 610
loss of stock, 608
marine, 621
**Insurance Policy,**
depreciation fund with, 60
(*See* Surrender Value)
**Intangible Assets,** 4
**Interest,**
capital, interest on partners', 129
debenture, 239, 244, 245, 247, 249, 279
drawings, interest on, 130
hire-purchase, 575 *et seq.*
investment accounts, in, 623 *et seq.*
paid out of capital, 273
rate varying with profits, 126
**Interim Dividends,** 302
**Interpretation of Accounts,** 320 *et seq.*
**Investment Grants,**
recommendation of Institute of Chartered Accountants, as to treatment of, 314
**Investments,**
classification in Balance Sheet, 287, 294

**Investments** (*continued*)
finance company's books, 666
income from, in accounts, 278
income from, franked and unfranked, 306
ledger accounts for, 623
purchase of, 624
quoted, 287, 294
recommendation of Institute of Chartered Accountants, as to treatment of, 294
unquoted, 287
valuation of, 295
**Invoice,**
*pro forma* (consignment), 98, 101
use of, as posting medium, 520,

**Joint Stock Bank,** 620
balance sheet, 620, Appendix I
functions of, 618
**Joint Venture,**
definition of, 187
entries in books relating to, 187 *et seq.*
**Journal,**
description of, 5, 13 *et seq.*
form for entries in, 13
narrative in, 13
rectification of errors through, 14
transfer, 32
use of, 13

**Lease,**
depreciation of, 54, 57
dilapidations arising under, 65
long and short, definition of, 287
**Ledger,**
accounts, kinds of, 2
card, 16
hotel visitors', 633
loose-leaf, 16
personal, methods of dispensing with, 26
plant, 634
purchases day book, combined with, 632
rental, 632
self-balancing, 36
share, 203, 231
summary book for entries in, 36
tabular, 631
types of, 16
**Ledger Posting Machines,**
accounting routine, 520
analysis by accounting machines, 526
control accounts, 522
detection and prevention of errors, 521
double run, 523
pre-listing, 522
sources of error, 521
**Letters of Allotment,** 216
**Letters of Regret,** 216
**Liabilities,**
contingent, 301
kinds of, 4
outstanding, 43
proposed dividends shown as, 302
secured, 285
**Life Assurance,** 662
**Life Policy,**
to provide for part payment of share of deceased partner, 146
**Limited Company.**
(*See* Company)

**Limited Partnerships Act, 1907,** 164
**Liquid Assets,** 3
**Liquidation Accounts,** 568, Appendices III F & III G
compulsory liquidation:
liquidators' accounts, in, 566, Appendix III E
statement of affairs, in, 557 *et seq.*
preferential creditors, in, 557 *et seq.*
return to shareholders, 569
statement of account, in voluntary liquidation, 566 *et seq.*
statement of affairs, 557 *et seq.*
voluntary liquidation, 566 *et seq.*
**Loans,**
directors', in balance sheet, 290
officers, to, disclosure of, 287, 290
partners, by, 133
repayment of, by sinking fund, 66
retired partner's capital left as, 156
secured by issue of debentures, 249
to partnership at interest varying with profits, 125, 156
**Long-Term Liabilities,** 4
**Loose-Leaf Books,**
ledgers, 16
minute books, 17, 204
**Loose Plant and Tools,**
depreciation by revaluation, 61
**Loss of Profits (Consequential Loss) Insurance,** 609

**Machine Hour,**
depreciation by, 62
**Magnetic Card/Tape Typewriter,** 512
**Maintenance Provision Account,** 65
**Make-up Price,** 637
**Management Shares,** 211
**Manufacturing Account,** 72 *et seq.*
**Marine Insurance Accounts,** 621
**Material,**
recommendation of Institute of Chartered Accountants, as to interpretation of, 296
**Mechanized Accounting,**
adding machines, 514
adding-listing machines, 516
calculating machines, 518
copying and writing devices, 509 *et seq.*
duplex machines, 517
full-keyboard machines, 514
half-keyboard machines, 516
ledger-posting machines (*q.v.*), 520 *et seq.*
principles, 508
punched card systems (*q.v.*), 523 *et seq.*
report of Institute of Chartered Accountants, as to, 508
ten-key keyboard, 516
writing and copying devices, 509 *et seq.*
**Members,**
register of, 203, 231
**Memorandum of Association,** 202
**Mine,**
depreciation for, 61
minimum rent and royalties, 600 *et seq.*
**Minimum Subscription,** 215
**Minority Interests,** 402, 432
indirect, 418
**Minute Books,** 207
loose-leaf, 17, 207

**Miscellaneous Accounts,** 575 *et seq.*
**Mortgage,**
  balance sheet, in, 238
  building societies, details in accounts of, 672, 675
  debentures, 238
  definition of, 237
  entries in register of charges, 204, 238
**Movement of Funds Statements,** 336 *et seq.*

**Name,**
  company, of, 202
  partnership, of, 126
  registration of, 126
**Negotiable Instruments,** 107
**Nominal Accounts,**
  definition of, 2
**No par value,**
  shares of, 213

**Obsolescence,**
  distinguished from depreciation, 45
  treatment of, 47
**Ordinary Shares,** 211
  deferred ordinary, 211
  preferred ordinary, 211
**Outgoing Partner,**
  amount due to, methods of settling, 153 *et seq.*
  deficiency of, 168, 170, 172
  *Elliot* v. *Elliot,* 153
  *Garner* v. *Murray,* 168, 172
  goodwill affecting, 135, 142
  holding out, 155
  liability of, 155
  life policy to provide for repayment of, 146
**Outstanding Costs,**
  of professional men, 657
**Outstanding Liabilities,** 43
**Overriding Commission,** 234

**Packages and Empties,** 668
**Partner,**
  advances by, 128, 133, 166
  agent of other partners, 125
  capital of, repayment by annuity, 157
  duties of a, 128
  general, 164
  incoming, 135, 137
  limited, 164
  outgoing (*q.v.*), 153 *et seq.*
  quasi, 164
  rights and duties of, 128, 164
  sleeping, 164
**Partnership,**
  agreement, 127
  at will, 126
  bankruptcy of, 554
  co-ownership, distinguished from, 125
  definition of, 125
  dissolution (*q.v.*), 166 *et seq.*
  holding out, 155, 164
  limited, 164
  limited company, conversion to, 184
  limited company, difference from, 196
  name, 126
  novation by creditors, 155
  number of partners restricted, 125, 196

**Partnership** (*continued*)
  realization account, on dissolution of, 167 *et seq.*
  registration of a, 126
  rights and duties in absence of agreement, 128
  when sharing of profits does not constitute, 125
**Partnership Accounts,**
  absence of agreement, rules in, 128
  adjustments, miscellaneous, 150
  agreement, usual clauses in, 127
  amalgamation of sole traders, 182
  bankruptcy, 554
  capital accounts of partners, 133
  change of personnel, adjustments on, 159
  current accounts of partners, 134
  dissolution, 166 *et seq.*
  goodwill in, 134 *et seq.*
  interest – on capital, 129
            on drawings, 130
  joint ventures, 187 *et seq.*
  life policy, to provide for share of deceased partner, 146
  loans by partners, 133
  outgoing partner (*q.v.*), 153 *et seq.*
  piecemeal realization, 174
  profit-sharing ratio, change in, 143
  salaries of partners, 130
  sale to limited company, 184 *et seq.*, 251 *et seq.*
**Payments in Advance,** 44
**Peg-Board Methods,** 513
**Personal Accounts,**
  definition of, 2
**Petty Cash,**
  columnar form of book, 10
  imprest system, 11
**Photographic Copying,** 510
**Plant,**
  depreciation of, 45 *et seq.*
  ledger, 634
  register, 49
**Preference Shares,**
  arrears of dividends on, 286
  consolidated balance sheet, treatment in, 412
  participating, 211
  redeemable, 211, 222
  reduction of capital, in, 377, 379
**Preferential Creditors,**
  bankruptcy, in, 546
  liquidation, in, 558 *et seq.*
**Preliminary Expenses,**
  balance sheet, on, 233, 289
  description of, 233
  fictitious asset, 3
**Premium,**
  debentures issued at, 239
  debentures, repayable at, 241
  insurance, 663
  redemption of redeemable preference shares, on, 222
  shares issued at, 219
**Prepayments,** 44
**Prime Entry, Books of,** 5 *et seq.*
**Private Company,**
  certificate required from, 201
  definition of, 200
  exempt, 201
  privileges of, 201

**Professional Accounts,** 648
**Profit,**
calculation for life assurance companies, 664
claims for loss of, 609
pre-acquisition (holding company), 429
prior to incorporation, apportionment of, 258 *et seq.*
**Profit and Loss Account,**
company, 276, 278 *et seq.*, 295
consolidated (*q.v.*), 428 *et seq.*
definition of, 19
exemptions for special classes of companies, 290
illustrations of company, 314 *et seq.*, Appendix I
Institute of Chartered Accountants, recommendations of, 293 *et seq.*
**Pro Forma Invoice,**
consignments, 98, 101
**Promissory Note,**
days of grace, 107
definition of, 106
forms of, 109
joint, 109
joint and several, 109
parties to, 106
stamp duties on, 107
**Prospectus,**
application letters, with, 213
discount on shares, 222
minimum subscription, 215
**Provisions,**
bad debts, for, 39
balance sheet, in, 277, 284, 293
cash discounts, for, 42
definition of, 39, 277
depreciation, for, 44 *et seq.*
outstanding liabilities for, 43
profit and loss account, in, 279
repairs, for, 65
unrealized profit, for, 77, 414, 430, 488, 593
**Published Accounts,**
specimens of, 678 *et seq.*
**Punched Card Accounting,**
analysis and tabulation, 525, 529
applications to invoicing and ledger posting, 526 *et seq.*
cards, 523
description, 523
electronic calculator, 525
flow chart, 530
interpolator, 526
interpreter, 526
punching the cards, 524
reproducing punch, 525
sorting, 524
summary card punch, 526
tabulating, 525
verifying, 524
**Purchases Day Book,**
columnar, 12, 35
combined with ledger, 632
departmental, 446
form of, 11, 12
outstanding liabilities, entered in, 44

**Quantity Stock Accounts of Agents,** 102
**Quasi-Partner,** 164

**Quoted Investments,**
balance sheet, in, treatment of, 287, 294
definition of, 287
profit and loss account in, treatment of income from, 278

**Ratios, Accounting,** 325 *et seq.*
capital, 330
capital gearing, 330
dividend cover, 331
earnings, 331
price/earnings, 332
primary, 326
production, 335
quick assets, 329
sales, 332
secondary, 328
solvency, 328
stock, 334
working capital, 328
**Real Accounts,**
definition of, 2
**Realization Account,**
dissolution of partnership, 167 *et seq.*
sale of company, 365
**Rebated Bills,** 124
**Receipts and Expenditure Account,**
definition of, 79
professional man, of, 658
**Receipts and Payments Account,**
definition of, 78
distinguished from an income and expenditure account, 78
form of, 80
receiver, of, 572, 574
statutory report, in, 210
trustee of a deed of arrangement, of, 556
**Receivership Accounts,** 572
**Reconciliation Statement,**
bank pass book with cash book, 8
**Reconstruction of a Company,** 382
**Redeemable Preference Shares,**
balance sheet, in, 223
conditions of redemption, 222
issue of, 222
journal entries on redemption, 224
stamp duty on new issue at redemption, 223
**Redeemable Short Workings,** 600 *et seq.*
**Reduction in Share Capital,** 374 *et seq.*
**Register,**
of charges, 204, 238
of debenture holders, 204
of directors and secretaries, 207
of directors' service contracts, 209
of directors' shareholdings etc., 208
of large shareholdings, 209
of members, 203
of transfers, 232
plant, 49
**Registration of Business Names,** 126
**Rental Ledger,** 632
**Repairs, Renewals and Replacement,**
provision for, 65
recommendation of Institute of Chartered Accountants as to replacement, having regard to rising costs, 48
treatment of, 64 *et seq.*
**Reserve,**
balance sheet, in, 284, 293

**Reserve** (*continued*)
 capital, 39
 definition of, 39
 fund, 39
 profit and loss account, in, 279
 secret, 68
**Reserve Fund,**
 capital redemption reserve fund, 223, 284
 definition of, 39
**Retired Bills,** 121
**Return Day Books,** 12
**Return of Allotments,** 217
**Return to Shareholders, in Liquidation,** 569
**Revaluation,**
 ascertaining outgoing partner's share, 159
 assets of subsidiary, 415
 change of personnel, on, 159
 depreciation by, 61
 loose plant and tools, 61
**Revenue Account,**
 definition of, 19
 insurance companies' accounts, 662, 664
**Revenue Expenditure,**
 definition of, 4
 distinguished from capital expenditure, 4
**Rights,**
 issue of, 628
**Royalties and Minimum Rents,** 600 *et seq.*

**Sale or Return,**
 goods sent out on, 89 *et seq.*
**Sales Day Book,**
 columnar, 35
 entries in, 12
**Schemes for Capital Reduction,** 378
**Scrip Profits,** 666
**Secret Reserves,** 68
**Secretaries and Directors,**
 register of, 207
**Sectional Balancing,** 36
**Self-Balancing Ledgers,** 36
**Share Books,**
 register of members, 203
 register of transfers, 232
 share ledger, 203, 231
**Share Capital,**
 application and allotment of, 213 *et seq.*
 classes of, 210 *et seq.*
 payment of interest out of, 273
 reduction of, 374 *et seq.*
 return of, in liquidation, 569
 stock and shares, distinction between, 212
**Share Certificate,** 217
 balance certificate, or ticket, 232
**Shareholders,**
 voting rights of, 212
**Share Premium Account,** 219, 284
**Share Profits,**
 treatment of, 666
**Shares,**
 application for and allotment of, 213 *et seq.*
 bonus, 271, 627
 calls on, 217
 commission on placing, 237
 deferred, 211
 deferred ordinary shares, 211
 definition of, 212
 discount, issued at, 222
 dividends on amount paid up, 302

**Shares** (*continued*)
 forfeiture of, 226
 founders', 211
 fractions, dealing with, 272, 361
 issue of, 218
 management, 211
 no par value, 213
 ordinary, 211
 participating preference, 211
 preference, 211
 preference shares of subsidiaries, 412
 preferred ordinary shares, 211
 premium, issued at, 219, 368
 redeemable preference, 211, 222, 284
 signatories', 217
 stock, distinguished from, 212
 transfer, 232
 underwriting commission on, 234
 valuation of, on amalgamation, 349 *et seq.*
  368
 vendors, 217
**Shipping Accounts,**
 marine insurance, 621
 voyage accounts, 620
**Short Bills,** 123
**Short Workings,** 600 *et seq.*
**Signatories' Shares,** 217
**Single Entry,**
 accounts from, 81
 definition of, 81
 statement of affairs under, 87
**Sinking Fund,**
 repayment of debentures, for, 241 *et seq.*
 repayment of loans, for, 66
**Sleeping Partner,** 164
**Sole Traders,**
 accounts of, 21
 amalgamation of, 182
 bankruptcy of, 543, 549 *et seq.*
**Solicitors' Accounts,** 648
 accounts on a cash basis, 657
 disbursements on behalf of clients, 656
 outstanding costs at the balance sheet date,
  657
 solicitors' accounts rules, 648 *et seq.*
**Split Platen Typewriters,** 512
**Stamp Duties,**
 bills of exchange, 107
 debentures, 239
 limited partner's capital, 165
 promissory notes, 107
 relief from, on amalgamation, 359 *et seq.*, 371
 share capital, 200
**Standard Accounting Practice,**
 statements of, *re* the results of associated
  companies, Appendix IV
**Statement of Affairs,**
 bankruptcy, 543, 549, 552, 555
 deed of arrangement, 556
 from incomplete records, 87
 illustration, 549 *et seq.*, 555 *et seq.*, 562
 liquidation, 557 *et seq.*
 receiver, must be sent to, 572
**Statutory Books and Returns of Companies,**
 203, *et seq.*
 allotments, 217
 annual return, 205
 books of account, 275
 minute books, 207

**Statutory Books and Returns of Companies**
(*continued*)
register of charges, 204, 238
register of debenture holders, 204
register of directors and secretaries, 207
register of directors' shareholdings, 208
register of members, 203, 231
statutory report, 209
**Statutory Forms of Account,**
building societies, 675
**Statutory Meeting and Report,** 209
directors' report, 209
**Stencil Copying,** 510
**Stock,**
definition of, 212
distinguished from shares, 212
**Stock Exchange Transactions,** 635 *et seq.*
**Stock-in-Trade,**
agents, accounts for, 102
branches, sent to, 452 *et seq.*
consignment stock, 95
consolidated accounts, adjustment of, 414, 430
fire claim for, 608
hire-purchase, out on, 591
quantity accounts, 102, 454
recommendations of Institute of Chartered Accountants as to, 297 *et seq.*
sale or return on, 92
valuation of –
consignment accounts, 95
trading accounts, 297 *et seq.*
**Subsidiary Companies.**
(*See* Holding Companies)
**Super Profits,**
goodwill, valuation on basis of, 136
**Surrender of Shares,**
reduction of capital, as, 377
**Surrender Value,** 665
insurance policy, adjustment to, 60, 61, 147, 148, 149, 665
**Suspense Account,**
annuity, 157
debtors' and creditors', where not taken over by company, 262
difference on books, 70

**Table 'A',**
application of, 203
provision regarding –
calls, 217
dividends, 302
forfeiture, 226
transfers, 232
**Table 'E',** 202
**Tabular Ledgers,** 631
**Tangible Assets,** 4
**Taxation,**
amount set aside to prevent undue fluctuations, for, 277, 285
recommendations of Institute of Chartered Accountants, as to treatment of, 310 *et seq.*
treatment of, in accounts, 305 *et seq.*
**Tax Reserve Certificates,** 310
**Tools and Loose Plant,**
treatment on revaluation of, 61
**Total (or Control) Accounts,**
branch debtors for, 457, 465
cash account, 8

**Total (or Control) Accounts** (*continued*)
creditors, 31, 83
debtors, 30, 83
definition of, 29
location of errors by, 29, 37
mechanized accounting, in, 522
reasons for raising, 29
**Trade Discount,**
definition of, 6
**Trading Account,**
compilation of, 18 *et seq.*
deeds of arrangement, trustee in, of, 556
definition of, 18
quantities in connection with, 18
trustee in bankruptcy, of, 556
**Transfer of Shares,**
certified transfer, 232
form of transfer, 232
procedure, 232
register of transfers, 233
**Trial Balance,**
currency, conversion of, 494 *et seq.*
definition of, 17
difference on, suspense account for, 70
errors not disclosed by, 17
location of errors in, 37 *et seq.*
**Trustee,**
bankruptcy, in, 556
debenture holders, for, 238
deed of arrangement, under, 556

**Uncompleted Work,**
accounts of professional men, 657
**Underwriters' Accounts,**
insurance, 621
scrip profits, treatment of, 666
shares, 234 *et seq.*
**Underwriting Commission,**
balance sheet, disclosure in, 237
definition of, 234
'over-riding', 234
**Unfranked Investment Income,**
definition of, 306
set off of income tax on, 308
treatment of income tax on, in balance sheet, 307
**Unlimited Companies,** 202
**Unquoted Investments,**
balance sheet, in, treatment of, 287
profit and loss account, in, treatment of income from, 278
**Unrealized Profit,**
provision for, 77, 414, 430, 488, 593

**Valuation Balance Sheet,** 664
**Valuation of Assets,**
goodwill, 135
statement of affairs, for, 547
stock-in-trade, 297 *et seq.*
**Vendors' Shares,** 217
**Voyage Accounts,** 620

**Wasting Assets,** 3
**Wear and Tear,** 45
**Working Capital,** 3, 4
maintenance of, by sinking fund, 66
**Work in Progress,**
manufacturing account, in, 75
professional man, of, 657
valuation of, 297 *et seq.*